REA: THE LEADER IN CLEP® TEST PREP

CLEP® GENERAL EXAMS

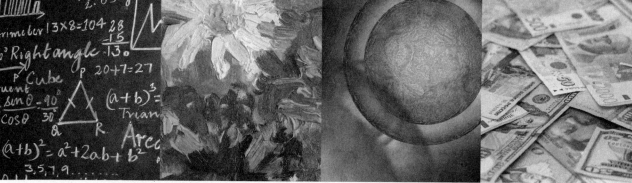

Humanities
Edited by Patricia Van Arnum, M.S.

College Mathematics
Mel Friedman, M.S.
Stu Schwartz, B.S.

Natural Sciences
Laurie Ann Callihan, Ph.D.
David Callihan, M.S.

Social Sciences & History
Scott Dittloff, Ph.D.

Research & Education Association
Visit our website at: www.rea.com

Research & Education Association
61 Ethel Road West
Piscataway, New Jersey 08854
Email: info@rea.com

CLEP® General Exams with Online Practice Tests, 9th Edition

Printed in the United States of America

Library of Congress Control Number 2017950770

ISBN-13: 978-0-7386-1231-7
ISBN-10: 0-7386-1231-6

 REA® is a registered trademark of
Research & Education Association, Inc.

CONTENTS

ACKNOWLEDGMENTS

We would like to thank Pam Weston, Publisher, for setting the quality standards for production integrity and managing the publication to completion; John Paul Cording, Vice President, Technology, for coordinating the design and development of the REA Study Center; Larry B. Kling, Vice President, Editorial, for his overall direction; Diane Goldschmidt, Managing Editor, for coordinating development of this edition; and Transcend Creative Services (TCS) for typesetting this edition; and Jennifer Calhoun, Graphic Designer, for designing our cover and file preparation.

In addition we would like to thank Ellen Gong for proofreading; Mary Berlinghieri for technically reviewing our College Mathematics manuscript; Miriam Perkoff, M.M. for editing our Music review; and Bernard Yanelli for editing our Social Sciences & History practice exams.

■ INTRODUCTION
PASSING THE CLEP GENERAL EXAMS

Congratulations! You're joining the millions of people who have discovered the value and educational advantage offered by the College Board's College-Level Examination Program, or CLEP. This test prep focuses on what you need to know to succeed on the four CLEP general exams. These exams correspond to the core courses required by most colleges and include Humanities, College Mathematics, Natural Sciences, and Social Sciences and History.

HOW TO USE THIS BOOK + ONLINE PREP

There are many different ways to prepare for a CLEP exam. What's best for you depends on how much time you have to study and how comfortable you are with the subject matter. To score your highest, you need a system that can be customized to fit you: your schedule, your learning style, and your current level of knowledge.

This book, and the online tools that come with it, allow you to create a personalized study plan for **each of the four CLEP general exams** through three simple steps: assessment of your knowledge, targeted review of exam content, and reinforcement in the areas where you need the most help.

Let's get started and see how this system works.
Follow this study plan for each of the four CLEP general exams.

Test Yourself and Get Feedback	Assess your strengths and weaknesses. The score report from your online diagnostic exam gives you a fast way to pinpoint what you already know and where you need to spend more time studying.
Review with the Book	Armed with your diagnostic score report, review the parts of the book where you're weak and study the answer explanations for the test questions you answered incorrectly.
Ensure You're Ready for Test Day	After you've finished reviewing with the book, take our full-length practice tests. Review your score reports and re-study any topics you missed. We give you two full-length practice tests to ensure you're confident and ready for test day.

THE REA STUDY CENTER

The best way to personalize your study plan is to get feedback on what you know and what you don't know. At the online REA Study Center (*www.rea.com/studycenter*), you can access two types of assessment for each of the four CLEP general exams: a diagnostic exam and full-length practice exams. Each of these tools provides true-to-format questions and delivers a detailed score report that follows the topics and assesses the skills set by the College Board.

DIAGNOSTIC EXAM – 1 FOR EACH CLEP GENERAL EXAM

Before you begin your review with the book, take the online diagnostic exam. Use your score report to help evaluate your overall understanding of the subject, so you can focus your study on the topics where you need the most review.

FULL-LENGTH PRACTICE EXAMS – 2 FOR EACH CLEP GENERAL EXAM

Our full-length practice tests give you the most complete picture of your strengths and weaknesses. After you've finished reviewing with the book, test what you've learned by taking the first of the two online practice exams. Review your score report, then go back and study any topics you missed. Take the second practice test to ensure you have mastered the material and are ready for test day.

If you're studying and don't have Internet access, you can take Practice Test 1 which is also included in this book. This is the same practice test offered at the REA Study Center, but without the added benefits of timed testing conditions and diagnostic score reports. Because the actual exam is Internet-based, we recommend you take at least one practice test online to simulate test-day conditions.

CLEP AND TECHNOLOGY-ENHANCED QUESTIONS

While most of the questions you will find on your CLEP exam will be standard multiple-choice questions, the College Board is now incorporating some technology-enhanced questions. These new question types include: filling in a numeric answer; shading areas of an object; or putting items in the correct order. In addition, several exams now have an optional essay section.

If you're familiar with basic computer skills, you'll have no trouble handling these question types if you encounter them on your exam.

ALL ABOUT THE CLEP PROGRAM

WHAT IS CLEP?

More adult learners use CLEP than any other credit-by-examination program in the United States. The CLEP program's 33 exams span five subject areas. The exams assess the material commonly required in an introductory-level college course. Based on recommendations from the American Council on Education, a passing score can earn you at least three credits per exam at more than 2,900 colleges and universities in the U.S. and abroad. Policies vary, so check with your school on the exams it accepts and the scores it requires. For a complete list of the CLEP subject examinations offered, visit the College Board website: *www.collegeboard.org/clep*.

WHO TAKES CLEP EXAMS?

CLEP exams are typically taken by people who have acquired knowledge outside the classroom and wish to bypass certain college courses and earn college credit. The CLEP program is designed to reward examinees for prior learning—no matter where or how that knowledge was acquired.

Although many CLEP examinees are adults returning to college, high school students, home-schooled students, traditional-age college students, military personnel, veterans, and international students take CLEP exams to earn college credit. There are no prerequisites, such as age or educational status, for taking CLEP examinations.

Because policies on granting credits vary among colleges, you should contact the particular institution from which you wish to receive CLEP credit. Be aware that some credit-awarding colleges may require that CLEP general exams be taken no later than your *first* semester.

HOW IS MY CLEP SCORE DETERMINED?

Your CLEP score is based on two calculations. First, your CLEP raw score is figured; this is just the total number of test items you answer correctly. After the test is administered, your raw score is converted to a scaled score through a process called *equating*. Equating adjusts for minor variations in difficulty across test forms and among test items, and ensures that your score accurately represents your performance on the exam regardless of when or where you take it, or on how well others perform on the same test form.

Your scaled score is the number your college will use to determine if you've performed well enough to earn college credit. Scaled scores for the CLEP exams are delivered on a 20–80 scale. Institutions can set their own scores for granting college credit, but a good passing estimate (based on recommendations from the American Council on Education) is generally a scaled score of 50, which usually requires getting roughly 66% of the questions correct.

For more information on scoring, contact the institution where you wish to be awarded the credit.

WHO ADMINISTERS THE EXAM?

CLEP exams are developed by the College Board, administered by Educational Testing Service (ETS), and involve the assistance of educators from throughout the United States. The test development process is designed and implemented to ensure that the content and difficulty level of the test are appropriate.

WHEN AND WHERE IS THE EXAM GIVEN?

CLEP exams are administered year-round at more than 1,800 test centers in the United States and abroad. To find the test center nearest you and to register for the exam, contact the CLEP Program:

CLEP Services
P.O. Box 6600
Princeton, NJ 08541-6600
Phone: (800) 257-9558 (8 a.m. to 6 p.m. ET)
Fax: (610) 628-3726
Website: *www.collegeboard.org/clep*

THE CLEP iBT PLATFORM

To improve the testing experience for both institutions and test-takers, the College Board's CLEP Program has transitioned its 33 exams from the eCBT platform to an Internet-based testing (iBT) platform. All CLEP test-takers may now register for exams and manage their personal account information through the "My Account" feature on the CLEP website. This new feature simplifies the registration process and automatically downloads all pertinent information about the test session, making for a more streamlined check-in.

OPTIONS FOR MILITARY PERSONNEL AND VETERANS

CLEP exams are available free of charge to eligible military personnel as well as eligible civilian employees. All the CLEP exams are available at test centers on college campuses and military bases. Contact your Educational Services Officer or Navy College Education Specialist for more information. Visit the DANTES or College Board websites for details about CLEP opportunities for military personnel.

Eligible U.S. veterans can claim reimbursement for CLEP exams and administration fees pursuant to provisions of the Veterans Benefits Improvement Act of 2004. For details on eligibility and submitting a claim for reimbursement, visit the U.S. Department of Veterans Affairs website at *www.gibill.va.gov.*

CLEP can be used in conjunction with the Post-9/11 GI Bill, which applies to veterans returning from the Iraq and Afghanistan theaters of operation. Because the GI Bill provides tuition for up to 36 months, earning college credits with CLEP exams expedites academic progress and degree completion within the funded timeframe.

SSD ACCOMMODATIONS FOR CANDIDATES WITH DISABILITIES

Many test candidates qualify for special accommodations when taking CLEP exams. Accommodations include, among other things, extra time, screen magnification, modifiable screen colors, and untimed rest breaks that don't cut into test time. You must make arrangements for these accommodations in advance. For information, contact:

College Board Services for Students with Disabilities (SSD)
P.O. Box 8060
Mt. Vernon, IL 62864-0060
Phone: (609) 771-7137 (Monday through Friday, 8 a.m. to 6 p.m. ET)
TTY: (609) 882-4118
Fax: (866) 360-0114
Website: *http://student.collegeboard.org/services-for-students-with-disabilities*
E-mail: *ssd@info.collegeboard.org*

TEST-TAKING TIPS

Know the format of the test. Familiarize yourself with the CLEP computer screen beforehand by logging on to the College Board website. Waiting until test day to see what it looks like in the pretest tutorial risks injecting needless anxiety into your testing experience. Also, familiarizing yourself with the directions and format of the exam will save you valuable time on the day of the actual test.

Read all the questions—completely. Make sure you understand each question before looking for the right answer. Reread the question if it doesn't make sense.

Read all of the answers to a question. Just because you think you found the correct response right away, do not assume that it's the best answer. The last answer choice might be the correct answer.

Use the process of elimination. Stumped by a question? Don't make a random guess. Eliminate as many of the answer choices as possible. By eliminating just two answer choices, you give yourself a better chance of getting the item correct, since there will only be three choices (two choices in college mathematics) left from which to make your guess. Remember, your score is based only on the number of questions you answer correctly.

Don't waste time! Don't spend too much time on any one question. Your time is limited, so pacing yourself is very important. Work on the easier questions first. Skip the difficult questions and go back to them if you have the time. Taking our timed practice tests online at the REA Study Center will help you learn how to budget your time.

Look for clues to answers in other questions. If you skip a question you don't know the answer to, you might find a clue to the answer elsewhere on the test.

Be sure that your answer registers before you go to the next item. Look at the screen to see that your mouse-click causes the pointer to darken the proper oval. If your answer doesn't register, you won't get credit for that question.

THE DAY OF THE EXAM

On test day, you should wake up early (after a good night's rest, of course) and have breakfast. Dress comfortably, so you are not distracted by being too hot or too cold while taking the test. (Note that "hoodies" are not allowed.) Arrive at the test center early. This will allow you to collect your thoughts and relax before the test, and it will also spare you the anxiety that comes with being late. As an added incentive, keep in mind that no one will be allowed into the test session after the test has begun.

Before you leave for the test center, make sure you have your admission form and another form of identification, which must contain a recent photograph, your name, and signature (i.e., driver's license, student identification card, or current alien registration card). You will not be admitted to the test center if you do not have proper identification.

You may not wear a digital watch (wrist or pocket), alarm watch, or wristwatch camera. In addition, no cell phones, dictionaries, textbooks, notebooks, briefcases, or packages will be permitted, and drinking, smoking, and eating are prohibited.

Good luck on the CLEP general exams!

PART I

CLEP Humanities

About Our Editor

This CLEP Humanities review was edited by Patricia Van Arnum, M.S. Ms. Van Arnum is editorial director of the Drug, Chemical and Associated Technologies Association. She is a former senior editor at REA, publishers of the CLEP General Exams (9th edition) test prep.

An Overview of the Exam

The CLEP Humanities exam consists of approximately 140 multiple-choice questions, each with five possible answer choices, to be answered in 90 minutes.

The exam tests general knowledge of literature, art, and music. The test covers all periods, from classical to contemporary and covers poetry, prose, philosophy, history of art, music, dance and theater. The questions are drawn from the entire history of Western art and culture and are fairly evenly divided among the following periods: Classical, Medieval and Renaissance, and the seventeenth through twentieth centuries. Some questions could be based on African and Asian cultures.

The approximate breakdown of topics is as follows:

50% Literature

10%	Drama
10%–15%	Poetry
15%–20%	Fiction
10%	Nonfictions (including philosophy)

50% Fine Arts

20%	Visual arts (painting, sculpture, etc.)
15%	Music
10%	Performing arts (film, dance, etc.)
5%	Architecture

6-Week Study Plan

Our study plan is designed to be used in the six weeks before your exam. Be sure to set aside enough time—at least two hours each day—to study. The more time you spend studying, the more prepared and relaxed you will feel on the day of the exam.

Week	Activity
1	Take the Diagnostic Exam at the online REA Study Center. (*www.rea.com/studycenter*). Your score report will identify topics where you need the most review.
2–4	Study the review, focusing on the topics you missed (or were unsure of) on the Diagnostic Exam.
5	Take Practice Test 1 at the REA Study Center. Review your score report and re-study any topics you missed.
6	Take Practice Test 2 at the REA Study Center to see how much your score has improved. If you still got a few questions wrong, go back to the review and study the topics you missed.

REVIEW OUTLINE

■LITERATURE REVIEW

PROSE

GENERAL RULES AND IDEAS

Why do people write prose? Certainly such a question has a built-in counter: As opposed to writing what, poetry? One possible answer is that the writer is a poor poet. The requirements and restrictions of the various genres make different demands upon a writer; most writers find their niche and stay there, secure in their private "comfort zone." Shakespeare did not write essays; Hemingway did not write poetry. If either did venture outside of his literary domain, the world took little note.

Students are sometimes confused as to what exactly is prose. Basically, prose is **not** poetry. **Prose** is what we write and speak most of the time in our everyday intercourse: unmetered, unrhymed language. Which is not to say that prose does not have its own rhythms—language, whether written or spoken, has cadence and balance. And certainly prose can have instances of rhyme or assonance, alliteration or onomatopoeia. Language is, after all, **phonic**.

Fiction and Non-fiction

Furthermore, prose may be either **fiction** or **non-fiction**. A novel (like a short story) is fiction; an autobiography is non-fiction. While a novel (or short story) may have autobiographical elements, an autobiography is presumed to be entirely factual. Essays are usually described in other terms: expository, argumentative, persuasive, critical, or narrative. Essays may have elements of either fiction or non-fiction, but are generally classed as a separate subgenre.

Satire, properly speaking, is not a genre at all, but rather a **mode**, elements of which can be found in any category of literature—from poetry and drama to novels and essays. Satire is a manifestation of authorial attitude (tone) and purpose. Our discussion of satire will be limited to its use in prose.

But we have not addressed the initial question: "Why do people write prose?" The answer depends, in part, on the writer's intent. If he wishes to tell a rather long story, filled with many characters and subplots, interlaced with motifs, symbols, and themes, with time and space to develop interrelationships and to present descriptive passages, the writer generally chooses the novel as his medium. If he believes he can present his story more compactly and less complexly, he may choose the novella or the short story.

These subgenres require from the reader a different kind of involvement than does the essay. The essay, rather than presenting a story from which the reader may discern meaning through the skillful analysis of character, plot, symbol, and language, presents a relatively straightforward account of the writer's opinion(s) on an endless array of topics. Depending upon the type of essay, the reader may become informed (expository), provoked (argumentative), persuaded, enlightened (critical), or, in the case of the narrative essay, better acquainted with the writer who wishes to illustrate a point with his story, whether it is autobiographical or fictitious.

Encountering satire in prose selections demands that the reader be sensitive to the nuances of language and form, that he detect the double-edged sword of irony, and that he correctly assess both the writer's tone and his purpose.

Reading Prose

Readers of prose, like readers of poetry, seek aesthetic pleasure, entertainment, and knowledge, not necessarily in that order. Fiction offers worlds—real and imagined—in which characters and ideas, events and language, interact in ways familiar and unfamiliar. As readers, we take delight in the wisdom we fancy we have acquired from a novel or short story. Non-fiction offers viewpoints which we may find comforting or horrifying, amusing or sobering, presented by the author rather than by his once-removed persona. Thus, we are tempted to believe that somehow the truths presented in non-fiction are more "real" than the truths revealed by fiction. But we must resist! **Truth** is not genre-specific.

Reading prose for the CLEP Humanities exam is really no different from reading prose for your own purposes, except for the time constraints, of course! Becoming a competent reader is a result of practicing certain skills. Probably most important is acquiring a broad reading base. Read widely; read eclectically; read actively; read avidly. The idea is not that you might stumble onto a familiar prose selection on the CLEP and have an edge in writing about it. Instead, it's about building your familiarity with many authors and works so you have a foundation upon which to build your understanding of **whatever** prose selection you encounter on the CLEP Humanities exam. So read, read, read!

READING NOVELS

Most literary handbooks will define a novel as an extended fictional prose narrative, derived from the Italian *novella*, meaning "tale, piece of news." The term "novelle," meaning short tales, was applied to works such as Boccaccio's *The Decameron*, a collection of stories which had an impact on later works such as Chaucer's *Canterbury Tales*. In most European countries, the word for **novel** is **roman**, short for **romance**, which was applied to longer verse narratives (Malory's *Le Morte d'Arthur*), which were later written in prose. Early romances were associated with "legendary, imaginative, and poetic material"—tales "of the long ago or the far away or the imaginatively improbable"; novels, on the other hand, were felt to be "bound by the facts of the actual world and the laws of probability" (*A Handbook to Literature*, C. Hugh Holman, p. 354).

The novel has, over some 600 years, developed into many special forms which are classified by subject matter: detective novel, psychological novel, historical novel, regional novel, picaresque novel, Gothic novel, stream-of-consciousness novel, epistolary novel, and so on. These terms, of course, are not exhaustive nor mutually exclusive. Furthermore, depending on the conventions of the author's time period, his style, and his outlook on life, his *mode* may be termed **realism**, **romanticism**, **impressionism**, **expressionism**, **naturalism**, or **neo-classicism** (Holman, p. 359).

Our earlier description of a novel ("...a rather long story, filled with many characters and subplots, interlaced with motifs, symbols, and themes, with time and space to develop interrelationships and to present descriptive passages") is satisfactory for our purposes here. The works generally included on the CLEP are those which have stood the test of time in significance, literary merit, and reader popularity. New works are incorporated into the canon, which is a reflection of what works are being taught in literature classes. And teachers begin to teach those works which are included frequently among the test questions you will encounter on the CLEP. So the process is circular, but the standards remain high for inclusion on the exam.

Plots

Analyzing novels is a bit like asking the journalist's five questions: what? who? why? where? and how? The **what** is the story, the narrative, the plot and subplots. Most students are familiar with Freytag's Pyramid, originally designed to describe the structure of a five-act drama but now widely used to analyze fiction as well. The stages generally specified are **introduction** or **exposition**, **complication**, **rising action**, **climax**, **falling action**, and **denouement** or **conclusion**. As the novel's events are charted, the "change which structures the story" should emerge. There are many events in a long narrative; but generally only one set of events comprises the "real" or "significant" story.

However, subplots often parallel or serve as counterpoints to the main plot line, serving to enhance the central story. Minor characters sometimes have essentially the same conflicts and goals as the major characters, but the consequences of the outcome seem less important. Sometimes the parallels involve reversals of characters and situations, creating similar yet distinct differences in the outcomes. Nevertheless, seeing the parallels makes understanding the major plot line less difficult.

Sometimes an author divides the novel into chapters—named or unnamed, perhaps just numbered. Or he might divide the novel into "books" or "parts," with chapters as subsections. Readers should take their cue from these divisions; the author must have had some reason for them. Take note of what happens in each larger section, as well as within the smaller chapters. Whose progress is being followed? What event or occurrence is being foreshadowed or prepared for? What causal or other relationships are there between sections and events? Some writers, such as Steinbeck in *The Grapes of Wrath*, use intercalary chapters, alternating between the "real" story (the Joads) and peripheral or parallel stories (the Okies and migrants in general). Look for the pattern of such organization; try to see the interrelationships of these alternating chapters.

Characters

Of course, plots cannot happen in isolation from characters, the **who** element of a story. Not only are there major and minor characters to consider; we need to note whether the various characters are **static** or **dynamic**. Static characters do not change in significant ways—that is, in ways which relate to the story which is structuring the novel. A character may die, i.e., change from alive to dead, and still be static, unless his death is central to the narrative. For instance, in Golding's *Lord of the Flies*, the boy with the mulberry birthmark apparently dies in a fire early in the novel. Momentous as any person's death is, this boy's death is not what the novel is about. However, when Simon is killed, and later Piggy, the narrative is directly impacted because the reason for their deaths is central to the novel's theme regarding man's innate evil. A dynamic character may change only slightly in his attitudes, but those changes may be the very ones upon which the narrative rests. For instance, Siddhartha begins as a very pure and devout Hindu but is unfulfilled spiritually. He eventually does achieve spiritual contentment, but his change is more a matter of degree than of substance. He is not an evil man who attains salvation, nor a pious man who becomes corrupt. It is the process of his search, the stages in his pilgrimage, which structure the novel *Siddhartha*.

We describe major characters or "actors" in novels as **protagonists** or **antagonists**. Built into those two terms is the Greek word **agon**, meaning "struggle." The *pro*tagonist struggles **toward** or for someone or something; the *ant(i)*agonist struggles **against** someone or something. The possible conflicts are usually cited as man against himself, man against man, man against society, or man against nature. Sometimes more than one of these conflicts appears in a story, but usually one is dominant and is the structuring device.

A character can be referred to as **stock**, meaning that he exists because the plot demands it. For instance, a Western with a gunman who robs the bank will require a number of **stock** characters: the banker's lovely daughter, the tough but kindhearted barmaid, the cowardly white-shirted citizen who sells out the hero to save his own skin, and the young freckle-faced lad who shoots the bad guy from a second-story hotel window.

Or a character can be a **stereotype**, without individuating characteristics. For instance, a sheriff in a small Southern town; a football player who is all brawn; a librarian clucking over her prized books; the cruel commandant of a POW camp.

Characters often serve as **foils** for other characters, enabling us to see one or more of them better. A classic example is Tom Sawyer, the romantic foil for Huck Finn's realism. Or, in Lee's *To Kill a Mockingbird*, Scout as the naïve observer of events which her brother Jem, four years older, comes to understand from the perspective of the adult world.

Sometimes characters are **allegorical**, standing for qualities or concepts rather than for actual personages. For instance, Jim Casey (initials "J. C.") in *The Grapes of Wrath* is often regarded as a Christ figure, pure and self-sacrificing in his aims for the migrant workers. Or Kamala, Siddhartha's teacher in the art of love, whose name comes from the tree whose bark is used as a purgative; she purges him of his ascetic ways on his road to self-hood and spiritual fulfillment.

Other characters are fully three-dimensional, "rounded," "mimetic" of humans in all their virtue, vice, hope, despair, strength, and weakness. This verisimilitude aids the author in creating characters who are credible and plausible, without being dully predictable and mundane.

Themes

The interplay of plot and characters determines in large part the **theme** of a work, the **why** of the story. First of all, we must distinguish between a mere topic and a genuine theme or thesis; and then between a theme and contributing *motifs*. A **topic** is a phrase, such as "man's inhumanity to man"; or "the fickle nature of fate." A **theme**, however, turns a phrase into a statement: "Man's inhumanity to man is barely concealed by 'civilization,'" or "Man is a helpless pawn, at the mercy of fickle fate." Many writers may deal with the same topic, such as the complex nature of true love; but their themes may vary widely, from "True love will always win out in the end," to "Not even true love can survive the cruel ironies of fate."

To illustrate the relationship between plot, character, and theme, let's examine two familiar fairy tales. In "The Ugly Duckling," the structuring story line is "Once upon a time there was an ugly duckling, who in turn became a beautiful swan." In this case, the duckling did nothing to merit either his ugliness or his eventual transformation; but he did not curse fate. He only wept and waited, lonely and outcast. And when he became beautiful, he did not gloat; he eagerly joined the other members of his flock, who greatly admired him. The theme here essentially is: "Good things come to him who waits," or "Life is unfair—you don't get what you deserve, nor deserve what you get." What happens to the theme if the ugly duckling remains an ugly duckling: "Some guys just never get a break"?

Especially rewarding to examine for the interdependence of plot and theme is "Cinderella": "Once upon a time, a lovely, sweet-natured young girl was forced to labor for and serve her ugly and ungrateful stepmother and two stepsisters. But thanks to her fairy godmother, Cinderella and the Prince marry, and live happily ever after."

We could change events (plot elements) at any point, but let's take the penultimate scene where the Prince's men come to the door with the single glass slipper. Cinderella has been shut away so that she is not present when the other women in the house try on the slipper. Suppose that the stepmother or either of the two stepsisters tries on the slipper—and it fits! Cinderella is in the back room doing the laundry, and her family waltzes out the door to the palace and she doesn't even get an invitation to the wedding. And imagine the Prince's dismay when the ugly, one-slippered lady lifts her wedding veil for the consummating kiss! Theme: "There is no justice in the world, for those of low or high station" or "Virtue is not its own reward."

Or let's say that during the slipper-test scene, the stepsisters, stepmother, and finally Cinderella all try on the shoe, but to no avail. And then in sashays the fairy godmother, who gives them all a knowing smirk, puts out her slipper-sized foot and cackles hysterically, like the mechanical witch in the penny arcade. Theme: "You can't trust anybody these days" or, a favorite statement of theme, "Appearances can be deceiving." The link between plot and theme is very strong, indeed.

Motifs

Skilled writers often employ **motifs** to help unify their works. A motif is a detail or element of the story which is repeated throughout, and which may even become symbolic. Television shows are ready examples of the use of motifs. A medical show, with many scenes alternately set in the hospital waiting room and operating room, uses elements such as the pacing, anxious parent or loved one, the gradually filling ashtray, the large wall clock whose hands melt from one hour to another. And in the operating room, the half-masked surgeon whose brow is frequently mopped by the nurse; the gloved hand open-palmed to receive scalpel, sponge, and so on; the various oscilloscopes giving read-outs of the patient's very fragile condition; the expanding and collapsing bladder manifesting that the patient is indeed breathing; and, again, the wall clock, assuring us that this procedure is taking forever. These are all **motifs**, details which in concert help convince the reader that this story occurs in a hospital, and that the mood is pretty tense, that the medical team is doing all it can, and that Mom and Dad will be there when Junior or Sissy wakes up.

But motifs can become symbolic. The oscilloscope line quits blipping, levels out, and gives off the ominous hum. And the doctor's gloved hand sets down the scalpel and shuts off the oscilloscope. In the waiting room, Dad crushes the empty cigarette pack; Mom quits pacing and sinks into the sofa. The door to the waiting room swings shut silently behind the retreating doctor. All these elements signal "It's over, finished."

This example is very crude and mechanical, but motifs in the hands of a skillful writer are valuable devices. And in isolation, and often magnified, a single motif can become a controlling image with great significance. For instance, Emma Bovary's shoes signify her obsession with material things; and when her delicate slippers become soiled as she crosses the dewy grass to meet her lover, we sense the impurity of her act as well as its futility. Or when wise Piggy, in *Lord of the Flies,* is reduced to one lens in his specs, and finally to no specs at all, we see the loss of insight and wisdom on the island, and chaos follows.

Settings in Novels

Setting is the **where** element of the story. But setting is also the **when** element: time of day, time of year, time period or year; it is the dramatic moment, the precise intersection of time and space when this story is being told. Setting is also the atmosphere: positive or negative ambiance, calm, chaotic, Gothic, Romantic. The question for the reader to answer is whether the setting is ultimately essential to the plot/theme, or whether it is incidental; i.e., could this story/theme have been told successfully in another time and/or place? For instance, could the theme in *Lord of the*

Flies be made manifest if the boys were not on an island? Could they have been isolated in some other place? Does it matter whether the "war" which they are fleeing is WWII or WWIII or some other conflict, in terms of the theme?

Hopefully, the student will see that the four elements of plot, character, theme, and setting are intertwined and largely interdependent. A work must really be read as a whole, rather than dissected and analyzed in discrete segments.

Style

The final question, **how?**, relates to an author's style. Style involves language (word choice), syntax (word order, sentence type, and length), the balance between narration and dialogue, the choice of narrative voice (first person participant, third person with limited omniscience), use of descriptive passages, and other aspects of the actual words on the page which are basically irrelevant to the first four elements (plot, character, theme, and setting). Stylistic differences are fairly easy to spot among such diverse writers as Jane Austen, whose style is—to today's reader—very formal and mannered; Mark Twain, whose style is very casual and colloquial; William Faulkner, whose prose often spins on without punctuation or paragraphs far longer than the reader can hold either the thought or his breath; and Hemingway, whose dense but spare, pared-down style has earned the epithet, "Less is more."

READING SHORT STORIES

The modern short story differs from earlier short fiction, such as the parable, fable, and tale, in its emphasis on character development through scenes rather than summary: through *showing* rather than *telling*. Gaining popularity in the nineteenth century, the short story generally was realistic, presenting detailed accounts of the lives of middle-class personages. This tendency toward realism dictates that the plot be grounded in *probability*, with causality fully in operation. Furthermore, the characters are human with recognizable human motivations, both social and psychological. Setting—time and place—is realistic rather than fantastic. And, as Poe stipulated, the elements of plot, character, setting, style, point of view, and theme all work toward a single *unified* effect.

However, some modern writers have stretched these boundaries and have mixed in elements of nonrealism—such as the supernatural and the fantastic—sometimes switching back and forth between realism and nonrealism, confusing the reader who is expecting conventional fiction. John Barth's "Lost in the Funhouse" and Woody Allen's "The Kugelmass Episode" are two stories which are not, strictly speaking, *realistic*. However, if the reader will approach and accept this type of story on its own terms, he will be better able to understand and appreciate them fully.

Unlike the novel, which has time and space to develop characters and interrelationships, the short story must rely on flashes of insight and revelation to develop plot and characters. The "slice of life" in a short story is of necessity much narrower than that in a novel; the time span is much shorter, the focus much tighter. To attempt anything like the panoramic canvas available to the novelist would be to view fireworks through a soda straw: occasionally pretty, but ultimately not very satisfying or enlightening.

Point of View

The elements of the short story are those of the novel, discussed earlier. However, because of the compression of time and concentration of effect, probably the short story writer's most important decision is **point of view**. A narrator may be *objective*, presenting information without bias or comment. Hemingway frequently uses the objective *third-person* narrator, presenting scenes almost dramatically, i.e., with a great deal of dialogue and very little narrative, none of which directly reveals the thoughts or feelings of the characters. The third-person narrator may, however, be less objective in his presentation, directly revealing the thoughts and feelings, of one or more of the characters, as Chopin does in "The Story of an Hour." We say that such a narrator is fully or partially *omniscient*, depending on how complete his knowledge is of the characters' psychological and emotional makeup. The least objective narrator is the *first-person* narrator, who presents information from the perspective of a single character who is a participant in the action. Such a narrative choice allows the author to present the discrepancies between the writer's/reader's perceptions and those of the narrator.

One reason the choice of narrator, the point of view from which to tell the story, is immensely important in a short story is that the narrator reveals character and event in ways which affect our understanding of theme. For instance, in Faulkner's "A Rose for Emily," the unnamed narrator who seems to be a townsperson recounts the story out of chronological order, juxtaposing events whose causality and significance are uncertain. The narrator withholds information which would explain events being presented, letting the reader puzzle over Emily Grierson's motivations, a device common in detective fiction. In fact, the narrator presents contradictory information, making the reader alternately pity and resent the spinster. When we examine the imagery and conclude that Miss Emily and her house represent the decay and decadence of the Old South which resisted the invasion of "progress" from the North, we see the importance of setting and symbol in relation to theme.

Similarly, in Mansfield's "Bliss," the abundant description of setting creates the controlling image of the lovely pear tree. But this symbol of fecundity becomes ironic when Bertha Young belatedly feels sincere and overwhelming desire for her husband. The third-person narrator's omniscience is limited to Bertha's thoughts and feelings; otherwise we would have seen her husband's infidelity with Miss Fulton.

In O'Connor's "Good Country People," the narrator is broadly omniscient, but the reader is still taken by surprise at the cruelty of the Bible salesman who seduces Joy-Hulga. That he steals her artificial leg is perhaps poetic justice, since she (with her numerous degrees) had fully intended to seduce him ("just good country people"). The story's title, the characters' names—Hopewell, Freeman, Joy; the salesman's professed Christianity, the Bibles hollowed out to hold whiskey and condoms, add to the irony of Mrs. Freeman's final comment on the young man: "Some can't be that simple… I know I never could."

Examples of Initiation Stories

The *initiation story* frequently employs the first-person narrator. To demonstrate the subtle differences which can occur in stories which ostensibly have the same point of view and general theme, let's look at three: "A Christmas Memory" (Capote), "Araby" (Joyce), and "A & P" (Updike).

Early in "A Christmas Memory," Capote's narrator identifies himself:

> The person to whom she is speaking is myself. I am seven; she is sixty-something. We are cousins, very distant ones, and we have lived together—well, as long as I can remember. Other people inhabit the house, relatives; and though they have power over us, and frequently make us cry, we are not, on the whole, too much aware of them. We are each other's best friend. She calls me Buddy, in memory of a boy who was formerly her best friend. The other Buddy died in the 1880s, when she was still a child. She is still a child.

Buddy and his cousin, who is called only "my friend," save their meager earnings throughout the year in order to make fruitcakes at Christmas to give mainly to "persons we've met maybe once, perhaps not at all… Like President Roosevelt…. Or Abner Packer, the driver of the six o'clock bus from Mobile, who exchanges waves with us everyday…." Their gifts to one another each year are always handmade, often duplicates of the year before, like the kites they present on what was to be their last Christmas together.

Away at boarding school, when Buddy receives word of his friend's death, it "merely confirms a piece of news some secret vein had already received, severing from me an irreplaceable part of myself, letting it loose like a kite on a broken string. That is why, walking across a school campus on this particular December morning, I keep searching the sky. As if I expected to see, rather like hearts, a lost pair of kites hurrying toward heaven."

Buddy's characterizations of his friend are also self-revelatory. He and she are peers, equals, despite their vast age difference. They are both totally unselfish, joying in the simple activities mandated by their economic circumstances. They are both "children."

The story is told in present tense, making the memories from the first paragraphs seem as "real" and immediate as those from many years later. And Buddy's responses from the early years ("Well, I'm disappointed. Who wouldn't be? With socks, a Sunday school shirt, some handkerchiefs, a hand-me-down sweater and a year's subscription to a religious magazine for children, *The Little Shepherd*. It makes me boil. It really does.") are as true to his seven-year-old's perspective, as his observations when he, much older, has left home ("I have a new home too. But it doesn't count. Home is where my friend is, and there I never go.").

The youthful narrator in "A & P" also uses present tense, but not consistently, which gives his narrative a very colloquial, even unschooled flavor. Like Buddy, Sammy identifies himself in the opening paragraph: "In walks these three girls in nothing but bathing suits. I'm in the third check-out slot, with my back to the door, so I don't see them until they're over by the bread." And later, "Stokesie's married, with two babies chalked up on his fuselage already, but as far as I can tell that's the only difference. He's twenty-two, and I was nineteen this April." The girls incur the wrath of the store manager, who scolds them for their inappropriate dress. And Sammy, in his adolescent idealism, quits on the spot. Although he realizes that he does not want to "do this" to his parents, he tells us "… it seems to me that once you begin a gesture it's fatal not to go through with it." But his *beau geste* is ill-spent: "I look around for my girls, but they're gone, of course…. I could see Lengel in my place in the slot, checking the sheep through. His face was dark gray and his back stiff, as if he'd just had an injection of iron, and my stomach kind of fell as I felt how hard the world was going to be to me hereafter."

Like Buddy, Sammy tells his story from a perch not too distant from the events he recounts. Both narrators still feel the immediacy of their rites of passage very strongly. Buddy, however, reveals himself to be a more admirable character, perhaps because his story occurs mainly when he is seven—children tend not to be reckless in the way that Sammy is. Sammy was performing for an audience, doing things he knew would cause pain to himself and his family, for the sake of those three girls who never gave him the slightest encouragement and whom he would probably never even see again.

In "Araby," the unnamed narrator tells of a boyhood crush he had on the older sister of one of his chums: "I thought little of the future. I did not know whether I would ever speak to her or not or, if I spoke to her, how I could tell her of my confused adoration. But my body was like a harp and her words and gestures were like fingers running upon the wires." She asks the boy if he is going to Araby, a "splendid bazaar," and reveals that she cannot. He promises to go himself and bring her something. But his uncle's late homecoming delays the boy's excursion until the bazaar is nearly closed for the night, and he is unable to find an appropriate gift. Forlornly, "I turned away slowly and walked down the middle of the bazaar…. Gazing up into the darkness I saw myself as a creature driven and derided by vanity, and my eyes burned with anguish and anger." This narrator is recounting his story from much further away than either Buddy or Sammy tells his own. The narrator of "Araby" has the perspective of an adult, looking back at a very important event in his boyhood. His "voice" reflects wisdom born of experience. The incident was very painful then, but its memory, while poignant, is no longer devastating. Like Sammy, this narrator sees the dichotomy between his adolescent idealism and the mundane reality of "romance." However, the difference is in the narrator's ability to turn the light on himself. Sammy is still so close to the incident that he very likely would whip off his checker's apron again if the girls returned to the A & P. The "Araby" narrator has "mellowed" and can see the futility—and the necessity—of adolescent love.

READING ESSAYS

Categories of Essays

Essays fall into four rough categories: **speculative**, **argumentative**, **narrative**, and **expository**. Depending on the writer's purpose, his essay will fit more or less into one or these groupings.

The **speculative** essay is so named because, as its Latin root suggests, it *looks* at ideas—explores them rather than explains them. While the speculative essay may be said to be *meditative*, it often makes one or more points. But the thesis may not be as obvious or clear-cut as that in an expository or argumentative essay. The writer deals with ideas in an associative manner, playing with ideas in a looser structure than he would in an expository or argumentative essay. This "flow" may even produce *intercalary* paragraphs, which present alternately a narrative of sorts and thoughtful responses to the events being recounted, as in White's "The Ring of Time."

The purposes of the **argumentative** essay, on the other hand, are always clear: to present a point and provide evidence, which may be factual or anecdotal, and to support it. The structure is usually very formal, as in a debate, with counterpositions and counterarguments. Whatever the organizational pattern, the writer's intent in an argumentative essay is to persuade his reader of the validity of some claim, as Bacon does in "Of Love."

Narrative and **expository** essays have elements of both the speculative and argumentative modes. The narrative essay may recount an incident or a series of incidents and is almost always autobiographical, in order to make a point, as in Orwell's "Shooting an Elephant." The informality of the storytelling makes the narrative essay less insistent than the argumentative essay, but more directed than the speculative essay.

Students are probably most familiar with the **expository** essay, the primary purpose of which is to explain and clarify ideas. While the expository essay may have narrative elements, that aspect is minor and subservient to that of explanation. Furthermore, while nearly all essays have some element of persuasion, argumentation is incidental in the expository essay. In any event, the four categories—speculative, argumentative, narrative, and expository—are neither exhaustive nor mutually exclusive.

Elements of Essays

As non-fiction, essays have a different set of elements from novels and short stories: **voice**, **style**, **structure**, and **thought**.

Voice in non-fiction is similar to the narrator's tone in fiction, but the major difference is in who is "speaking." In fiction, the author is not the speaker—the **narrator** is the speaker. Students sometimes have difficulty with this distinction, but it is necessary if we are to preserve the integrity of the fictive "story." In an essay, however, the author speaks directly to the reader, even if he is presenting ideas which he may not actually espouse personally—as in a satire. This directness creates the writer's **tone**, his attitude toward his subject.

Style in non-fiction derives from the same elements as style in fiction: word choice, syntax, balance between dialogue and narration, voice, use of description—those things specifically related to words on the page. Generally speaking, an argumentative essay will be written in a more formal style than will a narrative essay, and a meditative essay will be less formal than an expository essay. But such generalizations are only descriptive, not prescriptive.

Structure and **thought**, the final elements of essays, are so intertwined as to be inextricable. We must be aware that to change the structure of an essay will alter its meaning. For instance, in White's "The Ring of Time," to abandon the *intercalary* paragraph organization, separating the paragraphs which narrate the scenes with the young circus rider from those which reflect on the circularity and linearity of time, would alter our understanding of the essay's thesis. Writers signal structural shifts with alterations in focus, as well as with visual clues (spacing), verbal clues (e.g., *but, therefore, however*), or shifts in the kind of information being presented (personal, scientific, etc.).

Thought is perhaps the single element which most distinguishes non-fiction from fiction. The essayist chooses his form not to tell a story but to present an idea. Whether he chooses the speculative, narrative, argumentative, or expository format, the essayist has something on his mind that he wants to convey to his readers. And it is this idea which we are after when we analyze his essay.

Example of the Structure of an Essay

Often anthologized is Orwell's "Shooting an Elephant," a narrative essay recounting the writer's (presumably) experience in Burma as an officer of the British law that ruled the poverty-ridden people of a small town. Orwell begins with two paragraphs which explain that, as a white, European authority figure, he was subjected to taunts and abuse by the natives. Ironically, he sympathized with the Burmese and harbored fairly strong anti-British feelings regarding the imperialists as the oppressors rather than the saviors. He tells us that he felt caught, trapped between his position of authority which he himself resented and the hatred of those he was required to oversee.

The body of the essay—some 11 paragraphs—relates the incident with an otherwise tame elephant gone "must," or mad, bringing chaos and destruction to the village. Only occasionally does Orwell interrupt the narrative to reveal his reactions directly, but his descriptions of the Burmese are sympathetically drawn. The language is heavily connotative, revealing the helplessness of the villagers against both the elephant and the miserable circumstances of their lives.

Orwell recounts how, having sent for an elephant gun, he found that he was compelled to shoot the animal, even though its destruction was by now unwarranted and even ill-advised, given the value of the elephant to the village. But the people expected it, demanded it; the white man realized that he did not have dominion over these people of color after all. They were in charge, not him.

To make matters worse, Orwell bungles the "murder" of the beast, which takes half an hour to die in great agony. And in the aftermath of discussions of the rightness or wrongness of his action,

Orwell wonders if anyone realizes he killed the elephant only to save face. It is the final sentence of the final paragraph which directly reveals the author's feelings, although he has made numerous indirect references to them throughout the essay. Coupled with the opening paragraphs, this conclusion presents British imperialism of the period in a very negative light: "the unable doing the unnecessary to the ungrateful."

Having discovered Orwell's main idea, we must look at the other elements (voice, style, structure) to see *how* he communicates it to the reader. The voice of the first-person narrative is fairly formal, yet remarkably candid, using connotation to color our perception of the events. Orwell's narrative has many complex sentences, with vivid descriptive phrases in series, drawing our eye along the landscape and through the crowds as he ponders his next move. Structurally, the essay first presents a premise about British imperialism, then moves to a gripping account of the officer's reluctant shooting of the elephant, and ends with an admission of his own culpability as an agent of the institution he detests. Orwell frequently signals shifts between his role as officer and his responses as a humane personage with *but*, or with dashes to set off his responses to the events he is recounting.

READING SATIRE

Satire is a *mode* which may be employed by writers of various genres: poetry, drama, fiction, non-fiction. It is more a perspective than a product.

Satire mainly exposes and ridicules, derides and denounces vice, folly, evil, stupidity, as these qualities manifest themselves in persons, groups of persons, ideas, institutions, customs, or beliefs. While the satirist has many techniques at his disposal, there are basically only two types of satire: gentle or harsh, depending on the author's intent, his audience, and his methods.

Role of Satire

The terms *romanticism*, *realism*, and *naturalism* can help us understand the role of *satire*. Romanticism sees the world idealistically, as perfectible if not perfect. Realism sees the world as it is, with healthy doses of both good and bad. Naturalism sees the world as imperfect, with evil often triumphing over good. The satirist is closer to the naturalist than he is to the romantic or realist, for both the satirist and the naturalist focus on what is wrong with the world, intending to expose the foibles of man and his society. The difference between them lies in their techniques. The naturalist is very direct and does not necessarily employ humor; the satirist is more subtle, and does.

For instance, people plagued with overpopulation and starvation is not, on first glance, material for humor. Many works have treated such conditions with sensitivity, bringing attention to the plight of the world's unfortunate. Steinbeck's *Grapes of Wrath* is such a work. However, Swift's "A Modest Proposal" takes essentially the same circumstances and holds them up for our amused examination. How does the satirist make an un-funny topic humorous? And why would he do so?

Techniques of Satire

The satirist's techniques—his weapons—include **irony**, **parody**, **reversal** or **inversion**, **hyperbole**, **understatement**, **sarcasm**, **wit**, and **invective**. By exaggerating characteristics, by saying the opposite of what he means, by using his cleverness to make cutting or even cruel remarks at the expense of his subject, the writer of satire can call the reader's attention to those things he believes are repulsive, despicable, or destructive.

Whether he uses more harsh (Juvenalian) or more gentle (Horatian) satire depends upon the writer's attitude and intent. Is he merely flaunting his clever intellect, playing with words for our amusement or to inflate his own sense of superiority? Is he probing the psychological motivations for the foolish or destructive actions of some person(s)? Is he determined to waken an unenlightened or apathetic audience, moving its members to thought or action? Are the flaws which the satirist is pointing out truly destructive or evil, or are they the faults we would all recognize in ourselves if we glanced in the mirror, not admirable but not really harmful to ourselves or society? Is the author amused, sympathetic, objective, irritated, scornful, bitter, pessimistic, mocking? The reader needs to identify the satirist's purpose and tone. Its subtlety sometimes makes satire a difficult mode to detect and to understand.

Irony

Irony is perhaps the satirist's most powerful weapon. The basis of irony is inversion or reversal, doing or saying the opposite or the unexpected. Shakespeare's famous sonnet beginning "My mistress' eyes are nothing like the sun…" is an ironic tribute to the speaker's beloved, who, he finally declares is "as rare/As any she belied with false compare." At the same time, Shakespeare is poking fun at the sonnet form as it was used by his contemporaries—himself included—to extol the virtues of their ladies. By selecting a woman who, by his own description, is physically unattractive in every way imaginable, and using the conventions of the love sonnet to present her many flaws, he has inverted the sonnet tradition. And then by asserting that she compares favorably with any of the other ladies whose poet-lovers have lied about their virtues, he presents us with the unexpected twist. Thus, he satirizes both the love sonnet form and its subject by using irony.

Poetic Satires

Other notable poetic satires include Koch's "Variations on a Theme by William Carlos Williams," in which he parodies Williams' "This Is Just to Say." Koch focuses on the simplicity and directness of Williams' imagery and makes the form and ideas seem foolish and trivial. In "Boom!," Nemerov takes issue with a pastor's assertion that modern technology has resulted in a concomitant rise in religious activities and spiritual values. Nemerov catalogues the instant, disposable, and extravagant aspects of Americans' lifestyles, which result in "pray as you go… pilgrims" for whom religion is another convenience, commercial rather than spiritual.

Satire in Drama

Satire in drama is also common. Wilde's "The Importance of Being Earnest" is wonderfully funny in its constant word play (notably on the name *Ernest*) and its relentless ridiculing of the superficiality which Wilde saw as characteristic of British gentry. Barrie's "The Admirable Chrichton" has a similar theme, with the added assertion that it is the "lower" or servant class which is truly superior—again, the ironic reversal so common in satire. Both of these plays are mild in their ridicule; the authors do not expect or desire any change in society or in the viewer. The satire is gentle; the satirists are amused, or perhaps bemused at the society whose foibles they expose.

Satire in Classic Novels

Classic novels which employ satire include Swift's *Gulliver's Travels* and Voltaire's *Candide*, both of which fairly vigorously attack aspects of the religions, governments, and prevailing intellectual beliefs of their respective societies. A modern novel which uses satire is Heller's *Catch-22*, which is basically an attack on war and the government's bureaucratic bungling of men and material, specifically in World War II. But by extension, Heller is also viewing with contempt the unmotivated, illogical, capricious behavior of all institutions which operate by that basic law: "catch-22." Like Swift and Voltaire, Heller is angry. And although his work, like the other two, has humor, wit, exaggeration, and irony, his purpose is more than intellectual entertainment for his readers. Heller hopes for reform.

Heller's attack is frontal, his assault direct. Swift had to couch his tale in a fantastic setting with imaginary creatures in order to present his views with impunity. The audience, as well as the times, also affect the satirist's work. If the audience is hostile, the writer must veil his theme; if the audience is indifferent, he must jolt them with bitter and reviling language if he desires change. If he does not fear reprisals, the satirist may take any tone he pleases.

We can see satire in operation in two adaptations of the biblical story of King Solomon, who settled the dispute between two mothers regarding an infant: Cut the baby in two and divide it between you, he told them. The rightful mother protested and was promptly awarded the child. The story is meant to attest to the King's wisdom and understanding of parental love, in this case.

However, Twain's Huck Finn has some difficulty persuading runaway slave Jim that Solomon was wise. Jim insists that Solomon, having fathered "'bout five million chillen," was "waseful.... *He* as soon chop a chile in two as a cat. Dey's plenty mo'. A chile er two, mo' er less, warn't no consekens to Solermun, dad fetch him!" Twain is ridiculing not only Jim's ingenuousness, as he does throughout the novel; he is also deflating time-honored beliefs about the Bible and its traditional heroes, as he earlier does with the account of Moses and the "bulrushers." While Twain's tone is fairly mild, his intent shows through as serious. Twain was disgusted with traditional Christianity and its hypocritical followers, as we see later in *Huck Finn* when young Buck Grangerford is murdered in the feud with the Shepherdsons: "I wished I hadn't ever come ashore that night to see such things."

A second satiric variation on the Solomon theme appears in Asprin's *Myth Adventures*, in the volume *Hit or Myth*. Skeebe, the narrator, realizes that he, as king pro-tem, must render a decision regarding the ownership of a cat. Hoping to inspire them to compromise, he decrees that they divide the cat between them: "Instead they thanked me for my wisdom, shook hands, and left smiling, presumably to carve up their cat." He concludes that many of the citizens of this realm "don't have both oars in the water," a conclusion very like Huck's: "I never see such a nigger. If he got a notion in his head once, there warn't no getting it out again." The citizens' unthinking acceptance of the infallibility of authority is as laughable as Jim's out-of-hand rejection of Solomon's wisdom because no wise man would "want to live in the mids' er sich a blim-blammin' all de time" as would prevail in the harem with the King's "million wives."

POETRY

Opening a book to study for an examination is perhaps the worst occasion on which to read poetry, or about poetry, because above all, poetry should be enjoyed; it is definitely "reading for pleasure." This last phrase seems to have developed recently to describe the reading we do other than for information or for study. Perhaps you personally would not choose poetry as pleasure reading because of the bad name poetry has received over the years. Some students regard the "old" poetry such as Donne's or Shelley's as effete (for "wimps" and "nerds" only, in current language), or modern poetry as too difficult or weird. It is hard to imagine that poetry was the "current language" for students growing up in the Elizabethan or Romantic eras. Whereas in our world information can be retrieved in a nanosecond, in those worlds time was plentiful to sit down, clear the mind, and let poetry take over. Very often the meaning of a poem does not come across in a nanosecond and for the modern student this proves very frustrating. Sometimes it takes years for a poem to take on meaning—the reader simply knows that the poem sounds good and it provokes an emotional response that cannot be explained. With time, more emotional experience, more reading of similar experiences, more life, the reader comes to a meaning of that poem that satisfies for the time being. In a few more years that poem may take on a whole new meaning.

READING POETRY FOR AN EXAMINATION

This is all very well for reading for pleasure, but you are now called upon, in your present experience, to learn poetry for an important examination. Perhaps the first step in the learning process is to answer the question, "Why do people write poetry?" An easy answer is that they wish to convey an experience, an emotion, an insight, or an observation in a startling or satisfying way, one that remains in the memory for years. But why not use a straightforward sentence or paragraph? Why wrap up that valuable insight in fancy words, rhyme, paradox, meter, allusion, symbolism, and all the other seeming mumbo-jumbo that explicators of poetry use? Why not just come right out and say it like "normal people" do? An easy answer to these questions is that poetry is not a vehicle for conveying meaning alone. Gerard Manley Hopkins, one of the great innovators of rhythm in poetry, claimed that poetry should be "heard for its own sake and interest even over and above its interest or meaning." Poetry provides intellectual stimulus of course. One of the best ways of studying a poem is to consider it a jigsaw puzzle presented to you whole, an integral work of art, which can be taken apart piece by piece (word by word), analyzed scientifically, labelled, and put back together again into a whole, and then the meaning is complete. But people write poetry to convey more than meaning.

MEANINGS IN POETRY

T. S. Eliot maintained that the meaning of the poem existed purely to distract us "while the poem did its work." One interpretation of a poem's "work" is that it changes us in some way. We see the world in a new way because of the way the poet has seen it and told us about it. Maybe one of the reasons people write poetry is to encourage us to *see* things in the first place. Simple things like daffodils take on a whole new aspect when we read the way Wordsworth saw them. Why did Wordsworth write that poem? His sister had written an excellent account of the scene in her journal. Wordsworth not only evokes nature as we have never seen it before, alive, joyous, exuberant, he shows nature's healing powers, its restorative quality as the scene flashes "upon that inward eye/ Which is the bliss of solitude." Bent over your books studying, how many times has a similar quality of nature's power in the memory come to you? Maybe for you a summer beach scene rather than daffodils by the lake is more meaningful, but the poet captures a moment that we have all experienced. The poet's magic is to make that moment new again.

If poets enhance our power of sight they also awaken the other senses as powerfully. We can hear Emily Dickinson's snake in the repeated "s" sound of the lines:

His notice sudden is—
The Grass divides as with a Comb—
A spotted shaft is seen—

and because of the very present sense of sound, we experience the indrawn gasp of breath of fear when the snake appears. We can touch the little chimneysweep's hair "that curled like a lamb's back" in William Blake's poetry, and because of that tactile sense we are even more shocked to read that the child's hair is all shaved off so that the soot will not spoil its whiteness. We can smell the poison gas as Wilfred Owen's soldiers fumble with their gas masks; we can taste the blood gurgling in the poisoned lungs.

Poets write, then, to awaken the senses. They have crucial ideas, but the words they use are often more important than the meaning. More important still than ideas and sense awakening is the poet's appeal to the emotions. And it is precisely this area that disturbs a number of students. Our modern society tends to block out emotions—we need reviews to tell us if we enjoyed a film or a critic's praise to see if a play or novel is worth our time. We hesitate to laugh at something in case it is not the "in" thing to do. We certainly do not cry—at least in front of others. Poets write to overcome that blocking (very often it is their own blocking of emotion they seek to alleviate), but that is not to say that poetry immediately sets us laughing, crying, loving, or hating. The important fact about the emotional release in poetry is that poets help us explore our own emotions, sometimes by shocking us, sometimes by drawing attention to balance and pattern, and sometimes by cautioning us to move carefully in this inner world.

Poets tell us nothing really new. They tell us old truths about human emotions that we begin to restructure anew, to reread our experiences in light of theirs, to reevaluate our world view. Whereas a car manual helps us understand the workings of a particular vehicle, a poem helps us understand the inner workings of human beings. Poets frequently write to help their emotional life—the writing then becomes cathartic, purging or cleansing the inner life, feeding that part of us that separates us from the animal. Many poets might paraphrase Byron, who claimed that he had to write or go mad. Writer and reader of poetry enter into a collusion, each helping the other to find significance in the human world, to find safety in a seemingly alien world.

REASONS FOR READING POETRY

This last point brings any reader of poetry to ask the next question: Why read poetry? One might contend that a good drama, novel, or short story might provide the same emotional experience. But a poem is much more accessible. Apart from the fact that poems are shorter than other genres, there is a unique directness to them which hinges purely on language. Poets can say in one or two lines what may take novelists and playwrights entire works to express. For example, Keats' lines—

>   Beauty is truth, truth beauty,—that is all
>   Ye know on earth, and all ye need to know—

studied, pondered, and opened to each reader's interpretations, linger in the memory with more emphasis than George Eliot's *Middlemarch*, or Ibsen's *The Wild Duck*, which endeavor to make the same point.

In your reading of poems remember that poetry is perhaps the oldest art and yet surrounds us without our even realizing it. Listeners thrilled to Homer's poetry; tribes chanted invocations to their gods. Today we listen to pop-song lyrics and find ourselves, sometimes despite ourselves, repeating certain rhythmic lines. Advertisements we chuckle over or say we hate still have a way of embedding themselves in our minds with their catchy phrases or snappy repetition. Both lyricists and advertisers cleverly use language, playing on the reader's/listener's/watcher's ability to pick up on a repeated sound or engaging rhythm or inner rhyme. Think of a time as a child when you thoroughly enjoyed poetry: nursery rhymes, ball-game rhythms, jump-rope patterns. Probably you had no idea of the meaning of the words ("Little Miss Muffet sat on a tuffet..." a tuffet?!) but you responded to the sound, the pattern. As adults we read poetry for that sense of sound and pattern. With more experience at reading poetry there is an added sense of pleasure as techniques are recognized: alliteration, onomatopoeia; forms of poetry become obvious—the sonnet, the rondelle. Even greater enjoyment comes from watching a poet's development, tracing themes and ideas, analyzing maturity in growth of imagery, use of rhythm.

To the novice reader of poetry, a poem can speak to the reader at a particular time and become an experience in itself. A freshman's experience after her mother's death exemplifies this. Shortly after the death, the student found Elizabeth Jennings' poem "Happy Families." Using the familiar names of the cards, Mrs. Beef and Master Bun, the poet describes how strangers try to help the family carry on their lives normally although one of the "happy family" is "missing." The card game continues even though no one wants it to. At the end the players go back to their individual rooms and give way to their individual grief. The student described the relief at knowing that someone else had obviously experienced her situation where everyone in the family was putting up a front, strangers were being very kind, and a general emptiness prevailed because of that one missing family member. The poem satisfied. The student saw death through another's eyes; the experience was almost the same, yet helped the reader to reevaluate, to view a universal human response to grief as well as encourage her to deal with her own.

On reading a poem the brain works on several different levels: it responds to the sounds; it responds to the words themselves and their connotations; it responds to the emotions; it responds to the insights or learning of the world being revealed. For such a process poetry is a very good training ground—a boot camp—for learning how to read literature in general. All the other genres have elements of poetry within them. Learn to read poetry well and you will be a more accomplished reader, even of car manuals! Perhaps the best response to reading poetry comes from a poet herself, Emily Dickinson, who claimed that reading a book of poetry made her feel "as if the top of [her] head were taken off!"

Before such a process happens to you, here are some tips for reading poetry before and during the examination.

TIPS FOR PREPARATION

1) Make a list of poets and poems you remember; analyze poems you liked, disliked, loved, hated, and were indifferent to. Find the poems. Reread them and for each one analyze your *feelings*, first of all, about the poetry itself. Have your feelings changed? Now what do you like or hate? Then paraphrase the *meaning* of each poem. Notice how the "magic" goes from the poem, i.e., "To Daffodils"—the poet sees many daffodils by the side of a lake and then thinks how the sight of them later comforts him.

2) Choose a poem at random from an anthology or one mentioned in this introduction. Read it a couple of times, preferably aloud, because the speaking voice will automatically grasp the rhythm and that will help the meaning. Do not become bogged down in individual word connotation or the meaning of the poem—let the poetry do its "work" on you; absorb the poem as a whole jigsaw puzzle.

3) Now take the puzzle apart. Look carefully at the title. Sometimes a straightforward title helps you focus. Sometimes a playful title helps you get an angle on the meaning. "Happy Families," of course, is an ironic title because the family playing the card game of that name is not happy.

4) Look carefully at the punctuation. Does the sense of a line carry from one to another? Does a particular mark of punctuation strike you as odd? Ask why that mark was used.

5) Look carefully at the words. Try to find the meaning of words with which you are not familiar within the context. Familiar words may be used differently: ask why that particular use. Having tapped into your memory bank of vocabulary and you are still at a loss, go to a dictionary. Once you have the *denotation* of the word, start wondering about the *connotation*. Put yourself in the poet's position and think why that word was used.

6) Look carefully at all the techniques being used. You will gain these as you progress through this section and through the test preparation. As soon as you come across a new idea—"caesura" perhaps—learn the word, see how it applies to poetry, where it is used. Be on the lookout for it in other poetry. Ask yourself questions such as why the poet used alliteration here; why the rhythm changes there; why the poet uses a sonnet form and which sonnet form is in use. Forcing yourself to ask the WHY questions, and answering them, will train the brain to read more perceptively. Poetry is not accidental; poets are deliberate people; they do things for specific reasons. Your task under a learning situation is to discover WHY.

7) Look carefully at the speaker. Is the poet using another persona? Who is that persona? What is revealed about the speaker? Why use that particular voice?

8) Start putting all the pieces of the puzzle together. The rhythm helps the meaning. The word choice helps the imagery. The imagery adds to the meaning. Paraphrase the meaning. Ask yourself simple questions: What is the poet saying? How can I relate to what is being said? What does this poem mean to me? What does this poem contribute to human experience?

9) Find time to read about the great names in poetry. Locate people within time areas and analyze what those times entailed. For example, the Elizabethans saw a contest between secular love and love of God. The Romantics (Wordsworth, Coleridge, Keats, Shelley, Byron) loved nature and saw God within nature. The Victorians (Tennyson, Blake) saw nature as a threat to mankind and God, being replaced by the profit cash-nexus of the Industrial Age. The moderns (T. S. Eliot, Pound, Yeats) see God as dead and man as hollow, unwanted, and unsafe in an alien world. The Post-Moderns see life as "an accident," a comic/cosmic joke, fragmented, purposeless—often their topics will be political: apartheid, abortion, unjust imprisonment.

10) Write a poem of your own. Choose a particular style; use the sonnet form; parody a famous poem; express yourself in free verse on a crucial, personal aspect of your life. Then analyze your own poetry with the above ideas.

TIPS FOR TEST-TAKING

You will have established a routine for reading poetry, but when you sit for the CLEP exam you will be under pressure, will have to work quickly, and will have no access to a dictionary. In the CLEP testing center you cannot read aloud, but you can do the following:

1) Internalize the reading—hear the reading in your head. Read through the poem two or three times following the absorbing procedure.

2) If the title and poet are supplied, analyze the title as before and determine the era of the poetry. Often this pushes you toward the meaning.

3) Look carefully at the questions which should enable you to "tap into" your learning process. Answer the ones that are immediately clear to you: form, technique, language perhaps.

4) Go back for another reading for those questions that challenge you—theme or meaning perhaps—analyze the speaker or the voice at work— paraphrase the meaning— ask the simple question, "What is the poet saying?"

5) If a question asks you about a specific line, metaphor, opening, or closing lines, mentally highlight or underline them to force your awareness of each crucial word. Internalize another reading emphasizing the highlighted area—analyze again the options you have for your answers.

6) Do not waste time on an answer that eludes you. Move onto another section and let the poetry do its "work." Very often the brain will continue working on the problem on another level of consciousness. When you go back to the difficult question, it may well become clear.

7) If you still are not sure of the answer, choose the option that you *think* is the closest to correct.

VERSE AND METER

Verse

As children reading or learning poetry in school, we referred to each section of a poem as a verse. We complained we had ten verses to learn for homework. In fact the word **verse** strictly refers to a line of poetry, perhaps from the original Latin word "versus": a row or a line, and the notion of turning, "vertere," to turn or move to a new idea. In modern use we refer to poetry often as "verse" with the connotation of rhyme, rhythm, and meter; but we still recognize verse because of the positioning of lines on the page, the breaking of lines that distinguish verse from prose.

The verses we learned for homework are in fact known as **stanzas**: a grouping of lines with a metrical order and often a repeated rhyme which we know as the **rhyme scheme**. Such a scheme is shown by letters to show the repeating sounds. Byron's "Stanzas" will help you recall the word, see the use of a definite rhyme, and how to mark it:

"Stanzas"

(When a man hath no freedom to fight for at home)

When a man hath no freedom to fight for at home,	*a*
Let him combat for that of his neighbors;	*b*
Let him think of the glories of Greece and of Rome,	*a*
And get knocked on the head for his labors.	*b*
To do good to mankind is the chivalrous plan,	*c*
And is always as nobly requited;	*d*
Then battle for freedom wherever you can,	*c*
And, if not shot or hanged, you'll get knighted.	*d*

The rhyme scheme is simple: *abab* and your first question should be "Why such a simple, almost sing-song rhyme?" The simplicity reinforces the **tone** of the poem: sarcastic, cryptic, cynical. There is almost a sneer behind the words "And get knocked on the head for his labors." It is as if the poet sets out to give a lecture or at least a homily along the lines of: "Neither a lender nor a borrower be," but then undercuts the seriousness. The **irony** of the poem rests in the fact that Byron joined a freedom fighting group in Greece and died, not gloriously, but of a fever. We shall return to this poem for further discussion.

Forms of Rhymes

Certain types of rhyme are worth learning. The most common is the end rhyme, which has the rhyming word at the end of the line, bringing the line to a definite stop but setting up for a rhyming word in another line later on, as in "Stanzas": home… Rome, a perfect rhyme. **Internal rhyme** includes at least one rhyming word within the line, often for the purpose of speeding the rhythm or making it linger. Look at the effect of Byron's internal rhymes mixed with half-rhymes: "combat… for that"; "Can/And… hanged" slowing the rhythm, making the reader dwell on the harsh long "a" sound, prolonging the sneer which almost becomes a snarl of anger. **Slant rhyme**, sometimes referred to as half, off, near, or approximate rhyme, often jolts a reader who expects a perfect rhyme; poets thus use such a rhyme to express disappointment or a deliberate let-down. **Masculine rhyme** uses one-syllable words or stresses the final syllable of polysyllabic words, giving the feeling of strength and impact. **Feminine rhyme** uses a rhyme of two or more syllables, the stress not falling upon the last syllable, giving a feeling of softness and lightness; one can see that these terms for rhyme were written in a less enlightened age! The terms themselves for the rhymes are less important than realizing or at least appreciating the effects of the rhymes.

If the lines from "Stanzas" had been unrhymed and varying in metrical pattern, the verse would have been termed **free**, or to use the French term, *"Vers libre,"* not to be confused with **blank verse**, which is also unrhymed but has a strict rhythm. The Elizabethan poets Wyatt and Surrey introduced blank verse, which Shakespeare uses to such good effect in his plays, and later, Milton in the great English epic *Paradise Lost*. Free verse has become associated with "modern" poetry, often adding to its so-called obscurity because without rhyme and rhythm, poets often resort to complicated syntactical patterns, repeated phrases, awkward cadences, and parallelism. Robert Frost preferred not to use it because, as he put it, "Writing free verse is like playing tennis with the net down," suggesting that free verse is easier than rhymed and metrical. However, if you have ever tried writing such verse, you will know the problems. (Perhaps a good exercise after you learn about meter is to write some "free" verse.) T. S. Eliot, who uses the form most effectively in "The Journey of the Magi," claimed that no *"vers"* is *"libre"* for the poet who wanted to do a good job.

Meter

Such a claim for the artistry and hard work behind a poem introduces perhaps the most difficult of the skills for a poet to practice and a reader to learn: meter. This time the Greeks provide the meaning of the word from *"metron,"* meaning measure. **Meter** simply means the pattern or measure of stressed or accented words within a line of verse. When studying meter a student should note where stresses fall on syllables—that is why reading aloud is so important, because it catches the natural rhythm of the speaking voice—and if an absence of stressed syllables occurs there is always an explanation why. We "expect" stressed and unstressed syllables because that is what we use in everyday speech. We may stress one syllable over another for a certain effect, often using the definite article "THE well known author..." or the preposition "Get OUT of here!" Usually, however, we use a rising and falling rhythm, known as **iambic rhythm**. A line of poetry that alternates stressed and unstressed syllables is said to have **iambic meter**. A line of poetry with ten syllables of rising and falling stresses is known as **iambic pentameter**, best used by Shakespeare and Milton in their blank verse. The basic measuring unit in a line of poetry is called a **foot**. An **iambic foot** has one unstressed syllable followed by a stressed marked by u. Pentameter means "five-measure." Therefore, **iambic pentameter** has five groups of two syllables, or ten beats, to the line. Read aloud the second and fourth, sixth and eighth lines of "Stanzas," tapping the beat on your desk or your palm, and the ten beat becomes obvious. Read again with the stresses unstressed and stressed (or soft and loud, short or long, depending on what terminology works for you) and the iambic foot becomes clear.

Tapping out the other alternate lines in this poem you will not find ten beats but twelve. The term for this line is hexameter, or six feet, rather than five. Other line-length names worth learning are:

monometer	one foot	**dimeter**	two feet
trimeter	three feet	**tetrameter**	four feet
heptameter	seven feet	**octameter**	eight feet

Other foot names worth learning are:

the **anapest** marked u u /, the most famous anapestic line being:

u u / u u / u u / u u /

"Twas the night before Christmas, when all through the house…"

the **trochee**, marked / u, the most memorable trochaic line being:

/ u / u / u / u

"Double double toil and trouble…"

and the **dactyl** marked / u u, the most often quoted dactylic line being:

/ u u / u u

"Take her up tenderly…"

Accentual Meter

Old English poetry employs a meter known as **accentual meter**, with four stresses to the line without attention to the unstressed syllables. Contemporary poets tend not to use it, but one of the greatest innovators in rhythm and meter, Gerard Manley Hopkins, used it as the "base line" for his counterpointed "Sprung Rhythm." Living in the nineteenth century, Hopkins produced poetry that even today strikes the reader as "modern," in that the rhymes and rhythms often jar the ear, providing stressed syllables where we expect unstressed and vice versa. The rhythm was measured by feet of from one to four syllables, and any number of unstressed syllables. Underneath the rhythm we hear the "regular" rhythm we are used to in speech, and an intriguing counterpoint develops. One stanza from "The Caged Skylark" will show the method at work:

> As a dare-gale skylark scanted in a dull cage
> Man's mounting spirit in his bone-house, mean house, dwells—
> That bird beyond the remembering his free fells;
> This in drudgery, day-labouring-out life's age.

The stress on "That" and "This" works particularly well to draw attention to the two captives: the skylark and Man. The accentual meter in the second line reinforces the wretchedness of the human condition. No reader could possibly read that line quickly, nor fail to put the full length of the syllable on "dwells." The dash further stresses the length and the low pitch of the last word.

If at first the terms for meter are new and strange, remember that what is most important is not that you mindlessly memorize the terminology but are able to recognize the meter and analyze why the poet has used it in the particular context of the poem. For example, Shakespeare did not want the lyrical fall and rise of the iamb for his witches around the cauldron, so he employs the much more unusual trochee to suggest the gloom and mystery of the heath in "Macbeth."

Many poets will "mix and match" their meter and your task as a student of poetry is to analyze why. Perhaps the poet sets up the regular greeting card meter, rising and falling rhythm, regular end-stopped rhyme. If the poet abruptly changes that pattern, there is a reason. If the poet subtly moves from a disruptive meter into a smooth one, then analyze what is going on in the meaning. If the poet is doing "a good job" as T. S. Eliot suggested, then the rhyme, rhythm, and meter should all work together in harmony to make the poem an integral whole. Answer the test essay questions to practice the points in this section and the integrity of a poem as a single unit will become clearer.

FIGURATIVE LANGUAGE AND POETIC DEVICES

It will start becoming ever more obvious that a poem is not created from mere inspiration. No doubt the initial movement for a poem has something of divine intervention: the ancients talked of being visited by the Muse of Poetry; James Joyce coined the word "epiphany" for the clear moment of power of conception in literature, but then the poet sets to working at the expression to make it the best it can be.

Perhaps what most distinguishes poetry from any other genre is the use of figurative language—figures of speech—used through the ages to convey the poet's own particular world-view in a unique way. Words have **connotation** and **denotation**, **figurative** and **literal** meanings. We can look in the dictionary for denotation and literal meaning, but figurative language works its own peculiar magic, tapping into shared experiences within the psyche. A simple example involves the word "home." If we free-associated for awhile among a group of 20 students, we would find a number of connotations for the word, depending on what the idea of "home" represented for us in our experiences: comforting, scary, lonely, dark, creepy, safety, haven, hell…. However, the denotation is quite straightforward: a house or apartment or dwelling that provides shelter for an individual or family. Poets include in their skill various figures of speech to "plug into" the reader's experiences, to prompt the reader to say "I would have never thought of it in those terms but now I see!"

Metaphors and Similes

The most important of these skills is perhaps the **metaphor**, which compares two unlike things, feelings, or objects, and the **simile**. Metaphors are more difficult to find than **similes**, which also compare two dissimilar things but always use the words "as if" (for a clause) or "like" (for a word or phrase). Metaphors suggest the comparison; the meaning is implicit. An easy way to distinguish between the two is the simple example of the camel. **Metaphor**: the camel is the ship of the desert. **Simile**: a camel is like a ship in the desert. Both conjure up the camel's almost sliding across the desert, storing up its water as a ship must do for survival for its passengers, and the notion of the vastness of the desert parallels the sea. The metaphor somehow crystallizes the image. Metaphors can be *extended* so that an entire poem consists of a metaphor, or unfortunately they can be *mixed*. The latter rarely happens in poetry unless the poet is deliberately playing with his readers and provoking humor.

Start thinking of how many times you use similes in your own writing or speech. The secret is, as Isaac Babel once said, that similes must be "as precise as a slide rule and as natural as the smell of dill." The precision and naturalness coming together perfectly often set up an equation of comparison. A student once wrote, "I felt torn apart by my loyalty to my mother and grandmother, like the turkey wishbone at Thanksgiving." We have all experienced divided loyalties. Using the graphic wishbone-tearing idea, something we have all done or have seen done at Thanksgiving lets us more easily relate to the student's experience. Another student wrote of his friends waiting for the gym class to begin "like so many captive gazelles." Again, the visual point of comparison is important but also the sense of freedom in the idea of gazelle, the speed, the grace; juxtaposing that freedom with the word "captive" is a master stroke that makes a simile striking.

The same student went on to an *extended simile* to state precisely and naturally his feelings upon going into a fistfight: "I was like the kid whose parents were killed by the crooked sheriff, waiting for high noon and the showdown that would pit a scared kid with his father's rusty old pistol against the gleaming steel of a matched pair, nestled in the black folds of the sheriff's holsters. I knew there was no way out. Surrounded by friends, I marched out into the brilliant sun, heading for the back fields of the playground, desperately trying to polish the rusty old gun." Although this student was writing in prose, his use of figurative language is poetic. He plugs into readers' movie experience with the central idea of the showdown at high noon, an **allusion** that involves the reader on the same plane as the writer. The notion of the black holster extends the allusion of the old cowboy films where the "baddies" wore black hats and rode black horses. The use of the word "nestled" provokes some interesting connotations of something soft and sweet like a kitten nestling into something. But then the gun is an implement of destruction and death; maybe "nestles" takes on the connotation of how a snake might curl in the sun at the base of a tree. The metaphor then ends with the child going out into the sun. The "rusty gun" in context of the essay was in fact the outmoded ideas and morals his father and old books had inculcated in him. All in all a very clever use of figurative language in prose. If the same concept had been pursued in poetry, the metaphor would have moved more speedily, more subtly—a poet cannot waste words—and of course would have employed line breaks, rhythm, and meter.

Personification

Personification is a much easier area than metaphor to detect in poetry. Usually the object that is being personified—referred to as a human with the personal pronoun sometimes, or possessing human attributes—is capitalized, as in this stanza from Thomas Gray's "Ode on a Distant Prospect of Eton College":

> Ambition this shall tempt to rise,
> Then whirl the wretch from high,
> o bitter Scorn a sacrifice,
> And grinning Infamy.
> The stings of Falsehood those shall try,
> And hard Unkindness' altered eye,

That mocks the tear it forced to flow;
And keen Remorse with blood defiled,
And moody Madness laughing wild
Amid severest woe.

As the poet watches the young Eton boys, he envisions what the years have to offer them, and the qualities he sees he gives human status. Thus, Ambition is not only capable of tempting, an amoral act, but also of "whirling," a physical act. Scorn is bitter, Infamy grinning, and so on. Coleridge employs a more visual personification in "The Rime of the Ancient Mariner," for the sun whom he describes as:

…the Sun (was) flecked with bars
(Heaven's Mother send us grace!)
As if through a dungeon-grate he peered
With broad and burning face.

More so than with Gray's more formal personification, Coleridge's supplies an image that is precise—we can see the prisoner behind the bars, and what's more this particular prisoner has a broad and burning face… of course because he is the sun! The personification brings us that flash of recognition when we can say "Yes, I see that!"

Image

The word **image** brings us to another important aspect of figurative language. Not a figure of speech in itself, the image plays a large role in poetry because the reader is expected to **imagine** what the poet is evoking, through the senses. The image can be **literal**, wherein the reader has little adjustment to make to see or touch or taste the image; a **figurative image** demands more from readers, almost as if they have to be inside the poet's imagination to understand the image. Very often this is where students of poetry, modern poetry particularly, find the greatest problems because the poetry of **imagism**, a term coined by Ezra Pound, is often intensely personal, delving into the mind of the poet for the comparison and connection with past memories that many readers cannot possibly share. Such an image is referred to as *free*, open to many interpretations. This concept suits the post-modern poet who feels that life is fragmented, open to multi-interpretations—there is no fixed order. Poets of the Elizabethan and Romantic eras saw the world as whole, steady, *fixed*, exactly the word used for their type of images. Readers of this poetry usually share the same response to the imagery. For example, the second stanza of Keats's "Ode to a Nightingale" sets up the taste imagery of a

draught of vintage that hath been
Cooled a long age in the deep-delvéd earth,
Tasting of Flora and the country green,
Dance, and Provençal song, and sunburnt mirth!
O for a beaker of the warm South,
Full of the true, the blushful Hippocrene,

> With beaded bubbles winking at the brim,
> And purple-stainéd mouth;

Even though Flora and Hippocrene are not names we are readily familiar with, the image of the cool wine, the taste, the look, the feeling evoked of the South and warmth, all come rushing into our minds as we enter the poet's imagination and find images in common.

Blake's imagery in "London" works in a similar way but as readers we have to probe a little harder, especially for the last line of the last stanza:

> But, most thro' midnight streets I hear
> How the youthful Harlot's curse
> Blasts the new-born Infant's tear,
> And blights with plagues the Marriage hearse.

Notice how the "Marriage hearse" immediately sets up a double image. Marriage we associate with happiness and joy; hearse we associate with death and sorrow. The image is troubling. We go back to the previous lines. The harlot curses her newborn—the curse of venereal disease. She also foresees that the child ultimately will wed and carry the disease into marriage. Does marriage then becomes death? The image is intriguing and open to interpretation.

Symbol

Image in figurative language inevitably leads to **symbol**. When an object, an image, or a feeling takes on a larger meaning outside of itself, then a poet is employing a symbol, something which stands for something greater. Because mankind has used symbols for so long, many have become **stock** or **conventional**: the rose standing for love; the flag standing for patriotism, love of one's country (thus the controversy over flag-burning today); the color yellow standing for corruption (hence Gatsby's Daisy Buchanan—the white-dressed virginal lady with the center core of careless-ness); the bird for freedom; the sea for eternity; the cross for suffering and sacrifice. If you are not versed in the Christian tradition, it might be useful to read its symbols because the older poetry dwells on the church and the trials of loving God and loving Woman—the latter also has become a symbol deteriorating over the ages from Eve to the Madonna to Whore.

If the symbol is not conventional, then it may carry with it many interpretations, depending on the reader's insight. Some students "get carried away" with symbolism, seeing more in the words than the poets do! If the poet is "doing a good job," the poetry will steer you in the "right" direction of symbolism. Sometimes we are unable to say what "stands for" what, but simply that the symbol evokes a mood; it suggests an idea to you that is difficult to explain. The best way to approach symbolism is to understand a literal meaning first and then shift the focus, as with a dif-ferent camera lens, and see if the poet is saying something even more meaningful. Blake again supplies an interesting example. In his poem "The Chimney Sweeper" he describes the young child's dream of being locked up in "coffins of black." Literally, of course, coffins are brown wood; the color of mourning is black. Shift the focus then to the young child chimney sweeper, so young he can barely lisp the street cry "Sweep" so it comes out "'weep! 'weep! 'weep! 'weep!" (a symbolic line in itself). Your reading of the Industrial Age's cruelty to children who were exploited as cheap, plentiful, and an expendable labor force will perhaps have taught you that children were used as chimney brushes—literally thrust up the thin black chimneys of Victorian houses and factories, where very often they became trapped, suffocated, sometimes burned to death if fires were set by unknowing owners. Now the black coffins stand for the black-with-soot chimneys the little children had to sweep, chimneys which sometimes became their coffins. The realization of the symbol brings a certain horror to the poem. In the dream an Angel releases the children who then run down "a green plain leaping, laughing.../And wash in a river, and shine in the sun." The action is of course symbolic in that in real life the children's movements were restricted, living in monstrous cities where green plains would be enjoyed only by the rich, and totally limited by the size of the chimneys. They were always black with soot. They rarely saw the sun, never mind shone in it! Again, the symbolism adds something to the poem. In many students there have been reactions of tears and anger when they *see* the symbolism behind such simple lines.

Allusion

The idea of reading about the Industrial Age brings us to an important part of figurative language, briefly mentioned before: **allusion**. Poets tap into previous areas of experience to relate their insights, to draw their readers into shared experiences. Remember how the student writer alluded to old cowboy movies, the classic "high noon." Poets will refer to history, myth, other older poems, plays, music, heroes, famous people. Allusion is becoming more and more difficult for the modern student because reading is becoming more and more a lost art. Core courses in schools have become hotbeds of controversy about what students should know. Fortunately, modern poets are shifting their allusions so that contemporary readers can appreciate and join in with their background of knowledge. However, be aware that for the examination in poetry it will be useful to have a working knowledge of the traditional canon of literature. Think of areas of history that were landmarks: the burning of Carthage; Hannibal's elephants; Caesar's greatness; Alexander the Great; the First World War and its carnage of young men; the Second World War and the Holocaust. Think of the great Greek and Roman myths: the giving of fire to the world; the entrance of sin into the world; the labyrinth; the names associated with certain myths (Daedalus, Hercules, the Medusa). You may never have a question on the areas you read but your background for well-rounded college study will already be formulated.

Alliteration: the repetition of consonants at the beginning of words that are next to each other or close by. The Hopkins stanza quoted earlier provides some fine examples: "<u>sk</u>ylark <u>sc</u>anted"; "<u>M</u>an's <u>m</u>ounting... <u>m</u>ean house"; "<u>f</u>ree <u>f</u>ells"; "<u>d</u>rudgery, <u>d</u>ay-<u>l</u>abouring-out <u>l</u>ife's age." Always try to understand the reason for the alliteration. Does it speed or slow the rhythm? Is it there for emphasis? What does the poet want you to focus on?

Apostrophe: the direct address of someone or something that is not present. Many odes begin this way. Consider Keats's "Ode on a Grecian Urn," for example: "Thou still unravished bride of quietness," and "Ode to Psyche": "O Goddess! hear these tuneless numbers."

Assonance: the repetition of vowel sounds usually internally rather than initially. "Her goodly eyes like sapphires shining bright." Here the poet, Spenser, wants the entire focus on the blue eyes, the crispness, and the light.

Bathos: deliberate anticlimax to make a definite point or draw attention to a falseness. The most famous example is from Pope's "Rape of the Lock": "Here thou, great Anna! whom three realms obey, /Dost sometimes counsel take—and sometimes tea."

The humor in the bathos is the fact that Anna is the Queen of England—she holds meetings in the room Pope describes but also indulges in the venerable English custom of afternoon tea. The fact that tea should rhyme with obey doubles the humor as the elongated vowel of the upper-class laconic English social group is also mocked.

Caesura: the pause, marked by punctuation (/) or not within the line. Sometimes the caesura (sometimes spelled cesura) comes at an unexpected point in the rhythm and gives the reader pause for thought.

Conceits: very elaborate comparisons between unlikely objects. The metaphysical poets such as John Donne were criticized for "yoking" together outrageous terms, describing lovers in terms of instruments, or death in terms of battle.

Consonance: similar to slant rhyme—the repetition of consonant sounds without the vowel sound repeated. Hopkins again frequently uses this as in "Pied Beauty": "All things counter, original, spare, strange;… adazzle, dim."

Diction: the word for word choice. Is the poet using formal or informal language? Does the poetry hinge on slang or a dialect? If so what is the purpose? Are the words "highfalutin" or lowbrow? As always, the diction needs examining and questions like these answering.

Enjambment: the running-on of one line of poetry into another. Usually the end of lines are rhymed so there is an end-stop. In more modern poetry, without rhyme, poets often use run-on lines to give a speedier flow, the sound of the speaking voice or a conversational tone.

Hyperbole: is an obvious and intentional exaggeration. Donne's instruction to the woman he is trying to seduce not to kill the flea, by contrasting her reluctance with "a marriage" of blood within a flea, reinforces the hyperbole used throughout the poem:

> Oh stay, three lives in one flea spare,
> Where we almost, yea, more than married are.

This couplet is also a good example of an unexpected caesura for emphasis at the second pause.

Irony: plays an important role in voice or tone, inferring a discrepancy between what is said and what is meant. A famous example is Shelley's "Ozymandias," which tells of the great ruler who thought that he and his name would last forever, but the traveller describes the huge statue in ruins with the inscription speaking truer than the ruler intended: "My name is Ozymandias, king of kings: /Look on my works, ye Mighty, and despair!"

Metonymy: a figure of speech in which a term is used to evoke or stand for a related idea. Example: "The pen is mightier than the sword." <u>Pen</u> and <u>sword</u> are metonymical designations for (the artful use of) words and (engagement in) physical battle.

Onomatopoeia: a device in which the word captures the sound. In many poems the words are those in general use: the whiz of fireworks; the crashing of waves on the shore; the booming of water in an underground seacave.

Oxymoron: a rhetorical device of epigrammatic form in which incongruous or contradictory terms are conjoined. Examples: "painful pleasure," "sweet sorrow."

Paradox: a situation, action, or statement that appears to be contradictory but that nevertheless holds true.

Pun: a play on words often for humorous or sarcastic effect. The Elizabethans were very fond of them; many of Shakespeare's comedies come from punning. Much of Donne's sexual taunting involves the use of the pun.

Sarcasm: when verbal irony is too harsh, it moves into the sarcastic realm. It is the "lowest form of wit" of course but can be used to good effect in the tone of a poem. Browning's dramatic monologues make excellent use of the device.

Synecdoche: when a part of an object is used to represent the entire thing or vice versa. When we ask someone to give us a hand, we would be horrified if they cut off their hand; what we want is the person's help, from all of the body!

Syntax: the ordering of words into a particular pattern. If a poet shifts words from the usual word order, you know you are dealing with an older style of poetry (Shakespeare, Milton) or a poet who wants to shift emphasis onto a particular word.

Tone: the voice or attitude of the speaker. Remember that the voice need not be that of the poet's. He or she may be adopting a particular tone for a purpose. Your task is to analyze if the tone is angry, sad, conversational, abrupt, wheedling, cynical, affected, satiric, etc. Is the poet including you in a cozy way by using "you," or is he accusing "you" of what he is criticizing? Is the poet keeping you at a distance with coldness and third person pronouns. If so, why? The most intriguing of voices is Browning's in his **dramatic monologues**: poems that address another person who remains silent. Browning brought this type of poetry to an art. Think of all the variations of voices and attitudes and be prepared to meet them in poetry.

TYPES OF POETRY

Having begun to grasp that poetry contains a great deal more than what initially meets the eye, you should now start thinking about the various types of poetry. Of course, when reading for pleasure, it is not vital to recognize that the poem in hand is a sonnet or a villanelle, but for the exam you may well be asked to determine what sort of poem is under scrutiny. Knowing the form of poem may dictate certain areas of rhyme or meter and may enhance the meaning.

Form

The pattern or design of a poem is known as **form**, and even the strangest, most experimental poetry will have some type of form to it. Allen Ginsberg's "A Supermarket in California" caused a stir because it didn't read like poetry, but on the page there is a certain form to it. Some poets even try to match the shape of the poem to the subject. Find in anthologies John Hollander's "Swan and Shadow" and Dorthi Charles' "Concrete Cat." Such visual poems are not just fun to look at and read but the form adds to the subject and helps the reader appreciate the poet's world view. **Closed form** will be immediately recognizable because lines can be counted and shape determined. The poet must keep to the recognized form, in number of lines, rhyme scheme, and/or meter. **Open form** developed from "vers libre," which name some poets objected to as it suggested that there was little skill or craft behind the poem, simply creativity, as the name suggests, gives a freedom of pattern to the poet.

Sonnets

The most easily recognized closed form of poetry is the **sonnet**, sometimes referred to as a **fixed form**. The sonnet always has 14 lines, but there are two types of sonnets, the Petrarchan (or Italian), and the Shakespearean (or English). The word sonnet in fact comes from the Italian word "sonnetto" meaning a "little song." Petrarch, the fourteenth century Italian poet, took the form to its peak with his sonnets to his loved one, Laura. This woman died before he could even declare his love, and such poignant, unrequited love became the theme for many Elizabethan sonnets. As a young man might telephone a young woman for a date in today's society, the Elizabethan would send a sonnet. The Petrarchan sonnet is organized into two groups: eight lines and six—the **octave** and the **sestet**. Usually the rhyme scheme is abbaabba-cdecde, but the sestet can vary in its pattern. The octave may set up a problem or a proposition, and then the answer or resolution follows in the sestet after a turn or a shift. The Shakespearean sonnet organizes the lines into three groups of four lines: **quatrains** and a **couplet** (two rhyming lines). The rhyming scheme is always abab cdcd efef gg, and the turn or shift can happen at one of three places or leave the resolution or a "twist in the tail" at the end.

Couplets

The couplet, mentioned earlier, leads us to a closed form of poetry that is very useful for the poet. It is a two-line stanza that usually rhymes with an end rhyme. If the couplet is firmly end-stopped and written in iambic pentameter, it is known as an **heroic couplet**, after the use was made of it in the English translations of the great classical or heroic epics such as *The Iliad* and *The Odyssey*. Alexander Pope became a master of the heroic couplet, sometimes varying to the 12-syllable line from the old French poetry on Alexander the Great. The line became known as the **Alexandrine**. Pope gained fame first as a translator of the epics and then went on to write **mock-heroic** poems like "The Rape of the Lock," written totally in heroic couplets which never become monotonous, as a succession of regularly stepped-out couplets can, because he varied the place of the caesura and masterfully employed enjambment.

Epics

Rarely in an exam will you be presented with an **epic** because part of the definition of the word is vastness of size and range. You may, however, be confronted with an excerpt and will need to recognize the structure. The translation will usually be in couplets and the meter regular with equal line lengths, because originally these poems were sung aloud or chanted to the beat of drums. Because of their oral quality, repetition plays an important part, so that if the bard, or singer, forgot the line, the audience, who had heard the stories many times before, could help him out. The subject deals with great deeds of heroes: Odysseus (Ulysses), Hector, and Aeneus, their adventures and their trials; the theme will be of human grief or pride, divided loyalties—but all "writ large." The one great English epic, *Paradise Lost*, is written by Milton and deals with the story of Adam and Eve and the Fall. Adam thus becomes the great hero. The huge battle scenes of *The Iliad* are emulated in the War of the Heavens when Satan and his crew are expelled into Hell; the divided loyalties occur when Adam must choose between obedience to God and love for his wife.

Ballads

On much simpler lines are the **ballads**, sometimes the earliest poems we learn as children. Folk or popular ballads were first sung as early as the fifteenth century and then handed down through generations until finally written down. Usually the ballads are anonymous and simple in theme, having been composed by working folk who originally could not read or write. The stories—a ballad is a story in a song—revolve around love and hate and lust and murder, often rejected lovers, knights, and the supernatural. As with the epic, and for the same reason, repetition plays a strong part in the ballad and often a repeated refrain holds the entire poem together. The form gave rise to the **ballad stanza**, four lines rhyming *abcb* with lines 1 and 3 having eight syllables and lines 2 and 4 having six. Poets who later wrote what are known as **literary ballads** kept the same pattern. Read Coleridge's "The Rime of the Ancient Mariner" and all the elements of the ballad come together as he reconstructs the old folk story but writes it in a very closed form.

Lyrics

The earlier poetry dealt with narrative. The "father of English poetry," Geoffrey Chaucer, told stories within a story for the great *Canterbury Tales*. The Elizabethans turned to love and the humanistic battle between love of the world and love of God. Wordsworth and Coleridge marked a turning point by not only using "the language of men" in poetry but also by moving away from the narrative poem to the **lyric**. The word comes again from the Greek, meaning a story told with the poet playing upon a lyre. Wordsworth moves from story to emotion, often "emotion recollected in tranquillity" as we saw in "Daffodils." Although sometimes a listener is inferred, very often the poet seems to be musing aloud.

Part of the lyric "family" is the **elegy**, a lament for someone's death or the passing of a love or concept. The most famous is Thomas Gray's "Elegy Written in a Country Churchyard," which mourns not only the passing of individuals but of a past age and the wasted potential within every human being, no matter how humble. Often **ode** and elegy become synonymous, but an ode, also part of the lyric family, is usually longer, dealing with more profound areas of human life than simply death. Keats's odes are perhaps the most famous and most beloved in English poetry.

Specialized Types of Poetry

More specialized types of poetry need mentioning so that you may recognize and be able to explicate how the structure of the poem enhances the meaning or theme. For example the **villanelle**: a courtly love poem structure from medieval times, built on five three-line stanzas known as **tercets**, with the rhyme scheme aba, followed by a four-line stanza, and a **quatrain** which ends the poem abaa. As if this were not pattern and order enough, the poem's first line appears again as the last line of the 2nd and 4th tercets; *and* the third line appears again in the last line of the 3rd and 5th tercets; *and* these two lines appear again as rhyming lines at the end of the poem! The most famous and arguably the best villanelle, as some of the older ones can be so stiff in their pattern that the meaning is inconsequential, is Dylan Thomas's "Do not go gentle into that good night." The poem stands on its own with a magisterial meaning of mankind raging against death, but when one appreciates the structure also, the rage is even more emphatic because it is so controlled. A poem well worth finding for "reading for pleasure." In James Joyce's *A Portrait of the Artist as a Young Man*, writing a villanelle on an empty cigarette packet turns the young boy, Stephen Dedalus, dreaming of being an artist, into a poet, a "real" artist.

Said to be the most difficult of all closed forms is the **sestina**, also French, sung by medieval troubadours, a "song of sixes." The poet presents six six-line stanzas, with six end-words in a certain order, then repeats those six repeated words in any order in a closing tercet. Find Elizabeth Bishop's "Sestina" or W.H. Auden's "Hearing of Harvests Rotting in the Valleys" and the idea of six images running through the poet's head and being skillfully repeated comes across very clearly. You might even try working out a sestina for yourself.

Perhaps at this stage an **epigram** might be more to your liking and time scale because it is short, even abrupt, a little cynical and always to the point. The cynical Alexander Pope mastered the epigram, as did Oscar Wilde centuries later. Perhaps at some stage we have all written **doggerel**, rhyming poetry that becomes horribly distorted to fit the rhymes, not through skill but the opposite. In contrast, **limericks** are very skilled: five lines using the anapest meter with the rhyme scheme: aabba. Unfortunately, they can deteriorate into types such as "There was a young lady from….," but in artful hands such as Shakespeare's (see Ophelia's mad song in *Hamlet*: "And will he not come again?") and Edward Lear's, limericks display fine poetry. Finally, if you are trying to learn all the different types of closed-form poetry, you might try an **aubade**—originally a song or piece of music sung or played at dawn—a poem written to the dawn or about lovers at dawn—the very time when poetic creation is extremely high!

Although the name might suggest open-form, **blank verse** is in fact closed-form poetry. As we saw earlier, lines written in blank verse are unrhymed and in iambic pentameter. Open-form poets can arrange words on the page in any order, not confined by any rhyme pattern or meter. Often it seems as if words have spilled onto the page at random with a direct address to the readers, as if the poets are cornering them in their room, or simply chatting over the kitchen table. The lines break at any point—the dash darts in and out—the poets are talking to the audience with all the "natural" breaks that the speaking voice will demonstrate. Open-form poets can employ rhyme, but sometimes it seems as if the rhyme has slipped into the poem quite easily—there is no wrenching of the word "to make it rhyme." Very often there is more internal rhyme as poets play with words, often giving the sensation they are thinking aloud. Open-form poetry is usually thought of as "modern," at least post-World War I, but the use of space on the page, the direct address of the voice, and the use of the dash clearly marks Emily Dickinson as an open-form poet, even though she lived from 1830–1886.

DRAMA AND THEATER

The Glass Menagerie by Tennessee Williams begins when one of its four characters, Tom, steps into the downstage light and addresses the audience directly as though he were the chorus from a much earlier play. "I have tricks in my pocket, I have things up my sleeve," says Tom. "But I am the opposite of a stage magician. He gives you illusion that has the appearance of truth. I give you truth in the pleasant disguise of illusion."

To sit among the audience and watch a skillful production of *The Glass Menagerie* is to visit Tom's paradoxical world of theater, a magic place in which known imposters and stagecraft trickery create a spectacle which we know is illusion but somehow recognize as truth. Theater, as a performed event, combines the talents and skills of numerous artists and craftspersons, but before the spectacle must come the playwright's work, the pages of words designating what the audience sees and hears. These words, the written script separate from the theatrical performance of them, is what we call *drama*, and the words give the spectacle its significance because without them the illusion has neither frame nor content. Truth requires boundaries and substance. When Shakespeare's Hamlet advises actors just before their performance, he places careful emphasis on the importance of the words, cautioning the players to speak them "trippingly on the tongue." If all actions are not suited to the words, Hamlet adds, the performance will fail because the collaborative purpose combining the dramatist's literary art and the actors' performing art "is to hold as 'twere the mirror up to Nature."

COMPARISON OF DRAMA TO PROSE AND POETRY

Although drama is literature written to be performed, it closely resembles the other genres. In fact, both poetry and prose also can be performed, but as captivating as these public readings sometimes are, only performed drama best creates the immediate living "illusion as truth" Tom promises. Like fiction and narrative poetry, drama tells a tale—that is, it has plot, characters, and setting—but the author's voice is distant, heard only through the stage directions and perhaps some supplementary notes. With rare exceptions, dialogue dominates the script. Some drama is poetry, such as the works of Shakespeare and Molière, and all plays resemble poems as abstractions because both forms are highly condensed, figurative expressions. Even in Henrik Ibsen's social realism, the dramatic action is metaphorical.

A scene set inside a house, for instance, requires a room with only three walls. No audience complains, just as no movie audience feels betrayed by film characters' appearing ridiculously large. Without a thought, audiences employ what Samuel Taylor Coleridge called "a willing suspension of disbelief"; in other words, they know that the images before them are not real but rather representations, reflections in the mirror of which Hamlet speaks, not the real world ("Nature").

A play contains conflict which can be enacted immediately on the stage without any alterations in the written word. **Enacted** means performed by an actor or actors free to use the entire stage and such theatrical devices as sets, costumes, makeup, special lighting, and props for support. This differs from the oral interpretation of prose or poetry. No matter how animated, the public reader is not acting. This is the primary distinction between drama and other literary forms. Their most obvious similarity is that any form of literature is a linguistic expression. There is, however, one other feature shared by all kinds of narratives: the pulsating energy which pushes the action along is generated by human imperfection. We speak of tragic characters as having "flaws," but the same is true about comic characters as well. Indeed, nothing is more boring either on a stage or in a written text than a consistently flawless personality, because such characters can never be congruent with the real people of our everyday experiences. The most fundamental human truth is human frailty.

Although it can be argued that a play, like a musical composition, must be performed to be realized, the script's linguistic foundation always gives the work potential as a literary experience. Moreover, there is never a "definitive" interpretation. The script, in a sense, remains unfinished because it never stops inviting new variations, and among those invited to participate are individual readers whose imaginations should not be discounted. For example, when *Death of a Salesman* was originally produced, Lee J. Cobb played Willy Loman. Aside from the character's age, Dustin Hoffman's Willy in a revival 40 years later bore hardly any physical resemblance to Cobb's. Yet both portrayals "worked." The same could be said about the Willys created by the minds of the play's countless readers. Quite capable of composing its own visions and sounds, the human imagination is the original mirror, the place where all human truths evolve from perceived data.

Mimesis

Hamlet's mirror and Tom's truthful illusions are figures of speech echoing drama's earliest great critic, Aristotle, who believed art should create a **mimesis**, the Greek word for "imitation." For centuries this "mimetic theory" has asserted that a successful imitation is one which reproduces natural objects and actions in as realistic portrayal as possible. Later, this notion of imitation adopted what has been called the "expressive theory," a variation allowing the artist a freer, more individual stylized approach. A drama by Ibsen, for example, attempts to capture experience as unadorned raw sense, the way it normally appears to be. This is realistic imitation. As twentieth century drama moved toward examinations of people's inner consciousness as universal representations of some greater human predicament, new expressive styles emerged. The diversity in the works of Eugene O'Neill, Samuel Beckett, and Harold Pinter illustrate how dramatists' imitations can disrupt our sense of the familiar as their plays become more personally expressive. But the theater of Aristotle's time was hardly "realistic" in today's objective sense. Instead, it was highly stylized and full of conventions derived from theater's ritualistic origins. The same is true of medieval morality plays and the rigid formality of Japanese Kabuki theater, yet these differ greatly from each other and from ancient Greek and Roman dramas. In other words, imitating "what's out there" requires only that the form be consistent with itself, and any form is permissible.

PLOT STRUCTURE

Exposition

As with other narrative types, a play's **plot** is its sequence of events, its organized collection of incidents. At one time it was thought that all the actions within a play should be contained within a single 24-hour period. Few lengthy plays have plots which cover only the period of time enacted on the stage. Most plays condense and edit time much as novels do. Decades can be reduced to two hours. Included in the plot is the **exposition,** the revealing of whatever information we need in order to understand the impending conflict. This exposed material should provide us with a sense of place and time (**setting**), the central participants, important prior incidents, and the play's overall mood. In some plays such as Shakespeare's, the exposition comes quickly. Notice, for instance, the opening scenes in *Macbeth, Hamlet,* and *Romeo and Juliet*: not one presents us with a central character, yet each—with its witches or king's ghost or street brawl—clearly establishes an essential tension heralding the main conflict to come. These initial expositions attack the audience immediately and are followed by subsequent events in chronological order. Sophocles' *Oedipus Rex* works somewhat differently, presenting the central character late in the myth from which the play is taken. The exposition must establish what has come previously, even for an audience familiar with the story, before the plot can advance. Like Shakespeare, Sophocles must start his exposition at the beginning, but he takes a longer (though not tedious) time revealing the essential facts. Arthur Miller, in his *Death of a Salesman*, continuously interrupts the central action with dislocated expositions from earlier times as though the past were always in the present. He carefully establishes character, place, mood, and conflict throughout the earliest scenes; however, whatever present he places on stage is always caught in a tension between the audience's anticipation of the future and its suspicions of the past. The plots in plays like *Oedipus Rex* and *Death of a Salesman* tend not to attack us head-on but rather to surround us and gradually close in, the circle made tighter by each deliberately released clue to a mysterious past.

Complication and Crisis

Conflict requires two opposing forces. We see, for instance, how King Lear's irresponsible abdication and conceited anger are countered by Goneril and Regan's duplicity and lusts for power. We also see how Creon's excessive means for restoring order in Thebes is met by Antigone's allegiance to personal conscience. Fairly soon in a play we must experience some incident that incites the fundamental conflict when placed against some previously presented incident or situation. In most plays the conflict's abrasive conditions continuously chafe and even lacerate each other. The play's tempo might provide some interruptions or variations in the pace; nevertheless, conflicts generate the actions which make the characters' worlds worse before they can get better. Any plot featuring only repetitious altercations, however, would soon become tiresome. Potentially, anything can happen in a conflict. The **complication** is whatever presents an element capable of altering the action's direction. Perhaps some new information is discovered or a previously conceived scheme fails, creating a reversal of what had been expected. The plot is not a series of similar events but rather a compilation of related events leading to a culmination, a **crisis**.

Resolution

In retrospect we should be able to accept a drama's progression of actions leading to the crisis as inevitable. After the crisis comes the **resolution** (or **denouement**), which gives the play its concluding boundary. This does not mean that the play should offer us solutions for whatever human issues it raises. Rather, the playwright's obligation is to make the experience he presents to us seem filled within its own perimeters. George Bernard Shaw felt he had met this obligation when he ended *Pygmalion* with his two principal characters, Higgins and Eliza, utterly incapable of voicing any romantic affection for each other; and the resolution in Ibsen's *A Doll's House* outraged audiences a hundred years ago and still disturbs some people today, even though it concludes the play with believable consequences.

Terms such as **exposition**, **complication**, **crisis**, and **resolution**, though helpful in identifying the conflict's currents and directions, at best only artificially define how a plot is molded. If the play provides unity in its revelations, these seams are barely noticeable. Moreover, any successful creative composition clearly shows that the artist accomplished much more than merely plugging components together to create a finished work. There are no rules which all playwrights must follow, except the central precept that the play's unified assortment of actions be complete and contained within itself. *Antigone*, for instance, depicts the third phase of Sophocles' *Oedipus* trilogy, although it was actually written and performed before *Oedipus Rex* and *Oedipus at Colonus*. And although a modern reader might require some background information before starting, *Antigone* gives a cohesive dramatic impact independent from the other two plays.

CHARACTER

Examples of Characters from Hamlet

Essential to the plot's success are the characters who participate in it. Midpoint in *Hamlet* when Elsinore Castle is visited by the traveling theater company, the prince joyously welcomes the players, but his mood quickly returns to bitter depression shortly after he asks one actor to recite a dramatic passage in which the speaker recalls the fall of Troy and particularly Queen Hecuba's response to her husband's brutal murder. The player, caught by the speech's emotional power, becomes distraught and cannot finish. Left alone on stage, Hamlet compares the theatrical world created by the player with Hamlet's "real" world and asks: "What's Hecuba to him, or he to Hecuba,/That he should weep for her!" Under ordinary circumstances Hamlet's anxiety would not overshadow his Renaissance sensibilities, because he knows well that fictional characters always possess the potential to move us. As though by instinct, we know the same. We read narratives and go to the theater precisely because we want to be shocked, delighted, thrilled, saddened, titillated, or invigorated by "a dream of passion." Even though some characters are more complex and interesting than others, they come in countless types as the playwright's delegates to our imaginations and as the imitations of reality seeking our response.

Examples of Characters from Antigone

Antigone begins with two characters, Antigone and Ismene, on stage. They initiate the exposition through their individual reactions to a previous event, King Creon's edict following the battle in which Thebes defeated an invading army. Creon has proclaimed Eteocles and the others who recently died defending Thebes as heroes worthy of the highest burial honors; in addition, Creon has forbidden anyone, on penalty of death, from burying Polyneices and the others who fell attacking the city. Since Antigone, Ismene, Polyneices, and Eteocles are the children of Oedipus and Iocaste, the late king and queen, conflict over Creon's law seems imminent. These first two characters establish this inevitability. They also reveal much about themselves as individuals.

ANTIGONE:... now you must prove what you are:
A true sister, or a traitor to your family.
ISMENE: Antigone, are you mad! What could I possibly do?

ANTIGONE: You must decide whether you will help me or not.

ISMENE: I do not understand you. Help you in what?

ANTIGONE: Ismene, I am going to bury him. Will you come?

ISMENE: Bury him! You have just said the new law forbids it.

ANTIGONE: He is my brother. And he is your brother, too.

ISMENE: But think of the danger! Think what Creon will do!

ANTIGONE: Creon is not strong enough to stand in my way.

ISMENE: Ah sister!
Oedipus died, everyone hating him
For what his own search brought to light, his eyes
Ripped out by his own hand; and Iocaste died,
His mother and wife at once: she twisted the cords
That strangled her life; and our two brothers died,
Each killed by the other's sword. And we are left:
But oh, Antigone,
Think how much more terrible than these
Our own death would be if we should go against Creon
And do what he has forbidden! We are only women,
We cannot fight with men, Antigone!
The law is strong, we must give in to the law
In this thing, and in worse. I beg the Dead
To forgive me, but I am helpless: I must yield
To those in authority. And I think it is dangerous business
To be always meddling.

ANTIGONE: If that is what you think,
I should not want you, even if you asked to come.
You have made your choice, you can be what you want to be.
But I will bury him; and if I must die,
I say that this crime is holy: I shall lie down
With him in death, and I shall be as dear
To him as he to me.
It is the dead,
Not the living, who make the longest demands:
We die for ever...
You may do as you like,
Since apparently, the laws of the gods mean nothing to you.

ISMENE: They mean a great deal to me; but I have no strength
To break laws that were made for the public good.

ANTIGONE: That must be your excuse, I suppose. But as for me,
I will bury the brother I love.

ISMENE: Antigone, I am so afraid for you!

ANTIGONE: You need not be:
You have yourself to consider, after all.

ISMENE: But no one must hear of this, you must tell no one!
I will keep it a secret, I promise!

ANTIGONE: Oh tell it! Tell everyone!
Think how they'll hate you when it all comes out
If they learn that you knew about it all the time!

ISMENE: So fiery! You should be cold with fear.

ANTIGONE: Perhaps. But I am doing only what I must.

ISMENE: But can you do it? I say that you cannot.

ANTIGONE: Very well: when my strength gives out, I shall do no more.

ISMENE: Impossible things should not be tried at all.

ANTIGONE: Go away, Ismene:
I shall be hating you soon, and the dead will too,
For your words are hateful. Leave me my foolish plan:
I am not afraid of the danger; if it means death,
It will not be the worst of deaths—death without honor.

ISMENE: Go then, if you feel that you must.
You are unwise,
But a loyal friend to those who love you.

[Exit into the palace. ANTIGONE goes off...]

READING THE PLAY

All we know about Antigone and Ismene in this scene comes from what they say; therefore, we read their spoken words carefully. However, we must also remain attentive to dramatic characters, propensity for not revealing all they know and feel about a given issue, and often characters do not recognize all the implications in what they say. We might be helped by what one says about the other, yet these observations are not necessarily accurate or sincere. Even though the previous scene contains fewer ambiguities than some others in dramatic literature, we would be oversimplifying to say the conflict here is between one character who is "right" and another who is "wrong." Antigone comes out challenging, determined and unafraid, whereas Ismene immediately reacts fearfully. Antigone brims with the self-assured power of righteousness while Ismene expresses vulnerability. Yet Antigone's boast that "Creon is not strong enough to stand in my way" suggests a rash temperament. We might admire her courage, but we question her judgment. Meanwhile, Ismene can evoke our sympathies with her burden of family woes, at least until she confesses her helplessness and begs the Dead to forgive her, at which point we realize her objections stem from cowardice and not conscience.

Although we might remain unsettled by Antigone's single-mindedness, we soon find ourselves sharing her disdain for Ismene's trepidation, particularly when Ismene rationalizes her position as the more responsible and labels unauthorized intervention in royal decisions as "meddling" against the "public good." Soon, as we realize the issue here demands moral conscience, we measure

Ismene far short of what is required. Quickly, though, Ismene is partly redeemed by her obvious concern for Antigone's well-being: "I am so afraid for you." Unaffected, Antigone retorts with sarcasm and threats, but her demeanor never becomes so impetuously caustic that we dismiss her as a conceited adolescent. In fact, we are touched by her integrity and devotion, seeing no pretensions when she says: "I am not afraid of the danger: if it means death,/It will not be the worst of deaths—death without honor." Ismene's intimation that loyalty and love are unwise counters Antigone's idealism enough to make us suspect that the stark, cruel world of human imperfection will not tolerate Antigone's solitary rebellion, no matter how selfless her motivation. At the same time we wonder how long Ismene could remain neutral if Antigone were to clash with Creon.

What immediately strikes us about Antigone and Ismene is that each possesses a sense of self, a conscious awareness about her existence and her connection with forces greater than herself. This is why we can identify with them. It may not always feel reassuring, yet we too can define our existence by saying "I am, and I am not alone." As social creatures, a condition about which they have had no choice, both Antigone and Ismene have senses of self which are touched by their identification with others: each belongs to a family, and each belongs to a civil state. Indeed, much of the play's conflict focuses on which identification should be stronger. Another connection influences them as well—the unbreakable tie to truth. This truth, or ultimate reality, will vary from play to play, and not all characters ever realize it is there, and few will define it the same way. Still, the universe which characters inhabit has definition, even if the resolution suggests a great human absurdity in our insufficient capacity to grasp this definition or, worse, asserts the only definition is the absence of an ultimate reality. With Antigone, we see how her sense of self cannot be severed from its bonds to family obligations and certain moral principles.

Theme

Characters with a sense of self and an identity framed by social connections and unmitigated truths dwell in all good narratives. As readers we wander within these connecting perimeters, following the plot and sensing a commentary about life in general. This commentary, the **theme,** places us within the mirror's image along with the characters and their actions. We look and see ourselves. The characters' universe is ours, the playwright would have us believe, for a while at least. If his art succeeds, we do believe him. But reading literary art is no passive experience; it requires active work. And since playwrights seldom help us decide *how* characters say what they do or interrupt to explain *why* they say what they do, what personal voice he gives through stage directions deserves special attention, because playwrights never tell as much as novelists; instead they show. Our reading should focus on the tone of the dialogue as much as on the information in what is said. Prior to the nineteenth century, dramatists relied heavily on poetic diction to define their characters. Later playwrights provided stage directions which detail stage activities and modify dialogue. Modern writers usually give precise descriptions for the set and costume design and even prescribe particular background music. But no matter when a play was written or what its expressive style is, our role as readers and audience is to make judgments about characters in action, just as we make judgments about Antigone and Ismene the first time we see them. We should strive to be "fooled" by the truthful illusion by activating our sensitivities to human imperfections and the potential conflicts such flaws can generate. And, finally, as we peer into the playwright's mirror, we seek among the populated reflections shadows of ourselves.

Types of Plays

When Polonius presents the traveling players to Hamlet, he reads from the theater company's license, which identifies them as

> The best actors in the world, either for tragedy, comedy, history, pastoral, pastoral-comical, historical-pastoral, tragical-historical, tragical-comical-historical-pastoral, scene individable or poem unlimited…

Shakespeare's sense of humor runs through this speech which sounds like a parody of the license granted Shakespeare's own company by James I, authorizing "the Arte and faculty of playing Comedies, Tragedies, histories, Enterludes, moralls, pastoralls, Stageplaies and Such others…" for the king's subjects and himself. The joke is on those who think all plays somehow can be categorized according to preconceived definitions, as though playwrights follow literary recipes. The notion is not entirely ridiculous, to be sure, since audiences and readers can easily tell a serious play from a humorous one, and a play labeled "tragedy" or "comedy" will generate certain valid expectations from us all, regardless of whether we have read a word by Aristotle or any other literary critic. Still, if beginning playwrights had to choose between writing according to some rigid strictures designating the likes of a "tragical-comical-historical-pastoral" or writing a play unrestricted by such rules (a "poem unlimited"), they would probably choose the latter.

Thought

All plays contain thought—its accumulated themes, arguments, and overall meaning of the action—together with a mood or tone, and we tend to categorize dramatic thought into three clusters: the serious, the comic, and the seriocomic. These distinctions echo the primitive rites from which theater evolved, religious observances usually tied to seasonal cycles. In the course of a year numerous situations could arise which would initiate dramatic, communal prayers of supplication or thanksgiving. Indeed, for humanity to see its fate held by the will of a god is to see the intricate unity of flesh and spirit, a paradox ripe for representation as dramatic conflict. And if winter's chill brings the pangs of tragedy and summer's warmth the delight of comedy, the year becomes a metaphor for the overall human condition, which contains both. Thus, in our attempts to interpret life's complexities, it is tempting to place the art forms representing it in precise, fixed designations. From this can come critical practices which ascertain how well a work imitates life by how well it adheres to its designated form. Of course, such a critical system's rigidity would limit the range of possible human experiences expressed on stage to a narrow few, but then the range could be made elastic enough to provide for possible variations and combinations. Like the old Ptolemaic theories which held that the Earth was the center of the Solar System, these precepts could work for a while. After a few centuries, though, it would become clear that there is a better way of explaining what a play's form should be—not so much fixed as organic. In other words, we should think of a play as similar to a plant's growing and taking shape according to its own design. This analogy works well because the plant is not a mechanical device constructed from a predetermined plan, yet every plant is a species and as such contains qualities which identify it with others. So just as Shakespeare could ridicule overly precise definitions for dramatic art, he could still write dramas which he clearly identified as tragedies, comedies, or histories, even though he would freely mix two or more of these together in the same play. For the purpose of understanding some of the different perspectives available to the playwright's examining eye, we will look at plays from different periods which follow the three main designations Shakespeare used, followed by a fourth which is indicative of modern American drama. A knowledge of *The Importance of Being Earnest*, *Othello*, *A Man for All Seasons*, and *Death of a Salesman* will be helpful.

COMEDY

Forms of Comedy

The primary aim of comedy is to amuse us with a happy ending, although comedies can vary according to the attitudes they project, which can be broadly identified as either **high** or **low**, terms having nothing to do with an evaluation of the play's merit. Generally, the amusement found in comedy comes from an eventual victory over threats or ill fortune. Much of the dialogue and plot development might be laughable, yet a play need not be funny to be comic. **Farce** is low comedy intended to make us laugh by means of a series of exaggerated, unlikely situations that depend less on plot and character than on gross absurdities, sight gags, and coarse dialogue. The "higher" a comedy goes, the more natural the characters seem and the less boisterous their behavior. The plots become more sustained, and the dialogue shows more weighty thought. As with all dramas, comedies are about things that go wrong. Accordingly, comedies create deviations from accepted normalcy, presenting incongruities which we might or might not see as harmless. If these incongruities make us judgmental about the involved characters and events, the play takes on the features of **satire**, a rather high comic form implying that humanity and human institutions are in need of reform. If the action triggers our sympathy for the characters, we feel even less protected from the incongruities as the play tilts more in the direction of **tragi-comedy**. In other words, the action determines a figurative distance between the audience and the play. Such factors as characters' personalities and the plot's predictability influence this distance. The farther away we sit, the more protected we feel and usually the funnier the play becomes. Closer proximity to believability in the script draws us nearer to the conflict, making us feel more involved in the action and less safe in its presence. It is a rare play that can freely manipulate its audience back and forth along this plane and still maintain its unity. Shakespeare's *The Merchant of Venice* is one example.

Example of a Comedy

A more consistent play is Oscar Wilde's *The Importance of Being Earnest*, which opened in 1895. In the following scene, Lady Bracknell questions Jack Worthing, who has just announced that Lady Bracknell's daughter, Gwendolyn, has agreed to marry him. Being satisfied with Jack's answers concerning his income and finding his upper-class idleness and careless ignorance about world affairs an asset, she queries him about his family background. In grave tones, the embarrassed Jack reveals his mysterious lineage. His late guardian, Thomas Cardew—"an old gentleman of a very charitable and kindly disposition"—had found the baby Jack in an abandoned handbag.

LADY BRACKNELL: A hand-bag?

JACK (very seriously): Yes, Lady Bracknell. I was in a hand-bag—a somewhat large, black leather hand-bag, with handles to it—an ordinary hand-bag in fact.

LADY BRACKNELL: In what locality did this Mr. James, or Thomas, Cardew come across this ordinary hand-bag?

JACK: In the cloak-room at Victoria Station. It was given him in mistake for his own.

LADY BRACKNELL: The cloak-room at Victoria Station?

JACK: Yes. The Brighton line.

LADY BRACKNELL: The line is immaterial, Mr. Worthing. I confess I feel somewhat bewildered by what you have just told me. To be born, or at any rate bred, in a hand-bag, whether it had handles or not, seems to me to display a contempt for the ordinary decencies of family life that reminds one of the worst excesses of the French Revolution. And I presume you know what that unfortunate movement led to? As for the particular locality in which the hand-bag was found, a cloak-room at a railway station might serve to conceal a social indiscretion—has probably, indeed, been used for that purpose before now—but it could hardly be regarded as an assured basis for recognized position in good society.

JACK: May I ask you then what would you advise me to do? I need hardly say I would do anything in the world to ensure Gwendolyn's happiness.

LADY BRACKNELL: I would strongly advise you, Mr. Worthing, to try and acquire some relations as soon as possible, and to make a definite effort to produce at any rate one parent, of either sex, before the season is over.

JACK: Well, I don't see how I could possibly manage to do that. I can produce the hand-bag at any moment. It is in my dressing-room at home. I really think that should satisfy you, Lady Bracknell.

LADY BRACKNELL: Me, sir! What has it to do with me? You can hardly imagine that I and Lord Bracknell would dream of allowing our only daughter—a girl brought up with the utmost care—to marry into a cloak-room, and form an alliance with a parcel. Good morning, Mr. Worthing!

(LADY BRACKNELL sweeps out in majestic indignation.)

This dialogue between Lady Bracknell and Jack is typical of what runs throughout the entire play. It is full of exaggerations, in both the situation being discussed and the manner in which the characters, particularly Lady Bracknell, express their reactions to the situation. Under other circumstances a foundling would not be the focus of a comedy, but we are relieved from any concern for the child since the adult Jack is obviously secure, healthy, and, with one exception, carefree. Moreover, we laugh when Lady Bracknell exaggerates Jack's heritage by comparing it with the excesses of the French Revolution. On the other hand, at the core of their discussion is the deeply ingrained and oppressive notion of English class consciousness, a mentality so flawed it almost begs to be satirized. Could there be more there than light, witty entertainment?

TRAGEDY

Terms

The term "tragedy" when used to define a play has historically meant something very precise, not simply a drama which ends with unfortunate consequences. This definition originated with Aristotle, who insisted that the play be an imitation of complex actions which should arouse an emotional response combining fear and pity. Aristotle believed that only a certain kind of plot could generate such a powerful reaction. Comedy, as we have seen, shows us a progression from adversity to prosperity. Tragedy must show the reverse; moreover, this progression must be experienced by a certain kind of character, says Aristotle, someone whom we can designate as the **tragic hero**. This central figure must be basically good and noble: "good" because we will not be aroused to fear and pity over the misfortunes of a villain, and "noble" both by social position and moral stature because the fall to misfortune would not otherwise be great enough for tragic impact. These virtues do not make the tragic hero perfect, however, for he must also possess **hamartia**—a tragic flaw—the frailty which leads him to make an error in judgment which initiates the reversal in his fortunes, causing his death or the death of others or both. These dire consequences become the hero's **catastrophe**. The most common tragic flaw is **hubris**, an excessive pride that adversely influences the protagonist's judgment.

Often the catastrophic consequences involve an entire nation because the tragic hero's social rank carries great responsibilities. Witnessing these events produces the emotional reaction Aristotle believed the audience should experience, the **catharsis**. Although tragedy must arouse our pity for the tragic hero as he endures his catastrophe and must frighten us as we witness the consequences of a flawed behavior which anyone could exhibit, there must also be a purgation, "a cleansing," of these emotions which should leave the audience feeling not depressed but relieved and almost elated. The assumption is that while the tragic hero endures a crushing reversal somehow he is not thoroughly defeated as he gains new stature though suffering and the knowledge that comes with suffering. Classical tragedy insists that the universe is ordered. If truth or universal law is ignored, the results are devastating, causing the audience to react emotionally; simultaneously, the tragic results prove the existence of truth, thereby reassuring our faith that existence is sensible.

Example of a Tragedy

Sophocles' plays give us some of the clearest examples of Aristotle's definition of tragedy. Shakespeare's tragedies are more varied and more modern in their complexities. *Othello* is one of Shakespeare's most innovative and troublesome extensions of tragedy's boundaries. The title character commands the Venetian army and soon becomes acting governor of Cypress. He is also a Moor, a dark-skinned African whose secret marriage to the beautiful Desdemona has infuriated her father, a wealthy and influential Venetian, whose anger reveals a racist element in Venice which Othello tries to ignore. Iago hates Othello for granting a promotion to Cassio which Iago believes should rightfully be his. With unrelenting determination and malicious deception, Iago attempts to persuade Othello that Desdemona has committed adultery with Cassio. The following excerpt catches Iago in the early stages of his successful manipulation:

IAGO: In Venice they [wives] do let heaven see pranks
They dare not show their husbands; their best conscience
Is not to leave 't undone, but keep 't unknown.

OTHELLO: Dost thou say so?

IAGO: She did deceive her father, marrying you;
And when she seem'd to shake and fear your looks,
She lov'd them most.

OTHELLO: And so she did.

IAGO: Why, go to, then;
She that so young could give out such a seeming,
To see her father's eyes up close as oak,
He thought 'twas witchcraft; but I am much to blame;
I humbly do beseech you of your pardon
For too much loving you.

OTHELLO: I am bound to thee forever.

IAGO: I see, this hath a little dash'd your spirits.

OTHELLO: Not a jot, not a jot.

IAGO: I' faith, I fear it has.
I hope you will consider what is spoke
Comes from my love. But I do see you're mov'd;
I am to pray you not to strain my speech
To grosser issues nor to larger reach
Than to suspicion.

OTHELLO: I will not.

IAGO: Should you do so, my lord,
My speech should fall into such vile success
As my thoughts aim not at. Cassio's my worthy friend—
My lord, I see you're mov'd.

OTHELLO: No, not much mov'd:
I do not think but Desdemona's honest.

IAGO: Long live she so! and long live you to think so!

OTHELLO: And yet, how nature erring from itself,—

IAGO: Ay, there's the point: as, to be bold with you,
Not to affect many proposed matches
Of her own clime, complexion, and degree,
Whereto, we see, in all things nature tends;
Foh! one may smell in such, a will most rank,
Foul disproportion, thoughts unnatural.
But pardon me; I do not in position
Distinctly speak of her, though I may fear
Her will, recoiling to her better judgment,
May fall to match you with her country forms
And happily repent.

OTHELLO: Farewell, farewell:
If more thou dost perceive, let me know more;
Set on thy wife to observe. Leave me, Iago.

IAGO: My lord, I take my leave. (Going)

OTHELLO: Why did I marry? This honest creature, doubtless,
Sees and knows more, much more, than he unfolds.

Notice that Iago speaks much more than Othello. This is typical of their conversations, as though Iago were the superior of the two. Dramatically, for Iago's machinations to compel our interests we must perceive in Othello tragic proportions, both in his strengths and weaknesses; otherwise, *Othello* would slip into a malevolent tale about a rogue and his dupe. Much of the tension in this scene emanates from Othello's reluctance either to accept Iago's innuendos immediately or to dismiss them. This confusion places him on the rack of doubt, a torture made more severe because he questions his own desirability as a husband. Consequently, since Iago is not the "honest creature" he appears to be and Othello is unwilling to confront openly his own self-doubts, Iago becomes the dominant personality—a situation which a flawless Othello would never tolerate.

HISTORY

The playwright's raw data can spring from any source. A passion play, for instance, is a dramatic adaptation of the Crucifixion as told in the gospels. A history play is a dramatic perspective of some event or series of events identified with recognized historical figures. Television docudramas are the most recent examples. Among the earliest histories were the chronicle plays which flourished during Shakespeare's time and often relied on *Chronicles* by Raphael Holinshed, first published in 1577. Holinshed's volumes and similar books by others glorified English history and were very popular throughout the Tudor period, especially following the defeat of the Spanish Armada. Similarly, Shakespeare's *Henry V* and *Henry VIII* emphasize national and religious chauvinism in their treatments of kings who, from a more objective historical perspective, appear less than nobly motivated. These plays resemble romantic comedies with each one's protagonist defeating some adversary and establishing national harmony through royal marriage. *King Lear* and *Macbeth*, on the other hand, movingly demonstrate Shakespeare's skill at turning historical figures into tragic heroes.

Example of a History Play

Ever since the sixteenth century history plays have seldom risen above the level of patriotic whitewash and political propaganda. Of course there are notable exceptions to this trend: Robert Bolt's *A Man for All Seasons* is one. The title character, Sir Thomas More, is beheaded at the play's conclusion, following his refusal to condone Henry VIII's break from the Roman Catholic Church and the king's establishment of the Church of England with the monarch as its head. Henry wants More to condone these actions because the Pope will not grant Henry a divorce from Queen Catherine so that he can marry Anne Boleyn, who the king believes will bear him the male heir he desperately wants. The central issue for us is not whether More's theology is valid but whether any person of conscience can act freely in a world dominated by others far less principled. In Henry's only scene he arrives at Sir Thomas's house hoping his Lord Chancellor will not disappoint him:

[music in background]

HENRY: Son after son she's borne me, Thomas, all dead at birth, or dead within a month; I never saw the hand of God so clear in anything… I have a daughter, she's a good child, a well-set child—But I have no son. (He flares up). It is my bounden duty to put away the Queen, and all the Popes back to St. Peter shall not come between me and my duty! How is it that you cannot see? Everybody else does.

MORE: (Eagerly) Then why does Your Grace need my poor support?

HENRY: Because you are honest. What's more to the purpose, you're known to be honest… There are those like Norfolk who follow me because I wear the crown, and there are those like Master Cromwell who follow me because they are jackals with sharp teeth and I am their lion, and there is a mass that follow me because it follows anything that moves—and there is you.

MORE: I am sick to think how much I must displease Your Grace.

HENRY: No, Thomas, I respect your sincerity. Respect? Oh, man, it's water in the desert... How did you like our music? That air they played, it had a certain—well, tell me what you thought of it.

MORE: (Relieved at this turn; smiling) Could it have been Your Grace's own?

HENRY: (Smiles back) Discovered! Now I'll never know your true opinion. And that's irksome, Thomas, for we artists, though we love praise, yet we love truth better.

MORE: (Mildly) Then I will tell Your Grace truly what I thought of it.

HENRY: (A little disconcerted) Speak then.

MORE: To me it seemed—delightful.

HENRY: Thomas—I chose the right man for Chancellor.

MORE: I must in fairness add that my taste in music is reputably deplorable.

(From *A Man for All Seasons* by Robert Bolt. Copyright © 1960, 1962 by Robert Bolt. Reprinted by permission of Random House, Inc.)

To what extent Henry and More discussed the king's divorce and its subsequent events nobody knows, let alone what was actually said, although we can be certain they spoke an English distinctively different from the language in the play. Bolt's imagination, funneled through the dramatist's obligation to tell an interesting story, presides over the historical data and dictates the play's projections of More, Henry, and the other participants. Thus, we do not have "history"; instead, we have a dramatic perception of history shaped, altered, and adorned by Robert Bolt, writing about sixteenth century figures from a 1960 vantage point. But as the scene above shows, the characters' personalities are not simple reductions of what historical giants should be. Henry struts a royal self-assurance noticeably colored by vanity and frustration; yet although he lacks More's wit and intelligence, the king clearly is no fool. Likewise, as troubled as More is by the controversy before him, he projects a formidable power of his own. *A Man for All Seasons* succeeds dramatically because Bolt provides only enough historical verisimilitude to present a context for the characters' development while he allows the resultant thematic implications to touch all times, all seasons. When we read any history play, we should search for similar implications; otherwise, the work can never become more than a theatrical précis with a narrow, didactic focus.

MODERN DRAMA
Forms of Modern Drama

From the 1870s to the present, the theater has participated in the artistic movements reflecting accumulated theories of science, social science, and philosophy which attempt to define reality and the means we use to discern it. First caught in a pendulum of opposing views, modern drama eventually synthesized these perspectives into new forms, familiar in some ways and boldly original in others. Henrik Ibsen's plays began the modern era with their emphasis on **realism**, a seeking of truth through direct observation using the five senses. As objectively depicted, contemporary life received a closer scrutiny than ever before, showing everyday people in everyday situations. Before Ibsen, theatrical sets were limited, with rare exceptions, to castles and country estates. After Ibsen the farmhouse and city tenement were suitable for the stage. Ibsen's work influenced many others, and from realism came two main variations. The first, **naturalism**, strove to push realism towards a direct transformation of life on stage, a "slice of life" showing how the scientific principles of heredity and environment have shaped society, especially in depicting the plights of the lower classes. The second variation, **expressionism**, moved in a different direction and actually denied realism's premise that the real world could be objectively perceived; instead—influenced by Sigmund Freud's theories about human behavior's hidden, subconscious motivations and by other modernist trends in the arts, such as James Joyce's fiction and Picasso's paintings—expressionism imitated a disconnected dream-like world filled with psychological images at odds with the tangible world surrounding it. While naturalism attempts to imitate life directly, expressionism is abstract and often relies on symbols.

A modern play can employ any number of elements found in the spectrum between these extremes as well as suggest divergent philosophical views about whether humanity has the power to change its condition or whether any of its ideas about the universe are verifiable. Moreover, no work of art is necessarily confined within a particular school of thought. It is quite possible that seemingly incongruent forms can appear in the same play and work well. *The Glass Menagerie, A Man for All Seasons*, and *Death of a Salesman* feature characters and dialogue indicative of realistic drama, but the sets described in the stage directions are expressionistic, offering either framed outlines of places or distorted representations. Conventions from classical drama are also available to the playwright. As previously noted, Tom acts as a Greek chorus as well as an important character in his play; the same is true of the Common Man, whose identity changes from scene to scene. Playwrights Eugene Ionesco and Harold Pinter have created characters speaking and behaving in extraordinary ways while occupying sets which are typically realistic. In short, anything is possible in modern drama, a quality which is wholly compatible with the diversity and unpredictability of twentieth century human experiences.

Example of a Modern Drama

In a sense all good drama is modern. No label about a play's origin or form can adequately describe its content. Establishing the people, places, and thought within the play is crucial to our understanding. For the characters to interest us, we must perceive the issues that affect their lives, and eventually we will discover why the characters' personalities and backgrounds, together with their social situations, inevitably converge with these issues and create conflicts. We must also stay aware of drama's kinship with lyric poetry's subjective mood and tone, a quality dominating all plays regardless of the form. *Death of a Salesman* challenges the classical definitions of tragedy by giving us a modern American, Willy Loman, who is indeed a "low man," a person of little social importance and limited moral fiber. His delusionary values have brought him at age 64 to failure and despair, yet more than ever he clings to his dreams and painted memories for solace and hope.

Late one night, after Willy has returned from an aborted sales trip, his rambling conversation with his wife Linda returns to the topic which haunts him the most, his son Biff.

WILLY: Biff is a lazy bum!

LINDA: They're sleeping. Get something to eat. Go on down.

WILLY: Why did he come home? I would like to know what brought him home.

LINDA: I don't know. I think he's still lost, Willy. I think he's very lost.

WILLY: Biff Loman is lost. In the greatest country in the world a young man with such—personal attractiveness, gets lost. And such a hard worker. There's one thing about Biff—he's not lazy.

LINDA: Never.

WILLY (with pity and resolve): I'll see him in the morning; I'll have a nice talk with him. I'll get him a job selling. He could be big in no time. My God! Remember how they used to follow him around in high school? When he smiled at one of them their faces lit up. When he walked down the street… (He loses himself in reminiscences.)

LINDA (trying to bring him out of it): Willy, dear, I got a new kind of American-type cheese today. It's whipped.

WILLY: Why do you get American cheese when you know I like Swiss?

LINDA: I just thought you'd like a change—

WILLY: I don't want change! I want Swiss cheese. Why am I always being contradicted?

LINDA (with a covering laugh): I just thought it would be a surprise.

WILLY: Why don't you open a window in here, for God's sake?

LINDA (with infinite patience): They're all open dear.

WILLY: The way they boxed us in here. Bricks and windows, windows and bricks.

LINDA: We should have bought the land next door.

WILLY: The street is lined with cars. There's not a breath of fresh air in the neighborhood. The grass don't grow any more, you can't raise a carrot in the backyard. They should've had a law against apartment houses. Remember those two beautiful elms out there? When I and Biff hung the swing between them?

LINDA: Yeah, like a million miles from the city.

WILLY: They should've arrested the builder for cutting those down. They massacred the neighborhood. (Lost) More and more I think of those days, Linda. This time of year it was lilac and wisteria. And then the peonies would come out, and the daffodils. What fragrance in this room!

LINDA: Well, after all, people had to move somewhere.

WILLY: No, there's more people now.

LINDA: I don't think there's more people. I think—

WILLY: There's more people! That's what's ruining this country! Population is getting out of control. The competition is maddening! Smell the stink from that apartment house! And another on the other side... How can they whip cheese?

In Arthur Miller's stage directions for *Death of a Salesman*, the Loman house is outlined by simple framing with various floors represented by short, elevated platforms. Outside the house the towering shapes of the city angle inward presenting the crowded oppressiveness Willy complains about. First performed in 1949, the play continues to make a powerful commentary on modern American life. We see Willy as more desperate than angry about his condition, which he defines in ways as contradictory as his assessments of Biff. In his suffocating world so nebulously delineated, Willy gropes for peace while hiding from truth; and although his woes are uniquely American in some ways, they touch broader, more universal human problems as well.

DRILL: LITERATURE

1. Though often considered a work for children, this nineteenth century classic continues to amuse and amaze adults interested in puzzles, poems, and hidden meanings.

   (A) *The Cat in the Hat Comes Back*
   (B) *Lord of the Rings*
   (C) *Alice in Wonderland*
   (D) *Gulliver's Travels*

2. Which of the following presents a series of entertaining monologues and bawdy tales told by individuals with a common purpose?

   (A) *The Canterbury Tales*
   (B) *The Martian Chronicles*
   (C) *Tales from the Twilight Zone*
   (D) *The Complete Works of Edgar Allan Poe*

3. Which of the following is generally recognized as the most accurate literary representation of American soldiers in battle?

   (A) Heller's *Catch-22*
   (B) Remarque's *All's Quiet on the Western Front*
   (C) Mailer's *The Naked and the Dead*
   (D) Crane's *Red Badge of Courage*

4. In which of the following works does the author deal with his or her blindness?

   (A) Dickinson's "My Life Closed Twice Before Its Close"
   (B) Malory's *Le Morte d'Arthur*
   (C) Milton's "When I Consider How My Light Is Spent"
   (D) Asimov's *Nightfall*

5. Which of the following can be seen as a fable in which the main characters represent political personages engaged in the conflict of political systems?

   (A) *Gulliver's Travels*
   (B) *The Time Machine*
   (C) *1984*
   (D) *Animal Farm*

6. Which of the following presents a fascinating survey of English life at the time of William the Conqueror?

    (A) *Edwin Drood*
    (B) *The Battle of Malden*
    (C) *Twickenham Garden*
    (D) *The Domesday Book*

7. Many of Shakespeare's works are based on which of the following philosophical and literary constructs?

    (A) The Platonic Ideal
    (B) The Great Chain of Being
    (C) The Duality of Man
    (D) Man's Inhumanity to Man

8. Which of the following was written by Charles Dodgson under a pen name?

    (A) *Tom Sawyer*
    (B) *The Heart of Darkness*
    (C) *Alice in Wonderland*
    (D) *Locksley Hall*

9. Which of the following poets is known for dramatic monologues such as "Andrea del Sarto"?

    (A) Alfred Tennyson
    (B) Robert Browning
    (C) S.T. Coleridge
    (D) P.B. Shelley

10. Which of the following American novelists was known for his love of deep sea fishing and bullfighting?

    (A) Norman Mailer
    (B) Theodore Dreiser
    (C) John Steinbeck
    (D) Ernest Hemingway

11. Which of the following novels revolved around the bureaucratic aspects of the pursuit of war?

    (A) Steinbeck's *Grapes of Wrath*
    (B) Heller's *Catch-22*
    (C) Remarque's *All Quiet on the Western Front*
    (D) Mailer's *The Naked and the Dead*

12. John Donne is considered one of the

    (A) decadents.
    (B) Beat poets.
    (C) metaphysicals.
    (D) restoration poets.

13. Considered one of the greatest expressions of Existentialism, this play by Beckett chiefly involves only two characters.

    (A) *The American Dream*
    (B) *The Zoo Story*
    (C) *The Fantasticks*
    (D) *Waiting for Godot*

14. Which of the following modern novels portrays a New England prep school as America is about to go to war?

    (A) *The Catcher in the Rye*
    (B) *A Separate Peace*
    (C) *Being There*
    (D) *Goodbye, Mr. Chips*

15. Which famous ship is the subject of a novel about World War II mutiny?

    (A) HMS *Bounty*
    (B) USS *Nautilus*
    (C) USS *Caine*
    (D) *Golden Hinde*

16. Which nineteenth century novel ends with a hanging at sea?

    (A) Melville's *Billy Budd*
    (B) Capote's *In Cold Blood*
    (C) Clark's *The Oxbow Incident*
    (D) Bierce's *An Occurrence at Owl Creek Bridge*

17. Some of Shakespeare's sonnets are presumed to be written to someone critics call

    (A) Lady Ruffles.
    (B) Dark Lady.
    (C) Lady Jane.
    (D) Lady Juliet.

Question 18 refers to the following verse:

The Silkworm and the Spider Houses make,
All their materials from their Bowels take…
Yet they are Curious, built with Art and Care,
Like Lovers, who build Castles in the Air,
Which ev'ry puff of Wind is apt to break,
As imaginations, when Reason's weak.

18. The poem is written in

    (A) iambic pentameter.
    (B) iambic pentameter and rhyming couplets.
    (C) iambic pentameter and concrete language.
    (D) feminine rhyme.

19. What are the rules for a villanelle?

    (A) A fixed form of 14 lines with a concluding couplet
    (B) Six stanzas of six lines each
    (C) A free-form poem of five tercets
    (D) A fixed form with five tercets and a quatrain

20. An aubade is a poem that greets

    (A) the moon.
    (B) the sun.
    (C) nightfall.
    (D) the dawn.

LITERATURE REVIEW

Answer Key

1.	(C)	6.	(D)	11.	(B)	16.	(A)
2.	(A)	7.	(B)	12.	(C)	17.	(B)
3.	(D)	8.	(C)	13.	(D)	18.	(A)
4.	(C)	9.	(B)	14.	(B)	19.	(D)
5.	(D)	10.	(D)	15.	(C)	20.	(D)

DETAILED EXPLANATIONS OF ANSWERS
DRILL: LITERATURE

1. **(C)** Lewis Carroll's *Alice in Wonderland*, written in the 1870s, has long been considered a children's book—though critics have spoken about it for years as a work of intricate imagination and always in need of revised analysis (as in the new work *The Annotated Alice*). Some have considered it a compendium of playful games—reversed poems, anagrams, riddles, and gibberish rhymes. Others see in the book drug references, psychological allegories, and a fantastic map of the unconscious.

   Each possible answer has been considered at some time a children's book, although *Gulliver's Travels* (D) is a political satire. Seuss's *The Cat in the Hat* (A) is of course very popular with adults, but only insofar as it provides fun tongue-twisters and the like. The storyline clearly is aimed at the younger set. Tolkien's work (B) may have been interpreted well by animators, but is certainly too difficult to be considered children's material.

2. **(A)** The key to this answer is the word "bawdy." Many students who have only a cursory knowledge of Chaucer's "Canterbury Tales" (A) do not realize that many of his stories ("The Wife of Bath's Tale," for example) are risqué, and, if written in modern English instead of Middle, and if composed by a writer of less importance, would probably be avoided by many high schools, and even some colleges. Chaucer's unifying premise is that the monologues and stories within stories are being told by travelers on a pilgrimage to the church of Canterbury. Poe (D) is certainly horrifying, but not bawdy. The same may be said about Rod Serling's wonderful stories (C). Bradbury's *Martian Chronicles* (B) is certainly a collection in which the stories have a singular purpose (describing the colonization of Mars by Earthmen), but, again, "bawdy" does not apply.

3. **(D)** This question may pose some difficulties, as all the choices are well-known war novels. The operative phrase here is "generally recognized," and for this, the student must be aware of the particular strength of Crane's *Red Badge of Courage* (D) as well as the recognized critical viewpoint that perhaps no other war story so accurately portrays the heat of battle. This point is always emphasized when *Red Badge* is taught, for two reasons. Crane was a Realist writer who believed that his works should record sound, sight, and sensation as much as any painter would. Secondly, Crane was a newspaper reporter who was born after the Civil War (the subject of *Red Badge)*, and who never witnessed battle until after the book was published! Even so, veterans of the Civil War and other wars since regularly cite *Red Badge* for its accuracy.

   Catch-22 (A) discusses the dizzying aspects of bureaucratized war; *All Quiet* (B) is certainly vivid in its portrayal of German soldiers during World War I. Mailer's *The Naked and the Dead* (C) has enjoyed great popularity by veterans of World War II, but is not recognized for the attention to the universality of emotions that suffuse all soldiers in battle.

4. **(C)** Though all of the choices here deal with different ways to experience darkness, this question requires specific biographical knowledge of John Milton (C). His famous short poem which speaks of "this dark world" and his desire in remaining years to serve "my Maker" contains the famous line: "They also serve who only stand and wait." While the title of Asimov's science fiction classic work (D) is tantalizing, *Nightfall* deals with darkness of a different kind: an eclipse.

Malory's work (B), as its title indicates, deals with the death of the legendary King Arthur. The American poet Dickinson (A) is generally considered to be speaking about a lost love.

5. **(D)** Orwell's *Animal Farm* is perhaps the most artful of his works, because it combines fable with political commentary. Swift's *Travels* (A) does the same, but without a consistent representation of political systems in conflict, as in *Animal Farm,* in which Marxist-Leninism, Monarchy, and Western Democracy play out their conflict according to Orwell's interpretation of history from the Russian Revolution to World War II. Orwell's other great work, *1984* (C), is a more straightforward explication of the dangers of totalitarianism. H. G. Wells's work (B) offers intriguing possibilities: there are animal-like characters, and political systems in conflict, but one would be hard put to construe this novel as a fable.

6. **(D)** *The Domesday Book*, commissioned by William the Conqueror, which surveyed manor farms throughout England around the year 1086 CE, presents the most accurate picture we have today of the early feudal society that William governed. Population estimates, lists of individuals and their trades, and a general mapping of the main cities, marketplaces, and monasteries create a vivid picture. Donne's poem (C) was written in the 1600s. *Edwin Drood* (A) was Dickens' unfinished novel. *The Battle of Malden* (B) would be an interesting choice, but that it speaks of a specific Viking invasion of Britain in 991 CE.

7. **(B)** Shakespeare respected a fundamental Elizabethan world construct: The Great Chain of Being. The Chain conjectured a world in which all the creatures of the Earth—including man—were set forth in increasing importance and decreasing distance to the angels and to God. Mankind was closest to the angels, but within our species was further ordering: kings, for example, were of a higher order than regular workmen, with lesser royalty somewhere in-between. Shakespeare's writings have regularly been seen to respect this order. Revolution is punished. Rash and irrational acts result in equally brutal retribution.

Platonism (A) holds that the real world is but a shadow of the ideal. Duality (C)—the existence of good and evil in the same individual—is not a keynote Shakespearean characterization, and Man's Inhumanity to Man (D) is a rather modern concept—far different in perspective from Shakespearean justice where those who disrupt the proper order of things get all the bad things they deserve.

8. **(C)** Lewis Carroll was the pen name of Charles Dodgson, the Oxford Don who wrote *Alice in Wonderland* for Alice Liddle ("Little Alice"), the daughter of a friend. It has been suggested that a pen name was a must for an Oxford mathematician with an academic reputation to uphold. The novel *Tom Sawyer* (A) was written by an author under the pen name Mark Twain. Tennyson's poetic work (D) was authored without the use of a pseudonym. Joseph Conrad (author of *Heart of Darkness*) is an anglicization of Jozef Konrad Korzeniowski.

9. **(B)** Robert Browning is known for his dramatic monologues, in which the poem takes the form of a speech by the subject—and in so doing, elucidates the personality of the individual. "Andrea del Sarto" is perhaps one of Browning's most famous poems in this form—a form which Browning is credited with developing. Tennyson (A), Shelley (D), and Coleridge (C) did not employ this technique.

10. **(D)** Ernest Hemingway was a very active sportsman, and was considered to personify "machismo" in both his personal and literary life. *The Old Man and the Sea*, for example, was based on his experience deep-sea fishing off the coast of Cuba. Later research has tended to contradict this once

popular conception of the author. Mailer (A) has also pursued sports like boxing, but not deep sea fishing or bullfighting. Dreiser (B) and Steinbeck (C) are not known as sportsmen, nor do they concentrate upon sport in their writing.

11. **(B)** Heller's famous novel about American bomber pilots flying out of Sicily during World War II is based on a fundamental but changing principle of the battle group Catch-22. Briefly put, in order to be pulled off combat duty, a soldier would have to be crazy, but, of course, anyone who wanted to be removed could surely not be crazy, because the business of war is crazy. Remarque's novel (C) is about trench warfare during World War I; Mailer's (D) is about jungle warfare during World War II. Steinbeck's novel (A) has nothing to do with war, though its title might indicate that it does.

12. **(C)** John Donne is considered the leader of the Metaphysical poets of the seventeenth century, which include Crashaw and Crowley. The Decadents (A) were writers at the end of the last century; the Beats (B) were Greenwich Village poets of the 1950s; Restoration poets (D), like Dryden, are of the period after 1660.

13. **(D)** Beckett's play uses the conversation of two "bums" as they wait for Godot. Beckett's own beliefs (he and Sartre are considered fraternal Existentialists) and the content and interpretation of the play indicate Existentialist influence. Albee's plays—(A) and (B)—do not involve only two characters. *The Fantasticks* (C) is not Existentialist.

14. **(B)** John Knowles' autobiographical work depicts the Devon School (actually St. Paul's in New Hampshire) just before and during the early stages of World War II. The impending war came to profoundly affect life "inside" the prep school, as teachers were called up, and then students began to help the war effort by volunteering in town. Salinger's work (A) took place at a Pennsylvania prep school in the late 1940s, and there are no references to war. (D) *Goodbye, Mr. Chips* is a famous story about an English prep school. Kosinski's work (C) is not relevant here.

15. **(C)** *The Caine Mutiny* is based on a real incident that took place on an American minesweeper in the South Pacific during World War II. The tyrannical Captain Queeg is replaced by his first officers for incompetence during battle. One of the most famous mutinies in the British navy occurred on the *Bounty* (A). Drake's ship (D) of the 1500s and the first atomic submarine (B) were never objects of mutiny.

16. **(A)** All of the novels but one presented here involve a hanging, but only *Billy Budd* involves a hanging at sea. Billy, a foretopman aboard the HMS *Indomitable*, is sentenced to death for inadvertently killing John Claggart, the evil master at arms. (B) Capote's work involves the hanging of a murderer in the 1950s, Clark's (C) deals with a hanging in the Wild West, and Bierce's (D) an impromptu execution during the Civil War.

17. **(B)** About one-third of Shakespeare's 108 known sonnets are written to someone who has come to be known as the "Dark Lady of the Sonnets." The themes of these poems are many, but consistent: love that endures through time; love of an older man for a younger woman; testimonials to beauty that endures even after death. There has been some discussion as to whether these poems are simply formulaic: that Shakespeare had no specific person in mind. Many of Shakespeare's sonnets are addressed to a young boy. The other possibilities here are simply incorrect, although Lady Juliet (D) is clearly meant to trip up the reader with a specific reference. (C) is a reference to a Yeats poem, and (A) is an invention.

18. **(A)**   Through your review you will now be familiar with all the various terms for meter and rhyme; note that iambic pentameter is the form favored by Shakespeare and Milton, easily recognized by the ten beat, stressed/unstressed syllabic line. (B) is incorrect because the poem is not entirely composed of rhyming couplets. Concrete language (C) is present early in the poem, but it moves to abstract language after line 3 for the contrast. Although some of the rhymes are feminine, the opening couplet is masculine, so (D) is incorrect.

19. **(D)**   You may not be familiar with this term so work your way through what you do know—pull in other works you have read: Stephen Dedalus in *Portrait of the Artist as a Young Man* demonstrates his skill as a young budding poet by writing a villanelle in a few minutes on the back of a cigarette packet! Choices (A), (B), and (C) do not meet the requirements of a villanelle, so they are incorrect choices.

20. **(D)**   Learn the various poetry forms from glossaries in anthologies—they may not cover all the terms but then you can distinguish and eliminate all those you do know that do not fit the definition. If the poem had greeted (A) the moon, (B) the sun, or (C) nightfall, then it would not be an aubade. Thus, all of these choices are incorrect.

■ VISUAL ARTS AND ARCHITECTURE REVIEW

◼ CLASSICAL PERIOD

More than 20,000 years before the start of recorded history, humans were creating art. In an effort to master their environment, Paleolithic artists painted graceful and realistic animals on the walls of caves (Paleolithic sites of Lascaux in France and Altimira in Spain) and carved stone statuettes of females, symbols of fecundity (the "Venus" figures of Willendorf, Lespugue, and Lausell, named for their European discovery sites). Neolithic people erected megalithic structures (Stonehenge in England) of huge stones to create an environment for religious ritual and the sophisticated measurement and tracking of celestial bodies.

With the rise of the great cities, stable agricultural communities, trade, political systems, and organized religion, art and architecture became the powerful tools of kings, priests, and commerce. An obsession with the afterlife caused the ancient Egyptians to build lavish tombs, especially for their pharaohs, or god-kings. These tombs appeared first in the form of pyramids, like the Great Pyramid of Khufu at Giza (c. 2500 BCE), and later as mortuary temples built into the sides of cliffs, like that for Queen Hatshepsut at Deir El-Bahri (c. 1500 BCE). The Egyptians also constructed magnificent temples at Karnak and Luxor, which are characterized by massive stone columns and heavy walls organized along a central axis. The monuments and carvings of the Mesopotamian kingdom of the Assyrians (about 1500–612 BCE) recorded in powerful visual terms the warrior-kings' victories over rival nations and in the hunt. An extraordinary example of these stylized and meticulously decorative relief carvings (sculptural images only slightly raised from their stone surfaces) and the nearly naturalistic depiction of animals are the Lion-Hunting Reliefs of the palace of King Assurbanipal (Nineveh, c. 645–640 BCE). Their exciting energy provides a striking contrast to the stately repose of most Egyptian art.

The classical period of architecture and art begins with, and is best represented by the civilization of the ancient Greeks, the city-state of Athens being the most dominant. The accomplishments of Athenian architecture, drama, philosophy, government, science, and sculpture laid the foundation for all of western European culture. The Greeks of the classical period were fascinated by physical beauty: their Olympian gods were fashioned in the human image, and a universe of perfection, guided by a master plan, was re-created in their idealized and gracefully proportioned sculptures, architecture, and paintings.

The amazing innovations of classical Greek art had their origins in earlier "Greek" civilizations—the Minoans of Crete and the people of mainland Mycenae. The Minoans flourished about

2500–1400 BCE. Their palace at Knossos is known for the lively, sinuous forms of their characteristic wall paintings, revealing a people enamored of acrobatics, leisure, and the beauty of the sea. The Minoans produced increasingly sophisticated terracotta and bronze figurines and painted vases. Both Crete and Mycenae were sources for many of the heroic tales of the ancient Greeks. For example, in the mazelike complex of the palace at Knossos, frescoes of bull-leaping games can be found, suggesting a basis for the Greek legend of the battle of Theseus with the Minotaur in the labyrinth. The Mycenaeans on mainland Greece were more warlike, but they traded with the Minoans, whose culture they adapted after the destruction of Crete by a natural disaster about 1450 BCE. The Mycenaeans produced beautiful work in gold, such as face masks, and artistically adopted the Minoans' ritual animal, the bull, but with a more aggressive character. Much of their best ornamentation was reserved for weapons. The culture of the Mycenaeans was destroyed about 1100 BCE. Only after three more centuries was a revitalized mainland-Greek culture able to spread trade (and settle colonies) throughout the Mediterranean, and organize into a system of city-states.

The earliest period of Greek city-state civilization, the Archaic, boasted exemplary art in the form of vase paintings, whose simple, precise, linear decoration evolved from the earlier, geometric style of the ninth and eighth centuries BCE—zigzag, meandering, and triangular designs—to include, by the end of the eighth century, lively animals and humans. By the sixth century the dominant method of painting black figures as silhouettes on vases gave way to red figures with drawn-in details on a black background; pictured were heroes, athletes, feasts, weddings, and genre scenes. Contact with Egyptian culture in the mid-seventh century encouraged development of marble statuary in Greece: *The Lady of Auxerre* prefigures the standard forms of Greek *korai* and *kouroi* (life-sized draped female and nude male figures), and in its stylized pose resembles Egyptian statues. The emphasis on nakedness in the *kouros* led quickly to the virtuosic treatment of naturalistic representation. The *Kouros of Anavysos* (Attica, 540–515 BCE) retains the static Egyptian pose but already displays great subtlety in muscular modeling. The famous *Kritios Boy* (c. 490-480 BCE) marks the apogee of Archaic sculpture, with an elegance and naturalism of form and relatively relaxed pose that befitted a culture increasingly dedicated to exalting beauty. It epitomizes the elements that were to characterize the spirit of ancient Greek art: respect for and re-creation of visual reality; a love of beauty in itself; and the application of rules and formulas to achieve representations of ideal beauty. The philosopher Plato's emphasis on the existence, in the spiritual realm or mind of God, of ideal forms for everything on earth was the basis of much artistic creativity in both art and architecture.

The Greek temple developed as a columnar structure, with sculptures on the pediments (triangular space just below the roof) and relief sculpture (usually of narrative action) on the rectangular panels of the friezes (metopes) that banded the buildings above the columns. The most perfect example of classical proportions is found in the great Greek temples on the Athenian Acropolis. In the Parthenon (fifth century BCE), the architect Ictinus created a structure that represented the striving for perfection and ideal beauty in Athenian culture; refinement and perfect proportions are achieved by subtle curvatures in the relation of vertical elements and the tapering of the Doric columns. The style and elements of the Parthenon and other Greek buildings (such as the Erechtheion and the Temple of Athene Nike, also on the Acropolis) provided the forms—from the three major classical orders of columns (Doric, Ionic, and Corinthian) to pediments and sculptural friezes (relief sculptures in realistic narratives)—for two millennia of Western architecture.

The turning point for Greek sculpture came with the preeminence of Athens, after that city's victory over the Persians in the early fifth century. The classical period of the next hundred years boasted the great tragic playwrights Euripides, Aeschylus, and Sophocles, the historians Thucydides and Herodotus, and the moral philosophers Plato and Aristotle. Pericles established Athenian democracy and built a massive complex on the Acropolis, including the Parthenon (447–432 BCE). Under the direction of the sculptor Phydias (d. 432 BCE) there were created ninety-two figures in high relief on the metopes, in mythological combat scenes; sculptural figures on the pediments are characterized by fluid movement and dynamic drapery. Many Greek sculptures are known through Roman marble copies, notably Myron's *Discobolos* (c. 400 BCE), a masterpiece of ideal grace and potential action.

In the fourth century the Greek city-states warred upon one another, and Macedonia prevailed, first under Philip II, then under his son Alexander, who by 323 BCE had expanded the Greek empire to include Persia. The art of this period is characterized by greater naturalism, a wider variety of poses and of emotional display, and the intricate play of drapery. Praxiteles (*Hermes and the Infant Dionysus,* c. 350–330 BCE) was skilled in portraying the human body in a rhythmic curve; he produced the first free-standing life-size female nude, *The Cnidian Aphrodite* (known from a marble copy; originally c. 350–330 BCE). Scopus was known for his naturalistic portraiture, notably the statues on the tomb of Mausolos at Halicarnassus (c. 353 BCE).

During the Hellenistic period (323–31 BCE), Greek culture spread throughout the Mediterranean. Art was characterized by new freedoms, insistent naturalism, more genre subjects (not merely heroic figures, but old women, sportsmen, etc.), less symmetry, and emphasis on technical virtuosity and the depiction of movement. Examples are the Altar of Zeus at Pergamum (180–150 BCE), especially the *Battle of the Gods and Giants* frieze—a tour-de-force of light and shade, whirling movement, and expressive musculature and gestures. One of the most famous of Hellenistic sculptures is also from Pergamum: *The Dying Gaul* (c. 200 BCE), an ultranaturalistic genre piece, with its shaggy hair and palpable agony. Few examples of Greek painting survive, but notable painters were Apelles and Nikias in the fourth century BCE. Many works, however, survive in later mosaic copies, such as the Alexander painting by Philoxenos (about 300 BCE), found at Pompeii in a mosaic copy (90 BCE): it depicts Alexander the Great's dramatic meeting with the Persian king Darius in battle—and brilliantly conveys depth, light, and shade.

The Romans adopted much of the art and architectural forms of ancient Greece. The culture of Rome excelled in engineering and building, whose purpose it was to efficiently organize a vast empire and to provide an aesthetic environment for private and public use. The Romans built temples, roads, bath complexes, civic buildings, palaces, and aqueducts.

The cult of individual prestige and power was of major significance in Roman culture, and thus many of the statues were personalized and realistic. Greek ideal beauty was replaced by monuments and portraiture exalting specific personalities. The decoration of homes and public places by paintings and mosaics reflects the importance of a leisure-oriented "consumer" lifestyle. The paintings of Pompeii and Herculaneum (both towns victims of the Mt. Vesuvius eruption in 79 CE) reveal the Roman mastery of realistic form and modeling, of inspired decorative elements, and attempts at convincing spatial relationships. Roman architecture's strides emanated from the value placed on engineering and include innovations important for later centuries. The first-century development of the dome—a major engineering and artistic contribution to world architecture— for public buildings was important for the Renaissance and later periods, when the writings of the great Roman architect Vitruvius (first century BCE) were widely studied. The Roman basilica (an oblong building ending in a semicircular apse) was the basis for church architecture during the early Christian and medieval periods (300–1300).

Roman culture dates from the time of the mythical founding of Rome by Romulus and Remus in 753 BCE. Roman territory gradually expanded to include the Etruscan, or native Italian, culture in the fourth century, the Greek colonies in southern Italy in the third, and continuous expansion throughout the Mediterranean world until the height of Roman power in 100 CE under the emperor Trajan. Roman art was heavily influenced by the Greeks, especially after the sack of Syracuse in 212 BCE, when Greek artistic treasures—including the artists themselves—began pouring into Rome. While Greek forms were adopted, Greek ideas of beauty and perfection were not: Roman art served to provide luxury, as status symbols, and to enhance social position. Portraiture became very important, and the Romans eagerly adopted the innovation of the portrait bust from the Etruscans. Significant early busts are the *Capitoline Brutus* (third century BCE) and *Pompey* (c. 50 BCE), the earliest realistic likeness of a major Roman historical figure. In the Augustan age (first century CE), Greek prototypes were readopted to portray an idealized emperor. One of the most famous sculptures of the Roman empire is the *Laocoon* (first century CE), usually attributed to three Greek artists from Rhodes (Agesander, Athenodorus, and Polydorus): in this masterful, energetic, and dynamic composition (in the Hellenistic style of Pergamum), serpents sent by Apollo slay Laocoon and his sons. Examples of Roman painting fortunately still exist, due to their preservation by the hardened volcanic ashes of the destroyed southern towns of Pompeii and Herculaneum. The decorative paintings at Pompeii, such as those at the House of the Vettii (before 79 CE), depict realistically modeled humans in convincing landscapes, portraits of real characters, and the Roman fondness for trompe l'oeil —painting intended to fool the eye into believing one is seeing real three-dimensional objects, architectural details, or natural vistas.

The major Roman artistic statements were related to monumental architecture and sculpture. The Arch of Titus (c. 81 CE) describes the emperor's triumph and the spoils of Jerusalem in deep relief sculpture, a narrative of real events with lively poses. Trajan's Column (98–117 CE) is unlike any previous carved record: its story of Trajan's campaigns against the Dacians winds unbroken for more than 650 feet up the shaft of the 125-foot-high marble column; in low relief, like most ancient sculpture it was originally heightened with color. In the golden age of the empire, the emperor Hadrian (reigned 117–138 CE), an admirer of Greek culture, built extensively. His villa at Tivoli is a magnificent complex of baths, temples, gardens, and pavilions, and he commissioned the rebuilding of the greatest achievement of Roman architecture, the Pantheon in Rome. The relatively plain exterior of this temple "of all the gods" belies the astonishing technical accomplishment and interior decorative details. Inside, the wall of the main circular section of the building is characterized by rectangular niches and apses, small tabernacles, and a wealth of variously colored marble panels. A massive concrete dome is broken by a central oculus, or hole, that lets in an ever-moving shaft of light. Another imperial monument, to the emperor Marcus Aurelius, is the best surviving equestrian statue from antiquity, and the inspiration for the revival of the form in Renaissance Italy by Donatello.

The late classical era overlaps the early Christian period. Beginning with the monuments in the age of Constantine—the first Roman emperor to embrace Christianity—a new emphasis can be seen, more on spiritual meaning and symbolism, less on the realistic depiction of the world and personal accomplishments. The commanding bust of Constantine (c. 313 CE) is a large (eight feet high) head expressive of personality and majesty, but its huge eyes already represent the medieval Christian concept of "windows of the soul" to express inner being. In the Arch of Constantine, celebrating the emperor's victory over Maxentius in 312, there is little attempt at a cohesive style or realism, with many sculptural elements from other architecture physically incorporated. Already the familiar medieval large heads and squat figures are apparent. Similar de-emphasis of the real world and a burgeoning Christian iconography (salvation of souls, divine intervention, miracles) can be found in the art of the Catacombs, underground burial chambers outside Rome (200-400 CE); the image of Apollo was adopted to represent Christ in a small wall painting, *The Good Shepherd,* in the Catacomb of Priscilla.

MEDIEVAL AND RENAISSANCE PERIODS

During the Middle Ages, the Romans' cultural and artistic legacy lived on in the Byzantine empire, whose capital was the magnificent city of Constantinople (modern Istanbul, in Turkey). This empire lasted for a thousand years after the fall of the western Roman empire. Perhaps the greatest of the Byzantine emperors was Justinian (527–565 CE), who reaffirmed the empire and made Ravenna, a northeast Italian city on the Adriatic coast, the government center of the West. In Ravenna the important surviving art in the Byzantine style is at its finest. There, the seventh-century church of San Vitale echoes the mosaic mastery of the eastern Roman, or Byzantine, empire in Constantinople: its grandiose apse mosaics of glittering gold and sparkling color include walls depicting Emperor Justinian and Empress Theodora. The Byzantine style was meant to convey a supernatural, otherworldly effect. The most important church in Constantinople was Hagia Sophia, designed by the architects Isidorus and Anthemius—a magical, soaring structure with a beautiful dome, commissioned along with many other buildings by the Emperor Justinian in the mid-sixth century.

During the Dark Ages (about fifth to eighth centuries), Celtic artists of Ireland, Scotland, and northern Britain, especially in the monasteries, kept Western art alive in stone carvings and crosses with interlace patterns, and in magnificent illuminated manuscripts, whose design was influenced by Celtic metalwork. Among these manuscripts are the Book of Durrow (680), the Lindisfarne

Gospels (c. 690), and the Book of Kells (c. 800—the most sophisticated and flamboyant, with four hundred decorative initial letters). The end of the Dark Ages was officially marked by the coronation of the Frankish king Charlemagne as Holy Roman Emperor by the pope on Christmas Day 800. Charlemagne, whose capital was at Achen (Aix-la-Chapelle), aspired to create an empire that rivaled the Roman empire as well as reviving classical culture and learning. He acquired ancient Roman sculptures, established schools, gathered around him the scholars Alcuin and Theodulf, and commissioned illuminated manuscripts. Some of the finest of the early ninth-century manuscripts are the Utrecht Psalter, the Ebbo Gospels, and the Lorsch Gospels. The empire lapsed after Charlemagne but was revived by Otto the Great (after his 955 victory over the Hungarians). This period is marked by a revival of early Christian, Carolingian, and Byzantine art (Echternach Gospels, bronze doors at Hildesheim).

The Romanesque style of art and architecture was preeminent in the eleventh and twelfth centuries. A great expansion of building and sculpture occurred. It was the era of the First Crusade. Europe was more secure and settled, and there were more professional artisans, who traveled all over Europe. By then many local styles, including the decorative arts of the Byzantines, the Near East, and the German and Celtic tribes, were contributing to European culture. Common features of Romanesque churches are round arches, vaulted ceilings, and heavy walls that are profusely decorated—primarily with symbolic figures of Christianity, the realism of which for its creators had become less and less important and was, instead, subordinate to the message. Examples of the style are the abbey church in Cluny, France; Worms Cathedral (St. Peter's) in Germany; and Durham Cathedral in England. Sculpture, usually relief in stone, was an integral part of church architecture on portals (doorways) and capitals (column crowns). In France, prominent sculptural areas were around the door jambs and the semicircular area above the door, the tympanum. Romanesque sculpture grew out of the church almost organically, and was decoratively sophisticated. Examples are the tympanums at Sainte Foy in Conques and the Abbey of Moissac near Toulouse (the *Apocalypse*). The Great Tympanum depicting *Christ in Majesty* and the *Last Judgment* at St. Lazare (Autun Cathedral) is the work of Gislebertus, who signed his name. It is marked by an overall unity of design and an inventive use of narrative detail; it contains biblical scenes, allegories, and imagery from the mystery plays. One of the finest free-standing Romanesque sculptural works is the brass baptismal font of Renier de Huy, a work whose figures display realistic proportions and classical influence, thus pointing the way to the innovations of the Gothic and early Renaissance styles.

Gothic art flourished in Europe from the twelfth through the fifteenth centuries and was primarily a French and northern European style. The cathedrals in this style are some of the purest expressions of an age: they combine a continued search for engineering and structural improvement with features that convey a relentless verticality, a reach toward heaven, and the unbridled adoration of God. Soaring and airy, these cathedrals were constructed using such elements as flying buttresses and pointed arches and vaults, and are decorated by a profusion of sculptures and stained-glass windows that were, for the worshippers, visual encyclopedias of Christian teachings and stories. The first major Gothic church was Abbot Suger's Church of St. Denis, outside Paris (begun 1137–1144). The finest example of the Gothic use of stained glass is the decoration of Sainte Chapelle (c. 1245) in Paris, whose walls of stained glass create a jewel-like flood of heavenly light. Gothic art emphasized greater spirituality, as well as greater humanity and tenderness, than previous Christian art; its most important religious figure is the Virgin Mary. The style in sculpture displays grace and realism, and figures are often elongated to match the skyward-stretching form of the architecture. Rheims Cathedral, one of the masterpieces of the northern Gothic style, boasts some two thousand sculptures (c. 1230-1240). Other important Gothic cathedrals are Chartres, Beauvais, Bourges, and Amiens in France, and in England, Salisbury and Wells.

The work of Nicholas of Verdun at the end of the twelfth century reveals a classical style; the awakening of the spirit of humanism in Gothic art led to a new interest in the natural world and a revival of the classical tradition. The thirteenth and fourteenth centuries were a vital and exciting period that came to be considered both Gothic and proto-Renaissance. In northern Europe, life itself became more festive, the artisan and merchant classes achieved some status—among richer courts, tales of knights, and the great romances—all of which inspired the colorful and realistic paintings of the sumptuous books of hours (the Limbourg Brothers: *Les Très Riches Heures du Duc de Berry,* 1413–1416).

The Italian school of this period—from 1250 onward—provides the first glimmers of the Renaissance—in a new naturalism, plus an emphasis on wall decoration in fresco and the painting of altarpieces (panels—the forerunners of the easel paintings). The Florentine painter Cimabue (active 1272–1302) produced tempera paintings that signaled a clear movement toward the naturalistic treatment of human figures (*San Trinita Madonna*). Duccio (active 1278–1318) of Sienna painted the *Rucellai Madonna*, in which Mary is portrayed as a real human in real space, shown from the side. And Duccio's *Virgin in Majesty* (from the *Maesta* altarpiece, 1308–1311, for Siena Cathedral) has figures of even greater solidity, clearly inhabiting realistic space. Giotto (c. 1267–1337) was famed and successful in his lifetime; his work is often regarded as the beginning of Renaissance art in Florence. He is known for his ability to depict physical beings, dramatic and realistic details and gestures, human reactions, and real spatial arrangements. His *Ognissanti Madonna* shows real people beneath the drapery, as well as delicacy and grace and convincing spatial relationships. His Arena Chapel paintings in Padua depict the life story of the Virgin and Christ in a series of independent but continuous-narrative pictures, full of drama and psychological nuance. Giotto's other works include *The Life of St. Francis* paintings in the Bardi Chapel, Santa Croce, Florence (1316–1320) and *The Life of St. John the Baptist* in the Peruzzi Chapel. In the fourteenth century, Sienese painters were among the leaders in innovation in the new realism: Simone Martini (1285–1344; *The Annunciation*) and Ambrogio Lorenzetti (active first half of the fourteenth century; *The Presentation in the Temple* and *The Allegory of Good Government* and other frescoes in the Palazzo Publico in Sienna).

Lines were often blurred between the Gothic and the early Renaissance in sculpture. In Pisa, innovations were made in the thirteenth and fourteenth centuries by Nicola Pisano (active 1258–1284) and his son Giovanni. Nicola created the marble pulpit for the Baptistery at Pisa (he signed and dated it); based on classical models, it has crowded figures, multiple poses, and realistic movement. His pulpit for Sienna Cathedral is marked by even more animated movement. Giovanni's Pisa Cathedral pulpit (1302–1310) contains a naked female figure and merges Gothic and classical influences.

In fifteenth-century Florence, first among all the newly rich and independent Italian cities, wealthy patrons, merchants, and nobles consciously revived classical art and philosophy, set humankind at the center of life, and made celebrations of civic pride of the highest importance. The technical discovery of proportion was used in architecture and art, and the great artists of the Renaissance often combined talents in all fields. Architecture, in the hands of Filippo Brunelleschi and Leon Battista Alberti, revived the Greco-Roman elements and took a scientific, ordered approach, one similarly expressed in painting with the emphasis on the calculated composition of figures in space known as perspective. Brunelleschi (1377–1440) invented single-vanishing-point perspective, and the dome he designed for Florence Cathedral (added 1420–36) was a symbol of both technical and classical rebirth. Alberti (1404–1472) was an important early Renaissance architect (Palazzo Rucellai, Florence, 1446–55) and wrote on the mathematics of perspective in *On Painting* (1435). Michelozzo (1396–1472) designed the first great Renaissance palace, the Palazzo Medici in Florence. In Rome, Donato Bramante (1444–1514) designed—in addition to ambitious plans for rebuilding St. Peter's—a structure for the spot where St. Peter was crucified, the Tempietto (San Pietro in Montorio, 1502). It is the first Renaissance building created in imitation of a circular Roman temple and is vaulted by a hemispherical dome and encircled by classical columns. Andrea Palladio (1508–1580), the writer of the most influential treatise on architecture for centuries *(The Four Books of Architecture)*, created in the Villa Rotonda in Vincenza (begun 1567–69) a perfect unity of geometric forms: four temple fronts face the four compass points and surround an inner cube of rooms; the central dome provides a symbol of unity.

The sculptor Lorenzo Ghiberti won the 1401 competition for the bronze doors of the Florence Baptistery—his relief-sculpted panels boast graceful, realistic, classical figures. Other important sculptors were Nanni di Banco and Jacopo della Quercia. The greatest of the early Renaissance sculptors, however, was Ghiberti's pupil Donatello (1386–1466), whose work was not only classically inspired and realistic, but highly theatrical and full of psychological undertones. *St. George* is a life-size marble statue of a handsome hero, full of earthly life and potential power. His *David,* one of the most famous Renaissance bronze sculptures, marks the revival of the classical free-standing nude male—sinuous in form, in an elegant, almost impish pose. His *Gattamelata* (1443–48) revived the free-standing equestrian statue, based on the ancient Marcus Aurelius statue in Rome.

The first great painter of the Renaissance was Masaccio (1401–c. 1428). In the *Holy Trinity* fresco for the Church of Santa Maria Novella in Florence, he used perspective based on Brunelleschi's ideas; there is a clear light source that unifies the whole, plus classical details, such as the Corinthian pilasters framing Ionic columns. In the *Tribute Money* (fresco for the Brancacci Chapel in Santa Maria Carmine in Florence) real characters in expressive poses inhabit a realistic landscape (based on the hills east of Florence), all united by Brunelleschian perspective. Other important early Renaissance painters were Paolo Uccello, who was obsessed by perspective *(The Battle of San Romano,* c. 1455); Fra Angelico (c. 1395–1455), whose work was colorful and calmly sweet *(The Deposition; The Annunciation)*; Fra Filippo Lippi (1406–1469; *The Madonna and Child with Two Angels);* and Piero della Francesca (c. 1416–1492; *The Flagellation of Christ; The Resurrection* [with its foreshortened sleeping soldiers]). More than any other painter, Botticelli (c. 1445–1510) epitomized the spirit of the early Renaissance. A favorite of the Medicis, his work is intensely religious and allegorical and insistent on recalling the images of classical antiquity. He painted many Madonnas (which since the nineteenth century have been admired for their sweet countenances), as well as humanist allegories of classical inspiration: *The Birth of Venus* (the ultimate symbolic depiction of the period's rebirth) and *Primavera* (a visual celebration of spring). Other notable artists of this period were Andrea Mantegna (known for his bold experiments in perspective), who worked in Mantua (Ducal Palace paintings), and Giovanni Bellini of Venice (*St. Francis in Ecstasy*).

The three pillars of the High Renaissance of the early sixteenth century are Leonardo da Vinci, Michelangelo, and Raphael. Leonardo's intellectual curiosity led him to make scientific deductions (and sketch out inventions such as flying machines) based on observed reality; these he recorded in his famous Notebooks. In addition to *The Last Supper* (1495–98) and the *Mona Lisa* (1503), he painted *The Virgin of the Rocks* (1483–85), which epitomizes his artistic approach: strange and metaphysical, suffused with mysterious light, the picture uses the technique of sfumato, a smoky-shadowy way of modeling form.

Michelangelo, too, excelled in many fields: he was a poet, painter, sculptor, and architect. In addition to his architectural designs of the Medici Chapel in San Lorenzo and the Laurentian Library, he redesigned St. Peter's in Rome, adding an enormous dome and completing the work previously planned by Bramante and Raphael. His sculptures (*David; Moses;* the Tomb of Giuliano de' Medici), which are powerful and heroic, seek to portray bodily perfection, and convey a perfect synthesis of the human and the divine—the epitome of the Neoplatonic philosophy of the Renaissance (that is, the body expresses the spirit). The Sistine Chapel frescoes in the Vatican in Rome are his masterpieces: in painting a complex system of dynamic figures full of raw human power and divine spirit, Michelangelo created some of the world's most unforgettable artistic images (*The Creation of Adam; The Creation of Eve;* the Sybils; the Prophets; *The Creation of the World,* all on the ceiling [1508–12], as well as *The Last Judgment,* on the wall [1534–41]). For centuries the paintings of Raphael (1483–1520) have been the measure of artistic perfection. Raphael's Madonnas are both spiritual ideals and clear personalities, set against a serene landscape, and represent perfect compositional balance (*The Madonna and Child with St. John* [c. 1506] and *The Sistine Madonna* [1512]). In *The School of Athens* at the Stanza della Segnatura in the Vatican (1509–11), Raphael combines, in a massive composition of figures and architecture, elements of major Renaissance paintings—obvious perspective, classically inspired architecture, portraits of ancient philosophers, and even likenesses of Leonardo, Michelangelo, and himself. His *Transfiguration,* with its dramatic lighting, mixture of heavenly and earthly spheres, and floating figures in clouds, crowns the Renaissance ideal of art and is a blueprint for the pictorial elements used in Baroque art.

Venetian and northern Italian painters worked in highly personal styles, leading toward the style called Baroque. The Mannerists of the first half of the sixteenth century produced work full of exaggerations: floating angels, the confusion of illusion and reality, contorted and elongated figures, awkward spatial relationships, and strange lighting effects. The great Mannerists were Parmagianino (*The Madonna with the Long Neck*), Pontormo (*The Deposition*), and Bronzino (*Venus,*

Cupid, Folly, and Time). Giulio Romano painted the fantastic Sala dei Giganti in Mantua's Palazzo del Te, a structure he designed with typical Mannerist wildness: amidst classical perfection in form, massive stones jut out like monstrous ruins. In Parma, Correggio created pre-Baroque art full of drama and mysterious light, and incorporated floating angels (*The Adoration of the Shepherds*). Among the great Venetians were Bellini (the San Zaccaria Altarpiece) and Giorgione (an innovator in "mood painting": of pastoral classical worlds, a favorite subject of the Baroque and later Rococo artists; *The Tempest; Venus*). The giant among the Venetians is Titian (active c. 1500–1576), whose brilliant color and dynamic brushwork made him one of the most admired artists of his time and made his name synonymous with great art through the succeeding centuries. There are plenty of floating clouds and cherubs in Titian's paintings, and the importance of the female nude is evident in *The Rape of Europa, Sacred and Profane Love,* and *The Venus of Urbino* (significant because this female nude is not associated with a classical/mythological theme). Among his religious masterpieces are *The Assumption of the Virgin* and the *Pesary Madonna*. Drawing ever closer to the Baroque spirit were two other Venetians: Veronese, who specialized in vast pageants unfolding in a single, grand painting (*The Feast in the House of Levi*), and Tintoretto, whose unique canvases team with vibrant life and dramatic incident, from the intimate *Susanna and the Elders* (c. 1557) to the astonishing, turbulent, glowing scene of *The Last Supper* (1592–1594).

The northern European Renaissance also displayed a renewed interest in the visible world, and works by Albrecht Dürer, Lucas Cranach, Matthias Grünewald, and Albrecht Altdorfer reveal an emphasis on the symbolism of minutely observed details and an accurate realism based on observation of reality rather than on prescribed rules. This unique northern emphasis can be seen as far back as the fifteenth century. Northern art, particularly in the Netherlands (later Flanders and Holland) and Germany, pursued a parallel course to that in Italy from the Gothic period to the Baroque era—but with a clear difference: the reawakening to the material world was less intellectual and less based on classical models than in the south. Rather, it was a realism based on the tastes of a rising wealthy merchant and middle class, delighting in their everyday lives. This joyous visual naturalism was marked by jewel-like color in painting. In sculpture, Claus Sluter (d. 1406) carved the Well of Moses, an innovative masterpiece of realism and human characterization. Jan van Eyck (c. 1385–1441) exemplified the continuous northern insistence on the symbolism of objects, on a naturalism so precious in its details and observation of reality that all paintings, whether portraits or religious scenes, seem to have real-life bourgeois persons and their possessions as subjects. Among van Eyck's vibrantly colored masterpieces are the *Madonna with Chancellor Rolin* (c. 1435) and *The Arnolfini Marriage* (1434). Other important Flemish painters of the fifteenth century were Rogier van der Weyden (*The Last Judgment* [c. 1450] and *Portrait of a Young Woman* [c. 1440]); Hugo van der Goes (the Portinari Altarpiece) and Hans Memling (c. 1430–1494). In the work of Hieronymus Bosch (active 1470–1516), the symbolism of the north is taken to its most extreme in his bizarre and highly personal mystical masterwork, *The Garden of Earthly Delights* (c. 1505–1510).

In Germany the Renaissance produced many outstanding painters: Dürer, Grünewald, and Altdorfer, as well as Lucas Cranach, Hans Holbein, and Pieter Bruegel. By far the greatest of these was Albrecht Dürer (1471–1528), in many ways equal to Michelangelo in stature and innovation. Dürer traveled extensively and was influenced by the art of the Venetians; his scientific curiosity about the natural world was nearly equal to Leonardo's. Dürer lavished the same meticulous attention on lowly subjects (*The Piece of Turf; Hare*) that he did on major paintings (*The Four Apostles; The Adoration of the Trinity*). Dürer's fame spread throughout Europe because of his prolific and groundbreaking work in the area of printmaking (*The Great Passion* and *The Apocalypse* series; *Adam and Eve; Melancolia I*); as a virtuoso in the art of the woodcut (multiple copies printed from a raised surface) and metal engraving (multiple copies printed from an incised surface), Dürer has never been surpassed. The masterpiece of Grünewald (c. 1475–1528) is the Isenheim Altarpiece of 1515; Lucas Cranach the Elder (1472–1553) painted several portraits of Martin Luther, as well as *Adam and Eve* (1526); Albrecht Altdorfer depicted majestic landscapes, full of power and mystery, that dwarf the people in them (*St. George and the Dragon; The Battle of Alexander and Darius on the Issus*). One of the finest painters of the sixteenth century was Hans Holbein the Younger (1497–1543), who continued the northern emphasis on symbolic detail and highly finished realism, particularly in the area of portraiture. When he moved to London he became court painter to Henry VIII (*The Ambassadors* of 1553; *Sir Thomas More;* portraits of the king), and he is also known for his woodcut series *The Dance of Death.* The Flemish artist Pieter Bruegel specialized in robust depictions of peasants and ordinary people at work and play (*The Hunters in the Snow; The Peasant Wedding; The Corn Harvest*), often in landscape vistas viewed from a height.

THE SEVENTEENTH AND EIGHTEENTH CENTURIES

Presaged by the works of the Venetian artist Tintoretto (the radiating *Last Supper*) and El Greco in Spain (the visionary *Toledo; The Immaculate Conception*), the Baroque period of the seventeenth century produced artists who added heightened drama to the forms of Renaissance art. Bernini (1598–1680) was the giant of the style in Italy and enjoyed papal patronage, working in sculpture and architecture to create some of the most dynamic and personal statements of art. His architectural triumph was the design for the Piazza of St. Peter's in Rome, which united the various buildings of two centuries in two colonnaded galleries resembling outstretched arms. Bernini's sculpture is equally innovative and startling: his *David* is not an elegant, noble youth, but a powerful, angry warrior in motion; *St. Peter's Chair* is a complex sculpture of bronze, marble, stained glass, and stucco that grows out of the architecture of the church, incorporates the light of the oval stained glass, and overlaps the surrounding pilasters and walls with protruding shafts of bronze light-rays, clouds, and cherubs. *The Vision of the Ecstasy of St. Teresa* (Cornaro Chapel, Santa Maria della Vittoria in Rome) is a mesmerizing portrayal of mystical ecstasy, from the bronze shafts of heavenly light to the agitated and quirky folds of the saint's garment. Bernini's rival was Francesco Borromini, the other great Italian architect of the Baroque; his masterpieces in Rome include the Oratorio di San Filippo Neri, with its marriage of curved and triangular pediments, and

Sant'Ivo della Sapienza, with its plan based on two interlocking equilateral triangles forming a six-pointed star with a single domed center.

In France, Baroque splendor was carried to its grandest at Versailles, a complex supervised by Charles Le Brun. Vast terraces, water gardens, fountains, and the gallery of mirrors were all calculated to equate Louis XIV, the Sun King, with the god Apollo. In England, however, the seventeenth century marked the beginning of a new classicism, particularly through the influential writings of Palladio. The designs of Inigo Jones (1573–1652) were sober, grand, classical (the Banqueting House and Queen's Chapel in London). Christopher Wren (1632–1723) rebuilt much of London after the fire of 1666 in a new style of Baroque energy, classical elements, and even a touch of Gothic. The Palladian/classical "revival" in architecture—neoclassicism—continued throughout the eighteenth and early nineteenth centuries. Examples in England are William Kent's Mereworth Castle (1723); Lord Burlington's Chiswick House (1720–25); and Robert Adam's Syon House in Isleworth (1762–69), with its interior of green marble and gilt copies of famous ancient classical statues. In America, the author of the Declaration of Independence and third U.S. president, Thomas Jefferson, designed his Monticello estate in Virginia according to Palladian principles.

In painting, the most significant proponent of the Italian Baroque was Caravaggio (1571–1610), whose models were ordinary people, and whose use of contrasting shadow and light was revolutionary and made for works of bold drama (*The Calling of Saint Matthew; The Conversion of Saint Paul*). The Flemish masters Peter Paul Rubens (1577–1640; *Marie de Medici Lands at Marseilles; The Raising of the Cross; The Descent from the Cross)* and Jacob Jordaens portrayed figures in constant motion, draperies of agitated angles, and effects of lighting and shadow that amplified emotional impact and mystery. In this spirit followed such painters of court life and middle-class portraiture as Velazquez (1599–1660; *The Infanta Margarita; The Maids of Honor*) in Spain; Anthony Van Dyck *(Charles I Hunting)* in England; and in Holland, Frans Hals (1581–1666; *The Laughing Cavalier*) and Rembrandt van Rijn. Rembrandt (1601–1669), one of the greatest artists of all time, used expressive brushwork and mysterious light contrasts to enliven religious and genre painting and portraiture, particularly of groups. Rembrandt's influence has remained consistently potent throughout the centuries, since his art appears to impart universal truths, and sections of his compositions glow with a mysterious inner light (*The Night Watch; The Descent from the Cross; The Anatomy Lesson of Dr. Nicolaes Tulp;* many self-portraits). Rembrandt also set the standard for perfection in the art of etching (printing from a metal plate with incised lines that have been etched away by acid; *Christ Healing the Sick*).

The art of the early eighteenth century is often called Rococo. Painters like Jean Antoine Watteau (*Embarkation for Cythera*, 1717), Giambattista Tiepolo (frescoes of the Wurzberg Residenz), François Boucher (*Diana Bathing*, 1742), and Jean Honoré Fragonard (*Women Bathing*, 1777), often creating decorative wall and ceiling schemes, turned the agitated drama of the Baroque into light, pastel-toned, swirling compositions that seem placed in an idyllic land of a golden age. Rococo style in architecture is marked by a profusion of elegant and fantastic decorative elements, often employing representations of shells, scrolls, and leaves. The influence of Versailles, with its mirrors radiating light and theatricality, is seen in the stucco fantasies covering Rococo interiors like living organisms, the relentless vegetation often supported by floating cherubs (the Zimmermann brothers, Church of Die Wies, Bavaria). The major Rococo palaces are the Residenz at Wurzburg by Balthasar Neumann, and the Munich Residenz, Amalienburg Pavilon, and Residenz Theater, all designed by François Cuvillies in the 1730s.

In the seventeenth and eighteenth centuries, European artists also responded to middle-class life and everyday objects to create genre paintings: Jan Vermeer (1632–1675; *The Artist's Studio; The Head of a Girl)*; Adriaen van Ostade; Jean Baptiste Chardin (1699–1779; *The House of Cards; Saying Grace*). Jean Baptiste Greuze in France (*The Broken Pitcher)* and William Hogarth (*The Rake's Progress* and *Marriage ala Mode* series) in England endowed their everyday subjects with a wealth of narrative detail that aimed to impart a specific moral message. Such narrative art combined in the late eighteenth and early nineteenth centuries with romantic literature—Goethe, Byron, Shelley, Scott, Wordsworth, and others—and political events to produce works with a political point of view or a story to tell, in a variety of styles. Jacques Louis David (1748–1825) used a severe classical sculptural style (Neoclassicism) in his paintings to revive antique art and ennoble images of the French Revolution and Napoleon's empire (*The Death of Marat; The Oath of the Horatii; Napoleon in His Study*). The spiritual godfather of Neoclassicism is Nicholas Poussin (1593–1665), whose paintings of the seventeenth century are perfectly balanced, severe, idealized, and sculptural models of pristine classicism (*The Holy Family on the Steps; The Poet's Inspiration)*. Neoclassical sculpture in the late eighteenth century revived the aloof severity and perfection of form of ancient art. Leading sculptors were Jean Antoine Houdon (*Voltaire; George Washington*), Antonio Canova (*Pauline Borghese as Venus Victrix*), and Bertal Thorvaldsen (*Hebe*). In England, the draughtsman and engraver John Flaxman produced engraved outline illustrations reminiscent of Greek vase paintings for illustrations to the *Illiad;* his work was the basis for the enduring style of Wedgwood pottery.

THE NINETEENTH CENTURY

In the late eighteenth century, with the rise of democracy and republics, the revolutions in France and America, and the discovery of the preserved Roman city of Pompeii, there occurred a full-blown revival of Greek and Roman design. Important architectural examples are the Bank of England by John Soane, Canova's Temple of Possagno—which combines elements of both the Parthenon and the Pantheon—and the Virginia State Capitol in Richmond, designed by Thomas Jefferson to resemble a Roman temple. Another revival stressed the Gothic style, championed by architect Augustus Pugin and writer John Ruskin—inspiring numerous Victorian Gothic buildings in England (Charles Barry's Houses of Parliament in London, 1840–65) and America (Richard Upjohn's Trinity Church in New York).

Political and other national events were important subjects for the romantic-realist painters of the early nineteenth century. The Spanish painter Francisco de Goya commented powerfully on political events in his painting *May 3, 1808*. In France, Eugene Delacroix (1798–1863; *The Death of Sardanapalus; Liberty Leading the People*) and Theodore Gericault (1791–1824; *The Raft of the Medusa*) imbued subjects from literature, the Bible, exotic lands, and current events with dramatic, heroic intensity. The grandeur and transcendence of nature, the emotional reaction to inner dreams, and metaphysical truths of romanticism are seen in the work of such mystical artists as England's William Blake (a master of innovative printmaking), Henry Fuseli, and John Martin, and America's Thomas Cole. Caspar David Friedrich in Germany and the English Pre-Raphaelites (William Holman Hunt, John Everett Millais, Dante Gabriel Rossetti, Ford Madox Brown, Arthur Hughes, and others) endowed their keenly observed, minutely detailed works with a romantic spirit of poetic yearning and literary references, and accurately re-created the natural world in brilliantly colored landscapes.

In the first half of the nineteenth century, landscape painting in England reached a zenith with the works of John Constable (1776–1837; *The White Horse; The Haywain*) and Joseph Mallord William Turner (1775–1851; *The Slave Ship; Snowstorm: Hannibal Crossing the Alps*). Turner's awe-inspiring landscapes, revolutionary in their lighting effects achieved through bold, expressive brushwork, form a bridge between the spirit of romanticism and the expressionistic brushwork and realism of the Barbizon School in France, whose chief painters were Charles Daubigny and Jean Baptiste Camille Corot. Beginning with Barbizon, the French painters of the nineteenth century concentrated more and more on the reporter-like depiction of everyday life and the natural environment in a free, painterly (gestural brushwork) style. The realist pioneers Gustave Courbet (*The Stone Breakers; A Burial at Ormans*), Jean Francois Millet (*The Sower; The Angelus*), and Honoré Daumier (*The Third-Class Carriage*)—renowned as a political caricaturist, Daumier's chief medium was the lithograph—paved the way for the stylistic and subject innovations of the Impressionists.

In Impressionism, traditional means of composing a picture—academic methods of figure modeling, of color relations, and accurate and exact rendering of people and objects—were rejected in favor of an art that emphasized quickly observed and sketched moments from life, the relation of shapes and forms and colors, the effects of light, and the act of painting itself. Beginning with Edouard Manet (*Le Déjeuner sur l'Herbe; Olympia*) in the 1860s, French artists continually blurred the boundaries of realism and abstraction. The great Impressionist painters concentrated on landscapes and scenes of everyday life. Claude Monet (1840–1926) painted *Ladies in the Garden, Gare St. Lazare* (a steam-drenched train station), and multiple views of haystacks and Rouen Cathedral in varying daylight conditions. Auguste Renoir (1841–1919) painted people from contemporary life as well as robust female nudes (*Umbrellas; The Luncheon Party; The Bathers*). Like Manet and many other French artists, Edgar Degas (1834–1917) was influenced by the compositional techniques of Japanese prints; he delighted in achieving spontaneity by depicting his subjects from unusual angles and with figures seemingly arbitrarily cut off at the edge. Degas specialized in scenes of Parisian life and horses, nudes, and dancers (*The Glass of Absinthe; Ballet Rehearsal*). Other important Impressionist painters are Camille Pissarro, Alfred Sisley, Frederic Bazille, and Mary Cassatt—an American whose domestic interiors were greatly influenced by the flatness and coloring of Japanese prints. Auguste Rodin (1840–1917; *The Burghers of Calais; The Thinker; Honoré de Balzac)* produced powerful sculptures with the freedom of Impressionist style, and Degas also depicted his favored ballet dancers in bronze.

By the 1880s pure Impressionism gave way to the more experimental arrangements of form and color of the Post-impressionists—Japanese prints held much allure for Paul Gauguin (1848–1903), who arbitrarily placed almost garish colors in compositions where design and shape took precedence over any sense of perspective or proportion (*Vision After the Sermon,* which shows Jacob wrestling with the angel); and two works inspired by his stay in Tahiti: *Nevermore* and the woodcut *Noa Noa.* Vincent van Gogh (1853–1890) was the exception that seems to have become a rule: the misunderstood, struggling, emotionally disturbed genius whose art was only recognized after his death. Van Gogh adopted Gauguin's harsh and unusual color schemes that were unrelated to the reality of a scene, and painted with an innovative, personal, expressive brushwork of thick swirling lines—which paved the way for twentieth-century expressionism (*The Night Café; Sunflowers; Starry Night).* Georges Seurat (1859–1891) produced noble and serene compositions in a style called pointillism, which allowed the viewer to visually mix the colors of a painting that had been applied in minute individual dots (*La Grande Jatte; The Circus*). Henri de Toulouse-Lautrec, more than any other French artist, concentrated on themes of night life and entertainment and employed thick outlines and the flatness of shapes and color of Japanese prints, especially in his many color lithographic posters. Paul Cézanne, considered by many to be the father of modern art, used the lessons of Impressionism to make the subjectivity of the artist paramount. He bent his subjects' shapes and contours away from realistic proportions and relationships, and assigned colors based on harmonious balance in the picture. Cézanne (1839–1906; numerous self-portraits; *The Great Bathers; Still Life with Onions*) was able to break apart and re-form reality, and make the act of painting itself significant, and in so doing he was able to usher in the achievements of twentieth-century Cubism and abstract art.

Other important groups in the last two decades of the nineteenth century that distorted reality and pursued sinewy forms or abstract patterning were the Nabis (Pierre Bonnard and Edouard Vuillard); the art nouveau artists (Toulouse-Lautrec, Aubrey Beardsley [illustrations for *Le Morte d'Arthur* and *Salome*], and Gustav Klimt [*The Kiss*]), the early expressionists (James Ensor [*The Entry of Christ into Brussels*] and Edvard Munch [*The Scream*]), and the Symbolists (Gustave Moreau, Odilon Redon, Puvis de Chavannes, and Edward Burne-Jones).

The most significant innovations in nineteenth-century architecture were related to technical accomplishment; the possibility of construction on a large scale in metal, iron, and glass allowed for revolutionary skeletal structures. The Crystal Palace, built for London's Great Exhibition in 1851 by Joseph Paxton, was 1600 feet long, and basically a glass building. A famous metal monument of no apparent purpose other than to symbolize another world's fair (in Paris in 1889) was Gustave Eiffel's tower. English railway stations had similar designs, using metal and glass vaulted roofs (John Dobson's Central Railway Station, Newcastle-upon-Tyne). And in America, the steel-skeleton structure dictated no-nonsense, stripped-down, functional city buildings by Daniel H. Burnham and John W. Root (Reliance Building, Chicago, 1890-1894) and Louis Sullivan (Wainwright Building, St. Louis, 1890-1891). The curves and vegetal ornamentation of the art nouveau style were employed in the buildings of Hector Guimard, Victor Horta, and Antonio Gaudi.

The Twentieth Century

Architecture in the twentieth century announced a clean break with the past, building upon the technical and structural innovations of such nineteenth-century masters as Joseph Paxton and Louis Sullivan. Frank Lloyd Wright (1867–1959) was perhaps the new century's greatest innovator, who transformed both commercial and residential architecture into structures that perfectly matched their surroundings, broke with the decorative language of the past, and offered functionalism in working and living spaces. Such private residences as the Robie house (1909) in Illinois and Fallingwater (the Kaufman house) in Pennsylvania brilliantly and innovatively mingle interior and exterior space. In the 1920s, the Bauhaus school of design in Dessau, Germany, championed abstract art, geometric design, machine-age elements, and restricted ornament. The director was the important architect Walter Gropius, whose design for the Bauhaus school building featured glass facades—pure line and geometric shapes. In Berlin in the 1920s Mies van der Rohe abandoned the ornamental vocabulary of the past for glass and steel skyscrapers and concrete office blocks. In America, Mies van der Rohe's apartment buildings on Chicago's Lake Shore Drive are rectangular blocks (1948–51), and his Seagram building in New York (1954–58) is perhaps the most famous example of the trend of skyscraper glass rectangles. This American glass-box aesthetic is also seen in Wright's Johnson Wax building (1936–39) in Racine, Wisconsin; the Lever Brothers and Pepsi-Cola buildings in New York by the firm of Skidmore, Owings, and Merrill; the presidential Palace of the Alvorada in Brasilia (1958) by Oscar Neimeyer; and Le Corbusier's United Nations design. This style of technology-driven, unadorned, stripped-to-essentials architecture in the industrialized nations since the 1930s has been called International Style or simply modernism. In the last twenty years, the austerity of modernism has been redirected into a more decorative and humanistic style, often termed postmodernism, which incorporates cultural influences, imaginative decorative touches, and historical architectural elements into designs appropriate to modern technology and uses. Among the architects working in the style are Robert Venturi and Michael Graves.

Sculpture and painting, from the beginning of the twentieth century, built upon the rejection of realistic proportions and naturalistic depiction, substituting a breakup of forms and a play of shape and color such as employed by Gauguin, Van Gogh, Cézanne, the Nabis, and others. The new freer form of art centered around the personality of the artist and celebrated personal style and the manipulation of two-dimensional pictorial elements. In the late nineteenth and early twentieth centuries this evolved in a number of directions. Some artists turned inward to explore mystical, symbolic, and psychological truths: Symbolists, expressionists, and exponents of art nouveau, such as Odilon Redon, Jan Toorop, Edvard Munch, James Ensor, and Gustav Klimt. The German Expressionists portrayed disturbing psychological truths through highly personal styles and disjointed compositions, and they frequently worked in woodcut. These German artists banded together from 1905 to 1913 in a group called Die Brucke; their aims were unabashedly revolutionary, and their work was often meant to shock. Die Brucke's members were Ernst Kirchner, Karl Schmidt-Ruttluff, Erich Heckel, Otto Mueller, Max Pechstein, and Emil Nolde—all of whose compositions emphasized distortion, angular and contorted figures, sometimes screaming color, and outrageous themes. In the face of the horrors of World War I, shock value and humor were the artistic weapons of choice for the Dada artists (Francis Picabia, Man Ray, Hans Arp, Kurt Schwitters, Marcel Duchamp, Max Ernst), whose "antiart" or "nonart" works often assembled any materials available ("found objects"), from newspaper clippings and photographs to bicycle wheels (Marcel Duchamp's *Ready-made,* 1913, a wooden stool with a bicycle wheel attached).

Among the artists who pursued formal innovations were Henri Matisse, Pablo Picasso, Georges Braque, and Juan Gris. Matisse (1869–1954) was the leading figure of the Fauves (dubbed "wild beasts" because of their relentlessly unreal use of color). Matisse's most important works reduced a picture to its essentials—flat color and line (*The Dance; Le Luxe II*). Other Fauves were Andre Derain, Georges Braque, Maurice Vlaminck, and peripherally, Georges Rouault, whose art was distinctly religious. The most revolutionary and far-reaching art movement of the twentieth century was Cubism—which, by its blatant visual decomposition and reassemblage of observed reality, seemed the most direct call for the total destruction of realistic depiction and for abstraction. The greatest Cubist artist and one of the most important figures in the history of art was Pablo Picasso (1881–1973; *Les Demoiselles d'Avignon; Three Musicians; Ma Jolie*). His use of African and Oceanic tribal art, and his emphasis on taking objects apart and reassembling them—thus showing a subject's multiplicity of aspects and dissolving time and space—led to similar experiments by Georges Braque, Juan Gris, Fernand Léger, Marcel Duchamp (*Nude Descending a Staircase,* 1912), the sculptors Alexander Archipenko and Jacques Lipchitz, and the Italian Futurist Umberto Boccioni (*Unique Forms of Continuity in Space,* sculpture, 1913, and *The City Rises,* painting, 1911).

In the first decades of the twentieth century, pure abstraction, with little or no relation to the outside world, was approached in the more emotional, expressionistic, and color-oriented paintings of Wassily Kandinsky (with Franz Marc, a proponent of the Blue Rider school), Robert Delaunay, and Paul Klee. More cerebral arrangements of abstract geometrical shapes and colors were the mark of Kasimir Malevich (his Suprematist compositions), Piet Mondrian, and the Bauhaus School of Design in Germany (Klee, Kandinsky, Joseph Albers, Walter Gropius, Laszlo Moholy-Nagy; where Marcel Breuer originated the first tubular steel chair, a standard of mid-century "modern" furniture design). The Bauhaus's simplified and usually geometric-oriented aesthetic influenced architecture, industrial and commercial design, sculpture, and the graphic arts for half a century. In architecture can be seen the most obvious results of this new tradition, the simplified, sleek structures of Mies van der Rohe, Walter Gropius, Le Corbusier, and Frank Lloyd Wright.

Inspired by the psychoanalytic writings of Sigmund Freud and Carl Jung, the subconscious and the metaphysical became another important element in art, especially in the work of the Surrealist artists Salvador Dali (*The Persistence of Memory*), Giorgio de Chirico, Max Ernst, René Magritte, Joan Miró, and Yves Tanguy. Important sculptors who manipulated abstract shapes and/or were influenced by tribal arts in the twentieth century include Constantin Brancusi (*The Kiss*, 1910), Henry Moore (influenced by American Pre-Columbian art; *Mother and Child*, 1924; *Reclining Figure*, 1929), Hans Arp, and Alberto Giacometti. Alexander Calder created floating assemblies called mobiles, and Louise Nevelson made constructions and wall sculptures from scraps of every-day objects.

Obsession with self and with abstraction also led to the major American art movement after World War II, Abstract Expressionism, whose chief exponents were Clyfford Still, Jackson Pollock ("drip" paintings), Willem de Kooning, Franz Kline, and Robert Motherwell. Other Americans took this movement into the area of color-field painting, a cooler, more reserved formalism of simple shapes and experimental color relationships: Mark Rothko, Barnett Newman, Joseph Albers, and Ad Reinhardt.

Other important trends in American art in the twentieth century were reflective of a democratic and consumer society. The muralists and social realists during the first half of the century created art that was dynamically realistic—representative of a youthful and vigorous America—and whose subjects were accessible to the average person. John Sloan, George Bellows (*Stag at Sharkey's*, 1909), Edward Hopper (the new life in the lonely city, noble, quiet, stark: *The Automat*, 1927; *Nighthawks*, 1942), Thomas Hart Benton, Grant Wood, and John Stuart Curry were among those who celebrated the American scene in paintings, and frequently in murals for public buildings and through widely available fine prints. The great Mexican muralists, who usually concentrated on political themes—Diego Rivera, José Clemente Orozco, and David Siqueiros—brought their work to the public both in Mexico and in the United States.

The icons of American popular culture found their way, in the movement known as Pop art, into canvases by Andy Warhol (the multiplied silk-screened images of Campbell Soup cans and Marilyn Monroe), Robert Indiana, Larry Rivers, Jasper Johns (use of the American flag), Roy Lichtenstein (enlarged comic book panels), and Robert Rauschenberg. Other developments during the last thirty years include: Kinetic art (works that move or produce an illusion of movement) and Op art (manipulation of abstract color and repetitive patterns to play tricks on the eye [Victor Vasarely; Bridget Riley]); Minimal art (the work reduced to essentials) and Conceptual art (the idea itself, rather than the technical accomplishment); and the actual movement of, or covering of, land and monuments on a massive scale (Christo: *The Arco della Pace Wrapped*, 1970; *Running Fence*, 1972–76, a 24.5-mile-long nylon fence along the hills of Sonoma and Marin counties in northern California). Super- or Photorealism is the style of the sculptor Duane Hanson and the painters Chuck Close, Richard Estes, and Philip Pearlstein.

DRILL: VISUAL ARTS AND ARCHITECTURE

1. Pop artists used recognizable imagery from the mass media such as commercial products, comics, and celebrities because

    (A) they wanted to criticize the superficiality and consumerism of American culture.
    (B) they wanted to celebrate the images of their time.
    (C) they wanted to take advantage of new techniques and materials to present new products.
    (D) None of the above.

2. The Minimalists sought to

    (A) reduce shape and form to its simplest, purest state.
    (B) remove all evidence of the human hand's part in the construction of their work.
    (C) imitate industrial production in the slickness and coldness of their work.
    (D) All of the above.

3. Andy Warhol, the first artist to truly make use of the mass media, worked in which of the following media?

    (A) television.
    (B) film.
    (C) sculpture.
    (D) All of the above.

4. Warhol often repeated the same image many times within a single painting because

    (A) he was imitating the way the media saturates us with an image.
    (B) he wanted to show how we become numb to an image after seeing it so many times.
    (C) it was easy.
    (D) All of the above.

5. Which of the following is NOT considered by artists to be a technique of forming clay "by hand"?

    (A) Throwing
    (B) Coiling
    (C) Slab building
    (D) Modeling

6. "Form Follows Function" is an expression coined by

    (A) Frank Lloyd Wright.
    (B) Louis Sullivan.
    (C) Le Corbusier.
    (D) Mies van der Rohe.

7. Which of the following architects were founding members of the Bauhaus School of architecture?

    (A) Walter Gropius and Ludwig Mies van der Rohe
    (B) I.M. Pei and Robert Venturi
    (C) Theo van Doesburg and Le Corbusier
    (D) Benjamin Latrobe and Louis Sullivan

8. The Ionic Order of Greek architecture is characterized primarily by

    (A) cushion-shaped capitals.
    (B) volute-shaped capitals.
    (C) bell-shaped capitals.
    (D) fluted columns.

9. Giacomo della Porta's design for the facade of the Church of II Gesu in Rome dates from which of the following periods of art history?

    (A) Early Christian
    (B) Romanesque
    (C) Northern Renaissance
    (D) Baroque

10. The central vertical supporting pillar of Romanesque and Gothic portals is called a

    (A) lintel.
    (B) jamb.
    (C) column.
    (D) trumeau.

11. The twentieth-century movement in architecture which immediately succeeded the International Style, and which was defined largely by the writings of Robert Venturi, is

    (A) Modernism.
    (B) Postmodernism.
    (C) Constructivism.
    (D) Romanticism.

12. The staircase in the Hotel van Eetvelde, designed by Victor Horta in 1895, illustrates which one of the following art historical styles?

    (A) Art Nouveau
    (B) Postmodernism
    (C) Neoclassicism
    (D) Post-Impressionism

13. The earliest known example of town planning in the history of architecture is

    (A) Forum of Caesar, Rome.
    (B) Stonehenge, England.
    (C) Acropolis, Athens.
    (D) Catal Huyuk, Turkey.

14. The dome of Florence Cathedral was built in the fifteenth century according to which of the following architect's designs?

    (A) Leonardo da Vinci
    (B) Filippo Brunelleschi
    (C) Leon Battista Alberti
    (D) Giuliano da Sangallo

15. Supports used in post-and-lintel architecture that are carved in imitation of female figures are called

    (A) sirens.
    (B) caryatids.
    (C) atlantes.
    (D) Corinthian columns.

16. The central dome of St. Mark's in Venice rests on curved triangular supports called

    (A) squinches.
    (B) pendentives.
    (C) corbelled arches.
    (D) fan vaults.

17. Reinforced concrete, also known as ferroconcrete, is defined as concrete that is

    (A) covered with brick facing.
    (B) combined with stone masonry blocks.
    (C) embedded with iron rods or mesh.
    (D) mixed with a water repellent.

18. The plan of Charlemagne's Palace Chapel at Aachen is often compared to that of which of the following buildings?

    (A) Hagia Sophia, Istanbul
    (B) The Pantheon, Rome
    (C) Sant'Apollinare in Classe, Ravenna
    (D) San Vitale, Ravenna

VISUAL ARTS AND ARCHITECTURE REVIEW

Answer Key

1.	(D)	6.	(B)	11.	(B)	16.	(B)
2.	(D)	7.	(A)	12.	(A)	17.	(C)
3.	(D)	8.	(B)	13.	(D)	18.	(D)
4.	(D)	9.	(D)	14.	(B)		
5.	(A)	10.	(D)	15.	(B)		

DETAILED EXPLANATIONS OF ANSWERS
DRILL: VISUAL ARTS AND ARCHITECTURE

1. **(D)** Pop artists wanted neither to criticize nor celebrate American culture, but simply to take pieces of it, hold up a mirror and reflect it back to the society which produced it. (A) is incorrect. This is too simplistic a reading of Pop art and there is no evidence to show this intent. (B) is incorrect. This is also too simplistic a reading of Pop art. There is no evidence to show this intent over any other. (C) is incorrect because the pop artists employed already-established techniques such as silk screening and lithograph for their works.

2. **(D)** Choices (A), (B), and (C) are all goals of minimalism.

3. **(D)** The correct answer is (D), all of the above. (A) is incorrect because Warhol had a short-lived TV show on MTV called *Andy Warhol's Fifteen Minutes*. (B) is incorrect because Warhol made many films including the experimental *Sleep*, an eight-hour-long shot of a man sleeping. (C) is incorrect because Warhol worked in sculpture from the 1960s onward. His most famous pieces are the *Brillo Boxes* from the early part of that decade.

4. **(D)** Choices (A), (B), and (C) are all true, according to statements which Warhol himself made.

5. **(A)** Coiling, slab building, and modeling are all methods of forming clay strictly by hand. "Throwing" clay involves the use of a potter's wheel, and thus is not technically considered a method of hand-forming clay.

6. **(B)** Louis Sullivan, an architect best known for his late nineteenth century skyscrapers, promoted the idea that a building's form should follow its function. His slogan "form follows function" became one of the Great Truths for modern architects of the twentieth century, among them Gropius and Mies van der Rohe.

7. **(A)** Walter Gropius and Ludwig Mies van der Rohe helped found the Bauhaus School in Germany in the 1920s but later moved to the United States, where they exerted profound influence on twentieth-century American architecture. I.M. Pei and Robert Venturi (B) were active

as architects in the later twentieth century (especially in the 1970s), well after the founding of the Bauhaus. Theo van Doesburg and Le Corbusier (C) were architectural contemporaries of the Bauhaus founders, but were not themselves involved in the school. Benjamin Latrobe and Louis Sullivan (D) were architects working in the nineteenth century, thus pre-dating the founding of the Bauhaus. Inigo Jones, the first of the great English architects, precedes the Bauhaus, having lived and worked in the seventeenth century.

8. **(B)** Volute-shaped capitals, whose circular spiral motifs, or volutes, are carved on the corners of the capitals at the tops of each column, are the distinguishing characteristic of the Ionic order. Cushion-shaped capitals (A) characterize the Doric order of Greek architecture; and bell-shaped capitals (C), usually adorned with acanthus tendrils, identify the Corinthian order. Fluted columns (D) appear in all Greek architectural orders and are not used as criteria to identify the individual order.

9. **(D)** The two-storied facade, the levels of which are unified by the large flanking scrolls; the paired columns; and the pedimented windows and niches were widely imitated in the Baroque period to varying degrees on other buildings. The dramatic effect of the building's overtly anti-classical design was typical of Baroque-era architecture. Early Christian (A) and Romanesque (B) churches were designed with much simpler, more austere facades; and there are no comparable facades in the architecture of the (C) Northern Renaissance.

10. **(D)** Trumeau, which is often in imitation of human or animal forms. A lintel (A) is the horizontal beam that rests upon the (B) jambs (frames) of a doorway. A column (C) refers to any simple cylindrical support; however, simple columns were not used as central supports in such doorways.

11. **(B)** Postmodernism was the period of architectural history that was formulated in the 1970s. The definition of Postmodern architecture is complex, and the phrase is rejected by many modern architectural historians; loosely defined, it refers to contemporary architecture that seeks to challenge and re-examine traditional methods of architectural expression. Modernismo (A) refers to the Spanish version of Art Nouveau. (C) Constructivism is a term used to define the works (both sculptural and architectural) of a group of early twentieth century Russian artists. Romanticism (D) is a nineteenth-century movement in architecture, in which architects sought to imitate architectural styles of past eras, including those of classical Greece and Rome and medieval Europe.

12. **(A)** Art Nouveau is distinguished by the use of such curvilinear, decorative details of interior design. Postmodernism (B) is a later period in the history of architecture, and is not defined by such decorative elements. Neoclassicism (C), a nineteenth-century era of architecture, is characterized by the use of classical Greek and Roman architectural details, which are more austere in nature Post Impressionism (D) is a movement in painting, which has no equivalent in the history of architectural design.

13. **(D)** Catal Huyuk, Turkey, which dates from ca. 6000 BCE, revealed upon excavation multiple dwelling units and structures apparently designed for worship, indicating that the complex was designed for the dwelling of a large number of persons. The Forum of Caesar, Rome (A) dates from the first century BCE. Stonehenge, England (B) dates from c. 2000 BCE and is not believed to have served as living space. The Periclean Acropolis, Athens (C) dates from the fifth century BCE.

14. **(B)** Filippo Brunelleschi, whose dome (built 1420–1436) was unprecedented in design. To span the 140-foot space, Brunelleschi designed his dome with an avoid profile (to reduce the thrust at the dome's base), and with a double shell and 24 ribs to lighten the weight yet provide the dome

with sufficient stability. Leonardo da Vinci (A) is not known to have designed a comparable dome, nor has any such construction been attributed to him. Leone Battista Alberti (C) was much influenced by Brunelleschi, but had no part in the design of the dome of Florence Cathedral, nor did Giuliano da Sangallo (D), who succeeded Brunelleschi as an architect.

15. **(B)**   The correct choice is (B) Caryatids. Sirens (A) are female *characters* from Greek mythology, not an architectural form. Atlantes (C) are supports in post-and-lintel architecture which are carved in imitation of *male* figures; they are the counterparts of caryatids. Corinthian columns (D) are an order of Greek architecture, and are distinguished by bell-shaped capitals carved with acanthus tendrils.

16. **(B)**   The correct choice is (B) pendentives. Squinches (A) are also utilized to support domes, but these are block-like members laid across the corners of a structural unit to support a dome of similar structure. Corbelled arches (C) are arches formed by stepping stones outward from a base until the stones meet at midpoint. Fan vaults (D) are elaborate groin vaults, with tracery defining their wedge-shaped forms.

17. **(C)**   Embedded with iron rods or mesh, as indicated by the term *"ferro*concrete." Concrete that is (A) covered with brick facing or (B) used with stone masonry blocks, is simply concrete that is combined with other building materials. Concrete mixed with a water repellent (D) is referred to as an *ad*mixture.

18. **(D)**   San Vitale, Ravenna, which is also a centrally-planned building with central nave and encircling ambulatory. It is commonly believed that Charlemagne either visited Ravenna and viewed the plan of San Vitale, or that he was made familiar with its plan through architects at his court. Hagia Sophia in Istanbul (A), the Pantheon in Rome (B), and the Orthodox Baptistery in Ravenna are all centrally-planned buildings, but in size, interior elevation, and division of interior space, they are not comparable to Charlemagne's Palace Chapel. The church of Sant'Apollinare in Classe in Ravenna is not centrally-planned, but designed along a longitudinal axis.

PHILOSOPHY REVIEW

ANCIENT PHILOSOPHERS

All of the Greek philosophers before Socrates are known as the pre-Socratics. Pythagoras was a sixth century BCE pre-Socratic philosopher and mathematician. Pythagoras, who made many scientific and mathematical discoveries, believed in the transmigration of souls.

Thales, a sixth and fifth century BCE pre-Socratic philosopher, is sometimes called "the father of Western philosophy." Thales held that the first principle, or substance, that everything in the universe is made out of is water.

Parmenides was a pre-Socratic philosopher in the fifth and fourth century BCE. He denied the existence of time, plurality, and motion. He is considered the founder of metaphysics.

Heraclitus, in the fourth century BCE, was a pre-Socratic philosopher. Heraclitus was said to have believed that everything is in a continuous state of flux. He was opposed to the idea of a single ultimate reality.

Zeno was a pre-Socratic philosopher in the fourth century BCE and a disciple of Parmenides. He was famous for a set of paradoxes, which are intended to show that plurality and motion do not really exist.

Socrates was an Athenian fourth century BCE philosopher. He supposedly wrote down none of his views, because he believed writing distorted ideas. His ideas have survived only through the writings of his followers, most notably Plato. It is unclear to what extent the views attributed to Socrates' character in Plato's dialogues were the views of the actual historical Socrates.

Atomism is the belief that matter consists of atoms. Both Leucippus, a fourth century BCE Greek philosopher, and Democritus, a fourth and third century BCE Greek philosopher, were atomists. They both concluded atoms are different-shaped bits of matter.

Plato, who lived from 427 to 347 BCE, was a Greek philosopher. Plato wrote dialogues, many of which contain Socrates as the main character. These dialogues provided the starting point for many later developments in various areas, for example: ethics, the study of morals; epistemology, the study of knowledge; and metaphysics, the study of reality. Plato's best known theory is the theory of Forms (or Ideas). According to this theory, the objects of knowledge are universals, such as The Good and The Just. Because specific things in this world, such as a just person, are mere reflections of the Forms, they can only be the objects of opinion.

Aristotle, who lived in the third century BCE, was an extremely influential Greek philosopher. Aristotle, who criticized Plato's theory of Forms, was the first to systematize logic. The medieval study and development of Aristotle's philosophy is known as Aristotelianism.

PHILOSOPHERS OF THE FIRST MILLENNIUM

Neoplatonism was the dominant philosophy in Europe from 250 through 1250 CE. Begun by Plotinus, a third century CE philosopher, Neoplatonism is a combination of Plato's ideas with those of other philosophers, such as Aristotle and Pythagoras. Another Neoplatonist was Augustine, a fourth and fifth century bishop and philosopher. Augustine had a profound effect on medieval religious thought.

St. Anselm, an eleventh century philosopher, was an Italian monk who became archbishop of Canterbury. He founded Scholasticism. Anselm was best known for his ontological argument for the existence of God.

St. Thomas Aquinas, a thirteenth century philosopher, was best known for his "Five Ways," five proofs of the existence of God. The philosophy of Aquinas and his followers is called Thomism. He is considered the greatest thinker of the Scholastic School. His ideas were made the official Catholic philosophy in 1879.

Ockham was a fourteenth century English philosopher and cleric. He was famous for the dictum "Do not multiply entities beyond necessity."

Hobbes (1588–1679) was a British materialist. One of his famous works is *Leviathan,* in which he argues that men are selfish by nature. Because of this belief, Hobbes felt that a powerful absolute ruler is necessary.

Rationalism is the view that knowledge of the external world can be derived from reason alone, without recourse to experience. Notable rationalists include Descartes, Leibniz, and Spinoza. Descartes (1596–1650) was an extremely influential French philosopher and mathematician. He held a view of the relation between the mind and body which has come to be known as Cartesian dualism. In this view, the mind and body are two distinct, though interactive, entities. Descartes is famous for the statement "*cogito ergo sum*," or "I think therefore I am."

Two other well known Rationalists were Gottfried Wilhelm von Leibniz and Benedict Spinoza. Leibniz (1646–1716) was a German philosopher who argued, in his *Theodicy*, that this is the best of all possible worlds. He is considered one of the greatest minds of all times. Spinoza (1632–1677), a Dutch-born philosopher, is best known for his *Tractacus Theologico-Politicus*. He felt mind and body are aspects of a single substance, which he called God or Nature.

Blaise Pascal (1623–1662) was a French philosopher, mathematician, and theologian. He is most famous for an argument called "Pascal's Wager," which provides prudent reasons for believing in God. His work, *Pensées* (Thoughts), published after his death, argues that reason is by itself insufficient for man's spiritual needs and cannot bring man to God.

Empiricism is the view that all knowledge is derived from experience. Three well-known empiricists are Locke, Berkeley, and Hume. John Locke (1632–1704) was an English philosopher. In his *Essay Concerning Human Understanding*, Locke attempted to present an empiricist account of the origins, nature, and limits of human reason. Berkeley (1685–1753), another empiricist, was an Irish philosopher and an idealist. Idealism is the view that the so-called "external world" is actually a creation of the mind (another well-known idealist is Hegel). Finally, David Hume (1711–1776) was a Scots philosopher. An empiricist, Hume drew attention to the problem of induction.

Jean-Jacques Rousseau (1712–1778) was a German-born political philosopher and a philosopher of education. His major work was *The Social Contract* (1762). Rousseau emphasized man's natural goodness.

Adam Smith (1723–1790) was a Scots philosopher and political economist. He wrote *The Wealth of Nations*. Smith has had an enormous impact on economics into the present day.

Immanuel Kant (1724–1804) was a German idealist philosopher. He was most famous for the categorical imperative—"Act only on that maxim which you can at the same time will to become a universal law"—as a test of moral principles. Kant is also well known for his epistemological work, including his ideas of the Noumenon and Phenomenon.

Jeremy Bentham (1748–1832) was a British philosopher and a lawyer. He was one of the founders of utilitarianism. He was a powerful reformer of the British legal, judicial, and prison system.

Georg Wilhelm Friedrich Hegel (1770–1831), a German idealist philosopher, is famous for his theory of the dialectic. According to the theory, a dialectic is a process of argument which proceeds from a thesis and its antithesis to a synthesis of the two. His idealistic system of metaphysics was highly influential.

James Mill (1773–1836) was a Scots philosopher and economist. Mill was also the father of the better-known philosopher J.S. Mill (1806–1873), who was an English empiricist philosopher. J.S. Mill is best known both for his *System of Logic* and for his ethical writings, including *Utilitarianism* and *On Liberty*.

Arthur Schopenhauer (1788–1860), a German philosopher, was a Kantian best known for *The World as Will and Idea*. Schopenhauer believed that only art and contemplation could offer escape from determinism and pessimism. Schopenhauer had a strong influence on Freud, Nietzsche, Proust, Tolstoy, and Thomas Mann.

Søren Kierkegaard (1813–1855), a Danish philosopher, was probably the first existentialist. Existentialism is the view that the subject of philosophy is *being*, which cannot be made the subject of objective inquiry but can only be investigated by reflection on one's own existence. Sartre is another notable existentialist.

Karl Marx (1818–1883), author of *Das Kapital*, was a German social theorist. Engels (1820–1895), Marx's collaborator, was a dialectical materialist. Dialectical materialism is the metaphysical doctrine originally propounded by Engels. According to the doctrine, matter, rather than the mind, is primary. Matter, also, is governed by dialectical laws in this view. Dialectical materialism is included in Marxism, the body of doctrines originally held by Marx and Engels.

Brentano (1838–1917) was a German philosopher and psychologist who is remembered for his "doctrine of intentionality."

Charles Peirce (1839–1914), an American philosopher, was the founder of pragmatism. As used by Peirce, pragmatism was originally a theory of meaning. Later, William James (1842–1910), an American (empiricist) philosopher and psychologist, used pragmatism as a theory of truth according to which "ideas become true just so far as they help us get into satisfactory relations with other parts of our experience."

Friedrich Wilhelm Nietzsche (1844–1900), a German philosopher, is best known for introducing the concept of the *Übermensch,* or the Overman. As a moralist, he rejected Christian values.

Bradley (1846–1924) was an English philosopher. An idealist, Bradley wrote *Appearance and Reality*.

Frege (1848–1925) was a German philosopher and mathematician. Frege is considered the founding father of modern logic, philosophy of mathematics, and philosophy of language.

Edmund Husserl (1859–1938), a German philosopher, developed phenomenology. Phenomenology is a method of inquiry which begins with the scrupulous inspection of one's own conscious thought processes. Husserl's goal was to create a completely accurate description of consciousness and conscious experience.

John Dewey (1859–1952) was an American pragmatist philosopher and educational theorist. Dewey developed the views of William James and Charles Peirce into his own version of pragmatism. He emphasized the importance of inquiry into acquiring knowledge. George Santayana (1863–1952) was an American Platonist philosopher, novelist, and poet. Santayana was a student of James. He attempted to reconcile Platonism and materialism.

Bertrand Russell (1872–1970) was a British philosopher. Along with Whitehead, he was the author of the extremely influential *Principia Mathematica*. Russell, in such seminal papers as "On Denoting" and "The Principles of Logical Atomism," argued that the structure of the world can be revealed by the proper analysis of language.

G.E. Moore (1873–1958), a British philosopher, is best known for his *Principia Ethica*. Moore emphasized the common sense view of the reality of material objects.

Logical positivism, a radical empiricist position, is the doctrine that the meaning of a proposition consists in the method of its verification. Logical positivism is also known as "logical empiricism." A group of logical positivists, known as the Vienna Circle, centered around the University of Vienna in the 1920s and 1930s. Founded by Schlick (1882–1936), a logical positivist philosopher, the Vienna Circle also included Neurath (1882–1945), an Austrian logical positivist philosopher, and Carnap (1891–1970), a German logical positivist philosopher.

Ludwig Wittgenstein (1889–1951), a Viennese-born philosopher, has had an enormous influence on the later philosophy of language. *Tractatus Logico-Philosophicus*, his first and most famous work, was a defense of a picture theory of meaning. This work contains such often quoted aphorisms as "The world is everything that is the case."

Martin Heidegger (1889–1976), a German philosopher, is commonly regarded, despite his objections, as an existentialist. Heidegger studied with Husserl and was influenced by Kierkegaard. Heidegger's own philosophy emphasized the need to understand "being."

Alfred Tarski (1902–1993) was a logician and mathematician. He is famous for his definition of the concept of truth for formal logical languages, which has been used extensively by philosophers of language as a basis for theories of meaning for natural language.

Sir Karl Popper (1902–1994), a philosopher of science, wrote *The Logic of Scientific Discovery*. He is best known for his claim that falsifiability is the hallmark of science.

Jean-Paul Sartre (1905–1980) was a French philosopher. Sartre was a founder of Marxism and existentialism. Sartre believed man is condemned to be free and to bear the responsibility of making free choices.

Hempel (1905–1997) was a German empiricist philosopher of science. His theories of confirmation and explanation have been extremely influential. Goodman (1906–1998), an American philosopher, was a nominalist. Goodman wrote, most notably, *Fact Fiction and Forecast* and *Languages of Art*.

Merleau-Ponty (1908–1961) was a French philosopher who worked on ethics and problems of consciousness. Willard Van Orman Quine (1908–2000) was an American empiricist philosopher of language and a logician. Sir Alfred Jules Ayer (1910–1989), an English philosopher, is a logical positivist and member of the Vienna Circle. He wrote *Language, Truth and Logic*. Austin (1911–1960) was a British philosopher of language. He developed the speech act theory. P. F. Strawson (1919–2006), a British philosopher of language and a metaphysician, is best known for arguing, in "On Referring," that some meaningful sentences have no truth value. John Rawls (1921–2002), an American political philosopher, is best known for *A Theory of Justice*. Noam Chomsky (1928–   ) is an influential American linguist and philosopher. Chomsky argues that there is an innate universal grammar. Donald Davidson (1917–2003) is an American philosopher of language and the mind. He holds a theory of the mind called anomalous monism. Saul Kripke (1941–   ) is an American philosopher of language, philosopher of the mind, and logician. His most influential work, "Naming and Necessity," launched the causal theory of reference. His theory, in part, deals with the distinction between a statement's sense and its reference.

DRILL: PHILOSOPHY

1. It is not surprising that Rationalists like Leibniz, Spinoza, and Hegel all accepted some version of the Coherence theory of truth because the main alternative, the Correspondence theory, places too much weight on

    (A) innate ideas.
    (B) experience.
    (C) the relations among ideas.
    (D) knowledge.

2. Benjamin Franklin, Thomas Jefferson, and George Washington all rejected theism, but were not atheists. This is because they were

    (A) deists.
    (B) skeptics.
    (C) Christians.
    (D) immoralists.

3. Sextus Empiricus was the codifier of Greek skepticism, a view that held we cannot give our firm assent to any

    (A) creed.
    (B) dogma.
    (C) belief.
    (D) moral code.

4. Jealousy and envy are often conflated or confused, but cases of jealousy and envy differ in at least one important respect:

    (A) Jealousy involves more than two people.
    (B) Envy can be expressed.
    (C) Jealousy involves a belief.
    (D) Jealousy is sexual.

PHILOSOPHY REVIEW

Answer Key

1.   (B)
2.   (A)
3.   (C)
4.   (A)

DETAILED EXPLANATIONS OF ANSWERS
DRILL: PHILOSOPHY

1. **(B)**   Choice (B) identifies the Correspondence theory with experience. Hence, the Correspondence theory is mainly identified with Empiricism, the main rival to Rationalism. Choice (A) cannot be correct because Empiricists do not accept a doctrine of innate ideas, nor do they think truth is a function of the relations among ideas (C). Both Empiricists and Rationalists are concerned with (D) knowledge. However, they approach these matters differently.

2. **(A)**   The early Americans rejected theism but were not atheists because they believed in a God, but not the God of theism. Their God was a Creator but otherwise an "absentee God" of the sort proclaimed by Voltaire and other deists. Choice (B) is too vague, for it does not specify what the skepticism concerned. Choice (C) is incorrect because some Christians were theists while others were deists. None of the three was (D) an immoralist.

3. **(C)**   The Skeptics differed from the dogmatists who believed that certain knowledge was possible but also differed from those who dogmatically asserted that knowledge is impossible. Sextus recommended suspending judgment about all beliefs, preferring to remain an open-minded inquirer. The correct answer is (C), since his skepticism was sweeping. All the other terms are too narrow to capture the scope of his view. One might suspend judgment about a (B) dogma, or (A) creed, or (D) moral code without suspending judgment about all beliefs. Sextus does not claim these are all false, but only that we are not in a position to know that they are true. He thus thinks other skeptics went too far in claiming falsehood.

4. **(A)**   A person can envy his neighbor's good fortune, but jealousy involves more than two people since it typically involves a response to the belief that another person is paying too much attention to a third person. Thus, Tom may be jealous of Jane's attention to Fred, but not envious of Jane's attention to Fred. The other answers all mention a feature that is common to jealousy and envy, as various philosophies of emotion have shown. Both jealousy and envy involve belief (C), and envy could be sexual (D), since, for example, one might envy someone's sexual prowess.

◼ Music Review

Music is the organization of sound in time. Because it exists only in time, what some people call the fourth dimension, rather than in three-dimensional space, music is one of the more elusive art forms. Given this abstract quality and the enormous variety of music that exists in the world, it is surprising to realize that there are only four ways that one sound can differ from another. Each individual tone has four properties that give it a particular character: duration, frequency, intensity, and timbre. Musicians make choices within each of these categories to create the effect they hope their music will have on its listeners.

Duration refers to how long a sound or a silence lasts and the rate at which one sound succeeds another. **Rhythm** is based on this fundamental property of sound and is essential to our perception of time. Rhythm is built into the natural world. There is rhythm in the movement of the stars, in the cycle of seasons, in the alternation of day and night, in our very heartbeats and breathing. If there were no rhythm, we would not be aware that time was happening.

Most of the music that we hear and all music to which we dance or march has a steady beat, a regular **pulse** that underlies the melody. Whereas the pulse is steady with an unchanging note value, melodic rhythm involves a variety of note values. If you sing any song and clap the pulse, you will notice that some of the beats have more than one melodic note to them and some melodic notes extend over several beats. For instance, in "Happy Birthday to You," both of the notes of "happy" occur on a single beat while "you" extends over two beats.

Tempo refers to the speed of the pulse. The designation for different tempi are in Italian. Thus, if the beats are in the range of our heartbeats, around 72 pulses a minute, the tempo is *moderato* (moderate). If the beats are faster than our heartbeats, the tempo is *vivace*, or if very much faster, it is *presto*. If the beats are slower than our heartbeats, the tempo is *lento* or *largo*. A fast tempo conveys a mood of energy and excitement; a slow tempo produces a more somber or thoughtful feeling.

As rhythm in nature involves repeated patterns, such as the tide moving in and out twice a day, so the beat in music is most often organized into patterns. Patterns are formed when some beats are regularly stronger than others. Music organized in this fashion is said to be **metric**. In order to have meter, there must be both a steady pulse and a pattern of accented and unaccented beats. Music that does not have a steady pulse (such as recitative in operas or some atonal music), or music that has a steady pulse but no accents at all (such as Gregorian chant) or has unpredictable accents that do not form a recognizable pattern (such as Stravinsky's *Rite of Spring*) is said to be **ametric**. Most of the music in the world, however, is metric.

In Western music, we have only two basic patterns. A strong beat followed by a weak beat (ONE two, ONE two) or a strong beat followed by three weak beats (ONE two three four) is said to be **duple meter.** This is a meter you can walk and march to; it has a left - right, left - right straight-ahead sort of feeling. Almost all popular music is duple. The other pattern is **triple**, with a strong beat followed by two weak ones (ONE two three, ONE two three). Triple meter has a more swaying, side-to-side feeling and is used for waltzing, skating, or skipping. Some triple-meter songs are "Happy Birthday to You," "The Star-Spangled Banner," and "My Country 'Tis of Thee."

In notated music, each occurrence of the pattern constitutes a **measure** or **bar** and is set off by vertical bar lines. The meter itself is denoted by a **time signature** placed at the beginning of the music. This consists of two numbers positioned vertically. The upper number indicates how many beats are in a measure and the lower number identifies which kind of note gets the beat. For example, if the time signature is 3/4, there are three beats per bar and each bar will have the equivalent of three quarter notes.

Duple and triple refer to how beats are joined together. Beats can also be subdivided, that is, a single beat may carry several melodic notes. If the beat is subdivided into two or multiples of two, the meter is said to be **simple.** Duple simple meter is counted 1 & 2 & / 1 & 2 &, and triple simple meter is counted 1 & 2 & 3 & / 1 & 2 & 3 &. Sometimes, however, there are three melodic notes evenly spread over a single beat. In this case, the meter is said to be **compound.** "Row, row, row your boat" is in duple compound meter, counted 1 & a 2 & a / 1 & a 2 & a. This is evident in the words "merrily, merrily, merrily, merrily." Compound triple meter, counted 1 & a 2 & a 3 & a, also exists, but is less common. A beautiful example is J. S. Bach's "Jesu, Joy of Man's Desiring."

Sometimes there is a strong underlying meter, but the melodic accents come where you don't expect them — between the beats or on weak rather than strong beats, as in 1 & 2 **&**. This is called **syncopation** and is the means by which jazz conveys a feeling of swing.

Meter in much of the rest of the world is more complex than it is in even the most sophisticated Western music. In the music of India and the Arab world, for instance, the patterns might extend for over 20 beats, in contrast to our simple two- or three-beat patterns. In the music of Africa, many different patterns are heard simultaneously, creating a layering of patterns that produces a dense, highly complex meter.

Sound happens when something that is capable of vibrating, such as a taut string or a vocal chord, is set in motion by the movement of air. If the vibrations are irregular, the result is noise, such as the sound of wind in the trees, a car engine, or a cough. If the vibrations are regular, the result is a tone that has the property of pitch. Pitch refers to how high or low the ear perceives the tone to be. Frequency determines pitch and measures the number of regular vibrations per second. These are too fast to see; 440 vibrations per second produces the pitch to which instrumentalists tune, which is the note "A." The higher the frequency, the more vibrations per second and the higher the pitch; fewer vibrations per second produce a lower pitch.

When the number of vibrations is doubled or halved, the pitch that is produced is the same, but in a different register. That is to say, as pitches rise or descend, they repeat at a regular distance. Since 440 vibrations per second produce a note called "A," 220 will also produce an "A" but in a lower register; 880 will produce an "A" but in a higher register, and so on. An **interval** is the distance between two pitches. The interval from one pitch to its next repetition, for example from A220 to A440, is called an **octave.**

There are several ways of dividing up the octave into smaller intervals. In music of the Arab world and India, for example, the octave is divided into two dozen different pitches producing quarter-steps. In Western music, the octave is divided into only twelve intervals of equal size. These are called **half steps** and are the smallest intervals possible in Western music.

We name the pitches according to the alphabet, from A to G, at which point the pitches repeat. On a piano keyboard, pitch ascends as we move from left to right. Only the white keys are given alphabet names:

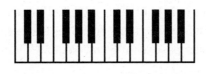

C D E F G A B C D E F G A B

Notice that the black keys are arranged in a pattern of alternating twos and threes. This asymmetrical arrangement helps in identifying the pitches. The white key between the pair of black keys is always D. The black keys are named according to their relationship to the white keys. When the black key is named in relationship to the white key on its left, it raises the pitch of that key a half step and is called a **sharp.** The symbol for a sharp is ♯. When the same black key is considered in relationship to the white key on its right, its pitch is a half step lower and is called a **flat.** The symbol for a flat is ♭. Thus the same pitch may have two different names, depending on the context. For example, C♯ is the same pitch as D♭.

On a keyboard, a half step is between adjacent keys, such as between a black key and its neighboring white key. There are also two places on the keyboard where half steps exist between two white keys that have no intervening black key: between E and F, and between B and C. A whole step consists of two half steps, for instance the distance from C to D, and from C♯ to D♯, and so on.

The arrangement of pitches within an octave is called a **scale**, which comes from the Italian *scala*, meaning ladder. Pitches are like the rungs of a ladder going from one level to the next. There are many different kinds of scales. A scale which contains all twelve half steps, that is, one that uses every key on the piano, is called a **chromatic** scale. A scale consisting only of whole steps is called a whole tone scale. Most scales, however, are a mixture of whole and half steps, and some have augmented 2nds, which is an interval of three half steps.

Almost all Western music is based on **diatonic** scales, that is, scales that use each letter name only once, and thus have seven different pitches. Not all scales are diatonic. A **pentatonic** scale has, as its name suggests, only five different pitches and therefore skips some letter names. Using only the black keys on the piano, you can produce a pentatonic scale. Much Japanese, Indonesian, Scottish, and folk music is based on pentatonic scales, as is the well-known hymn "Amazing

Grace." A **blues scale** has six different pitches, but one letter name is repeated and two are skipped: G B♭ C C♯ D F G.

There are two forms of diatonic scales: **major** and **minor**. If you play a scale from one C to the next using only white notes, you will produce a major scale. It consists of half steps between the 3rd and 4th notes and between the 7th and 8th notes. All other steps are whole steps. As long as this arrangement is kept intact: 1 - 2 - 3 4 - 5 - 6 - 7 8, a major scale can be built from any note. A scale built on D would be spelled: D - E - F♯ G - A - B - C♯ D. One on F would be: F - G - A B♭- C - D - E F. Notice that each letter name is used only once. In the scale on F, although A♯ would produce the same pitch as B♭, we have already used an A and may not skip the letter B.

The scale that a piece of music is built on is indicated in notated music by a **key signature** at the beginning of the music, just after the time signature. For example, in the scale built on D, the key signature would have two sharps, one on F and one on C. For the scale on F, the key signature would have one flat on B.

A diatonic scale in the **minor** mode is found on the white keys beginning on A. Here the half steps are between 2 and 3 and between 5 and 6 to produce the arrangement:

1 - 2 3 - 4 - 5 6 - 7 - 8. It may seem like a small detail, whether the third note of the scale is two whole steps or a whole step and a half step above the starting pitch, but the difference in effect is big. To most people, music using a major scale sounds bright and happy compared to music in a minor key, which sounds darker and sadder. Perhaps that is why most popular music is in a major mode.

The note on which a diatonic scale is built is called the **tonic**. Music that uses a diatonic scale is said to be **in the key of** the tonic note upon which the scale is built. Thus, music that uses the white notes beginning on C is said to be **in the key of** C major. Music that uses the scale beginning on C but with half-steps between 2 & 3 and 5 & 6 (C - D E♭ - F - G A♭ - B♭ - C) is said to be **in the key of** C minor. In both cases, C is the tonic, the home note, the goal of the music. Music that is in C major or C minor will not sound finished until it arrives on its tonic note of C. All the other notes of the diatonic scale are named in relation to this most important note. The note an interval of a 5th above the tonic (G in C major) is called the **dominant**. The one a 5th below the tonic (F in C major) is called the **subdominant**. The note between the tonic and the dominant (E in C major) is the **mediant**; that between the subdominant and the tonic is the **submediant**. The second step of the scale is the **supertonic**. And the note a half-step below the tonic in a major scale is called the **leading tone.** The notes can also be identified by solfege syllables:

Tonic	Supertonic	Mediant	Subdominant	Dominant	Mediant	Leading Tone	Tonic
Do	Re	Mi	Fa	Sol	La	Ti	Do

When three or more notes are sounded simultaneously, the result is a **chord**. The most prevalent chord is a **triad**. As the name suggests, a triad is a three-note chord comprised of alternating scale degrees. Examples are C - E - G; D - F - A; E - G - B, and so on. The tonic triad in C major is spelled C - E - G. C is the root of the triad; E is the third and G the fifth of the triad.

From C to E are two whole steps, which is called the interval of a **major 3rd (M3rd)**. From E to G are a whole step and a half step, an interval of a **minor 3rd (m3rd)**. The distance from the root to the fifth is three and a half steps, the interval of a **perfect 5th (P5th)**. This is the definition of a major triad: M3rd on bottom; m3rd on top; P5th from root to fifth. There are four possible kinds of triads, depending on the arrangement of major and minor thirds:

Quality of triad	MAJOR	MINOR	DIMINISHED	AUGMENTED
Root to Third	Major	Minor	Minor	Major
Third to Fifth	Minor	Major	Minor	Major
Root to Fifth	Perfect	Perfect	Diminished	Augmented

Triads may be built on each step of the scale. Their position and quality are identified by roman numerals: upper case for major, lower case for minor, a small circle for diminished, and a plus sign (+) for augmented. For example, a tonic triad is indicated by the roman numeral I. In a major scale, the triads built on the first, fourth, and fifth steps of the scale are major, hence the upper-case roman numerals. The triads built on the second, third, and sixth steps of the scale are minor, hence the lower-case roman numerals. And that built on the seventh step is diminished:

	Tonic	Supertonic	Mediant	Subdominant	Dominant	Mediant	Leading Tone	Tonic
Major scale:	I	ii	iii	IV	V	vi	vii°	I
Minor scale:	i	ii°	III	iv	v	VI	VII	i

The most common triads are I, IV, and V. With only these three chords, many songs can be accompanied.

Chords are pitches that happen simultaneously, or vertically. Pitches that occur horizontally, that is, in succession over time, create melody. **Melody** is a succession of pitches in a particular rhythmic pattern. Melody is a broad term that includes music that we may not consider very melodic. Melodies we can remember easily are "tunes." Each of us has hundreds of tunes stored in our memories.

Melodic direction refers to the shape of the arrangement of pitches. A melody may be mostly ascending, mostly descending, may seem to curl around itself, or, as is most often the case, use a mixture of all three. **Range** refers to how far the highest note is from the lowest note in a given melody. The wider the range, the more energy the music seems to have.

Melodic motion is how a tune gets from one pitch to the next. If the melody moves by small steps, it is said to be using conjunct motion. If it moves by leaps, it is using disjunct motion. All of these factors together produce the mood of a melody. If a composer wants to portray happy excitement, she will probably use much disjunct motion that mostly ascends over a wide range. Gloomy disappointment would be portrayed by conjunct motion, limping downward within a very narrow range.

Melodies are organized according to the principle of repetition and contrast. If a melody has too much repetition, it is dull; too much contrast sounds chaotic and unmemorable. So a good melody has the right balance between the two. As an example, "Twinkle, twinkle, little star" is in four musical phrases. The second and fourth phrases are exactly like the first —repetition. The third is different—contrast. So the phrases of this simple tune could be diagrammed as: a a b a. Large symphonic movements are more complex and happen over a larger space of time, but are in musical forms organized according to this same principle.

Texture refers to how melodies are presented. If there is only a single melody with no accompaniment at all, the texture is monophonic. This is true even if many performers and singers are playing the same melody. For instance, the famous opening notes of Beethoven's fifth symphony, "ta ta ta dum," are monophonic. If two or more melodies are happening at the same time and seem to be of equal interest and to be competing for the listener's attention, as happens when people sing a round beginning at different times, the texture is polyphonic. If there is a single melody in the foreground with subsidiary melodies or chords accompanying it in the background, the texture is homophonic. The use of harmony to accompany melody is what sets Western music apart from other kinds of music. Most of the music in much of the non-Western world is monophonic, but in the West the most prevalent texture is homophony.

Intensity refers to how loud or soft a tone is. The musical term for this is **dynamics**. As with tempo markings, the names for dynamics are in Italian. Ranging from softest to loudest they are:

pianissimo	*piano*	*mezzopiano*	*mezzoforte*	*forte*	*fortissimo*
pp	**p**	**mp**	**mf**	**f**	**ff**

Dynamics are a big factor in contributing to the effect of a piece of music. The louder the music, the more extroverted and energetic; softer music is more intimate and tender. Music can also gradually go from loud to soft (*decrescendo*) or from soft to loud (*crescendo*). It can be in a *piano* dynamic and suddenly become loud (*subito forte*), or in a *forte* dynamic and suddenly get soft (*subito piano*).

Timbre refers to the source of the musical sound, which instrument or what kind of voice is producing the music. Timbre has to do with the physics of sound, specifically what overtones are present and in what proportions. The concept is difficult to explain, but easy to hear. It's why we can tell the difference between a trumpet and a flute or a piano and how we can recognize our friends' voices.

The earliest musical instrument was undoubtedly the human voice. Using our voices in a musical manner seems to be universal in the human community. Voices are classified partly according to their range and partly according to their tone color. The lowest male voice is a bass, the highest a tenor, and in between the two is the baritone. The comparable female voices are alto, soprano, and mezzosoprano.

Instruments are categorized according to two different systems. One method is based on how the sound is produced and is useful for many different kinds of music. Chordophones produce sound when a taut string or chord is set in motion, by either bowing, hammering, or plucking. Violins, pianos, harpsichords, and guitars are chordophones. Aerophones are instruments that confine a column of air that is set in motion by breath. They include flutes, trumpets, and whistles. Membranophones produce sound when a membrane that is stretched across a hollow cavity is struck.

These are drums of all kinds. Idiophones are instruments that themselves vibrate when struck, such as bells, cymbals, and rattles.

The second method classifies instruments according to families in a symphony orchestra and is appropriate only for Western music. The string family includes violins, violas, cellos, and double basses. The wind family includes flutes, single-reed instruments like the clarinet, and double-reed instruments like the oboe and bassoon. The brass family comprises trumpets, French horns, trombones, and tubas. The percussion section includes all drums and anything that is struck, such as the xylophone.

Timbre is particularly important in the music of China. The Chinese have a large assortment of instruments that are classified according to the material of which they are made, such as silk, bamboo, brass, clay, wood, and so forth. Each timbre and each musical tone carries an extra-musical significance that is more important than any purely musical considerations. For example, a single tone may carry the connotation of autumn, water, and the north.

We have seen, in passing, that in different cultures, certain aspects of music are emphasized more than others. In Western music, harmony is treated in a sophisticated manner, while rhythm and melody remain relatively simple. In the music of Africa, rhythm is given a highly complex treatment, while harmony and melody are less developed. In the music of the Arab world and India, both melody and rhythm are more intricate, but there is little, if any, harmony. And in China, the emphasis is placed on subtleties of timbre.

WESTERN MUSIC

The history of Western music is divided into six periods, each with recognizably distinct characteristics: Medieval, Renaissance, Baroque, Classical, Romantic, and Twentieth Century. The pattern seemed to be that a musical style emerged, and, over a period of time, grew more and more intricate. There is then a reaction against that complexity, resulting in a new stylistic period.

The **MEDIEVAL** period begins with the earliest music in Europe for which any notated music survives and ends around the year 1450. Gradually during this period, musical notation was developed. It came about because monks in monasteries were required to learn an enormous body of chants that required some sort of *aide memoire*. At first only the direction of the melodic motion was indicated. Then, over time, a more precise method was devised for fixing pitches: noteheads were placed on ledger lines, which numbered anywhere from two to ten before finally settling into today's five-line staff. These fixed a relative, but not absolute, pitch. For that, a clef sign was needed to identify a single pitch from which the others could be derived. Clef signs therefore are designed to resemble letter names: the G-clef is our soprano clef; the F-clef our bass clef. There are also C-clefs, which are used by voices and violas. Finally, late in the period, a method was devised for indicating durations of notes, thus allowing rhythmic variety.

Paper was precious and expensive, and very few people could write words, let alone music. The only music that was notated was liturgical chant—that is, music that was performed as part of a religious service. Although this is the only music from the early part of this period that has come down to us, we can be sure that secular, popular music did, in fact, exist, but because it was not written down, we don't really know what it was like. We do know that there were nomadic poet-musicians known as troubadours and trouvères who sang songs of chivalric devotion and crusader feats as well as pilgrim songs, and that these were monophonic.

The liturgical music was called plainchant, or more commonly, albeit misleadingly, Gregorian chant. It was performed *a capella*—that is, voices only with no instrumental accompaniment or doubling, and was monophonic. Beginning around the tenth century, a stunning innovation took place. Perhaps emerging because boys and men sing at different octaves, or because some monks sang "out of tune," medieval polyphony gradually came about. At first the accompanying lines were mere drones, but little by little a second independent melodic line was achieved, and this eventually laid the foundation for the development of harmony.

By the twelfth century, Paris was the most important cultural center in Europe, and it is there that we have the first named composers. The cathedral of Notre Dame, then in the process of being built, had attached to it musicians who constituted the School of Notre Dame. **Leonin** (c. 1135–1201) composed the first complete annual cycle of chants for the mass in two parts. His successor **Perotin** (fl. 1190–c. 1225) did the same in four parts.

The fourteenth century was a turbulent period that saw the Hundred Years War, the Black Death, and great corruption in the church. Because of advances in musical notation, especially in the area of rhythm, music got enormously complex. Musicians of the time, as **Guillaume Machaut**, self-consciously called themselves *Ars Nova*, to set themselves apart from what they considered old-fashioned, conservative musical practices. In some secular music, as in the *Roman de Fauvel*, which was a cynical critique of both church and government, the voices simultaneously have different texts, often in different languages, and different melodic lines. Two or more of the voices would be quite active and independent of one another while one or more other voices would hold long drone notes. The inevitable reaction against an excess of complexity led to the next stylistic musical period.

The **RENAISSANCE** period in music begins around 1450 and extends to 1600. The word literally means "rebirth." It was a time of renewed confidence and a flowering of the arts influenced in part by the discovery of classical Greek philosophy. Renaissance musicians, inspired by the Greeks' belief in the power of music to shape one's soul and of words to express emotions and influence actions, had a great reverence for the importance of text when combined with music. In what was a new urge toward cohesion, all the voices have the same text set to the same music, although not sung at the same time, as the voices enter one after the other. Unlike *Ars Nova* polyphony, all the voices are of equal value; none is relegated to drone status. This new kind of texture, called **imitative polyphony,** is the most characteristic feature of Renaissance music.

As the church had reformed itself, there was a renewed emphasis on sacred compositions. Whereas Medieval composers had set mainly the Propers of the mass, those sections which change from day to day such as the Gradual and the Introit, Renaissance composers concentrated on the Ordinary of the mass, the Kyrie, Gloria, Credo, Sanctus and Benedictus, and Agnus Dei, that never vary from day to day. These, being sacred and for liturgical use, were in Latin, and were sung *a capella* in imitative polyphony. Free standing religious compositions, called **motets**, have the same characteristics as mass settings. Renaissance composers also wrote secular (non-religious) compositions called **madrigals.** They are similar to mass movements and motets, except they are in the vernacular—such as Italian or English—rather than Latin and tend to be in a livelier style.

Renaissance musical instruments were of two kinds: softer "indoor" instruments like the viol and lute, and louder "outdoor" ones like shawms, crumhorns, and sackbuts. The indoor instruments tended to be used for instrumental music that was modeled on vocal forms to create a text-less imitative polyphony. Outdoor instruments were used for movement, such as processionals and dances, and were therefore more obviously metrical.

The most outstanding composer of the Renaissance period was **Josquin Desprez** (1440–1521). Martin Luther, the moving spirit behind the Reformation, said of Josquin that he was master of the notes, whereas the reverse was true for other composers. During the period of the Counter-Reformation, when the Catholic church was again trying to reform itself from within, the decision was taken at the Council of Trent to ban polyphony from church services. Legend has it that **Giovanni Palestrina** (c. 1525–1594) saved Catholic church music by demonstrating to the cardinals at the Council of Trent that music could be polyphonic and yet be clearly understood with his Pope Marcellus Mass. Music written for the Roman Catholic church has been conservative ever since.

Experimentation was, however, taking place in the area of secular vocal music. Composers like **Carlo Gesualdo** (c. 1561–1613) wrote madrigals that displayed daring harmonic dissonances, but had a precious, mannered approach to the text. Each separate word was given its own illustrative treatment, making nonsense of the text as a whole. The reaction to this practice not only ushered in a new stylistic period, but led to the creation of an entirely new musical genre.

The **BAROQUE** period begins around 1600 with the invention of **opera** and ends around 1750 with the death of Johann Sebastian Bach. In the last decade of the sixteenth century, a group of intellectuals in Italy called the "Florentine Camerata" once again looked back to classical Greece for inspiration to reform music. Whereas at the beginning of the Renaissance, it was Greek philosophy that influenced music, for the Florentine Camerata it was Greek drama. They conceived of the idea that drama could be sung throughout with the simplest of accompaniments, and thus **opera** was created.

This produced far-reaching changes in musical style. The Renaissance ideal sound was three to six equal voices with no instrumental accompaniment. Each vocal line was conceived of horizontally, as a melodic line. In early opera, the ideal was a solo voice with a light instrumental accompaniment. The latter consisted of a bass line with a system of numbers over certain bass notes to indicate vertical harmony. A sustaining instrument such as a cello played the bass line while the harmony was improvised by a harpsichord or lute player. This was called **basso continuo** and is characteristic of almost all Baroque music. The Baroque ideal sound was a solo melodic line supported by a strong bass line with the space between the two filled in by harmony—in other words, a more vertical approach to musical organization. It was during this period that **functional tonal harmony** using major and minor diatonic scales was established.

Another difference in style between the Renaissance and Baroque has to do with rhythm. Except for instrumental music expressly written for the dance, Renaissance music is free-flowing and almost without accents, hence not quite metric. Baroque music, on the other hand, is strongly metrical. Baroque music, of all kinds and for whatever purpose, dances. Very often in Baroque music, once a rhythmical pattern is established, it persists throughout the entire piece or movement, reflecting an urge toward cohesion and unity.

The first great opera composer was **Claudio Monteverdi** (1567–1643), whose *Orfeo* is still performed today. But the most famous composer of Italian *opera seria* was a German who spent most of his creative life in London: **George Frideric Handel** (1685–1759). As the name suggests, *opera seria* deals with serious topics borrowed from Roman mythology or from ancient history. The elements of Italian opera are an instrumental overture, then alternating vocal recitative and arias. **Recitative** is like heightened speech and occurs in that part of the drama where action is carried forward. It is in prose with only basso continuo accompaniment. An **aria** is more akin to poetry and has a fuller orchestral accompaniment. When London audiences turned against Italian opera as an "irrational and exotic entertainment," Handel gave them unstaged opera in English using biblical stories as his subject matter and adding the new ingredient of the chorus: the **oratorio.** His *Messiah* is one of the most beloved musical works of all time.

An exact contemporary of Handel's whose music is the epitome of the High Baroque style is **Johann Sebastian Bach** (1685–1750). Bach never wrote an opera, but he wrote **cantatas** and The St. John and St. Matthew **passions** for the Lutheran church that, like Handel's oratorios, have all the characteristics of opera. Bach included in them the Lutheran chorale, a form of congregational hymn-singing introduced by Martin Luther.

During the Baroque period, instrumental music for the first time came to be as important as vocal music. This was the beginning of **absolute music**—that is, abstract instrumental music that is not dependent on words or movement for its form. Composers therefore had to look within the music itself, to the principles of repetition and contrast, to create musical forms. The rapidly developing tonal system also contributed to the creation of form, which essentially consists of establishing the tonic, moving away from the tonic, and returning to the tonic.

The most important of the new instruments was the violin, made popular by, among others, **Arcangelo Corelli** (1653–1713), who wrote exclusively for the violin in the genres of solo sonatas (one solo instrument plus continuo), and trio sonatas (two solo instruments plus continuo), and **Antonio Vivaldi** (1678–1741), who established the three-movement instrumental concerto (one or more solo instruments plus orchestra), as in his famous *The Four Seasons*, a set of four concerti with each one representing a season of the year.

Keyboard music was also important. The harpsichord was essential to almost all Baroque music as part of the *basso continuo*, but was also used extensively as a solo instrument. Bach, who was the greatest organist of his day, wrote **fugues** for organ and harpsichord as well as for vocal chorus. "Fugue" comes from the Italian *"fuga,"* meaning to chase. As in imitative polyphony, different voices sing the same melody at different times. In Renaissance imitative polyphony, however, each phrase is given its own music. In the Baroque fugue, a single musical idea, called the fugue subject, appears throughout, first in the tonic, then in other key areas, and finally in the tonic again. The repetition of the fugue subject provides unity; its appearance in different keys provides contrast.

The **CLASSICAL** period, dating from the death of J. S. Bach in 1750 until the 1820s, came about because of great changes taking place in society. The traditional sources of musical patronage, the aristocracy and the church, were losing ground to the emerging middle classes. Quality music was no longer limited to the privileged few. This period saw the proliferation of public concerts, which anybody could attend for the price of a ticket. Music publishing flourished, meaning the latest compositions were quickly available for the amateur music market. Composers therefore had to find ways of appealing to a broader public. They imbued their music with clarity, naturalness, and a pleasing variety, all hallmarks of the newly emerging Classical style.

The beginnings of the new style are found in what happened to opera late in the Baroque period. Italian *opera seria* comprised three acts. In the first half of the eighteenth century, a two-act *opera buffa* (comic opera) was often inserted between the acts to entertain the audience. In *opera seria*, the drama was less important than beautiful and bravura singing, and the characters were lofty historical figures. *Opera buffa* was about real people in everyday situations, such as problems between servants and their bourgeois masters. The emphasis was on fast-moving dramatic action, clever dialogue, and lightly accompanied and appealing arias. In time, *opera buffa* became so popular that it was detached from *opera seria* and became a genre in its own right, eventually eclipsing *opera seria* entirely. The best known examples are Mozart's *Marriage of Figaro, Don Giovanni,* and *Cosi fan tutte.*

Franz Josef Haydn (1732–1809) did much to develop two new classical instrumental genres, and **Wolfgang Amadeus Mozart** (1756–1791) further perfected them. The **symphony**, a work for full orchestra, and the **string quartet** (two violins, viola, and cello) are generally in four movements. The first movement is usually in **sonata** form, which is more of a dynamic process than a form. It comprises three sections that correspond to three acts of a drama. In the **exposition,** a musical idea is presented in the tonic key. There is then a transition to a new key area and, usually, contrasting thematic ideas. There is thus tension between the two key areas. In the **development** section, the plot thickens as material presented in the exposition is broken apart, combined in new ways, and taken to more distant key areas. The denouement in the **recapitulation** is brought about by repeating the exposition, but this time keeping everything in the tonic—the home key—to provide a resolution. Sonata form was so fundamental to the classical approach that it influenced other forms as well.

The second movement of symphonies and quartets is often a slow movement. It might be in sonata form, or theme and variations, or ternary form. The latter has three parts diagrammed as A B A: the first is in the tonic, the middle section presents contrasting material in a different key, and the third is a repetition of the first. The third movement, paired dances that hark back to the Baroque suite, is also in ternary form, with the A sections being a minuet or scherzo and the contrasting B section a trio. The fourth movement is usually fast and may be in sonata form, theme and variations, or rondo-sonata. Rondo form, inherited from the Baroque period, is an extension of the ternary idea with several contrasting sections, each in a different key, alternating with the A section, which is always in the tonic, for example A B A C A D A. In rondo-sonata form, the D section is replaced by the B section, which is now resolved in the tonic.

The classical **concerto** for soloist and orchestra omits the fourth movement, but is otherwise organized in the same manner, as is the classical **piano sonata,** for which the number of movements is more variable. The *fortepiano* was invented around the middle of the eighteenth century. Because it was capable of producing a wide range of dynamics, the piano rapidly replaced the softer-voiced harpsichord as the keyboard instrument of choice for solos, concerti, and chamber music that was performed in ever larger public concert halls.

Unlike Haydn and Mozart, **Ludwig van Beethoven** (1770–1827) was born late enough to have been influenced by the French Revolution. His music is considered revolutionary, not because he overthrew existing practices, but because he expanded all the elements of the classical style and enlarged the range of expression. His nine symphonies, for example, are longer and for larger performing forces than Haydn's or Mozart's. His dynamic range is wider, his rhythm more propulsive, and his harmonic resources greatly extended.

Rather than reacting against the Classical style, composers of the **ROMANTIC** period, which extends through the end of the nineteenth century, carried Beethoven's innovations even further to new levels of expressiveness. Where Classical composers aimed at clarity, Romantic composers sought ambiguity. Rhythm became more complex through the use of shifting meters and *rubato*, a surging forward or holding back of the pulse. Tonal harmony was obscured through the increasing use of *chromaticism*, which is the inclusion of notes that are foreign to the key, and through a tendency to defer a sense of resolution by seeming to evade arrival at the tonic. Phrases became longer and less clearly articulated. The symphony orchestra was enlarged and included a greater variety of wind and brass instruments.

Music during the Romantic period tended toward the grandiose, and audiences prized showy virtuosity. The pianist and composer **Franz Liszt** (1811–1886) and the violinist **Niccolo Paganini** (1782–1840) enjoyed the kind of adulation we associate with today's rock stars. **Program music** grew in importance during this period. Program music, in contrast to absolute music, is instrumental music that depends for its inspiration and its understanding on something external to music—a landscape, as in the *Hebrides Overture* by **Felix Mendelssohn** (1809–1847); drama, as in the symphonic overture *Romeo and Juliet* by the Russian composer **Peter Ilyich Tchaikovsky** (1840–1893); nature, as in the piano character piece *Papillons* (butterflies) by **Robert Schumann** (1810–1856); or even the composer's autobiography, as in the *Symphonie Fantastique* by the French composer **Hector Berlioz** (1803–1869). One composer who resisted the trend was

Johannes Brahms (1833–1897). His symphonies, concerti, and chamber music adhere to abstract musical principles.

In an age when bigger seemed to be better, it is surprising to find two new intimate genres. *Lieder*, which is German for art songs, is poetry set to music for a solo singer with piano accompaniment. **Franz Schubert** (1797–1828) wrote hundreds of *lieder,* including one written when he was only eighteen, his well-known setting of Goethe's ballad-poem *Der Erlkönig*. Like *lieder*, piano character pieces are one-movement miniatures that aim to set a mood in a brief space of time. Most Romantic composers wrote in many genres, but one, **Frederic Chopin** (1810–1849), wrote exclusively for the piano. His solo piano works include polonaises, études, and impromptus.

Opera during the nineteenth century was dominated by two composers. The Italian **Giuseppe Verdi** (1813–1901) wrote 28 operas, including some of the most beloved in the repertoire: *Rigoletto, La Traviata, Aida,* and *Otello*. His exact German contemporary, **Richard Wagner** (1813–1883), wrote his own *libretti* drawing on German mythic legends. His masterpiece, *Der Ring des Nibelungen*, is a cycle of four operas.

By the end of the nineteenth century, the romantics had stretched the elements of Western music so far that there was a reaction against what was viewed as emotional excess. Composers experimented with new techniques of composition and explored new directions for their music. Music of the **twentieth century** is therefore not distinguished by a single style. Instead we find several different approaches, none of which seem to have firmly caught hold. Most have in common an abandonment of tonality.

In the period preceding the first world war, contemporary movements in painting inspired three distinct musical styles. Impressionist painters, such as Monet, fragmented the visual into its elements of color and shape. **Impressionism** in music tried to do the same thing by careful attention to tone color and the manipulation of melodic fragments. An example is the three-movement orchestral work, *La Mer*, by the French composer **Claude Debussy** (1862–1918). **Expressionist** painters and composers were influenced by the work of Sigmund Freud on the irrational subconscious. They depict the outer world through a sort of deranged subjectivity. *Pierrot Lunaire* is a song cycle for soprano and five instrumentalists by the German composer **Arnold Schönberg** (1874–1951) that depicts the increasing lunacy of "Pierrot." The soprano uses *sprechstimme*, a style of performing characterized by wide, angular, unpredictable intervals where the exact pitches of the notes are not indicated. **Primitivism** was influenced by the Spanish painter Pablo Picasso, who painted the sets for the ballet *Sacre du Printemps* depicting the fertility rites of early Slavic tribes with music by the Russian composer **Igor Stravinsky** (1882–1971). This music is characterized by powerful dissonances; *ostinatos* in which Stravinsky obsessively repeats fragments taken from Russian folk songs; and an enlarged percussion section that was given unprecedented prominence.

In the 1920s, Arnold **Schönberg** devised a new method for organizing atonal music. He called it the *twelve-tone* method or *serialism*, whereby the composer makes a pre-compositional decision about the order in which the twelve notes of the chromatic scale will be heard. This was called the *tone row.* Once the composer sets the tone row, the pitches may only come in that order, although the row may be inverted (turned upside down) or played retrograde (backwards). Other composers, such as the American **Milton Babbitt** (1916–2011), took this even further and "serialized" duration and dynamic level as well as pitch.

Diametrically opposed to such total control was **chance music**, which also had parallels in the other arts such as participatory theater and art events known as "happenings." The ultimate example of this is *4'33"* by the American composer **John Cage** (1912–1992), wherein the performers sit in silence for the entire piece, drawing attention to ambient sounds in the environment. With advances in technology, some composers experimented with computer-generated music, such as *poème électronique* of the French composer **Edgard Varèse** (1883–1965). **Minimalism**, a more recent movement, represents a return to tonality and meter, but with a minimum of musical ideas obsessively repeated, for example *Glassworks* by the American composer **Philip Glass** (b. 1937). Composers today find inspiration from music of the distant past, from other cultural traditions, and from other fields, such as jazz.

Many people consider **JAZZ** to be America's only original contribution to music. It originated in American black culture around the beginning of the twentieth century. Some of its roots are found in the **call and response** of "field hollers," work songs where a leader sings a line and the others respond sympathetically, a technique that is still heard in African folk songs; **blues** songs; **gospel** singing; and the **ragtime** piano style of black artists like **Scott Joplin** (1868–1917).

Jazz is more of a performer's than a composer's art since the music is improvised rather than read from a score or memorized. This means that the performers agree on a tune, key, tempo, and form, then, based on that, make up what they play as they go along in a spontaneous way. Syncopation—putting an accent where one doesn't expect it—is an important element in jazz. This happens at two levels: the rhythm section provides a steady "back-beat" (one TWO one TWO) over which the melody instruments move a fraction of a beat ahead or behind the pulse. When this happens, the music is said to swing.

In its brief history, jazz has gone through several styles. The earliest is **New Orleans** style, also called Dixieland. Small ensembles consisted of a rhythm section of drums, piano, and/or bass and two or more soloists on trumpet, saxophone, clarinet, trombone, or voice. **Louis Armstrong** (1900–1971) played trumpet and sang in a style called "scat," where the voice, singing syllables rather than words, is used as another instrument. During the Depression years of the early 1930s, solo piano came to the fore with **stride** and **boogie woogie**. In the late 1930s and early 1940s during World War II, **swing** or **big-band** jazz "crossed over" and became widely popular. Swing bands were large ensembles of ten to twenty performers playing under the direction of a leader from written-out arrangements called "charts," which left less room for improvisation. One of the greatest of the swing band leaders was the pianist and composer **Duke Ellington** (1899–1974).

After the war years, when the popularity of the big bands collapsed as the mass market turned to rock and roll, jazz performers returned to the emphasis on improvisation afforded by smaller ensembles. But they did so with a new virtuosity and more sophisticated, complex harmonies in a style called **bebop**. Some of the outstanding performers of bebop were the alto saxophonist

Charlie Parker (1920–1955) and the trumpeter **Miles Davis** (1926–1991). Bebop has been succeeded by many different jazz styles, such as the more laid back cool jazz and free jazz (total improvisation), as well as a nostalgic return to the "classical" New Orleans style. As in art music, jazz musicians are currently looking to other fields, such as rap, Afro-Cuban music, and the music of other cultures, to produce a blended style called **fusion.**

DRILL: MUSIC

1. Which of the following are examples of musical scales?

   I.   Chromatic
   II. Octatonic
   III. Blues
   IV. Raga

   (A) I only
   (B) I and III
   (C) I and II
   (D) All of the above.

2. Which of the following is an example of ametric music?

   (A) African drumming
   (B) Gregorian chant
   (C) Jazz
   (D) Rap music

3. A major diatonic scale has half-steps between

   (A) 1-2 and 5-6.
   (B) 2-3 and 5-6.
   (C) 3-4 and 7-8.
   (D) 4-5 and 7-8.

4. A major triad has

   (A) two major thirds.
   (B) a minor third below a major third.
   (C) two minor thirds.
   (D) a minor third above a major third.

5. An important innovation during the Medieval period was

   I.   notation.
   II. serialism.
   III. opera.
   IV. polyphony.

   (A) I and IV
   (B) I only
   (C) I and II
   (D) I and III

6. An important characteristic of Renaissance music is

   (A) compound meter.
   (B) *sprechstimme.*
   (C) imitative polyphony.
   (D) recitative.

7. Which of the following is an example of absolute music?

   (A) Bach's *St. John Passion*
   (B) Beethoven's Symphony
   (C) Brahms' Piano Concerto No. 1
   (D) Tchaikovsky's *Swan Lake* No. 6

8. Swing, in jazz, has to do with

   (A) stop time.
   (B) improvisation.
   (C) 32-bar chorus.
   (D) rhythm.

9. J.S. Bach never wrote for which of the following instruments?

   I.   Viola da gamba
   II. Clarinet
   III. Fortepiano
   IV. Oboe de caccia

   (A) I and III
   (B) III and IV
   (C) II and III
   (D) I and II

10. Which of the following does not belong with the others?

    (A) Mozart's *The Magic Flute*
    (B) Stravinsky's *Firebird*
    (C) Tchaikovsky's *The Nutcracker Suite*
    (D) Prokofiev's *Romeo and Juliet*

11. Which of the following contributed to the development of Rock and Roll in the 1950s?

    I.   Economic prosperity
    II. Country and Western
    III. Tin Pan Alley
    IV. Rhythm and Blues

    (A) II and IV
    (B) II, III, and IV
    (C) I and II
    (D) All of the above.

12. Which of the following is not a genre typical of the Romantic period?

    (A) Tone poem
    (B) Concerto grosso
    (C) Symphonic overture
    (D) Song cycle

MUSIC REVIEW

Answer Key

1.	(D)	4.	(D)	7.	(C)	10.	(A)
2.	(B)	5.	(A)	8.	(D)	11.	(D)
3.	(C)	6.	(C)	9.	(C)	12.	(B)

DETAILED EXPLANATIONS OF ANSWERS
DRILL: MUSIC

1. **(D)**   All are examples of scales. The chromatic scale is one that uses every note in the Western octave and consists only of half-steps. The octatonic scale is one devised by Igor Stravinsky and consists of alternating half and whole steps. The blues scale is a particular arrangement of pitches (it has two augmented 2nds, two half steps, and two whole steps) that gives the blues its distinctive sound. Raga refers to both the arrangement of pitches within the octave and to the musical form of classical Indian music.

2. **(B)**   Metric music has both a steady pulse and a pattern of regular accents. Gregorian chant is ametric because, although it has a steady pulse, it has no accents. Rap music, which is essentially poetic, is strongly metric. In African drumming, several meters occur simultaneously, producing polymeters. Jazz exhibits rhythmic complexity in having a great deal of syncopation, but this occurs over and within a strong, underlying meter.

3. **(C)**   A major scale has half-steps between the third and fourth notes and the seventh and eighth notes. (B) is where the half-steps occur in a diatonic minor scale. The other two arrangements are of medieval modes; (A) is the phrygian mode, beginning on the pitch E, and (D) is the lydian mode, beginning on F. The other medieval modes are dorian (half-steps between 2-3 and 6-7, beginning on D) and mixolydian (half-steps between 3-4 and 6-7, beginning on G).

4. **(D)**   A major triad consists of a major third between the root and middle note and a minor third between the middle note and the upper note, producing a perfect fifth between the outer notes. If their position is reversed, with the minor third on the bottom, the result is a minor triad. If both thirds are major, the resulting fifth is augmented, and the triad is an augmented triad. If both thirds are minor, the fifth is diminished, and the triad is a diminished triad.

5. **(A)**   Both the notation of music and the development of medieval polyphony had their beginnings before 1000 CE. Opera was invented around 1600 and serialism, also called the twelve-tone method, in the 1920s.

6. **(C)**   The Renaissance sound ideal was *a capella* voices singing the same text to the same melody but entering at different times—imitative polyphony. The rhythm was flexible, without strong accents and therefore not strongly metric. Recitative refers to those sections of baroque and classical operas that were written in heightened speech style with a minimum of instrumental accompaniment. *Sprechstimme* was a singing style developed by Arnold Schönberg, wherein the direction of the melodic motion, but not exact pitches, is indicated.

7. **(C)**   Absolute music is abstract instrumental music that is not based on extra-musical references, such as Brahms's two piano concertos. Most of Beethoven's symphonies are examples of absolute music, but the sixth is not. Beethoven entitled it *Symphonie Pastorale* and gave each of its five movements a descriptive heading. This particular symphony is thus an example of program music. Bach's two Passions are for voices as well as instruments. Tchaikovsky's *Swan Lake* is ballet music.

8. **(D)**   Swing is the essential rhythmic component of jazz. Trumpeter Wynton Marsalis says jazz swings when the bass player is walking his instrument and the drummer is riding the cymbals. The

rhythm section is then providing a steady beat over which the lead instruments are free to syncopate around the beat. Improvisation is equally essential to jazz. The performers embellish a given tune, adding notes and continuously varying the melody as they go along, making it up on the spot. The 32-bar chorus is one of several jazz forms. It consists of four phrases of which is each eight bars long: A A B A. The first phrase is repeated, probably in a varied style; the third phrase is a contrasting one called the bridge; the fourth phrase is again a repetition of the first. In the last two bars of the second and fourth phrases, the rhythm section falls silent to allow the lead performer to improvise freely. This is called stop-time.

9. **(C)** Bach wrote for both the viola da gamba and the oboe da caccia. The viola da gamba is a bowed, fretted, six-string instrument tuned like a guitar that was widely used during the Renaissance. Little is known of the oboe da caccia. The conjecture is that it was an alto oboe that had a curved shape like a hunting horn. The fortepiano, a keyboard instrument with a hammer action, was invented in 1709. Bach had the opportunity to try one out in the 1730s, but was unimpressed with it. In the following decades, rapid technological improvements gained the fortepiano broad favor. The clarinet, a single-reed woodwind instrument, was not invented until the mid-eighteenth century.

10. **(A)** Mozart's *The Magic Flute* is an opera, or more appropriately a *singspiel*, meaning it is in the German language with sung arias interspersed with spoken dialogue. The other three are all ballets.

11. **(D)** The postwar prosperity of the 1950s in America meant that, for the first time ever, enough young people had sufficient disposable income to constitute a separate, lucrative market for music. Tin Pan Alley, shorthand for the popular music consumer industry and so called because it was centered in a noisy street full of shops with player pianos in New York City, aimed for as broad an appeal as possible, including cross-generational. Tin Pan Alley composers ranged from hacks to George Gershwin. Rhythm and Blues came about with the southern migration of blacks to the cities. It is an urbanized version of the country blues, often more energetic and with an electric guitar. Muddy Waters, John Lee Hooker and Howlin' Wolf were some of the great rhythm and blues singers. Country and Western was, in the beginning, southern, white, and rural. When Sam Phillips signed Elvis Presley because he was a white man who sounded like a black man, Phillips brought together the two strains of black and white popular music to create rock and roll.

12. **(B)** The concerto grosso is a baroque genre. It is a multi-movement work for two or more soloists. The passages for the soloists alternate with *tutti* sections where all the performers participate. The *tutti* passages are called *ritornelli* because they generally "return" to the opening theme while the *soli* passages usually contain contrasting material. Both the Tone Poem and the Symphonic Overture are one-movement orchestral works and are almost always examples of program music. Liszt was particularly associated with the former. His *Les Préludes* was inspired by the French Romantic poet Lamartine. An overture was historically used to introduce something—a drama, opera, or ballet. But the Romantic symphonic overture lost that function and is heard in concert as a free-standing work. An example is Brahms's *Academic Festival Overture*.

PERFORMING ARTS REVIEW

THEATER REVIEW

ORIGINS OF THEATER

As long as humans have been capable of communication, they have probably employed some form of drama and performance. Cave paintings supply evidence for the early use of costumes and masks to bolster mimetic performances, which, either as magic or prayer, functioned to encourage the productivity of nature.

THEATER IN GREECE

In keeping with this tradition, the earliest Greek plays were probably ritualistic performances that might involve, for instance, a conflict between winter and summer, and that would include a combat, a death, and a resurrection. These simple plays may have evolved into the dithyramb, a frenzied and impassioned hymn performed by a chorus of 50 men costumed in goatskins. The purposes and concerns of the earliest plays were reflected in the first **dithyrambs**, which celebrated Dionysus, the god of the abundance of nature. Aristotle described the dithyramb as the forerunner of tragedy, and the gradual development from dithyramb to tragic drama began as spoken lines were inserted into the lyrics, causing the leader of the chorus to become a solo performer.

According to legend, the fundamental changes that brought these early performances to the level of drama were made by Thespis, a poet and actor from whose name we derive the word *thespian*. He is known as the founder of classical **tragedy**. He is credited with inventing a new breed of performer, the actor, who would engage the audience by impersonating one or more characters between the dances of a chorus. Thespis also came up with the notion of a prologue to the choral narrative. With the creation of the actor to tell the story, the reaction of the chorus assumed greater importance, for it served to offer commentary on the struggles of the narrative's hero. Thespis is also credited with directing the emotional scope of Classical drama to concentrate on the hero's faults, on the obstacles facing the hero, and ultimately on the hero's death—i.e., the elements of tragedy.

Aeschylus, another actor and author of a trilogy of plays entitled the *Oresteia*, further refined the form and content of the Greek tragedy. Among the many improvements attributed to him is the addition of a second and third actor, which allowed for conflict between the characters. Conflict, requiring resolution, provoked a more developed sense of plot, and Aeschylus heightened this by providing a structure with which to organize the narrative episodes. He also introduced the concept of choice, providing the hero with a decision he or she must make, which frequently leads to his or her downfall.

By the fifth century BCE, the form of Greek tragedy had taken on a recurring structure. Most plays began with a prologue, spoken by a single actor in iambic verse, which described the events leading up to the action of the play. This was usually followed by the entrance of the chorus, a body of 15 people who chanted in anapestic meter to introduce the action and to create the desired mood in the audience. This was followed by a series of alternating **episodes** (scenes of action) and **stasima** (lyric songs sung by the chorus). The play was concluded by the **exodos**, during which the chorus continued to chant as the characters departed.

Aside from Aeschylus, there are only two other playwrights of this period from whom we have a substantial amount of work extant. Sophocles (496?–406 BCE) is thought to have written nearly 125 plays, among them *Oedipus Tyrannus, Antigone*, and *Electra*. His plays deal with men and women whose flaws lead to suffering and destruction, but ultimately result in increased wisdom and divine retribution. Euripides (480?–406 BCE) is the author of nineteen extant plays, including: *The Trojan Women, Medea*, and *The Bacchae*. Euripides is known for the dramatic realism of his plays, achieved by complex plots, increasingly natural speech, and the combination of good and evil found in all of his characters, be they human or divine.

Greek drama was a seasonal event, performed only at certain times of year during specific festivals. The plays were performed in competition with each other, as part of the festival. All dramatists were required, along with mastering the art of creating tragic trilogies, to perfect at least one comic form. Very few comedies survived, so little is known about the form of Classical Greek Comedy. It is thought that there were three forms of comedy—Old, Middle, and New. The Old Comic form probably employed three actors, contained burlesque, parody, and farce, and was wild and bawdy. Old Comedies always featured music, and frequently made use of fantastical subjects and settings. Old Comedy had a rigid structure similar to that of Classical Tragedy, combining lyrical, prosaic, and choral passages. Aristophanes (450–385 BCE), as the only Old Comedian whose work survived intact, is considered the father of Greek comedy. His plays include *The Clouds* and *The Birds*.

Middle Comedy, the primary dramatic form between 400 and 338 BCE, was far less obscene than Old Comedy, and led to the much more refined and sophisticated New Comedy. New Comedies were usually comedies of manners designed for an educated leisure class. They involved a number of stock scenes and stock characters and followed a five-act structure. The only New Comedies that survive are those of Menander of Athens (c. 342–c. 292 BCE), including *The Grouch*.

Greek tragic actors wore large masks that covered their whole faces and made them appear much taller than they actually were. Actors would wear several masks during a performance, to allow them to play a variety of roles. Characters might require a number of different masks to represent the changes that they undergo over the course of the play. The weight and size of the masks contributed to an emphasis on the study of movement, which tended to be slow, graceful, and stately, and to emphasize a number of standard gestures. The costumes for comedy were more colorful and fantastic than those for tragedy, and tended to exaggerate certain parts of the actors' bodies. Comedians, too, wore masks; however, comedic masks portrayed a larger variety of characters than the tragic masks.

THEATER IN CHINA

The first performances in China were recorded about 1500 BCE, during the Shang Dynasty. Dance, music, and ritual were important elements in Chinese life. Temples were associated with performers and records of a raised stage were found by archaeologists.

The Han Dynasty (206 BCE–CE 221) actively encouraged the arts and founded the Imperial Office of Music in 104 BCE, which functioned to organize entertainment and to promote dance and music.

Chinese Shadow Puppets (c. 121 BCE) were first used to materialize departed gods or souls, but later evolved into a source of entertainment.

Marionettes, puppets moved by string or hand, were created between CE 265 and CE 420. Many festivals and plays continued to spread through China around CE 610.

Emperor Hsuan Tsung established "The Pear Garden," a school for dancers, singers, and various court entertainers that stressed current forms of performance. Storytelling using puppets became a popular dramatic form from CE 960–CE 1279.

Historians in the 1920s uncovered the oldest surviving Chinese plays, *Chang Hsieh* and *The Doctor of Letters*, which consisted of a prologue and a main story.

Stage direction was practiced in Chinese theaters by the fourteenth century. The stage was usually stripped bare, with a door on either side for exits and entrances and an embroidered decorative wall hanging between the two doors as a backdrop. Both men and women performed in productions, and swords and fans were used as props during performances.

Drama began to emerge from the south. The southern plays tended to be long and formal, usually consisting of 50 or more acts, each of which had its own title. Theater in China was influenced by Western drama early in the twentieth century and gradually became less formal.

MEDIEVAL PERIOD

Medieval theater originally began as a springtime religious observance. It was a communal and public event that drew large audiences to celebrate the teachings of the Old and New Testaments of the Bible. Religious theater was restricted by such elements as the liturgy, church calendar, and ecclesiastical dress.

In England during the Middle Ages, pageant plays known as **cycles** were created using biblical and religious literature. The cycles were performed by a troupe of actors who traveled from town to town in wagons that also served as stages for performances. The double-decker wagon was narrow with two vertical levels that were utilized to demonstrate scenes of heaven and hell. Curtains concealed the wagon's undercarriage and served as the dressing area for the actors.

Morality plays were also performed during this time. They represented the conscience of the Middle Ages. After approximately 200 years, drama moved out of the church because the troupes were too restricted by the church's ruling.

Medieval producers made use of special effects such as trap doors in stages that were movable or fixed. The stages were set against buildings at outdoor festivals, and a stage wagon transported background scenery. This type of stage made special effects easy to perform.

The playwrights in the Medieval period wrote anonymously. Historians document that women never performed in medieval plays for two reasons. First, male-dominated, rigidly hierarchical groups like clergy, craftsmen, and merchants predominated. Secondly, it was believed that boys with trained voices could produce more volume than women.

Medieval audiences consisted of local and neighboring citizens. There was no fee charged to spectators of English cycle plays.

ELIZABETHAN THEATER IN ENGLAND

During the Elizabethan era in England, theater was used for the first time as a commercial enterprise. Philip Henslowe of London was the best-known theatrical manager. The stage became lavish with detailed scenery and colorful costumes. There were two basic types of costumes, contemporary and symbolic. Symbolic costumes were worn to distinguish the important characters from the ordinary people.

Theater companies acquired new plays by request from freelancers and from actor/playwrights. Notable playwrights of the Elizabethan era include Christopher Marlowe (1564–1593), author of a number of plays including *The Jew of Malta* and *Edward II,* and Ben Jonson (1573–1637), satirist, critic, and author of plays ranging from comedy and satire to court masques and tragedy, including *Every Man in His Humour* and *The Devil Is an Ass.* Ben Jonson said of his contemporary William Shakespeare that "He was not of an age but for all time!" It is certainly true that in his more than thirty tragedies, histories, and comedies, Shakespeare created enduring characters and addressed timeless questions that still resonate for us today. It would be impossible in a short space to describe Shakespeare's contribution to poetry, drama, and language.

THEATER IN ITALY

The Romans, borrowing architectural design from the Greeks, built amphitheaters of permanent stone. These theaters were built for a variety of entertainment, such as dancing, acrobatics, and gladiatorial events.

Italy's professional theater evolved from *commedia dell'arte* in the mid-1500s. *Commedia dell'arte* was a popular form of entertainment akin to street theater, designed to appeal to a mass audience. The plays, performed by a number of traveling troupes, were largely improvisational, though their plots were usually limited to the misadventures of a set of stock characters whose actions were commented on by a chorus of clowns or *zannis*. Many of the characters' names, personalities, and costumes are still familiar today—among them Harlequin, Pulcinella, Pantalone, Dottore, and Scaramuccia.

Throughout Europe in the late fifteenth century, audiences were entertained between the acts of larger comedies by short dramatic and musical works. In Italy, these became known as Intermezzi, and became more and more centered around spectacle. Eventually, dialogue was almost entirely phased out in favor of elaborate presentation. These works usually involved music, and as the entr'acte spectacles became longer and more important than the acts themselves, opera was born.

THEATER IN SEVENTEENTH-CENTURY FRANCE

French playwright/actor/director, Jean Baptiste Poquelin (1622–1673), also known as Molière, wrote and acted in *Tartuffe*, *The Misanthrope*, *The Doctor in Spite of Himself*, *The Miser*, and *The Imaginary Invalid*. Molière's comedies weigh follies of humanity against common good sense. Two other famous playwrights at this time were Pierre Corneille (1606–1684) and Jean Racine (1639–1699). Corneille's most successful play was entitled *The Cid*. Racine's most widely performed plays were *Phaedra* and *Iphigenie en Aulide*.

Costumes, hairstyles, and makeup on the French stage mirrored popular fashions on the street or at court. The audience in Parisian theaters varied from valets, soldiers, and pickpockets to nobility, gentlemen, and merchants. Respectable women usually did not attend the theater in the early 1600s. Women who did attend wore masks and sat in loges.

The first proscenium arch stage, which resembled a picture frame, was built in France in 1618 by Teatro Farnese. The proscenium was a wall with one large center opening that divided the theater-goers from the raised stage.

RESTORATION PERIOD

During the Interregnum period in England (1649–1660), theater and acting were banned due to political upheavals at the command of Oliver Cromwell. Once theaters were reopened, Charles II (1630–1685) marked the start of the modern proscenium playhouse, and repertory companies flourished. Two official theatrical companies, the King's Company and the Duke's Company, were started at this time.

Popular playwrights of the Restoration period were John Dryden, Richard Steele, William Wycherley, William Congreve, George Farquhar, George Etherege, and Richard Brinsley Sheridan. The term "comedy of manners" describes the majority of the Restoration prose plays. They were witty in dialogue and revolved around sexual intrigue.

CONTEMPORARY THEATER

Many successful playwrights emerged from nineteenth-century Europe. Henrik Ibsen, Johann Wolfgang Goethe, and August Strindberg are a few among many popular writers. These playwrights introduced stage realism and naturalism. English naturalist Charles Darwin and French philosopher Auguste Comte were two major influences on the theater of realism. Contemporary theater emerged from this emphasis on naturalism and realism.

In Russia, Konstantin Stanislavsky (1863–1938) developed an acting technique that came to be called "The Method" on account of its broad impact on the schooling of Western actors. Stanislavsky's approach to actor-training was essentially psychological. Cheryl Crawford, Harold Clurman, Lee Strasberg, and Stella Adler taught acting technique using "**The Method.**" In 1931 they formed the Group Theater in America, which consisted of actors and directors who provided actor-training workshops in New York City.

Playwright Eugene O'Neill brought to American drama a powerful insight into human passion and suffering. Other accomplished American playwrights of the twentieth century include Arthur Miller, Tennessee Williams, and Lillian Hellman. Their plays are produced on and off-Broadway. Experimental shows are generally produced in off-off Broadway theaters.

In Britain, the **Fringe theater** was considered equivalent to America's off-off Broadway theater. **Mobile theater** (the Fun Bus) and **avant-garde theater** brought the arts into urban communities and bridged the gap between nations and classes.

There were a number of significant off-off Broadway companies. La Mama theater, for example, provided a showcase for new playwrights. The Circle Repertory Company stressed the development of new plays by its own performing group. The Manhattan Theatre Club opened three theaters to assist playwrights through readings and productions. The New York Shakespeare Festival Public Theatre was founded by Joseph Papp in 1954. Papp's goal was to make theater more accessible. Papp established free summer performances at the Delacorte Theatre in Central Park, New York City.

In 1968, censorship of British theater was abolished. The rock musical *Hair*, which contained nudity and obscenity, was produced in London. Plays with homosexual themes, such as John Osborne's *A Patriot for Me,* were performed. Meanwhile, in the United States during the late 1960s, musicals like *Oh, Calcutta*, which included various scenes involving nudity, and *Che!,* which displayed explicit sexual acts, challenged theater audiences.

DANCE REVIEW

ORIGINS OF DANCE

Archaeologists have studied ancient drawings depicting dancing hunters costumed as animals wearing make-up and masks. Egyptian dance paintings were found that depict religious dancing in funeral processions. War dances, hunting dances, medicine dances, dances for health, and fertility dances were performed as a form of sympathetic magic or medicine. There were dances for death, birth, peace, and courtship.

The emergence of dance was evident in early Greek culture. Plato believed that dance was not solely an exercise for the body, but an art form given to us by the gods so we could please them. The Greeks themselves used dance accompanied by music in the intermezza of a performance event. Dance was a communal activity, enjoyed as entertainment and religious ritual.

For the Romans, dance was a vehicle for spectacle rather than for a classic dramatic presentation, and commonly included acrobatics. As Christian emperors became more powerful, the church became more controlling, and pagan rituals, spectacles, and gladiatorial combats were forbidden.

Dancing was incorporated in Christian services until the twelfth century at which time theologians decided that dancing was distracting and impious. In 1207, the Pope banned the clergy from wearing masks and dancing because theologians felt that these practices might cause the mind to wander from God. Later, music and acting were banned by the church.

FORMS OF DANCE

The first major ballet, entitled *The Ballet Comique de la Reine,* was choreographed by an Italian named Balthasar de Beaujoyeux (formerly Baldassari de Belgiojoso) in 1581. This event was commissioned by Catherine de' Medici in France, who was the daughter of one of the greatest families.

In France, Louis XIV, who was an accomplished dancer himself, and a great champion of ballet in particular, was known as a patron of the arts. His passion for dance favored court ballets. In 1661, he established a school which produced the best and most experienced dance masters. This school was called the Academie Royale de Danse.

The establishment of the five positions of the feet became the foundation of ballet technique. In the first position, legs are turned out away from the hips and heels and knees touch each other. The feet are to be out so as to form a straight line. Similar to first position, the legs remain turned out away from the hips during the second position, but the heels must be approximately 10 to 12 inches apart. During the third position, the heel of each foot is touching the middle of the other foot while one foot is placed directly in front of the other. The legs must be turned out away from the hips. In the fourth position, one foot is in front of the other with about eight inches separating the two feet. In the fifth position, the legs are turned out from the hips, and one foot is directly in front of the other. The heel of the front foot should also be placed at the joint to the toe of the rear foot. Correct weight and body balance, arm control, and attitude are essential in ballet.

Marius Petipa (1822–1910), often referred to as the father of classic ballet, transplanted the glory of the Romantic ballet from France to Russia. This was a turning point at the birth of a new era. Petipa reached success with one five-act ballet entitled *La Fille du Pharaon*. Petipa made Russia the leading country of ballet, and he raised the standard of dance technique with assistance from Swedish dancer Christian Johansson, Italian dancer Enrico Cecchetti, and Russian dancer Lev Ivanov. His other works include *La Bayadère* and *Sleeping Beauty*.

Isadora Duncan (1878–1927) contributed greatly to the creation of Modern Dance. She believed dancing was an expression of one's whole self, including body, mind, and soul. She wanted to be free of the control of ballet and desired to let the body rather than the mind dictate movement. She took off her ballet slippers and danced barefoot, wearing loose-fitting clothing so her body was not restricted. Her works were based on Greek art. Duncan founded schools in Berlin, Paris, and Moscow. In modern dance, there are no established patterns or steps. It requires the dancer to create his or her own, emanating from the natural movement of the body. Other contributors to modern dance were Agnes de Milles, Martha Graham, Ruth St. Denis, and Ted Shawn.

American dancer and choreographer Martha Graham's technique begins with the center of the body and follows contractions and releases of muscles when movement occurs. Ultimately, her technique is based on breath rhythms and is recognized for sharpness and preciseness.

Choreographer Doris Humphrey's movement technique was softer and more lyrical than Graham's. Humphrey's technique was created from natural observations of human movement. She examined rhythms of breath, weight shifts, motion, and successional flow.

The bridge between classical ballet and modern dance was connected under Agnes de Mille's direction. She stressed the understanding that dance is movement, and the body is its instrument. Choreographers worked with time, force, and space. De Mille believed that a personal exploration must be completed to understand and use the body.

Jazz dancing is a controlled style of dancing, though it is creative and allows free body movements. It is characterized by parallel feet, flat-footed steps, undulating torso, body isolation, and syncopated rhythms. Jazz became a popular form of dance in American musicals.

Ballet troupes and opera houses were established in America, among them the New York City Ballet, the Metropolitan Opera, Lincoln Center for the Performing Arts, and the American Ballet Theater. Edward Villella, Jacques d'Amboise, Arthur Mitchell, Diana Adams, Tanaquil Le Clerq, and Maria Tallchief became well-known dancers in New York City. In the 1950s, 18-year-old Darci Kistler became the youngest principal dancer in the City Ballet's history.

In the 1960s, Americans flocked to clubs and dance halls. Ballroom dancing, the foxtrot, the samba, and the salsa became popular. In the 1970s, choreographers added jazz to the most successful American musicals, such as *West Side Story, Fiddler on the Roof, 42nd Street, Chicago,*

A Chorus Line, and *Evita.* A few famous choreographers and directors were Jerome Robbins, Gower Champion, Bob Fosse, Michael Bennett, and Harold Prince.

A form of dance known as body art became popular in the 1970s, which emerged from the general mood of most Americans, which at the time was irritated and angry. This form of dance was used to demonstrate at political rallies. The artists were costumed or appeared nude and performed in galleries and small performance spaces.

American dancing has gone through many styles. Popular dances of the 1930s were the Peabody and the foxtrot. In the 1940s, they danced the jitterbug. The 1950s brought about the stroll, the mashed potato, and the cha-cha. The salsa, the monkey, and the pony were created in the 1960s. In the 1970s, two new types of dances were born—the hustle and the boogie, which became American favorites. In the 1980s, head banging to heavy metal rock and roll music emerged and faded away. With each new decade, dance styles change and vibrant new forms emerge.

FILM REVIEW

ORIGIN OF FILM

The creation of film was the result of a centuries-old fascination with the control and capture of movement. There is no one moment of history and no one inventor who can be credited with the creation of cinema as we know it today. A series of inventions and ideas, from Plato's shadows on the cave wall to magic lanterns and zoetropes, by means of curiosity, ingenuity, and accident, by the turn of the twentieth century we could reproduce movement. This new invention, which hung somewhere between a science and an art, was to capture the international imagination as a means to entertain, to shock, and increasingly, to earn money.

Around 1889, Thomas Alva Edison and his assistant, W.K.L. Dickinson, combined a number of existing inventions to create the **kinetoscope**, the original motion picture machine. This machine was designed as a cabinet that held revolving spools of film. When a coin was inserted, an electric light was projected on the rear of the cabinet. To view the movie, one would look through a small peephole. The average film ran for one minute and was 50 feet in length. Edison usually filmed action or movement, such as an animal eating or a person dancing.

Edison believed that films were simply a passing fad. Consequently, he did not develop a way to project films on screen. This task was performed by the Lumière brothers, Louis and Auguste. The Lumière brothers developed their own camera, which also served as a developing machine and projector. The Lumières held the first public showing of motion pictures projected on a screen at the Grand Café in Paris. The Lumière brothers helped to develop the form cinema would take.

Edison soon abandoned kinetoscopes to form his own production company to make films for theaters. Edison founded the first motion picture studio, "The Black Maria," in West Orange,

New Jersey. In the studio, **vaudeville** entertainers and celebrities performed for the camera. There were several actors who later gained fame in the early days of motion picture, among them Mme. Bertholdi, a contortionist; Annie Oakley; and Colonel William Cody, the original Buffalo Bill.

In 1895, the Lumière brothers produced their first experimental film entitled *L'Arroseur Arrosé*. Previously, the cinema had consisted of mainly newsreel footage, but narrative form quickly entered. The brothers understood the profit to be made from narrative films, so they perfected their experiment. The first two French production houses were established by Charles Pathé and Léon Gaumont. Their competitor was Georges Méliès. The Lumière brothers wanted to catch nature in the act, but Méliès, who was fascinated with the art of illusion, was considered "the creator of cinematic spectacle." Méliès constructed the first cinema set building that was completely made of glass for daylight shooting purposes.

The first American motion picture theater, established on April 16, 1902, was called "The Electric." Because each show cost a nickel, movie theaters were nicknamed "**nickelodeons**." Meanwhile, in France, Méliès created a film entitled *Trip to the Moon*. In America, Edwin Porter made *The Great Train Robbery*, an early prototype for the classic American Western. As motion pictures prospered, American and French companies regularly employed actors, and more theaters and nickelodeons were built.

Vitagraph, Edison's motion picture company, began producing one-reel films of Shakespearean plays like *Richard III*, *Antony and Cleopatra*, *The Merchant of Venice*, and *Romeo and Juliet*. Edison's determination to exploit the cinema for residuals led to his attempt to force competing filmmakers out of business by bringing lawsuits against them for violation of patents. Several companies, particularly Biograph, managed to survive by inventing cameras that differed from those Edison had patented. In 1908, Edison brought these companies under control by forming the Motion Pictures Patents Company (MPPC), a group of ten firms based primarily in Chicago, New York, and New Jersey. The MPPC never succeeded in eliminating its competition. Many independent companies were formed throughout this period. D.W. Griffith, considered to be Biograph's most important director, formed his own company in 1913. The U.S. government brought a lawsuit against the MPPC in 1912, and in 1915 it was declared a monopoly.

In France, the first Theatre Pathé was built in 1901. It was later rebuilt to hold larger audiences. The progress of French cinema was becoming paralyzed at the time of World War I. France, Germany, and Russia became influenced by realism used in theater. Most Soviet silent films dealt with themes of conflict and revolution.

In the 1920s, America, which did not experience the post–World War I depression as strongly as European countries, became dominant in film production. Particularly in Hollywood, the star system controlled the medium, causing it to become superficial and commercial. After 1912, old nickelodeons were outdated and new theaters were rapidly being built.

German actor/director/writer/set and costume designer Erich von Stroheim brought eroticism, brutality, and cynicism to American cinema after 1920. Stroheim's first films were entitled *Blind Husbands*, *The Devil's Passkey*, and *Foolish Wives*.

THE HOLLYWOOD ERA

After 1910, film companies began moving to a small town outside of Los Angeles, California, known as Hollywood. Some film historians feel that the independent companies moved west to avoid the wrath of the MPPC. In addition, filming in Hollywood had many advantages—the climate permitted year-round shooting, and California provided a great number of locations, from mountains to ocean to desert. By the 1920s, large studios were being built.

The Academy of Motion Picture Arts and Sciences (AMPAS) was founded in 1927 by Louis B. Mayer and other film industry innovators, including Cecil B. DeMille, Douglas Fairbanks, and Mary Pickford. The purpose of the AMPAS was to raise the educational, cultural, and technical standards of American movies. The Academy of Motion Picture Arts and Sciences was pioneered by writers, actors, producers, and directors.

INTRODUCTION OF SOUND IN FILM

Sound was introduced in 1926 with the release of *Don Juan*, a film with an orchestral accompaniment, sound effects, and a series of vaudeville shorts. Warner Brothers, in an attempt to promote the concept of films with sound, released *The Jazz Singer* (1927), a part sound/part silent film that was a huge success. In the same year, Warner Brothers decided that all of its silent films would include musical accompaniment and announced plans to purchase one major theater in every large American city. In 1928, Walt Disney produced *Steamboat Willie*, his first musical cartoon, contributing to the sound film genre and introducing to the world the beloved character, Mickey Mouse. By 1930, most American theaters were wired for sound. Silent films became part of film history by the late 1930s.

INTRODUCTION OF COLOR

During the 1930s, color film became widely used for the first time. Although photographic color had been used in various forms since 1908, only a few films in the 1920s had **Technicolor** sequences, because the process was too expensive to use on a large-scale basis. However, by the mid-1930s, three-strip Technicolor proved to be economically feasible. After the release of the all-color feature-length film, *Becky Sharp,* in 1935, and the release of *The Trail of the Lonesome Pine* in 1936, film studios began using Technicolor extensively.

THE ACADEMY AWARDS

The main function of the AMPAS is the annual presentation of the Academy Awards, or "Oscars," for distinguished film achievement in the previous year. The first film to win an academy award was *Wings* in 1928. *Gone with the Wind* won the most academy awards in a single year in 1939, and featured Oscar winners Vivien Leigh (Best Actress) and Hattie McDaniel (Best Supporting Actress). *Gone with the Wind* also marked the first time a black actor or actress (McDaniel) won an academy award. Other Best Picture winners of the 1930s and 1940s included *Grand Hotel*

(1932), *It Happened One Night* (1934), *You Can't Take It with You* (1938), *Mrs. Miniver* (1942), *Casablanca* (1943), *The Lost Weekend* (1945), and *All the King's Men* (1949). Best Actor winners of the 1930s and 1940s included Clark Gable, Spencer Tracy, James Stewart, Bing Crosby, Ray Milland, and Laurence Olivier. Best Actress winners of the 1930s and 1940s included Bette Davis, Katharine Hepburn, Ginger Rogers, Ingrid Bergman, Joan Crawford, and Olivia de Havilland.

TELEVISION, COLOR, AND FILM

Television affected box-office sales. Americans who owned television sets stayed home rather than go to the cinema and spend money. As a result, profits were not being generated. Hollywood fought back by exploiting the technological advantages which film possessed— the vast size of the images and the capacity to produce the images in color. As a result of the competition between television and films, Hollywood made a rapid conversion from black-and-white to color production between 1952 and 1955. In 1947, only 12 percent of American feature films were made in color. By 1954, the figure rose to over 50 percent.

The transition was made possible largely through a 1950 anti-trust decree which disassembled the Technicolor Corporation's monopoly on color cinematography and ordered it to release its basic patents to all producers. When this occurred, new color systems were developed quickly, aided by the war-time development of a new type of color film stock called "integral tripak." By 1952, the Eastman Kodak Corporation had developed the Eastmancolor system. Although the system has since come to be known by the trade names of the studios who pay to use it or the laboratories that process it, it was Kodak Eastmancolor that initiated and maintained the full-color age with dye-coupler printing. By 1975, even the Technicolor Corporation had changed to an Eastman-based process. Ninety-six percent of all American feature films by 1979 were being made in color.

FILMS IN THE 1950s AND 1960s

Hollywood's mania for producing films on a large scale in the 1950s damaged the conventional dramatic film. First, the standard length of a feature film rose from 90 minutes to an average of three hours before settling at a more manageable two hours in the mid-1960s. Second, there was a tendency on behalf of the studios to package every A-class film as a dazzling, big-budget spectacle, whether or not this format suited the material of the film. From 1955 to 1965, most traditional American genres experienced an inflation of production values that destroyed their original forms and caused them to be recreated into new ones. These genres included **musicals, comedies, Westerns, science fiction, gangster** and **anti-communist** films.

The musical genre underwent a period of great change in the 1950s and 1960s. Hollywood abandoned original scripts in favor of successful stage plays. This tendency peaked with the release in 1965 of *The Sound of Music*, which grossed more money than any other film had before. Comedy suffered in the early 1950s due to a focus on production values rather than verbal or visual humor. By the 1960s, the genre shifted to big-budget sex comedies concerned with strategies of seduction (*Sex and the Single Girl*, 1965, *A Guide for the Married Man*, 1967), which reflected the sexual revolution of the decade, and to corporate comedies, which dealt with business fraud and government deceit in a humorous light. American comedy became increasingly sophisticated in the 1950s and 1960s.

The Western experienced major changes in attitude and theme in correspondence to changes in American society. The heroic, idealized epic westerns of John Ford and his imitators remained popular in the 1950s but were gradually replaced by the adult Western which concentrated on the psychological and moral conflicts of the hero in society. Furthermore, by the 1960s, the portrayal of the Native American changed from one of hostile savages to one of intelligent, gentle people who were murdered by the U.S. military.

Science fiction emerged as a distinct genre in the 1950s. The common theme in the science fiction films of the 1950s was some form of a world-threatening crisis, usually produced by nuclear war or alien invasion. Another popular theme was the arrival of a dangerous creature from another planet, as in *The Thing* (1951).

In the 1960s, low-budget monster films were replaced by medium-to-high budget science fiction films, including *The Time Machine* (1960) and *Planet of the Apes* (1967). Serious filmmakers, including Stanley Kubrick (*2001: A Space Odyssey*, 1968), became interested in science fiction.

The gangster film re-emerged in the late 1940s after being replaced by domestic espionage films during the war. Two types of gangster films appeared in the 1950s—the caper film and the anti-communist film. The caper film concentrated on a plan to pull off a big heist, which could be either serious or humorous. The first caper film was John Huston's *The Asphalt Jungle* in 1950. The anti-communist film was a centered, original form that appeared only in the early 1950s. In these films, the criminal figure was a Communist spy and the syndicate was the international Communist conspiracy. However, the traditional concept of the gangster film was preserved. Although the anti-communist films appeared only in the 1950s, the theme of these movies can be seen in the James Bond espionage thrillers and imitations in the 1960s. These films replaced the gangster genre in the early 1960s by presenting criminal conspiracy on a world-wide scale and offering violence on the part of both the conspirators and the hero.

Academy Award-winning films in the 1950s and 1960s included *All About Eve* (1950), *From Here to Eternity* (1953), *The Bridge on the River Kwai* (1957), *Ben-Hur* (1959), *West Side Story* (1961), *My Fair Lady* (1965), *The Sound of Music* (1965), and *Midnight Cowboy* (1969). Best Actor winners in the 1950s and 1960s included Gary Cooper, William Holden, Yul Brynner, Charlton Heston, Rod Steiger, and John Wayne. Best Actress winners included Audrey Hepburn, Grace Kelly, Joanne Woodward, Susan Hayward, Anne Bancroft, Elizabeth Taylor, and Sophia Loren. In 1963, Sidney Poitier won an academy award for Best Actor for his performance in *Lilies of the Field*. Nineteen sixty-eight marked the occurrence of the first tie in the Best Actress category. Both Katharine Hepburn, for her performance in *The Lion in Winter*, and Barbra Streisand, for her performance in *Funny Girl*, shared the Oscar.

FILMS IN THE 1970s AND 1980s

The enormous success in 1970 of two conventional films, *Love Story* and *Airport*, restored Hollywood's faith in the big-budget feature. Production costs of American films were the largest in the industry's history. Between 1972 and 1977, the average production budget for a film increased by 178 percent. By the end of 1979, average production costs had nearly doubled the 1977 figure to reach the sum of $7.5 million per feature film. Profits were based on the film's success, so the financial risks of production multiplied. Consequently, fewer and fewer films were made every year, and there was a steady increase in the amount spent on advertising campaigns to ensure the success of the film. Often, the price for advertising would cost twice as much as the production cost of the film itself.

With fewer than 70 major films being produced each year, compared to 538 in 1937, there were serious questions about the creative spirit of the American cinema. However, the 1970s could be considered a renaissance of creative talent, as a result of many young directors who studied at American film schools, compared to the directors of the 1960s who were trained in television. Some of the directors of this renaissance were Francis Ford Coppola, George Lucas, Martin Scorsese, Steven Spielberg, and Brian De Palma. Coppola's epic of organized crime in the United States, *The Godfather Parts I, II*, and *III,* is one of the most significant American cinematic achievements of the 1970s. Lucas's *Star Wars* and Spielberg's *Jaws* (1975) and *Close Encounters of the Third Kind* (1977) were historically important for their use of dazzling special effects. De Palma directed some of the most stylish horror films of the 1970s, including *Carrie* (1976), while Scorsese directed *Taxi Driver* (1976). Not only were these films critically acclaimed, but they were financially successful. *Star Wars* grossed over $200 million, *Jaws* over $130 million, and *Close Encounters of the Third Kind*, over $83 million.

Some of the academy award winners for Best Picture in the 1970s were *The Godfather* (1972), *The Godfather II* (1974), *One Flew over the Cuckoo's Nest* (1975), *The Deer Hunter* (1978), and *Kramer vs. Kramer* (1979). Some of the Best Actress winners were Jane Fonda, Ellen Burstyn, Faye Dunaway, Diane Keaton, and Sally Field. Some of the Best Actor winners were Gene Hackman, Jack Lemmon, Jack Nicholson, Richard Dreyfuss, and Jon Voight. Two Best Actor winners, George C. Scott for his role in *Patton* in 1970, and Marlon Brando for his role in *The Godfather* in 1972, made history by refusing their awards.

FILM IN THE PRESENT

As in the 1950s with the invention of television, in the 1980s Hollywood was again faced with technological advances that would affect box office sales. **Cable television** services and **video cassette recorders** (VCRs) brought theatrical movies into the home for a monthly subscription or rental fee, transforming the entire system of film distribution. However, the speculation that movie theaters would become obsolete and that all films would one day be distributed through some form of home video technology remains a theory in the 1990s. People are still going to the movies in theaters and paying rising prices for tickets to experience the spectacle of the big screen. Directors like Allison Anders, Spike Lee, and Jim Jarmusch have produced innovative work and introduced new film techniques in the 1980s and 1990s.

Some of the Best Picture winners for the 1980s and 1990s were *Ordinary People* (1980), *Gandhi* (1982), *Amadeus* (1984), *Platoon* (1986), *Rainman* (1988), *Schindler's List* (1993), *Forrest Gump* (1994), and *Braveheart* (1995). Some of the Best Actor winners included Robert De Niro, William Hurt, Michael Douglas, Paul Newman, Dustin Hoffman, Sir Anthony Hopkins, Tom Hanks, and Nicholas Cage. Some of the Best Actress winners included Sissy Spacek, Meryl Streep, Shirley MacLaine, Cher, Jodie Foster, Jessica Tandy, Emma Thompson, Jessica Lange, and Susan Sarandon.

DRILL: PERFORMING ARTS

1. American choreographer Martha Graham often used sets designed by which of the following sculptors?

    (A) Henry Moore
    (B) Isamu Noguchi
    (C) David Smith
    (D) Louise Nevelson

2. Which of the following contemporary filmmakers sees a connection between Marxist politics and gender relations?

    (A) Werner Herzog
    (B) Woody Allen
    (C) John Ford
    (D) Lina Wertmüller

3. Igor Stravinsky's ballet *Petrouchka* drew heavily on which of the following influences?

    (A) Renaissance dance music
    (B) Russian folklore and tradition
    (C) Medieval mystery plays
    (D) Eighteenth-century Italian opera

4. Which of the following films was the work of the visionary German director Werner Herzog?

    (A) *Love and Anarchy*
    (B) *Reds*
    (C) *Aguirre, The Wrath of God*
    (D) *Love and Death*

5. Which film tells the story of a totalitarian society in which books are banned and burned?

    (A) *A Clockwork Orange*
    (B) *1984*
    (C) *Fahrenheit 451*
    (D) *Brazil*

6. Which of the following individuals would be out of place in the musical and theatrical circles of 1920s Paris?

    (A) Stravinsky
    (B) Satie
    (C) Nijinsky
    (D) Shostakovich

7. John Ford's 1939 epic Western *Stagecoach* featured which actor as the classic American male?

    (A) Humphrey Bogart
    (B) Gary Cooper
    (C) John Wayne
    (D) David Wayne

8. Which of the following directors is not associated with the French "New Wave" cinema?

    (A) Abel Gance
    (B) Louis Malle
    (C) Alain Resnais
    (D) Jean-Luc Godard

9. Composer Stephen Sondheim scored all of the following musicals EXCEPT

    (A) *Company.*
    (B) *A Little Night Music.*
    (C) *Sunday in the Park with George.*
    (D) *Pippin.*

10. Which Wagner opera tells the story of a legendary, doomed love affair?

    (A) *Parsifal*
    (B) *Tristan and Isolde*
    (C) *Siegfried*
    (D) *Die Meistersinger*

11. Which of the following operas tells the tragic story of a young Japanese bride?

    (A) *La Bohème*
    (B) *Tosca*
    (C) *Aida*
    (D) *Madama Butterfly*

12. Which of the following best describes *opera buffa*?

    (A) Tragedy
    (B) Serial
    (C) Melodrama
    (D) Comedy

13. Which film established James Dean as an icon of American youth?

    (A) *East of Eden*
    (B) *Rebel Without a Cause*
    (C) *The Wild One*
    (D) *Giant*

14. The popular Broadway show *West Side Story* was loosely based on the play

    (A) *Measure for Measure.*
    (B) *The Taming of the Shrew.*
    (C) *A Midsummer Night's Dream.*
    (D) *Romeo and Juliet.*

15. The controversial practice developed during the 1960s in which artists confronted or interacted with spectators, or used their own bodies as an artistic medium is called

    (A) Pop art.
    (B) minimalism.
    (C) video sculpture.
    (D) performance art.

16. Which modern choreographer, based in New York City and featuring a company of young black, white, and Asian dancers, used dance as a means to explore and interpret the American black experience?

    (A) Paul Taylor
    (B) Alwin Nikolais
    (C) Merce Cunningham
    (D) Alvin Ailey

PERFORMING ARTS REVIEW

Answer Key

1.	(B)	5.	(C)	9.	(D)	13.	(B)
2.	(D)	6.	(D)	10.	(B)	14.	(D)
3.	(B)	7.	(C)	11.	(D)	15.	(D)
4.	(C)	8.	(A)	12.	(D)	16.	(D)

DETAILED EXPLANATIONS OF ANSWERS
DRILL: PERFORMING ARTS

1. **(B)** Japanese-American sculptor Isamu Noguchi (1904–1988) collaborated with Martha Graham on such abstract ballet sets as *Frontier* in 1935. Neither Henry Moore (A), David Smith (C), nor Louise Nevelson (D) are known for their theater designs.

2. **(D)** Italian director Lina Wertmüller, a student of Federico Fellini, often analyzes sex in terms of Marxist politics in works such as *Love and Anarchy* (1973) and *Swept Away* (1974). Werner Herzog (A) is the proponent of German visionary cinema, while Woody Allen (B) directs modern urban comedies and dramas. John Ford (C) was an American director who often made westerns and adventure films.

3. **(B)** Stravinsky's *Petrouchka*, produced by Diaghilev's Ballet Russe in 1911 in Paris, draws its narrative from the story of a Russian country fair at which Petrouchka is one of the three dolls brought to life by a magician. Although Stravinsky was an eclectic composer with a strong religious strain, he drew neither from Renaissance dance (A), medieval mystery (C), nor Italian opera (D).

4. **(C)** Herzog's *Aguirre, The Wrath of God* (1972) tells the heavily symbolic tale of an obsessive Spanish conquistador's journey into the Amazonian jungle to find the mystical city El Dorado. *Love and Anarchy* (A) is a political film by the Italian Lina Wertmüller, while *Love and Death* (D) is a Woody Allen spoof of Tolstoy's novels. *Reds* (B) is Warren Beatty's film about the Russian Revolution.

5. **(C)** Francois Truffaut's 1966 film *Fahrenheit 451* was adapted from the Ray Bradbury novel, in which a repressive future world employs firemen not to stop fires, but to burn books. *A Clockwork Orange* (A) is Stanley Kubrick's version of Anthony Burgess's book set in an anarchistic future England, while *1984* (B) was based on George Orwell's prophetic novel of the same name. *Brazil* (D), by director Terry Gilliam, is a futuristic fantasy with a heavy debt to Orwell.

6. **(D)** Dmitri Shostakovich (1906–1975) was the Russian composer whose mature career coincided with the Stalinist regime in the Soviet Union, and whose works were often circumscribed by the Soviet party line. He was never a member of the musical/theatrical avant garde in 1920s Paris, where composer Igor Stravinsky (A) and dancer Vaslav Nijinsky (C) were all associated with the *Ballet Russe*. Eric Satie (B) was the irreverent leader of the *Les Six*.

7. **(C)** John Wayne starred as the Ringo Kid in John Ford's *Stagecoach*, the 1939 film shot in Monument Valley which featured spectacular scenery as a major element in the action, and which set the tone for decades of Westerns to come. Humphrey Bogart (A) created an image of the cynical, laconic American male in such films as *The Treasure of the Sierra Madre*, while Gary Cooper (B) developed a similar persona in *High Noon*. David Wayne (D) portrayed more intellectualized heroes.

8. **(A)** Abel Gance (1889–1981) was the French film director of the 1920s, whose masterpiece was *Napoleon* (1927), a grand, sweeping epic which used such devices as a triple screen and early color to mythologize the French dictator. All of the other directors listed were members of the generation which reached maturity in post World War II France, and whose films explored new levels of social, political, and psychological complexity.

9. **(D)** *Pippin*, the fictionalized story of the youngest son of Charlemagne, was composed by the young American Stephen Schwarz. All of the other musicals were hits written by Stephen Sondheim.

10. **(B)** Wagner's 1865 opera *Tristan and Isolde*, his most fully developed treatment of romantic love and passion, is drawn from a medieval legend of Celtic origin, and tells the story of two people fated to die because of their love. *Parsifal* (A) is Wagner's version of the Holy Grail legend, *Siegfried* (C) is a section of Wagner's enormous Ring cycle, and *Die Meistersinger* (D) tells of a medieval German guild of singers.

11. **(D)** Giacomo Puccini (1858–1924) wrote *Madama Butterfly* in 1904; in it he dramatized the tale of a young Japanese bride first wooed and then abandoned by an American naval lieutenant. *La Bohème* (A) is Puccini's opera about a colony of poor artists, and *Tosca* (B), also by Puccini, is about a nineteenth-century singer in Rome. *Aida* (C) is Verdi's lavish opera about an African princess in Egypt.

12. **(D)** *Opera buffa* was the Italian comic opera of the early eighteenth century which, with its emphasis on humor, farcical plots, frivolity, and catch musical numbers, closely parallels modern musical comedy. "Tragedy" (A) and "melodrama" (C) would best describe Wagner's Romantic works, while "serial" (B) would define a work such as Alban Berg's 12-tone *Wozzeck*.

13. **(B)** Nicholas Ray's 1955 film *Rebel Without a Cause* cast the young James Dean as a searching, alienated youth who rejects both the hypocritical values of his middle-class parents and the competitive violence of his peers. *East of Eden* (A) and *Giant* (D) were films which reinforced Dean's star status, while *The Wild One* (C) featured Marlon Brando as a cynical, rebellious youth.

14. **(D)** *Romeo and Juliet* provided the source for *West Side Story*, which was written by Jerome Robbins, Arthur Laurents, Leonard Bernstein, and Stephen Sondheim, and which opened on Broadway in 1957. Shakespeare's story of the doomed young lovers from feuding families was updated as the tale of New York City teenagers Tony and Maria.

15. **(D)** Performance art is a broad ranging term which includes environments and happenings, staged by such artists as Jim Dine, Claes Oldenburg, and Yves Klein in order to bombard the spectator with sensations and experiences which were extreme, bewildering, and often, subversive, of the social status quo. Pop art (A) was a predecessor of performance; minimalism (B) is a non-objective style; and video sculpture (C) exploits the kinetic imagery of television sets.

16. **(D)** Black choreographer Alvin Ailey (1931–1989) formed his own dance company in 1958, and drew a whole new kind of audience to modern dance with works such as *Revelations*, which used Negro spiritual music or blues and jazz to express the experience of the American black. Each of the other figures listed is also a prominent contemporary choreographer.

PRACTICE TEST

CLEP Humanities

Also available at the REA Study Center (*www.rea.com/studycenter*)

This practice test is also offered online at the REA Study Center (*www.rea.com/studycenter*). Since all CLEP exams are administered on computer, we recommend that you take the online version of the test to receive these added benefits:

- **Timed testing conditions** – Gauge how much time you can spend on each question.
- **Automatic scoring** – Find out how you did on the test, instantly.
- **On-screen detailed explanations of answers** – Learn not just the correct answers, but also why the other answer choices are incorrect.
- **Diagnostic score reports** – Pinpoint where you're strongest and where you need to focus your study.

Need more practice? Go to the REA Study Center and take Practice Test 2.

PRACTICE TEST

CLEP HUMANITIES

(Answer sheet can be found on page 179.)

TIME: 90 Minutes
Approximately 140 Questions

DIRECTIONS: Each of the questions or incomplete statements below is followed by five possible answers or completions. Select the BEST choice in each case and fill in the corresponding oval on the answer sheet.

1. In ancient Egyptian architecture, the large, sloping walls which flank the entrance to a temple complex are called

   (A) pyramids
   (B) mastabas
   (C) tombs
   (D) pylons
   (E) obelisks

2. An improvised performance, usually held in churchyards or city squares, that was performed in a circle and involved playing the role of redeemers, by the act of scourging and whipping themselves, which made them move and gesture, was performed by

   (A) fools
   (B) flagellants
   (C) minnesingers
   (D) mimes
   (E) joculators

3. An *a priori* truth is known to be true

   (A) independently of experience.
   (B) after careful experimentation or observation.
   (C) as a result of mathematical calculation.
   (D) only by God.
   (E) because its denial is a contradiction.

4. The fourth degree of a major scale is given what name?

   (A) Tonic
   (B) Dominant
   (C) Leading tone
   (D) Subdominant
   (E) Mediant

5. A natural minor scale contains five whole steps and two half steps. Between which scale degrees do the half steps occur?

   (A) 2-3, 5-6
   (B) 3-4, 7-8
   (C) 1-2, 7-8
   (D) 2-3, 7-8
   (E) 3-4

6. An example of the use of primitivism can be found in which musical selection?

   (A) "Prélude á l'après-midi d'un faune"
   (B) "Le Sacre du Printemps"
   (C) "Salome"
   (D) "Wozzeck"
   (E) "The Liberty Bell"

7. Which of the following is the earliest and clearest demonstration of the principles of romanticism?

   (A) Pope's "The Rape of the Lock"
   (B) Rousseau's *The Social Contract*
   (C) Blake's *Songs of Innocence and Experience*
   (D) James's *Daisy Miller*
   (E) Shakespeare's *Romeo and Juliet*

8. Which of the following works is known for defining the parameters of existentialism?

   (A) *L'Étranger*
   (B) *Le Morte D'Arthur*
   (C) *Candide*
   (D) *Saint Joan*
   (E) *Le Misanthrope*

9. Which American classic is known for its comprehensive description of frontier families' lives in the Midwest during the nineteenth century?

   (A) *The Last of the Mohicans*
   (B) *The History of the Dividing Line*
   (C) *On Plymouth Plantation*
   (D) *My Antonia*
   (E) *Huckleberry Finn*

10. Which of the following is a "coming of age" novel that utilizes the concept of the anti-hero?

    (A) *Tom Sawyer*
    (B) *Martin Chuzzlewit*
    (C) *Catcher in the Rye*
    (D) *The Great Gatsby*
    (E) *Sister Carrie*

11. Of the following poems, which is known as one of the most poignant elegies to President Abraham Lincoln?

    (A) "Elegy Written in a Country Churchyard"
    (B) "When Lilacs Last in the Dooryard Bloomed"
    (C) "After Death"
    (D) "Howl"
    (E) "Elegiac Stanzas"

QUESTION 12 refers to the following.

12. Which of the following is an important feature of the building pictured above?

    (A) A dependence on rectilinear lines and angles
    (B) An emphasis on the structural framework of the building
    (C) An interplay of large and small geometric shapes
    (D) The use of curvilinear forms to suggest organic growth or motion
    (E) An orderly, classically inspired floor plan

QUESTIONS 13–15 refer to the following illustrations (A) through (E).

(A)

(B)

(C)

(D)

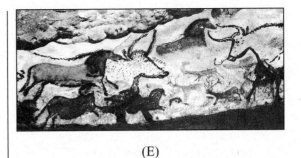

(E)

13. Which example is intent on a naturalistic rendering of an animal's anatomy?

14. Which example uses animals as a metaphor for human behavior?

15. In which example are animals seen in a magic or ritual context?

QUESTION 16 refers to the following.

16. The example pictured above most likely presents which of the following?

(A) A passage from a classical epic
(B) A scene from a Wagnerian opera
(C) An eighteenth-century satire on human foibles
(D) An episode from a Shakespearean drama
(E) An incident from the French Revolution

17. Which of the following lines is an example of iambic pentameter?

∪ / ∪ / ∪ / ∪ /
(A) Her deck / once red / with he/roes' blood /

/ ∪ / ∪ / ∪ / ∪
(B) Here goes / the try / I've al/ways know /

/ ∪ / ∪ ∪ / ∪ ∪
(C) She loves the / way I hold / her hand/

/ / ∪ / / ∪ / /
(D) Although I/ knew the road / led home/

∪ / ∪ / / ∪ / /
(E) As I lay / wait ing / for the / morn

QUESTIONS 18 and 19 refer to the following verses.

O God, do you hear it, this persecution,
These my sufferings from this hateful
Woman, this monster, murderess of children?
Still what I can do that I will do:
I will lament and cry upon heaven,
Calling the gods to bear me witness
How you have killed my boys to prevent me from
Touching their bodies or giving them burial.
I wish I never begot them to see them
Afterward slaughtered by you.

18. These lines are spoken by

(A) the murderer.
(B) the father of the dead children.
(C) one of the gods.
(D) a bystander.
(E) a judge.

19. It can be inferred from this passage that

(A) the woman had a right to kill her children.
(B) the man deserved to lose his children.
(C) the rites and ceremonies of burial are extremely important.

(D) the gods decreed the death of the children.
(E) the woman will get away with the murders.

QUESTIONS 20–22 refer to the following verses (A) through (E).

(A) For shade to shade will come too drowsily,
And drown the wakeful anguish of the soul.
(B) Rocks, caves, lakes, fens, bogs, dens, and shades of death.
(C) 'Twas brillig, and the slithy toves
Did gyre and gimble in the wabe
(D) Because I could not stop for Death—
He kindly stopped for me—
(E) … yet from these flames
No light, but rather darkness visible

20. Which passage contains an oxymoron?

21. Which passage uses assonance?

22. Which passage is written in iambic pentameter?

23. Which of the following are African-American playwrights who won awards and critical recognition for their plays in the 1920s?

(A) August Wilson and Lorraine Hansberry
(B) Charles Gordone and Imamu Amiri Baraka
(C) Ed Bullins and Sonia Sanchez
(D) Zora Neale Hurston and Marita Bonner
(E) Eugene O'Neill and Clifford Odets

24. A well-made play may have all of the following EXCEPT

    (A) a tight and logical construction.
    (B) a plot based on a withheld secret.
    (C) a misplaced letter and documents.
    (D) an obligatory scene.
    (E) an episodic structure.

25. Frank Lloyd Wright was the original architect/designer of which of the following twentieth-century museums?

    (A) Solomon R. Guggenheim Museum, New York
    (B) East Wing, National Gallery of Art, Washington, D.C.
    (C) Museum of Architecture, Frankfurt-am-Main
    (D) The High Museum of Art, Atlanta
    (E) None of the above.

QUESTIONS 26–28 refer to the following ballet definitions.

(A) Quick springing movement that resembles a cat walk by alternating feet.

(B) Placing and applying body weight to one foot that is against the floor while sliding the other foot into fifth position.

(C) Positioning one foot in front of the other while the feet remain one step apart.

(D) Weight proportioned incorrectly, creating the body to shift and lean in that direction.

(E) One left leg lifted at a 45-degree angle rotating from front to outer side, from back to inner side.

26. Which description describes glissade?

27. Which description describes improper balance?

28. Which description is fourth position crossed?

29. The predecessor of the modern-day piano is the _____

    (A) lute.
    (B) harpsichord.
    (C) synthesizer.
    (D) harp.
    (E) xylophone.

30. A poem set to music is a(n) _____

    (A) madrigal.
    (B) art song.
    (C) opera.
    (D) aria.
    (E) symphony.

31. A high male voice is classified as a(n)

    (A) soprano.
    (B) tenor.
    (C) bass.
    (D) baritone.
    (E) alto.

32. Which of the following well-known writers is famous for his verses about the struggle for Irish independence?

    (A) James Joyce
    (B) J. P. Donleavy
    (C) W. B. Yeats
    (D) G. B. Shaw
    (E) John O'Hara

33. The idea of evolution is propounded by which of the following English writers?

    (A) Alfred Lord Tennyson
    (B) Dr. Samuel Johnson
    (C) Charles Darwin
    (D) Robert Browning
    (E) Thomas Henry Huxley

34. Which of the following early American novels deals with the author's personal attempt to exorcise many of the negative aspects of his Puritan heritage?

    (A) Irving's *The History of New York*
    (B) Melville's *Moby Dick*
    (C) Brown's *Wieland*
    (D) Cooper's *The Pathfinder*
    (E) Hawthorne's *The Scarlet Letter*

35. Though once condemned as indecent and controversial, this modern English autobiographical novel is now acclaimed for its originality.

    (A) *The Metamorphosis*
    (B) *Sons and Lovers*
    (C) *Time and Again*
    (D) *Heart of Darkness*
    (E) *Ethan Frome*

36. Known for its transcendentalist underpinnings, this early American work also emphasizes the importance of self-reliance.

    (A) *The Scarlet Letter*
    (B) *The Open Boat*
    (C) *Walden*
    (D) *The Last of the Mohicans*
    (E) *The Red Badge of Courage*

QUESTIONS 37–39 refer to illustrations (A) through (E).

(B)

(A)

(C)

(D)

(E)

37. Which example characterizes a culture which values logic and order?

38. In which example are architectural forms and materials used for a whimsical effect?

39. Which example best characterizes a culture which values technological precision and efficiency?

QUESTION 40 refers to the following.

40. In the building pictured above, the cantilevered horizontal forms do all of the following EXCEPT

(A) echo the natural waterfall's rock ledge.
(B) emphasize the structural framework of the building.
(C) deny the mass and weight of the materials.
(D) integrate the building with the natural setting.
(E) rely on industrial construction materials.

QUESTION 41 refers to the following.

41. The architect of the building pictured above probably relied primarily on which of the following?

(A) Steel
(B) Concrete
(C) Wood
(D) Stone masonry and mortar
(E) Sheet glass

QUESTIONS 42 and 43 refer to the following poem.

The Sick Rose
O Rose, thou art sick.
The invisible worm
That flies in the night
In the howling storm

Has found out thy bed
Of crimson joy,
And his dárk sécret love
Does thy life destroy.
— *William Blake*

42. The imagery in this poem is mainly

(A) religious.
(B) sexual.
(C) animal.
(D) light.
(E) darkness.

43. The word "life" in line 8 means

(A) passion.
(B) spirit.
(C) love.
(D) beauty.
(E) memory.

QUESTIONS 44–46 refer to the following poem.

Apparently with no surprise
To any happy flower
The Frost beheads it at its play
In accidental power.
The blonde Assassin passes on,
The Sun proceeds unmoved
To measure off another Day
For an Approving God.

44. Line 3 demonstrates

(A) alliteration.
(B) personification.
(C) onomatopoeia.
(D) assonance.
(E) conceit.

45. "The blonde Assassin" in line 5 refers to

(A) fate.
(B) disease.
(C) the frost.
(D) the sun.
(E) an approving god.

46. Which of the following best describes the meaning of the poem?

(A) The cruelty of God
(B) The inevitability of death
(C) The indifference of God
(D) The happiness of flowers
(E) The inevitability of winter

47. Poetic drama is best described as

    (A) poetry in dialogue.
    (B) a poem in dialogue written for
        performance.
    (C) ancillary to action.
    (D) a one-act play.
    (E) a play with no well-defined scenes.

48. *The Threepenny Opera* is best described as

    (A) an adaptation of John Gay's *The
        Beggar's Opera.*
    (B) a melodrama.
    (C) a comedy.
    (D) an epic drama.
    (E) historification.

49. The belief that a human being has an absolute
    power to choose his or her own destiny is a
    hallmark of

    (A) existentialism.
    (B) essentialism.
    (C) pragmatism.
    (D) Marxism.
    (E) Platonism.

50. "Cyclopean" is a term which is often used to
    refer to the masonry building of which of the
    following civilizations?

    (A) Ancient Egyptian
    (B) Mesopotamian
    (C) Aztec
    (D) Roman
    (E) Mycenaean

51. Descartes used his *cogito* argument ("I think;
    therefore, I am") to establish

    (A) an indubitable foundation for
        knowledge.
    (B) the basis of personal identity.
    (C) metaphysics on a firm footing.
    (D) the existence of God.
    (E) the foundation of mathematics.

52. Which analysis represents a through-com-
    posed form?

    (A) AB
    (B) ABA
    (C) ABCDE
    (D) ABACA
    (E) A

53. Which of the following can be a synonym for
    Gregorian chant?

    (A) plainchant
    (B) motet
    (C) canon
    (D) aria
    (E) fugue

54. Which composer is best known for his tech-
    nique of weaving favorite melodies, often pa-
    triotic, into his compositions?

    (A) Sousa
    (B) Ives
    (C) Bernstein
    (D) Stravinsky
    (E) Haydn

55. Which of the following is perhaps the most
    curious – even hilarious – novel written in the
    eighteenth century?

    (A) *Tristram Shandy*
    (B) *Don Quixote*
    (C) *Candy*
    (D) *Catch-22*
    (E) *Where the Bee Sucks There Suck I*

56. Which Shakespeare play is considered by
    many critics to be the Bard's finest study of
    guilt and conscience following a crime?

    (A) *Julius Caesar*
    (B) *Macbeth*
    (C) *Hamlet*
    (D) *A Midsummer Night's Dream*
    (E) *Love's Labor Lost*

57. In which of the following tales is a house presented as a personification of a family?

    (A) *Anne of Green Gables*
    (B) *The House of Morgan*
    (C) *The Young Housewife*
    (D) *The House of the Seven Gables*
    (E) *An Angel on the Porch*

58. Which of the following is a twentieth-century novel about the Wild West written in the tradition of realistic movement?

    (A) *Huckleberry Finn*
    (B) *The Bird Comes to Yellow Sky*
    (C) *The Oxbow Incident*
    (D) *The Occurrence at Owl Creek Bridge*
    (E) *The Red Badge of Courage*

59. Which of the following poets is known as an American original who experimented with extensive works of detailed images and free verse?

    (A) Alexander Pope
    (B) Samuel Langhorne Clemens
    (C) Walt Whitman
    (D) Emily Dickinson
    (E) Anne Bradstreet

QUESTION 60 refers to the following.

60. The pose of the horse in the sculpture pictured above serves to express

    (A) physical aging and decay.
    (B) stability.
    (C) strength.
    (D) lightness and motion.
    (E) moral fortitude.

QUESTION 61 refers to the following.

61. Which of the following best describes the example pictured above?

    (A) Monumental architecture dominates the scene.
    (B) The scene is viewed from the window of a passing train.
    (C) Human drama is the artist's main concern.
    (D) The composition has a dramatic central focus.
    (E) The scene is viewed as though from a second-story window.

QUESTION 62 refers to the following.

62. Which of the following is probably true of the sculpture pictured above?

(A) The artist modelled it with his hands.
(B) The artist poured it into a mold.
(C) The artist shaped his materials with a blowtorch and welding tools.
(D) The artist shaped natural materials with a chisel.
(E) The artist used industrial forms as he found them.

QUESTION 63 refers to the following.

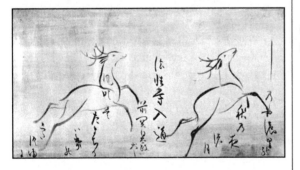

63. Which of the following is the most important artistic device in the example shown above?

(A) Line
(B) Tone
(C) Perspective
(D) Volume
(E) Hue

QUESTION 64 refers to the following.

64. Which of the following does NOT contribute to order and regularity in the example pictured on the previous page?

(A) The repeated second-story window design
(B) A facade which lacks deep recesses and voids
(C) The use of columns at the center and corners of the building
(D) A subtle use of the arch
(E) The balustrade running across the roof line

QUESTIONS 65 and 66 refer to the following stanza.

When my mother died I was very young
And my father sold me while yet my tongue
Could scarcely cry "'weep! 'weep! 'weep! 'weep!"
So your chimneys I sweep, and in soot I sleep.

65. The above stanza was taken from a longer poem written by which of the following?

(A) Shakespeare
(B) Milton
(C) Chaucer
(D) Blake
(E) Hardy

66. Which of the following best explains the use of the word "'weep!" in line 3 of the stanza?

(A) The child is so young he cannot yet pronounce the word.
(B) The child has a speech impediment because of neglect.
(C) The child is weeping because he was sold as a chimney sweep.
(D) The child wants to make you feel guilty about sweeping your chimneys.
(E) The child is so young he is upset at having to sweep chimneys.

QUESTIONS 67–71 refer to the following epic poem.

> A whole day's journey high but wide remote
> From this Assyrian garden, where the Fiend
> Saw undelighted all delight, all kind
> Of living creatures new to sight and strange:
> Two of far nobler shape erect and tall,
> God-like erect, with native honor clad
> In naked majesty seemed lords of all,
> And worthy seemed, for in their looks divine
> The image of their Maker shone,
>
> …
>
> For contemplation he and valor formed,
> For softness she and sweet attractive grace,
> He for God only, she for God in him:

67. The term "epic" refers to

(A) a long poem written in rhyming couplets about a hero.
(B) a long poem translated from Latin.
(C) a long poem written about heroic actions.
(D) a long poem written by Virgil.
(E) a long poem about death.

68. The above lines are from

(A) Dante's *Inferno*.
(B) Virgil's *Aeneid*.
(C) *The Iliad*.
(D) *Arabian Nights*.
(E) *Paradise Lost*.

69. The viewpoint of the lines is

(A) Faust's.
(B) God's.
(C) Scheherazade's.
(D) Satan's.
(E) Dante's.

70. Which best describes the couple in lines 4-6?

(A) Beowulf and Grendel's mother before the crucial fight.
(B) Grendel and Grendel's mother after the crucial fight.
(C) Adam and Eve before "The Fall."
(D) Hector and his wife before the crucial battle.
(E) Adam and Eve after "The Fall."

71. Which best describes the poet's views on the roles of men and women?

(A) Men and women are equal.
(B) Men are made for thoughtful action and women for beauty.
(C) Women must be submissive to the god in men.
(D) Men must be powerful and women soft.
(E) Men are reasonable and strong and women soft and graceful.

72. Which of the following plays focuses on a marriage built on a lie and problems with eyesight?

(A) *The Wild Duck*
(B) *Oedipus*
(C) *Electra*
(D) *Antigone*
(E) *Andromache*

73. *Tartuffe* is best described as a play about

   (A) the downfall of a noble king.
   (B) the problems of a marriage.
   (C) a man of considerable stature duped by a hypocrite.
   (D) individuals who wait and do not act.
   (E) children who are ingrates.

74. An *insula* refers to a(n)

   (A) Greek public meeting square.
   (B) multi-storied Roman apartment block.
   (C) western portion of a Carolingian church.
   (D) Greek cross plan.
   (E) vertical groove on the surface of a column.

75. Berkeley's famous dictum, "Esse est percipi" ("To be is to be perceived"), is associated most strongly with the outlook known as

   (A) idealism.
   (B) pragmatism.
   (C) empiricism.
   (D) rationalism.
   (E) phenomenology.

76. Which jazz saxophonist was named "Bird"?

   (A) Charlie Parker
   (B) John Coltrane
   (C) Dizzy Gillespie
   (D) Paul Desmond
   (E) Stan Getz

77. Which jazz tenor saxophonist is famous for his "Giant Steps"?

   (A) Charlie Parker
   (B) Stan Getz
   (C) John Coltrane
   (D) Coleman Hawkins
   (E) Ornette Coleman

78. A collaboration between Aaron Copland and the dance-choreographer Agnes de Mille resulted in the creation of which ballet suite?

   (A) "West Side Story"
   (B) "Rodeo"
   (C) "Porgy and Bess"
   (D) "Phantom of the Opera"
   (E) "Salome"

79. Which of the following novels of adventure presents the most detailed picture of eighteenth-century English manorial and city life?

   (A) *Great Expectations*
   (B) *Moby Dick*
   (C) *Jane Eyre*
   (D) *Tom Jones*
   (E) *Silas Marner*

80. Which of the following is among the most famous of English works by the group of writers called the "Decadents"?

   (A) Coleridge's "Rime of the Ancient Mariner"
   (B) Lawrence's *Sons and Lovers*
   (C) Fielding's *Joseph Andrews*
   (D) Wilde's *The Picture of Dorian Gray*
   (E) Joyce's *The Dubliners*

81. The important literary concept of the "pathetic fallacy" was first set forth in

   (A) Ruskin's *Modern Painters*.
   (B) Emerson's *Nature*.
   (C) Shakespeare's *As You Like It*.
   (D) Thomas Lodge's *Rosalynde*.
   (E) Samuel Johnson's *Dictionary*.

82. A reaction against utilitarianism – the theory of ethics formulated in England in the eighteenth century – can be seen in nineteenth-century literature, such as

   (A) Eliot's *Middlemarch*.
   (B) Dreiser's *Sister Carrie*.
   (C) Melville's *Billy Budd*.
   (D) James's *Washington Square*.
   (E) Dickens' *David Copperfield*.

83. Which of the following writers participated energetically in the Celtic Revival of the eighteenth century?

   (A) James Joyce
   (B) John O'Hara
   (C) J. P. Donleavy
   (D) James Macpherson
   (E) W. B. Yeats

QUESTION 84 refers to the following.

84. In the painting illustrated above, all of the following are important compositional devices EXCEPT

   (A) the perspective grid of the checkerboard floor.
   (B) the strong highlighting of the foreground figures.
   (C) the arcade of arches in the background.
   (D) the vigorous movement of the main figure group.
   (E) the intersecting lines of the arms and the swords.

QUESTION 85 refers to the following.

85. The building pictured above was produced in which of the following countries?

   (A) Japan
   (B) Indonesia
   (C) Easter Island
   (D) Greece
   (E) Nigeria

QUESTIONS 86–88 refer to the following illustrations (A) through (E) below.

(A)

(B)

(E)

(C)

(D)

86. Which example seeks to give a schematic representation of a ceremonial event?

87. In which example is the human figure most stylized and repeated in order to fit its container?

88. In which example do the figures show the greatest tendency toward rhythmic calligraphy?

QUESTIONS 89–91 refer to the following lines.

> As when in the sky the stars about the
>   moon's shining
> are seen in all their glory, when the air
>   has fallen to stillness.
> and all the high places of the hills are
>   clear, and the shoulders
> out-jutting,
> and the deep ravines, as endless bright air
>   spills from the heavens
> and all the stars are seen, to make glad
>   the heart of the shepherd:
> such in their numbers blazed the watch-
>   fires the Trojans were burning
> between the waters of Xanthos and the
>   ships, before Ilion.

89. The lines above are an example of

   (A) a Homeric simile.
   (B) an extended metaphor.
   (C) Augustan couplets.
   (D) English heroic verse.
   (E) Miltonic free verse.

90. What is being described as what?

   (A) The stars are like hills.
   (B) The stars are like shepherds.
   (C) The stars are like rivers.
   (D) The Trojan fires are like the stars.
   (E) The Trojan ships are like the stars.

91. The shepherd is introduced in line 5 in order to

   (A) humanize the description.
   (B) give some humor to the description.
   (C) give some depth to the description.
   (D) give some gladness to the description.
   (E) glamorize the description.

QUESTIONS 92–95 refer to lines (A) through (E) below.

   (A) As soon as April pierces to the root
        The drought of March, and bathes each
        bud and shoot
        …
   (B) Of man's first disobedience, and the
        fruit
        Of that forbidden fruit whose mortal
        taste
        …
   (C) My heart leaps up when I behold
        A rainbow in the sky;
        …
   (D) I placed a jar in Tennessee,
        And round it was, upon a hill.
        …
   (E) Because I could not stop for Death—
        He kindly stopped for me—

92. Which is written by a woman?

93. Which is by Chaucer?

94. Which represents the Romantic period?

95. Which represents the epic?

96. As Gregor Samsa awoke one morning from an uneasy dream he found himself transformed into a gigantic insect.

   This opening line is

   (A) Genet's
   (B) Sartre's
   (C) Ionesco's
   (D) Kafka's
   (E) Tolstoy's

97. The best definition for the original use of scapegoat is

   (A) a table ornament used when royalty was unable to appear.
   (B) a fur-bearing animal that was used to provide milk.
   (C) an animal tethered to lure animals terrorizing the village.
   (D) a victim sacrificed for the redemption of the tribe being driven into the wilderness.
   (E) a royal personage like Oedipus who went into exile.

98. Which of the following types of ancient Roman architecture most directly influenced the development of early Christian church planning?

   (A) Temple
   (B) Basilica
   (C) Bath
   (D) Forum
   (E) Villa

99. Dance was originated by

    (A) religious groups.
    (B) Egyptians.
    (C) Greeks.
    (D) Romans.
    (E) savage hunters.

100. The logical fallacy involved in concluding that the universe itself must have a cause because every event in the universe has cause is

    (A) the fallacy of composition.
    (B) the fallacy of division.
    (C) the slippery slope fallacy.
    (D) the *ad hominem* fallacy.
    (E) the fallacy of ignorance.

101. The themes of many musical compositions are often that of folk music. Which composer is most famous for his folk music settings for wind ensemble?

    (A) Sousa
    (B) Grainger
    (C) Beethoven
    (D) Strauss
    (E) Haydn

QUESTIONS 102–105 refer to the following musical notation.

102. What is the key of this excerpt?

    (A) B flat
    (B) F
    (C) C
    (D) D
    (E) A

103. The time signature for the above excerpt is not noted. What should it be?

    (A) $\frac{4}{4}$

    (B) $\frac{2}{4}$

    (C) $\frac{6}{8}$

    (D) $\frac{3}{4}$

    (E) $\frac{12}{8}$

104. How many measures are present?

    (A) 1
    (B) 2
    (C) 3
    (D) 0
    (E) 5

105. What is the arrow pointing towards?

    (A) Key signature
    (B) Clef sign
    (C) Double bar
    (D) Repeat sign
    (E) Time signature

106. Which of the following is considered among the "American Ethnic" body of literature?

    (A) James's *Daisy Miller*
    (B) Poe's *Cask of Amontillado*
    (C) Roth's *Goodbye, Columbus*
    (D) Updike's *Rabbit Redux*
    (E) Hawthorne's *Scarlet Letter*

107. One of the most famous and prophetic descriptions of settlements in the young American nation was

    (A) *The Journals of Lewis and Clark.*
    (B) *Main Street.*
    (C) *Letters From an American Farmer.*
    (D) *The Last of the Mohicans.*
    (E) *The Diary of Captain John Smith.*

108. Which of the following modern novels describes the difficulties faced by African-Americans in twentieth-century America?

    (A) *As I Lay Dying*
    (B) *Ethan Frome*
    (C) *Heart of Darkness*
    (D) *The Metamorphosis*
    (E) *The Invisible Man*

109. Which of the following nineteenth-century novels was used as an accurate travel guide well into this century?

    (A) *Journey to the Center of the Earth*
    (B) *The Mysterious Island*
    (C) *Robinson Crusoe*
    (D) *20,000 Leagues Under the Sea*
    (E) *Gulliver's Travels*

110. Which of the following novels recalls a time of medieval chivalry?

    (A) Eliot's *Middlemarch*
    (B) Scott's *Ivanhoe*
    (C) Poe's *The Fall of the House of Usher*
    (D) King's *The Shining*
    (E) West's *The Dreamlife of Balso Snell*

111. It has been said that Victorian poetry is essentially a continuation of the poetry of the romantic movement. This can be seen in

    (A) Hemingway's veneration for Eliot.
    (B) Tennyson's veneration for Browning.
    (C) Arnold's veneration for Wordsworth.
    (D) Rossetti's veneration for Browning.
    (E) Wordsworth's veneration for Scott.

112. Which of the following is one of the most hilarious stories in *Huckleberry Finn* – one which demonstrates both the accepting nature and eventual canniness of the heartland Americans?

    (A) *The Duke and the Dauphin*
    (B) Tom Sawyer and his painted fence
    (C) Huck's escape from Pap
    (D) Jim's escape to freedom
    (E) Huck "lighting out for the territories"

QUESTION 113 refers to the following.

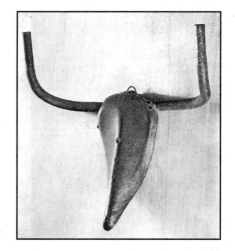

113. In combining found objects to make the sculpture shown above, the artist sought to create

    (A) a contrast of line and tone.
    (B) a religious symbol.
    (C) a visual analogy to a living creature.
    (D) a metaphor for human experience.
    (E) a functional device.

QUESTIONS 114–116 refer to the following illustrations (A) through (E)

(A)

(B)

(C)

(D)

(E)

114. In which example do carefully rendered decorative details in the painting help to visually relate the main subject to the background?

115. In which example is an off-center subject cropped to produce the effect of a casual photograph?

116. In which example does the subject's off-center position lead the viewer's eye out of the picture?

QUESTION 117 refers to the following.

117. The staircase in the Hotel van Eetvelde, designed by Victor Horta in 1895, illustrates which one of the following art historical styles?

(A) Surrealism
(B) Post-Modernism
(C) Neo-Classicism
(D) Post-Impressionsim
(E) Art Nouveau

QUESTIONS 118 and 119 refer to the following illustrations (A) through (D) below.

(A)

(B)

(C)

(D)

118. Which is Gothic?

(A) Building (A)
(B) Building (B)
(C) Building (C)
(D) Building (D)
(E) None of the above.

119. Which was NOT constructed as a place of religious worship?

(A) Building (A)
(B) Building (B)
(C) Building (C)
(D) Building (D)
(E) None of the above.

QUESTIONS 120 and 121 refer to the following verse.

> On the one-ton temple bell
> a moonmoth, folded into sleep,
> sits still.

120. The above is an example of

(A) hyperbole.
(B) an ode.
(C) haiku.
(D) an epigram.
(E) doggerel.

121. The original work above was written in

(A) French.
(B) Japanese.
(C) Chinese.
(D) British English.
(E) Persian.

122. Which of the following best defines the term *bathos*?

(A) A gross exaggeration
(B) A build to a climax
(C) An abrupt fall from climax
(D) An abrupt fall from the beautiful to the funny
(E) An abrupt build to a climax

123. Which poet gave us the term "negative capability"?

(A) William Carlos Williams
(B) T. S. Eliot
(C) William Wordsworth
(D) e. e. cummings
(E) John Keats

124. If all tragedies are finished by death, and all comedies by a marriage, then which of the following is the best example of tragedy?

(A) *A Death of a Salesman*
(B) *A Midsummer Night's Dream*
(C) *Oedipus*
(D) *The Tempest*
(E) *The Bad-Tempered Man*

QUESTIONS 125–127 refer to what happens when:

(A) misunderstandings are cleared up.
(B) action not intended by the main character takes place.
(C) the public is aided in its discovery of the villain.
(D) the main character whispers an "aside" to the audience.
(E) the hero's understanding of the true nature of the situation and the self changes.

125. Which of the choices best defines *anagnorisis*, the Greek word for "recognition" or "discovery"?

126. Which choice best describes Mark Antony's intent in the public oration that he makes regarding Julius Caesar's death?

127. Which choice is best used to characterize Othello's description of himself as "one that loved not wisely, but too well"?

128. "So the whole ear of Denmark / Is by a forged process of my death / Rankly abused."

    The speaker is

    (A) the Royal Dane.
    (B) King Lear.
    (C) Puck.
    (D) Falstaff.
    (E) Caliban.

129. The unglazed opening in the center of the dome of the Pantheon in Rome is called a(n)

    (A) window.
    (B) oculus.
    (C) splayed window.
    (D) stained-glass window.
    (E) clerestory.

130. Parallel feet, flat-footed steps, undulating torso, body isolation, and syncopated rhythms refer to

    (A) beledi dance (abdominal dance).
    (B) jazz dance.
    (C) danse mora (Flamenco dance).
    (D) tap dance.
    (E) country dance.

131. Suppose two theories are equally powerful in explaining certain phenomena, but one of them (**X**) postulates a larger number of unobservable entities than the other (**Y**). Which is preferable and why?

    (A) **Y**, because of Occam's Razor
    (B) **Y**, because of the Principle of Plenitude
    (C) **X**, because of the Open Question Argument
    (D) **X**, because of Underdetermination
    (E) **Y**, because of Scientific Realism

132. The hero of what nineteenth century novel states that "...vanity is a weakness indeed. But pride– where there is a real superiority of mind, pride will be always under good regulation."

    (A) *Silas Marner*
    (B) *Emma*
    (C) *Gone with the Wind*
    (D) *Pride and Prejudice*
    (E) *Gulliver's Travels*

133. A trumpet can play different notes by adjusting the lip or by doing what?

    (A) Pressing down a valve
    (B) Striking a string
    (C) Covering a hole
    (D) Using an octave key
    (E) Using a slide

QUESTIONS 134 and 135 refer to the following musical notation.

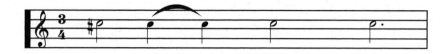

134. The diagram is an example of

    (A) hemiola.
    (B) paradiddle.
    (C) fermata.
    (D) crescendo.
    (E) glissando.

135. The C in measure 1 is a C sharp. Therefore, the C in measure 2 is a

    (A) C natural.
    (B) C sharp.
    (C) C flat.
    (D) B.
    (E) D.

136. What is another name for the bass clef?

    (A) F clef
    (B) G clef
    (C) Tenor clef
    (D) Treble clef
    (E) Alto clef

137. One of the greatest modern chronicles of a famous incident during the Civil War is

    (A) Hoover's *None Dare Call It Treason.*
    (B) Wouk's *Caine Mutiny.*
    (C) Mailer's *The Naked and the Dead.*
    (D) Catton's *A Stillness at Appomatox.*
    (E) Crane's *Red Badge of Courage.*

138. Which of the following is Edward Albee's memorable drama of the trials and tribulations of a university professor and his wife?

    (A) *Troilus and Cressida*
    (B) *Who's Afraid of Virginia Woolf*
    (C) *The American Dream*
    (D) *Brighton Beach Memoirs*
    (E) *A View from the Bridge*

139. One of the greatest diarists of the Restoration was

    (A) Sir Laurence Olivier.
    (B) Laurence Sterne.
    (C) O. E. Rolvaag.
    (D) Samuel Pepys.
    (E) Jonathan Swift.

140. In the early 1800s, which American minister and writer promoted the philosophical and literary movement called transcendentalism?

    (A) Jonathan Edwards
    (B) Sir William Pitt
    (C) Ralph Waldo Emerson
    (D) Henry David Thoreau
    (E) Dr. Samuel Fuller

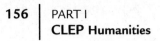

ANSWER KEY

1.	(D)	36.	(C)	71.	(E)	106.	(C)
2.	(B)	37.	(A)	72.	(A)	107.	(C)
3.	(A)	38.	(D)	73.	(C)	108.	(E)
4.	(D)	39.	(B)	74.	(B)	109.	(A)
5.	(A)	40.	(B)	75.	(A)	110.	(B)
6.	(B)	41.	(D)	76.	(A)	111.	(C)
7.	(C)	42.	(B)	77.	(C)	112.	(A)
8.	(A)	43.	(D)	78.	(B)	113.	(C)
9.	(D)	44.	(B)	79.	(D)	114.	(B)
10.	(C)	45.	(C)	80.	(D)	115.	(C)
11.	(B)	46.	(B)	81.	(A)	116.	(D)
12.	(D)	47.	(B)	82.	(E)	117.	(E)
13.	(D)	48.	(D)	83.	(D)	118.	(C)
14.	(A)	49.	(A)	84.	(D)	119.	(A)
15.	(E)	50.	(E)	85.	(A)	120.	(C)
16.	(C)	51.	(A)	86.	(A)	121.	(B)
17.	(A)	52.	(C)	87.	(C)	122.	(D)
18.	(B)	53.	(A)	88.	(D)	123.	(E)
19.	(C)	54.	(B)	89.	(A)	124.	(A)
20.	(E)	55.	(A)	90.	(D)	125.	(E)
21.	(B)	56.	(B)	91.	(A)	126.	(C)
22.	(A)	57.	(D)	92.	(E)	127.	(E)
23.	(D)	58.	(C)	93.	(A)	128.	(A)
24.	(E)	59.	(C)	94.	(C)	129.	(B)
25.	(A)	60.	(C)	95.	(B)	130.	(B)
26.	(B)	61.	(E)	96.	(D)	131.	(A)
27.	(D)	62.	(C)	97.	(D)	132.	(D)
28.	(C)	63.	(A)	98.	(B)	133.	(A)
29.	(B)	64.	(D)	99.	(E)	134.	(A)
30.	(B)	65.	(D)	100.	(A)	135.	(A)
31.	(B)	66.	(A)	101.	(B)	136.	(A)
32.	(C)	67.	(C)	102.	(B)	137.	(D)
33.	(C)	68.	(E)	103.	(D)	138.	(B)
34.	(E)	69.	(D)	104.	(C)	139.	(D)
35.	(B)	70.	(C)	105.	(D)	140.	(C)

PRACTICE TEST
DETAILED EXPLANATIONS OF ANSWERS

1. **(D)** Pylons serve as large "gates" to ancient Egyptian temple complexes. Pyramids (A), mastabas (B), and tombs (C) were burial sites and were not as a rule located near the entrances of temples. (E) Obelisks, while positioned near the entrance to many Egyptian temple complexes, are tall, narrow, vertical shafts, which are physically quite unlike wide, massive pylon walls.

2. **(B)** The group of performers who used such techniques for the purpose of displaying power were called flagellants. Fools used crude jokes and quick wit in their technique (A). Minnesingers were a group of entertainers who sang about war, political issues, and love (C). The mimes mimicked and acted out a situation without speech (D). Joculators were seen as actors and jesters, dancing mimes, acrobats, poets, and musicians (E).

3. **(A)** Although the definition of an *a priori* truth is not altogether clear, it is usually said that such truths are known independently of experience or "from the first." Thus, (B) cannot be correct. Mathematical calculation can count as a kind of experience, so (C) is incorrect. Human beings are believed to know truth "from the first" by many philosophers; thus, (D) is incorrect. A truth whose denial is a contradiction (E) is called an "analytic" truth.

4. **(D)** The fourth degree of a major scale is called the subdominant. Each degree is given a name to show its relation within the scale. Choice (D) is correct. The tonic is the first step of a scale; choice (A) is incorrect. The dominant is the fifth degree of the scale; choice (B) is incorrect. The leading tone is the seventh degree of the scale; choice (C) is incorrect. The mediant is the third degree of a scale; choice (E) is incorrect.

5. **(A)** A minor scale ascends from the tonic in the following pattern: $w \frac{1}{2} w\ w\ \frac{1}{2}\ w\ w$. Therefore, the half steps occur between the 2-3 and 5-6 scale degree, so choice (A) is correct. Half steps between steps 3-4 and 7-8 are found in a major scale, $w\ w\ 2\ w\ w\ w\ 2$. Choice (B) is incorrect. Half steps between steps 1-2 and 7-8 and 2-3 and 7-8 are not defined scales; choices (C) and (D) are incorrect. A half step between the third and fourth degrees of a scale is found in the blues scale; choice (E) is incorrect.

6. **(B)** Stravinsky's "Le Sacre du Printemps" is an example of the use of primitivism – employing rhythms that are explosive and powerful; choice (B) is correct. Debussy employs impressionism for "Prélude á l'après-midi d'un faune"; choice (A) is incorrect. "Salome" is a tone poem by Richard Strauss which experiments with atonality. Choice (C) is incorrect. "Wozzeck" is a 12-tone opera by Alban Berg; choice (D) is incorrect. "The Liberty Bell" is a march composed by John Phillip Sousa; choice (E) is incorrect.

7. **(C)** William Blake (1757-1827) has been described as "the first clear voice of romanticism." Perhaps his greatest work was *Songs of Innocence and Experience* (C), in which many of the characteristics of romantic poetry can be seen: the poetry expresses the poet's personal feelings, not

the actions of other men; spontaneity and freedom; natural scenes and pictures of flora and fauna. Pope's (A) "hero-comical" poem from the seventeenth century demonstrates none of the above. *The Social Contract* (B) is a sociological and philosophical essay. *Romeo and Juliet* (E), while commonly understood to be a romance between two teenagers, is not "romantic," and, in fact, predates romanticism by 200 years. James's novel (D) belongs to the American realist period.

8. **(A)** The titles presented here, of course, are mostly in French (except for (D) which is about a French historical figure) – the language of Albert Camus, the father of existentialism. Camus' *L'Étranger (The Stranger)* – the story of an expatriate Frenchman in Algeria – presents many of the precepts of existentialism: an emphasis on existence rather than essence, and the inadequacy of human reason to explain the enigma of the universe. *Le Morte D'Arthur* (B) was written in English by Tennyson; *Candide* (C) was by Voltaire and *Le Misanthrope* (E) was a comedy of the 1700s by Molière. While the latter title might indicate existential estrangement, the work appears 200 years before the literary movement. *Saint Joan* (D), a dramatic tragedy by G. B. Shaw, is biographical.

9. **(D)** All of the writings listed here describe life on an American frontier – but only *My Antonia* deals with frontier life in the Midwest during the nineteenth century – the rough weather, the difficulties of farm life, and the blossoming of romance in harsh conditions. Cooper's famous work (A), while written during that century, refers to upstate New York during the eighteenth century. William Byrd's work (B) deals with defining the border between Virginia and North Carolina during the late eighteenth century. Bradford's diary (C) is a Pilgrim document written in colonial Massachusetts, and Twain's classic (E), while it tangentially involves Illinois and the shores of Iowa on the Mississippi River, does not deal with the Midwest per se.

10. **(C)** Salinger's work is recognized as a coming of age novel in which his main character, Holden Caulfield, is an "antihero" – a character whose appeal is that his flaws are dominant. *Tom Sawyer* (A) has always been viewed by critics as a children's novel, because Tom can be seen as the "All-American Boy," unlike Huck Finn, Twain's later, more complicated creation. Dickens' work (B) does not deal with coming of age. Dreiser's *Sister Carrie* (E), on the other hand, does concern itself with changes in the protagonist through time, but Carrie is more a classic heroine in her rigid self-reliance and conquest over adversity. Fitzgerald (D) creates a number of interesting figures – some, like Gatsby, who have anti-heroic qualities – but all have basically "come of age" before the summer in which the story takes place.

11. **(B)** Whitman's poem is one of four elegies, entitled "Memories of President Lincoln," which were made part of *Drum-Taps* after Lincoln's death in 1864. Whitman, who volunteered as a male nurse in Washington during the Civil War – like so many Americans – mourned greatly for the president. The Englishman Gray's "Elegy" (A) is of a much earlier vintage (late 1700s). Christina Rossetti's "After Death" (C) is not an elegy, nor is Allen Ginsberg's "Howl" (D). Wordsworth's work (E) deals with the death of Sir George Beaumont, the poet's patron.

12. **(D)** The architect of the building illustrated was intent on avoiding traditional building forms in the search for a new, expressive use of space. The design pictured, therefore, carefully avoids all reminders of the symmetrical, balanced floor plans of classical and Renaissance architecture. It also dispenses with a conventional structural framework and with the geometric forms and angles of traditional buildings. Instead, it exploits fully the potential of a new material – in this case, poured concrete – to create dynamic, curving forms whose arcs and spirals echo both the shape of growing organisms and the motion of wind and water.

13. **(D)**   Answer choices (A), (B), and (E) each contain images of animals which are based to some degree on naturalistic observation. In each case, however, the animals are presented either as black-and-white line drawings or as schematic, two-dimensional renderings, with no attempt to model the forms of the animals; and in each case, the imagery functions in either a narrative or magical context and does not intend to explore anatomy. Answer choice (C) presents a basically realistic, well-modelled animal, based on naturalistic observation and with close attention to detail, but the addition of the wings adds a fantastic touch and the animal as a whole is elegantly designed and positioned to act as the functional handle of a jar. Only answer choice (D) explores the expressive forms of the animal's musculature, here conveying a sense of untamed emotion and animal energy through the tensed, swelling muscles of the crouched jaguar.

14. **(A)**   Answer choices (B) and (E) each present somewhat schematic representations of animals, the first in order to document the character and activities of an Egyptian noble, and the second to fulfill a magical, ritual function. The animal in answer choice (C) exists solely as a decorative detail on a purely functional object. Answer choice (D) shows animal behavior which might be called analogous to human behavior – i.e., the violence of the strong over the weak – but the image itself does not intend to comment directly on human life. Only answer choice (A) uses animal imagery to directly caricature human behavior. In this case, the Japanese scroll employs monkeys, frogs, hares, and foxes to mimic Buddhist religious practices.

15. **(E)**   Answer choice (E) presents animal images with a high degree of naturalism in a sophisticated, abstract, almost "modern" style. The artist, however, despite his naturalism, was not concerned with perspective or with conventional pictorial space, and concentrated solely on the overlapping images of the animals, which have no narrative function. He has included a view of the animals ascending, possibly to indicate a magical essence of these animals. These paintings were executed on the walls of a cave in what appears to be a sacred precinct, and seem to function as magical images to ensure success in the hunt.

16. **(C)**   The example pictured, by the English painter William Hogarth, satirizes eighteenth-century English life in a comic way. In telling the story of the human characters illustrated in the work, the picture uses a wealth of carefully chosen detail which the viewer is to "read" in a novelistic manner. The period details, therefore (as of dress, architecture, furnishings, etc.), and the attitudes and actions of the figures (the exasperated look, for instance, of the servant on the left) tell us that this is a human comedy set in the eighteenth century. Of the other answer choices, (A), (B), and (D) would be both historically anachronistic and weightier in subject matter. Answer choice (E) would fall roughly within the correct period, but it, too, would likely present a more dramatic context.

17. **(A)**   Choice (A) is the only correctly scanned line. It contains five iambic feet and is an example of iambic pentameter. The other examples have incorrectly marked accents and feet.

18. **(B)**   This passage comes from the Greek play *Medea* by Euripides. Medea, a woman who is being cast aside so her husband, Jason, can marry a princess, kills their two sons in retaliation. This passage shows Jason lamenting over the boys' deaths and invoking the gods to punish his ex-wife.

19. **(C)**   In the passage, Jason mourns that Medea killed the boys "to prevent me from/Touching their bodies or giving them burial." In Greek society, the dead were honored by elaborate burial rites and ceremonies. To be buried without ceremony was considered to be dishonorable to the dead, especially when they were related to great warriors, such as Jason.

20. **(E)** An oxymoron is an apparent contradiction in terms, such as "jumbo shrimp," "cruel kindness," or "peace force." Passage (E) contains an oxymoron because it mentions flames give "No light, but rather darkness." Choice (E) is the correct answer.

21. **(B)** Assonance is the repetition of vowel sounds in a single line of poetry. Passage (B) contains three examples of assonance: the words "Rocks" and "bogs," the words "caves," "lakes," and "shades," and the words "fens" and "dens." Thus, passage (B) is the correct answer.

22. **(A)** Iambic pentameter refers to the meter, or rhythm, of a line of poetry composed of five feet, each of which is an iamb, having one unstressed syllable followed by a stressed syllable. A line of poetry written in iambic pentameter is ten syllables long. Passage (A) contains two lines of poetry written in iambic pentameter. When read aloud, the unstressed-stressed pattern emerges: "For SHADE to SHADE will COME too DROWsiLY, / And DROWN the WAKEful ANGuish OF the SOUL." Thus, choice (A) is the correct answer.

23. **(D)** Zora Neale Hurston and Marita Bonner won awards and recognition for their plays in the 1920s. (A) Wilson and Hansberry are of different generations; Wilson is a contemporary playwright and Hansberry wrote her plays between 1961 and 1964. (B) Gordone and Baraka were best known in the 1970s. Ed Bullins was a novelist/poet who came to prominence in the late 1960s, too late for this question. Sonia Sanchez is a contemporary poet and is also too late to be considered as a correct answer for this question. O'Neill and Odets (E) are not African-American playwrights.

24. **(E)** A well-made play is characterized by (A) tight and logical construction, (B) a plot based on a withheld secret, (C) misplaced letters or documents, and (D) an obligatory scene. (E) Episodic structure is antithetical and characterized by little more than a series of incidents and has little logical arrangement; therefore, (E) is the exception to the well-made play and is the best answer.

25. **(A)** Solomon R. Guggenheim Museum, New York. The (B) East Wing of the National Gallery of Art in Washington, D.C., was designed by I.M. Pei. O.M. Ungers designed the (C) Museum of Architecture in Frankfurt-am-Main. Richard Meier was the architect of the (D) High Museum of Art in Atlanta.

26. **(B)** To brush one foot against the floor is to glissade. Pas de chat is a quick "cat-like" step (A), feet positioned in front of one another with a step separating them and legs turned out is fourth position crossed (C), body weight shifted incorrectly is improper balance (D), and a pointed foot and extended leg moving in a circular motion is a demi-rond de jambe (E).

27. **(D)** Weight and body shifted incorrectly is improper balance. Choices pas de chat (A), glissade (B), fourth position crossed (C), and demi-rond de jambe (E) are specific ballet movements.

28. **(C)** One foot in front of the other with a step separating them describes fourth position crossed. Pas de chat (A) and glissade (B) are steps in motion, improper balance is incorrect body alignment caused by uneven weight distribution (D), and demi-rond de jambe is a circular foot motion (E).

29. **(B)** The harpsichord is the predecessor of the piano, also called a spinet. The strings of the harpsichord were plucked with quills; this limited dynamics and tone colors. The piano was called the piano forte because it could play dynamics based on the performer's force. The harpsichord was widely used during the baroque period; choice (B) is correct. The lute is similar to the guitar; choice (A) is incorrect. The synthesizer is an electronic keyboard using analog and/or digital

technology to produce sound; choice (C) is incorrect. The harp is a stringed instrument that is plucked with the fingers; choice (D) is incorrect. The xylophone is a percussion instrument which is struck with a mallet; choice (E) is incorrect.

30. **(B)** An art song, or "lieder," is a poem set to music, for solo voice and piano; choice (B) is correct. A madrigal is verse set to music for two or more voices, which often follows a prescribed form; choice (A) is incorrect. An opera is a theatrical drama which is sung, often with instrumental accompaniment; choice (C) is incorrect. An aria is a solo for voice with accompaniment, occurring during a longer form such as an opera; choice (D) is incorrect. A symphony is a three or four movement work for orchestra; choice (E) is incorrect.

31. **(B)** A tenor is a high male voice; choice (B) is correct. The range of voices is classified from high to low; that is, soprano, alto, tenor, baritone, bass. A soprano is a high female voice; choice (A) is incorrect. A bass is the lowest male voice; choice (C) is incorrect. A baritone has a range between the tenor and the bass; choice (D) is incorrect. An alto is a medium female voice; choice (E) is incorrect.

32. **(C)** W. B. Yeats, the famous Irish poet and essayist of the early twentieth century, is always remembered for his devotion to Irish nationalism — most specifically in his volumes of collected poems such as "In the Seven Woods" and "The Green Helmet and Other Poems." James Joyce (A) is known for his depiction of Irish life, and dramatist George B. Shaw (D) is generally regarded more in a strictly literary and not political tradition. The other two choices — Donleavy (B) and O'Hara (E) — are modern American writers, whose literary interests tend more to romance and mystery than Irish nationalism and unification.

33. **(C)** Charles Darwin's *On the Origin of Species* helped shape Victorian English thought as well as considerations of natural history throughout the world. Tracing the origin of man from mammals, and species before them, was a monumental scientific effort and a shock so great to the religious community that many still attempt to deny Darwin's Theory of Evolution. Tennyson (A) referred to Darwin's theory of evolution in some of his major poems. English scientist and essayist Huxley (E) was a proponent of Darwin's theories. Dr. Johnson's (B) degree was not in science; his work as an essayist, commentator, and lexicographer remains an enormous contribution to arts and letters. Browning's (D) wonderful poetic monologues, while written during the Victorian Age, in no way represent a suitable answer to the question.

34. **(E)** *The Scarlet Letter.* While much writing is autobiographical, some works are known more than others for serving particular personal purposes. Hawthorne's work is among them. Hawthorne, a descendant of Judge John Hathorne (no *w*), one of the three judges who presided over the Salem Witch Trial, believed that a curse on male members of his family was still a matter of personal concern during his life in the early 1800s. He changed the spelling of his name and wrote *The Scarlet Letter,* in which Puritan justice is seen as harsh, overreactive, and heartless. In this and other ways, he hoped to atone for the cruelty of his ancestors. Irving (A) was an entertaining historian with no such worries. Melville (B) and Cooper (D) were great tale tellers, and Charles Brockden Brown's (C) main claim to fame is as the first American novelist.

35. **(B)** Lawrence's *Sons and Lovers* shocked an entire generation of critics when it was published in the early 1900s. Its passionate prose and erotic evocations will still shock the more innocent contemporary reader. Kafka's story (A) about a man who changes into an insect is dense with philosophy. Conrad's great work (D) is vivid in its natural descriptions, but hardly a novel to be "banned in Boston." Jack Finney's (C) modern novel of dimensional travel is also tame by any comparison, as most certainly is Edith Wharton's (E).

36. **(C)** Thoreau's *Walden* most clearly engages his friend Emerson's precepts of rugged individualism which the minister set down in his essay "Self Reliance." Thoreau writes about his month-long sojourn living off the land in a cabin near Walden Pond in Massachusetts. Hawthorne's work (A), while written at about the same time, demonstrates few of these concerns. Crane's works (B) and (E) are brilliant descriptions of an accident and warfare, and great stories – as is Cooper's (D) – but none is based in transcendentalist theory – a reliance on individual and conscience – and expressed powerfully through prose.

37. **(A)** Answer choices (C), (D), and (E) illustrate buildings which employ arching, curving, cylindrical, and circular forms, often in elaborate, complex combinations, and suggest the play of emotion, fantasy, or romance, but do not seem founded on any general cultural need for logic and order. Choice (B) shows a modern building whose design certainly proceeds from logical precepts, but, of the principles offered in the answer choices, technological precision seems to best characterize this example. Choice (A), however, the famous fifth century BCE Parthenon in Athens, presents a building whose design reflects perfectly the logical philosophies which defined Classical Greek culture. The Parthenon's architects were careful to construct a building of simple, refined forms, methodically repeated according to calculated ratios of size and space. The result is an effect of perfect balance and order which would be undermined by altering any one of the building's essential components.

38. **(D)** Choices (A) and (B) illustrate structures whose severe, regularized forms seem to deny the possibility of humor and whimsy. Choice (C), a Gothic cathedral interior, uses soaring arches and strong vertical thrust to express spirituality and religious fervor, while choice (E), an Italian baroque church exterior, conveys a sense of intellectual, nervous agitation through a contrast of convex and concave curves and the use of an overabundance of ornamental detail. Only choice (D), a nineteenth-century English pleasure pavilion, combines a fanciful assortment of playful, whimsical shapes – as in the "Islamic" domes and minarets – to create an effect of exotic fantasy and underscore its function as a place of recreation.

39. **(B)** Alone among the five answer choices, example (B) pares its structural forms to an absolute minimum, stressing the industrial materials – the steel of its framework and its extensive window glass – to achieve an effect of absolute structural logic and clarity. This "international style" architecture typifies the skyscrapers in large cities throughout the industrial world and reflects the high cultural value placed on industrial and commercial efficiency in the modern urbanized society.

40. **(B)** In the example, the 1939 "Fallingwater" house by the American architect Frank Lloyd Wright, the horizontal forms which project dramatically over the small waterfall do not emphasize the building's structural framework but, rather, deny the presence of a structural support altogether and seem almost to defy gravity. All of the other observations offered in the answer choices are valid. Consistent with Wright's conception of an "organic" architecture, the cantilevered forms echo the horizontal axis of the waterfall's rock shelf, and, even though they are rigidly cubic in form, help to merge the

house with its setting. This bold construction was only possible to the architect through the use of such modern, industrial-strength building materials as poured, pre-stressed concrete, whose great strength and flexibility made possible the long projecting forms supported at one end only.

41. **(D)**   The building pictured in the example is the *Abbaye-aux Hommes at Caen*. It was built and dedicated to Saint Stephen by William the Conqueror and is a good example of the Norman Romanesque style. Though the church was founded in the eleventh century, the vaults are a reconstruction from the first half of the twelfth century. The original building was wooden-roofed, but stone masonry is the most important element. All of the other materials listed in the answer choices are industrial-age materials which were unavailable to the medieval architect.

42. **(B)**   The rose has, for centuries, been a symbol of virginal love and beauty. By calling the rose "sick," the poet is implying that somehow this virginal beauty has been lost. This is due to, as the poet states, an "invisible worm," that has found the rose's "bed/Of crimson joy." The loss of virginity has been equated with "sickness," and the sex act causing the loss is alluded to in terms of "worms" and "beds of crimson joy."

43. **(D)**   Because of the "worm," the "rose" is "sick"; choice (D) is the best answer because it addresses the archetypical symbol of the rose as virginal love and beauty. Since the rose is "sick," this beauty is gone. Some of the other choices may adequately answer the question, but not as well as (D).

44. **(B)**   Personification means an object or emotion has been made into a person with human attributes – here the frost is seen beheading as if in battle as a show of power. Easily detected, the personified word is frequently capitalized. Alliteration (A) is a device that repeats the initial consonants (or vowels) as in "crowing cocks" or "weeping widows." Onomatopoeia (C) uses verbs that sound like the action, as in "ooze" or "hiss" or "swish." Assonance repeats the vowel sounds in a line or sentence. In fact, lines 6-8 demonstrate assonance in the words "unmoved," "another," and "approving," but for the technique in line 3 (D) is incorrect. Conceit (E) is a term connected with the metaphysical poets like John Donne where outrageous comparisons are made between unlike objects – the most famous is Donne's use of a drawing compass to link two people saying goodbye. Here frost is referred to as a killer of flowers, not compared to a weed-whacker. Study hint: find a glossary in the back of a poetry anthology and learn these figures of speech.

45. **(C)**   The frost has already been described as a killer beheading the flowers in line 3; it is a clear connection to see frost as blonde or icy white and the whole point of the poem is the killing power as of an assassin. Go through each of the possible suggestions and analyze the closest meaning of the line: fate (A) is part of the poem's *interpretation* but not the meaning of this particular line; disease (B) is not mentioned, rather, random acts of violence; the sun (D) follows the act of frost and is not involved in the killing; it is "unmoved." An approving god (E) watches but is not the assassin here. (C) is the best possible answer.

46. **(B)**   Although the other choices have something to do with the meaning of the poem, the "best," meaning the central or core description of what the poem is about, is that death comes to everyone; it cannot be planned for nor avoided. Certainly a cruelty is indicated in the frost's action but that is not (A) God's cruelty. God is shown not to be indifferent, but in fact approving, so (C) is incorrect. The flowers being happy (D) suggests that we put human experience into plants, but this is not the poem's central theme, nor is the fact that we know winter comes each year, so (E) is likewise an idea that is in the poem but is not the central point.

47. **(B)** Note that what is required here is both a knowledge of drama as well as an awareness of qualifying terms in both the question stem and answer. You are asked what poetic drama is "best" described as, while (A) asks for a value judgment; (B) is a full description incorporating both the fact that poetic drama is comprised of poetry and performance. (C) demonstrates value judgment; (D) is too limiting; so, too, is (E).

48. **(D)** Bertolt Brecht described his work as (D) epic drama, not (B) melodrama. It was based on (A) John Gay's *The Beggar's Opera*, but this is not the most important fact. The major characteristic of *The Threepenny Opera* is that Brecht's adaptation of it corresponds with his view of what drama should be. Brecht was concerned about defamiliarizing his audience with what they felt they knew. He thought that theaters should make things strange through (E) historification, the use of material drawn from other times and places, which allowed the audience to view the performance in a detached manner. This method of alienating the audience was the most important criterion for the development of an "epic" (meaning narrative, or non-dramatic) work. Since drama is antithetical to comedy, (C) should be eliminated immediately.

49. **(A)** Existentialism is a philosophy that arose in France and Germany in the late nineteenth century, which claims that "existence precedes essence" or that what one becomes is a matter of choice and not something usually called "human nature" or "essence." Essentialism (B) is thus incorrect because it is the opposite of existentialism. Pragmatism (C) is a distinctively American philosophy that the worth of an idea is its "cash value" or power to solve a problem. Marxism (D) depends on the supposition that humans have an essence or nature, as does Platonism (E). Platonists are clear examples of essentialism.

50. **(E)** The ancient Greeks, upon viewing the massive masonry blocks used in much Mycenaean construction, believed that they could only have been placed by giants; thus they are referred to as "cyclopean" after the giant Cyclops of Greek mythology. Although (A) ancient Egyptian, (B) Mesopotamian, (C) Aztec, and (D) Roman methods of construction often included the use of very large, heavy stone blocks, the term "cyclopean" is never used to identify them.

51. **(A)** The *cogito* resolves Descartes' methodological doubt and establishes a firm foundation for knowledge. He does not question the basis of personal identity (B) in the way that, say, Locke does. Descartes uses a separate argument to establish the existence of God (D). He then uses his proof of God's existence to put metaphysics (C) and mathematics (E) on firm foundations. The *cogito* is the foundation for his epistemology.

52. **(C)** Through-composed form is represented by ABCDE. This is because new music is created for each verse; choice (C) is correct. AB is binary form that starts in the tonic key and may modulate before the end. This is considered an open structure; choice (A) is incorrect. ABA is ternary form in which both A sections are in the tonic and the B section modulates and contains new material; choice (B) is incorrect. ABACA is a rondo form that contains multisections. These utilize modulations with new material and return to the tonic; choice (D) is incorrect. A form of A would only contain one musical idea; choice (E) is incorrect.

53. **(A)** Gregorian chant is often referred to as plainchant. Plainchant is monophonic vocal music, which was primarily used in church; choice (A) is correct. A motet is a polyphonic vocal composition used in church music for two or more voices; choice (B) is incorrect. A canon is imitated polyphonic vocal composition consisting of two or more voices; choice (C) is incorrect. An aria is

a vocal solo with accompaniment found in a larger composition; choice (D) is incorrect. A fugue is imitative polyphony with variations; choice (E) is incorrect.

54. **(B)**   Charles Ives mastered the technique of weaving bits of patriotic melodies within his compositions; choice (B) is correct. Sousa popularized patriotic marches; choice (A) is incorrect. Bernstein worked in many genres using classical and jazz elements; choice (C) is incorrect. Stravinsky explored primitivism and tonalities; choice (D) is incorrect. Franz Joseph Haydn was a composer of the classical period; choice (E) is incorrect.

55. **(A)**   *Tristram Shandy* was written by Laurence Sterne, a parish clergyman and small landowner. His sometimes bawdy, often hilarious novel demonstrated an extraordinary playfulness with the language, and with concepts of space and time in storytelling. Cervantes' (B) work was amusing, but the gentleman author was Spanish. *Candy* (C) is an American bawdy novel of the 1960s not to be confused with the French novel *Candide*. *Catch-22* (D) is at least as funny as the others, but is of the same vintage as the previous novel; and (E), though possessed of an amusing title, is a Shakespearean song.

56. **(B)**   Shakespeare's *Macbeth* deals with the powerful influence of guilt and conscience after the fact of an illicit deed. Lady Macbeth sleepwalks and tries to wash the imagined blood of King Duncan off of her hands, and Macbeth himself sees the ghost of the bloodied Banquo during a public celebration, thereby providing one more clue to the populace that he and his wife were responsible of the death of the rightful king. *Julius Caesar* (A) deals with many political themes including ambition – but conscience does not seem prominent. *Hamlet* (C) demonstrates the restraining power of conscience – even in the face of seeking revenge for a vile act. The fantasy (D) and the comedy (E) are artful treatments of happier themes.

57. **(D)**   Hawthorne's famous work is well known for its personification of the fading fortunes of the Pyncheon family in the famous seven gabled structure still to be visited in Salem, Massachusetts. The imploding and collapse of the structure at the end of the novel represents the end of the family that had been cursed during the witchcraft trials 150 years before. (A) of course, is a delightful children's book. (B), by Dos Passos, is a twentieth century description of the banking family. William Carlos Williams wrote the brief poem (C); and (E) was the first piece of fiction published by Thomas Wolfe, but does not deal with the subject in question.

58. **(C)**   The 1940 book deals with a hanging in the fictional Western town of Bridger's Wells. While Realism was a nineteenth-century movement, Clark employs Realistic techniques – accurate usage of concrete details to raise interest or create an effect – in relating his compelling story. Twain's famous story (A) had realistic elements in it, but was written during the nineteenth century – though only in one section can he be said to deal with the Wild West. Crane's work (B) was realistic and was about the Wild West, but was a short story also written in the nineteenth century. Bierce's tale (D) – though again in a similar tradition, and while it also deals with a hanging – also takes place during the Civil War.

59. **(C)**   Walt Whitman's poetry, including "Song of Myself" and "The Sleepers," presented American critics with a new American voice: one not bounded by the constraints of rhyme schemes and meter. His long listing of examples of American characters and prototypes are so detailed that they provide us with an accurate picture of the mid-nineteenth century nation of Whitman's day. The Englishman Pope (A) does not qualify for reason of nationality alone. Clemens (B) is the novelist

Mark Twain's real name. Emily Dickinson (D) is known for short, rhyming verse, and Anne Bradstreet (E) – perhaps our first American poet – wrote in traditional rhyme schemes and meter.

60. **(C)** This is an example from Donatello, one of the most representative sculptors of the early Renaissance. This piece, the equestrian statue of Gattamelta, is his first from Padua. It expresses strength, not lightness and motion, stability, and completely denies any suggestion of physical decay. Additionally, this sculpture does not allude in any specific way to moral fortitude.

61. **(E)** This city view by the French Impressionist Camille Pissarro is one of many in which the artist painted the scenes he saw beneath his second- or third-story Paris hotel windows; the correct answer is (E). The tilted perspective, with diagonal street axes and no horizon line, may owe a debt to photography, to Japanese prints, or to the example of his Impressionist peers. The resulting composition lacks not only a central focal point, but any single focal point at all; likewise, the only architecture visible does not dominate the scene, but, rather, acts as incidental local detail. The anonymous figures in the crowds below the artist's window share this lack of focus: they are busy in normal daily activity, without the least suggestion of drama. Finally, the idea that this scene was recorded from the window of a train lacks evidence: the scene is distinctly urban, not rural, and it is unlikely that a train would either pass through the crowded centers of a city or that it would be elevated to this height.

62. **(C)** In the work pictured, the American sculptor David Smith used power tools to cut, weld, and polish industrial-strength steel to create an ensemble in which the heavy, cubic forms balance in arrested motion. The sculptor obviously neither modelled the materials with his hands nor poured them into a mold: these forms have a rigid, machinelike, technological perfection to them and lack any such irregularities as those resulting from the molding action of human fingers. This same cubic perfection, and the gleaming, reflective surfaces, refute the idea of chisel work as well. And, finally, the erroneous suggestion that the artist merely joined ready-made industrial forms as he found them stems from this same sense of rigid, cubic perfection in the work's individual components.

63. **(A)** The seventeenth-century Japanese ink-on-paper scroll painting shown in the example relies almost exclusively on the qualities of line to convey the graceful forms of two leaping deer. In this painting, called *Deer and Calligraphy,* both the animals and the scripted characters share the same quality of fluid, rhythmic, spontaneous "writing." Gradations of tone are unimportant here, since the images are defined by black line on white, and volume, too, is absent, since these forms show no shading or modulation of tone. Perspective is not an issue here since this drawing does not attempt to reproduce a third dimension.

64. **(D)** The arch, whether rounded or pointed, is completely absent from the building pictured in the example, even though the alternating use of windows with rounded pediments in the lower story seems to suggest the presence of arches. Otherwise, all of the other features listed in the answer choices do help regularize the design of this seventeenth-century English Renaissance structure. The uniform second-story windows assert a regularity over the alternating window designs below them; they also emphasize a strong horizontal thrust across the building's facade, which is repeated in the balustrade at roof-level. The nearly flush front surface of the building is broken only by the window openings and by the engaged columns at the building's center and the pilasters at the outer

corners. Both of these features project just enough to establish a vertical contrast to the horizontal facade, but not enough to create a system of alternating solids and voids.

65. **(D)** You may not have come across this poem by William Blake so you need to look at the language and the topic. Blake often writes about the ugliness and horror of the Industrial Revolution – you may know "The Tiger." The topic of child labor gives you an immediate clue. Shakespeare (A), Milton (B), and Chaucer (C) may be familiar, so you can see the difference in their rhyme schemes and language. This rhyme and meter suggest a more modern style than the older writers. Hardy (E) often uses a similar simple rhyme and rhythm but his topics are more of fate and destiny, war and lost loves. By such a process of elimination, you should come to (D) as the correct answer.

66. **(A)** The word is cleverly used because it does suggest the child's weeping but the meaning of the line carries on from the opening line when he was sold before he could clearly say the chimney sweeper's cry for business: "Sweep! Sweep!" – not because of neglect (B), but because he is so young he still lisps on the "s" sound. The other suggestions all deal with emotions conjured up by the child's plight – of course he is upset at being sold (C); "the your" pronoun does make for guilt (D) but you are looking for the reason the poet chose this word, not the "message" of the poem. Of course he hates cleaning chimneys (E), but analyze the word's usage in the line itself and the best answer is (A).

67. **(C)** The epic is long and tells of heroes engaged in battles and actions involving valor. Look at the rhyme scheme and analyze. There are no rhyming couplets (A), epics are not all written in Latin (B), nor by Virgil (D), and although death (E) is usually featured, epics are not just about death.

68. **(E)** If you do not know *Paradise Lost,* a look at the context reveals a great deal – the garden idea, the noble couple made in God's image. Dante would be describing Hell so (A) is incorrect. Virgil (B) deals with family and honor in Latinate verse; *The Iliad* (C) deals with battles and the Greek gods; and *The Arabian Nights* (D) tells fantastic stories, so none of these apply.

69. **(D)** The key word here is "viewpoint" – but from which not the poem or story is told. Even if you do not know *Paradise Lost,* you will no doubt have heard of the fiend – place that fiend in a garden and the answer is Satan; not Faust (A), which is another story; not God (B) – the fiend is watching God's creation; not Scheherazade (C), who tells of magical things not people in a garden; and not Dante (E), who watches fiends in hell – he is not a fiend himself.

70. **(C)** The situation in the Garden is idyllic; the couple is naked – all such signs point to before the Fall. The references to God and "the image of their maker" eliminate both (A) and (B); the fiend is not a Homeric character, so (D) is incorrect; as stated, the idyllic setting indicates that this is before the Fall, so (E) is also incorrect.

71. **(E)** The last three lines need to be carefully equated with each of the options: equality is not possible if she sees God in the man (A); women are not just made for beauty but softness and grace (B); and (C) and (D) tell only half the meaning of the lines.

72. **(A)** is the correct answer. (B) *Oedipus* is also a play about a man who kills his father and blinds himself. In *The Wild Duck* Gregers returns home to find that Gina, who was once a maid in his family, is now married to Hjalmar. Gregers believes that Gina was impregnated by his father, Old

Werle, who is slowly losing his eyesight. Gregers believes that Gina and Hjalmar's marriage is based on a lie. Old Werle's diminished eyesight may be read symbolically, but it does not hold the same significance as Oedipus' blinding. The eyesight motif joins *The Wild Duck* and *Oedipus* and makes it easier to eliminate the other three answer choices. Both Sophocles and Euripides wrote plays they titled *Electra;* Sophocles also wrote *Antigone* and Euripides, *Andromache.* Basically, these answers are meant to confuse; therefore, (C), (D), and (E) should be eliminated immediately.

73. **(C)**   Orgon is rich, middle class, and middle-aged. He is duped by Tartuffe, who assumes a mask of religious piety. This question is testing your ability to recognize the situation of each play. For example, (A) is too vague, as the downfall of a king is a frequent theme in plays. (B) is also vague, as are (D) and (E).

74. **(B)**   A multi-storied Roman apartment block, the type which existed in large numbers in urban areas of the Roman Empire. A Greek public meeting square (A) is called an *agora;* the western portion of a Carolingian church (C) is referred to as a *westwerk.* A Greek cross-plan (D) is that of a centrally planned church whose four arms are all of equal length. A vertical groove on the surface of a column (E) is called a *flute.*

75. **(A)**   Berkeley held, in his famous dictum, that "to be is to be perceived," or that only ideas are real. Hence, the view expressed is known as (A) idealism. Pragmatism (B) is the view that ideas which work should be believed true. Empiricism (C) and rationalism (D) are broad tendencies to answer a question about the source of knowledge either as in experience or in the mind itself. Phenomenology (E) is a position in metaphysics that takes a special view of experience. Berkeley is perhaps the clearest advocate of idealism in the history of philosophy.

76. **(A)**   Charlie Parker was nicknamed "Bird" due to his rapid alto saxophone Bebop figures. Choice (A) is correct. John Coltrane was a master of the tenor and soprano saxophone; choice (B) is incorrect. Dizzy Gillespie was a master of the trumpet; choice (C) is incorrect. Paul Desmond was the alto saxophonist in the Dave Brubeck Quartet, which played classical jazz styles; choice (D) is incorrect. Stan Getz was a tenor saxophonist of the "cool" jazz style; choice (E) is incorrect.

77. **(C)**   John Coltrane made a lasting impact on the jazz scene with his album "Giant Steps." Choice (C) is correct. Charlie Parker played alto, not tenor saxophone, and performed such works as "Ko-ko" and "YardBird Suite"; choice (A) is incorrect. Stan Getz is the tenor saxophone player famous for his work on "The Girl from Ipanema"; choice (B) is incorrect. Coleman Hawkins is considered the father of jazz tenor saxophone; choice (D) is incorrect. Ornette Coleman experimented with "free jazz" on the alto saxophone; choice (E) is incorrect.

78. **(B)**   "Rodeo" is the result of a collaboration between Aaron Copland and Agnes de Mille. It incorporated music with dance; choice (B) is correct. "West Side Story" is a musical by Leonard Bernstein. It is a modern-day version of "Romeo and Juliet"; choice (A) is incorrect. "Porgy and Bess" is an opera with music by George Gershwin, portraying the struggles of black Americans in the South; choice (C) is incorrect. "The Phantom of the Opera" is a novel by Gaston LeRoux that has been adapted for film, stage, and most recently, a Broadway musical. Choice (D) is incorrect. "Salome" was a composition of Strauss; choice (E) is incorrect.

79. **(D)**   *Tom Jones,* Henry Fielding's (1707-1754) wonderful and raucous novel, is the only response option both written in and about the eighteenth century. Tom's travels take him from the seat of manorial propriety to the very bawdiest of tumbletown inns. Known for its wanton characterization

and surprising turns of plot, it is considered by many to be one of the most picturesque of the picaresque novels (defined as the "life story of a rascal of low degree... consisting of a series of thrilling incidents"). Dickens' work (A) is about England in the following century, as are Brontë's *Jane Eyre* (C) and George Eliot's *Silas Marner* (E). *Moby Dick* (B) is an American work by Melville.

80. **(D)**   Oscar Wilde's famous work is in the well-known tradition of the Decadents – a group of writers in the late nineteenth and early twentieth century in France, England, and America. One of their major precepts was that the finest beauty was that of dying or deteriorating things. Thus, Dorian – a character of low virtues – ages grotesquely and supernaturally on a canvas, while the actual person seems to be forever young. The Mariner (A) may be aging, but the lengthy romantic poem is not in the Decadent tradition, nor written at that time. Fielding's work (C) may be about decadence, but was written 100 years earlier than the movement. The same might be said about Lawrence's mid-twentieth century work (B), and Joyce's *Dubliners* (E), which is even less a possibility.

81. **(A)**   Ruskin in *Modern Painters* actually introduced the phrase "pathetic fallacy" to denote a tendency of some poets and writers to credit nature with the emotions of human beings – as in the phrase "the cruel, crawling foam." Nowadays it has come to mean writing that is false in its emotionalism – even if the topic considered is not nature. Emerson's work (B) is about the importance and reality of the natural world. Shakespeare's comedy (C) has nothing whatsoever to do with the topic, except that its plot does involve deception and falseness. Lodge's 1590 work (D) is considered a pastoral romance – in that it sets forth a romance in a beautiful natural setting. Johnson's *Dictionary* (E) could not have listed the term, as it was published over 50 years before Ruskin invented it.

82. **(E)**   Dickens' *David Copperfield* is one of his many works that present an opposing argument to utilitarianism – the powerful argument from the former century that defined utility in government and society as "the greatest happiness for the greatest number." The theory was proposed in the eighteenth century by Jeremy Bentham, and was modified and promoted in the nineteenth by James Mill and his son John Stuart Mill. Dickens' England is a place where misery counts – even for a statistical minority of orphans, waifs, and honest, if impoverished, men and women of the working class. Elliot's *Middlemarch* world (A) is the antithesis – as is James's *Washington Square* (D). Dreiser (B) does write about the seedier side of nineteenth century American life, but does not seem to "take sides" as far as the economic system itself is concerned. *Billy Budd* (C), of course, is an adventure novel by Melville.

83. **(D)**   While all of the writers suggested might claim Celtic origins, James Macpherson, the eighteenth-century composer of the poems "Fingal" (1762) and "Temora" (1763) is the most likely candidate. Macpherson invented, recorded, and reinterpreted Gaelic pieces preserved in the Scottish Highlands and published translations of the great early Celtic poet Ossian. His works, along with those of Thomas Gray, influenced many minor poets of the late eighteenth century. Joyce (A) and Yeats (E) were Irishmen of the twentieth century. O'Hara (B) and Donleavy (C) are contemporary American writers.

84. **(D)**   The late eighteenth-century neoclassical painting shown in the example illustrates an episode from ancient Roman legend and attempts to simulate the static, balanced, monumental character of much classical relief sculpture. The men in the main figure group, therefore, are represented in statuesque, absolutely motionless poses, and the correct answer choice here is (D). The

compositional devices listed in all of the other answer choices are important to the painting. The figures stand within a shallow pictorial space, which is marked off by the arches in the background; these arches also serve to place the focus on the man in the center. This shallow space, however, is modified somewhat by the checkerboard floor, which creates a slight perspective recession into the background and makes the figures' space seem logical and convincing. The strong highlighting on the foreground figures accentuates their static, sculptural quality, even as it pulls them to the absolute front of the picture. The intersecting lines of arms and swords establish the central focal point of the composition.

85. **(A)** This question asks you to consider both geographical proximity and some general characteristics of Eastern architecture in order to logically determine who would have the most direct influence on Japanese style. Of the answer choices, Greece and Nigeria fall well outside the Asian sphere both in distance and in building styles, while Easter Island, a Pacific site, is not known for a distinctive native architecture. Indonesian temple buildings may share something of the exotic, heavily ornamented character of the structure pictured but the most representative Indonesian buildings are both much larger and are constructed of stone. The seventh-century building pictured, in fact, illustrates the strong dependence of Japan on the arts of China. The Chinese character of the structure is visible in the distinctive silhouette of the roof, with its long sweeping pitch and upturned corners in the heavy tiled roof, and in the wealth of elaborate brackets which support the dramatically projecting eaves.

86. **(A)** Three of the answer choices – (B), (C), and (D) – show groups of figures engaged in activities which might be interpreted as ceremonial. Choice (C) illustrates a column of soldiers marching across the midsection of a ceramic vessel; while they could be marching in a ceremonial function such as a parade or assembly, they are most likely intended to be shown advancing into battle, and, in any case, their primary function on this vase is decorative. Choice (D) shows figures engaged in music-making activities in formally arranged groups, but here, too, the illustrations serve the secondary purpose of amplifying the accompanying text. Only answer choice (A), an ancient Persian relief sculpture, uses a rigidly schematized, formal composition and style to record an actual ceremonial event. Here, the clear-cut, well-defined figures are strictly arranged in three horizontal tiers, and each carries an accessory or attribute which identifies his role within this state occasion.

87. **(C)** Only answer choices (A) and (C) repeat the simplified forms of the human figure within a sculptural or ceramic context. Choice (A) appears to continually repeat a series of nearly identical figures arranged on three horizontal levels, but close inspection reveals several types of figures here, each marked by a variety of detail in posture, costume, accessories, etc. Further, the figures are sculpted in a softly rounded, convincing style. The figures in choice (C), in contrast, are grouped in a horizontal sequence which appears to show variety and movement; close examination, however, shows that the artist here has simply repeated figures whose clothing, weapons, postures, positions, and facial features are identical. While this serves to illustrate an anonymous mass of marching soldiers, it is even more important in helping the group of figures fit neatly, conveniently, and decoratively into its allotted space on the round "belly" of the vase.

88. **(D)** Calligraphy, or "fine writing," implies a two-dimensional or graphic format. Three of the possible answer choices, (A), (B) and (E), are forms of sculpture or sculptural relief, and therefore contain no drawn, calligraphic elements. Choice (C) presents a flat, two-dimensional illustration

painted in black and white and minimal color. However, the images here are rigidly formalized and static, and display none of the rhythmic curves or flourishes of artistic penmanship. Only choice (D), a ninth-century manuscript illustration, links calligraphy with figure drawing in the same rhythmic, linear style. In this illustration of the Bible's Psalm 150, the text written in ink above accompanies the figures below. Each is drawn in the same bold, agitated black-and-white line, with a sketchy spontaneity that creates an animated, nervous tension.

89. **(A)** If you familiarize yourself with *The Iliad* and *Odysseus*, you will see how Homer uses the simile with the long-extended idea clinched at the end – look out for the words "such" or "so" which signal the last clause of the simile. An extended metaphor (B) is close except that the metaphor never has the signal words *as when, as if, like*; (C) is not an option as the verse is "free form" rather than rhymed couplets; the other options mix terms. Be on the lookout for terms that sound reasonable but, upon analysis, are gibberish.

90. **(D)** This is a case of working your way through the simile until you come to the signal word "such," which cues the image of the watchfires. The stars are not compared to hills (A), shepherds (B), rivers (C), or ships (E), so these are all incorrect choices.

91. **(A)** Again, the more familiar you become with Homer, the more you will see touches like this to humanize the lofty, godlike themes and characters, so the answer is (A). If this had been a medieval English piece, humor of a coarse, ribald kind, especially in the drama, might have been the answer, but there is no humor here (B). Depth in Homer comes from the poetry itself rather than the people who figure in the poetry (C). Gladness (D) takes a back seat to the power of the simile and in any poetry shepherds never glamorize (E)!

92. **(E)** Questions such as these rely on identification of famous lines; read through anthologies and see the often repeated poems. If you do not recognize Emily Dickinson (the use of the long dash often gives her away – it is one of her "trademarks"), work your way through and eliminate each choice in its turn. Obviously this is not Chaucerian since the language is stark and modern (A); nor is the passage epic in its voice or theme: think of lofty topics and rhythm and rhyme – this is conversational and choppy in its rhythm (B). However, (B) does fit all the criteria of epic so save that for the last answer. Wordsworth is taught in most high-school poetry classes and this opening line is much quoted – even if you do not recall the poem itself, you might recall that Wordsworth was not a woman (the Romantic males dominated the field of poetry), so the answer cannot be (C). The jar and Tennessee is unique and should immediately make you think of one of the most famous modern male American poets, Wallace Stevens, so (D) is incorrect.

93. **(A)** This is the famous opening line of *The Canterbury Tales*; it would be worth looking over the poem (this is in translation from the middle English language), as Chaucer is said to be the "father of English poetry." If you do not recognize the lines, look again at each of the answers and, as for the previous explanation, eliminate: (B) sounds too modern and conversational, as does (C) and (E), so eliminate both those on voice alone. (D) Tennessee did not exist in Chaucer's time and is definitely not the answer.

94. **(C)** Even if you do not recognize Wordsworth, the idea of a love of nature would clue you to the Romantics, who looked upon nature as a rejuvenating force for the human spirit. You are working your way through the process of elimination, narrowing down your field through language and topic, so none of the other possibilities apply.

95. **(B)** If you recognize the opening of *Paradise Lost*, this is straightforward; if not, think of epics that you have read with the lofty, heroic subjects – none of the others fit this category.

96. **(D)** In your reading, be very aware of opening and closing lines in whatever genre. Kafka's famous opener from *Metamorphosis* sets symbol and theme for the entire work. All the other possibilities involve striking writers, but Genet and Ionesco are primarily playwrights, and Sartre and Tolstoy have less dramatic starting points. Even if you don't remember the first line of the *Metamorphosis*, recall that the story was about a man who awoke one morning as a bug.

97. **(D)** (A) refers to the coat of arms representing royal presence; (B) should be eliminated immediately because it is too vague; the same is true of (C). While (E) Oedipus did go into exile, he was not sacrificed for the redemption of the tribe.

98. **(B)** The basilica, a large, hall-like building with a minimum of internal supporting members, served a variety of public functions in the Roman era and was designed to accommodate large crowds. The basilican plan was thus an appropriate building type to contain large numbers of Christian worshippers. Roman temples (A) were not designed to regulate crowds, and, with their overt pagan associations, were not favored for use within a Christian context. Roman baths (C) consisted of several bathing rooms and facilities, and did not adhere to a specific type of plan. A Roman forum (D) is an open air, public city square, not a building type. A Roman villa (E) is a private domestic dwelling, composed of multiple rooms and courtyards, the design of which is inappropriate for the containment and regulation of communal worship.

99. **(E)** Dance began with the savage hunters. Religious groups (A), Egyptians (B), Greeks (C), and Romans (D) succeeded the savage hunters and created their own style of dance for self-expression, religious and political rituals, and entertainment.

100. **(A)** The fallacy of composition (A), as the name suggests, consists in thinking that what is true of the parts of something must be true of the whole composed by those parts. For instance, it would be fallacious to think that because every member of a team is outstanding, the team must be outstanding, since teamwork is involved in the performance of the team in a way that it isn't with respect to its members individually. The fallacy of division (B) is just the opposite: what is true of the whole is incorrectly reasoned to be true of the parts. The slippery-slope fallacy (C) is committed when one thinks small differences never add up to a significant difference, while the *ad hominem* fallacy (D) involves personal attacks. The fallacy of ignorance (E) is committed when one reasons that because something has not been proven false, it is true.

101. **(B)** Percy Grainger wrote extensively for wind ensemble. Most of his compositions were based on folk songs such as "Country Gardens" and "Ye Banks and Braes o' Bonnie Doon"; choice (B) is correct. Sousa composed primarily for military band; choice (A) is incorrect. Beethoven composed many works, including symphonies for orchestra and piano concertos. Choice (C) is incorrect. Strauss is famous for his tone poems; choice (D) is incorrect. Franz Joseph Haydn composed for the orchestra; choice (E) is incorrect.

102. **(B)** The key signature of this excerpt is F major. The key signature of F major contains a B flat, which can be determined by using the Circle of Fifths and proceeding counterclockwise from C to the scale with one flat, F. Choice (B) is correct. The B flat scale contains B flat and E flat; choice (A) is incorrect. The key of C contains no flats or sharps; choice (C) is incorrect. The key of D

contains an F sharp and a C sharp; choice (D) is incorrect. The key signature of A major contains an F#, C#, and G#. Choice (E) is incorrect.

103. **(D)** The time signature of this excerpt should be $\frac{3}{4}$. The total number of beats in each measure is three, and a quarter note would equal one beat. Choice (D) is correct. A time signature of $\frac{4}{4}$ would require four beats in each measure; choice (A) is incorrect. A time signature of $\frac{2}{4}$ would require two beats in each measure; choice (B) is incorrect. A time signature of $\frac{6}{8}$ would have six beats in each measure; choice (C) is not correct. A time signature of $\frac{12}{8}$ would have 12 beats in each measure. Choice (E) is incorrect.

104. **(C)** The excerpt is divided into three measures. The measures are divided by the number of beats found in each and marked by a vertical line through the staff; choice (C) is correct. The following choices, one measure, two measures, and zero measures (choices (A), (B), and (D)) are incorrect. Five measures cannot be calculated from the material presented; choice (E) is incorrect.

105. **(D)** The arrow is pointing at the repeat sign. This directs the musician to repeat the selection; choice (D) is correct. The key signature is the B flat symbol; choice (A) is incorrect. The clef sign is the G clef; choice (B) is incorrect. The double bar is a symbol which denotes the end of the music; choice (C) is incorrect. The time signature is not in the figure. The time signature would be $\frac{4}{4}$. Choice (E) is incorrect.

106. **(C)** Philip Roth's *Goodbye, Columbus* was a big literary hit in the late 1950s ushering in the age of the American Ethnic novelist. Roth's novel deals with the rocky road of young romance within a suburban New York Jewish-American context. It is both an American success story, and a recollection of transformation for generations between immigrant and native born. James's (A) novel concerns a pre-"recent" immigrant America of 100 years ago. Hawthorne's work (E) concerns the earliest Pilgrim immigrants, but ethnic Pilgrim has long been recognized as "ruling class standard." Updike's novels (D) of midwest suburbia do not involve "ethnics" so much as the descendants of Hawthorne's folk – and Poe's famous short story (B) takes place in Italy, not America.

107. **(C)** Alexis de Tocqueville's *Letters From an American Farmer* is considered one of the most perceptive and accurate portraits of the newly independent American nation. The Frenchman, who later became a citizen of the U.S. and a property owner, traveled widely and recorded his observations and perceptions. Lewis and Clark (A), the famed adventurers, explored the uninhabited West under orders from President Thomas Jefferson. Sinclair Lewis's novel (B) deals with the early decades of this century. Cooper's *Mohicans* (D) describes the frontier of New York State 200 years ago. Smith's *Diary* (E) predates the establishment of the United States by almost 200 years.

108. **(E)** Ralph Ellison's powerful novel defined for America of the 1950s the second-class status of African-Americans and is still referred to as a great work of literature that galvanized a nation at the height of the battle for civil rights. Faulkner's work (A), while it may have a seemingly appropriate title, does not deal with this subject – neither does Wharton's (B), about a white man in New England. Conrad's (C) powerful novel deals with Africa, and Kafka's (D) strange story superficially deals with a man's transformation into a bug.

109. **(A)** *Journey to the Center of the Earth* by Jules Verne has a remarkable history. Though its subject deals with a phenomenon – a hollow Earth – that apparently does not exist, the description it gives of Iceland is so accurate that travelers there were urged to take the book with them well into

the 1950s. Ironically, Verne rarely left Paris, never traveled to Iceland, and did all his research for the book in the libraries of the French capital. Stevenson's island (B) is invented, as is Defoe's (C). Verne's other work, listed as choice (D), is not focused in its description of a single spot. Swift's "travel" novel (E) is not one at all, but rather a well-known political satire.

110. **(B)**   Sir Walter Scott's famous nineteenth century romance *Ivanhoe* deals with the thirteenth century – now recognized by many scholars such as Barbara Tuchman as a dreadful period in history – but until recently it was thought of as the flower of the Middle Ages, replete with knights in shining armor and damsels in distress. Eliot's work (A) is a picture of manorial England in the nineteenth century and Poe's (C) of a formerly wealthy family in America at approximately the same time. King's terrifying book (D) is modern and also American, as is West's hilarious short novel (E).

111. **(C)**   Like many Victorian poets, Matthew Arnold venerated the works of Wordsworth. In Arnold's preface to the "Poems" of 1853, he pleads for poets to turn to the epic or drama – as epitomized, perhaps, by Wordsworth in lyrical ballads such as "The Ruined Cottage." The major problems with the other possible answers here is one of time sequence. Hemingway and Eliot (A) are modern, not Victorian. Tennyson and Browning (B) are Victorian contemporaries, as are Rossetti and Browning (D). Wordsworth and Scott (E) are Romantic contemporaries.

112. **(A)**   In the *Duke and the Dauphin,* Twain relates the story of a bogus pretender to the French throne and his accompli who perform what they hope will pass as Shakespeare to frontier audiences. Initially taken by the idea, the settlers get wise to their scam and chase them out of town. The famous fence-painting scene (B) took place in *Tom Sawyer.* Huck's escape from Pap (C) does not prove the quote; neither does Jim seeking freedom (D). At the end of the famous novel, Huck "lights out for the territories" (E). The West certainly represented a future of promise to Huck and Twain, but again, clearly does not prove the point.

113. **(C)**   In the example shown, the *Bull's Head* of 1943, the Spanish artist Pablo Picasso joined a bicycle seat and a set of handlebars in a clever, unexpected combination to produce a sculptural analogy to an actual bull. Thus, the artist was concerned here with form and substance, not with a contrast of line and tone and, even though the resulting artwork resembles a hat- or coat-rack the sculptor's first purpose was not to produce a functional device. Likewise, even though the bull has mythological connotations and figures prominently in many ancient religions, the artist was intent not on creating a religious symbol, but in exploring the visual unity of common objects brought together in new ways. The result is a strictly visual, sculptural effect, and in no way provides a metaphor for human experience.

114. **(B)**   Three of the answer choices, (A), (C) and (E), illustrate Impressionist paintings, which tend to suppress or eliminate secondary or decorative detail in the search for a quick, spontaneous, and optically "true" impression of the subject. None can be said to concentrate on details pointedly. Choice (D) shows a work of exhaustive detail, in which each tree branch, leaf, and grass stem, and the details and textures of clothing, stand out with stark realism. The main figure subject, however, far from merging into the background detail, is dramatically set off against it, especially in the face, neck, and arms. Only choice (B), by the American James MacNeill Whistler, accentuates decorative detail at the expense of the subject. In this case, the details of tiny flowers running up the back of the woman's dress connect visually to the delicate floral details in the wallpaper to the left, while the pale form of the woman's figure shades and merges into the background and almost reduces her to a flat pattern.

115. **(C)** Two of the answer choices crop, or cut off, the main subject, much as the arbitrary framing of a photograph might do. Choice (E), a study of two women and a child by the American Impressionist Mary Cassatt, pulls the figures to the very front of the picture plane, and cuts them off abruptly at the bottom edge and right side of the picture. The result seems to be an unposed, accidental image produced by a moment's glance. These figures, however, are firmly centered within the picture's borders, with a definite focal point in the image of the child with the book at center. Choice (C), by contrast, presents an extremely random composition in which the human subject is so far off-center and so dramatically cropped that she barely retains pictorial "presence" in the composition. This picture by the French Impressionist Edgar Degas produces an effect of seemingly unplanned, immediate realism which resembles a casually aimed photographic snapshot.

116. **(D)** Only two of the answer choices, (C) and (D), create their desired effect by positioning the primary subject noticeably off-center, thereby undermining the pictures formal visual balance. Choice (C), by the French painter Degas, shows a woman seated at a table on which rests an enormous bouquet of flowers. Even though the woman, apparently the main subject or sitter, glances out of the picture to the right and invites the viewer's gaze to follow, the huge bunch of flowers dominates the picture and calls the viewer's eye continually back to the painting's focal center. Answer choice (D), however, by the French Realist Bastien-Lepage, clearly positions the primary subject off-center, as she stares and steps to the right with her arm outstretched. The figure seems to have just left the empty center of the picture and is about to exit the painting at the right. Her glance, her pose, and her position create a strongly directional thrust which draws the viewer's eye out of the picture as the figure moves.

117. **(E)** Art Nouveau is the correct answer. Art Nouveau is distinguished by the extensive use of such curvilinear, decorative details of interior design. Post-Modernism (B) is a later period in the history of architecture, and is not defined by such decorative elements. Neo-Classicism (C), a nineteenth-century era of architecture, is characterized by the use of classical Greek and Roman architectural details, which are more austere in nature. Post-Impressionism (D) and surrealism (A) are movements in painting that have no equivalents in the history of architectural design.

118. **(C)** Reims Cathedral (ca. 1211–1260) is an example of the High Gothic style. The sheer verticality of the twin towers, the overall upward movement, and the multitude of pinnacles are identifying characteristics of the Gothic style and would most clearly set Reims apart from the most closely related structure in this group, St. Peter's (D), a work of the late Renaissance in Rome. (A) The Taj Mahal, Agra, India, (1630–1648) is incorrect because it is the finest example of Mughal architecture, a mix of Indian, Persian, and Islamic styles. (B) The Parthenon, Acropolis, Athens (448–432 BCE), is incorrect because it represents the classical phase of Greek architecture. (D) St. Peter's, Rome (1546-1564), by Michelangelo is incorrect because it is an example of the colossal order in Renaissance architecture. It has a symmetrical plan crowned by a central dome, very different from the longitudinal emphasis of the Gothic cathedral. St. Peter's Basilica lacks the exterior ornamentation of Reims, but its monumental dome creates a dramatic exterior profile.

119. **(A)** The Taj Mahal was built by Shah Jahan, one of the Moslem rulers of India, as a home for his wife. She died before it was finished and so in its completion the Taj Mahal became a memorial to her. (B) is incorrect because the Parthenon has served as a place of worship for four different faiths. It was originally built by the Greeks to honor the Goddess Athena. In Christian times it became the first Byzantine church, then a Catholic cathedral, and, finally, under Turkish rule, a mosque. (C) is incorrect because the Reims Cathedral is a Catholic church. (D) is incorrect because St. Peter's is a Roman Catholic church. (E) is incorrect because (A) was not constructed as a place of worship.

120. **(C)** Become aware of different types of poems: this is the short 17-syllable form that is highly evocative. Hyperbole (A) is characterized by exaggeration, which is not present. Odes (B) honor or exalt a specific person or subject, also not present. An epigram (D) is usually a witty expression of a particular idea. Doggerel (E) describes loose, inferior verse.

121. **(B)** If you are not aware of the original language of the form, start discounting the others – French and Chinese would be more symbolic; British English would not be so succinct and evocative; Persian would be on topics of love or religion.

122. **(D)** If you are not aware of the term, it is a useful one to learn – Pope uses it frequently to attain humor. Eliminate the other terms by what you know: (A) is hyperbole; (B) is crescendo; (C) is anticlimax; and (E) is not related to the question. Analyze that a climax suggests a building toward or upward.

123. **(E)** As well as learning meter, rhyme, and rhythm, look into what poets themselves say about poetry. Keats had a lot to say, especially about the ways to read and the use of the imagination, as did Wordsworth and Coleridge, but they frequently spoke of poetry being of and for the common man: this phrase often bemuses the "average" man so (C) is incorrect. T. S. Eliot wrote copiously on the art of writing poetry but his comments are not so easily captured in a phrase, except perhaps "objective correlative," but this phrase can only be fit into a long explanation – definitely not (B). If you are not aware of the term, think of the sorts of poetry the others wrote: Keats is the only one here who wants the mystery (of something like the "Grecian Urn" for example); neither William Carlos Williams nor e.e. cummings wanted mystery, preferring to have cryptic to-the-point statements about their art, so clearly neither (A) nor (D) are correct.

124. **(A)** is the correct answer. Though you may disagree with the quotation, you must make your selection based on the quotation. (B) *A Midsummer Night's Dream* is a comedy. *Oedipus* (C) is indeed a tragedy, but it does not fit the requirements for tragedy as established in the quotation. *Oedipus the King* is not completed by a death. Jocasta commits suicide, but Oedipus, the central character, remains within the walls of the city for many years before he is exiled. *Oedipus the King* is thus eliminated on the basis of this argument. (D) Shakespeare's *The Tempest* and (E) Menander's *The Bad-Tempered Man* should also be eliminated because both are comedies.

125. **(E)** *Anagnorisis* means recognition or discovery. Therefore, when the hero's understanding of the true nature of the situation and the self is evident in drama or fiction, then this is an example of *anagnorisis*. As a complete definition, this differs from (A), which is vague.

126. **(C)** After the idealistic Brutus tells the people that he participated in Caesar's murder because he loved Rome more, he and the other conspirators make the mistake of allowing the wily Mark Antony to speak. Antony must aid the public, or rabble, in understanding the villainy of the murder of Caesar, no matter the motivation. Thus, the statement he makes is ironic as what he wishes to do is arouse the people to act against Caesar's murderers.

127. **(E)** Othello's great weakness is his inability to recognize Iago's villainy and Desdemona's innocence. Iago is able to convince Othello that Desdemona is not the "chaste and heavenly true" wife she appears to be. Not until after he kills Desdemona does Othello understand the true nature of the situation and his own weakness.

128. **(A)** Though all of the characters listed are from plays by Shakespeare, "Dane" and "Denmark" are the contextual clues here. One who comes from or resides in Denmark is a Dane.

129. **(B)**   Oculus, meaning "eye," refers to the round opening in the dome, which is without glass and thus open to the sky. The terms (A) "window," (C) "splayed window," and (D) "stained-glass window" are all defined as wall openings that are glazed in some form, which is not applicable here. A clerestory (E) refers to the upper portion of a building whose walls are pierced with windows and which emits light to the remainder of the building below; this type of construction refers to fenestrated walls only.

130. **(B)**   The basic rules to jazz dance are parallel feet, flat-foot steps, undulating torso, body isolation, and syncopated rhythms. Beledi dance (abdominal dance) (A), danse mora (Flamenco dance) (C), tap dance (D), and country dance (E) each have their own different specific rules.

131. **(A)**   Occam's Razor contends that one should not multiply entities beyond necessity: since both theories are equally powerful, choose the simpler one. The Plenitude Principle (B) says that the universe contains as many types of things as possible. The Open Question Argument (C) applies to claims about the nature of goodness, not theories in general. The Underdetermination Principle (D) involves the notion that a given set of facts is compatible with many theories. Scientific Realism (E) is the view that the entities postulated by science actually exist.

132. **(D)**   Jane Austen's *Pride and Prejudice* is the source of this quote. The word *pride*, found in both the quote and the title, should give you a clue to the correct answer, even if you have not read these books. (B) Austen's *Emma* and (C) Margaret Mitchell's *Gone with the Wind* also deal with the issues of pride and vanity, although to a lesser extent than does *Pride and Prejudice*. However, neither of these is the source of the quote. In addition, Mitchell's novel, although set in the nineteenth century, was written in 1936. (A) George Eliot's *Silas Marner*, written in 1861, is a story of an old linen-weaver and his adopted daughter. (E) Jonathan Swift's *Gulliver's Travels* describes the four voyages of Lemuel Gulliver; it was written in the 1720s.

133. **(A)**   A trumpet can play different notes by pressing a valve down. A trumpet has three valves that, when combined in different prescribed combinations, help produce various notes; choice (A) is correct. Violins and pianos use strings to produce sound; choice (B) is incorrect. By covering and uncovering holes, the clarinet can change notes; choice (C) is incorrect. Saxophones use octave keys to change octaves; choice (D) is incorrect. Trombones use a slide to change pitches; choice (E) is incorrect.

134. **(A)**   The diagram is an example of a hemiola. The hemiola is a rhythmic term that is used to define three notes of a given value occupying the space of two notes of the same value. It is also referred to as three against two; choice (A) is correct. A paradiddle is a percussion roll that follows a pattern such as RLRR LRLL; choice (B) is incorrect. A fermata, ⌢•, directs a musician to hold the note until the conductor cuts it off; choice (C) is incorrect. A crescendo, <, indicates to increase in volume; choice (D) is incorrect. A glissando is sliding through the pitches quickly; choice (E) is incorrect.

135. **(A)**   The C in measure one is sharp because the accidental makes it sharp. This accidental affects all C's in the given measure. As a result, the C in measure two is C natural because there are no accidentals before the note; choice (A) is correct. Consequently, the C is not sharp, flat, or a B. Choices (B), (C), and (D) are incorrect. A D would be located on the fourth line, choice (E) is incorrect.

136. **(A)** The bass clef is also referred to as the F clef. The symbol locates F below middle C, which is the fourth line; choice (A) is correct. The G clef and treble clef locate the G above middle C; choice (B) and (D) are incorrect. The tenor clef is used for cello, bassoon, and trombone to locate middle C; choice (C) is incorrect. The alto clef is used primarily by the viola; choice (E) is incorrect.

137. **(D)** Catton's work about the surrender of Lee at Appomatox stands as one of the great Civil War accounts, though it was written almost 100 years after the incident. The temptation here is to respond with (E) Crane's work, but *Red Badge* was written during the last century. Mailer's war novel (C) concerned Word War II in the Pacific, as did Wouk's novel (B). That leaves Hoover's anti-Communist screed (A) written during the 1950s.

138. **(B)** Albee's 1960 popular play was made into a movie starring Richard Burton and Elizabeth Taylor as the university professor and his wife, who display their troubled marriage to a young faculty couple who they had invited to their home for a visit. Albee's *American Dream* (C) does not concern itself with this subject matter. Miller's work (E) concerns longshoremen and immigrants in Red Hook, Brooklyn. Neil Simon's reflective comedy (D) also relates the experience of growing up in a distinctly blue- collar immigrant world. (A) is a medieval play.

139. **(D)** Pepys' diary, written during the restoration of the Stuarts and Charles II in 1660, is still compelling material, especially his account of the Great Fire of London. Many critics consider that Pepys pioneered the form as literature, though he was not the first by any means to keep a diary. The time factor alone eliminates from consideration the satirists Swift (E) and Sterne (B), who wrote in the 1700s. O. E. Rolvaag (C) is a twentieth-century Swedish novelist. Sir Laurence (A), of course, is the recent star of stage and screen whose work included iconic Shakespearean performances.

140. **(C)** Ralph Waldo Emerson, Unitarian Minister, writer, and philosopher, is generally considered the chief promoter of transcendentalism. His influence was widely felt – on no less a personage than Henry David Thoreau (D) – with whom, eventually, Emerson had a falling out due to the inappropriate attentions Thoreau was said to have paid to Emerson's wife. Jonathan Edwards (A) was a New England minister of the early 1700s. Pitt (B) was a British parliamentarian of the American Revolutionary period. Dr. Samuel Fuller (E) was the only doctor to accompany the pilgrims to Massachusetts in 1620.

HUMANITIES PRACTICE TEST

ANSWER SHEET

1. Ⓐ Ⓑ Ⓒ Ⓓ Ⓔ	36. Ⓐ Ⓑ Ⓒ Ⓓ Ⓔ	71. Ⓐ Ⓑ Ⓒ Ⓓ Ⓔ	106. Ⓐ Ⓑ Ⓒ Ⓓ Ⓔ
2. Ⓐ Ⓑ Ⓒ Ⓓ Ⓔ	37. Ⓐ Ⓑ Ⓒ Ⓓ Ⓔ	72. Ⓐ Ⓑ Ⓒ Ⓓ Ⓔ	107. Ⓐ Ⓑ Ⓒ Ⓓ Ⓔ
3. Ⓐ Ⓑ Ⓒ Ⓓ Ⓔ	38. Ⓐ Ⓑ Ⓒ Ⓓ Ⓔ	73. Ⓐ Ⓑ Ⓒ Ⓓ Ⓔ	108. Ⓐ Ⓑ Ⓒ Ⓓ Ⓔ
4. Ⓐ Ⓑ Ⓒ Ⓓ Ⓔ	39. Ⓐ Ⓑ Ⓒ Ⓓ Ⓔ	74. Ⓐ Ⓑ Ⓒ Ⓓ Ⓔ	109. Ⓐ Ⓑ Ⓒ Ⓓ Ⓔ
5. Ⓐ Ⓑ Ⓒ Ⓓ Ⓔ	40. Ⓐ Ⓑ Ⓒ Ⓓ Ⓔ	75. Ⓐ Ⓑ Ⓒ Ⓓ Ⓔ	110. Ⓐ Ⓑ Ⓒ Ⓓ Ⓔ
6. Ⓐ Ⓑ Ⓒ Ⓓ Ⓔ	41. Ⓐ Ⓑ Ⓒ Ⓓ Ⓔ	76. Ⓐ Ⓑ Ⓒ Ⓓ Ⓔ	111. Ⓐ Ⓑ Ⓒ Ⓓ Ⓔ
7. Ⓐ Ⓑ Ⓒ Ⓓ Ⓔ	42. Ⓐ Ⓑ Ⓒ Ⓓ Ⓔ	77. Ⓐ Ⓑ Ⓒ Ⓓ Ⓔ	112. Ⓐ Ⓑ Ⓒ Ⓓ Ⓔ
8. Ⓐ Ⓑ Ⓒ Ⓓ Ⓔ	43. Ⓐ Ⓑ Ⓒ Ⓓ Ⓔ	78. Ⓐ Ⓑ Ⓒ Ⓓ Ⓔ	113. Ⓐ Ⓑ Ⓒ Ⓓ Ⓔ
9. Ⓐ Ⓑ Ⓒ Ⓓ Ⓔ	44. Ⓐ Ⓑ Ⓒ Ⓓ Ⓔ	79. Ⓐ Ⓑ Ⓒ Ⓓ Ⓔ	114. Ⓐ Ⓑ Ⓒ Ⓓ Ⓔ
10. Ⓐ Ⓑ Ⓒ Ⓓ Ⓔ	45. Ⓐ Ⓑ Ⓒ Ⓓ Ⓔ	80. Ⓐ Ⓑ Ⓒ Ⓓ Ⓔ	115. Ⓐ Ⓑ Ⓒ Ⓓ Ⓔ
11. Ⓐ Ⓑ Ⓒ Ⓓ Ⓔ	46. Ⓐ Ⓑ Ⓒ Ⓓ Ⓔ	81. Ⓐ Ⓑ Ⓒ Ⓓ Ⓔ	116. Ⓐ Ⓑ Ⓒ Ⓓ Ⓔ
12. Ⓐ Ⓑ Ⓒ Ⓓ Ⓔ	47. Ⓐ Ⓑ Ⓒ Ⓓ Ⓔ	82. Ⓐ Ⓑ Ⓒ Ⓓ Ⓔ	117. Ⓐ Ⓑ Ⓒ Ⓓ Ⓔ
13. Ⓐ Ⓑ Ⓒ Ⓓ Ⓔ	48. Ⓐ Ⓑ Ⓒ Ⓓ Ⓔ	83. Ⓐ Ⓑ Ⓒ Ⓓ Ⓔ	118. Ⓐ Ⓑ Ⓒ Ⓓ Ⓔ
14. Ⓐ Ⓑ Ⓒ Ⓓ Ⓔ	49. Ⓐ Ⓑ Ⓒ Ⓓ Ⓔ	84. Ⓐ Ⓑ Ⓒ Ⓓ Ⓔ	119. Ⓐ Ⓑ Ⓒ Ⓓ Ⓔ
15. Ⓐ Ⓑ Ⓒ Ⓓ Ⓔ	50. Ⓐ Ⓑ Ⓒ Ⓓ Ⓔ	85. Ⓐ Ⓑ Ⓒ Ⓓ Ⓔ	120. Ⓐ Ⓑ Ⓒ Ⓓ Ⓔ
16. Ⓐ Ⓑ Ⓒ Ⓓ Ⓔ	51. Ⓐ Ⓑ Ⓒ Ⓓ Ⓔ	86. Ⓐ Ⓑ Ⓒ Ⓓ Ⓔ	121. Ⓐ Ⓑ Ⓒ Ⓓ Ⓔ
17. Ⓐ Ⓑ Ⓒ Ⓓ Ⓔ	52. Ⓐ Ⓑ Ⓒ Ⓓ Ⓔ	87. Ⓐ Ⓑ Ⓒ Ⓓ Ⓔ	122. Ⓐ Ⓑ Ⓒ Ⓓ Ⓔ
18. Ⓐ Ⓑ Ⓒ Ⓓ Ⓔ	53. Ⓐ Ⓑ Ⓒ Ⓓ Ⓔ	88. Ⓐ Ⓑ Ⓒ Ⓓ Ⓔ	123. Ⓐ Ⓑ Ⓒ Ⓓ Ⓔ
19. Ⓐ Ⓑ Ⓒ Ⓓ Ⓔ	54. Ⓐ Ⓑ Ⓒ Ⓓ Ⓔ	89. Ⓐ Ⓑ Ⓒ Ⓓ Ⓔ	124. Ⓐ Ⓑ Ⓒ Ⓓ Ⓔ
20. Ⓐ Ⓑ Ⓒ Ⓓ Ⓔ	55. Ⓐ Ⓑ Ⓒ Ⓓ Ⓔ	90. Ⓐ Ⓑ Ⓒ Ⓓ Ⓔ	125. Ⓐ Ⓑ Ⓒ Ⓓ Ⓔ
21. Ⓐ Ⓑ Ⓒ Ⓓ Ⓔ	56. Ⓐ Ⓑ Ⓒ Ⓓ Ⓔ	91. Ⓐ Ⓑ Ⓒ Ⓓ Ⓔ	126. Ⓐ Ⓑ Ⓒ Ⓓ Ⓔ
22. Ⓐ Ⓑ Ⓒ Ⓓ Ⓔ	57. Ⓐ Ⓑ Ⓒ Ⓓ Ⓔ	92. Ⓐ Ⓑ Ⓒ Ⓓ Ⓔ	127. Ⓐ Ⓑ Ⓒ Ⓓ Ⓔ
23. Ⓐ Ⓑ Ⓒ Ⓓ Ⓔ	58. Ⓐ Ⓑ Ⓒ Ⓓ Ⓔ	93. Ⓐ Ⓑ Ⓒ Ⓓ Ⓔ	128. Ⓐ Ⓑ Ⓒ Ⓓ Ⓔ
24. Ⓐ Ⓑ Ⓒ Ⓓ Ⓔ	59. Ⓐ Ⓑ Ⓒ Ⓓ Ⓔ	94. Ⓐ Ⓑ Ⓒ Ⓓ Ⓔ	129. Ⓐ Ⓑ Ⓒ Ⓓ Ⓔ
25. Ⓐ Ⓑ Ⓒ Ⓓ Ⓔ	60. Ⓐ Ⓑ Ⓒ Ⓓ Ⓔ	95. Ⓐ Ⓑ Ⓒ Ⓓ Ⓔ	130. Ⓐ Ⓑ Ⓒ Ⓓ Ⓔ
26. Ⓐ Ⓑ Ⓒ Ⓓ Ⓔ	61. Ⓐ Ⓑ Ⓒ Ⓓ Ⓔ	96. Ⓐ Ⓑ Ⓒ Ⓓ Ⓔ	131. Ⓐ Ⓑ Ⓒ Ⓓ Ⓔ
27. Ⓐ Ⓑ Ⓒ Ⓓ Ⓔ	62. Ⓐ Ⓑ Ⓒ Ⓓ Ⓔ	97. Ⓐ Ⓑ Ⓒ Ⓓ Ⓔ	132. Ⓐ Ⓑ Ⓒ Ⓓ Ⓔ
28. Ⓐ Ⓑ Ⓒ Ⓓ Ⓔ	63. Ⓐ Ⓑ Ⓒ Ⓓ Ⓔ	98. Ⓐ Ⓑ Ⓒ Ⓓ Ⓔ	133. Ⓐ Ⓑ Ⓒ Ⓓ Ⓔ
29. Ⓐ Ⓑ Ⓒ Ⓓ Ⓔ	64. Ⓐ Ⓑ Ⓒ Ⓓ Ⓔ	99. Ⓐ Ⓑ Ⓒ Ⓓ Ⓔ	134. Ⓐ Ⓑ Ⓒ Ⓓ Ⓔ
30. Ⓐ Ⓑ Ⓒ Ⓓ Ⓔ	65. Ⓐ Ⓑ Ⓒ Ⓓ Ⓔ	100. Ⓐ Ⓑ Ⓒ Ⓓ Ⓔ	135. Ⓐ Ⓑ Ⓒ Ⓓ Ⓔ
31. Ⓐ Ⓑ Ⓒ Ⓓ Ⓔ	66. Ⓐ Ⓑ Ⓒ Ⓓ Ⓔ	101. Ⓐ Ⓑ Ⓒ Ⓓ Ⓔ	136. Ⓐ Ⓑ Ⓒ Ⓓ Ⓔ
32. Ⓐ Ⓑ Ⓒ Ⓓ Ⓔ	67. Ⓐ Ⓑ Ⓒ Ⓓ Ⓔ	102. Ⓐ Ⓑ Ⓒ Ⓓ Ⓔ	137. Ⓐ Ⓑ Ⓒ Ⓓ Ⓔ
33. Ⓐ Ⓑ Ⓒ Ⓓ Ⓔ	68. Ⓐ Ⓑ Ⓒ Ⓓ Ⓔ	103. Ⓐ Ⓑ Ⓒ Ⓓ Ⓔ	138. Ⓐ Ⓑ Ⓒ Ⓓ Ⓔ
34. Ⓐ Ⓑ Ⓒ Ⓓ Ⓔ	69. Ⓐ Ⓑ Ⓒ Ⓓ Ⓔ	104. Ⓐ Ⓑ Ⓒ Ⓓ Ⓔ	139. Ⓐ Ⓑ Ⓒ Ⓓ Ⓔ
35. Ⓐ Ⓑ Ⓒ Ⓓ Ⓔ	70. Ⓐ Ⓑ Ⓒ Ⓓ Ⓔ	105. Ⓐ Ⓑ Ⓒ Ⓓ Ⓔ	140. Ⓐ Ⓑ Ⓒ Ⓓ Ⓔ

PART II

CLEP College Mathematics

About Our Authors

This CLEP College Mathematics review was written by Mel Friedman, M.S., and Stu Schwartz, B.S.

Mr. Friedman is a former college mathematics professor who also worked as a test-item writer for Educational Testing Service.

Mr. Schwartz is a former AP teacher who has been teaching mathematics for over four decades. He is a recipient of the Presidential Award for Excellence in Mathematics and Science Teaching, America's highest honor for K-12 math and science teachers.

An Overview of the Exam

The CLEP College Mathematics exam consists of approximately 60 multiple-choice questions, each with four possible answer choices, to be answered in 90 minutes.

The exam covers the material one would find in a college-level class for non-mathematics majors in fields not requiring knowledge of advanced mathematics.

The approximate breakdown of topics is as follows:

20% Algebra and Functions

10% Counting and Probability

15% Data Analysis and Statistics

20% Financial Mathematics

10% Geometry

15% Logic and Sets

10% Numbers

The exam places little emphasis on arithmetic and calculators are not allowed to be brought into the testing area. A scientific (nongraphing) calculator is integrated into the exam software, and is available to students during the entire testing time. The scientific calculator, together with a brief video tutorial, is available to students as a free download for a 30-day trial period. Visit *www.collegboard.org/clep* for more information.

6-Week Study Plan

Our study plan is designed to be used in the six weeks before your exam. Be sure to set aside enough time—at least two hours each day—to study. The more time you spend studying, the more prepared and relaxed you will feel on the day of the exam.

Week	Activity
1	Take the Diagnostic Exam at the online REA Study Center (*www.rea.com/studycenter*). Your score report will identify topics where you need the most review.
2–4	Study the review, focusing on the topics you missed (or were unsure of) on the Diagnostic Exam.
5	Take Practice Test 1 at the REA Study Center. Review your score report and re-study any topics you missed.
6	Take Practice Test 2 at the REA Study Center to see how much your score has improved. If you still got a few questions wrong, go back to the review and study the topics you missed.

REVIEW OUTLINE

■ NUMBERS

Real numbers provide the basis for most precalculus mathematics topics.

> **Real numbers** are all of the numbers on the **number line** (see Figure 2-1).

In fact, a nice way to visualize real numbers is that they can be put in a one-to-one correspondence with the set of all points on a line. Real numbers include positives, negatives, square roots, π (pi), and just about any number you have ever encountered.

Figure 2-1

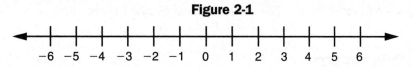

PROPERTIES OF REAL NUMBERS

Real numbers have several properties that you should know. You have used some of these properties ever since you could count. You intuitively know that $3 + 2$ gives the same result as $2 + 3$, or that if you add 0 to a number it remains unchanged, or if you multiply 79×194, you get the same result as 194×79 without actually multiplying the numbers. These properties deal with addition and multiplication. They do not work for subtraction and division. For example, you also intuitively know that $3 - 2$ is not the same as $2 - 3$.

Perhaps you are not familiar with the names of these properties. The following list provides the names for these properties. Learn them—you will encounter these property names in the next chapter and on mathematics tests. The examples use the numbers 2, 3, and 4, but the rules apply to any real numbers.

COMMUTATIVE PROPERTY

The numbers *commute*, or move:

Addition $2 + 3 = 3 + 2$
Multiplication $2 \times 3 = 3 \times 2$

ASSOCIATIVE PROPERTY

The numbers can be grouped, or *associated*, in any order:

Addition $\qquad$ $2 + (3 + 4) = (2 + 3) + 4$
Multiplication $\qquad$ $2 \times (3 \times 4) = (2 \times 3) \times 4$

Later in this chapter, you will see that operations in parentheses are always done first, but the associative property says that you can move the parentheses and it won't make a difference.

DISTRIBUTIVE PROPERTY

The first number gets *distributed* to the ones in parentheses:

$$2 \times (3 + 4) = (2 \times 3) + (2 \times 4)$$

The following properties have to do with the special numbers 0 and 1:

IDENTITY PROPERTY

Adding 0 or multiplying by 1 doesn't change the original value:

Addition $\qquad$ $3 + 0 = 3$
Multiplication $\qquad$ $3 \times 1 = 3$

INVERSE PROPERTY

Adding a number plus its *additive inverse* gives zero. Multiplying a number by its *multiplicative inverse* gives 1.

The additive inverse to 3 is -3 because $3 + (-3) = 0$.

The multiplicative inverse to 3 is $\dfrac{1}{3}$ because $3 \times \dfrac{1}{3} = 1$.

Note that there is no multiplicative inverse for 0 because there is no number that can be multiplied by 0 to get 1.

COMPONENTS OF REAL NUMBERS

The set of all real numbers (designated as R) has various components:

$N = \{1, 2, 3, \ldots\}$, the set of all **natural numbers** (sometimes called counting numbers)

$W = \{0, 1, 2, 3, \ldots\}$, the set of all **whole numbers**

$I = \{\ldots, -3, -2, -1, 0, 1, 2, 3, \ldots\}$, the set of all **integers**

$Q = \left\{ \text{all fractions in the form } \dfrac{a}{b}, \ a \text{ and } b \text{ integers with } b \neq 0 \right\}$, the set of all **rational numbers**

Examples of rational numbers include 2, $\dfrac{1}{2}$ and $\dfrac{3}{4}$. Numbers that have repeating decimals are also rational. 0.222 can be written as $0.\overline{2}$.

$6.797979\ldots$ can be written as $6.\overline{79}$.

$S = \{\text{all numbers that are not rational}\}$, the set of **irrational numbers**. These include numbers with decimals that do not terminate and do not have a repeating block of numbers.

Examples of irrational numbers include $0.1010010001\ldots$, π, and $\sqrt{2}$.

A natural number is also a whole number, a whole number is also an integer, and an integer is also rational. But a similar relationship does not hold between Q and S. A number is either rational or irrational.

All real numbers are normally represented by R. Every real number is either rational or irrational.

FRACTIONS

All rational numbers can be displayed as **fractions**, which consist of a numerator (on the top) and a denominator (on the bottom).

> **Proper fractions** are numbers between -1 and $+1$; the numerator is less than the denominator. Examples of proper fractions are $\dfrac{1}{2}$, $\dfrac{3}{4}$, and $\dfrac{17}{19}$.
>
> **Improper fractions** are all other rational numbers; the numerator is greater than or equal to the denominator.

Improper fractions are also called mixed numbers because they can be written as a whole number with a fractional part. Examples of improper fractions are $\dfrac{2}{1}$, $\dfrac{4}{3}$, and $\dfrac{19}{17}$. The first of these is actually a whole number (2); the others are equivalent to the mixed numbers $1\dfrac{1}{3}$ and $1\dfrac{2}{17}$, respectively.

ODD AND EVEN NUMBERS

All integers are either even or odd. The formal definition of an even number is one that is evenly divisible by 2. Odd numbers are not evenly divisible by 2. Zero is an even number as it is divisible by 2. When dealing with odd and even numbers, keep in mind the following:

Adding:

even + even = even

odd + odd = even

even + odd = odd

Multiplying:

even × even = even

even × odd = even

odd × odd = odd

FACTORS AND DIVISIBILITY NUMBERS

> Any counting number that divides into another number with no remainder is called a **factor** of that number.

The factors of 20 are 1, 2, 4, 5, 10, and 20.

> Multiplying a counting number by 1, 2, 3, ... are called multiples of that number.

Examples of multiples of 20 are 20, 40, 60, 80, etc.

PROBLEM

List the factors and multiples of 28.

SOLUTION

The factors of 28 are 1, 2, 4, 7, 14, and 28. Some multiples of 28 are 28, 56, 84, and 112. Note that the list of multiples is endless.

ABSOLUTE VALUE

> The **absolute value** of a number, denoted by two vertical lines surrounding the number, is the size of the number without regard to its sign.

The formal definition of the absolute value of a real number A is as follows:

$$|A| = \begin{cases} A \text{ if } A \geq 0 \\ -A \text{ if } A < 0 \end{cases}$$

Examples:

$$|5| = 5$$
$$|-8| = 8$$

The size of –8 without regard to its sign is 8. By the definition, $|-8| = -(-8) = 8$.

Absolute values follow the given rules:

1. $|-A| = |A|$

2. $|A| \geq 0$, equality holding only if $A = 0$

3. $\left|\dfrac{A}{B}\right| = \dfrac{|A|}{|B|}, B \neq 0$

4. $|AB| = |A| \times |B|$

5. $|A|^2 = A^2$

PROBLEM

Calculate the value of each of the following expressions:

1. $||2 - 5| + 6 - 14|$

2. $|-5| \times |4| + \dfrac{|-12|}{4}$

SOLUTION

Before solving this problem, one must remember the order of operations: parentheses, multiplication and division, addition and subtraction.

1. $||-3| + 6 - 14| = |3 + 6 - 14| = |9 - 14| = |-5| = 5$

2. $(5 \times 4) + \dfrac{12}{4} = 20 + 3 = 23$

INTEGERS

There are various subsets of I, the set of all integers:

NEGATIVE INTEGERS

The set of integers starting with -1 and decreasing:

$$\{-1, -2, -3, \ldots\}.$$

EVEN INTEGERS

The set of integers divisible by 2:

$$\{\ldots, -4, -2, 0, 2, 4, 6, \ldots\}.$$

ODD INTEGERS

The set of integers not divisible by 2:

$$\{\ldots, -3, -1, 1, 3, 5, 7, \ldots\}.$$

CONSECUTIVE INTEGERS

The set of integers starting with n, that differ by 1:

$$\{n, n + 1, n + 2, \ldots\} \ (n = \text{an integer}).$$

PRIME NUMBERS

The set of positive integers greater than 1 that are divisible only by 1 and themselves:

$$\{2, 3, 5, 7, 11, \ldots\}.$$

COMPOSITE NUMBERS

The set of integers, other than 0 and ± 1, that are not prime.

PROBLEMS

Classify each of the following numbers into as many different sets as possible.

Example: real, integer …

1. 0	3. $\sqrt{6}$	5. $\dfrac{2}{3}$	7. 11
2. 9	4. $\dfrac{1}{2}$	6. 1.5	

SOLUTIONS

1. 0 is a whole number, an even number, an integer, a rational number, and a real number.

2. 9 is a natural number, a whole number, an odd number, a composite number, a rational number, and a real number.

3. $\sqrt{6}$ is an irrational number and a real number.

4. $\dfrac{1}{2}$ is a rational number and a real number.

5. $\dfrac{2}{3}$ is a rational number and a real number.

6. 1.5 is a rational number and a real number.

7. 11 is a natural number, a whole number, an odd number, a prime number, a rational number, and a real number.

INEQUALITIES

> An **inequality** is a statement in which the value of one quantity or expression is greater than (>), less than (<), greater than or equal to (≥), less than or equal to (≤), or not equal to (≠) that of another.

If x and y are real numbers, then one and only one of the following statements is true:

$$x > y, x = y, \text{ or } x < y.$$

This is the **order property of real numbers**.

If a, b, and c are real numbers, the following statements are true:

$$\text{If } a < b \text{ and } b < c, \text{ then } a < c.$$

$$\text{If } a > b \text{ and } b > c, \text{ then } a > c.$$

This is the **transitive property of inequalities**.

If a, b, and c are real numbers and $a > b$, then $a + c > b + c$ and $a - c > b - c$. This is the **addition property of inequality**.

Example:

$5 > 4$. This expression means that the value of 5 is greater than the value of 4.

The **graph of an inequality** in one variable is represented by either a ray or a line segment on the real number line.

The endpoint is not a solution if the variable is strictly less than or greater than a particular value. In those cases, the endpoint is indicated by an open circle.

Example:

$x > 2$

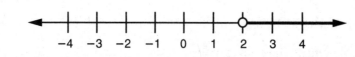

2 is not a solution and should be represented as shown.

The endpoint is a solution if the variable is either (1) less than or equal to or (2) greater than or equal to a particular value. In those cases, the endpoint is indicated by a closed circle.

Example:

$2 \leq x < 5$

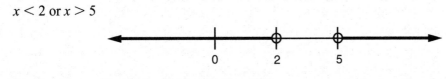

In this case, 2 is a solution and 5 is not a solution, and the solution should be represented as shown.

Example:

$x < 2$ or $x > 5$

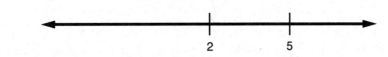

In this case, neither 2 nor 5 is a solution. Thus, an open circle must be shown at $x = 2$ and at $x = 5$.

Example:

$x \leq 2$ and $x \geq 5$

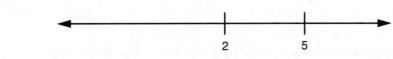

In this case, there is no solution. It is impossible for a number to be less than or equal to 2 and

greater than or equal to 5, both at the same time.

Example:

$x \geq 2$ or $x \leq 5$

In this case, the solution is all real numbers. Any number *must* belong to at least one of these inequalities. Some numbers, such as 3, belong to both inequalities. If you graph these inequalities separately, you will notice two rays going in opposite directions and which overlap between 2 and 5, inclusive.

Intervals on the number line represent sets of points that satisfy the conditions of an inequality.

An **open** interval does not include any endpoints.

Example:

$\{x \mid x > -3\}$, read as "the set of values x such that $x > -3$." The graph would appear as:

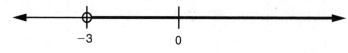

Example:

$\{x \mid x < 4\}$. The graph would appear as:

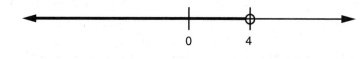

Example:

$\{x \mid 2 < x < 6\}$. The graph would appear as:

Example:

$\{x \mid x$ is any real number$\}$. The graph would appear as:

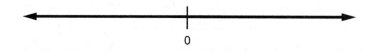

A **closed** interval includes two endpoints.

Example:

$\{x \mid -5 \leq x \leq 2\}$. The graph would appear as:

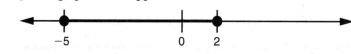

A **half-open** interval includes one endpoint.

Example:

$\{x \mid x \geq 3\}$. The graph would appear as:

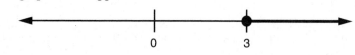

Example:

$\{x \mid x \le 6\}$. The graph would appear as:

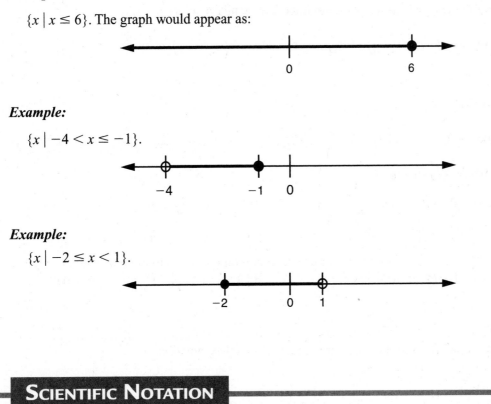

Example:

$\{x \mid -4 < x \le -1\}$.

Example:

$\{x \mid -2 \le x < 1\}$.

SCIENTIFIC NOTATION

It is possible that some of the numbers or answers you encounter on the CLEP College Math exam may be in **scientific notation**. While we use standard notation for most numbers we encounter, we use scientific notation when working with numbers that are either very large or very small. The number of cells in the human body is estimated to be 150,000,000,000,000 (read 150 trillion) and is written as 1.5×10^{14}. The length of time it takes light to travel 1 meter is approximately 0.000000003 second and is written as 3×10^{-9}.

The form for a number in scientific notation is $a \times 10^n$ where $1 \le a < 10$ and n is an integer.

SCIENTIFIC NOTATION TO STANDARD NOTATION

To convert a number in scientific notation to standard notation, we add zeros to it. If n is positive, we add zeros to the right. If n is negative, we add zeros to the left.

So to convert 1.2×10^5, we need to move our decimal point 5 places to the right. There is already one decimal place to the right of the decimal point so we add 4 zeros. So $1.2 \times 10^5 =$ 120000. We usually write 120000 as 120,000, making it easier to read.

PROBLEMS

Change the following scientific notation numbers to standard notation.

(A) 3.7×10^4

(B) 9.92×10^2

(C) 1.005×10^9

SOLUTIONS

(A) $3.7 \times 10^4 = 37,000$

(B) $9.92 \times 10^2 = 992$

(C) $1.005 \times 10^9 = 1,005,000,000$

To convert 4.7×10^{-4}, we need to move our decimal point 4 places to the left. There is already 1 decimal place to the left of the decimal point so we add 3 zeros. So $4.7 \times 10^{-4} = 0.00047$.

PROBLEMS

Change the following scientific notation numbers to standard notation.

(A) 5.1×10^{-3}

(B) 2.27×10^{-6}

(C) 8.004×10^{-5}

(D) 4.2×10^0

SOLUTIONS

(A) $5.1 \times 10^{-3} = 0.0051$

(B) $2.27 \times 10^{-6} = 0.00000227$

(C) $8.004 \times 10^{-5} = 0.00008004$

(D) $4.2 \times 10^0 = 4.2$

STANDARD NOTATION TO SCIENTIFIC NOTATION

To convert numbers to scientific notation, we focus on large numbers (numbers greater than 1) or small numbers (numbers less than 1).

Large numbers: To convert 34,320 to scientific notation, we place a caret after the first non-zero digit, the 3. We then count the number of decimal places from the caret to the real decimal point, which is at the end of the number. There are 4 decimal places. So our answer is 34,320 = 3.432×10^4.

If the number is 25,460,000,000, we place we place a caret after the first non-zero digit, the 2. We then count the number of decimal places from the caret to the real decimal point, which is at the end of the number. There are 10 decimal places. So our answer is 25,460,000,000 = 2.546×10^{10}.

Small numbers: To convert 0.000073 to scientific notation, place a caret after the first non-zero digit, the 7. We then count the number of decimal places from the caret to the real decimal point, which is to the left. There are 5 decimal places, so our answer is 0.000073 = 7.3×10^{-5}.

If the number is 0.01503, we place a caret after the first non-zero digit, the 1. We then count the number of decimal places from the caret to the real decimal point, which is to the left. There are 2 decimal places, so our answer is 0.01503 = 1.503×10^{-2}.

PROBLEMS

Change the following standard notation numbers to scientific notation.

(A) 600,000,000,000

(B) 2,450

(C) −10,080,000

(D) 0.79

(E) − 0.000005505

SOLUTIONS

(A) 600,000,000,000 = 6×10^{11}

(B) 2,450 = 2.45×10^3

(C) −10,080,000 = $- 1.008 \times 10^7$

(D) 0.79 = 7.9×10^{-1}

(E) − 0.000005505 = $- 5.505 \times 10^{-6}$

MULTIPLICATION AND DIVISION OF NUMBERS IN SCIENTIFIC NOTATION

To multiply two numbers in scientific notation, we multiply the numbers and add the exponents of the 10's. So $(a \times 10^m) (b \times 10^n) = ab \times 10^{m + n}$. This method works whether the exponents m and n are positive or negative. So $(4 \times 10^4) (2 \times 10^5) = 4(2) \times 10^{4 + 5} = 8 \times 10^9$. If when we multiply a times b, it is possible that this number is greater than 10. If so, change it to scientific notation as well.

PROBLEMS

Multiply the following.

(A) $(3 \times 10^8)(1.4 \times 10^7)$

(B) $(-7 \times 10^4)(1.1 \times 10^{-6})$

(C) $(-1.2 \times 10^{-2})^2$

(D) $(-3 \times 10^{10})(-5 \times 10^{-4})$

SOLUTIONS

(A) $(3 \times 10^8)(1.4 \times 10^7) = 4.2 \times 10^{15}$

(B) $(-7 \times 10^4)(1.1 \times 10^{-6}) = -7.7 \times 10^{-2}$

(C) $(-1.2 \times 10^{-2})^2 = (-1.2 \times 10^{-2})(-1.2 \times 10^{-2}) = 1.44 \times 10^{-4}$

(D) $(-3 \times 10^{10})(-5 \times 10^{-4}) = 15 \times 10^6 = 1.5 \times 10^1 \times 10^6 = 1.5 \times 10^7$

To divide two numbers in scientific notation, we divide the numbers and subtract the exponents of the 10's (numerator exponent minus denominator exponent). So $\dfrac{a \times 10^m}{b \times 10^n} = \dfrac{a}{b} \times 10^{m-n}$.

This method works whether the exponents m and n are positive or negative. So, $\dfrac{6 \times 10^9}{2 \times 10^4} = \dfrac{6}{2} \times 10^{9-4} = 3 \times 10^5$. When we divide a by b, it is possible that this number is less than 1. If so, change it to scientific notation as well.

PROBLEMS

Find the following.

(A) $\dfrac{3.2 \times 10^{15}}{2 \times 10^7}$

(B) $\dfrac{7.5 \times 10^4}{2.5 \times 10^{-2}}$

(C) $\dfrac{1.21 \times 10^{-3}}{-1.1 \times 10^{-6}}$

(D) $\dfrac{-2 \times 10^{-3}}{-8 \times 10^{-2}}$

SOLUTIONS

(A) $\dfrac{3.2\times10^{15}}{2\times10^{7}}=1.6\times10^{15-7}=1.6\times10^{8}$

(B) $\dfrac{7.5\times10^{4}}{2.5\times10^{-2}}=3\times10^{4-(-2)}=3\times10^{6}$

(C) $\dfrac{1.21\times10^{-3}}{-1.1\times10^{-6}}=-1.1\times10^{-3-(-6)}=-1.1\times10^{3}$

(D) $\dfrac{-2\times10^{-3}}{-8\times10^{-2}}=0.25\times10^{-3-(-2)}=2.5\times10^{-1}\times10^{-1}=2.5\times10^{-2}$

UNIT CONVERSIONS

Length and liquid measurement units are usually given in the Imperial (or Standard) system (which you are used to) or the Metric system (which is used in just about all countries except the United States). The relationships below are ones that you should know. If it is necessary to change from an imperial measurement to a metric measurement, you will be given the relationship (ex: 1 meter = 39.37 inches). There are basic relationships that you should know when you change from one unit to another.

Length

Imperial system
1 foot = 12 inches
1 yard = 3 feet
1 mile = 5,280 feet

Metric system
1 meter = 100 centimeters
1 meter = 1,000 millimeters
1 kilometer = 1,000 meters

Weight

Imperial system
1 pound = 16 ounces
1 ton = 2,000 pounds

Metric system
1 gram = 1,000 milligrams
1 kilogram = 1,000 grams

Liquid

Imperial system
1 pint = 16 ounces
1 quart = 2 pints
1 gallon = 4 quarts

Metric system
1 liter = 1,000 milliliters

Time

1 minute = 60 seconds
1 hour = 60 minutes
1 day = 24 hours
1 year = 365 days

To change from one unit to another, we can divide either side of a conversion relationship by the other and always get 1.

For example:

$$1 \text{ yard} = 3 \text{ feet} \Rightarrow \frac{1 \text{ yard}}{3 \text{ feet}} = 1 \text{ or } 1 \text{ gallon} = 4 \text{ quarts} \Rightarrow \frac{4 \text{ quarts}}{1 \text{ gallon}} = 1.$$

Since we can multiply any quantity by one, we can easily change measurements from one unit to another. So to convert 8 feet to inches, we multiply 8 feet by $\frac{12 \text{ inches}}{1 \text{ feet}}$. The feet cancel out to get 8(12) = 96 inches.

PROBLEMS

(A) Convert 15 kilometers to meters.

(B) Convert 6 pints to gallons.

(C) Convert 80 years to seconds.

SOLUTIONS

(A) $15 \text{ kilometers} \cdot \dfrac{1,000 \text{ meters}}{1 \text{ kilometers}} = 15,000 \text{ meters}$

(B) $6 \text{ pints} \cdot \dfrac{1 \text{ quart}}{2 \text{ pints}} \cdot \dfrac{1 \text{ gallon}}{4 \text{ quarts}} = \dfrac{3}{4} \text{ gallon}$

(C) $80 \text{ years} \cdot \dfrac{365 \text{ days}}{1 \text{ year}} \cdot \dfrac{24 \text{ hours}}{1 \text{ day}} \cdot \dfrac{60 \text{ minutes}}{1 \text{ hour}} \cdot \dfrac{60 \text{ seconds}}{1 \text{ minute}} = 2,522,880,000 \text{ seconds}$

PROBLEM

If 1 kilogram = 2.2 pounds, convert 180 pounds to kilograms.

SOLUTION

$$180 \text{ pounds} \cdot \frac{1 \text{ kilogram}}{2.2 \text{ pounds}} = 81.8 \text{ kilograms}$$

PROBLEM

The speed limit for a Canadian road is 80 kilometers per hour. If a car is traveling at 60 mph, is it speeding? (1 mile = 1.6 kilometer).

SOLUTION

$$\frac{60 \text{ miles}}{\text{hour}} \cdot \frac{1.6 \text{ kilometers}}{1 \text{ mile}} = 96 \frac{\text{kilometers}}{\text{hour}} \text{ so the car is speeding.}$$

PROBLEM

Convert 12 feet per second to miles per hour.

SOLUTION

$$\frac{12 \text{ feet}}{\text{second}} \cdot \frac{1 \text{ mile}}{5,280 \text{ feet}} \cdot \frac{60 \text{ seconds}}{1 \text{ minute}} \cdot \frac{60 \text{ minutes}}{1 \text{ hour}} = 8.18 \frac{\text{miles}}{\text{hour}}$$

DRILL QUESTIONS

1. If c is any odd integer, which one of the following must be an even integer?

    (A) $\dfrac{c}{2}$

    (B) $3c - 1$

    (C) $c^2 + 2$

    (D) $2c + 1$

2. What is the value of $|7 - 13| - |-2 - 9|$?

    (A) 16

    (B) 5

    (C) −5

    (D) −16

3. Which one of the following is an irrational number whose value lies between 7 and 8?

   (A) $\sqrt[3]{400}$

   (B) $7.\overline{2}$

   (C) $\sqrt{65}$

   (D) $\dfrac{25}{3}$

4. Which one of the following numbers is a prime number between 90 and 100?

   (A) 91
   (B) 94
   (C) 95
   (D) 97

5. Which one of the following inequalities describes a graph on the number line that includes all real numbers?

   (A) $x \geq 1$ and $x \leq 4$
   (B) $x \geq 1$ or $x \leq 4$
   (C) $x \leq 1$ or $x \geq 4$
   (D) $x \leq 1$ and $x \geq 4$

6. If 15 is a factor of x, which one of the following is true for any x?

   (A) 30 must be a factor of x.
   (B) Each of 3 and 5 must be factors of x.
   (C) x must be a prime number greater than 15.
   (D) The only prime factors of x are 3 and 5.

7. The number $0.\overline{4}$ is equivalent to which fraction?

   (A) $\dfrac{4}{5}$

   (B) $\dfrac{4}{7}$

   (C) $\dfrac{4}{9}$

   (D) $\dfrac{4}{11}$

8. The number 0.00000482 is equivalent to

   (A) 4.82×10^{-5}
   (B) 4.82×10^{-6}
   (C) 4.82×10^{-7}

   (D) $\dfrac{4.82}{10^{-7}}$

9. Convert 10 miles per hour to meters per second if 1 meter = 3.28 feet.

   (A) 4.47 meters/sec
   (B) 22.36 meters/sec
   (C) 48.11 meters/sec
   (D) 268.28 meters/sec

10. Which one of the following has no solution for x?

    (A) $|x| > 0$
    (B) $|x| = 0$
    (C) $|x| = -x$
    (D) $|x| < 0$

ANSWERS TO DRILL QUESTIONS

1. **(B)**   The product of 3 and an odd integer must be an odd integer. The difference of an odd integer and 1 must be an even integer. For example, suppose $c = 5$. Then $3c - 1 = (3)(5) - 1 = 15 - 1 = 14$, which is an even integer.

2. **(C)**   Recall that the absolute value of any quantity must be nonnegative. Then $|7 - 13| = |-6| = 6$ and $|-2 - 9| = |-11| = 11$. Then $6 - 11 = 6 + (-11) = -5$.

3. **(A)** $\sqrt[3]{400}$ is irrational because we cannot find any integer whose cube is exactly 400. Note that since $7^3 = 343$ and $8^3 = 512$, we know that $\sqrt[3]{400}$ has a value between 7 and 8. (It is approximately 7.368.) $\sqrt{65}$ is also irrational, but since $\sqrt{64} = 8$ and $\sqrt{81} = 9$, $\sqrt{65} > 8$.

4. **(D)**   A prime number can be divided by only two numbers, itself and 1. The number 97 is prime because it is divisible by only 1 and 97.

5. **(B)**   The inequality $x \geq 1$ includes all numbers greater than or equal to 1. The inequality $x \leq 4$ includes all numbers less than or equal to 4. Every number must satisfy at least one of these conditions. (Some numbers, such as 2, satisfy both conditions.) Thus, the graph of $x \geq 1$ or $x \leq 4$ includes all numbers on the number line.

6. **(B)**   If 15 is a factor of x, then x must be divisible by 15 and by any factor of 15. Each of 3 and 5 is a factor of 15. Let $x = 30$. Note that 15 is a factor of 30, since $30 \div 15 = 2$. In addition, we note that each of 3 and 5 is a factor of 30, since $30 \div 3 = 10$ and $30 \div 5 = 6$.

7. **(C)**   Let $N = 0.\overline{4}$, so that $10N = 4.\overline{4}$. By subtracting the first equation from the second equation, we get 9N = 4. For students not familiar with this technique, an easy way to determine the answer is trial and error. For each choice, divide the denominator into the numerator and see which gives a repeating 4.

8. **(B)**   Placing the carat after the 4, work backwards 6 places to the true decimal point so 0.00000482 $= 4.82 \times 10^{-6}$.

9. **(A)** $\dfrac{10 \text{ miles}}{\text{hour}} \cdot \dfrac{5280 \text{ feet}}{1 \text{ mile}} \cdot \dfrac{1 \text{ meters}}{3.28 \text{ feet}} \cdot \dfrac{1 \text{ hour}}{60 \text{ minutes}} \cdot \dfrac{1 \text{ minute}}{60 \text{ seconds}} = 4.47 \dfrac{\text{meters}}{\text{second}}$.

10. **(D)**   The absolute value of any number must be nonnegative. This means that $|x|$ must be greater than or equal to zero. Thus, $|x| < 0$ has no solution. Note that choice (C) is possible. For instance, if $x = -3$, $|-3| = -(-3) = 3$.

ALGEBRA AND FUNCTIONS

EQUATIONS

> An **equation** is defined as a statement that two separate expressions are equal. A **solution** to an equation containing a single variable is a number that makes the equation true when it is substituted for the variable.

For example, in the equation $3x = 18$, 6 is the solution since $3(6) = 18$. Depending on the equation, there can be more than one solution. Equations with the same solutions are said to be **equivalent equations**. An equation without a solution is said to have a solution set that is the **empty** or **null** set, represented by ϕ.

Replacing an expression within an equation by an equivalent expression will result in a new equation with solutions equivalent to the original equation. For example, suppose we are given the equation

$$3x + y + x + 2y = 15.$$

By combining like terms, we get

$$3x + y + x + 2y = 4x + 3y.$$

Since these two expressions are equivalent, we can substitute the simpler form into the equation to get

$$4x + 3y = 15$$

Performing the same operation to both sides of an equation by the same expression will result in a new equation that is equivalent to the original equation.

ADDITION OR SUBTRACTION

$$y + 6 = 10$$

We can add (-6) to both sides:

$$y + 6 + (-6) = 10 + (-6)$$

$$y + 0 = 10 - 6 = 4$$

MULTIPLICATION OR DIVISION

$$3x = 6$$

We can divide both sides by 3:

$$\frac{3x}{3} = \frac{6}{3}$$

$$x = 2$$

So $3x = 6$ is equivalent to $x = 2$.

PROBLEM

Solve for x, justifying each step.

$$3x - 8 = 7x + 8$$

SOLUTION

$3x - 8 = 7x + 8$	
$3x - 8 + 8 = 7x + 8 + 8$	Add 8 to both sides
$3x + 0 = 7x + 16$	Additive inverse property
$3x = 7x + 16$	Additive identity property
$3x - 7x = 7x + 16 - 7x$	Add $(-7x)$ to both sides
$-4x = 7x - 7x + 16$	Commutative property
$-4x = 0 + 16$	Additive inverse property

$$-4x = 16 \qquad \text{Additive identity property}$$

$$\frac{-4x}{-4} = \frac{16}{-4} \qquad \text{Divide both sides by } -4$$

$$x = -4$$

CHECK YOUR WORK!

Replacing x with -4 in the original equation:

$$3x - 8 = 7x + 8$$

$$3(-4) - 8 = 7(-4) + 8$$

$$-12 - 8 = -28 + 8$$

$$-20 = -20$$

LINEAR EQUATIONS

A **linear equation** with one unknown is one that can be put into the form $ax + b = 0$, where a and b are constants, and $a \neq 0$.

To solve a linear equation means to transform it into the form $x = \dfrac{-b}{a}$.

A. If the equation has unknowns on both sides of the equality, it is convenient to put similar terms on the same sides. Refer to the following example:

$$4x + 3 = 2x + 9$$

$$4x + 3 - 2x = 2x + 9 - 2x \qquad \text{Add } -2x \text{ to both sides}$$

$$(4x - 2x) + 3 = (2x - 2x) + 9 \qquad \text{Commutative property}$$

$$2x + 3 = 0 + 9 \qquad \text{Additive inverse property}$$

$$2x + 3 - 3 = 0 + 9 - 3 \qquad \text{Add } -3 \text{ to both sides}$$

$$2x = 6 \qquad \text{Additive inverse property}$$

$$\frac{2x}{2} = \frac{6}{2} \qquad \text{Divide both sides by 2}$$

$$x = 3$$

B. If the equation appears in fractional form, it is necessary to transform it using cross-multi-plication, and then repeat the same procedure as in (A). For example,

$$\frac{3x + 4}{3} = \frac{7x + 2}{5}$$

Cross-multiply as follows:

$$\frac{3x + 4}{3} \bowtie \frac{7x + 2}{5}$$

to obtain:

$$3(7x + 2) = 5(3x + 4).$$

This is equivalent to:

$$21x + 6 = 15x + 20,$$

which can be solved as in (A).

$$21x + 6 = 15x + 20$$

$$21x - 15x + 6 = 15x - 15x + 20 \qquad \text{Add } -15x \text{ to both sides}$$

$$6x + 6 - 6 = 20 - 6 \qquad \text{Combine like terms and add } -6 \text{ to both sides}$$

$$6x = 14 \qquad \text{Combine like terms}$$

$$\frac{6x}{6} = \frac{14}{6} \qquad \text{Divide both sides by 6}$$

$$x = \frac{7}{3}$$

Of course, to solve such equations we skip obvious steps, do some of the work in our heads, and don't write the reasons for each step. The solution is quickly found:

$$\frac{3x + 4}{3} = \frac{7x + 2}{5}$$

$$21x + 6 = 15x + 20$$

$$21x - 15x = 20 - 6$$

$$6x = 14$$

$$x = \frac{14}{6} = \frac{7}{3}$$

FACTOR THEOREM

> If $x = c$ is a solution of the equation $f(x) = 0$, then $(x - c)$ is a **factor** of $f(x)$.

Example:

Let $f(x) = 2x^2 - 5x - 3$. By inspection, we can determine that $2(3)^2 - (5)(3) - 3 = (2)(9) - (5)(3) - 3 = 0$. In this example, $c = 3$, so $(x - 3)$ is also a factor of $2x^2 - 5x - 3$.

Example:

Let $f(x) = x^3 + 3x^2 - 4$. By inspection, we can determine that $(-2)^3 + 3(-2)^2 - 4 = -8 + (3)(4) - 4 = 0$. In this example, $c = -2$, so $(x + 2)$ is also a factor of $x^3 + 3x^2 - 4$.

REMAINDER THEOREM

> If a is any constant and if the polynomial $p(x)$ is divided by $(x - a)$, the **remainder** is $p(a)$.

Example:

Given a polynomial $p(x) = 2x^3 - x^2 + x + 4$, divided by $x - 1$, the remainder is $p(1) = 2(1)^3 - (1)^2 + 1 + 4 = 6$.

That is, $2x^3 - x^2 + x + 4 = q(x) + \dfrac{6}{(x - 1)}$, where $q(x)$ is a polynomial.

Note that in this case $a = 1$.

Also, by using long division, we get $q(x) = 2x^2 + x + 2$.

Example:

Given a polynomial $p(x) = x^4 + x - 50$ divided by $x + 3$, the remainder is $p(-3) = 28$.

That is, $x^4 + x - 50 = q(x) + \dfrac{28}{(x + 3)}$, where $q(x)$ is a polynomial.

Note that in this case $a = -3$.

Also, by using long division, we get $q(x) = x^3 - 3x^2 + 9x - 26$.

SIMULTANEOUS LINEAR EQUATIONS

Two or more equations of the form $ax + by = c$, where a, b, c are constants and a, $b \neq 0$ are called **linear equations** with two unknown variables, or **simultaneous equations**.

Equations with more than one unknown variable are solvable only if you have as many equations as unknown variables.

There are several ways to solve systems of linear equations with two variables. Three of the basic methods are:

Method 1: **Substitution**—Find the value of one unknown in terms of the other. Substitute this value in the other equation and solve.

Method 2: **Addition or subtraction**—If necessary, multiply the equations by numbers that will make the coefficients of one unknown in the resulting equations numerically equal. If the signs of equal coefficients are the same, subtract the equations; otherwise add. The result is one equation with one unknown; we solve it and substitute the value into the other equations to find the unknown that we first eliminated.

Method 3: **Graph**—Graph both equations. The point of intersection of the drawn lines is a simultaneous solution for the equations, and its coordinates correspond to the answer that would be found by substitution or addition/subtraction.

> A system of linear equations is **consistent** if there is only one solution for the system.
>
> A system of linear equations is **inconsistent** if it does not have any solutions.

Inconsistent equations represent parallel lines, which are discussed later in this chapter.

PROBLEM

Solve the system of equations.

1. $x + y = 3$
2. $3x - 2y = 14$

SOLUTION

Method 1 (Substitution): From equation (1), we get $y = 3 - x$. Substitute this value into equation (2) to get

$$3x - 2(3 - x) = 14$$
$$3x - 6 + 2x = 14$$
$$5x = 20$$
$$x = 4$$

Substitute $x = 4$ into either of the original equations to find $y = -1$.

The answer is $x = 4$, $y = -1$.

Method 2 (Addition or subtraction): If we multiply equation (1) by 2 and add the result to equation (2), we get

$$
\begin{aligned}
2x + 2y &= 6 \\
+\ 3x - 2y &= 14 \\
\hline
5x + 0 &= 20 \\
x &= 4
\end{aligned}
$$

Then, as in Method 1, substitute $x = 4$ into either of the original equations to find $y = -1$.

The answer is $x = 4$, $y = -1$.

Method 3 (Graphing): Find the point of intersection of the graphs of the equations. To graph these linear equations, solve for y in terms of x. The equations will be in the form $y = mx + b$, where m is the slope and b is the intercept on the y-axis. This is the **slope-intercept form** of the equation.

$$x + y = 3$$

Subtract x from both sides:

$$y = 3 - x$$

$$3x - 2y = 14$$

Subtract $3x$ from both sides:

$$-2y = 14 - 3x$$

Divide by -2:

$$y = -7 + \frac{3}{2}x$$

The graph of each of the linear functions can be determined by plotting only two points. For example, for $y = 3 - x$, let $x = 0$, then $y = 3$. Let $x = 1$, then $y = 2$. The two points on this first line are $(0, 3)$ and $(1, 2)$. For $y = -7 + \dfrac{3}{2}x$, let $x = 0$, then $y = -7$. Let $x = 2$, then $y = -4$. The two points on this second line are $(0, -7)$ and $(2, -4)$.

To find the point of intersection P of the two lines, graph them.

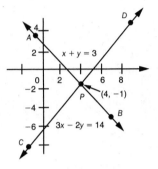

AB is the graph of equation (1), and CD is the graph of equation (2). The point of intersection P of the two graphs is the only point on both lines. The coordinates of P satisfy both equations and represent the desired solution of the problem. From the graph, P seems to be point $(4, -1)$. These coordinates satisfy both equations, and hence are the exact coordinates of the point of intersection of the two lines.

CHECK YOUR WORK!

To show that $(4, -1)$ satisfies both equations, substitute this point into both equations.

$x + y = 3$	$3x - 2y = 14$
$4 + (-1) = 3$	$3(4) - 2(-1) = 14$
$4 - 1 = 3$	$12 + 2 = 14$
$3 = 3$	$14 = 14$

DEPENDENT EQUATIONS

> **Dependent equations** are equations that represent the same line; therefore, every point on the line of a dependent equation represents a solution.

Since there are an infinite number of points on a line, there are an infinite number of simultaneous solutions.

Example:

$$2x + y = 8$$

$$4x + 2y = 16$$

These equations are dependent. Since they represent the same line, all points that satisfy either of the equations are solutions of the system.

PROBLEM

Solve the equations $2x + 3y = 6$ and $y = -\dfrac{2x}{3} + 2$ simultaneously.

SOLUTION

We have two equations and two unknowns:

$$2x + 3y = 6$$

and

$$y = -\frac{2x}{3} + 2$$

As with all simultaneous equations, there are several methods of solution. Since equation (2) already gives us an expression for y, we use the method of substitution.

Substitute $-\dfrac{2x}{3} + 2$ for y in equation (1):

$$2x + 3\left(-\frac{2x}{3} + 2\right) = 6$$

Distribute:

$$2x - 2x + 6 = 6$$

$$6 = 6$$

Although the result $6 = 6$ is true, it indicates no single solution for x. No matter what real number x is, if y is determined by equation (1), then equation (1) will always be satisfied.

The reason for this peculiarity may be seen if we take a closer look at the equation $y = -\dfrac{2x}{3} + 2$. It is equivalent to $3y = -2x + 6$, or $2x + 3y = 6$.

In other words, the two equations are equivalent, and thus dependent. Any pair of values of x and y that satisfies one satisfies the other.

It is hardly necessary to verify that in this case the graphs of the given equations are identical lines, and that there are an infinite number of simultaneous solutions to these equations.

PARALLEL LINES

Given two linear equations in x, y, their graphs are **parallel** lines if their slopes are equal. If the lines are parallel, they have no simultaneous solution.

Example:

Line $l_1 : 2x - 7y = 14$, Line $l_2 : 2x - 7y = 56$

In the slope-intercept form, the equation for l_1 is $y = \frac{2}{7}x - 2$ and the equation for l_2 is $y = \frac{2}{7}x - 8$. Each line has a slope of $\frac{2}{7}$.

PROBLEM

Solve the equations $2x + 3y = 6$ and $4x + 6y = 7$ simultaneously.

SOLUTION

We have two equations and two unknowns:

$$2x + 3y = 6$$

and

$$4x + 6y = 7$$

Again, there are several methods to solve this problem. We have chosen to multiply each equation by a different number so that when the two equations are added, one of the variables drops out. Thus,

Multiply equation (1) by 2:	$4x + 6y = 12$	(3)
Multiply equation (2) by -1:	$+\ -4x - 6y = -7$	(4)
Add equations (3) and (4):	$0 = 5$	

We obtain a peculiar result!

Actually, what we have shown in this case is that there is no simultaneous solution to the given equations because $0 \neq 5$. Therefore, there is no simultaneous solution to these two equations, and hence no point satisfying both.

The straight lines that are the graphs of these equations must be parallel if they never intersect, but not identical, which can be seen from the graph of these equations.

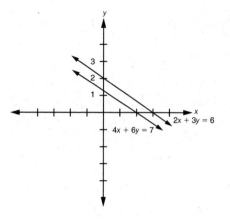

PERPENDICULAR LINES

> If the slopes of the graphs of two lines are negative reciprocals of each other, the lines are **perpendicular** to each other.

An example of two numbers that are negative reciprocals of each other are 2 and $-\frac{1}{2}$. (Remember: $2 = \frac{2}{1}$.)

Example:

l_3: $5x + 6y = 30$, l_4: $6x - 5y = 90$

In the slope-intercept form, the equation for l_3 is $y = -\frac{5}{6}x + 5$ and the equation for l_4 is $y = \frac{6}{5}x - 18$. The slope of l_3, which is $-\frac{5}{6}$, is the negative reciprocal of the slope of l_4, which is $\frac{6}{5}$. Therefore, l_3 is perpendicular to l_4.

To summarize:

- Parallel lines have slopes that are equal.

- Perpendicular lines have slopes that are negative reciprocals of each other.

ABSOLUTE VALUE EQUATIONS

The **absolute value** of a, denoted $|a|$, is defined as

$|a| = a$ when $a > 0$,

$|a| = -a$ when $a < 0$,

$|a| = 0$ when $a = 0$.

When the definition of absolute value is applied to an equation, the quantity within the absolute value symbol may have two values. This value can be either positive or negative before the absolute value is taken. As a result, each absolute value equation actually contains two separate equations.

When evaluating equations containing absolute values, proceed as follows:

$|5 - 3x| = 7$ is valid if either

$$5 - 3x = 7 \qquad \text{or} \qquad 5 - 3x = -7$$
$$-3x = 2 \qquad\qquad\qquad -3x = -12$$
$$x = -\frac{2}{3} \qquad\qquad\qquad x = 4$$

The solution set is therefore $x = \left\{ -\frac{2}{3}, 4 \right\}$.

Remember, the absolute value of a number cannot be negative. So the equation $|5x + 4| = -3$ would have no solution.

INEQUALITIES

The solution of a given inequality in one variable x consists of all values of x for which the inequality is true.

A **conditional inequality** is an inequality whose validity depends on the values of the variables in the sentence. That is, certain values of the variables will make the sentence true, and others will make it false.

The sentence $3 - y > 3 + y$ is a conditional inequality for the set of real numbers, since it is true for any replacement less than 0 and false for all others, or $y < 0$ is the solution set.

> An **absolute inequality** for the set of real numbers means that for *any* real value for the variable, x, the sentence is always true.

The sentence $x + 5 > x + 2$ is an absolute inequality because the expression on the left is greater than the expression on the right.

> A sentence is **inconsistent** if it is always false when its variables assume allowable values.

The sentence $x + 10 < x + 5$ is inconsistent because the expression on the left side is always greater than the expression on the right side.

The sentence $5y < 2y + y$ is inconsistent for the set of non-negative real numbers. For any y greater than or equal to zero, the sentence is always false.

Two inequalities are said to have the same **sense** if their signs of inequality point in the same direction.

The sense of an inequality remains the same if both sides are multiplied or divided by the same *positive* real number.

Example:

For the inequality $4 > 3$, if we multiply both sides by 5, we will obtain:

$$4 \times 5 > 3 \times 5$$

$$20 > 15$$

The sense of the inequality does not change.

If each side of an inequality is multiplied or divided by the same *negative* real number, however, the sense of an inequality changes direction.

Example:

For the inequality $4 > 3$, if we multiply both sides by -5, we would obtain:

$$4 \times (-5) < 3 \times (-5)$$

$$-20 < -15.$$

The sense of the inequality changes direction.

If $a > b$ and a, b, and n are positive real numbers, then

$$a^n > b^n \text{ and } a^{-n} < b^{-n}$$

Example

$4^2 > 3^2$ as $16 > 9$ so $4^{-2} < 3^{-2}$ as $\dfrac{1}{16} < \dfrac{1}{9}$

If $x > y$ and $q > p$, then $x + q > y + p$.

If $x > y > 0$ and $q > p > 0$, then $xq > yp$.

Example

Since $7 > 5$ and $3 > 1$, $7 + 3 > 5 + 1$ as $10 > 6$

Also, $7(3) > 5(1)$ as $21 > 5$

Inequalities that have the same solution set are called **equivalent inequalities**.

PROBLEM

Solve the inequality $2x + 5 > 9$.

SOLUTION

$$2x + 5 > 9$$

Add -5 to both sides: $\qquad 2x + 5 + (-5) > 9 + (-5)$

Additive inverse property: $\qquad 2x + 0 > 9 + (-5)$

Additive identity property: $\qquad 2x > 9 + (-5)$

Combine terms: $\qquad 2x > 4$

Multiply both sides by $\dfrac{1}{2}$ (this is the same as dividing both sides by 2):

$$\dfrac{1}{2}(2x) > \dfrac{1}{2} \times 4$$
$$x > 2$$

The solution set is $\{x \mid x > 2\}$

(that is, all x, such that x is greater than 2).

LINEAR INEQUALITIES

Linear inequalities are graphed by shading a section of the coordinate plane. The line is graphed using a solid line if the line is included ($\leq$ or $\geq$) and a dashed line if the line is not included ($<$ or $>$). Shading will be on either side of the line. If the inequality is in the form of $y > mx + b$ or $y \geq mx + b$, the shading is above the line and if the inequality is in the form of $y < mx + b$ or $y \leq mx + b$, the shading is below the line.

PROBLEM

Graph $y \geq 3x - 1$.

SOLUTION

We graph the line $y = 3x - 1$ and make it solid. Since the inequality is $\geq$, we shade above the line.

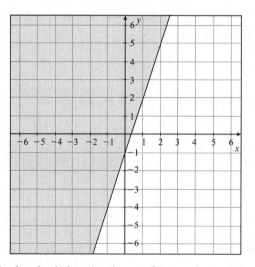

This means every point in the shaded region is true for $y \geq 3x - 1$. Let's check one random point $(-3, 1)$, to show this is correct. We get $1 \geq 3(-3) - 1 = -10$. Is $1 \geq -10$? Yes, so it checks out.

PROBLEM

Graph $x + 2y < 4$.

SOLUTION

$$2y < -x + 4$$
$$y < -\frac{1}{2}x + 2$$

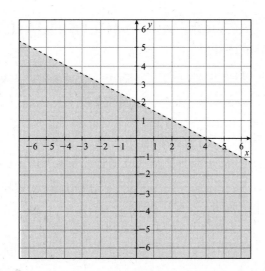

We graph the line $x + 2y = 4$ and make it a dashed line because it is not included in the inequality. Because the inequality for y is < 0, we shade below the line.

To check, we can use the origin $(0, 0)$ since it is in the shaded region. We use the original inequality $x + 2y = 4$. Is $0 + 2(0) < 4$? Since $0 < 4$, it checks out.

COMPLEX NUMBERS

As indicated above, real numbers provide the basis for most precalculus mathematics topics. However, on occasion, real numbers by themselves are not enough to explain what is happening. As a result, complex numbers were developed.

> A **complex number** is a number that can be written in the form $a + bi$, where a and b are real numbers and $i = \sqrt{-1}$. The number a is the **real part**, and the number bi is the **imaginary part** of the complex number.

Returning momentarily to real numbers, the square of a real number cannot be negative. More specifically, the square of a positive real number is positive, the square of a negative real number is positive, and the square of 0 is 0.

i is defined to be a number with a property that $i^2 = -1$. Obviously, i is not a real number. C is then used to represent the set of all complex numbers:

$$C = \{a + bi \,|\, a \text{ and } b \text{ are real numbers}\}.$$

ADDITION, SUBTRACTION, AND MULTIPLICATION OF COMPLEX NUMBERS

Here are the definitions of addition, subtraction, and multiplication of complex numbers.

Suppose $x + yi$ and $z + wi$ are complex numbers. Then (remembering that $i^2 = -1$):

$$(x + yi) + (z + wi) = (x + z) + (y + w)i$$

$$(x + yi) - (z + wi) = (x - z) + (y - w)i$$

$(x + yi) \times (z + wi)$ is handled as a FOIL type problem such as

$$(x + 4)(x + 3) = x^2 + 3x + 4x + 12 = x^2 + 7x + 12$$

PROBLEM

Simplify $(3 + i)(2 + i)$.

SOLUTION

$$(3+i)(2+i) = 6 + 3i + 2i + i^2$$
$$= 6 + 5i + (-1)$$
$$= 5 + 5i$$

DIVISION OF COMPLEX NUMBERS

Division of two complex numbers is usually accomplished with a special procedure that involves the conjugate of a complex number. The conjugate of $a + bi$ is denoted by $\overline{a + bi}$ and defined by $\overline{a + bi} = a - bi$.

Also,

$$(a + bi)(a - bi) = a^2 + b^2$$

The usual procedure for division is to multiply both the numerator and the denominator by the conjugate of the denominator. This is allowable as you are multiplying the fraction by 1, and thus not changing it.

$$\frac{4+5i}{2+3i} = \frac{4+5i}{2+3i} \times \frac{2-3i}{2-3i}$$

$$= \frac{8 - 12i + 10i - 15i^2}{4 - 6i + 6i - 9i^2}$$

$$= \frac{8 - 2i - 15(-1)}{4 - 9(-1)}$$

$$= \frac{23 - 2i}{13}$$

If a is a real number, then a can be expressed in the form $a = a + 0i$. So every real number is a complex number, but not every complex number is a real number.

All the properties of real numbers carry over to complex numbers, so those properties will not be stated again.

QUADRATIC EQUATIONS

Consider the polynomial:

$ax^2 + bx + c = 0$, where $a \neq 0$.

This type of equation is called a **quadratic equation**.

Values of x that satisfy this equation are called **solutions** or **roots**.

There are several methods to solve quadratic equations, some of which are highlighted here. The first two are based on the fact that if the product of two factors is 0, either one or the other of the factors equals 0. The equation can be solved by setting each factor equal to 0. If you cannot see the factors right away, however, the quadratic formula, which is the last method presented, *always* works.

SOLUTION BY FACTORING

We are looking for two binomials that, when multiplied together, give the quadratic trinomial

$$ax^2 + bx + c = 0$$

This method works easily if $a = 1$ and you can find two numbers whose product equals c and sum equals b. The signs of b and c need to be considered:

- If c is positive, the factors are going to both have the same sign, which is b's sign.

- If c is negative, the factors are going to have opposite signs, with the larger factor having b's sign.

Once you have the two factors, insert them in the general factor format $(x + \_)(x + \_) = 0$.

To solve the quadratic equation, set each factor equal to 0 to yield the solution set for x.

PROBLEM

Solve the quadratic equation $x^2 + 7x + 12 = 0$.

SOLUTION

We need two numbers whose product is $+12$ and sum is $+7$. They would be $+3$ and $+4$, and the quadratic equation would factor to $(x + 3)(x + 4) = 0$.

Therefore, $x + 3 = 0$ or $x + 4 = 0$ would yield the solutions, which are $x = -3$, $x = -4$.

CHECK YOUR WORK!

Substitute the values into the original quadratic equation:

For $x = -3$, $(-3)^2 + 7(-3) + 12 = 0$, or $9 + (-21) + 12 = 0$. So $x = -3$ is a solution.

Likewise, for $x = -4$, $(-4)^2 + 7(-4) + 12 = 0$, or $16 + (-28) + 12 = 0$. So $x = -4$ is a solution.

PROBLEM

Suppose the quadratic equation is similar to the previous example, but the sign of b is negative. Solve the quadratic equation $x^2 - 7x + 12 = 0$.

SOLUTION

We need two numbers whose product is $+12$ and sum is -7. They would be -3 and -4, and the quadratic would factor to $(x - 3)(x - 4) = 0$.

Therefore, $x - 3 = 0$ or $x - 4 = 0$ would yield the solutions, which are $x = 3$, $x = 4$.

CHECK YOUR WORK!

Substitute the values into the original quadratic equation:

For $x = 3$, $(3)^2 - 7(3) + 12 = 0$, or $9 - 21 + 12 = 0$. So $x = 3$ is a solution.

Likewise, for $x = 4$, $(4)^2 - 7(4) + 12 = 0$, or $16 - 28 + 12 = 0$. So $x = 4$ is a solution.

PROBLEM

As a final example, solve the quadratic equation $x^2 + 4x - 12 = 0$.

SOLUTION

We need two numbers whose product is -12 and sum is $+4$. They would be $+6$ and -2 (note that the larger numeral gets the $+$ sign, the sign of b). The quadratic equation would factor to $(x + 6)(x - 2) = 0$.

Therefore, $x + 6 = 0$ or $x - 2 = 0$ would yield the solutions, which are $x = -6$, $x = 2$.

CHECK YOUR WORK!

Substitute the values into the original quadratic equation:

For $x = -6$, $(-6)^2 + 4(-6) - 12 = 0$, or $36 + (-24) - 12 = 0$. So $x = -6$ is a solution.

Likewise, for $x = 2$, $(2)^2 + 4(2) - 12 = 0$, or $4 + 8 - 12 = 0$. So $x = 2$ is a solution.

DIFFERENCE OF TWO SQUARES

If the quadratic consists of the difference of only two terms, each of which is a perfect square, the factors are simply the sum and the difference of the square roots of the two terms.

PROBLEM

Solve the quadratic equation $x^2 - 16 = 0$.

SOLUTION

This is the difference of two perfect squares, x^2 and 16, whose square roots are x and 4. So the factors are $(x + 4)(x - 4) = 0$, and the solution is $x = \pm 4$.

CHECK YOUR WORK!

For $x = 4$, $(4)^2 - 16 = 16 - 16 = 0$.

For $x = -4$, $(-4)^2 - 16 = 16 - 16 = 0$.

PROBLEM

Solve the quadratic equation $9x^2 - 36 = 0$.

SOLUTION

This is the difference of two perfect squares, $9x^2$ and 36, whose square roots are $3x$ and 6. So the factors are $(3x + 6)(3x - 6) = 0$, then $3x + 6 = 0$ or $3x - 6 = 0$, and the solution is $x = \pm 2$.

CHECK YOUR WORK!

For $x = 2$, $9(2)^2 - 36 = 36 - 36 = 0$.

For $x = -2$, $9(-2)^2 - 36 = 36 - 36 = 0$.

QUADRATIC FORMULA

If the quadratic equation does not have obvious factors, the roots of the equation can always be determined by the **quadratic formula** in terms of the coefficients a, b, and c as shown below:

$$x = \frac{-b \pm \sqrt{b^2 - 4ac}}{2a}$$

where $(b^2 - 4ac)$ is called the **discriminant** of the quadratic equation.

- If the discriminant is less than zero $(b^2 - 4ac < 0)$, the roots are complex numbers, since the discriminant appears under a radical and square roots of negatives are imaginary numbers. A real number added to an imaginary number yields a complex number.

- If the discriminant is equal to zero $(b^2 - 4ac = 0)$, the roots are real and equal.

- If the discriminant is greater than zero $(b^2 - 4ac > 0)$, then the roots are real and unequal. The roots are rational if and only if a and b are rational and $(b^2 - 4ac)$ is a perfect square; otherwise, the roots are irrational.

PROBLEMS

Compute the value of the discriminant and then determine the nature of the roots of each of the following four equations:

1. $4x^2 - 12x + 9 = 0$
2. $3x^2 - 7x - 6 = 0$
3. $5x^2 + 2x - 9 = 0$
4. $x^2 + 3x + 5 = 0$

SOLUTIONS

1. $4x^2 - 12x + 9 = 0$

Here, a, b, and c are integers:

$a = 4$, $b = -12$, and $c = 9$.

Therefore,

$b^2 - 4ac = (-12)^2 - 4(4)(9) = 144 - 144 = 0$

Since the discriminant is 0, the roots are rational and equal.

2. $3x^2 - 7x - 6 = 0$

   Here, a, b, and c are integers:

   $a = 3, b = -7$, and $c = -6$.

   Therefore,

   $b^2 - 4ac = (-7)^2 - 4(3)(-6) = 49 + 72 = 121 = 11^2.$

   Since the discriminant is a perfect square, the roots are rational and unequal.

3. $5x^2 + 2x - 9 = 0$

   Here, a, b, and c are integers:

   $a = 5, b = 2$, and $c = -9$

   Therefore,

   $b^2 - 4ac = 2^2 - 4(5)(-9) = 4 + 180 = 184.$

   Since the discriminant is greater than zero, but not a perfect square, the roots are irrational and unequal.

4. $x^2 + 3x + 5 = 0$

   Here, a, b, and c are integers:

   $a = 1, b = 3$, and $c = 5$

   Therefore,

   $b^2 - 4ac = 3^2 - 4(1)(5) = 9 - 20 = -11$

   Since the discriminant is negative, the roots are complex.

PROBLEM

Solve the equation $x^2 - x + 1 = 0$.

SOLUTION

In this equation, $a = 1, b = -1$, and $c = 1$. Substitute into the quadratic formula.

$$x = \frac{-(-1) \pm \sqrt{(-1)^2 - 4(1)(1)}}{2(1)}$$

$$= \frac{1 \pm \sqrt{1 - 4}}{2}$$

$$= \frac{1 \pm \sqrt{-3}}{2}$$

$$= \frac{1 \pm i\sqrt{3}}{2}$$

$$x = \frac{1 + i\sqrt{3}}{2} \text{ or } x = \frac{1 - i\sqrt{3}}{2}$$

ADVANCED ALGEBRAIC THEOREMS

A. Every polynomial equation $f(x) = 0$ of degree greater than zero has at least one root either real or complex. This is known as the **fundamental theorem of algebra**.

B. Every polynomial equation of degree n has exactly n roots.

C. If a polynomial equation $f(x) = 0$ with real coefficients has a root $a + bi$, then the conjugate of this complex number $a - bi$ is also a root of $f(x) = 0$.

D. If $a + \sqrt{b}$ is a root of polynomial equation $f(x) = 0$ with rational coefficients, then $a - \sqrt{b}$ is also a root, where a and b are rational and $\sqrt{b}$ is irrational.

E. If a rational fraction in lowest terms $\dfrac{b}{c}$ is a root of the equation $a_n x^n + a_{n-1} x^{n-1} + \ldots + a_1 x + a_0 = 0$, $a_0 \neq 0$, and the a_i are integers, then b is a factor of a_0 and c is a factor of a_n.

F. Any rational roots of the equation $x^n + q_1 x^{n-1} + q_2 x^{n-2} + \ldots + q_{n-1} x + q_n = 0$ must be integers and factors of q_n. Note that $q_1, q_2, \ldots, q_n$ are integers.

RELATIONS AND GRAPHS

An **ordered pair** is commonly called a point. It is in the form of (x, y) where x and y are real numbers. A **relation** is a set of points.

PROBLEM

In relation $R = \{(0, 0), (1, 0), (0, 1), (1, 1), (2, 0), (2, 1), (1, 2), (0, 2), (2, 2)\}$, list the set of ordered pairs for which the 2nd member is greater than the first member.

SOLUTION

$(0, 1), (1, 2), (0, 2)$

The **domain** of a relation is the set of all first members of the relation. If a member is repeated, it is listed once.

The **range** of a relation is the set of all second members of the relation. If a member is repeated, it is listed once.

PROBLEM

List the domain and range of the relation

$R = \{(-2, -2), (-1, 0), (-1, -2), (-1, 0)\}$

SOLUTION

Domain: $\{-2, -1\}$ Range: $R = \{-2, 0\}$

FUNCTIONS: DEFINITION AND NOTATION

A **function** is a relation, a set of points (x, y), such that for every x, there is one and only one y. In short, in a function, the x-values cannot repeat while the y-values can. On the CLEP test, almost all of your graphs will come from functions.

PROBLEM

Which of the following relations are functions?

$A = \{(8, 0), (-6, -3), (1, -2), (2, -10)\}$
$B = \{(5, 1), (7, f), (5, 0), (-3, p)\}$
$C = \{(1, 5), (-1, -7), (0, 5), (1, -1), (-1, -2)\}$
$D = \{(3, 4), (5, 4), (8, 4), (1, 4), (12, 4), (0, 4)\}$

SOLUTION

A and D are functions. B is not a function as the 5 repeats. C is not a function as both the 1 and -1 repeat.

If a graph is given, you can quickly determine whether it is a function by the **vertical line test**. If it is possible for a vertical line to intersect a graph at more than one point, then the graph is not a function.

PROBLEM

Use the vertical line test to determine which of the following graphs are functions.

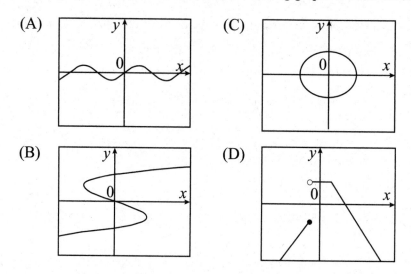

SOLUTION

(A) is a function as any vertical line would only intersect the graph in one location. Choices (B) and (C) are not functions as it is possible to draw a vertical line that will intersect the graph in more than one location. Choice (D) is a function. The open dot indicates the graph does not contain the point while the closed dot indicates the graph does include the point. Thus, a vertical line will intersect the graph in only one location.

Functions can be represented in three different ways. First is the **numerical representation** where functions are given by the set of points: $F = \{(-1, 1), (0, 2), (1, 3), (2, 4), (3, 5)\}$ is an example of a function given numerically. A **graphical representation** gives a picture of the function. In the problem on the previous page, (A) and (D) show functions graphically.

The most common way to represent a function is **symbolically**. We use a special function notation. This notation is either in the form of "$y =$" or "$f(x) =$". In the $f(x)$ notation, we are stating a rule to find y given a value of x. Using this notation, it is easy to **evaluate the function**—plugging in a value of x to find y.

PROBLEMS

If $f(x) = x^2 - 5x + 8$, find

(A) $f(-6)$

(B) $f\left(\dfrac{3}{2}\right)$

(C) $f(a)$

SOLUTIONS

(A) $f(-6) = (-6)^2 - 5(-6) + 8$
   $36 + 30 + 8$
   74

(B) $f\left(\dfrac{3}{2}\right) = \left(\dfrac{3}{2}\right)^2 - 5\left(\dfrac{3}{2}\right) + 8$
   $\dfrac{9}{4} - \dfrac{15}{2} + 8$
   $\dfrac{11}{4}$

(C) $f(a) = a^2 - 5a + 8$

COMPOSITION OF FUNCTIONS

One concept that is tested on the CLEP exam is composition of functions. If we have two functions f and g, we can find $f(g(a))$ or $g(f(a))$, which are different than $f(a) \cdot g(a)$. To find a composition of functions: plug a value into one function, determine an answer, and plug that answer into a second function. $f(g(x))$ can also be written as $(f \circ g)(x)$.

PROBLEMS

If $f(x) = x^2 - x + 1$ and $g(x) = 2x - 1$, find

(A) $f(-1) \cdot g(-1)$

(B) $f(g(-1))$

(C) $g(f(-1))$

(D) $(g \circ f)(x)$

SOLUTIONS

(A) $f(-1) \cdot g(-1) = (1+1+1)(-2-1) = 3(-3) = -9$

(B) $g(-1) = 2(-1) - 1 = -3$ so $f(-3) = 9 + 3 + 1 = 13$

(C) $f(-1) = 1 + 1 + 1 = 3$ so $g(3) = 6 - 1 = 5$

(D) $(g \circ f)(x) = g(f(x)) = 2(x^2 - x + 1) - 1 = 2x^2 - 2x + 2 - 1 = 2x^2 - 2x + 1$

PROBLEM

The graph of $g(x)$ is given in the figure below. Find the value of $g(g(-1))$.

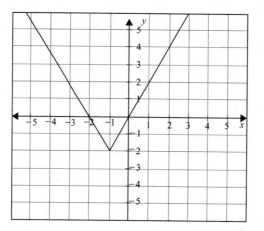

SOLUTION

$g(-1) = -2.$

$g(-2) = 0$

Piecewise functions

A **piecewise function** is one where there are two or more rules, based on the value of x.

PROBLEMS

If $f(x) = \begin{cases} x^2 - 3, & x \geq 0 \\ 2x + 1, & x < 0 \end{cases}$, find

(A) $f(4)$

(B) $f(3) - f(-1)$

(C) $f(f(0))$

SOLUTIONS

(A) $f(4) = 16 - 3 = 13$

(B) $f(3) - f(-1) = (9 - 3) - (-2 + 1)$
    $= 6 - (-1) = 7$

(C) $f(0) = 0 - 3 = -3$

$f(-3) = -6 + 1 = -5$

LINEAR FUNCTIONS

The type of function which appears most on the CLEP College Mathematics exam are **linear** or **first-degree functions**. The graph of any linear equation is a straight line. The **slope** of a line is a number that measures its steepness. The ratio of the change in y to the change in x is the slope of the line. It is commonly referred to as rise over run.

Slope: Given two points (x_1, y_1) and (x_2, y_2), the slope of the line passing through the points can be written as:

$$m = \frac{\text{rise}}{\text{run}} = \frac{y_2 - y_1}{x_2 - x_1} \ .$$

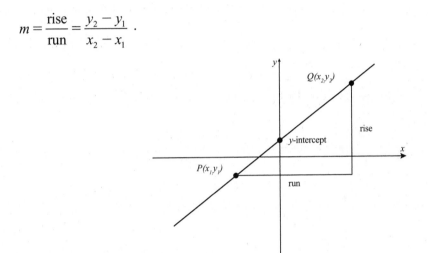

Lines that go up to the right have a positive slope, while lines that go up to the left have a negative slope.

PROBLEMS

Find the slope of the lines passing through the following two points:

(A)   (2, 3) and (4, 7)

(B)   (−5, 2) and (1, −3)

SOLUTIONS

(A) $m = \dfrac{7-3}{4-2} = \dfrac{4}{2} = 2$

(B) $m = \dfrac{-3-2}{1+5} = \dfrac{-5}{6}$

HORIZONTAL AND VERTICAL LINES

Horizontal lines: Lines that are horizontal are in the form: $y = $ constant. Horizontal lines have zero slope. In the formula for slope, $y_2 - y_1 = 0$, so the slope is always zero.

PROBLEM

Find the slope of the line passing through (4, –8) and (–2, –8).

SOLUTION

$$m = \frac{-8+8}{4+2} = \frac{0}{6} = 0 \quad \text{This is a horizontal line.}$$

Vertical lines: Lines that are vertical are said to have no slope (it is so steep that we cannot give a value to its steepness). In the formula for slope, $x_2 - x_1 = 0$, and division by zero is impossible, making the slope undefined.

PROBLEM

Find the equations of the two lines in the figure below.

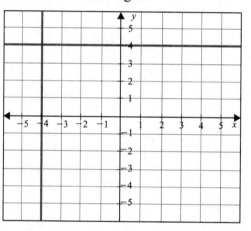

SOLUTION

The horizontal line is $y = 4$. The vertical line is $x = -4$.

LINEAR EQUATIONS

The equations of lines can have several forms, each having its own particular use.

General Form

The general form of an equation is $Ax + By + C = 0$ where A, B, and C are integers. This is the least useful form of a linear equation but it has no fractions in it. An equation in this form often has to be put into the other forms, described below, to get more information about the line, such as its slope. Sometimes answers on the CLEP exam will be placed into general form.

Slope-Intercept Form

All lines except vertical lines will have a **y-intercept**, the point in the form of $(0, b)$ at which the line crosses the y-axis. The equation of a line with slope m and y-intercept b is given by $y = mx + b$. If we are given the slope m and the y-intercept b, it is easy to write the equation of a line.

PROBLEM

Find the equation of the line in the figure below.

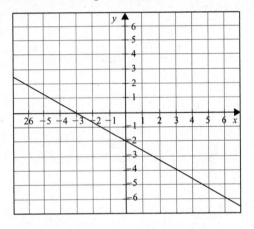

SOLUTION

We see that the y-intercept is $b = -2$. The line goes down 2 units for every 3 units it goes to the right, so the rise is -2 for a run of 3. Therefore, the slope is $m = \dfrac{-2}{3}$. So the equation is $y = \dfrac{-2}{3}x - 2$. To transform this equation to general form, clear the equation of fractions by multiplying each term by 3 to get $3y = -2x - 6$ or $2x + 3y + 6 = 0$.

Point-Slope Form

The equation of a line with slope m and passing through the point (x_1, y_1) is given by $y - y_1 = m(x - x_1)$.

If we are given two points, this is the easiest way to find the equation of the line. We need to find the slope first, then plug in either point into the point-slope formula.

PROBLEM

Find the equation passing through the points $(3, -2)$ and $(-1, 4)$.

SOLUTION

The slope $m = \dfrac{4+2}{-1-3} = \dfrac{6}{-4} = -\dfrac{3}{2}$. Choosing $(-1, 4)$ as the point, the point-slope form gives

$y - 4 = -\dfrac{3}{2}(x+1)$ or $\left(\text{multiplying by 2}\right)$, $2y - 8 = -3x - 3$ General form: $3x + 2y - 5 = 0$.

PROBLEM

Find the equation passing through the points $\left(\dfrac{3}{4}, 2\right)$ and $\left(\dfrac{1}{8}, -\dfrac{1}{2}\right)$.

SOLUTION

The slope $m = \dfrac{2 + \dfrac{1}{2}}{\dfrac{3}{4} - \dfrac{1}{8}}$. Multiply the numerator and denominator by the LCD of 8

to clear the fractions. Then $m = \dfrac{16+4}{6-1} = \dfrac{20}{5} = 4$. Choosing $\left(\dfrac{3}{4}, 2\right)$ as the point,

$y - 2 = 4\left(x - \dfrac{3}{4}\right)$ or $y - 2 = 4x - 3$ which gives $y = 4x - 1$.

The general form is thus $4x - y - 1 = 0$.

Intercept Form

In intercept form, the equation of a line with x-intercept a and y-intercept b is given by $\dfrac{x}{a} + \dfrac{y}{b} = 1$. If we know these intercepts, we can immediately write the equation of the line.

PROBLEM

Find the equation passing through the points $(0,4)$ and $(-3,0)$.

SOLUTION

We can use the intercept form above, $\dfrac{x}{a} + \dfrac{y}{b} = 1$, where point $(0, 4)$ says the y-intercept is 4 and $(-3,0)$ says the x-intercept is –3. Since we know the intercepts, we can write the equation directly:

$\dfrac{x}{-3} + \dfrac{y}{4} = 1$. Clearing the equation of fractions by multiplying through by the LCD $= 12$ gives

$-4x + 3y = 12$, which in general form is $4x - 3y + 12 = 0$.

TRANSFORMATION OF GRAPHS

A curve in the form $y = f(x)$, which is one of the basic common functions, can be transformed in a variety of ways. The shape of the resulting curve stays the same but x- and y-intercepts might change and the graph could be reversed. The table below describes transformations to a general function $y = f(x)$ with the graph $f(x) = x^2$ as an example.

Notation	How $f(x)$ changes	Example with $f(x) = x^2$
$f(x) + a$	Moves graph up a units.	
$f(x) - a$	Moves graph down a units.	
$f(x + a)$	Moves graph a units left.	
$f(x - a)$	Moves graph a units right.	

Notation	How $f(x)$ changes	Example with $f(x) = x^2$
$a \cdot f(x)$	$a > 1$: Vertical stretch	
$a \cdot f(x)$	$0 < a < 1$: Vertical shrink	
$f(ax)$	$a > 1$: Horizontal compression (for this curve, same effect as vertical stretch)	
$f(ax)$	$0 < a < 1$: Horizontal elongation (for this curve, same effect as vertical shrink)	
$-f(x)$	Reflection across x-axis	

Notation	How $f(x)$ changes	Example with $f(x) = x^2$
$f(-x)$	Reflection across y-axis	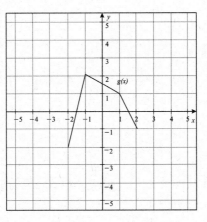

PROBLEMS

Let $g(x)$ be the curve shown in the figure below. Sketch the result of the following transformations.

(A) $g(x) + 2$ (B) $g(x) - 1$

(C) $2g(x)$ (D) $-g(x)$

(E) $g(x - 3)$ (F) $g(x + 2) + 1$

(G) $g(2x)$ (H) $g\left(\dfrac{1}{2}x\right)$

SOLUTIONS

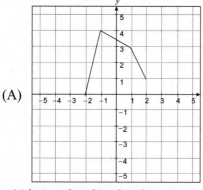

(A)

g(x) is translated up 2 units

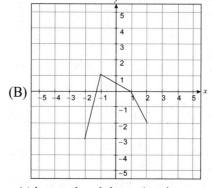

(B)

g(x) is translated down 1 unit

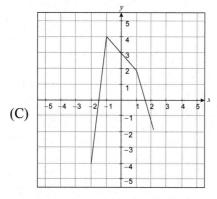

(C)

g(x) is vertically stretched 2 units.

It goes twice as high and twice as low.

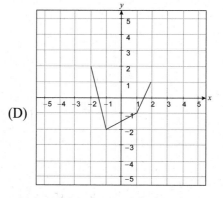

(D)

g(x) is reflected across the *x* axis.

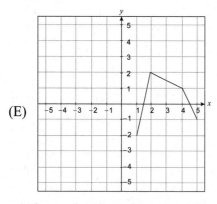

(E)

g(x) is translated 3 units to the right.

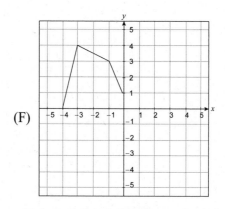

(F)

g(x) is translated 2 units to the left and one unit up.

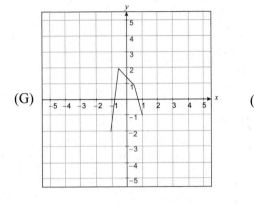

(G)

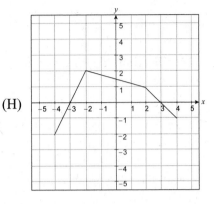

(H)

g(x) is horizontally compressed by a factor of 2.

g(x) is horizontally elongated by a factor of 2.

> A 90° **rotation** of a function moves each point P to a new point P′ so that OP = OP′ and $\overline{OP}$ is perpendicular to $\overline{OP'}$.

The letter O represents the origin, which is located at (0, 0). If the rotation is *counterclockwise*, each point (x, y) becomes (−y, x). If the rotation is *clockwise*, each point (x, y) becomes (y, −x).

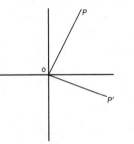

PROBLEM

Suppose a function contains the point (4, 3). What are the new coordinates of this point if the function is rotated 90° counterclockwise?

SOLUTION

(4, 3) will become (−3, 4).

PROBLEM

Suppose a function contains the point (4, 3). What are the new coordinates of (4, 3) if the function is rotated 90° clockwise?

SOLUTION

(4, 3) will become (3, −4).

> A **reflection** of a function is simply the mirror image of the function.

A reflection about the *x*-axis changes point (*x*, *y*) into point (*x*, −*y*). A reflection about the *y*-axis changes point (*x*, *y*) into point (−*x*, *y*). A reflection about the line *y* = *x* will move each point *P* to a new point *P′* so that the line *y* = *x* is the perpendicular bisector of $\overline{PP'}$. Each point (*x*, *y*) becomes (*y*, *x*) after the reflection.

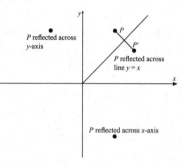

PROBLEM

A function contains the point (−6, 3). If this function is reflected about the line *y* = *x*, what will be the new coordinates for (−6, 3)?

SOLUTION

(−6, 3) will become (3, −6).

EXPONENTS

> When a number is multiplied by itself a specific number of times, it is said to be **raised to a power**. The way this is written is $a^n = b$, where *a* is the number or base; *n* is the **exponent** or **power** that indicates the number of times the base appears when multiplied by itself; and *b* is the **product** of this multiplication.

In the expression 3^2, 3 is the base and 2 is the exponent. This means that 3 appears 2 times when multiplied by itself (3×3), and the product is 9.

An exponent can be either positive or negative. A negative exponent implies a fraction, such that if n is a negative integer

$$a^{-n} = \frac{1}{a^n}, a \neq 0$$

$$\text{So, } 2^{-4} = \frac{1}{2^4} = \frac{1}{16}$$

> The **reciprocal** of a number is 1 divided by that number. The exception is 0, since $\frac{1}{0}$ is undefined.

We see that a negative exponent yields a fraction that is the reciprocal of the original base and exponent, with the exponent now positive instead of negative. Essentially, any quantity raised to a negative exponent can be "flipped" to the other side of the fraction bar and its exponent changed to a positive exponent. For example,

$$4^{-3} = \frac{1}{4^3} = \frac{1}{64}$$

An exponent that is 0 gives a result of 1, assuming that the base itself is not equal to 0.

$$a^0 = 1, a \neq 0$$

An exponent can also be a fraction. If m and n are positive integers,

$$a^{\frac{m}{n}} = \sqrt[n]{a^m}$$

The numerator remains the exponent of a, but the denominator tells what root to take. For example,

$$4^{\frac{3}{2}} = \sqrt[2]{4^3} = \sqrt{64} = 8$$

$$3^{\frac{4}{2}} = \sqrt[2]{3^4} = \sqrt{81} = 9$$

If a fractional exponent is negative, the operation involves the reciprocal as well as the roots. For example,

$$27^{\frac{-2}{3}} = \frac{1}{27^{\frac{2}{3}}} = \frac{1}{\sqrt[3]{27^2}} = \frac{1}{729} = \frac{1}{9}$$

PROBLEMS

Simplify the following expressions:

1. -3^{-2}

2. $(-3)^{-2}$

3. $\dfrac{-3}{4^{-1}}$

4. $-16^{-\frac{1}{2}}$

SOLUTIONS

1. Here the exponent applies only to 3. Since

$$x^{-y} = \frac{1}{x^y}, \text{ so } -3^{-2} = -(3)^{-2} = -\left(\frac{1}{3^2}\right) = -\frac{1}{9}$$

2. In this case, the exponent applies to the negative base. Thus,

$$(-3)^{-2} = \frac{1}{(-3)^2} = \frac{1}{(-3)(-3)} = \frac{1}{9}$$

3. $\dfrac{-3}{4^{-1}} = \dfrac{-3}{\left(\dfrac{1}{4}\right)^1} = \dfrac{-3}{\dfrac{1^1}{4^1}} = \dfrac{-3}{\dfrac{1}{4}} = \dfrac{-3}{1} \times \dfrac{4}{1} = -12$

4. $-16^{-\frac{1}{2}} = \dfrac{-1}{16^{\frac{1}{2}}} = -\dfrac{1}{\sqrt{16}} = -\dfrac{1}{4}$

GENERAL LAWS OF EXPONENTS

$a^p a^q = a^{p+q}$, bases must be the same

$$4^2 4^3 = 4^{2+3} = 4^5 = 1{,}024$$

$(a^p)^q = a^{pq}$

$$(2^3)^2 = 2^6 = 64$$

$\dfrac{a^p}{a^q} = a^{p-q}$, bases must be the same, $a \neq 0$

$$\frac{3^6}{3^2} = 3^{6-2} = 3^4 = 81$$

$(ab)^p = a^p b^p$

$$(3 \times 2)^2 = 3^2 \times 2^2 = (9)(4) = 36$$

$$\left(\frac{a}{b}\right)^p = \frac{a^p}{b^p}, b \neq 0$$

$$\left(\frac{4}{5}\right)^2 = \frac{4^2}{5^2} = \frac{16}{25}$$

EXPONENTIAL EQUATIONS

Most of the CLEP College Mathematics exam is about linear and polynomial functions, as discussed earlier in this chapter. However, **exponential functions**, in the form of $y=b^x$, are also tested on the exam.

The constant b is called the **base**, where b is a positive number. An exponential graph tends to increase or decrease rapidly because x is in the exponent. The following graphs are examples of exponential curves.

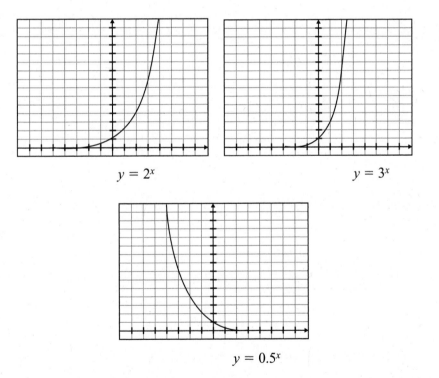

$$y = 2^x$$

$$y = 3^x$$

$$y = 0.5^x$$

A **growth curve** occurs when $b > 1$, and the larger b is, the steeper the growth curve is.

A **decay curve** occurs if $0 < b < 1$, as shown in the last graph above.

All exponential curves in the form of $y = b^x$, whether growth or decay, have certain features. The domain of the function is $(-\infty, \infty)$ since the exponent can be any number. However, the range of exponential functions is $(0, \infty)$ as any positive number raised to a positive power is positive and a positive number raised to a negative power creates a positive fraction. All exponential functions in the form of $y = b^x$ pass through the point (0, 1) as any base b raised to the zero power is one.

Solving basic exponential equations can be accomplished by using the fact that if $b^x = b^y$, then $x = y$. If the bases are the same, the powers must also be equal.

PROBLEM

Solve for x: $2^{x+1} = 8$

SOLUTION

We need to write 8 as a power of 2 so the bases are the same. We know $8 = 2^3$ so we have $2^{x+1} = 2^3$.

Thus $x + 1 = 3$, and $x = 2$.

PROBLEM

Solve for x: $3^{2x-3} = 9$

SOLUTION

$$3^{2x-3} = 3^2$$
$$2x - 3 = 2$$
$$2x = 5$$
$$x = \frac{5}{2}$$

PROBLEM

Solve for x: $3^{4x-1} = \frac{1}{3}$

SOLUTION

$$3^{4x-1} = 3^{-1}$$
$$4x - 1 = -1$$
$$x = 0$$

By using the facts for operations with exponents earlier in the chapter, we can solve more complicated exponential equations.

PROBLEM

Solve for x: $4^{3x-3} = 8^{x+2}$

SOLUTION

We cannot write 8 as a power of 4 but we can write both 4 and 8 as powers of 2.

$$\left(2^2\right)^{3x-3} = \left(2^3\right)^{x+2}$$

(Remember that powers raised to powers means to multiply the powers.)

$2^{6x-6} = 2^{3x+6}$

$6x - 6 = 3x + 6$

$3x = 12$

$x = 4$

LOGARITHMS

Solving exponential equations like the ones above are fairly easy when each side of the equation has common bases. But that technique doesn't work with $3^{x-1} = 6$ as we cannot write 6 as a power of 3.

To solve problems of this type, we introduce **logarithms** (also referred to as **logs**). A logarithm is the inverse of an exponential function. We know that when we find an inverse, we interchange x and y. So if $y = b^x$, the inverse is $x = b^y$. The use of logarithms helps us to solve exponential functions for y, since the notation $\log_b y = x$ is the same as $b^x = y$. The base b cannot be negative.

What you need to know about logarithms for the CLEP exam is this:

$\log_b y = x$ is the same thing as saying $b^x = y$.

When you are asked to find a logarithm (the abbreviation of *logarithm* is *log*), call it x. Then write the expression as an exponential and solve it using the technique above.

PROBLEM

Find $\log_2 8$.

SOLUTION

We do not know $\log_2 8$, so we write $\log_2 8 = x$.

Now we can write write the statement exponentially as $2^x = 8$.

Then write the right side as a power of 2: $2^x = 2^3$

Then $x = 3$. So, $\log_2 8 = 3$.

PROBLEM

Find $\log_3 81$.

SOLUTION

$\log_3 81 = x$

$3^x = 81$

$3^x = 3^4$

$x = 4$

PROBLEM

Find $\log_4 32$.

SOLUTION

$\log_4 32 = x$

$4^x = 32$

$2^{2x} = 2^5$

$2x = 5$

$x = \dfrac{5}{2}$

PROBLEM

Find $\log_8 \sqrt{2}$.

SOLUTION

$\log_8 \sqrt{2} = x$

$8^x = \sqrt{2}$

$2^{3x} = 2^{\frac{1}{2}}$

$3x = \dfrac{1}{2}$

$x = \dfrac{1}{2}\left(\dfrac{1}{3}\right) = \dfrac{1}{6}$

PROBLEM

Find $\log_9 1$.

SOLUTION

$\log_9 1 = x$

$9^x = 1$

$x = 0$

Common Logarithms

If the base is not specified, it is assumed to be 10. A logarithm with a base of 10 is called a **common logarithm**. The notations $\log_{10} x$ and $\log x$ are the same.

PROBLEM

Find $\log 1000$.

SOLUTION

$\log 1000 = x$

Since this is the same as $\log_{10} 1000 = x$,

$10^x = 1000$

$10^x = 10^3$

$x = 3$, or $\log 1000 = 3$

PROBLEM

Find $\log 1$.

SOLUTION

$\log 1 = x$

$10^x = 1$

$10^x = 10^0$

$x = 0$

Logarithm Rules

There are three basic rules for operations with logarithms that are important. These rules work with logs to any base. They are as follows:

Rule 1. $\log a + \log b = \log(a \cdot b)$

Rule 2. $\log a - \log b = \log\left(\dfrac{a}{b}\right)$

Rule 3. $\log a^b = b \log a$

PROBLEM

Find the value of $\log 25 + \log 4$.

SOLUTION

Even though we cannot find the log of 25 or the log of 4, we can use rule 1 to say

$\log 25 + \log 4 = \log(25 \cdot 4) = \log 100$

$\log 100 = x$

$10^x = 100$

$10^x = 10^2$

$x = 2$, or $\log 25 + \log 4 = 2$

PROBLEM

Find the value of $\log_2 80 - \log_2 5$.

SOLUTION

Even though we cannot find the $\log_2 80$ or $\log_2 5$, we can use rule 2 to say

$\log_2 80 - \log_2 5 = \log_2\left(\dfrac{80}{5}\right) = \log_2 16$

$\log_2 16 = x$

$2^x = 16$

$2^x = 2^4$

$x = 4$, or $\log_2 80 - \log_2 5 = 4$

PROBLEM

Find $\log 10^{35}$.

SOLUTION

We can use rule 3 to say $\log 10^{35} = 35 \log 10$

$\log 10 = x$

$10^x = 10$

$x = 1$

Since $35(1) = 35$, $\log 10^{35} = 35$.

LINEAR AND EXPONENTIAL GROWTH

LINEAR GROWTH

Linear equations and functions are used to model situations in which a quantity y grows or declines the same amount over the same time step or change in x. The graph of a linear growth model will be a straight line. We will usually be given the slope m and the y-intercept b and the linear function is given by $f(x)=mx+b$.

PROBLEM

Suppose that a car uses 0.03 gallons of gas per mile and the fuel tank, which holds 15 gallons of gas, is full. Using this information, we can determine a linear model for the remaining amount of fuel in the gas tank after driving x miles.

SOLUTION

Recall that a linear function is one that can be written in the form $f(x)=mx+b$, where m is the slope of the line and b is the y-intercept. The slope is the rate at which the car is using gas, 0.03 gallons per mile. Because the car is using the fuel, the amount of fuel in the tank is decreasing. Therefore, the slope is negative, and we have $m = -.03$.

When $x = 0$ (before the car drives away from the pump), there are 15 gallons of gas in the tank. The y-intercept is (0, 15).

So our function in the form of $f(x)=mx+b$ can be written as $f(x)=-0.03x+15$. We can graph this function as shown below.

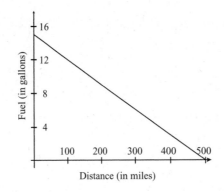

To find how far the car can travel on a tank of gas, we set the function $f(x) = -0.03x + 15$ equal to zero because when there are 0 gallons of fuel, the car cannot go any further.

$f(x) = -0.03x + 15 = 0$

$15 = 0.03x$

$x = \dfrac{15}{0.03} = 500$ miles

The car can go 500 miles on a full tank of gas.

A problem like this is a **linear decay** problem.

PROBLEM

A cellular phone company offers several different service options. One option, for people who plan on using the phone only in emergencies, costs the user $8.95 a month plus $0.33/minute for each minute the phone is used. Write a linear growth function for the monthly cost of the phone in terms of the number of minutes the phone is used. If the phone is used a total of 25 minutes, what would be the monthly cost?

SOLUTION

If x represents the number of minutes used, the cost is $8.95 + 0.33x$.

$f(x) = 0.33x + 8.95$

$f(25) = 0.33(25) + 8.95 = 17.20$

It will cost $17.20 for 25 minutes of cell phone use.

EXPONENTIAL GROWTH

Exponential equations and functions are used to model situations in which the rate of change of y increases faster over the same time step or change in x. When the rate of change is positive, it is called **exponential growth** and when the rate of change is negative, it is called **exponential decay**. The graph of an exponential growth or decay model will be an exponential curve. The equation is in the form of $f(x) = a \cdot b^x$ and the values of a and b are generally given.

Example:

A diamond merchant has determined the values of several white diamonds that have different weights, measured in carats, but are similar in quality. The value of these diamonds is given in the chart below.

Weight (carats)	0.50	0.75	1.00	1.25	1.50	1.75	2.00	3.00	4.00
Value	$4,700	$5,200	$5,800	$6,300	$7,000	$7,700	$8,500	$12,400	$18,300

The exponential growth function that models the value of the diamonds as a function of their weights is $\text{Value} = 3912(1.47)^{\text{carat weight}}$. We can use this model to approximate the value of a 2.5-carat diamond: $\text{Value} = 3912(1.47)^{2.5} = \$10,249$. The Millennium Star is one of the world's largest diamonds at 203 carats. We should not expect to use the $\text{Value} = 3912(1.47)^{\text{carat weight}}$ equation because the Millennium Star is a different type of diamond and a much greater weight than the equation that modeled it. But if it were applied, the cost of this diamond would be $\text{Value} = 3912(1.47)^{203} = \$3.6 \times 10^{37}$. That is why these rare gems are priceless.

PROBLEM

The table below shows the decreasing cost of hard-disk storage space.

Year	1992	1997	2002	2007	2012
Cost per megabyte	$915	$50.39	$2.78	$0.15	$0.01

The exponential decay function is given by $\text{Cost per megabyte} = 915 \times 0.56^{\text{year} - 1992}$. What was the approximate cost per megabyte of disk storage in the year 2005? What will be the approximate cost per megabyte of disk storage in the year 2020?

SOLUTION

In the year 2005, the

$$\text{Cost per megabyte} = 915 \times 0.56^{2005-1992} = 915 \times 0.56^{13} = 0.487 \approx \$0.49.$$

It isn't advisable to use this formula for the year 2020 as no one can forecast whether the cost of hard disk space will adhere to this formula in the future. But the value is given by:

$$\text{Cost per megabyte} = 915 \times 0.56^{2020-1992} = 915 \times 0.56^{28} = 8.14 \times 10^{-5} = \$0.0000814.$$

DRILL QUESTIONS

1. Which one of the following is an equation of a line parallel to the graph of $5x + 9y = 14$?

   (A) $y = -\dfrac{5}{9}x + 14$

   (B) $y = -\dfrac{5}{9}x - 20$

   (C) $y = \dfrac{5}{9}x + 14$

   (D) $y = -\dfrac{9}{5}x - 14$

2. The solution set of the inequality $5 - 7x \geq -9$ is

   (A) $\{x \mid x \leq 2\}$
   (B) $\{x \mid x \geq 2\}$
   (C) $\left\{x \mid x \leq \dfrac{4}{7}\right\}$
   (D) $\left\{x \mid x \geq \dfrac{4}{7}\right\}$

3. Place the following in order from largest to smallest.

   I. $\log 5000 - \log 5$

   II. $\log 50 + \log 2$

   III. $\log 10^4$

   (A) I, II, III
   (B) II, I, III
   (C) III, I, II
   (D) I, III, II

4. The graph below is described by what inequality?

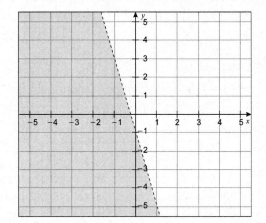

   (A) $y > 1 - 4x$
   (B) $y \geq 1 - 4x$
   (C) $y < -4x - 1$
   (D) $y \leq -4x - 1$

5. What is the solution set for x in the following inequality?

   $$-6 < \dfrac{2}{3}x + 6 < 2$$

   (A) $-12 < x < 0$
   (B) $-6 < x < 0$
   (C) $-18 < x < -12$
   (D) $-18 < x < -6$

6. What is the simplified expression for $-5i^7 + (2i)(i^2 - 2)$?

   (A) $11i$
   (B) $-11i$
   (C) i
   (D) $-i$

7. If $x + 2$ is a factor of $3x^3 - x + k$, what is the value of k?

   (A) 22
   (B) 16
   (C) −16
   (D) −22

8. A piece of lumber that is 28 inches in length is divided into three pieces. The length of the first piece is x inches and the length of the second piece is four times the length of the first piece. Which expression represents the length of the third piece?

   (A) $28 - 4x$
   (B) $28 - 5x$
   (C) $4x - 28$
   (D) $5x - 28$

9. What is the value of y in the following system of equations?

   $4x + 2y = 5$

   $3x + 5y = 9$

   (A) $\dfrac{1}{2}$
   (B) $\dfrac{3}{2}$
   (C) $\dfrac{5}{2}$
   (D) $\dfrac{7}{2}$

10. $2^5 = 32$ is equivalent to which logarithmic expression?

   (A) $\log_5 32 = 2$
   (B) $\log_{32} 5 = 2$
   (C) $\log_2 32 = 5$
   (D) $\log_2 5 = 32$

11. If $f(x) = 2x + 3$ and $g(x) = x^3 - 5$, what is the value of $f(g(-3))$?

   (A) −61
   (B) −32
   (C) 25
   (D) 47

12. If $h(x) = \dfrac{5}{x-2}$, which of the following is equivalent to the inverse of $h(x)$?

   (A) $\dfrac{x-2}{5}$
   (B) $\dfrac{5}{x+2}$
   (C) $\dfrac{2x-5}{5}$
   (D) $\dfrac{2x+5}{5}$

13. What is the domain of $f(x) = \sqrt{6-3x}$?

   (A) $x \geq 2$
   (B) $x \leq 2$
   (C) $x \geq -2$
   (D) $x \leq -2$

14. If $\{(4, -1), (5, -3), (6, -9), (\_\_, -16)\}$ represents a function, which one of the following *cannot* be used to fill in the blank space?

   (A) 5
   (B) 3
   (C) −4
   (D) −9

15. Each point of the function $f(x) = x^2 + 10$ is moved 3 units to the left and 2 units down to create a new function $g(x)$. What would be the y-coordinate of a point on the graph of $g(x)$ whose x-coordinate is −1 on the graph of $f(x)$?

   (A) 6
   (B) 7
   (C) 8
   (D) 9

16. If $f(x)$ is a linear function such that $f(1) = 5$ and $f(4) = -7$, then what is the value of $f(-1)$?

    (A) 11
    (B) 12
    (C) 13
    (D) 14

17. The function $g(x)$ is known to have a range of all real numbers except zero. Which one of the following expressions could represent $g(x)$?

    (A) $4x^2 - 4$

    (B) $\dfrac{4}{x}$

    (C) $\dfrac{4}{x^2}$

    (D) $-\sqrt{x^2 - 4}$

18. A builder estimates that the cost to build a new home is $50,000 plus $90 per square foot of floor space in the house. Use a linear model to determine the size of a house that can be built for $500,000.

    (A) 500
    (B) 2,000
    (C) 5,000
    (D) 6,111

19. The point $(-2, -3)$ is rotated 90° clockwise about the origin. What is its new location?

    (A) $(-3, 2)$
    (B) $(-3, -2)$
    (C) $(3, -2)$
    (D) $(3, 2)$

20. For which one of the following functions is $f(1) = f(-1) = 2$?

    (A) $f(x) = x^2 - 3x + 4$
    (B) $f(x) = 4x^2 - 2$
    (C) $f(x) = x^2 - 2x - 1$
    (D) $f(x) = 3x^2 - x$

ANSWERS TO DRILL QUESTIONS

1. **(B)** Rewrite the equation $5x + 9y = 14$ in slope-intercept form. Then $9y = -5x + 14$, which leads to $y = -\frac{5}{9}x + \frac{14}{9}$, where $-\frac{5}{9}$ is the slope and $\frac{14}{9}$ is the y-intercept. The equation of any line parallel to the graph of $5x + 9y = 14$ must also have a slope of $-\frac{5}{9}$. Only choice (B) satisfies this condition. Choice (A) is the line itself.

2. **(A)** Subtract 5 from each side of $5 - 7x \geq -9$, so that $5 - 7x - 5 \geq -9 - 5$, which simplifies to $-7x \geq -14$. Next, divide each side by -7. Since we are dividing by a negative number, we must switch the order of the inequality. Then $\frac{-7x}{-7} \leq \frac{-14}{-7}$, which becomes $x \leq 2$. This is equivalent to $X = \{x \mid x \leq 2\}$.

3. **(C)** I. $\log 5000 - \log 5 = \log \frac{5000}{5} = \log 1000 \colon 10^x = 1000 \Rightarrow x = 3$

   II. $\log 50 + \log 2 = \log(50 \times 2) = \log 100 \colon 10^x = 100 \Rightarrow x = 2$

   III. $\log 10^4 = 4 \log 10 = 4(1) = 4$

4. **(C)** The slope is -4 and the y-intercept is -1. Since the shading is below the line and the line is dashed, the inequality is $y < -4x - 1$.

5. **(D)** Subtract 6 from each part of the double inequality to get $-6 - 6 < \frac{2}{3}x + 6 - 6 < 2 - 6$, which simplifies to $-12 < \frac{2}{3}x < -4$. Now divide each expression by $\frac{2}{3}$, which is equivalent to multiplying by $\frac{3}{2}$. Thus, $(-12)\left(\frac{3}{2}\right) < \left(\frac{2}{3}x\right)\left(\frac{3}{2}\right) < (-4)\left(\frac{3}{2}\right)$, which leads to $-18 < x < -6$.

6. **(D)** Using the Distributive Law, $-5i^7 + (2i)(i^2 - 2) = -5i^7 + 2i^3 - 4i$. Recall that the powers of i are cyclical in groups of 4, which means that $i = i^5 = i^9 = \ldots, -1 = i^2 = i^6 = i^{10} = \ldots, -i = i^3 = i^7 = i^{11} = \ldots$, and $1 = i^4 = i^8 = i^{12} = \ldots$ Thus, $-5i^7 + 2i^3 - 4i = (-5)(-i) + (2)(-i) - 4i = 5i - 2i - 4i = -i$.

7. **(A)** Based on the Factor Theorem, if $x + 2$ is a factor of $3x^3 - x + k$, then -2 must be a solution for x in the equation $3x^3 - x + k = 0$. This means that $(3)(-2)^3 - (-2) + k = 0$. This equation simplifies to $(3)(-8) + 2 + k = 0$. Thus, $k = 24 - 2 = 22$.

8. **(B)** The length of the first piece is x and the length of the second piece is $4x$. The length of the third piece is found by adding the first two pieces and subtracting this sum from the total of 28 inches. The sum of the first two pieces is $5x$, so the length of the third piece must be $28 - 5x$.

9. **(B)** We can eliminate the variable x from the given system of equations as follows: Multiply the first equation by 3 to get $12x + 6y = 15$. Next, multiply the second equation by 4 to get $12x + 20y = 36$. Now, by the subtraction property of equalities, $(12x + 6y) - (12x + 20y) = 15 - 36$. This equation simplifies to $-14y = -21$. Thus, $y = \dfrac{-21}{-14} = \dfrac{3}{2}$.

10. **(C)** By definition, the expression $\log_b x = y$ is equivalent to $b^y = x$. Substituting 2 for b, 32 for x, and 5 for y, we conclude that $2^5 = 32$ is equivalent to $\log_2 32 = 5$.

11. **(A)** $g(-3) = (-3)^3 - 5 = -27 - 5 = -32$. Thus, $f(g(-3)) = f(-32) = (2)(-32) + 3 = -64 + 3 = -61$.

12. **(D)** The inverse of a function is found by reversing the roles of the two variables, then solving for the new dependent variable. Let $y = h(x)$ so that the initial function can be written as $x = \dfrac{5}{y-2}$. Interchanging the x and y, we get $x = \dfrac{5}{x-2}$. Multiply this equation by $y - 2$ to get $(x)(y - 2) = 5$. This equation simplifies to $xy - 2x = 5$. Next, add $2x$ to each side to get $xy - 2x + 2x = 5 + 2x$, which becomes $xy = 5 + 2x$. Finally, divide both sides by x to get $y = \dfrac{5+2x}{x}$. The right side of this equation, which is equivalent to $\dfrac{2x+5}{x}$, represents the expression for the inverse of $h(x)$.

13. **(B)** The domain of $f(x) = \sqrt{6 - 3x}$ is defined as the allowable values of x. The square root of any function must be at least zero in order to represent a real value. The domain is found by solving $6 - 3x \geq 0$. Subtracting 6 from each side leads to $-3x \geq -6$. Finally, divide both sides by -3 and reverse the order of the inequality. Thus, $\dfrac{-3x}{-3} \leq \dfrac{-6}{-3}$, which becomes $x \leq 2$.

14. **(A)** The definition of a function, as it relates to a set of ordered pairs, is that any specific first number must be associated with a single second number. This implies that a set of ordered pairs is not a function if two ordered pairs contain the same first number but a different second number. The given set contains the elements $(4, -1)$, $(5, -3)$, $(6, -9)$, and $(\_, -16)$. In order for this set to qualify as a function, we cannot repeat 4, 5, or 6 as a first number of the last ordered pair.

15. **(D)** Substitute -1 for x in the function $f(x)$ to get $(-1)^2 + 10 = 1 + 10 = 11$. The corresponding point on the graph of $f(x)$ is $(-1, 11)$. In order to find the corresponding point for $g(x)$, this point will be moved 3 units to the left and 2 units down. Thus, the point $(-1, 11)$ will become the point $(-4, 9)$ on the graph of $g(x)$. So, the y-coordinate becomes 9.

16. **(C)** The points on the graph of this linear function are $(1, 5)$ and $(4, -7)$. The slope of the line is $m = \dfrac{5+7}{1-4} = \dfrac{12}{-3} = -4$. Using the point-slope formula with the point $(1, 5)$, we get $y - 5 = -4(x - 1)$ which simplifies to $y = -4x + 9$. This is the same as $f(x) = -4x + 9$ and $f(-1) = -4(-1) + 9 = 13$.

17. **(B)** The range is represented by the $g(x)$ values. For $g(x) = \frac{4}{x}$, $g(x)$ can assume any value (including negative numbers) except zero. Also, note that $x \neq 0$. A graph of $g(x) = \frac{4}{x}$ would also confirm that the range is all numbers except zero. (C) $\frac{4}{x^2}$ has a range of only positive real numbers.

18. **(C)** Price $= 50000 + 90(\text{square feet}) = 500000$

    $90(\text{square feet}) = 450000$

    $\text{square feet} = \dfrac{450000}{90} = 5000$

19. **(A)** If the point (x, y) is rotated 90° clockwise about the origin, its new location is given by $(y, -x)$. Let $x = -2$ and $y = -3$. Then for the point $(-2, -3)$, its new location after being rotated 90° clockwise about the origin is found by interchanging the coordinates, then switching the sign of the new second coordinate. The correct answer is $(-3, 2)$.

20.

	$f(1)$	$f(-1)$
(A)	$1 - 3 + 4 = 2$	$1 + 3 + 4 = 8$
(B)	$4 - 2 = 2$	$4 - 2 = 2$
(C)	$1 - 2 - 1 = -2$	$1 + 2 - 1 = 2$
(D)	$3 - 1 = 2$	$3 + 1 = 4$

COUNTING AND PROBABILITY

SAMPLE SPACES AND COUNTING

In an event or activity that has a few or many possible outcomes, a sample space lists all of those possible outcomes.

Example:

A coin is tossed. The sample space is {heads, tails}.

Example:

A woman is expecting a delivery of a sofa between 1pm and 2pm. In terms of delivery time, the sample space is {early, on time, late, no show}.

PROBLEM

A die is rolled. Write the sample space.

SOLUTION

$$\{1, 2, 3, 4, 5, 6\}$$

PROBLEM

A piggy bank contains many nickels, dimes, and quarters. Two coins are chosen at random. Write the sample space of possible sums.

SOLUTION

$$\{0.10, 0.15, 0.30, 0.20, 0.35, 0.50\}$$

THE COUNTING PRINCIPLE

When dealing with the occurrence of more than one event or activity, it is important to be able to quickly determine how many outcomes exist, rather than listing them all in the sample space. If there are "*m* ways" for one activity to occur and "*n* ways" for a second activity to occur, the counting principle states that there are "*m* · *n* ways" for both to occur.

Example:

A vending machine sells snacks and soft drinks. If there are 8 different snacks and 5 different soft drinks, there are 8 · 5 = 40 different ways to choose a snack and a soft drink.

Example:

A popular car comes in 10 different colors, 4 different interiors, 3 engine sizes, and with or without a navigation system. There are 10 · 4 · 3 · 2 = 240 configurations of the car that are possible.

PROBLEM

The menu for a ship's dining room has 6 different appetizers, 6 different entrées, and 4 different desserts. How many different 3-course meals can a passenger order?

SOLUTION

$$6 \cdot 6 \cdot 4 = 144 \text{ meals}$$

PROBLEM

When a new area code is introduced, how many more 7-digit telephone numbers are available, assuming that the first digit cannot start with a 0 or a 1?

SOLUTION

$$8(10)(10)(10)(10)(10)(10) = 8{,}000{,}000 \text{ telephone numbers}$$

FACTORIAL

The factorial of a positive integer n, written as $n!$, is the product of all positive integers less than or equal to n.

$5! = 5 \cdot 4 \cdot 3 \cdot 2 \cdot 1 = 120$

$8! = 8 \cdot 7 \cdot 6 \cdot 5 \cdot 4 \cdot 3 \cdot 2 \cdot 1 = 40{,}320$

$\dfrac{6!}{3!} = \dfrac{6 \cdot 5 \cdot 4 \cdot 3 \cdot 2 \cdot 1}{3 \cdot 2 \cdot 1} = 120$

$0!$ is defined as 1.

PROBLEMS

Find the following:

(A) $6!$ (B) $\dfrac{7!}{3!}$ (C) $\dfrac{10!}{9!}$ (D) $\dfrac{10!}{5!\,5!}$

SOLUTIONS

(A) $6! = 6(5)(4)(3)(2)(1) = 720$

(B) $\dfrac{7!}{3!} = \dfrac{(7)(6)(5)(4)(3)(2)(1)}{(3)(2)(1)} = 840$

(C) $\dfrac{10!}{9!} = \dfrac{10(9)(8)(7)(6)(5)(4)(3)(2)(1)}{9(8)(7)(6)(5)(4)(3)(2)(1)} = 10$

(D) $\dfrac{10!}{5!5!} = \dfrac{10(9)(8)(7)(6)(5)(4)(3)(2)(1)}{5(4)(3)(2)(1)(5)(4)(3)(2)(1)} = 252$

PERMUTATIONS

A **permutation** is a set of objects in which position (or order) is important. An example is a "combination" to a safe, which is really a permutation. If the "combination" is 5-7-8, the order is important. 8-5-7 will not open the safe: it has to be exactly 5-7-8.

Permutations with repetition: An object *can* be repeated. In the lock example, it is possible for a "combination" to be 4-4-2 or 9-9-9. If we have n possibilities to choose from each time, the counting principle says that there will be $n \cdot n \cdot n \dots$ permutations.

Example:

In the lock example, there are 10 possibilities (0, 1, … 9) and we want 3 of them. There are $10 \cdot 10 \cdot 10 = 10^3 = 1,000$ permutations. Note that this assumes that it is possible for a number to repeat.

Permutations without repetition: An object cannot be repeated. Once we choose it, it can no longer be chosen.

Example:

In the lock example above, suppose that you cannot use a number over again. Once you use it, you cannot re-use it. The first number has a choice of 10. Once you use it, you now have only 9 choices for the second number. Once you use it, you only have 8 choices for the third number. So there are $10 \cdot 9 \cdot 8 = 720$ permutations. This asks for a permutation of 8 things taken 3 at a time. The notation for this is $_8P_3$.

PROBLEM

An ice cream shop has 25 flavors. If a person orders a triple-decker cone, how many different cones are possible if (A) it is allowed to repeat a flavor and (B) no repetition of flavors is allowed?

SOLUTIONS

(A) $25(25)(25) = 15,625$

(B) $25(24)(23) = 13,800$

PROBLEM

A computer password has 5 characters. Digits and letters (both lowercase and uppercase) can be used. How many different passwords are available if (A) it is allowed to repeat a character and (B) no repetition of characters is allowed? Do not actually compute the answer.

SOLUTIONS

There are 26 upper case letters, 26 lower case letters, and 10 digits. So there are 62 characters for each position of the password.

(A) $62(62)(62)(62)(62)$

(B) $62(61)(60)(59)(58)$

COMBINATIONS

A combination is a set of objects in which position (or order) is *not* important. An example would be a fruit salad that is a combination of cantaloupe, honeydew, and watermelon. We don't care what order the fruits are in. Watermelon, cantaloupe, and honeydew is the same fruit salad as honeydew, watermelon, and cantaloupe.

The best way to determine the number of combinations possible is to use a formula. When you have "n" objects and we wish to choose "r" of them, there are $_nC_r = \dfrac{n!}{r!(n-r)!}$ combinations possible. An alternate notation for combinations is $\binom{n}{r}$. When calculating combinations using this formula, we can usually do cancellation to make the calculations easier.

Example:

A basketball team has 9 members and 5 players are on the floor. The number of combinations of team members on the floor that are possible is given by:

$$_9C_5 = \frac{9!}{5!(9-5)!} = \frac{9!}{5! \cdot 4!} = \frac{9 \cdot 8 \cdot 7 \cdot 6 \cdot 5 \cdot 4 \cdot 3 \cdot 2 \cdot 1}{5 \cdot 4 \cdot 3 \cdot 2 \cdot 1 \cdot 4 \cdot 3 \cdot 2 \cdot 1} = \frac{9 \cdot 8 \cdot 7 \cdot 6 \cdot 5 \cdot 4 \cdot 3 \cdot 2 \cdot 1}{5 \cdot 4 \cdot 3 \cdot 2 \cdot 1 \cdot 4 \cdot 3 \cdot 2 \cdot 1} = 126$$

Example:

7 boys are on a camping trip and have two tents. 4 boys go into one tent and 3 boys go into the other. The number of ways to divide the boys is given by:

$$_7C_4 = \frac{7!}{4!(7-4)!} = \frac{7!}{4! \cdot 3!} = \frac{7 \cdot 6 \cdot 5 \cdot 4 \cdot 3 \cdot 2 \cdot 1}{4 \cdot 3 \cdot 2 \cdot 1 \cdot 3 \cdot 2 \cdot 1} = \frac{7 \cdot 6 \cdot 5 \cdot 4 \cdot 3 \cdot 2 \cdot 1}{4 \cdot 3 \cdot 2 \cdot 1 \cdot 3 \cdot 2 \cdot 1} = 35$$

It is important to be able to determine whether a problem defines a permutation or a combination.

Permutation	Combination
Picking players to pitch, catch, and play shortstop from a group of players.	Picking three team members from a group of players.
In a dog show, choosing 1st place, 2nd place, and 3rd place from a group of dogs.	In a dog show, choosing 3 dogs that will go to the finals from a group of dogs.
From a color paint brochure, choosing a color for the walls and a color for the trim.	From a color paint brochure, choosing two colors to paint the room.

PROBLEM

An essay exam has 10 questions and students are instructed to answer exactly 4 of them. How many ways can this be done?

SOLUTION

$$_{10}C_4 \text{ or } \binom{10}{4} = \frac{10!}{4! \cdot 6!} = \frac{10 \cdot 9 \cdot 8 \cdot 7 \cdot 6 \cdot 5 \cdot 4 \cdot 3 \cdot 2 \cdot 1}{4 \cdot 3 \cdot 2 \cdot 1 \cdot 6 \cdot 5 \cdot 4 \cdot 3 \cdot 2 \cdot 1} = 210$$

PROBLEM

A law firm has 25 associate lawyers and 2 of them will be promoted to partner in the firm. How many ways can this be done?

SOLUTION

$$_{25}C_2 \text{ or } \binom{25}{2} = \frac{25!}{2! \cdot 23!} = \frac{25 \cdot 24 \cdot 23 \cdot 22 \cdot ... \cdot 3 \cdot 2 \cdot 1}{2 \cdot 1 \cdot 23 \cdot 22 \cdot ... \cdot 3 \cdot 2 \cdot 1} = \frac{25 \cdot 24}{2 \cdot 1} = 300$$

PROBLEM

A golfer owns 17 golf clubs. When he plays a tournament he is allowed only 14 clubs in his golf bag. How many ways can he select the clubs if one of the clubs must be a putter?

SOLUTION

Since one of the clubs is a putter, there are now 16 clubs available. And since the putter must be used, the golfer must choose 13 of them.

$$_{16}C_{13} \text{ or } \binom{16}{13} = \frac{16!}{13! \cdot 3!} = \frac{16 \cdot 15 \cdot 14 \cdot 13 \cdot 12 \cdot ... \cdot 3 \cdot 2 \cdot 1}{13 \cdot 12 \cdot ... \cdot 3 \cdot 2 \cdot 1 \cdot 3 \cdot 2 \cdot 1} = \frac{16 \cdot 15 \cdot 14}{3 \cdot 2 \cdot 1} = 560$$

PROBABILITY

Probability refers to how likely an event is to occur. The probability of an event is a number between 0 and 1 inclusive. A probability of 0 means the event cannot occur, a probability of 1 means the event must occur, and a probability of 0.5 means that the event is as likely to occur than not. Probability can be expressed as a fraction, decimal, or percent.

Example:

A coin having two heads is tossed. The probability of heads appearing is 1. The probability of tails appearing is 0.

Example:

A fair coin is tossed. The probability of heads occurring is 0.5. The probability of tails occurring is 0.5.

> In general, the probability of an event happening
>
> $$= \frac{\text{number of ways the event can happen}}{\text{total number of outcomes}}.$$

Example:

A class has 20 students with 14 boys and 6 girls. The teacher calls on a student at random. The probability that she chooses a boy is $\frac{14}{20} = \frac{7}{10} = 0.7 = 70\%$.

Example:

From a group of 15 whiteboard markers, 10 are dried up. If I choose a marker at random, the probability that I choose a marker that works is $\frac{5}{15} = \frac{1}{3} = 0.\overline{3} = 33.\overline{3}\%$.

Example:

5 people line up at random and one of them is named Jack. The probability that Jack is first in line is $\frac{1}{5}$.

A more difficult example using permutations

5 people line up at random. If Jack and Jill are boyfriend and girlfriend, they wish to find the probability that they will be next to each other

Probability that Jack and Jill are together

$$= \frac{\text{Number of ways Jack and Jill can be together}}{\text{Number of ways 5 people can line up}}$$

Number of ways 5 people can line up $= 5! = 5 \cdot 4 \cdot 3 \cdot 2 \cdot 1 = 120$

It is easy to simply generate all the possibilities with Jack and Jill together.

1	**2**	**3**	**4**	**5**
Jack	Jill			
	Jack	Jill		
		Jack	Jill	
			Jack	Jill

1	**2**	**3**	**4**	**5**
Jill	Jack			
	Jill	Jack		
		Jill	Jack	
			Jill	Jack

Probability that Jack and Jill are together $= \dfrac{8}{120} = \dfrac{1}{15} = 0.0\overline{6} = 6.\overline{6}\%$

A more difficult example with combinations

There are 5 ice cream flavors, two of which are chocolate and vanilla. I choose 3 different flavors at random. What is the probability that I have both chocolate and vanilla?

Probability of having chocolate and vanilla

$$= \dfrac{\text{Number of dishes with chocolate, vanilla, and 1 other flavor}}{\text{Number of dishes with 3 flavors}}$$

Number of dishes with chocolate, vanilla, and 1 other flavor $= 3$

Number of dishes with 3 flavors $= {}_5C_3 = \dfrac{5!}{3!\,2!} = \dfrac{5 \cdot 4 \cdot 3 \cdot 2 \cdot 1}{3 \cdot 2 \cdot 1 \cdot 2 \cdot 1} = 10$

Probability of having chocolate and vanilla $= \dfrac{3}{10} = 0.3 = 30\%$.

When there are relatively few outcomes possible, a sample space can be made and the probability of an event determined by counting the number of objects in the sample space as well as the number of objects in the sample space that have the characteristics you wish. For example, suppose a day is chosen at random. What is the probability that the day is on a weekend? The sample space is:

{Monday, Tuesday, Wednesday, Thursday, Friday, Saturday, and Sunday}. There are 7 objects in the sample space and 2 of them are on the weekend, so the probability is $\dfrac{2}{7}$.

Still, it can be easy to make a mistake. If we define the sample space as {weekday, weekend day}, you might think the probability of choosing a weekend day as $\dfrac{1}{2}$, which is incorrect. So if you use the sample space technique to determine probability, all elements in the sample space must be equally likely.

PROBLEM

A jar contains 5 red marbles, 8 green marbles, 10 blue marbles, and 4 white marbles. If I choose a marble at random what is the probability that it is:

(A) green   (B) red   (C) not white

SOLUTION

(A) $\dfrac{8}{27}$

(B) $\dfrac{5}{27}$

(C) $\dfrac{23}{27}$

PROBLEM

A month of the year is chosen at random. What is the probability that it contains the letter y?

SOLUTION

Of the 12 months, January, February, May, and July contain the letter y. The probability is $\dfrac{4}{12} = \dfrac{1}{3}$.

PROBLEM

Tickets numbered 1 to 50 are mixed up and a ticket chosen at random. What is the probability that the ticket drawn has a number divisible by 4?

SOLUTION

The numbers divisible by 4 are 4, 8, 12, ..., 48. There are 12 of them so the probability is $\dfrac{12}{50} = \dfrac{6}{25}$.

PROBLEM

A librarian shelves 9 books, one of which is an algebra book and one of which is a history book. What is the probability that both the algebra and history books are on the ends?

SOLUTION

There are 9! ways of arranging 9 books.

If the algebra book goes first and the history book goes last, there are 7! ways of arranging the other 7 books.

If the history book goes first and the algebra book goes last, there are 7! ways of arranging the other 7 books.

So the probability is

$$\frac{7!}{9!} + \frac{7!}{9!} = \frac{7 \cdot 6 \cdot 5 \ldots 1}{9 \cdot 8 \cdot 7 \cdot 6 \cdot 5 \ldots 1} + \frac{7 \cdot 6 \cdot 5 \ldots 1}{9 \cdot 8 \cdot 7 \cdot 6 \cdot 5 \ldots 1} = \frac{1}{72} + \frac{1}{72} = \frac{1}{36}$$

PROBLEM

If I draw two cards from a deck of 52 cards, what is the probability that both are aces?

SOLUTION

There are $_{52}C_2 = \dfrac{52!}{2! \cdot 50!} = \dfrac{52 \cdot 51 \cdot 50 \cdot 49 \cdot \ldots \cdot 3 \cdot 2 \cdot 1}{2 \cdot 1 \cdot 50 \cdot 49 \cdot \ldots \cdot 3 \cdot 2 \cdot 1} = \dfrac{52 \cdot 51}{2 \cdot 1} = 1,326$ ways of choosing 2 cards.

To get 2 aces, there are $_4C_2 = \dfrac{4!}{2! \cdot 2!} = \dfrac{4 \cdot 3 \cdot 2 \cdot 1}{2 \cdot 1 \cdot 2 \cdot 1} = 6$ combinations:

1) clubs, hearts, 2) clubs, diamonds, 3) clubs, spades,

4) hearts, diamonds, 5) hearts, spades, 6) diamonds, spades.

So the probability of 2 aces is $\dfrac{6}{1,326} = \dfrac{1}{221}$.

PROBLEM

A fair coin is tossed 3 times. What is the probability that 2 or more heads would show after the toss?

SOLUTION

Generate a sample space of all possibilities:

Toss 1	H	H	H	H	T	T	T	T
Toss 2	H	H	T	T	H	H	T	T
Toss 3	H	T	H	T	H	T	H	T

There are 8 possibilities and 4 of them show 2 or more heads.

So the probability is $\frac{4}{8} = \frac{1}{2}$

We can also do this without generating the sample space. There are $2^3 = 8$ possibilities and $_3C_2$ ways to get 2 heads and $_3C_3$ to get 3 heads. $_3C_2 = \frac{3!}{2! \cdot 1!} = 3$ and $_3C_3 = \frac{3!}{3! \cdot 0!} = 1$. So there are 4 ways to get 2 or more heads and its probability is $\frac{4}{8} = \frac{1}{2}$. (This method is easier when there are a large number of coins being tossed, making the sample space too cumbersome to create.)

ODDS

Probability and odds have the same meaning—the chance of a random event occurring. However, they are not expressed in the same way. While the probability of an event is the ratio of the number of successful ways the event can occur compared with the *total number* of ways the event can occur, the odds of an event occurring is the ratio that compares the number of ways the event can occur with the number of ways the event cannot occur:

The odds in favor—the ratio of the number of ways that an outcome can occur compared to how many ways it cannot occur:

Number of successes: Number of failures.

The odds against—the ratio of the number of ways that an outcome cannot occur compared to in how many ways it can occur:

Number of failures: Number of successes.

Example:

If I roll a die, the probability of rolling a 3 is $\frac{1}{6}$. Rolling a 3 is a success, while rolling a 1, 2, 4, 5, 6 are failures. So the odds in favor of rolling a 3 are 1 to 5. The odds against rolling a 3 is 5 to 1.

PROBLEM

The odds against being chosen for a committee are 7 to 2. What is the probability of being chosen for the committee?

SOLUTION

Since this is "odds against," there are 7 failures and 2 successes. So the probability of being chosen for the committee is $\frac{2}{2+7} = \frac{2}{9}$. In gambling, odds are usually stated as "odds against." If a horse has odds of 4 to 1 in a race, the probability of the horse winning is considered to be $\frac{1}{5}$.

MUTUALLY EXCLUSIVE AND COMPLEMENTARY EVENTS

Events that are mutually exclusive (also called disjoint) are events that cannot happen at the same time. Examples of choosing mutually exclusive events are:

- Choose one student in a group. You either choose a boy or a girl.

- Turn on a lamp. It either turns on or it doesn't.

- View the results of your favorite baseball team. The team either won or lost.

- You and a friend buy a raffle ticket. You and your friend cannot both win. Note that it is possible that neither of you will win, but you and your friend both winning are still disjoint events.

Two events are described as complementary if they are the only two possible outcomes. The first three examples above are complementary events. For any event A, the probability of A complement is given by $P(A^C) = 1 - P(A)$.

Example:

- If the probability of choosing a boy is 62%, the probability of choosing a girl is $1 - 0.62 = 38\%$.

- If the probability that a lamp turns on is 98%, the probability that it does not turn on is $1 - 0.98 = 2\%$.

- If the probability that a baseball team wins a game is said to be 45%; the probability that the team loses is $1 - 0.45 = 55\%$.

- If the probability that you win a raffle is 1%, the probability that your friend wins is not 99%. That is because although you and your friend winning are mutually exclusive events (you both cannot win at the same time), they are not complementary. That is because other people are also entered into the raffle as well.

If two events A and B are mutually exclusive, the probability of A or B = Prob(A) + Prob(B).

Example:

- If a cooler contains 5 Cokes, 8 Pepsis, 10 Sprites, and 7 waters, the probability of choosing a Coke or a Pepsi at random $= \dfrac{5}{30} + \dfrac{8}{30} = \dfrac{13}{30}$. The probability of not choosing water is $1 - \dfrac{7}{30} = \dfrac{23}{30}$. That is because choosing water and not choosing water are complementary events.

- People were asked what their favorite pet was. 69 said dogs, 53 said cats, 21 said fish, 5 said "other." 32 said they did not like pets. The probability of choosing someone who preferred a dog or a cat $= \dfrac{69}{180} + \dfrac{53}{180} = \dfrac{122}{180} = \dfrac{61}{90}$. Note that if the question asked the probability of choosing someone who *liked* dogs or cats, we could not answer. *Preferring* a dog or cat are mutually exclusive events—you either prefer one or the other. But *liking* dogs and cats are not mutually exclusive events as it is possible to like both.

Probability questions can be answered by examining a Venn diagram. In a school, students can only be in one fall sport. This Venn diagram shows how many students participate in soccer or football. The probability that a student is chosen who plays soccer or football

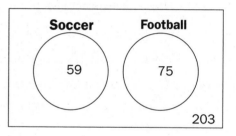

$= \dfrac{59 + 75}{59 + 75 + 203} = \dfrac{134}{337} = 39.8\%$. The probability of choosing a student who does not play soccer is $1 - \dfrac{59}{337} = \dfrac{278}{337}$ $= 82.5\%$ as playing soccer and not playing soccer are complementary events.

NON-MUTUALLY EXCLUSIVE EVENTS

If two events A and B are *not* mutually exclusive (meaning that they *can* occur at the same time), we use the general formula to find the probability of A or B occurring. The word "or" means "A or B" or both.

Probability of A or B occurring $=$ Prob(A) + Prob(B) $-$ Prob(both A and B occurring)

Problems asking for this probability are either expressed in a paragraph, a Venn diagram, or a table.

Example:

- In a class of 25 students, 15 are seniors, 12 have brown hair, and 8 are seniors with brown hair. We want the probability of choosing a senior *or* a student with brown hair. Note that being a senior and having brown hair are *not disjoint* events − they *can* happen at the same time. So

$$\text{Prob(senior or brown hair)} = \text{Prob(senior)} + \text{Prob(brown hair)} - \text{Prob(senior with brown hair)}$$

$$\text{Prob(senior or brown hair)} = \frac{15}{25} + \frac{12}{25} - \frac{8}{25} = \frac{19}{25} = 76\%.$$

- A poll was taken as to how people got to work. The result is shown in the Venn diagram. To find the probability that someone takes a car *or* a train (which are *not* mutually exclusive events), the easiest way is finding

$$\frac{120+15+55}{120+15+55+10} = \frac{190}{200} = 95\%.$$ This is not a violation

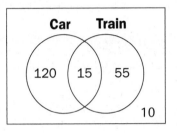

of the general formula as there are 135 people who drive a car, 70 people who take the train, and 15 people who do both.

$$\frac{135}{200} + \frac{70}{200} - \frac{15}{200} = \frac{190}{200} = 95\%.$$

- The pass/fail status of 30 students is shown in the following table:

	Passing	Failing	Total
Boy	15	3	18
Girl	7	5	12
Total	22	8	30

The probability of choosing a student who is a boy *and* passing is $\frac{15}{30} = \frac{1}{2} = 50\%$.

The probability of choosing a student who is a boy *or* passing is found by either

$$\frac{15+7+3}{30} = \frac{25}{30} = \frac{5}{6} = 83.3\% \quad \text{or} \quad \frac{22+18-15}{30} = \frac{25}{30} = \frac{5}{6} = 83.3\%.$$

PROBLEM

At a Florida road intersection, it is shown that 48% of the drivers go straight, 26% of the drivers turn right, 23% of the drivers turn left, and 3% of the drivers make U-turns. What is the probability that a driver turns right or left?

SOLUTION

Since these events are mutually exclusive, the probability that a driver turns right or left = 26% + 23% = 49%.

PROBLEM

A car rental lot has 35 Chevrolets, 44 Fords, 75 Toyotas, 68 Nissans, and 45 Hyundais. A car is chosen at random. What is the probability that the car is an American car?

SOLUTION

Since these events are mutually exclusive, the probability that the car is American is calculated as follows:

$$\frac{35 + 44}{267} = \frac{79}{267} = 29.6$$

PROBLEM

A number is chosen from 1 to 20. What is the probability that it is divisible by 2 or divisible by 3?

SOLUTION

Divisible by 2: 2, 4, 6, 8, 10, 12, 14, 16, 18, 20

Divisible by 3: 3, 6, 9, 12, 15, 18

There are 10 numbers divisible by 2, 6 numbers divisible by 3, but 6, 12, and 18 are counted twice.

So there are 13 numbers divisible by 2 or 3 and the probability is $\frac{13}{20}$.

PROBLEM

During a particular week, a doctor saw 125 patients. He treated 75 people with high blood pressure, 62 people with arthritis, and 41 people who had both. If a patient is chosen at random, what is the probability that the patient has arthritis or high blood pressure?

SOLUTION

Prob(arthritis or high BP) = Prob(arthritis) + Prob(high BP) − Prob(both)

$$\text{Prob(arthritis or high BP)} = \frac{75}{125} + \frac{62}{125} - \frac{41}{125} = \frac{96}{125}$$

PROBLEM

An Internet poll asks people whether they ever took a cruise, went on a bus tour, or both. The results are shown in the Venn diagram.

Find the probability of a person who went

(A) on a cruise only

(B) on a bus tour only

(C) on both a cruise and a bus tour

(D) on a cruise or a bus tour

(E) on a cruise or a bus tour, but not both

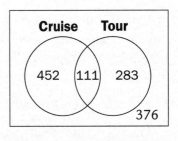

SOLUTIONS

(A) Prob(cruise only) $= \dfrac{452}{1222}$

(B) Prob(bus tour only) $= \dfrac{283}{1222}$

(C) Prob(both) $= \dfrac{111}{1222}$

(D) Prob(cruise or bus tour) $= \dfrac{452+111+283}{1222} = \dfrac{846}{1222}$

(E) Prob(cruise or bus tour but not both) $= \dfrac{452+283}{1222} = \dfrac{735}{1222}$

PROBLEM

The chart shows the on-time record of two airlines.

	On-time	Late
West Jet	52	75
United	38	60

Find the probability of a flight being from

(A) West Jet or on-time.

(B) United Airlines or late.

SOLUTIONS

(A) Prob(West Jet or on-time) $= \dfrac{52+75+38}{225} = \dfrac{165}{225} = \dfrac{11}{15}$

(B) Prob(United or late) $= \dfrac{38 + 60 + 75}{225} = \dfrac{173}{225}$

CONDITIONAL PROBABILITY

Florida is more likely to have rain if it is summer, rather than winter. The probability of rain in Florida is dependent on the month of the year. This is called conditional probability. Conditional probability is the probability event A occurs, given that event B occurs. We write this as Prob $(A|B)$.

Examples of conditional probability include:

Finding the probability that a student is on the honor roll, given that he plays a school sport.

Finding the probability that a student is absent, given that it is a Friday.

Finding the probability that a man watches basketball on TV, given that he plays basketball.

Finding the probability that a woman exercises, given that she is married.

Finding the probability that if a person goes to a seafood restaurant, he will order seafood.

Example:

Suppose we have a class composed of the following:

	Senior	Junior	Total
Boy	8	4	12
Girl	3	5	8
Total	11	9	20

A student is chosen at random.

The probability of choosing a boy is $\dfrac{12}{20} = \dfrac{3}{5} = 60\%$.

The probability of choosing a senior is $\dfrac{11}{20} = 55\%$.

The probability of choosing a boy and a senior is $\dfrac{8}{20} = \dfrac{2}{5} = 40\%$

The probability of choosing a boy or a senior is $\dfrac{8+4+3}{20} = \dfrac{15}{20} = \dfrac{3}{4} = 75\%$.

Note that all of these have a denominator of 20.

Suppose we wish the probability of choosing a senior *given* that we have chosen a boy. This is an example of conditional probability. The condition is choosing a boy. Since there are 12 boys and 8 of them are seniors, the denominator is no longer 20 but 12. So the probability of choosing a senior given that we have chosen a boy is Prob(Senior|Boy) $= \dfrac{8}{12} = \dfrac{2}{3} = 66.\overline{6}\%$. Since, as we saw above, the probability of choosing a senior is 55%, it is more likely to choose a senior, given that we choose a boy.

If we want the probability of choosing a boy *given* that we have chosen a senior, we see that there are 11 seniors and 8 of them are boys, so Prob(Boy|Senior) $= \dfrac{8}{11} = 72.7\%$.

PROBLEMS

	Senior	Junior	Total
Boy	8	4	12
Girl	3	5	8
Total	11	9	20

Using the chart, find

(A) the probability of choosing a girl given that we have chosen a junior.

(B) the probability of choosing a junior, given that we have chosen a girl.

SOLUTIONS

(A) Prob(Girl|Junior) $= \dfrac{5}{9}$

(B) Prob(Junior|Girl) $= \dfrac{5}{8}$

INDEPENDENT EVENTS

Two events are independent if knowing that one occurring does not change the probability of the other occurring. Flipping coins are independent events. If the first 5 flips are heads, the 6th coin has a 50% probability of being heads, assuming the coin is fair.

The weather in California today is independent of the weather in New York. If it is sunny in California, we are not willing to predict the weather in New York. However, the weather in Miami and the weather in Fort Lauderdale are not independent. Since the cities are only 20 miles apart, if it is raining in Miami, there is a good chance that it also will be raining in Fort Lauderdale.

Independent events are not the same as disjoint events. Disjoint events cannot happen at the same time. Independent events are events whose occurrences have no influence on each other.

To determine whether two events are independent we check to see whether Prob(A) · Prob(B) = Prob(both A and B occurring). If that is true, the events are independent.

Alternately, if Prob($A|B$) = Prob(A), the events are independent. If the probability of A given B is the same as the probability of A, then B has no impact on A, which is the definition of independence.

Example:

Using the chart, determine whether choosing a boy and choosing a senior are independent events.

	Senior	Junior	Total
Boy	8	4	12
Girl	3	5	8
Total	11	9	20

Prob(boy) Prob(senior) $\overset{?}{=}$ Prob(senior boy)

$$\frac{12}{20} \cdot \frac{11}{20} \overset{?}{=} \frac{8}{20} \quad 0.6 \cdot 0.55 \overset{?}{=} 0.4 \quad 0.33 \neq 0.4$$

Since 0.33 does not equal 0.4, choosing a boy and choosing a senior are not independent. This goes hand-in-hand with what we previously showed. It was more likely to choose a senior if we had chosen a boy. Gender makes a difference.

Alternately, we can check whether Prob(Boy|Senior) = Prob(Boy). Since $\frac{8}{11} \neq \frac{12}{20}$, choosing a boy and choosing a senior are not independent.

Determine whether choosing a girl and choosing a junior are independent events.

Prob(girl) · Prob(junior) $\overset{?}{=}$ Prob(junior girl)

$$\frac{8}{20} \cdot \frac{9}{20} \overset{?}{=} \frac{5}{20} \quad 0.4 \cdot 0.45 \overset{?}{=} 0.25 \quad 0.18 \neq 0.25$$

Since 0.18 does not equal 0.25, choosing a girl and choosing a junior are not independent. It is more likely to choose a junior if we had chosen a girl. Gender makes a difference.

PROBLEMS

In an office building, both lawyers and doctors rent offices. Some smoke and some do not smoke. A person is chosen at random.

	Smoker	Non-smoker
Lawyer	24	38
Doctor	6	32

Using the chart, find the following probabilities:

(A) choosing a lawyer

(B) choosing a doctor

(C) choosing a smoker

(D) choosing a non-smoker

(E) choosing a lawyer who smokes

(F) choosing a doctor who does not smoke

(G) choosing a lawyer or a smoker

(H) choosing a doctor or a non-smoker

(I) choosing a lawyer, given that you choose a smoker

(J) choosing a doctor, given that you choose a non-smoker

(K) choosing a smoker, given that you choose a lawyer

(L) choosing a non-smoker, given that you choose a doctor

(M) Are choosing a lawyer and choosing a doctor mutually exclusive?

(N) Are choosing a lawyer and choosing a smoker mutually exclusive?

(O) Determine whether choosing a lawyer and choosing a smoker are independent events.

SOLUTIONS

(A) $\text{Prob}(\text{lawyer}) = \dfrac{62}{100} = 62\%$

(B) $\text{Prob}(\text{doctor}) = \dfrac{38}{100} = 38\%$

(C) $\text{Prob}(\text{smoker}) = \dfrac{30}{100} = 30\%$

(D) $\text{Prob}(\text{non-smoker}) = \dfrac{70}{100} = 70\%$

(E) $\text{Prob}(\text{lawyer who smokes}) = \dfrac{24}{100} = 24\%$

(F) $\text{Prob}(\text{doctor who does not smoke}) = \dfrac{32}{100} = 32\%$

(G) $\text{Prob}(\text{lawyer or smoker}) = \dfrac{24 + 38 + 6}{100} = \dfrac{68}{100} = 68\%$

(H) $\text{Prob}(\text{doctor or non-smoker}) = \dfrac{6 + 32 + 38}{100} = \dfrac{76}{100} = 76\%$

(I) $\text{Prob}(\text{lawyer}|\text{smoker}) = \dfrac{24}{30} = \dfrac{4}{5} = 80\%$

(J) $\text{Prob}(\text{doctor}|\text{non-smoker}) = \dfrac{32}{70} = \dfrac{16}{35} = 45.7\%$

(K) $\text{Prob}(\text{smoker}|\text{lawyer}) = \dfrac{24}{62} = \dfrac{12}{31} = 38.7\%$

(L) $\text{Prob}(\text{non-smoker}|\text{doctor}) = \dfrac{32}{38} = \dfrac{16}{19} = 84.2\%$

(M) Yes. In this building, you cannot be a lawyer and doctor at the same time.

(N) No. In this building you can be a lawyer and a smoker at the same time.

(O) No. Prob(lawyer) · Prob(smoker) = 0.62(0.3) = 0.186. Prob(lawyer smoker) = 0.24

EXPECTED VALUE

When you flip a coin, you expect that the percentage of heads will be 50% and the percentage of tails will be 50%. Rarely will they be exactly 50%, especially if you flip the coin many times. We call this an expected value—what you expect will happen.

If an experiment has possible numerical outcomes $x_1, x_2, \ldots x_n$ each having probability $P_1, P_2, \ldots P_n$, and each mutually exclusive, the expected value will be $x_1 p_1 + x_2 p_2 + x_3 p_3 + \ldots + x_n p_n$. Using summation notation, we can express this as $\sum_{i=1}^{n} x_i p_i$. Expected value can also be thought of as an average value.

Example:

A drug is administered to sets of three patients. Over a period of time, it is determined that the probability of 3 cures, 2 cures, 1 cure, and no cures are .70, .20, .09, and .01 respectively. The expected number of cures that can be expected in a group of three is calculated:

$3(0.70) + 2(0.20) + 1(0.09) + 0(0.01) = 2.59.$

When we give this drug to 3 patients, we expect that 2.59 of them will be cured.

Note that we cannot get 2.59 cures. We get 2 cures or 3 cures. But the expected value is an average, just as saying the average family in a community has 2.4 children.

PROBLEM

When playing the Pick-3 lottery, you have to choose a 3-digit number. If you win, you get $500. If you lose, you get nothing. A lottery ticket costs $1. We wish to find the expected value of this lottery game. What should your expectation be when you buy a lottery ticket?

SOLUTION

There are only two results, winning and losing. Numerically, that means $500 or $0.

By the multiplication principle, there are $10 \cdot 10 \cdot 10 = 1,000$ possibilities so the probability of winning is $\frac{1}{1,000}$ and the probability of losing is $\frac{999}{1,000}$. So the expected value of the lottery is

$500\left(\frac{1}{1,000}\right) + 0\left(\frac{999}{1,000}\right) = \frac{1}{2} = 0.50$. So you will win 50 cents on average when you buy a lottery ticket. But since the lottery ticket costs $1, you will lose 50 cents on average every time you play the lottery. You can win the lottery but play it a lot of times and your expectation is losing 50 cents for every ticket you buy.

PROBLEM

In a community, the probability that a family will have a given number of cars (vehicles) is given by the chart below. What is the expected number of cars for a family in this community?

Cars	0	1	2	3	4
Probability	0.18	0.24	0.35	0.19	0.04

SOLUTION

Expected value $= 0(0.18) + 1(0.24) + 2(0.35) + 3(0.19) + 4(0.04) = 1.67$

The average family in the community owns 1.67 cars.

PROBLEM

Dollar-Dog-Night is a promotion that a professional baseball team runs several times during the season. They charge $1.00 for a hot dog and hope that people will eat more of them than they would if prices were normal. The chart below gives the probability that a person will purchase the indicated number of hot dogs.

Hot dogs	0	1	2	3	4	5
Probability	0.32	0.28	0.20	0.15	0.03	0.02

(A) Find the expected number of hot dogs that a fan at the game will eat.

(B) If the baseball team makes a profit of 40 cents per hot dog and 25,000 fans attend the game, how much profit will the team make?

SOLUTION

(A) Expected value = $0(0.32) + 1(0.28) + 2(0.20) + 3(0.15) + 4(0.03) + 5(0.02) = 1.35$
The average fan eats 1.35 hot dogs.

(B) The profit for 25,000 fans = $25{,}000(1.35)(0.40) = \$13{,}500$

1. All liberal arts students at Newton College must successfully complete one course taken from each of the following categories in order to graduate. In how many ways can a student satisfy the college requirement?

Science & Technology	Analysis	The Arts
Math	Political Science	Music
Physics	Philosophy	Art
Chemistry	Sociology	Photography
Astronomy	Logic	
Geology		
Programming		

  (A) 13
  (B) 30
  (C) 42
  (D) 72

2. Nine horses are in the Kentucky Derby. You wish to bet on the Trifecta. You need to predict which horse will win, which horse will come in 2nd, and which horse will come in 3rd. How many ways are there to do this?

  (A) 24
  (B) 504
  (C) 729
  (D) 362,880

3. In a meeting of 12 businesspeople, each shakes hands with the other. How many handshakes will there be?

  (A) 24
  (B) 66
  (C) 132
  (D) 12!

4. The letters in the word HEART are scrambled. What is the probability that the "H" will be first and the "T" will be last in the scrambled word?

  (A) $\frac{1}{20}$

  (B) $\frac{1}{6}$

  (C) $\frac{1}{40}$

  (D) $\frac{2}{5}$

5. A small class contains 3 boys and 6 girls. Their teacher chooses 3 students at random to serve on a committee. If Brian and Janice are boyfriend and girlfriend, what is the probability that they will both be chosen to be on the committee?

  (A) $\frac{2}{9}$

  (B) $\frac{1}{3}$

  (C) $\frac{1}{84}$

  (D) $\frac{1}{12}$

6. A study is done at a school on student lateness. The statistics taken on one day are shown in the table below. What is the probability that a student chosen either drove himself or herself or was late?

	On-time	Late
Drove themselves	54	8
Were driven	24	2
Took school bus	40	0

  (A) 0.50
  (B) 0.5625
  (C) 0.0625
  (D) 0.125

7. A study was done to determine whether people who purchase a particular brand of computer are more apt to switch to another brand of computer. The table below shows the results of the study for 100 people who originally purchased PC or Mac computers. A person is chosen at random.

	Stayed with computer	Switched computers	Total
Started with PC	44	20	64
Started with Mac	30	6	36
Total	74	26	100

Which statements are true?

I. It is more probable that the person originally purchased a PC than originally purchased a Mac.

II. It is more probable that the person originally purchased a PC and switched computers than originally purchased a Mac and switched computers.

III. Purchasing a PC and switching computers are independent events.

(A) I and II only
(B) I and III only
(C) II and III only
(D) I, II, and III

8. Frank is sorting through his Christmas lights. Some are defective. The chart below shows a summary of the classification of the lights.

	Defective	OK	Total
Red	2	6	8
Green	5	7	12
Total	7	13	20

Frank chooses a bulb at random. Arrange the following probabilities from highest to smallest.

I. He chooses a red bulb.

II. If he chooses a red bulb, it is defective.

III. If he chooses a defective bulb, it is red.

(A) I − II − III
(B) I − III − II
(C) II − III − I
(D) III − II − I

9. Suppose choosing a new car color is independent of choosing a car brand. If the probability of choosing a Toyota is 15% and the probability of choosing a white Toyota is 3%, find the probability of choosing a white car.

(A) 0.45%
(B) 16.7%
(C) 18%
(D) 20%

10. A charity is raffling off a 60-inch TV worth $2,000; two 32-inch TV's worth $500 each; and 5 iPods worth $230 each. A raffle ticket costs $10 and 1,000 tickets are sold. What is the mean expectation for raffle players?

(A) Loses $7.27
(B) Loses $5.85
(C) Wins $2.73
(D) Wins $4.15

Answers to Drill Questions

1. **(D)** $6(4)(3) = 72$

2. **(B)** $9(8)(7) = 504$

3. **(B)** This is a combination problem as A shaking hands with B is the same as B shaking hands with A.

   There are $_{12}C_2 = \dfrac{12!}{2! \cdot 10!} = \dfrac{12 \cdot 11 \cdot 10 \cdot 9 \cdot \ldots \cdot 3 \cdot 2 \cdot 1}{2 \cdot 1 \cdot 10 \cdot 9 \cdot \ldots \cdot 3 \cdot 2 \cdot 1} = \dfrac{12 \cdot 11}{2 \cdot 1} = 66$ handshakes.

4. **(A)** This is a permutation problem as order counts.
   There are $5! = 120$ ways to scramble the letters.

   If the H and T are in their proper positions, there are $3!$ ways to scramble the other 3 letters.

   So the probability that the H and the T will be in their proper positions is $\dfrac{3!}{5!} = \dfrac{3 \cdot 2 \cdot 1}{5 \cdot 4 \cdot 3 \cdot 2 \cdot 1} = \dfrac{1}{20}$.

5. **(D)** This is a combination problem as order doesn't count.

   There are $_9C_3 = \dfrac{9!}{3! \cdot 6!} = \dfrac{9 \cdot 8 \cdot 7 \cdot 6 \cdot 5 \cdot 4 \cdot 3 \cdot 2 \cdot 1}{3 \cdot 2 \cdot 1 \cdot 6 \cdot 5 \cdot 4 \cdot 3 \cdot 2 \cdot 1} = \dfrac{9 \cdot 8 \cdot 7}{3 \cdot 2 \cdot 1} = 84$ ways to choose the committee.

   If Brian and Janice are on the committee, there are 7 other people who can also be on the committee.

   So the probability that Brian and Janice will be on the committee is $\dfrac{7}{84} = \dfrac{1}{12}$.

6. **(A)** Total students: $54 + 24 + 40 + 8 + 2 + 0 = 128$

   Students who drove themselves or were late: $54 + 8 + 2 = 64$

   Probability that students drove themselves or were late: $\dfrac{64}{128} = 0.50$

7. **(A)** I. True: Prob (purchased PC) $= \dfrac{64}{100} = 0.64$

   Prob (purchased Mac) $= \dfrac{36}{100} = 0.36$

   II. True: Prob (Switch|Mac) $= \dfrac{20}{64} = 0.3125$

   Prob (Switch|Mac) $= \dfrac{6}{36} = 0.1667$

III. False: Prob(purchased PC) = 0.64

$$\text{Prob(Switch)} = \frac{26}{100} = 0.26$$

$$\text{Prob(purchased PC and switched)} = \frac{20}{100} = 0.20$$

$$0.64\,(0.26) = 0.1664 \neq 0.20$$

8. **(B)** I. $\text{Prob(Red)} = \dfrac{8}{20} = 0.4$

II. $\text{Prob(Defective|Red)} = \dfrac{2}{8} = 0.25$

III. $\text{Prob(Red|Defective)} = \dfrac{2}{7} = 0.286$

9. **(D)** When independent, Prob(Toyota) · Prob(White Car) = Prob(White Toyota)

$$0.15 \cdot \text{Prob(White Car)} = 0.03 \Rightarrow \text{Prob(White Car)} = \frac{0.03}{0.15} = 0.2 = 20\%$$

10. **(B)**

	60-inch TV	32-inch TV	iPod	Nothing
X	2000	500	230	0
Prob(X)	$\dfrac{1}{1000}$	$\dfrac{2}{1000}$	$\dfrac{5}{1000}$	$\dfrac{992}{1000}$

Expected Value (win)

$$= 2000\left(\frac{1}{1000}\right) + 500\left(\frac{2}{1000}\right) + 230\left(\frac{5}{1000}\right) + 0\left(\frac{992}{500}\right) = \frac{4150}{1000} = \$4.15$$

$$= 2000$$

Person wins $4.15 - $10.00 = -$5.85.

STATISTICS AND DATA ANALYSIS

MEASURES OF CENTRAL TENDENCY

Mean or average: The mean of a set of data is the average and is usually denoted $\bar{x}$. To find it, add up all the data and divide by the number of pieces of data.

Example:

8 people went out to dinner. The list below shows what they spent. Find the average cost.

$18.55, $21.35, $17.45, $20.50, $24.25, $14.75, $19.65 and $22.90.

$$\bar{x} = \frac{18.55 + 21.35 + 17.45 + 20.50 + 24.25 + 14.75 + 19.65 + 22.90}{8}$$

$$= \frac{159.40}{8} = \$19.93$$

PROBLEM

Find the average height of the starting 5 members of a basketball team whose heights are 6′6″, 6′10″, 5′11″, 7′1″, and 6′7″.

SOLUTION

To start, convert all heights to inches:

$$\bar{x} = \frac{78 + 82 + 71 + 85 + 79}{5} = \frac{395}{5} = 79$$

79 inches is equal to 6 feet 7 inches. Thus, the average height is 6 feet 7 inches.

PROBLEM

Sheldon averaged 88.5 over 4 rounds of golf. He shot 93 in his 2nd round, 84 in his 3rd round, and 90 in his 4th round. What was his first-round score?

SOLUTION

Let x be his first-round score:

$$\frac{x+93+84+90}{4}=88.5 \Rightarrow x+267=354 \Rightarrow x=87$$

Median: The median of a set of data is the middle score. To find the median, first put the data in increasing or decreasing order. Let n represent the number of pieces of data. If n is odd, the median is the data value: $\frac{n+1}{2}$. If n is even, take the average of data $\frac{n}{2}$ and the piece of data directly after it. When one of the data is much larger or smaller than the rest of the data, the mean can be strongly affected, while the median is not.

Example:

A small class is made up of the students with first names: Susie, Joe, Michael, Shawn, Caroline, Steve, Kurt, Jennifer, Matthew, and Jonathan. Find the median name length.

The lengths of the names are 5, 3, 7, 5, 8, 5, 4, 8, 7, and 8. When put in order we get: 3, 4, 5, 5, 5, 7, 7, 8, 8, 8. Since there are 10 pieces of data, the median is the average of the 5th and 6th pieces of data, which are 5 and 7. The median is 6. Note that it is possible that the median is not an actual data value.

PROBLEM

15 people entered a hot-dog eating contest. The number of hot dogs they ate are:

23, 14, 19, 21, 20, 12, 21, 24, 40, 19, 20, 23, 25, 12, and 15

(a) Find the mean and the median number of hot dogs eaten.

(b) If the person eating 40 hot dogs was disqualified, how would that affect the mean and the median?

SOLUTION

$$\bar{x}=\frac{23+14+19+21+20+12+21+24+40+19+20+23+25+12+15}{15}$$

$$=\frac{308}{15}=20.5\bar{3}$$

Data sorted: 12, 12, 14, 15, 19, 19, 20, 20, 21, 21, 23, 23, 24, 25, 40.

The median is the 8th score which is 20.

If 40 is eliminated, $\bar{x} = \dfrac{308 - 40}{14} = \dfrac{268}{14} = 19.14$

The median will be the average of the 7th and 8th score which is still 20.

Mode: The mode of a set of data is the data that occurs the most often. Mode is rarely used.

Example:

In the class mentioned above, since a name with 5 letters and a name with 8 letters both occur three times, more than any other number of letters, that set of data has two modes: 5 and 8. We call this bimodal.

PROBLEM

Movie patrons were asked to rate the movie they had just seen. They were asked to rate it with a 1 for strongly disliking the movie and a 5 for strongly liking it. Using tally marks to track the data, the chart that follows shows the results:

5	JHT JHT JHT III
4	JHT JHT JHT IIII
3	JHT JHT II
2	JHT II
1	III

Find the average score, the median score, and the mode.

SOLUTION

Score	Frequency
5	18
4	19
3	12
2	7
1	3

Mean: $\bar{x} = \dfrac{18(5) + 19(4) + 12(3) + 7(2) + 3(1)}{59} = \dfrac{219}{59} = 3.71$

Median is the 30th score, which is 4.

Mode is the most common score, which is 4.

COMPARING THE MEAN, MEDIAN, AND MODE IN A VARIETY OF DISTRIBUTIONS

It is sometimes useful to make comparisons about the relative values of the mean, median, and mode. This section presents steps to do that without having to calculate the exact values of these measures.

Step 1: If a bar graph is not provided, sketch one from the information given in the problem.

The graph will either be skewed to the left, skewed to the right, or approximately normal. A **skewed** distribution has one of its tails longer than the other.

- A graph skewed to the left will look like Figure 1; its left tail is longer. The order of the three measures is mean < median < mode (alphabetical order).

- A graph skewed to the right will look like Figure 2; its right tail is longer. The order of the three measures is mode < median < mean (reverse alphabetical order).

- A graph that is approximately normal (also called bell-shaped) will look like Figure 3, and the mean = median = mode.

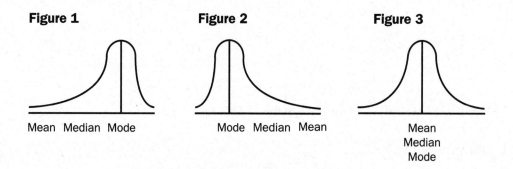

Step 2: Write the word "mode" under the highest column of the bar graph, because the mode is the most frequent. If the graph is skewed right or left, the positioning of the mode establishes the order for the remaining two terms according to the information provided above. If the graph is approximately symmetrical, the value of all three terms is approximately equivalent.

PROBLEM

On a trip to the Everglades, students tested the pH of the water at different sites. Most of the pH tests were at 6. A few read 7, and one read 8. Select the statement that is true about the distribution of the pH test results.

(A) The mode and the mean are the same.

(B) The mode is less than the mean.

(C) The median is greater than the mean.

(D) The median is less than the mode.

SOLUTION

Sketch a graph.

The graph is skewed to the right. The mode is furthest left. Thus, mode < median < mean.

Choices (A), (C), and (D) do not coincide with what has been established in terms of relative order. (B) is the only choice that does follow from our conclusions. Thus, (B) is the correct response.

PROBLEM

Estimate the median of each distribution shown below and describe how the mean compares to it.

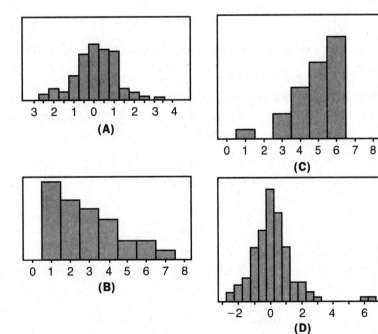

SOLUTION

Graph (A) is symmetric with a median at about 0. The mean will also be about 0, since it approximates a normal curve. Graph (B) is right-skewed with a median of about 3. The mean will be pulled more toward the values of $4-7$ than it will be toward $1-2$, so the mean will be greater than 3. Graph (C) is left-skewed with a median of about 5. The mean will be pulled toward the lower values, so it is less than 5. Graph (D) is symmetric with a few extreme high values. The median is about 0, and the mean will be just slightly larger due to the outliers (data far from the other given data values) around 6.

MEASURES OF VARIABILITY

While mean, median, and mode measure the center of a data set, they say nothing about how spread out the data is. We call this spread a measure of **variability**. A manufacturer of light bulbs would prefer small variability in the number of hours the bulbs will likely burn. A track coach who needs to decide which athletes go on to the finals may want larger variability in heat times because it will be easier to decide who are truly the fastest runners. There are two measures of variability: **range and standard deviation**.

Range: The range is the difference between the highest and lowest data values. Given all of the data, the range is easy to find. The larger the range, the greater the spread of the data.

Example:

If the heaviest person in a room is 205 pounds and the lightest person is 130 pounds, the range is $205 - 130 = 85$ pounds.

Variance and Standard Deviation: The standard deviation is a measure of how spread out the data is from the mean and is quite useful for data that is fairly symmetric. The greater the standard deviation, the greater the spread of the data from the mean.

The variance tells us how much variability exists in a distribution. It is the "average" of the squared differences between the data values and the mean. The variance s^2 is calculated with the formula

$$s^2 = \frac{1}{n-1}\sum\left(x_i - \bar{x}\right)^2$$

where n is the number of data points, $\sum$ refers to summation, x_i represents each data value, and $\bar{x}$ is the mean.

The formula for the standard deviation s is therefore $\sqrt{\text{variance}}$. Typically a calculator is needed to find the standard deviation of a data set. The standard deviation is used for most applications in statistics. It can be thought of as how far the typical observation lies from the mean.

Example:

Six movie reviewers rated a current movie on a star basis where 1 star is poor and 5 stars is excellent. If the ratings are

$$2, 5, 4, 5, 5, \text{ and } 3,$$

find the mean and the standard deviation.

The mean is $\bar{x} = \dfrac{2+5+4+5+5+3}{6} = \dfrac{24}{6} = 4$

The variance $s^2 = \dfrac{(2-4)^2 + (5-4)^2 + (4-4)^2 + (5-4)^2 + (5-4)^2 + (3-4)^2}{5}$

$$s^2 = \dfrac{4+1+0+1+1+1}{5} = \dfrac{8}{5} = 1.6$$

The standard deviation $s = \sqrt{1.6} = 1.26$

Outliers: An outlier is a score that is dramatically different from the other scores in a group of data. Outliers can have a huge effect on the mean and standard deviation and it is important to know whether the outlier is a true score and not a typographical error, or whether it occurred because of special circumstances.

At this stage of statistics, the standard deviation by itself tells us little about how the data is distributed. However, when two or more data sets are compared, the standard deviations of each allow us to compare the data sets.

Example:

The chart below shows exam scores of 4 classes of 5 students each. Each class has a mean of 80, but the data is quite different. The mean, median, range, and standard deviation of each class is also shown. Interpret the variability of the classes.

Class 1	Class 2	Class 3	Class 4
80	90	100	100
80	85	90	100
80	80	80	100
80	75	70	100
80	70	60	0
$\bar{x} = 80$	$\bar{x} = 80$	$\bar{x} = 80$	$\bar{x} = 80$
Median = 80	Median = 80	Median = 80	Median = 100
Range = 0	Range = 20	Range = 40	Range = 100
St. Dev = 0	St. Dev = 7.91	St. Dev = 15.81	St. Dev = 44.72

Class 1 has a standard deviation of 0 because there is no spread about the mean of 80. Classes 2, 3, and 4 have larger standard deviations meaning that there is a bigger spread about the mean. 0 is an outlier in class 4, which dramatically changes the mean and standard deviation.

PROBLEM

In a used car lot, the standard deviation of the car prices is $750. Suppose the cheapest car on the lot was originally $1,000 and the most expensive car was $10,000. If the owner raises the price of every car by $250, what would be the standard deviation of the revised car prices?

(A) $500

(B) $750

(C) $1,000

(D) Impossible to determine

SOLUTION

(B) Since the spread of the data does not change, the standard deviation remains the same. A $1,000 car will now cost $1,250 while a $10,000 car will now cost $10,250. The range will stay the same at $9,000.

PROBLEM

In another used car lot, the standard deviation of the car prices is $750. If the owner raises the cost of every car by 10%, what would be the standard deviation of the revised car prices?

(A) $450

(B) $750

(C) $825

(D) Impossible to determine

SOLUTION

(C) Multiplying each car price by 1.1 would increase the spread. A $1,000 car will now cost $1,100 while a $10,000 car will now cost $11,000. The range went from $9,000 to $9,900.

Thus, the standard deviation would likewise increase by 10%.

PROBLEM

The effect of global warming has not been higher temperatures, but bigger extremes in cold temperatures and warm temperatures. If the temperatures of cities in the United States were averaged in the years 1960 (pre-global warming) and 2015 (during global warming), what would be the approximate effect on the mean and standard deviation?

Mean:	Standard Deviation:
_____ Would go up	_____ Would go up
_____ Would stay the same	_____ Would stay the same
_____ Would go down	_____ Would go down

SOLUTION

If some cities got colder and others got warmer, there would not be a big difference in the means of the two years. However, if some cities got colder and others warmer, the spread from the mean would be greater, so the standard deviation would go up.

PROBLEM

Six people are standing on a subway platform. If the average position on the platform is measured, arrange the following choices in order from smallest to largest standard deviation.

SOLUTION

(A), (C), (D), (B)

In (A) all the people are standing at the end of the platform so the standard deviation should be close to zero. In (B), (C), and (D), the mean position is in the center of the platform. Choice (B) has the people furthest from the center so it will have the largest standard deviation.

PROBLEM

The standard deviation of rainfall in Seattle, Washington, during the summer is 0.8 inches. The standard deviation of rainfall in Miami, Florida, is 1.6 inches. Which of the following statements is true?

(A) It rains twice as much in Miami as in Seattle.

(B) It rains twice as much in Seattle as in Miami.

(C) Miami is more likely than Seattle to have days with no rain and days with a lot of rain.

(D) There are more rainy days in Miami than in Seattle.

SOLUTION

(C) With a larger standard deviation, there is a greater spread in Miami's rainfall than in Seattle's. So Miami is more likely to have days with no rain and others with a lot of rain. Seattle is more likely to have many days with moderate rain. The correct answer is (C).

PROBLEM

A large conference is held in a hotel and lunch is provided. Lunch consists of an 8-ounce sandwich, a 4-ounce cup of juice, and a package of cookies weighing 3 ounces. The meal is placed in a styrofoam container weighing 1 ounce. These styrofoam containers are placed in red boxes holding 12 containers or blue boxes holding 20 containers. If these boxes are completely filled with containers, which of the following statements is true?

I. There is no difference between the mean weight of the red boxes and the blue boxes.

II. There is no difference between the standard deviation weight of the red boxes and the blue boxes.

(A) I only

(B) II only

(C) I and II

(D) Neither I nor II

SOLUTION

(B) All of the red boxes weigh 12 pounds and all of the blue boxes weigh 20 pounds. The average weight of the red boxes is 12 and the average weight of the blue boxes is 20. Therefore, statement I is not true. Since all the red boxes weigh the same, the standard deviation is zero and the same can be said of the blue boxes. The correct answer is (B).

NORMAL DISTRIBUTIONS

One of the most important distributions in statistics is called the **normal distribution**. If a histogram is "smoothed out," many times its curve will appear symmetric, single-peaked, and bell-shaped. These are called *normal curves* or the *bell curve*. On the next page is a graph of a normal curve. Note how most of the data is in the center and it tails off symmetrically to the sides with little data at the far left and right.

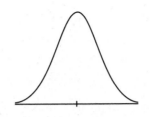

The reason these curves are so important in statistics is that so much of real-life statistics appears "normal." Here are some common examples:

- Heights: Most people are average height with fewer people being really short or really tall.

- Prices: Go to many markets and price a 2-liter bottle of the same brand of soda. The data will appear normal with most prices about average. Few prices will be cheaper and few will be more expensive.

- Wages: Most people earn an average amount of money while fewer people earn either a little money or a lot of money.

- Time it takes to get to work: Most days it might take 30 minutes to drive to work while fewer days it might take 20 minutes or 40 minutes.

- Grades: Collect GPAs for a class of students and many students will have an average GPA. Fewer will have either low GPAs or high GPAs.

The normal distribution follows an important rule called the **68-95-99.7% rule.** It states that in any normal distribution,

- 68% of the data lies within one standard deviation of the mean. In the figure below, we have a normal distribution with the mean $\overline{x}$ in the center. Going out one standard deviation to the left and right of $\overline{x}$ will represent 68% of the data.

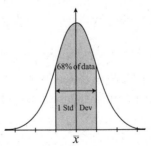

- 95% of the data lies within two standard deviations of the mean. In the figure that follows, we have a normal distribution with the mean $\overline{x}$ in the center. Going out two standard deviations to the left and right of $\overline{x}$ will represent 95% of the data.

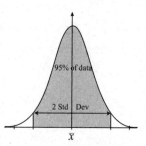

- 99.7% (or just about all) of the data lies within three standard deviations of the mean.

The more "normal" a distribution is, these relationships become closer to being perfectly true. No distribution is perfectly normal and, therefore, these relationships are approximations in most real-life settings.

Example:

The distribution of heights of adult American men is approximately normal with a mean of 69 inches and a standard deviation of 2.5 inches. On the normal curve below, we mark the values for the mean and 1, 2, and 3 standard deviations above and below the mean.

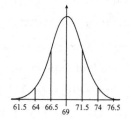

We can make the following observations:

- 68% of adult American men are between 66.5 and 71.5 inches (5'6.5" and 5'11.5") tall.

- 95% of adult American men are between 64 and 74 inches (5'4" and 6'2") tall.

- 99.7% of adult American men are between 61.5 and 76.5 inches (5'1.5" and 6'4.5") tall.

PROBLEM

The length of human pregnancies from conception to birth is approximately normally distributed with a mean of 284 days and a standard deviation of 11 days. Find the approximate percentage of pregnancies

(A) over 284 days

(B) over 295 days

(C) between 262 and 284 days

(D) less than 306 days

SOLUTION

The graph of the normal curve with standard deviation marks is shown below.

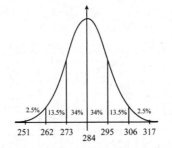

(A) Because of symmetry, 50% of pregnancies are greater than 284 days.

(B) 295 days is one standard deviation over the mean. 16% of pregnancies are greater than 295 days.

(C) 262 is two standard deviations below the mean. 47.5% of pregnancies are between 262 and 284 days.

(D) 306 is two standard deviations above the mean. 97.5% of pregnancies are below 306 days.

DATA ANALYSIS

Data analysis often involves putting numerical values into picture form, such as bar graphs, line graphs, and circle graphs. In this manner, we gain a more intuitive understanding of the given information.

BAR GRAPHS

Bar graphs are used to compare amounts of the same measurements. The following bar graph compares the number of bushels of wheat and corn produced on a farm from 1975 to 1985. The horizontal axis for a bar graph consists of categories (e.g., years, ethnicity, marital status) rather than values, and the widths of the bars are uniform. The emphasis is on the height of the bars. Contrast this with histograms, discussed next.

PROBLEM

According to the graph that follows, in which year was the least number of bushels of wheat produced?

**Number of Bushels (to the Nearest 5 Bushels) of
Wheat and Corn Produced by Farm RQS, 1975–1985**

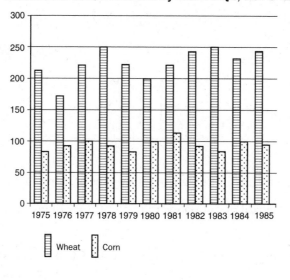

SOLUTION

By inspecting the graph, we find that the shortest bar representing wheat production is the one for 1976. Thus, the least number of bushels of wheat produced in 1975–1985 occurred in 1976.

HISTOGRAMS

A **histogram** is an appropriate display for quantitative data. It is used primarily for continuous data, but may be used for discrete data that have a wide spread. The horizontal axis is broken into intervals that do not have to be of uniform size. Histograms are also good for large data sets. The area of the bar denotes the value, not the height, as in a bar graph.

The histogram below shows the amount of money spent by passengers on a ship during a recent cruise to Alaska.

Example:

Passenger Spending During Cruise to Alaska

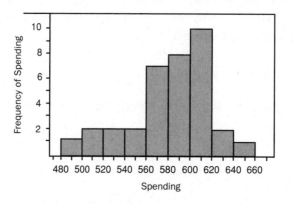

The intervals have widths of $20. One person spent between $480 and $500, two spent between $500 and $520, and so on. We cannot tell from the graph the precise amount each individual spent.

The distribution has a shape skewed to the left with a peak around $600 to $620. The data are centered at about $590. This is about where half of the observations will be to the left and half to the right. The range of the data is about $180, but the clear majority of passengers spent between $560 and $620. There are no extreme values present or gaps within the data.

LINE GRAPHS

Line graphs are very useful in representing data on two different but related subjects. Line graphs are often used to track the changes or shifts in certain factors. In the next problem, a line graph is used to track the changes in the amount of scholarship money awarded to graduating seniors at a particular high school over the span of several years.

PROBLEM

According to the line graph below, how much did the scholarship money increase between 1987 and 1988?

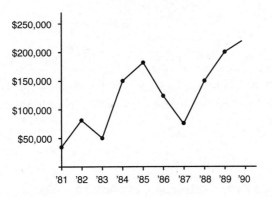

Amount of Scholarship Money Awarded to Graduating Seniors, West High, 1981–1990

SOLUTION

To find the increase in scholarship money from 1987 to 1988, locate the amounts for 1987 and 1988. In 1987, the amount of scholarship money is halfway between $50,000 and $100,000, or $75,000. In 1988, the amount of scholarship money is $150,000. The increase is thus $150,000 − 75,000 = $75,000.

PIE CHARTS

Circle graphs (or **pie charts**) are used to show the breakdown of a whole picture. When the circle graph is used to demonstrate this breakdown in terms of percents, the whole figure represents 100% and the parts of the circle graph represent percentages of the total. When added together, these percentages add up to 100%. The circle graph in the next problem shows how a family's budget has been divided into different categories by using percentages.

PROBLEM

Using the budget shown below, a family with an income of $3,000 a month would plan to spend what amount on housing?

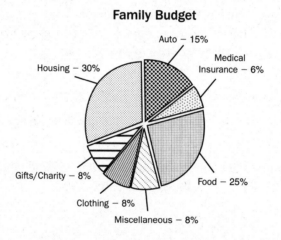

Family Budget

SOLUTION

To find the amount spent on housing, locate on the pie chart the percentage allotted to housing, or 30%. Then calculate 30% of $3,000 = $900. The family plans to spend $900 on housing.

STEMPLOTS

A **stemplot**, also called a stem-and-leaf plot, can be used to display univariate data as well. It is good for small sets of data (about 50 or less) and forms a plot much like a histogram. The stemplot on the next page represents test scores for a class of 32 students.

Test Scores

```
 3 | 3
 4 |
 5 |
 6 | 3 7 9
 7 | 2 2 5 7
 8 | 1 2 6 8 8 8 9 9 9
 9 | 0 0 0 1 3 3 4 5 5 6 7
10 | 0 0 0 0
```

Key: 6 | 3 represents a score of 63

The values on the left of the vertical bar are called the stems; those on the right are called leaves. Stems and leaves need not be tens and ones—they may be hundreds and tens, ones and tenths, and so on. A good stemplot always includes a key for the reader so that the values may be interpreted correctly.

PROBLEM

Describe the distribution of test scores for students in the class using the stemplot.

SOLUTION

The distribution of the test scores is skewed toward lower values (to the left). It is centered at about 89 with a range of 67. There is an extreme low value at 33, which appears to be an outlier. Without it, the range is only 37, about half as much. The test scores have a mean of approximately 85.4, a median of 89, and a mode of 100.

BIVARIATE DATA

Bivariate data examines the relationship between two variables. The two variables are called the **response variable** and the **explanatory variable**. The data is given as points (explanatory, response).

Response variable: measures the outcome of a study.

Explanatory variable: attempts to explain the response variable.

Examples:

How does studying affect the grade in a final exam? The explanatory variable is hours of study which explains the response variable, the grade. Someone who studies 8 hours and received a 94 would have the point (8, 94).

How does the average outside temperature affect your heating oil bill? The explanatory variable is average outside temperature in a month, which explains the response variable, the amount you spend for oil. A month whose average temperature was 34 degrees and in which the heating bill was $250 would have the point (34, 250).

PROBLEM

Charles works out on a treadmill that has many possible speeds. The treadmill also measures his pulse rate. Which is the explanatory variable and which is the response variable if his pulse rate was 125 when his speed was 7 mph? What would the data point be?

SOLUTION

The explanatory variable is speed and response variable is pulse rate. The point would be (7, 125).

A **scatter plot** shows the relationship between two quantitative variables measured on the same individuals.

The values of one variable appear on the horizontal (x) axis and the other variable appears on the vertical (y) axis. Each individual value appears as a point in the plot. The explanatory variable is placed on the x-axis and the response variable is placed on the y-axis.

Interpreting scatter plots

- Form – does the data appear linear or curved?

- Direction of association

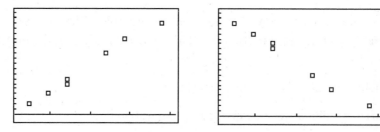

Positive association–data goes up to the right

Negative association–data goes down to the right

- Strength of an association – how closely the points follow a clear pattern. Both of the associations above are strongly linear.

Line of best fit (sometimes called the regression line):

The line of best fit is a straight line that describes how a response variable *y* changes as an explanatory variable *x* changes. Lines of best fit are used to predict the value of *y* for a given value of *x*. These lines require an explanatory variable and a response variable.

The closer the line of best fit comes to the data points, the stronger the association is:

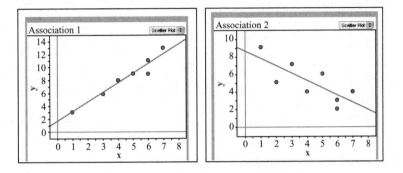

Strong positive association   Moderate negative association

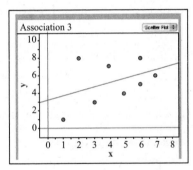

Weak positive association

- Meaning – an association between *x* and *y* means that as *x* changes, *y* changes. An association between *x* and *y* does not mean necessarily that *x* causes *y*.

Example:

There is a strong positive association between the number of firefighters sent to a fire and the amount of damage the fire does. However, sending firefighters to a fire does not cause damage.

The equation of the line of best fit describing data is in the familiar algebraic form $y = mx + b$ where *x* is the explanatory variable, *y* is the response variable, and *m* is the slope. Students are not responsible for calculating the line of best fit – it will be given. You simply need to interpret it.

Interpretation of slope *m*: For every unit increase in *x* (the explanatory variable), the *y* (the response variable) changes by *m*.

Example:

Over a 10-minute period in a busy bank, several tellers go to lunch and the line of customers becomes longer. The number of people in line at various times during that period is given in the table that follows and the scatter plot of the data is shown.

People in line

	time	people
1	0.0	12.0
2	1.5	18.0
3	3.0	17.0
4	4.0	19.0
5	6.5	23.0
6	8.0	27.0
7	10.0	34.0

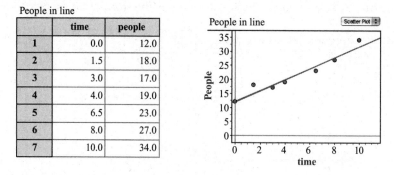

The association would be described as a strong positive linear association.

If the line of best fit equation is $y = 1.96x + 12.2$ where x represents the time and y represents the number of people in line, the slope of the line 1.96 is interpreted as: for every minute, the line increases by 1.96 people.

To predict the number of people in line at 7 minutes, we let $x = 7$ in the equation $y = 1.96x + 12.2$ and we get 25.92. So we predict that there were 26 people in line at 7 minutes. Since the association appears to be strong, we are fairly confident in our prediction. When we try to predict the value of y using a value of x between several given values of x, we call that **interpolation.**

To predict the number of people in line at 15 minutes, we let $x = 15$ in the equation $y = 1.96x + 12.2$ and we get 41.6. So we predict that there were 42 people in line at 15 minutes. However, even though the association is strong, we are less confident in that because nothing is known beyond the 10-minute mark. For instance, the tellers might come back from lunch and the line would be shorter. When we try to predict the value of y using a value of x outside the given values of x, we call that **extrapolation.**

PROBLEM

1. A study was done with 16 cars measuring their weight in pounds versus the mileage in miles per gallon. The scatter plot below shows the line of best fit.

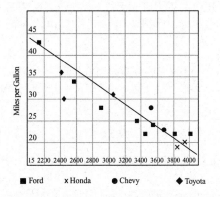

Which type of car has the greatest difference between its actual mileage and its predicted mileage?

(A) Honda

(B) Chevy

(C) Toyota

(D) Ford

2. Using the scatter plot above, if a new car was added to the study that weighed 3,750 pounds and got 40 miles to the gallon, how would the association be affected?

(A) becomes stronger with a steeper slope

(B) becomes weaker with a steeper slope

(C) becomes stronger with a more shallow slope

(D) becomes weaker with a more shallow slope

3. The line of best fit is: Miles per gallon = −0.01 Weight + 59.86. Interpret the slope of the line.

(A) For every mile to the gallon the car gets, the weight goes up by 100 pounds.

(B) For every extra 100 pounds of weight, the mileage goes down by 1 mile per gallon.

(C) For every extra pound of weight, the mileage goes down by 100 miles per gallon.

(D) The mileage goes down by 1/100 of the car's weight.

4. A car that weighs 1.5 tons would be expected to get how many miles to the gallon?

5. If a carmaker wants to build a car that gets 40 miles to the gallon, approximately how heavy should it be?

SOLUTIONS

1. **(C)** The make of car whose data point is farthest from the line weighs a little more than 2,400 pounds and gets 30 mpg. It is (C) Toyota.

2. **(D)** The new point would be to the upper right of the graph. It would weaken the relationship and it would act as a magnet to pull the line towards it, making the slope more shallow.

3. **(B)** The slope of −0.01 has the interpretation that for every additional pound, the mileage goes down by 0.01 mpg. For every additional 100 pounds, the mileage goes down by 1 MPG.

4. Mileage $= -0.01(3000) + 59.86 = 29.86$ MPG

5. $40 = -0.01x + 59.86 \Rightarrow 0.01x = 19.86 \Rightarrow x = \dfrac{19.86}{0.01} = 1{,}986$ lbs.

PROBLEM

Bears were anesthetized, tagged, and weighed. At different time intervals, the process was repeated to see the association between age in months and weight in pounds as shown in the scatter plot on the next page. The line of best fit is drawn in as well.

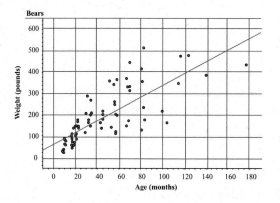

1. Which of the following values is closest to the monthly increase in weight of the bears?

(A) 2.5

(B) 5

(C) 10

(D) 20

2. Which of the following statements is true?

I. The line of best fit is a better predictor of weights of young bears rather than older bears.

II. If a new bear that is 15 years old and weighs 200 pounds is added to the study, the direction of the association will become negative.

(A) I only

(B) II only

(C) I and II

(D) neither I nor II

SOLUTIONS

1. **(A)** Choose two points that the line appears to pass through: (120, 400) and (160, 500).

    $$m = \frac{500 - 400}{160 - 120} = \frac{100}{40} = 2.5.$$

2. **(A)** Statement I is true. The points at the lower left are closer to the line than the ones further to the right. Statement II is false. The new point would be (180, 200). This point would be to the lower right of the graph. The association will not be negative, just less positive.

DRILL QUESTIONS

1. What is the difference between the mean and median of the following sample?

    {19, 15, 21, 24, 11, 18}

    (A) 0
    (B) 0.5
    (C) 1
    (D) 4

2. A car dealer asks its customers to rate their new car two months after they purchase it. They rate it on a 1—10 scale where 1 means very unhappy and 10 means very happy. The results are shown in the chart at right. Arrange the mean, median, and mode from highest to lowest.

Rating	Number
10	2
9	12
8	17
7	14
6	21
5	5
4	1
3	0
2	1
1	2

(A) mean – median – mode
(B) mode – median – mean
(C) mean – mode – median
(D) median – mean – mode

3. Mrs. Smith teaches a class of 150 students. On a recent exam she administered to her class, 100 students scored 90 or better; 40 students scored between 80 and 89; and the remaining

students scored between 70 and 79. Which of the following statements is correct concerning the students' exam scores?

(A) The median equals the mean.
(B) The mean is less than the mode.
(C) The median is greater than the mean.
(D) The median is greater than the mode.

4. What is the standard deviation of the data set: {−2, 0, 3, 5, 9}?

(A) 3.54
(B) 4.30
(C) 12.5
(D) 18.5

5. In a math class, the teacher curved an exam raising every student's score by 5 points. When the changed scores were compared to the original scores, which of the following would be 5 points higher?

(A) Mean, but not standard deviation
(B) Standard deviation, but not mean
(C) Both mean and standard deviation
(D) Neither mean nor standard deviation

6. A random sample of 25 people from the Sunnybrook Retirement Home were surveyed. The histogram below displays the ages of these residents.

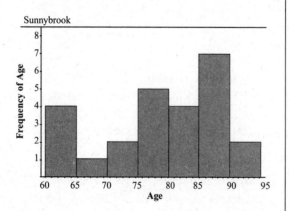

In which of the following intervals is the median age of these residents?

(A) 70 to less than 75
(B) 75 to less than 80
(C) 80 to less than 85
(D) 85 to less than 90

7. The number of years of experience in the sales department of a new-car dealer is shown by the stemplot below (where 1 | 5 corresponds to 15 years). What is the difference between the mean and median number of years?

0	112356778
1	02359
2	135589

(A) 0
(B) 1
(C) 2
(D) 3

8. A study was done to compare the percentage of men and women who purchase American, European, and Japanese cars. The first bar graph on the next page shows the make of each car and the percentage of males and females who prefer it. The second bar graph shows the preference of men and women regarding the different makes. Which of the following statements is true?

I. If I am a female, I am more likely to prefer a Japanese car.

II. If I prefer Japanese cars, I am more likely to be a female.

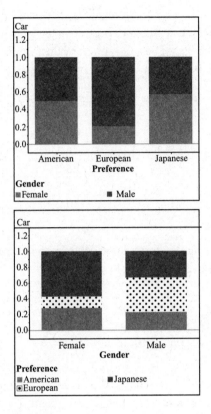

(A) I only
(B) II only
(C) I and II
(D) Neither

9. How many of the following sets of data would decidedly *not* graph a normal curve?

I. Lengths of great white sharks

II. The length of time it takes to do a transaction at a post office

III. Body temperatures of people

(A) 0
(B) 1
(C) 2
(D) 3

10. The amount of time students in a college statistics class study for the final exam is approximately normally distributed with $\bar{x} = 8$ and $s = 2.5$ hours. Which represents the greatest percentage?

(A) students studying less than 3 or more than 13 hours
(B) students studying more than 8 hours
(C) students studying less than 10.5 hours
(D) students studying between 5.5 and 13 hours

11. In a final exam given to 400 students, the mean score was 75 with a standard deviation of 5. If the top grade of an A is defined as 85 or higher and an F is defined as 65 or lower, how many students get either an A or fail the exam if the grades are normally distributed?

(A) 5
(B) 10
(C) 20
(D) 40

12. Which scatter plot has the strongest positive linear association?

(A)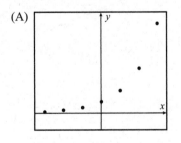

(B)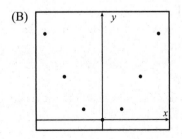

(C)
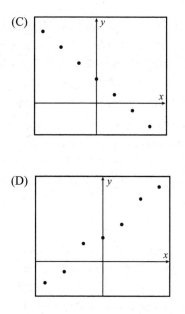

(D)

13. The depth of a diver ascending to the surface is shown in the scatter plot below. The line of best fit is Depth $= 228 - 0.3t$ where t is measured in seconds and depth is measured in feet. Interpret the slope of the line.

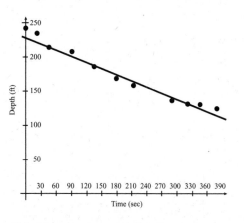

(A) For every second, the diver goes up 0.3 ft.
(B) For every foot, the diver needs 0.3 seconds.
(C) For every second, the diver goes down 0.3 ft.
(D) It takes 228 seconds for the diver to ascend.

14. The average remaining life expectancy for men in the United States is given in the table below. The line of best fit is given by the formula: Remaining years $= -0.88 \times$ current age $+ 73.4$.

Current age	Remaining years
0	74.9
15	60.6
35	42.1
50	26.3
65	16.8
74	10.2

Using this formula, which person is expected to live the longest?

(A) a 5-year-old
(B) a 25-year-old
(C) a 45-year-old
(D) a 70-year-old

15. Body Mass Index (BMI) is a calculation that relates a person's height and weight. The table below shows the percent of U.S. males age 18 years or older who were considered obese in the years indicated, judged on the basis of BMI. The line of best fit is given by the formula:

Percent obese $= 0.775 \cdot$ year $- 1529.3$.

Year	Percent obese
2003	22.7
2004	23.9
2005	24.9
2006	25.3
2007	26.5
2008	26.6
2009	27.6

In what year would we expect one-third of the U.S. male population age 18 or older to be considered obese?

(A) 2014
(B) 2015
(C) 2016
(D) 2017

ANSWERS TO DRILL QUESTIONS

1. **(B)** $\bar{x} = \dfrac{19+15+21+24+11+18}{6} = 18$

    Sorted data: {11, 15, 18, 19, 21, 24} Median is average of 18 and 19 which is 18.5. Difference: $18.5 - 18 = 0.5$

2. **(D)** $\bar{x} = \dfrac{2(10)+12(9)+17(8)+14(7)+21(6)+5(5)+1(4)+1(2)+2(1)}{6}$

    $= \dfrac{521}{75} = 6.95$

    Median is the data #38 $= 7$
    Mode $= 6$

3. **(C)** There were only $150 - 100 - 40 = 10$ students who scored 70–79.
    We know nothing about the mode. It could be that all 40 people scored an 80. But the distribution is skewed to the left which shows its mean is less than the median.

4. **(B)**

    $$\bar{x} = \frac{-2+0+3+5+9}{5} = \frac{15}{5} = 3$$

    $$s^2 = \frac{(-2-3)^2 + (0-3)^2 + (3-3)^2 + (5-3)^2 + (9-3)^2}{4}$$

    $$= \frac{25+9+0+4+36}{4} = \frac{74}{4} = 18.5$$

    $$s = \sqrt{18.5} = 4.30$$

5. **(A)** If there are n students, the sum of their scores will be $5n$ higher and the average is $\dfrac{5n}{n} = 5$

    points higher. The standard deviation is the spread of the data which has not changed.

6. **(C)** The median is in the 13th piece of data which occurs in the 80–85 grouping.

7. **(C)** The median is the average of the 10th and 11th pieces of data, 10 and 12, which is 11.

    $$\bar{x} = \frac{2(1)+2+3+5+6+2(7)+8+10+12+13+15+19+21+23+2(25)+28+29}{20}$$

    $$= \frac{260}{20} = 13$$

    Difference: $13 - 11 = 2$.

8. **(C)** I. Top bar graph, look at the female bar. About 60% of the females prefer Japanese cars.
    II. Bottom bar graph, look at the Japanese bar. About 55% of the people preferring Japanese cars are female.

9. **(B)**   I. Some sharks will be short, most will be medium length, and some are long. It should appear normal.

   II. Most transactions take little time. There are fewer that will take longer. The data is skewed right.

   III. Most people will be 98.6 with a small standard deviation. It should appear somewhat normal.

10. **(C)**   A. 5% B. 50% C. 84% D. 81.5%

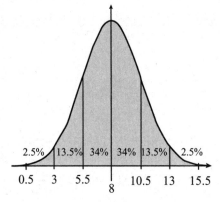

11. **(C)**   85 is 2 standard deviations above the mean so 0.25(400), 10 students get A's. 65 is 2 standard deviations above the mean so 0.25(400), 10 students get F's. 20 students either get an A or an F.

12. **(D)**   (A) and (B) are strong relationships, but not linear. (C) is a strong linear association, but negative.

13. **(A)**   The definition of slope m is every unit change in t, the response variable change by m. Since m is negative, the depth is getting smaller, meaning the diver is going up.

14. **(D)**
   (A) Projected age $= -0.88(5) + 73.4 + 5 = 74$
   (B) Projected age $= -0.88(25) + 73.4 + 25 = 76.4$
   (C) Projected age $= -0.88(45) + 73.4 + 45 = 78.8$
   (D) Projected age $= -0.88(70) + 73.4 + 70 = 81.8$

15. **(C)**   Percent obese $= 0.775$ year $- 1529.3 = 33.333$
   0.775 year $= 1562.633$
   Year $= 2016$

■ FINANCIAL MATHEMATICS

Percentages provide the basis for most problems involving financial situations. Percentages can be expressed as a percent, a fraction (usually over 100), or a decimal. Remember to include the leading zero for the decimal equivalent of percentages less than 10% (i.e., 5% = 0.05, not 0.5).

RATES

The word *rate* is used frequently in our everyday lives. Examples are *tax rates, hourly rates, inflation rates, vehicle accident rate,* and *consumption rate*. Rates are written as fractions.

Example:

A hybrid car travels 250 miles on 6 dollars of gas. The miles-to-dollars rate for this car is $\frac{250 \text{ miles}}{\$6}$.

An SUV travels 350 miles on 20 dollars of gas. The miles-to-dollars rate for this car is $\frac{350 \text{ miles}}{\$20}$.

A unit rate is a rate in which the denominator is 1. Unit rates make comparisons easier.

Example:

The hybrid car above gets $\frac{250}{6} = 41.67$ miles on $1 of gasoline while the SUV gets $\frac{350}{20} = 17.5$ miles on $1 of gasoline.

PROBLEM

A doctor's assistant earns $1,350 for working a 45-hour week. What is the assistant's hourly rate of pay?

SOLUTION

$\frac{\$1,350}{45 \text{ hr}} = \$30/\text{hr}.$

PROBLEM

A contractor is installing a bathroom and estimates that there will be 40 hours of labor to complete the project. He estimates the cost of the job at $13,250. When the work is actually done, there are 45 hours of labor. How much should he charge if the cost of materials is $8,000?

SOLUTION

The cost of labor will be $13,250 − $8,000 = $5,250. The unit rate is $\frac{\$5,250}{40 \text{ hr}} = \$131.25/\text{hr}$. For 45 hours, the labor cost will be $45(131.25) = \$5,906.25$. So the cost of the bathroom including materials and labor is $8,000 + $5906.25 = $13,906.25.

Consumers use unit pricing to determine the better buy. The more economical purchase is the product with the lower unit price, typically associated with a larger size or quantity. However, products with smaller unit prices can also cost more in total, depending upon the size offered. For example, a perishable product becomes a better deal only if you need all of it. A fifty-pack of batteries may cost much less per unit, but will cost much more in the long run if you seldom need batteries and most of them pass their sell-by date unused.

PROBLEM

Which is the more economical purchase: a 20-ounce bottle of ketchup at $1.49 or a 28-ounce bottle of ketchup at $1.89?

SOLUTION

$$\frac{\$1.49}{20 \text{ ounces}} = \$0.0745/\text{ounce}. \qquad \frac{\$1.89}{28 \text{ ounces}} = \$0.0675/\text{ounce}.$$

The $1.89 bottle of ketchup is the better deal.

PERCENTS

Problems involving percentages are best solved using basic equations. The word *is* translates to *equals*. The word *percent* is expressed as a fraction over 100, and the word *of* is expressed as multiplication. The unknown is expressed as x. 10% can be expressed as $\frac{10}{100}$ or 0.10, while 200% can be expressed as $\frac{200}{100}$ or 2.

PROBLEMS

1. What is 25% of 12?

2. 14 is 20% of what number?

3. 6 is what percent of 20?

SOLUTIONS

1. $\dfrac{25}{100} \cdot 12 = x \Rightarrow x = \dfrac{300}{100} = 3$

2. $14 = \dfrac{20}{100} \cdot x \Rightarrow 1400 = 20x \Rightarrow x = 70$

3. $6 = \dfrac{x}{100} \cdot 20 \Rightarrow 20x = 600 \Rightarrow x = 30$

There are many financial situations that involve increasing or decreasing an amount by a certain percentage.

% Increase − Find the difference between the new price and the original price and then determine what percent this is of the original price.

$$\% \text{ increase} = \frac{\text{New price } - \text{ Original price}}{\text{Original price}}$$

% Decrease − Find the difference between the original price and new price and then determine what percent this is of the original price.

$$\% \text{ decrease} = \frac{\text{Original price} - \text{New price}}{\text{Original price}}$$

PROBLEM

A house originally cost \$40,000. The house sold for \$150,000. By what percent did the house increase in value?

SOLUTION

$$\% \text{ increase} = \frac{150,000 - 40,000}{40,000} = 2.75 \text{. So the house increased in value by } 275\%.$$

PROBLEM

A new car costs $24,000. As a trade-in, the car would only be worth $15,000. By what percent did the car decrease in value?

SOLUTION

$$\% \text{ decrease} = \frac{24,000 - 15,000}{24,000} = \frac{9,000}{24,000} = 0.375$$

The car decreased in value by 37.5%.

PROBLEM

The cost of Internet service was $45 a month last year. This year, it is $50. What is the percent increase in price?

SOLUTION

$$\% \text{ increase} = \frac{50 - 45}{45} = \frac{5}{45} = 0.111.$$

There is an 11.1% increase in price.

PROBLEM

Your dream cellphone is on sale for 20% off the original price. If the original price is $280, what is the sale price?

SOLUTION

$$\% \text{ decrease} = \frac{20}{100} = \frac{280 - N}{280}$$

$$28,000 - 100N = 5,600 \Rightarrow 100N = 22,400 \Rightarrow N = \$224.$$

PROBLEM

A shirt is on sale for $30. The advertisement says that this price represents a 25% decrease in price. What was the shirt's original price?

SOLUTION

$$\% \text{ decrease} = \frac{25}{100} = \frac{x - 30}{x} \Rightarrow 100x - 3,000 = 25x \Rightarrow 75x = 3,000 \Rightarrow x = \$40.$$

TAXES

We all have to pay taxes. While few people relish paying taxes, everyone enjoys having good schools, roads, and services. In the end, taxes improve our overall quality of life. There are many types of taxes and usually they are computed as a percentage of some quantity. Here are some of the common ones:

- Sales tax: a tax on goods and services. Sales tax is determined by the state and can vary from state to state. As of this writing, the tax rate varies from 0% (Alaska, Delaware, Montana, New Hampshire and Oregon) to 7.25% (California).

- Property tax: paid by anyone who owns land.

- Capital gains taxes: paid by people who have investments that have appreciated (gained value over time) at the time they are sold. Examples include stocks, bonds, and real estate. You pay capital gains taxes on the difference between the purchase price and the sale price. If you sell the investment for less than you paid, you have a capital gains loss.

- Income tax: paid by people who earn income. Income tax is usually not paid by people who earn less than a certain income or who have special situations such as a disability. The amount of money that a person makes is called the **gross income**. When we deduct the income tax and other taxes, we are left with the **net income.** Everyone pays federal income tax. Depending on where you live, you may also pay state taxes and local taxes.

In 2015, the federal tax rates for individual taxpayers are as follows:

If taxable income is between	The tax due is
0 – $9,225	10% of the taxable income
$9,226 – $37,450	$923 + 15% of the amount over $9,225
$37,451 – $90,750	$5,156 + 25% of the amount over $37,450
$90,751 – $189,300	$18,481 + 28% of the amount over $90,750
$189,301 – $411,500	$46,075 + 33% of the amount over $189,300
$411,501 – $413,200	$119,401 + 35% of the amount over $411,500
$413,201 +	$119,996 + 39.6% of the amount over $413,200

Example:

Carrie is single and has a gross income (all taxable) of $50,000. Based on the federal tax rate table above, she is in the category of someone making between $37,451 and $90,750. She is in the 25% tax bracket (paying $5,156 + 25% of the amount over $37,450).

To determine her income tax, we first find the amount of her income that is over $37,450.

$50,000 - \$37,450 = \$12,550$

Carrie pays $5,156 + 0.25(12,550) = 5,156 + 3,137.50 = \$8,293.50$.

She ends up paying $\dfrac{8,293.50}{50,000} = 16.6\%$ of her salary in taxes.

PROBLEM

Wayne lives in Doylestown, Pennsylvania. Pennsylvania has a 3.07% personal income tax. Doylestown has a 1.025% local tax. If Wayne makes $110,000 a year, what is his net salary and what percent of his salary does he pay in taxes?

SOLUTION

Federal tax bracket: 28% $110,000 - 90,750 = 19,250$

Pay: $18,481 + 0.28(19,250) = 18,481 + 5,390 = \$23,871$

State Tax: $0.0307(110,000) = \$3,377$

Local Tax: $0.01025(110,000) = \$1,127.50$

Total Taxes: $23,871 + 3,377 + 1,127.50 = \$28,375.50$

Percentage taxes $= \dfrac{\$28,375.50}{110,000} = 25.8\%$

PROBLEM

Hans owns his own business and makes $175,000 a year in taxable income. He is considering taking on a new contract that would pay him an additional $50,000. What is the difference in federal taxes that he would pay with the additional income? What percentage of the additional $50,000 would be going to taxes?

SOLUTION

Income $= \$175,000$: Tax $= 18,481 + 0.28(175,000 - 90,750) = 18,481 + 0.28(84,250) = 18,481 + 23,590 = \$42,071$

Income $= \$225,000$: Tax $= 46,075 + 0.33(225,000 - 189,300) = 46,075 + 0.33(35,700) = 46,075 + 11,781 = \$57,856$

Difference: $57,856 - 42,071 = \$15,785$

Percent taxes: $\dfrac{15,785}{50,000} = 31.6\%$

MARKUPS AND MARKDOWNS

A **markup** is the difference in the amount the seller buys the product for and the amount at which the seller sells the product.

$$\text{Markup} = \text{Selling price} - \text{Cost} \quad \text{and} \quad \% \text{ Markup} = \frac{\text{Markup}}{\text{Cost}}.$$

All businesspeople mark up any merchandise they sell. (If they didn't, they wouldn't make money.) If a store owner bought a candy bar for 50 cents and sold it for a dollar, his markup would

be $1.00 - 0.50 = 0.50$. His percent markup would be $\dfrac{\text{Markup}}{\text{Cost}} = \dfrac{0.50}{0.50} = 100\%$.

A **markdown** is a reduction from the original selling price. There are many reasons that a retailer would mark down a product. For a car dealer, it could be the change in model year, and the dealer may need to sell all of the prior year's models to make room for the new year's models. In a supermarket, fruit is perishable. The retailer can either sell the fruit that's nearing its shelf-life limitations at a discount or throw it out. Many businesses will lure a customer in with a lower price in the hope that the customer will purchase other items at full price.

A markdown (or discount) is the amount the seller will take off the price of the product to give an incentive for a buyer to purchase it.

$$\text{Markdown} = \text{Original price} - \text{New price}.$$

The percentage markdown is $\dfrac{\text{Markdown}}{\text{Original Price}}$.

PROBLEM

A dealer sells a refrigerator at its list price of $1,200. The dealer's cost was $850. What is the markup and percentage markup?

SOLUTION

The markup is $1,200 - 850 = \$350$. His percentage markup is given by

$$\frac{\text{Markup}}{\text{Cost}} = \frac{350}{850} = 41.2\%.$$

PROBLEM

A new car dealer purchases a car for $25,000. The sticker price on the car (what the dealer tries to sell the car for) is $30,000. The dealer discounts the car by 5%. What is his percentage markup on the car?

SOLUTION

x is the discounted price

$$\frac{5}{100} = \frac{30,000 - x}{30,000} \Rightarrow 3,000,000 - 100x = 150,000 \Rightarrow 100x = 2,850,000 \Rightarrow$$
$$x = \$28,500$$

Markup $= \$28,500 - \$25,000 = \$3,500$ so percentage markup $=$

$$\frac{\text{Markup}}{\text{Cost}} = \frac{3,500}{25,000} = 14\%.$$

PROBLEM

A street vendor sells flowers for $10 a bunch. At the end of the day, he sells the flowers for $4 a bunch. What is the markdown and percentage markdown?

SOLUTION

The markdown is $10 − $4 = $6. The percentage markdown is

$$\frac{\text{Markdown}}{\text{Original Price}} = \frac{6}{10} = 60\%$$

When you operate a business or run a home, you either have a profit, a loss, or you break even.

If your sales (the money you take in) are greater than your expenses (the money you have to pay), you have a profit. If your expenses are greater than your sales, you have a loss. If your sale equals your expenses, you break even.

Suppose a car dealership has $100,000 in expenses per month. If the markup on a car is approximately $2,000, they would need to sell 50 cars a month to break even. If the dealership's goal is to have a $20,000 profit for the month, they would need to sell the 50 cars to break even and then another 10 cars for the $20,000 profit. So they would need to sell 60 cars for the month.

PROBLEM

It costs Mr. Meltzer $800 a week to run his household (rent, food, electricity, etc.). His salary is $40,000 annually. What percent raise will get him to the break-even point?

SOLUTION

$\dfrac{40,000}{52} = 769.23$ a week which is a loss of $30.77

$x\%$ of 769.23 is $30.77 \Rightarrow \dfrac{x}{100} - 769.23 = 30.77 \Rightarrow x = \dfrac{3,077}{769.23} = 4$.

If he gets a 4% raise, he will break even.

TYPES OF INTEREST

When you deposit money into a bank, you are allowing the bank to use your money. The bank may in turn lend that money to other customers to purchase a house or a car. The bank pays you for using your money. The amount that the bank pays you is called **interest**. If you use the bank for savings, the bank pays you interest. If you are the one who gets a loan from the bank, you pay the bank interest for the use of their money.

The amount you borrow from a bank or the money you deposit in a bank is called the **principal**. The amount of interest paid is usually a percent of the principal.

SIMPLE INTEREST

The simple interest formula is $I = P \times r \times t$ where P is the principal, r is the interest rate, and t is the time period.

The interest rate is usually given per year, called the **annual percentage rate** (APR). When r is given as a percentage per year, the time is also expressed in years. It is possible for the rate to be given in other time periods, such as months. In that case, time would have to be measured in months. Bank interest rates are usually given as an APR unless otherwise stated.

PROBLEM

Calculate the simple interest earned in two years on a deposit of $500 if the APR is 3%.

SOLUTION

$P = 500, r = 3\% = 0.03, t = 2$

$I = P \cdot r \cdot t = 500(0.03)(2) = 30$. So the simple interest is $30.

PROBLEM

Calculate the simple interest due on a 6-month loan of $2,500 if the APR is 4.5%.

SOLUTION

$$P = 2{,}500, \; r = 4.5\% = 0.045, \; t = \frac{6 \text{ months}}{1 \text{ year}} = \frac{6 \text{ months}}{12 \text{ months}} = \frac{1}{2}$$

$I = 2{,}500(0.045)(0.5) = 56.25$. So the simple interest is $56.25.

(Note that rather than work in years, we could work in months and still arrive at the same answer.)

$$P = 2{,}500, \; r = \frac{4.5\%}{\text{year}} = \frac{0.045}{12 \text{ months}}, \; t = 6 \text{ months}$$

$$I = 2{,}500 \left(\frac{0.045}{12} \right) (6) = \$56.25.$$

PROBLEM

If I earned $250 simple interest on a 3-year deposit of $5,000, what was the interest rate?

SOLUTION

$P = 5{,}000, \; I = 250, \; t = 3$

$$250 = 5{,}000(r)(3) \Rightarrow r = \frac{250}{15{,}000} = 0.0167 = 1.67\%$$

If the time period of a loan with an annual interest rate is given in days, it is necessary to convert the time period of the loan to a fractional part of a year. Usually, to simplify calculations, the value of t in years is divided by 360, an approximation to the number of days in the year (12 months times an average of 30 days per month).

PROBLEM

Calculate the simple interest on a 45-day loan of $4,000 if the interest rate is 7%.

SOLUTION

$$P = 4{,}000, \; r = 7\% = 0.07, \; t = \frac{45 \text{ days}}{360 \text{ days}} = \frac{45}{360}$$

$$I = 4{,}000(0.07) \left(\frac{45}{360} \right) = 35. \text{ So the simple interest due is } \$35.$$

COMPOUND INTEREST

Simple interest is given on the original principal only. Once interest is applied to the principal, however, the principal changes. It is only fair to give interest to the new principal. The process of applying interest to the original principal and to any interest that has occurred is called *compounding* and the interest is called **compound interest**.

PROBLEM

You deposit $1,000 in a savings account that earns 4% interest, compounded annually, for 4 years. How much will you have at the end of the 4 years?

SOLUTION

During the first year, the interest is given by $I = P \times r \times t = 1,000(0.04)(1) = \$40$. So at the end of the first year, the principal is now $1,040.

During the second year, the interest is given by $I = P \times r \times t = 1,040(0.04)(1) = \$41.60$. Instead of $40 interest, we have made $41.60 because our interest is based on a principal of $1,040 rather than $1,000. So at the end of the second year, the principal is now $1,081.60.

During the third year, the interest is given by $I = P \times r \times t = 1,081.60(0.04)(1) = \$43.26$. Our interest has gone up again and the principal is now $1,124.86.

Finally during the fourth year, the interest is given by $I = P \times r \times t = 1,124.86(0.04)(1) = \$44.99$. Our interest has gone up again and the maturity value (the value of your deposit at the end of the timeframe) is $1,169.85.

Using simple interest, we would only have received $40 interest for each of the 4 years and our maturity value would have been $1,160. Compounding gave us an extra $9.85. It's not much, but when interest is compounded for many years, when the interest rate is high, or the principal is high, compounding yields much greater amounts than simple interest does.

Compounding does not always occur annually. Interest can be given more frequently during the year. The frequency with which the interest is compounded is called the **compounding period**.

PROBLEM

Again you deposit $1,000 in a bank at 4% APR, but now the interest is **compounded quarterly**. This means that at the end of each quarter of a year (3 months), interest will be applied. Our interest will be given 4 times a year meaning that each quarter we will get $\frac{4\%}{4} = 1\%$. How much will we have at the end of one year?

SOLUTION

End of first quarter: $I = P \times r \times t = 1,000(0.01)(1) = \$10$
$$A = P + I = 1,000 + 10 = \$1,010$$

End of second quarter: $I = P \times r \times t = 1,010(0.01)(1) = \$10.10$
$$A = P + I = 1,010 + 10.10 = \$1,020.10$$

End of third quarter: $I = P \times r \times t = 1,020.10(0.01)(1) = \$10.20$
$$A = P + I = 1,020.10 + 10.20 = \$1,030.30$$

End of fourth quarter: $I = P \times r \times t = 1,030.30(0.01)(1) = \$10.30.$
$$A = P + I = 1,030.30 + 10.30 = \$1,040.60$$

Compared to the $1,040 amount when compounded annually, we have made an extra 60 cents when compounding quarterly. Compounding using even shorter periods of time can give savers more money, as we will soon see.

COMPOUND AMOUNT FORMULA

The compound amount formula is given by $A = P\left(1 + \dfrac{r}{n}\right)^{nt}$ where A is the compound amount, P is the principal, r is the APR, n is the number of compounding periods per year, and t is the number of years.

PROBLEM

Using the compounding periods listed below, find the future value of a $1,000 deposit invested for 10 years in a savings account earning 4% interest.

(A) Simple

(B) Annually

(C) Semiannually

(D) Quarterly

(E) Monthly

(F) Daily

SOLUTION

Interest compounded	n	Formula	A
(A) Simple — no compounding		$A = 1{,}000\left[1 + 0.04(10)\right]$	$1,400.00
(B) Annually	1	$A = 1{,}000\left(1 + \dfrac{0.04}{1}\right)^{1(10)}$	$1,480.24
(C) Semiannually	2	$A = 1{,}000\left(1 + \dfrac{0.04}{2}\right)^{2(10)}$	$1,485.95
(D) Quarterly	4	$A = 1{,}000\left(1 + \dfrac{0.04}{4}\right)^{4(10)}$	$1,488.86
(E) Monthly	12	$A = 1{,}000\left(1 + \dfrac{0.04}{12}\right)^{12(10)}$	$1,490.83
(F) Daily	360	$A = 1{,}000\left(1 + \dfrac{0.04}{360}\right)^{360(10)}$	$1,491.79

Note that the greater number of compound periods, the larger the interest amount becomes. No banks use simple interest and you cannot get a loan using simple interest. There is only about a $12 difference between the value of the principal when compounded annually and compounded daily. Still, when the principal and number of years are large, there can be quite a big difference in the future value using the different methods. We also see that as we increase the number of compounding periods, the larger the compound amount becomes. But it gets larger by a smaller amount. There is less than a one dollar difference between the amounts you receive by compounding daily as opposed to compounding monthly. Over 10 years, that amount is negligible. It is for that reason that most banks today compound daily.

FUTURE VALUE AND MATURITY VALUE

When you borrow money, the total amount to be repaid to the lender is the sum of the principal and interest. When you withdraw money from a bank, you will receive both the principal and the interest. We call this sum the **future value** or **maturity value**.

The future or maturity value for simple interest is given by $A = P + I$ where A is the amount after the interest, and I has been added to the principal, P. The formula can also be expressed as $A = P + P \times r \times t$ or $A = P(1 + rt)$.

PROBLEM

Calculate the maturity value of a simple interest, 15-month loan of $7,500 if the interest rate is 6.5%.

SOLUTION

$P = 7{,}500$, $r = 0.065$, $t = 15$ months $\cdot \dfrac{1 \text{ year}}{12 \text{ months}} = \dfrac{15}{12}$ years

$I = 7{,}500\,(0.065)\left(\dfrac{15}{12}\right) = \$609.38$

$A = 7{,}500 + 609.38 = 8{,}109.38$. The borrower needs to pay back $8,109.38.

PROBLEM

At the birth of their child, Greg, the Goldbergs place $5,000 into a simple interest account that earns 3.5% APR. When Greg graduates from high school at age 18, they plan to give him the money in the account. What is the future value of the deposit?

SOLUTION

$P = 5{,}000$, $r = 0.035$, $t = 18$

$I = P \cdot r \cdot t = 5{,}000(0.035)(18) = \$3{,}150$

$A = P + I = 5{,}000 + 3{,}150 = 8{,}150$. Greg will receive $8,150.

PROBLEM

The maturity value of a 3-month loan of $8,000 is $8,170. What is the simple interest rate?

SOLUTION

$A = 8{,}170$, $P = 8{,}000$, $t = 3$ months $\cdot \dfrac{1 \text{ year}}{12 \text{ months}} = \dfrac{3}{12} = \dfrac{1}{4}$ year

$A = P + I \Rightarrow 8{,}170 = 8{,}000 + I \Rightarrow I = 170$

$I = P \cdot r \cdot t \Rightarrow 170 = 8000\left(\dfrac{1}{4}\right)r$

$r = \dfrac{170}{2{,}000} = 0.085$. The interest rate is 8.5%.

PROBLEM

Your property tax bill is \$3,200. The county charges a penalty of 16% APR simple interest for late payments. How much would you pay if you pay the bill one month late?

SOLUTION

$P = 3,200, \ r = 0.16, \ t = 1 \text{ month} \cdot \dfrac{1 \text{ year}}{12 \text{ months}} = \dfrac{1}{12} \text{ years}$

$A = P(1 + rt) = 3,200\left[1 + 0.16\left(\dfrac{1}{12}\right)\right] = \$3,242.67.$

PROBLEM

At the birth of their child, Greg, the Goldbergs place \$5,000 into a compound interest account that earns 3.5% APR. When Greg graduates from high school at age 18, they plan to give him the money in the account. What is the difference in the future value of the deposit if it is compounded annually and compounded daily?

SOLUTION

Annually: $A = 5,000\left(1 + \dfrac{0.035}{1}\right)^{1(18)} = \$9,287.45$

Daily: $A = 5,000\left(1 + \dfrac{0.035}{360}\right)^{360(18)} = \$9,387.77$

Difference: \$100.32

PROBLEM

Ted, who is 25 years old, places \$2,500 into a retirement account that he will redeem at age 65. He has a choice of 6.5% APR compounded quarterly or 6.4% APR compounded daily. Which one will give him the larger future value?

SOLUTION

Quarterly: $A = 2,500\left(1 + \dfrac{0.065}{4}\right)^{4(40)} = \$32,963.20$

Daily: $A = 2,500\left(1 + \dfrac{0.064}{360}\right)^{360(40)} = \$32,332.19$

The 6.5% APR compounded quarterly will give him the larger future value.

PROBLEM

Ted purchases a $40,000 car. He puts a $10,000 down payment on the car and finances the remaining balance. What is the future value of the loan if he finances the car at 5.2% interest for 4 years compounded daily?

SOLUTION

$$A = 30,000\left(1 + \frac{0.052}{360}\right)^{360(4)} = 36,935.84$$

The value of the loan is $36,935.84 if he pays it back at the end of the loan period.

Since he makes monthly payments, he will actually pay back less money.

Some banking institutions advertise **continuous compounding,** which means the number of compounding periods per year gets very, very large. When compounding continuously, rather than use the formula $A = P\left(1 + \frac{r}{n}\right)^{nt}$, we use the formula $A = Pe^{rt}$ where e is approximately equal to 2.71828. Unless the principal is large and/or the length of time is large, continuous compounding yields little more than compounding daily does.

PROBLEM

Find the difference in the future value of a $10,000 investment for 30 years at 5% APR compounded daily and compounded continuously.

SOLUTION

Daily: $A = 10,000\left(1 + \frac{0.05}{360}\right)^{360(30)} = \$44,812.22$

Continuously: $A = 10,000(2.71828)^{0.05(30)} = \$44,816.85$

Difference: $4.63

When interest is compounded, the annual rate of interest (APR) is sometimes called the **nominal rate.** The **effective rate** is the simple interest rate that would yield the same amount of interest after one year. When a bank advertises a 3% annual interest rate compounded daily, yielding 3.05%, the nominal interest rate is 3% and the effective rate is 3.05%.

PROBLEM

Find the effective interest rate on an investment compounded quarterly with an APR of 4.25%.

SOLUTION

The principal amount makes no difference. Use $100 to make the numbers easy.

$$A = 100\left(1 + \frac{0.0425}{4}\right)^{4(1)} = \$104.32$$

$$I = A - P = 104.32 - 100 = \$4.32$$

So the compounded interest is $4.32, which means the effective interest rate is 4.32%.

PRESENT VALUE

The **present value** of an investment is the original principal investment, the value of the investment before it earns any interest. Therefore, it is the principal P in our compound interest formula. But we can also use present value to determine how much money must be invested today for an investment to have a specific value at a future date.

Our compound interest formula states that $A = P\left(1 + \frac{r}{n}\right)^{nt}$. Solving for P, we get $P = \dfrac{A}{\left(1 + \frac{r}{n}\right)^{nt}}$.

The present value formula is $P = \dfrac{A}{\left(1 + \frac{r}{n}\right)^{nt}}$ where P is the original principal (the present value), A is the compound amount, r is the APR, n is the number of compounding periods per year, and t is the number of years.

PROBLEM

The Hendricks wish to purchase a new car worth $20,000 for their newborn son, Charles, when he graduates high school at age 18. If they invest their money in an account compounded daily at 4.75% APR, how much should they invest when Charles is born?

SOLUTION

$$P = \frac{A}{\left(1 + \frac{r}{n}\right)^{nt}} = \frac{20,000}{\left(1 + \frac{0.0475}{360}\right)^{360(18)}} = \$8,506.14$$

They should invest $8,506.14. To do this calculation, it is easier to find the value of the denominator first and then divide that answer into 20,000.

PROBLEM

At age 25, Andrea received a large bonus from her employer. Rather than buy a house or a car, she decided to invest it. Her goal is to have $100,000 in a retirement account when she retires at age 65. If she gets an interest rate of 6.5% compounded monthly, how much should she invest?

SOLUTION

$$P = \frac{A}{\left(1 + \frac{r}{n}\right)^{nt}} = \frac{100,000}{\left(1 + \frac{0.065}{12}\right)^{12(40)}} = \$7,479.65$$

She should invest $7,479.65. Realize that because of inflation, in 40 years $100,000 won't have the same buying power as it does today.

INFLATION

When you invest money for a period of time in an interest-bearing account, you will have more money than you originally deposited. But that does not mean that you will be able to buy more with the compounded investment than you could have with the original investment. The reason is the effect of **inflation**. Inflation is an economic condition during which there are increases in the costs of goods and services. Inflation is usually expressed as an annual percentage rate. If the rate of inflation is greater than the compounding rate, an investor is actually losing money.

For example, suppose the price of a new computer is $2,000. You have enough money to purchase the computer, but decide to invest the $2,000 into an account paying 3.5% compounded quarterly. After one year, the compound amount is $2,070.92. If the rate of inflation is 4.5%, the cost of the computer is 2,000(1.045) = $2,090. Because $2,070.92 < $2,090, you have lost purchasing power. The compounded amount is not enough to pay for that same computer. Your money lost value because it buys less than it could one year before.

PROBLEM

You currently make $40,000. You want to know what an equivalent salary will be in 15 years if the inflation rate stays at 1.75%. You are finding a salary that will have the same purchasing power as today's salary.

SOLUTION

$P = 40,000$, $r = 0.0175$, $n = 1$ (since inflation is an annual rate), $t = 15$

$$A = P\left(1+\frac{r}{n}\right)^{nt} = 40,000\left(1+\frac{0.0175}{1}\right)^{1(15)} = \$51,889.11$$

15 years from now, you need to earn an annual salary of $51,889.11 to have the same purchasing power as today.

PROBLEM

In the year 2020, you purchase an insurance policy that will pay you $500,000 when you retire in the year 2050. Assuming an annual inflation rate of 3%, what will be the purchasing power of the $500,000 in the year 2050?

SOLUTION

$A = 500,000$, $r = 0.03$, $n = 1$ (since inflation is an annual rate), $t = 30$

$$P = \frac{A}{\left(1+\frac{r}{n}\right)^{nt}} = \frac{500000}{\left(1+\frac{0.03}{1}\right)^{1(30)}} = 205,993.38$$

The purchasing power of half a million dollars in 2050 is only $205,993.38.

DRILL QUESTIONS

1. 12 is what percent of 25?

   (A) 40
   (B) 48
   (C) 3
   (D) 300

2. 40 is 8% of what number?

   (A) 32
   (B) 3.2
   (C) 50
   (D) 500

3. Which of the following has the largest value?

   (A) 90% of 90%
   (B) 120% of 80%
   (C) 20% of 500%
   (D) 0.5% of 2,000%

4. Frederick purchased an airplane for $79,500. He sold the plane three years later for $92,000. If the capital gains tax rate is 15%, what is the capital gains tax on the sale of the plane?

   (A) $1,875
   (B) $5,850
   (C) $11,925
   (D) $13,800

5. Bernie is a single taxpayer who made $1 million this year. He pays $119,996 + 39.6% of the amount over $413,200 in taxes. What percentage of his income goes to taxes?

   (A) 28.3%
   (B) 31.7%
   (C) 35.2%
   (D) 39.6%

6. In his first job, Steve paid $1,600 in federal taxes. He is in the bracket that requires him to pay $923 + 15% of the amount his yearly pay is over $9,225. What is his yearly pay?

   (A) $10,667
   (B) $11,531
   (C) $12,745
   (D) $13,738

7. Ray received $13,550 for the trade-in of his car. He purchased a new car for $45,200. If the state charges 6% sales tax and $75 for tags, what is his total payment for the new car?

   (A) $30,912
   (B) $33,624
   (C) $34,362
   (D) $34,437

8. A car dealership advertises that for one day only, the cost of a $15,000 car will be reduced to $14,000. What is the percent decrease in price?

   (A) 2.1%
   (B) 6.7%
   (C) 7.1%
   (D) 93.3%

9. The list price for a men's suit is $350. The store bought it for $200. What is the store's percentage markup?

   (A) 64.6%
   (B) 57.1%
   (C) 42.9%
   (D) 75%

10. An electronics store purchases a television for $1,000 and marks it up 30%. When the new models come out, they discount the price of the old models by 30%. What is the store's net on the sale of this TV?

    (A) Store broke even
    (B) Store lost $90
    (C) Store made $30
    (D) Store lost $300

11. Furniture store A discounts a sofa 50% while furniture store B discounts the same sofa 30% and then 20%. Which store offers the best deal?

    (A) Store A
    (B) Store B
    (C) They give the same deal.
    (D) It depends on the price of the sofa.

12. John's parents lend him $12,000 to buy a used car that he can drive to work. He promises to pay them back in 200 days at 3% simple interest. How much will he pay them back?

    (A) $200
    (B) $12,036
    (C) $12,200
    (D) $12,360

13. What is the approximate interest paid on a 5-year $15,000 certificate of deposit at 4.25% APR compounded quarterly?

    (A) $3,531
    (B) $3,470
    (C) $18,470
    (D) $18,531

14. To the nearest $50, what is the dollar difference in the future value of an investment of $25,000 over 10 years at 3.4% compounded annually and compounded daily?

    (A) $50
    (B) $100
    (C) $200
    (D) $9,250

15. You take out a loan for $50,000 and plan to pay it back in 8 years. You have a choice of different payback plans. Which one is the most advantageous to you?

    (A) 5.2% at simple interest
    (B) 4.5% compounded annually
    (C) 4.4% compounded semi-annually
    (D) 4.3% compounded monthly

16. Different banks offer nominal interest rates for their large investors. Which bank gives the highest effective interest rate?

    (A) 5.9% compounded annually
    (B) 5.8% compounded quarterly
    (C) 5.7% compounded monthly
    (D) 5.6% compounded continuously

17. Diane is 40 years old and wins $100,000 in a lottery after taxes. She decides to spend some on a car and a vacation and to invest the rest. She wants the amount that she invests to grow to the value of $100,000 at the time of her early retirement at age 62. How much money would she have to spend on the car and vacation if she invests her money at 4.8% compounded daily?

    (A) $34,787
    (B) $5,101
    (C) $94,899
    (D) $65,213

18. Ian puts the same amount of money into two different banks, each with a variable rate account. Bank A gives 4% APR the first year and then 3% APR the next year, each compounded quarterly. Bank B gives 3% APR the first year and 4% APR the second year, each compounded quarterly. Which bank gives a higher future value?

    (A) Bank A
    (B) Bank B
    (C) They both have the same future value.
    (D) It depends on the principal.

19. The cost of medical school is approximately $70,000 a year. A medical student has to borrow the money to pay for it. For each of 4 years, he borrows $70,000 at 4% interest compounded monthly. If no money is paid back until the end of the 4th year, how much is owed?

    (A) $280,000
    (B) $291,200
    (C) $309,705
    (D) $328,496

20. A gallon of milk costs $3.83. If the inflation rate stays at 4.3%, how much more will a gallon of milk cost 10 years from now?

    (A) $0.17
    (B) $2.01
    (C) $4.00
    (D) $5.84

ANSWERS TO DRILL QUESTIONS

1. **(B)** $12 = \dfrac{x}{100}(25) \Rightarrow 25x = 1{,}200 \Rightarrow x = 48$

2. **(D)** $40 = \dfrac{8}{100}x \Rightarrow 8x = 4{,}000 \Rightarrow x = 500$

3. **(C)**

    (A) $09(0.9) = 0.81 = 81\%$

    (B) $1.2\,(0.8) = 0.96 = 96\%$

    (C) $0.2(5) = 1 = 100\%$

    (D) $0.005\,(20) = 0.1 = 10\%$

4. **(A)** $0.15(92{,}000 - 79{,}500) = 0.15(12{,}500) = \$1{,}875$

5. **(C)**

    Tax $= 119{,}996 + 0.396(1{,}000{,}000 - 413{,}200) = 119{,}996 + 0.396(586{,}800) = 119{,}996 + 232{,}373 = 352{,}369$

    Percent in taxes: $\dfrac{352{,}369}{1{,}000{,}000} = 35.2\%$

6. **(D)**

    Tax $= 923 + 0.15(x - 9{,}225) = 1{,}600$

    $923 + 0.15x - 1383.75 = 1{,}600 = 0.15x = 2{,}060.75$

    $x = \dfrac{2{,}060.75}{0.15} = \$13{,}738.33$, which rounds to $13,738.

    Note that this problem can also be done by trial and error.

7. **(B)**

Tax $= 0.06(45{,}200 - 13{,}550) = 0.06(31{,}650) = \$1{,}899$

Car cost $= 31{,}650 + 1{,}899 + 75 = \$33{,}624$

8. **(B)**

$$\% \text{ decrease} = \frac{\text{Original price} - \text{New price}}{\text{Original price}} = \frac{15{,}000 - 14{,}000}{15{,}000}$$

$$= \frac{1{,}000}{15{,}000} = 0.667 = 6.7\%$$

9. **(D)** Markup $=$ Selling price $-$ Cost $= 350 - 200 = 150$

$$\text{Percentage markup} = \frac{\text{Markup}}{\text{Cost}} = \frac{150}{200} = 75\%$$

10. **(B)** Price $= 1{,}000 + 0.30(1{,}000) = 1{,}000 + 300 = \$1{,}300$

Discount $= 0.30(1{,}300) = 390$

Discounted price $= 1{,}300 - 390 = \$910$

Store: Discounted price $-$ Cost $= 910 - 1{,}000 = -\$90$

11. **(A)** Suppose the sofa's price is \$1,000. Store A will sell it for \$500.
Store B discounts it \$300, making the price \$700 and then discounts it \$140 making the price \$560. Store A is better for the buyer.

If the price is x, Store A sells it for $0.5x$. Store B sells it for $0.8(0.7x) = 0.56x$.

12. **(C)**

$$P = 12{,}000, \; r = 3\% = 0.03, \; t = \frac{200 \text{ days}}{360 \text{ days}} = \frac{200}{360}$$

$$A = P + P \cdot r \cdot t = 12{,}000 + 12{,}000(0.03)\left(\frac{200}{360}\right) = 12{,}000 + 200 = \$12{,}200$$

13. **(A)**

$$P = 15{,}000, r = 0.0{,}425, n = 4, t = 5$$

$$A = 15{,}000\left(1 + \frac{0.0425}{4}\right)^{4(5)} = \$18{,}530.71$$

$$I = A - P = 18{,}530.71 - 15{,}000 = 3{,}530.71 \approx \$3{,}531$$

14. **(C)**

$$\text{Annually}: 25{,}000\left(1 + \frac{.034}{1}\right)^{1(10)} = \$34{,}925.72$$

$$\text{Daily}: 25{,}000\left(1 + \frac{.034}{360}\right)^{360(10)} = \$35{,}123.13$$

Difference $: 35{,}123.13 - 34{,}925.72 = 197.41 \approx \$200$

15. **(D)**   With a loan, you want to pay back the least amount.

(A) $50,000 + 50,000(0.052)(8) = \$70,800$

(B) $50,000\left(1 + \dfrac{.045}{1}\right)^{1(8)} = \$71,105.03$

(C) $50,000\left(1 + \dfrac{.044}{2}\right)^{2(8)} = \$70,824.64$

(D) $50,000\left(1 + \dfrac{.043}{12}\right)^{12(8)} = \$70,485.58$

16. **(B)**

(A) $100\left(1 + \dfrac{.059}{1}\right)^{1} = 105.9 \ (5.9\% \ \text{Effective interest})$

(B) $100\left(1 + \dfrac{.058}{4}\right)^{4} = \$105.93 \ (5.93\% \ \text{Effective interest})$

(C) $100\left(1 + \dfrac{.057}{12}\right)^{12} = \$105.85 \ (5.96\% \ \text{Effective interest})$

(D) $100(2.71828)^{0.056} = \$105.76 \ (5.76\% \ \text{Effective interest})$

17. **(D)**

$A = 100,000, \ r = 0.048, \ n = 360, \ t = 22$

$P = \dfrac{A}{\left(1 + \dfrac{r}{n}\right)^{nt}} = \dfrac{100,000}{\left(1 + \dfrac{0.048}{360}\right)^{360(22)}} = 34,786.89$

She can spend about $\$100,000 - \$34,787 = \$65,213$ on the car and vacation.

18. **(C)**

Bank A: $P\left(1 + \dfrac{.04}{4}\right)^{1(4)}\left(1 + \dfrac{.03}{4}\right)^{1(4)}$

Bank B: $P\left(1 + \dfrac{.03}{4}\right)^{1(4)}\left(1 + \dfrac{.04}{4}\right)^{1(4)}$

These are the same no matter the value of P.

19. **(C)**

Year 1's money is borrowed for 4 years: $70,000\left(1+\dfrac{.04}{12}\right)^{12(4)} = \$82,124$

Year 2's money is borrowed for 3 years: $70,000\left(1+\dfrac{.04}{12}\right)^{12(3)} = \$78,909$

Year 3's money is borrowed for 2 years: $70,000\left(1+\dfrac{.04}{12}\right)^{12(2)} = \$75,820$

Year 4's money is borrowed for 1 year: $70,000\left(1+\dfrac{.04}{12}\right)^{12(1)} = \$72,852$

Total: $82,124 + 78,909 + 75,820 + 72,852 = \$309,705$

20. **(B)**

$P = 3.83$, $r = 0.043$, $n = 1$ (since inflation is an annual rate), $t = 10$

$A = P\left(1+\dfrac{r}{n}\right)^{nt} = 3.83\left(1+\dfrac{0.043}{1}\right)^{1(10)} = \$5.84$

$5.84 - 3.83 = \$2.01$

■ GEOMETRY TOPICS

Plane geometry refers to two-dimensional shapes (that is, shapes that can be drawn on a sheet of paper), such as triangles, parallelograms, trapezoids, and circles. Three-dimensional objects (that is, shapes with depth) are the subjects of solid geometry.

TRIANGLES

> A closed three-sided geometric figure is called a **triangle**. The points of the intersection of the sides of a triangle are called the **vertices** of the triangle.

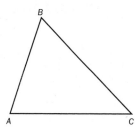

A **side** of a triangle is a line segment whose endpoints are the vertices of two angles of the triangle. The perimeter of a triangle is the sum of the measures of the sides of the triangle.

An **interior angle** of a triangle is an angle formed by two sides and includes the third side within its collection of points. The sum of the measures of the interior angles of a triangle is 180°.

A **scalene triangle** has no equal sides.

An **isosceles triangle** has at least two equal sides. The third side is called the **base** of the triangle, and the base angles (the angles opposite the equal sides) are equal.

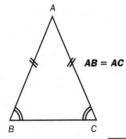

An **equilateral triangle** has all three sides equal. $\overline{AB} = \overline{AC} = \overline{BC}$. An equilateral triangle is also **equiangular**, with each angle equaling 60°.

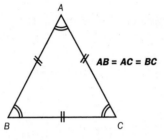

An **acute triangle** has three acute angles (less than 90°).

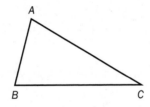

An **obtuse triangle** has one obtuse angle (greater than 90°).

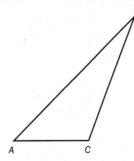

A **right triangle** has a right angle. The side opposite the right angle in a right triangle is called the **hypotenuse** of the right triangle. The other two sides are called the **legs** of the right triangle. By the **Pythagorean Theorem**, the lengths of the three sides of a right triangle are related by the formula

$$c^2 = a^2 + b^2$$

where c is the hypotenuse and a and b are the other two sides (the legs). The Pythagorean Theorem is discussed in more detail in the next section.

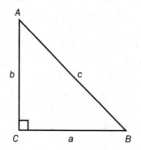

An **altitude**, or **height**, of a triangle is a line segment from a vertex of the triangle perpendicular to the opposite side. For an obtuse triangle, the altitude sometimes is drawn as a perpendicular line to an extension of the opposite side.

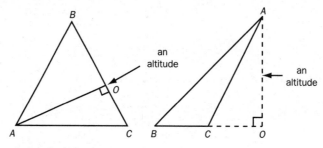

The **area** of a triangle is given by

$$A = \frac{1}{2}bh$$

where h is the altitude and b is the base to which the altitude is drawn.

A line segment connecting a vertex of a triangle and the midpoint of the opposite side is called a **median** of the triangle.

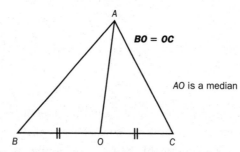

A line that bisects and is perpendicular to a side of a triangle is called a **perpendicular bisector** of that side.

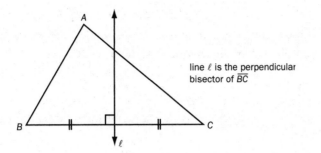

line ℓ is the perpendicular bisector of $\overline{BC}$

An **angle bisector** of a triangle is a line that bisects an angle and extends to the opposite side of the triangle.

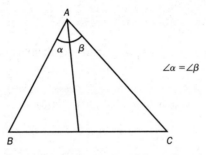

$\angle\alpha = \angle\beta$

The line segment that joins the midpoints of two sides of a triangle is called a **midline** of the triangle.

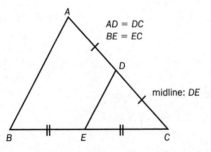

AD = DC
BE = EC

midline: DE

An **exterior angle** of a triangle is an angle formed outside a triangle by one side of the triangle and the extension of an adjacent side.

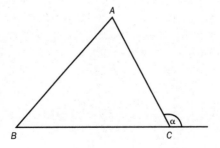

PROBLEM

The measure of the vertex angle of an isosceles triangle exceeds the measure of each base angle by 30°. Find the value of each angle of the triangle.

SOLUTION

In an isosceles triangle, the angles opposite the congruent sides (the base angles) are, themselves, congruent and of equal value.

Therefore,

1. Let x = the measure of each base angle

2. Then $x + 30$ = the measure of the vertex angle

We can solve for x algebraically by keeping in mind that the sum of all the measures of the angles of a triangle is 180°.

$$x + x + (x + 30) = 180$$
$$3x + 30 = 180$$
$$3x = 150$$
$$x = 50$$

Therefore, the base angles each measure 50°, and the vertex angle measures 80°.

THE PYTHAGOREAN THEOREM

The **Pythagorean Theorem** pertains to a right triangle, which, as we saw, is a triangle that has one 90° angle. The Pythagorean Theorem tells you that the square of the hypotenuse of a right triangle is equal to the sum of the squares of the other two sides, or

$$c^2 = a^2 + b^2$$

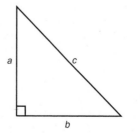

The Pythagorean Theorem is useful because if you know the length of any two sides of a right triangle, you can figure out the length of the third side.

PROBLEM

In a right triangle, one leg is 3 inches and the other leg is 4 inches. What is the length of the hypotenuse?

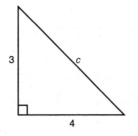

SOLUTION

$$c^2 = a^2 + b^2$$

$$c^2 = 3^2 + 4^2$$

$$c^2 = 9 + 16$$

$$c^2 = 25$$

$$c = 5$$

PROBLEM

If one leg of a right triangle is 6 inches, and the hypotenuse is 10, what is the length of the other leg?

SOLUTION

First, write down the equation for the Pythagorean Theorem. Next, plug in the information you are given. The hypotenuse c is equal to 10 and one of the legs, b, is equal to 6. Solve for a.

$$c^2 = a^2 + b^2$$

$$a^2 = c^2 - b^2$$

$$a^2 = 10^2 - 6^2$$

$$a^2 = 100 - 36$$

$$a^2 = 64$$

$$a = 8 \text{ inches}$$

PROBLEM

What is the value of *b* in the right triangle shown below?

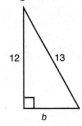

SOLUTION

To answer this question, you need to use the Pythagorean Theorem. The problem is asking for the value of the missing leg.

$$c^2 = a^2 + b^2$$

$$b^2 = c^2 - a^2$$

$$b^2 = 13^2 - 12^2$$

$$b^2 = 169 - 144$$

$$b^2 = 25$$

$$b = 5$$

Triangle Inequality: In any triangle with sides *a*, *b*, and *c*, $a+b>c$, $a+c>b$, and $b+c>a$. This states that the sum of any two sides must be greater than the third side.

So a triangle with sides 1, 4, and 9 is impossible as $1 + 4 < 9$. A triangle with sides 6, 12, and 6 is also impossible as $6 + 6 = 12$. To be possible, the third side must be greater than 12.

QUADRILATERALS

A **polygon** is any closed figure with straight line segments as sides. A **quadrilateral** is any polygon with four sides. The points where the sides meet are called **vertices** (singular: **vertex**).

PARALLELOGRAMS

A **parallelogram** is a quadrilateral whose opposite sides are parallel.

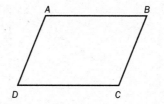

Two angles that have their vertices at the endpoints of the same side of a parallelogram are called **consecutive angles**. So $\angle A$ is consecutive to $\angle B$; $\angle B$ is consecutive to $\angle C$; $\angle C$ is consecutive to $\angle D$; and $\angle D$ is consecutive to $\angle A$.

The perpendicular segment connecting any point of a line containing one side of a parallelogram to the line containing the opposite side of the parallelogram is called the **altitude** of the parallelogram.

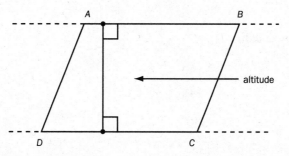

A **diagonal** of a polygon is a line segment joining any two nonconsecutive vertices. The area of a parallelogram is given by the formula $A = bh$, where b is the base and h is the height drawn perpendicular to that base. Note that the height is the same as the altitude of the parallelogram.

Example:

The area of the parallelogram below is:

$$A = bh$$

$$A = (10)(3)$$

$$A = 30$$

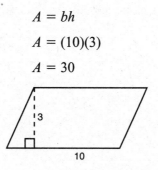

RECTANGLES

A **rectangle** is a parallelogram with right angles.

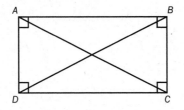

- The diagonals of a rectangle are equal, $\overline{AC} = \overline{BD}$.

- If the diagonals of a parallelogram are equal, the parallelogram is a rectangle.

- If a quadrilateral has four right angles, then it is a rectangle.

- The area of a rectangle is given by the formula $A = lw$, where l is the length and w is the width.

Example:

The area of the rectangle below is:

$$A = lw$$

$$A = (4)(9)$$

$$A = 36$$

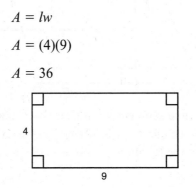

RHOMBI

A **rhombus** (plural: **rhombi**) is a parallelogram that has two adjacent sides that are equal.

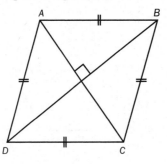

- All sides of a rhombus are equal.

- The diagonals of a rhombus are perpendicular bisectors of each other.

- The area of a rhombus can be found by the formula $A = \frac{1}{2}(d_1 \times d_2)$, where d_1 and d_2 are the diagonals.

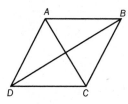

ABCD is a rhombus. $AC = 4$ and $BD = 7$. The area of the rhombus is

$$\left(\frac{1}{2}\right)(AC)(BD) = \left(\frac{1}{2}\right)(4)(7) = 14.$$

- The diagonals of a rhombus bisect the angles of the rhombus.

- If the diagonals of a parallelogram are perpendicular, the parallelogram is a rhombus.

- If a quadrilateral has four equal sides, then it is a rhombus.

- A parallelogram is a rhombus if either diagonal of the parallelogram bisects the angles of the vertices it joins.

SQUARES

A **square** is a rhombus with a right angle.

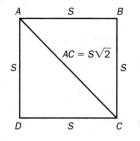

- A square is an equilateral quadrilateral.

- A square has all the properties of rhombi and rectangles.

- In a square, the measure of either diagonal can be calculated by multiplying the length of any side by the square root of 2.

- The area of a square is given by the formula $A = s^2$, where s is the side of the square.

- Since all sides of a square are equal, it does not matter which side is used.

Example:

The area of the square shown below is:

$$A = s^2$$

$$A = 6^2$$

$$A = 36$$

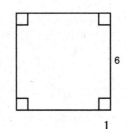

The area of a square can also be found by taking $\frac{1}{2}$ the product of the length of the diagonal squared. This comes from a combination of the facts that the area of a rhombus is $\left(\frac{1}{2}\right) d_1 d_2$ and that $d_1 = d_2$ for a square.

Example:

The area of the square shown below is:

$$A = \frac{1}{2}d^2$$

$$A = \frac{1}{2}(8)^2$$

$$A = 32$$

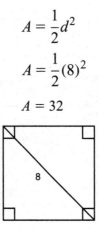

TRAPEZOIDS

A **trapezoid** is a quadrilateral with two and only two parallel sides. The parallel sides of a trapezoid are called the **bases**. The **median** of a trapezoid is the line joining the midpoints of the nonparallel sides.

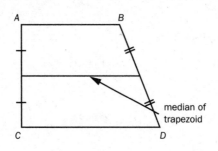

median of trapezoid

The perpendicular segment connecting any point in the line containing one base of the trapezoid to the line containing the other base is the **altitude** of the trapezoid.

A pair of angles including only one of the parallel sides is called a pair of **base angles**.

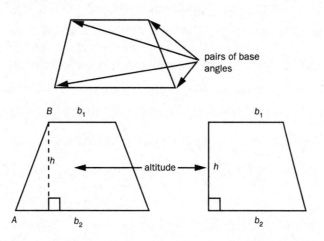

- The median of a trapezoid is parallel to the bases and equal to one-half their sum.

- The area of a trapezoid equals one-half the altitude times the sum of the bases, or $\frac{1}{2}h(b_1 + b_2)$.

- An **isosceles trapezoid** is a trapezoid whose non-parallel sides are equal. A pair of angles including only one of the parallel sides is called a pair of base angles.

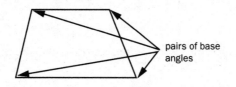

- The base angles of an isosceles trapezoid are equal.

- The diagonals of an isosceles trapezoid are equal.

- The opposite angles of an isosceles trapezoid are supplementary.

SIMILAR POLYGONS

> Two polygons are **similar** if there is a one-to-one correspondence between their vertices such that all pairs of corresponding angles are congruent and the ratios of the measures of all pairs of corresponding sides are equal.

Note that although similar polygons must have the same shape, they may have different sizes.

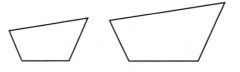

Theorem 1

The perimeters of two similar polygons have the same ratio as the measure of any pair of corresponding line segments of the polygons.

Theorem 2

The ratio of the lengths of two corresponding diagonals of two similar polygons is equal to the ratio of the lengths of any two corresponding sides of the polygons.

Theorem 3

The areas of two similar polygons have the same ratio as the square of the measures of any pair of corresponding sides of the polygons.

Theorem 4

Two polygons composed of the same number of triangles similar to each, and similarly placed, are similar. Thus, $ABCD$ is similar to $A'B'C'D'$. Note that when naming similar polygons, the corresponding letters must match: A to A', B to B', C to C', and D to D'.

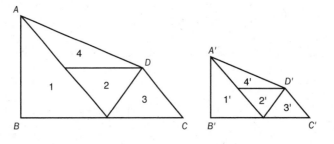

PROBLEM

The lengths of two corresponding sides of two similar polygons are 4 and 7. If the perimeter of the smaller polygon is 20, find the perimeter of the larger polygon.

SOLUTION

We know, by theorem, that the perimeters of two similar polygons have the same ratio as the measures of any pair of corresponding sides.

If we let s and p represent the side and perimeter of the smaller polygon and s' and p' represent the corresponding side and perimeter of the larger one, we can then write the proportion

$$s : s' = p : p'; \text{ or } \frac{s}{s'} = \frac{p}{p'}$$

By substituting the given values, we can solve for p'.

$$\frac{4}{7} = \frac{20}{p'}$$

$$4p' = 140$$

$$p' = 35$$

Therefore, the perimeter of the larger polygon is 35.

CIRCLES

A **circle** is a set of points in the same plane equidistant from a fixed point, called its **center**. Circles are often named by their center point, such as circle **O** below.

A **radius** of a circle is a line segment drawn from the center of the circle to any point on the circle.

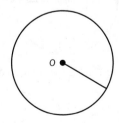

The **circumference** of a circle is the length of its outer edge, given by

$$C = \pi d = 2\pi r$$

where r is the radius, d is the diameter, and π (pi) is a mathematical constant approximately equal to 3.14.

> The **area** of a circle is given by
>
> $$A = \pi r^2$$

A full circle is 360°. The measure of a semicircle (half a circle) is 180°.

A line that intersects a circle in two points is called a **secant**.

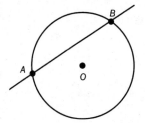

A line segment joining two points on a circle is called a **chord** of the circle.

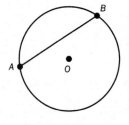

> A chord that passes through the center of the circle is called a **diameter** of the circle. The length of the diameter is twice the length of the radius, $d = 2r$.

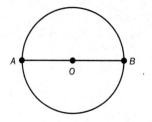

The line passing through the centers of two (or more) circles is called the **line of centers**.

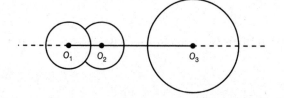

An angle whose vertex is on the circle and whose sides are chords of the circle is called an **inscribed angle** ($\angle BAC$ in the diagrams).

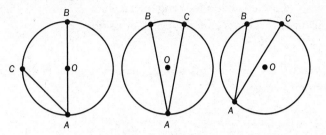

An angle whose vertex is at the center of a circle and whose sides are radii is called a **central angle**. The portion of a circle cut off by a central angle is called an **arc** of the circle.

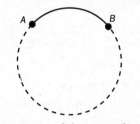

The measure of a minor arc is the measure of the central angle that intercepts that arc. The measure of a semicircle (half a circle) is 180°.

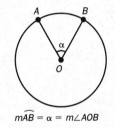

$$m\widehat{AB} = \alpha = m\angle AOB$$

The length of an arc intercepted by a central angle has the same ratio to the circle's circumference as the measure of the arc is to 360°, the full circle. Therefore, arc length is given by $\frac{n}{360} \times 2\pi r$, where n = measure of the central angle.

A sector is the portion of a circle between two radii (sector AOB here). Its area is given by $A = \frac{n}{360}(\pi r^2)$, where n is the central angle formed by the radii.

The distance from an outside point P to a given circle is the distance from that point to the point where the circle intersects with a line segment with endpoints at the center of the circle and point P. The distance of point P to the diagrammed circle with center O is the line segment $\overline{PB}$, part of line segment $\overline{PO}$.

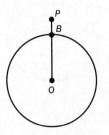

A line that has one and only one point of intersection
with a circle is called a **tangent** to that circle, and their
common point is called a **point of tangency**.

In the diagram, Q and P are each points of tangency. A tangent is always perpendicular to the
radius drawn to the point of tangency.

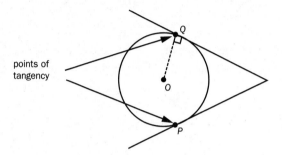

In geometry, we study **congruency**. Sides are congruent when they have the same length.
Angles are congruent when they have the same measurement. Shapes are congruent when you
can turn, flip, and/or slide one so it fits exactly on the other. The notation for congruency is $\cong$.
Congruent circles are circles whose radii are congruent.

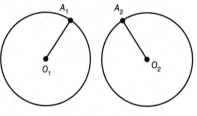

If $O_1A_1 \cong O_2A_2$, then $O_1 \cong O_2$.

Circles that have the same center and unequal radii are called **concentric circles**.

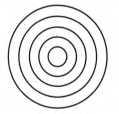

A **circumscribed circle** is a circle passing through all the vertices of a polygon. The polygon is
said to be **inscribed** in the circle.

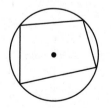

PROBLEM

A and B are points on a circle Q such that $\triangle AQB$ is equilateral. If the length of side $\overline{AB} = 12$, find the length of arc AB.

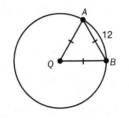

SOLUTION

To find the length of arc AB, we must find the measure of the central angle $\angle AQB$ and the measure of radius $\overline{QA}$. $\angle AQB$ is an interior angle of the equilateral triangle $\triangle AQB$. Therefore, $m\angle AQB = 60°$.

Similarly, in the equilateral $\triangle AQB$, $\overline{AQ} = \overline{AB} = \overline{QB} = 12 = r$.

Given the radius, r, and the central angle, n, the arc length is given by

$$\frac{n}{360} \times 2\pi r = \frac{60}{360} \times 2\pi \times 12 = \frac{1}{6} \times 2\pi \times 12 = 4\pi.$$

Therefore, the length of arc $AB = 4\pi$.

FORMULAS FOR AREA AND PERIMETER

Figures

Area (A) of a:

Areas

square	$A = s^2$; where s = side
rectangle	$A = lw$; where l = length, w = width
parallelogram	$A = bh$; where b = base, h = height
triangle	$A = \frac{1}{2}bh$; where b = base, h = height
circle	$A = \pi r^2$; where π = 3.14, r = radius
sector	$A = \left(\dfrac{n}{360}\right)(\pi r^2)$; where n = central angle, r = radius, π = 3.14
trapezoid	$A = \left(\dfrac{1}{2}\right)(h)(b_1 + b_2)$; where h = height, b_1 and b_2 = bases

<u>**Figures**</u>

Perimeter (P) of a:

square

rectangle

triangle

circumference (C)

of a circle

<u>**Perimeters**</u>

$P = 4s$; where s = side

$P = 2l + 2w$; where l = length, w = width

$P = a + b + c$; where a, b, and c are the sides

$C = \pi d = 2\pi r$; where $\pi = 3.14$, d = diameter, and r = radius.

PROBLEM

Points P and R lie on circle Q, $m \angle PQR = 120°$, and $PQ = 18$. What is the area of sector PQR?

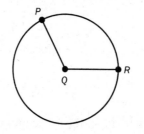

SOLUTION

$$\frac{120°}{360°} = \frac{\text{Area of sector } PQR}{\text{Area of circle } Q}$$

Letting X = area of sector PQR, and replacing area of circle Q with $\pi(18^2) = 324\pi$, we get

$$\frac{120°}{360°} = \frac{X}{324\pi}$$

$$\text{Then } X = \frac{(120°)(324\pi)}{360°} = 108\pi$$

DRILL QUESTIONS

1. What is the area of the following right triangle?

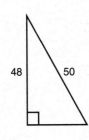

(A) 1200
(B) 672
(C) 336
(D) 112

2. Parallelogram *RSTU* is similar to parallelogram *WXYZ*. If $\angle RST = 60°$, $\angle XYZ =$

(A) 60°
(B) 90°
(C) 120°
(D) Not enough information is given

3. The center of circle *O* is at the origin, as shown. Point (2, 2) is on the circle. What is the circumference of circle *O*?

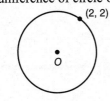

(A) 4π
(B) $4\pi\sqrt{2}$
(C) 2π
(D) $2\pi\sqrt{2}$

4. If the short side of a rectangle measures 3 inches, and its long side is twice as long, what is the length of a diagonal of a square with the same area as this rectangle?

(A) $3\sqrt{2}$
(B) 6
(C) 18
(D) 36

5. Which of the following *cannot* be the lengths of the sides of a triangle?

(A) 2, 5, 6
(B) 3, 4, 5
(C) 4, 5, 6
(D) 4, 5, 10

6. Find the length of the missing side in this right triangle.

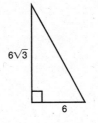

(A) 6
(B) $\sqrt{66}$
(C) 12
(D) $\sqrt{306}$

7. Given the intersecting lines and angle measurement in the figure, $x =$

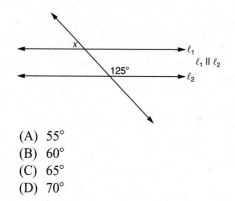

(A) 55°
(B) 60°
(C) 65°
(D) 70°

8. This figure shows sector *AOB* equal to a quarter of a circle, circumscribed about a square. What is the area of the shaded region?

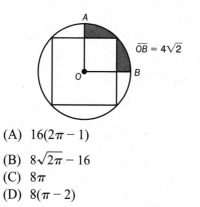

$$\overline{OB} = 4\sqrt{2}$$

(A) $16(2\pi - 1)$
(B) $8\sqrt{2\pi} - 16$
(C) 8π
(D) $8(\pi - 2)$

9. An isosceles right triangle has angles of

(A) 30°, 60°, 90°
(B) 45°, 45°, 90°
(C) 0°, 90°, 90°
(D) 60°, 60°, 60°

10. An angle of measure of 180° is termed

(A) straight
(B) supplementary
(C) obtuse
(D) reflex

ANSWERS TO DRILL QUESTIONS

1. **(C)** Let x represent the length of the horizontal base of this triangle. By the Pythagorean theorem, $x^2 + 48^2 = 50^2$. Then $x^2 + 2{,}304 = 2{,}500$, which means that $x^2 = 2{,}500 - 2{,}304 = 196$. So $x = \sqrt{196} = 14$. The area of the triangle is one-half the product of the base and the height. Thus, the required area is $\left(\dfrac{1}{2}\right)(14)(48) = \left(\dfrac{1}{2}\right)(672) = 336$.

2. **(C)** Corresponding angles of similar geometric figures must be congruent. This means that $\angle XYZ$ in parallelogram $WXYZ$ must be congruent to $\angle STU$ in parallelogram $RSTU$. We note that $\angle RST$ and $\angle STU$ are consecutive angles in $RSTU$ and the sum of any two consecutive angles in a parallelogram is 180°. Since $\angle RST = 60°$, $\angle STU = 180° - 60° = 120°$. Thus, $\angle XYZ = 120°$.

3. **(B)** The length of the radius of this circle is found by the distance between point O which is located at (0, 0) and the point (2, 2). The distance between (0, 0) and (2, 2) is $\sqrt{(0-2)^2 + (0-2)^2} = \sqrt{(-2)^2 + (-2)^2} = \sqrt{4+4} = \sqrt{8}$. Note that we can write $\sqrt{8}$ as $\left(\sqrt{4}\right)\left(\sqrt{2}\right) = 2\sqrt{2}$. Finally, the circumference equals the product of 2π and the radius, which is $\left(2\pi\right)\left(2\sqrt{2}\right) = 4\pi\sqrt{2}$.

4. **(B)** The long side of the rectangle measures (2)(3) = 6 inches, so its area is (6)(3) = 18 square inches. Then the area of the square is also 18 square inches. Then each side of the square is $\sqrt{18}$ inches. The diagonal of a square can represent the hypotenuse of a triangle whose two legs are consecutive sides of the square. Let d represent the length of the diagonal. By the Pythagorean theorem, $d^2 = \left(\sqrt{18}\right)^2 + \left(\sqrt{18}\right)^2 = 18 + 18 = 36$. Thus, $d = \sqrt{36} = 6$.

5. **(D)** The sum of any two sides of a triangle must exceed the length of the third side. This means that a triangle *cannot* have sides with lengths of 4, 5, and 10 because $4 + 5 < 10$.

6. **(C)** The missing side represents the hypotenuse of this triangle. Let x represent its length. By the Pythagorean theorem, $x^2 = 6^2 + \left(6\sqrt{3}\right)^2$. This equation simplifies to $x^2 = 36 + (36)(3) = 144$. Thus, $x = \sqrt{144} = 12$.

7. **(A)** When a transversal intersects two parallel lines, corresponding angles are congruent. By definition, x and the angle represented by 125° are corresponding angles. As such, $x = 125°$. Now note that the angle represented by x and 125° are adjacent angles that form a straight line. This means that $x + 125° = 180°$. Thus, $x = 180° - 125° = 55°$.

8. **(D)** The diagonal of the square $\overline{OD}$ is a radius of the circle, so its length is equal to $\overline{OB}$, which is $4\sqrt{2}$. Let x represent the length of each side of the square. By the Pythagorean theorem, $\left(\overline{OC}\right)^2 + \left(\overline{CD}\right)^2 = \left(\overline{OD}\right)^2$. Then $x^2 + x^2 = \left(4\sqrt{2}\right)^2 = (16)(2) = 32$. This equation can be simplified to $2x^2 = 32$, which further simplifies to $x^2 = 16$. This means that the area of the square is 16. The area of the quarter-circle formed by the points A, O, and B is one-fourth the area of the circle. This area is found by the expression $\left(\frac{1}{4}\right)(\pi)\left(r^2\right)$, where r is the length of the radius. Since we know the radius length to be $4\sqrt{2}$, the area of the quarter-circle is $\left(\frac{1}{4}\right)(\pi)\left(4\sqrt{2}\right)^2 = \left(\frac{1}{4}\right)(\pi)(16)(2) = \left(\frac{1}{4}\right)(\pi)(32) = 8\pi$. Finally, the area of the shaded region is the difference between the area of the quarter-circle and the area of the square, which is $8\pi - 16$. This is equivalent to $8(\pi - 2)$.

9. **(B)** An isosceles right triangle must consist of a 90° angle and two acute congruent angles whose sum is 90°. The only set of numbers that satisfies these conditions are angle measures of 45°, 45°, 90°.

10. **(A)** By definition, an angle whose measure is 180° is called a straight angle.

LOGIC AND SETS

LOGIC

The topic of logic encompasses a wealth of subjects related to the principles of reasoning. Here, we will be concerned with logic on an elementary level, and you will recognize the principles introduced here because not only have you been using them in your everyday life, you also have seen them in one form or another in this book. The chapter is designed to familiarize you with the terminology you might be expected to know as well as thought processes that you can use in everyday life.

Sentential calculus is the "calculus of sentences," a field in which the truth or falseness of assertions is examined by using algebraic tools. We will approach logic from a "true" or "false" perspective here. This chapter contains many examples of sentences to illustrate the terms that are defined.

SENTENCES

> A **sentence** is any expression that can be labeled either true or false.

Examples:

Expressions to which the terms "true" or "false" can be assigned include the following:

1. "It is raining where I am standing."

2. "My name is George."

3. "$1 + 2 = 3$"

Examples:

Expressions to which the terms "true" or "false" cannot be assigned include the following:

1. "I will probably be healthier if I exercise."

2. "It will rain on this day, one year from now."

3. "What I am saying at this instant is a lie."

Sentences can be combined to form new sentences using the connectives **AND, OR, NOT**, and **IF-THEN**.

Examples:

The sentences

1. "John is tired."

2. "Mary is cooking."

. . .*can be combined to form*. . .

1. "John is tired AND Mary is cooking."

2. "John is tired OR Mary is cooking."

3. "John is NOT tired."

4. "IF John is tired, THEN Mary is cooking."

LOGICAL PROPERTIES OF SENTENCES

Consistency

A sentence is **consistent** if and only if it is *possible* that it is true. A sentence is **inconsistent** if and only if it is not consistent; that is, if and only if it is *impossible* that it is true.

Example:

"At least one odd number is not odd" is an inconsistent sentence.

Logical Truth

A sentence is **logically true** if and only if it is *impossible* for it to be false; that is, the denial of the sentence is inconsistent.

Example:

Either Mars is a planet or Mars is not a planet.

Logical Falsity

A sentence is **logically false** if and only if it is *impossible* for it to be true; that is, the sentence is inconsistent.

Example:

Mars is a planet and Mars is not a planet.

Logical Indeterminacy (Contingency)

A sentence is **logically indeterminate** (contingent) if and only if it is neither logically true nor logically false.

Example:

Einstein was a physicist and Pauling was a chemist. Certainly one could check the Internet to determine whether this statement is true, but truth cannot be determined by pure logic.

Logical Equivalent of Sentences

Two sentences are **logically equivalent** if and only if it is *impossible* for one of the sentences to be true while the other sentence is false; that is, if and only if it is impossible for the two sentences to have different truth values.

Example:

"Chicago is in Illinois and Pittsburgh is in Pennsylvania" is logically equivalent to "Pittsburgh is in Pennsylvania and Chicago is in Illinois."

STATEMENTS

A **statement** is a sentence that is either true or false, but not both.

The following terms and their definitions should become familiar to you. Their logic is probably familiar, even though you haven't as yet given it a label.

CONJUNCTION

If a and b are statements, then a statement of the form "a and b" is called the **conjunction** of a and b, denoted by $a \wedge b$.

DISJUNCTION

The **disjunction** of two statements a and b is shown by the compound statement "a or b," denoted by $a \vee b$.

NEGATION

The **negation** of a statement q is the statement "not q," denoted by $\sim q$.

IMPLICATION

The compound statement "if a, then b," denoted by $a \rightarrow b$, is called a **conditional statement** or an **implication**. "If a" is called the **hypothesis** or **premise** of the implication, and "then b" is called the **conclusion** of the implication. Further, statement a is called the **antecedent** of the implication, and statement b is called the **consequent** of the implication.

CONVERSE

The **converse** of $a \rightarrow b$ is $b \rightarrow a$.

CONTRAPOSITIVE

The **contrapositive** of $a \rightarrow b$ is $\sim b \rightarrow \sim a$.

INVERSE

The **inverse** of $a \rightarrow b$ is $\sim a \rightarrow \sim b$.

BICONDITIONAL

The statement of the form "*p* if and only if *q*," denoted by $p \leftrightarrow q$, is called a **biconditional** statement.

VALIDITY

An argument is **valid** if the truth of the premises means that the conclusions must also be true.

INTUITION

Intuition is the process of making generalizations on insight.

PROBLEMS

Write the inverse for each of the following statements. Determine whether the inverse is true or false.

1. If a person is stealing, he is breaking the law.

2. If a triangle with sides *a*, *b*, and *c* (the largest side) is a right triangle, then $c^2 = a^2 + b^2$.

3. Dead men tell no tales.

SOLUTIONS

The inverse of a given conditional statement is formed by negating both the hypothesis and conclusion of the conditional statement.

1. The hypothesis of this statement is "a person is stealing"; the conclusion is "he is breaking the law." The negation of the hypothesis is "a person is not stealing." The inverse is "if a person is not stealing, he is not breaking the law."

   The inverse is false, since there are more ways to break the law than by stealing. Clearly, a murderer may not be stealing but he is surely breaking the law.

2. This statement is the Pythagorean Theorem. Its inverse is "If a triangle with sides *a*, *b*, and *c* (the largest side) is not a right triangle, then $c^2 \neq a^2 + b^2$." The inverse is true as the only type of triangle that obeys the Pythagorean Theorem is a right triangle.

3. This statement is not written in if-then form, which makes its hypothesis and conclusion more difficult to see. The hypothesis is implied to be "the man is dead"; the conclusion is implied to be "the man tells no tales." The inverse is, therefore, "If a man is not dead, then he will tell tales."

   The inverse is false. Many witnesses to crimes are still alive but they have never told their stories to the police, probably out of fear or because they didn't want to get involved.

BASIC PRINCIPLES, LAWS, AND THEOREMS

1. Any statement is either true or false. (The Law of the Excluded Middle)

2. A statement cannot be both true and false. (The Law of Contradiction)

3. The converse of a true statement is not necessarily true.

4. The converse of a definition is always true.

5. For a theorem to be true, it must be true for all cases.

6. A statement is false if one false instance of the statement exists.

7. The inverse of a true statement is not necessarily true.

8. The contrapositive of a true statement is true and the contrapositive of a false statement is false.

9. If the converse of a true statement is true, then the inverse is true. Likewise, if the converse is false, the inverse is false.

10. Statements that are either both true or both false are said to be **logically equivalent**.

NECESSARY AND SUFFICIENT CONDITIONS

Let P and Q represent statements. "If P, then Q" is a conditional statement in which P is a sufficient condition for Q, and similarly Q is a necessary condition for P.

Example:

Consider the statement: "If it rains, then Jane will go to the movies." "If it rains" is a sufficient condition for Jane to go to the movies. "Jane will go to the movies" is a necessary condition for rain to have occurred.

Note that for the statement given, "If it rains" may not be the only condition for which Jane goes to the movies; however, it is a *sufficient* condition. Likewise, "Jane will go to the movies" will certainly not be the only result from a rainy weather condition (for example, "the ground will get wet" is another likely conclusion). However, knowing that Jane went to the movies is a *necessary* condition for rain to have occurred.

In the biconditional statement "P if and only if Q," P is a necessary and sufficient condition for Q, and vice versa.

Example:

Consider the statement "Rick gets paid if and only if he works." "Rick gets paid" is both a sufficient and necessary condition for him to work. Also, Rick's working is a sufficient and necessary condition for him to get paid.

Thus, we have the following basic principles to add to our list of ten from the preceding section:

11. If a given statement and its converse are both true, then the conditions in the hypothesis of the statement are both necessary and sufficient for the conclusion of the statement.

12. If a given statement is true but its converse is false, then the conditions are sufficient but not necessary for the conclusion of the statement.

13. If a given statement and its converse are both false, then the conditions are neither sufficient nor necessary for the statement's conclusion.

DEDUCTIVE REASONING

An arrangement of statements that would allow you to deduce the third one from the preceding two is called a **syllogism**. A syllogism has three parts:

1. The first part is a general statement concerning a whole group. This is called the **major premise**.

2. The second part is a specific statement which indicates that a certain individual is a member of that group. This is called the **minor premise**.

3. The last part of a syllogism is a statement to the effect that the general statement which applies to the group also applies to the individual. This third statement of a syllogism is called a **deduction**.

Example:

This is an example of a properly deduced argument.

A. Major Premise: All birds have feathers.

B. Minor Premise: An eagle is a bird.

C. Deduction: An eagle has feathers.

The technique of employing a syllogism to arrive at a conclusion is called **deductive reasoning**.

If a major premise that is true is followed by an appropriate minor premise that is true, a conclusion can be deduced that must be true, and the reasoning is valid. However, if a major premise that is true is followed by an *inappropriate* minor premise that is also true, a conclusion cannot be deduced.

Example:

This is an example of an improperly deduced argument.

A. Major Premise: All people who vote are at least 18 years old.

B. Improper Minor Premise: Jane is at least 18.

C. Illogical Deduction: Jane votes.

The flaw in this example is that the major premise in statement A makes a condition on people who vote, not on a person's age. If statements B and C are interchanged, the resulting three-part deduction would be logical.

In the following we will use capital letters X, Y, Z, ... to represent sentences, and develop algebraic tools to represent new sentences formed by linking them with the above connectives. Our connectives may be regarded as operations transforming one or more sentences into a new sentence. To describe them in greater detail, we introduce symbols to represent them. You will find that different symbols representing the same idea may appear in different references.

TRUTH TABLES AND BASIC LOGICAL OPERATIONS

The **truth table** for a sentence X is the exhaustive list of possible logical values of X.

The **logical value** of a sentence X is true (or T) if X is true, and false (or F) if X is false.

NEGATION

If X is a sentence, then $\sim X$ represents the **negation**, the opposite, or the contradiction of X. Thus, the logical values of $\sim X$ are as shown in Table 2-1, where $\sim$ is called the **negation operation** on sentences.

Table 2-1 Truth Table for Negation

X	$\sim X$
T	F
F	T

Example:

For X = "Jane is eating an apple," we have
$\sim X$ = "Jane is *not* eating an apple."

The negation operation is called *unary*, transforming a sentence into a unique image sentence.

IFF

We use the symbol **IFF** to represent the expression "if and only if."

AND

For sentences X and Y, the conjunction "X AND Y," represented by $X \wedge Y$, is the sentence that is true IFF both X and Y are true. The truth table for $\wedge$ (or AND) is shown in Table 2-2, where $\wedge$ is called the **conjunction operator**.

Table 2-2 Truth Table for AND

X	Y	$X \wedge Y$
T	T	T
T	F	F
F	T	F
F	F	F

The conjunction $\wedge$ is a *binary* operation, transforming a pair of sentences into a unique image sentence.

Example:

For X = "Jane is eating an apple" and Y = "All apples are sweet," we have $X \wedge Y$ = "Jane is eating an apple AND all apples are sweet."

AND/OR

For sentences X and Y, the disjunction "X AND/OR Y," represented by $X \vee Y$, denotes the sentence that is true if either or both X and Y are true. The truth table for $\vee$ is shown in Table 2-3, where $\vee$ is called the **disjunction operator**.

Table 2-3   Truth Table for AND/OR

X	Y	X ∨ Y
T	T	T
T	F	T
F	T	T
F	F	F

As with the conjunction operator, the disjunction is a *binary* operation, transforming the pair of sentences X, Y into a unique image sentence $X \vee Y$.

Example:

For X = "Jane is eating the apple" and Y = "Marvin is running," we have $X \vee Y$ = "Jane is eating the apple AND/OR Marvin is running."

IF-THEN

For sentences X and Y, the **implication** $X \rightarrow Y$ represents the statement "IF X THEN Y." $X \rightarrow Y$ is false IFF X is true and Y is false; otherwise, it is true. The truth table for $\rightarrow$ is shown in Table 2-4. $\rightarrow$ is referred to as the **implication operator**.

Table 2-4   Truth Table for IF-THEN

X	Y	X → Y
T	T	T
T	F	F
F	T	T
F	F	T

Implication is a *binary* operation, transforming the pair of sentences X and Y into a unique image sentence $X \rightarrow Y$.

LOGICAL EQUIVALENCE

For sentences X and Y, the **logical equivalence** $X \leftrightarrow Y$ is true IFF X and Y have the same truth value; otherwise, it is false. The truth table for $\leftrightarrow$ is shown by Table 2-5, where $\leftrightarrow$ represents logical equivalence, "IFF."

Table 2-5   Truth Table for Equivalence

X	Y	$X \leftrightarrow Y$
T	T	T
T	F	F
F	T	F
F	F	T

Example:

For X = "Jane eats apples" and Y = "apples are sweet," we have $X \leftrightarrow Y$ = "Jane eats apples IFF apples are sweet."

Equivalence is a *binary* operation, transforming pairs of sentences X and Y into a unique image sentence $X \leftrightarrow Y$. The two sentences X, Y for which $X \leftrightarrow Y$ are said to be logically equivalent.

LOGICAL EQUIVALENCE VERSUS "MEANING THE SAME"

Logical equivalence ($\leftrightarrow$) is not the same as an equivalence of meanings. Thus, if Jane is eating an apple and Barbara is frightened of mice, then for X = "Jane is eating an apple" and Y = "Barbara is frightened of mice," X and Y are logically equivalent, since both are correct. However, they do not have the same meaning. Statements having the same meaning are, for example, the double negative $\sim\sim X$ (not-not) and X itself.

THEOREM 1—Double Negation Equals Identity

For any sentence X,
$\sim\sim X \leftrightarrow X$.

FUNDAMENTAL PROPERTIES OF OPERATIONS

THEOREM 2—Properties of Conjunction Operation

For any sentences X, Y, Z, the following properties hold:

1. Commutativity: $X \wedge Y \leftrightarrow Y \wedge X$

2. Associativity: $X \wedge (Y \wedge Z) \leftrightarrow (X \wedge Y) \wedge Z$

THEOREM 3—Properties of Disjunction Operation

For any sentences X, Y, Z, the following properties hold:

1. Commutativity: $X \vee Y \leftrightarrow Y \vee X$

2. Associativity: $X \vee (Y \vee Z) \leftrightarrow (X \vee Y) \vee Z$

THEOREM 4—Distributive Laws

For any sentences X, Y, Z, the following laws hold:

1. $X \vee (Y \wedge Z) \leftrightarrow (X \vee Y) \wedge (X \vee Z)$

2. $X \wedge (Y \vee Z) \leftrightarrow (X \wedge Y) \vee (X \wedge Z)$

THEOREM 5—De Morgan's Laws for Sentences

For any sentences X, Y, the following laws hold:

1. $\sim(X \wedge Y) \leftrightarrow (\sim X) \vee (\sim Y)$

2. $\sim(X \vee Y) \leftrightarrow (\sim X) \wedge (\sim Y)$

Proof of Part 1 of Theorem 5

We can prove $\sim(X \wedge Y) \leftrightarrow (\sim X) \vee (\sim Y)$ by developing a truth table over all possible combinations of X and Y and observing that all values assumed by the sentences are the same. To this end, we first evaluate the expression $\sim(X \wedge Y)$ in Table 2-6a.

Table 2-6a   Truth Table for Negation of Conjunction

X	Y	$X \wedge Y$	$\sim(X \wedge Y)$
T	T	T	F
T	F	F	T
F	T	F	T
F	F	F	T

Now we evaluate $(\sim X) \vee (\sim Y)$ in Table 2-6b.

Table 2-6b   Truth Table for Disjunction of Negation

X	Y	$\sim X$	$\sim Y$	$(\sim X) \vee (\sim Y)$
T	T	F	F	F
T	F	F	T	T
F	T	T	F	T
F	F	T	T	T

The last columns of the truth tables coincide, proving our assertion.

THEOREM 6—Two Logical Identities

For any sentences X, Y, the sentences X and $(X \wedge Y) \vee (X \wedge \sim Y)$ are logically equivalent. That is,

$$(X \wedge Y) \vee (X \wedge \sim Y) \leftrightarrow X$$

This is proven in Table 2-7a.

Table 2-7a   Truth Table for (X $\wedge$ Y) $\vee$ (X $\wedge$ ~Y) $\leftrightarrow$ X

X	Y	~Y	X $\wedge$ Y	X $\wedge$ ~Y	(X $\wedge$ Y) $\vee$ (X $\wedge$ ~ Y)
T	T	F	T	F	T
T	F	T	F	T	T
F	T	F	F	F	F
F	F	T	F	F	F

For any sentences X, Y, the sentences X and $X \vee (Y \wedge \sim Y)$ are logically equivalent. That is

$$X \vee (Y \wedge \sim Y) \leftrightarrow X$$

This is proven in Table 2-7b.

Table 2-7b   Truth Table for X $\vee$ (Y $\wedge$ ~Y) $\leftrightarrow$ X

X	Y	~Y	Y $\wedge$ ~Y	X $\vee$ (Y $\wedge$ ~ Y)
T	T	F	F	T
T	F	T	F	T
F	T	F	F	F
F	F	T	F	F

For any sentences X, Y, $(X \rightarrow Y)$ and $(\sim X \vee Y)$ are logically equivalent.

This is proven in Table 2-7c.

Table 2-7c

X	Y	X $\rightarrow$ Y	~X	~ X $\vee$ Y
T	T	T	F	T
T	F	F	F	F
F	T	T	T	T
F	F	T	T	T

THEOREM 7—Proof by Contradiction

For any sentences X, Y, the following holds:

$$X \rightarrow Y \leftrightarrow \sim Y \rightarrow \sim X$$

To prove this, we consider Table 2-8.

Table 2-8   Truth Table for Proof by Contradiction

X	Y	X $\rightarrow$ Y	~Y	~X	~ Y $\rightarrow$ ~ X
T	T	T	F	F	T
T	F	F	T	F	F
F	T	T	F	T	T
F	F	T	T	T	T

SENTENCES, LITERALS, AND FUNDAMENTAL CONJUNCTIONS

We have seen that logically equivalent sentences may be expressed in different ways, the simplest examples being that a sentence is equal to its double negation,

$$\sim\sim X \leftrightarrow X,$$

and by De Morgan's theorem,

$$X \vee Y \leftrightarrow \sim(\sim X \wedge \sim Y)$$

The significance of sentential calculus and the algebra of logic is that it provides us with a method of producing a "standard" form for representing a statement in terms of the literals. This is indeed unique and, although usually the simplest representation, it does serve as a standard form for comparison and evaluation of sentences.

SETS

You have seen the topics of set theory in most of the chapters of this book; in fact, you use set theory in many of your everyday activities. But since it is not labeled as "set theory" in most cases, you are unaware that set theory is the basis for most of your mathematical and logical thought. In this section you'll find the set theory vocabulary you should know as well as such topics as Venn diagrams for the union and intersection of sets (used in logic), laws of set operations (similar to those for operations on the real number system), and Cartesian products (used in graphs of linear functions). Let's set the stage for sets.

> A **set** is defined as a collection of items. Each individual item belonging to a set is called an **element** or **member** of that set.
>
> Sets are usually represented by capital letters, and elements by lowercase letters. If an item k belongs to a set A, we write $k \in A$ ("k is an element of A"). If k is not in A, we write $k \notin A$ ("k is not an element of A").

The order of the elements in a set does not matter:

$$\{1, 2, 3\} = \{3, 2, 1\} = \{1, 3, 2\}, \text{ etc.}$$

A set can be described in two ways:

1. element by element.

2. a rule characterizing the elements.

For example, given the set A of the whole numbers starting with 1 and ending with 9, we can describe it either as $A = \{1, 2, 3, 4, 5, 6, 7, 8, 9\}$ or as $A = \{$whole numbers greater than 0 and less than 10$\}$. In both methods, the description is enclosed in brackets. A kind of shorthand is often used for the second method of set description, so instead of writing out a complete sentence between the brackets, we can write instead

$$A = \{k \mid 0 < k < 10, k \text{ a whole number}\}$$

This is read as "the set of all elements k such that k is greater than 0 and less than 10, where k is a whole number."

A set not containing any members is called the **empty** or **null** set. It is written either as ϕ or $\{\ \}$.

A set is **finite** if the number of its elements can be counted.

Example:

$\{2, 3, 4, 5\}$ is finite since it has four elements.

Example:

$\{3, 6, 9, 12, ..., 300\}$ is finite since it has 100 elements.

Note: The empty set, denoted by ϕ, is finite since we can count the number of elements it has, namely zero.

Any set that is not finite is called **infinite**.

Example:

$\{1, 2, 3, 4, ...\}$

Example:

$\{..., -7, -6, -5, -4\}$

Example:

$\{x \mid x \text{ is a real number between 4 and 5}\}$

SUBSETS

> Given two sets A and B, A is said to be a **subset** of B if every member of set A is also a member of set B.

A is a *proper* subset of B if B contains at least one element not in A. We write $A \subseteq B$ if A is a subset of B, and $A \subset B$ if A is a proper subset of B.

Two sets are **equal** if they have exactly the same elements; in addition, if $A = B$, then $A \subseteq B$ and $B \subseteq A$.

Example:

Let $A = \{1, 2, 3, 4, 5\}$

$B = \{1, 2\}$

$C = \{1, 4, 2, 3, 5\}$

1. A equals C, and A and C are subsets of each other, but not proper subsets.

2. $B \subseteq A$, $B \subseteq C$, $B \subset A$, $B \subset C$ (B is a subset of both A and C. In particular, B is a proper subset of A and C).

Two sets are **equivalent** if they have the same *number* of elements.

Example:

$O = \{3, 7, 9, 12\}$ and $E = \{4, 7, 12, 19\}$. O and E are equivalent sets, since each one has four elements.

Example:

$F = \{1, 3, 5, 7, ..., 99\}$ and $G = \{2, 4, 6, 8, ..., 100\}$. F and G are equivalent sets, since each one has 50 elements.

Note: If two sets are equal, they are automatically equivalent.

A **universal set** U is a set from which other sets draw their members. If A is a subset of U, then the complement of A, denoted A', is the set of all elements in the universal set that are not elements of A.

Example:

If $U = \{1, 2, 3, 4, 5, 6, ...\}$ and $A = \{1, 2, 3\}$, then $A' = \{4, 5, 6, ...\}$.

Figure 2-1 illustrates this concept through the use of a simple **Venn diagram**. A number is either in A or A'. Together A and A' comprise U.

Figure 2-1

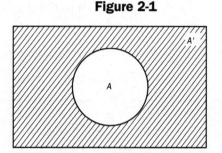

A Venn diagram is a visual way to show the relationships among or between sets that share something in common. Usually, the Venn diagram consists of two or more overlapping circles, with each circle representing a set of elements, or members. If two circles overlap, the members in the overlap belong to both sets; if three circles overlap, the members in the overlap belong to all three sets. Although Venn diagrams can be formed for any number of sets, you will probably encounter only two or three sets (circles) when working with Venn diagrams. As shown in Figure 2-1, the circles are usually drawn inside a rectangle called the universal set, which is the set of all possible members in the universe being described.

Venn diagrams are organizers. They are used to organize similarities (overlaps) and differences (non-overlaps of circles) visually, and they can pertain to any subject. For example, if the universe is all animals, Circle A may represent all animals that live in the water, and Circle B may represent all mammals. Then whales would be in the intersection of Circles A and B, but lobsters would be only in Circle A, humans would be only in Circle B, and scorpions would be in the part of the universe that was outside of Circles A and B. These relationships are shown in Figure 2-2.

Figure 2-2

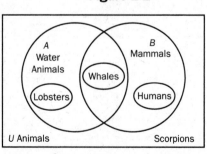

UNION AND INTERSECTION OF SETS

The **union** of two sets A and B, denoted $A \cup B$, is the set of all elements that are either in A or B or both.

Figure 2-3 is a Venn diagram for $A \cup B$. The shaded area represents the given operation.

Figure 2-3

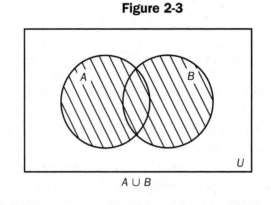

$A \cup B$

The **intersection** of two sets A and B, denoted $A \cap B$, is the set of all elements that belong to both A and B.

Figure 2-4 is a Venn diagram for $A \cap B$. The shaded area represents the given operation.

If $A = \{1, 2, 3, 4, 5\}$ and $B = \{2, 3, 4, 5, 6\}$, then $A \cup B = \{1, 2, 3, 4, 5, 6\}$ and $A \cap B = \{2, 3, 4, 5\}$.

If $A \cap B = \phi$, A and B are **disjoint**.

Figure 2-4

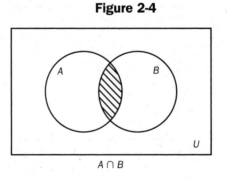

$A \cap B$

LAWS OF SET OPERATIONS

If U is the universal set, and A, B, C are any subsets of U, then the following hold for union, intersection, and complement:

Identity Laws

1a. $A \cup \phi = A$

1b. $A \cap \phi = \phi$

2a. $A \cup U = U$

2b. $A \cap U = A$

Idempotent Laws

3a. $A \cup A = A$

3b. $A \cap A = A$

Complement Laws

4a. $A \cup A' = U$

4b. $A \cap A' = \phi$

5a. $\phi' = U$

5b. $U' = \phi$

Commutative Laws

6a. $A \cup B = B \cup A$

6b. $A \cap B = B \cap A$

Associative Laws

7a. $(A \cup B) \cup C = A \cup (B \cup C)$

7b. $(A \cap B) \cap C = A \cap (B \cap C)$

Figures 2-5 and 2-6 illustrate the associative law for intersections. In Figure 2-5, the intersection of A and B is done first, and then the intersection of this result with C. In Figure 2-6, the intersection of B and C is done first, and then the intersection of this result with A. In both cases, the end result (double-hatched region) is the same.

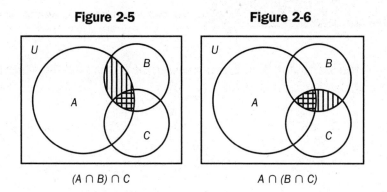

Figure 2-5   Figure 2-6

$(A \cap B) \cap C$ $A \cap (B \cap C)$

Distributive Laws

8a. $A \cup (B \cap C) = (A \cup B) \cap (A \cup C)$

8b. $A \cap (B \cup C) = (A \cap B) \cup (A \cap C)$

De Morgan's Laws

9a. $(A \cup B)' = A' \cap B'$

9b. $(A \cap B)' = A' \cup B'$

> The **difference** of two sets, A and B, written as $A - B$, is the set of all elements that belong to A but do not belong to B.

Example:

$J = \{10, 12, 14, 16\}, K = \{9, 10, 11, 12, 13\}$

$J - K = \{14, 16\}$. Note that $K - J = \{9, 11, 13\}$.

In general, $J - K \neq K - J$.

Example:

$T = \{a, b, c\}, V = \{a, b, c, d, e, f\}$.

$T - V = \phi$, whereas $V - T = \{d, e, f\}$.

Note, in this example, that T is a proper subset of V. In general, whenever set A is a proper subset of set B, $A - B = \phi$.

If set P is any set, then $P - \phi = P$ and $\phi - P = \phi$. Also if P and Q are any sets, $P - Q = P \cap Q'$.

CARTESIAN PRODUCT

> Given two sets M and N, the **Cartesian product**, denoted $M \times N$, is the set of all ordered pairs of elements in which the first component is a member of M and the second component is a member of N.

Often, the elements of the Cartesian product can be found by making a table with the elements of the first set as row headings and the elements of the second set as column headings, and the elements of the table the pairs formed from these elements.

Example:

$M = \{1, 3, 5\}, N = \{2, 8\}$

The Cartesian product $M \times N = \{(1, 2), (1, 8), (3, 2), (3, 8), (5, 2), (5, 8)\}$

We can easily see that these are all of the elements of $M \times N$ and the only elements of $M \times N$ by looking at Table 2-9:

Table 2-9   M × N

	2	8
1	1, 2	1, 8
3	3, 2	3,8
5	5, 2	5, 8

Example:

$W = \{a, b, c\}, Y = \{a, g, h\}$

The Cartesian product $W \times Y = \{(a, a), (a, g), (a, h), (b, a), (b, g), (b, h), (c, a), (c, g), (c, h)\}$

The elements for this Cartesian product are shown in Table 2-10.

Table 2-10   W × Y

	a	g	h
a	a, a	a, g	a, h
b	b, a	b, g	b, h
c	c, a	c, g	c, h

In the first example above, since M has 3 elements and N has 2 elements, $M \times N$ has $3 \times 2 = 6$ elements. In the second example above, since W has 3 elements and Y has 3 elements, $W \times Y$ has $3 \times 3 = 9$ elements. In general, if the first set has x elements and the second set has y elements, the Cartesian product will have xy elements.

DRILL QUESTIONS

1. If P and Q represent statements, which one of the following is equivalent to "Not P and not Q"?

   (A) Not P or not Q
   (B) Not P or Q
   (C) Not (P or Q)
   (D) Not (P and Q)

2. Let R and S represent statements. Consider the following:

   I.   If R then S
   II. Not R and S
   III. If S then R

   Which of the above statements is (are) equivalent to the statement "R is a necessary condition for S"?

   (A) Only I
   (B) I and II
   (C) II and III
   (D) Only III

3. What is the inverse of the statement "If it is snowing, then people stay indoors"?

   (A) If people stay indoors, then it is snowing.
   (B) If it is not snowing, then people do not stay indoors.
   (C) If people do not stay indoors, then it is not snowing.
   (D) If it is not snowing, then people stay indoors.

4. What is the negation for the statement "Image is important or personality matters"?

   (A) Image is important and personality does not matter.
   (B) Image is not important or personality does not matter.
   (C) Image is important or personality does not matter.
   (D) Image is not important and personality does not matter.

5. Given any two statements P and Q, where Q is a false statement, which one of the following *must* be false?

   (A) Not P and Q
   (B) Not (P and Q)
   (C) P or not Q
   (D) P implies Q

6. "All of P is in Q and some of R is in P." Based on the previous statement, which one of the following is a valid conclusion?

   (A) Some of R is not in Q.
   (B) All of R is in Q.
   (C) Some of R is in Q.
   (D) None of R is in Q.

7. Given three statements, P, Q, and R, suppose it is known that R is true. Which one of the following must be true?

   (A) $(P \wedge Q) \to R$
   (B) $R \to (P \vee Q)$
   (C) $(P \to Q) \wedge R$
   (D) $(R \to Q) \vee P$

8. Suppose that set K has 12 elements and set L has 3 elements. How many elements are there in the Cartesian product $K \times L$?

   (A) 4
   (B) 9
   (C) 15
   (D) 36

9. If $A = \{x \mid x$ is an even integer less than 10$\}$ and $B = \{$all negative numbers$\}$, which one of the following describes $A \cap B$?

   (A) {all negative numbers and all positive even integers}
   (B) {all negative numbers}
   (C) {all negative even integers}
   (D) {all negative odd integers}

10. Consider the Venn diagram shown below. Which one of the following correctly describes the shading?

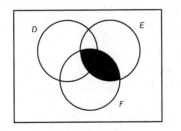

   (A) $E \cap F$
   (B) $D \cap E \cap F$
   (C) $D \cap E$
   (D) $D \cap F$

11. Which one of the following is an example of disjoint sets?

   (A) $\{0, 1, 2, 3\}$ and $\{3, 2, 1, 0\}$
   (B) $\{0, 2, 4, 6\}$ and $\{2, 4, 6, 8\}$
   (C) $\{0, 3, 6, 9\}$ and $\{9, 16, 25, 36\}$
   (D) $\{0, 4, 8, 12\}$ and $\{6, 10, 14, 18\}$

12. If the universal set $U = \{x \mid x$ is a positive odd integer less than 30$\}$, $R = \{1, 5, 7\}$, and $S = \{1, 3, 7, 11, 13\}$, how many elements are in $(R \cap S)'$?

   (A) 15
   (B) 13
   (C) 7
   (D) 2

13. If $P \subseteq Q$, which one of the following conclusions must be true?

   (A) P is either equal to Q or P is a proper subset of Q.
   (B) P is a proper subset of Q.
   (C) Q is a proper subset of P.
   (D) P is either equal to Q or P is the empty set.

14. Given any two sets F and G, which one of the following is not necessarily true?

   (A) $F \cup G = G \cup F$
   (B) $F \cap G = G \cap F$
   (C) $F - G = G - F$
   (D) $F \cap F' = \phi$

15. Consider the Venn diagram shown below.

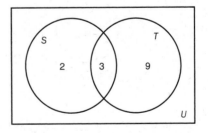

   If the given numbers represent the number of elements in each region, how many elements are in $T - S$?

   (A) 10
   (B) 9
   (C) 7
   (D) 6

ANSWERS TO DRILL QUESTIONS

1. **(C)** One of De Morgan's Laws for sentences is $\sim(X \vee Y) \leftrightarrow -X \wedge \sim Y$. Substituting P for X and Q for Y, we have $\sim(P \vee Q) \leftrightarrow \sim P \wedge \sim Q$. This statement is read as follows: "Not (P or Q)" is equivalent to "Not P and not Q."

2. **(D)** If R is a necessary condition for S, then by definition S implies R. Also, the statement that "S implies R" is equivalent to the statement "If S then R," which represents item III. Neither of items I or II is equivalent to the given statement.

3. **(B)** The inverse of "If P then Q" is "If not P then not Q." Let P represent the statement "It is snowing" and let Q represent the statement "People stay indoors." By substitution, for the statement "If it is snowing, then people stay indoors," the inverse statement is "If it is not snowing, then people do not stay indoors."

4. **(D)** The negation of $(P \vee Q)$ is $\sim(P \vee Q)$. By one of De Morgan's Laws, the statement $\sim(P \vee Q)$ is equivalent to $\sim P \wedge \sim Q$. Let P represent the statement "Image is important" and let Q represent the statement "Personality matters." Then the negation for "Image is important or personality matters" is "Not (Image is important or personality matters)." This latter statement is equivalent to "Image is not important and personality does not matter."

5. **(A)** Given that Q is a false statement, the statement "Not P and Q" must be false. Any compound statement with the conjunction operator (which is "and") is false unless both component parts are true.

6. **(C)** Here are the three possible diagrams for sets P, Q, and R.

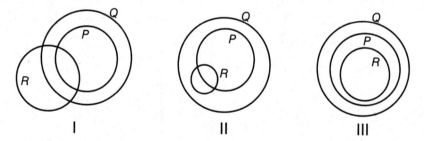

I   II   III

The statement "Some of R is in Q" is true for each of diagrams I, II, and III. Choice (A) is incorrect because it is false for diagrams II and III. Choice (B) is incorrect because it is false for diagram I. Choice (D) is incorrect because it is false for all three diagrams. Note that the statement "Some of R is in P" is true even if all of R is actually in P. The word "some" means "at least one."

7. **(A)** A conditional statement "$X \rightarrow Y$" is true in all instances except when X is true and Y is false. Let X be represented by $P \wedge Q$ and let Y be represented by R. Since R is known to be true and we do not know the truth value of "$P \wedge Q$," we have either "True $\rightarrow$ True" or "False $\rightarrow$ True." In either case "$(P \wedge Q) \rightarrow R$" must be true.

8. **(D)**   Given two sets K and L, the Cartesian product $K \times L$ is the set consisting of all ordered pairs in which the first element is chosen from K and the second element is chosen from L. For example, if set K contains the element a and set L contains the element b, then one of the elements of $K \times L$ is (a, b). Since we know that K has 12 elements and L has 3 elements, we conclude that there are (12)(3) = 36 different ordered pairs for $K \times L$.

9. **(C)**   In roster form, $A = \{...,-8,-6,-4,-2,0,2,4,6,8\}$. Although we cannot write set B in roster form, we can determine that the elements common to both A and B can be represented as $\{...,-8,-6,-4,-2\}$, which is the set of all negative even integers.

10. **(A)**   The shaded region represents all elements common to both sets E and F. This is the definition of the intersection of sets E and F, written as $E \cap F$. Note that the presence of set D becomes incidental, and does not affect the correct answer choice.

11. **(D)**   Disjoint sets are those that do not contain any common elements, such as {0, 4, 8, 12} and {6, 10, 14, 18}.

12. **(B)**   Written in roster form, U = {1, 3, 5, 7, ..., 29}, which contains 15 elements. $R \cap S$ represents the elements common to both R and S, so $R \cap S = \{1, 7\}$. Finally, $(R \cap S)'$ represents the elements in U that do not belong to $R \cap S$. Thus, $(R \cap S)'$ must contain $15 - 2 = 13$ elements.

13. **(A)** $P \subseteq Q$ means that each element of set P is also an element of set Q. This implies that either (a) P and Q are identical, or (b) Q contains all the elements of P, plus at least one element not found in P. By definition, if part (b) applies, then P is a proper subset of Q.

14. **(C)** $F - G$ represents the set of elements in F that do not belong to G, whereas $G - F$ represents the set of elements in G that do not belong to F. Unless these sets are equivalent, $F - G \neq G - F$. For example, let $F = \{1, 3, 6\}$ and let $G = \{1, 5, 8, 9\}$. Then $F - G = \{3, 6\}$, but $G - F = \{5, 8, 9\}$.

15. **(B)** $T - S$ is the set of elements in T that do not belong to S. According to the given Venn Diagram, there are 9 elements that fit this description.

PRACTICE TEST

CLEP College Mathematics

Also available at the REA Study Center (*www.rea.com/studycenter*)

This practice test is also available online at the REA Study Center. The CLEP College Mathematics test is only offered as a computer-based exam; therefore, we recommend that you take the online version of the practice test to receive these added benefits:

- **Timed testing conditions** – Gauge how much time you can spend on each question.
- **Automatic scoring** – Find out how you did on the test, instantly.
- **On-screen detailed explanations of answers** – Learn not just the correct answer, but also why the other answer choices are incorrect.
- **Diagnostic score reports** – Pinpoint where you're strongest and where you need to focus your study.

Need more practice? Go to the REA Study Center and take Practice Test 2.

■ PRACTICE TEST

CLEP COLLEGE MATHEMATICS

(Answer sheet can be found on page 408.)

TIME: 90 Minutes
Approximately 60 Questions

> **Directions:** An online scientific calculator will be available for the questions in this test.
>
> Some questions will require you to select from among four choices. For these questions, select the BEST of the choices given.
>
> Some questions will require you to type a numerical answer in the box provided.
>
> **Notes:** (1) Unless otherwise specified, the domain of any function f is assumed to be the set of all real numbers x for which $f(x)$ is a real number.
>
> (2) i will be used to denote $\sqrt{-1}$
>
> (3) Figures that accompany questions are intended to provide information useful in answering the questions. All figures lie in a plane unless otherwise indicated. The figures are drawn as accurately as possible EXCEPT when it is stated in a specific question that the figure is not drawn to scale.

1. Which one of the following is equivalent to the negation of the statement "Cats are friendly and Bob has a hamster"?

   (A) If cats are friendly, then Bob does not have a hamster.
   (B) If Bob has a hamster, then cats are friendly.
   (C) If cats are not friendly, then Bob has a hamster.
   (D) If Bob does not have a hamster, then cats are not friendly.

2. 50 miles per hour is the same as

   I.   73.33 ft/sec
   II. 1,466.67 yards/min

   (A) I only
   (B) II only
   (C) Both I and II
   (D) Neither I nor II

3. If x is an odd integer and y is even, then which of the following must be an even integer?

   I. $2x + 3y$
   II. xy
   III. $x + y - 1$

   (A) I only
   (B) II only
   (C) I, II, and III
   (D) II and III only

4. An ordinary six-sided cube, with its sides numbered 1 through 6, is rolled twice. The probability of rolling any of the six numbers is equally likely. What is the probability that on two consecutive rolls of the cube, a number less than 3 appears on the first roll and the number 5 appears on the second roll?

5. Not counting the empty set, how many proper subsets are there for $R = \{2, 3, 4\}$?

   (A) 5
   (B) 6
   (C) 7
   (D) 8

6. The average size of a house in 2010 was 2,463 ft². This is 145% of the average size of a house in 1980. What was the average size of a house in 1980?

   (A) 1,108 ft²
   (B) 1,589 ft²
   (C) 1,699 ft²
   (D) 3,572 ft²

7. Let P, Q, and R represent statements where P is true, Q is false, and R is false. Which one of the following is a true statement?

   (A) (P and R) or Q
   (B) (P implies Q) and Not R
   (C) Not P or (Q and R)
   (D) Not P implies (Q and R)

8. Given that $i = \sqrt{-1}$, what is the simplified expression for $3i^3 - 4i^2 + 5i$?

   (A) $-2i - 4$
   (B) $-2i + 4$
   (C) $2i - 4$
   (D) $2i + 4$

9. The federal debt is the amount the government owes after borrowing the money it needs to pay for its expenses. It measures how much of government spending is financed by debt rather than taxation. If the federal debt was 3.21 trillion dollars in 1990 and 13.79 trillion dollars in 2010, find the approximate percentage increase in the federal debt from 1990 to 2010.

   (A) 3%
   (B) 23%
   (C) 77%
   (D) 330%

10. Payday lending has been legalized in some states. It involves lending money, usually at a very high interest rate, until a borrower can pay it off with his paycheck. If a borrower secures a payday loan of $625 for 15 days at 450% APR simple interest, to the nearest dollar, how much must he pay back?

    (A) $117
    (B) $636
    (C) $742
    (D) $906

11. A highway study of 15,000 vehicles that passed by a checkpoint found that their speeds were normally distributed with a mean of 59 mph and a standard deviation of 6 mph. How many of the vehicles had speeds greater than 65 mph?

    (A) 375
    (B) 2,400
    (C) 5,100
    (D) 9,900

12. You win $2 million in the lottery. You invest half that money in Bank M at 3.02% interested compounded daily while the other half is invested in Bank N at 3.05% interest compounded quarterly. What is the approximate difference between the interest earned in the two banks after the first year?

    (A) $0
    (B) $192
    (C) $264
    (D) $300

13. If $m^x \cdot m^7 = m^{28}$ and $(m^5)^y = m^{15}$, what is the value of $x + y$?

    (A) 31
    (B) 24
    (C) 14
    (D) 12

14. Which is largest?

    (A) $\log_6 4 + \log_6 9$
    (B) $\log_5 15 - \log_5 3$
    (C) $\log_4 \dfrac{1}{4}$
    (D) $\log 100^{1/4}$

15. Suppose $S = \{5, 6, 9\}$ and $T = \{7, 8, 9\}$. Which one of the following ordered pairs is *NOT* in the Cartesian Product of $T \times S$?

    (A) $(9, 9)$
    (B) $(8, 5)$
    (C) $(6, 8)$
    (D) $(7, 6)$

16. The future value of an investment 75 years from now is $75,000. It was invested at 5% compounded semi-annually. What is the present value (rounded to the nearest dollar)?

    (A) $1,000
    (B) $1,777
    (C) $1,847
    (D) $2,102

17. A fair coin is tossed 4 times. What are the odds of getting exactly two heads?

    (A) 3:8
    (B) 8:3
    (C) 5:3
    (D) 3:5

18. Given the following list of six numbers:

    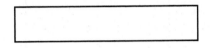
    $$\pi, \sqrt{5}, \sqrt{\frac{4}{25}}, -.212, 5\frac{2}{7}, \text{ and } .1\overline{8}$$

    How many of these numbers are irrational?

19. The mean of Sheila's five exam scores is 78. She will be taking three more exams. Assuming that each exam is given the same weight, what must her mean score be on the remaining exams in order to attain a mean score of 84 on all 8 exams?

    (A) 94
    (B) 92
    (C) 90
    (D) 88

20. Look at the triangle below.

    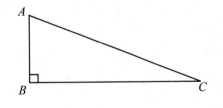

    AB is perpendicular to BC. $AB = 10$ and $AC = 26$. What is the area of the triangle?

    (A) 260
    (B) 240
    (C) 130
    (D) 120

21. Which graph does NOT represent a function $y = f(x)$?

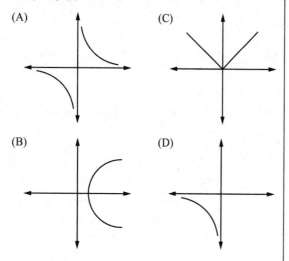

(A)

(C)

(B)

(D)

22. The cost of a men's shirt at a department store is $15. The store marks up the price 80% and then has a sale advertising a 30% markdown. What is the percentage markup of the shirt when it is sold at the sale price?

(A) 14.4%
(B) 26%
(C) 30%
(D) 50%

23. Which one of the following has the lowest value?

(A) $|-8| - |3|$
(B) $-|-8 - 3|$
(C) $|-3 + 8| - |-8 + 3|$
(D) $-|3 - 8|$

24. Let $U = \{$cat, dog, frog, goat, horse, pig, tiger$\}$, $A = \{$dog, frog, horse, pig$\}$, and $B = \{$dog, goat, pig, tiger$\}$. Define A' as the elements in set U that are not in set A. Which of the following completely describes $A' \cap B$?

(A) $\{$cat, goat, tiger$\}$
(B) $\{$goat, tiger$\}$
(C) $\{$dog, pig$\}$
(D) $\{$dog, goat, pig$\}$

25. In the figure below, the hypotenuse of the right triangle is 4. What is the area of the shaded region?

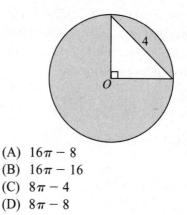

(A) $16\pi - 8$
(B) $16\pi - 16$
(C) $8\pi - 4$
(D) $8\pi - 8$

26. On a cruise ship, movies are shown at night. Popcorn and soft drinks are available. 100 people attend a showing of a movie and the number of people having popcorn and a soft drink are shown in the Venn diagram below. Classify the two events: having popcorn and having a soft drink.

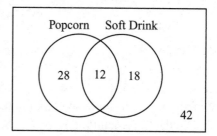

(A) Mutually exclusive and independent
(B) Mutually exclusive but not independent
(C) Independent but not mutually exclusive
(D) Neither mutually exclusive nor independent

27. If $A \subset C$ and $B \subset C$, which of the following statements is true?

(A) The set $A \cup B$ is also a subset of C.
(B) The complement of A is also a subset of C.
(C) The complement of B is also subset of C.
(D) The union of $\overline{A}$ and $\overline{B}$ is also a subset of C.

28. Which one of the following is equivalent to the statement "If Joan sings, then I will play my guitar"?

 (A) Joan sings and I will play my guitar.
 (B) Joan does not sing and I will not play my guitar.
 (C) Joan sings or I will not play my guitar.
 (D) Joan does not sing or I will play my guitar.

29. During the 1970s the number of people in the U.S. military began to decrease. The chart below shows the number of military personnel, in thousands, in each of the 4 branches of the military between 1970 and 1975. Which branch had the biggest percentage decrease?

	Army	Navy	Air Force	Marines
1975	784	535	612	196
1980	777	527	578	188

 (A) Amy
 (B) Navy
 (C) Air Force
 (D) Marines

30. A floor that measures 10 feet by 20 feet is to be tiled with square tiles that are 36 square inches in area. How many tiles are needed to cover the entire floor?

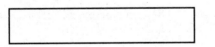

31. During a sale in an appliance store, 250 people came into the store. 55 people were interested in looking at washers, 45 were interested in looking at dryers, and 25 were interested in both. What is the probability that a customer chosen at random was interested in either washers or dryers?

 (A) 4%
 (B) 10%
 (C) 30%
 (D) 40%

32. An analysis of commercial airplanes compares the number of seats and the rate of fuel consumption in gallons per hour as shown by the scatter plot below. The regression line is drawn. Which of the following is closest to the increase in fuel consumption for each seat added?

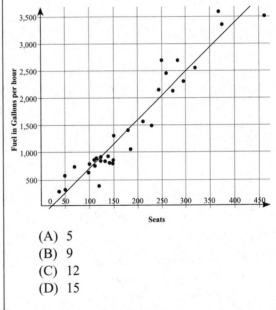

 (A) 5
 (B) 9
 (C) 12
 (D) 15

33. What is the domain of the function given by
$f(x) = \dfrac{x^2 + 1}{x + 3}$?

 (A) All numbers except -3
 (B) All numbers except -1
 (C) All numbers except 1
 (D) All numbers except 3

34. In the figure below, the lines are extensions of the triangle. Find the value of $x + y - z$.

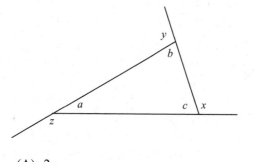

(A) $2a$
(B) $2a + 2c$
(C) $360°$
(D) $720°$

35. What is the median of the following data?

2, 24, 7, 10, 15, 8

(A) 7.5
(B) 8.5
(C) 9
(D) 11

36. Which one of the following is a valid argument?

(A) All rainy days are cloudy.
Yesterday was not cloudy.
Yesterday was not rainy.
(B) All trees have brown leaves.
This plant has brown leaves.
This plant is a tree.
(C) Some wolves are vicious.
This animal is vicious.
This animal is a wolf.
(D) Some people have stocks and bonds.
Charles has stocks.
Charles has bonds.

37. A nightclub has a target amount of $10 for the average amount each customer spends on drinks. They find that the average amount each customer spends is $8. So the nightclub reduces prices by 10% in the hope that customers will purchase more drinks. By what percent must customers increase their spending with the new pricing structure for the nightclub to reach its goal?

(A) 72%
(B) 172%
(C) 39%
(D) 139%

38. Which one of the following groups of data has exactly two modes?

(A) 1, 1, 3, 4, 4, 5, 5, 5
(B) 1, 1, 1, 2, 2, 2, 2
(C) 1, 2, 3, 3, 4, 4, 5, 5
(D) 1, 3, 3, 3, 4, 4, 4

39. If f is defined by $f(x) = \dfrac{5x - 8}{2}$ for each real number x, find the solution set for $f(x) > 2x$.

(A) $\{x \mid x > 6\}$
(B) $\{x \mid x > 8\}$
(C) $\{x \mid x < 8\}$
(D) $\{x \mid 6 < x < 8\}$

40. Look at the following Venn Diagram, for which a Roman numeral has been assigned to each region.

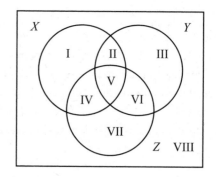

Which region(s) would include $(X \cup Y)'$?

(A) VII and VIII
(B) Only VII
(C) V, VII, and VIII
(D) Only VIII

41. The sample standard deviation s of a group of data is given by the formula

$$ s = \sqrt{\frac{\sum_{i=1}^{n}(X_i - \overline{X})^2}{n-1}} , \text{ where } X_i \text{ represents} $$

each data, $\overline{X}$ represents the mean, and n represents the number of data. What is the sample standard deviation for the following data? 4, 5, 6, 9, 11. (Round off your answer to the nearest hundredth.)

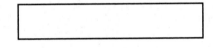

42. For federal income tax, a person whose salary is between $9,226 and $37,450 pays $923 + 15% of the amount his salary is over $9,225. If a person makes exactly $37,450, what percentage of his salary goes to taxes?

(A) 11.3%
(B) 13.8%
(C) 15%
(D) 17.5%

43. If g is a linear function such that $g(4) = 6$ and $g(10) = 21$, what is the value of $g(8)$?

(A) 19
(B) 18
(C) 16
(D) 10

44. A real estate broker receives a commission of 6% of the selling price of a house. If the broker received a commission of $16,250 on the sale of the house, and the commission is taken off the price of the house at settlement, how much does the seller receive for the house?

(A) $254,583
(B) $270,833
(C) $287,083
(D) $300,433

45. A supermarket is having a sale on its store brand of soda, selling a 48-ounce bottle for $0.99. It also sells 12-ounce cans for $0.40 and sells its 2-liter (67.6 ounces) bottle for $1.39. Arrange the three types from lowest to highest unit price.

(A) 2-liter – 48-ounce – can
(B) 48-ounce – 2-liter – can
(C) 48-ounce – can – 2-liter
(D) can – 48-ounce – 2-liter

46. Write $(6 \times 10^{-3})(8 \times 10^{-1})$ in standard notation.

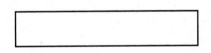

47. A bike wheel has a radius of 12 inches. How many revolutions will it take to cover one mile? (Use 1 mile = 5,280 feet, and $\pi = \frac{22}{7}$.)

(A) 70
(B) 84
(C) 120
(D) 840

48. For which one of the following groups of data are the mean and median identical?

    (A) 2, 2, 5, 6, 8, 8, 11
    (B) 2, 3, 6, 6, 6, 8, 12
    (C) 2, 4, 5, 6, 8, 11
    (D) 2, 5, 5, 7, 8, 12

49. Which one of the following is an equation of a line containing the point $(2, -1)$ and is perpendicular to the graph of $x + 3y = 4$?

    (A) $x + 3y = -1$
    (B) $3x - y = 7$
    (C) $3x + y = 5$
    (D) $x - 3y = 5$

50. A study was done as to the height in inches of children in a school aged 9 through 16. The data is broken up by gender. The scatter plot and the two lines of best fit are shown in the figure below. What conclusion about the school can be made from this graph?

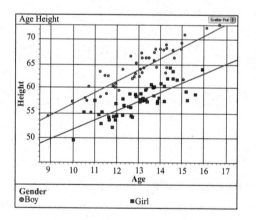

    (A) There are more girls than boys
    (B) There is a greater standard deviation in boy heights than girl heights
    (C) Boys grow faster than girls
    (D) None of these

51. The figure below is comprised of a parallelogram and a trapezoid. If the parallelogram and trapezoid have the same areas, find the value of the altitude h of the trapezoid.

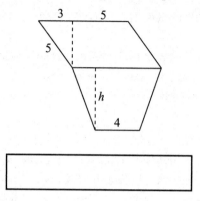

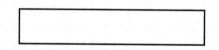

52. The function $f(x)$ is defined as follows:

$$f(x) = \begin{cases} 4x - 1, x \leq -5 \\ 5x + 1, x > -5 \end{cases}$$

What is the value of $f(-7) + f(10)$?

53. Given a collection of nine books, in how many different ways can any four of them be lined up on a shelf?

    (A) 262,144
    (B) 60,480
    (C) 6,561
    (D) 3,024

54. On January 1, 2015, Jerry receives a royalty check in the sum of $2,000 for a book he wrote. He deposits it in a bank account at 3% APR compounded daily. Six months later, he receives another royalty check for $3,000 and deposits it in the same account at the same interest rate. To the nearest dollar, how much money is in the account January 1, 2016?

(A) $5,106
(B) $5,126
(C) $5,152
(D) $5,311

55. In the figure on the next page, the graph of $f(x)$ is shown as the solid line. Which of the following is the equation of the transformation of $f(x)$ shown by the dashed line?

(A) $y = f(x + 3) - 3$
(B) $y = f(x + 3) + 3$
(C) $y = f(x - 3) - 3$
(D) $y = f(x - 3) + 3$

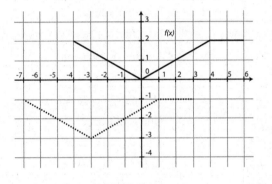

56. A charity is raffling off a 60-inch TV worth $2,000, two 32-inch TV's worth $500 each and five iPods worth $230 each. A chance costs $10 and 1,000 chances are sold. What is your mean expectation for the raffle?

(A) winning $4.15
(B) losing $5.85
(C) winning $2.73
(D) losing $7.27

57. A rectangle and a square have the same perimeter. The side of the square is 9 and the length of the rectangle is 13. What is the width of the rectangle?

58. Ed purchases a stock whose value y grows linearly as a function of time t while Noreen purchases a stock that grows exponentially according to the formula $y = 250(2^{\,t+1})$ as shown by the following figure where t is measured in years. How many of the following statements are true?

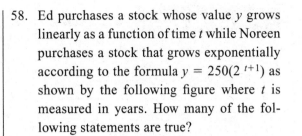

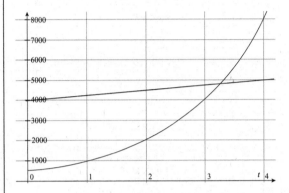

I. If they both sell their stock after 2 years, Ed's stock value will be greater.

II. When $t = 0$, the difference in the value of Ed's stock and Noreen's stock is $4,000.

III. When $t = 4$, Noreen's stock is worth 60% more than Ed's stock.

(A) 3
(B) 2
(C) 1
(D) 0

59. The number $0.\overline{8}$ is equivalent to what reduced fraction?

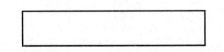

60. In a room of 20 people, if each person shakes hands with every other person, how many different handshakes are possible?

(A) 40
(B) 190
(C) 380
(D) 400

ANSWER KEY

#	Answer	Chapter	#	Answer	Chapter
1.	A	8. Logic & Sets	31.	C	4. Probability & Counting
2.	C	2. Numbers	32.	B	5. Statistics & Data Analysis
3.	C	2. Numbers	33.	D	3. Algebra & Functions
4.	1/18	4. Probability & Counting	34.	A	7. Geometry
5.	B	8. Logic & Sets	35.	C	5. Statistics & Data Analysis
6.	C	6. Financial Math	36.	A	8. Logic & Sets
7.	D	8. Logic & Sets	37.	C	6. Financial Math
8.	D	3. Algebra & Functions	38.	D	5. Statistics & Data Analysis
9.	D	6. Financial Math	39.	B	3. Algebra & Functions
10.	C	6. Financial Math	40.	A	8. Logic & Sets
11.	B	5. Statistics & Data Analysis	41.	2.92	5. Statistics & Data Analysis
12.	B	6. Financial Math	42.	B	6. Financial Math
13.	B	3. Algebra & Functions	43.	C	3. Algebra & Functions
14.	A	3. Algebra & Functions	44.	A	6. Financial Math
15.	C	8. Logic & Sets	45.	A	6. Financial Math
16.	C	6. Financial Math	46.	0.0048	2. Numbers
17.	C	4. Probability & Counting	47.	D	7. Geometry
18.	2	2. Numbers	48.	A	5. Statistics & Data Analysis
19.	A	5. Statistics & Data Analysis	49.	B	3. Algebra & Functions
20.	D	7. Geometry	50.	C	5. Statistics & Data Analysis
21.	B	3. Algebra & Functions	51.	5.33	7. Geometry
22.	B	6. Financial Math	52.	22	3. Algebra & Functions
23.	B	2. Numbers	53.	D	4. Probability & Counting
24.	B	8. Logic & Sets	54.	A	6. Financial Math
25.	C	7. Geometry	55.	A	3. Algebra & Functions
26.	C	4. Probability & Counting	56.	B	4. Probability & Counting
27.	A	8. Logic & Sets	57.	5	7. Geometry
28.	D	8. Logic & Sets	58.	B	3. Algebra & Functions
29.	C	6. Financial Math	59.	8/9	2. Numbers
30.	800	7. Geometry	60.	B	4. Probability & Counting

PRACTICE TEST
DETAILED EXPLANATIONS OF ANSWERS

1. **(A)** When a statement is in the form "If P, then Q," the equivalent statement is in the form "Not P or Q." The negation of "Not P or Q" is the statement "P and not Q." Let P represent the statement "Cats are friendly." Let "not Q" represent the statement "Bob has a hamster." Then the given statement in the stem of this question is written in the form "P and not Q," so the negation will be in the form "If P, then Q." Note that Q represents the statement "Bob does not have a hamster."

2. **(C)**

   I.
$$\frac{50 \text{ miles}}{\text{hour}} \cdot \frac{5280 \text{ feet}}{1 \text{ mile}} \cdot \frac{1 \text{ hour}}{60 \text{ minutes}} \cdot \frac{1 \text{ minutes}}{60 \text{ seconds}} = 73.33 \frac{\text{feet}}{\text{second}}$$

   II.
$$\frac{50 \text{ miles}}{\text{hour}} \cdot \frac{5280 \text{ feet}}{1 \text{ mile}} \cdot \frac{1 \text{ yard}}{3 \text{ feet}} \cdot \frac{1 \text{ hour}}{60 \text{ minutes}} = 1,466.67 \frac{\text{yards}}{\text{minute}}$$

3. **(C)**

   I.   An odd integer times two will become an even integer. An even integer times any number will remain even. The sum of two even numbers is also an even number. Therefore, $2x + 3y$ must be even.

   II.   An even integer times any number will remain even. Therefore, xy must be even.

   III. The sum of an odd integer and an even integer is odd. An odd integer minus one will become even. Therefore, $x + y - 1$ must be even.

4. The correct answer is $\frac{1}{18}$. A number less than 3 means 1 or 2. The probability of 1 or 2 appearing on the first roll is $\frac{2}{6} = \frac{1}{3}$. The probability of 5 appearing on the second roll is $\frac{1}{6}$. Since these events are independent, the probability that both will occur is the product of these probabilities, which is $\frac{1}{3} \cdot \frac{1}{6} = \frac{1}{18}$.

5. **(B)** Given a set of n elements, the number of proper subsets is given by the expression $2^n - 1$. The set of proper subsets does not include the set itself. However, the expression $2^n - 1$ does include the empty set. Thus, the answer is $2^n - 2 = 2^3 - 2 = 6$.

6. **(C)** We want to answer the question: 145% of what number is 2,463?

$$\frac{145}{100}x = 2463 \Rightarrow 145x = 246{,}300$$

$$x = \frac{246300}{145} = 1698.62$$

The average size of a house in 1980 was 1,699 ft².

7. **(D)** Not P becomes false. Q and R is also false. A statement that reads "False implies false" is always true. Answer choice (A) is wrong because P and R is false, so it reads "False or False." Answer choice (B) is wrong because P implies Q is false, so it reads "False and True," which is false. Answer choice (C) is wrong because Q and R is false, so it reads "False or False."

8. **(D)**

$$i^2 = -1 \text{ and } i^3 = i^2 (i) = (-1)(i) = -i. \text{ So, } 3i^3 - 4i^2 + 5i$$
$$= (3)(-i) - (4)(-1) + 5i = 5i - 3i + 4 = 2i + 4.$$

9. **(D)** % increase $= \dfrac{\text{New debt} - \text{Original debt}}{\text{Original debt}} = \dfrac{13.79 - 3.21}{3.21} = 3.295 \approx 330\%$

10. **(C)** $P = 625, \ r = 450\% = 4.5, \ t = \dfrac{15 \text{ days}}{360 \text{ days}} = \dfrac{15}{360}$

$$I = 625(4.5)\left(\frac{15}{360}\right) = 117.19 \ \text{ So the simple interest due is \$117.19.}$$

$$A = P + I = 625 + 117 = \$742$$

11. **(B)** 65 mph is one standard deviation above the mean. Since there is 68% of the data within one standard deviation of the mean, there is 34% of data between the mean and 65 mph. So there is 16% of the data above one standard deviation. 0.16(15,000) = 2,400.

12. **(B)** Bank M: $A = 1000000\left(1 + \dfrac{0.0302}{360}\right)^{360(1)} = \$1{,}030{,}659 \Rightarrow$

Interest = \$30,659

Bank N: $A = 1000000\left(1 + \dfrac{0.0305}{4}\right)^{360(4)} = \$1{,}030{,}851 \Rightarrow$

Interest = \$30,851

Difference: 30,851 − 30,659 = \$192.

13. **(B)** For the first equation, $x + 7 = 28$, so $x = 21$. For the second equation, $5y = 15$, so $y = 3$. Then $x + y = 24$.

14. **(A)** $\log_6 4 + \log_6 9 = \log_6(4 \cdot 9) = \log_6 36 \Rightarrow 6^x = 36 \Rightarrow x = 2$

$\log_5 15 - \log_5 3 = \log_5 \dfrac{15}{3} = \log_5 5 \Rightarrow 5^x = 5 \Rightarrow x = 1$

$\log_4 \dfrac{1}{4} = x \Rightarrow 4^x = \dfrac{1}{4} \Rightarrow x = -1$

$\log 100^{1/4} = \dfrac{1}{4}\log 100 = \dfrac{1}{4}(2) = \dfrac{1}{2}$

15. **(C)** The Cartesian Product of $T \times S$ consists of all ordered pairs, where the first element is chosen from T and the second element is chosen from S. The correct answer choice $(6, 8)$ is not a member of $T \times S$. It is a member of $S \times T$.

16. **(C)** $P = \dfrac{A}{\left(1 + \dfrac{r}{n}\right)^{nt}} = \dfrac{75,000}{\left(1 + \dfrac{0.05}{2}\right)^{2(75)}} = 1847.06.$

An investment of \$1,847 will be worth \$75,000 in 75 years.

17. **(C)**

Coin 1	Coin 2	Coin 3	Coin 4	Coin 1	Coin 2	Coin 3	Coin 4
H	H	H	H	T	H	H	H
H	H	H	T	⇒T	H	H	T
H	H	T	H	⇒T	H	T	H
⇒H	H	T	T	T	H	T	T
H	T	H	H	⇒T	T	H	H
⇒H	T	H	T	T	T	H	T
⇒H	T	T	H	T	T	T	H
H	T	T	T	T	T	T	T

Of the 16 possibilities, 6 have exactly 2 heads. The probability is $\dfrac{6}{16} = \dfrac{3}{8}$

so the odds are 8–3 to 3 or 5:3.

Or: for each toss, there are two possibilities, heads or tails. With four tosses,

there are $2^4 = 16$ possible outcomes.

The number of ways to choose two heads from 4 tosses is $_4C_2 = \dfrac{4!}{2!2!} = \dfrac{4 \cdot 3 \cdot 2 \cdot 1}{2 \cdot 1 \cdot 2 \cdot 1} = 6.$

18. The correct answer is 2. The irrational numbers are π and $\sqrt{5}$. Irrational numbers cannot be written as a quotient of two integers. The other four numbers can be written as a quotient of integers.

$$\sqrt{\frac{4}{25}} = \frac{2}{5}, \ -.212 = -\frac{212}{1000}, \ 5\frac{2}{7} = \frac{37}{7}, \ \text{and} \ .1\overline{8} = \frac{17}{90}.$$

19. **(A)** The total number of points on Sheila's five exams is $(5)(78) = 390$. In order to attain a mean score of 84 on all the exams, she will need a total of $(8)(84) = 672$ points. Thus, she needs a total of $672 - 390 = 282$ points on the next three exams. Finally $282 \div 3 = 94$.

20. **(D)** Using the Pythagorean Theorem, $AB^2 + BC^2 = AC^2$. By substitution, $10^2 + BC^2 = 26^2$. Then $BC^2 = 676 - 100 = 576$, so $BC = 24$. The area of the triangle is given by the formula $\left(\frac{1}{2}\right)(AB)(BC) = \left(\frac{1}{2}\right)(10)(24) = 120$.

21. **(B)** To determine whether or not a graph represents a function, it is possible to apply the "vertical line test." If any vertical line to the graph intersects it in more than one point, the graph is not a function. The only graph for which a vertical line passes through more than one point is (B). A relation is a function if for any x there is one and only one y.

22. **(B)** % Markup $= \dfrac{\text{markup}}{\text{Cost}} \Rightarrow 0.8 = \dfrac{\text{markup}}{15} \Rightarrow \text{markup} = \$12$

Markup $=$ selling price $-$ cost $\Rightarrow 12 =$ selling price $- 15 \Rightarrow$ selling price $= 27$

% Markdown $= \dfrac{\text{markdown}}{\text{selling price}} \Rightarrow 0.3 = \dfrac{\text{markdown}}{27} \Rightarrow$ markdown $= \$8.10$

Markdown $=$ original price $-$ new price $\Rightarrow 8.10 = 27 -$ new price $\Rightarrow$ new price $= \$18.90$

Markup $=$ new selling price $-$ cost $\Rightarrow 18.90 - 15 = 3.90$

% Markup $= \dfrac{\text{markup}}{\text{cost}} \Rightarrow \dfrac{3.90}{15} = 26\%$

23. **(B)** $-|-8 - 3| = -|-11| = -11$. The values of answer choices (A), (C), and (D) are 5, 0, and -5, respectively.

24. **(B)** In this example, $A' = \{\text{cat, goat, tiger}\}$.
Then, $A' \cap B = \{\text{cat, goat, tiger}\} \cap \{\text{dog, goat, pig, tiger}\} = \{\text{goat, tiger}\}$.

25. **(C)** Each leg is the radius r. $r^2 + r^2 = 16 \Rightarrow r^2 = 8$.

Area of circle is $\pi r^2 = 8\pi$. Area of triangle $= \frac{1}{2}\left(\sqrt{8}\right)^2 = 4$.

Area of shaded region is $8\pi - 4$.

26. **(C)** The events are not mutually exclusive. They can occur at the same time. To be independent, Prob(Popcorn) $\cdot$ Prob(Soft drink) $=$ Prob(Both).

Since $\left(\dfrac{40}{100}\right)\left(\dfrac{30}{100}\right)=\dfrac{12}{100}$ as $(0.4)(0.3)=0.12$, having popcorn and a soft drink are independent.

Alternately: To be independent, Prob(Popcorn|Soft drink) = Prob(Popcorn) ⇒

$\dfrac{12}{30}=\dfrac{40}{100}$ or $0.4=0.4$.

27. **(A)** The set $A \cup B$ contains all elements which belong to either set A or set B. Since all elements, which belong to set A or set B, also belong to C, the set $A \cup B$ is a subset of C.

28. **(D)** Given a conditional statement in the form "If P then Q," an equivalent statement is in the form "Not P or Q." In this example, P is the statement "Joan sings" and Q is the statement "I will play my guitar."

29. **(C)**

$$\% \text{ decrease} = \frac{1975 \text{ Personnel} - 1980 \text{ Personnel}}{1975 \text{ Personnel}}$$

$$\text{Army: } \% \text{ decrease} = \frac{784-777}{784} = 0.89\%$$

$$\text{Navy: } \% \text{ decrease} = \frac{535-527}{535} = 1.50\%$$

$$\text{Air Force: } \% \text{ decrease} = \frac{612-578}{612} = 5.56\%$$

$$\text{Marines: } \% \text{ decrease} = \frac{196-188}{196} = 4.08\%$$

30. The answer is 800. The floor that measures 10 ft. by 20 ft. has an area of $10 \times 20 = 200$ sq. ft. The tiles with 36 sq. in. of area must measure 6 in. by 6 in. or $\dfrac{1}{2}$ ft. by $\dfrac{1}{2}$ ft. for $\dfrac{1}{4}$ sq. ft. of area. Because it would take four tiles to cover 1 sq. ft., $4 \times (200 \text{ sq. ft.}) = 800$ tiles would be needed to cover the entire floor.

31. **(C)** Prob(Washer or Dryer) = Prob(Washer + Prob(dryer) − Prob(Both)

$$\text{Prob}\left(\text{Washer or Dryer}\right)=\frac{55}{250}+\frac{45}{250}-\frac{25}{250}=\frac{75}{250}=\frac{3}{10}=30\%$$

32. **(B)** Choosing two approximate points that the line passes through: (200, 1,600), (300, 2,500), the slope of the line is $\dfrac{2500-1600}{300-200}=\dfrac{900}{100}=9$.

33. **(D)** The domain refers to all allowable values of x. In this example, the only value(s) of x that are not allowed are those for which the denominator is zero. If $x + 3 = 0$, then $x = -3$. Thus, -3 is the only value that is not allowed in the domain.

34. **(A)** Since $x + c = a + b + c = 180°$, $x = a + b$
Since $y + b = a + b + c = 180°$, $y = a + c$
Since $z + a = a + b + c = 180°$, $z = b + c$
So $x + y - z = a + b + a + c - (b + c) = 2a + b + c - b - c = 2a$

35. **(C)** To find the median, first arrange the data in ascending order. The data will then appear as
follows: 2, 7, 8, 10, 15, 24. The median will be the average of the two middle numbers. Thus, the
median is $\dfrac{8 + 10}{2} = 9$.

36. **(A)** An argument is valid if given that the premises are true, then the conclusion *must* be true.
Only answer choice (A) would satisfy this definition. Answer choice (B) is wrong because other
objects besides trees may have brown leaves. Answer choice (C) is wrong because animals other
than wolves may be vicious. Answer choice (D) is wrong because people may own only stocks, only
bonds, both stocks and bonds, or neither stocks nor bonds.

37. **(C)** 10% of $8 is $0.80. So with the new prices, a customer averages $7.20.

x% of $7.20 = 10 \Rightarrow \dfrac{x}{100} \cdot 7.20 = 10 \Rightarrow 7.20x = 1000 \Rightarrow x = 138.89$

The average customer must increase his spending by about 39%.

38. **(D)** The correct answer (D) has exactly two modes, namely 3 and 4. Answer choice (A) has a
single mode of 5. Answer choice (B) has a single mode of 2. Answer choice (C) has three modes,
namely 3, 4, and 5.

39. **(B)** To find the solution set of $f(x) > 2x$, we proceed as follows:

$$\frac{5x - 8}{2} > 2x$$

$$5x - 8 > 4x$$

$$-8 > -x$$

which implies $x > 8$.

40. **(A)** $(X \cup Y)'$ means the regions that are *not* included by X, by Y, or by both X and Y. Note that
answer choice (C) is wrong because it includes region V, which is in all three of X, Y, and Z.

41. The correct answer is 2.92. The value of $\overline{X}$ is $(4 + 5 + 6 + 9 + 11) \div 5 = 7$.

The value of $\displaystyle\sum_{i=1}^{n} (X_i - \overline{X})^2$ can be found by computing

$$(4 - 7)^2 + (5 - 7)^2 + (6 - 7)^2 + (9 - 7)^2 + (11 - 7)^2$$

$$= 9 + 4 + 1 + 4 + 16 = 34.$$

Then $s = \sqrt{\dfrac{34}{4}} = \sqrt{8.5} \approx 2.92$

42. **(B)**   Tax $= 923 + 0.15(37,450 - 9,225) = 923 + 4,234 = \$5,157.$

$$\%\text{Tax} = \frac{5,157}{37,450} = 0.1377 = 13.8\%$$

43. **(C)**   Since g is a linear function, we can use the point-slope formula with the points $(4, 6)$ and $(10, 21)$ to generate its equation:

$$m = \frac{21-6}{10-4} = \frac{15}{6} = \frac{5}{2}$$

$$y - 6 = \frac{5}{2}(x-4) \text{ or } 2y - 12 = 5x - 20 \text{ so } 2y = 5x - 8$$

$$y = g(x) = \frac{5}{2}x - 4 \text{ and } g(8) = \frac{5}{2}(8) - 4 = 20 - 4 = 16$$

44. **(A)** x = selling price $\Rightarrow 0.06x = 16,250 \Rightarrow x = \$270,833.$

Money at settlement: $270,833 - 16,250 = \$254,583$

45. **(A)**   Can: $\dfrac{0.40}{12} = \$0.0333/\text{ounce}$

48-ounce: $\dfrac{0.99}{48} = \$0.02063/\text{ounce}$

2-liter: $\dfrac{1.39}{67.6} = \$0.02056/\text{ounce}$

46. The correct answer 0.0048.

$(6 \times 10^{-3})(8 \times 10^{-1}) = 48 \times 10^{-4} = 4.8 \times 10^{-3} = 0.0048$

47. **(D)**   The circumference of the wheel is:

$$C = 2\pi(1 \text{ ft.})$$

$$C = 2\left(\frac{22}{7}\right) = \frac{44}{7} \text{ ft.}$$

To find the number of revolutions the wheel takes, calculate:

$$5,280 \div \frac{44}{7} = 5,280 \times \frac{7}{44}$$

$$= 120 \times 7 = 840 \text{ revolutions}$$

48. **(A)** The mean and the median are each 6. For answer choice (B), the median is 6 but the mean is $\frac{43}{7}$. For answer choice (C), the mean is 6 but the median is 5.5. For answer choice (D), the median is 6 but the mean is 6.5.

49. **(B)** Rewriting $x + 3y = 4$ as $y = -\frac{1}{3}x + \frac{4}{3}$, we can identify the slope as $-\frac{1}{3}$. A line that is perpendicular to the graph of this line must have a slope that is the negative reciprocal of $-\frac{1}{3}$, which is 3. When answer choice (B) is rewritten as $y = 3x - 7$, the slope can be identified as 3. Note also that $y = 3x - 7$ contains the point $(2, -1)$. The slopes for answer choices (A), (C), and (D) are $-\frac{1}{3}$, -3, and $\frac{1}{3}$, respectively.

50. **(C)** Without seeing any of the data, we know nothing about the number and standard deviation. But since the slope of the boy line of best fit is slightly greater than the slope of the girl line of best fit, we can conclude that boys grow faster than girls in this school.

51. The correct answer is 5.33. By the Pythagorean Theorem, the height of the parallelogram is 4 and the area of the parallelogram is $4(8) = 32$. The area of the trapezoid is $\frac{1}{2}h(8 + 4) = 6h$. So $6h = 32$ and $h = \frac{16}{3} = 5.33$.

52. The correct answer is 22. $f(-7) = (4)(-7) - 1 = -29$ and $f(10) = (5)(10) + 1 = 51$. Then $-29 + 51 = 22$.

53. **(D)** There are 9 selections for the first spot on the shelf, 8 selections for the second spot, 7 selections for the third spot, and 6 selections for the fourth spot. The number of different ways is $(9)(8)(7)(6) = 3024$. This is a permutation of 9 items taken 4 at a time.

54. **(A)** The first $2,000 is in the bank for 1 year:
$$A = 2000\left(1 + \frac{0.03}{360}\right)^{360\cdot1} = \$2,060.91$$

The second $3,000 is in the bank for half a year:
$$A = 3000\left(1 + \frac{0.03}{360}\right)^{360\cdot0.5} = \$3,045.34$$

Total $= 2060.91 + 3045.34 = \$5,106.25$

55. **(A)** $f(x)$ is shifted 3 units to the left and 3 units down so $y = f(x + 3) - 3$.

56. **(B)**

	60-inch TV	32-inch TV	iPod	Nothing
X	2,000	500	230	0
Prob(X)	$\dfrac{1}{1,000}$	$\dfrac{2}{1,000}$	$\dfrac{5}{1,000}$	$\dfrac{992}{1,000}$

$$\text{Expected Value(win)} = 2000\left(\frac{1}{1000}\right) + 500\left(\frac{2}{1000}\right) + 230\left(\frac{5}{1000}\right) + 0\left(\frac{992}{500}\right)$$

$$= \frac{4150}{1000} = \$4.15$$

Person wins $\$4.15 - \$10.00 = -\$5.85$. A person can expect to lose $\$5.85$.

57. The correct answer is 5. The perimeter of the square is $(4)(9) = 36$, which is the same as the perimeter of the rectangle. The perimeter of a rectangle is twice the length plus twice the width. Twice the length is 26, so twice the width must be 10. Thus, the width is 5.

58. **(B)** I. True. The line is above the exponential curve at $t = 2$.

   II. False. Ed's stock is worth $\$4,000$ at $t = 0$. Noreen's stock is worth $250(2) = \$500$. The difference is $\$3,500$.

   III. True, Ed's stock is worth $\$5,000$ at $t = 4$. Noreen's stock is worth $250(32) = \$8,000$.
   60% of $\$5,000 = \$3,000$ and $\$5,000 + \$3,000 = \$8,000$.

59. The correct answer is $\frac{8}{9}$. Let $N = 0.\overline{8}$. Multiply both sides of the equation by 10 to get $10N = 8.\overline{8}$. Subtract $N = 0.\overline{8}$ from $10N = 8.\overline{8}$ to get $9N = 8$. Then $N = \frac{8}{9}$.

60. **(B)** Each handshake involves two people, so the number of handshakes for 20 people is given by the expression $_{20}C_2 = (20)(19) \div 2 = 190$.

■ PRACTICE TEST

ANSWER SHEET

1. Ⓐ Ⓑ Ⓒ Ⓓ
2. Ⓐ Ⓑ Ⓒ Ⓓ
3. Ⓐ Ⓑ Ⓒ Ⓓ
4. ☐
5. Ⓐ Ⓑ Ⓒ Ⓓ
6. Ⓐ Ⓑ Ⓒ Ⓓ
7. Ⓐ Ⓑ Ⓒ Ⓓ
8. Ⓐ Ⓑ Ⓒ Ⓓ
9. Ⓐ Ⓑ Ⓒ Ⓓ
10. Ⓐ Ⓑ Ⓒ Ⓓ
11. Ⓐ Ⓑ Ⓒ Ⓓ
12. Ⓐ Ⓑ Ⓒ Ⓓ
13. Ⓐ Ⓑ Ⓒ Ⓓ
14. Ⓐ Ⓑ Ⓒ Ⓓ
15. Ⓐ Ⓑ Ⓒ Ⓓ
16. Ⓐ Ⓑ Ⓒ Ⓓ
17. Ⓐ Ⓑ Ⓒ Ⓓ
18. ☐
19. Ⓐ Ⓑ Ⓒ Ⓓ
20. Ⓐ Ⓑ Ⓒ Ⓓ

21. Ⓐ Ⓑ Ⓒ Ⓓ
22. Ⓐ Ⓑ Ⓒ Ⓓ
23. Ⓐ Ⓑ Ⓒ Ⓓ
24. Ⓐ Ⓑ Ⓒ Ⓓ
25. Ⓐ Ⓑ Ⓒ Ⓓ
26. Ⓐ Ⓑ Ⓒ Ⓓ
27. Ⓐ Ⓑ Ⓒ Ⓓ
28. Ⓐ Ⓑ Ⓒ Ⓓ
29. Ⓐ Ⓑ Ⓒ Ⓓ
30. ☐
31. Ⓐ Ⓑ Ⓒ Ⓓ
32. Ⓐ Ⓑ Ⓒ Ⓓ
33. Ⓐ Ⓑ Ⓒ Ⓓ
34. Ⓐ Ⓑ Ⓒ Ⓓ
35. Ⓐ Ⓑ Ⓒ Ⓓ
36. Ⓐ Ⓑ Ⓒ Ⓓ
37. Ⓐ Ⓑ Ⓒ Ⓓ
38. Ⓐ Ⓑ Ⓒ Ⓓ
39. Ⓐ Ⓑ Ⓒ Ⓓ
40. Ⓐ Ⓑ Ⓒ Ⓓ

41. ☐
42. Ⓐ Ⓑ Ⓒ Ⓓ
43. Ⓐ Ⓑ Ⓒ Ⓓ
44. Ⓐ Ⓑ Ⓒ Ⓓ
45. Ⓐ Ⓑ Ⓒ Ⓓ
46. ☐
47. Ⓐ Ⓑ Ⓒ Ⓓ
48. Ⓐ Ⓑ Ⓒ Ⓓ
49. Ⓐ Ⓑ Ⓒ Ⓓ
50. Ⓐ Ⓑ Ⓒ Ⓓ
51. ☐
52. ☐
53. Ⓐ Ⓑ Ⓒ Ⓓ
54. Ⓐ Ⓑ Ⓒ Ⓓ
55. Ⓐ Ⓑ Ⓒ Ⓓ
56. Ⓐ Ⓑ Ⓒ Ⓓ
57. ☐
58. Ⓐ Ⓑ Ⓒ Ⓓ
59. ☐
60. Ⓐ Ⓑ Ⓒ Ⓓ

PART III

CLEP Natural Sciences

About Our Authors

This CLEP Natural Sciences review was written by Laurie Callihan, Ph.D., and David Callihan, M.S.

Dr. Callihan is a veteran science author, researcher, and widely recognized CLEP test-prep expert. She earned a University Fellowship at Florida State University, one of FSU's most prestigious graduate awards. She managed a $3.5 million National Science Foundation grant-funded project promoting science among English language learners.

Mr. Callihan is an experienced science teacher and CLEP aficionado who earned recognition in the classroom for his students' academic performance. He has worked with the NASA Florida Space Grant Consortium and the Centers for Ocean Sciences Education Excellence.

AN OVERVIEW OF THE EXAM

The CLEP Natural Sciences exam consists of approximately 120 multiple-choice questions, each with five possible answer choices, to be answered in 90 minutes.

The exam covers the material one would find in a freshman or sophomore general science survey course covering biology and physical science. It is meant for students who are non-science majors. The exam stresses basic facts and principles as well as general theoretical approaches used by scientists.

The approximate breakdown of topics is as follows:

50% Biological Science

10%   Origin and evolution of life, classification of organisms

10%   Cell organization, cell division, chemical nature of the gene, bioenergetics, biosynthesis

20%   Structure, function, and development in organisms; patterns of heredity

10%   Concepts of population biology with emphasis on ecology

50% Physical Science

7%   Atomic and nuclear structure and properties, elementary particles, nuclear reactions

10%   Chemical elements, compounds and reactions, molecular structure and bonding

12%   Heat, thermodynamics, and states of matter; classical mechanics; relativity

4%   Electricity and magnetism, waves, light, and sound

7%   The universe: galaxies, stars, the solar system

10%   The Earth: atmosphere, hydrosphere, structure features, geologic processes, and history

6-WEEK STUDY PLAN

Our study plan is designed to be used in the six weeks before your exam. Be sure to set aside enough time—at least two hours each day—to study. The more time you spend studying, the more prepared and relaxed you will feel on the day of the exam.

Week	Activity
1	Take the Diagnostic Exam at the online REA Study Center (*www.rea.com/studycenter*). Your score report will identify topics where you need the most review.
2—4	Study the review, focusing on the topics you missed (or were unsure of) on the Diagnostic Exam.
5	Take Practice Test 1 at the REA Study Center. Review your score report and re-study any topics you missed.
6	Take Practice Test 2 at the REA Study Center to see how much your score has improved. If you still got a few questions wrong, go back to the review and study the topics you missed.

REVIEW OUTLINE

■ SECTION 1: BIOLOGICAL SCIENCE

■ EVOLUTION AND CLASSIFICATION

DARWINIAN CONCEPT OF NATURAL SELECTION

Current theories of evolution have their basis in the work of Charles Darwin and one of his contemporaries, Alfred Russell Wallace. Darwin's book, *The Origin of Species by Means of Natural Selection*, served to catalyze the study of evolution across scientific disciplines. A synopsis of Darwin's ideas follows.

From a study of populations, we know that population growth and maintenance of a species is dependent on limiting factors. Individuals within the species that are unable to acquire the minimum requirement of resources are unable to reproduce. The ecosystem can support only a limited number of organisms—known as the carrying capacity (K).

Once the carrying capacity is reached, a competition for resources ensues. Darwin considered this competition to be the basic *struggle for existence*. Some of the competitors will fail to survive. Within every population, there is variation among traits. Darwin proposed that those individuals who win the competition for resources pass those successful traits on to their children. Clearly, only the well adapted survive, and only the surviving competitors reproduce successfully and thus pass on traits generation after generation. Therefore, traits providing the competitive edge will be represented most often in succeeding generations.

MODERN CONCEPT OF NATURAL SELECTION

Although the concepts of natural selection put forth by Darwin still form the basis of evolutionary theory today, Darwin had no real knowledge of genetics when he presented his ideas.

Several years after Darwin's writings, Mendel's work (on experimental genetics) was rediscovered independently by three scientists. The laws of genetics served to support the suppositions Darwin had made. Over the next 40 years, the study of genetics included not only individual organisms but also population genetics (how traits are preserved, changed, or introduced within a population of organisms). Progress in the studies of biogeography and paleontology of the early 1900s also served to reinforce Darwin's basic observations.

The modern concept of natural selection emerged from Darwin's original ideas, with additions and confirmations of genetics, population studies, and paleontology. This **modern synthesis** focused on the concept that evolution was a process of gradual adaptive change in traits among populations and communities (over thousands or hundreds of thousands of generations). Evolution was not a process of individual-by-individual change, but change that occurred in entire populations within communities due to major environmental events.

THE ORIGIN OF LIFE

EVOLUTION OF THE FIRST CELLS

The modern theory of the evolution of life on Earth suggests that the earliest forms of life began approximately four billion years ago. Theories suggest that conditions on Earth were very different from conditions today. The atmosphere of the early Earth was likely chemically reducing (accepting electrons), composed mainly of methane (CH_4), ammonia (NH_3), hydrogen sulfide (H_2S), carbon dioxide (CO_2) or carbon monoxide (CO), and phosphate (PO_{43-}). The pre-life Earth environment was also plenteous in water (H_2O). There was little or no free oxygen (O_2) and ozone (O_3). In order for life to arise on Earth, organic molecules such as amino acids (the building blocks of proteins), sugars, acids, and bases would need to have formed from these available chemicals.

Over the last century there has been much research into plausible mechanisms for the origin of life. The **Oparin Hypothesis** is one theory developed by a Russian scientist (A.I. Oparin) in 1924. Oparin proposed that the Earth was formed approximately 4.6 billion years ago, stating that the early Earth had a reducing atmosphere, meaning there was very little free oxygen present. Instead there was an abundance of ammonia, hydrogen, methane, and steam (H_2O), all escaping from volcanoes. The Earth was in the process of cooling down, so there was a great deal of heat energy available, as well as a pattern of recurring violent lightning storms providing a source of energy in addition to sunlight. During this cooling of the Earth, much of the steam surrounding the Earth would condense, forming hot seas. In the presence of abundant energy, the synthesis of simple organic molecules from the available chemicals would be possible. These organic substances then collected in the hot, turbulent seas (sometimes referred to as the "primordial soup").

As the concentration of organic molecules became very high, they formed into larger, charged complex molecules. Oparin called these highly absorptive molecules "coacervates." Coacervates theoretically had the ability to divide.

Oparin's research involved experimental findings of evidence to support his ideas that amino acids could combine to form proteins under early Earth conditions. Oparin knew proteins were catalysts, so they could encourage further change and development of early cells.

Stanley Miller provided support for Oparin's hypotheses in experiments where he exposed simple inorganic molecules to electrical charges similar to lightning. Miller recreated conditions as they were supposed to have existed in early Earth history, and was successful in his attempts to produce complex organic molecules including amino acids under these conditions. Miller's experiments served to support Oparin's hypotheses.

Sidney Fox, a major evolution researcher of the 1960s, conducted experiments that proved ultraviolet light may induce the formation of dipeptides from amino acids. Under conditions of moderate dry heat, Fox showed formation of proteinoids—polypeptides of up to 18 amino acids. He also showed that poly-phosphoric acid could increase the yield of these polymers, a process that simulates the modern role of ATP in protein synthesis. These proteins formed small spheres known as microspheres that showed similarities to living cells.

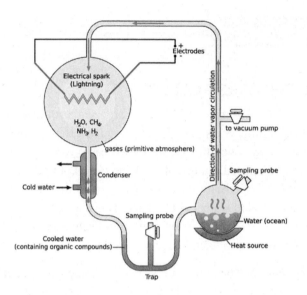

Fig. 3–1   Setup of the Miller-Urey Experiment.

Further strides were made by researcher Cyril Ponnamperuma who demonstrated that small amounts of guanine formed from the thermal polymerization of amino acids. He also demonstrated the synthesis of adenine and ribose from long-term treatment of reducing atmospheric gases with electrical current.

Once organic compounds had been synthesized, it is theorized that primitive cells developed that used ATP for energy and contained genetic material in the form of RNA (or possibly DNA). These primitive cells, called prokaryotes, were similar to some bacteria now found on Earth.

The endosymbiont theory suggests that original prokaryotic cells absorbed other cells that performed various tasks. For instance, an original cell could absorb several symbiotic bacteria that then evolve into mitochondria. Several cells that lived in symbiosis would have combined and evolved to form a single eukaryotic cell.

EVOLUTION OF LIFE

PLANT EVOLUTION

The evolution of plant species is still a matter of considerable research and discovery. Most theories indicate that the first plants derived from heterotrophic prokaryotic cells (cells that got their energy from other cells). Since it is presumed that the early Earth's atmosphere was lacking in oxygen, early cells were anaerobic. Over time, some bacteria evolved the ability to carry on photosynthesis (most likely the cyano-bacteria), thus becoming autotrophic (making their own food/

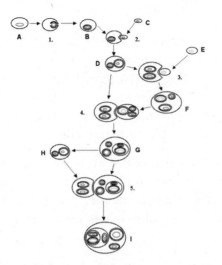

Fig. 3–2   Endosymbiont Theory. Step (1) Two prokaryotic cells (A and B) combine to form a new cell that is more complex since the functions of the ingested cell can continue within the first. The new cell combines with C to form D and so on. Eventually they form a eukaryotic cell (I) with diverse membrane-bound organelles performing specified functions within that single cell.

energy), which in turn introduced significant amounts of oxygen into the atmosphere. Oxygen is poisonous to most anaerobic cells, however, a new niche opened up: cells became able to survive in the presence of oxygen, and were also able to use oxygen for metabolism.

Cyanobacteria were incorporated into larger aerobic cells, which then evolved into photosynthetic eukaryotic cells. Cellular organization increased as nuclei and membranes formed, and cell specialization occurred, leading to multicellular photosynthetic organisms—that is, plants.

Clearly, this is a very abbreviated and simplified version of a very prolonged and extremely complex process. Each and every step along the way has been researched and questioned, and is still under the scrutiny of research. Scientists simply do not yet have enough evidence, to know with certainty whether one pathway of evolution was the one and only pathway or whether another or possibly several pathways converged.

Scientists do know with high levels of certainty that the earliest plants were aquatic, but as niches filled in marine and freshwater environments, plants began to move onto land. Anatomical changes occurred over time, allowing plants to survive in a non-aqueous environment. Cell walls thickened and tissues to carry water and nutrients developed. As plants continued to adapt to land conditions, differentiation of tissues continued, resulting in the evolution of stems, leaves, roots, and seeds. The development of the seed was a key factor in the survival of land plants. Asexual reproduction dominated in early species, but sexual reproduction developed over time, increasing the possibilities of diversity.

Processes of adaptive radiation, genetic drift, and natural selection continued over long periods of time to produce the incredible diversity seen in the plant world today.

ANIMAL EVOLUTION

The evolution of animals is thought to have begun with marine protists (one-celled living organisms). Although there is no fossil record going back to the protist level, animal cells bear the most similarity to marine protist cells. Fossilized burrows from multicellular organisms begin to appear in the geological record approximately 700 million years ago, during the Precambrian period. These multicellular animals had only soft parts—no hard parts, which could be fossilized. We can only see the remains of their life—the burrows they made.

During the Cambrian period (the first period of the Paleozoic Era), beginning about 570 million years ago, the fossil record begins to show multicellular organisms with hard parts, exoskeletons. The fossil record at this time includes fossil representations from all modern day (and some extinct) phyla. This sudden appearance of multitudes of differentiated animal forms is known as the **Cambrian explosion.**

At the end of the Paleozoic Era, the fossil record attests to several mass extinction events. These combined events resulted in the extinction of about 95% of animal species developed to that point. Fossils indicate that many organisms, such as Trilobites, which were numerous in the Cambrian era, did not survive to the end of the Paleozoic Era.

Approximately 505 million years ago marked the beginning of the Ordovician period, which lasted until about 440 million years ago. The Ordovician period was marked by diversification among species that survived past the Cambrian extinctions. The Ordovician is also known for the development of land plants. Early forms of fish arose in the Cambrian, but developed during the Ordovician, these being the first vertebrates to be seen in the fossil record. Again, the end of the Ordovician is marked by vast extinctions, but these extinctions allowed the opening of ecological situations, which in turn encouraged adaptive radiation.

Adaptive radiation is the evolutionary mechanism (see section on evolutionary mechanisms) credited with the development of new species in the next period, the Silurian, from 440 to 410 million years ago. The Silurian period is marked by widespread colonization of landmasses by plants and animals. Large numbers of insect fossils are recognizable in Silurian geologic sediments, as well as fish and early amphibians. The mass movement onto land by formerly marine animals required adaptation in numerous areas, including gas exchange, support (skeletal), water conservation, circulatory systems, and reproduction.

In the study of animal evolution, attention is paid to two concepts, homology and analogy. Structures that exist in two different species because they share a common ancestry are called **homologous**. For instance, the forelimbs of a salamander and an opossum are similar in structure because of common ancestry. **Analogous** structures are similar because of their common function, although they do not share a common ancestry. Analogous structures are the product of **convergent evolution**. For instance, birds and insects both have wings, although they are not relatives. Rather, the wings evolved as a result of convergence. Convergence occurs when a particular characteristic evolves in two unrelated populations. Wings of insects and birds are analogous structures (they are similar in function regardless of the lack of common ancestors).

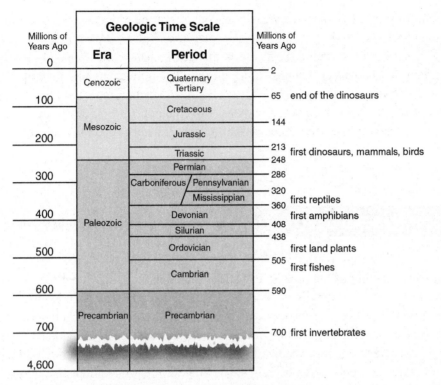

Fig. 3–3   Geologic Time Scale.

The process of **extinction** has played a large part in the direction evolution has taken. Extinctions occur at a generally low rate at all times. It is presumed that species that face extinction have not been able to adapt appropriately to environmental changes. However, there have also been several "extinction events" that have wiped out up to 95% of the species of their time. These events served to open up massive ecological niches, encouraging evolution of multitudes of new species.

Approximately 400 million years ago, the first amphibians gave rise to early reptiles that then diversified into birds, then mammals. One branch of mammals developed into the tree-dwelling primates, considered the ancestors of humans.

HUMAN EVOLUTION

Humans evolution theories are still in development, but current research states that *Homo sapiens sapiens* (modern humans) have evolved from primates who over time developed larger brains. A branch of bipedal primates gave rise to the first true hominids about 4.5 million years ago. The earliest known hominid fossils were found in Africa in the 1970s. The well-known "Lucy" skeleton was named *Australopithecus afarensis*. It was determined from the skeleton of *Australopithecus* that it was a biped. It had a human-like jaw and teeth, but a skull that was more similar to that of a small ape. The arms were proportionately longer than humans, indicating the ability to still be motile in trees.

The fossilized skull of *Homo erectus,* who is considered the oldest known fossil of the human genus, is thought to be about 1.8 million years old. The skull of *Homo erectus* was quite a lot larger than *Australopithecus,* about the size of a modern human brain. *Homo erectus* was thought to walk upright and had facial features more closely resembling humans than apes. The oldest fossils to be designated *Homo sapiens* are also called Cro-Magnon man, with brain size and facial features essentially the same as modern humans. Cro-Magnon *Homo sapiens* are thought to have evolved in Africa and migrated to Europe and Asia approximately 100,000 years ago.

MECHANISMS OF EVOLUTION

Modern understanding of the process of natural selection recognizes that there are some basic mechanisms that support evolutionary change. Mutations happen only in individuals, and Darwin focused on natural selection that happened to individuals. However, modern theories focus on the change that occurs among populations within communities, not on individuals. The mutations that occur produce traits that affect individuals that then pass down traits through their genes. This then has an impact on a population of individuals after several generations. Natural selection that impacts evolution is the selection of genetic traits that make a population of a species more fit to survive and to reproduce in the community.

All evolution is dependent upon genetic change. The entire collection of genes within a given population is known as its **gene pool**. Individuals in the population will have only one pair of alleles (variations of a gene type) for a particular single-gene trait. Yet, the gene pool may contain dozens or hundreds of alleles for this trait. Evolution does not occur through changes from individual to individual, but rather as the gene pool changes through one of a number of possible mechanisms.

One mechanism that drives the changing of traits over time in a community is **differential reproduction**. Natural selection exists due to the fact that some individuals within a population are more suited for survival, given environmental conditions. Differential reproduction occurs because those individuals within a population that are most adapted to the environment are also the most likely individuals to reproduce successfully. Therefore, the reproductive processes tend to strengthen the frequency of expression of desirable traits across the population. Differential reproduction increases the number of alleles for desirable traits in the gene pool. This trend will be established and strengthen gradually over time, eventually producing a population where the desirable trait becomes rampant, if environmental conditions remain the same.

Another mechanism of genetic change is mutation. A **mutation** is a change of the DNA sequence of a gene, resulting in a change of the trait. Although a mutation can cause a very swift change in the genotype (genetic code) and possibly phenotype (expressed trait) of the offspring, mutations do not necessarily produce a trait desirable for a particular environment. Mutation is a much more random occurrence than differential reproduction.

Although mutations occur quickly, the change in the gene pool is minimal, so change in the community occurs very slowly (over multiple generations). Mutation does provide a vehicle of introducing new genetic possibilities; genetic traits, which did not exist in the original gene pool, can be introduced through mutation.

A third mechanism recognized to influence the evolution of new traits is known as **genetic drift**. Over time, a gene pool (particularly in a small population) may experience a change in frequency of particular genes simply due to chance fluctuations. In a finite population, the gene pool may not reflect the entire number of genetic possibilities of the larger genetic pool of the species population. Over time, the genetic pool within this finite population changes, and evolution has occurred. Genetic drift has no particular tie to environmental conditions, and thus the random change in gene frequency is unpredictable. The change of gene frequency may produce a small or a large change, depending on what traits are affected. The process of genetic drift, as opposed to mutation, actually causes a reduction in genetic variety.

Genetic drift occurs within finite separated populations, allowing each population to develop its own distinct gene pool. However, occasionally an individual from an adjacent population of the same species may immigrate and breed with a member of the previously locally isolated group. The introduction of new genes from the immigrant results in a change of the gene pool, known as **gene migration**. Gene migration is also occasionally successful between members of different, but related, species. The resultant hybrids succeed in adding increased variability to the gene pool.

The study of genetics shows that in a situation where random mating is occurring within a population (which is in equilibrium with its environment), gene frequencies and genotype ratios will remain constant from generation to generation. This law is known as the **Hardy-Weinberg Law of Equilibrium**, named after the two men (G.H. Hardy and Wilhelm Weinberg, c. 1909) who first studied this principle in mathematical studies of genetics. The Hardy-Weinberg Law is a mathematical formula that shows why recessive genes do not disappear over time from a population.

According to the Hardy-Weinberg Law, the sum of the frequencies of all possible alleles for a particular trait is 1. That is,

$$p + q = 1.0$$

where the frequency of one allele is represented by **p** and the frequency of another is **q**. It then follows mathematically that the frequency of genotypes within a population can be represented by the equation:

$$p^2 + 2pq + q^2 = 1$$

where the frequency of homozygous dominant genotypes is represented by p^2, the homozygous recessive by q^2, and the heterozygous genotype by $2pq$.

For instance, in humans the ability to taste the chemical phenylthiocarbamide (PTC) is a dominant inherited trait. If **T** represents the allele for tasting PTC and **t** represents the recessive trait (inability to taste PTC), then the possible genotypes in a population would be **TT**, **Tt**, and **tt**. If the frequency of non-tasters in a particular population is 4% or 0.04 (that is, $q^2 = 0.04$), then the frequency of the allele **t** equals the square root of 0.04 or 0.2. It is then possible to calculate the frequency of the dominant allele, **T**, in the population using the equation:

$$p + 0.2 = 1 \text{ so, } p = 0.8$$

The frequency of the allele for tasting PTC is 0.8. The frequency of the various possible genotypes (**TT**, **Tt**, and **tt**) in the population can also be calculated since the frequency of the homozygous dominant is p^2 or 0.64 or 64%. The frequency of the heterozygous genotype is $2pq$.

$$2pq = 2(0.8)(0.2) = 0.32 = 32\%.$$

$$\text{Frequency of TT} = 64\%, \text{Tt} = 32\%, \text{tt is } 4\% \ldots \text{totaling } 100\%$$

$$\text{or } 0.64 + 0.32 + 0.04 = 1$$

In order for Hardy-Weinberg equilibrium to occur, the population in question must meet the following conditions: random mating (no differential reproduction) must be taking place and no migration, mutation, selection, or genetic drift can be occurring. When these conditions are met, Hardy-Weinberg equilibrium can occur, and there will be no changes in the gene pool over time. Hardy-Weinberg is important to the evolutionary process because it shows that alleles that have no current selective value will be retained in a population over time.

MECHANISMS OF SPECIATION

A species is an interbreeding population that shares a common gene pool and produces viable offspring. Up to this point we have been considering mechanisms that produce variation within species. It is apparent that to explain evolution on a broad scale we must understand how genetic change produces new species. There are two mechanisms that produce separate species: allopatric speciation and sympatric speciation.

In order for a new species to develop, substantial genetic changes must occur between populations, which prohibit them from interbreeding. These genetic changes may result from genetic drift or from mutation that take place separately in the two populations. **Allopatric speciation** occurs when two populations are geographically isolated from each other. For instance, a population of squirrels may be geographically separated by a catastrophic event such as a volcanic eruption. Two populations (separated by the volcanic flow) continue to reproduce and experience genetic drift and/or mutation over time. This limits each population's gene pool and produces changes in expressed traits. Later, the geographical separation may be eliminated as the volcanic flow subsides; even so, the two populations have now experienced too much change to allow them to successfully interbreed again. The result is the production of two separate species.

Speciation may also occur without a geographic separation when a population develops members with a genetic difference, which prevents successful reproduction with the original species. The genetically different members reproduce with each other, producing a population, which is separate from the original species. This process is called **sympatric speciation**.

As populations of an organism in a given area grow, some will move into new geographic areas looking for new resources or to escape predators. (In this case, a natural event does not separate the population; instead, part of the population moves.) Some of these adventurers will discover new niches and advantageous conditions. Traits possessed by this traveling population will grow more common over several generations through the process of natural selection. Over time the species will specially adapt to live more effectively in the new environment. Through this process, known as **adaptive radiation**, a single species can develop into several diverse species over time. If the separated populations merge again and are able to successfully interbreed, then by definition new species have not been developed. Adaptive radiation is proven to have occurred when the species remerge and do not interbreed successfully.

All of the above evolutionary mechanisms are dependent upon reproduction of organisms over a long period of time, a very gradual process. **Punctuated equilibrium** is an entirely different method of explaining speciation. Punctuated equilibrium is a scientific model that proposes that adaptations of species arise suddenly and rapidly. Punctuated equilibrium states that species undergo a long period of equilibrium, which at some point is upset by environmental forces causing a short period of quick mutation and change.

Punctuated equilibrium was first proposed as paleontologists studied the fossil record. Gradualism would produce slowly changing and adapting species over many generations. However, the fossil record seems to show that organisms in general survive many generations in many areas with very little change over long periods of geologic time. New species appear in the fossils suddenly, without transitional forms, though "sudden" in this context needs to be understood on a geologic time scale.

Scientists still do not agree on the degree to which gradualism, punctuated equilibrium, or a combination of these processes is responsible for speciation.

CLASSIFICATION OF LIVING ORGANISMS

The study of **taxonomy** seeks to organize living things into groups based on morphology, or more recently, genetics.

Carolus Linnaeus, who published his book *Systema Naturae* in 1735, first developed our current methods of taxonomy. Linnaeus based his taxonomic keys on the morphological (outward anatomical) differences seen among species. Linnaeus designed a system of classification for all known and unknown organisms according to their anatomical similarities and differences.

Linnaeus used two Latin-based categories—*genus* and *species*—to name each organism. Every genus name could include one or more types of species. We refer to this two-word naming of species as **binomial nomenclature** (literally meaning "two names" in Latin). For example, Linnaeus named humans *Homo sapiens* (literally "man who is wise"). *Homo* is the genus name and *sapiens* the species name. *Homo sapiens* is the only extant species left from the genus *Homo.*

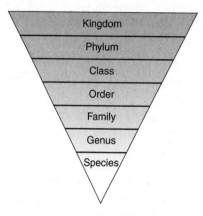

Fig. 3–4 Organism Classification System.

Beyond genus and species, Linnaeus further categorized organisms in a total of seven levels. Every **species** also belongs to a **genus, family, order, class, phylum,** and **kingdom**. *Kingdom* is the most general category, *species* the most limited. Taxonomists now also add "sub" and "super" categories to give even more opportunity for grouping similar organisms, and have added categories even more general than kingdom (that is, **domains**).

When considering the classification of living organisms, and as you look at Figure 3–4, you should realize that the organisms within the classification layers as you go down the upside-down pyramid are going to be more and more alike to each other. For example, organisms within the same kingdom will be more alike than those in another kingdom, but organisms in the same genus will be much more alike than those sharing only a family, but not a genus.

Although Linnaeus's system was designed before evolution was understood, the system he designed remains in use because it is based on similarities of species. An evolutionary classification system would use these same criteria. However, today the classification system also serves to show relationships between organisms. When one constructs a **phylogenetic tree** (an evolutionary family tree of species) the result will generally show the same relationships represented with Linnaeus's taxonomy.

The most modern classification system contains three domains: the **Archaea**, the **Eubacteria**, and the **Eukaryota**. The organisms of the domain Archaea are prokaryotic, have unique RNA, and are able to live in the extreme ecosystems on Earth. The domain Archaea includes methane-producing organisms, and organisms able to withstand extreme temperatures and high salinity. The domain Eubacteria contains the prokaryotic organisms we call bacteria.

It should be noted that some taxonomists still use a system including five kingdoms and no domains. In this case, the kingdom Monera would include organisms that are considered by other taxonomists to be included within the domains Archaea and Eubacteria.

The domain Eukaryota includes all organisms that possess eukaryotic cells. The domain Eukaryota includes the four kingdoms: **Kingdom Protista, Kingdom Fungi, Kingdom Animalia, and Kingdom Plantae**. The following chart gives the major features of the four kingdoms of the Eukaryota:

Fig. 3–5   Four Kingdoms of the Eukaryota.

Kingdom	No. of Known Phyla/Species	Nutrition	Structure	Included Organisms
Protista	27/250,000 +	photosynthesis, some ingestion and absorption	large eukaryotic cells	algae & protozoa
Fungi	5/100,000 +	absorption	multicellular (eukaryotic) filaments	mold, mushrooms, yeast, smuts, mildew
Animalia	33/1,000,000 +	ingestion	multicellular, specialized eukaryotic motile cells	various worms, sponges, fish, insects, reptiles, amphibians, birds, and mammals
Plantae	10/250,000 +	photosynthesis	multicellular, specialized eukaryotic nonmotile cells	ferns, mosses, woody and non-woody flowering plants

There are nine major phyla within the **Kingdom Animalia**. (Each phylum is further broken down, but the focus here will be on the phylum Chordata.) The Phyla are as follows:

1. **Porifera**—the sponges

2. **Cnidaria**—jellyfish, sea anemones, hydra, etc.

3. **Platyhelminthes**—flat worms

4. **Nematoda**—round worms

5. **Mollusca**—snails, clams, squid, etc.

6. **Annelida**—segmented worms (earthworms, leeches, etc.)

7. **Arthropoda**—crabs, spiders, lobster, millipedes, insects

8. **Echinodermata**—sea stars, sand dollars, etc.

9. **Chordata**—fish, amphibians, reptiles, birds, mammals, lampreys

Vertebrates are within the phylum Chordata, which is split into three subphyla, the **Urochordata** (animals with a tail cord such as tunicates), the **Cephalochordata** (animals with a head cord such as lampreys), and **Vertebrata** (animals with a backbone).

The subphylum Vertebrata is divided into two **superclasses**, the **Aganatha** (animals with no jaws), and the **Gnathostomata** (animals with jaws). The Gnathostomata includes six classes with the following major characteristics:

a. **Chondrichthyes**—fish with a cartilaginous endoskeleton, two-chambered heart, 5–7 gill pairs, no swim bladder or lung, and internal fertilization (sharks, rays, etc.).

b. **Osteichthyes**—fish with a bony skeleton, numerous vertebrae, swim bladder (usually), two-chambered heart, gills with bony gill arches, and external fertilization (herring, carp, tuna).

c. **Amphibia**—animals with a bony skeleton, usually with four limbs having webbed feet with four toes, cold-blooded (ectothermic), large mouth with small teeth, three-chambered heart, separate sexes, internal or external fertilization, amniotic egg (salamanders, frogs, etc.).

d. **Reptilia**—horny epidermal scales, usually have paired limbs with five toes (except limbless snakes), bony skeleton, lungs, no gills, most have three-chambered heart, cold-blooded (ecothermic), internal fertilization, separate sexes, mostly egg-laying (oviparous), eggs contain extraembryonic membranes (snakes, lizards, alligators).

e. **Aves**—spindle-shaped body (with head neck, trunk, and tail), long neck, paired limbs, most have wings for flying, four-toed foot, feathers, leg scales, bony skeleton, bones with air cavities, beak, no teeth, four-chambered heart, warm blooded (endothermic), lungs with thin air sacs, separate sexes, egg-laying, eggs have hard calcified shell (birds, ducks, sparrows, etc.).

f. **Mammalia**—body covered with hair, glands (sweat, scent, sebaceous, mammary), teeth, fleshy external ears, usually four limbs, four-chambered heart, lungs, larynx, highly developed brain, warm-blooded, internal fertilization, live birth (except for the egg-laying monotremes), milk-producing (cows, humans, platypus, apes, etc.).

CELLULAR AND MOLECULAR BIOLOGY

THE STRUCTURE AND FUNCTION OF CELLS

The **cell** is the smallest and most basic unit of most living things **(organisms)**. Many species have only a single cell, others are multicellular. (Although viruses are sometimes considered to be living, they are non-cellular and cannot fulfill the characteristics of life without invading the cell of another organism.) Cell structure varies according to the function of the cell and the type of living thing.

There are two main types of cells: prokaryotic and eukaryotic. **Prokaryotes** have no nucleus or any other membrane-bound **organelles** (cell components that perform particular functions). The DNA in prokaryotic cells usually forms a single chromosome which is circular or loop-like and which floats within the cytoplasm. Prokaryotic organisms have only one cell and include all bacteria. Plant, fungi, and animal cells, as well as protozoa, are **eukaryotic**. Eukaryotic cells contain membrane-bound intracellular organelles, including a nucleus. The DNA within eukaryotes is organized into chromosomes.

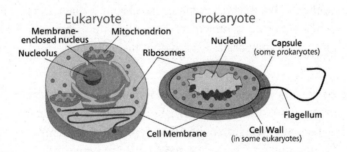

Fig. 3–6   Comparison of Eukaryote and Prokaryote Cells.

A single organism can be *unicellular* (consisting of just one cell), or *multicellular* (consisting of many cells). A multicellular organism may have many different types of cells that differ in structure to serve different functions. Individual cells may contain organelles that assist them with specialized functions. For example, muscle cells tend to contain more mitochondria (organelles that make energy available to the cells) since muscle requires the use of extra energy.

Animal cells differ in structure and function from photosynthetic cells, which are found in plants and some protists. Photosynthetic cells have the added job of producing food so they are equipped with specialized photosynthetic organelles. Plant cells also have a central vacuole and cell walls, structures not found in animal cells.

Note: Some prokaryotes are photosynthetic as well, but don't "contain" photosynthetic cells. They simply have developed photosynthetic ability (i.e., cyanobacteria).

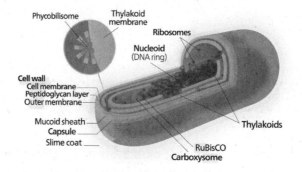

Fig. 3–7   Cyanobacteria (Photosynthetic Prokaryote).

CELL ORGANELLES OF PLANTS AND ANIMALS

The light microscope is useful in examining most cells and some cell organelles (such as the nucleus). However, many cell organelles are very small and require the magnification and resolution power of an **electron microscope**.

All cells are enclosed within the **cell membrane** (or plasma membrane). Near the center of each eukaryotic cell is the **nucleus**, which contains the chromosomes. Between the nucleus and the cell membrane, the cell contains a region called the **cytoplasm**. Since all of the organelles outside the nucleus but within the cell membrane exist within the cytoplasm, they are all called **cytoplasmic organelles**.

The shape and size of cells can vary widely. The longest nerve cells (neurons) may extend over a meter in length with an approximate diameter of only 4-100 micrometers (1 millimeter = 1,000 micrometers [μm]). A human egg cell may be 100 micrometers in diameter. The average size of a bacterium is 0.5 to 2.0 micrometers. However, most cells are between 0.5 and 100 micrometers in diameter. The size of a cell is limited by the ratio of its volume to its surface area. In the illustration below, note the variation of shape of cells within the human body:

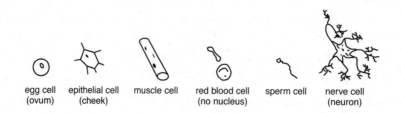

Fig. 3–8   Varying Cell Types. The six sketches of human cell types show some of the diversity in shape and size among cells with varying functions. The sketches are not sized to scale.

Animal Cells (See Fig. 3–10.)

1. The **cell membrane (1a)** encloses the cell and separates it from the environment. It may also be called a plasma membrane. This membrane is composed of a double layer (bilayer) of phospholipids with globular proteins embedded within the layers. These proteins span all layers of the membrane connecting the inside of the cell with the outside world. The membrane is extremely thin (about 80 angstroms; 10 million angstroms = 1 millimeter) and elastic. The combination of the lipid bilayer and the proteins embedded within it allow the cell to determine what molecules and ions can enter and leave the cell, and regulate the rate at which they enter and leave.

Endocytic vesicles (1b) form when the plasma membrane of a cell surrounds a molecule outside the membrane, then releases a membrane-bound sack containing the desired molecule or substance into the cytoplasm. This process allows the cell to absorb larger molecules than would be able to pass through the cell membrane, or that need to remain packaged within the cell.

2. Microvilli are projections of the cell extending from the cell membrane. Microvilli are found in certain types of cells—for example, those involved in absorption (such as the cells lining the intestine). These filaments increase the surface area of the cell membrane, increasing the area available to absorb nutrients. They also contain enzymes involved in digesting certain types of nutrients.

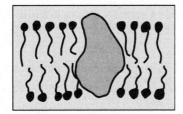

Fig. 3–9   Cell Membrane. A phospholipid bilayer with embedded globular proteins.

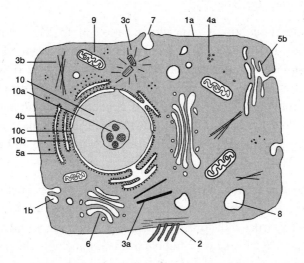

Fig. 3–10   A Generalized Animal Cell (cross-section). Since there are many types of animal cells, this diagram is generalized. In other words, some animal cells will have all of these organelles, others will not. However, this illustration will give you a composite picture of the organelles within the typical animal cell. It is also important to note the function of each organelle. Each labeled component is explained by the corresponding text.

3. The **cytoskeleton** provides structural support to a cell. **Microtubules (3a)** are long, hollow, cylindrical protein filaments, which give structure to the cell. These filaments are scattered around the edges of a cell and form a sort of loose skeleton or framework for the cytoplasm. Microtubules also are found at the base of cilia or flagella (organelles which allow some cells to move on their own) and give these organelles the ability to move. **Microfilaments (3b)** are double-stranded chains of proteins, which serve to give structure to the cell. Together with the larger microtubules, microfilaments form the cytoskeleton, providing stability and structure. **Centrioles (3c)** are structural components of many cells, and are particularly common in animal cells. Centrioles are tubes constructed of a geometrical arrangement of microtubules in a pinwheel shape. Their function includes the formation of new microtubules, but is primarily the formation of structural skeleton around which cells split during mitosis and meiosis. Basal bodies are structurally similar to centrioles, but their function is to anchor and aid in the movement of flagella or cilia.

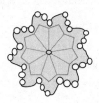

Fig. 3–11 Cross-section of a Centriole. Centrioles are tubes constructed of a geometrical arrangement of microtubules in a pinwheel shape.

4. **Ribosomes** are the site of protein synthesis within cells. Ribosomes are composed of certain protein molecules and RNA molecules (ribosomal RNAs, or rRNAs). **Free ribosomes (4a)** float unattached within the cytoplasm. The proteins synthesized by free ribosomes are made for use in the cytoplasm, not within membrane-bound organelles. **Attached ribosomes (4b)** are attached to the ER (see No. 5). Proteins made at the site of attached ribosomes are destined for use within the membrane-bound organelles.

5. The **endoplasmic reticulum,** a large organization of folded membranes, is responsible for the delivery of lipids and proteins to certain areas within the cytoplasm (a sort of cellular highway). **Rough endoplasmic reticulum or RER (5a)** has attached ribosomes. In addition to packaging and transport of materials within the cell, the RER is instrumental to protein synthesis. **Smooth endoplasmic reticulum or SER (5b)** is a network of membranous channels. Smooth endoplasmic reticulum does not have attached ribosomes. The endoplasmic reticulum is responsible for processing lipids, fats, and steroids, which are then packaged and dispersed by the Golgi apparatus.

6. The **Golgi apparatus** (also known as Golgi bodies, or the Golgi complex) is instrumental in the storing, packaging, and shipping of proteins. The Golgi apparatus looks much like stacks of hollow pancakes and is constructed of folded membranes. Within these membranes, cellular products are stored or packaged by closing off a bubble of membrane with the proteins or lipids inside. These packages are shipped (via the endoplasmic reticulum) to the part of the cell where they will be used or to the cell membrane for secretion from the cell.

7. **Secretory vesicles** are packets of material packaged by either the Golgi apparatus or the endoplasmic reticulum. Secretory vesicles carry substances produced within the cell (a protein, for example) to the cell membrane. The vesicle membrane fuses with the cell membrane in a process called **exocytosis**, allowing the substance to escape the cell.

8. **Lysosomes** are membrane-bound organelles containing digestive enzymes. Lysosomes digest unused material within the cell, damaged organelles, or materials absorbed by the cell for use.

9. **Mitochondria** are centers of cellular respiration (the process of breaking up covalent bonds within sugar molecules with the intake of oxygen and release of ATP, adenosine triphosphate). ATP molecules store energy that is later used in cell processes. Mitochondria (plural of mitochondrion) are more numerous in cells requiring more energy (muscle, etc.). Mitochondria are self-replicating, containing their own DNA, RNA, and ribosomes. Mitochondria have a double membrane; the internal membrane is folded. Cellular respiration reactions occur along the folds of the internal membrane (called **cristae**). Mitochondria are thought to be an evolved form of primitive bacteria (prokaryotic cells) that lived in a symbiotic relationship with eukaryotic cells more than 2 billion years ago. This concept, known as the **endosymbiont hypothesis**, is a plausible explanation of how mitochondria, which have many of the necessary components for life on their own, became an integral part of eukaryotic cells.

10. The **nucleus** is an organelle surrounded by two lipid bilayer membranes. The nucleus contains chromosomes, nuclear pores, nucleoplasm, and nucleoli. The **nucleolus (10a)** is a rounded area within the nucleus of the cell where ribosomal RNA is synthesized. This rRNA is incorporated into ribosomes after exiting the nucleus. Several nucleoli (plural of nucleolus) can exist within a nucleus. The **nuclear membrane (10b)** is the boundary between the nucleus and the cytoplasm. The nuclear membrane is actually a double membrane, which allows for the entrance and exit of certain molecules through the nuclear pores. **Nuclear pores (10c)** are points at which the double nuclear membrane fuses together, forming a passageway between the inside of the nucleus and the cytoplasm outside the nucleus. Nuclear pores allow the cell to selectively move molecules in and out of the nucleus. There are many pores scattered about the surface of the nuclear membrane.

Plant Cells

The structure of plant cells differs noticeably from animal cells with the addition of three organelles: the cell wall, the chloroplasts, and the central vacuole. In Fig. 3–12, the organelles numbered 1 to 7 function the same way in plant cells as in animal cells (see below).

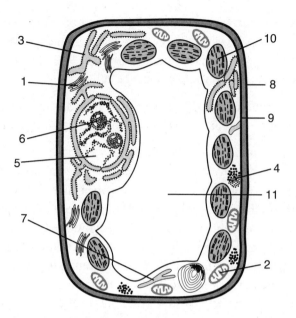

Fig. 3–12   A Typical Plant Cell.

1. **Golgi apparatus**

2. **Mitochondria**

3. **Rough endoplasmic reticulum**

4. **Ribosome**

5. **Nucleus**

6. **Nucleolus**

7. **Smooth endoplasmic reticulum**

8.   **Cell walls** surround plant cells. (Bacteria also have cell walls.) Cell walls are made up of cellulose and lignin, making them strong and rigid (whereas the cell membrane is relatively weak and flexible). The cell wall encloses the cell membrane providing strength and protection for the cell. The cell wall allows plant cells to store water under relatively high concentration. The combined strength of a plant's cell walls provides support for the whole organism. Dry wood and cork are essentially the cell walls of dead plants. The structure of the cell wall allows substances to pass through it readily, so transport in and out of the cell is still regulated by the cell membrane.

9.   The **cell membrane** (or plasma membrane) functions in plant and animal cells in the same way. However, in some plant tissues, channels connect the cytoplasm of adjacent cells.

10.   **Chloroplasts** are found in plant cells (and also in some protists). Chloroplasts are the site of photosynthesis within plant cells. **Chlorophyll** pigment molecules give the chloroplast their green color, although the chloroplasts also contain yellow and red carotenoid pigments. In the fall, as chloroplasts lose chlorophyll, these pigments are revealed giving leaves their red and yellow

colors. The body (or **stroma**) of the chloroplast contains embedded stacked disk-like plates (called **grana**), which are the site of photosynthetic reactions.

11. The **central vacuole** takes up much of the volume of plant cells. It is a membrane-bound (this particular membrane is called the **tonoplast**), fluid-filled space, which stores water and soluble nutrients for the plant's use. The tendency of the central vacuole to absorb water provides for the rigid shape (turgidity) of some plant cells. (Animal cells may also contain vacuoles for varying purposes, and these too are membrane-bound fluid-filled spaces. For instance, contractile vacuoles perform the specific function of expelling waste and excess water from single-celled organisms.)

PROPERTIES OF CELL MEMBRANES

The cell membrane is an especially important cell organelle with a unique structure, which allows it to control movement of substances into and out of the cell. Made up of a fluid phospholipid bilayer, proteins, and carbohydrates, this extremely thin (approximately 80 angstroms) membrane can only be seen clearly with an electron microscope. The selective permeability of the cell membrane serves to manage the concentration of substances within the cell. Substances can cross the cell membrane by passive transport, facilitated diffusion, and active transport. During **passive transport**, substances freely pass across the membrane without the cell expending any energy. **Facilitated diffusion** does not require added energy, but it cannot occur without the help of specialized proteins. Transport requiring energy output from the cell is called **active transport**.

Simple diffusion is one type of passive transport. **Diffusion** is the process whereby molecules and ions flow through the cell membrane from an area of higher concentration to an area of lower concentration (thus tending to equalize concentrations). Where the substance exists in higher concentration, collisions occur, which tend to propel them away toward lower concentrations. Diffusion generally is the means of transport for ions and molecules that can slip between the lipid molecules of the membrane. Diffusion requires no added energy to propel substances through a membrane.

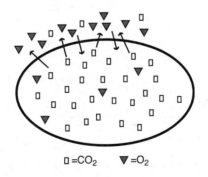

$\square = CO_2$ $\blacktriangledown = O_2$

Fig. 3–13   Diffusion. CO_2 diffuses out of the cell since its concentration is higher inside the cell. O_2 diffuses into the cell because its concentration is higher outside. Molecules diffuse from areas of high concentration to areas of lower concentration.

Another type of passive transport is **osmosis**, a special process of diffusion occurring only with water molecules. Osmosis does not require the addition of any energy, but occurs when the water concentration inside the cell differs from the concentration outside the cell. The water on the side of the membrane with the highest water concentration will move through the membrane until the concentration is equalized on both sides. When the water concentration is equal inside and outside the cell, it is called isosmotic or isotonic. For instance, a cell placed in a salty solution will tend to lose water until the solution outside the cell has the same concentration of water molecules as the cytoplasm (the solution inside the cell).

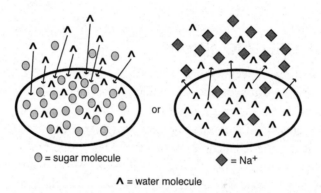

$\bigcirc$ = sugar molecule $\blacklozenge$ = Na$^+$

$\wedge$ = water molecule

Fig. 3–14   Osmosis. Water crosses the membrane into a cell that has a higher concentration of sugar molecules than the surrounding solution. Water crosses the membrane to leave the cell when there is a higher concentration of Na$^+$ ions outside the cell than inside the cell.

Facilitated diffusion is another method of transport across the cell membrane. Facilitated diffusion allows for transfer of substances across the cell membrane with the help of specialized proteins. These proteins, which are embedded in the cell membrane, are able to pick up specific molecules or ions and transport them through the membrane. The special protein molecules allow the diffusion of molecules and ions that cannot otherwise pass through the lipid bilayer.

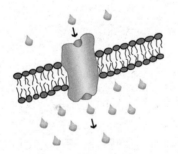

Fig. 3–15   Facilitated Diffusion. Specialized proteins embedded in the cell membrane (and crossing the entire membrane) permit passage of substances of a particular shape and size.

Active transport, like facilitated diffusion, requires membrane-bound proteins. Unlike facilitated diffusion, active transport uses energy to move molecules across a cell membrane against a concentration gradient (in the opposite direction than they would go under normal diffusion circumstances).

With the addition of the energy obtained from ATP, a protein molecule embedded in the membrane changes shape and moves a molecule across the membrane against the concentration gradient.

Large molecules are not able to pass through the cell membrane, but may be engulfed by the cell membrane. **Endocytosis** is the process whereby large molecules (i.e., some sugars or proteins) are taken up into a pocket of membrane. The pocket pinches off, delivering the molecules, still inside a membrane sack, into the cytoplasm. This process, for instance, is used by white blood cells to engulf bacteria. **Exocytosis** is the reverse process, exporting substances from the cell.

ENERGY TRANSFORMATIONS (BIOENERGETICS)

All living things require energy. Ultimately, the source of most energy for life on Earth is the sun. Photosynthetic organisms (plants, some protists, and some bacteria) are able to harvest solar energy and transform it into chemical energy eventually stored within covalent bonds of molecules (such as carbohydrates, fats, and proteins). These organisms are called primary producers. Consumers eat producers and utilize the chemical energy stored in them to carry on the functions of life. Other organisms then consume the consumers. In each of these steps along the food chain, some energy is lost as heat (see discussion of thermodynamic laws in Chapter 8).

Cellular metabolism is a general term that includes all types of energy transformation processes, including photosynthesis, respiration, growth, movement, etc. Energy transformations occur as chemicals are broken apart or synthesized within the cell. The process whereby cells build molecules and store energy (in the form of chemical bonds) is called **anabolism**. **Catabolism** is the process of breaking down molecules and releasing stored energy.

ATP

Energy from the sun is transformed by photosynthetic organisms into chemical energy in the form of ATP. **ATP (adenosine triphosphate)** is known as the energy currency of cellular activity. While energy is stored in the form of carbohydrates, fats, and proteins, the amount of energy contained within the bonds of any of these substances would overwhelm (and thus kill) a cell if released at once. In order for the energy to be released in small packets usable to a cell, large molecules need to be broken down in steps. ATP is an efficient storage molecule for the energy needed for cellular processes. ATP consists of a nitrogenous base (adenine), a simple sugar (ribose), and three phosphate groups. When a cellular process requires energy, a molecule of ATP can be broken down into ADP (adenosine diphosphate) plus a phosphate group. Even more energy is released when ATP is decomposed into AMP (adenosine monophosphate) and two phosphate groups. These energy-releasing reactions are then coupled with energy-absorbing reactions.

PHOTOSYNTHESIS

The process of **photosynthesis** includes a crucial set of reactions. These reactions convert the light energy of the sun into chemical energy usable by living things. Photosynthetic organisms carry out photosynthesis. They use the converted energy for their own life processes, and also store energy that may be used by organisms that consume them.

Although the process of photosynthesis actually occurs through many small steps, the entire process can be summed up with the following equation:

$6CO_2 + 6H_2O + \text{light energy} \rightarrow C_6H_{12}O_6 + 6O_2$

(carbon dioxide + water → glucose + oxygen)

Chlorophyll is a green pigment (a pigment is a substance that absorbs light energy). Photosynthesis occurs in the presence of chlorophyll, as the chlorophyll is able to absorb a photon of light. Chlorophyll is contained in the grana of the chloroplast (see discussion of plant cells earlier in this chapter). Photosynthesis can only occur where chlorophyll is present. It is not used up in the photosynthetic process, but must be present for the reactions to occur.

There are two phases of the photosynthetic process, the light reaction, or **photolysis**, and the dark reaction, or **CO_2 fixation.** During photolysis, the chlorophyll pigment absorbs a photon of light, leaving the chlorophyll in an excited (higher energy) state. The light reaction is a decomposition reaction, which separates water molecules into hydrogen and oxygen atoms utilizing the energy from the excited chlorophyll pigment. Oxygen, which is not needed by the cell, combines to form O_2 (gas) and is released into the environment. The free hydrogen is grabbed and held by a particular molecule (called the hydrogen acceptor) until it is needed. The excited chlorophyll also supplies energy to a series of reactions that produce ATP from ADP and inorganic phosphate (Pi).

The dark reaction (CO_2 fixation) then occurs in the stroma of the chloroplast. This second phase of photosynthesis does not require light; however, it does require the use of the products of photolysis (hydrogen and energy in the form of ATP). In this phase, six CO_2 molecules are linked with hydrogen (produced in photolysis) forming glucose (a six-carbon sugar). This is a multi-step process, which requires energy, the ATP produced in the photolysis phase. Glucose molecules can link to form polysaccharides (starch or sugar), which are then stored in the cell.

Cellular Respiration

Unlike photosynthesis (which only occurs in photosynthetic cells), respiration occurs in all cells. Respiration is the process that releases energy for use by the cell. There are several steps involved in cellular respiration. Some require oxygen (that is, they are **aerobic)** and some do not (that is, they are **anaerobic** reactions).

Glycolysis is the breaking down of the six-carbon sugar (glucose) into smaller carbon-containing molecules yielding ATP (glyco = sugar, lysis = breakdown). It is the first step in all respiration pathways and occurs in the cytoplasm of all living cells. Each molecule of glucose (six carbons) is broken down into two molecules of pyruvic acid (or pyruvate with three carbons each), two ATP molecules, and two hydrogen atoms (attached to NADH, nicotinamide adenine dinucleotide). This is an **anaerobic reaction** (no oxygen is required). After glycolysis has occurred, respiration will continue on one of two pathways, depending upon whether oxygen is present or not.

The process of cellular respiration is summarized by the following chemical equation:

$$C_6H_{12}O_6 + 6O_2 \rightarrow 6CO_2 + 6H_2O + ATP$$

(glucose + oxygen → carbon dioxide + water + energy)

CHEMICAL NATURE OF THE GENE

Watson and Crick were responsible for explaining the structure of the DNA molecule, research that laid the foundation of our current understanding of the function of chromosomes and genes. Today, through the discoveries of these two scientists, and through the collaborative work of scientists worldwide, the study of chromosomes and genetic inheritance has proceeded to discover the intricacies of the **genomes** (sum total of genetic information) of many organisms, including humans.

DNA, deoxyribonucleic acid, is a polymer biological molecule (made up of a string of monomers). Each monomer is made up of three major components. Deoxyribose is a sugar. (RNA, ribonucleic acid, is a close relative that uses the sugar ribose.) In addition to the sugar, each DNA nucleotide has a phosphate group and one of four bases named A, C, G, or T. (In RNA, they are A, C, G, and U.)

The bases form hydrogen bonds, A with T and C with G (in RNA, U replaces T), and the monomers are linked with covalent bonds—sugar, phosphate, sugar, phosphate. The space between the outer bonds pulls the structure into a spiral formation as shown in Fig. 3–16.

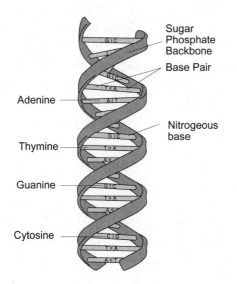

Fig. 3–16   Structure of DNA.

DNA encodes all the information needed for differentiating cells to form an organism and to produce proteins to keep an organism functioning. This information is encoded into genes that exist on the DNA molecules. A **gene** is a length of DNA that encodes a particular protein. Each protein the cell synthesizes performs a specific function in the cell. The function of one protein, or the function of a group of proteins, is called a trait (i.e., hair color, production of an enzyme, specialization of a cell type, etc.).

DNA REPLICATION

In order to replicate, a portion of a DNA molecule unwinds, separating the two halves of the double helix. (This separation is aided by the enzyme helicase.) Another enzyme (DNA polymerase) binds to each strand and moves along them as it collects nucleotides using the original DNA strands as templates. The new strand is complementary to the original template and forms a new double helix with one of the parent strands. If no errors occur during DNA synthesis, the result is two identical double helix molecules of DNA.

DNA carries the information for making all the proteins a cell can make. The DNA information for making a particular protein can be called the gene for that protein. Genetic traits are expressed and specialization of cells occurs, as a result of the combination of proteins encoded by the DNA of a cell. Protein synthesis occurs in two steps called transcription and translation.

Transcription refers to the formation of an RNA molecule, which corresponds to a gene. The DNA strand "unzips" and replicates; individual RNA nucleotides are strung together to match the DNA sequence by the enzyme RNA polymerase. The new RNA strand (known as messenger RNA or **mRNA)** migrates from the nucleus to the cytoplasm, where it is modified in a process known as **post-transcriptional processing**. This processing prepares the mRNA for protein synthesis by removing the non-coding sequences. In the processed RNA, each unit of three nucleotides or **codon** encodes a particular amino acid.

The next phase of protein synthesis is called **translation**. In order for the protein synthesis process to continue, a second type of RNA is required transfer RNA or **tRNA**. Transfer RNA is the link between the "language" of nucleotides (codon and anticodon) and the "language" of amino acids (hence the word "translation"). Transfer RNA is a chain of about 80 nucleotides. At one point along the tRNA chain, there are three unattached bases, which are called the anticodon. This anticodon will line up with a corresponding codon during translation. Each tRNA molecule also has an attached specific amino acid.

Translation occurs at the ribosomes. A ribosome is a structure composed of proteins and ribosomal RNA (rRNA). A ribosome attaches to the mRNA strand at a particular codon known as the start codon. This codon is only recognized by a particular initiator tRNA. The ribosome continues to add tRNA whose anticodons make complementary bonds with the next codon on the mRNA string, forming a peptide bond between amino acids as each amino acid is held in place by a tRNA. At the end of the translation process, a terminating codon stops the synthesis process and the protein is released.

MUTATIONS

Mutations can and do occur in the DNA replication and protein synthesis process all the time. All the DNA of every cell of every organism is copied repeatedly to form new cells for growth, repair, and reproduction. A mutation can result from an error that randomly occurs during replication. Mutations can also result from damage to DNA caused by exposure to certain chemicals, such as some solvents or the chemicals in cigarette smoke, or by radiation, such as ultraviolet radiation in sunlight or x-rays. In many cases, the living organism has mechanisms to recognize and destroy dysfunctional mutated cells, or proteins. Some mutations develop into malformations (i.e., a freckle or a mole) or diseases, such as cancer, and cause damage to the living organism. However, these mutated traits are never passed on to offspring unless the mutation happens within the gametes (sex cells) that are produced in the sex organs (ovaries or testes).

STRUCTURAL AND REGULATORY GENES

Genes encode proteins of two varieties. **Structural genes** code proteins that form organs and structural characteristics. **Regulatory genes** code proteins that determine functional or physiological events, such as growth. These proteins regulate when other genes start or stop encoding proteins, which in turn produce specific traits.

CELL DIVISION

The process of cell reproduction is called **cell division**. The process of cell division centers on the replication and separation of strands of **DNA**.

STRUCTURE OF CHROMOSOMES

Chromosomes are long chains of subunits called **nucleosomes.** Each nucleosome is composed of a short length of DNA wrapped around a core of small proteins called **histones**. The combination of DNA with histones is called **chromatin**. Each nucleosome is about 11 nm in diameter (a nanometer is one billionth of a meter) and contains a central core of eight histones with the DNA double helix wrapped around them. Each gene spans dozens of nucleosomes. The DNA plus histone strings are then tightly packed and coiled, forming chromatin.

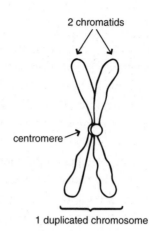

Fig. 3–17   A Chromosome.

In a cell that is getting ready to divide, each strand of chromatin is duplicated. The two identical strands (called **chromatids)** remain attached to each other at a point called the **centromere**. During cell division, the chromatin strands become more tightly coiled and packed forming a chromosome, which is visible in a light microscope. At this stage, a chromosome consists of two identical chromatids, held together at the centromere, giving each chromosome an **X** shape.

Within the nucleus, each chromosome pairs with another of similar size and shape. These pairs are called **homologs**. Each set of homologous chromosomes has a similar genetic constitution, but the genes are not necessarily identical. Different forms of corresponding genes are called **alleles**.

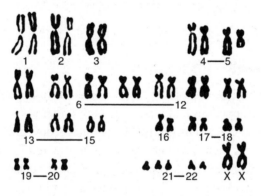

Fig. 3–18   Paired Homologous Chromosomes.

The Cell Cycle

A cell that is going to divide progresses through a particular sequence of events ending in cell division, which produces two daughter cells. This is known as the **cell cycle** (see Fig. 3–19). The time taken to progress through the cell cycle differs with different types of cells, but the sequence is the same. Cells in many tissues never divide.

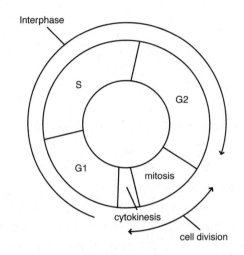

Fig. 3–19   The Cell Cycle. Interphase includes the Gl, S, and G2 phases. The cell division phase includes mitosis and cytokinesis.

There are two major periods within the cell cycle: interphase and mitosis (also called the M phase or cell division phase). **Interphase** is the period when the cell is active in carrying on its function. Interphase is divided into three phases. During the first phase, the **G$_1$ phase**, metabolism and protein synthesis are occurring at a high rate, and most of the growth of the cell occurs at this time. The cell organelles are produced (as necessary) and undergo growth during this phase. During the second phase, the **S phase**, the cell begins to prepare for cell division by replicating the DNA and proteins necessary to form a new set of chromosomes. In the final phase, the **G2** phase, more proteins are produced, which will be necessary for cell division, and the centrioles (which are integral to the division process) are replicated as well. Cell growth and function occur through all the stages of interphase.

MITOSIS

Mitosis is the process by which a cell distributes its duplicated chromosomes so that each daughter cell has a full set of chromosomes. Mitosis progresses through four phases: prophase, metaphase, anaphase, and telophase (see Fig. 3–20).

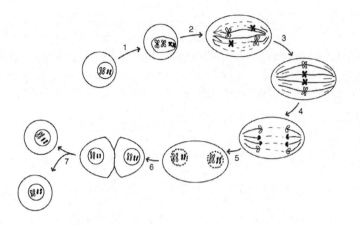

Fig. 3–20   Mitosis. See explanations of numbered steps below.

During **prophase (1, 2)**, the first stage of mitosis, the chromatin condenses into chromosomes within the nucleus and becomes visible through a light microscope. The centrioles move to opposite ends of the cell, and **spindle fibers** begin to extend from the centromeres of each chromosome toward the center of the cell. At this point, although the chromosomes become visible, the nucleolus no longer is. During the second part of prophase, the nuclear membrane dissolves and the spindle fibers attach to the centromeres forming a junction called a **kinetochore.** The chromosomes then begin moving in preparation for the next step, metaphase.

During **metaphase (3)**, the spindle fibers pull the chromosomes into alignment along the equatorial plane of the cell, creating the metaphase plate. This arrangement ensures that one copy of each chromosome is distributed to each daughter cell.

During **anaphase (4)**, the chromatids are separated from each other when the centromere divides. Each former chromatid is now called a chromosome. The two identical chromosomes move along the spindle fibers to opposite ends of the cell. **Telophase (5)** occurs as nuclear membranes form around the chromosomes. The chromosomes disperse through the new nucleoplasm, and are no longer visible as chromosomes under a standard microscope. The spindle fibers disappear. After telophase, the process of **cytokinesis (6)** produces two separate cells (7).

Cytokinesis differs somewhat in plants and animals. In animal cells, a ring made up of the protein actin surrounds the center of the cell and contracts. As the actin ring contracts, it pinches the cytoplasm into two separate compartments. Each cell's plasma membrane seals, making two distinct daughter cells. In plant cells, a cell plate forms across the center of the cell and extends out towards the edges of the cell. When this plate reaches the edges, a cell wall forms on either side of the plate, and the original cell then splits into two.

Mitosis, then, produces two nearly identical daughter cells. (Cells may differ in distribution of mitochondria or because of DNA replication errors, for example.) Organisms (such as bacteria) that reproduce asexually, do so through the process of mitosis.

MEIOSIS

Meiosis is the process of producing four daughter cells, each with single unduplicated chromosomes **(haploid)**. The parent cell is **diploid**, that is, it has a normal set of paired chromosomes. Meiosis goes through a two-stage process resulting in four new cells, rather than two (as in mitosis). Each cell has half the chromosomes of the parent. Meiosis occurs in reproductive organs, and the resultant four haploid cells are called **gametes** (egg and sperm). When two haploid gametes fuse during the process of fertilization, the resultant cell has one chromosome set from each parent, and is diploid. This process allows for the huge genetic diversity available among species.

Two distinct nuclear divisions occur during meiosis, reduction (or meiosis 1, steps **1 to 5** in Fig. 3–21), and division (or meiosis 2, steps **6 to 10**). **Reduction** affects the **ploidy** (referring to haploid or diploid) level, reducing it from 2n to n (i.e., diploid to haploid). **Division** then distributes the remaining set of chromosomes in a mitosis-like process.

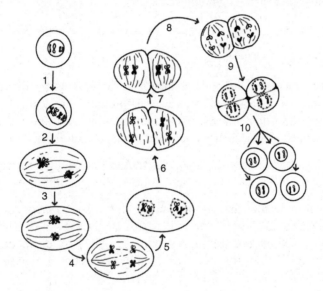

Fig. 3–21   Meiosis. See explanations of numbered steps in text.

The phases of meiosis 1 are similar to the phases of mitosis, with some notable differences. As in mitosis, chromosome replication (**1**) occurs before prophase; then during prophase 1 (**2**), homologous chromosomes pair up and join at a point called a **synapse** (this happens only in meiosis). The attached chromosomes are now termed a tetrad, a dense four-stranded structure composed of the four chromatids from the original chromosomes. At this point, some portions of the chromatid may break off and reattach to another chromatid in the tetrad. This process, known as **crossing over**, results in an even wider array of final genetic possibilities.

The nuclear membrane disappears during late prophase (or prometaphase). Each chromosome (rather than each chromatid) develops a kinetochore, and as the spindle fibers attach to each chromosome, they begin to move.

In metaphase 1 (**3**), the two chromosomes (a total of four chromatids per pair) align themselves along the equatorial plane of the cell. Each homologous pair of chromosomes contains one chromosome from the mother and one from the father from the original sexual production of that organism. When the homologous pairs orient at the cell's center in preparation for separating, the chromosomes randomly sort. The resulting cells from this meiotic division will have a mixture of chromosomes from each parent. This increases the possibilities for variety among descendent cells.

Anaphase 1 (**4**) occurs next as the chromosomes move to separate ends of the cell. This phase differs from the anaphase of mitosis where one of each chromosome pair (rather than one chromatid) separates. In telophase 1 (**5**), the nuclear envelope may or may not form, depending on the type of organism. In either case, the cell then proceeds to meiosis 2.

The nuclear envelopes dissolve (if they have formed) during prophase 2 (**6**) and spindle fibers form again. All else proceeds as in mitosis, through metaphase 2 (**7**), anaphase 2 (**8**), and telophase 2 (**9**). Again, as in mitosis, each chromosome splits into two chromatids. The process ends with cytokinesis (**10**), forming four distinct gamete cells.

BIOSYNTHESIS

Biosynthesis is the process of producing chemical compounds by living things. Organisms need to produce membranes and organelles as well as proteins that regulate cellular activity and molecules that store energy. Biosynthesis takes reactant molecules and with added energy (and often the action of enzymes) produces the products that are needed for cell or organism function.

Protein synthesis, as described earlier, involves DNA, RNA, and the processes of transcription and translation. Protein synthesis is a biosynthetic process vital to all life functions.

Enzymes are protein molecules that act as catalysts for organic reactions. (A catalyst is a substance that lowers the activation energy of a reaction. A catalyst is not consumed in the reaction.) Enzymes do not make reactions possible that would not otherwise occur under the right energy conditions, but they lower the activation energy, which increases the rate of the reaction.

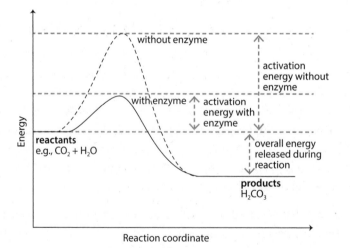

Fig. 3–22   Effect of Enzyme on a Reaction. Adding an enzyme lowers the activation energy for a reaction.

Enzymes are named ending with the letters *-ase*, and usually begin with a syllable describing the catalyzed reaction (i.e., hydrolase catalyzes hydrolysis reactions, lactase catalyzes the breakdown of the sugar lactose). Thousands of reactions occur within cells, each controlled by one or more enzymes. Enzymes are synthesized within the cell at the ribosomes, as all proteins are.

Enzymes are effective catalysts because of their unique shapes. Each enzyme has a uniquely shaped area, called its **active site**. For each enzyme, there is a particular substance known as its **substrate**, which fits within the active site (like a hand in a glove). When the substrate is seated in the active site, the combination of two molecules is called the **enzyme-substrate complex**. An enzyme can bind to two substrates and catalyze the formation of a new chemical bond linking the two substrates. An enzyme may also bind to a single substrate and catalyze the breaking of a chemical bond releasing two products. Once the reaction has taken place, the unchanged enzyme is released.

The operation of enzymes lowers the energy needed to initiate cellular reactions. However, the completion of the reaction may either require or release energy. Reactions requiring energy are called endothermic reactions. Reactions that release energy are called exothermic reactions. Endothermic reactions can take place in a cell by being coupled to the breakdown of ATP or a similar molecule. Exothermic reactions are coupled to the production of ATP or another molecule with high-energy chemical bonds.

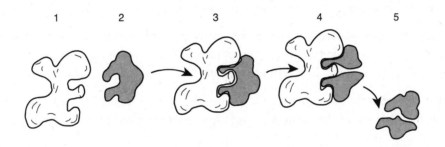

Fig. 3–23   Enzyme Reaction. 1: enzyme; 2: substrate; 3 & 4: enzyme-substrate complex; 5: products.

Environmental conditions within the cell, such as high temperature or acidity, may inhibit an enzymatic reaction. These conditions may change the shape of the active site and render the enzyme ineffective.

■STRUCTURE AND FUNCTION OF PLANTS AND ANIMALS; GENETICS

PLANTS (BOTANY)

Most of us commonly recognize plants as organisms that produce their own food through the process of photosynthesis. (Some bacteria are also photo-synthetic.) However, the plant kingdom is divided into several classifications according to physical characteristics.

Vascular plants (tracheophytes) have tissue organized in such a way as to conduct food and water throughout their structure. These plants include some that produce seeds (such as corn or roses) as well as those that do not produce any seeds (such as ferns). **Nonvascular** plants (bryophytes), such as mosses, lack special tissue for conducting water or food. They produce no seeds or flowers and are generally only a few centimeters in height.

Another method of classifying plants is according to their method of reproduction. **Angiosperms** are plants that produce flowers as reproductive organs. **Gymnosperms**, on the other hand, produce seeds without flowers. These include conifers (cone-bearers) and cycads.

Plants that survive only through a single growing season are known as **annuals**. Other plants are **biennial**; their life cycle spans two growing seasons. **Perennial** plants continue to grow year after year.

PLANT ANATOMY

Plants have structures with attributes that equip them to thrive in their environment. Angiosperms and Gymnosperms differ mostly in the structure of their stems and reproductive organs. Gymnosperms are mostly trees, with woody instead of herbaceous stems. Gymnosperms do not produce flowers; instead they produce seeds in cones or cone-like structures.

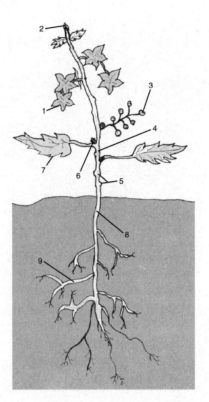

Fig. 3–24   A Typical Flowering Plant (angiosperm).
See descriptions of numbered structures in text.

Angiosperms

The shoot system of angiosperms includes the **stem (4)**, **leaves (7)**, **flowers (1)**, and **fruit (3)**, as well as growth structures such as **nodes (5)** and **buds (6)** and the **shoot apex (2)** (see Fig. 4–1). In addition, the **primary root (8)** and **secondary root (9)** provide nourishment of water and minerals and structural support for the plant as it grows. The signature structure of an angiosperm is the **flower (1)** (see Fig. 3–25), the primary reproductive organ. Before the flower blooms, it is enclosed within the **sepals (1-a)**, small, green, leaf-like structures, which fold back to reveal the flower **petals (1-b)**. The petals usually are brightly colored; their main function is to attract insects and birds, which may be necessary to the process of pollination. The short branch of the stem, which supports the flower, is called the **pedicel (1-c)**.

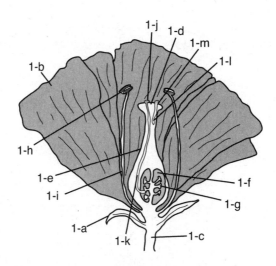

Fig. 3–25 Typical Flower. See numbered explanations in text.

Usually (but depending on the species), a single flower will have both male and female reproductive organs. The **pistil** is the female structure, and includes the stigma, style, ovary, and ovules. The **stigma (1-d)** is a sticky surface at the top of the pistil, which traps pollen grains. The stigma sits above a slender vase-like structure, the **style (1-e)**, which encloses the ovary. The **ovary (1-f)** is the hollow, bulb-shaped structure in the lower interior of the pistil. (After seeds have formed, the ovary will ripen and become fruit.) Within the ovary are the **ovules (1-g)**, small round cases each containing one or more egg cells. (If the egg is fertilized, the ovule will become a seed.) In the process of meiosis in the ovule, an egg cell is produced, along with smaller bodies known as polar nuclei. The polar nuclei will develop into the endosperm of the seed when fertilized by sperm cells.

The male structure is the stamen, consisting of the **anther (1-h)** atop the long, hollow **filament (1-i)**. The anther has four lobes and contains cells (microspore mother cells) that become pollen. Some mature **pollen grains (1-j)** are conveyed (usually by wind, birds, or insects) to a flower of a compatible species, where they stick to the stigma. The stigma produces chemicals, which stimulate the pollen to burrow into the style, forming a hollow **pollen tube (1-k)**. This tube is produced by the tube **nucleus (1-l)**, which has developed from a portion of the pollen grain. The pollen tube extends down toward the ovary. Behind the tube nucleus are two **sperm nuclei (1-m)**. When the sperm nuclei reach the ovule, one will join with an egg cell, fertilizing it to become a zygote (the beginning cell of the embryo). The other sperm nucleus merges with the polar bodies forming the endosperm, which will feed the growing embryo.

Fruit is a mature ovary, which contains the seeds (mature fertilized ovules). The fruit provides protection for the seeds, as well as a method to disburse them. For instance, when ripened fruit is eaten by animals the seeds are discarded or excreted in the animal's waste, transferring the seed to a new location for germination.

Each **seed** contains a tiny embryonic plant, stored food, and a seed coat for protection. When the seed is exposed to proper moisture, temperature, and oxygen, it germinates (begins to sprout and grow into a new plant). Stored food in a seed is found in the cotyledon.

The **stem** is the main support structure of the plant. The stem produces leaves and lateral (parallel with the ground) branches. The stem is also the main organ for transporting food and water to and from the leaves. In some cases the stem also stores food; for instance, a potato is a tuber (stem) that stores starch. The stem also contains meristem tissue.

Most of the stem tissue is made up of **vascular tissue**, including two varieties—**xylem** and **phloem**. Xylem tissue is composed of long tubular cells, which transport water up from the ground to the branches and leaves. Phloem tissue, made of stacked cells connected by sieve plates (which allow nutrients to pass from cell to cell), transports food made in the leaves (by photosynthesis) to the rest of the plant.

The **leaf** is the primary site of photosynthesis in most plants. Most leaves are thin, flat, and joined to a branch or stem by a petiole (a small stem-like extension). The petiole houses vascular tissue, which connects the veins in the leaf with those in the stem.

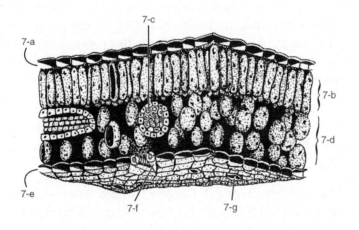

Fig. 3–26   Cross Section of a Leaf.

The **cuticle**, which maintains the leaf's moisture balance, covers most leaf surfaces. Considering a cross-section of a leaf (Fig. 3–26), the outermost layer is the **epidermis (7-a, e)**. The epidermis is generally one cell thick. It secretes the waxy cuticle and protects the inner tissue of the leaf.

The mesophyll is composed of several layers of tissue between the upper and lower epidermis. The uppermost, the **palisade layer (7-b)**, contains vertically aligned cells with numerous chloroplasts. The arrangement of these cells maximizes the potential for exposure of the chloroplasts to needed sunlight. Most photosynthesis occurs in this layer.

The sugars produced by photosynthesis are transported throughout the plant via the **vascular bundles (7-c)** of xylem and phloem. The vascular bundles make up the veins in the leaf.

The next layer beneath the palisade cells is the **spongy layer (7-d)**, a layer of parenchyma cells separated by large air spaces. The air spaces allow for the exchange of gases (carbon dioxide and oxygen) for photosynthesis.

On the underside of the leaf there are openings ringed by **guard cells (7-f)**. The openings are called stomata **(7-g)** (or stomates). The stomata serve to allow moisture and gases (carbon dioxide and oxygen) to pass in and out of the leaf, thus facilitating photosynthesis.

PLANT PHYSIOLOGY

Water and Mineral Absorption and Transport

Although plants produce their own sugars and starches for food, they must obtain water, carbon dioxide, and minerals from their environment. Vascular plants have well-developed systems for absorption and transport of water and minerals.

Water is essential to all cells of all plants, so plants must have the ability to obtain water and transport water molecules throughout their structure. Most water is absorbed through the plant's root system, then makes its way in one of two pathways toward the xylem cells, which will transport water up the stem and to the leaves and flowers. The first pathway is for water to seep between the epidermal cells of the roots and between the parenchyma cells of the cortex. When water reaches the endodermal tissue, it enters the cells and is pushed through the vascular tissue toward the xylem.

A second pathway is for the water to pass through the cell wall and plasma membrane. Water travels along this intracellular route through channels in the cell membranes (plasmodesmata), until it reaches the xylem.

Once water reaches the xylem, hydrogen bonding between water molecules (known as **cohesion**) causes tension that pulls water through the water column up through the stem and on to the leaves (known as the **cohesion-tension process**). Some water that has traveled up through the plant to the leaves is evaporated in a process known as **transpiration**. As water is evaporated it causes a siphoning effect (like sucking on a straw), which continues to pull water up from the root xylem, through the length of the plant and to the leaves.

Food Translocation and Storage

Food is manufactured by photosynthesis mostly in the leaves. The rest of the plant must have this food (carbohydrates) imported from the leaves. The leaves have source cells, which store the manufactured sugars. The food molecules are transferred from the source cells to phloem tissue through active transport (energy is expended to move molecules across the plasma membrane against the concentration gradient—from low concentration to high concentration). Once in the phloem, the sugars begin to build up, causing osmosis to occur (water enters the phloem lowering the sugar concentration). The entrance of water into the phloem causes pressure, which pushes the water-sugar solution through **sieve plates** that join the cells. This pressure thrusts the water-sugar solution to all areas of the plant, making food available to all cells in the plant.

PLANT REPRODUCTION AND DEVELOPMENT

The reproductive cycle of plants occurs through the alternation of haploid (n) and diploid (2n) phases. Haploid cells have one complete set of chromosomes (n). Diploid cells have two sets of chromosomes (2n). Diploid and haploid stages are both capable of undergoing mitosis in plants. The diploid generation is known as a **sporophyte**. The reproductive organs of the sporophyte produce **gametophytes** through the process of meiosis. Gametophytes may be male or female and are haploid. The male gametophyte produces **sperm (male gamete)**; the female produces an **egg cell (female gamete)**. When a sperm cell **fertilizes** an egg cell (haploid cells join to form a diploid cell) they produce a **zygote**. The zygote will grow into an **embryo**, which resides within the growing seed.

Asexual Plant Reproduction

Some plants may also reproduce through **vegetative propagation**—an asexual process. Asexual reproduction occurs through mitosis only (it does not involve gametes), and produces offspring genetically identical to the parent. While sexual reproduction leads to genetic variation and adaptation, asexual reproduction of a plant with a desirable set of genetic traits preserves these intact in successive generations. Many plants reproduce through a combination of sexual and asexual reproduction, reaping the advantages of each.

ANIMALS (ZOOLOGY)

The animal kingdom includes a wide variety of phyla that have a range of body plans. This range includes certain invertebrates with relatively simple body plans as well as highly complex vertebrates (including humans). There are specific characteristics that differentiate animals from other living things. Organisms in the animal kingdom share the following traits:

1. Animal cells do not have cell walls or plastids.

2. Adult animals are multicellular with specialized tissues and organs.

3 Animals are heterotrophic (they do not produce their own food).

4. Animal species are capable of sexual reproduction, although some are also capable of asexual reproduction (ex. hydra).

5. Animals develop from embryonic stages.

In addition to the above traits, most adult animals have a symmetrical anatomy. Adult animals can have either radial symmetry (constituent parts are arranged radiating symmetrically about a center point) or bilateral symmetry (the body can be divided along a center plane into equal, mirror-image halves). There are a few exceptions to this rule, including the adult sponge whose body is not necessarily symmetrical. While there is wide variation in the physical structure of animals, the animal kingdom is usually divided into two broad categories—invertebrates and vertebrates. There are many more species of invertebrates than vertebrates.

Invertebrates are those species having no internal backbone structure; **vertebrates** have internal backbones. Invertebrates include sponges and worms, which have no skeletal structure at all, and arthropods, mollusks, crustaceans, etc., which have exoskeletons. In fact, there are many more species of invertebrates than vertebrates (about 950,000 species of invertebrates and only about 40,000 species of vertebrates).

ANIMAL ANATOMY

Tissues

Like all multicellular organisms, animal bodies contain several kinds of tissues, made up of different cell types. Differentiated cells may organize into specialized tissues performing particular functions. There are eight major types of animal tissue:

1. **Epithelial tissue** consists of thin layers of cells. Epithelial tissue makes up the layers of skin, lines ducts, and the intestine, and covers the inside of the body cavity. Epithelial tissue forms the barrier between the environment and the interior of the body.

2. **Connective tissue** covers internal organs and composes ligaments and tendons. This tissue holds tissues and organs together, stabilizing the body structure.

3. **Muscle tissue** is divided into three types—smooth, skeletal, and cardiac. **Smooth** muscle makes up the walls of internal organs and functions in involuntary movement (breathing, etc.). **Skeletal** muscle attaches bones of the skeleton to each other and surrounding tissues. Skeletal muscle's function is to enable voluntary movement. **Cardiac** muscle is the tissue forming the walls of the heart. Its strength and electrical properties are vital to the heart's ability to pump blood.

4. **Bone tissue** is found in the skeleton and provides support, protection for internal organs, and ability to move as muscles pull against bones.

5. **Cartilage tissue** reduces friction between bones, and supports and connects them. For example, it is found at the ends of bones and in the ears and nose.

6. **Adipose tissue** is found beneath the skin and around organs providing cushioning, insulation, and fat storage.

7. **Nerve tissue** is found in the brain, spinal cord nerves, and ganglion. It carries electrical and chemical impulses to and from organs and limbs to the brain. Nerve tissue in the brain receives these impulses and sustains mental activity.

8. **Blood tissue** consists of several cell types in a fluid called plasma. It flows through the blood vessels and heart, and is essential for carrying oxygen to cells, fighting infection, and carrying nutrients and wastes to and from cells. Blood also has clotting capabilities, which preserve the body's functions in case of injury.

Tissues are organized into organs, and organs function together to form systems, which support the life of an organism. Studying these systems allows us to understand how organisms thrive within their ecosystem.

SYSTEMS

Many different body plans exist amongst animals, and each type of body plan includes systems necessary for the organism to live. Our discussion of systems here focuses on those found in most vertebrates. Vertebrates are highly complex organisms with several systems working together to perform the functions necessary to life. These include the digestive, gas exchange, skeletal, nervous, circulatory, excretory, and immune systems.

Digestive System

The **digestive system** (see Fig. 3–27) serves as a processing plant for ingested food. The digestive system in animals generally encompasses the processes of **ingestion** (food intake), **digestion** (breaking down of ingested particles into molecules that can be absorbed by the body), and **egestion** (the elimination of indigestible materials). In most vertebrates, the digestive organs are divided into two categories, the **alimentary canal**, and the **accessory organs**. The alimentary canal is also known as the **gastrointestinal** (or **GI**) **tract** and includes the mouth, pharynx, esophagus, stomach, small intestine, large intestine, rectum, and anus. The accessory organs include the teeth, tongue, salivary glands, liver, gallbladder, and pancreas.

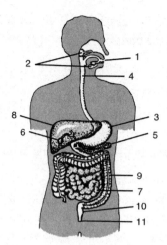

Fig. 3–27 Human Digestive System.

The **mouth** (oral cavity, **1**) is the organ of ingestion and the first organ of digestion in the GI tract. The first step in digestion in many vertebrates occurs as food is chewed. Chewing is the initial step in breaking down food into particles of manageable size. Chewing also increases the surface area of the food and mixes it with saliva, which contains the starch-digesting enzyme amylase. Saliva is secreted by the **salivary glands (2)**. Chewed food is then swallowed and moved toward the **stomach (3)** by peristalsis (muscle contraction) of the **esophagus (4)**. The stomach is a muscular organ that stores incompletely digested food. The stomach continues the mechanical and chemical breakdown of food particles begun by the chewing process. The lining of the stomach secretes mucous to protect it from the strong digestive chemicals necessary in the digestive process. The stomach also secretes digestive enzymes and hydrochloric acid which continue the digestive process to the point of producing a watery soup of nutrients, which then proceeds through the pyloric sphincter into the small intestine (the duodenum). The **pancreas (5)** and **gall bladder (6)** release more enzymes into the small intestine, the site where the final steps of digestion and most absorption occurs. The cells lining the **small intestine (7)** have protrusions out into the lumen of the intestine called **villi**. Villi provide a large surface area for absorption of nutrients. Nutrients move into the capillaries through or between the cells making up the villi. The enriched blood travels to the **liver (8)**, where some sugars are removed and stored. The indigestible food proceeds from the small intestine to the **large intestine (9)** where water is absorbed back into the body. The waste (feces) is then passed through the **rectum (10)** and excreted from the **anus (11)**.

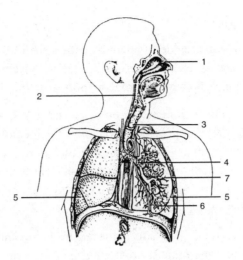

Fig. 3–28   Human Respiratory System.

Respiratory or Gas Exchange System

Also known as the **respiratory system** (see Fig. 3–28), the **gas exchange system** is responsible for the intake and processing of gases required by an organism, and for expelling gases produced as waste products. In humans, air is taken in primarily through the **nose** (although gases may be inhaled through the mouth, the nose is better at filtering out pollutants in the air). The **nasal passages (1)** have a mucous lining to capture foreign particles. This lining is surrounded by epithelial tissue with embedded capillaries, which serve to warm the entering air. Air then passes through the **pharynx (2)** and into the **trachea (3)**. The trachea includes the windpipe or **larynx** in its upper portion, and the **glottis**, an opening allowing gases to pass into the two branches known as the bronchi. The glottis is guarded by a flap of tissue, the **epiglottis**, which prevents food particles from entering the bronchial tubes. The **bronchi (4)** lead to the two **lungs (5)** where they branch out in all directions into smaller tubules known as **bronchioles (6)**. The bronchioles end in **alveoli (7)**, thin-walled air sacs, which are the site of gas exchange. The bronchioles are surrounded by capillaries, which bring blood with a high density of carbon dioxide and a low concentration of oxygen from the pulmonary arteries. At the alveoli, the carbon dioxide diffuses from the blood into the alveoli and oxygen diffuses from the alveoli into the blood. The oxygenated blood is carried away to tissues throughout the body.

All living organisms require the ability to exchange gases, and there are several variations to the means and organs utilized for this life process. Invertebrates such as the earthworm are able to absorb gases through their skin. Insects rely on the diffusion of gases through holes in the exoskeleton known as spiracles. In single-celled organisms such as the amoeba, diffusion of gases occurs directly through the plasma membrane.

Musculoskeletal System

The **musculoskeletal system** provides the body with structure, stability, and the ability to move. By definition, the musculoskeletal system is unique to vertebrates, although some invertebrates (such as mollusks and insects) have external support structures (exoskeletons) and muscle.

In humans, the musculoskeletal system is composed of joints, ligaments, cartilage, muscle groups, and 206 bones. The skeleton provides protection for the soft internal organs, as well as structure and stability allowing for an upright stature and movement. Bones also perform the important function of storing calcium and phosphates, and producing red blood cells within the bone marrow. The 206 bones forming the human skeleton are linked with movable joints, and joined by muscle systems controlling movement.

Skeletal muscles are voluntary—they are activated by command from the nervous system. **Smooth muscle** lines most internal organs, protecting their contents and function, and generally contracting without conscious intent. For instance, the involuntary (automatic) contraction of smooth muscle in the esophagus and lungs facilitates digestion and respiration. **Cardiac muscle** is unique to the heart. It is involuntary muscle (like smooth muscle), but cardiac muscle also has unique features, which cause it to "beat" rhythmically. Cardiac muscle cells have branched endings that interlock with each other, keeping the muscle fibers from ripping apart during their strong contractions. In addition, electrical impulses travel in waves from cell to cell in cardiac muscle, causing the muscle to contract in a coordinated way with a rhythmic pace.

Nervous System

The **nervous system** is a communication network that connects the entire body of an organism, and provides control over bodily functions and actions. Nerve tissue is composed of nerve cells known as **neurons**. Neurons carry impulses via electrochemical responses through their **cell body** and **axon** (long root-like appendage of the cell). Nerve cells exist in networks, with axons of neighbor neurons interacting across small spaces **(synapses)**. Chemical neurotransmitters send messages along the nerve network causing responses specific to varying types of nerve tissue. The nervous system allows the body to sense stimuli and conditions in the environment and respond with necessary reactions. **Sensory organs**—skin, eyes, nose, ears, etc.—transmit signals in response to environmental stimuli to the **brain**, which then conveys messages via nerves to glands and muscles, which produce the necessary response.

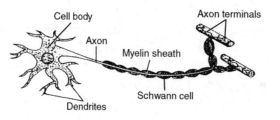

Fig. 3–29   A Typical Neuron.

The human nervous system (and that of many mammals) is anatomically divided into two systems—the central nervous system and the peripheral nervous system. The following outline shows the components of each portion of the nervous system:

I. **Central Nervous System** (CNS)—two main components, the **brain** and the **spinal cord**. These organs control all other organs and systems of the body. The spinal cord is a continuation of the brain stem, and acts as a conduit of nerve messages.

II. **Peripheral Nervous System** (PNS)—a network of nerves throughout the body.

   A. **Sensory Division**

      1. **visceral sensory nerves**—carry impulses from body organs to the CNS

      2. **somatic sensory nerves**—carry impulses from body surface to the CNS

   B. **Motor Division**

      1. **somatic motor nerves**—carries impulses to skeletal muscle from the CNS

      2. **autonomic**

         a. **sympathetic** nervous system—carries impulses that stimulate organs

         b. **parasympathetic** nervous system—carries impulses back from organs

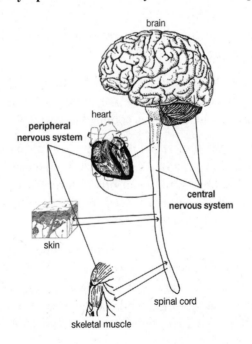

Fig. 3–30   Human Nervous System.

The brain of vertebrates has three major divisions: the forebrain, midbrain, and hindbrain. The **forebrain** is located most anterior, and contains the **olfactory lobes** (sense of smell), **cerebrum** (controls sensory and motor responses, memory, speech, and most factors of intelligence), as well as the **thalamus** (integrates senses), **hypothalamus** (involved in hunger, thirst, blood pressure, body temperature, hostility, pain, pleasure, etc.), and **pituitary gland** (releases various hormones). The **midbrain** is between the forebrain and hindbrain and contains the **optic lobes** (visual center connected to the eyes by the optic nerves). The **hindbrain** consists of the **cerebellum** (controls balance, equilibrium, and muscle coordination) and the **medulla oblongata** (controls involuntary response such as breathing and heartbeat).

Within the brain, nerve tissue is grayish in color and is called **gray matter**. The nerve cells, which exist in the spinal cord and throughout the body, have insulation covering their axons. This insulation (called the **myelin sheath)** speeds electrochemical conduction within the axon of the nerve cell. Since the myelin sheath gives this tissue a white color, it is called **white matter**. The myelin sheath is made up of individual cells called Schwann cells.

The nervous systems of vertebrates and some invertebrates are highly sophisticated, providing conscious response and unconscious controls. However, the nervous systems of some species of invertebrates (such as jellyfish) are relatively simple networks of neurons that control only some aspects of their body functions.

Circulatory System

The **circulatory system** is the conduit for delivering nutrients and gases to all cells and for removing waste products from them.

In invertebrates, the circulatory system may consist entirely of diffusion in the gastrovascular cavity, or it may be an **open circulatory system** (where blood directly bathes the internal organs), or a **closed circulatory system** (where blood is confined to vessels).

Closed circulatory systems are also typical of vertebrates. In vertebrates, **blood** flows throughout the circulatory system within **vessels.** Vessels include **arteries, veins**, and **capillaries**. The pumping action of the **heart** (a hollow, muscular organ) forces blood in one direction throughout the system. In large animals, valves within the heart, and some of the vessels in limbs, keep blood from flowing backwards (being pulled downward by gravity).

Blood carries many products to cells throughout the body, including minerals, infection-fighting white blood cells, nutrients, proteins, hormones, and metabolites. Blood also carries dissolved gases (particularly oxygen) to cells and waste gases (mainly carbon dioxide) away from cells. The process of cellular metabolism is a fundamental process of life and cannot proceed without a continuous supply of oxygen to every living cell within the body.

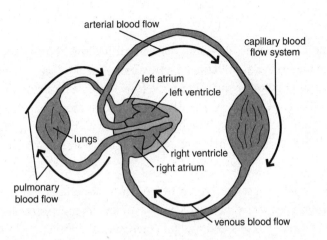

Fig. 3–31   Human Circulatory System. Blood flows from the heart through arteries to the capillaries throughout the body and returns via the veins.

Capillaries (tiny vessels) surround all tissues of the body and exchange carbon dioxide for oxygen. Oxygen is carried by **hemoglobin** (containing iron) in red blood cells. Oxygen enters the blood in the lungs and travels to the heart, then through **arteries** (larger vessels that carry blood away from the heart), then **arterioles** (small arteries), to capillaries. The blood picks up carbon dioxide waste from the cells and carries it through capillaries, then **venules** (small veins) and **veins** (vessels that carry blood toward the heart), back to the heart and on to the lungs. Thus, blood is continually cycled.

Excretory System

The **excretory system** is responsible for collecting waste materials and transporting them to organs that expel them from the body. There are many types of waste that must be expelled from the body, and there are many organs involved in this process.

The primary excretory organs of most vertebrates are the kidneys. The **kidneys** filter metabolic wastes from the blood and excrete them as **urine** into the urinary tract. The urinary tract carries the fluid that is eventually expelled from the body. Urine is typically 95% water, and may contain urea (formed from breakdown of proteins), uric acid (formed from breaking down nucleic acids), creatinine (a by-product of muscle contraction), and various minerals and hormones.

The **liver** produces **bile** from broken-down pigments and chemicals (often from pollutants and medications) and secretes it into the small intestine, where it proceeds to the large intestine and is expelled in the feces. The liver also breaks down some nitrogenous molecules (including some proteins), excreting them as urea.

The **lungs** are the sites of excretion for carbon dioxide. The **skin** is an accessory excretory organ; salts, urea, and other wastes are secreted with water from sweat glands in the skin.

Immune System

The **immune system** functions to defend the body from infection by bacteria and viruses. The **lymphatic system** is the principal infection-fighting component of the immune system. The organs of the lymphatic system in humans and other higher invertebrates include the lymph, lymph nodes, spleen, thymus, and tonsils. **Lymph** is a collection of excess fluid that is absorbed from between cells into a special system of vessels, which circulates through the lymphatic system and finally dumps into the bloodstream. Lymph also collects plasma proteins that have leaked into interstitial fluids.

Lymph nodes are small masses of lymph tissue whose function is to filter lymph and produce lymphocytes. **Lymphocytes** and other cells are involved in the immune system. Lymphocytes begin in bone marrow as stem cells and are collected and distributed via the lymph nodes. There are two classes of lymphocytes: B cells, and T cells. **B cells** emerge from the bone marrow mature, and produce **antibodies**, which enter the bloodstream. These antibodies find and attach themselves to foreign **antigens** (i.e., toxins, bacteria, foreign cells, etc.). The attachment of an antibody to an antigen marks the pair for destruction.

The **spleen** contains some lymphatic tissue, and is located in the abdomen. It filters larger volumes of lymph than nodes can handle. The **tonsils** are a group of lymph cells connected together and located in the throat.

The **thymus** is another mass of lymph tissue, which is active only through the teen years, fighting infection and producing T cells. **T cells** mature in the thymus gland. Some T cells (like B cells) patrol the blood for antigens, but T cells are also equipped to destroy antigens themselves. T cells also regulate the body's immune responses.

HOMEOSTATIC MECHANISMS

All living cells, tissues, organs, and organisms must maintain a tight range of physical and chemical conditions in order for them to live. Conditions such as temperature, pH, water balance, sugar levels, and so on, must be monitored and controlled in order to keep them within the accepted ranges that will not inhibit life. When the conditions of an organism are within acceptable ranges, it is said to be in **homeostasis**. Organisms have a special set of mechanisms that serve to keep them in homeostasis. Homeostasis is a state of dynamic equilibrium, which balances forces tending toward change with forces acceptable for life functions.

Homeostasis is achieved mostly by actions of the sympathetic and parasympathetic nervous systems by a process known as **feedback control**. For instance, when the body undergoes physical activity, muscle action causes a rise in temperature. If not checked, rising temperature could destroy cells. In this instance, the nervous system detects rising temperature and reacts with a response that causes sweat glands to produce sweat. The evaporation of sweat cools the body.

There are many instances of feedback control. These take effect when any situation arises that may drive levels outside the normal acceptable range. In other words, the homeostatic mechanism is a reaction to a stimulus. This reaction, called a **feedback response**, is the production of some counterforce that levels the system.

HORMONAL CONTROL IN HOMEOSTASIS AND REPRODUCTION

Hormones are chemicals produced in the endocrine glands of an organism, which travel through the circulatory system and are taken up by specific targeted organs or tissues, where they modify metabolic activities.

Hormonal control occurs through one of two processes. The first is the **mobile receptor mechanism**. A hormone is manufactured in response to a particular **stimulus**. The hormone (for instance, a **steroid**) enters the bloodstream from one of the ductless endocrine glands that manufacture hormones. The steroid passes through the cell membrane of the targeted cell and enters the cytoplasm. The hormone combines with a particular protein known as a receptor, creating the **hormone-receptor complex**. This complex enters the nucleus and binds to a DNA molecule causing a gene to be transcribed. The mRNA molecule leaves the nucleus for the endoplasmic reticulum, where it encodes a particular protein. The protein migrates to the site of the stimulus and counteracts the source of the stimulus. The result is homeostasis, a balance of the counterproductive forces.

The second process targets receptors on a cell's membrane. A particular **receptor** exists on the membrane when the cell is in a particular condition (for instance, containing an excess of glucose). When the hormone binds with the receptor on the membrane, the receptor changes its form. This triggers a chain of events within the cytoplasm resulting in the production or destruction of proteins, thus moderating the conditions.

Hormones control many physiological functions, from digestion, to conscious responses and thinking, to reproduction. In humans, for instance, women of childbearing age have a continuous cycle of hormones. The hormone cycle causes the release of eggs at specific times. If the egg is fertilized a different combination of hormones stimulates a chain of events that promotes the development of the embryo.

ANIMAL REPRODUCTION AND DEVELOPMENT

Reproduction in multicellular animals is a complex process that generally proceeds through the steps of **gametogenesis** (gamete formation) and then **fertilization**.

Gametes are the sex cells formed in the reproductive organs—sperm and eggs. When a sperm of one individual combines with the egg cell of another, the resulting cell is known as a **zygote**. A **zygote** then develops into a new individual. In the case of **spermatogenesis** (sperm formation), diploid **primary spermatocytes** are formed from special cells (**spermatogonia**) in the testes. The primary spermatocytes then undergo meiosis I, forming haploid **secondary spermatocytes** with a single chromosome set. (Please see the section on meiosis.) The secondary spermatocytes go through meiosis II, forming **spermatids**, which are haploid. These spermatids then develop into the **sperm cells**.

In human female reproductive organs, egg cells are formed through a similar process known as **oogenesis. Primary oocytes** are typically present in great number in the female's ovaries at birth. Primary oocytes undergo meiosis I, forming one **secondary oocyte** and one smaller **polar body**. Both the secondary oocyte and the polar body undergo meiosis II; the polar body producing two polar bodies (not functional cells), and the oocyte producing one more polar body and one haploid **egg cell**. The egg cell is now ready for fertilization, and if there are sperm cells present, the egg may be fertilized forming a diploid cell with a new combination of chromosomes, the zygote.

PRINCIPLES OF HEREDITY (GENETICS)

The process by which characteristics pass from one generation to another is known as **inheritance**. The study of the principles of heredity (now called genetics) advanced greatly through the experimental work of **Gregor Mendel** (c. 1865). Mendel studied the relationships between traits expressed in parents and offspring, and the hereditary factors that caused expression of traits.

Mendel systematically bred pea plants to determine how certain hereditary traits passed from generation to generation. First, he established true-breeding plants, which produce offspring with the same traits as the parents. For example, the seeds of pea plants with yellow seeds would grow into plants that produced yellow seeds. Green seeds grow into plants that produce green seeds. Mendel named this first generation of true-breeding plants the parent or P_1 **generation**; he then bred the plant with yellow seeds and the plant with green seeds. Mendel called the first generation of offspring the F_1 **generation**. The F_1 generation of Mendel's yellow seed/green seed crosses contained only yellow seed offspring.

Mendel continued his experiment by crossing two individuals of the F_1 **generation** to produce an F_2 **generation**. In this generation, he found that some of the plants (one out of four) produced green seeds. Mendel performed hundreds of such crosses, studying some 10,000 pea plants, and was able to establish the rules of inheritance from them. The following are Mendel's main discoveries:

- Parents transmit hereditary factors (now called **genes**) to offspring. Genes then produce a characteristic, such as seed-coat color.

- Each individual carries two copies of a gene, and the copies may differ.

- The two genes an individual carries act independently, and the effect of one may mask the effect of the other. Mendel coined the terms geneticists still use: "dominant" and "recessive."

MODERN GENETICS

We now know that **chromosomes** carry all the genetic information in most organisms. Most organisms have corresponding pairs of chromosomes that carry genes for the same traits. These pairs are known as **homologous chromosomes**. Genes that produce a given trait exist at the same position (or **locus**) on homologous chromosomes. Each gene may have different forms, known as **alleles**. For instance, yellow seeds and green seeds arise from different alleles of the same gene. A gene can have two or more alleles, which differ in their nucleotide sequence. That difference can translate into proteins that function differently, resulting in variations of the trait.

Sexual reproduction (meiosis) produces gamete cells with one-half the genetic information of the parents (paired chromosomes are separated and sorted independently). Therefore, each gamete may receive one of any number of combinations of each parent's chromosomes.

In addition, a trait may arise from one or more genes. (However, because one-gene traits are easiest to understand, we will use them for most of our examples.) If a trait is produced from a gene or genes with varying alleles, several possibilities for traits exist. The combination of alleles that make a particular trait is the **genotype**, while the trait expressed is the **phenotype**.

An allele is considered **dominant** if it masks the effect of its partner allele. The allele that does not produce its trait when present with a dominant allele is **recessive**. That is, when a dominant allele pairs with a recessive allele, the expressed trait is that of the dominant allele.

A **Punnett square** is a notation that allows us to easily predict the results of a genetic cross. In a Punnett square, a letter is assigned to each gene. Uppercase letters represent dominant traits, while lowercase letters represent recessive traits (a convention begun by Mendel). The possible alleles from each parent are noted across the top and side of a box diagram; then the possible offspring are represented within the internal boxes. If we assign the allele that produces yellow seeds the letter **Y**, and the allele that produces green seeds y, we can represent Mendel's first cross between pea plants (**YY** $\times$ **yy**) by the following Punnett square:

	Y	Y
y	Yy	Yy
y	Yy	yy

One parent pea plant had green seeds (green seeds is its phenotype), so it must not have had any of the dominant genes for yellow seeds (**Y**); therefore it must have the genotype **yy**. If the second parent had one allele for yellow and one for green, then some of the offspring would have inherited two genes for green. Since Mendel started with true-breeding plants, we may deduce that one parent had two genes for green seeds (**yy**) and the other two genes for yellow seeds (**YY**).

When both alleles for a given gene are the same in an individual (such as **YY** or **yy**), that individual is **homozygous** for that trait. Furthermore, the individual's genotype can be called homozygous. Both of the above parents (**P₁**) were homozygous. The children in the **F₁** generation all have one dominant gene (**Y**) and one recessive gene (**y**), their phenotype is yellow, and their genotype is Yy. When the two alleles for a given gene are different in an individual (**Yy**), that individual is said to be **heterozygous** for that trait; its genotype is heterozygous.

Breeding two **F₁** offspring from the example above produces the following Punnett square of a double heterozygous (both parents **Yy**) cross:

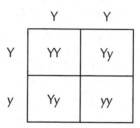

Through this Punnett square, we can determine that three-fourths of the offspring will produce yellow seeds. This is consistent with Mendel's findings. However, there are two different genotypes represented among the yellow seed offspring. One-half of the offspring were heterozygous yellow (**Yy**), while one-fourth were homozygous yellow (**YY**).

The previous example shows a **monohybrid cross**—a cross between two individuals where only one trait is considered. Mendel also experimented with crossing two parents while considering two separate traits, a **dihybrid cross**.

The laws investigated by Mendel form the basis of modern genetics. However, Mendel's laws now incorporate modern terminology (i.e., "genes" rather than "hereditary factors," etc.).

THE LAW OF SEGREGATION

The first law of Mendelian genetics is the **law of segregation**. The law of segregation states that traits are expressed from a pair of genes in the individual (on homologous chromosomes). Each parent provides one chromosome of every pair of homologous chromosomes. Paired chromosomes (and thus corresponding genes) separate and randomly recombine during gamete formation.

THE LAW OF DOMINANCE

Mendel determined that one gene was usually dominant over the other. This is the **law of dominance**, Mendel's second law of inheritance. In Mendel's experiments, the first generation produced no plants with green seeds, leading him to recognize the existence of genetic dominance. The yellow-seed allele was clearly dominant.

THE LAW OF INDEPENDENT ASSORTMENT

Mendel also investigated whether genes for one trait always were linked to genes for another. In other words, Mendel experimented not only with pea seed-coat color, but also with pea-plant height (and a number of other traits in peas and other plants). He wanted to determine whether if the parent plant had green seeds and was tall, all plants with green seeds would be tall. These dihybrid cross experiments demonstrated that most traits were independent of one another. That is, a pea plant could be green and tall or green and short, yellow and tall, or yellow and short. In most cases, genes for traits randomly sort into pairs (although some genes lie close to others on a chromosome and can therefore be inherited together). Since homologous chromosomes separate and independently sort in gamete formation, alleles are also separated and independently sorted, an assertion known as the **law of independent assortment**.

The following Punnett square demonstrates independent assortment. **Y** stands for the allele for yellow color, **y** for the allele for green, **T** for the allele tall, and **t** for short:

	TY	Ty	tY	ty
TY	TTYY	TTYy	TtYY	TtYy
Ty	TTYy	TTyy	TtYy	Ttyy
tY	TtYY	TtYy	ttYY	ttYy
ty	TtYy	Ttyy	ttYy	ttyy

INCOMPLETE DOMINANCE

Some traits have no genes that are dominant and instead produce offspring that are a mix of the two parents. For instance, in snapdragons a plant with red flowers crossed with a plant with white flowers produces offspring with pink flowers. This is known as **incomplete dominance**. Neither white nor red is dominant over the other. In incomplete dominance, the conventional way to symbolize the alleles is with a capital letter designating the trait (in this case C for color) and a superscript designating the allele choices (in this case ^{R} for red, ^{w} for white), making the possible alleles C^R and C^W. The following Punnett square represents the incomplete dominance of the allele for red flowers (C^R), the allele for white as (C^W), and the combination resulting in pink as ($C^R C^W$).

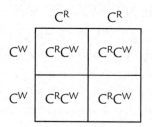

	C^R	C^R
C^W	$C^R C^W$	$C^R C^W$
C^W	$C^R C^W$	$C^R C^W$

In this case, two plants, one with white flowers, one with red, cross to form all pink flowers. If two of the heterozygous offspring of this cross are then bred, the outcome of this cross ($\mathbf{C^R C^W} \times \mathbf{C^R C^W}$) will be:

	C^R	C^W
C^R	$C^R C^R$	$C^R C^W$
C^W	$C^R C^W$	$C^W C^W$

One-fourth of the offspring will be red one-half pink, and one-fourth white, a 1:2:1 ratio.

MULTIPLE ALLELES

In the instances above, two possible alleles exist in a species, so the genotype will be a combination of those two alleles. There are some instances where more than two choices of alleles are present. For instance, for human blood types there is a dominant allele for type A blood, another dominant allele for type B blood as well as a recessive allele for neither A nor B, known as O blood. There are three different alleles and they may combine in any way. In multiple-allele crosses, it is conventional to denote the chromosome by a letter (in this case **I** for dominant, **i** for recessive), with a subscript letter representing the allele types (in this case **A**, **B**, or **O**). The alleles for A and B blood are codominant, while the allele for O blood is recessive. The possible genotypes and phenotypes, then, are as follows:

genotype	phenotype
$I^A I^A$	Type A blood
$I^B I^B$	Type B blood
$I^B i^O$	Type B blood
$I^A i^O$	Type A blood
$I^A I^B$	Type AB blood
$i^O i^O$	Type O blood

[Note: There is another gene responsible for the Rh factor that adds the + or− to the blood type.]

LINKAGE

While Mendel had established the law of independent assortment, later study of genetics by other scientists found that this law was not always true. In studying fruit flies, for instance, it was found that some traits are always inherited together; they were not independently sorted. Traits that are inherited together are said to be **linked**. Genes are portions of chromosomes, so most traits produced by genes on the same chromosome are inherited together. (The chromosomes are independently sorted not the individual genes.)

However, an exception to this rule complicates the issue. During metaphase of meiosis I, when homologous chromosomes line up along the center of the dividing cell, some pieces of the chromosomes break off and move from one chromosome to another (change places). This random breaking and reforming of homologous chromosomes allows genes to change the chromosome they are linked to, thus changing the genome of that chromosome. This process, known as **crossing over**, adds even more possibility of variation of traits among species. It is more likely for crossing over to occur between genes that do not lie close together on a chromosome than between those that lie close together.

Gender is determined in an organism by a particular homologous pair of chromosomes. The symbols **X** and **Y** denote the sex chromosomes. In mammals and many insects, the male has an **X** and **Y** chromosome **(XY)**, while the female has two **X**'s **(XX)**. Genes that are located on the gender chromosome **Y** will only be seen in males. It would be considered a **sex-limited trait**. An example of a sex-limited trait is bar coloring in chickens that occurs only in males.

Some traits are **sex-linked**. In sex-linked traits, more males **(XY)** develop the trait because males have only one copy of the **X** chromosome. Females have a second **X** gene, which may carry a gene coding for a functional protein for the trait in question that may counteract a recessive trait. These traits (for example, hemophilia and colorblindness) occur much more often in males than females.

Still other traits may be **sex-influenced**. In this case, the trait is known as autosomal—it only requires one recessive gene to be expressed if there is no counteracting dominant gene. A male with one recessive allele will develop the trait, whereas a female would require two recessive genes to develop it. An example of a sex-influenced trait is male-pattern baldness.

POLYGENIC INHERITANCE

While the best-studied genetic traits arise from alleles of a single gene, most traits, such as height and skin color, are produced from the expression of more than one set of genes. Traits produced from interaction of multiple sets of genes are known as **polygenic traits**. Polygenic traits are difficult to map and difficult to predict because of the varied effects of the different genes for a specific trait.

ECOLOGY AND POPULATION BIOLOGY

ECOLOGY

Ecology is the study of how organisms interact, and how they influence or are influenced by their physical **environment**. The word "ecology" is derived from the Greek term *oikos* (meaning "home" or "place to live") and *ology* (meaning "the study of"), so ecology is a study of organisms in their home. This study has revealed a number of patterns and principles that help us understand how organisms relate to their environment. First, however, it is important to grasp some basic vocabulary used in ecology.

The study of ecology centers on the ecosystem. An **ecosystem** is a group of populations found within a given locality, plus the inanimate environment around those populations. A **population** is the total number of a single species of organism found in a given ecosystem. Typically, there are many populations of different species within a particular ecosystem. The term **organism** refers to an individual of a particular species. Each species is a distinct group of individuals that are able to interbreed (mate), producing viable offspring. Although species are defined by their ability to reproduce, they are usually described by their morphology (their anatomical features).

Populations that interact with each other in a particular ecosystem are collectively termed a **community**. For instance, a temperate forest community includes pine trees, oaks, shrubs, lichen, mosses, ferns, squirrels, deer, insects, owls, bacteria, fungi, etc.

The part of the Earth that includes all living things is called the **biosphere**. The biosphere also includes the **atmosphere** (air), the **lithosphere** (ground), and the **hydrosphere** (water).

A habitat refers to the physical place where a species lives. A species' habitat must include all the factors that will support its life and reproduction. These factors may be **biotic** (i.e., living – food source, predators, etc.) and **abiotic** (i.e., nonliving – weather, temperature, soil features, etc.).

A species' **niche** is the role it plays within the ecosystem. It includes its physical requirements (such as light and water) and its biological activities (how it reproduces, how it acquires food, etc.). One important aspect of a species' niche is its place in the food chain.

ECOLOGICAL CYCLES

Every species within an ecosystem requires resources and energy in varying forms. The interaction of organisms and the environment can be described as cycles of energy and resources that allow the community to flourish. Although each ecosystem has its own energy and nutrient cycles, these cycles also interact with each other to form bioregional and planetary biological cycles.

The **energy cycle** supports life throughout the environment. There are also several **biogeochemical cycles** (the water cycle, the carbon cycle, the nitrogen cycle, the phosphorous cycle, the rock cycle, etc.), which are also important to the health of ecosystems. A biogeochemical cycle is the system whereby the substances needed for life are recycled and transported throughout the environment.

Carbon, hydrogen, oxygen, phosphorous, and nitrogen are called macronutrients; they are used in large quantities by living things. Micronutrients—those elements utilized in trace quantities in organisms—include iodine, iron, zinc, and copper.

Energy Cycle (Food Chain)

Since all life requires the input of energy, the **energy cycles** within the ecosystem are central to its well-being. On Earth, the Sun provides the energy that is the basis of life in most ecosystems. (An exception is the hydrothermal vent communities that derive their energy from the heat of the Earth's core.) Without the constant influx of solar energy into our planetary ecosystem, most life would cease to exist. Energy generally flows through the entire ecosystem in one direction—from producers to consumers and on to decomposers (consumers may also consume decomposers) through the **food chain**.

Photosynthetic organisms—such as plants, some protists, and some bacteria—are the first link in most food chains; they use the energy of sunlight to combine carbon dioxide and water into sugars, releasing oxygen gas (O_2). Photosynthetic organisms are called producers, since they synthesize sugar and starch molecules using the Sun's energy to link the carbons in carbon dioxide. Primary consumers (also known as herbivores) are species that eat photosynthetic organisms. Consumers utilize sugars and starches stored in cells or tissues for energy. Secondary consumers feed on primary consumers, and on the chain goes, through tertiary, quaternary (etc.) consumers. Finally, decomposers (bacteria, fungi, some animals) are species that recycle the organic material found in dead plants and animals back into the food chain.

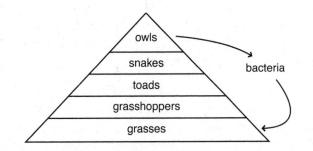

Fig. 3–32 A Food Chain Pyramid.

Animals that feed only on other animals are called **carnivores** (meat-eaters), whereas those that consume both photosynthetic organisms and other animals are known as **omnivores**.

The energy cycle of the food chain is subject to the laws of thermodynamics. Energy can neither be created nor destroyed. However, every use of energy is less than 100% efficient; about 10% is lost as heat. When we call photosynthetic organisms producers, we mean that they produce food using the Sun's energy to form chemical bonds in sugars and other biomolecules. Other organisms can use the energy stored in the bonds of these biomolecules.

The steps in the food chain are also known as **trophic levels**. Consider the pyramid diagram (Fig. 3–32) as one example of a food chain with many trophic levels. Grasses are on the bottom of the pyramid; they are the producers, the first trophic level. Producers are also known as **autotrophs**, as they produce their own food. Each trophic level is greater in **biomass** (total mass of organisms) than the level above it.

Grasshoppers represent the **second trophic level**, or primary consumers in this example of a food chain. Grasshoppers consume plants and are consumed (in this example) by toads, the secondary consumers, which represent the **third trophic level**. Snakes consume toads, and are in turn consumed by owls— making these the **fourth and fifth trophic levels**. In this example, bacteria are the decomposers that recycle some of the nutrients from dead owls (and other levels) to be reused by the first trophic level.

The pyramid illustrates a food chain; however, in nature it is never actually as simple as shown. Owls consume snakes, but they may also consume toads (a lower level in the pyramid) and fish (from an entirely different pyramid). Thus, within every ecosystem there may be numerous food chains interacting in varying ways to form a **food web**. Furthermore, all organisms produce waste products that feed decomposers. The food web represents the cycling and recycling of both energy and nutrients within the ecosystem. The productivity of the entire web is dependent upon the amount of photosynthesis carried out by photosynthesizers.

Water Cycle

The availability of water is crucial to the survival of all living things. Water vapor circulates through the biosphere in a process called the **hydrologic cycle**. Water is evaporated via solar radiation from the ocean and other bodies of water into clouds. Water is also released into the atmosphere from vegetation (leaves) by transpiration. Some water is also evaporated directly from soil, but most water in the ground flows into underground aquifers, which eventually empty into the oceans. Water above ground flows into waterways, which also eventually flow into the ocean (a process known as runoff). Water vapor is then redistributed over land (and back into oceans as well) via clouds, which release water as precipitation.

The water cycle also has a profound effect on Earth's climate. Clouds reflect the Sun's radiation away from the Earth, causing cool weather. Water vapor in the air also acts as a **greenhouse gas,** reflecting radiation from the Earth's surface back toward the Earth, and therefore trapping heat. The water cycle also intersects nearly all the other cycles of elements and nutrients.

Nitrogen Cycle

Nitrogen is another substance essential to life processes, since it is a key component of amino acids (components of proteins) and nucleic acids. The nitrogen cycle recycles nitrogen. Nitrogen is the most plentiful gas in the atmosphere, making up 78% of the air. However, neither photosynthetic organisms nor animals are able to use nitrogen gas (N_2), which does not readily react with other compounds, directly from the air. Instead a process known as nitrogen fixing makes nitrogen available for absorption by the roots of plants. **Nitrogen fixing** is the process of combining nitrogen with either hydrogen or oxygen, mostly by **nitrogen-fixing bacteria**, or to a small degree by volcanoes and **lightning**.

These nitrogen-fixing bacteria fill a unique and vital niche, by living in the soil and performing the task of combining gaseous nitrogen from the atmosphere with hydrogen, forming ammonium (NH_4^+ ions). (Some cyanobacteria, also called blue-green bacteria, are also active in this process.) Ammonium ions are then absorbed and used by plants. Other types of nitrogen-fixing bacteria live in symbiosis on the nodules of the roots of legumes (beans, peas, clover, etc.), supplying the roots with a direct source of ammonia.

Some plants are unable to use ammonia, instead they use **nitrates**. Some bacteria perform **nitrification**, a process, which further breaks down ammonia into nitrites (NO_2^-), and yet again another type of bacteria converts nitrites into nitrates (NO_3^-).

Nitrogen compounds (such as ammonia and nitrates) are also produced by natural, physical processes such as volcanic activity. Another source of usable nitrogen is lightning, which reacts with atmospheric nitrogen to form nitrates.

In addition, nitrogen passes along through the food chain, and is recycled through decomposition processes. When plants are consumed, the amino acids are recombined and used in a process that passes the nitrogen-containing molecules on through the food chain or web. Animal waste products, such as urine, release nitrogen compounds (primarily ammonia) back into the environment, yet another source of nitrogen. Finally, large amounts of nitrogen are returned to the Earth by bacteria and fungi, which decompose dead plant and animal matter into ammonia (and other substances), a process known as **ammonification**.

Various species of bacteria and fungi are also responsible for breaking down excess nitrates, a process known as **denitrification**, which releases nitrogen gas back into the air. The nitrogen cycle involves cycling nitrogen through both living and non-living entities.

Carbon Cycle

The carbon cycle is the route by which carbon is obtained, used, and recycled by living things. Carbon is an important element contained in the cells of all species. The study of organic chemistry is the study of carbon-based molecules.

Earth's atmosphere contains large amounts of carbon in the form of carbon dioxide (CO_2). Photosynthetic organisms require the intake of carbon dioxide for the process of photosynthesis, which is the foundation of the food chain. Most of the carbon within organisms is derived from the production of carbohydrates through photosynthesis. The process of photosynthesis also releases oxygen molecules (O_2), which are necessary to animal respiration. Animal respiration releases carbon dioxide back into the atmosphere in large quantities.

Since plant cells consist of molecules containing carbon, animals that consume photosynthetic organisms are consuming and using carbon from the photosynthetic organisms. Carbon is passed along the food chain as these animals are then consumed. When animals and photosynthetic organisms die, decomposers, including the detritus feeders, bacteria, and fungi, break down the organic matter. Detritus feeders include worms, mites, insects, and crustaceans, which feed on dead organic matter, returning carbon to the cycle through chemical breakdown and respiration.

Carbon dioxide (CO_2) is also dissolved directly into the oceans, where it is combined with calcium to form calcium carbonate, which is used by mollusks to form their shells. When mollusks die, the shells break down and often form limestone. Limestone is then dissolved by water over time and some carbon may be released back into the atmosphere as CO_2, or used by new ocean species.

Finally, organic matter that is left to decay, may, under conditions of heat and pressure, be transformed into coal, oil, or natural gas (the **fossil fuels**). When fossil fuels are burned for energy, the combustion process releases carbon dioxide back into the atmosphere, where it is available to plants for photosynthesis.

Phosphorus Cycle

Phosphorus is another mineral required by living things. Unlike carbon and nitrogen, which cycle through the atmosphere in gaseous form, phosphorus is only found in solid form, within rocks and soil. Phosphorus is a key component in ATP, NADP (a molecule that, like ATP, stores energy in its chemical bonds), and many other molecular compounds essential to life.

Phosphorus is found within rocks and is released by the process of erosion. Water dissolves phosphorus from rocks, and carries it into rivers and streams. Here phosphorus and oxygen react to form phosphates, which end up in bodies of water. Phosphates are absorbed by photosynthetic organisms in and near the water and are used in the synthesis of organic molecules. As in the carbon and nitrogen cycles, phosphorus is then passed up the food chain and returned through animal wastes and organic decay.

New phosphorous enters the cycle as undersea sedimentary rocks. These rocks are thrust up during the shifting of the Earth's tectonic plates. New rock containing phosphorus is then exposed to erosion and enters the cycling process.

POPULATION GROWTH AND REGULATION

The population growth of a species is regulated by limiting factors that exist within the species' environment. Population growth maintains equilibrium in all species under normal conditions because of these limiting factors. A population's overall growth rate is affected by the birth rate (**natality**) and death rate (**mortality**) of the population. The rate of increase within a population is represented by the birth rate minus the death rate. When the birth rate within a population equals the death rate, the population remains at a constant level.

There are two models of population growth, the exponential curve (or J-curve) and the logistic curve (or the S-curve). The exponential curve represents populations in which there is no environmental or social limit on population size, so the rate of growth accelerates over time. Exponential population growth exists only during the initial population growth in a particular ecosystem, since as the population increases the limiting factors become more influential. In other words, a fish population introduced into a pond would experience exponential population growth until food and space supplies began to limit the population.

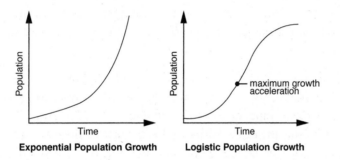

Exponential Population Growth   **Logistic Population Growth**

The logistic curve reflects the effects of limiting factors on population size, where growth accelerates to a point, then slows down. The logistic curve shows population growth over a longer period of time, and represents population growth under normal conditions.

Population growth is directly related to the life characteristics of the population such as the age at which an individual begins to reproduce, the age of death, the rate of growth, etc. For instance, species that grow quickly, mature sexually at an early age, and live a long life would have a population growth rate that exceeds that of species with a short life span and short reproductive span.

In general, most populations have an incredible ability to increase in numbers. A population without limiting factors could overpopulate the world in several generations. It is the limits existing within each ecosystem that keep this from happening.

LIMITING FACTORS

Many factors affect the life of an ecosystem, which may be permanent or temporary. Populations within an ecosystem will be affected by changes in the environment from **abiotic factors** (physical, non-living factors such as fire, pollution, sunlight, soil, light, precipitation, availability of oxygen, water conditions, and temperature) and **biotic factors** (biological factors, including availability of food competition, predator-prey relationships, symbiosis, and overpopulation).

These biotic and abiotic factors are known as **limiting factors** since they will determine how much a particular population within a community will be able to grow. For instance, the resource in shortest supply in an ecosystem may limit population growth. As an example, we know that photosynthetic organisms require phosphorous in order to thrive, so the population growth will be limited by the amount of phosphorous readily available in the environment. Conversely, growth may be limited by having more of an element (such as heat or water) than it can tolerate. For example, plants need carbon dioxide to grow; however, a large concentration of carbon dioxide in the atmosphere is toxic.

Ecologists now commonly combine these two ideas to provide a more comprehensive understanding of how conditions limit growth of populations. It may be stated that the establishment and survival of a particular organism in an area is dependent upon both (1) the availability of necessary elements in at least the minimum quantity, and (2) the controlled supply of those elements to keep it within the limits of tolerance.

Limiting factors interact with each other and generally produce a situation within the ecosystem that supports homeostasis (a steady-state condition). **Homeostasis** is a dynamic balance achieved within an ecosystem functioning at its optimum level. Homeostasis is the tendency of the ecological community to stay the same. However, the balance of the ecosystem can be disturbed by the removal, or decrease, of a single factor or by the addition, or increase, of a factor.

Populations are rarely governed by the effect of a single limiting factor; instead many factors interact to control population size. Changes in limiting factors have a domino effect in an ecosystem, as the change in population size of one species will change the dynamics of the entire community. The number of individuals of a particular species living in a particular area is called the population **density** (number of organisms per area).

Both abiotic and biotic limiting factors exist in a single community; however, one may be dominant over the other. Abiotic limiting factors are also known as **density-independent factors**. That is, they are independent of population density. For instance, the populations around Mount St. Helens were greatly affected by its eruption in 1980, and this effect had nothing to do with the population levels of the area before the eruption. In this situation, the density-independent physical factors dominated the population changes that took place.

Pollution is a major density-independent factor in the health of ecosystems. Pollution is usually a by-product of human endeavors and affects the air or water quality of an ecosystem with secondary effects. In addition to producing pollution, humans may deliberately utilize chemicals such as pesticides or herbicides to limit growth of particular species. Such chemicals can damage the homeostatic mechanisms within a community, causing a long-term upset in the balance of an ecosystem.

In other situations, biotic factors, called **density-dependent factors** may be the dominant influence on population in a given area. Density-dependent factors include population growth issues and interactions between species within a community.

Within a given area, there is a maximum level the population may reach at which it will continue to thrive. This is known as the **carrying capacity** of the environment. When an organism has reached the carrying capacity of the ecosystem, the population growth rate will level off and show no net growth. Populations also occupy a particular geographic area with suitable conditions. This total area occupied by a species is known as the **range**. Typically, populations will have the greatest density in the center of their range, and lower density at the edges. The area outside the range is known as the area of intolerance for that species, since it is not able to survive there. Environmental changes will affect the size and location of the range, making it a dynamic characteristic.

Over time, species may move in or out of a particular area, a process known as **dispersion**. Dispersion occurs in one of three ways—through **emigration** (permanent one way movement out of the original range), **immigration** (permanent one way movement into a new range), and **migration** (temporary movement out of one range into another, and back). Migration is an important process to many species and communities, since it allows animals that might not survive year round in a particular ecosystem to temporarily relocate for a portion of the year. Therefore, migration gives the opportunity for greater diversity of species in an ecosystem.

Two or more species living within the same area and that overlap niches (their function in the food chain) are said to be in **competition** if the resource they both require is in limited supply. If the niche overlap is minimal (other sources of food are available), then both species may survive. In some cases, one of the species may be wiped out in an area due to competition, a situation called **competitive exclusion**. This is a rare but plausible occurrence.

A predator is simply an organism that eats another. The organism that is eaten is known as the **prey**. The **predator/prey** relationship is one of the most important features of an ecosystem. As seen in our study of the energy cycle, energy is passed from lower trophic levels to higher trophic levels, as one animal is consumed by another. This relationship not only provides transfer of energy up the food chain, it also is a population control factor for the prey species. In situations where natural predators are removed from a region, the overpopulation occurring amongst the prey species can cause problems in the population and community. For instance, the hunting and trapping of wolves in the United States has led to an overpopulation of deer (the prey of wolves), which in turn has caused a shortage of food for deer in some areas, causing these deer populations to starve.

When two species interact with each other within the same range, it is known as **symbiosis**. **Amensalism** is one type of symbiosis where one species is neither helped nor harmed while it inhibits the growth of another species. **Mutualism** is another form of symbiosis where both species benefit. **Parasitism** is symbiosis in which one species benefits, but the other is harmed. (Parasites are not predators, since the parasitic action takes a long period of time and may not actually kill the host.)

When the entire population of a particular species is eliminated, it is known as **extinction**. Extinction may be a local phenomenon, the elimination of a population of one species from one area. However, species extinction is a worldwide phenomenon, where all members of all populations of a species die.

The extinction of a single species may also cause a chain reaction of secondary extinctions if other species depend on the extinct species. Conversely, the introduction of a new species into an area can also have a profound effect on other populations within that area. This new species may compete for the niche of native population or upset a predator/prey balance. For example, the brown tree snake (native to Australia) was introduced into islands in the Pacific years ago. (They probably migrated on ships.) The brown snake has caused the extinction of several species of birds on those Pacific islands. The bird populations could not withstand the introduction of this new predator.

Ultimately, the survival of a particular population is dependent on maintaining a **minimal viable population** size. When a population is significantly diminished in size, it becomes highly susceptible to breeding problems and environmental changes that may result in extinction.

COMMUNITY STRUCTURE

Community structure refers to the characteristics of a specified community including the types of species that are dominant, major climatic trends of the region, and whether the community is open or closed. A **closed community** is one whose populations occupy essentially the same range with very similar distributions of density. These types of communities have sharp boundaries called **ecotones** (such as a pond aquatic ecosystem that ends at the shore). An **open community** has indefinite boundaries, and its populations have varying ranges and densities (such as a forest). In an open community, the species are more widely distributed and animals may actually travel in and out of the area.

An open community is often more able to respond to calamity and may be therefore more resilient. Since the boundaries are subtler, the populations of a forest, for instance, may be able to move as necessary to avoid a fire. If, however, a closed community is affected by a traumatic event (for example, a pond being polluted over a short period of time) it may be completely wiped out.

Communities do grow and change over time. Some communities are able to maintain their basic structure with only minor variations for very long periods of time. Others are much more dynamic, changing significantly over time from one type of ecosystem to another. When one community completely replaces another over time in a given area, it is called **succession**. Succession occurs both in terrestrial and aquatic biomes.

Succession may occur because of small changes over time in climate or conditions, the immigration of a new species, disease, or other slow-acting factors. It may also occur in direct response to cataclysmic events such as fire, flood, or human intervention (for example, clearing a forest for farmland). The first populations that move back into a disturbed ecosystem tend to be hardy species that can survive in bleak conditions. These are known as **pioneer communities**.

An example of terrestrial succession occurs when a fire wipes out a forest community. The first new colonization will come from quick growing species such as grasses, which will produce over time a grassland ecosystem. The decay of grasses will enrich the soil, providing fertile ground for germination of seeds for shrubs brought in by wind or animals. The shrubs will further prepare the soil for germination of larger species of trees, which over time will take over the shrub-land and produce a forest community once again.

When succession ends in a stable community, the community is known as the **climax community**. The climax community is the one best suited to the climate and soil conditions, and one that achieves a homeostasis. Generally, the climax community will remain in an area until a catastrophic event (fire, flood, etc.) destroys it.

■ SECTION 2: PHYSICAL SCIENCE
■ ATOMIC CHEMISTRY

STRUCTURE OF THE ATOM

The study of matter is known as **chemistry**. All matter is made up of **atoms**. The properties of matter are a result of the structure of atoms and their interaction with each other. An **element** is a substance that cannot be broken down into any other substances. The simplest unit of an element that retains the element's characteristics is known as an **atom**. Each atom of a given element has a nucleus containing a unique number of **protons** and usually a similar number of **neutrons**. The nucleus is surrounded by **electrons**.

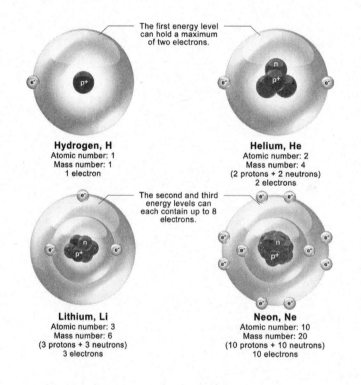

The first energy level can hold a maximum of two electrons.

Hydrogen, H
Atomic number: 1
Mass number: 1
1 electron

Helium, He
Atomic number: 2
Mass number: 4
(2 protons + 2 neutrons)
2 electrons

The second and third energy levels can each contain up to 8 electrons.

Lithium, Li
Atomic number: 3
Mass number: 6
(3 protons + 3 neutrons)
3 electrons

Neon, Ne
Atomic number: 10
Mass number: 20
(10 protons + 10 neutrons)
10 electrons

Fig. 3–33 Atom Illustrations.

Elements are listed by atomic number on the **Periodic Table of the Elements**. The **atomic number** is the number of protons found in the nucleus of an atom of that element. In an uncharged atom, the number of protons is equal to the number of electrons.

Fig. 3-34   The Periodic Table of the Elements. Elements are listed by atomic number.

PERIODIC TABLE
Atomic Properties of the Elements

NIST
National Institute of
Standards and Technology
U.S. Department of Commerce

Physics Laboratory
physics.nist.gov

Standard Reference Data
www.nist.gov/srd

Frequently used fundamental physical constants

For the most accurate values of these and other constants, visit physics.nist.gov/constants
1 second = 9 192 631 770 periods of radiation corresponding to the transition
between the two hyperfine levels of the ground state of ^{133}Cs

speed of light in vacuum	c	299 792 458 m s^{-1} (exact)
Planck constant	h	6.6261 × 10^{-34} J s ($\hbar = h/2\pi$)
elementary charge	e	1.6022 × 10^{-19} C
electron mass	m_e	9.1094 × 10^{-31} kg
	$m_e c^2$	0.5110 MeV
proton mass	m_p	1.6726 × 10^{-27} kg
fine-structure constant	α	1/137.036
Rydberg constant	R_∞	10 973 732 m^{-1}
	$R_\infty c$	3.289 842 × 10^{15} Hz
	$R_\infty hc$	13.6057 eV
Boltzmann constant	k	1.3807 × 10^{-23} J K^{-1}

Solids
Liquids
Gases
Artificially Prepared

NIST SP 966 (September 2010)

For a description of the data, visit physics.nist.gov/data

Atomic Number — 58
Symbol — Ce
Name — Cerium
Atomic Weight[1] — 140.116
Ground-state Configuration — [Xe]4f5d6s^2
Ground-state Level — $^1G_4$
Ionization Energy (eV) — 5.5387

[1]Based upon ^{12}C. ( ) indicates the mass number of the longest-lived isotope.

Group / Period

Period 1

1 $^2S_{1/2}$ H Hydrogen 1.00794 1s 13.5984

2 $^1S_0$ He Helium 4.002602 1s^2 24.5874

Period 2

3 $^2S_{1/2}$ Li Lithium 6.941 1s^{2}2s 5.3917

4 $^1S_0$ Be Beryllium 9.012182 [He]2s^2 9.3227

5 $^2P_{1/2}$ B Boron 10.81 1s^{2}2s^{2}2p 8.2980

6 $^3P_0$ C Carbon 12.0107 1s^{2}2s^{2}2p^2 11.2603

7 $^4S_{3/2}$ N Nitrogen 14.0067 1s^{2}2s^{2}2p^3 14.5341

8 $^3P_2$ O Oxygen 15.9994 [He]2s^{2}2p^4 13.6181

9 $^2P_{3/2}$ F Fluorine 18.9984032 [He]2s^{2}2p^5 17.4228

10 $^1S_0$ Ne Neon 20.1797 [He]2s^{2}2p^6 21.5645

Period 3

11 $^2S_{1/2}$ Na Sodium 22.98976928 [Ne]3s 5.1391

12 $^1S_0$ Mg Magnesium 24.3050 [Ne]3s^2 7.6462

13 $^2P_{1/2}$ Al Aluminum 26.9815386 [Ne]3s^{2}3p 5.9858

14 $^3P_0$ Si Silicon 28.0855 [Ne]3s^{2}3p^2 8.1517

15 $^4S_{3/2}$ P Phosphorus 30.973762 [Ne]3s^{2}3p^3 10.4867

16 $^3P_2$ S Sulfur 32.065 [Ne]3s^{2}3p^4 10.3600

17 $^2P_{3/2}$ Cl Chlorine 35.453 [Ne]3s^{2}3p^5 12.9676

18 $^1S_0$ Ar Argon 39.948 [Ne]3s^{2}3p^6 15.7596

Period 4

19 $^2S_{1/2}$ K Potassium 39.0983 [Ar]4s 4.3407

20 $^1S_0$ Ca Calcium 40.078 [Ar]4s^2 6.1132

21 $^2D_{3/2}$ Sc Scandium 44.955912 [Ar]3d4s^2 6.5615

22 $^3F_2$ Ti Titanium 47.867 [Ar]3d^{2}4s^2 6.8281

23 $^4F_{3/2}$ V Vanadium 50.9415 [Ar]3d^{3}4s^2 6.7462

24 $^7S_3$ Cr Chromium 51.9961 [Ar]3d^{5}4s 6.7665

25 $^6S_{5/2}$ Mn Manganese 54.938045 [Ar]3d^{5}4s^2 7.4340

26 $^5D_4$ Fe Iron 55.845 [Ar]3d^{6}4s^2 7.9024

27 $^4F_{9/2}$ Co Cobalt 58.933195 [Ar]3d^{7}4s^2 7.8810

28 $^3F_4$ Ni Nickel 58.6934 [Ar]3d^{8}4s^2 7.6399

29 $^2S_{1/2}$ Cu Copper 63.546 [Ar]3d^{10}4s 7.7264

30 $^1S_0$ Zn Zinc 65.38 [Ar]3d^{10}4s^2 9.3942

31 $^2P_{1/2}$ Ga Gallium 69.723 [Ar]3d^{10}4s^{2}4p 5.9993

32 $^3P_0$ Ge Germanium 72.64 [Ar]3d^{10}4s^{2}4p^2 7.8994

33 $^4S_{3/2}$ As Arsenic 74.92160 [Ar]3d^{10}4s^{2}4p^3 9.7886

34 $^3P_2$ Se Selenium 78.96 [Ar]3d^{10}4s^{2}4p^4 9.7524

35 $^2P_{3/2}$ Br Bromine 79.904 [Ar]3d^{10}4s^{2}4p^5 11.8138

36 $^1S_0$ Kr Krypton 83.798 [Ar]3d^{10}4s^{2}4p^6 13.9996

Period 5

37 $^2S_{1/2}$ Rb Rubidium 85.4678 [Kr]5s 4.1771

38 $^1S_0$ Sr Strontium 87.62 [Kr]5s^2 5.6949

39 $^2D_{3/2}$ Y Yttrium 88.90585 [Kr]4d5s^2 6.2173

40 $^3F_2$ Zr Zirconium 91.224 [Kr]4d^{2}5s^2 6.6339

41 $^6D_{1/2}$ Nb Niobium 92.90638 [Kr]4d^{4}5s 6.7589

42 $^7S_3$ Mo Molybdenum 95.96 [Kr]4d^{5}5s 7.0924

43 $^6S_{5/2}$ Tc Technetium (98) [Kr]4d^{5}5s^2 7.28

44 $^5F_5$ Ru Ruthenium 101.07 [Kr]4d^{7}5s 7.3605

45 $^4F_{9/2}$ Rh Rhodium 102.90550 [Kr]4d^{8}5s 7.4589

46 $^1S_0$ Pd Palladium 106.42 [Kr]4d^{10} 8.3369

47 $^2S_{1/2}$ Ag Silver 107.8682 [Kr]4d^{10}5s 7.5762

48 $^1S_0$ Cd Cadmium 112.411 [Kr]4d^{10}5s^2 8.9938

49 $^2P_{1/2}$ In Indium 114.818 [Kr]4d^{10}5s^{2}5p 5.7864

50 $^3P_0$ Sn Tin 118.710 [Kr]4d^{10}5s^{2}5p^2 7.3439

51 $^4S_{3/2}$ Sb Antimony 121.760 [Kr]4d^{10}5s^{2}5p^3 8.6084

52 $^3P_2$ Te Tellurium 127.60 [Kr]4d^{10}5s^{2}5p^4 9.0096

53 $^2P_{3/2}$ I Iodine 126.90447 [Kr]4d^{10}5s^{2}5p^5 10.4513

54 $^1S_0$ Xe Xenon 131.293 [Kr]4d^{10}5s^{2}5p^6 12.1298

Period 6

55 $^2S_{1/2}$ Cs Cesium 132.9054519 [Xe]6s 3.8939

56 $^1S_0$ Ba Barium 137.327 [Xe]6s^2 5.2117

57 $^2D_{3/2}$ La Lanthanum 138.90547 [Xe]5d6s^2 5.5769

72 $^3F_2$ Hf Hafnium 178.49 [Xe]4f^{14}5d^{2}6s^2 6.8251

73 $^4F_{3/2}$ Ta Tantalum 180.94788 [Xe]4f^{14}5d^{3}6s^2 7.5496

74 $^5D_0$ W Tungsten 183.84 [Xe]4f^{14}5d^{4}6s^2 7.8640

75 $^6S_{5/2}$ Re Rhenium 186.207 [Xe]4f^{14}5d^{5}6s^2 7.8335

76 $^5D_4$ Os Osmium 190.23 [Xe]4f^{14}5d^{6}6s^2 8.4382

77 $^4F_{9/2}$ Ir Iridium 192.217 [Xe]4f^{14}5d^{7}6s^2 8.9670

78 $^3D_3$ Pt Platinum 195.084 [Xe]4f^{14}5d^{9}6s 8.9588

79 $^2S_{1/2}$ Au Gold 196.966569 [Xe]4f^{14}5d^{10}6s 9.2255

80 $^1S_0$ Hg Mercury 200.59 [Xe]4f^{14}5d^{10}6s^2 10.4375

81 $^2P_{1/2}$ Tl Thallium 204.3833 [Hg]6p 6.1082

82 $^3P_0$ Pb Lead 207.2 [Hg]6p^2 7.4167

83 $^4S_{3/2}$ Bi Bismuth 208.98040 [Hg]6p^3 7.2855

84 $^3P_2$ Po Polonium (209) [Hg]6p^4 8.414

85 $^2P_{3/2}$ At Astatine (210) [Hg]6p^5

86 $^1S_0$ Rn Radon (222) [Hg]6p^6 10.7485

Period 7

87 $^2S_{1/2}$ Fr Francium (223) [Rn]7s 4.0727

88 $^1S_0$ Ra Radium (226) [Rn]7s^2 5.2784

89 $^2D_{3/2}$ Ac Actinium (227) [Rn]6d7s^2 5.3807

104 Rf Rutherfordium (265) [Rn]5f^{14}6d^{2}7s^2 6.07

105 Db Dubnium (268)

106 Sg Seaborgium (271)

107 Bh Bohrium (272)

108 Hs Hassium (277)

109 Mt Meitnerium (276)

110 Ds Darmstadtium (281)

111 Rg Roentgenium (280)

112 Cn Copernicium (285)

113 Uut Ununtrium (284)

114 Uuq Ununquadium (289)

115 Uup Ununpentium (288)

116 Uuh Ununhexium (293)

117 Uus Ununseptium (294)

118 Uuo Ununoctium (294)

Lanthanides

58 $^1G_4$ Ce Cerium 140.116 [Xe]4f5d6s^2 5.5387

59 $^4I_{9/2}^o$ Pr Praseodymium 140.90765 [Xe]4f^{3}6s^2 5.473

60 $^5I_4$ Nd Neodymium 144.242 [Xe]4f^{4}6s^2 5.5250

61 $^6H_{5/2}^o$ Pm Promethium (145) [Xe]4f^{5}6s^2 5.582

62 $^7F_0$ Sm Samarium 150.36 [Xe]4f^{6}6s^2 5.6437

63 $^8S_{7/2}^o$ Eu Europium 151.964 [Xe]4f^{7}6s^2 5.6704

64 $^9D_2^o$ Gd Gadolinium 157.25 [Xe]4f^{7}5d6s^2 6.1498

65 $^6H_{15/2}^o$ Tb Terbium 158.92535 [Xe]4f^{9}6s^2 5.8638

66 $^5I_8$ Dy Dysprosium 162.500 [Xe]4f^{10}6s^2 5.9389

67 $^4I_{15/2}^o$ Ho Holmium 164.93032 [Xe]4f^{11}6s^2 6.0215

68 $^3H_6$ Er Erbium 167.259 [Xe]4f^{12}6s^2 6.1077

69 $^2F_{7/2}^o$ Tm Thulium 168.93421 [Xe]4f^{13}6s^2 6.1843

70 $^1S_0$ Yb Ytterbium 173.054 [Xe]4f^{14}6s^2 6.2542

71 $^2D_{3/2}$ Lu Lutetium 174.9668 [Xe]4f^{14}5d6s^2 5.4259

Actinides

90 $^3F_2$ Th Thorium 232.03806 [Rn]6d^{2}7s^2 6.3067

91 $^4K_{11/2}$ Pa Protactinium 231.03588 [Rn]5f^{2}6d7s^2 5.89

92 $^5L_6^o$ U Uranium 238.02891 [Rn]5f^{3}6d7s^2 6.1939

93 $^6L_{11/2}$ Np Neptunium (237) [Rn]5f^{4}6d7s^2 6.2657

94 $^7F_0$ Pu Plutonium (244) [Rn]5f^{6}7s^2 6.0260

95 $^8F_{1/2}^o$ Am Americium (243) [Rn]5f^{7}7s^2 5.9738

96 $^9D_2^o$ Cm Curium (247) [Rn]5f^{7}6d7s^2 5.9914

97 $^6H_{15/2}^o$ Bk Berkelium (247) [Rn]5f^{9}7s^2 6.1979

98 $^5I_8$ Cf Californium (251) [Rn]5f^{10}7s^2 6.2817

99 $^5I_{15/2}^o$ Es Einsteinium (252) [Rn]5f^{11}7s^2 6.3676

100 $^3H_6$ Fm Fermium (257) [Rn]5f^{12}7s^2 6.50

101 $^2F_{7/2}^o$ Md Mendelevium (258) [Rn]5f^{13}7s^2 6.58

102 $^1S_0$ No Nobelium (259) [Rn]5f^{14}7s^2 6.65

103 $^2P_{1/2}^o$ Lr Lawrencium (262) [Rn]5f^{14}7s^{2}7p? 4.9?

The mass of an atom consists of the cumulative mass of all the particles in the atom, which includes protons, neutrons, and electrons. The mass of the electrons is insignificant relative to the mass of protons or neutrons. Therefore, the **atomic mass** is calculated by adding up the masses of the protons and neutrons. For example, a helium atom consists of two protons and two electrons. In addition, most helium atoms also have 2 neutrons giving it an atomic mass of 4 amu (atomic mass units—the mass of one proton or neutron).

ATOMIC PARTICLE CHART		
NAME	**CHARGE**	**MASS**
Proton	+	1 AMU
Electron	-	~ 0 AMU
Neutron	0	1 AMU

Atoms with the same number of protons but different numbers of neutrons are called **isotopes** of one another. For example, carbon-12 and carbon-14 are the same element (carbon), which is defined as having 6 protons. The difference in the **mass numbers** indicates that carbon-12 has 6 neutrons, while carbon-14 has 8 neutrons. In nature, elements naturally occur as a combination of more than one isotope. The average mass number takes into account the relative frequencies of the different isotopes. The average mass number is also called the **atomic weight**. This number is also the **molar mass** of the element, or the mass in grams of one mole of atoms.

Electrons have a charge of -1, while protons have a charge of $+1$. Neutrons have no charge. The number of protons in the nucleus of an atom carries a positive charge equal to this number; that is, if an atom's nucleus contains 4 protons, the charge is $+4$. Since positive and negative charges attract, the positive charges of the nucleus attract an equal number of negatively charged electrons.

Electrons travel freely in a three-dimensional space that may be called an **electron cloud.** Current models of the atom follow the principles of **quantum mechanics**, which predict the probabilities of an electron being in a certain area at a certain time. The orbital represents a probability of finding an electron at a particular location.

Each electron cloud has a particular amount of energy related to it, and is therefore also referred to as an **energy level**. Each energy level has a limited capacity for holding electrons and each energy level requires a different number of electrons to fill it. Lower energy levels (closer to the nucleus) have less capacity for electrons than those farther from the nucleus.

Since electrons are attracted to the nucleus, electrons fill the electron shells closest to the nucleus (lowest energy levels) first. Once a given level is full, electrons start filling the next level out. The outermost occupied energy level of an element is called the **valence shell.** The number of electrons in the valence shell will determine the combinations that this atom will be likely to make with other atoms. Atoms are more stable when every electron is paired and are most stable when their valence shell is full. The tendency for an atom toward stability means that elements having unpaired or partially-filled valence shells will easily gain or lose electrons in order to obtain the most stable configuration.

Electrons give off energy in the form of **electromagnetic radiation** when they move from a higher level, or an excited state, to a lower level. The energy represented by light, using Planck's equation, represents the difference between the two energy levels of the electron.

NUCLEAR REACTIONS AND EQUATIONS

An element is radioactive when the nuclei of its atoms are unstable and spontaneously release one of a variety of subatomic particles in order to form nuclei with higher stability.

Alpha decay occurs when the nucleus of an atom emits a package of two protons and two neutrons, called an **alpha particle** (α), which is equivalent to the nucleus of a helium atom. This usually occurs with elements that have a mass number greater than 60. Alpha decay causes the atom's atomic mass to decrease by four units and the atomic number by two units. For example:

$$\overset{\text{Mass \#}}{\underset{\text{\#Protons}}{}} \quad {}^{238}_{92}U \longrightarrow {}^{234}_{90}Th + \overset{\text{Alpha Particle}}{{}^{4}_{2}He}$$

Beta decay occurs in two forms, positive and negative. A **Beta particle** (β) is a high speed, high energy electron or positron (same particle as an electron but with a reversed – negative – charge). This usually occurs with elements that have a mass number greater than their atomic weight. Beta decay causes the mass number to remain the same but either increases or decreases the atomic number by one. Beta decay converts a neutron into a proton and releases a Beta particle. For example:

Carbon emits a β– gains a proton and becomes Nitrogen.

$$\overset{}{} {}^{14}_{6}C \rightarrow {}^{14}_{7}N + \overset{\text{electron}}{e^{-}} + \overset{}{\bar{v}_{e}}\,\,{\text{electron neutrino}}$$

Magnesium emits a β– loses a proton and becomes Sodium.

$$\underset{\text{positron neutrino}}{\underset{\nwarrow}{^{23}_{12}\text{Mg} \rightarrow \,^{23}_{11}\text{Na} + \overset{\overset{\text{positron}}{\nwarrow}}{e^+} + \nu_e}}$$

Gamma radiation consists of *gamma rays* (γ), which are high-frequency, high-energy electromagnetic radiation that are usually given off in combination with alpha and beta decay. Gamma decay can occur when a nucleus undergoes a transformation from a higher-energy state to a lower-energy state. The resulting atom may or may not be radioactive. Gamma rays are photons, which have neither mass nor charge.

RATE OF DECAY; HALF-LIFE

Half-life is the time it takes for 50 percent of an isotope to decay. Nuclear decay represents a "first-order" reaction in that it depends on the amount of material and the rate constant. For example:

Strontium-85 has a half-life of 65.2 days. How long will it take for 20 grams of strontium-85 to decay into five grams of strontium-85?

Solution:

It takes two half-lives to decrease the amount of strontium-85 from 20 grams to 5 grams.

20 grams decays to 10g in 65.2 days. It takes another 65.2 days for half of that 10g to decay to 5 grams.

Elements such as Uranium are constantly decaying according to their half lives. The quantity of these elements is replenished by the elements with higher atomic numbers decaying down into them.

CHEMISTRY OF REACTIONS

COMMON ELEMENTS

Some elements on the Periodic Table of the Elements are more commonly found on Earth than others, and some are more likely to interact with other elements. Properties of each element, such as mass, electronegativity, valence electrons, etc., make a particular element fit for interaction with other elements in a variety of ways. The most common elements encountered in chemical reactions are found on the following table:

Table 3–1.   Most Common Elements Found in Chemical Reactions.

Atomic Number	Symbol	Common Name
1	H	Hydrogen
2	He	Helium
6	C	Carbon
7	N	Nitrogen
8	O	Oxygen
11	Na	Sodium
12	Mg	Magnesium
14	Si	Silicon
15	P	Phosphorus
16	S	Sulphur
17	Cl	Chlorine
19	K	Potassium
20	Ca	Calcium
24	Cr	Chromium
26	Fe	Iron
29	Cu	Copper
30	Zn	Zinc
47	Ag	Silver
53	I	Iodine
79	Au	Gold
80	Hg	Mercury
82	Pb	Lead
88	Ra	Radium

CHEMICAL BONDS

Valence properties of atoms provide opportunities for them to bond with other atoms. As discussed in Chapter 6, "Atoms are more stable when every electron is paired and are most stable when the valence shell is full. The tendency for an atom toward stability means that elements having unpaired or partially-filled valence shells will easily gain or lose electrons in order to obtain the most stable configuration." Therefore, certain atoms are easily available to make certain types of bonds under the right conditions with other atoms.

A **covalent bond** between atoms is formed when atoms share electrons. For instance, hydrogen has only one electron, which is unpaired leaving the first valence shell lacking one electron. Oxygen has 6 electrons in the valence shell; it needs 2 more electrons in the valence shell for that shell to be full. It is easy for 2 hydrogen atoms to share their electrons with the oxygen, making the effective valence shells of the oxygen and each hydrogen atom full. The result of the bonding of these three atoms is one molecule of water (H_2O).

A **molecule** is two or more atoms held together by shared electrons (covalent bonds). For example, two hydrogen atoms can join together covalently to form a H_2 molecule. In fact, hydrogen in the air is in the form of H_2. A **compound** is formed when two or more different elemental atoms bond together chemically to form a unique substance (i.e., H_2O, CH_4). These compounds are also molecules. Therefore, all compounds are molecules, but not all molecules are compounds. A covalent bond is the strongest bond due to the sharing of electrons.

Charged atoms are called **ions**. An atom that loses one or more electrons becomes a positively charged particle, or a positive ion. We call this positively charged ion a **cation**. An atom that gains one or more electrons becomes a negative ion, or an **anion**. Positive and negative ions are attracted to each other in an **ionic bond**. An ionic bond is a weak bond, and in fact is considered more of an attraction. Na^+Cl^- (sodium chloride or table salt) is an example of a substance held together by ionic bonds. Na^+Cl^- is considered an ionic substance rather than a molecule since it will quickly dissociate in water.

Some molecules (covalently bonded) have a weak, partial negative charge at one region of the molecule and a partial positive charge in another region. Molecules that have regions of partial charge are called **polar molecules**. For instance, water molecules (which have a net charge of 0) have a partial negative charge near the oxygen atom and a partial positive charge near each of the hydrogen atoms. Thus, when water molecules are close together, their positive regions are attracted to the negatively charged regions of nearby molecules; the negative regions are attracted to the positively charged regions of nearby molecules. The force of attraction between water molecules is called a **hydrogen bond**. A hydrogen bond is a weak chemical bond between molecules.

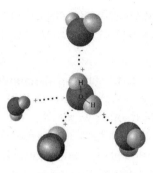

Fig. 3–35   Hydrogen Bond.

CHEMICAL REACTIONS

Chemical reactions occur when molecules interact with each other to form one or more molecules of another type. There are several categories of chemical reactions. Chemical reactions are symbolized by an equation where the reacting molecules **(reactants)** are shown on one side and the newly formed molecules **(products)** on the other, with an arrow between indicating the direction of the reaction. Some chemical reactions are simple, such as the breakdown of a compound into its components (a **decomposition** reaction):

$$AB \rightarrow A + B$$

A simple **combination** reaction is the reverse of decomposition:

$$A + B \rightarrow AB$$

When one compound breaks apart and forms a new compound with a free reactant, it is called a **replacement** reaction:

$$AB + C \rightarrow AC + B$$

When two compounds break apart and exchange components it is called a double replacement reaction:

$$AB + CD \rightarrow AC + BD$$

Chemical reactions may require an input of energy or they may release energy. Reactions that require energy are called **endothermic** reactions. Reactions that release energy are termed **exothermic**.

All chemical reactions are subject to the **laws of thermodynamics**. The first law of thermodynamics (also known as the law of conservation of matter and energy) states that matter and energy can neither be created nor destroyed. In other words, the sum of matter and energy of the reactants must equal that of the products. The second law of thermodynamics, or the law of increasing disorder (or **entropy**), asserts that all reactions spread energy, which tends to diminish its availability. So, although we know from the first law that the energy must be equal on both sides of a reaction equation, reaction processes also tend to degrade the potential energy into a form that cannot perform any useful work.

PHYSICS

HEAT

Heat is energy that flows from an object that is warm to an object that is cooler. It is important to understand the difference between heat and temperature. **Temperature** is the measure of the **average kinetic energy** of a substance. The atoms and molecules of all substances are constantly in motion. The energy of the motion of the atoms and molecules in a substance is called its kinetic energy. Temperature is a measure of that energy. The faster the particles in a substance move (more energy), the higher the temperature will be. The slower the particles move (less energy), the lower the temperature.

The theoretical temperature at which particle motion stops is called **absolute zero** (or 0 Kelvin). This temperature has never been reached by any known substance.

When substances come in contact, the hotter (greater energy) substance transfers kinetic energy to the cooler (lower energy) one and heat is expended. Heat is measured in calories or joules.

Energy (including heat) may be transferred from one object to another by three processes—radiation, conduction, and convection. **Radiation** is the transfer of energy via waves. Radiation can occur through matter, or without any matter present. Radiation from the Sun passes through space (very low density of matter) to reach Earth. **Convection** involves the movement of energy by the movement of matter, usually through currents. For instance, convection moves warm air up, while cool air sinks. (Cool air is more dense.) In a fluid the heat will move with the fluid. **Conduction** is movement of energy by transfer from particle to particle. Conduction can only occur when objects are touching. A pan on a stove heats water by conduction. An oven cooks by convection—warming food by movement of hot air. A microwave cooks by radiation—waves travel into food, adding kinetic energy.

SPECIFIC HEAT

Different substances have different capacities for storing energy. For example, it may take twenty minutes to heat water to 75°C. The same mass of aluminum might require five minutes and the same amount of copper may take only two minutes to reach the same temperature. However, water will retain the kinetic energy (stay hot) longer than the aluminum or copper. The measure of a substance's ability to retain energy is called **specific heat**. Specific heat is measured as the amount of heat needed to raise the temperature of one gram of a substance by one degree Celsius.

THE LAWS OF THERMODYNAMICS

The Laws of Thermodynamics explain the interaction between heat and work (energy) in the universe. The First Law says that matter and energy can neither be created nor destroyed. This law is also known as the **Law of Conservation of Matter and Energy**. The Second Law is known as the **Law of Entropy** and states that whenever energy is exchanged some energy becomes unavailable for use (entropy increases). The Third Law or the **Law of Absolute Zero** says that absolute zero cannot be attained in any system (that is, energy of motion of particles cannot be stopped). The **Zeroth Law of Thermodynamics** is so named because it was accepted by scientists after the first three laws were named but it underlies them all—thus the name "zeroth." The Zeroth Law says that when two bodies are in contact that they will move toward a state of thermodynamic equilibrium—where both bodies eventually reach the same temperature.

STATES OF MATTER

All matter has physical properties that can be observed. These properties affect the way substances react with each other under various conditions. Physical properties include color, odor, taste, strength, hardness, density, and state.

SOLIDS, LIQUIDS, GASES, PLASMA

Matter exists in one of four fundamental states—solid, liquid, gas, or plasma. Under most conditions elements will be in the solid, liquid, or gas phase. Plasma only exists in the case of extreme heat and ionization—in this state ions and electrons move about freely, giving plasma properties different from the other three states. The center of the Sun and stars are in the plasma state.

A solid has molecules in fixed positions giving the substance definite shape. Solids have a definite volume. In a solid the molecules are packed and bonded together. The strength of the bonds determines the strength of the solid and its melting point. When heat energy is applied to the bonds, they break apart, the molecules can move about and the substance becomes a liquid.

A liquid has definite volume but not definite shape since the molecules are loosely attracted. The loose attractions between molecules allow for the shape of the substance to mold to its surroundings. When a liquid is cooled, the molecules become bonded and the substance becomes a solid. Heat energy is lost since the molecules are moving less. When heat energy is added to a liquid, the weak attractions holding the molecules together break apart, causing the molecules to move about randomly and the liquid to become a gas.

A gas is a substance with relatively (relative to solids and liquids) large distances and little attraction between molecules. The molecules are free to move about randomly. Gases have no definite shape or volume since temperature and pressure can impact the density.

Different substances have different conditions under which they exist in a solid liquid or gas. The state that a substance exists in at room temperature depends on how the molecules are bonded together.

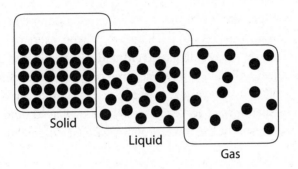

Solid

Liquid

Gas

Fig. 3–36   Solids, liquids, and gases differ in the arrangement and density of molecules.

The following are some terms that are important to know related to substances and their states:

— **melting point**—temperature at which a substance changes from solid to liquid form

— **heat of fusion**—heat required to melt 1 kg of a solid at its melting point (also known as enthalpy of fusion)

— **freezing point**—temperature at which a substance changes from liquid to solid

— **boiling point**—temperature at which a substance changes from liquid to gas

— **heat of vaporization**—amount of energy required to change 1 kg of liquid of a substance to a gas (also known as enthalpy of vaporization)

— **evaporation**—escape of individual particles of a substance into gaseous form

— **condensation**—change of a gaseous substance to liquid form

— **diffusion**—mixing of particles in a gas or liquid

DENSITY

Density is the measure of how much matter exists in a given volume. The density of a substance is determined by measuring the mass of a substance and dividing it by the volume $\left(D = \dfrac{m}{v}\right)$. Substances that are less dense will float when placed in a denser substance. Denser substances will sink in a less dense liquid. It is important to understand that density is a function of mass (amount of matter), not weight (attraction of gravity on mass). Density has to do with how tightly packed the atoms in a substance are.

Consider this: Which weighs more, a pound of lead or a pound of feathers? Neither. A pound is a pound; but the volume of a pound of feathers will be much greater than a pound of lead.

Pressure is a measure of the amount of force applied per unit of area. Pressure exerted on a gas may affect its density, by compressing its volume. Liquids and solids are much less responsive to pressure. **Pascal's principle** states that the pressure exerted on any point of a confined fluid is transmitted unchanged throughout the fluid. Therefore, if you exert pressure on a liquid it will exert that same pressure on its surroundings. **Archimedes' principle** states that when an object is placed in a fluid the object will have a buoyant force equal to the weight of the displaced fluid. Archimedes' principle results in **buoyancy**, a decrease in the measured apparent weight of an object in a fluid due to the net upward force caused by the displaced fluid. This apparent decrease in weight of the object is a result of the force of the displaced fluid acting in an upward direction opposing the object.

GRAVITY

The **mass** of an object refers to the amount of matter that is contained by the object; however, the **weight** of an object is the force of gravity acting upon that object. Mass is related to how much material is there while weight refers to the pull of the Earth (or any other planet or object) upon that material.

The mass of an object (measured in kg) will be the same no matter where in the universe the object is located. Mass is never altered by location, the pull of gravity, speed or even the existence of other forces. A 51 kg object will have a mass of 51 kg whether it is located on Earth, the Moon, or anywhere else. The amount of mass and the gravitational field of the Earth (or the Moon, etc.) imparts weight to an object. The weight of an object, however, will vary according to where in the universe the object is. Weight depends upon the mass of the celestial body that is exerting the gravitational field and the distance from the center of the gravitational field of the body upon the mass experiencing the field.

Gravity is a property of all matter; all matter exerts a gravitational force on all other matter. Gravity acts at a distance and attracts bodies of matter toward each other. The gravity of the Moon affects the water in the Earth's oceans, causing the tides. In the study of atomic particles, there is even a weak force of gravity between all particles.

The gravity on the Earth is greater than the gravity on the Moon, since the Earth has much more matter or mass than the Moon. The force of gravity on an object caused by the mass of the Earth equals the mass of the object (m) times the acceleration caused by gravity (g). The equation is:

$$F = mg$$

This acceleration caused by gravity on Earth, g (more commonly called the acceleration of gravity) equals 9.8 m/s² in the metric system and 32 ft/s² in the English system.

The weight of an object is the measurement of the force of gravity on that object. When you weigh something on a scale, the weight is actually the force of gravity on that object:

$$Weight = mg$$

The mass of the Moon is less than the mass of the Earth, so the acceleration of gravity (g) is less on the Moon than the Earth. If you put an object on the Moon and weighed it, its weight would be $\frac{1}{6}$ the weight on Earth. In other words, a 180-pound man would only weigh 30 pounds on the Moon.

The fundamental units of measure used in the metric system are the meter, kilogram, and second or mks system. To get the weight of an object in the metric system, you multiply the mass in kilograms by the acceleration of gravity (9.8 m/s²), resulting in the units of kg • m/s² or Newtons.

The universal gravitational law, first described by Sir Isaac Newton, states that *the force of gravity between two objects is proportional to the product of the masses of the objects and inversely proportional to the square of the distance between them*—in simple English—as objects get further apart, the effect of gravity drops dramatically. The equation below shows this relationship . . . the mass of one body is designated as M, the mass of a second as m, and the distance between them is r; the force of attraction between the two bodies is F.

$$F = G\frac{Mm}{r^2}$$

where G is the universal gravitational constant $G = 6.67 \times 10^{-11}$ N$\left(\frac{m^2}{kg^2}\right)$ (Newton-meter squared per kilogram squared).

If you drop an object relatively near the Earth, it will speed up according to the acceleration of gravity (g). When you let go of the object, its velocity is zero. Since g = 32 ft/s² = 9.8 m/s², the velocity will be 32 ft/s² (9.8 m/s²) after one second. Because the object is accelerating, the velocity after 2 seconds will be 2 s $\times$ 32 ft/s/s = 64 ft/s² (19.6 m/s²). After 10 seconds, the velocity will be 10 s $\times$ 32 ft/s/s = 320 ft/s or 98 m/s².

Although a falling object will continue to accelerate until it is made to stop (when it hits the ground), air resistance will slow down that acceleration. Air resistance is approximately proportional to the square of the velocity, so as the object falls faster, the air resistance increases until it equals the force of gravity. The point at which these forces are equal is called its **terminal velocity.** For instance, a falling baseball reaches 94 miles per hour or 42 meters/second; it would remain at that velocity and no longer accelerate. A penny dropped from a high building will accelerate until it reaches around 230 mph.

The acceleration of the force of gravity on falling bodies is independent of the mass of the falling object. Therefore, a 15-pound weight would fall at the same rate as a 2-pound weight and would hit the ground at the same time if dropped from the same height. In addition, gravity of the mass of an object is also *independent of the velocity* of the object parallel to the ground. For example, two bullets are positioned at the same initial height. One is shot from a gun horizontal to the surface. The other bullet is dropped at the exact same time as the bullet is fired from the gun. Both bullets will hit the ground at the exact same time, if no incidental air resistance or friction exists.

$$F = ma$$

Since *force = mass times acceleration,* the universal gravity equation implies that as objects are attracted and get closer together, the force increases and the acceleration between them also increases.

CLASSICAL MECHANICS

Mechanics is the study of things in motion. **Classical mechanics** involves particles bigger than atoms and slower than light. **Newton's Laws of Motion** form the basis of most of our understanding of things in motion. These three laws are:

#1 Law of Inertia: A particle at rest will stay at rest and a particle in motion will stay in motion until acted upon by an outside force;

#2 Law of Force versus Mass: The rate of change of a particle is directly proportional to its mass and the force that is exerted on it, or

$$F = m \times a \quad or \quad F = ma$$
(where F is force, m is mass, and a is acceleration);

#3 Law of Action and Reaction: Mutual interactions between bodies produce two forces that are equal in magnitude and opposite in direction; one body exerts a force on the second and the second body exerts an equal force on the first.

The study of classical mechanics is predominately involved with evaluating relationships of motion using equations. When studying relationships in classical mechanics, we usually identify quantities in terms of both their magnitude and direction. These mathematical quantities are called **vectors**. A vector recognizes both the size and direction of the dimension being considered. For example, velocity involves both a speed and a direction of the object. The formula for momentum (p) would then be written as $p = mv$, where p and v are both vector quantities, that is, they represent both a quantity of magnitude (or size) and a direction in which the object is moving. Vectors are identified with either bold letters or an arrow over the letter that indicates direction. It is important to understand how to do vector multiplication in standard physics courses. However, it will not be necessary to practice with vectors in a basic physics course, except to know that this is a standard procedure that may be described in some physics problems you may encounter as you study the material.

The following definitions and equations are those central to the general study of classical mechanics:

— **Work** is the movement of a mass over a distance:

$$\text{Work} = \text{Force} \times \text{Distance}$$
$$W = F \times d \ or \ W = Fd$$

— **Speed** is the rate of change of an object's distance traveled.

$$s = \frac{d}{t}$$

— **Displacement** measures the change in position of an object, using the starting point and ending point and noting the direction. Consider that displacement may be in some cases the same as distance, but in other cases very different. For instance, if a biker traveled from point A to B to C to D in the following diagram, the distance would equal A + B + C + D. However, the displacement would be 0 since the biker started and ended at the same location (ending with no displacement).

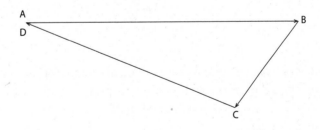

— **Velocity** is the rate of change of displacement; it includes both speed and direction.

$$v = \frac{d}{t}$$

(where v is velocity and has a directional component of plus or minus; d is displacement, t is time)

— **Friction** is the rubbing force that acts against motion between two touching surfaces. Friction between any two objects depends upon the surface attractions or the roughness or smoothness of the two surfaces. The measurement of the amount of friction between any two given objects can be determined experimentally and is designated by the Greek symbol mu, μ, called the coefficient of friction. There are tables that give standard coefficients of friction for some objects that have already been determined experimentally. If μ approaches zero, then there is very little friction. As the value for μ increases, it indicates that there is increasing friction between the objects. For example, tires with worn tread on an icy road would have a low coefficient of friction (μ), and therefore a car with such tires would likely skid. Tires with heavy tread would have a higher coefficient of friction (the addition of sand on the road or chains on the tires would increase this even further) and greatly decrease the likelihood of the car skidding on an icy road.

— **Acceleration** is the rate of change of velocity; it can act in the direction of motion, at an angle, or opposite to the direction of motion.

$$a = \frac{v_2 - v_1}{t_2 - t_1}$$

— **Momentum** is the product of mass and velocity; the quantity of motion for an object.

$$p = mv$$

(where p = momentum)

— **Force** is the push or pull exerted on an object.

$$F = ma$$

$$F = \frac{w}{d}$$

It is also important to note measurements related to mechanics. In science, all measurements are recorded and reported in **metric** units, known as the Système Internationale (International System) or **SI** units:

Mass—measure in kilograms

Length—measured in meters

Time—measured in seconds

Volume—measured in liters

THEORY OF RELATIVITY

Classical mechanics and its resultant laws and equations hold true for systems where we can recognize certain frames of reference. For instance, when a person is traveling on a train going east and walking toward the rear of the train (to the west) while tossing a ball in the air, each of the movements can be described within their own frame of reference whether that be in reference to a point on the ground such as a GPS point (the ball is moving east at x velocity), a spot on the train (the ball is moving west at x velocity), or the person (the ball is moving upward at x velocity).

In 1905, Albert Einstein expanded on the work of Faraday, Lorentz, and Maxwell to propose his **"Special Theory of Relativity."** He stated it in the following two postulates again in 1954:

1. ". . . the same laws of electrodynamics and optics will be valid for all frames of reference for which the equations of mechanics hold good. . . . A coordinate system that is moved uniformly and in a straight line relative to an inertial system is likewise an inertial system. By the 'special principle of relativity' is meant the generalization of this definition to include any natural event whatever: thus, every universal law of nature which is valid in relation to a coordinate system C must also be valid as it stands, in relation to a coordinate system C which is in uniform translatory motion relative to C."

2. "The second principle, on which the special theory of relativity rests, is the 'principle of constant velocity of light in vacuo.' This principle asserts that light in a vacuum always has a definite velocity of propagation (independent of the state of motion of the observer or of the source of the light). The confidence which physicists place in this principle springs from the successes achieved by the electrodynamics of Maxwell and Lorentz." *

In basic terms, Einstein's Special Relativity states that

- the speed of light is a constant,
- the laws of physics are the same in all inertial (non-accelerating) reference frames.

The famous equation that resulted from this theory is

$$E = mc^2$$

where E is energy, m is the mass of an object and c is the speed of light.

What these two postulates logically say is that if you measure the velocity of light c to have a particular value, then no matter which inertial (non-accelerated) reference frame you are moving in, you will always measure it to have the same value; this is an experimental fact. It follows that the velocity of light will be the same regardless of the motion of the object against which it is being measured.

---

*Albert Einstein (1954). *Ideas and Opinions*. Crown Trade Paperbacks.

Classical mechanics "works" because for objects at speeds not approaching the speed of light and at masses much greater than atomic particles, the equations are appropriate. However, Einstein postulated that the speed of light was the only true constant, and that time and distance would always be made relative in order to maintain the speed of light as a constant. In other words, if a plane is traveling toward a given point at 500 miles per hour and shoots a missile forward at 100 mph, you would presume the missile to be traveling at 600 mph at takeoff. The light that is leaving from the plane's warning beacons is presumably also traveling at 500 miles per hour plus the speed of light when it leaves the plane. However, according to Einstein's special theory of relativity, since the speed of light is always constant, the light is actually traveling at the constant speed for light, not that plus 500 mph.

Einstein proposed several experiments to test his special theory of relativity which required equipment and technology unavailable during his time, but which have now been carried out and verified. The experiments have served to confirm Einstein's proposed theories. The theory of special relativity poses questions as to how distance and time might be distorted by travel at the speed of light or by travel in high gravitational fields, which may mimic the effect of speed of light travel. In addition, the special theory of relativity has also added understanding to the field of *quantum mechanics*—the world of very small objects, namely, subatomic particles. Scientists have long known through experimentation that subatomic particles did not follow the laws of classical mechanics, but rather have their own rules for motion. Quantum mechanics explains these classical discrepancies adequately to allow us to work at the subatomic level.

ENERGY

ELECTRICITY AND MAGNETISM

Electrical charges consist of **electrons** (with their negative charge) gathered on the surface of an object. When the electrical charges are not moving, it is called *static electricity*. When a positively charged ion attracts the electron, a spark may occur, which is a transfer or discharge of the electrical charge.

Electrical charges may also move through substances that are called **conductors**. A flow of electrons through a conductor is an **electrical current**. Some elements are good conductors (such as metals); others are poor conductors (called **insulators**). Plastic, rubber, glass, and wood are insulators.

An electrical **circuit** is the path that an electric current follows. Every electric circuit has four parts—

1. a *source of charge* (voltage) [a battery, generator, or AC source],

2. a *set of conductors* [wires],

3. a *load* [light, meter, appliance, etc.], and

4. a *switch.*

A **closed circuit** is one that has a continuous path for electron flow (no interruptions). An **open circuit** has no flow of electrons because the pathway is interrupted (by a switch, disconnection, etc.).

Voltage refers to the electromotive force that pushes electrons through the circuit. **Amperage** is the measure of the amount of electron flow or current. **Resistance** is a hindrance to current due to objects that deter the current by their size, shape, or type of conductor.

SERIES AND PARALLEL CIRCUITS

In a series circuit, there is only one path along which the electrons may flow, moving around the circuit along this single pathway from the positive to the negative pole of the battery (source). The current flows through each component in succession. Linking this group of electric cells in a series means that the voltage of the circuit will be equal to the sum total of the voltages in each cell added together.

In a parallel circuit, the electrical devices are connected to provide two or more paths through which the current may flow. Linking electrical cells in parallel will increase the amperage of the circuit (the current of the circuit will equal the sum of the currents in each cell).

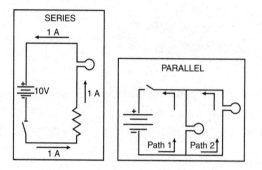

Fig. 3–37   Series and Parallel Circuits.

MAGNETISM

Magnetism is defined as the ability of a substance to produce a magnetic field. The magnetic field acts like point charges (in electricity) producing north (N) and south (S) poles. When magnets are placed in close proximity to each other, the similar poles repel, while opposite poles attract. Magnets can be either permanent or temporary. Permanent magnets are ones that contain natural magnetic ore, such as iron, cobalt or nickel, the three natural elements with magnetic properties. Temporary magnets are ones that can be induced to carry a magnetic field but will not hold the magnetic field permanently. Electromagnets are electrically induced magnets usually created by wrapping coils of wire around an iron core.

WAVES: SOUND AND LIGHT

The study of waves is very important in science. Many things in nature travel in waves, including sound, light, and water. A wave has no mass of its own; it is simply movement within a medium, a disturbance that does not cause the medium itself to move significantly.

There are different types of waves with different types of movement. Light and ocean waves travel in transverse waves. A **transverse wave** causes particles to move up and down while the wave moves forward (perpendicular to the wave motion). Sound and some earthquake waves travel as longitudinal (compression) waves. In a **longitudinal wave** the particles move back and forth but in the same direction as (parallel with) the wave motion.

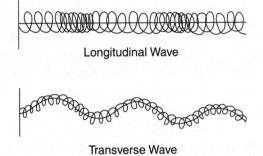

Fig. 3–38 Longitudinal and Transverse Waves.

Properties of waves are described with the following terms. The **wavelength** of a wave is defined as the distance from one crest (or top) of a wave to the next crest on the same side. The **frequency** of a wave is the number of wavelengths that pass a point in a second.

Waves also interact with each other in various ways. Wave **interference** can occur between waves. Interference can increase wave amplitude if the crests and troughs of the waves coincide. If the crest and trough of two waves coincide, they can cancel each other or reduce the amplitude. Waves can also be **reflected** when they hit a surface.

The speed of a wave can be described by the equation: $v = f\lambda$, where v = the speed of the wave, f = frequency of the wave, λ = wavelength of the wave.

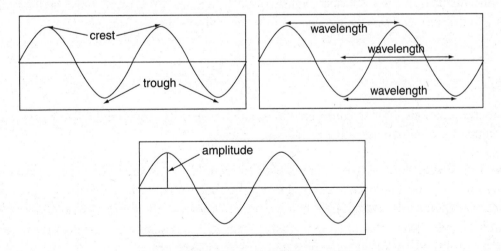

Fig. 3–39 Properties of Waves.

SOUND

Sound travels in longitudinal waves. Sound waves are made when an object vibrates and causes air molecules to take on a compression wave motion. This motion is picked up by our eardrums and translated in our brains into sounds. Changes in amplitude account for volume changes, while changes in frequency result in pitch changes.

Anyone who has stood beside a train track and heard the sound of the train whistle or horn has noticed that it sounds the same as the train approaches. As soon as the train passes by, however, the pitch of the horn begins to drop at a regularly reducing pattern as the train moves away from the listener. This phenomenon is known as the "Doppler effect." What is happening here?

As the train approaches, the sound coming to the ear is being pushed by compression waves so that it arrives at the speed of sound, which is the sum of the speed of sound in air plus the speed of the train. Since the sound wave hits the ear drum at the speed of sound or greater, it maintains its regular pitch. However, as the train passes the ear, the speed of the sound wave will begin to decrease proportionately to the ratio of the speed of sound divided by the speed of sound minus the train's speed away from the listener. This results in a lowering of the horn's pitch according to the following equation:

$$f_0 = \left(\frac{v}{v - v_s}\right) f_s$$

where the frequency of the detected sound will be f_o, v is the velocity of sound in air, vs is the velocity of the train, and fs is the frequency of the emitted sound wave from the train.

LIGHT

In many situations, light is considered to travel in waves. However, light also has characteristics indicative of a particle, rather than simply a wave.

The Light Spectrum—A spectrum is used to identify the arrangement of the components of a light wave according to wavelength. The visible spectrum of light is the arrangement of the visible wavelengths in a beam of light in the order red orange, yellow, green, blue, violet. Different kinds of light have different spectra. Fluorescent light has sharper bands than incandescent light (light bulb). Sunlight has more blue and violet in its spectrum.

Light travels in straight lines until it hits an object. In order to see an object your eye must intercept a ray of light traveling straight from it. To understand how light affects how things are seen, it is important to understand the ways that light moves by reviewing the following terms:

Diffraction—the bending of a light wave around an obstacle

Reflection—the bouncing of a wave of light off an object

Refraction—the change of direction of a wave as it passes from one medium to another

■ THE UNIVERSE

ASTRONOMY

GALAXIES

A **galaxy** is a system that contains stars, star systems (like our solar system), dust, and any other objects within range of the gravitation of its star systems. While all galaxies are massive in scale, the galaxy our solar system resides in, the Milky Way, is thought to be of average size. It is known to contain hundreds of billions of stars including our Sun. Galaxies come in a myriad of shapes and take on various overall colors, but ours is a rotating spiral of milky white. It is theorized that at the center of most galaxies is a black hole. Recent data from space probes and telescopes has given scientists important insights into the nature of black holes. Scientists theorize that these incredibly dense areas of matter arise from remnants of a large star (or the collision of stars) that implodes after a supernova explosion. Once the mass of the star becomes large enough, it collapses under the force of its own gravity. As it collapses, the surface of the star nears an imaginary surface called the "event horizon," as time on the star becomes slower than the time kept by observers far away. When the surface reaches the event horizon, time stands still, and the star can collapse no more. This object contains enough gravity to pull entire star systems into its grasp.

Fig. 3–40   Center of Milky Way Galaxy orbiting a black hole.
Courtesy of NASA

STARS

The core of our Sun, along with most stars, begins with hydrogen. With the core temperature of stars being over 10 million Kelvin, and the tremendous pressures they contain, protons can fuse together to produce helium, gamma ray energy, positrons and neutrinos. These neutrinos are nearly massless and charge-less. They do not interact with other matter very much and flow almost unimpeded throughout the universe. It is speculated that neutrinos produced in the center of the Sun sweep through the average human's body here on Earth at a rate of billions per second.

Stars are huge masses of plasma with colossal amounts of energy and gravity. Many stars are held in by magnetic fields, but particles slip through occasional holes in the fields. The atoms are so hot, the protons, neutrons, and electrons move rapidly and react with each other, thus releasing energy. This energy moves out from stars in electromagnetic waves, producing heat and light. We are too far from most stars to notice their heat, but their light still reaches us.

The stars consist of incredible amounts of matter. Since we know all matter has gravity, stars have very large gravitational forces. Many stars have their own systems, like our solar system with planets, asteroids, and moons orbiting them.

The stars are arrayed in the sky in patterns that ancient people named for various creatures and objects (scales, scorpions, archers, etc.). We call these the zodiac. Travelers have used the zodiac for navigation since biblical times. In addition, Polaris, the North Star, sits directly over our North Pole so it can be used to determine directions on the Earth.

Current scientific theory, including the theory of the **Big Bang**, describes the birth of our universe as a massive explosion occurring approximately fifteen billion years ago. The matter and energy that became the universe was compacted into an infinitely small area. It then began an expansion process at an explosive rate that slowed down over time but that is theorized to still be occurring. The simplest components of matter—protons, neutrons, electrons—came into being and over time condensed into particles of matter. Over hundreds of thousands of years of expansion and cooling, gases condensed and stars were formed, then galaxies, and much later solar systems.

Since the beginning of the universe, stars have been forming and dying. Stars begin as large masses of dust and cosmic gases that collapse together due to gravitational forces. This process of collapse may take millions of years, and during this time the mass is called a nebulae or a proto-star. Over time a process of nuclear fusion of hydrogen (and later helium) atoms begins to power the star at its core, and this will fuel it as a main sequence star for the rest of its life. As the star grows in size, powered by the nuclear fusion reactor at its core, it eventually reaches a red giant phase. Our Sun is a red giant. Eventually, the star will consume its supply of nuclear fuel, and the core will collapse on itself due to its own gravity. At this point it is called a white dwarf. Very large stars may explode into supernovas then coalesce into a dense neutron star or a black hole.

THE SUN

Our Sun is a mid-size star that emits heat and light energy. There are stars much larger than our Sun and stars that are smaller. Our Sun is about ten times more massive than the largest planet in the solar system (Jupiter) and 109 times larger than the Earth's diameter.

The Sun releases incredible amounts of energy as protons interact with each other (nuclear fusion). The energy is in the form of heat and light radiation, providing heat and light for life on Earth.

THE SOLAR SYSTEM

Our solar system consists of all of the common celestial bodies such as planets, moons, asteroids, and various types of space debris that orbit the Sun.

A planet is a celestial body that (a) is in orbit around the Sun, (b) has sufficient mass for its self-gravity to assume a nearly round shape, and (c) has cleared the neighborhood around its orbit.

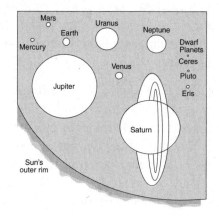

Fig. 3–41   Approximate relative sizes of planets in relation to the Sun.

The characteristics of the planets vary greatly because of their size, composition, and distance from the Sun. It is easy to remember the eight planets in order, starting with the closest to the Sun, by learning the following sentence: <u>M</u>y <u>V</u>ery <u>E</u>ducated <u>M</u>other <u>J</u>ust <u>S</u>erved <u>U</u>s <u>N</u>oodles. The beginning letter of each word in this sentence is the beginning letter of a planet (Mercury, Venus, Earth, Mars, Jupiter, Saturn, Uranus, and Neptune).

Planet	Type of Planet	Size (to nearest thousand)	Average Distance from Sun (in Miles/Km)	Number of Moons
Mercury	Terrestrial	3,000 mi (5,000 km)	36 million miles (58 million km)	0
Venus	Terrestrial	8,000 mi (12,000 km)	67 million miles (108 million km)	0
Earth	Terrestrial	8,000 mi (13,000 km)	93 million mi. (150 million km)	1

Planet	Type of Planet	Size (to nearest thousand)	Average Distance from Sun (in Miles/Km)	Number of Moons
Mars	Terrestrial	4,000 mi (7,000 km)	142 million mi. (228 million km.)	2
Jupiter	Gas Giant	89,000 mi (143,000 km)	483 million mi. (778 million km.)	67
Saturn	Gas Giant	75,000 mi (120,000 km)	885 million mi. (1,426 million km.)	62
Uranus	Gas Giant	32,000 mi (51,000 km)	1,787 million mi. (2,877 milion km.)	27
Neptune	Gas Giant	31,000 mi (50,000 km)	2,800 million mi. (4.508 million km.)	13

From the table above, you can note several trends about the planets of our solar system. The **terrestrial planets** are so named because they are composed of solid elements. As distance from the Sun increases, so does the size of the planet, and from that information you can infer that the mass of the planet also increases. The planets inside the asteroid belt (which lies outside Mars) are significantly larger and have more mass. The composition of these planets is also different. Being farther from the Sun, they are much colder and are composed of mostly gases with huge atmospheric layers. They are called the **Gas Giants**. Their distance from the Sun means their orbital around the Sun is much longer, making their year much longer. These planets also have much stronger gravitational attraction, since gravity is a function of mass. Therefore, they have captured many more moons into their orbit than the smaller terrestrial planets.

In addition to the planets orbiting our Sun, our solar system also has asteroids and several other minor planets and other space objects. Asteroids are irregular masses of rock and metal that are smaller than planets. There is an asteroid belt between Mars and Jupiter and another beyond the orbit of Neptune.

The outer Solar System is home to comets, masses of frozen gas that travel in orbital patterns. At times, comets travel near the Sun, where the tail of the comet begins to melt and form a stream of gas giving them a long extended look.

Fig. 3–42 Halley's Comet.
Courtesy of NASA

Our calendar year is a measure of the time the Earth takes to orbit the Sun. Each year Earth completes one trip around the Sun in about 365 days. The seasons we experience on Earth are a result of the inclination of the Earth on its axis. That is, if you were to draw a line through the Earth's poles, the line would not be perpendicular with the Earth's orbit around the Sun (see Fig. 10–4).

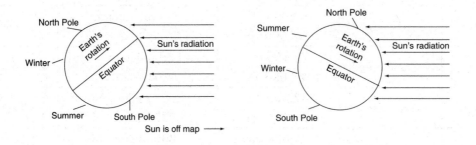

Fig. 3–43   Tilt of the Earth and seasons.

The Earth's axis tilts at an angle of twenty-three and one-half degrees with its orbit. The tilt means that the Northern Hemisphere will be tilted toward the Sun for half the orbit, and the Southern Hemisphere will be tilted for the other half (half-a-year). The hemisphere tilted toward the Sun absorbs more of the solar radiation during that half of the year and experiences summer. The hemisphere tilted away from the Sun experiences winter.

The orbit of the Moon around the Earth occurs approximately every twenty-nine days. This is the origin of our months. A day is the time the Earth takes to rotate one time on its axis. An hour is simply a division of the rotation of the Earth (one day) obtained by dividing the globe into twenty-four time zones.

THE MOON

Our view of the Moon is constantly changing as the Moon orbits Earth and as Earth rotates on its axis. Our daily view of the Moon changes as it moves around Earth along its regular orbital path. The changes we see in the shape and location of the Moon are regular in their occurrence because of the regular nature of the rotation and orbit. The Moon orbits around the Earth once approximately every twenty-nine days (one lunar month). The Moon's rotation on its axis is synchronous with its orbit, so we always see the same side of the Moon reflecting the sunlight.

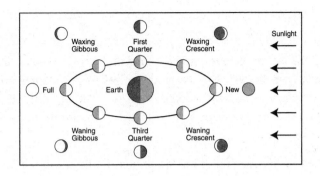

Fig. 3–44   The Phases of the Moon.

The Moon does not emit any of its own light, but reflects the light from the Sun. Our daily view of the Moon changes during its orbit of the Earth. The phases that we see are a result of the angle between the Earth, Moon, and Sun as viewed by us from Earth.

A *new moon* occurs when the Moon is directly between the Earth and the Sun. At this point, the Moon will rise at about 6:00 a.m. and set at about 6:00 p.m. (on standard, not daylight saving, time). The lighted side of the Moon is toward the Sun, so our view is of the dark side only (we don't see it at all).

Following the new moon, the Moon (continuing its orbit) moves so that we see an increasing portion of the lit side each night. We call this the *waxing crescent moon.*

In about a week, the angle between the Earth, Sun, and Moon is 90°, allowing us to see half its lighted surface, the *first quarter*. This 90° angle means the Moon rises halfway through the day at about noon, and sets at about midnight.

For the following week, we see more of the Moon's surface each night (*waxing gibbous*) until the full moon, which marks the middle of the lunar orbit (and the lunar month).

During the *full moon*, the Earth/Moon/Sun angle is 180°, meaning the Earth is between the Sun and the Moon so we see the entire bright half of its surface. The full moon rises near sundown and sets near sunrise, opposite the Sun (see Fig. 10–6).

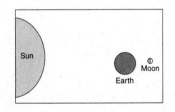

Fig. 3–45   Positioning of Full Moon.

During the remaining two weeks of the lunar month, the Moon wanes through another gibbous moon to the third quarter (the other half of the Moon's lit surface is visible rising around midnight and setting at noon). It wanes through another crescent moon and on until it returns to the beginning of the orbital—the new moon.

We view the Moon "rising" in the east and "setting" in the west as the Earth rotates on its axis. The Moon's orbit is nearly in the same plane as the orbits of the planets around the Sun, so we view the Moon near that plane in the sky called the *ecliptic*. The tilt of the Earth on its axis means the ecliptic is visible (to those in the northern hemisphere of the Earth) in the southern sky at varying heights through the seasons.

At most times, the angle between the Sun, Moon, and Earth at full and new moon is such that there is no blockage of the view of the Moon or Sun. However, when, during a full moon, the Earth lies directly in the path between the Earth viewer and the Moon, it is called a lunar eclipse, since the Earth blocks the light of the Sun from reaching the Moon for a period of time.

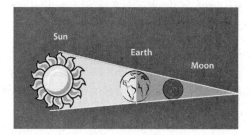

Fig. 3–46   Lunar Eclipse.

▪EARTH

▪ATMOSPHERE

The atmosphere is comprised of several layers of gases immediately surrounding the Earth. Earth's atmosphere is an essential feature that allows our planet to sustain life. It extends approximately 560 km (350 miles) from the surface of the Earth, though the actual thickness varies from place to place. Our atmosphere makes Earth a habitable planet for people, plants, and animals by absorbing the Sun's energy, recycling and preserving water and chemicals needed for life, and by moderating our weather patterns. The atmosphere is attracted to and maintained by the force of gravity of the Earth.

Without the protection of our atmosphere, Earth would be subjected to the extreme freezing temperatures found in the vacuum of space. The Earth would also be bombarded by dangerous amounts of radiant energy from the Sun. Our atmosphere is specifically formulated to provide us with an environment suited to our needs.

Earth's atmosphere (Fig. 3–47) is made up of about 78% nitrogen, 21% oxygen, slightly less than 1% argon, and the remaining fraction of 1% contains small amounts of other gases (including carbon dioxide, helium, hydrogen, krypton, methane, neon, nitrogen dioxide, nitrous oxide, ozone, sulfur dioxide, water vapor, and xenon).

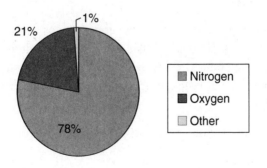

Fig. 3–47 Atmospheric Composition.

We identify five distinct layers (called strata) of atmosphere: the troposphere, stratosphere, mesosphere, thermosphere, and exosphere. Each layer differs from the others by its temperature, density, and chemical composition. Four transition zones separate the four atmospheric layers: the tropopause, stratopause, mesopause, and thermopause.

The **troposphere** is the atmospheric layer closest to the Earth's surface. It extends to an altitude of approximately 8 to 15 kilometers (5 to 9 miles). The force of gravity is strongest nearest the surface of the Earth, thus the number of gas molecules per area (density) is greatest at the lowest altitudes. In addition, the density of gas molecules decreases as altitude increases. Therefore, the troposphere is the densest atmospheric layer, accounting for most of the mass of the atmosphere.

The troposphere contains 99% of the water vapor found in the atmosphere. Water vapor in the air absorbs solar energy and absorbs heat that radiates back from the Earth's surface. The water vapor concentration within the troposphere is greatest near the equator and lowest at the poles.

Nearly all weather phenomena experienced on Earth are caused by the interactions of gases (including water vapor) within the troposphere. The temperature of the troposphere decreases as altitude increases from about 16°C (60°F) nearest Earth's surface to –65°C (–85°F) at the tropopause. (Temperatures are averages of all the temperatures over the surface of the Earth and across all seasons.) For every kilometer in altitude above the Earth, the temperature drops approximately 6°C within the troposphere.

The troposphere is separated from the next layer (the stratosphere) by the tropopause.

The **stratosphere** is above the troposphere. The stratosphere extends from the tropopause (found approximately 14 km or 9 miles above the Earth's surface) to approximately 48 km (30 miles) above the Earth's surface. The stratosphere contains much less water vapor than the troposphere. The gases of the stratosphere are much less dense than in the troposphere as well.

The temperature within the lower stratosphere (up to about 25 km altitude) is mostly constant. In the upper stratosphere, the temperature rises gradually with increased altitude to a temperature of approximately 3°C. The rising temperatures are caused by the absorption of ultraviolet radiation from the Sun by ozone molecules.

Ozone (O_3) molecules form the ozone layer at the upper ranges of the stratosphere. Ozone molecules absorb solar ultraviolet radiation, which is converted to kinetic energy (heat). This process accounts for the increased temperature levels as altitude increases within the stratosphere. The ozone layer also performs the crucial function of protecting organisms from the harmful effects of too much ultraviolet radiation.

The stratosphere is separated from the next atmospheric layer (the mesosphere) by the stratopause.

The **mesosphere** is the atmospheric layer found at approximately 50–80 km altitude. The mesosphere is characterized by temperatures decreasing with increased altitude from about 3°C at the stratopause to –110°C at 80 km. The mesosphere has a low density of molecules with very little ozone or water vapor. The atmospheric gases of the upper mesosphere separate into layers of gases according to molecular mass. This phenomenon is caused by the weakened effects of gravity on the gas molecules (because of distance from Earth). Lighter (low molecular mass) gases are found at the higher altitudes.

The **mesopause** separates the stratosphere from the next layer, the thermosphere.

The **thermosphere** is found at altitudes of approximately 80 to 480 kilometers. Gas molecules of the thermosphere are widely separated, resulting in very low gas density. The absorption of solar radiation by oxygen molecules in the thermosphere causes the temperature to rise to approximately 1980°C at the upper levels of the thermosphere.

The final layer, the **exosphere** extends from the **thermopause** at approximately 480 km to an altitude of 960 to 1000 kilometers. The exosphere, however, is difficult to define and is more of a transitional area between Earth and space than a distinct layer. The low gravitational forces at this altitude hold only the lightest molecules, mostly hydrogen and helium. Even these are at very low densities.

In addition to the names of the five atmospheric layers, some other terms describe various levels of the atmosphere. The troposphere and tropopause together are sometimes referred to as the "lower atmosphere." The stratosphere and mesosphere are sometimes called the "middle atmosphere," while the thermosphere and exosphere are together known as the "upper atmosphere." Still other scientists call the entire lower area of Earth's atmosphere, embracing the troposphere, mesosphere, and stratosphere together as the "homosphere," and term the thermosphere and exosphere together the "heterosphere."

The **ionosphere** includes portions of the mesosphere and thermosphere. The term *ionosphere* refers to the portion of the atmosphere where ultraviolet radiation causes excitation of atoms resulting in extreme temperatures. Under extreme temperature conditions, electrons are actually separated from the atoms. The highly excited atoms are left with a positive charge. Charged atoms (ions) form layers within the thermosphere. The charged layers are referred to as the ionosphere. The charged particles within the ionosphere deflect some radio signals. While some radio frequencies are not affected by the ionosphere, others are. This reflection of some radio signals causes some radio frequencies (particularly AM transmissions) to be received far from their origination point.

Solar flares create magnetic storms in the thermosphere near Earth's poles. These storms temporarily strip electrons from atoms. When the electrons rejoin the atoms, brilliant light (in green and red) is emitted as they return to their normal state. These lights are called **auroras,** or the Northern and Southern lights.

The total weight of the atmosphere exerts force on the Earth. This force is known as **atmospheric pressure** and can be measured with a **barometer.**

EARTH'S LAYERS

The **geosphere** is the solid or mineral part of the Earth. It consists of layers, from the outer crust down to the inner core separated according to density and temperature. There are two ways to classify the composition of the geosphere:

1. chemically, into crust, mantle, and core, or

2. functionally, into lithosphere and asthenosphere.

CRUST, MANTLE, AND CORE

The density of the Earth averages three times that of water. This density varies depending upon the layer of the Earth being considered.

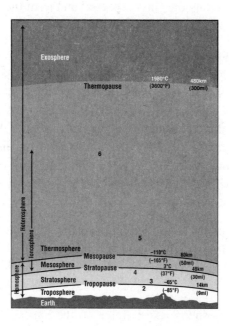

Fig. 3–48   Layers of the Atmosphere. 1: Mt. Everest; 2: Commercial Jet; 3: Fighter Jet; 4: Ozone Layer; 5: Auroras; 6: Space Shuttle.

The **crust** is the outermost layer of the geosphere, what we think of as "the Earth." It includes the mountains, valleys, continents, ocean beds, etc. The crust is rich in oxygen, silicon, and aluminum, with lesser amounts of other elements like iron, nickel, etc. It has low density (2.5 to 3.5 gm/cm^3), that allows it to float on the denser mantle. It is brittle and breaks relatively easily. It is made up mostly of sedimentary rocks resting on a base of igneous rocks. Several separate tectonic plates float beneath it on the surface of the mantle.

It is estimated that the entire surface of the Earth can re-form in about 500 million years through erosion and subsequent re-creation through tectonic activity.

The **mantle** is the complex middle layer of the geosphere. It is a broad layer of dense rock and metal oxides that lies between the molten core and the crust and extends to a depth of between 40 and 2,900 kilometers. It accounts for around 82% of the Earth's volume and is thought to be made up mostly of iron, magnesium, silicon, and oxygen. Analysis of seismic waves shows that the material that makes up the mantle behaves as aplastic—a substance with the properties of a solid but which flows under pressure. More precisely, the mantle consists of rigid and plastic zones.

The **core** is the innermost layer of the geosphere, composed of mostly iron and nickel. It extends from a depth of about 2,900 kilometers to nearly 6,400 kilometers (1,800 to 3,900 miles). It is extremely hot, even after thousands (to millions) of years of cooling. The core has two layers, the liquid **outer core,** and the solid iron **inner core** at the Earth's center. Even with the high temperatures at the center (up to 7,500K, hotter than the Sun's surface), this layer is solid due to the immense pressure of the overlying layers.

The material that makes up the Earth's interior is similar to that of liquid steel, but it maintains a fluidic consistency. This results in the migration of Earth's material toward the equator due to angular momentum caused by the spinning of the Earth. The effect is that the equatorial radius is about 21 kilometers larger than the polar radius, which results in its oblate spheroid shape.

Another way to classify the layers is into the lithosphere and asthenosphere. The rigid outermost layer of the geosphere (from the Greek *lithos*—stone) is called the **lithosphere.** The upper layer of the lithosphere is the crust. Beneath the crust is a layer of rigid mantle. The **asthenosphere** is the molten plastic outer mantle of hot silicate rock beneath the lithosphere (from the Greek *asthenos*—devoid of force).

THE DISCONTINUITIES

The **Mohorovicic** discontinuity or **Moho** is the sharp boundary between the crust and mantle. The **Gutenberg** discontinuity separates the mantle from the core.

THE HYDROSPHERE

The Earth is unique among planets in the solar system because of the large quantities of water that cover its surface. This water is responsible for much of its formation and dynamics. The interconnections between climate and geophysical processes due to hydrology are complex. Two-thirds of the planet's surface is covered by water at an average ocean depth of 3.9 kilometers (12,795 feet). The water area is 3.6×10^8 square kilometers (nearly 140 million square miles).

THE MAGNETOSPHERE

The magnetic field that surrounds the Earth extends thousands of miles into outer space. It mimics a bar magnet with the poles being approximately located at the north and south poles and a neutral area at the equator. The poles shift slightly over time. The power of the Earth's magnet is not very strong, being approximately .5 Gauss at the surface of the Earth.

The location of the North Magnetic Pole was determined in 1996 by a Canadian expedition and certified by magnetometer and theodolite at 78°35.7′N 104°11.9′W. In 2005, the location was at 82.7°N 114.4°W, slightly west of Ellesmere Island in Northern Canada. It is clear that the magnetic field moves over time.

The Geologic Column

The estimated age of Earth is determined by radiometric dating and geological estimates to be about 4.6 billion years. The geologic column represents the layers of the Earth near the surface that contain fossils and various types of sediment. The geologic column is currently used as a tool of evolutionary uniformitarian scientists to display a "progression" of life from simple species in the deepest (oldest) layers to more complex species in the layers closer to the surface (younger). The layers are categorized into Eras, Periods, and Epochs. Fig. 3–49 represents the general arrangement of the geologic column.

Geologic Time Scale

Eon	Era	Period	Epoch	Age (my)
Phanerozoic (Visible Life)	Cenozoic (Recent Life) (Age of Mammals)	Quaternary	Holocene	0.01
			Pleistocene	1.6
		Tertiary	Pliocene	5.3
			Miocene	23.7
			Oligocene	36.6
			Eocene	57.8
			Paleocene	66.4
	Mesozoic (Middle Life) (Age of Reptiles)	Cretaceous		144
		Jurassic		208
		Triassic		245
	Paleozoic (Ancient Life)	Permian		286
		Pennsylvanian		320
		Mississippian		360
		Devonian		408
		Silurian		438
		Ordovician		505
		Cambrian		570
Proterozoic (Early Life)				
Archean		Oldest Known Life		2500
Hadean		Oldest Known Rocks		3900
		Age of Earth		4600

Fig. 3–49   Geologic Column.

PRACTICE TEST

CLEP Natural Sciences

Also available at the REA Study Center (*www.rea.com/studycenter*)

This practice test is also available online at the REA Study Center. The CLEP Natural Sciences test is only offered as a computer-based exam; therefore, we recommend that you take the online version of the practice test to receive these added benefits:

- **Timed testing conditions** – Gauge how much time you can spend on each question.
- **Automatic scoring** – Find out how you did on the test, instantly.
- **On-screen detailed explanations of answers** – Learn not just the correct answer, but also why the other answer choices are incorrect.
- **Diagnostic score reports** – Pinpoint where you're strongest and where you need to focus your study.

Need more practice? Go to the REA Study Center and take Practice Test 2.

PRACTICE TEST

CLEP NATURAL SCIENCES

(Answer sheet can be found on page 541.)

TIME: 90 Minutes
Approximately 120 Questions

> **DIRECTIONS:** Each of the following groups of questions consists of five lettered terms followed by a list of numbered phrases or sentences. For each numbered phrase or sentence, select the one choice that is most clearly related to it. Each choice may be used once, more than once, or not at all. Fill in the corresponding oval on the answer sheet.

Questions 1–5

    (A) Secretory vesicle
    (B) Smooth endoplasmic reticulum
    (C) Microvilli
    (D) Nucleolus
    (E) Nuclear pore

1. _____ Communication channel between the cytoplasm and nucleoplasm

2. _____ Extensions that provide extra surface area for absorption

3. _____ Contain digestive enzymes

4. _____ Packets that carry substances (hormones, fats, etc.) synthesized within the cell

5. _____ Network of membranes that deliver lipids and proteins throughout the cytoplasm

Questions 6–8

    (A) KCl
    (B) NaF
    (C) Cu
    (D) SiC
    (E) $HC_2H_3O_2$

6. _____ Atoms are held together with network covalent attraction.

7. _____ Atoms are held together with covalent attraction.

8. _____ Atoms are held together with metallic attraction.

Questions 9–13

    (A) Nodes
    (B) Nonvascular plants
    (C) Angiosperms
    (D) Gymnosperms
    (E) Lateral buds

9. _____ Bryophytes

10. _____ Flowering plants

11. _____ Shoots and roots

12. _____ Produce seeds without flowers

13. _____ Conifers and cycads

Questions 14–16

    (A) Radiation
    (B) Convection
    (C) Irradiation
    (D) Conduction
    (E) Diffusion

14. _____ An athlete with a sore shoulder places a warm compress on it to transfer energy to soothe the muscle.

15. _____ On a cold February morning, a blower system in a car warms up after several minutes and blows air through vents in the floor, dashboard, and windshield. Eventually, the driver is able to unbutton his coat and stay warm when the outside temperature is still 23°F.

16. _____ Getting ready for a fall cruise inspires a young lady to spend a couple of weeks going to a local spa and reclining under a tanning lamp. However, such practices might result in dangerous overexposure to ultraviolet rays that can lead to cancer or premature aging of the skin.

Questions 17–19

    (A) H_2
    (B) $KMnO_4$
    (C) MgO
    (D) KCI
    (E) Fe_2O_3

17. _____ This substance is a very strong oxidizing agent.

18. _____ The metal in this substance has an oxidation number of +2.

19. _____ The oxidation potential of this substance is zero.

Questions 20–24

    (A) Natality
    (B) J-curve
    (C) Population rate of growth
    (D) Mortality
    (E) S-curve

20. _____ Exponential population growth curve; population growth accelerates

21. _____ Birth rate minus death rate

22. _____ Death rate

23. _____ Birth rate

24. _____ Logistic population growth curve; population growth accelerates and then slows down because of limits

DIRECTIONS: Each of the questions or incomplete statements below is followed by five possible answers or completions. Select the best choice in each case and fill in the corresponding oval on the answer sheet.

25. Starting from rest, the distance a freely falling object will fall in 0.5 seconds is about

    (A) 0.5 m.
    (B) 1.0 m.
    (C) 1.25 m.
    (D) 5.0 m.
    (E) 5.25 m.

26. Which of the following mechanisms of evolution can produce genetic changes in a community that did not originally exist in the gene pool?

    (A) genetic drift
    (B) allopatric speciation
    (C) sympatric speciation
    (D) mutation
    (E) natural selection

27. Which of the following statements is NOT correct when cells undergo meiosis?

    (A) Meiosis ensures that the chromosome number remains constant generation after generation.
    (B) Meiosis ensures that each generation has a different genetic makeup than the previous one.
    (C) Meiosis ensures that each newly-formed daughter cell receives the same number and kinds of chromosomes.
    (D) Meiosis results in four daughter cells.
    (E) Meiosis occurs in the production of egg and sperm cells in animals.

28. Which of the following classification groups is known for radial symmetry in most of its species?

    (A) felidae
    (B) echinodermata
    (C) platyhelminthes
    (D) chondrichthyes
    (E) Astralopithicus

29. Which of the following processes results in genetic variation?

    (A) interphase
    (B) meiosis
    (C) metaphase
    (D) prophase
    (E) mitosis

30. The evolution of plant species is considered to have begun with

    (A) autotrophic prokaryotic cells
    (B) heterotrophic eukaryotic cells
    (C) aerobic eukaryotic cells
    (D) pre-nucleic eukaryotic cells
    (E) aerobic prokaryotic cells

31. What type of a wave is a sound wave?

    (A) Compression
    (B) Transverses
    (C) Inverse
    (D) Converse
    (E) Convex

32. Salinity is a measure of dissolved solids in water. On average, 1,000 g of typical sea water contains 35 g of salt. The level of salinity is below average in areas where large amounts of freshwater enter the ocean and above average in hot, arid climates. The Mediterranean and the Red seas are adjacent to deserts. The water in these two seas would be expected to have

(A) above-average salinity
(B) below-average salinity
(C) average salinity
(D) no salt content
(E) cold temperatures

33. The discoveries of Galileo Galilei (1564–1642) and Isaac Newton (1642–1727) precipitated the scientific revolution of the seventeenth century. Stressing the use of detailed measurements during experimentation enabled them to frame several universal laws of nature and to overthrow many of Aristotle's (384–322 BCE) erroneous ideas about motion, which were based on sheer reasoning alone. One of these universal laws is now known as the law of inertia or Newton's first law of motion. According to this law, objects in motion tend to stay in motion and objects at rest tend to stay at rest unless acted upon by an external force. The more mass (inertia) an object has, the more resistance it offers to changes in its state of motion. According to the law of inertia, which of the following would offer the greatest resistance to a change in its motion?

(A) A pellet of lead shot
(B) A golf ball
(C) A large watermelon
(D) A feather
(E) A sheet of notebook paper

34. The site of transfer for nutrients, water, and waste between a mammalian mother and embryo is the

(A) yolk sac membrane
(B) uterus
(C) placenta
(D) umbilical membrane
(E) ovary

35. The process of genetic inheritance was first investigated and explained by

(A) Robert Hooke
(B) Dmitri Mendeleev
(C) Theodor Schwann
(D) Matthias Schleiden
(E) Gregor Mendel

36. The first cells to evolve on Earth were most likely NOT

(A) anaerobic
(B) specialized
(C) prokaryotic
(D) aquatic
(E) small

37. Which of the following best represents the sequence of human evolution?

(A) *Australopithecus afarensis*, Cro-Magnon, *Homo erectus*, *Homo sapiens*, Modern man
(B) Cro-Magnon, *Australopithecus afarensis*, *Homo erectus*, *Homo sapiens*
(C) *Homo sapiens*, *Australopithecus afarensis*, *Homo erectus*, Cro-Magnon
(D) *Australopithecus afarensis*, *Homo erectus*, Cro-Magnon, Modern man
(E) Cro-Magnon, *Homo erectus*, *Australopithecus afarensis*, Modern man

38. Which of the following demonstrates pi bonding?

    (A) OH^2
    (B) H^1
    (C) C_2H_2
    (D) H_2S
    (E) KCl

39. The Sun crosses the celestial equator going north on March 21. This is known as the

    (A) solstice
    (B) lunar eclipse
    (C) solar eclipse
    (D) spring equinox
    (E) autumnal equinox

40. Cells of eukaryotes have all of the following EXCEPT

    (A) membraned organelles
    (B) DNA organized into chromosomes
    (C) a nucleus
    (D) DNA floating free in the cytoplasm
    (E) ribosomes

41. A small non-protein molecule such as iron that works with enzymes to promote catalysis is known as

    (A) a protein
    (B) an inorganic cofactor
    (C) a coenzyme
    (D) a hormone
    (E) a carbohydrate

42. Which of the following will NOT inhibit enzymatic reactions?

    (A) Temperature
    (B) pH level
    (C) Particular chemical agents
    (D) Lack of substrate
    (E) Large amount of enzyme

For questions 43–46, identify the answer that corresponds with the correct functional group.

(A)
$$R - \overset{\overset{\displaystyle H}{|}}{\underset{\underset{\displaystyle H}{|}}{C}} - OH$$

(D)
$$R - \overset{\overset{\displaystyle}{\|}}{\underset{\underset{\displaystyle O}{}}{C}} - R$$

(B)
$$R - \overset{\overset{\displaystyle}{\|}}{\underset{\underset{\displaystyle O}{}}{C}} - H$$

(E)
$$R - \overset{\overset{\displaystyle}{\|}}{\underset{\underset{\displaystyle O}{}}{C}} - OH$$

(C)
$$R - \overset{\overset{\displaystyle}{\|}}{\underset{\underset{\displaystyle O}{}}{C}} - O - \overset{\overset{\displaystyle H}{|}}{\underset{\underset{\displaystyle H}{|}}{C}} - R$$

43. _____ Ketone

44. _____ Alcohol

45. _____ Ester

46. _____ Aldehyde

47. The conversion of light energy into chemical energy is accomplished by

    (A) catabolism
    (B) oxidative phosphorylation
    (C) metabolism
    (D) protein synthesis
    (E) photosynthesis

48. Which of the following terms is defined as the increase in the statistical disorder of a physical system?

    (A) Enthalpy
    (B) Entropy
    (C) Epathy
    (D) Euprophy
    (E) Empathy

49. Which of the following evolutionary developments is out of sequence?

   (A) Formation of coacervates occurred in primordial seas.
   (B) Development of eukaryotic cells took place.
   (C) The process of photosynthesis was developed within single cells.
   (D) Amphibians diversified into birds, then mammals.
   (E) A branch of mammals developed into primates, the direct ancestors of man.

50. Energy flows through the food chain from

   (A) producers to consumers to decomposers
   (B) producers to secondary consumers to primary consumers
   (C) decomposers to consumers to producers
   (D) secondary consumers to producers
   (E) consumers to producers

51. If the Moon completely covers the sun as seen by an earthbound observer, there is a

   (A) total lunar eclipse
   (B) total solar eclipse
   (C) partial lunar eclipse
   (D) partial solar eclipse
   (E) parallax

52. The projection of the Earth's axis on the sky is the

   (A) celestial equator
   (B) zenith
   (C) celestial poles
   (D) ecliptic
   (E) zodiac

53. The process that releases energy for use by the cell is known as

   (A) photosynthesis
   (B) aerobic metabolism
   (C) anaerobic metabolism
   (D) cellular respiration
   (E) dark reaction

54. Which of the following is NOT a step in the translation portion of protein synthesis?

   (A) tRNA anticodons line up with corresponding mRNA codons
   (B) a ribosome attaches to the start codon on mRNA; ribosome adds tRNA whose anticodons complement the next codon on the mRNA string; and the process repeats to locate sequential amino acids
   (C) Ribosomal enzymes also link the sequential amino acids into a protein chain
   (D) As the protein chain is forming, rRNA moves along the sequence adding amino acids designated by codons on the mRNA
   (E) Terminating codon stops the synthesis process and releases the newly formed protein

55. Which of the following most closely represents the sequence leading to human evolution?

   (A) Coacervates, eukaryotes, plants, fish, amphibians, mammals, primates, man
   (B) Eukaryotes, plants, amphibians, fish, mammals, primates, man
   (C) Eukaryotes, coacervates, plants, fish, amphibians, mammals, primates, man
   (D) Coacervates, eukaryotes, plants, fish, amphibians, primates, mammals, man
   (E) Plants, eukaryotes, coacervates, fish, amphibians, mammals, primates, man

56. Water molecules are attracted to each other due to which of the following?

   (A) Polarity; partial positive charge near hydrogen atoms; partial negative charge near oxygen atoms
   (B) Inert properties of hydrogen and oxygen
   (C) Ionic bonds between hydrogen and oxygen
   (D) The crystal structure of ice
   (E) Brownian motion of hydrogen and oxygen atoms

57. The voltage across the terminal of a circuit containing a resistor is 12 V, and it contains a resistor connected to the circuit which reads 8 ohms. What is the amperage of the service?

(A) 1.5 A
(B) 48 A
(C) 0.67 A
(D) 15 A
(E) 96 A

58. The percentage of Earth's surface that is water is

(A) 10 percent
(B) 30 percent
(C) 50 percent
(D) 70 percent
(E) 90 percent

59. Traits that are produced by the expression of more than one set of genes are known as

(A) polygenic traits
(B) autosomal traits
(C) sex-limited traits
(D) monohybrid traits
(E) dihybrid crosses

60. The major driving force of the evolution of species is known as

(A) the Oparin Theory
(B) natural selection
(C) environmental determinism
(D) Hardy-Weinberg Equilibrium
(E) genetic drift

61. Which of the following items found on a bicycle is NOT a simple machine?

(A) tire
(B) pedal mechanism
(C) rear-wheel gear mechanism
(D) horn
(E) kickstand

62. Which of the following sets of quantum numbers (listed in order of n, l, ml, ms) describe the highest energy valence electron of nitrogen in its ground state?

(A) 2, 0, 0, 1½
(B) 2, 1, 1, 2½
(C) 2, 1, 1, 1½
(D) 2, 1, 21, 2½
(E) 2, 1, 21, 1½

63. The change of state from liquid to solid or solid to liquid involves a phase where the temperature remains constant. This phase is known as the

(A) transition phase
(B) heat of fusion
(C) heat of fission
(D) specific heat
(E) equilibrium

64. Which of the following solid crystals has, on average, one atom per cubic unit cell?

(A) Face-centered
(B) Body-centered
(C) Rhombic
(D) All cubic crystals
(E) Simple cubic crystals only

65. Which of the following is part of the alimentary canal?

(A) Artery
(B) Sinus
(C) Vagus nerve
(D) Bronchus
(E) Esophagus

66. Which of the following experimental evidence was NOT considered supportive of the Oparin Hypothesis?

(A) Amino acids can be produced in the laboratory by exposing simple inorganic molecules to electrical charge.
(B) Guanine can be formed in the laboratory by thermal polymerization of amino acids.
(C) Ultraviolet light induces the formation of dipeptides from amino acids in laboratory experiments.
(D) In the laboratory, proteins are not useful as catalysts, indicating that early proteins were stable.
(E) Phosphoric acid increases the yield of polymers in the laboratory, simulating the role of ATP in protein synthesis.

Questions 67–71

In snapdragons, a red flower crossed with a white flower produces a pink flower. In this illustration, R stands for red and W represents white. The Punnett square for a cross between a white snapdragon and a red snapdragon is shown here:

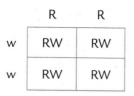

67. The cross illustrated in this Punnett square is an example of

(A) a sex-linked trait
(B) multiple alleles
(C) incomplete dominance
(D) a dihybrid cross
(E) complete dominance

68. The symbol RW represents which of the following?

(A) The allele for red
(B) The genotype for pink
(C) The phenotype for pink
(D) The allele for white
(E) The genotype for white

69. In this cross, both parents have genotypes that are

(A) heterozygous for color
(B) homozygous for color
(C) recessive for pink
(D) dominant for pink
(E) dominant for white

70. Which of the following statements about this cross must be true?

(A) Both parents of the red snapdragon must have had the genotype RR.
(B) One of the parents of the red snapdragon must have had the genotype RR.
(C) Both parents of the red snapdragon must have been pink.
(D) Neither parent of the red snapdragon could be white.
(E) One parent of the red snapdragon could have been white.

71. If two of the heterozygous offspring (RW) of this cross are bred, what will be the ratio of phenotypes of the offspring?

(A) 0 red: 4 pink: 0 white
(B) 2 red: 2 pink: 0 white
(C) 1 red: 1 pink: 1 white
(D) 2 red: 0 pink: 2 white
(E) 1 red: 2 pink: 1 white

72. The physical place where a particular organism lives is called a

    (A) niche
    (B) biosphere
    (C) lithosphere
    (D) habitat
    (E) ecosystem

73. What is the most likely explanation for the fact that a sample of solid nickel is attracted into a magnetic field, but a sample of solid zinc chloride is not?

    (A) There are unpaired outer electrons in nickel.
    (B) There is some iron mixed in with the nickel.
    (C) There are unpaired outer electrons in zinc.
    (D) The presence of chlorine keeps zinc from being attracted to the magnet.
    (E) Nickel does not produce a magnetic field to oppose the one that is attracting it.

74. The specific heat of water is 4.2 J/g °C. What mass of water will be heated by 10°C by 840J?

    (A) 0.5 g
    (B) 10 g
    (C) 20 g
    (D) 4.2 g
    (E) 840 g

75. A light-year represents the

    (A) total amount of light energy that travels past a point on Earth in one year
    (B) total distance that an object travels in space at the speed of light in one year
    (C) total amount of time that a photon of light travels in order to reach a star, planet, or other extraterrestrial object
    (D) speed at which light travels in a year
    (E) speed of a photon in a vacuum when it collides with an x-ray

76. The half-life of C 14 is 5,730 years. A piece of cypress is measured to have ¾ of the carbon to be C 12 and ¼ C 14. How many years old is this piece of wood likely to be?

    (A) 5,730
    (B) 2,865
    (C) 4,297
    (D) 11,460
    (E) 1,435

77. Igneous rock forms are commonly called

    (A) marble
    (B) limestone
    (C) cement
    (D) granite
    (E) sandstone

78. Which of the following statements is true?

    (A) Despite the contraction of space, galaxies appear to be static relative to each other when observed.
    (B) The expansion of space makes galaxies appear to be moving apart, causing the color of their spectral lines to shift when observed.
    (C) Galaxies themselves are moving apart from each other.
    (D) Hubble's law states that the redshift in light coming from a distant galaxy is inversely proportional to its distance from Earth.
    (E) The actual motion of galaxies is questionable due to variations in Hubble's constant.

79. All of the following are major structural regions of roots EXCEPT the

    (A) meristematic region
    (B) elongation region
    (C) root cap
    (D) epistematic region
    (E) maturation region

80. When a yellow pea plant is crossed with a green pea plant, all the offspring are yellow. The law that best explains this is the law of

    (A) intolerance
    (B) dominance
    (C) interference
    (D) relative genes
    (E) codominance

81. Which of the following statements is true about electrons?

    (A) Electrons have a positive charge.
    (B) Electrons have less mass than protons and neutrons.
    (C) Electrons are found within the nucleus of atoms.
    (D) The number of electrons is equal to the number of protons in an ion.
    (E) An atom's valence number is the number of electrons in its lowest energy level.

82. What is the energy-generating mechanism of the stars, including the Sun?

    (A) Fission
    (B) Fusion
    (C) Spontaneous generation
    (D) Combustion
    (E) Stellar explosion

83. When measuring the flow of heat in a system, a natural process that starts at one equilibrium state and flows to another will go in what direction for an irreversible process that is impacted by the entropy of the system plus the environment?

    (A) Increase
    (B) Decrease
    (C) Remain static
    (D) Fluctuate between increases and decreases in a constant pattern
    (E) Increase steadily and then drop off, similar to the conservation of momentum in a closed system

84. What is the resistance of an electric can opener if it takes a current of 10 A when plugged into a 120 V service?

    (A) 1,200 ohms
    (B) 0.083 ohms
    (C) 130 ohms
    (D) 12 ohms
    (E) 1.2 ohms

85. Photosynthesis would NOT proceed without which of the following that allow moisture and gases to pass in and out of the leaf?

    (A) Surface hairs
    (B) Stomata
    (C) Cuticles
    (D) Epidermal cells
    (E) Cilia

86. In ferns, the individual we generally recognize as an adult fern is really which structure?

    (A) A mature gametophyte
    (B) A prothallus
    (C) A mature sporophyte
    (D) A young sporophyte
    (E) A young gametophyte

87. Which of the following is the least polar molecule?

    (A) H_2
    (B) H_2O
    (C) H_2S
    (D) C_2H_2
    (E) NaH

88. Which state of matter does NOT have a definite shape or a definite volume?

    (A) Solid
    (B) Liquid
    (C) Gas
    (D) Plasma
    (E) Both (C) and (D)

89. A person who has been exercising vigorously begins to sweat and breathe rapidly. These reactions are involuntary responses known as

    (A) fight or flight responses
    (B) homeostatic mechanisms
    (C) equilibrium responses
    (D) stimulus receptors
    (E) hormone reactions

90. The nervous system is an integrated circuit with many functions. Which of the following parts of the nervous system are matched with the wrong function?

    (A) Forebrain — controls olfactory lobes (smell)
    (B) Cerebrum — controls the function of involuntary muscles
    (C) Hypothalamus — controls hunger and thirst
    (D) Cerebellum — controls balance and muscle coordination
    (E) Midbrain — contains optic lobes and controls sight

91. Fog is

    (A) the same as smog
    (B) caused when cold air moves over warm air
    (C) a collection of minute water droplets
    (D) associated with a tornado
    (E) Both (C) and (D)

92. Land and sea (or lake) breezes form because of

    (A) uneven heating of coastal environments
    (B) the pressure gradient force
    (C) the difference in temperature between land and water surfaces
    (D) solar radiation
    (E) a variety of factors involving temperature, pressure, and geographical components

93. An electric shock can restart a heart that has stopped beating. Which of the following statements is a valid reason for this fact?

    (A) Electric shock stimulates the nervous system.
    (B) Smooth muscle is affected by electric shock.
    (C) The electric shock pushes blood through the stopped heart.
    (D) Cardiac muscle of the heart responds to the electric shock.
    (E) Electric shock causes air to enter the lungs.

94. When a hamburger is consumed by an individual, it passes through all of the following organs EXCEPT the

    (A) mouth
    (B) esophagus
    (C) salivary glands
    (D) stomach
    (E) small intestine

95. Each ecosystem can support a certain number of organisms—a number usually designated by the letter K and known as

    (A) ecodensity
    (B) population
    (C) carrying capacity
    (D) a community
    (E) the biosphere

96. Which of the following parts of an atom is NOT a subatomic particle?

    (A) A quark
    (B) A boson
    (C) A neutrino
    (D) An electron
    (E) A positron

97. The function of the gallbladder and pancreas is to aid digestion by producing digestive enzymes and secreting them into the

   (A) small intestine
   (B) large intestine
   (C) stomach
   (D) esophagus
   (E) mouth

98. Many insects have special respiratory organs known as

   (A) spiracles
   (B) alveoli
   (C) cephalothorax
   (D) lungs
   (E) gills

99. Most of Earth's photosynthesis takes place in which one of the following biomes?

   (A) Oceans
   (B) Tundra
   (C) Deciduous forests
   (D) Deserts
   (E) Tropical rainforests

100. Which of the following chemical equations represents a replacement reaction?

   (A) $A + C \rightarrow AC + B$
   (B) $A + B \rightarrow AB$
   (C) $AB + C \rightarrow AC + B$
   (D) $AB \rightarrow A + B$
   (E) $AB + CD \rightarrow A + B + C + D$

101. The study of the interaction of organisms with their living space is known as

   (A) environmentalism
   (B) habitology
   (C) zoology
   (D) ecology
   (E) paleontology

102. What is the name of a distinct group of individuals that are able to mate and produce viable offspring?

   (A) A class
   (B) A community
   (C) A phylum
   (D) A family
   (E) A species

103. Which of the following is true concerning Einstein's theory of relativity?

   (A) As energy increases, the speed of light increases and mass is constant.
   (B) As energy increases, mass increases and the speed of light is constant.
   (C) As energy increases, the speed of light decreases and mass is constant.
   (D) As energy increases, mass decreases and the speed of light is constant.
   (E) As energy increases, the speed of light and mass will increase.

104. Which of the following is an autotroph?

   (A) *E. coli* bacteria
   (B) A Portuguese man-of-war
   (C) A portobello mushroom
   (D) An asparagus fern
   (E) A perch

105. The Michelson-Morley experiment in 1887 proved that the speed of light

   (A) is the same in all directions
   (B) can slow down in a vacuum
   (C) is slower in air than in liquid
   (D) is different on the Moon
   (E) continuously speeds up in a vacuum

106. Which of the following is NOT a fundamental geological principle?

(A) The principle of original horizontality
(B) The principle of supererogation
(C) The principle of lateral continuity
(D) The principle of fossil succession
(E) The principle of uniformitarianism

107. Astronomers observing the redshift of light from a faraway star means that the star is

(A) moving away from us
(B) moving toward us
(C) ready to explode
(D) a dwarf star
(E) a giant nova

108. The three most recent geological eras are

(A) Paleozoic, Proterozoic, Archean
(B) Mesozoic, Paleozoic, Cenozoic
(C) Cenozoic, Mesozoic, Paleozoic
(D) Cenozoic, Archean, Paleozoic
(E) Recent, Tertiary, Quaternary

109. A form of symbiosis in which one species is benefited while the other is harmed is called

(A) parasitism
(B) mutualism
(C) amensalism
(D) altruism
(E) commensalism

110. An axis is

(A) a connecting line at the equator
(B) a connecting line between the poles
(C) a connecting line between orbits
(D) a pole
(E) a connecting line at the tropical zones

111. In order of magnitude, how many galaxies are there in the universe?

(A) Hundreds
(B) Thousands
(C) Millions
(D) Billions
(E) Trillions

112. An astronaut is traveling in a spacecraft that is slowing down. To the astronaut inside the spacecraft, the apparent force inside the craft is directed

(A) backward
(B) forward
(C) sideways
(D) vertically only
(E) nowhere because there is no force

113. The cells of which of the following organisms are most likely to be prokaryotic?

(A) Mold
(B) Seaweed
(C) Blue-green algae
(D) Fern
(E) Hydra

114. The name for the imaginary object that centers on and surrounds Earth by which background stars are projected is called a(n)

(A) geodesic dome
(B) celestial sphere
(C) stellar ball
(D) Cartesian coordinate system
(E) equatorial coordinate system

115. Why is stratospheric ozone depletion (destruction of the ozone layer) a serious concern?

 (A) It is a major cause of the "greenhouse effect."
 (B) It will increase the amount of ultraviolet radiation reaching the ground.
 (C) It causes acid rain.
 (D) It is really nothing to worry about.
 (E) It leads to global warming as more radiation enters through the hole in the atmosphere.

116. Mountain and valley breezes form because of

 (A) gravity and the pressure gradient force
 (B) the pressure gradient force and heating
 (C) gravity and heating
 (D) the pressure gradient force and the Coriolis force
 (E) high pressure forming near the top of the mountain due to warm air expansion forcing air up the mountain from the valley below

117. As you go down the periodic table and to the left, which of the following traits increases?

 (A) Atomic radius
 (B) Electronegativity
 (C) Electron affinity
 (D) Ionization energy
 (E) Acidity of the oxides

118. According to Newton's laws of motion, the greater the mass of an object, the greater the force necessary to change its

 (A) position
 (B) force
 (C) state of motion
 (D) shape
 (E) density

119. The top or peak of a sine wave is called the

 (A) crest
 (B) trough
 (C) amplitude
 (D) period
 (E) frequency

120. A wave does not carry along the medium through which it travels. Thus, it follows that

 (A) molecules of water in the ocean are pushed to shore by waves
 (B) the ocean's water molecules are thoroughly mixed each day by waves
 (C) debris in the ocean is washed ashore by waves
 (D) individual water molecules do not travel toward shore, but wave peaks do
 (E) waves move water, not swimmers

ANSWER KEY

1.	(E)	31.	(A)	61.	(D)	91.	(C)
2.	(C)	32.	(A)	62.	(C)	92.	(E)
3.	(C)	33.	(C)	63.	(B)	93.	(D)
4.	(A)	34.	(C)	64.	(E)	94.	(C)
5.	(B)	35.	(E)	65.	(E)	95.	(C)
6.	(D)	36.	(B)	66.	(D)	96.	(D)
7.	(E)	37.	(D)	67.	(C)	97.	(A)
8.	(C)	38.	(C)	68.	(B)	98.	(A)
9.	(B)	39.	(D)	69.	(B)	99.	(A)
10.	(C)	40.	(D)	70.	(D)	100.	(C)
11.	(C)	41.	(B)	71.	(E)	101.	(D)
12.	(D)	42.	(E)	72.	(D)	102.	(E)
13.	(D)	43.	(D)	73.	(A)	103.	(B)
14.	(D)	44.	(A)	74.	(C)	104.	(D)
15.	(B)	45.	(C)	75.	(B)	105.	(A)
16.	(A)	46.	(B)	76.	(D)	106.	(B)
17.	(B)	47.	(E)	77.	(D)	107.	(A)
18.	(C)	48.	(B)	78.	(B)	108.	(C)
19.	(A)	49.	(C)	79.	(D)	109.	(A)
20.	(B)	50.	(A)	80.	(B)	110.	(B)
21.	(C)	51.	(B)	81.	(B)	111.	(D)
22.	(D)	52.	(C)	82.	(B)	112.	(B)
23.	(A)	53.	(D)	83.	(A)	113.	(C)
24.	(E)	54.	(A)	84.	(D)	114.	(B)
25.	(D)	55.	(A)	85.	(B)	115.	(B)
26.	(D)	56.	(A)	86.	(C)	116.	(C)
27.	(C)	57.	(A)	87.	(A)	117.	(A)
28.	(B)	58.	(D)	88.	(E)	118.	(C)
29.	(B)	59.	(A)	89.	(B)	119.	(A)
30.	(E)	60.	(B)	90.	(B)	120.	(D)

PRACTICE TEST
DETAILED EXPLANATIONS OF ANSWERS

1. **(E)** Nuclear pores are holes in the nuclear membrane where the double nuclear membrane fuses together, forming a break or hole, allowing the selective intake and excretion of molecules to or from the nucleus. Thus, nuclear pores are the channel of communication between the cytoplasm and the nucleoplasm.

2. **(C)** Microvilli are filaments that extend from the cell membrane, particularly in cells that are involved in absorption (such as in the intestine). These filaments increase the surface area of the cell membrane, thus increasing the area available to absorb nutrients.

3. **(C)** Microvilli also contain enzymes that are involved in digesting certain types of nutrients.

4. **(A)** Secretory vesicles are packets of material packaged by either the Golgi apparatus or the endoplasmic reticulum. The secretory vesicle carries the substance produced within the cell to the cell membrane. The vesicle membrane fuses with the cell membrane, allowing the substance to escape the cell.

5. **(B)** The smooth endoplasmic reticulum is a network of continuous membranous channels that connect the cell membrane with the nuclear membrane and is responsible for the delivery of lipids and proteins to certain areas within the cytoplasm. The smooth endoplasmic reticulum lacks attached ribosomes.

6. **(D)** Silicon carbide (SiC) is held together with network covalent bonds, which creates a crystal entirely from covalent bonds and confers unusual strength (and a high melting point) upon the crystal.

7. **(E)** Acetic acid is a molecular compound that is held together with covalent bonds, in which electrons are shared between atoms, so that both atoms in the bond end up having a full octet of electrons.

8. **(C)** As a metal, copper is held together by metallic bonds, which involve delocalized d-orbital electrons.

9. **(B)** Nonvascular plants are known as bryophytes (mosses). They lack tissue that will conduct water or food.

10. **(C)** Angiosperms are those plants that produce flowers as reproductive organs.

11. **(C)** Angiosperms (flowering plants) have two main systems—the shoot system, which is mainly above ground and the root system below ground.

12. **(D)** Gymnosperms produce seeds without flowers.

13. **(D)** Gymnosperms produce seeds without flowers, which include conifers (cone-bearers) and cycads.

14. **(D)** Conduction is the transfer of molecules by collisions, passing heat through one material into another.

15. **(B)** Convection is caused by the flow of heated liquid or gas through a volumetric medium.

16. **(A)** Radiation is waves traveling through space to transfer heat away from the energy source.

17. **(B)** The manganese ion in potassium permanganate has a +5 oxidation state, and is therefore readily reduced. When it is reduced, it forces another species to be oxidized. Therefore, the permanganate ion is a very strong oxidizing agent.

18. **(C)** The magnesium atom that is combined with oxygen has a +2 oxidation state. Oxygen carries a –2 oxidation state, and the sum of the oxidation states of oxygen and magnesium must total the charge on the compound, which is 0.

19. **(A)** Hydrogen gas by definition, since it is a standard, has an oxidation potential of 0.

20. **(B)** One of the modes of population growth is represented by the exponential curve (or J-curve). The rate of growth accelerates over time since there are no limiters of growth.

21. **(C)** The rate of increase within a population is represented by the birth rate minus the death rate.

22. **(D)** Mortality is the death rate within a population.

23. **(A)** Natality is the birth rate within a population.

24. **(E)** Another mode of population growth is represented by the logistic curve (or S-curve) for populations that encounter limiting factors in which acceleration occurs up to a point and then slows down.

25. **(D)** The acceleration due to gravity equals approximately 10 meters per second squared. Therefore, in 0.5 seconds (one half second) the ball will have traveled half of 10 meters, or 5 meters.

26. **(D)** The only answer that causes any change in the entire gene pool is mutation (D). A mutation adds or subtracts (or changes) a trait from the existing genes within the pool. Genetic drift, allopatric speciation, and sympatric speciation are all forms of natural selection that cause changes in populations of already expressed traits.

27. **(C)** All of the answers are true except choice (C) because meiosis does not ensure the same kinds of chromosomes; in fact it ensures that there is a variety in the genetic code of different chromosomal material.

28. **(B)** Echinodermata is the class including sea stars and sand dollars that clearly show radial symmetry (like pieces of pie). The rest of the choices show bilateral symmetry where sides are mirror images of the other (like humans).

29. **(B)** Meiosis results in genetic variation since there is a division and sorting of chromosomes resulting in a variety of eggs and sperm (or pollen) that can recombine in new patterns. Mitosis produces identical daughter cells, and metaphase and prophase are parts of that process. Interphase is the growth portion of the cell cycle.

30. **(E)** The evolution of plant species is considered to have begun with aerobic prokaryotic cells.

31. **(A)** A sound wave is a compression or longitudinal wave, which means that it compresses and rarefies as it moves through a medium. Transverse waves oscillate up and down as they move through a medium. The other three terms are not commonly used to label sound waves.

32. **(A)** The desert areas increase evaporation of the water that is present, causing a concentration of salts.

33. **(C)** The property of an object that determines the object's resistance to motion is its mass. A large watermelon has a far greater mass than the pellet of lead shot, the golf ball, the feather, or the sheet of notebook paper. The mass of an object never changes. Its mass is equal to the object's weight divided by the acceleration due to gravity (g) at its current position in space.

34. **(C)** The placenta is the connection between the mother and embryo; it is the site of transfer for nutrients, water, and waste between them.

35. **(E)** Gregor Mendel studied the relationships between traits expressed in parents and offspring, and the genes that caused the traits to be expressed.

36. **(B)** The first cells to evolve were most likely unspecialized. Since the Earth's atmosphere was most likely lacking in oxygen, it is presumed that preplant cells were also anaerobic. Early cells were also small, aquatic, and prokaryotic.

37. **(D)** A branch of bipedal primates gave rise to the first true hominids about 4.5 million years ago. The earliest known hominid fossils were found in Africa in the 1970s. The well-known "Lucy" skeleton was named Australopithecus afarensis. It was determined from the skeleton of Australopithecus that it was a biped that walked upright. It had a human-like jaw and teeth, but a skull that resembled that of a small ape. The arms were proportionately longer than humans', indicating the ability to still be motile in trees. The fossilized skull of Homo erectus, the oldest known fossil of the human genus, is thought to be about 1.8 million years old. The skull of Homo erectus was much larger than Australopithecus, about the size of a modern human brain. Homo erectus was thought to walk upright and had facial features more closely resembling men than apes. A third fossil, the oldest to be designated Homo sapiens, is also called Cro-Magnon man, with a brain size and facial features comparable to modern men. Cro-Magnon Homo sapiens are thought to have evolved in Africa and migrated to Europe and Asia approximately 100,000 years ago.

38. **(C)** Acetylene shows a triple bond between the two carbons, which contains two pi bonds. In multiple bonds, the first bond is a sigma bond in which electrons are shared along the internuclear axis. Any additional bonding is created by the sideways overlap of unhybridized p-orbitals above and below the internuclear axis. None of the other options for answers contain multiple covalent bonds between any two atoms.

39. **(D)** Equinoxes are described as the two points on the celestial sphere where the ecliptic crosses the celestial equator. Since the crossing occurs on March 21 in this question, it is the spring equinox. Solstices occur in the summer and winter, and correspond to the ecliptic being farthest from the celestial equator. In general, when this crossing occurs on March 21, the Moon is not necessarily aligned with the Earth and the Sun, so the odds of an eclipse occurring are very low. The autumnal equinox occurs at the other end of the celestial sphere, on September 22.

40. **(D)** The DNA of eukaryotes is organized into chromosomes within the nucleus.

41. **(B)** Inorganic cofactors are small non-protein molecules that promote proper enzyme catalysis. These molecules may bind to the active site or to the substrate itself. The most common inorganic cofactors are metallic atoms such as iron, copper, and zinc.

42. **(E)** Environmental conditions such as heat or acidity inhibit enzymatic reactions by changing the shape of the active site and rendering the enzyme ineffective. Certain chemicals inhibit enzymatic reactions by changing the shape of the enzyme's active site. If there is a lack of substrate, the enzyme will have no substance to affect. Thus, a large amount of enzyme is the only factor that will not inhibit enzymatic reactions.

43. **(D)** A ketone group has a double bond between oxygen and a carbon atom that is imbedded within a carbon chain.

44. **(A)** An alcohol group has a hydroxide group (OH) with the second bond from oxygen going to a carbon atom.

45. **(C)** An ester group is an ether with an additional double bond to an oxygen from an adjacent carbon.

46. **(B)** An aldehyde group has a double bond between an oxygen atom and a carbon that is one end of a carbon chain, or not otherwise bonded to any other carbons.

47. **(E)** The process of photosynthesis is the crucial reaction that converts the light energy of the Sun into chemical energy that is usable by living things.

48. **(B)** Entropy is defined as the new state variable that describes the increase of disorder in a system. Stated positively, it describes the amount of increase in the statistical disorder of a physical system.

49. **(C)** The development of photosynthetic cells took place before the development of eukaryotes. The first photosynthetic cells were prokaryotic.

50. **(A)** Energy flows through the entire ecosystem in one direction—from producers to consumers and on to decomposers through the food chain.

51. **(B)** The eclipse must be a solar eclipse because the Moon is between the Earth and the Sun. The solar eclipse is total because the Moon's disk covers the Sun from our view completely. Parallax has to do with the apparent displacement of a celestial object.

52. **(C)** The celestial poles are extensions of Earth's north and south geographic poles up into the sky. The celestial equator identifies the projection of Earth's equator. The zenith is the point directly overhead above an observer. The ecliptic is the line that describes the Sun's orbit across the celestial sphere. The zodiac is the name for the annual cycle of twelve stations along the ecliptic that the Sun and planets travel along the celestial sphere.

53. **(D)** Cellular respiration is the process that releases energy for use by the cell. There are several steps involved in cellular respiration; some require oxygen (aerobic) and some do not (anaerobic).

54. **(A)** When tRNA anticodons line up with corresponding mRNA codons, it is the last step in the transcription process before translation begins. Translation begins as a ribosome attaches to the mRNA strand at a particular codon known as the start codon. This codon is only recognized by a particular initiator tRNA. The ribosome continues to add tRNA whose anticodons complement the next codon on the mRNA string. A third type of RNA is utilized at this point, ribosomal RNA or rRNA. Ribosomal RNA exists in concert with enzymes as a ribosome. In order for the tRNA and mRNA to link up, enzymes connected to rRNA at the ribosome must be utilized. Ribosomal enzymes also are responsible for linking the sequential amino acids into a protein chain. As the protein chain is forming, the rRNA moves along the sequence, adding the amino acids that are designated by the codons on the mRNA. At the end of the translation process, a terminating codon stops the synthesis process, and the protein is released.

55. **(A)** The most likely sequence leading to human evolution begins with coacervates, then eukaryotes, plants, fish, amphibians, mammals, primates, and finally, man.

56. **(A)** The hydrogen atoms in water molecules have a partial positive charge, while the oxygen atoms in water have a partial negative charge, causing polarity. This polarity allows the oxygen of one water molecule to attract the hydrogen of another. The partial charges attract other opposite partial charges of other water molecules allowing for weak (hydrogen) bonds between the molecules. *Inert* means non-reactive; it does not explain the attraction between H and O. There are no ionic bonds within water molecules, only covalent bonds. A crystal structure forms in ice because of the attraction of hydrogen bonds; the crystal structure does not cause the attraction. Brownian motion is the random movement of atoms or particles caused by collisions between them; it does not explain the attraction between atoms or molecules.

57. **(A)** Using Ohm's law, V = IR, we solve for I=V/R with V = 12 V and R = 8 ohms. I = 12.0 V/8.0 ohms = 1.5 V/ohm = 1.5 A. The other answers are results of erroneous calculations or misapplications of Ohm's law.

58. **(D)** Earth is approximately 70 percent water. Most of the water is in the oceans. Land makes up the remaining 30 percent.

59. **(A)** Traits, such as height and skin color, are produced from the expression of more than one set of genes and are known as polygenic traits.

60. **(B)** Evolution is driven by the process of natural selection, a feature of population genetics first popularized by Charles Darwin in his book *The Origin of Species* (published in 1859).

61. **(D)** The horn is not a simple machine. Simple machines are mechanical devices that alter the magnitude and direction of a force. They are represented by the following six objects: (1) lever, (2) wheel and axle, (3) pulley, (4) inclined plane, (5) pulley, and (6) screw. On a bicycle, the tire is a type of wheel. The pedal mechanism is a wheel and axle as well as a gear mechanism (two simple machines). The rear wheel gear mechanism is obviously one of the simple machines. The kickstand is a lever.

62. **(C)** Since nitrogen is in the second row, its highest-energy electron is at n = 2, which is the first number. The second number signifies that its outer electron is in a *p*-orbital. The third number indicates the third *p*-orbital to receive an electron, since nitrogen is the third element in the *p*-block

in the periodic table. The last number is the magnetic spin quantum number and signifies that the highest energy electron is the only electron in the orbital.

63. **(B)** Although there is a transition from one state of matter to another, there is no term "transition phase" to describe this process. The term fission is used in nuclear physics to describe the breaking apart of nuclear particles. It is not used to describe changes of state of matter. Specific heat is the amount of energy in calories required to raise one gram of a substance by 1°C. Equilibrium is the state of a system or body at rest or lacking acceleration which results when all the forces acting upon it are equal to zero and the sum of all of the torques equals zero. In chemistry, it is the state of a reaction when all the products and reactants are balanced.

64. **(E)** A simple cubic crystal is the only unit cell mentioned that has, on average, one atom per unit cell. A simple cubic unit cell has one atom in each of the eight corners of the unit cell, but only one-eighth of each of those atoms is ascribed to that particular unit cell. A face-centered unit cell has four atoms per unit cell, while a body-centered unit cell has two atoms per unit cell.

65. **(E)** The alimentary canal is also known as the gastrointestinal (GI) tract and includes the mouth, pharynx, esophagus, stomach, small intestine, and large intestine.

66. **(D)** Proteins are catalysts in the laboratory, so the formation of proteins in the laboratory under conditions presumed to be representative of early Earth history is key evidence of the evolution of life on Earth. Stanley Miller provided support for Oparin's hypotheses in experiments in which he succeeded in producing amino acids by exposing simple inorganic molecules to electrical charges similar to lightning. Sidney Fox conducted experiments that proved ultraviolet light may induce the formation of dipeptides from amino acids. He also showed that polyphosphoric acid could increase the yield of these polymers, a process that simulates the modern role of ATP in protein synthesis. Researcher Cyril Ponnamperuma demonstrated that small amounts of guanine formed from the thermal polymerization of amino acids.

67. **(C)** This is known as incomplete dominance. Neither white nor red is dominant over the other.

68. **(B)** RW is a symbol for genotype. In this case, the RW genotype produces a pink phenotype. R and W represent the alleles for red and white, respectively.

69. **(B)** Both parents have two alleles that are the same; thus they have homozygous genotypes for color.

70. **(D)** While (A), (B), and (C) could have been true, a red snapdragon could have been produced by any of those choices. However, a white snapdragon cannot produce a red snapdragon as an offspring even if paired with a red snapdragon.

71. **(E)** If two of the heterozygous offspring of an incomplete dominant trait are bred, the Punnett square would be

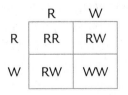

The phenotypic ratio of the offspring, then, is one-fourth red one-half pink, and one-fourth white, a 1:2:1 ratio—1 red: 2 pink: 1 white.

72. **(D)** A habitat refers to the physical place where an organism lives. A species' habitat must include all the factors that will support its life and reproduction.

73. **(A)** Nickel has an unpaired electron in its d-orbital, which induces a magnetic field and causes it to be attracted to another magnetic field. Zinc chloride does not have such an unpaired electron and is not attracted to a magnet.

74. **(C)** The heat absorbed by the water equals the mass of the water multiplied by the specific heat of water times the increase in temperature change. The 840 J added to the water is enough heat to raise the temperature of 20 g of water by 10°C.

75. **(B)** A light-year is a distance, not a speed or velocity. It is also not a time measurement. A light-year represents the measurement of the distance to one celestial body from another celestial body, measured as a multiple or fraction of the distance light travels in one year. It is equal to $(3.0 \times 10^8 \text{ m/s})(3.6 \times 10^3 \text{ s/hr})(2.4 \times 10^1 \text{ hr/day})(3.65 \times 10^2 \text{ days/yr})(1 \text{ yr}) = 95 \times 10^{14} \text{ m} = 9.5 \times 10^{15} \text{ m} = 9.5 \times 10^{12} \text{ km} = 9,500,000,000,000 \text{ km or } 9.5$ trillion kilometers.

76. **(D)** Since the half-life of C 14 is 5,730 years, that means it takes 5,730 years for half the C 14 to decay to C 12. Since the end sample has ¼ C 12, we see that two half-life periods would have occurred. The first would have decayed the sample to half of each type, and the second time period would degrade the half sample to a quarter sample. Two half-life periods is a total of 11,460 years.

77. **(D)** An example of igneous rock is granite. Marble is a metamorphic rock, while limestone, cement, and sandstone are all sedimentary rocks.

78. **(B)** Although it appears that galaxies are moving apart, Hubble's law explains that this apparent motion is the expansion of the space between them, not the motion of the galaxies themselves. Hubble's law states that the redshift in light coming from a distant galaxy is directly and linearly proportional to its distance from Earth.

79. **(D)** There is no epistematic region in plant roots. Roots have four major structural regions that run vertically from bottom to top. The root cap is composed of dead thick-walled cells and covers the tip of the root, protecting it as the root pushes through soil. The meristematic region is just above the root cap. It consists of undifferentiated cells that undergo mitosis, providing the cells that grow to form the elongation region. In the elongation region, cells differentiate, large vacuoles are formed, and cells grow. As the cells differentiate into various root tissues, they become part of the maturation region.

80. **(B)** Gregor Mendel determined that one gene is sometimes dominant over another gene for the same trait (i.e., it expressed itself over the other). This is known as the law of dominance, Mendel's second law of inheritance.

81. **(B)** Electrons have very small mass, much less than either protons or neutrons. They are found orbiting in a cloud surrounding the nucleus. Electrons are negatively charged. An ion is an atom with a greater or fewer number of electrons than the standard atom for the element, causing a charge of positive or negative due to the unequal number of protons and electrons. An atom's valence number is the number of electrons in its highest (not lowest) energy level.

82. **(B)**   Astrophysicists speculate that just 1/100 of a second after the big bang, the entire universe was filled with elementary particles (i.e., electrons, protons, positrons, nutrinos, photons, etc.). At 1 second, the temperature was 10^{10} K, which was still too hot for neutrons and protons to stay together in the nuclei by the strong nuclear force. After about 3 minutes, it had cooled to about 10^9 K. Electrons and positrons were annihilated, generating photons, neutrinos, anti-neutrinos, and a small number of neutrons and protons. The universe was now as hot and dense as the core of a star undergoing nuclear fusion. However, it wasn't until 300,000 years later that the nuclei could hold on to the electrons, clearing the vast fog. The process then continued to cool, coalesce, and expand through fusion, forming stars and galaxies in the visible universe. Fission does not occur until much later in stellar evolution. Spontaneous generation, disproven by Pasteur, has nothing to do with the evolution of stars. Combustion is common in various exothermic processes in a general way. Stellar explosions indicative of the latter stages of stellar evolution generally occur toward the end of a star's life, not at the origination.

83. **(A)**   The answer is that entropy increases as a natural process goes from one equilibrium state to another. This is the only direction that heat flow will go in an irreversible process.

84. **(D)**   Using Ohm's law, V = IR, solve for R=V/I with V = 120 V and I = 10 A. R = 120 V / 10 A = 12 V / A or 12 ohms. All of the other answer choices are results of erroneous calculations or misapplications of Ohm's law.

85. **(B)**   Stomata are openings in the leaf surface that allow for exchange of water and gases.

86. **(C)**   The individual we recognize as an adult fern is actually the mature sporophyte.

87. **(A)**   Hydrogen gas is the least polar because it is bonded to itself as a diatomic molecule. Therefore, there is no difference in electronegativity between the two atoms in the bond, and it is entirely nonpolar.

88. **(E)**   Both a gas and plasma have no defined shape or volume. A solid has a definite shape and volume. A liquid holds the shape of its container and thus has a definite volume. A plastic is not a state of matter and is confused with the fourth state of matter, plasma.

89. **(B)**   Conditions such as temperature, pH, water balance, and sugar levels must be monitored and controlled in order to keep them within the accepted ranges that will not inhibit life. Cells and living organisms have homeostatic mechanisms that serve to keep body conditions within normal ranges.

90. **(B)**   The cerebrum controls sensory and motor responses, memory, speech, and intelligence factors. It does not control involuntary muscles.

91. **(C)**   Fog consists of a visible collection of minute water droplets suspended in the atmosphere near the Earth's surface. It occurs when atmospheric humidity combines with a warm layer of air that is transported over a cold body of water or land surface.

92. **(E)**   Due to the high specific heat capacity of water, land surfaces will heat up more rapidly than water surfaces. Since warmer air is less dense than cooler air, this uneven heating along coastal areas causes vertical expansion of the isobaric field over the land and compression of the field

over the water. This forms an elevated area of high pressure over the land and an elevated area of low pressure over the water. The pressure gradient force acts on the air and moves it from higher pressure to lower pressure. The net movement of air toward the low pressure aloft induces an area of high pressure on the water surface, while the net movement of air away from the high pressure aloft induces an area of low pressure on the land surface. The pressure gradient force now begins to move the surface air from the higher pressure on the water surface towards the lower pressure on the land surface. It is this surface flow of air that is the sea (or lake) breeze. The greater the contrast is between water temperature and land temperature, the stronger the breeze. At night, the land will cool faster than the adjacent water, reversing the process and forming a land breeze from the land towards the water.

93. **(D)**   The electrical properties of cardiac muscle tissue cause the beating of the heart muscle that results in the pumping of blood through the body.

94. **(C)**   Ingested food does not pass through the salivary glands. The saliva secreted from these glands enters the digestive tract and helps digest the food.

95. **(C)**   Carrying capacity (designated by K) is the number of organisms that can be supported within a particular ecosystem.

96. **(D)**   Quarks, bosons, neutrinos, and positrons are all subatomic particles. An electron is an atomic particle that represents the negatively charged part of an atom.

97. **(A)**   Digestive enzymes are released by the pancreas and gall bladder into the small intestine.

98. **(A)**   Insects have spiracles that allow for gas exchange.

99. **(A)**   Over 70 percent of Earth's surface is covered by water. The great majority of Earth's photosynthesis takes place near the surface of the oceans, with 70 percent of the entire amount of it taking place in the euphoric zone to a depth of 100 m. Many people mistakenly think that the tropical rainforests and deciduous forests are responsible for most of the production of oxygen during photosynthesis, but this is not so. The tundra and deserts are even more obviously incorrect because the amount of plant life in these biomes is very sparse.

100. **(C)**   A replacement reaction occurs when a compound is broken down into its components and recombined with another reactant—as shown by the equation AB 1 C → AC 1 B. The reaction A 1 B → AB represents a combination reaction; AB → A 1 B and AB 1 CD → A 1 B 1 C 1 D are both decomposition reactions; and A 1 C → AC 1 B is not a possible reaction since it is not with the first law of thermodynamics, which states that matter cannot be created or destroyed in a chemical reaction. Since B was not a reactant, it cannot be a product.

101. **(D)**   Ecology is literally "the study of" (ology) a "place to live" (eco).

102. **(E)**   Each species is a distinct group of individuals that are able to mate and produce viable offspring.

103. **(B)**   Einstein's energy equation, $E = mc^2$, is based on the premise that the speed of light for all observers is constant, and that energy is directly proportional to mass. As energy increases, so does its mass. The speed of light is considered constant; the mass and energy values must increase or decrease directly and proportionately.

104. **(D)**   Plants that produce their own food through photosynthesis are known as autotrophs. (Mushrooms are fungi; they do not produce their own food.)

105. **(A)**   The speed of light is the same in all directions. In a vacuum, the speed of light remains constant. The speed of light in a liquid is slower than in air. The speed of light is the same on the Moon as it is on the Earth.

106. **(B)**   The principle of supererogation is completely fictitious, so this is the correct answer. The principle of original horizontality states that if rock layers are not laid horizontally, then something forced the structures to move. The principle of lateral continuity means that sediments are originally deposited in layers that extend laterally in all directions and eventually thin out. The principle of fossil succession says that if rocks are undisturbed, the oldest layers of rock should be on the bottom and will have older fossils in them. The principle of uniformitarianism states that present geological events explain former ones. It is popularly stated as the principle that "the present is the key to the past."

107. **(A)**   A redshift in the electromagnetic spectrum of the light from a faraway star means that the star is moving away from the observer. In the 1920s, Edwin Hubble (1889–1953) observed that galaxies around the Milky Way were moving away from us because of this redshift, and those farther away are moving away from us even more rapidly; it is not moving toward us. The redshift does not indicate that a star is ready to explode, is a dwarf star, or is a giant nova.

108. **(C)**   These eras are parts of the Phanerozoic Eon and represent the past 570 million years. Cenozoic represents "recent life," Mesozoic represents "middle life," and Paleozoic represents "old life." There were complex life-forms during all three of these eras.

109. **(A)**   Parasitism is symbiosis in which one species benefits, but the other is harmed.

110. **(B)**   An axis is defined as a line connecting two poles. Earth has an axis connecting the North Pole and the South Pole. The other choices are incorrect.

111. **(D)**   There are estimated to be about 100 billion stars in the universe. To count to a billion, if a person counted one number per second it would take over 34 years. To then count to 100 billion would take $34 \times 100 = 3,400$ years! In other words, a billion is a huge number.

112. **(B)**   The astronaut will feel as if he is being pushed forward toward the front of the spacecraft. The others are incorrect directions of motion. There is a negative acceleration (deceleration) and thus a negative force occurring since the vehicle is slowing down.

113. **(C)**   Blue-green algae is a prokaryotic organism in the Kingdom Monera. Prokaryotes have no nucleus-or-membrane-bound organelles.

114. **(B)**   The celestial sphere is an imaginary sphere centered on and surrounding Earth upon which the background stars are projected. The Sun, Moon, planets, and other celestial bodies seem to move relative to this background of fixed stars. It is a model used to describe positions and motions of astronomical bodies. A geodesic dome is not an astronomical tool, but is simply an architectural structure. A stellar ball is a made-up term. The Cartesian coordinate system is a mathematical system used to plot points on an x-y graph. The equatorial coordinate system is another mathematical

system used to plot specific celestial bodies in the sky using time and angular coordinates of right ascension and declination. It relates the stars to their apparent motion in the sky along the celestial sphere relative to the celestial equator. It is used to make measurements within the celestial sphere, but is not actually the sphere itself.

115. **(B)**   The "greenhouse effect" is the result of radiation being blocked from leaving the atmosphere because of the ozone layer. Depletion of the ozone layer would impact the "greenhouse effect," not cause it. The "greenhouse effect" is also caused mainly by other atmospheric gases such as water vapor and carbon dioxide. This depletion will increase radiation because the hole in the ozone layer will get larger. Acid rain is primarily caused by oxides of sulfur and nitrogen due to pollution. Photochemical reactions involving oxides of nitrogen and chlorofluorocarbons play a major role in ozone destruction. These chemicals react with ozone and lead to a net decrease in ozone concentration in the stratosphere. Since ozone is a strong absorber of incoming ultraviolet (UV) radiation, any decrease in ozone concentration will increase the amount of UV radiation reaching the surface. This will significantly increase the risk of skin cancer from exposure to the Sun. With this in mind it is easy so see why choice (D) is incorrect. However, the ozone depletion has no impact on global warming directly.

116. **(C)**   The pressure gradient force plays no significant role in vertical air circulations. Since temperature decreases with height, as the valley air warms during the day, it becomes less dense than the air along the adjacent hillsides and begins to flow up the surrounding slopes. At night, air in the hills cools faster than the air in the valleys. Gravity pulls the cooler, denser air down the hillsides into the valleys. It is low pressure near the top of the mountain that forces breezes up from the valley, so choice (E) is wrong.

117. **(A)**   Only the size of the atom increases as you move down and to the left in the periodic table.

118. **(C)**   The greater the mass of an object, the greater the force necessary to change its state of motion. Newton's first law of motion states that an object in motion will stay in motion and an object at rest will stay at rest until acted upon by an outside force. Since Newton's second law of motion states that Force = (mass)(acceleration), then in order to change its motion, as the object increases in mass, more force will be necessary to alter its acceleration. Its position may be changed slightly with the same amount of force as might be applied to a smaller object, so changing its position is not the correct answer. Greater force may not change its shape at all, and will not change its density.

119. **(A)**   The top of the sine wave is the crest. The bottom is the trough. The amplitude represents the height of the wave. The period is the wave's cycle length. The frequency is the number of cycles per second.

120. **(D)**   The water molecules, which are the medium, are not carried but the wave peaks do move toward shore. Answer choice (A) erroneously states the opposite of what is mentioned in the question. Although the ocean is somewhat mixed each day, this mixing is due to turbulence and currents, not waves. Similarly, debris washes ashore by turbulence and currents and not wave action. Waves also do not move swimmers, nor water; the waves travel through the water and the swimmer will bob up and down but will not be carried by the wave. Again, currents and turbulence are responsible for moving both the water and swimmers.

PRACTICE TEST

ANSWER SHEET

1. Ⓐ Ⓑ Ⓒ Ⓓ Ⓔ
2. Ⓐ Ⓑ Ⓒ Ⓓ Ⓔ
3. Ⓐ Ⓑ Ⓒ Ⓓ Ⓔ
4. Ⓐ Ⓑ Ⓒ Ⓓ Ⓔ
5. Ⓐ Ⓑ Ⓒ Ⓓ Ⓔ
6. Ⓐ Ⓑ Ⓒ Ⓓ Ⓔ
7. Ⓐ Ⓑ Ⓒ Ⓓ Ⓔ
8. Ⓐ Ⓑ Ⓒ Ⓓ Ⓔ
9. Ⓐ Ⓑ Ⓒ Ⓓ Ⓔ
10. Ⓐ Ⓑ Ⓒ Ⓓ Ⓔ
11. Ⓐ Ⓑ Ⓒ Ⓓ Ⓔ
12. Ⓐ Ⓑ Ⓒ Ⓓ Ⓔ
13. Ⓐ Ⓑ Ⓒ Ⓓ Ⓔ
14. Ⓐ Ⓑ Ⓒ Ⓓ Ⓔ
15. Ⓐ Ⓑ Ⓒ Ⓓ Ⓔ
16. Ⓐ Ⓑ Ⓒ Ⓓ Ⓔ
17. Ⓐ Ⓑ Ⓒ Ⓓ Ⓔ
18. Ⓐ Ⓑ Ⓒ Ⓓ Ⓔ
19. Ⓐ Ⓑ Ⓒ Ⓓ Ⓔ
20. Ⓐ Ⓑ Ⓒ Ⓓ Ⓔ
21. Ⓐ Ⓑ Ⓒ Ⓓ Ⓔ
22. Ⓐ Ⓑ Ⓒ Ⓓ Ⓔ
23. Ⓐ Ⓑ Ⓒ Ⓓ Ⓔ
24. Ⓐ Ⓑ Ⓒ Ⓓ Ⓔ
25. Ⓐ Ⓑ Ⓒ Ⓓ Ⓔ
26. Ⓐ Ⓑ Ⓒ Ⓓ Ⓔ
27. Ⓐ Ⓑ Ⓒ Ⓓ Ⓔ
28. Ⓐ Ⓑ Ⓒ Ⓓ Ⓔ
29. Ⓐ Ⓑ Ⓒ Ⓓ Ⓔ
30. Ⓐ Ⓑ Ⓒ Ⓓ Ⓔ
31. Ⓐ Ⓑ Ⓒ Ⓓ Ⓔ
32. Ⓐ Ⓑ Ⓒ Ⓓ Ⓔ
33. Ⓐ Ⓑ Ⓒ Ⓓ Ⓔ
34. Ⓐ Ⓑ Ⓒ Ⓓ Ⓔ
35. Ⓐ Ⓑ Ⓒ Ⓓ Ⓔ
36. Ⓐ Ⓑ Ⓒ Ⓓ Ⓔ
37. Ⓐ Ⓑ Ⓒ Ⓓ Ⓔ
38. Ⓐ Ⓑ Ⓒ Ⓓ Ⓔ
39. Ⓐ Ⓑ Ⓒ Ⓓ Ⓔ
40. Ⓐ Ⓑ Ⓒ Ⓓ Ⓔ

41. Ⓐ Ⓑ Ⓒ Ⓓ Ⓔ
42. Ⓐ Ⓑ Ⓒ Ⓓ Ⓔ
43. Ⓐ Ⓑ Ⓒ Ⓓ Ⓔ
44. Ⓐ Ⓑ Ⓒ Ⓓ Ⓔ
45. Ⓐ Ⓑ Ⓒ Ⓓ Ⓔ
46. Ⓐ Ⓑ Ⓒ Ⓓ Ⓔ
47. Ⓐ Ⓑ Ⓒ Ⓓ Ⓔ
48. Ⓐ Ⓑ Ⓒ Ⓓ Ⓔ
49. Ⓐ Ⓑ Ⓒ Ⓓ Ⓔ
50. Ⓐ Ⓑ Ⓒ Ⓓ Ⓔ
51. Ⓐ Ⓑ Ⓒ Ⓓ Ⓔ
52. Ⓐ Ⓑ Ⓒ Ⓓ Ⓔ
53. Ⓐ Ⓑ Ⓒ Ⓓ Ⓔ
54. Ⓐ Ⓑ Ⓒ Ⓓ Ⓔ
55. Ⓐ Ⓑ Ⓒ Ⓓ Ⓔ
56. Ⓐ Ⓑ Ⓒ Ⓓ Ⓔ
57. Ⓐ Ⓑ Ⓒ Ⓓ Ⓔ
58. Ⓐ Ⓑ Ⓒ Ⓓ Ⓔ
59. Ⓐ Ⓑ Ⓒ Ⓓ Ⓔ
60. Ⓐ Ⓑ Ⓒ Ⓓ Ⓔ
61. Ⓐ Ⓑ Ⓒ Ⓓ Ⓔ
62. Ⓐ Ⓑ Ⓒ Ⓓ Ⓔ
63. Ⓐ Ⓑ Ⓒ Ⓓ Ⓔ
64. Ⓐ Ⓑ Ⓒ Ⓓ Ⓔ
65. Ⓐ Ⓑ Ⓒ Ⓓ Ⓔ
66. Ⓐ Ⓑ Ⓒ Ⓓ Ⓔ
67. Ⓐ Ⓑ Ⓒ Ⓓ Ⓔ
68. Ⓐ Ⓑ Ⓒ Ⓓ Ⓔ
69. Ⓐ Ⓑ Ⓒ Ⓓ Ⓔ
70. Ⓐ Ⓑ Ⓒ Ⓓ Ⓔ
71. Ⓐ Ⓑ Ⓒ Ⓓ Ⓔ
72. Ⓐ Ⓑ Ⓒ Ⓓ Ⓔ
73. Ⓐ Ⓑ Ⓒ Ⓓ Ⓔ
74. Ⓐ Ⓑ Ⓒ Ⓓ Ⓔ
75. Ⓐ Ⓑ Ⓒ Ⓓ Ⓔ
76. Ⓐ Ⓑ Ⓒ Ⓓ Ⓔ
77. Ⓐ Ⓑ Ⓒ Ⓓ Ⓔ
78. Ⓐ Ⓑ Ⓒ Ⓓ Ⓔ
79. Ⓐ Ⓑ Ⓒ Ⓓ Ⓔ
80. Ⓐ Ⓑ Ⓒ Ⓓ Ⓔ

81. Ⓐ Ⓑ Ⓒ Ⓓ Ⓔ
82. Ⓐ Ⓑ Ⓒ Ⓓ Ⓔ
83. Ⓐ Ⓑ Ⓒ Ⓓ Ⓔ
84. Ⓐ Ⓑ Ⓒ Ⓓ Ⓔ
85. Ⓐ Ⓑ Ⓒ Ⓓ Ⓔ
86. Ⓐ Ⓑ Ⓒ Ⓓ Ⓔ
87. Ⓐ Ⓑ Ⓒ Ⓓ Ⓔ
88. Ⓐ Ⓑ Ⓒ Ⓓ Ⓔ
89. Ⓐ Ⓑ Ⓒ Ⓓ Ⓔ
90. Ⓐ Ⓑ Ⓒ Ⓓ Ⓔ
91. Ⓐ Ⓑ Ⓒ Ⓓ Ⓔ
92. Ⓐ Ⓑ Ⓒ Ⓓ Ⓔ
93. Ⓐ Ⓑ Ⓒ Ⓓ Ⓔ
94. Ⓐ Ⓑ Ⓒ Ⓓ Ⓔ
95. Ⓐ Ⓑ Ⓒ Ⓓ Ⓔ
96. Ⓐ Ⓑ Ⓒ Ⓓ Ⓔ
97. Ⓐ Ⓑ Ⓒ Ⓓ Ⓔ
98. Ⓐ Ⓑ Ⓒ Ⓓ Ⓔ
99. Ⓐ Ⓑ Ⓒ Ⓓ Ⓔ
100. Ⓐ Ⓑ Ⓒ Ⓓ Ⓔ
101. Ⓐ Ⓑ Ⓒ Ⓓ Ⓔ
102. Ⓐ Ⓑ Ⓒ Ⓓ Ⓔ
103. Ⓐ Ⓑ Ⓒ Ⓓ Ⓔ
104. Ⓐ Ⓑ Ⓒ Ⓓ Ⓔ
105. Ⓐ Ⓑ Ⓒ Ⓓ Ⓔ
106. Ⓐ Ⓑ Ⓒ Ⓓ Ⓔ
107. Ⓐ Ⓑ Ⓒ Ⓓ Ⓔ
108. Ⓐ Ⓑ Ⓒ Ⓓ Ⓔ
109. Ⓐ Ⓑ Ⓒ Ⓓ Ⓔ
110. Ⓐ Ⓑ Ⓒ Ⓓ Ⓔ
111. Ⓐ Ⓑ Ⓒ Ⓓ Ⓔ
112. Ⓐ Ⓑ Ⓒ Ⓓ Ⓔ
113. Ⓐ Ⓑ Ⓒ Ⓓ Ⓔ
114. Ⓐ Ⓑ Ⓒ Ⓓ Ⓔ
115. Ⓐ Ⓑ Ⓒ Ⓓ Ⓔ
116. Ⓐ Ⓑ Ⓒ Ⓓ Ⓔ
117. Ⓐ Ⓑ Ⓒ Ⓓ Ⓔ
118. Ⓐ Ⓑ Ⓒ Ⓓ Ⓔ
119. Ⓐ Ⓑ Ⓒ Ⓓ Ⓔ
120. Ⓐ Ⓑ Ⓒ Ⓓ Ⓔ

PART IV
CLEP Social Sciences and History

About Our Author

This CLEP Social Sciences and History review was written by Scott Dittloff, Ph.D. Dr. Dittloff is a professor in the Department of Government and International Affairs at the University of the Incarnate Word in San Antonio, Texas. He is the recipient of the Incarnate Word Presidential Teaching Award, given to faculty members who demonstrate extraordinary dedication to teaching that encourages student engagement. He is on the editorial board of the Journal of Social Sciences and was a longstanding member of the College Board's CLEP Social Sciences and History Test Development Committee.

AN OVERVIEW OF THE EXAM

The CLEP Social Sciences and History exam consists of 120 multiple-choice questions, each with five possible answer choices, to be answered in 90 minutes.

The exam covers the material one would find in college-level introductory classes in the following disciplines: United States history, western civilization, world history, government/political science, geography, and economics.

The approximate breakdown of topics is as follows:

40% History

   13%–15% United States History

   13%–15% Western Civilization

   13%–15% World History

60% Social Sciences

   20% Economics

   20% Geography

   20% Government/Political Science

6-WEEK STUDY PLAN

Our study plan is designed to be used in the six weeks before your exam. Be sure to set aside enough time—at least two hours each day—to study. The more time you spend studying, the more prepared and relaxed you will feel on the day of the exam.

Week	Activity
1	Take the Diagnostic Exam at the online REA Study Center (*www.rea.com/studycenter*). Your score report will identify topics where you need the most review.
2—4	Study the review, focusing on the topics you missed (or were unsure of) on the Diagnostic Exam.
5	Take Practice Test 1 at the REA Study Center. Review your score report and re-study any topics you missed.
6	Take Practice Test 2 at the REA Study Center to see how much your score has improved. If you still got a few questions wrong, go back to the review and study the topics you missed.

REVIEW OUTLINE

POLITICAL SCIENCE

INTRODUCTION TO POLITICAL SCIENCE

WHAT IS POLITICAL SCIENCE?

Political Science is the organized study of government and politics. It borrows from the related disciplines of history, philosophy, sociology, economics, and law. **Political scientists** explore such fundamental questions as: What are the philosophical foundations of modern political systems? What makes a government legitimate? What are the duties and responsibilities of those who govern? Who participates in the political process and why? What is the nature of relations among nations?

OVERVIEW OF POLITICAL PHILOSOPHY

In the 4th century BCE, the political writings of Plato and Aristotle sought to combine the realms of ethics and politics. Conjoining the two was especially urgent to Plato after he witnessed the tragic death of his great mentor, Socrates, at the hands of the self-serving political leaders of Athens in 399 BCE. Plato is most famous today for writing a series of dialogues in which Socrates played a prominent role. His most famous dialogue on politics is entitled *The Republic*. In it, he includes the timeless story of the "Allegory of the Cave," which inspired the hit movie *The Matrix*.

Aristotle was Plato's most famous student and also a tutor to Alexander the Great. Two of Aristotle's best known works are his *Politics* and *Nicomachean Ethics*, both of which remain important texts in political philosophy classes today. In both books, Aristotle articulates what he calls the "Golden Mean," where "a virtue is the midpoint between two extremes." In politics, Aristotle argues that the best type of government is the one ruled from the middle (class), because at either extreme—either rule by the rich or rule by the poor—negative consequences will occur: either the rich will exploit the poor, or the poor will seek to destroy the rich.

During the early 1500s, Niccolo Machiavelli wrote a famous political treatise entitled *The Prince*. In it, he argued that for a ruler, it is "better to be feared than loved." He also noted that rulers may have to separate politics from morality in order to achieve their ambitions. Today, Machiavelli's name is often used as an adjective. Thus, when someone accuses another person of being "Machiavellian," this typically means that the person in question is acting in an immoral manner, using "the ends" (whatever he or she wants) to "justify the means" (the tactics being used).

During the mid-1600s to the late 1700s, three thinkers emerged who made important contributions to the field of political philosophy—Thomas Hobbes, John Locke, and Jean-Jacques Rousseau. All three became known as "Social Contract" theorists, in that each one postulated a possible "social contract" that people entered into while still living in a hypothetical "state of nature," just prior to moving into an organized society.

The section below highlights some of their thoughts:

I. Thomas Hobbes / Principal Book: *The Leviathan* (1651)

Principal Concepts:

Hobbes had a pessimistic view toward humans. Accordingly, he famously argued that life in the state of nature was "solitary, poor, nasty, brutish, and short."

Hobbes assumed that, by nature, people are violently self-interested and, if necessary, they will kill others to get what they want. Hobbes thus envisioned a "social contract" whereby people gave up *all* their rights to the state (or government) in return for protection against a violent death. He thus promoted a totalitarian-style of government. The graphic novel and movie *V for Vendetta* dramatically depict a Hobbesian type of state.

II. John Locke / Principal Book: *Two Treatises on Government* (1690)

Principal Concepts:

Locke, who had a much more moderate view toward human behavior than Hobbes, believed that while humans are mostly self-interested, extreme self-interest could be held in check by enforcing a rigorous series of laws. Locke thus saw the "social contract" as one in which people gave up only some of their *natural rights* to the state. He further argued (unlike Hobbes) that if the politicians of a state became corrupt, the people had a right and obligation to overthrow them. A fundamental tenet of John Locke is that power forever resides in the people.

It should also be noted that Locke had a greater influence on America's founding fathers than any other political philosopher. For instance, the opening of Jefferson's Declaration of Independence is, in many ways, a paraphrasing of Locke's teachings.

III. Jean-Jacques Rousseau / Principal Book: *Social Contract* (1762)

Principal Concepts:

Rousseau had the most optimistic view toward human nature of the three Social Contract theorists. In that regard, he famously asserted that, "Man is born free, and everywhere he is in chains."

Rousseau argued for a very limited form of government, which was to be held in check by the loosely defined "General Will." Rousseau felt that, in the state of nature, mankind was uncorrupted, but once people entered into society, they were quickly tainted by the abuses of the corrupt church and state, both of which must be stripped of power so that mankind can return to its original, peaceful state of being.

PRINCIPAL SUBFIELDS OF POLITICAL SCIENCE

At the present time, the study of political science in the United States is concerned with the following broad subtopics or subfields:

Political Theory is an historical exploration of the major contributions to political thought from the ancient Greeks to the contemporary theorists. These theorists raise fundamental questions about the individual's existence and his relationship to the political community. **Political theory** also involves the philosophical and speculative consideration of the political world.

American Government and Politics is a survey of the origins and development of the political system in the United States from the colonial days to modern times with an emphasis on the Constitution, various political structures such as the legislative, executive, and judicial branches, the federal system, political parties, voter behavior, and fundamental freedoms.

Comparative Government is a systematic study of the structures of two or more political systems (such as those of Britain and the People's Republic of China) to achieve an understanding of how different societies manage the realities of governing. Also considered are political processes and behavior and the ideological foundations of various systems.

International Relations is a consideration of how nations interact with each other within the frameworks of law, diplomacy, and international organizations such as the United Nations.

THE DEVELOPMENT OF THE DISCIPLINE OF POLITICAL SCIENCE

Early History

Political science as a systematic study of government developed in the United States and in Western Europe during the nineteenth century as new political institutions evolved. Prior to 1850, during its classical phase, political science relied heavily on philosophy and utilized the deductive method of research.

Post–Civil War Period

The political science curriculum was formalized in the United States by faculty at Columbia and Johns Hopkins, who were deeply influenced by German scholarship on the nation-state and the formation of democratic institutions. Historical and comparative approaches to analysis of institutions were predominant. Emphasis was on constitutional and legal issues, and political institutions were widely regarded as factors in motivating the actions of individuals.

Twentieth-Century Trends

Political scientists worked to strengthen their research base, to integrate quantitative data, and to incorporate comparative studies of governmental structures in developing countries into the discipline.

American Political Science Association (APSA)

The APSA was founded in 1903 to promote the organized study of politics and to distinguish it as a field separate from history.

The Behavioral Period

From the early 1920s to the present, political science has focused on psychological interpretations and the analysis of the behavior of individuals and groups in a political context. Research has been theory-based, values-neutral, and concerned with predicting and explaining political behavior.

Contemporary Developments

Since the 1960s, interest has focused on such subtopics as African-American politics, public policy, urban and ethnic politics, and women in politics. Influenced by the leadership of Harold Lasswell, political scientists showed greater concern for using their discipline to solve social problems.

THE SCIENTIFIC METHOD OF RESEARCH IN POLITICAL SCIENCE

The modern method of scientific inquiry in the field aims to compile a body of data based on direct observation (**empirical knowledge**) that can be utilized both to explain what has been observed and to form valid generalizations. The scientific method in political science has resulted in three types of statements: **observational/evidential**, which describe the principal characteristics of what has been studied; **observational laws**, which are hypotheses based on what has been observed; and **theories**, which analyze the data that have been collected and offer plausible general principles that can be drawn from what has been observed.

Examples of Statements Based on the Scientific Method

- **Observational/evidential:** In 1992, 518 out of 535 members of the U.S. Congress were males. In the British Parliament, 550 of the 635 members were males. Eighteen of France's 20 cabinet ministers were males.

- **Observational law (hypothesis):** Legislative and executive bodies in modern democracies tend to be dominated by males.

- **Theory:** Political power in modern democracies is in male hands.

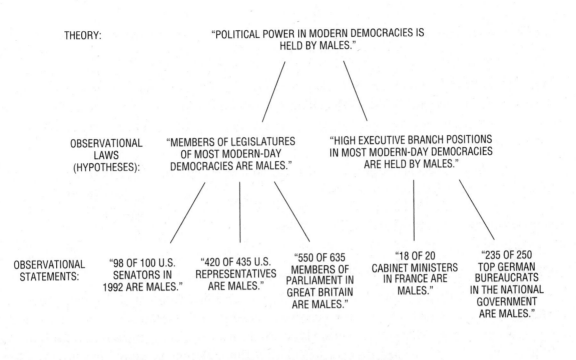

THEORY: "POLITICAL POWER IN MODERN DEMOCRACIES IS HELD BY MALES."

OBSERVATIONAL LAWS (HYPOTHESES): "MEMBERS OF LEGISLATURES OF MOST MODERN-DAY DEMOCRACIES ARE MALES." "HIGH EXECUTIVE BRANCH POSITIONS IN MOST MODERN-DAY DEMOCRACIES ARE HELD BY MALES."

OBSERVATIONAL STATEMENTS: "98 OF 100 U.S. SENATORS IN 1992 ARE MALES." "420 OF 435 U.S. REPRESENTATIVES ARE MALES." "550 OF 635 MEMBERS OF PARLIAMENT IN GREAT BRITAIN ARE MALES." "18 OF 20 CABINET MINISTERS IN FRANCE ARE MALES." "235 OF 250 TOP GERMAN BUREAUCRATS IN THE NATIONAL GOVERNMENT ARE MALES."

UNITED STATES GOVERNMENT AND POLITICS

CONSTITUTIONAL FOUNDATIONS

The government of the United States rests on a written framework created in an attempt to strengthen a loose confederation that was in crisis in the 1780s. The **Constitution** is a basic plan that outlines the structure and functions of the national government. Clearly rooted in Western political thought, it sets limits on government and protects both property and individual rights.

Historical Background

Following the successful revolt of the British colonies in North America against imperial rule, a plan of government was implemented that was consciously weak and ultimately ineffective: the **Articles of Confederation**. The Articles served as the national government from 1781–1787. The government under the Articles consisted of a **unicameral** (one-house) legislature that was clearly subordinate to the states. Representatives to the Congress were appointed and paid by their respective state legislatures, and their mission was to protect the interests of their home states. Each state, regardless of size, had one vote in Congress, which could request but not require states to provide financial and military support. **Key weaknesses of the Articles** included: their inability to regulate interstate and foreign trade, their lack of a chief executive and a national court system, and their rule that amendments must be approved by unanimous consent.

Dubbed the "**critical period**," the 1780s was a decade in the United States marked by internal conflict. The economy deteriorated as individual states printed their own currencies, taxed the products of their neighbors, and ignored foreign trade agreements. Inflation soared, small farmers lost their property, and states engaged in petty squabbles with one another. The discontent of the agrarian population reached crisis proportions in 1786 in rural Massachusetts when Revolutionary War veteran **Daniel Shays** led a rebellion of farmers against the tax collectors and the banks that were seizing their property. **Shays' Rebellion** symbolized the inability of the government under the Articles to maintain order. Bostonians subscribed money to raise an army, which successfully suppressed the rebels.

In response to the economic and social disorder and the dangers of foreign intervention, a series of meetings to consider reform of the Articles was held. In 1787, the **Constitutional Convention** was convened in **Philadelphia** ostensibly to revise the ineffective Articles. The result was an entirely new plan of government, the Constitution.

Philosophy and Ideology of the Founding Fathers

Among the distinguished men assembled at the Constitutional Convention in 1787 were **James Madison**, who recorded the debate proceedings; **George Washington**, president of the body; **Gouverneur Morris**, who wrote the final version of the document; and **Alexander Hamilton**, one of the authors of the *Federalist Papers* (1787–1788). This collection of essays, to which **Madison** and **John Jay** also contributed, expresses the political philosophy of the Founders and was instrumental in bringing about the ratification of the Constitution.

Clearly the framers of the Constitution were influenced by the ideological heritage of the Enlightenment of the seventeenth and eighteenth centuries in Western Europe. From Hobbes and Locke came the concept of the social contract. The latter had a marked influence upon **Thomas Jefferson**, who incorporated Locke's doctrines with respect to equality; government's responsibility to protect the life, liberty, and property of its constituency; and the right of revolution in his **Declaration of Independence** (1776). The Constitution itself includes Montesquieu's separation of powers and checks and balances. British documents, such as the **Magna Carta** (1215), the **Petition of Right** (1628), and the **Bill of Rights** (1689), all promoting the principle of limited government, were influential in shaping the final form of the Constitution.

Basic Principles of the Constitution

The authors of the Constitution sought to establish a government free from the tyrannies of both monarchs and mobs. Two of the critical principles embedded in the final document, **federalism** and **separation of powers**, address this concern.

The federal system established by the Founders divides the powers of government between the states and the national government. Local matters are handled on a local level, and those issues that affect the general populace are the responsibility of the federal government. Such a system is a natural outgrowth of the colonial relationship between the Americans and the mother country of England. American federalism is defined in the **Tenth Amendment** which declares: "those powers not delegated to the United States by the Constitution, nor prohibited by it to the States, are reserved to the States respectively, or to the people." In practice, the system may be confusing in that powers overlap (i.e., welfare). In cases where they conflict, the federal government is supreme.

The principle of separation of powers is codified in **Articles I**, **II**, and **III** of the main body of the Constitution. The national government is divided into three branches which have separate functions (**legislative**, **executive**, and **judicial**). Not entirely independent, each of these branches can check or limit in some way the power of one or both of the others (**checks and balances**). This system of dividing and checking powers is a vehicle for guarding against the extremes the Founders feared. Following are some examples of checks and balances:

- The legislative branch can check the executive by refusing to confirm appointments.

- The executive can check the legislature by vetoing its bills.

- The judiciary can check both the legislature and the executive by declaring laws unconstitutional.

Additional basic principles embodied in the Constitution include:

- The establishment of a representative government (**republic**).

- **Popular sovereignty** or the idea that government derives its power from the people. This concept is expressed in the **Preamble** which opens with the words, "**We the People.**"

- The enforcement of government with limits ("**rule of law**").

STRUCTURE AND FUNCTIONS OF THE NATIONAL GOVERNMENT

The national government consists of the three branches outlined in the Constitution as well as a huge bureaucracy comprised of departments, agencies, and commissions.

The Legislative Branch

Legislative power is vested in a **bicameral** (two-house) Congress which is the subject of Article I of the Constitution. The bicameral structure was the result of a compromise at the Constitutional Convention between the large states, led by Virginia, which presented a plan calling for a strong national government with representation favoring the larger states (**Virginia Plan**) and the smaller states, which countered with the **New Jersey Plan**. The latter would have retained much of the structure of the Articles of Confederation including equal representation of the states in Congress. Connecticut offered a solution in the form of the **Great Compromise**. It called for a two-house legislature with equal representation in the **Senate** and representation in the **House of Representatives** based on population.

The **expressed** or **delegated powers** of Congress are set forth in **Section 8** of Article I. They can be divided into several broad categories including economic, judicial, war, and general peace powers. **Economic powers** include:

- to lay and collect taxes
- to borrow money
- to regulate foreign and interstate commerce
- to coin money and regulate its value
- to establish rules concerning bankruptcy

Judicial powers include:

- to establish courts inferior to the Supreme Court
- to provide punishment for counterfeiting
- to define and punish piracies and felonies committed on the high seas

War powers include:

- to declare war
- to raise and support armies
- to provide and maintain a navy
- to provide for organizing, arming, and calling forth the militia

Peace powers include:

- to establish rules on naturalization
- to establish post offices and post roads
- to promote science and the arts by granting patents and copyrights
- to exercise jurisdiction over the seat of the federal government (**District of Columbia**)

The Constitution includes the so-called "**elastic clause**" which grants Congress **implied powers** to implement the delegated powers.

In addition, Congress maintains the power to discipline federal officials through **impeachment** (formal accusation of wrongdoing) and removal from office.

Article V empowers Congress to propose **amendments** (changes or additions) to the Constitution. A two-thirds majority in both houses is necessary for passage. An alternate method is to have amendments proposed by the legislatures of two-thirds of the states. In order for an amendment to become part of the Constitution, it must be **ratified** (formally approved) by three-fourths of the states (through their legislatures or by way of special conventions as in the case of the repeal of Prohibition).

Article I, **Section 9** specifically denies certain powers to the national legislature. Congress is prohibited from suspending the right of **habeas corpus** (writ calling for a party under arrest to be brought before the court where authorities must show cause for detainment) except during war or rebellion. Other prohibitions include: the passage of export taxes, the withdrawal of funds from the treasury without an appropriations law, the passage of **ex post facto** laws (make past actions punishable that were legal when they occurred), and favored treatment of one state over another with respect to commerce.

The work of the Congress is organized around a committee system. The **standing committees** are permanent and deal with such matters as agriculture, the armed services, the budget, energy, finance, and foreign policy. Special or **select committees** are established to deal with specific issues and usually have a limited duration. **Conference committees** iron out differences between the House and the Senate versions of a bill before it is sent on to the President.

One committee unique to the House of Representatives is the powerful **Rules Committee**. Thousands of bills are introduced each term, and the Rules Committee acts as a clearing house to weed out those that are unworthy of consideration before the full House. Constitutionally, all revenue-raising bills must originate in the House of Representatives. They are scrutinized by the powerful House **Ways and Means Committee**.

Committee membership is organized on party lines with **seniority** being a key factor, although in recent years, length of service has diminished in importance in the determination of chairmanships. The composition of each committee is largely based on the ratio of each party in the Congress as a whole. The party that has a **majority** is allotted a greater number of members on each committee. The chairman of the standing committees are selected by the leaders of the majority party.

The legislative process is at once cumbersome and time consuming. A **bill** (proposed law) can be introduced in either house (with the exception of **revenue bills**, which must originate in the House of Representatives). It is referred to the appropriate **committee** and then to a **subcommittee**, which will hold **hearings** if the members agree that it has merit. The bill is reported back to the **full committee**, which must decide whether or not to send it to the **full chamber** to be debated. If the bill passes in the full chamber, it is then sent to the **other chamber** to begin the process all over again. Any differences between the House and Senate versions of the bill must be resolved in a **conference committee** before it is sent to the **President** for consideration. Most of the thousands of bills introduced in Congress die in committee with only a small percentage becoming law.

Debate on major bills is a key step in the legislative process because of the tradition of attaching **amendments** at this stage. In the House, the rules of debate are designed to enforce limits necessitated by the size of the body (435 members). In the smaller Senate (100 members), unlimited debate (**filibuster**) is allowed. Filibustering is a delaying tactic that can postpone action indefinitely. **Cloture** is a parliamentary procedure that can limit debate and bring a filibuster to an end.

Constitutional qualifications for the House of Representatives state that members must be at least **25** years of age, must have been **U.S. citizens for at least seven years**, and must be **residents of the state** that sends them to Congress. According to the **Reapportionment Act of 1929**, the size of the House is fixed at **435** members. They serve terms of **two years** in length. The presiding officer and generally the most powerful member is the **Speaker of the House**, who is the leader of the political party that has a majority in a given term.

Constitutional qualifications for the Senate state that a member must be at least **30** years of age, must have been a **U.S. citizen for at least nine years**, and must be an **inhabitant of the state** that he/she represents. Senators are elected for terms of **six years** in length on a staggered basis so that one-third of the body is up for re-election in each national election. The president of the Senate is the **Vice President**. This role is largely symbolic, with the Vice President casting a vote only in the case of a tie. There is no position in the Senate comparable to that of the Speaker of the House, although the **Majority Leader** is generally recognized as the most powerful member.

The Executive Branch

The **President** is the head of the executive branch of the federal government. **Article II** of the Constitution deals with the powers and duties of the President or chief executive. Following are the President's principal **constitutional responsibilities**:

- serves as **Commander-in-Chief** of the armed forces

- negotiates treaties (with the approval of two-thirds of the Senate)

- appoints ambassadors, judges, and other high officials (with the consent of the Senate)

- grants pardons and reprieves for those convicted of federal crimes (except in impeachment cases)

- seeks counsel of department heads (Cabinet members)

- recommends legislation

- meets with representatives of foreign states

- sees that the laws are faithfully executed

Despite the attempts by the Founders to set clear limits on the power of the chief executive, the importance of the presidency has grown dramatically over the years. Recent trends to reassert the pre-eminence of the Congress notwithstanding, the President remains the most visible and powerful single member of the federal government and the only one (with the exception of the vice president) elected to represent all the people. He shapes foreign policy with his diplomatic and treaty-making powers and largely determines domestic policy. Presidents also possess the power to **veto** legislation. A presidential veto may be overridden by a two-thirds vote in both houses, but such a majority is not easy to build, particularly in the face of the chief executive's opposition. A

pocket veto occurs when the President neither signs nor rejects a bill, and the Congress adjourns within ten days of his receipt of the legislation. The fact that the President is the head of a vast federal bureaucracy is another indication of the power of the office.

Although the Constitution makes no mention of a formal **Cabinet** as such, since the days of George Washington, chief executives have relied on department heads to aid in the decision-making process. Washington's Cabinet was comprised of the secretaries of **state, war, treasury**, and an **attorney general**. Today there are 15 Cabinet departments, with **Homeland Security** being the most recently created post. Efforts to trim the federal government in the 1990s have resulted in suggestions to streamline and eliminate some Cabinet posts.

The **Executive Office of the President** is made up of agencies that supervise the daily work of the government. The **White House Staff** manages the President's schedule and is usually headed by a powerful **chief of staff**. Arguably the most critical agency of the Executive Office is the **Office of Management and Budget**, which controls the budget process for the national government. Other key executive agencies include the **Council of Economic Advisors** and the **National Security Council**, which advises the President on matters that threaten the safety of the nation and directs the **Central Intelligence Agency**.

The **Constitutional Requirements** for the office of President and Vice President are as follows: a candidate must be at least **35** years of age, must be a **natural-born** citizen, and must have **resided in the United States for a minimum of 14 years**. Article II provides for an **Electoral College** to elect the President and Vice President. Each state has as many votes in the Electoral College as it has members of Congress plus three additional electors from the District of Columbia—making a grand total of 538 electors. The Founding Fathers established the Electoral College to provide an **indirect** method of choosing the chief executive; as shown in the 2000 and 2016 elections, the Electoral College can still play a decisive role in determining the outcome of presidential elections.

The question of **presidential succession** has been addressed by both legislation and amendment. The Constitution states that if the President dies or cannot perform his duties, the "powers and duties" of the office shall "devolve" on the Vice President. The **Presidential Succession Act** (1947) placed the **speaker of the house** next in line if both the President and the Vice President were unable to serve. Until recently, when the Vice President assumed the office of President, his former position was left vacant. The **Twenty-Fifth Amendment** (1967) gives the President the power to appoint a new Vice President (with the approval of a majority of both houses of Congress). It also provides for the Vice President to serve as **Acting President** if the chief executive is disabled or otherwise unable to carry out the duties of the office. The **Twenty-Second Amendment** (1951) says, "No person shall be elected to the office of the President more than twice...." In addition, anyone who has served more than two years while filling out another person's term may not be elected to the presidency more than once.

The Judicial Branch

Article III of the Constitution establishes the **Supreme Court** but does not define the role of this branch as clearly as it does the legislative and executive branches. Yet our contemporary judicial branch consists of thousands of courts and is in essence a dual system, with each state having its own judiciary functioning simultaneously with a complete set of federal courts. The most significant piece of legislation with respect to establishing a network of federal courts was the **Judiciary Act of 1789**. This law organized the Supreme Court and set up the 13 **federal district courts**. The district courts have **original jurisdiction** (to hear cases in the first instance) for federal cases involving both civil and criminal law. Federal cases on appeal are heard in the **Courts of Appeal**. The decisions of these courts are final, except for those cases that are accepted for review by the Supreme Court.

The **Supreme Court** today is made up of a **Chief Justice** and eight **Associate Justices**. They are appointed for life by the President with the approval of the Senate.

In the early history of the United States, the Supreme Court was largely preoccupied with the relationship between the federal government and the states. In 1803, the process of **judicial review** (power to determine the constitutionality of laws and actions of the legislative and executive branches) was established under **Chief Justice John Marshall** in the case of *Marbury v. Madison*. This power has become the foundation of the American judicial system and underscores the deep significance of the courts in determining the course of United States history.

The Supreme Court chooses cases for review based on whether they address substantial federal issues. If four of the nine justices vote to consider a case, then it will be added to the agenda. In such cases, **writs of certiorari** (orders calling up the records from a lower court) are issued. The justices are given detailed briefs and hear oral arguments. Reaching a decision is a complicated process. The justices scrutinize the case with reference to the Constitution and also consider previous decisions in similar cases (**precedent**). When all of the justices agree, the opinion issued is **unanimous**. In the case of a split decision, a **majority opinion** is written by one of the justices in agreement. Sometimes a justice will agree with the majority but for a different principle, in which case he/she can write a **concurring opinion** explaining the different point of view. Justices who do not vote with the majority may choose to write **dissenting opinions** to air their conflicting arguments.

In addition to the Supreme Court, the federal District Courts, and the Courts of Appeal, several special courts at the federal level have been created by Congress. The **U.S. Tax Court** handles conflicts between citizens and the Internal Revenue Service. The **Court of Claims** was designed to hear cases in which citizens bring suit against the U.S. government. Other special courts include the **Court of International Trade**, the **Court of Customs**, and the **Court of Military Appeals**.

The Federal Bureaucracy

In addition to the President's Cabinet and the Executive Office, a series of independent agencies makes up the federal bureaucracy, the so-called "**fourth branch**" of the national government. Most of these agencies were established to protect consumers and to regulate industries engaged in interstate trade. Others were set up to oversee government programs. From the time of the establishment of the Interstate Commerce Commission in 1887, these departments grew in number and influence. Late in the 1970s, the trend began to reverse, as some agencies were cut back and others eliminated altogether.

Among the most important of these powerful agencies are the **regulatory commissions**. The President appoints their administrators with the approval of the Senate. Unlike Cabinet secretaries and other high appointees, they cannot be dismissed by the chief executive. This system protects the independent status of the agencies. Following are examples of some of the major regulatory agencies and their functions.

Agency	Regulatory Functions
Interstate Commerce Commission	Monitors surface transportation and some pipelines
Federal Reserve Board	Supervises the banking system, sets interest rates, and controls the money supply
Federal Trade Commission	Protects consumers by looking into false advertising and antitrust violations
Federal Communications Commission	Regulates interstate and international communications by radio, television, wire, satellite, and cable.
Securities and Exchange Commission	Protects investors by monitoring the sale of stocks and bonds
National Labor Relations Board	Oversees labor and management practices
Consumer Product Safety Commission	Sets standards of safety for manufactured products
Nuclear Regulatory Commission	Licenses and inspects nuclear power plants

Another category of the "fourth branch" of government is made up of the **independent executive agencies**. These were created by Congress and resemble Cabinet departments, but they do not enjoy Cabinet status. Nonetheless they are powerful entities. Some of the key executive agencies include the Civil Rights Commission, the Environmental Protection Agency, and the National Aeronautics and Space Administration. Their names are indicative of their functions. The top-level executives of these agencies are appointed by the President with the approval of the Senate.

Some of the independent agencies are actually **government corporations**. These are commercial enterprises created by Congress to perform a variety of necessary services. Their roots can be traced back to the **First Bank of the United States** established in 1791 by Secretary of the Treasury **Alexander Hamilton**. The **Federal Deposit Insurance Corporation** (FDIC), which insures bank deposits, is a more recent example. Under **Franklin Roosevelt's New Deal**, the **Tennessee Valley Authority** (TVA) was authorized to revive a depressed region of the nation. Today it oversees the generation of electric power throughout a vast region and maintains flood control programs as well. The largest of the government corporations and the most familiar to the general

HOW A BILL BECOMES A LAW

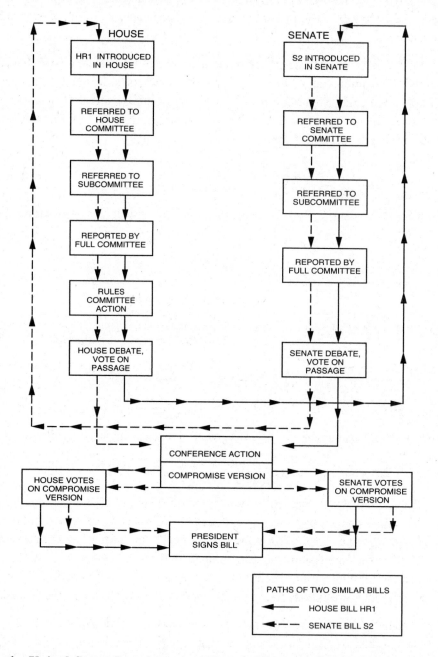

public is the **United States Postal Service**. The original Post Office Department was established in 1775 by the Second Continental Congress, and it enjoyed Cabinet status. It was reorganized in 1970 in hopes that it would eventually become self-supporting.

The large and powerful federal bureaucracy shapes and administers government policy. It is inherently political despite sporadic efforts throughout the years to maintain the integrity of the bureaucratic staff. Dating back to the administrations of **Andrew Jackson**, the practice of handing out government jobs in return for political favors (**spoils system**) had been the rule. The **Civil Service Act** (the **Pendleton Act**) was passed in 1883 in an attempt to reform the spoils system. Federal workers were to be recruited on the basis of merit determined by a competitive examination. Veterans were given preferential status. The Civil Service system was reorganized in the 1970s with the creation of the **Office of Personnel Management**. The OPM is charged with recruiting, training, and promoting government workers. Merit is the stated objective when hiring federal employees. A controversial policy of the OPM is affirmative action, a program to help groups discriminated against in the job market to find employment.

POLITICAL BELIEFS AND CHARACTERISTICS OF CITIZENS

The population of the United States, with its diverse components, is difficult to characterize with respect to political beliefs and attitudes. The process by which individuals form their political allegiances is called **political socialization**. Several factors (**cleavages**) are relevant to the formation of political opinions, including family, race, gender, class, religion, education, and region. Following are some generalizations as to the impact of these cleavages on an individual's political identification and activity.

Family – affiliation with a political party is commonly passed from one generation to another.

Race – African Americans tend to be more liberal than whites on economic, social, and public policy issues.

Gender – women tend to be more liberal than men.

Class – citizens from the middle and upper classes tend to be more politically active than those from the lower socioeconomic brackets. Low income voters tend to identify more with the liberal agenda.

Religion – Protestants tend to be more conservative than Catholics and Jews. Evangelical Protestants seem to be most conservative on ethical and moral issues.

Education – graduate-level education seems to have a liberalizing effect that remains potent after schooling is completed.

Region – Southerners tend to be most conservative, Midwesterners more liberal, and those living on the East and West coasts the most liberal of all.

Despite the categorization of Americans as either **liberals** or **conservatives**, most studies indicate that they do not follow clearly delineated **ideologies** (firm and consistent beliefs with respect to political, economic, and social issues). The terms *liberal* and *conservative* with reference to the political beliefs of Americans are difficult to define in precise terms. Liberals tend to favor change and to view government as a tool for improving the quality of life. Conservatives, on the other hand, are more inclined to view both change and government with suspicion. They emphasize individual initiative and local solutions to problems. A puzzling reversal is seen in the attitudes of liberals and conservatives when confronting moral issues such as abortion and school prayer. Here conservatives see a role for government in ensuring the moral climate of the nation while liberals stress the importance of individual choice.

POLITICAL INSTITUTIONS AND SPECIAL INTERESTS

Civic culture in the United States is dominated by the two major political parties and is heavily influenced by the activities of interest groups and the mass media. These latter forces, both directly and indirectly, are largely responsible for molding and swaying public opinion.

Political Parties

A **political party** is an organization that seeks to influence government by electing candidates to public office. The party provides a label for candidates, recruits and campaigns, and tries to organize and control the legislative and executive branches of government through a set of leaders.

The Constitution does not mention political parties, and the Founders in general were opposed to them. Yet they developed simultaneously with the organization of the new government in 1789. It was the initial conflict over the interpretation of the powers assigned to the new government by the Constitution that gave rise to the first organized American political parties.

The **Federalist Party** evolved around the policies of Washington's Secretary of the Treasury, **Alexander Hamilton**. He and his supporters favored a **"loose construction"** approach to the interpretation of the Constitution. They advocated a strong federal government with the power to assume any duties and responsibilities not prohibited to it by the text of the document. They generally supported programs designed to benefit banking and commercial interests, and in foreign policy, the Federalists were **pro-British**.

The **Democratic** or **Jeffersonian Republicans** formed in opposition to the Federalists. They rallied around Washington's Secretary of State, **Thomas Jefferson**. The Jeffersonians took a **"strict constructionist"** approach, interpreting the Constitution in a narrow, limited sense. Sympathetic to the needs of the "common man," the Democratic-Republicans were mistrustful of powerful centralized government. They saw the small farmers, shopkeepers, and laborers as the backbone of the nation. In the area of foreign affairs, the Democratic-Republicans were **pro-French**. The present-day Democratic Party traces its roots to the Jeffersonians.

By the 1820s, the Democrats had splintered into factions led by **Andrew Jackson** (the Democrats) and **John Quincy Adams** (National Republicans). The Jacksonians continued with Jefferson's tradition of supporting policies designed to enhance the power of the common man. Their support was largely agrarian. The National Republicans, like their Federalist predecessors, represented the interests of bankers, merchants, and some large planters. Eventually a new party, the **Whigs**, was organized from the remnants of the old Federalists and the National Republicans. The Whigs were prominent during the 1840s, but like their Democratic rivals, they fragmented during the 1850s over the divisive slavery issue. The modern **Republican Party** was born in 1854 as Whigs and anti-slavery Democrats came together to halt the spread of slavery. The Republicans built a constituency around the interests of business, farmers, workers, and the newly emancipated slaves in the post-Civil War era.

Political parties exert a variety of functions essential to the democratic tradition in the United States. Nominating candidates for local, state, and national office is their most visible activity. At the national level, this function has been diluted somewhat by the popularity of **primary elections** allowing voters to express their preference for candidates. Raucous conventions where party bosses chose obscure "**dark horse**" candidates in "smoke-filled rooms" are largely a thing of the past.

Political parties stimulate interest in public issues by highlighting their own strengths and maximizing the flaws of the opposition. They also provide a framework for keeping the machinery of government operating, most notably in their control of Congress and its organization, which is strictly along party lines.

American political parties appear in theory to be highly organized. The geographic size of the country coupled with the federal system of government keep the parties in a state of relative decentralization. At the local level, the fundamental unit of organization is the **precinct**. At this level, there is usually a captain or committee to handle such routine chores as registering voters, distributing party literature, organizing "**grass-roots**" meetings, and getting out the vote on election day.

State central committees are critical to the parties' fund-raising activities. They also organize the state party conventions. There is great variety from state to state regarding the composition and selection of the state committees, which often formulate policies independent from those of the national committee.

In presidential election years, the **national party committees** are most visible. They plan the **national nominating convention**, write the party **platforms** (summaries of positions on major issues), raise money to finance political activities, and carry out the election campaigns. Representatives from each state serve on the national committees, and the **presidential nominee** chooses the individual to serve as the **party chairperson**.

Although the two-party system is firmly established in the United States, over the years, "**third parties**" have left their marks. The national nominating conventions were introduced in the 1830s by the **Anti-Masonic Party** and were soon adopted by the Democrats and the Whigs. The **Prohibition Party** opposed the use of alcohol and worked for the adoption of the **Eighteenth Amendment**. In the 1890s, the **Populist Party** championed the causes of the farmers and workers and impacted the mainstream parties with its reform agenda. Among the Populist innovations were the **initiative petition** (a mechanism allowing voters to put proposed legislation on the ballot) and the **referendum** (allowing voters to approve or reject laws passed by their legislatures). The **Progressive** or **Bull Moose Party** was a **splinter party** (one that breaks away from an established party, in this case the Republican Party) built around the personality of Theodore Roosevelt.

Another party formed around the personality of a forceful individual was the 1992 **Reform Party** of **H. Ross Perot**. Perot did not capture any electoral votes but garnered 19 percent of the popular tally.

Elections

In comparison to citizens in other democratic systems, Americans elect a large number of public officials. Elections in the United States are largely regulated by **state** law. The Constitution does assign to Congress the responsibility for determining "the times, places, and manner of holding elections for Senators and Representatives." Article II establishes the Electoral College for presidential elections and specifies that they shall be held on the same day throughout the nation. Several of the Amendments deal with election procedures, voter qualifications, and **suffrage** (the right to vote) for target groups (former slaves, women, and those 18 years of age and older). Nonetheless, the principal responsibility for arranging and supervising elections rests with the states.

The actual election process consists of two phases: nominating the candidates and choosing the final officials. **Primary elections** screen and select the final party candidates. **Closed primaries** allow voters **registered** (legal procedure that must be completed before an individual can vote) in one of the political parties to express their preferences for the final candidate from among the field of hopefuls in that party. **Open primaries** allow voters to select their party affiliations on site. Some states allow "**crossover**" voting which permits voters registered in one party to vote for candidates in the other party. This practice can lead to the tactic of voting for the weakest choice in the opposition party to give an advantage in the final election to the candidate and the party the voter actually supports.

In **national elections** (those held in November of each even-numbered year to choose national officeholders), the **campaign** traditionally begins after Labor Day. **Off-year elections** are those in which only members of Congress are chosen and no presidential contest is held. In both presidential and off-year elections, candidates follow exhausting schedules and spend huge sums on media advertising. Their activities usually dominate the national and local news coverage, and debates are common forums for airing their differences. Funding for political campaigns comes from a variety of sources including the candidates' own resources, private supporters, **Political Action Committees** (PACs), and the federal government. In the election reform drive of the 1970s, the **Federal Election Commission** was created to ensure that laws concerning campaign financing are followed.

The cost of the elections themselves is borne by the state and local governments, which must prepare ballots, designate polling places, and pay workers who participate in administering the elections. **Registrars of voters** oversee the preparation of ballots, the establishment of polling places, and the tallying of the votes. In a close election, the loser may request a **recount**. Some states require them in closely contested races.

Voter Behavior

In recent years, attention has focused on the problem of voter apathy. Despite efforts to extend suffrage to all segments of the adult population, participation in the electoral process has been on the decline. Several theories have been advanced to explain this trend. There is widespread belief that Americans are dissatisfied with their government and mistrust all elected officials. Therefore, they refuse to participate in the electoral process. Some citizens do not vote in a given election, not because they are "turned-off" to the system, but because they are ill, homeless, away on business, or otherwise preoccupied on election day. College students and others away from their legal residences find registration and the use of **absentee ballots** cumbersome and inconvenient. Efforts were made in the 1990s to streamline the registration process with such legislation as the **"motor-voter" bill** that makes it possible for citizens to register at their local registries of motor vehicles.

While most attempts to explain voter apathy focus on negatives such as citizen apathy, some analysts disagree. They see disinterest in the ballot as a sign that the majority of Americans are happy with the system and feel no sense of urgency to participate in the political process.

Political participation is not limited to voting in elections. Working for candidates, attending rallies, contacting elected officials and sharing opinions about issues, writing letters to newspapers, marching in protest, and joining in community activities are all forms of political participation. While voter turnout has decreased in recent years, other forms of participation seem to be on the increase.

Interest Groups

American officials and political leaders are continually subjected to pressure from a variety of **interest groups** seeking to influence their actions. Such groups arise from bonds among individuals who share common concerns. Interest groups may be loosely organized (**informal**), with no clear structure or regulations. A good example of such an informal or ad hoc interest group was the "March of the Poor" on Washington, D.C., in 1963 to focus Congress's attention on the needs of the "underclass" in America. A group of neighbors united in opposition to a new shopping mall that threatens a wetland is an example of this type of group. Other interest groups are much more **formal** and permanent in nature. They may have suites of offices and large numbers of employees. Their political objectives are usually clearly defined. Labor unions, professional and public-interest groups, and single-issue organizations fall into this category. The National Rifle Association and the National Right to Life Organization are examples of **single-issue** pressure groups.

Interest groups employ a variety of tactics to accomplish their goals. Most commonly, they **lobby** (influence the passage or defeat of legislation) elected officials, particularly members of Congress. Lobbyists provide legislators with reports and statistics to persuade them of the legitimacy of their respective positions. They may present expert testimony at public hearings and influence the media to portray their causes in a favorable light. Lobbyists are required to register in

Washington and to make their positions public. They are barred from presenting false and misleading information and from bribing public officials. Regulatory legislation cannot, however, curb all the abuses inherent to a system of organized persuasion.

One particularly controversial brand of pressure group is the **Political Action Committee** (PAC). PACs were formed in the 1970s in an attempt to circumvent legislation limiting contributions to political campaigns. Critics see these interest groups as another means of diluting the influence individual voters may have on their elected officials. Some politicians refuse to accept PAC money.

Public Opinion

Public opinion refers to the attitudes and preferences expressed by a significant number of individuals about an issue that involves the government or the society at large. It does not necessarily represent the sentiments of all or even most of the citizenry. Nonetheless, it is an important component of a democratic society.

In today's technological society, the influence of the **mass media** on public opinion cannot be over-emphasized. The print and broadcast media can reach large numbers of people cheaply and efficiently, but the electronic media in particular have been criticized for over-simplifying complicated issues and reducing coverage of major events to brief sound bites. Both the print and broadcast media claim to present news in a fair and objective format, but both conservatives and liberals claim that coverage is slanted. In recent years, a number of partisan digital media have taken root on the Internet and in apps. **Paid political advertising** is another vehicle for molding public opinion. In this case, objectivity is neither expected nor attempted, as candidates and interest groups employ "hard-sell" techniques to persuade voters to support their causes.

Measuring the effects of the media on public opinion is difficult, as is gauging where the public stands on a given issue at a particular point in time. **Public opinion polls** have been designed to these ends. Pollsters usually address a **random sample** and try to capture a **cross-section** of the population. Their questions are designed to elicit responses that do not mirror the biases of the interviewer or the polling organization. Results are tabulated and analyzed, and summaries are presented to the media.

Although polls are more accurate today than in the past, they are still subject to criticism for oversimplifying complicated issues and encouraging pat answers to complex problems. Public opinion is constantly in a state of flux, and what may be a valid report today is passé tomorrow. Another criticism is that interviewees may not be entirely candid, particularly with respect to sensitive issues. They may answer as they think they should but not necessarily with full honesty.

A type of election poll that has been the target of sharp criticism is the **exit poll** in which interviewers question subjects about their votes as they leave the polling places. These polls may be accurate, but if the media present the results while voting is still in progress, the outcome may be affected. Predicting the winners before voters throughout the country have had the opportunity to cast their ballots in a national election robs a segment of the electorate of the sense that its participation is of any consequence. In the 2000 election, exit polls led to confusion as Florida results were projected prematurely; the television networks vowed to be more careful.

CIVIL RIGHTS AND INDIVIDUAL LIBERTIES

Civil rights are those legal claims that individuals have to protect themselves from discrimination at the hands of both the government and other citizens. They include the right to vote, equality before the law, and access to public facilities. **Individual** or **civil liberties** protect the sanctity of the person from arbitrary governmental interference. In this category belong the fundamental freedoms of speech, religion, press, and rights such as **due process** (government must act fairly and follow established procedures, as in legal proceedings).

The origin of the concept of fundamental rights and freedoms can be traced to the British constitutional heritage and to the theorists of the Enlightenment. Jefferson's **Declaration of Independence** contains several references to the crown's failure to uphold the civil rights that British subjects had come to value and expect. When fashioning the Constitution, the Founding Fathers included passages regarding the protection of civil liberties, such as the provision in Article I for maintaining the right of *habeas corpus*. One of the criticisms of the Constitution lodged by its opponents was that it did not go far enough in safeguarding individual rights. During the first session of Congress in 1789, the first ten amendments (the **Bill of Rights**) were adopted and sent to the states for ratification. These amendments contain many of the protections that define the ideals of American life. The Bill of Rights was meant to limit the power of the federal government to restrict the freedom of individual citizens. The **Fourteenth Amendment** of 1868 prohibits **states** from denying civil rights and individual liberties to their residents. The Supreme Court is charged with interpreting the law, particularly as it applies to civil rights and individual liberties cases. Not until the **Gitlow Case** in 1925 did the Supreme Court begin to exercise this function with respect to state enforcement of the Bill of Rights. States are now expected to conform to the federal standard of civil rights.

The Amendment that is most closely identified with individual liberty in the United States is the **First Amendment**, which protects freedom of religion, speech, press, assembly, and petition. The First Amendment sets forth the principle of **separation of Church and State** with its "**free exercise**" and "**establishment**" clauses. These have led the Supreme Court to rule against such practices as school prayer (***Engel v. Vitale**, 1962*) and Bible reading in public schools (***Abington Township v. Schempp,** 1963*).

The **Fourth Amendment**, which outlawed "**unreasonable searches and seizures**," mandates that warrants be granted only "**upon probable cause**," and affirms the "**right of the people to be secure in their persons**," is fundamental to the Court's interpretation of due process and the rights of the accused. The **Fifth Amendment**, which calls for a grand jury, outlawed **double jeopardy** (trying a person who has been acquitted of a charge for a second time) and states that a person may not be compelled to be a witness against himself, is also the basis for Supreme Court rulings that protect the accused. "**Cruel and unusual punishments**" are banned by the **Eighth Amendment**. This clause has been invoked by opponents of capital punishment to justify their position, but the Supreme Court has ruled that the death penalty can be applied if states are judicious and use equal standards in sentencing to death those convicted of capital crimes.

In the twentieth century, a major concern for litigation and review by the Supreme Court was the area of civil rights for minorities, particularly African Americans. When civil rights organizations such as the NAACP brought a series of cases before the courts under the **"equal protection clause"** of the **Fourteenth Amendment**, they began to enjoy some victories. Earlier when the Supreme Court enforced its **"separate but equal"** doctrine in the 1896 case *Plessy v. Ferguson*, it did not apply the equal protection standard and allowed segregation to be maintained. The Court reversed itself in 1954 in the landmark case *Brown v. Board of Education*, which ruled that separate but equal was unconstitutional. This ruling led to an end to most **de jure** (legally enforced) segregation, but **de facto** (exists in fact) segregation persisted, largely due to housing patterns and racial and ethnic enclaves in urban neighborhoods.

Landmark Supreme Court Cases

In addition to the previously cited Supreme Court rulings in civil rights and individual liberties cases, the following landmark decisions are notable for their relevance to the concepts of civil rights and individual freedoms:

- *Dred Scott v. Sandford* (1857) – ruled that as a slave Scott had no right to sue for his freedom, and further that Congressional prohibitions against slavery in U.S. territories were unlawful.

- *Near v. Minnesota* (1931) – states were barred from using the concept of prior restraint (outlawing something before it has taken place) to discourage the publication of objectionable material except during wartime or in the cases of obscenity or incitement to violence.

- *West Virginia Board of Education v. Barnette* (1943) – overturned an earlier decision and ruled that compulsory saluting of the flag was unconstitutional.

- *Korematsu v. United States* (1944) – upheld the legality of the forced evacuation of persons of Japanese ancestry during World War II as a wartime necessity.

- *Mapp v. Ohio* (1961) – extended the Supreme Court's exclusionary rule, which bars at trial the introduction of evidence that has not been legally obtained. The Court has modified this ruling, particularly with reference to drug cases, so that evidence that might not initially have been obtained legally, but which would eventually have turned up in lawful procedures, can be introduced.

- *Gideon v. Wainwright* (1963) – ruled that courts must provide legal counsel to poor defendants in all felony cases. A later ruling extended this right to all defendants facing possible prison sentences.

- *Escobedo v. Illinois* (1964) – extended the right to counsel to include consultation prior to interrogation by authorities.

- *Miranda v. Arizona* (1966) – mandated that all suspects be informed of their due process rights before questioning by police.

- *Tinker v. Des Moines School District* (1969) – defined the wearing of black armbands in school in protest against the Vietnam War as "symbolic speech" protected by the First Amendment.

- *New York Times v. United States* (1971) – allowed, under the First Amendment's freedom of the press protection, the publication of the controversial Pentagon Papers during the Vietnam War.

- *Roe v. Wade* (1973) – legalized abortion so long as a fetus is not viable (able to survive outside the womb).

- *Bakke v. Regents of the University of California* (1978) – declared the university's quota system to be unconstitutional while upholding the legitimacy of affirmative action policies in which institutions consider race and gender as factors when determining admissions.

- *Hazelwood School District v. Kuhlmeier* (1988) – ruled that freedom of the press does not extend to student publications that might be construed as sponsored by the school.

COMPARATIVE GOVERNMENT AND POLITICS

This subfield of government and politics includes two principal areas of scholarship and information: the theoretical frameworks for the government structures, functions, and political cultures of nations, and a comparative analysis of the political systems of a series of targeted nations or societies.

THEORETICAL FRAMEWORKS FOR GOVERNMENT STRUCTURES, FUNCTIONS, AND POLITICAL CULTURE

Environmental Factors

In order to understand the political institutions and civic life of any nation, several environmental factors need to be considered. Such questions as the **size, location, geographic features, economic strength, level of industrialization,** and **cultural diversity** of a society must be explored. Both the **domestic** and **international** contexts need to be examined as well as the level of **dependence** on or **independence** from the world community. The location of the United States in the Western Hemisphere, separated from both Europe and Asia by vast expanses of ocean, is a critical component in the development of its relatively independent political culture. Conversely, the location of Eastern European countries in the shadow of the post-World War II Soviet Union led to political dependence. The cultural diversity and traditional hostilities of the Balkan peoples are key elements in the political and military volatility of the region. Industrialization and economic stability are conditions that are commonly conducive to a highly developed political system.

The **age** and **historical traditions** of a nation have a great impact on its current political culture. France's contemporary unitary form of government can be viewed as an evolutionary manifestation of earlier traditions that centralized power in divine right monarchs and ambitious emperors. **Legitimacy** (acceptance by citizens) is quite another prospect in such places as Somalia and Haiti with their unstable political histories and economic vulnerability.

Government Structures and Functions

How a government is organized, its mechanisms for carrying out its mission, the scope of that mission, and how its structures and functions compare with other governments are prime considerations in comparative government.

The **geographic distribution of authority and responsibility** is a key variable. **Confederations**, such as the United States under the Articles of Confederation, have weak central governments and delegate principal authority to smaller units such as the states. **Federal systems**, on the other hand, divide sovereignty between a central government and those of their separate states. Brazil, India, and the United States are contemporary examples of federal republics. Highly centralized, **unitary** forms of government concentrate power and authority at the top, as in France and Japan.

Separation of governmental powers is another aspect of structure useful in comparing political systems. **Authoritarian** governments concentrate power in a single or collective executive, with the legislative and judicial bodies having little input. The former Soviet Union is an example. Great Britain typifies the **parliamentary** form of government. Here legislative and executive combine, with a prime minister and cabinet selected from within the legislative body. They maintain power only as long as the legislative assembly supports their major policies. The **democratic presidential** system of the United States clearly separates the legislative, executive, and judicial structures. The branches, particularly the executive and the legislative, must cooperate, however, in order for policy to be consistent and for government operations to be carried out smoothly.

A third aspect of governmental structure and function involves the **limits** placed on the power to govern. This facet of politics closely reflects the theoretical and ideological roots of a system. **Constitutional** systems limit the powers of government through written and/or unwritten sources. Law, custom, and precedent combine to protect individuals from the unchecked power of a central authority. The United States and Great Britain have constitutional governments. **Authoritarian** regimes, such as those found in China and the former Soviet Union, do not limit the power of the central authority over the lives of individuals. Those in control impose their values and their will on the society at large regardless of popular sentiments. Authoritarianism is associated with **fascism**, **Nazism**, and **totalitarianism** in general.

Political Culture, Parties, Participation, and Mechanisms for Change

Understanding a nation's **political culture** is key to analyzing the theoretical foundations, structure, and functions of its government. It can be defined as the aggregate values a society shares about how politics and government should operate. Some societies function from a **consensus** framework, while other political cultures are more **conflicted**. The Soviet Union's political culture after World War II, as contrasted with the post-Soviet situation there in the early 1990s, illustrates the difference between consensual and conflicted societies. The vehicles for transmitting the political culture and the social cleavages that characterize that culture will impact its system of governing and its legitimacy in the minds of its citizenry. Analysis of the extent to which citizens support their political systems is an important component of comparative government.

The methods citizens employ to have an impact upon their political system and the ease of their access to the power structure are the types of questions comparative politics examines. Do elections offer a **choice** between candidates with diverse programs and contrasting agendas, as is often the case in the United States, or do they present citizens the opportunity to show their support for the government in a **one party** system such as in China? The number, nature, and power of political parties are additional factors for analysis with respect to how the demands and concerns of citizens in various nations are represented and met. The presence and proliferation of other interest groups, such as labor unions and environmental activists, provide additional clues as to the values and methods of a political culture.

Beyond voting in elections and joining and supporting political parties and interest groups, **citizen participation** can take other forms. Contacting politicians, lobbying for legislation, and demonstrating in the streets are common vehicles for involvement in the political life of a nation. The degree to which such expressions are encouraged and tolerated by government officials is another facet of political culture that varies from society to society.

Comparative politics and government as a field is concerned with **mechanisms for change** in different nations. Can citizens effect reform through ballots, protest, public opinion polls, or revolts? The underlying factors precipitating the need for change are relevant to an understanding of the overall process.

INTERNATIONAL RELATIONS

THE THEORETICAL FRAMEWORK

The study of how nations interact with one another can be approached from a variety of perspectives including the following:

- A **traditional analysis** uses the descriptive process and focuses on such topics as global issues, international institutions, and the foreign policies of individual nation-states.

- The **strategists' approach** zeroes in on war and deterrence. Scholars in this camp may employ game theory to analyze negotiations, the effectiveness of weapons systems, and the likelihood of limited versus all-out war in a given crisis situation.

- The **middle range theorists** analyze specific components of international relations, such as the politics of arms races, the escalation of international crises, and the role of prejudice and attitudes toward other cultures in precipitating war and peace.

- A **world politics approach** takes into consideration such factors as economics, ethics, law, and trade agreements and stresses the significance of international organizations and the complexities of interactions among nations.

- The **grand theory** of international relations is presented by **Hans J. Morgenthau** in *Politics Among Nations* (1948). He argues for **realism** in the study of interactions on the international stage. Morgenthau suggests that an analysis of relations among nations reveals such recurring themes as "interest defined as power" and striving for equilibrium/balance of power as a means of maintaining peace.

- The **idealists** assume that human nature is essentially good; hence, people and nations are capable of cooperation and avoiding armed conflict. They highlight global organizations, international law, disarmament, and the reform of institutions that lead to war.

An analysis of international politics can be conducted at various levels by looking at the actions of individual statesmen, the interests of individual nations, and/or the mechanics of a whole system of international players. In studying the rise of Nazism and its role in precipitating World War II, the **individual** approach would focus on Hitler, the **state** approach would treat the German preoccupation with racial superiority and the need for expansion, and the **systemic** approach would highlight how German military campaigns upset the balance of power and triggered unlikely alliances, such as the linking of the democratic Britain and the United States with the totalitarian Soviet Union in a common effort to restore equilibrium.

FOREIGN POLICY PERSPECTIVES

International relations as a discipline is inextricably linked to the field of **foreign policy**. Foreign policy involves the objectives nations seek to gain with reference to other nations and the procedures in which they engage in order to achieve their objectives. The principal foreign policy goals of sovereign states or other political entities may include some or all of the following: independence, national security, economic advancement, encouraging their political values beyond their own borders, gaining respect and prestige, and promoting stability and international peace.

The **foreign policy process** involves the stages a government goes through in formulating policy and arriving at decisions with respect to courses of action. A variety of models have been identified in reference to the process of creating foreign policy. The **primary players** (nations, world organizations, multinational corporations, and non-state ethnic entities such as the Palestine Liberation Organization) are often referred to as **actors**.

The **unitary/rational actor model** assumes that all nations or primary players share similar goals and approach foreign policy issues in like fashion. The actions players take, according to this theory, are influenced by the actions of other players rather than by what may be taking place internally. The rational component in this model is based on the assumption that actors will respond on the world stage by making the best choice after measured consideration of possible alternatives. Maximizing goals and achieving specific objectives motivate the rational actor's course of action.

The **bureaucratic model** assumes that, due to the many large organizations involved in formulating foreign policy, particularly in powerful nation-states, final decisions are the result of struggle among the bureaucratic actors. In the United States, the bureaucratic actors include the Departments of State and Defense, as well as the National Security Council, the Central Intelligence Agency, the Environmental Protection Agency, the Department of Commerce, and/or any other agencies and departments whose agendas might be impacted by a foreign policy decision. While the bureaucratic model is beneficial in that it assumes the consideration of multiple points of view, the downside is that inter-agency competition and compromise often drive the final decision.

A third model assumes that foreign policy results from the intermingling of a variety of political factors including national leaders, bureaucratic organizations, legislative bodies, political parties, interest groups, and public opinion.

The **implementation of foreign policy** depends upon the tools a nation or primary player has at its disposal. The major instruments of foreign policy include **diplomacy**, **military strength/ actions**, and **economic initiatives**.

Diplomacy involves communicating with other primary players through official representatives. It might include attending conferences and summit meetings, negotiating treaties and settlements, and exchanging official communications. Diplomacy is an indispensable tool in the successful conduct of an entity's foreign policy.

The extent to which a player may rely on the **military** tool depends upon its technological strength, its readiness, and the support of both its domestic population and the international community. President George H. W. Bush's decision to engage in a military conflict with Iraq's Saddam Hussein in 1991, after Iraq's invasion of Kuwait, largely rested on positive assessments of those factors. Sometimes the buildup of military capabilities is in itself a powerful foreign policy tool and thus a deterrent to armed conflict—as was the case in the Cold War between the United States and the Soviet Union.

Economic development and the ability to employ economic initiatives to achieve foreign policy objectives are effective means by which a principal player can interact on the international scene. The Marshall Plan, through which the United States provided economic aid to a ravaged Europe after World War II, could be viewed as a tool to block Soviet expansion as well as a humanitarian gesture. It was a tool to resurrect the devastated economies of Europe which had been major trading partners and purchasers of U.S. exports before the war. Membership in an economic community such as OPEC (Organization of Petroleum Exporting Countries) or the EC (European Community) can drive the foreign policy of both member nations and those impacted by their decisions.

THE MODERN GLOBAL SYSTEM

International systems today evidence many of the global forces and foreign policy mechanisms formulated in Western Europe in the eighteenth and nineteenth centuries. Largely due to the influence of Western imperialism and colonialism, the less developed countries of modern times have, to a great extent, embraced ideological and foreign policy values that originated in Europe during the formative centuries. Such concepts as political autonomy, nationalism, economic advancement through technology and industrialization, and gaining respect and prestige in the international community move the foreign policies of major powers and many less developed countries as well.

Historical Context of the Modern Global System

The modern global system or network of relationships among nations owes its origins to the emergence of the nation-state. It is generally recognized that the **Peace of Westphalia** (1648), which concluded the Thirty Years' War in Europe and ended the authority of the Roman Catholic popes to exert their political dominance over secular leaders, gave birth to the concept of the modern nation-state. The old feudal order in Europe that allowed the Holy Roman Emperor to extend his influence over the territories governed by local princes was replaced by a new one in which distinct geographic and political entities interacted under a new set of principles. These allowed the nation-states to conduct business with each other, such as negotiating treaties and settling border disputes, without interference from a higher authority. Hence, the concept of sovereignty evolved.

The eighteenth century in Europe was notable for its relatively even distribution of power among the nation-states. With respect to military strength and international prestige, such nations as England, France, Austria, Prussia, and Russia were on the same scale. Some of the former major powers, such as Spain, the Netherlands, and Portugal, occupied a secondary status. Both the major and secondary players created alliances and competed with each other for control of territories beyond their borders. Alignments, based primarily on economic and colonial considerations, shifted without upsetting the global system. Royal families intermarried and professional soldiers worked for the states that gave them the best benefits without great regard for political allegiances.

Military conflicts in the eighteenth century tended to be conservative with the concept of the **balance of power** at play. Mercenaries and professionals controlled the action mindful of strategic maneuvers to bring about victory. Wiping out the enemy was not the principal goal. Major upheavals were avoided through the formation of alliances and a high regard for the authority of monarchs and the Christian Church. The eighteenth century has been dubbed the "**golden age of diplomacy**" because it was an era of relative stability in which moderation and shared cultural values on the part of the decision-makers were the rule.

Structural changes in the process and implementation of international relations occurred in the nineteenth and twentieth centuries due to major political, technological, and ideological developments.

The nation-state of the eighteenth century was a relatively new phenomenon. Statesmen of the era traded territory with little consideration of ethnic loyalties. This style of diplomacy was irrevocably altered by the French Revolution and the Napoleonic Wars that saw **nationality** emerge as a rallying point for conducting wars and for raising the citizens' armies necessary to succeed in military conflicts. The trend was exacerbated in the mid-nineteenth century by the European drive for unification of distinct ethnic groups and the creation of the Italian and German nation-states. The twentieth century saw a particularly impassioned link between nationalism and war.

The scientific and industrial revolutions of the eighteenth century gave rise to advancements in **military technology** in the nineteenth and twentieth centuries that dramatically altered the concept and the conduct of war. Replacing the eighteenth century conservative, play-by-the-rules approach was a new, fiercely violent brand of warfare that increasingly involved civilian casualties and aimed at utter destruction of the enemy. The World Wars of the twentieth century called for mass mobilization of civilians as well as of the military, prompting leaders to whip up nationalistic sentiments. The development of nuclear weapons in the mid-twentieth century rendered total war largely unfeasible. Nuclear arms buildups, with the goal of **deterrent capabilities** (the means to retaliate so swiftly and effectively that an enemy will avoid conflict) was viewed by the superpowers as the only safety net.

Another factor molding the structural changes in international relations that surfaced in the nineteenth and twentieth centuries was the **ideological component**. Again the French Revolution, anchored in the ideology of "liberty, equality, and fraternity," is viewed as the harbinger of future trends. Those conservative forces valuing legitimacy and monarchy fought the forces of the Revolution and Napoleon to preserve tradition against the rising tide of republican nationalism. In the twentieth century, with its binding "isms"—Communism, democratic republicanism, liberalism, Nazism, socialism—competing for dominance, ideological conflicts became more pronounced.

The Contemporary Global System

The values of the contemporary system are rooted in the currents of eighteenth and nineteenth century Europe, transplanted to the rest of the world through colonialism and imperialism. The forces of nationalism, belief in technological progress, and ideological motivations, as well as the desire for international respect and prestige, are evident worldwide. Principal players in Africa, Asia, Latin America, and the Middle East as often as not dominate the diplomatic arena.

The contemporary scene in international relations is comprised of a number of entities beyond the **nation-state**. These include: **non-state actors** or **principal players**, **nonterritorial transnational organizations**, and **nonterritorial intergovernmental** or **multinational organizations**.

Contemporary **nation-states** are legal entities occupying well-defined geographic areas and organized under a common set of governmental institutions. They are recognized by other members of the international community as sovereign and independent states.

Non-state actors or **principal players** are movements or parties that function as independent states. They lack sovereignty, but they may actually wield more power than some less developed nation-states. The **Palestine Liberation Organization (PLO)** is an example of a non-state actor that conducts its own foreign policy, purchases armaments, and has committed acts of terror with grave consequences for the contemporary international community. The **Irish Republican Army (IRA)** is another example of a non-state actor that has employed systematic acts of terror to achieve political ends.

Nonterritorial transnational organizations are institutions such as the Catholic Church that conduct activities throughout the world but whose aims are largely nonpolitical. A relatively new nonterritorial transnational organization is the **multi-national corporation (MNC)**, such as General Motors, Hitachi, or energy giant BP. These mammoth business entities have bases in a number of countries and exist primarily for economic profit. Despite their apparent nonpolitical agendas, multinational corporations can greatly impact foreign policy, as in the case of the United Fruit Company's suspect complicity in the overthrow of the government of Guatemala in the 1950s. Initially the MNC was largely an American innovation, but in recent years, Asian players, particularly the Chinese, Japanese, and South Koreans, have proliferated, changing the makeup of the scene.

An **intergovernmental organization**, such as the United Nations, NATO, or the European Community (EC), is made up of nation-states and can wield significant power on the international scene. While NATO is primarily a military intergovernmental organization and the EC is mainly economic, the UN is really a multipurpose entity. While its primary mission is to promote world peace, the UN engages in a variety of social, cultural, economic, health, and humanitarian activities.

The contemporary global system tends to classify nation-states based on power, wealth, and prestige in the international community. Such labels as **superpower**, **secondary power**, **middle power**, **small power**, and the like tend to be confusing because they are not based on a single set of criteria or a shared set of standards. Some countries may be strong militarily, as was Iraq prior to the Persian Gulf War, yet lack the wealth and prestige in the international community to classify them as superpowers or secondary powers. Others like Japan may have little in the way of military capabilities, but wide influence due to economic preeminence.

The **structure** of the contemporary global system during the Cold War was distinctly **bipolar**, with the United States and the Soviet Union assuming diplomatic, ideological, and military leadership for the international community. With the breakup of the Soviet Union and the reorganization of the Eastern bloc countries has come the disintegration of the bipolar system. Since the 1970s, when tensions between the United States and the Soviet Union eased, a **multipolar system**, in which new alignments are flexible and more easily drawn, has been emerging. President George H. W. Bush spoke of the **New World Order** at the end of the Cold War. This concept involves alliances that transcend the old bipolar scheme with its emphasis on ideology and military superiority and calls for multinational cooperation as seen in the Persian Gulf War. It also assumes greater non-military, transnational cooperation in scientific research and humanitarian projects. The multipolar system is less cohesive than the bipolar system of the recent past and the orders of the distant past, such as the **hierarchical system** (one unit dominates) of the Holy Roman Empire or the **diffuse system** (power and influence are distributed among a large number of units) of eighteenth-century Europe.

A set of fundamental rules has long governed international relations and, though often ignored, is still held as the standard today. These rules include **territorial integrity**, **sovereignty**, and the **legal equality of nation-states**. However, in an age of covert operations, mass media, multinational corporations, and shifting territorial boundaries, these traditional rules of international conduct are subject to both violation and revision.

INTERNATIONAL LAW

The present system of international law is rooted in the fundamental rules of global relations: territorial integrity, sovereignty, and legal equality of nation-states. It embodies a set of basic principles mandating what countries may or may not do and under what conditions the rules should be applied.

Historical Context

Despite evidence that the legal and ethical norms of modern international law may have guided interactions among political entities in non-Western pre-industrial systems, contemporary international law emanates from the Western legal traditions of Greece, Rome, and modern Europe. The development of the European nation-state gave rise to a system of legal rights and responsibilities in the international sphere that enlarged upon the religious-based code of the feudal era. In medieval Europe, the church's emphasis on hierarchical obligations, duty, and obedience to authority helped shape the notion of the "**just war**." **Hugo Grotius** (1583–1645), Dutch scholar and statesman, codified the laws of war and peace and has been called the "**father of international law**."

A new era was launched in 1648, with the Peace of Westphalia, that promulgated the idea of the treaty as the basis of international law. Multilateral treaties dominated the eighteenth century, while Britain, with its unparalleled sea power, established and enforced maritime law. By the nineteenth century, advances in military technology rendered the old standard of the "just war" obsolete. Deterrents, rather than legal and ethical principles, provided the means to a relatively stable world order. The concept of **neutrality** evolved during this period, defining the rights and responsibilities of both warring and neutral nations. These restraints helped prevent smaller conflicts from erupting into world wars.

Contemporary International Law

In the twentieth century, international law retreated theoretically from the tradition of using force as a legitimate tool for settling international conflicts. The **Covenant of the League of Nations** (1920), the **Kellogg-Briand Pact** (1929), and the **United Nations Charter** (1945) all emphasize peaceful relations among nations, but the use of force continues to be employed to achieve political ends. The **International Court of Justice**, the judicial arm of the United Nations, and its predecessor, the **Permanent Court of International Justice** represent concerted efforts to replace armed conflict with the rule of law. Unfortunately, the World Court has proven to be an ineffective organ. Nation-states are reluctant to submit vital questions to the Court, and there is a lack of consensus as to the norms to be applied. Members of the United Nations are members of the Court, but they are not compelled to submit their international disputes for consideration.

The UN Charter seeks to humanize the international scene in its admonition that all member nations assist victims of aggression. This approach negates the old idea of neutrality. It further dismisses the tradition of war as a legitimate tool for resolution of disputes between nation-states of equal legal status. Aggressive conflicts can be categorized as crimes against humanity, and individuals may be held personally accountable for launching them.

The concept of international law has been criticized on several fronts. The rise of **multiculturalism**, with its emphasis on multiple perspectives, has called into question the relevance of applying Western legal traditions to the global community. International law has been seen as an instrument of the powerful nations in pursuit of their aims at the expense of weaker nations. Strong nation-states are in a position to both enforce international law and to violate it without fear of reprisal. These observations have led some to conclude that international law is primarily an instrument to maintain the **status quo**.

International law can be effective if parties involved see some **mutual self-advantage** in compliance. **Fear of reprisal** is another factor influencing nations to observe the tenets of international law. **Diplomatic advantage** and **enhanced global prestige** may follow a nation's decisions to abide by international law. It can be argued that international law is valuable in that it seeks to impose **order** on a potentially chaotic system and sets expectations that, while not always met, are positive and affirming.

REVIEW QUESTIONS

1. All of the following are major differences between the Congress of the United States and the parliaments of Western Europe EXCEPT

   (A) campaigns of parliament members are more personalistic.
   (B) members of parliament are more likely to support the party after election.
   (C) Congress functions more separately from the executive than does parliament.
   (D) party discipline is tighter within parliament.

2. During which time period was power in the U.S. House of Representatives most centralized in the leadership?

   (A) 1860s
   (B) Late 1800s and early 1900s
   (C) 1930s
   (D) Today

3. During which period in U.S. history was the House of Representatives more powerful than the Senate?

   (A) The early 1800s
   (C) 1920s
   (B) 1870s
   (D) 1970s

4. The seniority system of choosing committee chairmen

   (A) is less important today than it was a few years ago.
   (B) has never been particularly important in reality.
   (C) was often opposed openly by powerful Speakers.
   (D) has existed since the early 1800s.

5. The most powerful leader(s) in the Senate is (are) the

   (A) party whips.
   (B) Speaker.
   (C) president *pro tempore*.
   (D) majority and minority leaders.

6. Which of the following powers did the U.S. president lack until 1994?

   (A) Pocket veto
   (B) Executive privilege
   (C) Commander-in-chief of the armed forces
   (D) Line item veto

7. What is the maximum number of terms for which one may be elected president of the U.S.?

   (A) Three terms
   (C) Three-and-a-half terms
   (B) Two terms
   (D) No limit

8. The number of bureaucrats in the U.S. government

   (A) has grown significantly since the end of World War II.
   (B) has not grown significantly, although the power of the bureaucracy has grown.
   (C) has not grown significantly, and the power of the bureaucracy has declined.
   (D) has grown significantly, as has the power of the bureaucracy.

9. The most important motivation for the limitation of civil liberties and civil rights early in the 20th century was

   (A) national security.
   (B) violence caused by early civil rights leaders.
   (C) the lower percentages of minority groups within the U.S. population.
   (D) the need to control the inequalities caused by an industrialized society.

10. A recently organized country is MOST likely to have problems with

    (A) structures not matching functions.
    (B) survival in the international environment.
    (C) a high GNP.
    (D) establishing legitimacy.

11. The process whereby political culture is transmitted to the citizens is

    (A) political communication.
    (C) political socialization.
    (B) domestic environment.
    (D) political recruitment.

12. In a consensual political culture,

    (A) citizens always agree with political leaders.
    (B) citizens consent to give all power to a dictator.
    (C) there is usually only one political party.
    (D) citizens are in general agreement about the basics of government.

13. The ways in which a political system encourages individuals to serve in leadership roles is known as

    (A) political socialization.
    (B) political communication.
    (C) a democratic political structure.
    (D) recruitment of elites.

14. The theoretical point of view that focuses on building an understanding of deterrence in the nuclear age is

    (A) traditional analysis.
    (B) the strategists' perspective.
    (C) grand theory.
    (D) middle range theory.

15. A scholar who develops a theory of arms races would MOST likely be studying international relations from which theoretical perspective?

    (A) Traditional analysis
    (B) The strategists' perspective
    (C) Grand theory
    (D) Middle range theory

16. The major purpose of operational definitions in a research design is

    (A) to generate more data.
    (B) to establish criteria for judging reality on a more common basis.
    (C) to prove a theory to be correct.
    (D) to define the relationship between hypotheses and theories.

17. The level of measurement that provides ONLY discreet categories for data is

    (A) nominal.
    (C) operational.
    (B) ordinal.
    (D) integral.

18. Which of the following is an example of ordinal categorization?

    (A) Republican/Democrat
    (B) Liberal Democrat/Conservative Democrat; Liberal Republican/Conservative Republican
    (C) Income levels per year: $10,000-$20,000; $20,000-$30,000; $30,000-$40,000; $40,000-$60,000
    (D) Democratic regime/totalitarian regime

19. Procedures that are repeatable and that yield similar readings on repeated applications are said to have

(A) validity.
(C) operationalism.
(B) reliability.
(D) empiricism.

20. A sample in which a random sample is selected from every sampling unit proportionate to the size of the sampling unit is called

(A) cluster sampling.
(B) systematic sampling.
(C) stratified sampling.
(D) multi-stage random sampling.

ANSWER KEY

1.	(A)	6.	(D)	11.	(C)	16.	(B)
2.	(B)	7.	(B)	12.	(D)	17.	(A)
3.	(A)	8.	(B)	13.	(D)	18.	(B)
4.	(A)	9.	(A)	14.	(B)	19.	(B)
5.	(D)	10.	(D)	15.	(D)	20.	(C)

DETAILED EXPLANATIONS OF ANSWERS

1. **(A)** Choice (A) is correct. Candidates can only be elected to parliament through the efforts of a political party, whereas Congressmen may have more personalistic campaigns that are only loosely supported by a party.

2. **(B)** Choice (B) is the correct answer. During the late 1800s and early 1900s, power in the House was centralized in the hands of Speakers Thomas B. Reed and Joseph Cannon.

3. **(A)** Choice (A) is the correct answer. In the early 1800s, the House of Representatives was more powerful than the Senate, and leadership was strongly centralized under House Speaker Henry Clay.

4. **(A)** Choice (A) is the correct answer. In the 1970s, a series of reforms weakened the seniority system, allowing election of chairmen by secret ballot, open committee meetings, and more authority to subcommittees and individual members.

5. **(D)** Choice (D) is the correct answer. The real leadership is in the hands of the majority and minority leaders.

6. **(D)** Choice (D) is correct. Congress granted the president the line item veto in 1994; however, it came under legal challenge by litigants who claimed it upsets the balance of power between the Executive and Legislative branches.

7. **(B)** Choice (B) is the correct answer. The Twenty-Second Amendment, ratified in 1951, says, "No person shall be elected to the office of the President more than twice...."

8. **(B)** Choice (B) is the correct answer. Although the number of bureaucrats has not grown significantly, the power of the bureaucracy has grown dramatically since the country's founding.

9. **(A)** Choice (A) is correct. Early in the twentieth century, the Supreme Court usually ruled to limit freedoms if national security was at stake.

10. **(D)** Choice (D) is the correct answer. A new country with a recently organized government may have trouble with legitimacy (acceptance by the citizens) because no centralization of power has existed before.

11. **(C)** Choice (C) is correct. Political socialization is the way in which children and adults learn political values and attitudes. Some governments emphasize political socialization as an important basis for establishing the legitimacy of the government.

12. **(D)** Choice (D) is correct. In consensual political culture, citizens are in general agreement about the basics of government. In contrast, in a conflictual political culture, citizens have conflicting points of view about the way the government should be run.

13. **(D)** Choice (D) is correct. Political recruitment defines the way in which a government encourages citizens to participate in government (citizen recruitment), and the ways in which it encourages individuals to serve in leadership roles (recruitment of elites).

14. **(B)** Choice (B) is the correct answer. The strategists' perspective was particularly strong during the Cold War era. Their main concern has been to understand deterrence in the nuclear age, to analyze the importance of new weapon systems, and to maximize national security and minimize the possibility of nuclear war.

15. **(D)** Choice (D) is correct. Middle range theorists believe that international relations may be best understood by developing more specific explanations, such as a theory of arms races or crisis decision making. A number of middle range theories focus on the study of war and peace. These theories highlight some of the processes leading to escalation of violence, the relationship between prejudice and national hostility, the economic consequences of disarmament, and the sources of public attitudes toward foreign cultures.

16. **(B)** Choice (B) is correct. Operational definitions are required to set agreement on common meanings. Giving a concept an operational definition means providing a set of instructions to indicate how to measure, label, or otherwise designate a given concept.

17. **(A)** Choice (A) is the correct answer. The nominal level of measurement is the simplest measurement, providing only discreet categories for data. There is no metric order in nominal data. There are simply categories.

18. **(B)** Choice (B) is correct. The ordinal level of measurement categorizes *and* orders. For example, an ideological ordering may be attached to the partisan categories of Democratic and Republican by using a liberal/conservative dimension. The ordinal level goes beyond mere categorization and is considered a higher and more meaningful level of measurement than is nominal categorization.

19. **(B)** Choice (B) is the correct answer. One way to assess the adequacy of a research design and its operational definitions and measurement procedures is to determine a measure's reliability. Procedures are deemed to have reliability if they are repeatable and if they yield similar readings on repeated applications.

20. **(C)** Choice (C) is correct. A stratified sample is drawn from different sub-groups of a theoretical population to ensure the overall sample's representativeness.

ECONOMICS

INTRODUCTION TO ECONOMICS

WHAT IS ECONOMICS?

Economics is "the study of how a society allocates scarce resources amidst unlimited human wants." As such, the concepts of *scarcity* and *human wants* are fundamentally important to the study of economics.

Macroeconomics is the study of the economy as a whole. Some of the topics considered include inflation, unemployment, and economic growth.

Microeconomics is the study of the individual parts that make up the economy. The parts include households, business firms, and government agencies, and particular emphasis is placed on how these units make decisions and the consequences of these decisions.

ECONOMIC ANALYSIS

Economic Theory—An economic theory is an explanation of why certain economic phenomena occur. For example, there are theories explaining the rate of inflation, how many hours people choose to work, and the amount of goods and services the U.S. will import. Stripped down to essentials, a theory is a set of statements about cause-and-effect relationships in the economy.

Models—A model is an abstract replica of reality and is the formal statement of a theory. The best models retain the essence of the reality, but do away with extraneous details. Virtually all economic analysis is done by first constructing a model of the situation the economist wants to analyze. The reason for this is because human beings are incapable of fully understanding reality. It is too complex for the human mind. Models, because they avoid many of the messier details of reality, can be comprehended, but good models are always "unrealistic."

It would not be inaccurate to say that economists do not analyze the economy; they analyze models of the economy. Almost every prediction that an economist makes, e.g., the impact of changes in the money supply on interest rates, the effect of the unemployment rate on the rate of inflation, the effect of increased competition in an industry on profits, is based on a model.

Models come in verbal, graphical, or mathematical form.

Empirical Analysis—All models yield predictions about the economy. For example, a widely held model predicts that increases in the rate of growth of the money supply will lead to higher inflation. In empirical analysis, economists compare predictions with the actual performance of the economy as measured by economic data. Good empirical analysis often requires mastery of sophisticated statistical and mathematical tools.

Positive Economics—Positive economics is the analysis of "what is." For example, positive economics tries to answer such questions as these: What will the effect be on the rate of inflation if the rate of growth of the money supply is raised by one percentage point? What will happen to hours of work of welfare recipients if welfare benefits are raised $500? What will the effect be on our trade balance if the exchange rate is devalued five percent? Many economists view positive economics as "objective" or "scientific," and believe their special training gives them the expertise to draw conclusions about these types of issues.

Normative Economics—Normative economics is the analysis of "what should be." For example, normative economics tries to answer such questions as these: What inflation rate should our economy strive for? Should welfare recipients be expected to work? Is reducing our trade deficit a desirable thing? Normative economics is clearly a subjective area. There is nothing in an economist's training that gives his or her opinions on these issues any more validity than anyone else's.

THE ECONOMIC WAY OF THINKING

Economics analysis is characterized by an emphasis on certain fundamental concepts.

Scarcity—Human wants and needs (for goods, services, leisure, etc.) exceed the ability of the economy to satisfy those wants and needs. This is true for the economy as a whole as well as each individual in the economy. In other words, there is never enough to go around. Individuals never have enough money to buy all they want. Business firms cannot pay completely satisfactory wages without cutting into profits, and vice versa. Government never has enough money to fund all worthwhile projects.

Opportunity Cost—The reality of scarcity implies that individuals, businesses, and governments must make choices, selecting some opportunities while foregoing others. Buying a car may mean foregoing a vacation; acquiring a new copy machine may mean canceling the company picnic; paying higher welfare benefits may require terminating a weapons system. The opportunity cost of a choice is the value of the best alternative choice sacrificed.

Individualism—Economic analysis emphasizes individual action. Most economic theories attempt to model the behavior of "typical" individuals. All groups, such as "society," business firms, or unions, are analyzed as a collection of individuals each acting in a particular way. In a sense, the preceding sentence represents an ideal. Not all economic theory achieves this goal.

Rational Behavior—Individuals are assumed to act rationally. This is the most misunderstood term in economics. It does not necessarily mean people are cold, calculating, and greedy. Rather, it means that given a person's goals and knowledge, people take actions likely to achieve those goals and avoid actions likely to detract from those goals. A greedy person acts rationally if she spends on herself and does not give to charity. She is irrational if she does the opposite. An altruistic person acts rationally if she gives her money to the needy and does not spend it on herself. Irrational behavior is the opposite.

Marginal Analysis—Economists assume that people make choices by weighing the costs and benefits of particular actions.

IMPORTANT ECONOMIC CONCEPTS AND TERMS

Specialization and Division of Labor—This is a strategy for producing goods and services. Division of labor means that different members of a team of producers are given responsibility for different aspects of a production plan. Specialization means that producers become quite apt at those aspects of production they concentrate on. Specialization and division of labor is alleged to lead to efficiency which facilitates economic growth and development.

THE ECONOMIC PROBLEM

UNIVERSALITY OF THE PROBLEM OF SCARCITY

Goods and Services—Goods and Services refers to anything that satisfies human needs, wants, or desires. Goods are tangible items, such as food, cars, and clothing. Services are intangible items, such as education, health care, and leisure. The consumption of goods and services is a source of happiness, well-being, satisfaction, or utility.

Resources (Factors of Production)—Resources refers to anything that can be used to produce goods and services. A commonly used classification scheme places all resources into one of six categories:

> **Land**—All natural resources, whether on the land, under the land, in the water, or in the air; e.g., fertile agricultural land, iron ore deposits, tuna fish, corn seeds, and quail.

> **Labor**—The work effort of human beings.

> **Capital**—Productive implements made by human beings, e.g., factories, machinery, and tools.

> **Entrepreneurship**—A specialized form of labor. Entrepreneurship is creative labor. It refers to the ability to detect new business opportunities and bring them to fruition. Entrepreneurs also manage the other factors of production.

> **Technology**—The practical application of scientific knowledge. Technology is typically combined with the other factors to make them more productive.

Scarcity—Economists assume that human wants and needs are virtually limitless while acknowledging that the resources to satisfy those needs are limited. Consequently, society is never able to produce enough goods and services to satisfy everybody, or most anyone, completely. Alternatively, resources are scarce relative to human needs and desires.

Scarcity is a problem of all societies, whether rich or poor. As a mental experiment, write down the amount of income you think a typical family needs to be "comfortable" in the United States today. Now compare your figure with the median family income in the United States ($51,939 in 2013). In most instances, what students think is necessary to be comfortable far exceeds median family income, which loosely implies that the typical family in the U.S. is not comfortable, even though the United States is the richest nation in the history of the world. If your figure is less than the median income, think again. Do you think you would really be "comfortable" at that level of income?

UNIVERSAL PROBLEMS CAUSED BY SCARCITY

A society without scarcity is a society without problems, and consequently one where there is no need to make decisions. In the real world, all societies must make three crucial decisions:

1. **What goods and services to produce and in what quantities.**

2. **How to produce the goods and services selected**—what resource combinations and production techniques to use.

3. **How to distribute the goods and services produced among people**—who gets how much of each good and service produced.

UNIVERSAL ECONOMIC GOALS

Allocative (Economic) Efficiency—A society achieves allocative efficiency if it produces the types and quantities of goods and services that most satisfies its people. Failure to do so wastes resources.

Technical Efficiency—A society achieves technical efficiency when it is producing the greatest quantity of goods and services possible from its resources. Failure to do so is also a waste of resources.

Equity—A society wants the distribution of goods and services to conform with its notions of "fairness."

Standards of Equity—Equity is not necessarily synonymous with equality. There is no objective standard of equity, and all societies have different notions of what constitutes equity. Three widely held standards are:

1. **Contributory standard**—Under a contributory standard, people are entitled to a share of goods and services based on what they contribute to society. Those making larger contributions receive correspondingly larger shares. The measurement of contribution and what to do about those who contribute very little or are unable to contribute (i.e., the disabled) are continuing issues.

2. **Needs standard**—Under a needs standard, a person's contribution to society is irrelevant. Goods and services are distributed based on the needs of different households. Measuring need and inducing people to contribute to society when goods and services are guaranteed are continuing issues.

3. **Equality standard**—Under an equality standard, every person is entitled to an equal share of goods and services, simply because they are a human being. Some of the ongoing issues with this theory are how to allow for needs and how to induce individuals to maximize their productivity when the reward is the same for everyone.

Economists remain divided over whether the goals of equity and efficiency (allocative and technical) are complementary or in conflict.

PRODUCTION POSSIBILITIES CURVE

The Production Possibilities Curve is a model of the economy used to illustrate the problems associated with scarcity. It shows the maximum feasible combinations of two goods or services that society can produce, assuming all resources are used in their most productive manner.

Assumptions of the Model

1. Society is only capable of producing two goods (guns and butter).

2. At a given point in time, society has a fixed quantity of resources.

3. All resources are used in their most productive manner.

Table 4–1 shows selected combinations of the two goods that can be produced given the assumptions.

Point	Guns	Butter
A	0	16
B	4	14
C	7	12
D	9	9
E	10	5
F	11	0

Table 4–1 Selected Combinations of Guns and Butter

Figure 4–1 is a graphical depiction of the Production Possibilities Curve (curve FA).

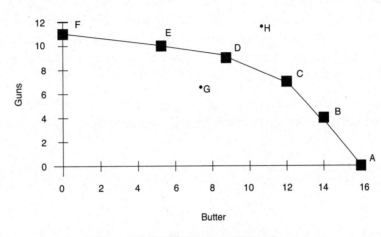

Figure 4–1 Production Possibilities Curve

Technical Efficiency—All points on the curve are points of technical efficiency. By definition, technical efficiency is achieved when more of one good cannot be produced without producing less of the other good. Find point D on the curve. Any move to a point with more guns (i.e., point E) will necessitate a reduction in butter production. Any move to a point with more butter (such as point C) will necessitate a reduction in guns production. Any point inside the curve (such as point G) represents technical inefficiency. Either inefficient production methods are being used or resources are not fully employed. A movement from G to the curve will allow more of one or both goods to be produced without any reduction in the quantity of the other good. Points outside the curve (such as H) are technically infeasible given society's current stock of resources and technological knowledge.

Opportunity Cost—Consider a move from D to E. Society gets one more unit of guns, but must sacrifice four units of butter. The four units of butter is the opportunity cost of the gun. One gun costs four units of butter.

Law of Increasing Costs—Starting from point A and moving up along the curve, note that the opportunity cost of guns increases. From point A to B, two butter are sacrificed to get four guns (one gun costs one-half butter); from point B to C, two butter are sacrificed to get three guns (one gun costs two-thirds butter); from C to D, three butter are sacrificed for two guns (one gun costs one-and-one-half butter); from D to E, one gun costs four butter; and from E to F, one gun costs five butter.

The law of increasing costs says that as more of a good or service is produced, its opportunity cost will rise. It is a consequence of resources being specialized in particular uses. Some resources are particularly good in gun production and not so good for butter production, and vice versa.

At the commencement of gun production, the resources shifted out of butter will be those least productive in butter (and most productive in guns). Consequently, gun production will rise with little cost in terms of butter. As more resources are diverted, those more productive in butter will be affected, and the opportunity cost will rise. This is what gives the production possibilities curve its characteristic convex shape.

If resources are not specialized in particular uses, opportunity costs will remain constant and the production possibilities curve will be a straight line (see Figure 4–2).

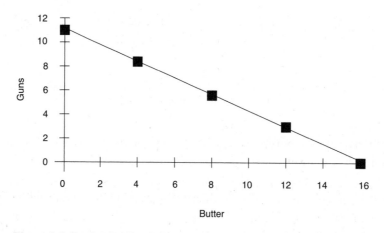

Figure 4–2 Production Possibilities Curve with No Specialized Resources

Allocative Efficiency—Allocative efficiency will be represented by the point on the curve that best satisfies society's needs and wants. It cannot be located without additional knowledge of society's likes and dislikes. A complicating factor is that the allocatively efficient point is not independent of society's distribution of income and wealth.

Economic Growth—Society's production of goods and services is limited by its resources. Economic growth, then, requires that society increases the amount of resources it has or makes those resources more productive through the application of technology. Graphically, economic growth is represented by an outward shift of the curve to IJ (see Figure 4–3). Economic growth will make more combinations of goods and services feasible, but will not end the problem of scarcity.

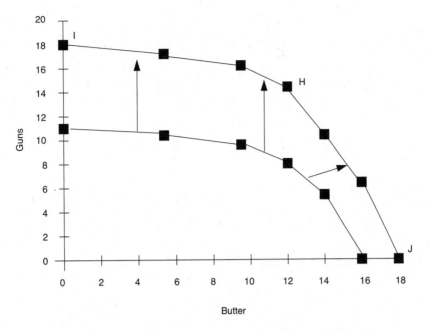

Figure 4–3 Production Possibilities Curve and Economic Growth

---

DEMAND AND SUPPLY

DEMAND

   Demand is a schedule or a graph showing the relationship between the price of a product and the amount consumers are willing and able to buy, *ceteris paribus*. The schedule or graph does not necessarily show what consumers actually buy at each price. The Law of Demand says there is an inverse relationship between price and quantity demanded; people will be willing and able to buy more if the product gets cheaper.

Ceteris Paribus

   All hypothetical relationships between variables in economics include a stated or implied assumption *ceteris paribus*. The term means "all other factors held constant." As we will see, there are many factors affecting the amount of a product people are willing and able to buy. The demand schedule shows the relationship between price and quantity demanded, holding all the other factors constant. This allows us to investigate the independent effect that price changes have on quantity demanded without worrying about the influence the other factors are having.

   Demand Schedule—Assume the product is widgets. Let *Qd* be quantity demanded and *P* be price.

Qd	P
48.0	1.00
47.5	1.25
47.0	1.50
46.5	1.75
46.0	2.00

Demand Graph

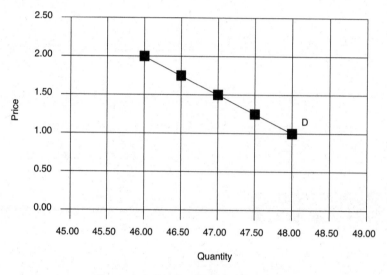

Figure 4–4 Graph of Demand Schedule

SUPPLY

Supply is a schedule or a graph showing the relationship between the price of a product and the amount producers are willing and able to supply, *ceteris paribus*. The schedule or graph does not necessarily show what producers actually sell at each price. There is generally a positive relationship between price and quantity supplied, reflecting higher costs associated with greater production.

Supply Schedule—Assume the product is widgets. Let Qs be quantity supplied.

Qs	P
46.0	1.00
46.5	1.25
47.0	1.50
47.5	1.75
48.0	2.00

Supply Graph

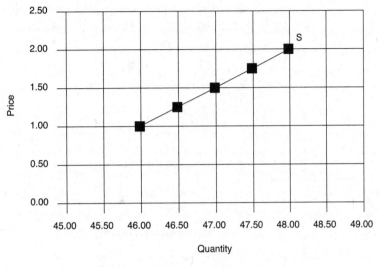

Figure 4–5 Graph of Supply Schedule

MARKET EQUILIBRIUM

The intersection of the demand and supply curves indicates the equilibrium price and quantity in the market (see Figure 4–6). The word *equilibrium* is synonymous with *stable*. The price and quantity in a market will frequently not be equal to the equilibrium, but if that is the case then the market will be adjusting, and, hence, not stable.

If the price of the product is $2.00, then the quantity supplied of the product (48) will be greater than the quantity demanded (46). There will be a surplus in the market of 48 – 46 = 2. The unsold product will force producers to lower their prices. A reduction in price will reduce the quantity supplied while increasing quantity demanded until the surplus disappears. Two dollars is not an equilibrium because the market is forced to adjust.

If the price of the product is $1.00, then the quantity supplied of the product (46) will be less than the quantity demanded (48). There will be a shortage in the market of 48 – 46 = 2. Unsatisfied customers will cause the price of the product to be bid up. The higher price will cause the quantity supplied to increase while decreasing the quantity demanded until the shortage disappears. One dollar is not an equilibrium because the market is forced to adjust.

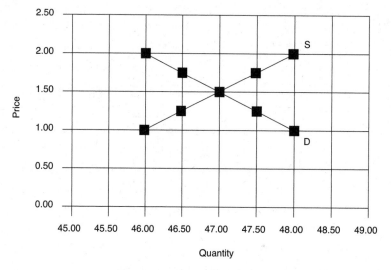

Figure 4–6 Market Equilibrium

If the price of the product is $1.50, then the quantity demanded (47) is just equal to the quantity supplied (47). Producers can sell all they want. Buyers can buy all they want. Since everyone is satisfied, there is no reason for the price to change. Hence, $1.50 is an equilibrium price and 47 is an equilibrium quantity.

ECONOMIC SYSTEMS

TYPES OF SYSTEMS

Every society must have some method for making the basic economic decisions.

Tradition—Traditional systems largely rely on custom to determine production and distribution questions. While not static, traditional systems are slow to change and are not well-equipped to propel a society into sustained growth. Traditional systems are found in many of the poorer Third World countries.

Command—Command economies rely on a central authority to make decisions. The central authority may be a dictator or a democratically constituted government.

Market—It is easier to describe what a market system is not than what it is. In a pure market system, there is no central authority and custom plays very little role. Every consumer makes buying decisions based on his or her own needs and desires and income. Individual self-interest rules. Every producer decides for him- or herself what goods or services to produce, what price to charge, what resources to employ, and what production methods to use. Producers are motivated solely by profit considerations. There is vigorous competition in every market.

Mixed—A mixed economy contains elements of each of the three systems defined above. All real-world economies are mixed economies, although the mixture of tradition, command, and market differs greatly. The U.S. economy has traditionally placed great emphasis on the market, although there is a large and active government (command) sector. The Soviet economy placed main reliance on government to direct economic activity, but there was a small market sector.

Capitalism—The key characteristic of a capitalistic economy is that productive resources are owned by private individuals.

Socialism—The key characteristic of a socialist economy is that productive resources are owned collectively by society. Alternatively, productive resources are under the control of government.

CIRCULAR FLOW

The Circular Flow is a model of economic relationships in a capitalistic market economy. Households, the owners of all productive resources, supply resources to firms through the resource markets, receiving monetary payments in return. Firms use the resources purchased (or rented, as the case may be) to produce goods and services, which are then sold to households and other businesses in the product markets. Household income not spent (consumed) may be saved in the Financial Markets. Firms may borrow from the financial markets to finance capital expansion (investment). Firm saving and household borrowing are not shown.

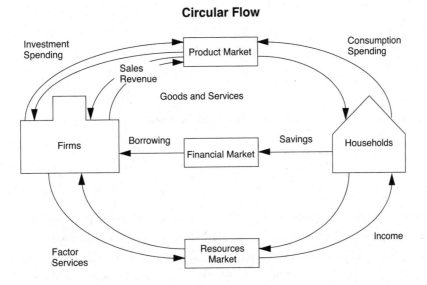

Figure 4–7 The Circular Flow

HOW A MARKET ECONOMY WORKS

Although the description of a market economy may suggest that chaos is the order of the day, economists believe that if certain conditions are met, a market economy is easily capable of achieving the major economic goals.

How a Market Economy Achieves Allocation Efficiency—Market forces will lead firms to produce the mix of goods most desired. Unforeseen events can be responded to in a rational manner.

CHANGE IN TASTES

Assume a change in consumer tastes from beef to chicken (see Figure 4–8). An increase in demand in the chicken market will be accompanied by a decrease in demand in the beef market. The higher price of chicken will attract more resources into the market and lead to an increase in the quantity supplied. The lower price of beef will induce a reduction in the quantity supplied and exit of resources to other industries.

Note that the change in the level of output of both goods occurred because it was in the economic self-interest of firms to do so. Greater demand in the chicken market increased the profitability of chicken; lower demand in the beef market decreased the profitability of beef. Chicken and beef producers responded to society's desires not out of a sense of public spiritedness, but out of self-interest.

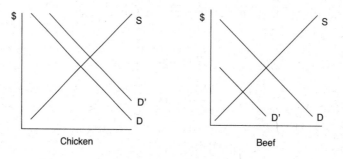

Figure 4–8 Changes in Tastes

SCARCITY

An unexpected freeze in Florida will cause a shift in the supply curve of orange juice, driving up its price, and causing consumers to cut back their purchases (see Figure 4–9). The higher price of orange juice will increase the demand for substitute products like apple juice, causing an increase in the quantity supplied of apple juice to take the place of orange juice.

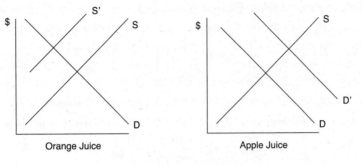

Figure 4–9 Freeze in Florida

As above, the reaction of market participants reflected their evaluation of their own self-interest. Consumers reduced their quantity demanded of orange juice because it was now more expensive. Apple juice producers expanded production because now it was more profitable.

Consumer Sovereignty—"The Consumer is King." Consumer sovereignty means that consumers determine what is produced in the economy. In a market economy, business must cater to the whims of consumer tastes or else go out of business.

How a Market Economy Achieves Technical Efficiency—Market forces will lead firms to produce output in the most efficient manner. The constant struggle for profits will stimulate firms to cut costs. Note that technical efficiency results from attention to self-interest, not the public interest.

The Importance of Competition—A market economy thrives on competition between firms. In their struggle for survival, firms will be forced to cater to consumer demand (leading to allocative efficiency) and force production costs down as far as possible (leading to technical efficiency).

How a Market Economy Achieves Full Employment—Full employment of resources is thought to be the normal state of affairs in a market economy. Resource surpluses will force down the resource's price, leading quickly to re-employment.

How a Market Economy Achieves Growth—Competition between firms for the consumer's dollar will force a constant search for better products and methods of production. The resulting technological change will lead to optimal growth.

The Market Economy and Equity—This is a problematic area for a market economy. Certainly there are financial rewards for those who produce the products that win consumer acceptance. There are losses for those who do not. Yet winners in a market economy are not necessarily the most virtuous of people—they just sell a better product. While consumer demand determines the pattern of production, those consumers with the most income exert the greatest influence on the pattern.

The Role of Prices in a Market Economy—In order for an economy to operate efficiently, there must be information and incentives. There must be information on what goods and services are in demand, which resources are scarce, and so on. There must be an incentive to produce the goods and services desired, conserve on scarce resources, and so on. Both information and incentives are provided by prices. High prices indicate goods and services in demand; low prices indicate goods and services that have lost favor. High prices indicate scarce resources; low prices indicate plentiful. Firms responding "properly" to high prices will earn profits; firms responding "properly" to low prices will avoid losses. Firms exploiting cheap resources will earn profits; firms conserving on expensive resources will avoid losses.

Prices always provide accurate information and appropriate incentives. Since traditional and command economies downplay the role of prices, they have a much more difficult time achieving allocational and technical efficiency.

CONDITIONS THAT MUST BE MET FOR A MARKET ECONOMY TO ACHIEVE ALLOCATIVE AND TECHNICAL EFFICIENCY

A market economy will automatically produce the optimum quantity of every good or service at the lowest possible cost if four conditions are met:

Adequate Information—Consumers must be well-enough informed about prices, quality and availability of products, and other matters so they can make intelligent spending decisions. Workers must be well-enough informed about wages and working conditions so they can choose wisely among job opportunities. Other segments of the economy must be similarly well-informed.

Competition—There must be vigorous competition in every market. Monopolistic elements will reduce output, raise prices, and allow inefficiency in particular markets.

No Externalities—Externalities exist when a transaction between a buyer and seller affects an innocent third party. An example would be if A buys a product from B that B produced under conditions that polluted the air that others breathe. (Not all externalities result in damage to society. Some are beneficial.) Where externalities are present, there is the possibility of over- or underproduction of particular goods and services.

No Public Goods—The market is unlikely to produce the appropriate quantity of public goods.

THE PUBLIC SECTOR IN THE AMERICAN ECONOMY

PUBLIC SECTOR

The Public Sector refers to the activities of government.

GOVERNMENT SPENDING

Government Expenditures on Goods and Services versus Transfer Payments—Government spending can be usefully broken down into two categories. One category is spending on goods and services. When government buys a battleship, a hammer, or the Space Shuttle, it is acquiring goods. When government pays the salary of a soldier, teacher, or bureaucrat, it is getting a service in return. The second category is transfer payments. Transfers are money or in-kind items given to individuals or businesses for which the government receives no equivalent good or service in return. Examples would be social security payments, welfare, or unemployment compensation.

GDP, GNP, AND MEASURING ECONOMIC PERFORMANCE

Gross Domestic Product (GDP) equals the total dollar value of all *final* goods and services produced *within* a country's borders in a given period (usually a quarter or a year). GDP *includes* foreign firms producing in the United States (such as Toyota in Kentucky) and *excludes* U.S. firms producing overseas (such as IBM in Japan).

GDP also excludes "intermediate" goods, such as tires produced by Goodyear but sold to Ford. These types of sales are excluded because Ford, as an automaker, will then install these tires on a car and sell that car to a consumer, which is considered the *final* good for sale.

The formula for GDP is:

Consumer Spending + Business Investment + Government Spending + Net Exports

$$(C + I + G + NX)$$

Consumer spending makes up roughly 70% of GDP.

Note: "Nominal" GDP does *not* take out the effects of inflation, whereas "Real" GDP does.

In contrast to GDP, **Gross National Product (GNP)** equals GDP *plus* all income earned *outside* of the United States by U.S. firms and citizens (such as IBM in Japan) and *less* income earned by foreign firms and citizens *in* the U.S. (such as Toyota in Kentucky).

Note: Given the significant influence that increased globalization has played on the United States' economy since the 1970s, the vast majority of economists today use GDP as the preferred measurement tool rather than GNP.

Technology and Productivity: The four factors of production are (i) land; (ii) labor; (iii) capital; and (iv) entrepreneurial ability. If a country's political and business leaders combine these factors effectively, then that country should have a productive economy.

The United States has the largest economy in the world for several reasons. These include the following elements: (i) ever-growing population; (ii) access to domestic and international capital (or money); (iii) history of technological innovation via a long line of talented entrepreneurs, including Ben Franklin, Thomas Edison, Henry Ford, Steve Jobs, Bill Gates, and Jeff Bezos; (iv) abundant natural resources; and (v) a large national market.

GDP per Capita equals GDP divided by the number of people in the country. For example, in 2016 the U.S. had a GDP of approximately $18.5 trillion and a population of 324 million people. Its GDP per Capita, therefore, was slightly over $57,000.

THE TWO PRIMARY SCHOOLS OF ECONOMIC THOUGHT

I. CLASSICAL SCHOOL

- **Key Person:** Adam Smith / **Principal Book:** *The Wealth of Nations* (1776)

- **Main Period of Influence:** late 1700s to early 1930s

- **Principal Concepts:**

  — **Laissez-faire:** Governments should severely limit their role in markets by taking a *laissez-faire* ("hands-off") approach.

  — **Invisible Hand:** Instead of government involvement, Smith argued that a combination of self-interest, competition, and the laws of supply and demand should direct how markets function. If a firm in a given market is successful in producing the right product at the right price at the right time, it will profit; if not, it will likely fail over time.

  — **Self-Correcting Markets:** In the "long run," markets will correct themselves without government interference.

  — **Labor Specialization:** The concept of labor specialization leads more people to be more efficient and productive, which in turn leads a country to achieving a higher national income (GDP).

— **Profit Motive/Self Interest:** Smith stated the "unintended consequences of intend actions" tend to benefit a society. He further asserted that, "It is not from the benevolence of the butcher, the brewer, or the baker that we expect our dinner, but from their regard to their own interest."

• **Perceived Strengths:** From the late 1700s through the end of the 1920s, Smith's theories led to long periods of prosperity in the United States. Moreover, a general adherence to Smith's key tenets allowed America to become the most dominant economic and industrial power in the world. If humans are mostly self-interested, then Smith's theories have some obvious merit. The lack of government interference, it should also be noted, led to balanced budgets.

• **Perceived Weaknesses:** Economic busts tend to follow economic booms. For example, there were five panics/depressions in the 1800s—1819, 1837, 1857, 1873, and 1893—and all were preceded by economic booms. The Panic of 1893 was the worst of the five, but its severe consequences were later surpassed by those of the Great Depression, which began with the Stock Market Crash in 1929. Smith's view that governments should not intervene in the business cycle lost favor during the prolonged Great Depression. As a result, by the mid-1930s the theories of John Maynard Keynes gradually took root. Most economists today would agree that Smith's policy of *laissez-faire* led to many excesses during the 1920s, which included both the overproduction of consumer goods and the overextension of credit to both businesses and consumers. Critics of Smith assert that his theories underestimate the human capacity for greed and corruption, which together can take markets to artificial highs before they come crashing back down.

II. KEYNESIAN SCHOOL

• **Key Person:** John Maynard Keynes / **Principal Book:** *The General Theory of Employment, Interest and Money* (1935)

• **Main Period of Influence:** mid-1930s to 1980

• **Principal Concepts:**

— A key role of a democratic form of government is to take away the rough edges of capitalism.

— "In the long run, we're all dead." Keynes agreed with Adam Smith that markets will correct themselves in the long run, but he also noted that, "In the long run, we're all dead." Because Keynes felt there would be too much human suffering during a severe recession, he argued that governments needed to intervene and smooth out the large swings in the business cycle.

— **Aggregate Demand:** In a severe economic recession, Keynes felt that it was the government's duty to "prime the pump," or increase government spending to lift GDP back up to a healthy level. In making his argument, Keynes provided the basis for fiscal policy (manipulating taxes and government spending) and monetary policy (manipulating interest rates and the money supply) to correct an economy that is surging or flailing.

— **"Animal Spirits":** Keynes lived through the horrors of World War I and thus concluded that people often act irrationally. To this end, he coined the term "animal spirits," which he defined as "a spontaneous urge to action rather than inaction." Keynes asserted that irrational emotions (such as greed and fear) tend to override our rational instincts at various times, and when they do so in the economic realm, booms and busts may occur.

— **"Paradox of Thrift":** During a boom time, many people get exuberant and spend all they earn, rather than saving. Conversely, during a recession, people tend to save extensively when governments need them to spend in order to boost national income (GDP).

- **Perceived Strengths:** Keynes' theories did not eliminate the business cycle, but when implemented, especially during the 1950s and 1960s, they did limit the cycle's large swings up and down. Keynes' theories also provided for a greater sense of equality in society, but this benefit was achieved by taking away a certain amount of individual liberty.

- **Perceived Weaknesses:** The implementation of Keynes' theories, critics argue, led to "stagflation"—a combination of high inflation and high unemployment—in the United States during the 1970s. While this is true, the OPEC oil embargo and the resulting surge in oil prices also played a major role in terms of causing stagflation.

- Critics of Keynes have also argued that his theories led to bloated government budgets and massive budget deficits. Moreover, they assert that Keynes was naïve about the role of government. For instance, Keynes argued that when an economy improves, political leaders are supposed to raise taxes and cut government spending to pay off any national debt incurred while propping up the economy. That said, when politicians do in fact raise taxes, they tend to get voted out of office, so there is little incentive for them to do so.

VARIOUS ECONOMIC POLICIES SINCE 1980

After Keynes lost favor around 1980, the "supply-side" economic theories of economist Arthur Laffer gained favor. Adopting a variation of the policies of Andrew Mellon—the U.S. Treasury Secretary during the 1920s—Laffer promoted reducing taxes on businesses and the wealthy in order to induce more production (or supply) of goods and services. In turn, this process would lead to the creation of more jobs. President Ronald Reagan embraced Laffer's theories, and his policies known as Reaganomics did stimulate the economy. These same policies, however, also led to high budget deficits and the tripling of the national debt under Reagan's presidency. A large increase in defense spending also played a major role in the increased budget deficits of the 1980s.

Since the 1980s, political leaders in the United States—in conjunction with the leaders of the Federal Reserve Bank—have used a variation of the theories put forth by both Adam Smith and John Maynard Keynes, including those of their various protégés. As the Great Recession of 2007-2009 recently showed, however, there is no one economic theory today that remains completely dominant in the United States during the various stages of the business cycle. During times of expansion, we tend to lean towards Adam Smith, while during times of economic turbulence, John Maynard Keynes tends to make a comeback.

MACROECONOMIC PROBLEMS OF THE AMERICAN ECONOMY

THE BUSINESS CYCLE

Business Cycles—Business cycles are the alternating periods of prosperity and recession that seem to characterize all market-oriented economies.

Four Phases of the Cycle—Every business cycle consists of four phases. The peak is the high point of business activity. It occurs at a specific point of time. The contraction is a period of declining business activity. It occurs over a period of time. The trough is the low point in business activity. It, too, occurs at a specific point in time. The expansion is a period of growing business activity. It takes place over a period of time.

Although the word "cycle" implies a certain uniformity, that is misleading. Each business cycle differs from every other in terms of duration of contractions and expansions, and height of peak and depth of trough.

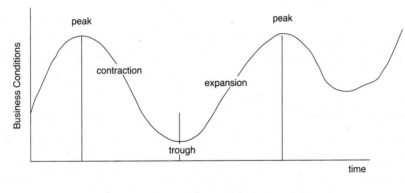

Figure 4–10 Phases of the Business Cycle

Seasonal Fluctuations—Seasonal fluctuations are changes in economic variables that reflect the season of the year. For example, every summer, ice cream sales soar. They decrease during winter. Every December, toy sales increase dramatically. They fall back during January.

Secular Trends—A secular trend is the long run direction of movement of a variable. For example, our economy has become dramatically richer over the past century. We can say that there was a secular upward trend in real GNP. Of course, growth was not steady. There were periods of faster than average followed by slower than average growth, which accounts for business cycles.

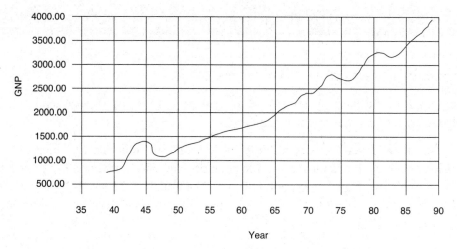

Figure 4–11 Secular Trend and Cycle in Real GNP, 1939–88

MONEY AND BANKING

WHAT MONEY IS AND DOES

Money is anything that is generally acceptable in exchange for goods and services and in payment of debts. Suppose you had something you wanted to sell. Few would be willing to part with their product for a commodity like a loaf of bread, a chicken, or an automobile hubcap. All would be willing to exchange their product for coins, currency, or a check. Therefore, these latter items are money because they are generally acceptable. Everybody is willing to accept them in exchange for what they want to sell.

Functions of Money—Money performs four particular functions:

1. **Medium of Exchange**—Money is used to facilitate exchanges of goods and services. Money makes buying and selling easier. Assume we had an economy where nothing was money. Such an economy is known as a **barter economy**. In a barter economy goods and services exchange directly for other goods and services. If you want an axe that someone is selling, you must find an item that person wants to trade for it. Barter requires a **double coincidence of wants**, each party must want what the other party has. If that condition does not hold, then exchange cannot take place, and valuable resources can be wasted in putting together trades. With money this problem never arises because **everyone always wants money**. Consequently, the resources used to facilitate exchanges can be put to more productive use.

2. **Unit of Value**—We use our monetary unit as the standard measure of value. We say a shirt is worth $25.00, not 14 chickens.

3. **Store of Value**—Money is one of the forms wealth can be stored in. Alternatives include stocks and bonds, real estate, gold, great paintings, and many others. One advantage of storing wealth in money form is that money is the most liquid of all assets. **Liquidity** refers to the ease with which an asset can be transformed into spendable form. Money is already in spendable form. The disadvantage of holding wealth in money form is that money typically pays a lower return than other assets.

4. **Standard of Deferred Payment**—Money is used in transactions involving payments to be made at a future date. An example would be building contracts where full payment is made only when the project is completed. This function of money is implicit in the three already discussed.

What Serves as Money?—Virtually anything can and has served as money. Gold, silver, shells, boulders, cheap metal, paper, and electronic impulses stored in computers are examples of the varied forms money has taken. The only requirement is that the item be generally acceptable. Money does **not** have to have intrinsic value (see below). Typically, the items that have served as money have had the following additional characteristics:

1. durability

2. divisibility

3. homogeneity (uniformity or standardization)

4. portability (high value-to-weight and value-to-volume)

5. relative stability of supply

6. optimal scarcity

What Makes Money Valuable?—Money is valuable if it can be used for or exchanged for something useful. Money's lack of intrinsic value means it cannot be used for anything useful. Why can it be exchanged for something useful? Sellers accept money because they know they can use it anywhere else in the country to buy goods and services and pay off debts. If they could not do that, they would not want it. What this means is that the substance that is used for money need not be valuable, and that money need not be backed by anything valuable. Such is the case. Our money is not backed by gold, silver, or anything else. It is just cheap metal, cheap paper, and electronic impulses stored in computers. Gold can be put to better use filling teeth!

THE UNITED STATES' MONEY SUPPLY

While there are many different definitions of the money supply available, the two most commonly used are M1 and M2.

M1—M1 consists of currency, demand deposits, other checkable deposits, and traveler's checks.

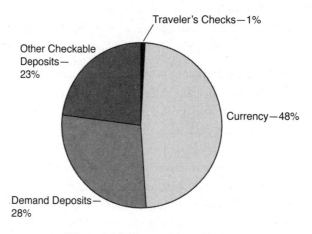

Figure 4–12 Composition of M1

Currency—coins and paper money.

Demand deposits—These are checking accounts held in commercial banks. Funds can be transferred from person to person by means of a check. Demand deposits are considered money because checks are generally acceptable.

Other checkable deposits—This category, includes all other financial institution deposits upon which checks can be written. Among these are NOW accounts, ATS accounts, and credit union share drafts.

Traveler's checks—Most traveler's checks are generally acceptable throughout much of the world.

M2—M2 includes all of M1 plus savings deposits, small-denomination time deposits, money-market mutual funds and deposit accounts, overnight repurchase agreements (known as repos), and Eurodollars.

Savings Deposits—These are the common passbook savings accounts. They do not provide check-writing privileges.

Small-denomination time deposits—Better known as certificates of deposits, or CDs. They typically do not provide check-writing privileges.

Money market mutual funds and deposit accounts—Both mutual funds and deposit accounts are investment funds. Large numbers of people pool their money to allow for diversification and professional investment management. Mutual funds are managed by private financial companies. Deposit accounts are managed by commercial banks. Investors earn a return on their investment and have limited check-writing privileges. Mutual funds are not afforded protection by the government, as is the case with FDIC-insured bank accounts.

Overnight repurchase agreements and Eurodollars—Overnight repos essentially are short-term (literally, overnight) loans. A corporation with excess cash may arrange to purchase a security from a bank with the stipulation that the bank will buy the security back the next day at a slightly higher price. The corporation receives a return on its money, and the bank gets access to funds. Eurodollars are dollar-denominated demand deposits held in banks outside the United States (not just in Europe). From the standpoint of M2, deposits held in Caribbean branches of Federal Reserve member banks are relevant. These deposits are easily accessed by U.S. residents. While both instruments are important in financial affairs, they are negligible in the totality of M2.

A significant proportion of M2 cannot be used as a medium of exchange. Why, then, are the items considered money? First, each of these items is highly liquid. Second, studies indicate that people's economic behavior is not very sensitive to their relative holdings of the various assets in question (see Figure 4–13).

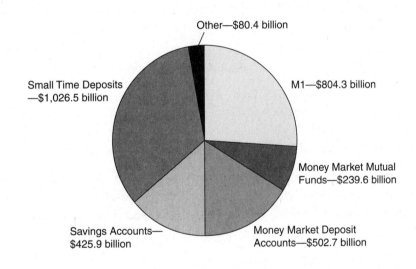

Figure 4–13 Composition of M2.

THE FINANCIAL SYSTEM

Financial Intermediaries—Financial intermediaries are organizations such as commercial banks, savings and loan institutions, credit unions, and insurance companies. They play an important role in facilitating the saving and investment process which helps the economy grow. Savers typically look to place their money where the combination of return, liquidity, and safety is best. Through the various types of deposits they offer, financial intermediaries compete for the saved funds. The money so obtained is used to finance borrowing. Through their ability to obtain large pools of money from many depositors, intermediaries are able to service the needs of large borrowers.

Balance Sheet of Typical Bank

Assets	Liabilities
Reserves	Demand Deposits
Loans	Savings Deposits
Securities	Time Deposits
Property	Other Deposits
Other Assets	Net Worth

Reserves—Reserves are a bank's money holdings. Most reserves are held in the form of demand deposits at other banks or the Federal Reserve System. The remainder is cash in the bank's vault. Reserves are held to meet the demand for cash on the part of depositors and to honor checks drawn upon the bank. The amount of reserves a bank must hold is based on the **required reserve ratio**. Set by the Federal Reserve System, the required reserve ratio is a number from 0 to 1.00 and determines the level of reserve holdings relative to the bank's deposits.

Required Reserves—Required reserves are the amount a bank is legally obligated to hold. Required reserves are calculated by multiplying the required reserve ratio by the amount of deposits.

$$\text{Required Reserves} = \text{Required Reserve Ratio} \times \text{Deposits}$$

The required reserve ratio does not make banks safe. In the absence of a requirement, most banks would voluntarily hold adequate reserves to be "safe." In fact, the level of reserves banks are required to hold is probably higher than what they need to be safe. The main purpose of the requirement is to give the Federal Reserve System some control over the banks.

Excess Reserves—Excess reserves are the difference between the amount of reserves a bank holds and what it is required to hold. All banks hold excess reserves at all times for reasons of financial prudence; however, greater excess reserves will be held during periods of financial uncertainty.

$$\text{Excess Reserves} = \text{Reserves} - \text{Required Reserves}$$

Why Can Banks Hold "Fractional" Reserves?—All banks constantly operate with reserve holdings only a fraction of deposit liabilities. This is known as **fractional reserve banking**. If all depositors tried to withdraw their money simultaneously, banks would not be able to honor the demands. Fortunately, this is unlikely to happen because people like to hold deposits because they are safe and convenient. On a normal business day, some withdrawals are made, but these are counterbalanced by new deposits. Reserve holdings need only be a small fraction of deposits for prudent operation.

MONETARY POLICY

THE FEDERAL RESERVE SYSTEM

The Federal Reserve System (known as the "Fed") is the central bank of the United States. Its responsibilities are to oversee the stability of the banking system and conduct monetary policy to the end of fighting inflation and unemployment and stimulating economic growth.

Structure—The Fed has an unusual structure. It consists of a Board of Governors, 12 regional banks, money subregional banks, and commercial banks that opt for membership in the system. Although it was created by an Act of Congress (in 1913), nominally the Fed is privately owned by the member banks. Members of the Board of Governors are appointed by the President and confirmed by the Senate for 14 year terms. The Chair of the Board is appointed by the President and confirmed by the Senate for a four year term. The Fed's budget is overseen by a committee of Congress, and it must report to Congress about its operations at least twice a year. To a large extent, the Fed can be considered an independent agency of the government.

The Fed's virtual independence has led to a continuing controversy. Is it wise to give the power to influence the state of the economy to an entity that is not directly accountable to the people? The "pro" side claims the Fed's independence puts it "above" politics and leads to decisions more in the "public interest." The "con" side says that in a democracy, the people should be given a voice in all decisions that affect them.

Functions—The major functions of the Fed are as follows:

1. **Bank Regulation**—The Fed has been given the responsibility of examining member banks to determine if they are financially strong and in conformity with the banking regulations. The Fed also approves mergers.

2. **Clearing Interbank Payments**—The Fed performs a service for member banks in operating the check clearing function. Banks receiving deposit checks drawn on other banks can present them to the Fed. The Fed will credit the receiving bank's reserve account, reduce the paying bank's reserve account, and send the check back to the paying bank. Banks do not universally avail themselves of this service. Local banks will frequently cooperate and establish their own check clearing process for local checks.

3. **Lender of Last Resort**—One of the original motivations for establishing the Fed was to have a bank that could act as a "lender of last resort."

Bank panics refer to situations where depositors lose faith in their bank and try to withdraw their money. Given the fractional reserve nature of modern banking, under which banks, by law, must set aside a fixed percent of their total deposits as reserves with the Fed, it is impossible for all depositors to withdraw their money simultaneously. The inability of depositors to withdraw their money from any one bank has the potential of scaring other depositors and starting a "run on the banks." By standing ready to loan reserves to banks experiencing difficulties, the Fed helps reduce the danger of panics.

Federal Deposit Insurance was established during the New Deal era. Federal Deposit Insurance provides government guarantees for bank deposits should a bank fail. Both commercial banks and savings and loans are insured. Panics were much more common in the days before the Fed and the Federal Deposit Insurance Corporation, but are not unknown today. Witness the widespread failures of savings and loan institutions in Ohio and Maryland (institutions which *lacked* federal insurance) in the 1980s and '90s.

4. **Monetary Policy—**

    Open Market Operations—Open market operations refers to the Fed's buying or selling of U.S. Government bonds in the open market. The purpose is to influence the amount of reserves in the banking system, and, consequently, the banking system's ability to extend credit and create money.

a. **To expand the economy**—The Fed would buy bonds in the open market. If $50 million in bonds was purchased directly from commercial banks, the banks' balance sheet would change as follows:

All Commercial Banks

R + 50 million	
Bonds – 50 million	

Banks are now holding an additional $50 million in excess reserves which they can use to extend additional credit. To induce borrowers, banks are likely to lower interest rates and credit standards. As loans are made, the money supply will expand. The additional credit will stimulate additional spending, primarily for investment goods.

The $50 million in bonds could be purchased directly from private individuals. The private individuals would then deposit the proceeds in their bank accounts. After the money was deposited, the balance sheet of all commercial banks would look as follows:

All Commercial Banks

R + 50 million	DD + 50 million

As above, the banks are now holding excess reserves which they can use to extend credit. Lower interest rates, a greater money supply, and a higher level of total expenditure will result.

b. **To contract the economy**—The Fed would sell bonds in the open market. If it sold $20 million in bonds directly to the commercial banks, the banks' balance sheet would change as follows:

All Commercial Banks

R	– 20 million	
Bonds	+ 20 million	

Banks are now deficient in reserves. They need to reduce their demand deposit liabilities, and will do so by calling in loans and making new credit more difficult to get. Interest rates will rise, credit requirements will be tightened, and the money supply will fall. Total spending in the economy will be reduced.

If the Fed sells the $20 million in bonds directly to private individuals, payment will be made with checks drawn against the private individuals' bank accounts. The banks' balance sheet will change as follows:

All Commercial Banks

R	– 20 million	DD	– 20 million

Again, banks are deficient in reserves. They are forced to reduce credit availability, which will raise interest rates, reduce the money supply, and lead to a drop in total spending.

Bonds are a financial instrument frequently used by government and business as a way to borrow money. Every bond comes with a par value (often $1,000), a date to maturity (ranging from 90 days to 30 years), a coupon (a promise to pay a certain amount of money each year to the bondholder until maturity), and a promise to repay the par value on the maturity date. The issuing government or business sells the bonds in the bond market for a price determined by supply and demand. The money received from the sale represents the principal of the loan, the annual coupon payment is the interest on the loan, and the principal is repaid at the date of maturity. There is also a secondary market in bonds.

Assume a bond carries a coupon of $100 and is sold for $1,000. Then the annual yield to the purchaser is roughly 10% ($100/$1,000). If the same bond was sold for $950, the yield would be roughly 10.5% ($100/$950). If the same bond was sold for $1,050, the yield would roughly be 9.5% ($100/$1,050). Note the inverse relationship between bond yield and price. Also note that the actual yield formulas are considerably more complicated than those used.

Reserve Ratio—The Fed can set the legal reserve ratio for both member and non-member banks. The purpose is to influence the level of excess reserves in the banking system, and consequently, the banking system's ability to extend credit and create money.

a. **To expand the economy**—The Fed would reduce the reserve requirement. Assume the reserve requirement is 8%, and all banks are "all loaned up."

If the Fed reduces the reserve requirement to 6%, required reserves fall to $30 million, and there are immediately $10 million in excess reserves. Banks will lower the interest rates they charge and credit requirements in an attempt to make more loans. As the loans are granted, the economy's money supply and total spending will rise.

All Commercial Banks

R	40 million	DD	50 million

b. **To contract the economy**—The Fed would raise the reserve requirement. Assume the reserve requirement is 8%, and all banks are "all loaned up."

All Commercial Banks

R	40 million	DD	50 million

If the Fed raises the reserve requirement to 10%, required reserves rise to $50 million, and banks are immediately $10 million deficient in reserves. Banks will raise the interest rates they charge and credit requirements to reduce the amount of money borrowed. They may also call in loans. As the loans are reduced, the economy's money supply and total spending will fall.

Discount Rate—One of the responsibilities of the Fed is to act as a "lender of last resort." Member banks needing reserves can borrow from the Fed. The interest rate the Fed charges on these loans is called the **discount rate**. By changing the discount rate, the Fed can influence the amount member banks try to borrow, and, consequently, the banking system's ability to extend credit and create money.

a. **To expand the economy**—The Fed would lower the discount rate. A lower discount rate would make it less "painful" for member banks to borrow from the Fed. Consequently, they will be more willing to lend money and hold a low level of excess reserves. A lower discount rate would lead to lower interest rates and credit requirements, a higher money supply, and greater total spending in the economy.

b. **To contract the economy**—The Fed would raise the discount rate. A higher discount rate would make it more "painful" for member banks to borrow from the Fed. Consequently, they will be less willing to lend money and more likely to hold a high level of excess reserves. A higher discount rate would lead to higher interest rates and more stringent credit requirements, a lower money supply, and lower total spending in the economy.

Monetary Policy Summary Table

Tool	Action	Effect on Interest Rates	Effect on Money Supply	Effect on Total Spending	Effect on GNP
Open Market	buy	lower	raise	raise	raise
Operations	sell	raise	lower	lower	lower
Reserve	raise	raise	lower	lower	lower
Ratio	lower	lower	raise	raise	raise
Discount	raise	raise	lower	lower	lower
Rate	lower	lower	raise	raise	raise

REVIEW QUESTIONS

1. In *The Wealth of Nations*, Adam Smith attempted to demonstrate which of the following about international trade?

   (A) Tariffs and quotas should be used to protect domestic industries.
   (B) Countries should produce only those commodities for which they have an absolute advantage.
   (C) When countries specialize and trade, world wealth is enhanced.
   (D) Countries should be self-sufficient and produce all commodities they consume.

2. If the Treasury required the central bank to buy bonds in the amount of $10 million, the effect on the money supply would be the same as the effect of

   (A) the sale of $10 million in bonds by the central bank to commercial banks.
   (B) the purchase of $10 million in U.S. bonds by foreigners.
   (C) the purchase of $10 million in bonds by the central bank from commercial banks.
   (D) the Treasury printing $10 million in new money.

3. Which of the following is NOT a factor that enhances an economy's growth potential?

   (A) Increasing levels of investment
   (B) Relatively high levels of training among the labor force
   (C) A relatively high capital to output ratio
   (D) New technologies

4. Conflicts between the goals of the Treasury and the Federal Reserve Bank exist when

   (A) the GNP is increasing, thus causing tax revenues to increase.
   (B) the Fed restrains money to reduce inflation and the Treasury needs to borrow.
   (C) the Fed follows an easy money policy to reduce unemployment, and the Treasury needs to borrow.
   (D) national debt and interest rates are decreasing due to fiscal restraint.

5. Which of the following represents monetary policy geared to increase the supply of money?

    (A) The purchase of bonds by the Federal Reserve Bank
    (B) The sale of bonds by the central bank
    (C) An increase in reserve requirements
    (D) An increase in the discount rate

6. Prices tend to be inflated during wartime because

    (A) guns cost more than butter.
    (B) there is competition for fully employed resources.
    (C) the Consumer Price Index is calculated differently in wartime.
    (D) the cost of government is not included in the CPI.

7. If people start eating more fish and chicken to reduce their intake of cholesterol, and the importation of Canadian pork is restricted due to a steroid problem, what will happen to meat prices in the U.S.?

    (A) The prices of chicken, pork, and fish will go down.
    (B) The prices of chicken, pork, fish, and beef will go up.
    (C) There will be no substantial effect on prices.
    (D) The price of pork will go down, while the prices of chicken and fish will go up.

8. Both Bank A and Bank B are required to meet a 20% legal reserve requirement. Bank A has excess reserves of $20,000. Bank B has no excess reserves but receives a deposit of $20,000. Which of the following statements is correct?

    (A) Each bank can make a loan of $20,000.
    (B) Bank A can make a loan of $20,000, but Bank B can make a loan of only $16,000.
    (C) Bank B can make a loan of $20,000, but Bank A can make a loan of $16,000.
    (D) The most each bank can loan is $16,000.

9. If the Fed wants to create a situation of "tight" money, which of the following actions would be taken?

    (A) Raise the discount rate, buy government securities, and lower the legal reserve requirement.
    (B) Raise the discount rate, buy government securities, and raise the legal reserve requirement.
    (C) Raise the discount rate, sell government securities, and raise the legal reserve requirement.
    (D) Lower the discount rate, buy government securities, and raise the legal reserve requirement.

10. An economist's definition of investment in human capital would be represented by

    (A) labor costs in producing an intermediate good.
    (B) labor costs in producing a final good.
    (C) federal government's expenses for unemployment compensation.
    (D) the expenditure by an individual on college tuition and other college expenses.

ANSWER KEY

1.	(C)	4.	(B)	7.	(B)	9.	(C)
2.	(D)	5.	(A)	8.	(B)	10.	(D)
3.	(C)	6.	(B)				

DETAILED EXPLANATIONS OF ANSWERS

1. **(C)** Choice (C) is correct. Adam Smith believed that each country producing what it does best, or relatively better, and trading for those commodities produced to advantage elsewhere, enhanced each nation's wealth and world wealth. Choices (A) and (D) would interfere with the types of specialization and trade described in choice (C). Smith stated that countries should produce those goods that they have an absolute and comparative advantage in, a comparative advantage being the least relative disadvantage.

2. **(D)** Choice (D) is the correct answer. If the central bank buys bonds in the amount of $10 million from the Treasury, it creates $10 million in "new money," the effect of which is identical to the Treasury printing this amount of money. Conversely, if the central bank buys $10 million in bonds from commercial banks, it creates less money because some must be used as reserves. Choices (A) and (B) reduce the supply of money.

3. **(C)** Choice (C) is correct. A growth formula derived from the Harrod-Domar model is:

$$\text{growth rate} = \frac{\text{average propensity to save}}{\text{capital/output ratio}}$$

It should be evident after inspection that as the capital to output ratio decreases, the growth rate increases. Choices (A), (B), and (D) enhance economic growth.

4. **(B)** Choice (B) is correct. The Treasury needs to borrow money to finance a debt and wants to do so at the lowest interest rates possible, but monetary restraint and tight money are inconsistent with this goal.

5. **(A)** Choice (A) is the correct answer. When the Fed purchases bonds, it pays for them with money which increases money supply. Choices (B), (C), and (D) are contractionary moves by the Fed.

6. **(B)** Choice (B) is correct. During wartime, the economy is working to produce more defense than in peacetime, which bids up prices. Choice (C) is false. Choice (D) is true, but if the government were included, it would probably cause more inflation.

7. **(B)** Choice (B) is the correct answer. The price of chicken and fish would be bid up by increased demand. The price of pork would go up due to controlled supply, and the price of beef would go up because it is a substitute for pork.

8. **(B)** Choice (B) is correct. A single commercial bank can make loans to the extent of its excess reserves. Therefore, Bank A can make loans of $20,000. Bank B, however, must hold 20% of the $20,000 deposit as federal reserve deposit. Therefore, Bank B can only make $16,000 of loans. The loans that banks make depend upon meeting the legal reserve requirements.

9. **(C)** Choice (C) is correct. Raising the discount rate raises the cost of commercial banks borrowing from the Fed. Selling government securities to commercial banks or the public takes money or potential money out of circulation. (Money becomes near money.) Raising the legal reserve requirement wipes out excess reserves and lowers the value of the money multiplier. All three of the actions described in (C) are consistent in creating a "tight" money situation.

10. **(D)** Choice (D) is the correct answer. When an economist speaks of human capital, the emphasis is on capital theory which includes investment as a large component. Investment is performed to obtain a return. Investment in human capital consists of those expenditures which an individual makes to improve earning power. The concept is very specific and all other answers are not appropriate.

GEOGRAPHY

INTRODUCTION TO GEOGRAPHY

WHAT IS GEOGRAPHY?

Geography is the study of the earth's surface, including such aspects as its climate, topography, vegetation, and population. **Physical geography** is a branch of geography concerned with the natural features of the earth's surface. Physical geography concentrates on such areas as land formation, water, weather, and climate.

Population geography is a form of geography that deals with the relationships between geography and population patterns, including birth and death rates. **Political geography** deals with the effect of geography on politics, especially on national boundaries and relations between states. **Economic geography** is a study of the interaction between the earth's landscape and the economic activity of the human population.

UNITED STATES

San Diego, California	1,394,928
Omaha, Nebraska	443,885
Baltimore, Maryland	621,849
Houston, Texas	2,296,224
Boston, Massachusetts	667,137
New York, New York	8,175,133

Table 4–1 U.S. City Populations, 2010 (U.S. Census Bureau est.)

Year	Population	Year	Population
1860	31,443,321	1950	151,325,798
1870	38,558,371	1960	179,323,175
1880	50,189,209	1970	203,302,031
1890	62,979,766	1980	226,547,082
1900	76,212,168	1990	248,790,925
1910	92,228,496	2000	282,171,936
1920	106,021,537	2010	308,745,538
1930	123,202,624	2017 (est.)	326,474,013
1940	132,164,569		

Table 4–2 Population of the United States

There are many sources of energy in the United States that are being developed to lessen the country's dependence on foreign oil. Some of these sources are solar energy, nuclear energy, gasohol, fossil fuels, and others. With the development of these sources of energy, more jobs will be made available and our economy will not be afflicted by adverse situations in oil-rich countries.

The United States is a relatively young country made up of immigrants from all over the world. This country serves as a leader of the free world and has many allies around the world.

It has helped many countries that needed financial help to rebuild their countries and continues to play an important part in world affairs.

The Middle Atlantic states, which include New York, West Virginia, Delaware, Maryland, New Jersey, and Pennsylvania, are a hub of activity. This area is highly industrialized and includes a skilled work force. The financial center of the nation is found in New York and cultural activities of all kinds are found in this area.

The states of North Dakota, South Dakota, Nebraska, Kansas, Minnesota, Iowa, Missouri, Wisconsin, Illinois, Michigan, Indiana, and Ohio make up the Plains states. This area is also referred to as the Midwest Region of the United States. It is known as a great agricultural region. Some of the crops grown are wheat, corn, and oats.

The Plains states are highly industrialized. Their location near waterways and the close proximity to coal and iron deposits have made it relatively easy for industries to develop. Skilled laborers are available and are necessary to work in manufacturing plants.

The South includes the following states: Texas, Oklahoma, Louisiana, Arkansas, Mississippi, Alabama, Florida, Georgia, South Carolina, North Carolina, Tennessee, Kentucky, and Virginia. This area is known for its relatively mild weather and good, rich soil. Agriculture and oil are two of the most important industries in the South. Some of the crops grown are cotton, corn, tobacco, peanuts, and rice. Cattle raising is also very important in some of these states. Five of these states border on the Gulf of Mexico.

Texas is the second-largest state in land area. It is composed of 267,000 square miles and 254 counties. It is broken up into many large physical regions such as piney woods, post oak belt, plains, rolling prairie, high plains, valley, coastal prairie, and West Texas. The estimated population of Texas in 2008 was 24.3 million. Texas is, without a doubt, one of the most geographically varied states in the United States.

The Pacific states include Washington, Oregon, and California, as well as tropical Hawaii. California has the largest population of any state in the United States. It is known for its agriculture and leads all other states in this regard. Oregon and Washington also are known for farming. All three states also have very developed industries.

Some of the major cities located in the Pacific states are Seattle, Spokane, Portland, Olympia, San Francisco, Los Angeles, Salem, and San Diego. Skiing, surfing, and national parks make tourism a major industry in this region.

The Mountain states are Montana, Idaho, Wyoming, Nevada, Utah, Colorado, Arizona, and New Mexico. These states are sparsely populated, even though the combined square mileage is over 800,000. The Rocky Mountains stretch through this area and most people feel they are a beautiful sight to behold.

The New England states include Maine, Massachusetts, New Hampshire, Vermont, Rhode Island, and Connecticut. Territorially, this is a very small region. The total size is about 67,000 square miles. The main industries in this area are fishing, shipping, manufacturing, and dairy farming.

MEXICO

Mexico borders the United States on the south and has about 107 million people. The land area is about 762,000 square miles. The capital is Mexico City. Some of the chief crops are coffee, cotton, corn, sugar cane, and rice.

Mexico has an abundance of natural resources, such as oil, gold, silver, and natural gas. Textiles, steel production, tourism, and petroleum are the major industries in Mexico.

CANADA

Canada is the United States' neighbor to the north. It includes the second-largest territory in the world. The current population is about 32 million people. The capital of Canada is Ottawa.

The United States and Canada are two sprawling countries that make up North America. Each country is an industrial giant and provides a very high standard of living for its population. The population of the United States is about nine or ten times larger than that of Canada.

The United States and Canada have large supplies of natural resources. In the United States, the minerals include coal, copper, gold, nickel, silver, zinc, and others. In Canada, the minerals found are nickel, gold, lead, silver, zinc, and others.

SOUTH AND CENTRAL AMERICA

Country	Population	Square Miles
Argentina	43,132,000	1,065,189
Brazil	204,579,000	3,286,470
Chile	18,006,000	292,257
Venezuela	30,620,000	352,143
Ecuador	16,279,000	109,483

Table 4–3 Selected South American Countries, 2015 est.

CENTRAL AMERICA

Central America is the connecting point between North and South America. The countries in Central America have an extremely long coastline. The main industry of this area is agriculture, and most people who live in this area are extremely poor. Bananas, coffee, and corn are some of their chief crops.

The seven nations that make up Central America are Belize, Guatemala, Honduras, El Salvador, Panama, Costa Rica, and Nicaragua.

SOUTH AMERICA

South America, lying entirely in the Western Hemisphere and mostly south of the Equator, has a Pacific shoreline on the west and an Atlantic shoreline east and north. South America connects with Central America and lies to the south and east of the Caribbean Sea and North America. It is the realm closest to Antarctica.

A few physical characteristics dominate the physiography of South America. The Andes Mountains stretch the length of the west coast while the Amazon Basin covers the north central part of the realm. The remaining parts of the realm consist mainly of plateaus.

Roughly half of the area and half of the population of South America are concentrated in Brazil.

The population of South America resides primarily on the periphery of the continent. The interior is only lightly populated. However, parts of the interior are undergoing extensive development with some population shifts.

Historically, the difficult terrain and the large distances separating the various states have limited the interchange between the different states on the continent. More recently, the states have increased their interconnections, particularly economically. Economic integration has become a significant factor throughout the continent, but primarily so in the southern part of the continent.

South America can be easily divided into four distinct regions: the North, the West, the Southern Cone, and Brazil.

The North consists of Colombia, Venezuela, Guyana, French Guiana, and Suriname. Each of the states has a Caribbean orientation both economically and culturally. All the states followed a plantation development model that involved the importation of slaves and contract laborers. Eventually, those immigrants were absorbed into the culture. While Guyana, French Guiana, and Suriname retained the culture from the colonial period, Colombia and Venezuela expanded into farming, ranching, mining, and oil and became much more diversified.

The West includes the Andean states Ecuador, Peru, Bolivia, and Paraguay. In addition to the influence of Andes, these states also share a strong Amerindian heritage.

The South, or Southern Cone, consists of Argentina, Chile, and Uruguay. These states have a strong European influence and little Amerindian influence.

Brazil distinguishes itself in two respects from the rest of South America. First is the influence of Portugal rather than Spain and second is the importance of Africans as opposed to Amerindians in both culture and demography.

Most states exhibit a marked degree of cultural pluralism. While there are a variety of ethnicities that are remnants of the colonial and slave heritage, these groups exist side by side without mixing. This pluralism is often expressed economically as well. Within the predominant economic activity, agriculture, commercial and subsistence farming exist side by side to a greater extent than any place else in the world. This, too, reflects the history of the continent, as commercial farming is associated with the land distribution of European landholders while subsistence farming is associated with the landholdings of indigenous, African, and Asian peoples.

Urban growth throughout the continent continues its rapid rise. Levels of urbanization overall today are equivalent to those in Europe and the United States.

EUROPE

Europe consists of 39 states and approximately 731 million people, according to the United Nations. On the north, west, and south, it has boundaries facing the Atlantic Ocean and the Mediterranean Sea, as well as a large number of other bodies of water. The eastern boundary is somewhat uncertain, with the line of demarcation lying along the border of Russia or along the Ural Mountains.

The physiography of Europe includes a wide range of topographic, climatic, and soil conditions which have had an impact on the cultural, political, and economic development.

In the south, the coastal areas have hot dry summers that required the development of specially adapted plants. Lacking the richness of natural resources of other regions, the southern region of Europe has nonetheless achieved a continuity of culture that has continuously depended on the exploitation of agriculture. As a result, the region tends to have a lower standard of living than other parts of Europe with the notable exception of Eastern Europe. While not as urbanized as Northern Europe, Southern Europe is actually more populous than Northern Europe.

Eastern Europe encompasses the largest region in Europe as well as the largest range of physiological, cultural, and political characteristics. This is a region of open plains, major rivers, lowlands, highlands, and mountains and valleys that provide key transit corridors. The result is that numerous peoples have converged on the area and kept this rich area in almost continuous conflict. The region is referred to as a shatter belt because of the unrelenting break up of existing orders. The term "balkanization" comes from this region where chronic division and fragmentation occurs.

Northern or Nordic Europe, one of the largest regions in terms of size is also one of the most poorly endowed regions in terms of natural resources. Cold climates with poor soil and limited mineral wealth combined with long distances over mountainous, remote terrain result in an isolated region, yet one that has succeeded economically as is evidenced by Norway's ranking as fourth-richest European country based on per capita income.

The British Isles, off the western coast of Europe consist of two main islands, Ireland and Britain as well as numerous small islands. While its isolation from continental Europe has protected it from attack, that isolation has led the United Kingdom to look outward to fulfill its economic needs. The United Kingdom had one of the largest empires in history and has become a hub of banking and industry.

Western Europe is at the heart of Europe. It provides the hub of economic power, which has led to its leadership in economic and political union.

Europe consists of strong regional distinctions in physical and cultural characteristics. The distinctions extend to functional specializations, thus helping to provide for extensive interchange.

The economy of Europe is well developed and depends in large part on manufacturing for its income. While Europe is considered to be overall highly productive and developed, the further east one goes, the lower the level of development.

Being at the western end of the Eurasian landmass, Europe is located in a prime position to facilitate contact with the rest of the world. Location as well as durable power cores provided necessary elements for the creation of wide ranging colonial empires.

Europe has an aging population that enjoys a high standard of living, is highly urbanized, and has a long life expectancy. The aging population coincides with a drop in fertility rates and thus a population decline in some states. Immigration partially offsets the population decline, but it is changing the cultural make up of the states, with some instability resulting.

Unlike most other parts of the world, Europe has made significant progress toward economic integration through the European Union. Political progress, although also a part of the developing and expanding European Union, has come much more slowly.

NORTH AFRICA

Northern Africa is the northern most part of Africa, separated from Sub-Saharan Africa by the Sahara Desert. Northern Africa is almost completely surrounded by water in all other directions, with only a small connection to Asia at the Sinai Peninsula of Egypt. Northern Africa is bordered by the Atlantic Ocean to the west, the Red Sea to the east, and the Mediterranean Sea to the north. The states of Algeria, Egypt, Libya, Morocco, Sudan, Tunisia, and Western Sahara make up the region. The dominant physical feature of Northern Africa is the Sahara Desert, which covers more than 90% of the region. The other physical feature of note is the Atlas Mountains, which extend across much of Morocco, northern Algeria, and Tunisia. The Atlas Mountains are part of the mountain system, which also runs through much of Southern Europe. The mountains become a steppe landscape as they transition into the Sahara Desert.

Farming has been the traditional economic base of the region, with Atlas Mountain valleys, the Nile valley and delta, and the Mediterranean coast providing good agricultural land. Cereals, rice, cotton, cedar, and cork are important crops. Olives, figs, dates, and citrus fruits are also grown here. The Nile Valley, being fertile and providing its own source of water, is particularly fertile, while elsewhere irrigation is essential to agricultural production. In the 20th century, the economies of Algeria and Libya were transformed by the discovery of oil and natural gas. Morocco depends on phosphates, agriculture, and tourism for its economy. Egypt and Tunisia also depend on tourism. Egypt, also has a varied industrial base, importing technology to develop its electronics and engineering industries.

The population of North Africa can be divided along the main geographic regions of North Africa: the Maghreb (northwest), the Nile Valley (northeast), and the Sahara (south).

SUB-SAHARAN AFRICA

Sub-Saharan Africa is the whole of the African continent south of the Sahara Desert. It is bordered to the north by the Sahara, the largest desert in the world, the Atlantic Ocean to the west, the Indian Ocean to the east, and the Atlantic and Indian Oceans meeting to border Africa to the south. Despite being geographically part of Sub-Saharan Africa, the Horn of Africa and large parts of Sudan show a strong Middle Eastern influence.

The landforms of Sub-Saharan Africa include rainforests, grasslands, and a few mountain ranges. Equatorial Africa, including the Sahel (a transitional zone just north of the equator between the Sahara and the tropical savanna), is covered by tropical rain forests while farther south there are grassy flat highlands leading to coastal plains. While Northern Africa has the Atlas Mountains, the Ruwenzri on the Uganda-Zaire border is the main mountain range in the Sub-Saharan region. Kilimanjaro, part of the Ruwenzri and Africa's highest mountain, is a dormant volcano. Further to the east is the Great Rift Valley, which contains several lakes. In addition to these landforms, Africa has some of the world's longest rivers, including the Nile, Niger, Zaire, and Zambezi. While there are many great lakes and large river systems, Africa has few natural sea harbors.

Sub-Saharan Africa is culturally rich and diverse with approximately 50 independent states and hundreds of ethnic groups. The large number of states is a legacy of the colonial occupation of Africa by European states. When African states were given their independence, state boundaries were drawn with little thought given to natural geographic boundaries. The result has been great instability that exists to the present day. Governmental fraud, mismanagement, and poor leadership as well as the highest number of refugees and displaced persons in the world compound the instability. In addition to the political instability, health and nutritional conditions in the region are poor. Many diseases remain uncontrolled, malnutrition is rampant, and the AIDS pandemic, which had its genesis in Africa, is a significant health crisis.

Despite the wide variety of cultures, most people in Sub-Saharan Africa depend on farming to earn a living. This is true despite the fact that Sub-Saharan Africa is rich in natural resources.

States such as Angola and Nigeria have oil reserves, while South Africa is known for diamonds. The patterns of resource exploitation and transportation still follow those established during the colonial period. Thus, the people of the region have little access to and largely do not benefit from the wealth of raw materials they possess.

RUSSIA

Russia, the largest state in terms of territory, spans most of the northern part of Eurasia. It is almost twice as large as the next biggest state, Canada. It is also the largest and most populous state that lies the farthest north in the world. Russia's climate is largely continental because of its large size and compactness. Most of its land is more than 200 miles from the sea, and the center is approximately 1,600 miles from the sea. Furthermore, Russia's mountain ranges, which are mostly to the south and the east, block moderating temperatures from the Indian and Pacific Oceans.

Despite its large size, comparatively speaking, Russia's population of approximately 143 million people is not very large. Most of that population lives west of the Ural Mountains and that population is very heterogeneous. Russia is a patchwork of many different ethnic groups, which formed the original basis for the 21 internal republics. As such, Russia is multicultural with a multifaceted political geography.

Despite having 80% of its land mass east of the Ural Mountains, most of the development, population, and infrastructure lie west of the Urals. The largest cities with the attendant industrial and transportation structure as well as the most productive farmland exist on the western 20% of Russia. What development does exist east of the Urals follows a narrow corridor near the southern border that reaches the Sea of Japan at Vladivostok. This corridor coincides with the Trans-Siberian Railway, which was built to reach one of the few seaports that is usable all year. Despite the fact that Russia is large, it is almost completely encircled by land within Eurasia.

While having extensive industrial development (at least regionally), Russia also holds the greatest mineral resource reserves in the world. The country is the most abundant in mineral fuels. It may contain up to half of the world's coal reserves and an even larger percentage of petroleum reserves. While Russia is blessed with plentiful resources, they are located in remote areas with extreme climates. For example, deposits of coal are scattered throughout the region, but the largest deposits are located in central and eastern Siberia, making them difficult to reach and expensive to mine.

Despite the wealth of natural resources, Russia has never been an exporter of manufactured goods, with the exception of weapons. Scarcity and low quality have limited the availability of Russian consumer goods outside of Russia (and, in many cases, inside as well).

With the collapse of Soviet Communism in the late 20th century, regions that have been associated with both Russia and the Soviet Union have begun to look outside of the Russian Federation for political, economic, and cultural connections.

SOUTH ASIA

South Asia is a clearly demarcated realm bounded by deserts in the west, the Himalayas to the north, mountains and dense forests to the east, and ocean to the south. Despite containing over 20 percent of the world's population, South Asia consists of only seven states: Bangladesh, Bhutan, India, the Maldives, Nepal, Pakistan, and Sri Lanka. The realm of South Asia is the most populous and densest in the world. The region has been beset by political instability and is the site of frequent military conflicts including wars between India and Pakistan, both of whom possess nuclear weapons.

The bulk of the region's territory is on the Indian subcontinent. Sections of all the states in the realm lie within the subcontinent on the Indian tectonic plate.

The climate varies considerably from area to area being influenced by altitude, proximity to the coast, and seasonal monsoons. The south is hot in summer and subject to vast quantities of rain during monsoon periods. The north is also hot in summer, but cools during winter. As the elevation increases in mountainous areas, the weather is colder and snow falls at higher altitudes in the Himalayas. However, on the plains at the foot of the Himalayas, the temperatures are much more moderate, as the mountains block the bitter winds that make Siberia so cold.

Despite the temperature variations, the climate of the region is called a monsoon climate. The weather is humid during the summer and dry during winter, resulting in two seasons rather than four: wet and dry. In the south, the climate is tropical monsoon while the north has a temperate monsoon climate. The impact of the monsoon climate can be seen on agriculture in the prevalence of jute, tea, rice, and other vegetables being grown in this region.

With more than half its population engaged in subsistence agriculture, it follows that South Asia has a high rate of poverty. Average incomes are low as are levels of education. Moreover, the low income and education levels contribute to poor overall health for the region. All of these factors paint a grim picture of economic prospects.

Sitting on only three percent of the land mass of the world, yet possessing over 22 percent of its population, South Asia has a high population density that will only continue to get worse as it also has one of the highest population growth rates. India, with over 1 billion people, is the world's largest federal republic. Despite having a representative government, economic gains for the majority of the population are limited.

With more than 2,000 ethnic groups, South Asia is one of the most ethnically diverse realms. Ethnic groups range in size from hundreds of millions to small tribal groups. Throughout its history South Asia has been invaded and settled by many ethnic groups. The fusion of the cultures of these different ethnic groups over the centuries has resulted in the creation of a common culture, traditions, and beliefs such as the religions of Hinduism, Jainism, Buddhism, and Sikhism. As a consequence, they share many similar cultural practices, festivals, and traditions.

Religion continues to play a major role in South Asia. Hindus in India, Muslims in Bangladesh and Pakistan, and Buddhists in Sri Lanka display fundamentalist and nationalist tendencies that exacerbate already tendentious religious relationships.

British colonialism created a politically unified South Asia. However, when Britain granted its South Asian colony independence, it split into numerous states along mainly cultural/religious lines. Political friction, particularly between India and Pakistan, remains a constant problem. The cultural and religious differences that contribute to conflict combine with ongoing border disputes between India and Pakistan and India and China to create a potentially disastrous situation, as all three countries possess nuclear weapons.

EAST ASIA

East Asia consists of four states and two other political entities. China, Japan, South Korea, and Mongolia are states, while Taiwan and North Korea cannot be classified as states because they lack general recognition by the states of the world. Taiwan, while considering itself independent, is viewed by the People's Republic of China as a temporarily insubordinate or wayward province. North Korea's political status is uncertain. It is not a full member of the United Nations and there are doubts as to whether the division of Korea into North and South is permanent.

Review Questions

Question 1 is based on Table 4–1 as shown on page 617.

1. Which city has the third-largest population?

    (A) Houston
    (B) Boston
    (C) San Diego
    (D) Baltimore

Questions 2 and 3 are based on Table 4–2 as shown on page 618.

2. How much did the population increase between 1970 and 1980?

    (A) By approximately 20,000
    (B) By approximately 200,000
    (C) By approximately 2,000,000
    (D) By approximately 20,000,000

3. The population of the United States has

    (A) steadily declined.
    (B) remained about the same.
    (C) dropped markedly.
    (D) steadily increased.

4. Two of the main industries of the South are

    (A) oil and agriculture.
    (B) oil and mining.
    (C) agriculture and fishing.
    (D) oil and cattle raising.

5. The Pacific states have one thing in common. They are

    (A) farming centers.
    (B) extremely cold in the winter.
    (C) located in the Southwest.
    (D) not highly populated.

6. Mexico has an abundance of

    (A) oil and gold.
    (B) natural gas and nickel.
    (C) nickel and diamonds.
    (D) diamonds and natural gas.

7. Canada

    (A) is the largest country in the world.
    (B) is located to the south of the United States.
    (C) includes the second-largest territory in the world.
    (D) is a part of the United States.

Question 8 is based on Table 4–3 as shown on page 620.

8. Which country in South America is the largest in both population and square miles?

    (A) Ecuador
    (B) Brazil
    (C) Venezuela
    (D) Argentina

9. One of the chief crops in Central America is

    (A) wheat.
    (B) bananas.
    (C) barley.
    (D) rice.

10. Which of the following is an example of climate?

    (A) Changes in the temperature from time to time
    (B) Long, extended periods of little or no rainfall in certain areas
    (C) A forecast of sunshine
    (D) An electrical storm

ANSWER KEY

1.	(C)	4.	(A)	7.	(C)	9.	(B)
2.	(D)	5.	(A)	8.	(B)	10.	(B)
3.	(D)	6.	(A)				

DETAILED EXPLANATIONS OF ANSWERS

1. **(C)** Choice (C) is the correct answer. San Diego has the third-largest population, with approximately 1.39 million people. New York City is first with 8.17 million; Houston is second with 2.29 million.

2. **(D)** Choice (D) is the correct answer. Between 1970 and 1980, the population increased by 23,245,051.

3. **(D)** Choice (D) is the correct answer. The population has increased every decade since 1860.

4. **(A)** Choice (A) is the correct answer. Oil and agriculture are two of the main industries in the South. Some of the crops grown in the South are cotton, corn, tobacco, peanuts, and rice.

5. **(A)** Choice (A) is the correct answer. Oregon and Washington are known for farming, and California leads all other states in agriculture.

6. **(A)** Choice (A) is the correct answer. Mexico has an abundance of natural resources, such as oil, gold, silver, and natural gas.

7. **(C)** Choice (C) is the correct answer. Choice (D) is incorrect because Canada is not part of the United States. Choice (B) is wrong because Canada is located north, not south, of the United States.

8. **(B)** Choice (B) is the correct answer. The population of Brazil is 204 million and its area is 3,286,470 square miles.

9. **(B)** Choice (B) is the correct answer. Some of Central America's chief crops are bananas, coffee, and corn.

10. **(B)** Choice (B) is the correct answer. Choices (A), (C), and (D) are incorrect because they refer to day-to-day conditions, not an overall condition over a period of time.

WESTERN CIVILIZATION AND WORLD HISTORY

THE ANCIENT AND MEDIEVAL WORLDS

THE APPEARANCE OF CIVILIZATION

Between 6000 and 3000 BCE, humans invented the plow, utilized the wheel, harnessed the wind, discovered how to smelt copper ores, and began to develop accurate solar calendars. Small villages gradually grew into populous cities. The invention of writing in Mesopotamia around 3500 BCE, in combination with heightened refinement in sculpture, architecture, and metal working from about 3000 BCE, marks the beginning of civilization and divides prehistoric from historic times.

MESOPOTAMIA

Sumer (4000 to 2000 BCE) included the city of Ur. The *Gilgamesh* is an epic Sumerian poem. The Sumerians constructed dikes and reservoirs and established a loose confederation of city-states. They probably invented writing (called "cuneiform" because of its wedge-shaped letters). The Amorites, or Old Babylonians (2000 to 1550 BCE), established a new capital at Babylon, known for its famous Hanging Gardens. King Hammurabi (reigned 1792–1750 BCE) promulgated a legal code that called for retributive punishment ("an eye for an eye") and provided that one's social class determined punishment for a crime.

The Assyrians (1100–612 BCE) conquered Syria, Palestine, and much of Mesopotamia. They controlled a brutal, militaristic empire. The Chaldeans, or New Babylonians (612–538 BCE), conquered the Assyrian territory, including Jerusalem. In 538 BCE, Cyrus, king of the southern Persians, defeated the Chaldeans. The Persians created a huge empire and constructed a road network. Their religion, Zoroastrianism, promoted worship of a supreme being in the context of a cosmic battle with the forces of evil. After 538 BCE, the peoples of Mesopotamia came under the rule of a series of different empires and dynasties.

EGYPT

During the end of the Archaic Period (5000–2685 BCE), Menes, or Narmer, unified Upper and Lower Egypt around 3200 BCE During the Old Kingdom (2685–2180 BCE), the pharaohs came to be considered living gods. The capital moved to Memphis during the Third Dynasty (ca. 2650 BCE). The pyramids at Giza were built during the Fourth Dynasty (ca. 2613–2494 BCE).

After the Hyksos invasion (1785–1560 BCE), the New Kingdom (1560–1085 BCE) expanded into Nubia and invaded Palestine and Syria, enslaving the Jews. King Amenhotep IV or Akhenaton (reigned c. 1372–1362 BCE) promulgated the idea of a single god, Aton, and closed the temples of all other Gods and Goddesses. His successor, Tutankhamen, reestablished pantheism in Egypt.

In the Post-Empire Period (1085–1030 BCE), Egypt came under the successive control of the Assyrians, the Persians, Alexander the Great, and finally, in 30 BCE, the Roman Empire. The Egyptians developed papyrus and made many medical advances. Other peoples would elaborate their ideas of monotheism and the notion of an afterlife.

PALESTINE AND THE HEBREWS

Phoenicians settled along the present-day coast of Lebanon (Sidon, Tyre, Beirut, Byblos) and established colonies at Carthage and in Spain. They spread Mesopotamian culture through their trade networks.

The Hebrews probably moved to Egypt around 1700 BCE and were enslaved about 1500 BCE. The Hebrews fled Egypt under Moses and around 1200 BCE returned to Palestine. Under King David (reigned ca. 1012–972 BCE), the Philistines were defeated and a capital established at Jerusalem. Ultimately, Palestine divided into Israel (10 tribes) and Judah (two tribes). The 10 tribes of Israel—also known as the Lost Tribes—disappeared after Assyria conquered Israel in 722 BCE.

The poor and less attractive state of Judah continued until 586 BCE, when the Chaldeans transported the Jews to Chaldea as advisors and slaves (Babylonian captivity). When the Persians conquered Babylon in 539 BCE, the Jews were allowed to return to Palestine. Alexander the Great conquered Palestine in 325 BCE. During the Hellenistic period (323–63 BCE), the Jews were allowed to govern themselves. Under Roman rule, Jewish autonomy was restricted. The Jews revolted in 66–70 CE. The Jews also revolted in 132–135 CE. These uprisings led to the Jews' loss of their Holy Land. The Romans quashed the revolt and ordered the dispersion of the Jews. The Jews contributed the ideas of monotheism and humankind's covenant and responsibility to God to lead ethical lives.

GREECE

Homer's *Iliad* and *Odyssey* were poems that dramatized for Ancient Greek civilization ideas like excellence (*arete*), courage, honor, and heroism. Hesiod's *Works and Days* summarized everyday life. His *Theogony* recounted Greek myths. Greek religion was based on their writings.

In the Archaic Period (800–500 BCE), Greek life was organized around the polis (city-state). Oligarchs controlled most of the polis until the end of the sixth century, when individuals holding absolute power (tyrants) replaced them. By the end of the sixth century, democratic governments replaced many tyrants.

Sparta, however, developed into an armed camp. Sparta seized control of neighboring Messenia around 750 BCE. To prevent rebellions, every Spartan entered lifetime military service (as hoplites) beginning at age 7. Around 640 BCE, Lycurgus promulgated a constitution. Around 540 BCE, Sparta organized the Peloponnesian League.

Athens was the principal city of Attica. Draco (ca. 621 BCE) first codified Athenian law. His Draconian Code was known for its harshness. Solon (ca. 630–560 BCE) reformed the laws in 594 BCE. He enfranchised the lower classes and gave the state responsibility for administering justice. Growing indebtedness of small farmers and insufficient land strengthened the nobles. Peisistratus (ca. 605–527 BCE) seized control and governed as a tyrant. In 527 BCE, Cleisthenes led a reform movement that established the basis of Athens's democratic government, including an annual assembly to identify and exile those considered dangerous to the state.

The Fifth Century (Classical Age)

The fifth century marked the high point of Greek civilization. It opened with the Persian Wars (490; 480–479 BCE) after which Athens organized the Delian League. Pericles (ca. 495–429 BCE) used League money to rebuild Athens, including construction of the Parthenon and other Acropolis buildings. Athens's dominance spurred war with Sparta.

The Peloponnesian War between Athens and Sparta (431–404 BCE) ended with Athens's defeat, but weakened Sparta as well. Sparta fell victim to Thebes, and the other city-states warred amongst themselves until Alexander the Great's conquest. It was his conquest that unified the Greek city-states in the fourth century BCE, the beginning of the Hellenistic Age.

A revolution in philosophy occurred in classical Athens. The Sophists emphasized the individual and his/her attainment of excellence through rhetoric, grammar, music, and mathematics. Socrates (ca. 470–399 BCE) criticized the Sophists' emphasis on rhetoric and emphasized a process of questioning, or dialogues, with his students. Like Socrates, Plato (ca. 428–348 BCE) emphasized ethics. His *Theory of Ideas or Forms* said that what we see is but a dim shadow of the eternal Forms or Ideas. Philosophy should seek to penetrate to the real nature of things. Plato's *Republic* described an ideal state ruled by a philosopher king.

Aristotle (ca. 384–322 BCE) was Plato's pupil. He criticized Plato, arguing that ideas or forms did not exist outside of things. He contended that it was necessary to examine four factors in treating any object: its matter, its form, its cause of origin, and its end or purpose.

Greek art emphasized the individual. In architecture, the Greeks developed the Doric and Ionian forms. Euripides (484–406 BCE) is often considered the most modern tragedian because he was so psychologically minded. In comedy, Aristophanes (ca. 450–388 BCE) was a pioneer who used political themes. The New Comedy, exemplified by Menander (ca. 342–292 BCE), concentrated on domestic and individual themes.

The Greeks were the first to develop the study of history. They were skeptical and critical and banished myth from their works. Herodotus (ca. 484–424 BCE), called the "father of history," wrote *History of the Persian War.* Thucydides (ca. 460–400 BCE) wrote *History of the Peloponnesian War.*

The Hellenistic Age and Macedonia

The Macedonians were a Greek people who were considered semibarbaric by their southern Greek relatives. They never developed a city-state system and had more territory and people than any of the polis.

In 359 BCE, Philip II (382–336 BCE) became king. To finance his state and secure a seaport, he conquered several city-states. In 338 BCE, Athens fell. In 336 BCE, Philip was assassinated.

Philip's son, Alexander the Great (356–323 BCE), killed or exiled rival claimants to his father's throne. He established an empire that included Syria and Persia and extended to the Indus River Valley. At the time of his death, Alexander had established 70 cities and created a vast trading network. With no succession plan, Alexander's realm was divided among three of his generals. By 30 BCE, all of the successor states had fallen to Rome.

ROME

The traditional founding date for Rome is 753 BCE. Between 800 and 500 BCE, Greek tribes colonized southern Italy, bringing their alphabet and religious practices to Roman tribes. In the sixth and seventh centuries, the Etruscans expanded southward and conquered Rome.

Late in the sixth century (the traditional date is 509 BCE), the Romans expelled the Etruscans and established an aristocratically based republic in place of the monarchy. In the early Republic, power was in the hands of the patricians (wealthy landowners). A Senate composed of patricians governed. The Senate elected two consuls to serve one-year terms. Roman executives had great power (the imperium). They were assisted by two quaestors, who managed economic affairs.

Rome's expansion and contact with Greek culture disrupted the traditional agrarian basis of life. Tiberius Gracchus (163–133 BCE) and Gaius Gracchus (153–121 BCE) led the People's party (or *Populares*). They called for land reform and lower grain prices to help small farmers. They were opposed by the *Optimates* (best men). Tiberius was assassinated. Gaius continued his work, assisted by the *Equestrians*. After several years of struggle, Gaius committed suicide.

Power passed into the hands of military leaders for the next 80 years. During the 70s and 60s, Pompey (106–48 BCE) and Julius Caesar (100–44 BCE) emerged as the most powerful men. In 73 BCE, Spartacus led a slave rebellion, which General Crassus suppressed.

In 60 BCE, Caesar convinced Pompey and Crassus (ca. 115–53 BCE) to form the First Triumvirate. When Crassus died, Caesar and Pompey fought for leadership. In 49 BCE, Caesar crossed the Rubicon, the stream separating his province from Italy, and a civil war followed. In 47 BCE, the Senate proclaimed Caesar as dictator, and later named him consul for life. Brutus and Cassius believed that Caesar had destroyed the Republic. They formed a conspiracy, and on March 15, 44 BCE (the Ides of March), Caesar was assassinated in the Roman Forum. His 18-year-old nephew and adopted son, Octavian, succeeded him. Caesar reformed the tax code and eased burdens on debtors. He instituted the Julian calendar, in use until 1582. The Assembly under Caesar had little power.

In literature and philosophy, Plautus (254–184 BCE) wrote Greek-style comedy. Terence, a slave (ca. 186–159 BCE), wrote comedies in the tradition of Menander. Catullus (87–54 BCE) was the most famous lyric poet. Lucretius's (ca. 94–54 BCE) *On the Nature of Things* described Epicurean atomic metaphysics, while arguing against the immortality of the soul. Cicero (106–43 BCE), the great orator and stylist, defended the Stoic concept of natural law. He was an important advocate of the Roman Republic and an opponent of Caesar. His *Orations* described Roman life. Roman religion was family-centered and more civic-minded than Greek religion.

The Roman Empire

After a period of struggle, Octavian (63 BCE–14 CE), named as Caesar's heir, gained absolute control while maintaining the appearance of a republic. When he offered to relinquish his power in 27 BCE, the Senate gave him a vote of confidence and a new title, "Augustus." Augustus ruled for 44 years (31 BCE–14 CE) He introduced many reforms, including new coinage, new tax collection, fire and police protection, and land for settlers in the provinces.

Between 27 BCE and 180 CE, Rome's greatest cultural achievements occurred under the Pax Romana. The period between 27 BCE and 14 CE is called the **Augustan Age**. Virgil (70–19 BCE) wrote the *Aeneid,* an account of Rome's rise. Horace (65–8 BCE) wrote the lyric *Odes.* Ovid (43 BCE–18 CE) published the *Ars Amatoria,* a guide to seduction, and the *Metamorphoses,* about Greek mythology. Livy (57 BCE–17 CE) wrote a narrative history of Rome based on earlier accounts.

The Silver Age lasted from 14–180 CE. Writings in this period were less optimistic. Seneca (5 BCE–65 CE) espoused Stoicism in his tragedies and satires. Juvenal (50–127 CE) wrote satire, Plutarch's (46–120 CE) *Parallel Lives* portrayed Greek and Roman leaders, and Tacitus (55–120 CE) criticized the follies of his era in his histories.

Stoicism was the dominant philosophy of the era. Epictetus (ca. 60–120 CE), a slave, and Emperor Marcus Aurelius were its chief exponents. In law, Rome made a lasting contribution. It distinguished three orders of law: civil law (*jus civile*), which applied to Rome's citizens, law of the people (*jus gentium*), which merged Roman law with the laws of other peoples of the Empire, and natural law (*jus naturale*), governed by reason.

After the Pax Romana, the third century was a period of great tumult for Rome. Civil war was nearly endemic in the third century. Between 235 and 284 CE, 26 "barracks emperors" governed, taxing the population heavily to pay for the Empire's defense.

Rome's frontiers were attacked constantly by barbarians. Emperors Diocletian (reigned 285–305 CE) and Constantine (reigned 306–337 CE) tried to stem Rome's decline. Diocletian divided the Empire into four parts and moved the capital to Nicomedia in Asia Minor. Constantine moved the capital to Constantinople.

Some historians argue that the rise of Christianity was an important factor in Rome's decline. Jesus was born around 4 BCE, and began preaching and ministering to the poor and sick at the age of 30. The Gospels provide the fullest account of his life and teachings. Saul of Tarsus, or Paul (10–67 CE), transformed Christianity from a small sect of Jews who believed Jesus was the Messiah into a world religion. Paul won followers through his missionary work. He also shifted the focus from the early followers' belief in Jesus' imminent return to concentrate on personal salvation. His *Epistles* (letters to Christian communities) laid the basis for the religion's organization and sacraments.

The Pax Romana allowed Christians to move freely through the Empire. In the Age of Anxiety, many Romans felt confused and alienated, and thus drawn to the new religion. And unlike other mystery religions, Christianity included women. By the first century, the new religion had spread throughout the Empire.

Around 312 CE, Emperor Constantine converted to Christianity and ordered toleration in the Edict of Milan (ca. 313 CE). In 391 CE, Emperor Theodosius I (reigned 371–395 CE) proclaimed Christianity as the Empire's official religion. By the second century, the church hierarchy had developed. Eventually, the Bishop of Rome came to have preeminence, based on the interpretation that Jesus had chosen Peter as his successor.

THE BYZANTINE EMPIRE

Emperor Theodosius II (reigned 408–450 CE) divided his empire between his sons, one ruling the East, the other the West. After the Vandals sacked Rome in 455 CE, Constantinople was the undisputed leading city of the Empire.

In 527 CE, Justinian I (483–565 CE) became emperor in the East and reigned with his controversial wife Theodora until 565 CE. The Nika revolt broke out in 532 CE and demolished the city. It was crushed by General Belisarius in 537 CE, after 30,000 had died in the uprising.

The Crusaders further weakened the state. In 1204 CE, Venice contracted to transport the Crusaders to the Near East in return for the Crusaders capturing and looting Constantinople. The Byzantines were defeated in 1204 CE. Though they drove out the Crusaders in 1261 CE, the empire never regained its former power. In 1453 CE, Constantinople fell to the Ottoman Turks.

ISLAMIC CIVILIZATION IN THE MIDDLE AGES

Mohammed was born about 570 CE and received a revelation from the Angel Gabriel around 610 CE. In 630 CE, Mohammed marched into Mecca. The Sharia (code of law and theology) outlines five pillars of faith for Muslims to observe. First is the belief that there is one God and that Mohammed is his prophet. The faithful must pray five times a day, perform charitable acts, fast from sunrise to sunset during the holy month of Ramadan, and make a *haj*, or pilgrimage, to Mecca. The Koran, which consists of 114 *suras* (verses), contains Mohammed's teachings. *Mullahs* (teachers) occupy positions of authority, but Islam did not develop a hierarchical system comparable to that of Christianity.

A leadership struggle developed after Mohammed's death. His father-in-law, Abu Bakr (573–634 CE), succeeded as caliph (successor to the prophet) and governed for two years, until his death in 634 CE. Omar succeeded him. Between 634 and 642 CE, Omar established the Islamic Empire.

The Omayyad caliphs, based in Damascus, governed from 661–750 CE. They called themselves Shiites and believed they were Mohammed's true successors. (Most Muslims were Sunnites, from *sunna*, oral traditions about the prophet.) They conquered Spain by 730 CE and advanced into France until they were stopped by Charles Martel (ca. 688–741 CE) in 732 CE at Poitiers and Tours. Muslim armies penetrated India and China. They transformed Damascus into a cultural center and were exposed to Hellenistic culture from the nearby Byzantine Empire.

The Abbasid caliphs ruled from 750–1258 CE. They moved the capital to Baghdad and treated Arab and non-Arab Muslims as equals. Islam assumed a more Persian character under their reign. In the late tenth century, the empire began to disintegrate. In 1055 CE, the Seljuk Turks captured Baghdad, allowing the Abbasids to rule as figureheads. Genghis Khan (ca. 1162–1227 CE) and his army invaded the Abbasids. In 1258 CE, they seized Baghdad and murdered the last caliph.

FEUDALISM IN JAPAN

Feudalism in Japan began with the arrival of mounted nomadic warriors from throughout Asia during the Kofun Era (300–710). Some members of these nomadic groups formed an elite class and became part of the court aristocracy in the capital city of Kyoto, in western Japan. During the Heian Era (794–1185), a hereditary military aristocracy arose in the Japanese provinces, and by the late Heian Era, many of these formerly nomadic warriors had established themselves as independent land owners, or as managers of landed estates *(shoen)* owned by Kyoto aristocrats. These aristocrats depended on these warriors to defend their *shoen,* and in response to this need, the warriors organized into small groups called *bushidan.*

As the years passed, these warrior clans grew larger, and alliances formed among them, led by imperial descendants who moved from the capital to the provinces. After victory in the Taira-Minamoto War (1180–1105), Minamoto no Yoritomo forced the emperor to award him the title of *shogun,* which is short for "barbarian subduing generalissimo." He used this power to found the Kamakura Shogunate which survived for 148 years. Under the Kamakura Shogunate, many vassals were appointed to the position of *jitro* or land steward, or the position of provincial governors *(shugo)* to act as liasons between the Kamakura government and local vassals.

By the fourteenth century, the *shugo* had augmented their power enough to become a threat to the Kamakura, and in 1333 lead a rebellion that overthrew the shogunate. Under the Ashikaga Shogunate, the office of *shogu* was made hereditary, and its powers were greatly extended. These new *shogu* turned their vassals into aggressive local warriors called *kokujin*, or *jizamurai*. Following this move, the Ashikaga shoguns lost a great deal of their power to political fragmentation, which eventually led to the Warring States Era (1467–1568).

By the middle of the sixteenth century, the feudal system had evolved considerably. At the center of this highly evolved system was the *daimyo*, a local feudal lord who ruled over one of the many autonomous domains.

Far-reaching alliances of *daimyo* were forged under the Tokugawa Shogunate, the final and most unified of the three shogunates. Under the Tokugawa, the *daimyo* were considered direct vassals of the shoguns, and were kept under strict control. The warriors were gradually transformed into scholars and bureaucrats under the *bushido*, or code of chivalry, and the principles of Neo-Confucianism. A merchant class, or *chonin* gained wealth as the samurai class began to lose power, and the feudal system effectively ended when power was returned to the emperor under the Meji Restoration of 1868, when all special privileges of the samurai class were abolished.

CHINESE AND INDIAN EMPIRES

The Harappan or Indus civilization was confined to the Indus basin. Around 1500 BCE, during the so-called Vedic age, India came to be ruled by the Indo-Aryans, a mainly pastoral people with a speech closely related to the major languages of Europe.

The religion of the Harappan peoples revolved around the god Siva, the belief in reincarnation, in a condition of "liberation" beyond the cycle of birth and death, and in the technique of mental concentration which later came to be called *yoga*. The religion of the Indo-Aryans was based on a pantheon of gods of a rather worldly type, and sacrifices were offered to them. The traditional hymns that accompanied them were the Vedas, which form the basic scriptures for the religion of Hinduism. Indian society also came to be based on a *caste* system.

In the third century BCE, the Indian kingdoms fell under the Mauryan Empire. The grandson of the founder of this empire, named Asoka, opened a new era in the cultural history of India by introducing the Buddhist religion. Buddha had disregarded the Vedic gods and the institutions of caste and had preached a relatively simple ethical religion that had two levels of aspiration—a monastic life of renunciation of the world and a high, but not too difficult morality for the layman. The two religions of Hinduism and Buddhism flourished together for centuries in a tolerant rivalry, and in the end Buddhism virtually disappeared from India by the thirteenth century CE.

Chinese civilization originated in the Yellow River Valley and gradually extended to the southern regions. Three dynasties ruled early China: the Xia or Hsia, the Shang (c. 1500 to 1122 BCE), and the Zhou (c. 1122 to 211 BCE). After the Zhous fell, China welcomed the teachings of Confucius, as warfare between states and philosophical speculation created circumstances ripe for such teachings. Confucius made the good order of society depend on an ethical ruler, who should be advised by scholar-moralists like Confucius himself.

In contrast to the Confucians, the Taoists professed a kind of anarchism; the best kind of government was none at all. The wise man did not concern himself with political affairs, but by means of mystical contemplation identified himself with the forces of nature.

SUB-SAHARAN KINGDOMS AND CULTURES

The Nok were a people that lived in the area now known as Nigeria. Artifacts indicate that they were peaceful farmers who built small communities consisting of houses of wattle and daub.

The people referred to as the Ghana lived about 500 miles from what we now call Ghana. The Ghana peoples traded with Berber merchants. The Ghana offered these traders gold from deposits found in the south of their territory. In the 1200s the Mali kingdom conquered Ghana and the civilization mysteriously disappeared.

The people known as the Mali lived in a huge kingdom that lay mostly on the savanna bordering the Sahara Desert. The city of Timbuktu, built in the thirteenth century, was a thriving city of culture where traders visited stone houses, shops, libraries, and mosques.

The Songhai lived near the Niger River and gained their independence from the Mali in the early 1400s. The major growth of the empire came after 1464 CE under the leadership of Sunni Ali, who devoted his reign to warfare and expansion of the empire.

The Bantu peoples, numbering about 100,000,000 lived across large sections of Africa. Bantu societies lived in tiny chiefdoms, starting in the third millennium BCE, and each group developed its own version of the original Bantu language.

CIVILIZATIONS OF THE AMERICAS

The great civilizations of early America were agricultural, and foremost of these was the Mayan, in Yucatan, Guatemala, and eastern Honduras.

Mayan history is divided into three parts, the Old Empire, Middle Period, and the New Empire. By the time the Spanish conquerors arrived, most of the Mayan religious centers had been abandoned and their civilization had deteriorated seriously, perhaps due to the wide gulf between the majority of the people, who were peasants, and the priests and nobles.

Farther north, in Mexico, there arose a series of advanced cultures that derived much of their substance from the Maya. Such peoples as the Zapotecs, Totonacs, Olmecs, and Toltecs evolved a high level of civilization. By 500 BCE, agricultural peoples had begun to use a ceremonial calendar and had built stone pyramids on which they performed religious observances.

The Aztecs then took over Mexican culture. A major feature of their culture was human sacrifice in repeated propitiation of their chief god. Aztec government was centralized, with an elective king and a large army. Like their predecessors, the Aztecs were skilled builders and engineers, accomplished astronomers and mathematicians.

Andean civilization was characterized by the evolution of beautifully made pottery, intricate fabrics, and flat-topped mounds called *huacas*.

The Incas, a tribe from the interior of South America who termed themselves "Children of the Sun," controlled an area stretching from Ecuador to central Chile. They were Sun worshippers, and believed themselves to be the vice regent on earth of the sun god; the Inca were all powerful; every person's place in society was fixed and immutable; the state and the army were supreme. They were at the apex of their power just before the Spanish conquest.

In the southwestern U.S. and northern Mexico, meanwhile, two ancient cultures are noteworthy. The Anasazi, who lived in the plateau region extending through today's northern Arizona and New Mexico, southern Utah and Colorado, developed adobe architecture, worked the land extensively, had a highly developed system of irrigation, and made cloth and baskets. Their time ran approximately from 100 to 1300 CE. The Hohokam, roughly contemporaneous to the Anasazi, built separate stone and timber houses around central plazas in the desert Southwest.

EUROPE IN ANTIQUITY

Between 486 and 1050 CE, Europe acquired a distinctive identity. In antiquity, much of Europe was occupied by Germanic tribes.

Nomadic tribes from the central Asian steppes invaded Europe and pushed Germanic tribes into conflict with the Roman Empire. Ultimately, in 410 CE, the Visigoths sacked Rome, followed by the Vandals in 455 CE. In 476 CE, the Ostrogoth king forced the boy emperor Romulus Augustulus to abdicate, ending the empire in the West.

The Frankish Kingdom was the most important medieval Germanic state. Under Clovis I (reigned 481–511 CE), the Franks conquered France and the Gauls in 486 CE. Clovis converted to Christianity and founded the Merovingian dynasty.

Pepin's son, known as Charles the Great or Charlemagne (reigned 768–814 CE), founded the Carolingian dynasty. In 800 CE, Pope Leo III named Charlemagne Emperor of the Holy Roman Empire. In the Treaty of Aix-la-Chapelle (812 CE), the Byzantine emperor recognized Charles's authority in the West.

The Holy Roman Empire was intended to reestablish the Roman Empire in the West. Charles vested authority in 200 counts, who were each in charge of a county. Charles's son, Louis the Pious (reigned 814–840 CE), succeeded him. On Louis's death, his three sons vied for control of the Empire. The three eventually signed the Treaty of Verdun in 843 CE. This gave Charles the Western Kingdom (France), Louis the Eastern Kingdom (Germany), and Lothair the Middle Kingdom, a narrow strip of land running from the North Sea to the Mediterranean.

In the ninth and tenth centuries, Europe was threatened by attacks from the Vikings in the north, the Muslims in the south, and the Magyars in the east. Under the leadership of William the Conqueror (reigned 1066–1087), the Normans conquered England in 1066 CE (Battle of Hastings).

Rome's collapse had ushered in the decline of cities, a reversion to a barter economy from a money economy, and a fall in agricultural productivity with a shift to subsistence agriculture.

Manorialism and feudalism developed in this period. Manorialism refers to the economic system in which large estates, granted by the king to nobles, strove for self-sufficiency. Large manors might incorporate several villages. The lands surrounding the villages were usually divided into long strips, with common land in-between. Ownership was divided among the lord and his serfs (also called villeins).

Feudalism describes the decentralized political system of personal ties and obligations that bound vassals to their lords. The nature of feudalism varied in different areas and changed over time. But at its base were serfs—peasants who were bound to the land. They worked on the demesne, or lord's property, three or four days a week in return for the right to work their own land. In difficult times, the nobles were supposed to provide for the serfs.

The church was the only institution to survive the Germanic invasions intact. The power of the popes grew in this period. Gregory I (reigned 590–604 CE) was the first member of a monastic order to rise to the papacy. He advanced the ideas of penance and purgatory. He centralized church administration and was the first pope to rule as the secular head of Rome. Monasteries preserved the few remnants of antiquity that survived the decline.

THE HIGH MIDDLE AGES (1050–1300)

The year 1050 CE marked the beginning of the High Middle Ages. Europe was poised to emerge from five centuries of decline. Between 1000 and 1350 CE, the population grew from 38 million to 75 million. Agricultural productivity grew, aided by new technologies, such as heavy plows, and a slight temperature rise, which produced a longer growing season. Horses were introduced into agriculture in this period, and the three-field system replaced the two-field system.

Enfranchisement, or freeing of serfs, grew in this period, and many other serfs simply fled their manors for the new lands.

THE HOLY ROMAN EMPIRE

Charlemagne's grandson, Louis the German, became Holy Roman Emperor under the Treaty of Verdun. Under the weak leadership of his descendants, the dukes in Saxony, Franconia, Swabia, Bavaria, and the Lorraine eroded Carolingian power. The last Carolingian died in 911 CE. The German dukes elected the leader of Franconia to lead the German lands. He was replaced in 919 CE by the Saxon dynasty, which ruled until 1024 CE. Otto became Holy Roman Emperor in 962 CE.

His descendants governed the Empire until 1024 CE, when the Franconian dynasty assumed power, reigning until 1125 CE.

When the Franconian line died out in 1125 CE, the Hohenstaufen family (Conrad III, reigned 1138–1152 CE) won power over a contending family. The Hapsburg line gained control of the Empire in 1273 CE.

The Romans abandoned their last outpost in England in the fourth century. Alfred the Great (ca. 849–899 CE) defeated the Danes who had begun invading during the previous century in 878 CE. In 959 CE, Edgar the Peaceable (reigned 959–975 CE) became the first king of all England.

William (reigned 1066–1087 CE) stripped the Anglo-Saxon nobility of its privileges and instituted feudalism. He ordered a survey of all property of the realm, which was recorded in the Domesday Book (1086 CE).

In 1215 CE, the English barons forced John I to sign the Magna Carta Libertatum, acknowledging their "ancient" privileges. The Magna Carta established the principle of a limited English monarchy. Henry III reigned from 1216–1272 CE. In 1272 CE, Edward I became king. His need for revenue led him to convene a parliament of English nobles, which would act as a check upon royal power.

In 710 CE, the Muslims conquered Spain from the Visigoths. Under the Muslims, Spain enjoyed a stable, prosperous government. The caliphate of Córdoba became a center of scientific and intellectual activity. Internal dissent caused the collapse of Córdoba and the division of Spain into more than 20 Muslim states in 1031 CE.

The Reconquista (1085–1340 CE) wrested control from the Muslims. Rodrigo Diaz de Bivar, known as El Cid (ca. 1043–1099 CE) was the most famous of its knights. The fall of Córdoba in 1234 CE completed the Reconquista, except for the small state of Granada.

Most of Russia and Eastern Europe was never under Rome's control, and it was cut off from Western influence by the Germanic invasions. Poland converted to Christianity in the tenth century, and after 1025 CE was dependent on the Holy Roman Empire. In the twelfth and thirteenth centuries, powerful nobles divided control of the country.

In Russia, Vladimir I converted to Orthodox Christianity in 988 CE. He established the basis of Kievian Russia. After 1054 CE, Russia broke into competing principalities. The Mongols (Tatars) invaded in 1221 CE, completing their conquest in 1245 CE, and cutting Russia's contact with the West for almost a century.

The Crusades were an attempt to liberate the Holy Land from infidels. There were seven major crusades between 1096 and 1300 CE. Urban II called Christians to the First Crusade (1096–1099 CE) with the promise of a plenary indulgence (exemption from punishment in purgatory). Younger sons who would not inherit their fathers' lands were also attracted. The Crusades helped to renew interest in the ancient world. But thousands of Jews and Muslims were massacred as a result of the Crusades, and relations between Europe and the Byzantine Empire collapsed.

Charlemagne mandated that bishops open schools at each cathedral, and founded a school in his palace for his court. The expansion of trade and the need for clerks and officials who could read and write spurred an 1179 CE requirement that each cathedral set aside enough money to support one teacher.

Scholasticism was an effort to reconcile reason and faith and to instruct Christians on how to make sense of the pagan tradition.

Peter Abelard (ca. 1079–1144 CE) was a controversial proponent of Scholasticism. In *Sic et Non* (Yes and No), Abelard collected statements in the Bible and by church leaders that contradicted each other. Abelard believed that reason could resolve the apparent contradictions between the two authorities, but the church judged his views as heretical.

Thomas Aquinas (ca. 1225–1274 CE) believed that there were two orders of truth. The lower, reason, could demonstrate propositions such as the existence of God, but on a higher level, some of God's mysteries such as the nature of the Trinity must be accepted on faith. Aquinas viewed the universe as a great chain of being, with humans midway on the chain, between the material and the spiritual.

Latin was the language used in universities. But the most vibrant works were in the vernacular. The *chansons de geste* were long epic poems composed between 1050 and 1150 CE. Among the most famous are the *Song of Roland,* the *Song of the Nibelungs,* the Icelandic *Eddas,* and *El Cid.*

The fabliaux were short stories, many of which ridiculed the clergy. Boccaccio (1313–1375 CE) and Chaucer (ca. 1342–1400 CE) belonged to this tradition. The work of Dante (1265–1321 CE), the greatest medieval poet, synthesized the pagan and Christian traditions.

In this period, polyphonic (more than one melody at a time) music was introduced. In architecture, Romanesque architecture (rounded arches, thick stone walls, tiny windows) flourished between 1000 and 1150 CE. After 1150 CE, Gothic architecture, which emphasized the use of light, came into vogue.

THE RENAISSANCE, REFORMATION, AND THE WARS OF RELIGION (1300–1648)

THE LATE MIDDLE AGES

The Middle Ages fell chronologically between the classical world of Greece and Rome and the modern world. The papacy and monarchs, after exercising much power and influence in the high Middle Ages, were in eclipse after 1300. During the late Middle Ages (1300–1500), all of Europe suffered from the Black Death. While England and France engaged in destructive warfare in northern Europe, in Italy the Renaissance had begun.

Toward the end of the period, monarchs began to assert their power and control. The major struggle, between England and France, was the Hundred Years' War (1337–1453).

The war was fought in France, though the Scots (with French encouragement) invaded northern England. A few major battles occurred—Crécy (1346), Poitiers (1356), Agincourt (1415)—although the fighting consisted largely of sieges and raids. Eventually, the war became one of attrition; the French slowly wore down the English. Technological changes during the war included the use of English longbows and the increasingly expensive plate armor for knights.

Joan of Arc (1412–1431), an illiterate peasant girl who said she heard voices of saints, rallied the French army for several victories. But she was captured by the Burgundians, allies of England, and sold to the English who tried her for heresy (witchcraft). She was burned at the stake at Rouen.

England lost all of its Continental possessions, except Calais. French farmland was devastated, with England and France both expending great sums of money. Population, especially in France, declined. In addition, both countries suffered internal disruption as soldiers plundered and local officials left to fight the war. Trade everywhere was disrupted and England's wool trade with the Low Countries slumped badly. To cover these financial burdens, heavy taxation was inflicted on the peasants.

Because of the war, nationalism grew. Literature also came to express nationalism, as it was written in the language of the people instead of in Latin. Geoffrey Chaucer portrayed a wide spectrum of English life in the *Canterbury Tales*, while François Villon (1431–1463), in his *Grand Testament*, emphasized the ordinary life of the French with humor and emotion.

THE NEW MONARCHS

The defeat of the English in the Hundred Years' War and of the duchy of Burgundy in 1477 removed major military threats. Trade was expanded, fostered by the merchant Jacques Coeur (1395–1456). Louis XI (1461–1483) demonstrated ruthlessness in dealing with his nobility as individuals and collectively in the Estates General.

The marriage of Isabella of Castile (reigned 1474–1504) and Ferdinand of Aragon (reigned 1474–1516) created a united Spain. The Muslims were defeated at Granada in 1492. Navarre was conquered in 1512.

THE BLACK DEATH AND SOCIAL PROBLEMS

The bubonic plague ("Black Death") is a disease affecting the lymph glands. It causes death quickly. Conditions in Europe encouraged the quick spread of disease. There was no urban sanitation, and streets were filled with refuse, excrement, and dead animals. Living conditions were overcrowded, with families often sleeping in one room or one bed. Poor nutrition was rampant. There was little personal cleanliness.

Carried by fleas on rats, the plague was brought from Asia by merchants, and arrived in Europe in 1347. The plague affected all of Europe by 1350 and killed perhaps 25 to 40 percent of the population, with cities suffering more than the countryside.

THE RENAISSANCE (1300–1600)

The Renaissance emphasized new learning, including the rediscovery of much classical material, and new art styles. Italian city-states, such as Venice, Milan, Padua, Pisa, and especially Florence, were the home to many Renaissance developments, which were limited to the rich elite.

LITERATURE, ART, AND SCHOLARSHIP

Humanists, as both orators and poets, were inspired by and imitated works of the classical past. The literature was more secular and wide-ranging than that of the Middle Ages.

Dante (1265–1321) was a Florentine writer whose *Divine Comedy*, describing a journey through hell, purgatory, and heaven, shows that reason can only take people so far and that God's grace and revelation must be used.

Petrarch (1304–1374) encouraged the study of ancient Rome, collected and preserved work of ancient writers, and produced much work in the classical literary style.

Boccaccio (1313–1375) wrote *The Decameron*, a collection of short stories in Italian, which were meant to amuse, not edify, the reader.

Artists also broke with the medieval past, in both technique and content. Renaissance art sometimes used religious topics, but often dealt with secular themes or portraits of individuals. Oil paints, chiaroscuro, and linear perspectives produced works of energy in three dimensions.

Leonardo da Vinci (1452–1519) produced numerous works, including *The Last Supper* and *Mona Lisa*. Raphael (1483–1520), a master of Renaissance grace and style, theory and technique, represented these skills in *The School of Athens*. Michelangelo (1475–1564) produced masterpieces in architecture, sculpture (*David*), and painting (the Sistine Chapel ceiling). His work was a bridge to a new, non-Renaissance style called Mannerism.

Renaissance scholars were more practical and secular than medieval ones. Manuscript collections enabled scholars to study the primary sources and to reject all traditions which had been built up since classical times. Also, scholars participated in the lives of their cities as active politicians.

Leonardo Bruni (1370–1444), a civic humanist, served as chancellor of Florence, where he used his rhetorical skills to rouse the citizens against external enemies.

Machiavelli (1469–1527) wrote *The Prince*, which analyzed politics from the standpoint of expedience. His work, amoral in tone, describes how a political leader could obtain and hold power by acting only in his own self-interest.

THE REFORMATION

The Reformation destroyed Western Europe's religious unity and introduced new ideas about the relationships between God, the individual, and society. Its course was greatly influenced by politics and led, in most areas, to the subjection of the church to the political rulers.

MARTIN LUTHER (1483–1546)

Martin Luther, to his personal distress, could not reconcile the problem of the sinfulness of the individual with the justice of God. How could a sinful person attain the righteousness necessary to obtain salvation? he wondered. During his studies of the Bible, especially of Romans 1:17, Luther came to believe that personal efforts—good works such as a Christian life and attention to the sacraments of the church—could not "earn" the sinner salvation, but that belief and faith were the only way to obtain grace. By 1515 Luther believed that "justification by faith alone" was the road to salvation.

On October 31, 1517, Luther nailed 95 theses, or statements, about indulgences, the cancellation of a sin in return for money, to the door of the Wittenberg church and challenged the practice of selling them. At this time he was seeking to reform the church, not divide it.

In 1519, Luther presented various criticisms of the church and was driven to say that only the Bible, not religious traditions or papal statements, could determine correct religious practices and beliefs. In 1521, Pope Leo X excommunicated Luther for his beliefs.

In 1521, Luther appeared in the city of Worms before a meeting (Diet) of the important figures of the Holy Roman Empire, including the Emperor, Charles V. He was again condemned. At the Diet of Worms Luther made his famous statement about his writings and the basis for them: "Here I stand. I can do no other." After this, Luther could not go back; the break with the pope was permanent.

Frederick III of Saxony, the ruler of the territory in which Luther resided, protected Luther in Wartburg Castle for a year. Frederick never accepted Luther's beliefs but protected him because Luther was his subject. The weak political control of the Holy Roman Emperor contributed to Luther's success in avoiding the pope's and the Emperor's penalties.

OTHER REFORMERS

Anabaptist (derived from a Greek word meaning to baptize again) is a name applied to people who rejected the validity of child baptism and believed that such children had to be rebaptized when they became adults. A prominent leader was Menno Simons (1496-1561).

Anabaptists sought to return to the practices of the early Christian church, which was a voluntary association of believers with no connection to the state. Anabaptists adopted pacifism and avoided involvement with the state whenever possible.

In 1536, John Calvin (1509–1564), a Frenchman, arrived in Geneva, a Swiss city-state which had adopted an anti-Catholic position. He left after his first efforts at reform failed. Upon his return in 1540, Geneva became the center of the Reformation. Calvin's *Institutes of the Christian Religion* (1536), a strictly logical analysis of Christianity, had a universal appeal.

Calvin emphasized the doctrine of predestination (God knew who would obtain salvation before those people were born) and believed that church and state should be united. Calvinism triumphed as the majority religion in Scotland, under the leadership of John Knox (ca. 1514–1572), and in the United Provinces of the Netherlands. Puritans in England and New England also accepted Calvinism.

REFORM IN ENGLAND

England underwent reforms in a pattern different from the rest of Europe. Personal and political decisions by the rulers determined much of the course of the Reformation there, when in 1533 Henry VIII defied the pope and turned to Archbishop Thomas Cranmer to dissolve his marriage to Catherine of Aragon.

Protestant beliefs and practices made little headway during Henry's reign, as he accepted transubstantiation, enforced celibacy among the clergy, and otherwise made the English church conform to most medieval practices.

Under Henry VIII's son, Edward VI (1547–1553), who succeeded to the throne at age 10, the English church adopted Calvinism. Clergy were allowed to marry, communion by the laity expanded, and images were removed from churches. Doctrine included justification by faith, the denial of transubstantiation, and only two sacraments.

Some reformers wanted to purify (hence "Puritans") the church of its remaining Catholic aspects. The resulting church, Protestant in doctrine and practice but retaining most of the physical possessions, such as buildings, and many of the powers, such as church courts, of the medieval church, was called Anglican.

THE COUNTER-REFORMATION

The Counter-Reformation brought changes to the portion of the Western church that retained its allegiance to the pope.

Ignatius of Loyola (1491–1556), a former soldier, founded the Society of Jesus in 1540 to lead the attack on Protestantism. Jesuits became the leaders of the Counter Reformation.

The Sack of Rome in 1527, when soldiers of the Holy Roman Emperor captured and looted Rome, was seen by many as a judgment of God against the lives of the Renaissance popes. In 1534, Paul III became pope and attacked abuses while reasserting papal leadership.

THE WARS OF RELIGION (1560–1648)

The period from approximately 1560 to 1648 witnessed continuing warfare, primarily between Protestants and Catholics. In the latter half of the sixteenth century, the fighting was along the Atlantic seaboard between Calvinists and Catholics; after 1600 the warfare spread to Germany, where Calvinists, Lutherans, and Catholics fought.

THE CATHOLIC CRUSADE

The territories of Charles V, the Holy Roman Emperor, were divided in 1556 between Ferdinand, Charles's brother, and Philip II (1556–1598), Charles's son. Ferdinand received Austria, Hungary, Bohemia, and the title of Holy Roman Emperor. Philip received Spain, Milan, Naples, the Netherlands, and the New World. It was Philip, not the pope, who led the Catholic attack on Protestants.

Spain dominated the Mediterranean following a series of wars led by Philip's half-brother, Don John, against Moslem (largely Turkish) forces. Don John secured the Mediterranean for Christian merchants with a naval victory over the Turks at Lepanto off the coast of Greece in 1571.

Portugal was annexed by Spain in 1580 following the death of the king without a clear successor. This gave Philip the only other large navy of the day as well as Portuguese territories around the globe.

ENGLAND AND SPAIN

England was ruled by two queens, Mary I (reigned 1553–1558), who married Philip II, and then Elizabeth I (reigned 1558–1603), while three successive kings of France from 1559 to 1589 were influenced by their mother, Catherine de' Medici (1519–1589).

Mary I sought to make England Catholic. She executed many Protestants, earning the name "Bloody Mary" from opponents. Mary married Philip II, king of Spain, and organized her foreign policy around Spanish interests. They had no children.

Elizabeth I, a Protestant, achieved a religious settlement between 1559 and 1563 which left England with a church governed by bishops and practicing Catholic rituals, but maintaining a Calvinist doctrine.

Catholics participated in several rebellions and plots. Mary, Queen of Scots, had fled to England from Scotland in 1568, after alienating the nobles there. In Catholic eyes, she was the legitimate queen of England. Several plots and rebellions to put Mary on the throne led to her execution in 1587. Elizabeth was formally excommunicated by the pope in 1570.

In 1588, as part of his crusade and to stop England from supporting the rebels in the Netherlands, Philip II sent the Armada, a fleet of more than 125 ships, to convey troops from the Netherlands to England as part of a plan to make England Catholic. The Armada was defeated by a combination of superior English naval tactics and a wind which made it impossible for the Spanish to accomplish their goal. A peace treaty between Spain and England was signed in 1604, but England remained an opponent of Spain.

THE THIRTY YEARS' WAR

Calvinism was spreading throughout Germany. The Peace of Augsburg (1555), which settled the disputes between Lutherans and Catholics, had no provision for Calvinists. Lutherans gained more territories through conversions and often took control of previous church-states—a violation of the Peace of Augsburg. A Protestant alliance under the leadership of the Calvinist ruler of the Palatinate opposed a Catholic League led by the ruler of Bavaria. Religious wars were common.

The war brought great destruction to Germany, leading to a decline in population of perhaps one-third, or more, in some areas. Germany remained divided and without a strong government until the nineteenth century.

After 1648, warfare, though often containing religious elements, would not be executed primarily for religious goals.

The Catholic crusade to reunite Europe failed, largely due to the efforts of the Calvinists. The religious distribution of Europe has not changed significantly since 1648.

Nobles, resisting the increasing power of the state, usually dominated the struggle. France, then Germany, fell apart due to the wars. France was reunited in the seventeenth century. Spain began a decline which ended its role as a great power of Europe.

THE GROWTH OF THE STATE AND THE AGE OF EXPLORATION

In the seventeenth century the political systems of the countries of Europe began dividing into two types, absolutist and constitutionalist. England, the United Provinces, and Sweden moved towards constitutionalism, while France was adopting absolutist ideas.

Overseas exploration, begun in the fifteenth century, expanded. Governments supported such activity in order to gain wealth and to preempt other countries.

ENGLAND

The English church was a compromise of Catholic practices and Protestant beliefs and was criticized by both groups. The monarchs, after 1620, gave leadership of the church to men with Arminian beliefs, a modified Calvinist creed that de-emphasized predestination.

Opponents to this shift in belief were called Puritans, a term that covered a wide range of beliefs and people. To escape the church in England, many Puritans began moving to the New World, especially Massachusetts.

In financial matters, inflation and Elizabeth's wars left the government short of money. Contemporaries blamed the shortage on the extravagance of the courts of James I and Charles I. The monarchs lacked any substantial source of income and had to obtain the consent of a Parliament to levy a tax.

Parliament met only when the monarch summoned it. Though Parliaments had existed since the Middle Ages, there were long periods of time between parliamentary meetings. Parliaments consisted of nobles and gentry, and a few merchants and lawyers. The men in a Parliament usually wanted the government to remedy grievances as part of the agreement to a tax.

Charles I inherited both the English and Scottish thrones at the death of his father, James I. He claimed a "divine right" theory of absolute authority for himself as king and sought to rule without Parliament. That rule also meant control of the Church of England.

Charles stumbled into wars with both Spain and France during the late 1620s. A series of efforts to raise money for the wars led to confrontations with his opponents in Parliament. A "forced loan" was collected from taxpayers with the promise it would be repaid when a tax was voted by a Parliament. Soldiers were billeted in subjects' houses during the wars. In 1628 Parliament passed the Petition of Right, which declared royal actions involving loans and billeting illegal. Charles ruled without calling a Parliament during the 1630s.

In August 1642 Charles abandoned all hope of negotiating with his opponents and instead declared war against them. Charles's supporters were called Royalists or Cavaliers. His opponents were called Parliamentarians or Roundheads, due to many who wore their hair cut short. This struggle is called the Puritan Revolution, the English Civil War, or the Great Rebellion.

Charles was defeated. His opponents had allied with the Scots who still had an army in England. Additionally, the New Model Army, with its general, Oliver Cromwell (1599–1658), was superior to Charles's army, and became a cauldron of radical ideas.

FRANCE

The regions of France had long had a large measure of independence, and local parliaments could refuse to enforce royal laws. The centralization of all government proceeded by replacing local authorities with intendants, civil servants who reported to the king.

Henry IV relied on the Duke of Sully (1560–1641), the first of a series of strong ministers in the seventeenth century. Sully and Henry increased the involvement of the state in the economy, acting on a theory known as mercantilism.

Louis XIII reigned from 1610 to 1643, but Cardinal Richelieu became the real power in France. The unique status of the Huguenots was reduced through warfare and the Peace of Alais (1629), when their separate armed cities were eliminated. The nobility was reduced in power through constant attention to the laws and the imprisonment of offenders.

Cardinal Mazarin governed while Louis XIV (reigned 1643–1715) was a minor. During the Fronde, from 1649 to 1652, the nobility controlled Paris, drove Louis XIV and Mazarin from the city, and attempted to run the government. Noble ineffectiveness, the memories of the chaos of the wars of religion, and the overall anarchy convinced most people that a strong king was preferable to a warring nobility.

Louis XIV saw the need to increase royal power and his own glory and dedicated his life to these goals. He steadily pursued a policy of "one king, one law, one faith."

EXPLORATIONS AND CONQUESTS

Portugal. Prince Henry the Navigator (1394–1460) supported exploration of the African coastline, largely in order to seek gold. Bartholomew Dias (1450–1500) rounded the southern tip of Africa in 1487. Vasco da Gama (1460–1524) reached India in 1498 and, after some fighting, soon established trading ports at Goa and Calicut. Albuquerque (1453–1515) helped establish an empire in the Spice Islands after 1510.

Spain. Christopher Columbus (1451–1506), seeking a new route to the (East) Indies, "discovered" the Americas in 1492. Ferdinand Magellan (1480–1521) circumnavigated the globe in 1521–1522. Conquests of the Aztecs by Hernando Cortes (1485–1547), and the Incas by Francisco Pizarro (ca. 1476–1541), enabled the Spanish to send much gold and silver back to Spain.

Other Countries. In the 1490s, the Cabots, John (1450–1498) and Sebastian (ca. 1483–1557), explored North America, and after 1570, various Englishmen, including Francis Drake (ca. 1540–1596), fought the Spanish around the world. Jacques Cartier (1491–1557) explored parts of North America for France in 1534.

Samuel de Champlain (1567–1635) and the French explored the St. Lawrence River, seeking furs to trade. The Dutch established settlements at New Amsterdam and in the Hudson River Valley. The Dutch founded trading centers in the East Indies, the West Indies, and southern Africa. Swedes settled on the Delaware River in 1638.

BOURBON, BAROQUE, AND THE ENLIGHTENMENT

Through the Treaty of Paris (1763), France lost all possessions in North America to Britain. (In 1762, France had ceded to Spain all French claims west of the Mississippi River and New Orleans.)

France entered the French-American Alliance of 1778 in an effort to regain lost prestige in Europe and to weaken her British adversary. In 1779, Spain joined France in the war, hoping to recover Gibraltar and the Floridas.

With the Treaty of Paris (1783) Britain recognized the independence of the United States of America and retroceded the Floridas to Spain. Britain left France no territorial gains by signing a separate and territorially generous treaty with the United States.

ECONOMIC DEVELOPMENTS

There were several basic assumptions of mercantilism: 1) Wealth is measured in terms of commodities, especially gold and silver, rather than in terms of productivity and income-producing investments; 2) Economic activities should increase the power of the national government in the direction of state controls; 3) Since a favorable balance of trade was important, a nation should purchase as little as possible from nations regarded as enemies. The concept of the mutual advantage of trade was not widely accepted; 4) Colonies existed for the benefit of the mother country, not for any mutual benefit that would be gained by economic development.

Absentee landlords and commercial farms replaced feudal manors, especially in England. Urbanization, increased population, and improvements in trade stimulated the demand for agricultural products.

The steam engine, developed by James Watt between 1765 and 1769, became one of the most significant inventions in human history. It was no longer necessary to locate factories on mountain streams where water wheels were used to supply power. Its portability meant that both steamboats and railroad engines could be built to transport goods across continents. Ocean-going vessels were no longer dependent on winds to power them. At the same time, textile machines revolutionized that industry.

BOURBON FRANCE

Louis XIV (reigned 1643–1715) believed in absolute, unquestioned authority. Louis XIV deliberately chose his chief ministers from the middle class in order to keep the aristocracy out of government.

Council orders were transmitted to the provinces by intendants, who supervised all phases of local administration (especially courts, police, and the collection of taxes).

Louis XIV never called the Estates General. His intendants arrested the members of the three provincial estates who criticized royal policy, and the *parlements* were too intimidated by the lack of success of the *Frondes* to offer further resistance.

Control of the peasants, who comprised 95 percent of the French population, was accomplished by numerous means. Some peasants kept as little as 20 percent of their cash crops after paying the landlord, the government, and the Church. Peasants also were subject to the *corvée*, a month's forced labor on the roads. People not at work on the farm were conscripted into the French army or put into workhouses. Finally, rebels were hanged or forced to work as galley slaves.

Under Louis XV (reigned 1715–1774) French people of all classes desired greater popular participation in government and resented the special privileges of the aristocracy. All nobles were exempt from certain taxes. Many were subsidized with regular pensions from the government. The highest offices of government were reserved for aristocrats. Promotions were based on political connections rather than merit.

There was no uniform code of laws and little justice. The king had arbitrary powers of imprisonment. Government bureaucrats were often petty tyrants, many of them merely serving their own interests. The bureaucracy became virtually a closed class. Vestiges of the feudal and manorial systems taxed peasants excessively compared to other segments of society. The *philosophes* gave expression to these grievances and discontent grew.

Louis XVI (reigned 1774–1792) married Marie Antoinette (1770), daughter of the Austrian Empress Maria Theresa. Louis XVI was honest, conscientious, and sought genuine reforms, but he was indecisive and lacking in determination. One of his first acts was to restore judicial powers to the French parlements. When he sought to impose new taxes on the undertaxed aristocracy, the parlements refused to register the royal decrees. In 1787, he granted toleration and civil rights to French Huguenots (Protestants).

In 1787, the king summoned the Assembly of the Notables, a group of 144 representatives of the nobility and higher clergy. Louis XVI asked them to tax all lands, without regard to privilege of family; to establish provincial assemblies; to allow free trade in grain; and to abolish forced labor on the roads. The Notables refused to accept these reforms and demanded the replacement of certain of the king's ministers.

The climax of the crisis came in 1788 when the king was no longer able to achieve either fiscal reform or new loans. He could not even pay the salaries of government officials. By this time one-half of government revenues went to pay interest on the national debt.

For the first time in 175 years, the king called for a meeting of the Estates General (1789). The Estates General formed itself into the National Assembly, and the French Revolution was underway.

ENGLAND, SCOTLAND, AND IRELAND

One of the underlying issues in this conflict was the constitutional issue of the relationship between the king and Parliament. In short, the question was whether England was to have a limited constitutional monarchy, or an absolute monarchy as in France and Prussia.

The theological issue focused on the form of church government England was to have. The episcopal form meant that the king, the Archbishop of Canterbury, and the bishops of the church would determine policy, theology, and the form of worship and service in the presbyterian form. Each congregation would have a voice in the life of the church, and a regional group of ministers, or "presbytery," would attempt to ensure "doctrinal purity."

The political implications for representative democracy were present in both issues. That is why most Presbyterians, Puritans, and Congregationalists sided with Parliament and most Anglicans and Catholics sided with the king.

The Parliament in effect bribed the king by granting him a tax grant in exchange for his agreement to the Petition of Right in 1628. It stipulated that no one should pay any tax, gift, loan, or contribution except as provided by an act of Parliament; no one should be imprisoned or detained without due process of law; all were to have the right to the writ of *habeas corpus;* there should be no forced billeting of soldiers in the homes of private citizens; and martial law was not to be declared in England.

In 1629, Charles I dissolved Parliament—for 11 years. Puritan leaders and leaders of the opposition in the House of Commons were imprisoned by the king, some for several years.

The established Church of England was the only legal church under Charles I, a Catholic. Archbishop of Canterbury William Laud (1573–1645) sought to enforce the king's policies vigorously. Arminian clergymen were to be tolerated, but Puritan clergymen silenced. Criticism was brutally suppressed. Several dissenters were executed.

The king, however, had no money, no army, and no popular support. He summoned the Parliament to meet in November 1640. With mobs in the street and rumors of an army enroute to London to dissolve Parliament, a bare majority of an underattended House of Commons passed a bill of attainder to execute the Earl of Strafford, one of the king's principal ministers. Fearing mob violence as well as Parliament itself, the king signed the bill and Strafford was executed in 1641. Archbishop William Laud was also arrested and eventually tried and executed in 1645.

The House of Commons passed a series of laws to strengthen its position and protect civil and religious rights. The Triennial Act (1641) provided that no more than three years should pass between Parliaments. Another act provided that the current Parliament should not be dissolved without its own consent. Various hated laws, taxes, and institutions were abolished: the Star Chamber, the High Commission, and power of the Privy Council to deal with property rights.

Men began identifying themselves as Cavaliers if they supported the king, or Roundheads if they supported Parliament.

The king withdrew to Hampton Court and sent the queen to France for safety. In March 1642 Charles II went to York, and the English Civil War began. Charles put together a sizeable force with a strong cavalry and moved on London, winning several skirmishes.

Oliver Cromwell (1599–1658) led the parliamentary troops to victory, first with his cavalry, which eventually numbered 1,100, and then as lieutenant general in command of the well-disciplined and well-trained New Model Army. He eventually forced the king to flee.

During the Civil War, under the authority of Parliament, the Westminster Assembly convened to write a statement of faith for the Church of England that was Reformed or Presbyterian in content. Ministers and laymen from both England and Scotland participated for six years and wrote the *Westminster Confession of Faith*, still a vital part of Presbyterian theology.

The army tried Charles Stuart, former king of England, and sentenced him to death for treason. After the execution of the king, Parliament abolished the office of king and the House of Lords. The new form of government was to be a Commonwealth, or Free State, governed by the representatives of the people in Parliament. This commonwealth lasted four years, between 1649 and 1653.

Royalists and Presbyterians both opposed Parliament for its lack of broad representation and for regicide. The army was greatly dissatisfied that elections were not held, as one of the promises of the Civil War was popular representation. Surrounded by foreign enemies, the Commonwealth became a military state with a standing army of 44,000. The North American and West Indian colonies were forced to accept the government of the Commonwealth.

When it became clear that Parliament intended to stay in office permanently, Cromwell agreed to serve as Lord Protector from 1653–1659, with a Council of State and a Parliament. The new government permitted religious liberty, except for Catholics and Anglicans.

The new Parliament restored the monarchy from 1660–1688, but the Puritan Revolution clearly showed that the English constitutional system required a limited monarchy. Parliament in 1660 was in a far stronger position in its relationship to the king than it ever had been before.

Two events in 1688 goaded Parliament to action. In May, James reissued the Declaration of Indulgence with the command that it be read on two successive Sundays in every parish church. On June 10, 1688, a son was born to the king and his queen, Mary of Modena. As long as James was childless by his second wife, the throne would go to one of his Protestant daughters, Mary or Anne. The birth of a son, who would be raised Roman Catholic, changed the picture completely.

A group of Whig and Tory leaders, speaking for both houses of Parliament, invited William and Mary to assume the throne of England.

On November 5, 1688, William and his army landed at Torbay in Devon. King James offered many concessions, but it was too late. He finally fled to France. William assumed temporary control of the government and summoned a free Parliament. In February 1689, William and Mary were declared joint sovereigns, with the administration given to William.

The English Declaration of Rights (1689) declared the following:

1) The king could not be a Roman Catholic.

2) A standing army in time of peace was illegal without Parliamentary approval.

3) Taxation was illegal without Parliamentary consent.

4) Excessive bail and cruel and unusual punishments were prohibited.

5) Right to trial by jury was guaranteed.

6) Free elections to Parliament would be held.

The Toleration Act (1689) granted the right of public worship to Protestant Nonconformists, but did not permit them to hold office. The Act did not extend liberty to Catholics or Unitarians, but normally they were left alone. The Trials for Treason Act (1696) stated that a person accused of treason should be shown the accusations against him and should have the advice of counsel. They also could not be convicted except upon the testimony of two independent witnesses. Freedom of the press was permitted, but with very strict libel laws.

Control of finances was to be in the hands of the Commons, including military appropriations. There would no longer be uncontrolled grants to the king. Judges were made independent of the Crown. Thus, England declared itself a limited monarchy and a Protestant nation.

RUSSIA UNDER THE MUSCOVITES AND THE ROMANOVS

In 1480, Ivan III (1440–1505), "Ivan the Great," put an end to Mongol domination over Russia. Ivan took the title of Caesar (Czar) as heir of the Eastern Roman Empire (Byzantine Empire). He encouraged the Eastern Orthodox Church and called Moscow the "Third Rome."

Ivan IV (1530–1584), "Ivan the Terrible," grandson of Ivan III, began westernizing Russia. A contemporary of Queen Elizabeth, he welcomed both the English and Dutch and opened new trade routes to Moscow and the Caspian Sea. English merchant adventurers opened Archangel on the White Sea and provided a link with the outer world free from Polish domination.

After a "Time of Troubles" following Ivan's death in 1584, stability returned to Russia in 1613 when the Zemsky Sobor (Estates General representing the Russian Orthodox church, landed gentry, townspeople, and a few peasants) elected Michael Romanov, who ruled as Czar from 1613 to 1645.

Under Michael Romanov, Russia extended its empire to the Pacific. Romanov continued westernization. By the end of the seventeenth century, 20,000 Europeans lived in Russia, developing trade and manufacturing, practicing medicine, and smoking tobacco, while Russians began trimming their beards and wearing Western clothing.

In 1649, three monks were appointed to translate the Bible for the first time into Russian. The Raskolniki (Old Believers) refused to accept any Western innovations or liturgy in the Russian Orthodox church and were severely persecuted as a result.

Peter I (reigned 1682–1725) was one of the most extraordinary people in Russian history. The driving ambitions of Peter the Great's life were to modernize Russia and to compete with the great powers of Europe on equal terms. By the end of Peter's reign, Russia produced more iron than England.

Peter built up the army through conscription and a 25-year term of enlistment. He gave flintlocks and bayonets to his troops instead of the old muskets and pikes. Artillery was improved and discipline enforced. By the end of his reign, Russia had a standing army of 210,000, despite a population of only 13 million. The Czar ruled by decree (*ukase*). Government officials and nobles acted under government authority, but there was no representative body.

All landowners owed lifetime service to the state, either in the army, the civil service, or at court. In return for government service, they received land and serfs to work their fields. Conscription required each village to send recruits for the Russian army. By 1709, Russia manufactured most of its own weapons and had an effective artillery.

After a series of largely ineffective rulers, Catherine II "the Great," (reigned 1762–1796) continued the westernization process begun by Peter the Great. The three partitions of Poland, in 1772, 1793, and 1795 respectively, occurred under Catherine II's rule. Russia also annexed the Crimea and warred with Turkey during her reign.

ITALY AND THE PAPACY

Italy in the seventeenth and eighteenth centuries remained merely a geographic expression divided into small kingdoms, most of which were under foreign domination. Unification of Italy into a national state did not occur until the mid-nineteenth century.

THE SCIENTIFIC REVOLUTION AND SCIENTIFIC SOCIETIES

Science and religion were not in conflict in the seventeenth and eighteenth centuries. Scientists universally believed they were studying and analyzing God's creation, not an autonomous phenomenon known as "Nature." There was no attempt, as in the nineteenth and twentieth centuries, to secularize science.

For the first time in human history, the eighteenth century saw the appearance of a secular worldview. This became known as the Age of the Enlightenment. In the past, some kind of a religious perspective had always been central to Western civilization. The philosophical starting point for the Enlightenment was the belief in the autonomy of man's intellect apart from God. The most basic assumption was faith in reason rather than faith in revelation.

The Enlightenment believed in the existence of God as a rational explanation of the universe and its form; "God" was a deistic Creator who made the universe and then was no longer involved in its mechanistic operation. That mechanistic operation was governed by "natural law."

Rationalists stressed deductive reasoning or mathematical logic as the basis for their epistemology (source of knowledge). They started with "self-evident truths," or postulates, from which they constructed a coherent and logical system of thought.

René Descartes (1596–1650) sought a basis for logic and thought he found it in man's ability to think. "I think; therefore, I am" was his most famous statement.

Benedict de Spinoza (1632–1677) developed a rational pantheism in which he equated God and nature. He denied all free will and ended up with an impersonal, mechanical universe.

Gottfried Wilhelm Leibniz (1646–1716) worked on symbolic logic and calculus, and invented a calculating machine. He, too, had a mechanistic world- and life-view and thought of God as a hypothetical abstraction rather than a persona.

Empiricists stressed inductive observation—the "scientific method"—as the basis for their epistemology.

John Locke (1632–1704) pioneered in the empiricist approach to knowledge and stressed the importance of environment in human development. He classified knowledge as 1) according to reason, 2) contrary to reason, or 3) above reason. Locke thought reason and revelation were both complementary and from God.

David Hume (1711–1776) was a Scottish historian and philosopher who began by emphasizing the limitations of human reasoning and later became a dogmatic skeptic.

The Enlightenment believed in a closed system of the universe in which the supernatural was not involved in human life, in contrast to the traditional view of an open system in which God, angels, and devils were very much a part of human life on earth.

The "Counter-Enlightenment" is a comprehensive term encompassing diverse and disparate groups who disagreed with the fundamental assumptions of the Enlightenment and pointed out its weaknesses.

Roman Catholic Jansenism in France argued against the idea of an uninvolved or impersonal God. Hasidism in Eastern European Jewish communities, especially in the 1730s, stressed a joyous religious fervor in direct communion with God.

CULTURE OF THE BAROQUE AND ROCOCO

The Baroque emphasized grandeur, spaciousness, unity, and emotional impact. The splendor of Versailles typifies the baroque in architecture; gigantic frescoes unified around the emotional impact of a single theme is Baroque art; the glory of Bach's *Christmas Oratorio* expresses the baroque in music. Although the Baroque began in Catholic Counter-Reformation countries to teach in a concrete, emotional way, it soon spread to Protestant nations as well, and some of the greatest Baroque artists and composers were Protestant (e.g., Johann Sebastian Bach and George Frideric Handel).

Characteristics of the Rococo can be found in the compositions of both Franz Josef Haydn (1732–1809) and Wolfgang Amadeus Mozart (1756–1791).

REVOLUTION AND THE NEW WORLD ORDER (1789–1848)

THE FRENCH REVOLUTION I (1789–1799)

Radical ideas about society and government were developed during the eighteenth century in response to the success of the "scientific" and "intellectual" revolutions of the preceding two centuries. Armed with new scientific knowledge of the physical universe, as well as new views of the human capacity to detect "truth," social critics assailed existing modes of thought governing political, social, religious, and economic life. Ten years of upheaval in France (1789–1799) further shaped modern ideas and practices.

Napoleon Bonaparte spread some of the revolutionary ideas about the administration of government as he conquered much of Europe. The modern world that came of age in the eighteenth century was characterized by rapid, revolutionary changes which paved the way for economic modernization and political centralization throughout Europe.

Influence of the Enlightenment (c. 1700–1800)

While they came from virtually every country in Europe, most of the famous social activists were French, and France was the center of this intellectual revolution. Voltaire, Denis Diderot, Baron de Montesquieu, and Jean-Jacques Rousseau were among the more famous philosophers.

The major assumptions of the Enlightenment were as follows:

- Human progress was possible through changes in one's environment; in other words: better people, better societies, better standard of living.

- Humans were free to use reason to reform the evils of society.

- Material improvement would lead to moral improvement.

- Natural science and human reason would discover the meaning of life.

- Laws governing human society would be discovered through application of the scientific method of inquiry.

- Inhuman practices and institutions would be removed from society in a spirit of humanitarianism.

- Human liberty would ensue if individuals became free to choose what reason dictated was good.

The Enlightenment's Effect on Society:

Religion. Deism or "natural religion" rejected traditional Christianity by promoting an impersonal God who did not interfere in the daily lives of the people. The continued discussion of the role of God led to a general skepticism associated with Pierre Bayle (1647–1706), a type of religious skepticism pronounced by David Hume (1711–1776), and a theory of atheism or materialism advocated by Baron d'Holbach (1723–1789).

Political Theory. John Locke (1632–1704) and Jean-Jacques Rousseau (1712–1778) believed that people were capable of governing themselves, either through a political (Locke) or social (Rousseau) contract forming the basis of society. However, most philosophes opposed democracy, preferring a limited monarchy that shared power with the nobility.

Economic Theory. The assault on mercantilist economic theory was begun by the physiocrats in France, who proposed a "laissez-faire" (nongovernmental interference) attitude toward land usage, and culminated in the theory of economic capitalism associated with Adam Smith (1723–1790) and his slogans of free trade, free enterprise, and the law of supply and demand.

Attempting to break away from the strict control of education by the church and state, Jean-Jacques Rousseau advanced the idea of progressive education, where children learn by doing and where self-expression is encouraged. This idea was carried forward by Johann Pestalozzi, Johann Basedow, and Friedrich Fröbel, and influenced a new view of childhood.

Psychological Theory. In the *Essay Concerning Human Understanding* (1690), John Locke offered the theory that all human knowledge was the result of sensory experience, without any pre-conceived notions.

Causes of the French Revolution

The rising expectations of "enlightened" society were demonstrated by the increased criticism directed toward government inefficiency and corruption, and toward the privileged classes. The clergy (First Estate) and nobility (Second Estate), representing only two percent of the total population of 24 million, were the privileged classes and were essentially tax exempt. The remainder of the population (Third Estate) consisted of the middle class, urban workers, and the mass of peasants, who bore the entire burden of taxation and the imposition of feudal obligations. As economic conditions worsened in the eighteenth century, the French state became poorer, and totally dependent on the poorest and most depressed sections of the economy for support at the very time this tax base had become saturated.

Designed to represent the three estates of France, the Estates General had only met twice, once at its creation in 1302 and again in 1614. When the French parlements insisted that any new taxes must be approved by this body, King Louis XVI reluctantly ordered it to assemble at Versailles by May 1789.

Election fever swept over France for the very first time. The election campaign took place in the midst of the worst subsistence crisis in eighteenth-century France, with widespread grain shortages, poor harvests, and inflated bread prices. Finally, on May 5, 1789, the Estates General met and argued over whether to vote by estate or individual. Each estate was ordered to meet separately and vote as a unit. The Third Estate refused and insisted that the entire assembly stay together.

Phases of Revolution

The National Assembly (1789–1791): After a six-week deadlock over voting methods, representatives of the Third Estate declared themselves the true National Assembly of France (June 17). Defections from the First and Second Estates then caused the king to recognize the National Assembly (June 27) after dissolving the Estates General. At the same time, Louis XVI ordered troops to surround Versailles.

The "Parisian" revolution began at this point. Angry because of food shortages, unemployment, high prices, and fear of military repression, the workers and tradespeople began to arm themselves.

The Legislative Assembly (1791–1792): While the National Assembly had been rather homogeneous in its composition, the new government began to fragment into competing political factions. The most important political clubs were republican groups such as the Jacobins (radical urban) and Girondins (moderate rural), while the *Sans-culottes* (working-class, extremely radical) were a separate faction with an economic agenda.

The National Convention (1792–1795): Meeting for the first time in September 1792, the Convention abolished monarchy and installed republicanism. Louis XVI was charged with treason, found guilty, and executed on January 21, 1793. Later the same year, the queen, Marie Antoinette, met the same fate.

The most notorious event of the French Revolution was the famous "Reign of Terror" (1793–1794), the government's campaign against its internal enemies and counterrevolutionaries.

The Directory (1795–1799): The Constitution of 1795 restricted voting and office holding to property owners. The middle class was in control. It wanted peace in order to gain more wealth and to establish a society in which money and property would become the only requirements for prestige and power. Despite rising inflation and mass public dissatisfaction, the Directory government ignored a growing shift in public opinion. When elections in April 1797 produced a triumph for the royalist right, the results were annulled, and the Directory shed its last pretense of legitimacy.

But the weak and corrupt Directory government managed to hang on for two more years because of great military success. French armies annexed the Austrian Netherlands, the left bank of the Rhine, Nice, and Savoy. The Dutch republic was made a satellite state of France. The greatest military victories were won by Napoleon Bonaparte, who drove the Austrians out of northern Italy and forced them to sign the Treaty of Campo Formio (October 1797), in return for which the Directory government agreed to Bonaparte's scheme to conquer Egypt and threaten English interests in the East.

THE FRENCH REVOLUTION II: THE ERA OF NAPOLEON (1799–1815)

Consulate Period, 1799–1804 (Enlightened Reform): The new government was installed on December 25, 1799, with a constitution which concentrated supreme power in the hands of Napoleon. His aim was to govern France by demanding obedience, rewarding ability, and organizing everything in orderly hierarchical fashion. Napoleon's domestic reforms and policies affected every aspect of society.

Empire Period, 1804–1814 (War and Defeat): After being made Consul for Life (1801), Napoleon felt that only through an empire could France retain its strong position in Europe. On December 2, 1804, Napoleon crowned himself emperor of France in Notre Dame Cathedral.

Militarism and Empire Building: Beginning in 1805 Napoleon engaged in constant warfare that placed French troops in enemy capitals from Lisbon and Madrid to Berlin and Moscow, and temporarily gave Napoleon the largest empire since Roman times. Napoleon's Grand Empire consisted of an enlarged France, satellite kingdoms, and coerced allies.

French-ruled peoples viewed Napoleon as a tyrant who repressed and exploited them for France's glory and advantage. Enlightened reformers believed Napoleon had betrayed the ideals of the Revolution. The downfall of Napoleon resulted from his inability to conquer England, economic distress caused by the Continental System (boycott of British goods), the Peninsular War with Spain, the German War of Liberation, and the invasion of Russia. The actual defeat of Napoleon was the result of the Fourth Coalition and the Battle of Leipzig ("Battle of Nations"). Napoleon was exiled to the island of Elba as a sovereign with an income from France.

After learning of allied disharmony at the Vienna peace talks, Napoleon left Elba and began the Hundred Days by seizing power from the restored French king, Louis XVIII. Napoleon's gamble ended at Waterloo in June 1815. He was exiled as a prisoner of war to the South Atlantic island of St. Helena, where he died in 1821.

THE POST-WAR SETTLEMENT: THE CONGRESS OF VIENNA (1814–1815)

The Congress of Vienna met in 1814 and 1815 to redraw the map of Europe after the Napoleonic era, and to provide some way of preserving the future peace of Europe. Europe was spared a general war throughout the remainder of the nineteenth century. But the failure of the statesmen who shaped the future in 1814–1815 to recognize the forces, such as nationalism and liberalism, unleashed by the French Revolution, only postponed the ultimate confrontation between two views of the world—change and accommodation, or maintaining the status quo.

The Vienna settlement was the work of the representatives of the four nations that had done the most to defeat Napoleon: England (Lord Castlereagh), Austria (Prince Klemens Von Metternich), Russia (Czar Alexander I), and Prussia (Karl Von Hardenberg).

Arrangements to guarantee the enforcement of the status quo as defined by the Vienna settlement included two provisions: The "Holy Alliance" of Czar Alexander I of Russia, an idealistic and unpractical plan, existed only on paper. No one except Alexander took it seriously. But the "Quadruple Alliance" of Russia, Prussia, Austria, and England provided for concerted action to arrest any threat to the peace or balance of power.

From 1815 to 1822, European international relations were controlled by the series of meetings held by the great powers to monitor and defend the status quo: the Congress of Aix-la-Chapelle (1818), the Congress of Troppau (1820), the Congress of Laibach (1821), and the Congress of Verona (1822).

THE INDUSTRIAL REVOLUTION

Twentieth-century English historian Arnold Toynbee came to refer to the period since 1750 as "the Industrial Revolution." The term was intended to describe a time of transition when machines began to significantly displace human and animal power in methods of producing and distributing goods, and an agricultural and commercial society converted into an industrial one.

These changes began slowly, almost imperceptibly, gaining momentum with each decade, so that by the middle of the nineteenth century, industrialism had swept across Europe west to east, from England to Eastern Europe. Few countries purposely avoided industrialization, because of its promised material improvement and national wealth. The economic changes that constitute the Industrial Revolution have done more than any other movement in Western civilization to revolutionize Western life.

Roots of the Industrial Revolution could be found in the following: 1) the Commercial Revolution (1500–1700), which spurred the great economic growth of Europe and brought about the Age of Discovery and Exploration, which in turn helped to solidify the economic doctrines of mercantilism; 2) the effect of the Scientific Revolution, which produced the first wave of mechanical inventions and technological advances; 3) the increase in population in Europe from 140 million people in 1750, to 266 million people by the mid-part of the nineteenth century (more producers, more consumers); and 4) the political and social revolutions of the nineteenth century, which began the rise to power of the "middle class," and provided leadership for the economic revolution.

The revolution occurred first in the cotton and metallurgical industries, because those industries lent themselves to mechanization. A series of mechanical inventions (1733–1793) would enable the cotton industry to mass-produce quality goods. The need to replace wood as an energy source led to the use of coal, which increased coal mining, and resulted ultimately in the invention of the steam engine and the locomotive. The development of steam power allowed the cotton industry to expand and transformed the iron industry. The factory system, which had been created in response to the new energy sources and machinery, was perfected to increase manufactured goods.

A transportation revolution ensued in order to distribute the productivity of machinery and deliver raw materials to the eager factories. This led to the growth of canal systems, the construction of hard-surfaced "macadam" roads, the commercial use of the steamboat (demonstrated by Robert Fulton, 1765–1815), and the railway locomotive (made commercially successful by George Stephenson, 1781–1848).

A subsequent revolution in agriculture made it possible for fewer people to feed the population, thus freeing people to work in factories, or in the new fields of communications, distribution of goods, or services like teaching, medicine, and entertainment.

The Industrial Revolution created a unique new category of people who were dependent on their job alone for income, a job from which they might be dismissed without cause. Until 1850 workers as a whole did not share in the general wealth produced by the Industrial Revolution. Conditions would improve as the century wore on, as union action combined with general prosperity and a developing social conscience to improve the working conditions, wages, and hours first of skilled labor, and later of unskilled labor.

The most important sociological result of industrialism was urbanization. The new factories acted as magnets, pulling people away from their rural roots and beginning the most massive population transfer in history. Cities made the working class a powerful force by raising consciousness and enabling people to unite for political action and to remedy economic dissatisfaction.

IMPACT OF THOUGHT SYSTEMS ("ISMS") ON THE EUROPEAN WORLD

Romanticism was a reaction against the rigid classicism, rationalism, and deism of the eighteenth century. Strongest between 1800 and 1850, the romantic movement differed from country to country and from romanticist to romanticist. Because it emphasized change, it was considered revolutionary in all aspects of life.

English literary Romantics like Wordsworth and Coleridge epitomized the romantic movement. Other romantics included Goethe of Germany, Hugo of France, and Pushkin of Russia. Romanticism also affected music and the visual arts.

Romantic philosophy stimulated an interest in Idealism, the belief that reality consists of ideas, as opposed to materialism. This school of thought (Philosophical Idealism), founded by Plato, was developed through the writings of Immanuel Kant, Johann Gottlieb Fichte, and Georg Wilhelm Friedrich Hegel, the greatest exponent of this school of thought. Hegel believed that an impersonal God rules the universe and guides humans along a progressive evolutionary course by means of a process called dialecticism; this is a historical process by which one thing is constantly reacting with its opposite (the thesis and antithesis), producing a result (synthesis) that automatically meets another opposite and continues the series of reactions.

Conservatism arose in reaction to liberalism and became a popular alternative for those who were frightened by the violence, terror, and social disorder unleashed by the French Revolution. Early conservatism was allied to the restored monarchical governments of Austria, Russia, France, and England. Support for conservatism came from the traditional ruling classes as well as the peasants who still formed the majority of the population. In essence, conservatives believed in order, society, and the state; faith and tradition.

The theory of liberalism was the first major theory in the history of Western thought to teach that the individual is a self-sufficient being whose freedom and well-being are the sole reasons for the existence of society. Liberalism was more closely connected to the spirit and outlook of the Enlightenment than to any of the other "isms" of the early nineteenth century. Liberalism was reformist and political rather than revolutionary in character.

Liberals also advocated economic individualism (i.e., laissez-faire capitalism), heralded by Adam Smith (1723–1790) in his 1776 economic masterpiece, *Wealth of Nations*.

The regenerative force of liberal thought in early nineteenth-century Europe was dramatically revealed in the explosive force of the power of nationalism. Raising the level of consciousness of people having a common language, soil, traditions, history, culture, and experience to seek political unity around an identity of what or who constitutes the nation, nationalism was aroused and made militant during the turbulent French Revolutionary era.

Nationalistic thinkers and writers examined the language, literature, and folkways of their people, thereby stimulating nationalist feelings. Emphasizing the history and culture of the various European peoples reinforced and glorified national sentiment.

SOCIALISM

The Utopian Socialists (from *Utopia*, Saint Thomas More's (1478–1535) book on a fictional ideal society) were the earliest writers to propose an equitable solution to improve the distribution of society's wealth. While they endorsed the productive capacity of industrialism, they denounced its mismanagement. Human society was to be organized as a community rather than a mixture of competing, selfish individuals. All the goods a person needed could be produced in one community.

The Anarchists rejected industrialism and the dominance of government.

"Scientific" Socialism, or Marxism, was the creation of Karl Marx (1818–1883), a German scholar who, with the help of Friedrich Engels (1820–1895), intended to replace utopian hopes and dreams with a militant blueprint for socialist working-class success. The principal works of this revolutionary school of socialism were *The Communist Manifesto* and *Das Kapital*.

The theory of dialectical materialism enabled Marx to explain the history of the world. By borrowing Hegel's dialectic, substituting materialism and realism in place of Hegel's idealism and inverting the methodological process, Marx was able to justify his theoretical conclusions. Marxism consisted of a number of key propositions: 1) An economic interpretation of history, i.e., all human history has been determined by economic factors (mainly who controls the means of production and distribution); 2) Class struggle, i.e., since the beginning of time there has been a class struggle between the rich and the poor or the exploiters and the exploited; 3) Theory of surplus value, i.e., the true value of a product was labor, and since the worker received a small portion of his just labor price, the difference was surplus value, "stolen" from him by the capitalist; and 4) Socialism was inevitable, i.e., capitalism contained the seeds of its own destruction (overproduction, unemployment, etc.); the rich would grow richer and the poor would grow poorer until the gap between each class (proletariat and bourgeoisie) is so great that the working classes would rise up in revolution and overthrow the elite bourgeoisie to install a "dictatorship of the proletariat." As modern capitalism was dismantled, the creation of a classless society guided by the principle "from each according to his abilities, to each according to his needs" would take place.

THE REVOLUTIONARY TRADITION

The year 1848 is considered the watershed of the nineteenth century. The revolutionary disturbances of the first half of the nineteenth century reached a climax in a new wave of revolutions that extended from Scandinavia to southern Italy, and from France to central Europe. Only England and Russia avoided violent upheaval.

The issues were substantially the same as they had been in 1789. What was new in 1848 was that these demands were far more widespread and irrepressible than ever. Whole classes and nations demanded to be fully included in society. Aggravated by rapid population growth and the social disruption caused by industrialism and urbanization, a massive tide of discontent swept across the Western world.

Generally speaking, the 1848 upheavals shared the strong influences of romanticism, nationalism, and liberalism, as well as a new factor of economic dislocation and instability.

Specifically, a number of similar conditions existed in several countries: 1) Severe food shortages caused by poor harvests of grain and potatoes (e.g., Irish potato famine); 2) Financial crises caused by a downturn in the commercial and industrial economy; 3) Business failures; 4) Widespread unemployment; 5) A sense of frustration and discontent among urban artisan and working classes as wages diminished; 6) A system of poor relief which became overburdened; 7) Living conditions, which deteriorated in the cities; 8) The power of nationalism in the Germanies, Italies and in Eastern Europe to inspire the overthrow of existing governments. Middle-class predominance within the unregulated economy continued to drive liberals to push for more government reform and civil liberty. They enlisted the help of the working classes to put more pressure on the government to change.

In France, working-class discontent and liberals' unhappiness with the corrupt regime of King Louis Philippe (reigned 1830–1848)—especially his minister Guizot (1787–1874)—erupted in street riots in Paris on February 22–23, 1848. With the workers in control of Paris, King Louis Philippe abdicated on February 24, and a provisional government proclaimed the Second French Republic.

The "June Days" revolt was provoked when the government closed the national workshop. This new revolution (June 23–26) was unlike previous uprisings in France. It marked the inauguration of genuine class warfare; it was a revolt against poverty and a cry for the redistribution of property. It foreshadowed the great social revolutions of the twentieth century. The revolt was extinguished after General Cavaignac was given dictatorial powers by the government. The June Days confirmed the political predominance of conservative property holders in French life.

The new Constitution of the Second French Republic provided for a unicameral legislature and executive power vested in a popularly elected president of the Republic. When the election returns were counted, the government's candidate was defeated by a "dark horse" candidate, Prince Louis Napoleon Bonaparte (1808–1873), a nephew of the great emperor. On December 20, 1848, Louis Napoleon was installed as president of the Republic. In December 1852 Louis Napoleon became Emperor Napoleon III (reigned 1852–1870), and France retreated from republicanism again.

Italian nationalists and liberals wanted to end Hapsburg (Austrian), Bourbon (Naples and Sicily), and papal domination and unite these disparate Italian regions into a unified liberal nation. A revolt by liberals in Sicily in January 1848 was followed by the granting of liberal constitutions in Naples, Tuscany, Piedmont, and the Papal States. Milan and Venice expelled their Austrian rulers. In March 1848 upon hearing the news of the revolution in Vienna, a fresh outburst of revolution against Austrian rule occurred in Lombardy and Venetia, with Sardinia-Piedmont declaring war on Austria. Simultaneously, Italian patriots attacked the Papal States, forcing the pope, Pius IX (1792–1878), to flee to Naples for refuge.

The temporary nature of these initial successes was illustrated by the speed with which the conservative forces regained control. In the north Austrian Field Marshal Radetzky (1766–1858) swept aside all opposition, regaining Lombardy and Venetia and crushing Sardinia-Piedmont. In the Papal States the establishment of the Roman Republic (February 1849) under the leadership of Giuseppe Mazzini and the protection of Giuseppe Garibaldi (1807–1882) would fail when French troops took Rome in July 1849 after a heroic defense by Garibaldi. Pope Pius IX returned to Rome cured of his liberal leanings. In the south and in Sicily the revolts were suppressed by the former rulers.

The immediate effect of the 1848 Revolution in France was a series of liberal and nationalistic demonstrations in the German states (March 1848), with the rulers promising liberal concessions. The liberals' demand for constitutional government was coupled with another demand—some kind of union or federation of the German states.

GREAT BRITAIN AND THE VICTORIAN COMPROMISE

The Victorian Age (1837–1901) is associated with the long reign of Queen Victoria, who succeeded her uncle King William IV at the age of 18, and married her cousin, Prince Albert. The early years of her reign coincided with the continuation of liberal reform of the British government, accomplished through an arrangement known as the "Victorian Compromise." The Compromise was a political alliance of the middle class and aristocracy to exclude the working class from political power. The middle class gained control of the House of Commons, the aristocracy controlled the government, the army, and the Church of England. This process of accommodation worked successfully.

Parliamentary reforms continued after passage of the 1832 Reform Bill. Laws were enacted abolishing slavery throughout the Empire (1833). The Factory Act (1831) forbade the employment of children under the age of nine. The New Poor Law (1834) required the needy who were able and unemployed to live in workhouses. The Municipal Reform Law (1835) gave control of the cities to the middle class. The last remnants of the mercantilistic age fell with the abolition of the Corn Laws (1846) and repeal of the old navigation acts (1849).

The revolutions of 1848 began with much promise, but all ended in defeat for a number of reasons. They were spontaneous movements which lost their popular support as people lost their enthusiasm. Initial successes by the revolutionaries were due less to their strength than to the hesitancy of governments to use their superior force. Once this hesitancy was overcome, the revolutions were smashed. They were essentially urban movements, and the conservative landowners and peasants tended, in time, to nullify the spontaneous actions of the urban classes. The middle class, who led the revolutions, came to fear the radicalism of their working-class allies. Divisions among national groups, and the willingness of one nationality to deny rights to other nationalities, helped to destroy the revolutionary movements in Central Europe.

However, the results of 1848–1849 were not entirely negative. Universal male suffrage was introduced in France; serfdom remained abolished in Austria and the German states; parliaments were established in Prussia and other German states, though dominated by princes and aristocrats;

and Prussia and Sardinia-Piedmont emerged with new determination to succeed in their respective unification schemes.

A new age followed the revolutions of 1848–1849, as Otto von Bismarck (1815–1898), one of the dominant political figures of the second half of the nineteenth century, was quick to realize. If the mistake of these years was to believe that great decisions could be brought about by speeches and parliamentary majorities, the sequel showed that in an industrial era new techniques involving ruthless force were all too readily available. The period of *Realpolitik*—of realistic, iron-fisted politics and diplomacy—followed.

REALISM AND MATERIALISM (1848–1914)

REALPOLITIK AND THE TRIUMPH OF NATIONALISM

After the collapse of the revolutionary movements of 1848, the leadership of Italian nationalism was transferred to Sardinian leaders Victor Emmanuel II (1820–1878), Camillo de Cavour (1810–1861), and Giuseppe Garibaldi (1807–1882). The new leaders did not entertain romantic illusions about the process of transforming Sardinia into a new Italian kingdom; they were practitioners of the politics of realism, *Realpolitik*.

In 1855, under Cavour's direction, Sardinia joined Britain and France in the Crimean War against Russia. At the Paris Peace Conference (1856), Cavour addressed the delegates on the need to eliminate the foreign (Austrian) presence in the Italian peninsula and attracted the attention and sympathy of the French Emperor, Napoleon III.

After being provoked, the Austrians declared war on Sardinia in 1859. French forces intervened and the Austrians were defeated in the battles of Magenta (June 4) and Solferino (June 24).

Napoleon III, without consulting Cavour, signed a secret peace treaty (The Truce of Villafranca) on July 11, 1859. Sardinia received Lombardy but not Venetia; the other terms indicated that Sardinian influence would be restricted and that Austria would remain a power in Italian politics. The terms of Villafranca were clarified and finalized with the Treaty of Zurich (1859).

In 1860, Cavour arranged the annexation of Parma, Modena, Romagna, and Tuscany into Sardinia. These actions were recognized by the Treaty of Turin between Napoleon III and Victor Emmanuel II; Nice and Savoy were transferred to France.

Giuseppe Garibaldi and his Red Shirts landed in Sicily in May 1860 and extended the nationalist activity to the south. Within three months, Sicily was taken and by September 7, Garibaldi was in Naples and the Kingdom of the Two Sicilies had fallen under Sardinian influence. Cavour distrusted Garibaldi, but Victor Emmanuel II encouraged him.

In February 1861, in Turin, Victor Emmanuel was declared King of Italy and presided over an Italian Parliament which represented the entire Italian peninsula with the exception of Venetia and the Patrimony of St. Peter (Rome). Cavour died in June 1861.

Venetia was incorporated into the Italian Kingdom in 1866 as a result of an alliance between Bismarck's Prussia and the Kingdom of Italy which preceded the Austro-Prussian War between Austria and Prussia. In return for opening a southern front against Austria, Prussia, upon its victory, arranged for Venetia to be transferred to Italy.

Bismarck was again instrumental in the acquisition of Rome into the Italian Kingdom in 1870. In 1870, the Franco-Prussian War broke out and the French garrison, which had been in Rome providing protection for the Pope, was withdrawn to serve on the front against Prussia. Italian troops seized Rome, and in 1871, as a result of a plebiscite, Rome became the capital of the Kingdom of Italy.

BISMARCK AND THE UNIFICATION OF GERMANY

In the period after 1815, Prussia emerged as an alternative to a Hapsburg-based Germany.

Otto von Bismarck (1810–1898) entered the diplomatic service of Wilhelm I as the Revolutions of 1848 were being suppressed. By the early 1860s, Bismarck had emerged as the principal adviser and minister to the king. Bismarck was an advocate of a Prussian-based (Hohenzollern) Germany.

In 1863, the Schleswig-Holstein crisis broke. These provinces, which were occupied by Germans, were under the personal rule of Christian IX (1818–1906) of Denmark. The Danish government advanced a new constitution which specified that Schleswig and Holstein would be annexed into Denmark. German reaction was predictable and Bismarck arranged for joint Austro-Prussian military action. Denmark was defeated and agreed (Treaty of Vienna, 1864) to give up the provinces, and Schleswig and Holstein were to be jointly administered by Austria and Prussia.

In 1870, deteriorating relations between France and Germany collapsed over the Ems Dispatch. Wilhelm I was approached by representatives of the French government who requested a Prussian pledge not to interfere on the issue of the vacant Spanish throne. Wilhelm I refused to give such a pledge and informed Bismarck of these developments through a telegram from Ems.

Bismarck exploited the situation by initiating a propaganda campaign against the French. Subsequently, France declared war and the Franco-Prussian War (1870–1871) commenced. Prussian victories at Sedan and Metz proved decisive; Napoleon III and his leading general, Marshal MacMahon, were captured. Paris continued to resist but fell to the Prussians in January 1871. The Treaty of Frankfurt (May 1871) concluded the war and resulted in France ceding Alsace-Lorraine to Germany and a German occupation until an indemnity was paid.

The German Empire was proclaimed on January 18, 1871, with Wilhelm I becoming the Emperor of Germany. Bismarck became the Imperial Chancellor. Bavaria, Baden, Württemberg, and Saxony were incorporated into the new Germany.

THE CRIMEAN WAR

The Crimean War originated in the dispute between two differing groups of Christians and their protectors over privileges in the Holy Land. During the nineteenth century, Palestine was part of the Ottoman Turkish Empire. In 1852, the Turks negotiated an agreement with the French to provide enclaves in the Holy Land to Roman Catholic religious orders; this arrangement appeared to jeopardize already existing agreements which provided access to Greek Orthodox religious orders. Czar Nicholas I (reigned 1825–1855), unaware of the impact of his action, ordered Russian troops to occupy several Danubian principalities; his strategy was to withdraw from these areas once the Turks agreed to clarify and guarantee the rights of the Greek Orthodox orders. In October 1853, the Turks demanded that the Russians withdraw from the occupied principalities. The Russians failed to respond, and the Turks declared war. In February 1854, Nicholas advanced a draft for a settlement of the Russo-Turkish War; it was rejected and Great Britain and France joined the Ottoman Turks and declared war on Russia.

With the exception of some naval encounters in the Gulf of Finland off the Aaland Islands, the war was conducted on the Crimean Peninsula in the Black Sea. In September 1854, more than 50,000 British and French troops landed in the Crimea, determined to take the Russian port city of Sebastopol. In December 1854, Austria reluctantly became a co-signatory of the Four Points of Vienna, a statement of British and French war aims. In 1855, Piedmont joined Britain and France in the war. In March 1855, Czar Nicholas I died and was succeeded by Alexander II (reigned 1855–1881), who was opposed to continuing the war. In December 1855, the Austrians, under excessive pressure from the British, French, and Piedmontese, sent an ultimatum to Russia in which they threatened to renounce their neutrality. In response, Alexander II indicated that he would accept the Four Points.

The resulting Peace of Paris had the following major provisions: Russia had to acknowledge international commissions to regulate maritime traffic on the Danube, recognize Turkish control of the mouth of the Danube, renounce all claims to the Danubian Principalities of Moldavia and Wallachia (which later led to the establishment of Romania), agree not to fortify the Aaland Islands, renounce its previously espoused position of protector of the Greek Orthodox residents of the Ottoman Empire, and return all occupied territories to the Ottoman Empire. The Straits Convention of 1841 was revised by neutralizing the Black Sea. The Declaration of Paris specified rules to regulate commerce during periods of war. Lastly, the independence and integrity of the Ottoman Empire were recognized and guaranteed by the signatories.

THE EASTERN QUESTION AND THE CONGRESS OF BERLIN

In 1876, Turkish forces under the leadership of Osman Pasha soundly defeated Serbian armies. In March 1878, the Russians and the Turks signed the Peace of San Stephano; implementation of its provisions would have resulted in Russian hegemony in the Balkans and dramatically altered the balance of power in the eastern Mediterranean.

Britain, under the leadership of Prime Minister Benjamin Disraeli (1804–1881), denounced the San Stephano Accord, dispatched a naval squadron to Turkish waters, and demanded that the San Stephano agreement be scrapped. The German Chancellor, Otto von Bismarck, intervened and offered his services as mediator.

The delegates of the major powers convened in Berlin in June and July 1878 to negotiate a settlement. Prior to the meeting, Disraeli had concluded a series of secret arrangements with Austria, Russia, and Turkey. The combined impact of these accommodations was to restrict Russian expansion in the region, reaffirm the independence of Turkey, and maintain British control of the Mediterranean.

The Russians, who had won the war against Turkey and had imposed the harsh terms of the San Stephano Treaty, found that they left the conference with very little (Kars, Batum, etc.) for their effort. Although Disraeli was the primary agent of this anti-Russian settlement, the Russians blamed Bismarck for its dismal results. Their hostility toward Germany led Bismarck (1879) to embark upon a new system of alliances which transformed European diplomacy and rendered any additional efforts of the Concert of Europe futile.

CAPITALISM AND THE EMERGENCE OF THE NEW LEFT (1848–1914)

During the nineteenth century, Europe experienced the full impact of the Industrial Revolution. The Industrial Revolution resulted in improving aspects of the physical lives of a greater number of Europeans; at the same time, it led to a factory system with undesirable working and living conditions and the abuses of child labor.

As the century progressed, the inequities of the system became increasingly evident. Trade-unionism and socialist political parties emerged which attempted to address these problems and improve the lives of the working class.

During the period from 1815 to 1848, Utopian Socialists such as Robert Owen (1771–1858), Saint Simon, and Charles Fourier advocated the establishment of a political-economic system which was based on romantic concepts of the ideal society. The failure of the Revolutions of 1848 and 1849 discredited the Utopian Socialists, and the new "Scientific Socialism" advanced by Karl Marx (1818–1883) became the primary ideology of protest and revolution. Marx stated that the history of humanity was the history of class struggle and that the process of the struggle (the dialectic) would continue until a classless society was realized. The Marxian dialectic was driven by the dynamics of materialism. The proletariat, or the industrial working class, needed to be educated and led towards a violent revolution which would destroy the institutions which perpetuated the struggle and the suppression of the majority. After the revolution, the people would experience the dictatorship of the proletariat, during which the Communist party would provide leadership. Marx advanced these concepts in a series of tracts and books including *The Communist Manifesto* (1848), *Critique of Political Economy* (1859), and *Capital* (1863–1864).

BRITAIN

In 1865, Lord Palmerston died, and during the next two decades significant domestic developments occurred which expanded democracy in Great Britain. The dominant leaders of this period were William Gladstone (1809–1898) and Benjamin Disraeli (1804–1881). As the leader of the Liberal party (until 1895), Gladstone supported Irish Home Rule, fiscal responsibility, free trade, and the extension of democratic principles. He was opposed to imperialism, the involvement of Britain in European affairs, and the further centralization of the British government. Disraeli argued for an aggressive foreign policy, the expansion of the British Empire, and, after opposing democratic reforms, the extension of the franchise.

THE SECOND FRENCH REPUBLIC AND THE SECOND EMPIRE

Louis Napoleon became the president of the Second French Republic in December 1848. During the three-year life of the Second Republic, Louis Napoleon demonstrated his skills as a gifted politician through the manipulation of the various factions in French politics. His deployment of troops in Italy to rescue and restore Pope Pius IX was condemned by the republicans, but strongly supported by the monarchists and moderates.

Louis Napoleon minimized the importance of the Legislative Assembly, capitalized on the developing Napoleonic Legend, and courted the support of the army, the Catholic church, and a range of conservative political groups. The Falloux Law returned control of education to the church. Further, Louis Napoleon was confronted with Article 45 of the constitution, which stipulated that the president was limited to one four-year term; he had no intention of relinquishing power. With the assistance of a core of dedicated supporters, Louis Napoleon arranged for a coup d'état on the night of December 1–2, 1851. The Second Republic fell and was soon replaced by the Second French Empire.

Louis Napoleon drafted a new constitution which resulted in a highly centralized government. On December 2, 1852, he announced that he was Napoleon III, Emperor of the French.

The Second Empire collapsed after the capture of Napoleon III during the Franco-Prussian War (1870–1871). After a regrettable Parisian experience with a communist type of government, the Third French Republic was established; it would survive until 1940.

IMPERIAL RUSSIA

The autocracy of Nicholas I's (reigned 1825–1855) regime was not threatened by the revolutionary movements of 1848. In 1848 and 1849, Russian troops suppressed disorganized Polish attempts to reassert Polish nationalism.

Russian involvement in the Crimean War met with defeat. Russian ambitions in the eastern Mediterranean had been thwarted by a coalition of Western European states. In 1855 Nicholas I died and was succeeded by Alexander II (reigned 1855–1881).

Fearing the transformation of Russian society from below, Alexander II instituted a series of reforms which altered the nature of the social contract in Russia. In 1861, Alexander II declared that serfdom was abolished. Further, he issued the following reforms: 1) The serf (peasant) would no longer be dependent upon the lord; 2) all people were to have freedom of movement and were free to change their means of livelihood; and 3) the serf could enter into contracts and could own property.

The last years of the reign of Alexander II witnessed increased political opposition, manifested in demands for reforms from an ever more hostile group of intellectuals, the emergence of a Russian populist movement, and attempts to assassinate the Czar. As the regime matured, greater importance was placed on traditional values. This attitude developed at the same time that nihilism, which rejected romantic illusions of the past in favor of a rugged realism, was being advanced by such writers as Ivan Turgenev in his *Fathers and Sons*.

The notion of the inevitability and desirability of a social and economic revolution was promoted through the Russian populist movement. Originally, the populists were interested in an agrarian utopian order. The populists had no national support. Government persecution of the populists resulted in the radicalization of the movement. In the late 1870s and early 1880s, leaders such as Andrei Zhelyabov and Sophie Perovskaya became obsessed with the need to assassinate Alexander II. In March 1881, the Czar was killed in St. Petersburg when his carriage was bombed. He was succeeded by Alexander III (reigned 1881–1894), who advocated a national policy based on "Orthodoxy, Autocracy, and Nationalism." Alexander III died in 1894 and was succeeded by the last of the Romanovs to hold power, Nicholas II (reigned 1894–1917). Nicholas II displayed lack of intelligence, wit, political acumen, and the absence of a firm will throughout his reign. From his ministers to his wife, Alexandra, to Rasputin (1872–1916), Nicholas was influenced by stronger personalities.

The opposition to the czarist government became more focused, and thus more threatening, with the emergence of the Russian Social Democrats and the Russian Social Revolutionaries. Both groups were Marxist. Vladimir Ilyich Ulyanov, also known as Lenin, became the leader of the Bolsheviks, a splinter group of the Social Democrats. By the winter of 1904–1905, the accumulated consequences of inept management of the economy and the prosecution of the Russo-Japanese War reached a critical stage. A group under the leadership of the radical priest Gapon marched on the Winter Palace in St. Petersburg (January 9, 1905) to submit a list of grievances to the Czar. Troops fired on the demonstrators and many casualties resulted on this "Bloody Sunday." In June 1905, naval personnel on the battleship *Potemkin* mutinied while the ship was in Odessa. In October 1905, Nicholas II issued the October Manifesto calling for the convocation of a Duma, or assembly of state, which would serve as an advisory body to the Czar, extending civil liberties to include freedom of speech, assembly, and press, and announcing that Nicholas II would reorganize his government.

The leading revolutionary forces differed in their responses to the manifesto. The Octobrists indicated that they were satisfied with the arrangements; the Constitutional Democrats, also known as the Kadets, demanded a more liberal representative system. The Duma convened in 1906 and, from its outset to the outbreak of the First World War, was paralyzed by factionalism which was exploited by the Czar's ministers. By 1907, Nicholas II's ministers had recovered the real power of government. Russia experienced a general though fragile economic recovery by 1909, which lasted until the war.

ORIGINS, MOTIVES, AND IMPLICATIONS OF THE NEW IMPERIALISM (1870–1914)

By the 1870s, the European industrial economies required external markets to distribute products which could not be absorbed within their domestic economies. Further, excess capital was available and foreign investment, while risky, appeared to offer high returns. Finally, the need for additional sources of raw materials served as a rationale and stimulant for imperialism. Politicians were also influenced by the numerous missionary societies which sought government protection, in extending Christianity throughout the world. European statesmen were also interested in asserting their national power overseas through the acquisition of strategic (and many not so strategic) colonies.

The focus of most of the European imperial activities during the late nineteenth century was Africa. Initially, European interest in these activities was romantic. With John Hanning Speke's discovery of Lake Victoria (1858), David Livingstone's surveying of the Zambezi, and Henry Stanley's work on the Congo River, Europeans became enraptured with the greatness and novelty of Africa south of the Sahara.

Disraeli was involved in the intrigue which would result in the British acquisition of the Suez Canal (1875), and during the 1870s and 1880s Britain was involved in a Zulu War and announced the annexation of the Transvaal, which the Boers regained after their great victory of Majuba Hill (1881). At about the same time, Belgium established its interest in the Congo; France, in addition to seizing Tunisia, extended its influence into French Equitorial Africa, and Italy established small colonies in East Africa. During the 1880s Germany acquired several African colonies including German East Africa, the Cameroons, Togoland, and German South West Africa. The Berlin Conference (1884–1885) resulted in an agreement which specified the following: 1) The Congo would be under the control of Belgium through an International Association; 2) More liberal use of the Niger and Congo rivers; and 3) European powers could acquire African territory through, first, occupation and, second, notifying the other European states of their occupation and claim.

British movement north of the Cape of Good Hope involved Europeans fighting one another rather than a native African force. The Boers had lived in South Africa since the beginning of the nineteenth century. With the discovery of gold (1882) in the Transvaal, many English Cape settlers moved into the region. The Boers, under the leadership of Paul Kruger, restricted the political and economic rights of the British settlers and developed alternative railroads through Mozambique which would lessen the Boer dependency on the Cape colony. The crisis mounted and, in 1899, the Boer War began. Until 1902, the British and Boers fought a war which was costly to both sides. Britain prevailed and by 1909, the Transvaal, Orange Free State, Natal, and the Cape of Good Hope were united into the Union of South Africa.

Another area of increased imperialist activity was the Pacific. In 1890, the American naval officer Captain Alfred Mahan published *The Influence of Sea Power Upon History*; in this book he argued that history demonstrated that nations which controlled the seas prevailed. During the 1880s and 1890s naval ships required coaling stations. While Britain, the Netherlands, and France demonstrated that they were interested in Pacific islands, the most active states in this region during the last 20 years of the nineteenth century were Germany and the United States. The United States acquired the Philippines in 1898. Germany gained part of New Guinea, and the Marshall, Caroline, and Mariana island chains. The European powers were also interested in the Asian mainland. Most powers agreed with the American Open Door Policy which recognized the independence and integrity of China and provided economic access for all the powers. Rivalry over China (Manchuria) was a principal cause of the outbreak of the Russo-Japanese War in 1904.

THE AGE OF BISMARCK (1871–1890)

During the period from the establishment of the German Empire in January 1871 to his dismissal as chancellor of Germany in March 1890, Otto von Bismarck dominated European diplomacy and established an integrated political and economic structure for the new German state. Bismarck established a statist system which was reactionary in political philosophy and based upon industrialism, militarism, and innovative social legislation.

During the 1870s and 1880s, Bismarck's domestic policies were directed at the establishment of a strong united German state which would be capable of defending itself from a French war of revenge designed to restore Alsace-Lorraine to France. Laws were enacted which unified the monetary system, established an Imperial Bank and strengthened existing banks, developed universal German civil and criminal codes, and required compulsory military service. All of these measures contributed to the integration of the German state.

In order to develop public support for the government and to minimize the threat from the left, Bismarck instituted a protective tariff, to maintain domestic production, and introduced many social and economic laws to provide social security, regulate child labor, and improve working conditions for all Germans.

Bismarck's foreign policy was centered on maintaining the diplomatic isolation of France. In the crisis stemming from the Russo-Turkish War (1877–1878), Bismarck tried to serve as the "Honest Broker" at the Congress of Berlin. Russia did not succeed at the conference and incorrectly blamed Bismarck for its failure. Early in the next year, a cholera epidemic affected Russian cattle herds, and Germany placed an embargo on the importation of Russian beef. The Russians were outraged by the German action and launched an anti-German propaganda campaign in the Russian press. Bismarck, desiring to maintain the peace and a predictable diplomatic environment, concluded a secret defensive treaty with Austria-Hungary in 1879. The Dual Alliance was very significant because it was the first "hard" diplomatic alliance of the era. A "hard" alliance involved the specific commitment of military support; traditional or "soft" alliances involved pledges of neutrality or to hold military conversations in the event of a war. The Dual Alliance, which had a five-year term and was renewable, directed that one signatory would assist the other in the event that one power was attacked by two or more states.

In 1882, another agreement, the Triple Alliance, was signed between Germany, Austria-Hungary, and Italy. In the 1880s, relations between Austria-Hungary and Russia became estranged over Balkan issues. Bismarck, fearing a war, intervened and by 1887, had negotiated the secret Reinsurance Treaty with Russia. This was a "hard" defensive alliance with a three-year term, which was renewable.

In 1888, Wilhelm I died and was succeeded by his son Friedrich III, who also died within a few months. Friedrich's son, Wilhelm II (reigned 1888–1918), came to power and soon found himself in conflict with Bismarck. Early in 1890, two issues developed which led ultimately to Bismarck's dismissal. First, Bismarck had evolved a scheme for a fabricated attempted coup by the Social Democratic Party (SDP); his intent was to use this situation to create a national hysteria through which he could restrict the SDP through legal action. Second, Bismarck intended to renew the Reinsurance Treaty with Russia to maintain his policy of French diplomatic isolation. Wilhelm II opposed both of these plans; in March 1890, Bismarck, who had used the threat of resignation so skillfully in the past, suggested that he would resign if Wilhelm II would not approve of these actions. Wilhelm II accepted his resignation; in fact, Bismarck was dismissed.

THE MOVEMENT TOWARD DEMOCRACY IN WESTERN EUROPE

Even after the reform measures of 1867 and 1884 to 1885, the movement toward democratic reforms in Great Britain continued unabated.

The most significant political reform of this long-lived Liberal government was the Parliament Act of 1911, which eliminated the powers of the House of Lords and resulted in the House of Commons becoming the unquestioned center of national power.

The most recurring and serious problem which Great Britain experienced during the period from 1890 to 1914 was the "Irish Question." The Irish situation became more complicated when the Protestant counties of the north started to enjoy remarkable economic growth from the mid-1890s; they were adamant in their rejection of all measures of Irish Home Rule. In 1914, an Irish Home Rule Act was passed by both the Commons and the Lords, but the Protestants refused to accept it. Implementation was deferred until after the war.

THE THIRD FRENCH REPUBLIC

In the fall of 1870, Napoleon III's Second Empire collapsed when it was defeated by the Prussian armies. Napoleon III and his principal aides were captured; later, he abdicated and fled to England. A National Assembly (1871–1875) was created and Adolphe Thiers was recognized as its chief executive. At the same time, a more radical political entity, the Paris Commune (1870–1871), came into existence and exercised extraordinary power during the siege of Paris. After the siege and the peace agreement with Prussia, the Commune refused to recognize the authority of the National Assembly. Led by radical Marxists, anarchists, and republicans, the Paris Commune repudiated the conservative and monarchist leadership of the National Assembly. From March to May 1871, the Commune fought a bloody struggle with the troops of the National Assembly. France began a program of recovery which led to the formulation of the Third French Republic in 1875. The National Assembly sought to 1) put the French political house in order; 2) establish a new constitutional government; 3) pay off an imposed indemnity and, in doing so, remove German troops from French territory; and 4) restore the honor and glory of France. In 1875 a constitution was adopted which provided for a republican government consisting of a president (with little power), a Senate, and a Chamber of Deputies, which was the center of political power. During the early years of the Republic, Leon Gambetta (1838–1882) led the republicans.

The most serious threat to the Republic came through the Dreyfus Affair. In 1894, Captain Alfred Dreyfus (1859–1935) was assigned to the French General Staff. A scandal broke when it was revealed that classified information had been provided to German spies. Dreyfus, a Jew, was charged, tried, and convicted. Later, it was determined that the actual spy was Commandant Marie Charles Esterhazy (1847–1923), who was acquitted in order to save the pride and reputation of the army. In 1906, the case was closed when Dreyfus was declared innocent and returned to the ranks. Rather than lead to the collapse of the Republic, the Dreyfus Affair demonstrated the intensity of anti-Semitism in French society, the level of corruption in the French army, and the willingness of the Catholic church and the monarchists to join in a conspiracy against an innocent man.

From 1905 to 1914 the socialists under Jean Jaurès gained seats in the Chamber of Deputies. The Third French Republic endured the crises which confronted it and, in 1914, enjoyed the support of the vast majority of French citizens.

INTERNATIONAL POLITICS AND THE COMING OF THE WAR (1890–1914)

During the late nineteenth century, the economically motivated "New Imperialism" resulted in further aggravating the relations among the European powers. The Fashoda Crisis (1898–1899), the Moroccan Crisis (1905–1906), the Balkan Crisis (1908), and the Agadir Crisis (1911) demonstrated the impact of imperialism in heightening tensions among European states and in creating an environment in which conflict became more acceptable.

In 1908, the decadent Ottoman Empire was experiencing domestic discord which attracted the attention of both the Austrians and the Russians. These two powers agreed that Austria would annex Bosnia and Herzegovina and Russia would be granted access to the Straits and thus the Mediterranean. Great Britain intervened and demanded that there be no change in the status quo in the Straits. Russia backed down from a confrontation, but Austria proceeded to annex Bosnia and Herzegovina.

On June 28, 1914, Archduke Franz Ferdinand (1863–1914), heir to the Austro-Hungarian throne, and his wife were assassinated while on a state visit to Sarajevo, the capital of Bosnia. The assassination resulted in a crisis between Austria-Hungary and Serbia. On July 23, Austria's foreign minister, Count Berchtold, sent a 10-point ultimatum to Serbia. Though the ultimatum was purposely drafted to inflame Serbia, the Serbians argued the validity of only one of its precepts.

German Chancellor Bethmann-Hollweg and British Foreign Secretary Sir Edward Grey attempted to mediate the conflict. It was too late. On July 28, Austria declared war on Serbia and by August 4, Britain, France, and Russia (The Allies) were at war with Germany and Austria-Hungary (The Central Powers); later, other nations would join one of the two camps.

The initial military actions did not proceed as planned. The German Schlieffen Plan failed to succeed in the West as a result of German tactical adjustments and the French and British resistance in the First Battle of the Marne (September 1914). In the East, the Germans scored significant victories over the numerically superior Russians at the battles of Tannenberg and Masurian Lakes (August–September 1914).

WORLD WAR I AND EUROPE IN CRISIS (1914–1935)

THE ORIGINS OF WORLD WAR I

The long-range roots of the origins of World War I can be traced to numerous factors, beginning with the creation of modern Germany in 1871. Achieved through a series of wars, the emergence of this new German state completely destroyed Europe's traditional balance of power, and forced its diplomatic and military planners back to their drawing boards to rethink their collective strategies.

From 1871 to 1890, balance of power was maintained through the network of alliances created by the German Chancellor, Otto von Bismarck, and centered around his *Dreikaiserbund* (League of the Three Emperors) that isolated France, and the Dual (Germany, Austria) and Triple (Germany, Austria, Italy) Alliances. Bismarck's fall in 1890 resulted in new policies that saw Germany move closer to Austria, while England and France (Entente Cordiale, 1904), and later Russia (Triple Entente, 1907), drew closer.

Germany's dramatic defeat of France in 1870–1871 coupled with Kaiser William II's decision in 1890 to build up a navy comparable to that of Great Britain created a reactive arms race. This, blended with European efforts to carve out colonial empires in Africa and Asia—plus a new spirit of nationalism and the growing romanticization of war—helped create an unstable international environment in the years before the outbreak of World War I.

IMMEDIATE CAUSE OF WORLD WAR I

The Balkans, the area which today comprises the former Yugoslavia, Albania, Greece, Bulgaria, Macedonia, and Romania, were notably unstable. Part of the rapidly decaying Ottoman (Turkish) Empire, it saw two main forces at work: (1) ethnic nationalism among the various small groups who lived there, and (2) an intense rivalry between Austria-Hungary and Russia over spheres of influence. Existing friction between Austria and Serbia heated up all the more. In 1912, with Russia's blessing, the Balkan League (Serbia, Montenegro, Greece, and Bulgaria) went to war with Turkey. Serbia, which sought a port on the Adriatic, was rebuffed when Austria and Italy backed the creation of an independent Albania. Russia, meanwhile, grew increasingly protective of its southern Slavic cousins, supporting Serbia's and Montenegro's claims to Albanian lands.

THE OUTBREAK OF THE WORLD WAR

As noted earlier, the match that would set Europe ablaze was struck on June 28, 1914, when Archduke Franz Ferdinand (1863–1914), heir to the Austrian throne, was assassinated by Gavrilo Princip, a young Serbian nationalist. Austria consulted with the German government on July 6 and received a "blank check" to take any steps necessary to punish Serbia. On July 23, 1914, the Austrian government presented Serbia with a 10-point ultimatum that required Serbia to suppress and punish all forms of anti-Austrian sentiment there with the help of Austrian officials. On July 25, 1914, three hours after mobilizing its army, the Serbians acceded to most of Austria's terms. In fact, they requested only that Austria's demand to participate in Serbian judicial proceedings be adjudicated by the International Tribunal at The Hague.

Austria immediately broke off official relations with Serbia and mobilized its army. On July 28, 1914, Austria went to war against Serbia, and began to bombard Belgrade the following day. At the same time, Russia gradually prepared for war against Austria and Germany, declaring full mobilization on July 30.

German military strategy, based in part on the plan of the Chief of the General Staff Count Alfred von Schlieffen, viewed Russian mobilization as an act of war. The Schlieffen Plan was based on a two-front war with Russia and France. It was predicated on a swift, decisive blow against France while maintaining a defensive position against slowly mobilizing Russia, which would be dealt with after France.

Germany demanded that Russia demobilize in 12 hours and appealed to the Russian ambassador in Berlin. Russia's offer to negotiate the matter was rejected, and Germany declared war on Russia on August 1, 1914. On August 3, Germany declared war on France. Berlin asked Belgium for permission to send its troops through its territory to attack France, which Belgium refused. On

August 4, England, which agreed in 1839 to protect Belgian neutrality, declared war on Germany; Belgium followed suit. Between 1914 and 1915, the alliance of the Central Powers (Germany, Austria-Hungary, Bulgaria, and Turkey) faced the Allied Powers of England, France, Russia, Japan, and in 1917, the United States. A number of smaller countries were also part of the Allied coalition.

THE WAR IN 1914

The Western Front: After entering Belgium, the Germans attacked France on five fronts in an effort to encircle Paris rapidly. However, the unexpected Russian attack in East Prussia and Galicia from August 17 to 20 forced Germany to transfer important forces eastward to halt the Russian drive.

To halt a further German advance, the French army, aided by Belgian and English forces, counterattacked. In the Battle of the Marne (September 5–9), they stopped the German drive and forced small retreats. Mutual outflanking maneuvers by France and Germany created a battlefront that would determine the demarcation of the Western Front for the next four years. It ran, in uneven fashion, from the North Sea to Belgium and from northern France to Switzerland.

The Eastern Front: The Germans retreated after their assault against Warsaw in late September. Hindenburg's attack on Lodz, 10 days after he was appointed Commander-in-Chief of the Eastern Front (Nov. 1), was a more successful venture; by the end of 1914 this important textile center was in German hands.

THE WAR IN 1915

The Western Front: Wooed by both sides, Italy joined the Allies and declared war on the Central Powers on May 23 after signing the secret Treaty of London (April 26). This treaty gave Italy Austrian provinces in the north and some Turkish territory.

The Eastern Front: On January 23, 1915, Austro-German forces began a coordinated offensive in East Russia and in the Carpathians. The two-pronged German assault in the north was stopped on February 27, while Austrian efforts to relieve their besieged defensive network at Przemyśl failed when it fell into Russian hands on March 22.

German forces, strengthened by troops from the Western Front under August von Mackensen, began a move on May 2 to strike at the heart of the Russian Front. By August 1915, much of Russian Poland was in German hands.

In an effort to provide direct access to the Turks defending Gallipoli, Germany and Austria invaded Serbia in the early fall, aided by their new ally, Bulgaria. On October 7, the defeated Serbian army retreated to Corfu.

THE EASTERN MEDITERRANEAN

Turkey entered the war on the Central Power side on October 28, 1914, which prevented the shipment of Anglo-French aid to Russians through the Straits.

THE WAR IN 1916

The Western Front: The Battle for Verdun lasted from February 21 to December 18, 1916. From February until June, German forces, aided by closely coordinated heavy artillery barrages, assaulted the forts around Verdun. The Germans suffered 281,000 casualties while the French, under Marshal Henri Pétain (1856–1951), lost 315,000 while successfully defending their position.

To take pressure off the French, an Anglo-French force mounted three attacks on the Germans to the left of Verdun in July, September, and November. After the Battle of the Somme (July 1–November 18), German pressure was reduced, but at great loss. Anglo-French casualties totaled 600,000.

The Eastern Front: Orchestrated by Aleksei Brusilov (1853–1926), The Brusilov Offensive (June 4–September 20) envisioned a series of unexpected attacks along a lengthy front to confuse the enemy. By late August, he had advanced into Galicia and the Carpathians.

Romania entered the war on the Allied side as a result of Russian successes and the secret Treaty of Bucharest (August 17). The ensuing Romanian thrust into Transylvania was pushed back, and on December 6, a German-Bulgarian army occupied Bucharest as well as the bulk of Romania.

The death of Austrian Emperor Franz Joseph (reigned 1848–1916) on November 21 prompted his successor, Charles I (1887–1922), to discuss the prospect of peace terms with his allies. On December 12, the four Central Powers, strengthened by the fall of Bucharest, offered four separate peace proposals based on their recent military achievements. The Allies rejected them on December 30 because they felt them to be insincere.

By the end of 1914, Allied fleets had gained control of the high seas, which caused Germany to lose control of its colonial empire. Germany's failure in 1914 to weaken British naval strength prompted German naval leaders to begin using the submarine as an offensive weapon to weaken the British. On February 4, Germany announced a war zone around the British Isles, and advised neutral powers to sail there at their own risk. On May 7, 1915, a German submarine sank the *Lusitania*, a British passenger vessel, because it was secretly carrying arms.

NEW MILITARY TECHNOLOGY

Germany, Russia, and Great Britain all had submarines, but the German U-boats were the most effective. Designed principally for coastal protection, they increasingly used them to reduce British naval superiority through tactical and psychological means.

By the spring of 1915, British war planners finally awoke to the fact that the machine gun had become the mistress of defensive trench warfare. In a search for a weapon to counter trench defenses, the British developed tanks as an armored "land ship," and first used them on September 15, 1916, in the battle of the Somme.

Airplanes were initially used for observation purposes in the early months of the war. As their numbers grew, mid-air struggles using pistols and rifles took place, until the Germans devised a synchronized propeller and machine gun on its Fokker aircraft in May 1915. The Allies responded with similar equipment and new squadron tactics during the early days of the Verdun campaign in February 1916, and briefly gained control of the skies. They also began to use their aircraft for bombing raids against Zeppelin bases in Germany. Air supremacy shifted to the Germans in 1917.

During the first year of the war, the Germans began to use Zeppelin airships to bomb civilian targets in England. Though their significance was neutralized with the development of the explosive shell in 1916, Zeppelins played an important role as a psychological weapon in the first two years of the war.

In the constant search for methods to counter trench warfare, the Germans and the Allied forces experimented with various forms of internationally outlawed gas. On October 27, 1914, the Germans tried a nose/eye irritant gas at Neuve-Chapelle, and by the spring of 1915 had developed a poison chlorine gas at the Battle of Ypres. That fall, the British countered with a similar chemical at the battles of Champagne and Loos.

THE RUSSIAN REVOLUTIONS OF 1917

The February Revolution

The government's handling of the war prompted a new wave of civilian unrest. Estimates are that 1,140 riots and strikes swept Russia in January and February 1917. Military and police units ordered to move against the mobs either remained at their posts or joined them.

Despite being ordered by the Czar not to meet until April, Duma leaders demanded dramatic solutions to the country's problems. Though dissolved on March 11, the Duma met in special session on March 13 and created a Provisional Committee of Elders to deal with the civil war. After two days of discussions, it decided that the Czar must give up his throne, and on March 15, 1917, President Mikhail Rodzianko and Aleksandr Ivanovich Guchkov, leader of the Octobrist Party, convinced the Czar to abdicate. He agreed, turning over the throne to his brother, the Grand Duke Mikhail, who himself abdicated the next day. Thus ended the three century-old Romanov dynasty.

The Bolshevik October Revolution

On October 23–24, Lenin returned from Finland to meet with the party's Central Committee to plan the coup. Though he met with strong resistance, the Committee agreed to create a Political Bureau (Politburo) to oversee the revolution.

Leon Trotsky (1879–1940), head of the Petrograd Soviet and its Military Revolutionary Committee, convinced troops in Petrograd to support Bolshevik moves. While Trotsky gained control of important strategic points around the city, Alexander Kerensky, Prime Minister of the Russian Provisional Government at the time, and well-informed of Lenin's plans, finally decided on November 6 to move against the plotters. In response, Lenin and Trotsky ordered their supporters to seize the city's transportation and communication centers. The Winter Palace was captured later that evening, along with most of Kerensky's government.

The Second Congress opened at 11 p.m. on November 7, with Lev Kamenev (1883–1936), a member of Lenin's Politburo, as its head. Soon after it opened, many of the moderate socialists walked out in opposition to Lenin's coup, leaving the Bolsheviks and the Left Socialist Revolutionaries in control of the gathering.

At the Congress, it was announced that the government's new Cabinet, officially called the Council of People's Commissars (Sovnarkom), and responsible to a Central Executive Committee, would include Lenin as Chairman or head of government, Trotsky as Foreign Commissar, and Josef Stalin as Commissar of Nationalities. The Second Congress issued two decrees on peace and land. The first called for immediate peace without any consideration of indemnities or annexations, while the second adopted the Socialist Revolutionary land program that abolished private ownership of land and decreed that a peasant could only have as much land as he could farm. Village councils would oversee distribution.

The Constituent Assembly

The Constituent Assembly, long promised by the Provisional Government as the country's first legally elected legislature, presented serious problems for Lenin, since he knew the Bolsheviks could not win a majority of seats in it. Regardless, Lenin allowed elections for it to be held on November 25 under universal suffrage. When the assembly convened on January 18 in the Tauride Palace, it voted down Bolshevik proposals and elected Victor Chernov, a Socialist Revolutionary, as president, and declared the country a democratic federal republic. The Bolsheviks walked out. The next day, troops dissolved the Assembly.

WORLD WAR I: THE FINAL PHASE (1917–1918)

Russia Leaves the War

As order collapsed among Russian units along the Eastern Front, the Soviet government began to explore cease-fire talks with the Central Powers. Leon Trotsky, now Commissar of Foreign

Affairs, offered general negotiations to all sides, and signed an initial armistice as a prelude to peace discussions with Germany at Brest-Litovsk on December 5, 1917.

The Soviets accepted terms that were integrated into the Treaty of Brest-Litovsk of March 3, 1918. According to its terms, in return for peace, Soviet Russia lost its Baltic provinces, the Ukraine, Finland, Byelorussia, and part of Transcaucasia. The area lost totaled 1,300,000 square miles and included 62 million people.

The American Presence: Naval and Economic Support

The United States, which had originally hoped that it could simply supply the Allies with naval and economic support, made its naval presence known immediately and helped Great Britain mount an extremely effective blockade of Germany and, through a convoy system, strengthened the shipment of goods across the Atlantic.

An initial token group, the American Expeditionary Force under General John J. Pershing (1860–1948), arrived in France on June 25, 1917, while by the end of April 1918, 300,000 Americans a month were placed as complete divisions alongside British and French units.

Stirred by the successes on the Marne, the Allies began their offensive against the Germans at Amiens on August 8, 1918. By September 3, the Germans retreated to the Hindenburg Line. On September 26, Foch began his final offensive, and took the Hindenburg Line the following day. Two days later, Ludendorff advised his government to seek a peace settlement. Over the next month, the French took St. Quetin (October 1), while the British occupied Cambrai, Le Cateau, and Ostend.

On September 14, Allied forces attacked in the Salonika area of Macedonia and forced Bulgaria to sue for peace on September 29. On September 19, General Allenby began an attack on Turkish forces at Megiddo in Palestine and quickly defeated them. In a rapid collapse of Turkish resistance, the British took Damascus, Aleppo, and finally forced Turkey from the war at the end of October. On October 24, the Italians began an assault against Austria-Hungary at Vitto Veneto and forced Vienna to sign armistice terms on November 3. Kaiser Wilhelm II, pressured to abdicate, fled the country on November 9, and a republic was declared. On November 11, at 11 a.m., the war ended, with Germany accepting a harsh armistice.

THE PARIS PEACE CONFERENCE OF 1919–1920

Preliminary Discussions

To a very great extent, the direction and thrust of the discussions at the Paris Peace Conference were determined by the destructive nature of the war itself and the political responsibilities, ideals, and personalities of the principal architects of the settlements at Paris. The sudden, unexpected end of the war, combined with the growing threat of communist revolution throughout Europe created an unsettling atmosphere at the conference. The "Big Four" of Wilson (U.S.), Clemenceau (France), Lloyd-George (England), and Orlando (Italy) took over the peace discussions. The delays caused by uncertainty over direction at the beginning of the conference, Wilson's insistence that the League of Nations be included in the settlement, and fear of European-wide revolution resulted in a hastily prepared, dictated peace settlement.

THE TREATY OF VERSAILLES

The treaty's war guilt statements were the justification for its harsh penalties. The former German king, Wilhelm II, was accused of crimes against "international morality and the sanctity of treaties," while Germany took responsibility for itself and for its allies for all losses suffered by the Allied Powers and their supporters as a result of German and Central Power aggression.

Germany had to return Alsace and Lorraine to France and Eupen-Malmedy to Belgium. France got Germany's Saar coal mines as reparations, while the Saar Basin was to be occupied by the major powers for 15 years, after which a plebiscite would decide its ultimate fate. Poland got a number of German provinces and Danzig, now a free city, as its outlet to the sea. Additionally, Germany lost all of its colonies in Asia and Africa.

The German Army was limited to 100,000 men and officers with 12-year enlistments for the former and 25 for the latter. The General Staff was also abolished. The Navy lost its submarines and most offensive naval forces, and was limited to 15,000 men and officers with the same enlistment periods as the army. Aircraft and blimps were outlawed. A Reparations Commission was created to determine Germany's war debt to the Allies, which it figured in 1921 to be $32.4 billion, to be paid over an extended period of time. In the meantime, Germany was to begin immediate payments in goods and raw materials.

The Allies presented the treaty to the Germans on May 7, 1919, but the Germans stated that its terms were too much for the German people, and that it violated the spirit of Wilson's Fourteen Points. After some minor changes were made, the Germans were told to sign the document or face an Allied advance into Germany. The treaty was signed on June 28, 1919, at Versailles.

TREATIES WITH GERMANY'S ALLIES

The Allied treaty with Austria legitimized the breakup of the Austrian Empire in the latter days of the war and saw Austrian territory ceded to Italy and the new states of Czechoslovakia, Poland, and Yugoslavia. The agreement included military restrictions and debt payments.

WEIMAR GERMANY (1918–1929)

The dramatic collapse of the German war effort in the second half of 1918 ultimately created a political crisis that forced the abdication of the kaiser and the creation of a German Republic on November 9.

From the outset, the Provisional Government, formed by a coalition of Majority and Independent Social Democratic Socialists, was beset by divisions from within and threats of revolution throughout Germany.

Elections for the new National Constituent Assembly, which was to be based on proportional representation, gave no party a clear majority. A coalition of the Majority Socialists, the Catholic Centre party, and the German Democratic party (DDP) dominated the new assembly. On February 11, 1919, the assembly met in the historic town of Weimar and selected Friedrich Ebert President of Germany. Two days later, Philip Scheidemann (1865–1939) formed the first Weimar Cabinet and became its first Chancellor.

On August 11, 1919, a new constitution was promulgated, which provided for a bicameral legislature.

POLITICS AND PROBLEMS OF THE WEIMAR REPUBLIC (1919–1923)

The territorial, manpower, and economic losses suffered during and after the war, coupled with the $32.4 billion reparations debt, had a severe impact on the German economy and society, and severely handicapped the new government's efforts to establish a stable governing environment.

In an effort of good faith based on hopes of future reparation payment reductions, Germany borrowed heavily and made payments in kind to fulfill its early debt obligations. The result was a spiral of inflation. After the Allied Reparations Commission declared Germany in default on its debt, the French and the Belgians occupied the Ruhr on January 11, 1923.

Chancellor Wilhelm Cuno (1876–1933) encouraged the Ruhr's Germans passively to resist the occupation, and printed worthless currency. The occupation ended on September 26, and helped prompt stronger Allied sympathy to Germany's payment difficulties, though the inflationary spiral had severe economic, social, and political consequences.

Weimar Politics (1919–1923): Germany's economic and social difficulties deeply affected its infant democracy. From February 1919 to August 1923, the country had six chancellors.

Growing right-wing discontent with the Weimar Government resulted in the assassination of the gifted head of the Catholic Center Party, Matthias Erzberger (1875–1921), on August 29, 1921, and the murder of Foreign Minister Walter Rathenau (1867–1922) on June 24, 1922. These were two of the most serious of over 350 political murders in Germany since the end of the war.

Following the death of President Ebert on February 28, 1925, two ballots were held for a new president, since none of the candidates won a majority on the first vote. On the second ballot on April 26, the Reichsblock, a coalition of Conservative parties, was able to get its candidate elected. War hero Paul von Hindenburg was narrowly elected.

The elections of May 20, 1928, saw the Social Democrats get almost one-third of the popular vote which, blended with other moderate groups, created a stable, moderate majority in the Reichstag, which chose Hermann Müller (1876–1931) as chancellor.

ITALY (1919–1925)

Benito Mussolini, capitalizing on the sympathy of unfulfilled war veterans, disaffected nationalists, and those fearful of communism, formed the Fascio Italiano di Combattimento (Union of Combat) in Milan on March 23, 1919. Initially, Mussolini's movement had few followers, and it did badly in the November 1919 elections. However, Socialist strikes and unrest enabled him to convince Italians that he alone could bring stability and prosperity to their troubled country.

The resignation of the Bonomi Cabinet on February 9, 1922, underlined the government's inability to maintain stability. In the meantime, the Fascists seized control of Bologna in May and Milan in August. In response, Socialist leaders called for a nationwide strike on August 1, 1922; it was stopped by Fascist street violence within 24 hours. On October 24, 1922, Mussolini told followers that if he was not given power, he would "March on Rome." Three days later, Fascists began to seize control of other cities, while 26,000 began to move towards the capital. On October 29, the king, Victor Emmanuel III (1869–1947), asked Mussolini to form a new government as Premier of Italy.

Beginning in 1925, Mussolini arrested opponents, closed newspapers, and eliminated civil liberties in a new reign of terror. On December 24, 1925, the legislature's powers were greatly limited, while those of Mussolini were increased as the new Head of State. Throughout 1926, Mussolini intensified his control over the country with legislation that outlawed strikes and created the syndicalist corporate system. A failed assassination attempt prompted the "Law for the Defense of the State" of November 25, 1926, that created a Special Court to deal with political crimes and introduced the death penalty for threats against the king, his family, or the Head of State.

Italian Foreign Policy

The nation's wish for post-war peace and stability saw Italy participate in all of the international developments in the 1920s aimed at securing normalcy in relations with its neighbors. Because Italy did not receive its desired portions of Dalmatia at the Paris Peace Conference, Italian nationalist Gabriele D'Annunzio seized Fiume on the Adriatic in the fall of 1919. D'Annunzio's daring gesture as well as his deep sense of Italian national pride deeply affected Mussolini. However, in the atmosphere of detente prevalent in Europe at the time, he agreed to settle the dispute with

Yugoslavia in a treaty on January 27, 1924, which ceded most of the port to Italy and the surrounding area to Yugoslavia.

In the fall of 1923, Mussolini used the assassination of Italian officials, who were working to resolve a Greek-Albanian border dispute, as a pretext to seize the island of Corfu. Within a month, however, the British and the French convinced him to return the island for an indemnity.

SOVIET RUSSIA (1922–1932)

The Civil War and "War Communism" had brought economic disaster and social upheaval throughout the country. On March 1, 1921, as the Soviet leadership met to decide on policies to guide the country in peace, a naval rebellion broke out at the Kronstadt naval base. The Soviet leadership sent Trotsky to put down the rebellion, which he did brutally by March 18.

Vladimir Ilyich Lenin, the founder of the Soviet State, suffered a serious stroke on May 26, 1922 and a second in December of that year. Lenin died on January 21, 1924.

Iosif Vissarionovich Dzhugashvili (Joseph Stalin, 1879–1953) took over numerous, and in some cases, seemingly unimportant party organizations after the Revolution and transformed them into important bases of power. Among them were Politburo (Political Bureau), which ran the country; the Orgburo (Organizational Bureau), which Stalin headed, and which appointed people to positions in groups that implemented Politiburo decisions, the Inspectorate (Rabkrin, Commissariat of the Workers' and Peasants' Inspectorate) which tried to eliminate party corruption, and the Secretariat, which worked with all party organs and set the Politburo's agenda. Stalin served as the party's General Secretary after 1921.

Lev Davidovich Bronstein (Trotsky, 1879–1940) was Chairman of the Petrograd Soviet, headed the early Brest-Litovsk negotiating team, served as Foreign Commissar, and was father of the Red Army. A brilliant organizer and theorist, Trotsky was also brusque and, some felt, overbearing.

In China the Soviets helped found a young Chinese Communist party (CCP) in 1921. When it became apparent that Sun Yat-sen's (1866–1925) revolutionary Kuomintang (KMT) was more mature than the infant CCP, the Soviets encouraged an alliance between its party and this movement. Sun's successor, Chiang Kai-shek (1887–1975), was deeply suspicious of the Communists and made their destruction part of his effort to militarily unite China.

Founded in 1919, the Soviet-controlled Comintern (Third International or Communist International) sought to coordinate the revolutionary activities of Communist parties abroad, though it often conflicted with Soviet diplomatic interests. It became an effectively organized body by 1924, and was completely Stalinized by 1928.

EUROPE IN CRISIS: DEPRESSION AND DICTATORSHIP (1929–1935)

In Great Britain in 1929, Ramsay MacDonald formed a minority Labour government that would last until 1931. The most serious problem facing the country was the Depression, which caused unemployment to reach 1,700,000 by 1930 and peaked at over 3 million, or 25 percent of the labor force, by 1932. To meet growing budget deficits caused by heavy subsidies to the unemployed, a special government commission recommended budget cuts and tax increases. Cabinet and labor union opposition helped reduce the total for the cuts but this could not help restore confidence in the government, which fell on August 24, 1931.

THE "NATIONAL GOVERNMENT" (1931–1935)

The following day, King George VI (1895–1952) helped convince MacDonald to return to office as head of a National Coalition cabinet made up of four Conservatives, four Labourites, and two Liberals. MacDonald's coalition swept the November 1931 general elections winning 554 of 615 seats.

The British government abandoned the gold standard on September 21, 1931, and adopted a series of high tariffs on imports. By 1934, unemployment had dropped to 2 million.

MacDonald resigned his position in June 1935 because of ill health and was succeeded by Stanley Baldwin, whose conservative coalition won 428 seats in new elections in November.

FRANCE: RETURN OF THE CARTEL DES GAUCHES (1932–1934)

France remained plagued by differences over economic reform between the Radicals and the Socialists. The latter advocated nationalization of major factories, expanded social reforms, and public works programs for the unemployed, while the Radicals sought a reduction in government spending. This instability was also reflected in the fact that there were six Cabinets between June 1932 and February 1934. The government's inability to deal with the country's economic and political problems saw the emergence of a number of radical groups from across the political spectrum.

GERMANY: THE DEPRESSION

The Depression had a dramatic effect on the German economy and politics. The country's national income dropped 20 percent between 1928 and 1932, while unemployment rose from 1,320,000 in 1929 to 6 million by January 1932. This meant that a staggering 43 percent of the German work force were without jobs (compared to one-quarter of the work force in the U.S.).

In 1919, Adolf Hitler joined the German Workers party (DAP), which he soon took over and renamed the National Socialist German Workers' party (NAZI). In 1920, the party adopted a 25-point program that included treaty revision, anti-Semitism, economic, and other social changes.

They also created a defense cadre of the *Sturm-abteilung* (SA)—"Storm Troopers" or "brown shirts"—which was to help the party seize power.

The Beer Hall Putsch (1923): In the midst of the country's severe economic crisis in 1923, the party, which now had 55,000 members, tried to seize power, first by a march on Berlin, and then, when this seemed impossible, on Munich. The march was stopped by police, and Hitler and his supporters were arrested. Though sentenced to five years imprisonment, he was released after eight months. While incarcerated, he dictated *Mein Kampf* (My Struggle) to Rudolf Hess.

Hitler's failed coup and imprisonment convinced him to seek power through legitimate political channels, which would require transforming the Nazi party. To do this, he reasserted singular control over the movement from 1924 to 1926. Party districts were set up throughout Germany, overseen by *gauleiters* personally appointed by Hitler.

Hindenburg's seven-year presidential term expired in 1932, and he was convinced to run for reelection to stop Hitler from becoming president on the first ballot of March 13. Hitler got only 30 percent of the vote (11.3 million) to Hindenburg's 49.45 percent (18.6 million).

On June 1, Chancellor Bruenig was replaced by Franz von Papen (1879–1969), who formed a government made up of aristocratic conservatives and others that he and Hindenburg hoped would keep Hitler from power.

Later in the year, Papen convinced Hindenburg to appoint Hitler as chancellor and head of a new coalition cabinet with three seats for the Nazis. Hitler dissolved the Reichstag and called for new elections on March 5. Using presidential decree powers, he initiated a violent anti-Communist campaign that included the lifting of certain press and civil freedoms. On February 27, the Reichstag burned, which enabled Hitler to get Hindenburg to issue the "Ordinances for the Protection of the German State and Nation," that removed all civil and press liberties as part of a "revolution" against communism. In the Reichstag elections of March 5, the Nazis only got 43.9 percent of the vote and 288 Reichstag seats but, through an alliance with the Nationalists, got majority control of the legislature.

Once Hitler had full legislative power, he began a policy of *Gleichschaltung* (coordination) to bring all independent organizations and agencies throughout Germany under his control. All political parties were outlawed or forced to dissolve, and on July 14, 1933, the Nazi party became the only legal party in Germany. In addition, non-Aryans and Nazi opponents were removed from the civil service, the court system, and higher education. On May 2, 1933, the government declared strikes illegal, abolished labor unions, and later forced all workers to join the German Labor Front (DAF) under Robert Ley. In 1934 the Reichsrat was abolished and a special People's Court was created to handle cases of treason. Finally, the secret police or Gestapo (*Geheime Staatspolizei*) was created on April 24, 1933, under Hermann Göring to deal with opponents and operate concentration camps. The party had its own security branch, the SD (*Sicherheitsdienst*) under Reinhard Heydrich.

From the inception of the Nazi state in 1933, anti-Semitism was a constant theme and practice in all *Gleichschaltung* and Nazification efforts. Illegal intimidation and harassment of Jews was coupled with rigid enforcement of civil service regulations that forbade employment of non-Aryans. This first wave of anti-Semitic activity culminated with the passage of the Nuremburg Laws on September 15, 1935, that deprived Jews of German citizenship and outlawed sexual or marital relations between Jews and other Germans, thus effectively isolating them from the mainstream of German society.

Hitler's international policies were closely linked to his rebuilding efforts to give him a strong economic and military base for an active, aggressive, independent foreign policy. The Reich simultaneously quit the League of Nations. On January 26, 1934, Germany signed a non-aggression pact with Poland, which ended Germany's traditional anti-Polish foreign policy and broke France's encirclement of Germany via the Little Entente. This was followed by the Saarland's overwhelming decision to return to Germany. The culmination of Hitler's foreign policy moves, though, came with his March 15, 1935, announcement that Germany would no longer be bound by the military restrictions of the Treaty of Versailles, that it had already created an air force (Luftwaffe), and that the Reich would institute a draft to create an army of 500,000 men.

ITALY (1926–1936)

Until Mussolini's accession to power, the pope had considered himself a prisoner in the Vatican. In 1926, Mussolini's government began talks to resolve this issue, which resulted in the Lateran Accords of February 11, 1929. Italy recognized the Vatican as an independent state, with the pope as its head, while the papacy recognized Italian independence. Catholicism was made the official state religion of Italy, and religious teaching was required in all secondary schools.

In an effort to counter the significance of France's Little Entente with Czechoslovakia, Yugoslavia, and Romania, Mussolini concluded the Rome Protocols with Austria and Hungary which created a protective bond of friendship between the three countries.

In response to Hitler's announcement of German rearmament in violation of the Treaty of Versailles on March 16, 1935, France, England, and Italy met at Stresa in northern Italy on April 11–14, and concluded agreements that pledged joint military collaboration if Germany moved against Austria or along the Rhine.

Ethiopia (Abyssinia) became an area of strong Italian interest in the 1880s. The coastal region was slowly brought under Italian control until the Italian defeat at Ethiopian hands at Adowa in 1894. In 1906, the country's autonomy was recognized and in 1923 it joined the League of Nations. Mussolini, who had been preparing for war with Ethiopia since 1932, established a military base at Wal Wal in Ethiopian territory. Beginning in December 1934, a series of minor conflicts took place between the two countries, which gave Mussolini an excuse to plan for the full takeover of the country in the near future.

On October 2, 1935, Italy invaded Ethiopia, while the League of Nations, which had received four appeals from Ethiopia since January about Italian territorial transgressions, finally voted to adopt economic sanctions against Mussolini. Unfortunately, the League failed to stop shipments of oil to Italy and continued to allow it to use the Suez Canal. On May 9, 1936, Italy formally annexed the country and joined it to Somalia and Eritrea, which now became known as Italian East Africa.

SOVIET RUSSIA (1933–1938)

The Second Five Year Plan (1933–1937) was adopted by the Seventeenth Party Congress in early 1934. Its economic and production targets were less severe than the First Plan, and thus, more was achieved. By the end of the Second Plan, Soviet Russia had emerged as a leading world industrial power, though at great cost. It gave up quality for quantity, and created tremendous social and economic discord that ramifies in the nations of the former Soviet Union even today.

In the spring of 1935, the recently renamed and organized secret police, the NKVD, oversaw the beginnings of a new, violent Purge that eradicated 70 percent of the 1934 Central Committee, and a large percentage of the upper military ranks. Stalin sent between 8 and 9 million to camps and prisons, and caused untold deaths before the Purges ended in 1938.

The period from 1929 to 1933 saw the U.S.S.R. retreat inward as the bulk of its energies were put into domestic economic growth. Regardless, Stalin remained sensitive to growing aggression and ideological threats abroad such as the Japanese invasion of Manchuria in 1931 and Hitler's appointment as Chancellor in 1933. As a result, Russia left its cocoon in 1934, joined the League of Nations, and became an advocate of "collective security" while the Comintern adopted Popular Front tactics, allying with other parties against fascism, to strengthen the U.S.S.R.'s international posture. Diplomatically, in addition to League membership, the Soviet Union completed a military pact with France.

INTERNATIONAL DEVELOPMENTS (1918–1935)

Efforts to create an international body to arbitrate international conflicts gained credence with the creation of a Permanent Court of International Justice to handle such matters at the First Hague Conference (1899). But no major efforts towards this goal were initiated until 1915, when pro-League of Nations organizations arose in the United States and Great Britain. Support for such a body grew as the war lengthened, and creation of such an organization became the cornerstone of President Woodrow Wilson's post-war policy, enunciated in his "Fourteen Points" speech before Congress on January 8, 1918.

The Preamble of the League's Covenant defined the League's purposes, which were to work for international friendship, peace, and security. To attain this, its members agreed to avoid war, maintain peaceful relations with other countries, and honor international law and accords.

Headquartered in Geneva, the League came into existence as the result of an Allied resolution on January 25, 1919, and the signing of the Treaty of Versailles on June 28, 1919. The League had the right, according to Article 8 of the League Covenant, to seek ways to reduce arms strength, while Articles 10 through 17 gave it the authority to search for means to stop war. It could recommend ways to stop aggression, and could suggest economic sanctions and other tactics to enforce its decisions, though its military ability to enforce its decisions was vague.

THE LOCARNO PACT (1925)

Signed on October 16, 1925, by England, France, Italy, Germany, and Belgium, the Locarno Pact guaranteed Germany's western boundaries and accepted the Versailles settlement's demilitarized zones. Italy and Great Britain agreed militarily to defend these lines if flagrantly violated.

In the same spirit, Germany signed arbitration dispute accords that mirrored the Geneva Protocol with France, Belgium, Poland, and Czechoslovakia, and required acceptance of League-determined settlements. Since Germany would only agree to arbitration and not finalize its eastern border, France separately signed guarantees with Poland and Czechoslovakia to defend their frontiers.

The Locarno Pact went into force when Germany joined the League on September 10, 1926, acquiring, after some dispute, the U.S.'s permanent seat on the Council. France and Belgium began to withdraw from the Rhineland, though they left a token force there until 1930.

THE PACT OF PARIS (KELLOGG-BRIAND PACT)

The Locarno Pact heralded a new period in European relations known as the "Era of Locarno" that marked the end of post-war conflict and the beginning of a more normal period of diplomatic friendship and cooperation. It reached its peak, with the Franco-American effort in 1928 to seek an international statement to outlaw war. On August 27, 1928, 15 countries, including the U.S., Germany, France, Italy, and Japan, signed this accord with some minor limitations, which renounced war as a means of solving differences and as a tool of national policy. Within five years, 50 other countries signed the agreement.

LEAGUE AND ALLIED RESPONSE TO AGGRESSION

On September 19, 1931, the Japanese Kwantung Army, acting independently of the government in Tokyo, began the gradual conquest of Manchuria after fabricating an incident at Mukden to justify their actions. Ultimately, they created a puppet state, Manchukuo, under the last Chinese emperor, Henry P'u-i. China's League protest resulted in the creation of an investigatory commission under the Earl of Lytton that criticized Japan's actions and recommended a negotiated settlement that would have allowed Japan to retain most of its conquest. Japan responded by resigning from the League on January 24, 1933.

Hitler's announcement on March 15, 1935, of Germany's decisions to rearm and to introduce conscription in violation of the Treaty of Versailles prompted the leaders of England, France, and

Italy to meet in Stresa, Italy (April 11–14). They condemned Germany's actions, underlined their commitment to the Locarno Pact, and re-affirmed the support they collectively gave for Austria's independence in early 1934. Great Britain's decision, however, to separately protect its naval strength vis-à-vis a German buildup in the Anglo-German Naval Treaty of June 18, 1935, effectively compromised the significance of the Stresa Front.

FROM WORLD WAR II TO THE POST-COMMUNIST ERA (1935–1996)

THE COURSE OF EVENTS

Using a Franco-Soviet agreement of the preceding year as an excuse, Hitler, on March 7, 1936, repudiated the Locarno agreements and reoccupied the Rhineland (an area demilitarized by the Versailles Treaty). Neither France (which possessed military superiority at the time) nor Britain was willing to oppose these moves.

The Spanish Civil War (1936–1939) is usually seen as a rehearsal for World War II because of outside intervention. The government of the Spanish Republic (established in 1931) caused resentment among conservatives by its programs, including land reform and anti-clerical legislation aimed at the Catholic church. Following an election victory by a popular front of republican and radical parties, right-wing generals in July began a military insurrection. Francisco Franco, stationed at the time in Spanish Morocco, emerged as the leader of this revolt, which became a devastating civil war lasting nearly three years.

The democracies, including the United States, followed a course of neutrality. Nazi Germany, Italy, and the U.S.S.R. did intervene despite non-intervention agreements negotiated by Britain and France. Spain became a battlefield for fascist and anti-fascist forces with Franco winning by 1939 in what was seen as a serious defeat for anti-fascist forces everywhere.

The Spanish Civil War was a factor in bringing together Mussolini and Hitler in a Rome-Berlin Axis. Already Germany and Japan had signed the Anti-Comintern Pact in 1936. Ostensibly directed against international communism, this was the basis for a diplomatic alliance between those countries, and Italy soon adhered to this agreement, becoming Germany's ally in World War II.

In 1938 Hitler pressured the Austrian chancellor to make concessions and when this did not work, German troops annexed Austria (the *Anschluss*). Again Britain and France took no effective action, and about six million Austrians were added to Germany.

Hitler turned next to Czechoslovakia. Three million persons of German origin lived in the Sudetenland, a borderland between Germany and Czechoslovakia given to Czechoslovakia in order to provide it with a more defensible boundary. In 1938, after a series of demands from Hitler, a four-power conference was held in Munich with Hitler, Mussolini, Chamberlain, and Daladier in attendance, at which Hitler's terms were accepted. Britain and France, despite the French alliance with Czechoslovakia, put pressure on the Czech government to force it to comply with German demands. Hitler signed a treaty agreeing to this settlement as the limit of his ambitions. At the same time the Poles seized control of Teschen, and Hungary (with the support of Italy and Germany and over the protests of the British and French) seized 7,500 square miles of Slovakia. By the concessions forced on her at Munich, Czechoslovakia lost its frontier defenses and was totally unprotected against any further German encroachments.

In March 1939, Hitler annexed most of the Czech state while Hungary conquered Ruthenia. At almost the same time Germany annexed Memel from Lithuania. In April, Mussolini, taking advantage of distractions created by Germany, landed an army in Albania and seized that Balkan state in a campaign lasting about one week.

Disillusioned by these continued aggressions, Britain and France made military preparations. Guarantees were given to Poland, Romania, and Greece. The two democracies also opened negotiations with the U.S.S.R. for an arrangement to obtain that country's aid against further German aggression. Hitler, with Poland next on his timetable, also began a cautious rapprochement with the U.S.S.R. On August 23, 1939, the world was stunned by the announcement of a Nazi-Soviet Treaty of Friendship. A secret protocol provided that in the event of a "territorial rearrangement" in Eastern Europe the two powers would divide Poland. In addition, Russia would have the Baltic states (Latvia, Lithuania, and Estonia) and Bessarabia (lost to Romania in 1918) as part of her sphere. Stalin agreed to remain neutral in any German war with Britain or France. World War II began with the German invasion of Poland on September 1, 1939, followed by British and French declarations of war against Germany on September 3.

WORLD WAR II

The German attack (known as the "blitzkrieg" or "lightning war") overwhelmed the poorly equipped Polish army, which could not resist German tanks and airplanes.

On September 17 the Russian armies attacked the Poles from the east. They met the Germans two days later. Stalin's share of Poland extended approximately to the Curzon Line. Russia also made demands on Finland. Later, in June 1940, while Germany was attacking France, Stalin occupied the Baltic states of Latvia, Lithuania, and Estonia.

The only military action of any consequence during the winter of 1939–1940 resulted from Russian demands made on Finland, especially for territory adjacent to Leningrad (then only 20 miles from the border). Finnish refusal led to a Russian attack in November 1939. The Finns resisted with considerable vigor, receiving some supplies from Sweden, Britain, and France, but eventually by March they had to give in to the superior Russian forces. Finland was forced to cede the Karelian Isthmus, Viipuri, and a naval base at Hangoe.

On May 10, the main German offensive was launched against France. Belgium and the Netherlands were simultaneously attacked. According to plan, British and French forces advanced to aid the Belgians. At this point the Germans departed from the World War I strategy by launching a surprise armored attack through Luxembourg and the Ardennes Forest (considered by the British and French to be impassable for tanks). The Dutch could offer no real resistance and collapsed in four days after the May 13 German bombing of Rotterdam.

Paris fell to the Germans in mid-June. The Pétain government quickly made peace with Hitler, who added to French humiliation by dictating the terms of the armistice to the French at Compiègne in the same railroad car used by Marshal Foch when he gave terms to the Germans at the end of the First World War. The complete collapse of France quickly came as a tremendous shock to the British and Americans.

Mussolini declared war on both France and Britain on June 10. Hitler's forces remained in occupation of the northern part of France, including Paris. He allowed the French to keep their fleet and overseas territories probably in the hope of making them reliable allies. Pétain and his chief minister Pierre Laval established their capital at Vichy and followed a policy of collaboration with their former enemies. A few Frenchmen, however, joined the Free French movement started in London by the then relatively unknown General Charles de Gaulle (1890–1970).

FROM THE FRENCH DEFEAT TO THE INVASION OF RUSSIA

By mid-summer 1940, Germany, together with its Italian ally, dominated most of Western and Central Europe. Germany began with no real plans for a long war, but continued resistance by the British made necessary the belated mobilization of German resources. Hitler's policy included exploiting areas Germany conquered. Collaborators were used to establish governments subservient to German policy. Germany began the policy of forcibly transporting large numbers of conquered Europeans to work in German war industries. Jews especially were forced into slave labor for the German war effort, and increasingly large numbers were rounded up and sent to concentration camps, where they were systematically murdered as the Nazis carried out Hitler's "final solution" of genocide against European Jewry. Although much was known about this during the war, the full horror of these atrocities was not revealed until Allied troops entered Germany in 1945.

With the fall of France, Britain remained the only power of consequence at war with the Axis. Hitler began preparations for invading Britain (Operation "Sea Lion"). Air control over the Channel was vital if an invasion force was to be transported safely to the English Coast. The German Air Force (Luftwaffe) under Herman Göring began its air offensive against the British in the summer of 1940. The Germans concentrated first on British air defenses, then on ports and shipping, and finally in early September they began the attack on London. The Battle of Britain was eventually a defeat for the Germans, who were unable to gain decisive superiority over the British, although they inflicted great damage on both British air defenses and major cities such as London. Despite the damage and loss of life, British morale remained high and necessary war production continued. German losses determined that bombing alone could not defeat Britain. "Operation Sea Lion" was postponed October 12 and never seriously taken up again, although the British did not know this and had to continue for some time to give priority to their coastal and air defenses.

During the winter of 1940–1941, having given up "Operation Sea Lion," Hitler began to shift his forces to the east for an invasion of Russia ("Operation Barbarossa"). Russian expansion towards the Balkans dismayed the Germans, who hoped for more influence there themselves.

The German invasion of Russia began June 22, 1941. The invasion force of three million included Finnish, Romanian, Hungarian, and Italian contingents along with the Germans and advanced on a broad front of about 2,000 miles. They surrounded the city of Leningrad (although they never managed to actually capture it) and came within about 25 miles of Moscow. In November the enemy actually entered the suburbs, but then the long supply lines, early winter, and Russian resistance (strong despite heavy losses) brought the invasion to a halt. During the winter a Russian counterattack pushed the Germans back from Moscow and saved the capital.

With the coming of the Great Depression and severe economic difficulties, Japanese militarists gained more and more influence over the civilian government. On September 18, 1931, the Japanese occupied all of Manchuria. On July 7, 1937, a full-scale Sino-Japanese war began with a clash between Japanese and Chinese at the Marco Polo Bridge in Peking (now Beijing). An indication of ultimate Japanese aims came on November 3, 1938, when Prince Fumimaro Konoye's (1891–1946) government issued a statement on "A New Order in East Asia." This statement envisaged the integration of Japan, Manchuria (now the puppet state of Manchukuo), and China into one "Greater East Asia Co-Prosperity Sphere" under Japanese leadership. In July 1940, the Konoye government was re-formed with General Hideki Tojo (1884–1948) (Japan's principal leader in World War I) as minister of war.

All of these events led to worsening relations between Japan and the two states in a position to oppose her expansion—the Soviet Union and the United States. Despite border clashes with the Russians, Japan avoided any conflict with that state, and Stalin wanted no war with Japan after he became fully occupied with the German invasion. In the few weeks after attacking the U.S. at Pearl Harbor, Japanese forces were able to occupy strategically important islands (including the Philippines and Dutch East Indies) and territory on the Asian mainland (Malaya, with the British naval base at Singapore, and all of Burma to the border of India).

The Japanese attack brought the United States not only into war in the Pacific, but resulted in German and Italian declarations of war which meant the total involvement of the United States in World War II.

American involvement in the war was ultimately decisive, for it meant that the greatest industrial power of that time was now arrayed against the Axis powers. The United States became, as President Roosevelt put it, "the arsenal of democracy." American aid was crucial to the immense effort of the Soviet Union. Lend-Lease aid was extended to Russia. By 1943 supplies and equipment were reaching Russia in considerable quantities.

The German forces launched a second offensive in the summer of 1942. This attack concentrated on the southern part of the front, aiming at the Caucasus and vital oil fields around the Caspian Sea. At Stalingrad on the Volga River the Germans were stopped. With the onset of winter, Hitler refused to allow the strategic retreat urged by his generals. As a result, the Russian forces crossed the river north and south of the city and surrounded 22 German divisions. On January 31,

1943, following the failure of relief efforts, the German commander Friedrich Paulus (1890–1957) surrendered the remnants of his army. From then on the Russians were almost always on the offensive.

After entering the war in 1940, the Italians invaded British-held Egypt. In December 1940, the British General Archibald Wavell (1883–1950) launched a surprise attack. The Italian forces were driven back about 500 miles and 130,000 were captured. Then Hitler intervened, sending General Erwin Rommel with a small German force (the Afrika Korps) to reinforce the Italians. Rommel took command and launched a counter-offensive which put his forces on the border of Egypt. By mid-1942 Rommel had driven to El Alamein, only 70 miles from Alexandria.

A change in the British high command now placed General Harold Alexander (1891–1969) in charge of Middle Eastern forces, with General Bernard Montgomery (1887–1976) in immediate command of the British Eighth Army. Montgomery attacked at El Alamein, breaking Rommel's lines and starting a British advance which was not stopped until the armies reached the border of Tunisia.

Meanwhile, the British and American leaders decided that they could launch a second offensive in North Africa ("Operation Torch") which would clear the enemy from the entire coast and make the Mediterranean once again safe for Allied shipping.

The landings resulted in little conflict with the French, and the French forces soon joined the war against the Axis. It was only a matter of time before German troops were forced into northern Tunisia and surrendered. American forces, unused to combat, suffered some reverses at the Battle of the Kasserine Pass, but gained valuable experience. The final victory came in May 1943, about the same time as the Russian victory at Stalingrad.

Relatively safe shipping routes across the North Atlantic to Britain were essential to the survival of Britain and absolutely necessary if a force was to be assembled to invade France and strike at Germany proper. New types of aircraft, small aircraft carriers, more numerous and better-equipped escort vessels, new radar and sonar (for underwater detection), extremely efficient radio direction finding, decipherment of German signals plus the building of more ships turned the balance against the Germans despite their development of improved submarines by early 1943, and the Atlantic became increasingly dangerous for German submarines.

Success in these three campaigns—Stalingrad, North Africa, and the Battle of the Atlantic—gave new hope to the Allied cause and made certain that victory was attainable. With the beginning of an Allied offensive in late 1942 in the Solomon Islands against the Japanese, 1943 became the turning point of the war.

At their conference at Casablanca in January 1943, Roosevelt and Churchill developed a detailed strategy for the further conduct of the war. Sicily was to be invaded, then Italy proper. Rome was not captured by the Allied forces until June 4, 1944. With a new Italian government now supporting the Allied cause, Italian resistance movements in northern Italy became a major force in helping to liberate that area from the Germans.

At the Teheran Conference, held in November 1943 and attended by all three major Allied leaders, the final decision reached by Roosevelt and Churchill some six months earlier to invade France in May 1944 was communicated to the Russians. Stalin promised to open a simultaneous Russian offensive.

The Normandy invasion (Operation "Overlord") was the largest amphibious operation in history. The landings actually took place beginning June 6, 1944. The first day, 130,000 men were successfully landed. Strong German resistance hemmed in the Allied forces for about a month. Then the Allies, now numbering about 1,000,000, managed a spectacular breakthrough. By the end of 1944, all of France had been seized. A second invasion force landed on the Mediterranean coast in August, freed southern France, and linked up with Eisenhower's forces. By the end of 1944, the Allied armies stood on the borders of Germany ready to invade from both east and west.

Stalin's armies crossed into Poland July 23, 1944, and three days later the Russian dictator officially recognized a group of Polish Communists (the so-called Lublin Committee) as the government of Poland. As the Russian armies drew near the eastern suburbs of Warsaw, the London Poles, a resistance group, launched an attack. Stalin's forces waited outside the city while the Germans brought in reinforcements and slowly wiped out the Polish underground army in several weeks of heavy street fighting. The offensive then resumed and the city was liberated by the Red Army, but the influence of the London Poles was now virtually nil. Needless to say, this incident aroused considerable suspicion concerning Stalin's motives and led both Churchill and Roosevelt to begin to think through the political implications of their alliance with Stalin.

By late summer of 1944, the German position in the Balkans began to collapse. The Red Army crossed the border into Romania, leading King Michael (1921–) to seize the opportunity to take his country out of its alliance with Germany and to open the way to the advancing Russians. German troops were forced to make a hasty retreat. At this point Bulgaria changed sides. The German forces in Greece withdrew in October.

From October 9–18, Winston Churchill visited Moscow to try to work out a political arrangement regarding the Balkans and Eastern Europe. Dealing from a position of weakness, he simply wrote out some figures on a sheet of paper: Russia to have the preponderance of influence in countries like Bulgaria and Romania, Britain to have the major say in Greece, and a fifty-fifty division in Yugoslavia and Hungary. Stalin agreed. The Americans refused to have anything to do with this "spheres of influence" arrangement.

In Greece, Stalin maintained a hands-off policy when the British used military force to suppress the Communist resistance movement and install a regent for the exiled government.

In early spring of 1945 the Allied armies crossed the Rhine. As the Americans and British and other Allied forces advanced into Germany, the Russians attacked from the east. While the Russian armies were fighting their way into Berlin, Hitler committed suicide in the ruins of the bunker where he had spent the last days of the war. Power was handed over to a government headed by Admiral Karl Dönitz (1891–1980). On May 7, General Alfred Jodl (1890–1946), acting for the German government, made the final unconditional surrender at General Eisenhower's headquarters near Reims.

The future treatment of Germany, and Europe in general, was determined by decisions of the "Big Three" (Churchill, Stalin, and Roosevelt).

The first major conference convened at Teheran on November 28, 1943, and lasted until December 1. Here the two Western allies told Stalin of the May 1944 date for the planned invasion of Normandy. In turn, Stalin confirmed a pledge made earlier that Russia would enter the war against Japan after the war with Germany was concluded. The Yalta Conference was the second attended personally by Stalin, Churchill, and Roosevelt. It lasted from the 4th to the 11th of February 1945. A plan to divide Germany into zones of occupation, which had been devised in 1943 by a committee under British Deputy Prime Minister Clement Attlee, was formally accepted with the addition of a fourth zone taken from the British and American zones for the French to occupy. Berlin, which lay within the Russian Zone, was divided into four zones of occupation also.

The third summit meeting of the Big Three took place at Potsdam outside Berlin after the end of the European war but while the Pacific war was still going on. The conference began July 17, 1945, with Stalin, Churchill, and the new American President Harry Truman attending. A Potsdam Declaration, aimed at Japan, called for immediate Japanese surrender and hinted at the consequences that would ensue if it were not forthcoming. While at the conference, American leaders received the news of the successful testing of the first atomic bomb in the New Mexico desert, but the Japanese were given no clear warning that such a destructive weapon might be used against them.

On August 6, 1945, the bomb was dropped by a single plane on Hiroshima and an entire city disappeared, with the instantaneous loss of 70,000 lives. In time many other persons died from radiation poisoning and other effects. Since no surrender was received, a second bomb was dropped on Nagasaki, obliterating that city. Even the most fanatical of the Japanese leaders saw what was happening and surrender came quickly. The only departure from unconditional surrender was to allow the Japanese to retain their emperor (Hirohito, 1901–1989), but only with the proviso that he would be subject in every respect to the orders of the occupation commander. The formal surrender took place September 2, 1945, in Tokyo Bay on the deck of the battleship *Missouri*, and the occupation of Japan began under the immediate control of the American commander, General Douglas MacArthur (1880–1964).

EUROPE AFTER WORLD WAR II: 1945 TO 1953

Anglo-American ideas about what the post-war world should be like were expressed by Roosevelt and Churchill at their meeting off the coast of Newfoundland in August 1941. The Atlantic Charter was a general statement of goals: restoration of the sovereignty and self-government of nations conquered by Hitler, free access to world trade and resources, cooperation to improve living standards and economic security, and a peace that would ensure freedom from fear and want and stop the use of force and aggression as instruments of national policy.

At the Casablanca Conference, the policy of requiring unconditional surrender by the Axis powers was announced. This ensured that at the end of the war, all responsibility for government of the defeated nations would fall on the victors, and they would have a free hand in rebuilding government in those countries. No real planning was done in detail before the time arrived to meet this responsibility. It was done for the most part as the need arose.

At Teheran, the Big Three did discuss in a general way the occupation and demilitarization of Germany. They also laid the foundation for a post-war organization—the United Nations Organization—which like the earlier League of Nations was supposed to help regulate international relations and keep the peace and ensure friendly cooperation between the nations of the world.

At Potsdam, agreement was reached to sign peace treaties as soon as possible with former German allies. A Council of Foreign Ministers was established to draft the treaties. Several meetings were held in 1946 and 1947 and treaties were signed with Italy, Romania, Hungary, Bulgaria, and Finland. These states paid reparations and agreed to some territorial readjustments as a price for peace. No agreement could be reached on Japan or Germany. In 1951, the Western powers led by the U.S. concluded a treaty with Japan without Russian participation. The latter made their own treaty in 1956. A final meeting of the Council of Foreign Ministers broke up in 1947 over Germany, and no peace treaty was ever signed with that country. The division of Germany for purposes of occupation and military government became permanent, with the three Western zones joining and eventually becoming the Federal Republic of Germany and the Russian zone becoming the German Democratic Republic.

Arrangements for the United Nations were confirmed at the Yalta Conference: the large powers would predominate in a Security Council, where they would have permanent seats together with several other powers elected from time to time from among the other members of the U.N. Consent of all the permanent members was necessary for any action to be taken by the Security Council (thus, giving the large powers a veto). The General Assembly was to include all members.

EASTERN EUROPE: 1945–1953

Much of European Russia had been devastated, and about 25 million people made homeless. In March 1946 a fourth five-year plan was adopted by the Supreme Soviet intended to increase industrial output to a level 50 percent higher than before the war. A bad harvest and food shortage in 1946 had been relieved by a good harvest in 1947, and in December 1947, the government announced the end of food rationing. At the same time a drastic currency devaluation was put through, which brought immediate hardship to many people but strengthened the Soviet economy in the long run. As a result of these and other forceful and energetic measures, the Soviet Union was able within a few years to make good most of the wartime damage and to surpass pre-war levels of production.

The fate of Eastern Europe (including Poland, Hungary, Romania, Bulgaria, Czechoslovakia, and the Russian zone of Germany) from 1945 on was determined by the presence of Russian armies in that area.

Communization of Eastern Europe and the establishment of regimes in the satellite areas of the Soviet Union occurred in stages over a three-year period following the end of the war. The timetable of events varied in each country.

As relations broke down between the four occupying powers, the Soviet authorities gradually created a Communist state in their zone. On October 7, 1948, a German Democratic Republic was established. In June 1950, an agreement with Poland granted formal recognition of the Oder-Neisse Line as the boundary between the two states. Economic progress was unsatisfactory for most of the population, and on June 16–17, 1953, riots occurred in East Berlin which were suppressed by Soviet forces using tanks. In East Germany, a program of economic reform was announced which eventually brought some improvement.

In Yugoslavia, Marshal Tito (1892–1980) and his Communist partisan movement emerged from the war in a strong position because of their effective campaign against the German occupation. Tito was able to establish a Communist government in 1945 despite considerable pressure from Stalin, and pursue a course independent of the Soviet Union unique among the countries of Eastern Europe.

WESTERN EUROPE: 1945–1953

The monarchy which had governed Italy since the time of unification in the mid-nineteenth century was now discarded in favor of a republic. King Victor Emmanuel III (1869–1947), compromised by his association with Mussolini, resigned in favor of his son, but a referendum in June 1946 established a republic. In simultaneous elections for a constituent assembly, three parties predominated: the Social Democrats, the Communists, and the Christian Democrats.

In the last two years of the war, France recovered sufficiently under the leadership of General Charles de Gaulle to begin playing a significant military and political role once again. In July 1944, the United States recognized de Gaulle's Committee of National Liberation as the de facto government of areas liberated from the German occupation.

In foreign affairs, France occupied Germany. In addition, the Fourth Republic was faced with two major problems abroad when it attempted to assert its authority over Indochina and Algeria. The Indochina situation resulted in a long and costly war against nationalists and Communists under Ho Chi Minh (1890–1969). French involvement ended with the Geneva Accords of 1954 and French withdrawal. The Algerian struggle reached a crisis in 1958 resulting in General de Gaulle's return to power and the creation of a new Fifth Republic.

In May 1945, when Germany surrendered unconditionally, the country lay in ruins. About three-quarters of city houses had been gutted by air raids, industry was in a shambles, and the country was divided into zones of occupation ruled by foreign military governors. Economic chaos was the rule, currency was virtually worthless, food was in short supply, and the black market flourished for those who could afford to buy in it. By the Potsdam agreements, Germany lost about one-quarter of its pre-war territory. In addition, some 12 million people of German origin driven from their homes in countries like Poland and Czechoslovakia had to be fed, housed, and clothed along with the indigenous population.

Demilitarization, denazification, and democratization were the initial goals of the occupation forces in Germany. All four wartime allies agreed on the imperative to try leading Nazis for a variety of war crimes and "crimes against humanity." An International Military Tribunal was established at Nuremburg to try 22 major war criminals, and lesser courts tried many others. Most of the defendants were executed, although a few like Rudolf Hess were given life imprisonment.

As relations between the three Western powers and the Soviets gradually broke down in Germany, East and West became separate states. In the West, the British and American zones were fused into one in 1946, with the French joining in 1948. Political parties were gradually re-established.

In February 1948, a charter granted further powers of government to the Germans in the American and British zones. Later that year, the Russians and East Germans, in an effort to force the Western powers out of their zones in Berlin, began a blockade of the city which was located within the Russian zone. The response was an allied airlift to supply the city, and eventually, after some months, the blockade was called off.

In 1951 a Conservative majority was returned in Great Britain, and Winston Churchill, who had been defeated in 1945, became prime minister again. The new regime immediately reversed the nationalization of iron and steel. Other measures survived, however, especially the universal health care program which proved to be one of the most popular parts of the Labour achievement. In April 1955, Churchill resigned for reasons of age and health and turned over the prime minister's office to Anthony Eden (1897–1977).

THE MARSHALL PLAN

European recovery from the effects of the war was slow for the first two or three years after 1945. The European Recovery Program (Marshall Plan, named after the American secretary of state and World War II army chief of staff) began in 1948 and showed substantial results in all the Western European countries that took part. The most remarkable gains were in West Germany. The Plan aimed to strengthen Western Europe's resistance to communism.

NATO

The United States joined eleven other states in the Atlantic region in a mutual defense pact called the North Atlantic Treaty Organization (NATO) in 1949. NATO was created to counterbalance the Soviet presence in Central and Eastern Europe.

BRITISH OVERSEAS WITHDRAWAL

Following World War II, there was a considerable migration of Jews who had survived the Nazi Holocaust to Palestine to join Jews who had settled there earlier. Conflicts broke out with the Arabs. The British occupying forces tried to suppress the violence and to negotiate a settlement between the factions. In 1948, after negotiations failed, the British, feeling they could no longer support the cost of occupation, announced their withdrawal. Zionist leaders then proclaimed the independent state of Israel and took up arms to fight the armies of Egypt, Syria, and other Arab states which invaded the Jewish-held area. The new Israeli state quickly proved its technological and military superiority by defeating the invaders.

The Jews of Israel created a modern parliamentary state on the European model with an economy and technology superior to their Arab neighbors. The new state was thought by many Arabs to be simply another manifestation of European imperialism made worse by religious antagonisms.

In 1967, Israel defeated Egypt, Syria, and Jordan in a six-day war, and the Israelis occupied additional territory including the Jordanian sector of the city of Jerusalem. An additional million Arabs came under Israeli rule as a result of this campaign.

Although defeated, the Arabs refused to sign any treaty or to come to terms with Israel. Palestinian refugees living in camps in states bordering Israel created grave problems. A Palestine Liberation Organization (PLO) was formed to fight for the establishment of an Arab Palestinian state on territory taken from Israel on the west bank of the Jordan River. The PLO resorted to terrorist tactics against both Israel and other states in support of their cause.

In October 1973, the Egyptians and Syrians launched an attack on Israel known as the Yom Kippur War. With some difficulty the attacks were repulsed. A settlement was mediated by American Secretary of State Henry Kissinger.

The government under King Farouk I (1920–1965) did little to alleviate the overriding problem of poverty after the war. In 1952, a group of army officers, including Gamal Abdel Nasser (1918–1970) and Anwar Sadat (1918–1981), plotted against the government, and on July 23 the king was overthrown. Colonel Nasser became premier in April 1954. A treaty with Britain later that year resulted in the withdrawal of all British troops from the Canal Zone.

India under Jawaharlal Nehru (1889–1964) and the Congress Party became a parliamentary democracy. The country made economic progress, but gains were largely negated by a population increase to 600 million from 350 million.

THE FRENCH IN INDOCHINA AND ALGERIA

Following World War II, the French returned to Indochina and attempted to restore their rule there. The opposition nationalist movement was led by the veteran Communist Ho Chi Minh. War broke out between the nationalists and the French forces. In 1954 their army was surrounded at

Dien Bien Phu and forced to surrender. This military disaster prompted a change of government in France.

This new government under Premier Pierre Mendès-France (1907–1982) negotiated French withdrawal at a conference held at Geneva, Switzerland in 1954. Cambodia and Laos became independent and Vietnam was partitioned at the 17th parallel. The North, with its capital at Hanoi, became a Communist state under Ho Chi Minh. The South remained non-Communist. Under the Geneva Accords, elections were to be held in the South to determine the fate of that area. However, the United States chose to intervene and support the regime of Ngo Dinh Diem (1901–1963), and elections were never held. Eventually a second Vietnamese war resulted, with the United States playing the role earlier played by France.

In a referendum, on January 8, 1961, the French people approved of eventual Algerian self-determination. In July 1962 French rule ended in Algeria. There was a mass exodus of Europeans from Algeria, but most Frenchmen were grateful to de Gaulle for ending the long Algerian conflict.

THE DUTCH AND INDONESIA

During World War II, the Japanese conquered the Dutch East Indies. At the end of the war, they recognized the independence of the area as Indonesia. When the Dutch attempted to return, four years of bloody fighting ensued against the nationalist forces of Achmed Sukarno (1901–1970). In 1949, the Dutch recognized Indonesian independence. In 1954, the Indonesians dissolved all ties with the Netherlands.

THE COLD WAR AFTER THE DEATH OF STALIN

Following Stalin's death in 1953, Russian leaders appeared more willing than Stalin to be conciliatory and to consider peaceful coexistence.

In the U.S. the atmosphere also changed with the election of President Dwight Eisenhower, and conciliatory gestures were not always automatically considered appeasement of the Communists. In 1955 a summit conference of Eisenhower, the British and French leaders, and Khrushchev (1894–1971) met at Geneva in an atmosphere more cordial than any since World War II. The "spirit of Geneva" did not last long, however.

After his return to power in France in 1958, General de Gaulle endeavored to make France a leader in European affairs with himself as spokesman for a Europe that he hoped would be a counter to the "dual hegemony" of the U.S. and U.S.S.R. His policies at times were anti-British or anti-American. Despite his prestige as the last great wartime leader, he did not have great success.

A NEW ERA BEGINS

Joseph Stalin died in March 1953. Eventually a little-known party functionary, Nikita Khrushchev, became Communist Party General Secretary in 1954. Khrushchev's policy of relaxing the regime of terror and oppression of the Stalin years became known as "The Thaw," after the title of a novel by Ilya Ehrenburg (1891–1967).

Change occurred in foreign affairs also. Khrushchev visited Belgrade and re-established relations with Tito, admitting that there was more than one road to socialism. He also visited the United States, met with President Eisenhower, and toured the country. Later, relations became more tense after the U-2 spy plane incident.

Following the loss of face sustained by Russia as a result of the Cuban Missile Crisis and the failure of Khrushchev's domestic agricultural policies, he was forced out of the party leadership and lived in retirement in Moscow until his death in 1971.

After Khrushchev's ouster, the leadership in the Central Committee divided power, making Leonid Brezhnev (1906–1982) party secretary and Aleksei Kosygin chairman of the council of ministers, or premier.

Stalin's successors rehabilitated many of Stalin's victims. They also permitted somewhat greater freedom in literary and artistic matters and even allowed some political criticism. Controls were maintained, however, and sometimes were tightened. Anti-Semitism was also still present, and Soviet Jews were long denied permission to emigrate to Israel.

Brezhnev occupied the top position of power until his death in 1982. He was briefly succeeded by Yuri Andropov (1914–1984) (a former secret police chief) and Konstantin Chenenko (1911–1985), then by Mikhail Gorbachev, who carried out a further relaxation of the internal regime. Gorbachev pushed disarmament and détente in foreign relations, and attempted a wide range of internal reforms known as *perestroika* ("restructuring"). Gorbachev resigned in 1991. Boris Yeltsin assumed control over the collapsing Soviet Union, which would later become known as the Commonwealth of Independent States, with Yeltsin as president.

Economic difficulties associated with a transition to a free economy, the mishandled repression of the Chechnya independence movement, and Yeltsin's dissolution of Russia's parliament in 1993 gave ammunition to his opponents. In the 1996 elections, Yeltsin retained office as president, but the poor state of his health, despite successful heart bypass surgery in the fall of 1996, eventually made him step down and yield leadership to Vladimir Putin in late 1999.

CHANGE IN EASTERN EUROPE

In the 1980s, the trade union movement known as Solidarity and its leader, Lech Walesa, emerged as a political force, organizing mass protests in 1980–1981 and maintaining almost continuous pressure on the government headed by General Wojciech Jaruzelski. Despite government efforts to maintain strong central control and suppress the opposition, the ruling Communists were forced to recognize the opposition and make concessions. In June 1989, after power had passed to the Polish Parliament, a national election gave Solidarity an overwhelming majority, and Walesa assumed the presidency. By 1993–94, economic problems resulted in a Communist majority and a change of administration, but there was no return to the old Communist dictatorship.

CHANGE IN WESTERN EUROPE

In March 1957, inspired chiefly by Belgian Foreign Minister Paul-Henri Spaak, two treaties were signed in Rome creating a European Atomic Energy Commission (Euratom) and a European Economic Community (the Common Market)—which eventually absorbed Euratom. The EEC was to be a customs union creating a free market area with a common external tariff for member nations. Toward the outside world, the EEC acted as a single bargaining agent for its members in commercial transactions, and it reached a number of agreements with other European and Third World states.

In 1973, the original six were joined by three new members: Britain, Ireland, and Denmark. The name was changed to "European Community." In 1979, there were three more applicants: Spain, Portugal, and Greece. These latter states were less well off and created problems of cheap labor, agricultural products, etc., which delayed their acceptance as members until 1986. With the acceptance of the Maastricht treaty in 1993, the group's name became the "European Union."

Relations with Northern Ireland proved a burden to successive British governments. The 1922 settlement had left Northern Ireland as a self-governing part of the United Kingdom. Of 1.5 million inhabitants, one-third were Roman Catholic and two-thirds were Protestant. Catholics claimed they were discriminated against and pressed for annexation by the Republic of Ireland. Activity by the Irish Republican Army brought retaliation by Protestant extremists. From 1969 on, there was considerable violence, causing the British to bring in troops to maintain order.

Under Prime Minister Margaret Thatcher in the 1980s, the British economy improved somewhat. London regained some of its former power as a financial center. In recent years, an influx of people from former colonies in Asia, Africa, and the West Indies has caused some racial tensions.

Prime Minister Thatcher was a partisan of free enterprise. She fought inflation with austerity and let economic problems spur British employers and unions to change for greater efficiency. She received a boost in popularity when Britain won a brief war with Argentina over the Falkland Islands. She stressed close ties with the Republican administration of Ronald Reagan in the U.S. A Conservative victory in the 1987 elections made Thatcher the longest-serving prime minister in modern British history.

In 1990, having lost the support of Conservatives in Parliament, Thatcher resigned and was replaced by Chancellor of the Exchequer John Major. Under Major's leadership, Conservatives had to deal with slow economic growth, unemployment, and racial tensions caused by resentment over the influx of immigrants from other parts of the Commonwealth. And there remains the seemingly intractable religious strife in Northern Ireland, with its Protestant-Catholic animosities. Tony Blair, prime minister from 1997 to 2007, made Northern Ireland peace a priority. In 2007, the hard-line Roman Catholic Sinn Fein and Protestant Democratic Unionist Party reached a historic power-sharing agreement. Blair also succeeded in achieving closer relations with the European Union, but in 2016, Britain reversed course with a vote to leave the EU— a vote that continued to stir turmoil through 2017.

France under de Gaulle saw a new constitution drafted and approved establishing the Fifth Republic with a much strengthened executive in the form of a president with power to dissolve the legislature and call for elections, to submit important questions to popular referendum, and if necessary to assume emergency powers. De Gaulle used all these powers in his 11 years as president.

In domestic politics, de Gaulle strengthened the power of the president by often using the referendum and bypassing the Assembly. De Gaulle was re-elected in 1965, but people became restless with what amounted to a republican monarch. Labor became restive over inflation and housing while students objected to expenditures on nuclear forces rather than education. In May 1968, student grievances over conditions in the universities caused hundreds of thousands to revolt. They were soon joined by some 10 million workers, who paralyzed the economy. De Gaulle survived by promising educational reform and wage increases. New elections were held in June 1968, and de Gaulle was returned to power. Promised reforms were begun, but in April 1969, he resigned and died about a year later.

De Gaulle's immediate successors were Georges Pompidou (1969–1974) and Valéry Giscard d'Estaing (1974–1981). Both provided France with firm leadership, and continued to follow an independent foreign policy.

In 1981 François Mitterand succeeded Giscard d'Estaing. He inherited a troubled economy. During his first year Mitterand tried to revitalize economic growth, granted wage hikes, reduced the work week, expanded paid vacations, and nationalized 11 large private companies and banks. The aim was to stimulate the economy by expanding worker purchasing power and confiscating the profits of large corporations for public investment. Loans were made abroad to finance this program. When results were poor, these foreign investors were reluctant to grant more credit. Mitterand then reversed his policy and began to cut taxes and social expenditures. By 1984, this had brought down inflation but increased unemployment.

Mitterand lost his Socialist majority in Parliament in 1986, but regained it in 1988. In 1995, an ailing Mitterand indicated he would retire at the end of his term. He died in January 1996. Out of the election of April 1995 emerged a fractured right-of-center bloc that came to coalesce around Jacques Chirac, the mayor of Paris and former two-time prime minister. Following a second-round runoff, Chirac won 52 percent of the vote. Facing a far-right challenger, Jean-Marie Le Pen, in 2002, Chirac won a decisive victory for re-election.

In Germany in November 1966, the Christian Democrats formed a so-called "great coalition" with the Social Democrats under Willy Brandt. Kurt Georg Kiesinger (1904–1988) became chancellor, and Brandt the Socialist took over as foreign minister. Brandt announced his intention to work step by step for better relations with East Germany, but found that in a coalition of two very dissimilar parties he could make no substantial progress.

Problems with the economy and the environment brought an end to Kiesinger's chancellorship and the rule of the Socialists in 1982. An organization called the Greens, which was a loosely organized coalition of environmentalists alienated from society, detracted from Socialist power. In 1982, the German voters turned to the more conservative Christian Democrats again, and Helmut Kohl became chancellor. Kohl served until 1998, when he was replaced by Social Democrat Gerhard Schroeder.

In Italy, the Christian Democrats, who were closely allied with the Roman Catholic Church, dominated the national scene. Their organization, though plagued by corruption, did provide some unity to Italian politics by supplying the prime ministers for numerous coalitions.

Italy advanced economically. Natural gas and some oil was discovered in the north and the Po valley area especially benefited. Unfortunately, business efficiency found no parallel in the government or civil service. Italy suffered from terrorism, kidnappings, and assassinations by extreme radical groups such as the Red Brigades. These agitators hoped to create conditions favorable to the overthrow of the democratic constitution. The most notorious terrorist act was the assassination in 1978 of Aldo Moro (1916–1978), a respected Christian Democratic leader.

In 1983, Bettino Craxi (Socialist) became prime minister at the head of an uneasy coalition that lasted four years—the longest single government in postwar Italian history. By the 1990s Italian industry and its economy had advanced to a point where Italy was a leading center in high-tech industry, fashion, design, and banking, but instability continued to mark Italian politics. Corruption within a system dominated by the Christian Democrats resulted in criminal trials in the 1990s that sent a number of high government officials to prison. In 1993 the electoral system for the Senate was changed from proportional representation to one that gives power to the majority vote-getting party. The 1994 elections for Parliament brought to power the charismatic, conservative Silvio Berlusconi and his *Forzia Italia* ("Let's go, Italy") movement.

In Portugal, Europe's longest right-wing dictatorship came to an end in September 1968, when a stroke incapacitated Antonio Salazar, who died two years later. A former collaborator, Marcelo Caetano (1906–1980), became prime minister, and an era of change began. Censorship was relaxed and some freedom was given to political parties.

In April 1974, the Caetano regime was overthrown and a "junta of national salvation" took over, headed by General Spinola, who later retired and went into exile. Portugal went through a succession of governments. Its African colonies of Mozambique and Angola were finally granted independence in 1975. Portugal joined the Common Market in 1986.

Spain's Francisco Franco, who had been ruler of a fascist regime since the end of the Civil War in 1939, held on until he was close to 70. He then designated the Bourbon prince, Juan Carlos, to be his successor. In 1975, Franco relinquished power and died three weeks later. Juan Carlos proved an able leader and took the country from dictatorship to constitutional monarchy. Basque and Catalan separatist movements, which had caused trouble for so long, were temporarily appeased by the granting of limited local autonomy. Spain also entered the European Community in 1986.

Under the Maastricht Treaties of 1991, all members of the EC began measured steps toward an economic and political union that would ultimately have its own common currency. In 1996, the 12 member nations of the European Union accounted for one-fifth of world trade.

REVIEW QUESTIONS

1. Renaissance Humanism was a threat to the Church because it

   (A) espoused atheism.
   (B) denounced scholasticism.
   (C) denounced neo-Platonism.
   (D) emphasized a return to the original sources of Christianity.

2. *Defense of the Seven Sacraments* was a tract

   (A) written by Thomas More in which the Church is attacked because of its sacramental theology.
   (B) written by Zwingli which argued that the Eucharist was a symbolic reenactment of the Last Supper.
   (C) in which Luther called upon the German nobility to accept responsibility for cleansing Christianity of the abuses which had developed within the Church.
   (D) written by Henry VIII in which the Roman Catholic Church's position on sacramental theology was supported.

3. Erasmus of Rotterdam was the author of

   (A) *The Praise of Folly.*
   (B) *The Birth of Venus.*
   (C) *Utopia.*
   (D) *The Prince.*

4. The Henrician reaffirmation of Catholic theology was made in the

   (A) Ten Articles of Faith.
   (B) Six Articles of Faith.
   (C) Forty-two Articles of Faith.
   (D) Act of Supremacy.

5. The Peace of Augsburg

   (A) recognized that Lutheranism was the true interpretation of Christianity.
   (B) recognized the principle that the religion of the leader would determine the religion of the people.
   (C) denounced the Papacy and Charles V.
   (D) resulted in the recognition of Lutheranism, Calvinism, and Catholicism.

6. The Catholic Counter-Reformation included all of the following EXCEPT

   (A) the *Index of Prohibited Books.*
   (B) the Council of Trent.
   (C) a more assertive Papacy.
   (D) a willingness to negotiate non-doctrinal issues with reformers.

7. Where did the Saint Bartholomew's Day Massacre occur?

   (A) France
   (B) England
   (C) Spain
   (D) The Netherlands

8. The Price Revolution of the 16th century was caused by

   (A) the establishment of monopolies.
   (B) the importation of silver and gold into the European economy.
   (C) a shortage of labor.
   (D) the wars of religion caused by the Reformation.

9. The Peace of Westphalia (1648)

    (A) transferred Louisiana from France to Britain.
    (B) recognized the independence of the Netherlands.
    (C) recognized the unity of the German Empire.
    (D) was a triumph of the Hapsburg polity to unity.

10. Sir Isaac Newton's intellectual synthesis was advanced in

    (A) *Principia.*
    (B) *Discourse on Method.*
    (C) *Novum Organum.*
    (D) *Three Laws of Planetary Motion.*

11. Richelieu served as "Prime Minister" to

    (A) Louis XII.
    (B) Henry IV.
    (C) Louis XIV.
    (D) Louis XIII.

12. In the Edict of Fontainebleau, Louis XIV

    (A) abrogated the Edict of Nantes.
    (B) abrogated the Edict of Potsdam.
    (C) announced his divorce from Catherine de Médici.
    (D) denounced Cardinal Mazarin.

13. In order to seize the Russian throne, Peter the Great had to overthrow his sister

    (A) Theodora.
    (B) Natalia.
    (C) Sophia.
    (D) Catherine.

14. Peter the Great's principal foreign policy achievement was

    (A) the acquisition of ports on the Black Sea.
    (B) the acquisition of ports on the Baltic Sea.
    (C) the Russian gains in the three partitions of Poland.
    (D) the defensive alliance with England.

Unemployment
(Numbers in thousands & percentage of appropriate workforce)

	Germany		Great Britain	
1930	3,076	15.3	1,917	14.6
1932	5,575	30.1	2,745	22.5
1934	2,718	14.9	2,159	17.7
1936	2,151	11.6	1,755	14.3
1938	429	2.1	1,191	13.3

15. The chart above indicates

    (A) that Germany and Great Britain recovered from the Depression at about the same level and rate.
    (B) that Hitler's Germany reduced unemployment at a remarkable rate during the period from 1936 and 1938.
    (C) that Britain was complacent about its double-digit unemployment during the 1930s.
    (D) that the German economic system was superior to that of Great Britain.

16. A moderate proposal which called on France to adopt a political system similar to Great Britain was an element espoused by Montesquieu in

    (A) *The Social Contract.*
    (B) *The Spirit of the Laws.*
    (C) *The Encyclopédie.*
    (D) *The Declaration of the Rights of Man and the Citizen.*

17. Which of the following chronological sequences on the French Revolution is correct?

    (A) Directory, Consulate, Legislative Assembly
    (B) Legislative Assembly, Convention, Directory
    (C) Convention, Consulate, Directory
    (D) National Assembly, Convention, Directory

18. Thomas Hobbes' political philosophy can be most clearly identified with the thought of which of the following?

    (A) Rousseau
    (B) Voltaire
    (C) Quesnay
    (D) Montesquieu

19. Who was the most important enlightened political ruler of the 18th century?

    (A) Catherine the Great
    (B) Louis XV
    (C) Maria Theresa
    (D) Frederick the Great

20. The reaction to the Peterloo Massacre was characteristic of the conservative policies advanced by the British government under

    (A) George Canning.
    (B) Robert Peel.
    (C) Lord Melbourne.
    (D) Lord Liverpool.

21. The Factory Act of 1833

    (A) established the five-day work week in Britain.
    (B) eliminated child labor in the mining of coal and iron.
    (C) required employers to provide comprehensive medical coverage for all employees.
    (D) alleviated some of the abuses of child labor in the textile industry.

22. The Anglo-French Entente (also known as the Entente Cordiale)

    (A) was a defensive treaty directed at containing German expansion in Europe.
    (B) was a defensive treaty directed at containing German expansion overseas.
    (C) resolved Anglo-French colonial disputes in Egypt and Morocco.
    (D) was a 19th century agreement which ended the diplomatic isolation of Britain.

23. Who was the most prominent British advocate for the abolition of slavery during the early 19th century?

    (A) William Pitt the Younger
    (B) the Duke of Wellington
    (C) William Wilberforce
    (D) William Wordsworth

24. English Utilitarianism was identified with the phrase

    (A) all power to the people.
    (B) from each according to his labor, to each according to his need.
    (C) universal reason.
    (D) the greatest good for the greatest number.

25. An economic philosophy identified with "bullionism" and the need to maintain a favorable balance of trade was

    (A) Utopian Socialism.
    (B) Marxism.
    (C) Capitalism.
    (D) Mercantilism.

26. Which British Prime Minister was closely associated with the Irish Home Rule bill?

    (A) Benjamin Disraeli
    (B) William Gladstone
    (C) Lord Salisbury
    (D) Joseph Chamberlain

27. The Balfour Declaration (1917)

   (A) denounced the use of chemicals by the Germans on the Western Front.
   (B) was a pledge of British support for the future.
   (C) was a mediation effort to resolve the Anglo-Irish crisis.
   (D) was an attempt to persuade the United States to abandon its neutrality.

28. The Boulanger Crisis

   (A) was a left-wing attempt engineered by Leon Gambetta to overthrow the Third French Republic.
   (B) involved a financial scandal associated with raising funds to build the Panama Canal.
   (C) was caused by a right-wing scheme to overthrow the Third French Republic and install General Georges Boulanger as the political leader.
   (D) broke when the Dreyfus affair became known to the French press.

29. All of the following were plots against Elizabeth I EXCEPT

   (A) the Babington Plot.
   (B) the Throckmorton Plot.
   (C) the Ridolfi Plot.
   (D) the Wisbech Stirs.

30. The map below indicates the partition of Africa in what year?

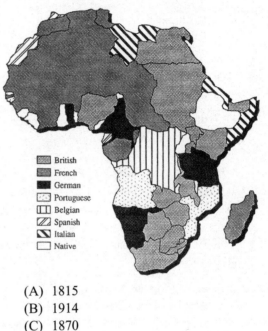

British
French
German
Portuguese
Belgian
Spanish
Italian
Native

   (A) 1815
   (B) 1914
   (C) 1870
   (D) 1960

31. The French essayist Montaigne was representative of which intellectual movement?

   (A) Enlightenment
   (B) Baroque
   (C) Positivism
   (D) Utopian Socialism

32. The Hundred Days was

   (A) the label given to the reactionary period which followed the Manchester riots in Britain.
   (B) an unsuccessful attempt by Napoleon to restore himself as a credible European leader.
   (C) the worst phase of the Reign of Terror.
   (D) a period which witnessed British defeats in Africa and the Low Countries.

33. Jeremy Bentham, James Mill, and John Stuart Mill were

    (A) Positivists.
    (B) Romantic Idealists.
    (C) Utilitarians.
    (D) Utopian Socialists.

34. The Russian blockade of Berlin in 1948–49 was a reaction to

    (A) the unification of the British, French, and American zones into West Germany.
    (B) the Truman Doctrine.
    (C) the Marshall Plan.
    (D) the formation of NATO.

35. The Heptarchy consisted of the following Anglo-Saxon states:

    (A) Essex, Wessex, Sussex, Kent, East Anglia, Mercia, and Northumbria
    (B) West Cornwall, Essex, Wessex, Sussex, East Anglia, Mercia, and Northumbria
    (C) Wales, West Anglia, Kent, Essex, Wessex, Sussex, and Mercia
    (D) The Danelaw, Cumbria, Essex, Wessex, Sussex, Kent, and East Anglia

36. All of the following were contributors in the Realist-Nominalist Controversy EXCEPT

    (A) Peter Abelard.
    (B) Peter Lombard.
    (C) Albertus Magnus.
    (D) Hildebrand.

37. The reasons for the formation of the Delian League included

    I. the Greek victory over Xerxes.
    II. the Athenian intent to develop a defensive and offensive alliance against Persia.
    III. Athenian strategy to control all of the eastern Mediterranean.

    IV. an imminent Spartan threat to Athens.
    V. more than twenty years of crisis caused by Persian aggression.

    (A) I and II only
    (B) I, II, and III only
    (C) II and III only
    (D) I, II, and V only

38. "Peasant" or "public" uprisings broke out in all of the following places on the dates listed EXCEPT

    (A) France in 1358.
    (B) Sicily in 1282.
    (C) Flanders in 1302.
    (D) Holy Roman Empire in 1190.

39. During the late 2nd century BCE, Roman political life was dominated by the

    (A) First Triumvirate.
    (B) prevailing political parties; *Populares, Optimates*, and *Equites*.
    (C) Gracchi.
    (D) end of the Punic Wars.

40. After the death of Alexander, which of the following Hellenistic kingdoms emerged?

    I. Antigonid Macedonia
    II. Seleucid Asia
    III. Ptolemaic Egypt
    IV. Bactria
    V. India

    (A) I and II only
    (B) I, II, and III only
    (C) I, II, III, and IV only
    (D) I, III, and IV only

ANSWER KEY

1.	(D)	11.	(D)	21.	(D)	31.	(B)
2.	(D)	12.	(A)	22.	(C)	32.	(B)
3.	(A)	13.	(C)	23.	(C)	33.	(C)
4.	(B)	14.	(B)	24.	(D)	34.	(A)
5.	(B)	15.	(B)	25.	(D)	35.	(A)
6.	(D)	16.	(B)	26.	(B)	36.	(D)
7.	(A)	17.	(B)	27.	(B)	37.	(D)
8.	(B)	18.	(B)	28.	(C)	38.	(D)
9.	(B)	19.	(D)	29.	(D)	39.	(B)
10.	(A)	20.	(D)	30.	(B)	40.	(B)

DETAILED EXPLANATIONS

1. **(D)** Renaissance Humanism was a threat to the Church because it (D) emphasized a return to the original sources of Christianity—the Bible and the writings of the Fathers of Church. In that light, the humanists tended to ignore or denounce the proceedings of Church councils and pontiffs during the Middle Ages. While many Renaissance humanists denounced scholasticism, there was no inherent opposition to it and many retained support of the late Medieval philosophy. Renaissance humanism did not espouse atheism nor did it advance an amoral philosophy; it tended to advance a neo-Platonism through the writings of such individuals as Pico Della Mirandola and Marsiglio.

2. **(D)** The *Defense of the Seven Sacraments* was a tract (D) written by Henry VIII in which the Roman Catholic Church's position on sacramental theology was supported. This 1521 publication repudiated Luther's views on the sacraments which he advanced in pamphlets during the preceding year. While some earlier authorities have asserted that the real author of the tract was Thomas More (A), contemporary scholarship has affirmed that, while More no doubt provided assistance, authorship should be attributed to Henry VIII. Zwingli (B) did maintain that the Eucharist was a symbolic reenactment of the Last Supper but he did not write this tract. Obviously, Luther (C), to whom it was directed, was not the author.

3. **(A)** Erasmus of Rotterdam was the author of (A) *The Praise of Folly* which was a criticism of the ambitions of the clergy. *The Birth of Venus* (B) was not a literary work. Thomas More was the author of *Utopia* (C); Niccolo Machiavelli wrote (D) *The Prince*.

4. **(B)** The Henrican reaffirmation of the Catholic Theology was made in the (B) Six Articles of Faith of 1539. In response to mounting criticism and the vague (A) Ten Articles of Faith (1536) and the dissolution of the monasteries, Henry VIII retreated from the movement toward Protestantism. The (D) Act of Supremacy was passed by the Reformation Parliament to decree and enforce Henry

VIII's authority over the Church in England. The Forty-two Articles of Faith (C) was a statement of Protestant doctrines developed by Thomas Cranmer during the early 1550s.

5. **(B)**   The Peace of Augsburg (1555) (B) recognized the principle that the religion of the leader would determine the religion of the people; it was a major victory for Lutheranism and a defeat of the Hapsburg aspirations to effectively control the Holy Roman Empire. Lutheranism (A) was not recognized as the true interpretation of Christianity. Calvinism (D) was not recognized until the Peace of Westphalia in 1648; (C) Charles V and the Papacy were negotiators in formulating the Peace of Augsburg.

6. **(D)**   The Catholic Counter-Reformation did not include (D) a willingness to negotiate non-doctrinal issues with reformers; indeed, the Catholic Church considered all confrontational issues to be doctrinal. The Council of Trent (B) was convened in three sessions from 1545 to 1564 and reaffirmed traditional Catholic doctrines; the papacy (C) became more assertive as can be seen in the issuing of the *Index of Prohibited Books* (A) in 1558–59.

7. **(A)**   The St. Bartholomew's Day Massacre occurred in 1572 in (A) France; it was the work of Queen Catherine De Medici and involved the execution of thousands of French Huguenots during the subsequent months. Obviously, this event did not transpire in (B) England, (C) Spain, or (D) the Netherlands.

8. **(B)**   The Price Revolution of the 16th century was caused by (B) the importation of silver and gold into the European economy; the influx of specie from Latin America resulted in eliminating the scarcity of money—the result was a general fourfold increase in prices. The establishment of monopolies (A) was an important element in 17th century mercantilism. While there were occasional labor shortages (C) and the wars of religion (D) did not disrupt economic activities, these developments did not have any substantive impact on the price revolution.

9. **(B)**   The Peace of Westphalia (1648) (B) recognized the independence of the Netherlands and Switzerland. Louisiana (A) was not transferred to Britain, and the Hapsburg plan (D) and (C) for a unified central Europe was destroyed.

10. **(A)**   Sir Isaac Newton's intellectual synthesis was advanced in (A) *Principia* in 1687; he established scientism as a credible alternative to preceding intellectual approaches and methods. *Discourse on Method* (B) was written by René Descartes in 1637; *Novum Organum* (C) was a work by Francis Bacon which addressed the issue of empiricism; Kepler developed the Three Laws of Planetary Motion (D).

11. **(D)**   Richelieu served as "Prime Minister" to (D) Louis XIII. For over two decades during the turbulence of the Thirty Years' War and the La Rochelle crisis with the Huguenots, Cardinal Richelieu administered France for Louis XIII. Henry IV (B) was Louis XIII's father; Louis XIV (C) was his son. Louis XII (A) was an earlier French monarch.

12. **(A)**   In the Edict of Fontainebleau (1685), Louis XIV (A) abrogated the Edict of Nantes of 1598 in which Henry IV had to extend some religious liberties to French Protestants. Fontainebleau directed that all Frenchmen would conform to Catholicism. The Edict of Potsdam (1686) (B)

was issued by Elector Frederick William of Brandenburg-Prussia; it invited French Protestants to migrate to Brandenburg. The Fontainebleau decree was not related to (C) Catherine de Médici or (D) Cardinal Mazarin.

13. **(C)**   In order to seize the Russian throne, Peter the Great had to overthrow (1689) his sister (C) Sophia. His mother, Natalia (B), served as regent until 1694 when Peter took over the government. Catherine (D) was a Russian leader in the 18th century. (A) Theodora was not a Romanov ruler.

14. **(B)**   Peter the Great's principal foreign policy achievement was (B) the acquisition of ports on the Baltic Sea. His efforts to acquire ports on the Black Sea (A) were not realized; later Catherine the Great would expand in this area at the expense of the Ottoman Turks. The partitions of Poland (C) occurred after Peter's death; Russia did not enter into any alliance with England (D) during this period.

15. **(B)**   This chart indicates (B) that Hitler's Germany reduced unemployment at a remarkable rate during the period from 1936 to 1938; the fascist economic controls facilitated this development. (A), (C), and (D) are incorrect; the German economy was not "superior" to Britain's nor was Britain content with excessive unemployment—while there is much to criticize about the manner in which the Labour and Conservative parties handled economic recovery, one must remember that free economies are naturally more difficult to direct than state controlled economic systems.

16. **(B)**   A moderate proposal which called on France to adopt a political system similar to that of Great Britain was an element espoused by Montesquieu in (B) *The Spirit of the Laws*. *The Social Contract* (A) was written by Jean-Jacques Rousseau; *The Encyclopédie* (C) was by Denis Diderot; *The Declaration of the Rights of Man and the Citizen* (D) was produced by the National Assembly in August 1789.

17. **(B)**   The correct chronological sequence is (B) Legislative Assembly (1791–92), Convention (1792–95), and Directory (1795–99). The National Assembly existed from 1789 to 1791; the Consulate from 1799 to 1804; and the Empire from 1804 to 1814.

18. **(B)**   Thomas Hobbes' political philosophy can be most clearly identified with the thought of (B) Voltaire. Voltaire maintained that Enlightened Despotism would be the best form of government for France; this position concurs with the Hobbesian view that people need to be governed, not government by the people; (C) Quesnay's program was similar though not as directly related. (A) Rousseau and (D) Montesquieu entertained political theories which were more revolutionary in the context of sovereign power and the exercise of that power.

19. **(D)**   The most prominent enlightened political ruler of the 18th century was (D) Frederick the Great of Prussia. He had a genuine interest in enlightened government and introduced a wide range of reforms. Catherine the Great (A) of Russia considered herself enlightened but her barbarism did not support that claim. Louis XV (B) and Maria Theresa (C) were opposed to the thought of the enlightenment.

20. **(D)**   The reaction to the Peterloo Massacre was characteristic of the conservative policies advanced by the British government under (D) Lord Liverpool. While George Canning (A) and

Robert Peel (B) were involved in the government, they were not very influential at this time. Melbourne (C) became Prime Minister during the 1830s.

21. **(D)** The Factory Act of 1833 (D) alleviated some of the abuses of child labor in the textile industry. The five-day work week (A) did not become a reality until the 20th century; reforms in the use of children in mining and heavy industry (B) were not implemented until later in the 19th century; employers were never required (C) to provide comprehensive medical coverage for all employees.

22. **(C)** The Anglo-French Entente (also known as the Entente Cordiale) (C) resolved Anglo-French colonial disputes in Egypt and Morocco; northeast Africa (Egypt and the Sudan) was recognized as a British sphere of influence, northwest Africa (Morocco and Algeria) was recognized as a French sphere of influence. This arrangement was not (A) directed at German expansion in Europe or (B) overseas; it was signed in 1904 and therefore was not (D) a 19th century agreement.

23. **(C)** The most prominent British advocate for the abolition of slavery during the early 19th century was (C) William Wilberforce. While Wordsworth (D) was sympathetic to abolitionism, he was not in the forefront of opposition to slavery. William Pitt the Younger (A) and the Duke of Wellington (B) were preoccupied with the Napoleonic Wars.

24. **(D)** English Utilitarianism was identified with the phrase (D) "the greatest good for the greatest number." Jeremy Bentham, James Mill, and John Stuart Mill were prominent Utilitarians. "All power to the people" (A) and "From each according to his labor, to each according to his need" (B) were elements in Lenin's rhetoric. "Universal reason" (C) is identified with Georg Wilhelm Hegel.

25. **(D)** Mercantilism was an economic philosophy identified with "bullionism" and the need to maintain a favorable balance of trade. Utopian Socialism (A) was an early 19th century philosophy which emphasized the need for a more equitable distribution of wealth; (B) Marxism was a leftist approach to economics and politics. (C) Capitalism was the developing condition in which mercantilism operated.

26. **(B)** The British Prime Minister who was associated closely with Irish Home Rule was (B) William Gladstone. Gladstone maintained through his four ministries that one of his principal tasks was "to pacify Ireland." Benjamin Disraeli (A), Lord Salisbury (C), and Joseph Chamberlain (D) were not particularly interested or sympathetic to the Irish.

27. **(B)** The Balfour Declaration (1917) (B) was a pledge of British support for the future establishment of a Jewish state. It was not related to (A) the German use of chemicals, (C) the Anglo-Irish crisis stemming from the Easter Rebellion, or (D) American neutrality.

28. **(C)** The Boulanger Crisis (C) was caused by a right-wing scheme to overthrow the Third French Republic and install General Georges Boulanger as the political leader; it was supported by monarchists and other rightist enemies of the republic. It was not (A) a left-wing scheme, nor was it related to the (B) Panama Canal or (D) the Dreyfus Affair.

29. **(D)** While the (A) Babington Plot, (B) the Throckmorton Plot, and (C) the Ridolfi Plot were attempts to overthrow Elizabeth I, the Wisbech Stirs of the late 1590s was a controversy among Catholics over control of the outlawed English Catholic Church.

30. **(B)**   The map indicates the partition of Africa in (B) 1914 after most of the European powers had participated in establishing colonial empires.

31. **(B)**   The French essayist Montaigne was representative of an intellectual movement known as (B) Baroque which was an intellectual quest for a new synthesis; it was caused by the chaos of the Reformation/Counter-Reformation era. The Enlightenment (A) developed in the 18th century and constituted an elaboration on the new scientific synthesis which emerged during the 17th century. (C) Positivism and (D) Utopian Socialism were 19th century intellectual movements.

32. **(B)**   The Hundred Days (1815) was (B) an unsuccessful attempt by Napoleon to restore himself as a credible European leader. The Hundred Days concluded in June 1815 at the Battle of Waterloo when Wellington's army defeated Napoleon. Obviously, the Hundred Days did not relate to (A) the reactionary period in Britain following the Manchester riots, (C) the Reign of Terror, or (D) British defeats in Africa and the Low Countries.

33. **(C)**   Jeremy Bentham, James Mill, and John Stuart Mill were (C) Utilitarians who argued the case "the greatest good for the greatest number." Auguste Comte established (A) Positivism; Fichte and Hegel were German Romantic Idealists (B); Robert Owen and Charles Fourier were Utopian Socialists (D).

34. **(A)**   The Russian blockade of Berlin in 1948–49 was a reaction to (A) the unification of the British, French, and American zones into West Germany. While the (B) Truman Doctrine was directed at preventing communist victories in Greece and Turkey, and the Marshall Plan (C) was designed to assist in accelerating the economic recovery of Europe, they were not the direct causes of the blockade. NATO (D) was formed after the blockade began.

35. **(A)**   During the 6th century, the Heptarchy of Anglo-Saxon England included Essex, Wessex, Sussex, Kent, East Anglia, Mercia, and Northumbria. By the end of the 6th century, Kent emerged as the primary power in Britain. West Cornwall (B), Wales (C), the Danelaw, and Cumbria (D) were not organized political entities during the 6th century and so were not part of the Heptarchy.

36. **(D)**   Hildebrand (D) was a medieval church reformer who became pope. Peter Abelard (A) (*Sic at Non*), Peter Lombard (B) (*Four Books of Sentences*) and Albertus Magnus (C) were all significant contributors to the Realist-Nominalist Controversy. While this controversy was initiated over Plato's Doctrine of Ideas, it was transformed into a discussion of whether truth obtained through reason was reconcilable with truth obtained through revelation.

37. **(D)**   The Delian League was established in 477 BCE after more than two decades of war (V) with Persian armies led by Darius and Xerxes (I). Under Athenian leadership, the Delian League was intended to provide a defensive and offensive alliance directed against Persia. Not until later was the Delian League interpreted as an Athenian attempt to dominate the Greek, not Mediterranean, world (III) for its own gain. The Spartan threat to Athens (IV) did not materialize until the early years of the Peloponnesian War in the late 430s.

38. **(D)**   In 1190, the Holy Roman Empire (D) was preoccupied with the Third Crusade and did not experience any peasant uprisings. A popular uprising known as the Jacquerie broke out in France in 1358 (A). The "Sicilian Vespers" took place in Sicily in 1282 (B) when the people rebelled

against French rule, and the peasants and laborers in Flanders in 1302 (C) followed the Sicilian example and expelled French rulers from Flanders.

39. **(B)** During the late 2nd century BCE, Roman political life was dominated by the prevailing political parties: Populares, the so-called "people's party"; Optimates, the "best men"; and the Equites, rich knights (B). The First Triumvirate (A) did not appear until the next century. The Gracchi (C), Tiberius and Gaius Gracchus, were significant public figures but did not hold substantive power. The Punic Wars (D) concluded in 146 BCE; they did not dominate Roman political life.

40. **(B)** After Alexander the Great's death in 323 BCE, his empire was divided into three major units: Antigonid Macedonia (I), with a monarchy limited by an armed population; Seleucid Asia (II), with a monarchy restricted by autonomous cities; and Ptolemaic Egypt (III), with an unrestricted monarchy. As the Seleucid Empire later disintegrated, Bactria (IV) emerged as a buffer against the barbarians of the East. Most of India (V) was not included in Alexander's empire, although he did penetrate northwest India during his campaigns.

■ UNITED STATES HISTORY

AMERICAN HISTORY: THE COLONIAL PERIOD (1500–1763)

THE AGE OF EXPLORATION

The Treaty of Tordesillas (1494) drew a line dividing the land in the New World between Spain and Portugal. Lands east of the line were Portuguese. As a result, Brazil eventually became a Portuguese colony, while Spain maintained claims to the rest of the Americas.

To conquer the Americas, the Spanish monarchs used their powerful army, led by independent Spanish adventurers known as conquistadores. The European diseases they unwittingly carried with them devastated the local Native American populations, who had no immunities against such diseases.

Spain administered its new holdings as an autocratic, rigidly controlled empire in which everything was to benefit the parent country. The Spaniards developed a system of large manors or estates (encomiendas), with Indian slaves ruthlessly managed for the benefit of the conquistadores. The encomienda system was later replaced by the similar but somewhat milder hacienda system. As the Indian population died from overwork and European diseases, Spaniards began importing African slaves to supply their labor needs.

ENGLISH AND FRENCH BEGINNINGS

In 1497, the Italian John Cabot (Giovanni Caboto, ca. 1450–1499), sailing under the sponsorship of the king of England in search of a Northwest Passage (a water route to the Orient through or around the North American continent), became the first European since the Vikings more than four centuries earlier to reach the mainland of North America, which he claimed for England. Beginning in 1534, Jacques Cartier (1491–1557), authorized by the king of France, mounted three expeditions to the area of the St. Lawrence River, which he believed might be the hoped for Northwest Passage. He explored up the river as far as the site of Montreal.

When the English finally began colonization, commercial capitalism in England had advanced to the point that the English efforts were supported by private rather than government funds, allowing English colonists to enjoy greater freedom from government interference.

THE BEGINNINGS OF COLONIZATION

Two groups of merchants gained charters from James I, Queen Elizabeth's successor. One group of merchants was based in London and received a charter to North America between what are now the Hudson and the Cape Fear rivers. The other was based in Plymouth and was granted the right to colonize in North America from the Potomac to the northern border of present-day Maine. They were called the Virginia Company of London and the Virginia Company of Plymouth, respectively. They were joint-stock companies that raised their capital by the sale of shares of stock.

The Virginia Company of London settled Jamestown in 1607. It became the first permanent English settlement in North America. During the early years of Jamestown, the majority of the settlers died of starvation, various diseases, or hostile actions by Native Americans. The colony's survival remained in doubt for a number of years.

Impressed by the potential profits from tobacco growing, King James I was determined to have Virginia for himself. In 1624, he revoked the London Company's charter and made Virginia a royal colony. This pattern was followed throughout colonial history; both company colonies and proprietary colonies tended eventually to become royal colonies.

The French opened a lucrative trade in fur with the Native Americans. In 1608, Samuel de Champlain established a trading post in Quebec, from which the rest of what became New France eventually spread. French exploration and settlement spread through the Great Lakes region and the valleys of the Mississippi and Ohio rivers. French settlements in the Midwest were generally forts and trading posts serving the fur trade.

In 1609, Holland sent an Englishman named Henry Hudson (d. 1611) to search for a Northwest Passage. In this endeavor, Hudson discovered the river that bears his name. Arrangements were made to trade with the Iroquois for furs. In 1624, Dutch trading outposts were established on Manhattan Island (New Amsterdam) and at the site of present-day Albany (Fort Orange).

Many Englishmen came from England for religious reasons. For the most part, these fell into two groups, Puritans and Separatists. Though similar in many respects to the Puritans, the Separatists believed the Church of England was beyond saving and so felt they must separate from it.

Led by William Bradford (1590–1657), a group of Separatists departed in 1620, having obtained from the London Company a charter to settle just south of the Hudson River. Driven by storms, their ship, the *Mayflower*, made landfall at Cape Cod in Massachusetts. This, however, put them outside the jurisdiction of any established government; and so before going ashore they drew up and signed the Mayflower Compact, establishing a foundation for orderly government based on the consent of the governed. After a number of years of hard work, they were able to buy out the investors who had originally financed their voyage, and thus gain greater autonomy.

The Puritans were far more numerous than the Separatists. Charles I determined in 1629 to persecute the Puritans aggressively and to rule without the Puritan-dominated Parliament. In 1629, they chartered a joint-stock company called the Massachusetts Bay Company. The charter neglected to specify where the company's headquarters should be located. Taking advantage of this unusual omission, the Puritans determined to make their headquarters in the colony itself, 3,000 miles from meddlesome royal officials.

Puritans saw their colony not as a place to do whatever might strike one's fancy, but as a place to serve God and build His kingdom. Dissidents would only be tolerated insofar as they did not interfere with the colony's mission.

One such dissident was Roger Williams (ca. 1603–1683). When his activities became disruptive he was asked to leave the colony. He fled to the wilderness around Narragansett Bay, bought land from the Indians, and founded the settlement of Providence (1636).

Another dissident was Anne Hutchinson (1591–1643), who openly taught things contrary to Puritan doctrine. She was banished from the colony. She also migrated to the area around Narragansett Bay and with her followers founded Portsmouth (1638).

In 1663, Charles II, having recently been restored to the throne moved to reward eight of the noblemen who had helped him regain the crown by granting them a charter for all the lands lying south of Virginia and north of Spanish Florida. The new colony was called Carolina, after the king.

In 1664, Charles gave his brother James, Duke of York, title to all the Dutch lands in America, provided James conquered them first. New Amsterdam fell almost without a shot and became New York.

THE COLONIAL WORLD

New England enjoyed a much more stable and well-ordered society than did the Chesapeake colonies. Puritans placed great importance on the family, which in their society was highly patriarchal. Puritans also placed great importance on the ability to read, since they believed everyone should be able to read the Bible. As a result, New England was ahead of the other colonies educationally and enjoyed extremely widespread literacy. Since New England's climate and soil were unsuited to large-scale farming, the region developed a prosperous economy based on small farming, home industry, fishing, and especially trade and a large shipbuilding industry. Boston became a major international port.

On the bottom rung of Southern society were the black slaves. During the first half of the 17th century, blacks in the Chesapeake made up only a small percentage of the population, and were treated more or less as indentured servants. Between 1640 and 1670 this gradually changed, and blacks came to be seen and treated as life-long chattel slaves whose status would be inherited by their children. By 1750, they composed 30 to 40 percent of the Chesapeake population.

While North Carolina tended to follow Virginia in its economic and social development (although with fewer great planters and more small farmers), South Carolina developed a society even more dominated by large plantations and chattel slavery.

Beginning around 1650, British authorities began to take more interest in regulating American trade for the benefit of the mother country. A key idea that underlay this policy was the concept of mercantilism. Each nation's goal was to export more than it imported (i.e., to have a "favorable balance of trade"). To achieve their goals, mercantilists believed economic activity should be regulated by the government. Colonies could fit into England's mercantilist scheme by providing staple crops, such as rice, tobacco, sugar, and indigo, and raw materials, such as timber, that England would otherwise have been forced to import from other countries. Parliament passed a series of Navigation Acts (1651, 1660, 1663, and 1673) to help accomplish these goals.

Pennsylvania was founded as a refuge for Quakers. One of a number of radical religious sects that had sprung up about the time of the English Civil War, the Quakers held many controversial beliefs. They believed all persons had an "inner light" which allowed them to commune directly with God, and therefore they placed little importance on the Bible. They were also pacifists and declined to show customary deference to those who were considered to be their social superiors.

Delaware, though at first part of Pennsylvania, was granted a separate legislature by Penn, but until the American Revolution, Pennsylvania's proprietary governors also functioned as governors of Delaware.

THE EIGHTEENTH CENTURY

America's population continued to grow rapidly, both from natural increases due to prosperity and a healthy environment and from large-scale immigration, not only of English but also of other groups such as Scots-Irish and Germans.

It was decided to found a colony as a buffer between South Carolina and Spanish-held Florida. In 1732, a group of British philanthropists, led by General James Oglethorpe (1696–1785), obtained a charter for such a colony, which was named Georgia.

England and France continued on a collision course, as France determined to take complete control of the Ohio Valley and western Pennsylvania. British authorities ordered colonial governors to resist this. George Washington (1732–1799), a young major of the Virginia militia, was sent to western Pennsylvania but was forced by superior numbers to fall back on his hastily built Fort Necessity and then to surrender.

While Washington skirmished with the French, delegates of seven colonies met in Albany, New York, to discuss common plans for defense. Delegate Benjamin Franklin proposed a plan for an intercolonial government. While the other colonies showed no support for the idea, it was an important precedent for the concept of uniting in the face of a common enemy.

Between 1756 and 1763 Britain and France fought the Seven Years' War (also known as the French and Indian War). By the Treaty of Paris of 1763, Britain gained all of Canada and all of what is now the United States east of the Mississippi River. France lost all of its North American holdings.

THE AMERICAN REVOLUTION (1763–1787)

THE COMING OF THE AMERICAN REVOLUTION

In 1763, George Grenville (1712–1770) became prime minister and set out to solve some of the empire's more pressing problems. Chief among these was the large national debt incurred in the recent war.

In 1764, Grenville pushed through Parliament the Sugar Act (also known as the Revenue Act), which aimed at raising revenue by taxing goods imported by the Americans.

The Stamp Act (1765) imposed a direct tax on Americans for the first time. It required Americans to purchase revenue stamps on everything from newspapers to legal documents, and would have created an impossible drain on hard currency in the colonies. Americans reacted first with restrained and respectful petitions and pamphlets in which they pointed out that "taxation without representation is tyranny." From there, resistance progressed to stronger protests that eventually became violent.

In October 1765, delegates from nine colonies met as the Stamp Act Congress, and passed moderate resolutions against the act, asserting that Americans could not be taxed without the consent of their representatives. The Stamp Act Congress showed that representatives of the colonies could work together, and gave political leaders in the various colonies a chance to become acquainted with each other.

Colonial merchants' boycott of British goods spread throughout the colonies and had a powerful effect on British merchants and manufacturers, who began clamoring for the act's repeal.

Meanwhile, the fickle King George III had dismissed Grenville over an unrelated disagreement and replaced him with a cabinet headed by Charles Lord Rockingham (1730–1782). In March 1766 Parliament repealed the Stamp Act. At the same time, however, it passed the Declaratory Act, which claimed the power to tax or make laws for the Americans "in all cases whatsoever."

The Rockingham ministry was replaced with a cabinet dominated by Chancellor of the Exchequer Charles Townshend (1725–1767). In 1766, Parliament passed his program of taxes on items imported into the colonies. These taxes came to be known as the Townshend duties.

American reaction was at first slow, but the sending of troops, aroused them to resistance. Nonimportation was again instituted, and soon British merchants were calling on Parliament to repeal the acts. In March 1770, Parliament, under the new prime minister, Frederick Lord North (1737–1792), repealed all of the taxes except that on tea, which was retained to prove Parliament had the right to tax the colonies if it so desired.

A relative peace was brought to an end by the Tea Act of 1773. In desperate financial condition—partially because the Americans were buying smuggled Dutch tea rather than the taxed British product—the British East India Company sought and obtained from Parliament concessions that allowed it to ship tea directly to the colonies rather than only by way of Britain. The result would be that East

India Company tea, even with the tax, would be cheaper than smuggled Dutch tea. The colonists would thus, it was hoped, buy the tea, tax and all. The East India Company would be saved, and the Americans would be tacitly accepting Parliament's right to tax them.

The Americans, however, proved resistant to this approach; rather than seem to admit Parliament's right to tax, they vigorously resisted the cheaper tea. Various methods, including tar and feathers, were used to prevent the collection of the tax on tea. In most ports, Americans did not allow the tea to be landed.

In Boston, however, pro-British Governor Thomas Hutchinson (1711–1780) forced a confrontation by ordering Royal Navy vessels to prevent the tea ships from leaving the harbor. After 20 days, this would, by law, result in the cargoes being sold at auction and the tax paid. The night before the time was to expire, December 16, 1773, Bostonians thinly disguised as Native Americans boarded the ships and threw the tea into the harbor.

The British responded with four acts collectively titled the Coercive Acts. First, the Boston Port Act closed the port of Boston to all trade until local citizens would agree to pay for the lost tea (they would not). Secondly, the Massachusetts Government Act greatly increased the power of Massachusetts's royal governor at the expense of the legislature. Thirdly, the Administration of Justice Act provided that royal officials accused of crimes in Massachusetts could be tried elsewhere, where chances of acquittal might be greater. Finally, a strengthened Quartering Act allowed the new governor, General Thomas Gage (1721–1787), to quarter his troops anywhere, including unoccupied private homes.

THE WAR FOR INDEPENDENCE

The British government paid little attention to the First Continental Congress, having decided to teach the Americans a military lesson. More troops were sent to Massachusetts, which was officially declared to be in a state of rebellion. Orders were sent to General Gage to arrest the leaders of the resistance, or failing that, to provoke any sort of confrontation that would allow him to turn British military might loose on the Americans.

Gage decided on a reconnaissance-in-force to find and destroy a reported stockpile of colonial arms and ammunition at Concord. Seven hundred British troops set out on this mission on the night of April 18, 1775, which resulted in skirmishes with the colonists at Lexington and Concord.

Open warfare had begun, and the myth of British invincibility was destroyed. Militia came in large numbers from all the New England colonies to join the force besieging Gage and his army in Boston. The following month the Americans tightened the noose around Boston by fortifying Breed's Hill (a spur of Bunker Hill).

The British determined to remove them by a frontal attack. Twice the British were thrown back, but they finally succeeded when the Americans ran out of ammunition. Over a thousand British soldiers were killed or wounded in what turned out to be the bloodiest battle of the war (June 17, 1775). Yet the British had gained very little and remained bottled up in Boston.

Meanwhile in May 1775, American forces under Ethan Allen (1738–1789) and Benedict Arnold (1741–1801) took Fort Ticonderoga on Lake Champlain.

While these events were taking place in New England and Canada, the Second Continental Congress met in Philadelphia in May 1775. Congress was divided into two main factions. One was composed mostly of New Englanders and leaned toward declaring independence from Britain. The other drew its strength primarily from the Middle Colonies and was not yet ready to go that far.

The Declaration of Independence was primarily the work of Thomas Jefferson (1743–1826) of Virginia. It was a restatement of political ideas by then commonplace in America and showed why the former colonists felt justified in separating from Great Britain. It was formally adopted by Congress on July 4, 1776.

The British landed that summer at New York City, where they hoped to find many loyalists. Washington narrowly avoided being trapped there (an escape partially due to Howe's slowness). Defeated again at the Battle of Washington Heights (August 29–30, 1776) in Manhattan, Washington was forced to retreat across New Jersey with the aggressive British General Lord Charles Cornwallis (1738–1805) in pursuit.

With his victory almost complete, General Howe decided to wait until spring to finish annihilating Washington's army. Scattering his troops in small detachments so as to hold all of New Jersey, he went into winter quarters.

Washington, with his small army melting away as demoralized soldiers deserted, decided on a bold stroke. On Christmas night 1776, his army crossed the Delaware River and struck the Hessians at Trenton. The Hessians, still groggy from their hard-drinking Christmas party, were easily defeated. A few days later, Washington defeated a British force at Princeton (January 3, 1777). Much of New Jersey was regained, and Washington's army was saved from disintegration.

Hoping to weaken Britain, France began making covert shipments of arms to the Americans early in the war. Shipments from France were vital for the Americans. The American victory at Saratoga convinced the French to join openly in the war against England. Eventually, the Spanish (1779) and the Dutch (1780) joined as well.

Howe was replaced by General Henry Clinton (1738–1795), who was ordered to abandon Philadelphia and march to New York. Clinton maintained New York as Britain's main base. In November 1778, the British easily conquered Georgia. Late the following year, Clinton moved on South Carolina and in May 1780 Charleston surrendered. Clinton then returned to New York, leaving Cornwallis to continue the Southern campaign.

In the west, George Rogers Clark (1752–1818), led an expedition down the Ohio River and into the area of present-day Illinois and Indiana, defeating a British force at Vincennes, Indiana, and securing the area north of the Ohio River for the United States.

In the south, Cornwallis began to move northward toward North Carolina, but on October 7, 1780, a detachment of his force was defeated by American frontiersmen at the Battle of Kings Mountain in northern South Carolina. Cornwallis unwisely moved north without bothering to secure South Carolina first. The result was that the British would no sooner leave an area than American militia or guerilla bands, such as that under Francis Marion "the Swamp Fox" (ca. 1732–1795), were once again in control.

American commander Nathaniel Greene's (1742–1786) brilliant southern strategy led to a crushing victory at Cowpens, South Carolina (January 17, 1781), by troops under Greene's subordinate, General Daniel Morgan (1736–1802) of Virginia. It also led to a near victory by Greene's own force at Guilford Court House, North Carolina (March 15, 1781).

The frustrated and impetuous Cornwallis now abandoned the southern strategy and moved north into Virginia, taking a defensive position at Yorktown. With the aid of a French fleet which took control of Chesapeake Bay and a French army which joined him in sealing off the land approaches to Yorktown, Washington succeeded in trapping Cornwallis. After three weeks of siege, Cornwallis surrendered (October 17, 1781).

News of the debacle at Yorktown brought the collapse of Lord North's ministry, and the new cabinet opened peace negotiations.

The final agreement became known as the Treaty of Paris of 1783. Its terms stipulated the following: 1) The United States was recognized as an independent nation by the major European powers, including Britain. 2) Its western boundary was set at the Mississippi River. 3) Its southern boundary was set at 31° north latitude (the northern boundary of Florida). 4) Britain retained Canada, but had to surrender Florida to Spain. 5) Private British creditors would be free to collect any debts owed by United States citizens. 6) Congress was to recommend that the states restore confiscated loyalist property.

THE CREATION OF NEW GOVERNMENTS

After the collapse of British authority in 1775, it became necessary to form new state governments. By the end of 1777, ten new state constitutions had been formed. Most state constitutions included bills of rights—lists of things the government was not supposed to do to the people.

In the summer of 1776, Congress appointed a committee to begin devising a framework for a national government. The end result preserved the sovereignty of the states and created a very weak national government.

The Articles of Confederation provided for a unicameral Congress in which each state would have one vote, as had been the case in the Continental Congress. Executive authority under the articles would be vested in a committee of 13, with one member from each state. In order to amend the articles, the unanimous consent of all the states was required.

The Articles of Confederation government was empowered to make war, make treaties, determine the amount of troops and money each state should contribute to the war effort, settle disputes between states, admit new states to the Union, and borrow money. But it was not empowered to levy taxes, raise troops, or regulate commerce.

Ratification of the Articles of Confederation was delayed by disagreements over the future status of the lands that lay to the west of the original 13 states. Maryland, which had no such claim, withheld ratification until, in 1781, Virginia agreed to surrender its western claims to the new national government.

THE UNITED STATES CONSTITUTION (1787–1789)

DEVELOPMENT AND RATIFICATION

As time went on, the inadequacy of the Articles of Confederation became increasingly apparent. It was decided in 1787 to call for a convention of all the states to meet in Philadelphia for the purpose of revising the Articles of Confederation.

The men who met in Philadelphia in 1787 were remarkably able, highly educated, and exceptionally accomplished. For the most part they were lawyers, merchants, and planters. Though representing individual states, most thought in national terms.

George Washington was unanimously elected to preside, and the enormous respect that he commanded helped hold the convention together through difficult times.

The delegates shared a basic belief in the innate selfishness of man, which must somehow be kept from abusing the power of government. For this purpose, the document that they finally produced contained many checks and balances, designed to prevent the government, or any one branch of the government, from gaining too much power.

Benjamin Franklin played an important role in reconciling the often heated debates and in making various suggestions that eventually helped the convention arrive at the "Great Compromise," proposed by Roger Sherman (1721–1793) and Oliver Ellsworth (1745–1807). The Great (or Connecticut) Compromise provided for a presidency, a Senate with all states represented equally (by two senators each), and a House of Representatives with representation according to population.

Another crisis involved North-South disagreement over the issue of slavery. Here also a compromise was reached. Slavery was neither endorsed nor condemned by the Constitution. Each slave was to count as three-fifths of a person for purposes of apportioning representation and direct taxation on the states (the Three-Fifths Compromise). The federal government was prohibited from stopping the importation of slaves prior to 1808.

The third major area of compromise was the nature of the presidency. The result was a strong presidency with control of foreign policy and the power to veto Congress's legislation. Should the president commit an actual crime, Congress would have the power to impeach him. Otherwise, the president would serve for a term of four years and be reelectable without limit. As a check to the possible excesses of democracy, the president was to be elected by an electoral college, in which each state would have the same number of electors as it did senators and representatives combined. The person with the second highest total in the electoral college would be vice president. If no one gained a majority in the electoral college, the president would be chosen by the House of Representatives.

The new Constitution was to take effect when nine states, through special state conventions, had ratified it. As the struggle over ratification got under way, those favoring the Constitution astutely named themselves Federalists (i.e., advocates of centralized power) and labeled their opponents Antifederalists.

By June 21, 1788, the required nine states had ratified, but the crucial states of New York and Virginia still held out. Ultimately, the promise of the addition of a bill of rights helped win the final states. In March 1789, George Washington was inaugurated as the nation's first president.

THE NEW NATION (1789–1824)

THE FEDERALIST ERA

Few Antifederalists were elected to Congress, and many of the new legislators had served as delegates to the Philadelphia Convention two years before.

George Washington received virtually all the votes of the presidential electors, and John Adams received the next highest number, thus becoming the vice-president. After a triumphant journey from Mount Vernon, Washington was inaugurated in New York City, the temporary seat of government (April 30, 1789).

Ten amendments were ratified by the states by the end of 1791 and became the Bill of Rights. The first nine spelled out specific guarantees of personal freedoms, and the Tenth Amendment reserved to the states all those powers not specifically withheld or granted to the federal government.

The Judiciary Act of 1789 provided for a Supreme Court with six justices, and invested it with the power to rule on the constitutional validity of state laws. It was to be the interpreter of the "supreme law of the land." A system of district courts was set up to serve as courts of original jurisdiction, and three courts of appeal were established.

Congress established three departments of the executive branch—state, treasury, and war—as well as the offices of attorney general and postmaster general.

WASHINGTON'S ADMINISTRATION (1789–1797)

Treasury Secretary Alexander Hamilton, in his "Report on the Public Credit," proposed the funding of the national debt at face value, federal assumption of state debts, and the establishment of a national bank. In his "Report on Manufactures," Hamilton proposed an extensive program for federal stimulation of industrial development through subsidies and tax incentives. The money needed to fund these programs would come from an excise tax on distillers and from tariffs on imports.

Thomas Jefferson, Secretary of State, and others objected to the funding proposal because they believed it would enrich a small elite group at the expense of the more worthy common citizen.

Hamilton interpreted the Constitution as having vested extensive powers in the federal government. This "implied powers" stance claimed that the government was given all powers that were not expressly denied to it. This is the "broad" interpretation.

Jefferson and Madison held the view that any action not specifically permitted in the Constitution was thereby prohibited. This is the "strict" interpretation, and the Republicans opposed the establishment of Hamilton's national bank based on this view of government. The Jeffersonian supporters, primarily under the guidance of James Madison, began to organize political groups in opposition to the Federalist program. They called themselves Republicans.

The Federalists, as Hamilton's supporters were called, received their strongest support from the business and financial groups in the commercial centers of the Northeast and from the port cities of the South. The strength of the Republicans lay primarily in the rural and frontier areas of the South and West.

FOREIGN AND FRONTIER AFFAIRS

The U.S. proclaimed neutrality when France went to war with Europe in 1792, and American merchants traded with both sides. In retaliation, the British began to seize American merchant ships and force their crews into service with the British navy.

John Jay negotiated a treaty with the British that attempted to settle the conflict at sea, as well as to curtail English agitation of their Native American allies on the western borders in 1794.

In the Pinckney Treaty, ratified by the Senate in 1796, the Spanish opened the Mississippi River to American traffic and recognized the 31st parallel as the northern boundary of Florida.

INTERNAL PROBLEMS

In 1794, western farmers refused to pay the excise tax on whiskey which formed the backbone of Hamilton's revenue program. When a group of Pennsylvania farmers terrorized the tax collectors, President Washington sent out a federalized militia force of some 15,000 men and the rebellion evaporated, thus strengthening the credibility of the young government.

JOHN ADAMS' ADMINISTRATION (1797–1801)

In the election of 1796, John Adams was the Federalist candidate, and Thomas Jefferson the Republican. Jefferson received the second highest number of electoral votes and became vice president.

REPRESSION AND PROTEST

The elections in 1798 increased the Federalists' majorities in both houses of Congress and they used their "mandate" to enact legislation to stifle foreign influences. The Alien Act raised new hurdles in the path of immigrants trying to obtain citizenship, and the Sedition Act widened the powers of the Adams administration to muzzle its newspaper critics.

Republican leaders were convinced that the Alien and Sedition Acts were unconstitutional, but the process of deciding on the constitutionality of federal laws was as yet undefined. Jefferson and James Madison decided that state legislatures should have that power, and they drew up a series of resolutions which were presented to the Kentucky and Virginia legislatures. They proposed that state bodies could "nullify" federal laws within those states. These resolutions were adopted only in these two states, and so the issue died, but the principle of states' rights would have great force in later years.

THE REVOLUTION OF 1800

Thomas Jefferson and Aaron Burr (1756–1836) ran on the Republican ticket against John Adams and Charles Pinckney (1746–1825) for the Federalists. The Republican candidates won handily, but both received the same number of electoral votes, thus throwing the selection of the president into the House of Representatives. After a lengthy deadlock, Alexander Hamilton threw his support to Jefferson, and Burr had to accept the vice-presidency, the result obviously intended by the electorate. Jefferson appointed James Madison as secretary of state and Albert Gallatin (1761–1849) to the treasury.

The Federalist Congress passed a new Judiciary Act early in 1801, and President Adams filled the newly created vacancies with party supporters, many of them with last-minute commissions. John Marshall (1755–1835) was then appointed chief justice of the United States Supreme Court, thus guaranteeing continuation of Federalist policies from the bench of the high court.

THE JEFFERSONIAN ERA

Thomas Jefferson and his Republican followers envisioned a nation of independent farmers living under a central government that exercised a minimum of control and served merely to protect the individual liberties guaranteed by the Constitution. This agrarian paradise would be free from the industrial smoke and urban blight of Europe, and would serve as a beacon light of Enlightenment rationalism to a world searching for direction. But Jefferson presided over a nation that was growing more industrialized and urban, and which seemed to need an ever-stronger president.

DOMESTIC AFFAIRS

The Twelfth Amendment was adopted and ratified in 1804, ensuring that a tie vote between candidates of the same party could not again cause the confusion of the Jefferson-Burr affair.

Following the Constitutional mandate, the importation of slaves was stopped by law in 1808.

The Louisiana Purchase: An American delegation purchased the trans-Mississippi territory from Napoleon for $15 million in April 1803, even though they had no authority to buy more than the city of New Orleans.

Exploring the West: Meriwether Lewis (1774–1809) and William Clark's (1770–1838) group left St. Louis in 1804 and returned two years later with a wealth of scientific and anthropological information. At the same time, Zebulon Pike and others had been traversing the middle parts of Louisiana and mapping the land.

MADISON'S ADMINISTRATION (1809–1817)

The Election of 1808: Republican James Madison won the election over Federalist Charles Pinckney, but the Federalists gained seats in both houses of the Congress.

The Native American tribes of the Northwest and the Mississippi Valley were resentful of the government's policy of pressured removal to the West, and the British authorities in Canada exploited their discontent by encouraging border raids against the American settlements.

At the same time, the British interfered with American transatlantic shipping, including impressing sailors and capturing ships.

The Congress in 1811 contained a strong pro-war group called the War Hawks led by Henry Clay (1777–1852) and John C. Calhoun (1782–1850). They gained control of both houses and began agitating for war with the British. On June 1, 1812, President Madison asked for a declaration of war and Congress complied.

After three years of inconclusive war, in 1815 the Treaty of Ghent provided for the acceptance of the status quo that had existed at the beginning of hostilities, and both sides restored their wartime conquests to the other.

The Federalists had increasingly become a minority party. They vehemently opposed the war, and Daniel Webster (1782–1852) and other New England congressmen consistently blocked the Administration's efforts to prosecute the war effort. On December 15, 1814, delegates from the New England states met in Hartford, Connecticut, and drafted a set of resolutions suggesting nullification—and even secession—if their interests were not protected against the growing influence of the South and the West.

Soon after the convention adjourned, the news of Andrew Jackson's victory over the British on January 8, 1815, at New Orleans was announced and their actions were discredited. The Federalist party ceased to be a political force from this point on.

POSTWAR DEVELOPMENTS

Protective Tariff (1816): The first protective tariff in the nation's history was passed in 1816 to slow the flood of cheap British manufactures into the country.

Rush-Bagot Treaty (1817): An agreement was reached in 1817 between Britain and the United States to stop maintaining armed fleets on the Great Lakes. This first "disarmament" agreement is still in effect.

The Adams-Onis Treaty (1819): Spain had decided to sell the remainder of the Florida territory to the Americans before they took it anyway. Under this agreement, the Spanish surrendered all their claims to Florida. The United States agreed to assume $5 million in debts owed to American merchants.

THE MONROE DOCTRINE

As Latin American nations began declaring independence, British and American leaders feared that European governments would try to restore the former New World colonies to their erstwhile royal owners.

In December 1823, President James Monroe (1758–1831) included in his annual message to Congress a statement that the peoples of the American hemisphere were "henceforth not to be considered as subjects for future colonization by any European powers."

INTERNAL DEVELOPMENT (1820–1830)

The years following the War of 1812 were years of rapid economic and social development, followed by a severe depression in 1819. But this slump was temporary, and it became obvious that the country was moving rapidly from its agrarian origins toward an industrial, urban future.

The Monroe Presidency (1817–1823): James Monroe, the last of the "Virginia dynasty," had been handpicked by the retiring Madison and he was elected with only one electoral vote opposed—a symbol of national unity.

THE MARSHALL COURT

John Marshall delivered the majority opinions in a number of critical decisions in these formative years, all of which served to strengthen the power of the federal government and restrict the powers of state governments.

Marbury v. Madison **(1803):** This case established the precedent of the Supreme Court's power to rule on the constitutionality of federal laws.

Gibbons v. Ogden **(1824):** In a case involving competing steamboat companies, Marshall ruled that commerce included navigation, and that only Congress has the right to regulate commerce among states. Thus, the state-granted monopoly was voided.

National Expansion

The Missouri Compromise (1820): The Missouri Territory, the first to be organized from the Louisiana Purchase, applied for statehood in 1819. Since the Senate membership was evenly divided between slaveholding and free states at that time, the admission of a new state would give the voting advantage either to the North or to the South.

As the debate dragged on, the northern territory of Massachusetts applied for admission as the state of Maine. The two admission bills were combined, with Maine coming in free and Missouri coming in as a slave state. To make the package palatable for the House, a provision was added that prohibited slavery in the remainder of the Louisiana Territory north of the southern boundary of Missouri (latitude 36° 30′).

JACKSONIAN DEMOCRACY AND WESTWARD EXPANSION (1824–1850)

THE ELECTION OF 1824

Although John Quincy Adams, through the controversial action of the House of Representatives, became president in the 1824 election, Andrew Jackson instigated a campaign for the presidency immediately. He won the election of 1828.

Jackson was popular with the common man. He seemed to be the prototype of the self-made Westerner: rough-hewn, violent, vindictive, with few ideas but strong convictions. He ignored his appointed cabinet officers and relied instead on the counsel of his "Kitchen Cabinet," a group of partisan supporters.

Jackson expressed the conviction that government operations could be performed by untrained, common folk, and he threatened to dismiss large numbers of government employees and replace them with his supporters.

He exercised his veto power more than any other president before him.

THE WAR ON THE BANK OF THE UNITED STATES

The Bank of the United States had operated under the direction of Nicholas Biddle (1786–1844) since 1823. He was a cautious man, and his conservative economic policy enforced conservatism among the state and private banks—which many bankers resented. In 1832, Jackson vetoed the Bank's renewal, and it ceased being a federal institution in 1836.

Jackson had handpicked his Democratic successor, Martin Van Buren (1782–1862) of New York. The opposition Whig party had emerged from the ruins of the National Republicans and other groups who opposed Jackson's policies.

Van Buren inherited all the problems and resentments generated by his mentor. He spent most of his term in office dealing with the financial chaos left by the death of the Second Bank. The best he could do was to eventually persuade Congress to establish an Independent Treasury to handle government funds. It began functioning in 1840.

THE ELECTION OF 1840

The Whigs nominated William Henry Harrison, "Old Tippecanoe," a western fighter against the Native Americans. Their choice for vice-president was John Tyler (1790–1862), a former Democrat from Virginia. The Democrats put up Van Buren again.

Harrison won but died only a month after the inauguration, having served the shortest term in presidential history.

THE MEANING OF JACKSONIAN POLITICS

The Age of Jackson was the beginning of the modern two-party system. Popular politics, based on emotional appeal, became the accepted style. The practice of meeting in mass conventions to nominate national candidates for office was established during these years.

The Democrats opposed big government and the requirements of modernization: urbanization and industrialization. Their support came from the working classes, small merchants, and small farmers.

The Whigs promoted government participation in commercial and industrial development, the encouragement of banking and corporations, and a cautious approach to westward expansion. Their support came largely from northern business and manufacturing interests and large southern planters. Calhoun, Clay, and Webster dominated the Whig party during the early decades of the nineteenth century.

REMAKING SOCIETY: ORGANIZED REFORM

The early antislavery movement advocated only the purchase and colonization of slaves. The American Colonization Society was organized in 1817, and established the colony of Liberia in 1830, but by that time the movement had reached a dead end.

In 1831, William Lloyd Garrison (1805–1879) started his paper, *The Liberator*, and began to advocate total and immediate emancipation. He founded the New England Anti-slavery Society in 1832 and the American Anti-slavery Society in 1833. Theodore Weld (1803–1895) pursued the same goals, but advocated more gradual means.

The movement split into two wings: Garrison's radical followers, and the moderates who favored "moral suasion" and petitions to Congress. In 1840, the Liberty party, the first national anti-slavery party, fielded a presidential candidate on the platform of "free soil" (nonexpansion of slavery into the new western territories).

DIVERGING SOCIETIES—LIFE IN THE NORTH

As the nineteenth century progressed, the states seemed to polarize more into the two sections we call the North and the South, with the expanding West becoming ever more identified with the North.

THE ROLE OF MINORITIES

The women's rights movement focused on social and legal discrimination, and women like Lucretia Mott (1793–1880) and Sojourner Truth (ca. 1797–1883) became well-known figures on the speakers' circuit.

By 1850, 200,000 free blacks lived in the North and West. Their lives were restricted everywhere by prejudice, and "Jim Crow" laws separated the races. Black citizens organized separate churches and fraternal orders. The economic security of the free blacks was constantly threatened by the newly arrived immigrants, who were willing to work at the least desirable jobs for lower wages. Racial violence was a daily threat.

THE GROWTH OF INDUSTRY

By 1850, the value of industrial output had surpassed that of agricultural production. The Northeast produced more than two-thirds of the manufactured goods. Between 1830 and 1850, the number of patents issued for industrial inventions almost doubled.

DIVERGING SOCIETIES—LIFE IN THE SOUTH

The southern states experienced dramatic growth in the second quarter of the nineteenth century. The economy grew more productive and more prosperous, but still the section called the South was basically agrarian, with few important cities and only scattered industry. The plantation system, with its cash-crop production driven by the use of slave labor, remained the dominant institution.

The most important economic phenomenon of the early decades of the nineteenth century was the shift in population and production from the old "upper South" of Virginia and the Carolinas to the "lower South" of the newly opened Gulf states of Alabama, Mississippi, and Louisiana. In the older Atlantic states, tobacco retained its importance, but shifted westward to the Piedmont. It was replaced in the East by food grains. The southern Atlantic coast continued to produce rice, and southern Louisiana and east Texas retained their emphasis on sugar cane. But the rich black soil of the new Gulf states proved ideal for the production of short-staple cotton, especially after the invention of the "gin." Cotton soon became the center of the southern economy.

CLASSES IN THE SOUTH

The large plantations growing cotton, sugar, or tobacco used the gang system, in which white overseers directed black drivers who supervised large groups of workers in the fields, all performing the same operation. In the culture of rice, and on the smaller farms, slaves were assigned specific tasks, and when those tasks were finished, the worker had the remainder of the day to himself.

House servants usually were considered the most favored since they were spared the hardest physical labor and enjoyed the most intimate relationship with the owner's family.

COMMERCE AND INDUSTRY

The lack of manufacturing and business development has frequently been blamed for the South's losing its bid for independence in 1861–1865. Actually, the South was highly industrialized for its day and compared favorably with most European nations in the development of manufacturing capacity. However, it trailed far behind the North, so much so that when war erupted in 1861, the northern states owned 81 percent of the factory capacity in the United States.

MANIFEST DESTINY AND WESTWARD EXPANSION

Although the term "Manifest Destiny" was not actually coined until 1844, the belief that the American nation was destined to eventually expand all the way to the Pacific Ocean, and to possibly embrace Canada and Mexico, had been voiced for years by many who believed that American liberty and ideals should be shared with everyone possible, by force if necessary. The rising sense of nationalism which followed the War of 1812 was fed by the rapidly expanding population, the reform impulse of the 1830s, and the desire to acquire new markets and resources for the burgeoning economy of "Young America."

The Adams-Onis Treaty of 1819 had set the northern boundary of Spanish possessions near the present northern border of California. The territory north of that line and west of the vague boundaries of the Louisiana Territory had been claimed over the years by Spain, England, Russia, France, and the United States. By the 1820s, all these claims had been yielded to Britain and the United States. The United States claimed all the way north to the 54°40′ parallel. Unable to settle the dispute, they had agreed on a joint occupation of the disputed land.

In the 1830s, American missionaries followed the traders and trappers to the Oregon country. They began to publicize the richness and beauty of the land. The result was the "Oregon Fever" of the 1840s, as thousands of settlers trekked across the Great Plains and the Rocky Mountains to settle the new Shangri-la.

Texas had been a state in the Republic of Mexico since 1822, following the Mexican revolution against Spanish control. The new Mexican government invited immigration from the north by offering land grants to Stephen Austin (1793–1836) and other Americans. By 1835, approximately 35,000 "gringos" were homesteading on Texas land.

The Mexican officials saw their power base eroding as the foreigners flooded in, so they moved to tighten control through restrictions on immigration and through tax increases. The Texans responded in 1836 by proclaiming independence and establishing a new republic. The ensuing war was short-lived. The Mexican dictator, Antonio López de Santa Anna (1794–1876), advanced north and annihilated the Texan garrisons at the Alamo and at Goliad. On April 23, 1836, Sam Houston (1793–1863) defeated him at San Jacinto, and the Mexicans were forced to let Texas go its way.

Houston immediately asked the American government for recognition and annexation, but President Andrew Jackson feared the revival of the slavery issue. He also feared war with Mexico and so did nothing. When Van Buren followed suit, the new republic sought foreign recognition and support, which the European nations eagerly provided, hoping thereby to create a counterbalance to rising American power and influence in the Southwest. France and England both quickly concluded trade agreements with the Texans.

The district of New Mexico had, like Texas, encouraged American immigration. Soon that state was more American than Mexican. The Santa Fe Trail, running from Independence, Missouri, to the town of Santa Fe, created a prosperous trade in mules, gold, silver, and furs, which moved north in exchange for manufactured goods. American settlements sprung up all along the route.

TYLER, POLK, AND CONTINUED WESTWARD EXPANSION

A states' rights southerner and a strict constitutionalist who had been placed on the Whig ticket to draw Southern votes, John Tyler, who became president in 1841 upon Harrison's death, rejected the entire Whig program of a national bank, high protective tariffs, and federally funded internal improvements (roads, canals, etc.). In the resulting legislative confrontations, Tyler vetoed a number of Whig-sponsored bills.

The Whigs were furious. In opposition to Tyler over the next few years, the Whigs, under the leadership of Clay, transformed themselves from a loose grouping of diverse factions to a coherent political party with an elaborate organization.

Rejected by the Whigs and without ties to the Democrats, Tyler was a politician without a party. Hoping to gather a political following of his own, he sought an issue with powerful appeal and believed he had found it in the question of Texas annexation. Tyler's new secretary of state, John C. Calhoun, negotiated an annexation treaty with Texas. Calhoun's identification with extreme pro-slavery forces and his insertion in the treaty of proslavery statements caused the treaty's rejection by the Senate (1844).

THE ELECTION OF 1844

Democratic front-runner Martin Van Buren and Whig front-runner Henry Clay agreed privately that neither would endorse Texas annexation, and that it would not become a campaign issue, but expansionists at the Democratic convention succeeded in dumping Van Buren in favor of James K. Polk (1795–1849). Polk, called "Young Hickory" by his supporters, was a staunch Jacksonian who opposed protective tariffs and a national bank, but favored territorial expansion, including not only annexation of Texas but also occupation of all the Oregon country (up to latitude 54° 40′) hitherto jointly occupied by the United States and Britain.

The Whigs nominated Clay, who continued to oppose Texas annexation. Later, sensing the mood of the country was against him, he began to equivocate.

The antislavery Liberty party nominated James G. Birney. Apparently because of Clay's wavering on the Texas issue, Birney was able to take enough votes away from Clay in New York to give that state, and thus the election, to Polk.

Tyler, as a lame-duck president, made one more attempt to achieve Texas annexation before leaving office. By means of a joint resolution, which unlike a treaty required only a simple majority rather than a two-thirds vote, he was successful in getting the measure through Congress. Texas was finally admitted to the Union in 1845.

As a good Jacksonian, Polk favored a low, revenue-only tariff rather than a high, protective tariff. This he obtained in the Walker Tariff (1846). He also opposed a national debt and a national bank and reestablished Van Buren's Independent Sub-Treasury system, which remained in effect until 1920.

By the terms of the Oregon Treaty (1846), a compromise with Great Britain was reached. The current United States-Canada boundary east of the Rockies (49°) was extended westward to the Pacific. Some northern Democrats were angered and felt betrayed by Polk's failure to insist on all of Oregon, but the Senate readily accepted the treaty.

Though Mexico broke diplomatic relations with the United States immediately upon Texas's admission to the Union, there was still hope of a peaceful settlement. In the fall of 1845, Polk sent John Slidell (1793–1871) to Mexico City with a proposal for a peaceful settlement.

Nothing came of these attempts at negotiation. Racked by coup and counter-coup, the Mexican government refused even to receive Slidell.

Polk thereupon sent United States troops into the disputed territory in southern Texas. A force under General Zachary Taylor (1784–1850) (who was nicknamed "Old Rough and Ready") took up a position just north of the Rio Grande. Eight days later, April 5, 1846, Mexican troops attacked an American patrol. When news of the clash reached Washington, Polk sought and received from Congress a declaration of war against Mexico on May 13, 1846.

Americans were sharply divided about the war. Some favored it because they felt Mexico had provoked the war, or because they felt it was the destiny of America to spread the blessings of freedom to oppressed peoples. Others, generally northern abolitionists, saw in the war the work of a vast conspiracy of southern slaveholders greedy for more slave territory.

Negotiated peace finally came about when the State Department clerk Nicholas Trist negotiated and signed the Treaty of Guadalupe-Hidalgo (February 2, 1848), ending the Mexican War. Under the terms of the treaty, Mexico ceded to the United States the southwestern territory from Texas to the California coast.

Although the Mexican War increased the nation's territory by one-third, it also brought to the surface serious political issues that threatened to divide the country, particularly the question of slavery in the new territories.

SECTIONAL CONFLICT AND THE CAUSES OF THE CIVIL WAR (1850–1860)

THE CRISIS OF 1850 AND AMERICA AT MID-CENTURY

The Mexican War had no more than started when, on August 8, 1846, freshman Democratic Congressman David Wilmot (1814–1868) of Pennsylvania introduced his Wilmot Proviso as a proposed amendment to a war appropriations bill. It stipulated that "neither slavery nor involuntary servitude shall ever exist" in any territory to be acquired from Mexico. It was passed by the House, and though rejected by the Senate, it was reintroduced again and again amid increasingly acrimonious debate.

The southern position was expressed by John C. Calhoun, now serving as senator from South Carolina. He argued that the territories were not the property of the United States federal government, but of all the states together, and therefore Congress had no right to prohibit in any territory any type of "property" (by which he meant slaves) that was legal in any of the states.

Antislavery northerners, pointing to the Northwest Ordinance of 1787 and the Missouri Compromise of 1820 as precedents, argued that Congress had the right to make what laws it saw fit for the territories, including, if it so chose, laws prohibiting slavery.

A compromise proposal favored by President Polk and many moderate southerners called for the extension of the 36° 30′ line of the Missouri Compromise westward through the Mexican Cession to the Pacific, with territory north of the line to be closed to slavery.

Another compromise solution, favored by northern Democrats such as Lewis Cass (1782–1866) of Michigan and Stephen A. Douglas (1813–1861) of Illinois, was known as "squatter sovereignty" and later as "popular sovereignty." It held that the residents of each territory should be permitted to decide for themselves whether to allow slavery.

THE ELECTION OF 1848

The Democrats nominated Lewis Cass, and their platform endorsed his middle-of-the-road popular sovereignty position with regard to slavery in the territories.

The Whigs dodged the issue even more effectively by nominating General Zachary Taylor, whose fame in the Mexican War made him a strong candidate. Taylor knew nothing of politics, had never voted, and liked to think of himself as above politics. He took no position at all with respect to slavery in the territories.

Some antislavery northern Whigs and Democrats, disgusted with their parties' failure to take a clear stand against the spread of slavery, deserted the party ranks to form an antislavery third party. Their party was called the Free Soil party, since it stood for keeping the soil of new western territories free of slavery. Its candidate was Martin Van Buren. The election excited relatively little public interest. Taylor won a narrow victory.

The question of slavery's status in the western territories was made more immediate when, on January 24, 1848, gold was discovered not far from Sacramento, California. The next year, gold seekers from the eastern United States and from many foreign countries swelled California's population from 14,000 to 100,000.

In September 1849, having more than the requisite population and being in need of better government, California petitioned for admission to the Union as a free state.

Southerners were furious. Long outnumbered in the House of Representatives, the South would now find itself, should California be admitted as a free state, also outvoted in the Senate.

At this point, the aged Henry Clay proposed an eight-part package. For the North, California would be admitted as a free state; the land in dispute between Texas and New Mexico would go to New Mexico; the New Mexico and Utah territories (all of the Mexican Cession outside of California) would not be specifically reserved for slavery, the status there would be decided by popular sovereignty; and the slave trade would be abolished in the District of Columbia.

For the South, a tougher Fugitive Slave Law would be enacted; the federal government would pay Texas's $10,000,000 pre-annexation debt; Congress would declare that it did not have jurisdiction over the interstate slave trade and would promise not to abolish slavery itself in the District of Columbia.

President Taylor died (apparently of gastroenteritis) on July 9, 1850, and was succeeded by Vice-President Millard Fillmore (1800–1874). In Congress, the fight for the Compromise was taken up by Senator Stephen A. Douglas of Illinois who broke Clay's proposal into its component parts so that he could use varying coalitions to push each part through Congress. The Compromise was adopted.

The 1852 Democratic convention deadlocked between Cass and Douglas and so settled on dark horse Franklin Pierce (1804–1869) of New Hampshire. The Whigs chose General Winfield Scott, a war hero with no political background.

The result was an easy victory for Pierce, largely because the Whig party, badly divided along North-South lines as a result of the battle over the Compromise of 1850, was beginning to come apart.

President Pierce expressed the nation's hope that a new era of sectional peace was beginning. He sought to distract the nation's attention from the slavery issue to an aggressive program of foreign economic and territorial expansion known as "Young America."

In 1853, Commodore Matthew Perry (1794–1858) led a United States naval force into Tokyo Bay on a peaceful mission to open Japan—previously closed to the outside world—to American diplomacy and commerce.

By means of the Reciprocity Treaty (1854), Pierce succeeded in opening Canada to greater United States trade.

From Mexico he acquired in 1853 the Gadsden Purchase, a strip of land in what is now southern New Mexico and Arizona along the Gila River. The purpose of this purchase was to provide a good route for a transcontinental railroad across the southern part of the country.

The chief factor in the economic transformation of America during the 1840s and 1850s was the dynamic rise of the railroads. They helped link the Midwest to the Northeast rather than just the South, as would have been the case had only water transportation been available.

The 1850s was the heyday of the steamboat on inland rivers, and the clipper ship on the high seas. The period also saw rapid and sustained industrial growth, especially in the textile industry.

In the North, the main centers of agricultural production shifted from the Mid-Atlantic states to the more fertile lands of the Midwest. Mechanical reapers and threshers came into wide use.

America's second two-party system, which had developed during the 1830s, was in the process of breaking down. The Whig party was now in the process of complete disintegration. This was partially the result of the slavery issue, which divided the party along North-South lines, and partially the result of the nativist movement.

The collapse of a viable two-party system made it much more difficult for the nation's political process to contain the explosive issue of slavery.

THE RETURN OF SECTIONAL CONFLICT

The strengthened Fugitive Slave Law enraged northerners. So violent was northern feeling against the law that several riots erupted as a result of attempts to enforce it. Some northern states passed personal liberty laws in an attempt to prevent the enforcement of the Fugitive Slave Law.

One northerner who was outraged by the Fugitive Slave Act was Harriet Beecher Stowe. She wrote *Uncle Tom's Cabin*, a novel depicting what she perceived as the evils of slavery. Furiously denounced in the South, the book became an overnight bestseller in the North, where it turned many toward active opposition to slavery.

All illusion of sectional peace ended abruptly in 1854 when Senator Stephen A. Douglas of Illinois introduced a bill in Congress to organize the area west of Missouri and Iowa as the territories of Kansas and Nebraska on the basis of popular sovereignty.

The Kansas-Nebraska Act aroused a storm of outrage in the North, where its repeal of the Missouri Compromise was seen as the breaking of a solemn agreement. It hastened the disintegration of the Whig party and divided the Democratic party along North-South lines.

In the North, many Democrats left the party and were joined by former Whigs and Know-Nothings in the newly created Republican party. Springing to life almost overnight as a result of northern fury at the Kansas-Nebraska Act, the Republican party included diverse elements whose sole unifying principle was the firm belief that slavery should be banned from all the nation's territories, confined to the states where it already existed, and allowed to spread no further.

For the next several years Kansas was in chaos, including at various times armed conflict, voter fraud, two governments, and a questionable constitution.

In *Dred Scott v. Sandford*, the Supreme Court attempted to finally settle the slavery question. The case involved a Missouri slave, Dred Scott (ca. 1795–1858), who had been encouraged by abolitionists to sue for his freedom on the basis that his owner had taken him for several years to a free state, Illinois, and then to a free territory, Wisconsin.

Under the domination of aging pro-southern Chief Justice Roger B. Taney of Maryland, the Court attempted to read the extreme southern position on slavery into the Constitution, ruling not only that Scott had no standing to sue in federal court, but also that temporary residence in a free state, even for several years, did not make a slave free, and that the Missouri Compromise (already a dead letter by that time) had been unconstitutional all along because Congress did not have the authority to exclude slavery from a territory. Nor did territorial governments have the right to prohibit slavery.

The 1858 Illinois senatorial campaign produced a series of debates that got to the heart of the issues that were threatening to divide the nation. Incumbent Democratic senator and front-runner for the 1860 presidential nomination Stephen A. Douglas was opposed by a Springfield lawyer, little known outside the state, by the name of Abraham Lincoln.

Lincoln, in a series of seven debates that the candidates agreed to hold during the course of the campaign, stressed that Douglas's doctrine of popular sovereignty failed to recognize slavery for the moral wrong it was.

Douglas, for his part, maintained that his guiding principle was democracy, not any moral standard of right or wrong with respect to slavery.

At the debate held in Freeport, Illinois, Lincoln pressed Douglas to reconcile the principle of popular sovereignty to the Supreme Court's decision in the Dred Scott case. How could the people "vote it up or vote it down," if, as the Supreme Court asserted, no territorial government could prohibit slavery? Douglas, in what came to be called his "Freeport Doctrine," replied that the people of any territory could exclude slavery simply by declining to pass any of the special laws that slave jurisdictions usually passed for their protection.

Douglas's answer was good enough to win him reelection to the Senate, although by the narrowest of margins, but hurt him in the coming presidential campaign.

For Lincoln, despite the failure to win the Senate seat, the debates were a major success, propelling him into the national spotlight, and strengthening the resolve of the Republican party to resist compromise on the free-soil issue.

THE COMING OF THE CIVIL WAR

On the night of October 16, 1859, John Brown, an abolitionist, led 18 followers in seizing the federal arsenal at Harpers Ferry, Virginia, taking hostages, and endeavoring to incite a slave uprising. Quickly cornered by Virginia militia, he was eventually captured by a force under the command of army Colonel Robert E. Lee (1807–1870).

Brown was quickly tried, convicted, sentenced, and on December 2, 1859, hanged. Many northerners looked upon Brown as a martyr.

Though responsible northerners such as Lincoln denounced Brown's raid as a criminal act which deserved to be punished by death, many southerners became convinced that the entire northern public approved of Brown's action and that the only safety for the South lay in a separate southern confederacy.

As the 1860 presidential election approached, two Democratic conventions failed to reach consensus, and the sundered halves of the party nominated separate candidates. The southern wing of the party nominated Buchanan's vice president, John C. Breckinridge of Kentucky, on a platform calling for a federal slave code in all the territories. What was left of the national Democratic party nominated Douglas on a platform of popular sovereignty.

A third presidential candidate was added by the Constitutional Union party, a collection of aging former Whigs and Know-Nothings from the southern and border states, plus a handful of moderate southern Democrats. It nominated John Bell of Tennessee on a platform that sidestepped the issues and called simply for the Constitution, the Union, and the enforcement of the laws.

The Republicans met in Chicago, confident of victory and determined to do nothing to jeopardize their favorable position. Accordingly, they rejected as too radical front-running New York Senator William H. Seward in favor of Illinois' favorite son Abraham Lincoln. The platform called for federal support of a transcontinental railroad and for the containment of slavery.

On election day, the voting went along strictly sectional lines. Breckinridge carried the Deep South; Bell, the border states; and Lincoln, the North. Douglas, although second in popular votes, carried only a single state and part of another. Lincoln led in popular votes, and though he was short of a majority in that category, he did have the needed majority in electoral votes and was elected.

THE SECESSION CRISIS

On December 20, 1860, South Carolina, by vote of a special convention, declared itself out of the Union. By February 1, 1861, six more states (Alabama, Georgia, Florida, Mississippi, Louisiana, and Texas) had followed suit.

Representatives of the seceded states met in Montgomery, Alabama, in February 1861 and declared themselves to be the Confederate States of America. They elected former Secretary of War and United States senator Jefferson Davis of Mississippi as president and Alexander Stephens (1812–1883) of Georgia as vice president. They also adopted a constitution for the Confederate states which, while similar to the United States Constitution in many ways, contained several important differences:

1) Slavery was specifically recognized, and the right to move slaves from one state to another was guaranteed.

2) Protective tariffs were prohibited.

3) The president was to serve for a single nonrenewable six-year term.

4) The president was given the right to veto individual items within an appropriations bill.

5) State sovereignty was specifically recognized.

THE CIVIL WAR AND RECONSTRUCTION (1860–1877)

HOSTILITIES BEGIN

In his inaugural address, Lincoln urged southerners to reconsider their actions, but warned that the Union was perpetual, that states could not secede, and that he would therefore hold the federal forts and installations in the South.

Only two remained in federal hands: Fort Pickens, off Pensacola, Florida; and Fort Sumter, in the harbor of Charleston, South Carolina. Lincoln soon received word from Major Robert Anderson, commander of the small garrison at Sumter, that supplies were running low. Desiring to send in the needed supplies, Lincoln informed the governor of South Carolina of his intention, but promised that no attempt would be made to send arms, ammunition, or reinforcements unless southerners initiated hostilities.

Confederate General P.G.T. Beauregard (1818–1893), acting on orders from President Davis, demanded Anderson's surrender. Anderson said he would surrender if not resupplied. Knowing supplies were on the way, the Confederates opened fire at 4:30 a.m. on April 12, 1861. The next day, the fort surrendered.

The day following Sumter's surrender, Lincoln declared an insurrection and called for the states to provide 75,000 volunteers to put it down. In response to this, Virginia, Tennessee, North Carolina, and Arkansas declared their secession.

The remaining slave states, Delaware, Kentucky, Maryland, and Missouri, wavered, but stayed with the Union.

The North enjoyed at least five major advantages over the South. It had overwhelming preponderance in wealth and was vastly superior in industry.

The North also had an advantage of almost three to one in manpower; and over one-third of the South's population was composed of slaves, whom Southerners would not use as soldiers. Unlike the South, the North received large numbers of immigrants during the war. The North retained control of the United States Navy, and thus, would command the sea and be able to blockade the South. Finally, the North enjoyed a much superior system of railroads.

The South did, however, have several advantages. It was vast in size, making it difficult to conquer. Its troops would be fighting on their own ground, a fact that would give them the advantage of familiarity with the terrain, as well as the added motivation of defending their homes and families. Its armies would often have the opportunity of fighting on the defensive, a major advantage in the warfare of that day.

Though Jefferson Davis had extensive military and political experience, Lincoln was much superior to Davis as a war leader, showing firmness, flexibility, mental toughness, great political skill, and, eventually, an excellent grasp of strategy.

At a creek called Bull Run near the town of Manassas Junction, Virginia, just southwest of Washington, D.C., the Union Army met a Confederate force under generals P.G.T. Beauregard and Joseph E. Johnston on July 21, 1861. In the First Battle of Bull Run (called First Manassas in the South), the Union army was forced to retreat in confusion back to Washington.

THE UNION IS PRESERVED

To replace the discredited McDowell, Lincoln chose General George B. McClellan (1826–1885). McClellan was a good trainer and organizer and was loved by the troops, but he was unable to effectively use the powerful army (now called the Army of the Potomac) he had built up.

Lee summoned General Thomas J. "Stonewall" Jackson (1824–1863) and his army from the Shenandoah Valley (where Jackson had just finished defeating several superior federal forces), and with the combined forces attacked McClellan.

After two days of bloody but inconclusive fighting, McClellan lost his nerve and began to retreat. In the remainder of what came to be called the Battle of the Seven Days, Lee continued to attack McClellan, forcing him back to his base, though at great cost in lives. McClellan's army was loaded back onto its ships and taken back to Washington.

Before McClellan's army could reach Washington, Lee took the opportunity to thrash Union General John Pope (1822–1892), who was in northern Virginia with another northern army, at the Second Battle of Bull Run.

West of the Appalachian Mountains, matters were proceeding differently. The northern commanders there, Henry W. Halleck (1815–1872) and Don Carlos Buell (1818–1898), were no more enterprising than McClellan, but Halleck's subordinate, Ulysses S. Grant, was.

With permission from Halleck, Grant mounted a combined operation—army troops and navy gunboats—against two vital Confederate strongholds, forts Henry and Donelson, which guarded the Tennessee and Cumberland rivers in northern Tennessee. When Grant captured the forts in February 1862, Johnston was forced to retreat to Corinth in northern Mississippi.

Grant pursued, but ordered by Halleck to wait until all was in readiness before proceeding, halted his troops at Pittsburg Landing on the Tennessee River, 25 miles north of Corinth. On April 6, 1862 General Albert Sidney Johnston, who had received reinforcements and been joined by General P.G.T. Beauregard, surprised Grant there, but in the two-day battle that followed (Shiloh) failed to defeat him. Johnston was among the many killed in what was, up to this point, the bloodiest battle in American history.

Grant was severely criticized in the North for having been taken by surprise. Yet with other Union victories and Farragut's capture of New Orleans, the North had taken all of the Mississippi River except for a 110-mile stretch between the Confederate fortresses of Vicksburg, Mississippi, and Port Hudson, Louisiana.

Many southerners believed Britain and France would rejoice in seeing a divided and weakened America. They also believed the two countries would likewise be driven by the need of their factories for cotton and thus intervene on the Confederacy's behalf.

This view proved mistaken. Britain already had a large supply of cotton, and had other sources besides the U.S. British leaders may also have weighed their country's need to import wheat from the northern United States against its desire for cotton from the southern states. Finally, British public opinion opposed slavery.

Skillful northern diplomacy had a great impact. In this, Lincoln had the extremely able assistance of Secretary of State William Seward, who took a hard line in warning Europeans not to interfere, and of ambassador to Great Britain Charles Francis Adams (1807–1886). Britain remained neutral, and other European countries, including France followed its lead.

Congress in 1862 passed two highly important acts dealing with domestic affairs in the North. The Homestead Act granted 160 acres of government land free of charge to any person who would farm it for at least five years. Much of the West was eventually settled under the provisions of this act. The Morrill Land Grant Act offered large amounts of the federal government's land to states that would establish "agricultural and mechanical" colleges. Many of the nation's large state universities were later founded under the provisions of this act.

THE EMANCIPATION PROCLAMATION

By mid-1862, Lincoln, under pressure from radical elements of his own party and hoping to create a favorable impression on foreign public opinion, determined to issue the Emancipation Proclamation, which declared free all slaves in areas still in rebellion as of January 1, 1863. At Seward's recommendation, Lincoln waited to announce the proclamation until the North won some sort of victory. This was provided by the Battle of Antietam (September 17, 1863).

After his victory at the Second Battle of Bull Run, Lee moved north and crossed into Maryland, where he hoped to win a decisive victory that would force the North to recognize southern independence.

The armies finally met along Antietam Creek, just east of the town of Sharpsburg in western Maryland. In a bloody but inconclusive day-long battle, known as Antietam in the North and Sharpsburg in the South, McClellan's timidity led him to miss another excellent chance to destroy Lee's cornered and badly outnumbered army. After the battle, Lee retreated to Virginia, and Lincoln removed McClellan from command.

To replace him, Lincoln chose General Ambrose E. Burnside (1824–1881), who promptly demonstrated his unfitness by blundering into a lopsided defeat at Fredericksburg, Virginia (December 13, 1862).

Lincoln then replaced Burnside with General Joseph "Fighting Joe" Hooker (1814–1879). He was soundly beaten at the Battle of Chancellorsville (May 5–6, 1863). At this battle, the brilliant Southern general "Stonewall" Jackson was accidentally shot by his own men and died several days later.

Lee received permission from President Davis to invade Pennsylvania. He was pursued by the Army of the Potomac, now under the command of General George G. Meade (1815–1872), who had replaced the discredited Hooker. They met at Gettysburg in a three-day battle (July 1–3, 1863) that was the bloodiest of the war. Lee, who sorely missed the services of Jackson and whose cavalry leader, the normally reliable J.E.B. Stuart (1833–1864), failed to provide him with timely reconnaissance, was defeated. However, he was allowed by the victorious Meade to retreat to Virginia with his army intact if battered, much to Lincoln's disgust.

Meanwhile, Grant moved on Vicksburg, one of the last two Confederate bastions on the Mississippi River. In a brilliant campaign, he bottled up the Confederate forces of General

John C. Pemberton (1814–1881) inside the city and placed them under siege. After six weeks, the defenders surrendered on July 4, 1863. Five days later, Port Hudson surrendered, giving the Union complete control of the Mississippi River.

After Union forces under General William Rosecrans (1819–1898) suffered an embarrassing defeat at the Battle of Chickamauga in northwestern Georgia (September 19–20, 1863), Lincoln named Grant overall commander of Union forces in the West.

Grant went to Chattanooga, Tennessee, where Confederate forces under General Braxton Bragg (1817–1876) were virtually besieging Rosecrans, and immediately took control of the situation. Gathering Union forces from other portions of the western theater and combining them with reinforcements from the East, Grant won a resounding victory at the Battle of Chattanooga (November 23–25, 1863), in which federal forces stormed seemingly impregnable Confederate positions on Lookout Mountain and Missionary Ridge. This victory put Union forces in position for a drive into Georgia, which began the following spring.

Early in 1864, Lincoln made Grant commander of all Union armies. Grant devised a coordinated plan for constant pressure on the Confederacy. General William T. Sherman would lead a drive toward Atlanta, Georgia, with the goal of destroying the Confederate army under General Joseph E. Johnston (who had replaced Bragg). Grant would accompany Meade and the Army of the Potomac in advancing toward Richmond with the goal of destroying Lee's Confederate army.

In a series of bloody battles (the Wilderness, Spotsylvania, Cold Harbor) in May and June of 1864, Grant drove Lee to the outskirts of Richmond. Still unable to take the city or get Lee at a disadvantage, Grant circled around, attacking Petersburg, Virginia, an important railroad junction just south of Richmond and the key to that city's—and Lee's—supply lines. Once again turned back by entrenched Confederate troops, Grant settled down to besiege Petersburg and Richmond in a stalemate that lasted some nine months.

Sherman had been advancing simultaneously in Georgia. He maneuvered Johnston back to the outskirts of Atlanta with relatively little fighting. At that point, Confederate President Davis lost patience with Johnston and replaced him with the aggressive General John B. Hood (1831–1879). Hood and Sherman fought three fierce but inconclusive battles around Atlanta in late July, and then settled down to a siege of their own during the month of August.

THE ELECTION OF 1864 AND NORTHERN VICTORY

Lincoln ran on the ticket of the National Union party, essentially the Republican party with loyal or "War" Democrats. His vice-presidential candidate was Andrew Johnson (1808–1875), a loyal Democrat from Tennessee.

The Democratic party's presidential candidate was General George B. McClellan, who ran on a platform labeling the war a failure, and calling for a negotiated peace settlement even if that meant southern independence.

In September 1864, word came that Sherman had taken Atlanta. The capture of this vital southern rail and manufacturing center brought an enormous boost to northern morale. Along with other northern victories that summer and fall, it ensured a resounding election victory for Lincoln and the continuation of the war to complete victory for the North.

To speed that victory, Sherman marched through Georgia from Atlanta to the sea, arriving at Savannah in December 1864 and turning north into the Carolinas, leaving behind a 60-mile-wide swath of destruction.

Lee abandoned Richmond (April 3, 1865) and attempted to escape with what was left of his army. Pursued by Grant, he was cornered and forced to surrender at Appomattox, Virginia (April 9, 1865). Other Confederate armies still holding out in various parts of the South surrendered over the next few weeks.

Lincoln did not live to receive news of the final surrenders. On April 14, 1865, he was shot in the back of the head while watching a play in Ford's Theatre in Washington.

THE ORDEAL OF RECONSTRUCTION

Reconstruction began well before the fighting of the Civil War came to an end. It brought a time of difficult adjustments in the South.

Among those who faced such adjustments were the recently freed slaves. To ease the adjustment for these recently freed slaves, Congress in 1865 created the Freedmen's Bureau to provide food, clothing, and education, and generally look after the interests of former slaves.

To restore legal governments in the seceded states, Lincoln developed a policy that made it relatively easy for southern states to enter the collateral process.

Tennessee, Arkansas, and Louisiana formed loyal governments under Lincoln's plan, but were refused recognition by a Congress dominated by Radical Republicans.

Radical Republicans such as Thaddeus Stevens (1792–1868) of Pennsylvania believed Lincoln's plan did not adequately punish the South, restructure southern society, or boost the political prospects of the Republican party.

Instead, the radicals in Congress drew up the more stringent Wade-Davis Bill which Lincoln killed with a "pocket veto," and the radicals were furious. When Lincoln was assassinated the radicals rejoiced, believing Vice President Andrew Johnson would be less generous to the South, or at least easier to control.

FOREIGN POLICY UNDER JOHNSON

In 1866, the Russian minister approached Seward with an offer to sell Alaska to the United States. In 1867, the sale went through and Alaska was purchased for $7,200,000.

CONGRESSIONAL RECONSTRUCTION

Determined to reconstruct the South as it saw fit, Congress passed a Civil Rights Act and extended the authority of the Freedmen's Bureau, giving it both quasi-judicial and quasi-executive powers.

Johnson vetoed both bills, claiming they were unconstitutional; but Congress overrode the vetoes. Fearing that the Supreme Court would agree with Johnson and overturn the laws, Congress approved and sent on to the states for ratification (June 1866) the Fourteenth Amendment, making constitutional the laws Congress had just passed. The Fourteenth Amendment defined citizenship and forbade states to deny various rights to citizens, reduced the representation in Congress of states that did not allow blacks to vote, forbade the paying of the Confederate debt, and made former Confederates ineligible to hold public office.

To control the president, Congress passed the Army Act, reducing the president's control over the army. Congress also passed the Tenure of Office Act, forbidding Johnson to dismiss cabinet members without the Senate's permission.

Johnson obeyed the letter but not the spirit of the Reconstruction acts, and Congress, angry at his refusal to cooperate, sought in vain for grounds to impeach him, until in August 1867 Johnson violated the Tenure of Office Act in order to test its constitutionality. The matter was not tested in the courts, however, but in Congress, where Johnson was impeached by the House of Representatives and came within one vote of being removed by the Senate.

THE ELECTION OF 1868 AND THE 15TH AMENDMENT

In 1868, the Republicans nominated, for president, Ulysses S. Grant, who had no political record and whose views—if any—on national issues were unknown.

The narrow victory of even such a strong candidate as Grant prompted Republican leaders to decide that it would be politically expedient to give the vote to all blacks, North as well as South. For this purpose, the 15th Amendment was drawn up and submitted to the states. Ironically, the idea was so unpopular in the North that it won the necessary three-fourths approval only with its ratification by southern states.

Though personally of unquestioned integrity, Grant naïvely placed his faith in a number of thoroughly dishonest men. His administration was rocked by one scandalous revelation of government corruption after another.

Many of the economic difficulties the country faced during Grant's administration were caused by the necessary readjustments from a wartime economy back to a peacetime economy. The central economic question was deflation versus inflation, or more specifically, whether to retire the unbacked paper money, greenbacks, printed to meet the wartime emergency, or to print more.

Early in Grant's second term, the country was hit by an economic depression known as the Panic of 1873. Brought on by the overexpansive tendencies of railroad builders and businessmen during the immediate postwar boom, the Panic was triggered by economic downturns in Europe, and more immediately, by the failure of Jay Cooke and Company, a major American financial firm.

The Panic led to clamor for the printing of more greenbacks. In 1874, Congress authorized a small new issue of greenbacks, but it was vetoed by Grant. Pro-inflation forces were further enraged when Congress in 1873 demonetized silver, going to a straight gold standard. Silver was becoming more plentiful due to western mining and was seen by some as a potential source of inflation. Pro-inflation forces referred to the demonetization of silver as the "Crime of '73."

In the election of 1876, the Democrats campaigned against corruption and nominated New York Governor Samuel J. Tilden (1814–1886), who had broken the Tweed political machine of New York City.

The Republicans passed over Grant and turned to Governor Rutherford B. Hayes (1822–1893) of Ohio. Like Tilden, Hayes was decent, honest, in favor of hard money and civil service reform, and opposed to government regulation of the economy.

Tilden won the popular vote and led in the electoral vote 184 to 165. However, 185 electoral votes were needed for election, and 20 votes, from the three Southern states still occupied by federal troops and run by Republican governments, were disputed.

A deal was made whereby those 20 votes went to Hayes in return for removal of federal troops from the South. Reconstruction was over.

INDUSTRIALISM, WAR, AND THE PROGRESSIVE ERA (1877–1912)

POLITICS OF THE PERIOD (1877–1882)

The presidencies of Abraham Lincoln and Theodore Roosevelt (1858–1919) mark the boundaries of a half century of relatively weak executive leadership and legislative domination by Congress and the Republican party.

"Stalwarts," led by New York senator Roscoe Conkling (1829–1888) favored the old spoils system of political patronage. "Half-Breeds," headed by Maine senator James G. Blaine (1830–1893), pushed for civil service reform and merit appointments to government posts.

THE ECONOMY (1877–1882)

Between 1860 and 1894, the United States moved from the fourth-largest manufacturing nation to the world's leader through capital accumulation, natural resources, especially in iron, oil, and coal, an abundance of labor helped by massive immigration, railway transportation, and communications and major technical innovations such as the development of the modern steel industry and electrical energy.

By 1880, northern capital erected the modern textile industry in the New South by bringing factories to the cotton fields.

SOCIAL AND CULTURAL DEVELOPMENTS (1877–1882)

In time, advocates of the "social gospel" such as Jane Addams (1860–1939) and Washington Gladden (1836–1918) urged the creation of settlement houses and better health and education services to accommodate the new immigrants. In 1881, Booker T. Washington (1856–1915) became president of Tuskegee Institute in Alabama, a school devoted to teaching and vocational education for African Americans.

THE ECONOMY (1882–1887)

Captains of industry such as John D. Rockefeller in oil, J. P. Morgan (1837–1919) in banking, Gustavus Swift (1839–1903) in meat processing, Andrew Carnegie in steel, and E. H. Harriman (1848–1909) in railroads put together major industrial empires.

The concentration of wealth and power in the hands of a relatively small number of giant firms led to a monopoly capitalism that minimized competition. This led to a demand by small businessmen, farmers, and laborers for government regulation of the economy in order to promote competition.

The Interstate Commerce Act (1887): Popular resentment of railroad abuses such as price-fixing, kickbacks, and discriminatory freight rates created demands for state regulation of the railway industry. The Interstate Commerce Act was passed, paving the way for a commission to be established to oversee fair and just railway rates, prohibit rebates, end discriminatory practices, and require annual reports and financial statements.

American Federation of Labor (1886): Samuel Gompers (1850–1924) and Adolph Strasser put together a combination of national craft unions to represent labor's concerns with wages, hours, and safety conditions. Although militant in its use of the strike and in its demand for collective bargaining in labor contracts with large corporations, it did not promote violence or radicalism.

Frederick W. Taylor (1856–1915), an engineer credited as the father of scientific management, introduced modern concepts of industrial engineering, plant management, and time and motion studies. This gave rise to a separate class of managers in industrial manufacturing—efficiency experts.

THE EMERGENCE OF A REGIONAL EMPIRE (1887–1892)

Despite a protective tariff policy, the United States became increasingly international as it sought to export surplus manufactured and agricultural goods. Foreign markets were viewed as a safety valve for labor employment problems and agrarian unrest.

THE ECONOMY (1887–1892)

Corporate monopolies (trusts) which controlled whole industries were subject to federal prosecution if they were found to be combinations or conspiracies in restraint of trade. Although supported by smaller businesses, labor unions, and farm associations, the Sherman Antitrust Act of 1890 was in time interpreted by the Supreme Court to apply to labor unions and farmers' cooperatives as much as to large corporate combinations. Monopoly was still dominant over laissez-faire, free-enterprise economics during the 1890s.

FOREIGN RELATIONS (1887–1892)

As secretary of state, James G. Blaine was concerned with international trade, political stability, and excessive militarism in Latin America. His international Bureau of American Republics was designed to promote a Pan-American customs union and peaceful conflict resolution. To achieve his aims, Blaine opposed U.S. military intervention in the hemisphere.

ECONOMIC DEPRESSION AND SOCIAL CRISIS (1892–1897)

The economic depression that began in 1893 brought about a collective response from organized labor, militant agriculture, and the business community. Each group called for economic safeguards and a more humane free-enterprise system which would expand economic opportunities in an equitable manner.

POLITICS OF THE PERIOD (1892–1897)

The most marked development in American politics was the emergence of a viable third-party movement in the form of the essentially agrarian Populist party.

Democrat Grover Cleveland (New York) regained the White House by defeating Republican president Benjamin Harrison (Indiana). Cleveland's conservative economic stand in favor of the gold standard brought him the support of various business interests. The Democrats won control of both houses of Congress.

The People's party (Populist) nominated James Weaver (Iowa) for president in 1892. The party platform called for the enactment of a program espoused by agrarians, but also for a coalition with urban workers and the middle class. Specific goals were the coinage of silver to gold at a ratio of 16 to 1; federal loans to farmers; a graduated income tax; postal savings banks; public ownership of railroads and telephone and telegraph systems; prohibition of alien land ownership; immigration restriction; a ban on private armies used by corporations to break up strikes; an eight-hour working day; a single six-year term for president and direct election of senators; the right of initiative and referendum; and the use of the secret ballot.

In the election of 1896, the Republicans nominated William McKinley (Ohio) for president on a platform which promised to maintain the gold standard and protective tariffs. The Democratic party repudiated Cleveland's conservative economics and nominated William Jennings Bryan (1860–1925) (Nebraska) for president on a platform similar to the Populists. Bryan delivered one of the most famous speeches in American history when he declared that the people must not be "crucified upon a cross of gold."

The Populist party also nominated Bryan. Having been outmaneuvered by the Silver Democrats, the Populists lost the opportunity to become a permanent political force.

McKinley won a hard-fought election by only about one-half million votes, as Republicans succeeded in creating the fear among business groups and middle-class voters that Bryan represented a revolutionary challenge to the American system. The Republicans retained control over Congress, which they had gained in 1894.

THE ECONOMY (1892–1897)

Homestead Strike (1892): Iron and steel workers went on strike in Pennsylvania against the Carnegie Steel Company to protest salary reductions.

The primary causes for the depression of 1893 were dramatic growth of the federal deficit, withdrawal of British investments from the American market and the outward transfer of gold, and loss of business confidence. Twenty percent of the workforce was eventually unemployed. The depression would last four years.

March of Unemployed (1894): The Populist businessman Jacob Coxey (1854–1951) led a march of hundreds of unemployed workers on Washington asking for a government work-relief program.

Pullman Strike (1894): Eugene Debs's (1855–1926) American Railway Union struck the Pullman Palace Car Co. in Chicago over wage cuts and job losses. The strikes were all ended by force.

Wilson-Gorman Tariff (1894): This protective tariff did little to promote overseas trade as a way to ease the depression.

Dingley Tariff (1897): The Dingley Tariff raised protection to new highs for certain commodities.

SOCIAL AND CULTURAL DEVELOPMENTS (1892–1897)

The Anti-Saloon League was formed in 1893. Women were especially concerned about the increase of drunkenness during the depression.

Immigration declined by almost 400,000 during the depression. Settlement houses helped poor immigrants. Such institutions also lobbied against sweatshop labor conditions, and for bans on child labor.

FOREIGN RELATIONS (1892–1897)

The Cuban revolt against Spain in 1895 threatened American business interests in Cuba. Sensational "yellow" journalism, and nationalistic statements from officials such as Assistant Secretary of the Navy Theodore Roosevelt (1858–1919), encouraged popular support for direct American military intervention on behalf of Cuban independence. President McKinley, however, proceeded cautiously through 1897.

THE SINO-JAPANESE WAR (1894–1895)

Japan's easy victory over China signaled to the United States and other nations trading in Asia that China's weakness might result in its colonization by industrial powers, and thus, in the closing of the China market. This concern led the United States to announce the Open Door policy with China, designed to protect equal opportunity of trade and China's political independence (1899 and 1900).

FOREIGN POLICY (1897–1902)

On March 27, President McKinley asked Spain to call an armistice, accept American mediation to end the war, and end the use of concentration camps in Cuba. Spain refused to comply. On April 21, Congress declared war on Spain with the objective of establishing Cuban independence (Teller Amendment). The first U.S. forces landed in Cuba on June 22, 1898 and by July 17 had defeated the Spanish forces.

On May 1, 1898, the Spanish fleet in the Philippines was destroyed, and Manila surrendered on August 13. Spain agreed to a peace conference to be held in Paris in October 1898, where it ceded the Philippines, Puerto Rico, and Guam to the United States, in return for a payment of $20 million to Spain for the Philippines. The Treaty of Paris was ratified by the Senate on February 6, 1900.

Filipino nationalists under Emilio Aguinaldo (1869–1964) rebelled against the United States (February 1899) when they learned the Philippines would not be given independence. The United

States used 70,000 men to suppress the revolutionaries by June 1902. A special U.S. commission recommended eventual self-government for the Philippines.

During the war with Spain, the United States annexed Hawaii on July 7, 1898. In 1900, the United States claimed Wake Island, 2,000 miles west of Hawaii.

Although Cuba was granted its independence, the Platt Amendment of 1901 guaranteed that it would become a virtual protectorate of the United States. Cuba could not: 1) make a treaty with a foreign state impairing its independence, or 2) contract an excessive public debt. Cuba was required to: 1) allow the United States to preserve order on the island, and 2) lease a naval base for 99 years to the United States at Guantanamo Bay.

POLITICS OF THE PERIOD (1900–1902)

The unexpected death of Vice President Garrett Hobart led the Republican party to choose the war hero and reform governor of New York, Theodore Roosevelt, as President William McKinley's vice-presidential running mate. Riding the crest of victory against Spain, the GOP platform called for upholding the gold standard for full economic recovery, promoting economic expansion and power in the Caribbean and the Pacific, and building a canal in Central America. The Democrats once again nominated William Jennings Bryan on a platform condemning imperialism and the gold standard. McKinley easily won reelection and the Republicans retained control of both houses of Congress.

While attending the Pan American Exposition in Buffalo, New York, the president was shot on September 6 by Leon Czolgosz, an anarchist. The president died on September 14. Theodore Roosevelt became the nation's 25th president, and at age 42, its youngest to date.

THEODORE ROOSEVELT AND PROGRESSIVE REFORMS (1902–1907)

President Roosevelt did much to create a bipartisan coalition of liberal reformers whose objective was to restrain corporate monopoly and promote economic competition at home and abroad.

The president pledged strict enforcement of the Sherman Antitrust Act (1890), which was designed to break up illegal monopolies and regulate large corporations for the public good.

Hepburn Act (1906): Membership of the Interstate Commerce Commission was increased from five to seven. The I.C.C. could set its own fair freight rates, had its regulatory power extended over pipelines, bridges, and express companies, and was empowered to require a uniform system of accounting by regulated transportation companies.

Pure Food and Drug Act (1906): This prohibited the manufacture, sale, and transportation of adulterated or fraudulently labeled foods and drugs in accordance with consumer demands.

Meat Inspection Act (1906): This provided for federal and sanitary regulations and inspections in meat packing facilities. Wartime scandals in 1898 involving spoiled canned meats were a powerful force for reform.

THE ECONOMY (1902–1907)

Antitrust Policy (1902): Attorney General P. C. Knox (1853–1921) first brought suit against the Northern Securities Company, a railroad holding corporation put together by J. P. Morgan (1837–1913), and then moved against Rockefeller's Standard Oil Company. By the time he left office in 1909, Roosevelt had indictments against 25 monopolies.

Department of Commerce and Labor (1903): A new cabinet position was created to address the concerns of business and labor. Within the department, the Bureau of Corporations was empowered to investigate and report on the illegal activities of corporations.

Coal Strike (1902): Roosevelt interceded with government mediation to bring about negotiations between the United Mine Workers union and the anthracite mine owners after a bitter strike over wages, safety conditions, and union recognition. This was the first time that the government intervened in a labor dispute without automatically siding with management.

A brief economic recession and panic occurred in 1907 as a result, in part, of questionable bank speculations, a lack of flexible monetary and credit policies, and a conservative gold standard. This event called attention to the need for banking reform which would lead to the establishment of the Federal Reserve System in 1913.

SOCIAL AND CULTURAL DEVELOPMENTS (1902–1907)

There was not one unified progressive movement, but a series of reform causes designed to address specific social, economic, and political problems. Progressive reforms might best be described as evolutionary change from above rather than revolutionary upheaval from below.

Muckrakers (a term coined by Roosevelt) were investigative journalists and authors who were often the publicity agents for reforms.

FOREIGN RELATIONS (1902–1907)

Panama Canal: Roosevelt engineered the separation of Panama from Colombia and the recognition of Panama as an independent country. The Hay-Bunau-Varilla Treaty of 1903 granted the United States control of the canal zone in Panama for $10 million and an annual fee of $250,000, beginning nine years after ratification of the treaty by both parties. Construction of the canal began in 1904 and was completed in 1914.

Roosevelt Corollary to the Monroe Doctrine: The United States reserved the right to intervene in the internal affairs of Latin American nations to keep European powers from using military force to collect debts in the Western Hemisphere. The United States by 1905 had intervened in the affairs of Venezuela, Haiti, the Dominican Republic, Nicaragua, and Cuba.

Taft-Katsura Memo (1905): The United States and Japan pledged to maintain the Open Door principles in China. Japan recognized American control over the Philippines, and the United States granted a Japanese protectorate over Korea.

Gentleman's Agreement with Japan (1907): After numerous incidents of racial discrimination against Japanese in California, Japan agreed to restrict the emigration of unskilled Japanese workers to the United States.

THE REGULATORY STATE AND THE ORDERED SOCIETY (1907–1912)

Deciding not to run for reelection, Theodore Roosevelt opened the way for William H. Taft (1857–1930) (Ohio) to run on a Republican platform calling for a continuation of antitrust enforcement, environmental conservation, and a lower tariff policy to promote international trade. The Democrats nominated William Jennings Bryan for a third time on an antimonopoly and low tariff platform. Taft easily won and the Republicans retained control of both houses of Congress. For the first time, the American Federation of Labor entered national politics officially with an endorsement of Bryan. This decision began a long alliance between organized labor and the Democratic party in the twentieth century.

Antitrust Policy: In pursuing anti-monopoly law enforcement, Taft chose as his attorney general George Wickersham (1858–1936), who brought 44 indictments in antitrust suits.

Taft was less successful in healing the Republican split between conservatives and progressives over such issues as tariff reform, conservation, and the almost dictatorial power held by the reactionary Republican Speaker of the House, Joseph Cannon (Illinois).

The 1912 election was one of the most dramatic in American history. President Taft's inability to maintain party harmony led Theodore Roosevelt to return to national politics. When denied the Republican nomination, Roosevelt and his supporters formed the Progressive (Bull Moose) party and nominated Roosevelt for president on a political platform nicknamed "The New Nationalism." It called for stricter regulation on large corporations, creation of a tariff commission, women's suffrage, minimum wages and benefits, direct election of senators, initiative, referendum and recall, presidential primaries, and prohibition of child labor. Roosevelt also called for a Federal Trade Commission to regulate the economy, a stronger executive, and more government planning. Theodore Roosevelt did not see big business as evil, but as a permanent development that was necessary in a modern economy.

The Republicans: President Taft and Vice President Sherman were nominated on a platform of "Quiet Confidence," which called for a continuation of the progressive programs pursued by Taft.

The Democrats: A compromise gave the nomination to New Jersey Governor Woodrow Wilson. Wilson, who had also served as president of Princeton University, called his campaign the "New Freedom"; it borrowed pieces from the Progressive and Republican platforms. Wilson called for breaking up large corporations rather than just regulating them. He differed from the other two party candidates by favoring independence for the Philippines, and by advocating the exemption from prosecution of labor unions under the Sherman Antitrust Act. Wilson also supported such measures as lower tariffs, a graduated income tax, banking reform, and direct election of senators.

The Republican split set the stage for Wilson's victory. Although a minority president, Wilson garnered the largest electoral majority in American history up to that time. Democrats won control of both houses of Congress.

THE WILSON PRESIDENCY

Before the outbreak of World War I in 1914, President Wilson, working with cooperative majorities in both houses of Congress, achieved much of the remaining progressive agenda, including lower tariff reform (Underwood-Simmons Act, 1913), the Sixteenth Amendment (graduated income tax, 1913), the Seventeenth Amendment (direct election of senators, 1913), the Federal Reserve banking system (which provided regulation and flexibility to monetary policy, 1913), the Federal Trade Commission (to investigate unfair business practices, 1914), and the Clayton Antitrust Act (improving the old Sherman Act and protecting labor unions and farm cooperatives from prosecution, 1914).

Other goals such as the protection of children in the work force (Keating-Owen Act, 1916), credit reform for agriculture (Federal Farm Loan Act, 1916), and an independent tariff commission (1916) came later. By the end of Wilson's presidency, the New Freedom and the New Nationalism had merged into one government philosophy of regulation, order, and standardization in the interest of an increasingly diverse nation.

SOCIAL AND CULTURAL DEVELOPMENTS (1907–1912)

In 1905, the African-American intellectual militant W.E.B. DuBois (1868–1963) founded the Niagara Movement which called for federal legislation to protect racial equality and for full rights of citizenship. The National Association for the Advancement of Colored People was organized in 1909.

A radical labor organization called the Industrial Workers of the World (I.W.W., or Wobblies, 1905–1924) was active in promoting violence and revolution. The I.W.W. organized effective strikes in the textile industry in 1912, and among a few western miners groups, but had little appeal to the average American worker. After the Red Scare of 1919, the government worked to smash the I.W.W. and deported many of its immigrant leaders and members.

FOREIGN RELATIONS (1907–1915)

President Taft sought to avoid military intervention, especially in Latin America, by replacing "big stick" policies with "dollar diplomacy" in the expectation that American financial investments would encourage economic, social, and political stability. This idea proved an illusion.

Wilson urged Huerta to hold democratic elections and adopt a constitutional government. Huerta refused, and Wilson invaded Mexico with troops at Veracruz in 1914. A second U.S. invasion came in northern Mexico in 1916.

The United States kept a military presence in the Dominican Republic and Haiti, and intervened militarily in Nicaragua (1911) to quiet fears of revolution and help manage foreign financial problems.

WILSON AND WORLD WAR I (1912–1920)

THE EARLY YEARS OF THE WILSON ADMINISTRATION

Wilson was only the second Democrat (Cleveland was the first) elected president since the Civil War. Key appointments to the cabinet were William Jennings Bryan as secretary of state and William Gibbs McAdoo (1863–1941) as secretary of the treasury.

The Federal Reserve Act of 1913: The law divided the nation into 12 regions, with a Federal Reserve bank in each region. Federal Reserve banks loaned money to member banks at interest less than the public paid to the member banks, and the notes of indebtedness of businesses and farmers to the member banks were held as collateral. This allowed the Federal Reserve to control interest rates by raising or lowering the discount rate.

The money loaned to the member banks was in the form of a new currency—Federal Reserve notes—which was backed 60 percent by commercial paper and 40 percent by gold. This currency was designed to expand and contract with the volume of business activity and borrowing.

The Federal Reserve system serviced the financial needs of the federal government. The system was supervised and policy was set by a national Federal Reserve Board composed of the secretary of the treasury, the comptroller of the currency, and five other members appointed by the president of the United States.

The Clayton Antitrust Act of 1914: This law supplemented and interpreted the Sherman Antitrust Act of 1890. Under its provisions, stock ownership by a corporation in a competing corporation was prohibited, and the same persons were prohibited from managing competing corporations. Price discrimination (charging less in some regions than in others to undercut the competition) and exclusive contracts which reduced competition were prohibited.

THE ELECTION OF 1916

The Democrats, the minority party nationally in terms of voter registration, nominated Wilson and adopted his platform calling for continued progressive reforms and neutrality in the European war.

The Republican convention bypassed Theodore Roosevelt and chose Charles Evans Hughes (1862–1948), an associate justice of the Supreme Court and formerly a progressive Republican governor of New York.

Wilson won the election.

SOCIAL ISSUES IN THE FIRST WILSON ADMINISTRATION

In 1913, Treasury Secretary William G. McAdoo and Postmaster General Albert S. Burleson segregated workers in some parts of their departments with no objection from Wilson. Many northern blacks and whites protested, especially black leader W.E.B. DuBois (1868–1963), who had supported Wilson in 1912.

Wilson opposed immigration restrictions and vetoed a literacy test for immigrants in 1915, but in 1917, Congress overrode a similar veto.

WILSON'S FOREIGN POLICY AND THE ROAD TO WAR

Wilson's Basic Foreign Policy Premise: Wilson promised a more moral foreign policy than that of his predecessors, denouncing imperialism and dollar diplomacy, and advocating the advancement of democratic capitalist governments throughout the world.

Wilson signaled his repudiation of Taft's dollar diplomacy by withdrawing American involvement from the six-power loan consortium of China.

In 1912, American marines had landed in Nicaragua to maintain order, and an American financial expert had taken control of the customs station. The Wilson administration kept the marines in Nicaragua and negotiated the Bryan-Chamorro Treaty of 1914, which gave the United States an option to build a canal through the country.

Claiming that political anarchy existed in Haiti, Wilson sent marines in 1915 and imposed a treaty making the country a protectorate, with American control of its finances and constabulary. The marines remained until 1934.

In 1916, Wilson sent marines to the Dominican Republic to stop a civil war and established a military government under an American naval commander.

Wilson feared in 1915 that Germany might annex Denmark and its Caribbean possession, the Danish West Indies or Virgin Islands. After extended negotiations, the United States purchased the islands from Denmark by treaty on August 4, 1916, for $25 million and took possession of them on March 31, 1917.

In 1913, Wilson refused to recognize the government of Mexican military dictator Victoriano Huerta, and offered unsuccessfully to mediate between Huerta and his Constitutionalist opponent, Venustiano Carranza. When the Huerta government arrested several American seamen in Tampico in April 1914, American forces occupied the port of Veracruz, an action condemned by both Mexican political factions. In July 1914, Huerta abdicated his power to Carranza, who was soon opposed by his former general Francisco "Pancho" Villa (1878–1923). Seeking American intervention as a means of undermining Carranza, Villa shot 16 Americans on a train in northern Mexico in January 1916 and burned the border town of Columbus, New Mexico, in March 1916, killing 19 people. Carranza reluctantly consented to Wilson's request that the United States be allowed to pursue and capture Villa in Mexico, but did not expect the force of about 6,000 army troops under the command of General John J. Pershing which crossed the Rio Grande on March 18. The force advanced more than 300 miles into Mexico, failed to capture Villa, and became, in effect, an army of occupation. The Carranza government demanded an American withdrawal, and several clashes with Mexican troops occurred. War threatened, but in January 1917 Wilson removed the American forces.

THE ROAD TO WAR IN EUROPE

When World War I broke out in Europe, Wilson issued a proclamation of American neutrality on August 4, 1914. The value of American trade with the Central Powers fell from $169 million in 1914 to almost nothing in 1916, but trade with the Allies rose from $825 million to $3.2 billion during the same period. In addition, the British and French had borrowed about $3.25 billion from American sources by 1917. The United States had become a major supplier of Allied munitions, food, and raw materials.

The sinking of the British liner *Lusitania* off the coast of Ireland on May 7, 1915, with the loss of 1,198 lives, including 128 Americans, brought strong protests from Wilson. Secretary of State Bryan, who believed Americans should stay off belligerent ships, resigned rather than insist on questionable neutral rights and was replaced by Robert Lansing.

The House-Grey Memorandum: Early in 1915, Wilson sent his friend and adviser Colonel Edward M. House on an unsuccessful visit to Europe to offer American mediation in the war. Late in the year, House returned to London to propose that Wilson call a peace conference; if Germany refused to attend or was uncooperative at the conference, the United States could enter the war on the Allied side. An agreement to that effect, called the House-Grey memorandum, was signed by the British foreign secretary, Sir Edward Grey, on February 22, 1916.

In an address to Congress on January 22, 1917, Wilson made his last offer to serve as a neutral mediator. He proposed a "peace without victory," based not on a "balance of power" but on a "community of power."

Germany announced on January 31, 1917, that it would sink all ships, belligerent or neutral, without warning in a large war zone off the coasts of the Allied nations in the eastern Atlantic and the Mediterranean. Wilson broke diplomatic relations with Germany on February 3. During February and March several American merchant ships were sunk by submarines.

The British intercepted a secret message from the German foreign secretary, Arthur Zimmermann, to the German minister in Mexico, and turned it over to the United States on February 24, 1917. The Germans proposed that, in the event of a war between the United States and Germany, Mexico attack the United States. After the war, the "lost territories" of Texas, New Mexico, and Arizona would be returned to Mexico. When the telegram was released to the press on March 1, many Americans became convinced that war with Germany was necessary. A declaration of war against Germany was signed by Wilson on April 6.

WORLD WAR I: THE MILITARY CAMPAIGN

The American force of about 14,500, which had arrived in France by September 1917, was assigned a quiet section of the line near Verdun. When the Germans mounted a major drive toward Paris in the spring of 1918, the Americans experienced their first important engagements. In June, they prevented the Germans from crossing the Marne at Chateau-Thierry, and cleared the area of Belleau Woods. In July, eight American divisions aided French troops in attacking the German line between Reims and Soissons. The American First Army, with over half a million men under Pershing's immediate command, was assembled in August 1918, and began a major offensive at St. Mihiel on the southern part of the front on September 12. Following the successful operation, Pershing began a drive against the German defenses between Verdun and Sedan, an action called the Meuse-Argonne offensive. He reached Sedan on November 7. During the same period the English in the north and the French along the central front also broke through the German lines. The fighting ended with the armistice on November 11, 1918.

MOBILIZING THE HOME FRONT

A number of volunteer organizations sprang up around the country to search for draft dodgers, enforce the sale of bonds, and report any opinion or conversation considered suspicious. Such groups publicly humiliated people accused of not buying war bonds, and persecuted, beat, and sometimes killed people of German descent. The anti-German and antisubversive war hysteria in the United States far exceeded similar public moods in Britain and France during the war.

The Espionage Act of 1917 provided for fines and imprisonment for persons who made false statements which aided the enemy, incited rebellion in the military, or obstructed recruitment or the draft. Printed matter advocating treason or insurrection could be excluded from the mails. The Sedition Act of May 1918 forbade any criticism of the government, flag, or uniform, even if there were not detrimental consequences, and expanded the mail exclusion. The laws were applied in ways that trampled on civil liberties. The Espionage Act was upheld by the Supreme Court in the case of *Schenck v. United States* in 1919. The opinion, written by Justice Oliver Wendell Holmes, Jr. (1841–1935), stated that Congress could limit free speech when the words represented a "clear and present danger," and that a person cannot cry "fire" in a crowded theater. The Sedition Act was similarly upheld in *Abrams v. United States* a few months later. Ultimately 2,168 persons were prosecuted under the laws, and 1,055 were convicted, of whom only 10 were charged with actual sabotage.

WARTIME SOCIAL TRENDS

Large numbers of women, mostly white, were hired by factories and other enterprises in jobs never before open to them. When the war ended, almost all returned to traditional "women's jobs" or to homemaking. Returning veterans replaced them in the labor market.

The labor shortage opened industrial jobs to Mexican-Americans and to African-Americans. W.E.B. DuBois, the most prominent African-American leader of the time, supported the war effort in the hope that the war would make the world safe for democracy and bring a better life for African-Americans in the United States. About half a million rural southern African-Americans migrated to cities, mainly in the North and Midwest, to obtain employment in war and other industries, especially in steel and meatpacking. In 1917, there were race riots in 26 cities in the North and South, with the worst in East St. Louis, Illinois.

In December 1917, a constitutional amendment to prohibit the manufacture and sale of alcoholic beverages in the United States was passed by Congress and submitted to the states for ratification.

PEACEMAKING AND DOMESTIC PROBLEMS (1918–1920)

From the time of the American entry into the war, Wilson had maintained that the war would make the world safe for democracy. He insisted that there should be peace without victory, meaning that the victors would not be vindictive toward the losers, so that a fair and stable international situation in the postwar world would ensure lasting peace. In an address to Congress on January 8, 1918, he presented his specific peace plan in the form of the Fourteen Points. The first five points called for open rather than secret peace treaties, freedom of the seas, free trade, arms reduction, and a fair adjustment of colonial claims. The next eight points were concerned with the national aspirations of various European peoples and the adjustment of boundaries. The fourteenth point, which he considered the most important and had espoused as early as 1916, called for a "general association of nations" to preserve the peace.

Wilson decided that he would lead the American delegation to the peace conference which opened in Paris on January 12, 1919. In doing so he became the first president to leave the country during his term of office. In the negotiations, which continued until May 1919, Wilson found it necessary to make many compromises in forging the text of the treaty.

Following a protest by 39 senators in February 1919, Wilson obtained some changes in the League of Nations structure to exempt the Monroe Doctrine and domestic matters from League jurisdiction. Then, on July 26, 1919, he presented the treaty with the League within it to the Senate for ratification. Almost all of the 47 Democrats supported Wilson and the treaty, but the 49 Republicans were divided. About a dozen were "irreconcilables" who thought that the United States should not be a member of the League under any circumstances. The remainder included 25 "strong" and 12 "mild" reservationists who would accept the treaty with some changes. The main objection centered on Article X of the League Covenant, where the reservationists wanted it understood that the United States would not go to war to defend a League member without the approval of Congress.

On September 3, 1919, Wilson set out on a national speaking tour to appeal to the people to support the treaty and the League and to influence their senators. He collapsed after a speech in Pueblo, Colorado, on September 25, and returned to Washington, where he suffered a severe stroke on October 2 which paralyzed his left side. He was seriously ill for several months, and never fully recovered. The treaty failed to get a two-thirds majority either with or without the reservationists.

Many people, including British and French leaders, urged Wilson to compromise on reservationists, including the issue of Article X. Many historians think that Wilson's ill health impaired his judgment, and that he would have worked out a compromise had he not had the stroke. The Senate took up the treaty again in February 1920, and on March 19 it was again defeated both with and without the reservationists. The United States officially ended the war with Germany by a resolution of Congress signed on July 2, 1921, and a separate peace treaty was ratified on July 25. The United States did not join the League.

DOMESTIC PROBLEMS AND THE END OF THE WILSON ADMINISTRATION

In January 1919, the Eighteenth Amendment to the Constitution prohibiting the manufacture, sale, transportation, or importation of intoxicating liquors was ratified by the states, and it became effective in January 1920. The Nineteenth Amendment providing for women's suffrage, which had been defeated in the Senate in 1918, was approved by Congress in 1919. It was ratified by the states in time for the election of 1920.

Americans feared the spread of the Russian Communist revolution to the United States, and many interpreted the widespread strikes of 1919 spurred by inflation as Communist-inspired and the beginning of the revolution. Bombs sent through the mail to prominent government and business leaders in April 1919 seemed to confirm their fears, although the origin of the bombs has never been determined. The anti-German hysteria of the war years was transformed into the anti-Communist and antiforeign hysteria of 1919 and 1920, and continued in various forms through the 1920s.

Attorney General A. Mitchell Palmer, who aspired to the 1920 presidential nomination, was one of the targets of the anonymous bombers in the spring of 1919. In August 1919, he named J. Edgar Hoover (1895–1972) to head a new Intelligence Division in the Justice Department to collect information about radicals. After arresting nearly 5,000 people in late 1919 and early 1920, Palmer announced that huge Communist riots were planned for major cities on May Day (May 1, 1920). Police and troops were alerted, but the day passed with no radical activity. Palmer was discredited and the Red Scare subsided.

White hostility based on competition for lower-paying jobs and black encroachment into neighborhoods led to race riots in 25 cities, with hundreds killed or wounded and millions of dollars in property damage. The Chicago riot in July was the worst. Fear of returning African-American veterans in the South led to an increase of lynchings from 34 in 1917 to 60 in 1918 and 70 in 1919. Some of the victims were veterans still in uniform.

THE ROARING TWENTIES AND ECONOMIC COLLAPSE (1920–1929)

THE ELECTION OF 1920

The Republican Convention: Senator Warren G. Harding (1865–1923) of Ohio was nominated as a dark-horse candidate, and Governor Calvin Coolidge (1872–1933) of Massachusetts was chosen as the vice presidential nominee. The platform opposed the League and promised low taxes, high tariffs, immigration restriction, and aid to farmers.

The Democratic Convention: Governor James Cox was nominated on the 44th ballot, and Franklin D. Roosevelt (1882–1945), an assistant secretary of the Navy and distant cousin of Theodore, was selected as his running mate. The platform endorsed the League, but left the door open for reservations.

THE TWENTIES: ECONOMIC ADVANCES AND SOCIAL TENSIONS

The principal driving force of the economy of the 1920s was the automobile. Automobile manufacturing stimulated supporting industries such as steel, rubber, and glass, as well as gasoline refining and highway construction. During the 1920s, the United States became a nation of paved roads. The Federal Highway Act of 1916 started the federal highway system and gave matching funds to the states for construction.

Unlike earlier boom periods, which had involved large expenditures for capital investments such as railroads and factories, the prosperity of the 1920s depended heavily on the sale of consumer products. Purchases of "big ticket" items such as automobiles, refrigerators, and furniture were made possible by installment or time payment credit. The idea was not new, but the availability of consumer credit expanded tremendously during the 1920s. Consumer interest and demand was spurred by the great increase in professional advertising, which used newspapers, magazines, radio, billboards, and other media.

There was a trend toward corporate consolidation during the 1920s. In most fields, an oligopoly of two to four firms dominated. This is exemplified by the automobile industry, where Ford, General Motors, and Chrysler produced 83 percent of the vehicles in 1929. Government regulatory agencies such as the Federal Trade Commission and the Interstate Commerce Commission were passive and generally controlled by persons from the business world.

There was also a trend toward bank consolidation. Because corporations were raising much of their money through the sale of stocks and bonds, the demand for business loans declined. Commercial banks then put more of their funds into real estate loans, loans to brokers against stocks and bonds, and the purchase of stocks and bonds themselves.

AMERICAN SOCIETY IN THE 1920S

By 1920, for the first time, a majority of Americans (51 percent) lived in an urban area with a population of 2,500 or more. A new phenomenon of the 1920s was the tremendous growth of suburbs and satellite cities, which grew more rapidly than the central cities. Streetcars, commuter railroads, and automobiles contributed to the process, as well as the easy availability of financing for home construction. The suburbs had once been the domain of the wealthy, but the technology of the 1920s opened them to working-class families.

Traditional American moral standards regarding premarital sex and marital fidelity were widely questioned for the first time during the 1920s. The automobile, by giving people mobility and privacy, was generally considered to have contributed to sexual license. Birth control, though illegal, was promoted by Margaret Sanger (1883–1966) and others and was widely accepted.

When it became apparent that women did not vote as a block, political leaders gave little additional attention to the special concerns of women. Divorce laws were liberalized in many states at the insistence of women. Domestic service was the largest job category. Most other women workers were in traditional female occupations such as secretarial and clerical work, retail sales, teaching, and nursing. Rates of pay were below those for men. Most women still pursued the traditional role of housewife and mother, and society accepted that as the norm.

The migration of southern rural African-Americans to the cities continued, with about 1.5 million moving during the 1920s. By 1930, about 20 percent of American blacks lived in the North, with the largest concentrations in New York, Chicago, and Philadelphia. While they were generally better off economically in the cities than they had been as tenant farmers, they generally held low-paying jobs and were confined to segregated areas of the cities.

A native of Jamaica, Marcus Garvey (1887–1940) founded the Universal Negro Improvement Association, advocating African-American racial pride and separatism rather than integration, and called for a return of African-Americans to Africa. In 1921, he proclaimed himself the provisional president of an African empire, and sold stock in the Black Star Steamship Line which would take migrants to Africa. The line went bankrupt in 1923, and Garvey was convicted and imprisoned for mail fraud in the sale of the line's stock and then deported. His legacy was an emphasis on African-American pride and self-respect.

Many writers of the 1920s were disgusted with the hypocrisy and materialism of contemporary American society. Often called the "Lost Generation," many of them, such as novelists Ernest Hemingway (1899–1961) and F. Scott Fitzgerald (1896–1940) and poets Ezra Pound (1885–1972) and T. S. Eliot (1888–1965), moved to Europe.

SOCIAL CONFLICTS

Many white Protestant families saw their traditional values gravely threatened. The traditionalists were largely residents of rural areas and small towns, and the clash of farm values with the values of an industrial society of urban workers was evident. The traditionalist backlash against modern urban industrial society expressed itself primarily through intolerance.

On Thanksgiving Day in 1915, the Knights of the Ku Klux Klan, modeled on the organization of the same name in the 1860s and 1870s, was founded near Atlanta by William J. Simmons. Its purpose was to intimidate African-Americans, who were experiencing an apparent rise in status during World War I. By 1923, the Klan had about five million members throughout the nation. The largest concentrations of members were in the South, the Southwest, the Midwest, California, and Oregon.

There had been calls for immigration restriction since the late nineteenth century. Labor leaders believed that immigrants depressed wages and impeded unionization. Some progressives believed that they created social problems. In June 1917, Congress, over Wilson's veto, had imposed a literacy test for immigrants and excluded many Asian nationalists. In 1921, Congress passed the Emergency Quota Act. In practice, the law admitted about as many as wanted to come from such nations as Britain, Ireland, and Germany, while severely restricting Italians, Greeks, Poles, and east European Jews. It became effective in 1922 and reduced the number of immigrants annually to about 40 percent of the 1921 total. Congress then passed the National Origins Act of 1924, which further reduced the number of southern and eastern Europeans, and cut the annual immigration to 20 percent of the 1921 figure. In 1927, the annual maximum was reduced to 150,000.

The Eighteenth Amendment, which prohibited the manufacture, sale, or transportation of intoxicating liquors, took effect in January 1920.

Fundamentalist Protestants, under the leadership of William Jennings Bryan, began a campaign in 1921 to prohibit the teaching of evolution in the schools, and thus protect belief in the literal biblical account of creation. The idea was especially well received in the South.

Sacco and Vanzetti: On April 15, 1920, two unidentified gunmen robbed a shoe factory and killed two men in South Braintree, Massachusetts. Nicola Sacco and Bartolomeo Vanzetti, Italian immigrants and admitted anarchists, were tried for the murders. After they were convicted and sentenced to death in July 1921, there was much protest in the United States and in Europe that they had not received a fair trial. After six years of delays, they were executed on August 23, 1927. Fifty years later, on July 19, 1977, the pair were vindicated by Governor Michael Dukakis.

GOVERNMENT AND POLITICS IN THE 1920S: THE HARDING ADMINISTRATION

Harding was a handsome and amiable man of limited intellectual and organizational abilities. He had spent much of his life as the publisher of a newspaper in the small city of Marion, Ohio. He recognized his limitations, but hoped to be a much-loved president.

Harding appointed some outstanding persons to his cabinet, including Secretary of State Charles Evans Hughes, a former Supreme Court justice and presidential candidate; Secretary of the Treasury Andrew Mellon (1855–1937), a Pittsburgh aluminum and banking magnate and reportedly the richest man in America; and Secretary of Commerce Herbert Hoover, a dynamic multimillionaire mine owner famous for his wartime relief efforts. Less impressive was his appointment of his cronies Albert B. Fall as secretary of the interior and Harry M. Daugherty as attorney general.

The Teapot Dome Scandal began when Secretary of the Interior Albert B. Fall in 1921 secured the transfer of several naval oil reserves to his jurisdiction. In 1922, he secretly leased reserves at Teapot Dome in Wyoming to Harry F. Sinclair of Monmouth Oil and at Elk Hills in California to Edward Doheny of Pan-American Petroleum. Sinclair and Doheny were acquitted in 1927 of charges of defrauding the government, but in 1929, Fall was convicted, fined, and imprisoned for bribery.

Vice President Calvin Coolidge became president upon Harding's death in 1923.

THE ELECTION OF 1924

The Republicans: Calvin Coolidge was nominated. The platform endorsed business development, low taxes, and rigid economy in government. The party stood on its record of economic growth and prosperity since 1922.

The Progressives: Robert M. La Follette, after failing in a bid for the Republican nomination, formed a new Progressive party, with support from Midwest farm groups, socialists, and the American Federation of Labor. The platform attacked monopolies, and called for the nationalization of railroads, the direct election of the president, and other reforms.

The Democrats: John W. Davis was nominated and presented little contrast with the Republicans.

THE ELECTION OF 1928

The Republicans: Coolidge did not seek another term, and the convention quickly nominated Herbert Hoover, the secretary of commerce, for president. The platform endorsed the policies of the Harding and Coolidge administrations.

The Democrats: Governor Alfred E. Smith (1873–1944) of New York, a Catholic and an anti-prohibitionist, controlled most of the nonsouthern delegations. Southerners supported his nomination with the understanding that the platform would not advocate repeal of prohibition. The platform differed little from the Republican, except in advocating lower tariffs.

THE GREAT DEPRESSION: THE CRASH

Herbert Hoover, an Iowa farm boy and an orphan, graduated from Stanford University with a degree in mining engineering. He became a multimillionaire from mining and other investments around the world. After serving as the director of the Food Administration under Wilson, he became secretary of commerce under Harding and Coolidge. He believed that cooperation between business and government would enable the United States to abolish poverty through continued economic growth.

Stock prices increased throughout the decade. The boom in prices and volume of sales was especially active after 1925, and was intensive during 1928–29.

Careful investors, realizing that stocks were overpriced, began to sell to take their profits. During October 1929, prices declined as more stock was sold. On "Black Thursday," October 24, 1929, almost 13 million shares were traded, a large number for that time, and prices fell precipitously. Investment banks tried to boost the market by buying, but on October 29, "Black Tuesday," the market fell about 40 points, with 16.5 million shares traded.

THE GREAT DEPRESSION AND THE NEW DEAL (1929–1941)

REASONS FOR THE DEPRESSION

A stock-market crash does not mean that a depression must follow. In 1929, a complex interaction of many factors caused the decline of the economy.

Many people had bought stock on a margin of 10 percent, meaning that they had borrowed 90 percent of the purchase price through a broker's loan and put up the stock as collateral. When the price of a stock fell more than 10 percent, the lender sold the stock for whatever it would bring and thus further depressed prices. The forced sales brought great losses to the banks and businesses that had financed the broker's loans, as well as to the investors.

There were already signs of recession before the market crash in 1929. The farm economy, which involved almost 25 percent of the population, had been depressed throughout the decade. Coal, railroads, and New England textiles had not been prosperous. After 1927, new construction declined and auto sales began to sag. Many workers had been laid off before the crash of 1929.

During the early months of the depression, most people thought it was just an adjustment in the business cycle which would soon be over. As time went on, the worst depression in American history set in, reaching its bottom point in early 1932.

HOOVER'S DEPRESSION POLICIES

The Agricultural Marketing Act: Passed in June 1929, before the market crash, this law, proposed by the president, created the Federal Farm Board. It had a revolving fund of $500 million to lend agricultural cooperatives to buy commodities, such as wheat and cotton, and hold them for higher prices.

The Hawley-Smoot Tariff: This law, passed in June 1930, raised duties on both agricultural and manufactured imports.

The Reconstruction Finance Corporation: Chartered by Congress in 1932, the RFC loaned money to railroads, banks, and other financial institutions. It prevented the failure of basic firms, on which many other elements of the economy depended, but was criticized by some as relief for the rich.

The Federal Home Loan Bank Act: This law, passed in July 1932, created home-loan banks to make loans to building and loan associations, savings banks, and insurance companies to help them avoid foreclosures on homes.

ELECTION OF 1932

The Republicans renominated Hoover while the Democrats nominated Franklin D. Roosevelt, governor of New York. Although calling for a cut in spending, Roosevelt communicated optimism and easily defeated Hoover.

THE FIRST NEW DEAL

In February 1933, before Roosevelt took office, Congress passed the Twenty-First Amendment to repeal prohibition, and sent it to the states. In March, the new Congress legalized light beer. The amendment was ratified by the states and took effect in December 1933.

When Roosevelt was inaugurated on March 4, 1933, the American economic system seemed to be on the verge of collapse. Roosevelt assured the nation that "the only thing we have to fear is fear itself," called for a special session of Congress to convene on March 9, and asked for "broad executive powers to wage war against the emergency." Two days later, he closed all banks and forbade the export of gold or the redemption of currency in gold.

LEGISLATION OF THE FIRST NEW DEAL

The special session of Congress, from March 9 to June 16, 1933, passed a great body of legislation which has left a lasting mark on the nation. The period has been referred to ever since as the "Hundred Days." Historians have divided Roosevelt's legislation into the First New Deal (1933–1935) and a new wave of programs beginning in 1935 called the Second New Deal.

The Emergency Banking Relief Act was passed on March 9, the first day of the special session. The law provided additional funds for banks from the RFC and the Federal Reserve, allowed the Treasury to open sound banks after 10 days and to merge or liquidate unsound ones, and forbade the hoarding or export of gold. Roosevelt, on March 12, assured the public of the soundness of the banks in the first of many "fireside chats," or radio addresses. People believed him, and most banks were soon open with more deposits than withdrawals.

The Banking Act of 1933, or the Glass-Steagall Act, established the Federal Deposit Insurance Corporation (FDIC) to insure individual deposits in commercial banks, and separated commercial banking from the more speculative activity of investment banking.

The Truth-in-Securities Act required that full information about stocks and bonds be provided by brokers and others to potential purchasers.

The Home Owners Loan Corporation (HOLC) had authority to borrow money to refinance home mortgages and thus prevent foreclosures. Eventually, it lent more than three billion dollars to more than one million home owners.

Gold was taken out of circulation following the president's order of March 6, and the nation went off the gold standard. Eventually, on January 31, 1934, the value of the dollar was set at $35 per ounce of gold, 59 percent of its former value. The object of the devaluation was to raise prices and help American exports.

The Securities and Exchange Commission was created in 1934 to supervise stock exchanges and to punish fraud in securities trading.

The Federal Housing Administration (FHA) was created by Congress in 1934 to insure long-term, low-interest mortgages for home construction and repair.

These programs, intended to provide temporary relief for people in need, were to be disbanded when the economy improved.

The Federal Emergency Relief Act appropriated $500 million for aid to the poor to be distributed by state and local governments. It also established the Federal Emergency Relief Administration under Harry Hopkins (1890–1946).

The Civilian Conservation Corps enrolled 250,000 young men aged 18 to 24 from families on relief to go to camps where they worked on flood control, soil conservation, and forest projects under the direction of the War Department.

The Public Works Administration, under Secretary of the Interior Harold Ickes, had $3.3 billion to distribute to state and local governments for building projects such as schools, highways, and hospitals.

In November 1933, Roosevelt established the Civil Works Administration to hire four million unemployed workers. The temporary and makeshift nature of the jobs, such as sweeping streets, brought much criticism, and the experiment was terminated in April 1934.

The Agricultural Adjustment Act of 1933 created the Agricultural Adjustment Administration (AAA). Farmers agreed to reduce production of principal farm commodities and were paid a subsidy in return. The money came from a tax on the processing of the commodities. Farm prices increased, but tenants and sharecroppers were hurt when owners took land out of cultivation. The law was repealed in January 1936 on the grounds that the processing tax was not constitutional.

The Federal Farm Loan Act consolidated all farm credit programs into the Farm Credit Administration to make low-interest loans for farm mortgages and other agricultural purposes.

The Commodity Credit Corporation was established in October 1933 by the AAA to make loans to corn and cotton farmers against their crops so that they could hold them for higher prices.

The Frazier-Lemke Farm Bankruptcy Act of 1934 allowed farmers to defer foreclosure on their land while they obtained new financing, and helped them to recover property already lost through easy financing.

National Industrial Recovery Act: This law was viewed as the cornerstone of the recovery program. It sought to stabilize the economy by preventing extreme competition, labor-management conflicts, and overproduction. A board composed of industrial and labor leaders in each industry or business drew up a code for that industry which set minimum prices, minimum wages, maximum work hours, production limits, and quotas. The antitrust laws were temporarily suspended.

The TVA, a public corporation under a three-member board, was proposed by Roosevelt as the first major experiment in regional public planning. Starting from the nucleus of the government's Muscle Shoals property on the Tennessee River, the TVA built 20 dams in an area of 40,000 square miles to stop flooding and soil erosion, improve navigation, and generate hydroelectric power. It also manufactured nitrates for fertilizer, conducted demonstration projects for farmers, engaged in reforestation, and attempted to rehabilitate the whole area.

The economy improved but did not recover. The GNP, money supply, salaries, wages, and farm income rose. Unemployment dropped from about 25 percent of nonfarm workers in 1933 to about 20.1 percent, or 10.6 million, in 1935.

THE SECOND NEW DEAL: OPPOSITION

The Share Our Wealth Society was founded in 1934 by Senator Huey "The Kingfish" Long (1893–1935) of Louisiana. Long was a populist demagogue who was elected governor of Louisiana in 1928, established a practical dictatorship over the state, and moved to the United States Senate in 1930. He supported Roosevelt in 1932, but then broke with him, calling him a tool of Wall Street for not doing more to combat the depression. Long called for the confiscation of all fortunes over five million dollars and a tax of one hundred percent on annual incomes over one million. His society had more than five million members when he was assassinated on the steps of the Louisiana Capitol on September 8, 1935.

THE SECOND NEW DEAL BEGINS

The Works Progress Administration (WPA) was started in May 1935, following the passage of the Emergency Relief Appropriations Act of April 1935. The WPA employed people from the relief rolls for 30 hours of work a week at pay double the relief payment but less than private employment.

The National Youth Administration (NYA) was established as part of the WPA in June 1935, to provide part-time jobs for high school and college students to enable them to stay in school, and to help young adults not in school to find jobs.

The Rural Electrification Administration (REA) was created in May 1935, to provide loans and WPA labor to electric cooperatives so they could build lines into rural areas not served by private companies.

The Social Security Act was passed in August 1935. It established a retirement plan for persons over age 65, which was to be funded by a tax on wages paid equally by employee and employer. The first benefits, ranging from $10 to $85 per month, were paid in 1942. Another provision of the act had the effect of forcing the states to initiate unemployment insurance programs.

The Banking Act of 1935 created a strong central Board of Governors of the Federal Reserve system with broad powers over the operations of the regional banks.

THE ELECTION OF 1936

Roosevelt had put together a coalition of followers who made the Democratic party the majority party in the nation for the first time since the Civil War. While retaining the Democratic base in the South and among white ethnics in the big cities, Roosevelt also received strong support from Midwestern farmers. Two groups that made a dramatic shift into the Democratic ranks were union workers and African-Americans.

THE LAST YEARS OF THE NEW DEAL

Frustrated by a conservative Supreme Court which had overturned much of his New Deal legislation, Roosevelt, in February 1937, proposed to Congress the Judicial Reorganization Bill, which would allow the president to name a new federal judge for each judge who did not retire by the age of $70\frac{1}{2}$. The appointments would be limited to a maximum of 50, with no more than six added to the Supreme Court. The president was astonished by the wave of opposition from Democrats and Republicans alike, but he uncharacteristically refused to compromise. In doing so, he not only lost the bill but control of the Democratic Congress, which he had dominated since 1933. Nonetheless, the Court changed its position, as Chief Justice Charles Evans Hughes and Justice Owen Roberts began to vote with the more liberal members.

Most economic indicators rose sharply between 1935 and 1937. Roosevelt decided that the recovery was sufficient to warrant a reduction in relief programs and a move toward a balanced budget. The budget for fiscal year 1938 was reduced from $8.5 billion to $6.8 billion, with the WPA experiencing the largest cut. During the winter of 1937–1938, the economy slipped rapidly and unemployment rose to 12.5 percent. In April 1938, Roosevelt requested and received from Congress an emergency appropriation of about $3 billion for the WPA, as well as increases for public works and other programs. In July 1938, the economy began to recover, and it regained the 1937 levels in 1939.

SOCIAL DIMENSIONS OF THE NEW DEAL ERA

Unemployment for African-Americans was much higher than for the general population, and before 1933 they were often excluded from state and local relief efforts. Roosevelt seems to have given little thought to the special problems of African-Americans, and he was afraid to endorse legislation such as an antilynching bill for fear of alienating the southern wing of the Democratic party. More African-Americans were appointed to government positions by Roosevelt than ever before, but the number was still small. Roosevelt issued an executive order on June 25, 1941, establishing the Fair Employment Practices Committee to ensure consideration for minorities in defense employment.

John Collier, the commissioner of the Bureau of Indian Affairs, persuaded Congress to repeal the Dawes Act of 1887 by passing the Indian Reorganization Act of 1934. The law restored tribal ownership of lands, recognized tribal constitutions and government, and provided loans to tribes for economic development.

LABOR UNIONS

Labor unions lost members and influence during the 1920s and early 1930s. The National Industrial Recovery Act gave them new hope when it guaranteed the right to unionize, and during 1933 about 1.5 million new members joined unions.

The passage of the National Labor Relations or Wagner Act in 1935 resulted in a massive growth of union membership, but at the expense of bitter conflict within the labor movement. The American Federation of Labor was made up primarily of craft unions. Some leaders wanted to unionize the mass-production industries, such as automobiles and rubber, with industrial unions. In November 1935, John L. Lewis and others established the Committee for Industrial Organization to unionize basic industries, presumably within the AFL. President William Green of the AFL ordered the CIO to disband in January 1936. When the rebels refused, they were expelled by the AFL in March 1937. The insurgents then reorganized the CIO as the independent Congress of Industrial Organizations.

During its organizational period, the CIO sought to initiate several industrial unions, particularly in the steel, auto, rubber, and radio industries. In late 1936 and early 1937, it used a tactic called the sit-down strike, with the strikers occupying the workplace to prevent any production. By the end of 1941, the CIO was larger than the AFL. Union members comprised about 11.5 percent of the work force in 1933 and 28.2 percent in 1941.

NEW DEAL DIPLOMACY AND THE ROAD TO WAR

Roosevelt and Secretary of State Cordell Hull continued the policies of their predecessors by endeavoring to improve relations with Latin American nations, and formalized their position by calling it the Good Neighbor Policy.

At the Montevideo Conference of American Nations in December of 1933, the United States renounced the right of intervention in the internal affairs of Latin American countries. In 1936, in the Buenos Aires Convention, the United States agreed to submit all American disputes to arbitration.

UNITED STATES NEUTRALITY LEGISLATION

Belief that the United States should stay out of foreign wars and problems began in the 1920s and grew in the 1930s. Examinations of World War I profiteering and revisionist history that asserted Germany had not been responsible for World War I and that the United States had been misled were also influential during the 1930s. A Gallup poll in April 1937 showed that almost two-thirds of those responding thought that American entry into World War I had been a mistake.

The Johnson Act of 1934: This law prohibited any nation in default on World War I payments from selling securities to any American citizen or corporation.

The Neutrality Acts of 1935: On outbreak of war between foreign nations, all exports of American arms and munitions to them would be embargoed for six months. In addition, American ships were prohibited from carrying arms to any belligerent, and the president was to warn American citizens not to travel on belligerent ships.

The Neutrality Acts of 1936: The laws gave the president authority to determine when a state of war existed, and prohibited any loans or credits to belligerents.

The Neutrality Acts of 1937: The laws gave the president authority to determine if a civil war was a threat to world peace and if it was covered by the Neutrality Acts. It also prohibited all arms sales to belligerents, and allowed the cash-and-carry sale of nonmilitary goods to belligerents.

THE AMERICAN RESPONSE TO THE WAR IN EUROPE

In August 1939, Roosevelt created the War Resources Board to develop a plan for industrial mobilization in the event of war. The next month, he established the Office of Emergency Management in the White House to centralize mobilization activities.

The Neutrality Act of 1939: Roosevelt officially proclaimed the neutrality of the United States on September 5, 1939. The Democratic Congress, in a vote that followed party lines, passed a new Neutrality Act in November. It allowed the cash-and-carry sale of arms and short-term loans to belligerents, but forbade American ships to trade with belligerents or Americans to travel on belligerent ships.

Almost all Americans recognized Germany as a threat. They were divided on whether to aid Britain or to concentrate on the defense of America. The Committee to Defend America by Aiding the Allies was formed in May 1940, and the America First Committee, which opposed involvement, was incorporated in September 1940.

In April 1940, Roosevelt declared that Greenland, a possession of conquered Denmark, was covered by the Monroe Doctrine, and he supplied military assistance to set up a coastal patrol there.

In May 1940, Roosevelt appointed a Council of National Defense, chaired by William S. Knudson (1879–1948), the president of General Motors, to direct defense production and to build 50,000 planes. The Office of Production Management was created to allocate scarce materials, and the Office of Price Administration was established to prevent inflation and protect consumers.

Congress approved the nation's first peacetime draft, the Selective Service and Training Act, in September 1940.

Roosevelt determined that to aid Britain in every way possible was the best way to avoid war with Germany. In September 1940, he signed an agreement to give Britain 50 American destroyers in return for a 99-year lease on air and naval bases in British territories in Newfoundland, Bermuda, and the Caribbean.

THE ELECTION OF 1940

The Republicans: The Republicans nominated Wendell L. Willkie (1892–1944) of Indiana, a dark-horse candidate. The platform supported a strong defense program, but severely criticized New Deal domestic policies.

The Democrats: Roosevelt was nominated for a third term, breaking a tradition which had existed since George Washington. The platform endorsed the foreign and domestic policies of the administration.

The Election: Roosevelt won by a much narrower margin than in 1936.

AMERICAN INVOLVEMENT WITH THE EUROPEAN WAR

The Lend-Lease Act: This let the United States provide supplies to Britain in exchange for goods and services after the war. It was signed on March 11, 1941.

In April 1941, Roosevelt started the American Neutrality Patrol. The American navy would search out but not attack German submarines in the western half of the Atlantic and warn British vessels of their location. Also in April, U.S. forces occupied Greenland, and in May, the president declared a state of unlimited national emergency.

American marines occupied Iceland, a Danish possession, in July 1941 to protect it from seizure by Germany. The American navy began to convoy American and Icelandic ships between the United States and Iceland.

On August 9, 1941, Roosevelt and Winston Churchill issued the Atlantic Charter.

Germany invaded Russia in June 1941, and in November the United States extended lend-lease assistance to the Russians.

The American destroyer *Greer* was attacked by a German submarine near Iceland on September 4, 1941. Roosevelt ordered the American military forces to shoot on sight any German or Italian vessel in the patrol zone. An undeclared naval war had begun. The American destroyer *Kearny* was attacked by a submarine on October 16, and the destroyer *Reuben James* was sunk on October 30, with 115 lives lost. In November, Congress authorized the arming of merchant ships.

THE ROAD TO PEARL HARBOR

In late July 1941, the United States placed an embargo on the export of aviation gasoline, lubricants, and scrap iron and steel to Japan, and granted an additional loan to China. In December, the embargo was extended to include iron ore and pig iron, some chemicals, machine tools, and other products.

In October 1941, a new military cabinet headed by General Hideki Tojo took control of Japan. The Japanese secretly decided to make a final effort to negotiate, and to go to war if no solution was found by November 25. A new round of talks followed in Washington, but neither side would make a substantive change in its position, and on November 26, Hull repeated the American demand that the Japanese remove all their forces from China and Indochina immediately. The Japanese gave final approval on December 1 for an attack on the United States.

The Japanese planned a major offensive to take the Dutch East Indies, Malaya, and the Philippines in order to obtain the oil, metals, and other raw materials they needed. At the same time, they would attack Pearl Harbor in Hawaii to destroy the American Pacific fleet to keep it from interfering with their plans.

The United States had broken the Japanese diplomatic codes and knew that trouble was imminent. Between December 1 and December 6, 1941, it became clear to administration leaders that Japanese task forces were being ordered into battle. American commanders in the Pacific were warned of possible aggressive action there, but not forcefully.

At 7:55 a.m. on Sunday, December 7, 1941, the first wave of Japanese carrier-based planes attacked the American fleet in Pearl Harbor. A second wave followed at 8:50 a.m. The United States suffered the loss of two battleships sunk, six damaged and out of action, three cruisers and three destroyers sunk or damaged, and a number of lesser vessels destroyed or damaged. All of the 150 aircraft at Pearl Harbor were destroyed on the ground. Worst of all, 2,323 American servicemen were killed and about 1,100 wounded. The Japanese lost 29 planes, five midget submarines, and one fleet submarine.

WORLD WAR II AND THE POSTWAR ERA (1941–1960)

DECLARED WAR BEGINS

On December 8, 1941, Congress declared war on Japan, with one dissenting vote. On December 11, Germany and Italy declared war on the United States. Great Britain and the United States then established the Combined Chiefs of Staff, headquartered in Washington, to direct Anglo-American military operations.

On January 1, 1942, representatives of 26 nations met in Washington, D.C., and signed the Declaration of the United Nations, pledging themselves to the principles of the Atlantic Charter and promising not to make a separate peace with their common enemies.

THE HOME FRONT

War Production Board: The WPD was established in 1942 by President Franklin D. Roosevelt for the purpose of regulating the use of raw materials.

Wage and Price Controls: In April 1942, the General Maximum Price Regulation Act froze prices and extended rationing. In April 1943, prices, wages, and salaries were frozen.

Revenue Act of 1942: The Revenue Act of 1942 extended the income tax to the majority of the population. Payroll deduction for the income tax began in 1944.

Social Changes: Rural areas lost population, while population in coastal areas increased rapidly. Women entered the work force in increasing numbers. African-Americans moved from the rural South to northern and western cities, with racial tensions often resulting, most notably in the June 1943 racial riot in Detroit.

Smith-Connolly Act: Passed in 1943, the Smith-Connolly Antistrike Act authorized government seizure of a plant or mine idled by a strike if the war effort was impeded. It expired in 1947.

Korematsu v. United States: In 1944, the Supreme Court upheld President Roosevelt's 1942 order that Issei (Japanese-Americans who had emigrated from Japan) and Nisei (native born Japanese-Americans) be relocated to concentration camps. The camps were closed in March 1946.

Presidential Election of 1944: President Franklin D. Roosevelt, together with new vice-presidential candidate Harry S. Truman (1884–1972) of Missouri, defeated his Republican opponent, Governor Thomas E. Dewey of New York.

Roosevelt died on April 12, 1945, at Warm Springs, Georgia. Harry S. Truman became president.

THE NORTH AFRICAN AND EUROPEAN THEATERS

The United States joined in the bombing of the European continent in July 1942. Bombing increased during 1943 and 1944 and lasted to the end of the war.

The Allied army under Dwight D. Eisenhower attacked French North Africa in November 1942. The Vichy French forces surrendered.

In the Battle of Kassarine Pass, North Africa, February 1943, the Allied army met General Erwin Rommel's Africa Korps. Although the battle is variously interpreted as a standoff or a defeat for the United States, Rommel's forces were soon trapped by the British moving in from Egypt. In May 1943, Rommel's Africa Korps surrendered.

Allied armies under George S. Patton (1885–1945) invaded Sicily from Africa in July 1943, and gained control by mid-August. Moving from Sicily, the Allied armies invaded the Italian mainland in September. The Germans, however, put up a stiff resistance, with the result that Rome did not fall until June 1944.

In March 1944, the Soviet Union began pushing into Eastern Europe.

On "D-Day," June 6, 1944, Allied armies under Dwight D. Eisenhower, now commander-in-chief of the Allied Expeditionary Forces, began an invasion of Normandy, France.

Allied armies liberated Paris in August. By mid-September, they had arrived at the Rhine, on the edge of Germany.

Beginning December 16, 1944, at the Battle of the Bulge, the Germans counterattacked, driving the Allies back about 50 miles into Belgium. By January, the Allies were once more advancing toward Germany. The Allies crossed the Rhine in March 1945. In the last week of April, Eisenhower's forces met the Soviet army at the Elbe. On May 7, 1945, Germany surrendered.

THE PACIFIC THEATER

By the end of December 1941, Guam, Wake Island, the Gilbert Islands, and Hong Kong had fallen to the Japanese. In January 1942, Raboul, New Britain, fell, followed in February by Singapore and Java, and in March by Rangoon, Burma. U.S. forces surrendered at Corregidor, Philippines, on May 6, 1942.

The Battle of the Coral Sea, May 7–8, 1942, stopped the Japanese advance on Australia.

The Battle of Midway, June 4–7, 1942, proved to be the turning point in the Pacific.

A series of land, sea, and air battles took place around Guadalcanal in the Solomon Islands from August 1942 to February 1943, stopping the Japanese.

The Allied strategy of island hopping, begun in 1943, sought to neutralize Japanese strongholds with air and sea power and then move on.

U.S. forces advanced into the Gilberts (November 1943), the Marshalls (January 1944), and the Marianas (June 1944). After the American capture of the Marianas, General Tojo resigned as premier of Japan.

The Battle of Leyte Gulf, October 25, 1944, resulted in Japan's loss of most of its remaining naval power. Forces under General Douglas MacArthur (1880–1964) liberated Manila in March 1945.

Between April and June 1945, in the battle for Okinawa, nearly 50,000 American casualties resulted from the fierce fighting, but the battle virtually destroyed Japan's remaining defenses.

THE ATOMIC BOMB

The Manhattan Engineering District was established by the army engineers in August 1942 for the purpose of developing an atomic bomb (it eventually became known as the Manhattan Project). J. Robert Oppenheimer directed the design and construction of a transportable atomic bomb at Los Alamos, New Mexico.

On December 2, 1942, Enrico Fermi (1901–1954) and his colleagues at the University of Chicago produced the first atomic chain reaction.

On July 16, 1945, the first atomic bomb was exploded at Alamogordo, New Mexico.

The *Enola Gay* dropped an atomic bomb on Hiroshima, Japan, on August 6, 1945, killing about 78,000 persons and injuring 100,000 more. On August 9, a second bomb was dropped on Nagasaki, Japan.

On August 8, 1945, the Soviet Union entered the war against Japan.

Japan surrendered on August 14, 1945. The formal surrender was signed on September 2.

DIPLOMACY

Casablanca Conference: On January 14–25, 1943, Franklin D. Roosevelt and Winston Churchill, prime minister of Great Britain, declared a policy of unconditional surrender for "all enemies."

Moscow Conference: In October 1943, Secretary of State Cordell Hull obtained Soviet agreement to enter the war against Japan after Germany was defeated, and to participate in a world organization after the war was over.

Declaration of Cairo: Issued on December 1, 1943, after Roosevelt met with General Chiang Kai-shek in Cairo from November 22 to 26, the Declaration of Cairo called for Japan's unconditional surrender and stated that all Chinese territories occupied by Japan would be returned to China and that Korea would be free and independent.

THE EMERGENCE OF THE COLD WAR AND CONTAINMENT

In 1947, career diplomat and Soviet expert George F. Kennan wrote an anonymous article for *Foreign Affairs* in which he called for a counterforce to Soviet pressures, for the purpose of "containing" communism.

Truman Doctrine: In February 1947, Great Britain notified the United States that it could no longer aid the Greek government in its war against Communist insurgents. The next month President Harry S. Truman asked Congress for $400 million in military and economic aid for Greece and Turkey. In what became known as the "Truman Doctrine," he argued that the United States must support free peoples who were resisting Communist domination.

Marshall Plan: Secretary of State George C. Marshall (1880–1959) proposed in June 1947 that the United States provide economic aid to help rebuild Europe. The following March, Congress passed the European Recovery Program, popularly known as the Marshall Plan, which provided more than $12 billion in aid.

After the United States, France, and Great Britain announced plans to create a West German Republic out of their German zones, the Soviet Union in June 1948 blocked surface access to Berlin. The United States then instituted an airlift to transport supplies to the city until the Soviets lifted their blockade in May 1949.

NATO

In April 1949, the North Atlantic Treaty Organization was signed by the United States, Canada, Great Britain, and nine European nations. The signatories pledged that an attack against one would be considered an attack against all. The Soviets formed the Warsaw Treaty Organization in 1955 to counteract NATO.

INTERNATIONAL COOPERATION

Representatives from Europe and the United States, at a conference held July 1–22, 1944, signed agreements for an international bank and a world monetary fund to stabilize international currencies and rebuild the economies of war-torn nations.

From April to June 1945, representatives from 50 countries met in San Francisco to establish the United Nations. The UN charter created a General Assembly composed of all member nations which would act as the ultimate policy-making body. A Security Council, made up of 11 members, including the United States, Great Britain, France, the Soviet Union, and China as permanent members and six additional nations elected by the General Assembly for two-year terms, would be responsible for settling disputes among UN member nations.

CONTAINMENT IN ASIA

General Douglas MacArthur headed a four-power Allied Control Council which governed Japan, allowing it to develop economically and politically.

Between 1945 and 1948, the United States gave more than $2 billion in aid to the Nationalist Chinese under Chiang Kai-shek, and sent George C. Marshall to settle the conflict between Chiang's Nationalists and Mao Tse-tung's Communists. In 1949, however, Mao defeated Chiang and forced the Nationalists to flee to Formosa (Taiwan). Mao established the People's Republic of China on the mainland.

KOREAN WAR

On June 25, 1950, North Korea invaded South Korea. President Truman committed U.S. forces commanded by General MacArthur, but under United Nations auspices. By October, the UN forces (mostly American) had driven north of the 38th parallel, which divided North and South Korea. Chinese troops attacked MacArthur's forces on November 26, pushing them south of the 38th parallel, but by spring 1951, the UN forces had recovered their offensive.

In June 1953, an armistice was signed, leaving Korea divided along virtually the same boundary that had existed prior to the war.

EISENHOWER-DULLES FOREIGN POLICY

Dwight D. Eisenhower, elected president in 1952, chose John Foster Dulles (1888–1959) as secretary of state. Dulles talked of a more aggressive foreign policy, calling for "massive retaliation" and "liberation" rather than containment. He wished to emphasize nuclear deterrents rather than conventional armed forces.

After several years of nationalist war against French occupation, France, Great Britain, the Soviet Union, and China signed the Geneva Accords in July 1954, dividing Vietnam along the 17th parallel. The North would be under Ho Chi Minh and the South under Emperor Bao Dai. Elections were scheduled for 1956 to unify the country, but Ngo Dinh Diem overthrew Bao Dai and prevented the elections from taking place. The United States supplied economic aid to South Vietnam.

Dulles attempted to establish a Southeast Asia Treaty Organization parallel to NATO, but was able to obtain only the Philippine Republic, Thailand, and Pakistan as signatories in September 1954.

President Eisenhower announced in January 1957 that the United States was prepared to use armed force in the Middle East against Communist aggression. Under this doctrine, U.S. marines entered Beirut, Lebanon, in July 1958 to promote political stability during a change of governments. The marines left in October.

The United States supported the overthrow of President Jacobo Arbenz Guzman of Guatemala in 1954 because he began accepting arms from the Soviet Union.

In January 1959, Fidel Castro overthrew Fulgencio Batista, dictator of Cuba. Castro soon began criticizing the United States and moved closer to the Soviet Union, signing a trade agreement with the Soviets in February 1960. The United States prohibited the importation of Cuban sugar in October 1960, and broke off diplomatic relations in January 1961.

THE POLITICS OF AFFLUENCE: DEMOBILIZATION AND DOMESTIC POLICY

Harry S. Truman, formerly a senator from Missouri and vice president of the United States, became president on April 12, 1945.

Congress created the Atomic Energy Commission in 1946, establishing civilian control over nuclear development and giving the president sole authority over the use of atomic weapons in warfare.

Taft-Hartley Act (1947): The Republicans, who had gained control of Congress in 1946, sought to control the power of the unions through the Taft-Hartley Act. This act made the "closed-shop" illegal; labor unions could no longer force employers to hire only union members. The act slowed down efforts to unionize the South, and by 1954, 15 states had passed "right to work" laws, forbidding the "union-shop."

In 1948, the president banned racial discrimination in federal government hiring practices and ordered desegregation of the armed forces.

The Presidential Succession Act of 1947 placed the Speaker of the House and the president pro tempore of the Senate ahead of the secretary of state and after the vice president in the line of succession. The Twenty-Second Amendment to the Constitution, ratified in 1951, limited the president to election to two terms.

ELECTION OF 1948

Truman was the Democratic nominee, but the Democrats were split by the States' Rights Democratic party (Dixiecrats) which nominated Governor Strom Thurmond of South Carolina, and the Progressive party, which nominated former Vice President Henry Wallace. The Republicans nominated Governor Thomas E. Dewey of New York. After traveling widely, and attacking the "do-nothing Congress," Truman won a surprise victory.

ANTICOMMUNISM

In 1950, Julius and Ethel Rosenberg and Harry Gold were charged with giving atomic secrets to the Soviet Union. The Rosenbergs were convicted and executed in 1953.

On February 9, 1950, Senator Joseph R. McCarthy (1908–1957) of Wisconsin alleged that he had a list of known Communists who were working in the State Department. He later expanded his attacks. After making unproved charges against the army, he was censured by the Senate in 1954.

EISENHOWER'S DYNAMIC CONSERVATISM

The Republicans nominated Dwight D. Eisenhower, most recently NATO commander, for the presidency. The Democrats nominated Governor Adlai E. Stevenson (1900–1965) of Illinois for president. Eisenhower won by a landslide; for the first time since Reconstruction, the Republicans won some southern states.

Eisenhower sought to balance the budget and lower taxes but did not attempt to roll back existing social and economic legislation. Eisenhower first described his policy as "dynamic conservatism," and then as "progressive moderation." The administration abolished the Reconstruction Finance Corporation, ended wage and price controls, and reduced farm price supports. It cut the budget and in 1954 lowered tax rates for corporations and individuals with high incomes; an economic slump, however, made balancing the budget difficult.

Social Security was extended in 1954 and 1956 to an additional 10 million people, including professionals, domestic and clerical workers, farm workers, and members of the armed services.

The Rural Electrification Administration announced in 1960 that 97 percent of American farms had electricity.

In 1954, Eisenhower obtained congressional approval for joint Canadian-U.S. construction of the St. Lawrence Seaway, which was to give oceangoing vessels access to the Great Lakes. In 1956, Congress authorized construction of the Interstate Highway System, with the federal government supplying 90 percent of the cost and the states 10 percent.

The launching of the Soviet space satellite *Sputnik* on October 4, 1957, created fear that America was falling behind technologically. Although the United States launched *Explorer I* on January 31, 1958, the concern continued. In 1958, Congress established the National Aeronautics and Space Administration (NASA) to coordinate research and development, and passed the National Defense Education Act to provide grants and loans for education.

On January 3, 1959, Alaska became the 49th state, and on August 21, 1959, Hawaii became the 50th.

CIVIL RIGHTS

Eisenhower completed the formal integration of the armed forces, desegregated public services in Washington, D.C., naval yards, and veteran's hospitals, and appointed a Civil Rights Commission.

Brown v. Board of Education of Topeka: In this 1954 case, NAACP lawyer Thurgood Marshall challenged the doctrine of "separate but equal" (*Plessy v. Ferguson*, 1896). The Court declared that separate educational facilities were inherently unequal. In 1955, the Court ordered states to integrate "with all deliberate speed."

Although he did not personally support the Supreme Court decision, Eisenhower sent 10,000 National Guardsmen and 1,000 paratroopers to Little Rock, Arkansas, to control mobs and enable African-Americans to enroll at Central High in September 1957.

On December 11, 1955, in Montgomery, Alabama, Rosa Parks, a black woman, refused to give up her seat on a city bus to a white person and was arrested. Under the leadership of Martin Luther King (1929–1968), an African-American pastor, African-Americans of Montgomery organized a bus boycott that lasted for a year, until in December 1956, the Supreme Court refused to review a lower court ruling that stated that separate but equal was no longer legal.

In 1959, state and federal courts nullified Virginia laws that prevented state funds from going to integrated schools. This proved to be the beginning of the end for "massive resistance."

On February 1, 1960, upon being denied service, four African-American students staged a sit-in at a Woolworth lunch counter in Greensboro, North Carolina. This inspired sit-ins by thousands elsewhere in the South and led to the formation of the Student Nonviolent Coordinating Committee.

THE ELECTION OF 1960

Vice President Richard M. Nixon won the Republican presidential nomination, and the Democrats nominated Senator John F. Kennedy (1917–1963) for the presidency, with Lyndon B. Johnson (1908–1973), majority leader of the Senate, as his running mate.

Kennedy won the election by slightly more than 100,000 popular votes and 94 electoral votes, based on majorities in New England, the Middle Atlantic, and the South.

THE NEW FRONTIER, VIETNAM, AND SOCIAL UPHEAVAL (1960–1972)

KENNEDY'S "NEW FRONTIER" AND THE LIBERAL REVIVAL

Kennedy was unable to get much of his program through Congress because of an alliance of Republicans and southern Democrats.

Kennedy did gain congressional approval for raising the minimum wage from $1.00 to $1.25 an hour and extending it to 3 million more workers.

The 1961 Housing Act provided nearly $5 billion over four years for the preservation of open urban spaces, development of mass transit, and the construction of middle-class housing.

CIVIL RIGHTS

In May 1961, blacks and whites boarded buses in Washington, D.C., and traveled across the South to New Orleans to test federal enforcement of regulations prohibiting discrimination. They met violence in Alabama but continued to New Orleans.

The Justice Department, under Attorney General Robert F. Kennedy (1925–1968), began to push for civil rights, including desegregation of interstate transportation in the South, integration of schools, and supervision of elections.

In the fall of 1962, President Kennedy called the Mississippi National Guard to federal duty to enable an African-American, James Meredith, to enroll at the University of Mississippi.

Kennedy presented a comprehensive civil rights bill to Congress in 1963. With the bill held up in Congress, 200,000 people marched, demonstrating on its behalf on August 28, 1963, in Washington, D.C. Martin Luther King gave his "I Have a Dream" speech.

THE COLD WAR CONTINUES

Under Eisenhower, the Central Intelligence Agency had begun training some 2,000 men for an invasion of Cuba to overthrow Fidel Castro, the left-leaning revolutionary who had taken power in 1959. On April 19, 1961, this force invaded at the Bay of Pigs, but was pinned down and forced to surrender. Some 1,200 men were captured.

In August 1961, Khrushchev closed the border between East and West Berlin and ordered the erection of the Berlin Wall.

The Soviet Union began the testing of nuclear weapons in September 1961. Kennedy then authorized resumption of underground testing by the United States.

On October 14, 1962, a U-2 reconnaissance plane brought photographic evidence that missile sites were being built in Cuba. Kennedy, on October 22, announced a blockade of Cuba and called on Khrushchev to dismantle the missile bases and remove all weapons capable of attacking the United States from Cuba. Six days later, Khrushchev backed down, withdrew the missiles, and Kennedy lifted the blockade.

In July 1963, a treaty banning the atmospheric testing of nuclear weapons was signed by all the major powers except France and China.

In 1961, Kennedy announced the Alliance for Progress, which would provide $20 million in aid to Latin America.

JOHNSON AND THE GREAT SOCIETY

On November 22, 1963, Kennedy was assassinated by Lee Harvey Oswald in Dallas, Texas. Jack Ruby, a nightclub owner, killed Oswald two days later.

Succeeding Kennedy, Lyndon B. Johnson had extensive experience in both the House and Senate, and as a Texan, was the first southerner to serve as president since Woodrow Wilson.

A tax cut of more than $10 billion passed Congress in 1964, and an economic boom resulted.

The 1964 Civil Rights Act outlawed racial discrimination by employers and unions, created the Equal Employment Opportunity Commission to enforce the law, and eliminated the remaining restrictions on black voting.

Michael Harrington's *The Other America* (1962) showed that 20 to 25 percent of American families were living below the governmentally defined poverty line. The Economic Opportunity Act of 1964 sought to address the problem by establishing a Job Corps, community action programs, educational programs, work-study programs, job training, loans for small businesses and farmers, and Volunteers in Service to America (VISTA), a "domestic peace corps." The Office of Economic Opportunity administered many of these programs.

ELECTION OF 1964

Lyndon Johnson was nominated for president by the Democrats. The Republicans nominated Senator Barry Goldwater, a conservative from Arizona. Johnson won more than 61 percent of the popular vote and could now launch his own "Great Society" program.

The Medicare Act of 1965 combined hospital insurance for retired people with a voluntary plan to cover physician's bills. Medicaid provided grants to states to help the poor below retirement age.

EMERGENCE OF BLACK POWER

In 1965, Martin Luther King announced a voter registration drive. With help from the federal courts, he dramatized his effort by leading a march from Selma to Montgomery, Alabama, between March 21 and 25. The Voting Rights Act of 1965 authorized the attorney general to appoint officials to register voters.

Seventy percent of African-Americans lived in city ghettos. In 1966, New York and Chicago experienced riots, and the following year there were riots in Newark and Detroit. The Kerner Commission, appointed to investigate the riots, concluded that they were directed at a social system that prevented African-Americans from getting good jobs and crowded them into ghettos.

Stokely Carmichael, in 1966, called for the civil rights movements to be "black-staffed, black-controlled, and black-financed." Later, he moved on to the Black Panthers, self-styled urban revolutionaries based in Oakland, California. Other leaders such as H. Rap Brown also called for Black Power.

On April 4, 1968, Martin Luther King was assassinated in Memphis by James Earl Ray. Riots in more than 100 cities followed.

THE NEW LEFT

Students at the University of California at Berkeley staged sit-ins in 1964 to protest the prohibition of political canvassing on campus. In December, police broke up a sit-in; protests spread to other campuses across the country.

Student protests began focusing on the Vietnam War. In the spring of 1967, 500,000 gathered in Central Park in New York City to protest the war, many burning their draft cards. Students for a Democratic Society (SDS) became more militant and willing to use violence.

More than 200 large campus demonstrations took place in the spring, culminating in the occupation of buildings at Columbia University to protest the university's involvement in military research and its poor relations with minority groups. Police wielding billy clubs eventually broke up the demonstration. In August, thousands gathered in Chicago to protest the war during the Democratic convention.

Beginning in 1968, SDS began breaking up into rival factions. By the early 1970s, the New Left had lost political influence, having abandoned its original commitment to democracy and nonviolence.

WOMEN'S LIBERATION

In *The Feminine Mystique* (1963), Betty Friedan argued that middle-class society stifled women and did not allow them to use their individual talents. She attacked the cult of domesticity.

Friedan and other feminists founded the National Organization for Women (NOW) in 1966, calling for equal employment opportunities and equal pay.

VIETNAM

After the French defeat in 1954, the United States sent military advisors to South Vietnam to aid the government of Ngo Dinh Diem. The pro-Communist Vietcong forces gradually grew in strength, partly because Diem failed to follow through on promised reforms. They received support from North Vietnam, the Soviet Union, and China.

In August 1964—after claiming that North Vietnamese gunboats had fired on American destroyers in the Gulf of Tonkin—Lyndon Johnson pushed the Gulf of Tonkin resolution through Congress, authorizing him to use military force in Vietnam. After a February 1965 attack by the Vietcong on Pleiku, Johnson ordered operation "Rolling Thunder," the first sustained bombing of North Vietnam. Johnson then sent combat troops to South Vietnam; under the leadership of General William C. Westmoreland, they conducted search and destroy operations. The number of troops increased to 184,000 in 1965, 385,000 in 1966, 485,000 in 1967, and 538,000 in 1968.

"Hawks" defended the president's policy and, drawing on containment theory, said that the nation had the responsibility to resist aggression. If Vietnam should fall, it was said, all Southeast

Asia would eventually go. The administration stressed its willingness to negotiate the withdrawal of all "foreign" forces from the war.

Opposition began quickly, with "teach-ins" at the University of Michigan in 1965 and a 1966 congressional investigation led by Senator J. William Fulbright. Antiwar demonstrations were gaining large crowds by 1967. "Doves" argued that the war was a civil war in which the United States should not meddle.

On January 31, 1968, the first day of the Vietnamese new year (Tet), the Vietcong attacked numerous cities and towns, American bases, and even Saigon. Although they suffered large losses, the Vietcong won a psychological victory, as American opinion began turning against the war.

THE ELECTION OF 1968

In November 1967, Senator Eugene McCarthy of Minnesota announced his candidacy for the 1968 Democratic presidential nomination, running on the issue of opposition to the war.

In February, McCarthy won 42 percent of the Democratic vote in the New Hampshire primary, compared with Johnson's 48 percent. Robert F. Kennedy then announced his candidacy for the Democratic presidential nomination.

Lyndon Johnson withdrew his candidacy on March 31, 1968, and Vice President Hubert H. Humphrey took his place as a candidate for the Democratic nomination.

After winning the California primary over McCarthy, Robert Kennedy was assassinated by Sirhan Sirhan, a young Palestinian. This event assured Humphrey's nomination.

The Republicans nominated Richard M. Nixon. Governor George C. Wallace of Alabama ran for the presidency under the banner of the American Independent party, appealing to fears generated by protestors and big government.

Johnson suspended air attacks on North Vietnam shortly before the election. Nonetheless Nixon, who emphasized stability and order, defeated Humphrey by a margin of 1 percent. Wallace's 13.5 percent was the best showing by a third-party candidate since 1924.

THE NIXON CONSERVATIVE REACTION

The Nixon administration sought to block renewal of the Voting Rights Act and delay implementation of court-ordered school desegregation in Mississippi.

In 1969, Nixon appointed Warren E. Burger, a conservative, as chief justice. Although more conservative than the Warren court, the Burger court did declare the death penalty, as used at the time, unconstitutional in 1972, and struck down state antiabortion legislation in 1973.

VIETNAMIZATION

The president turned to "Vietnamization," the effort to build up South Vietnamese forces while withdrawing American troops. In 1969, Nixon reduced American troop strength by 60,000, but at the same time ordered the bombing of Cambodia, a neutral country.

In April 1970, Nixon announced that Vietnamization was succeeding but a few days later, he sent troops into Cambodia to clear out Vietcong sanctuaries and resumed bombing of North Vietnam.

Protests against escalation of the war were especially strong on college campuses. After several students were killed during protests, several hundred colleges were closed down by student strikes, as moderates joined the radicals. Congress repealed the Gulf of Tonkin Resolution.

The publication in 1971 of classified Defense Department documents, called "The Pentagon Papers," revealed that the government had misled the Congress and the American people regarding its intentions in Vietnam during the mid-1960s.

Nixon drew American forces back from Cambodia but increased bombing. In March 1972, after stepped-up aggression from the North, Nixon ordered the mining of Haiphong and other northern ports.

In the summer of 1972, negotiations between the United States and North Vietnam began in Paris. A few days before the 1972 presidential election, Henry Kissinger, the president's national security advisor, announced that "peace was at hand."

Nixon resumed bombing of North Vietnam in December 1972, claiming that the North Vietnamese were not bargaining in good faith. In January 1973, the opponents reached a settlement in which the North Vietnamese retained control over large areas of the South and agreed to release American prisoners of war within 60 days. Nearly 60,000 Americans had been killed and 300,000 more wounded and the war had cost Americans $109 billion. On March 29, 1973, the last American combat troops left South Vietnam.

FOREIGN POLICY

With his national security advisor, Henry Kissinger, Nixon took some bold diplomatic initiatives. In February 1972, Nixon and Kissinger went to China to meet with Mao Tse-tung and his associates. The United States agreed to support China's admission to the United Nations and to pursue economic and cultural exchanges.

Nixon and Kissinger called their policy *détente*, a French term meaning a relaxation in the tensions between two governments.

THE ELECTION OF 1972

Richard M. Nixon, who had been renominated by the Republicans, won a landslide victory over the Democratic nominee, Senator George McGovern.

WATERGATE, CARTER, AND THE NEW CONSERVATISM, AND POST–COLD WAR CHALLENGES (1972–2008)

WATERGATE

What became known as the Watergate crisis began during the 1972 presidential campaign. Early on the morning of June 17, James McCord, a security officer for the Committee for the Re-Election of the President, and four other men broke into Democratic headquarters at the Watergate apartment complex in Washington, D.C., and were caught while going through files and installing electronic eavesdropping devices.

In March 1974, a grand jury indicted H.R. Haldeman, John Ehrlichman, former Attorney General John Mitchell, and four other White House aides and named Nixon an unindicted coconspirator.

Meanwhile, the House Judiciary Committee televised its debate over misconduct by the President, adopting three articles of impeachment. It charged the president with obstructing justice, misusing presidential power, and failing to obey the committee's subpoenas.

Before the House began to debate impeachment, Nixon announced his resignation on August 8, 1974, to take effect at noon the following day. Gerald Ford then became president.

THE FORD PRESIDENCY

Gerald Ford was in many respects the opposite of Nixon. Although a partisan Republican, he was well liked and free from any hint of scandal. Ford almost immediately encountered controversy when in September 1974 he offered to pardon Nixon. Nixon accepted the offer, although he admitted no wrongdoing and had not yet been charged with a crime.

VIETNAM

As North Vietnamese forces pushed back the South Vietnamese, Ford asked Congress to provide more arms for the South. Congress rejected the request, and in April 1975 Saigon fell to the North Vietnamese.

CARTER'S MODERATE LIBERALISM

Ronald Reagan, a former movie actor and governor of California, opposed Ford for the Republican presidential nomination, but Ford won by a slim margin. The Democrats nominated James Earl Carter, formerly governor of Georgia, who ran on the basis of his integrity and lack of Washington connections. Carter narrowly defeated Ford in the election.

Carter offered amnesty to Americans who had fled the draft and gone to other countries during the Vietnam War. He established the Departments of Energy and Education and placed the civil service on a merit basis. He created a "superfund" for cleanup of chemical waste dumps, established controls over strip mining, and protected 100 million acres of Alaskan wilderness from development.

CARTER'S FOREIGN POLICY

Carter negotiated a controversial treaty with Panama, affirmed by the Senate in 1978, that provided for the transfer of ownership of the canal to Panama in 1999 and guaranteed its neutrality.

Carter ended official recognition of Taiwan and in 1979 recognized the People's Republic of China. Conservatives called the decision a "sell-out."

In 1978, Carter negotiated the Camp David Agreement between Israel and Egypt. Israel promised to return occupied land in the Sinai to Egypt in exchange for Egyptian recognition, a process completed in 1982. An agreement to negotiate the Palestinian refugee problem proved ineffective.

THE IRANIAN CRISIS

In 1978, a revolution forced the shah of Iran to flee the country, replacing him with a religious leader, Ayatollah Ruhollah Khomeini. Because the United States had supported the shah with arms and money, the revolutionaries were strongly anti-American, calling the United States the "Great Satan."

After Carter allowed the exiled shah to come to the United States for medical treatment in October 1979, some 400 Iranians broke into the American embassy in Teheran on November 4, taking the occupants captive. They demanded that the shah be returned to Iran for trial and that his wealth be confiscated and given to Iran. Carter rejected these demands; instead, he froze Iranian assets in the United States and established a trade embargo against Iran.

THE ELECTION OF 1980

Republican Ronald Reagan defeated Carter by a large electoral majority, and the Republicans gained control of the Senate and increased their representation in the House.

After extensive negotiations with Iran, in which Algeria acted as an intermediary, American hostages were freed on January 20, 1981, the day of Reagan's inauguration.

THE REAGAN PRESIDENCY: ATTACKING BIG GOVERNMENT

An ideological though pragmatic conservative, Ronald Reagan acted quickly and forcefully to change the direction of government policy. He placed priority on cutting taxes. His approach was based on "supply-side" economics, the idea that if government left more money in the hands of the people, they would invest rather then spend the excess on consumer goods. The results would be greater production, more jobs, and greater prosperity, and thus more income for the government despite lower tax rates.

Reagan asked for a 30 percent tax cut, and despite fears of inflation on the part of Congress, in August 1983 obtained a 25 percent cut, spread over three years.

Congress passed the Budget Reconciliation Act in 1981, cutting $39 billion from domestic programs, including education, food stamps, public housing, and the National Endowments for the Arts and Humanities. While cutting domestic programs, Reagan increased the defense budget by $12 billion.

From a deficit of $59 billion in 1980, the federal budget was running $195 billion in the red by 1983.

Because of rising deficits, Reagan and Congress increased taxes in various ways. The 1982 Tax Equity and Fiscal Responsibility Act reversed some concessions made to business in 1981. Social Security benefits became taxable income in 1983. In 1984, the Deficit Reduction Act increased taxes by another $50 billion. But the deficit continued to increase.

Reagan ended ongoing antitrust suits against IBM and AT&T, thereby fulfilling his promise to reduce government interference with business.

ASSERTING AMERICAN POWER

Reagan took a hard line against the Soviet Union, calling it an "evil empire." He placed new cruise missiles in Europe, despite considerable opposition from Europeans.

Reagan also concentrated on obtaining funding for the development of a computer-controlled strategic defense initiative system (SDI), popularly called "Star Wars" after the widely seen movie, that would destroy enemy missiles from outerspace.

In Nicaragua, Reagan encouraged the opposition (*contras*) to the leftist Sandinista government with arms, tactical support, and intelligence, and supplied aid to the government of El Salvador in its struggles against left-wing rebels. In October 1983, the president also sent American troops into the Caribbean island of Grenada to overthrow a newly established Cuban-backed regime.

THE ELECTION OF 1984

Walter Mondale, a former senator from Minnesota and vice president under Carter, won the Democratic nomination. Mondale criticized Reagan for his budget deficits, high unemployment and interest rates, and reduction of spending on social services. However, Reagan was elected to a second term in a landslide.

SECOND-TERM FOREIGN CONCERNS

After Mikhail S. Gorbachev became the premier of the Soviet Union in March 1985 and took a more flexible approach toward both domestic and foreign affairs, Reagan softened his anti-Soviet stance.

Reagan and Gorbachev had difficulty in reaching an agreement on arms limitations at summit talks in 1985 and 1986. Finally, in December 1987, they signed an agreement eliminating medium-range missiles from Europe.

IRAN-CONTRA

In 1985 and 1986, several Reagan officials sold arms to the Iranians in hopes of encouraging them to use their influence in getting American hostages in Lebanon released. The profits from these sales were then diverted to the Nicaraguan *contras* in an attempt to get around congressional restrictions on funding the *contras*. The president was forced to appoint a special prosecutor, and Congress held hearings on the affair in May 1987.

SECOND-TERM DOMESTIC AFFAIRS: THE ECONOMY

The Tax Reform Act of 1986 lowered tax rates. At the same time, it removed many tax shelters and tax credits. The law did away with the concept of progressive taxation, the requirement that the percentage of income taxed increased as income increased.

The federal deficit reached $179 billion in 1985. At about the same time, the United States experienced trade deficits of more than $100 billion annually.

Black Monday: On October 19, 1987, the Dow Jones Industrial Average dropped more than 500 points. Between August 25 and October 20, the market lost over a trillion dollars in paper value.

NASA: The explosion of the shuttle *Challenger* soon after take-off on January 28, 1986, damaged NASA's credibility and reinforced doubts about the complex technology required for the SDI program.

Supreme Court: Reagan reshaped the Court in 1986, replacing Chief Justice Warren C. Burger with Associate Justice William H. Rehnquist, probably the most conservative member of the Court. Although failing in his nomination of Robert Bork for associate justice, Reagan did appoint other conservatives to the Court: Sandra Day O'Connor, Antonin Scalia, and Anthony Kennedy.

THE ELECTION OF 1988

Vice President George H. W. Bush won the Republican nomination. Bush easily defeated Michael Dukakis, the Democratic nominee, but the Republicans were unable to make any inroads in Congress.

THE BUSH ADMINISTRATION

Soon after Bush took office, the budget deficit for 1990 was estimated at $143 billion. In September, the administration and Congress agreed to increase taxes on gasoline, tobacco, and alcohol, establish an excise tax on luxury items, and raise Medicare taxes. Cuts were also to be made in medicare and other domestic programs. In a straight party vote, Republicans voting against and Democrats voting in favor, Congress in December transferred the power to decide whether new tax and spending proposals violated the deficit cutting agreement from the White House Office of Management and Budget to the Congressional Budget Office.

The Commission on Base Realignment and Closure proposed in December 1989 that 54 military bases be closed. In June 1990, Secretary of Defense Richard Cheney sent Congress a plan to cut military spending by 10 percent and the armed forces by 25 percent over the next five years. The following April, Cheney recommended the closing of 43 domestic military bases, plus many more abroad.

With the savings and loan industry in financial trouble in 1989, largely because of bad real-estate loans, Bush signed a bill which created the Resolution Trust Corporation to oversee the closure and merging of savings and loans, and which provided $166 billion over 10 years to cover the bad debts. Estimates of the total costs of the debacle were over $300 billion.

BUSH'S ACTIVIST FOREIGN POLICY

Panama: Since coming to office, the Bush administration had been concerned with Panamanian dictator Manuel Noriega because he allegedly served as an important link in the drug traffic between South America and the United States. After economic sanctions, diplomatic efforts, and an October 1989 coup failed to oust Noriega, Bush ordered 12,000 troops into Panama on December 20. The Americans installed a new government headed by Guillermo Endara, who had earlier won a presidential election that was promptly nullified by Noriega. On January 3, 1990, Noriega surrendered to the Americans and was taken to the United States to stand trial on drug trafficking charges; he was convicted and jailed for assisting the Medellín drug cartel. Twenty-three United States soldiers and three American civilians were killed in the operation. The Panamanians lost nearly 300 soldiers and more than 500 civilians.

Nicaragua: After years of civil war, Nicaragua held a presidential election in February 1990. Because of an economy largely destroyed by civil war and large financial debt to the United States, Violeta Barrios de Chamorro of the National Opposition Union defeated Daniel Ortega Saavedra of the Sandinistas, thereby fulfilling a long-standing American objective. The United States lifted its economic sanctions in March and put together an economic aid package for Nicaragua. In September 1991, the Bush administration forgave Nicaragua most of its debt to the United States.

China: After the death in April 1989 of reformer Hu Yaobang, formerly general secretary and chairman of the Chinese Communist party, students began pro-democracy marches in Beijing. By the middle of May, more than one million people were gathering on Beijing's Tiananmen Square, and other protestors elsewhere in China, calling for political reform. Martial law was imposed and in early June the army fired on the demonstrators. Estimates of the death toll in the wake of the nationwide crackdown on demonstrators ranged between 500 and 7,000. In July 1989, United States National Security Advisor Brent Scowcroft and Deputy Secretary of State Lawrence Eagleburger secretly met with Chinese leaders. When they again met the Chinese in December and revealed their earlier meeting, the Bush administration faced a storm of criticism for its policy of "constructive engagement" from opponents arguing that sanctions should be imposed. While establishing sanctions in 1991 on Chinese high-technology satellite-part exports, Bush continued to support renewal of Most Favored Nation trading status.

Africa: To rescue American citizens threatened by civil war, Bush sent 230 marines into Liberia in August 1990, evacuating 125 people. South Africa in 1990 freed Nelson Mandela, the most famous leader of the African National Congress, after 28 years of imprisonment. South Africa then began moving away from apartheid, and in 1991 Bush lifted economic sanctions imposed five years earlier. Mandela and his wife, Winnie, toured the U.S. in June 1990 to a tumultuous welcome, particularly from African-Americans. During their visit, they also addressed Congress.

COLLAPSE OF EAST EUROPEAN COMMUNISM

In August 1989 Hungary opened its borders with Austria. The following October, the Communists reorganized their party, calling it the Socialist party. Hungary then proclaimed itself a "Free Republic."

With thousands of East Germans passing through Hungary to Austria, after the opening of the borders in August 1989, Erich Honecker stepped down as head of state in October. On November 1, the government opened the border with Czechoslovakia and eight days later the Berlin Wall fell. On December 6, a non-Communist became head of state, followed on December 11 by large demonstrations demanding German reunification. Reunification took place in October 1990.

After anti-government demonstrations were forcibly broken up in Czechoslovakia in October 1989, changes took place in the Communist leadership the following month. Then, on December

8, the Communists agreed to relinquish power and Parliament elected Václav Havel, a playwright and anti-Communist leader, to the presidency on December 29.

When anti-government demonstrations in Romania were met by force in early December, portions of the military began joining the opposition which captured dictator Nicolae Ceauşescu and his wife, Elena, killing them on December 25, 1989. In May 1990 the National Salvation Front, made up of many former Communists, won the parliamentary elections.

In January 1990 the Bulgarian national assembly repealed the dominant role of the Communist party. A multi-party coalition government was formed the following December.

Albania opened its border with Greece and legalized religious worship in January 1990, and in July ousted hardliners from the government.

Amid the collapse of Communism in Eastern Europe, Bush met with Mikhail Gorbachev in Malta from December 1 through December 3, 1989; the two leaders appeared to agree that the Cold War was over. On May 30 and 31, 1990, Bush and Gorbachev met in Washington to discuss the possible reunification of Germany, and signed a trade treaty between the United States and the Soviet Union. The meeting of the two leaders in Helsinki on September 9 addressed strategies for the developing Persian Gulf crisis. At the meeting of the "Group of 7" nations (Canada, France, Germany, Italy, Japan, United Kingdom, and the United States) in July 1991, Gorbachev requested economic aid from the West. A short time later, on July 30 and 31, Bush met Gorbachev in Moscow where they signed the START treaty, which cut U.S. and Soviet nuclear arsenals by 30 percent, and pushed for Middle Eastern talks.

PERSIAN GULF CRISIS

Saddam Hussein of Iraq charged that Kuwait had conspired with the United States to keep oil prices low and began massing troops at the Iraq-Kuwait border.

On August 2, Iraq invaded Kuwait, an act that Bush denounced as "naked aggression." One day later 100,000 Iraqi soldiers were poised south of Kuwait City near the Saudi Arabian border. The United States quickly banned most trade with Iraq, froze Iraq's and Kuwait's assets in the United States, and sent aircraft carriers to the Persian Gulf. After the United Nations Security Council condemned the invasion, on August 6 Bush ordered the deployment of air, sea, and land forces to Saudi Arabia, dubbing the operation "Desert Shield." At the end of August there were 100,000 American soldiers in Saudi Arabia.

Bush encouraged Egypt to support American policy by forgiving Egypt its debt to the United States and obtaining pledges of financial support from Saudi Arabia, Kuwait, and Japan, among other nations, to help pay for the operation. On October 29, the Security Council warned Saddam Hussein that further actions might be taken if he did not withdraw from Kuwait. In November Bush ordered that U.S. forces be increased to more than 400,000. On November 29, the United Nations set January 15, 1991, as the deadline for Iraqi withdrawal from Kuwait.

On January 9, Iraq's foreign-minister, Tariq Aziz, rejected a letter written by Bush to Hussein. Three days later, after an extensive debate, Congress authorized the use of force in the Gulf. On January 17, an international force including the United States, Great Britain, France, Italy, Saudi Arabia, and Kuwait launched an air and missile attack on Iraq and occupied Kuwait. The U.S. called the effort "Operation Desert Storm." Under the overall command of Army General H. Norman Schwarzkopf, the military effort emphasized high-technology weapons, including F-15 E fighter-bombers, F-117 A stealth fighters, Tomahawk cruise missiles, and Patriot anti-missile missiles. Beginning on January 17, Iraq fired SCUD missiles into Israel in an effort to draw that country into the war and splinter the U.S.-Arabian coalition. On January 22 and 23, Hussein's forces set Kuwaiti oil fields on fire and spilled oil into the Gulf.

On February 23, the allied ground assault began. Four days later Bush announced that Kuwait was liberated and ordered offensive operations to cease. The United Nations established the terms for the cease-fire: Iraqi annexation of Kuwait to be rescinded, Iraq to accept liability for damages and return Kuwaiti property, Iraq to end all military actions and identify mines and booby traps, and Iraq to release captives.

On April 3, the Security Council approved a resolution to establish a permanent cease-fire; Iraq accepted U.N. terms on April 6. The next day the United States began airlifting food to Kurdish refugees on the Iraq-Turkey border who were fleeing the Kurdish rebellion against Hussein, a rebellion that was seemingly encouraged by Bush, who nonetheless refused to become militarily involved. The United States estimated that 100,000 Iraqis had been killed during the war while the Americans had lost about 115 lives.

On February 6, 1991, the United States had set out its postwar goals for the Middle East. These included regional arms control and security arrangements, international aid for reconstruction of Iraq and Kuwait, and resolution of the Israeli-Palestinian conflict. Immediately after cessation of the conflict, Secretary of State James Baker toured the Middle East attempting to promote a conference to address the problems of the region. After several more negotiating sessions, Saudi Arabia, Syria, Jordan, and Lebanon had accepted the U.S. proposal for an Arab-Israeli peace conference by the middle of July; Israel conditionally accepted in early August. Despite continuing conflict with Iraq, including United Nations inspections of its nuclear capabilities, and new Israeli settlements in disputed territory—which kept the conference agreement tenuous—the nations met in Madrid, Spain, at the end of October. Bilateral talks in early November between Israel and the Arabs concentrated on procedural issues.

BREAKUP OF THE SOVIET UNION

Following the collapse of Communism in Eastern Europe, the Baltic republic of Lithuania, which had been taken over by the Soviet Union in 1939 through an agreement with Adolf Hitler, declared its independence from the Soviet Union on March 11, 1990.

Two days later, on March 13, the Soviet Union removed the Communist monopoly of political power, allowing non-Communists to run for office. The process of liberalization went haltingly forward in the Soviet Union. Perhaps the most significant event was the election of Boris Yeltsin, who had left the Communist party, as president of the Russian republic on June 12, 1991.

On August 19, Soviet hard-liners attempted a coup to oust Gorbachev, but a combination of their inability to control communication with the outside world, a failure to quickly establish military control, and the resistance of Yeltsin, members of the military, and people in the streets of cities such as Moscow and Leningrad, ended the coup on August 21, returning Gorbachev to power.

In the aftermath of the coup, much of the Communist structure came crashing down, setting the stage for opposition parties to emerge. The remaining Baltic republics of Latvia and Estonia declared their independence, which was recognized by the United States several days after other nations had done so. Most of the other Soviet republics then followed suit in declaring their independence. The Bush administration wanted some form of central authority to remain in the Soviet Union; hence, it did not seriously consider recognizing the independence of any republics except the Baltics. Bush also resisted offering economic aid to the Soviet Union until it presented a radical economic reform plan to move toward a free market. However, humanitarian aid such as food was pledged in order to preserve stability during the winter.

In September 1991, George Bush announced unilateral removal and destruction of ground-based tactical nuclear weapons in Europe and Asia, removal of nuclear-armed Tomahawk cruise missiles from surface ships and submarines, immediate destruction of intercontinental ballistic missiles covered by START, and an end to the 24-hour alert for strategic bombers that the U.S. had maintained for decades. Gorbachev responded the next month by announcing the immediate deactivation of intercontinental ballistic missiles covered by START, removal of all short-range missiles from Soviet ships, submarines, and aircraft, and destruction of all ground-based tactical nuclear weapons. He also said that the Soviet Union would reduce its forces by 700,000 troops, and he placed all long-range nuclear missiles under a single command. Gorbachev's hold on the presidency progressively weakened in the final months of 1991, with the reforms he had put in place taking on a life of their own. The dissolution of the U.S.S.R. led to his resignation in December, making way for Boris Yeltsin, who had headed popular resistance. The United States was now the world's only superpower.

THE DEMOCRATS RECLAIM THE WHITE HOUSE

William Jefferson Clinton, governor of Arkansas, overcame several rivals to win the Democratic presidential nomination in 1992 and with his running mate, Senator Albert Gore of Tennessee, went on to win the White House. During the campaign, Clinton and independent candidate H. Ross Perot, a wealthy Texas businessman, emphasized jobs and the economy while attacking the mounting federal debt. The incumbent, Bush, stressed traditional values and his foreign policy accomplishments. In the 1992 election, Clinton won 43 percent of the popular vote and 370 electoral votes, defeating Bush and Perot. Perot took 19 percent of the popular vote, but was unable to garner any electoral votes.

Clinton came to be dogged by a number of controversies, ranging from alleged ill-gotten gains in a complex Arkansas land deal that came to be known as the Whitewater Affair to charges of sexual misconduct, brought by a former Arkansas state employee (with whom he would ultimately reach an out-of-court settlement), that dated to an incident she said had occurred when Clinton was governor. In December 1998 Clinton was impeached by the House on charges that stemmed from an adulterous affair with a White House intern, Monica Lewinsky. The affair had been uncovered by Independent Counsel Kenneth Starr in the course of a long-running investigation into alleged malfeasance by the president and his wife, Hillary, in the Whitewater land deal and other matters. Extraordinary detail about Clinton's encounters with Lewinsky was revealed in a voluminous report from Starr's office. Its release triggered the impeachment proceedings, which ended with Clinton's acquittal by the Senate in February 1999.

On the legislative front, Clinton was strongly rebuffed in an attempt during his first term to reform the nation's healthcare system. In the 1994 mid-term elections, in what Clinton himself considered a repudiation of his administration, the Republicans took both houses of Congress from the Democrats and voted in Newt Gingrich of Georgia as Speaker of the House. Gingrich had helped craft the Republican congressional campaign strategy to dramatically shrink the federal government and give more power to the states.

Clinton, however, was not without his successes, both on the legislative and diplomatic fronts. He signed legislation establishing a five-day waiting period for handgun purchases as well as a crime bill emphasizing community policing. He signed the Family and Medical Leave Act, which requires large companies to provide up to 12 weeks' unpaid leave to workers for family and medical emergencies. He also championed welfare reform (a central theme of his campaign), but made it clear that the legislation he signed into law in August 1996 radically overhauling FDR's welfare system disturbed him on two counts—its exclusion of legal immigrants from getting most federal benefits and its deep cut in federal outlays for food stamps; Clinton said these flaws could be repaired with further legislation. In foreign affairs, Clinton signed the North American Free Trade Agreement (NAFTA), which lifted most trade barriers with Mexico and Canada as of 1994. Clinton sought to ease tensions between Israelis and Palestinians, and he helped bring together Itzhak Rabin, prime minister of Israel, and Yasir Arafat, chairman of the Palestine Liberation Organization, for a summit at the White House. Ultimately, the two Middle East leaders signed an accord in 1994 establishing Palestinian self-rule in the Gaza Strip and Jericho. In October 1994 Israel and Jordan signed a treaty to begin the process of establishing full diplomatic relations. Rabin was assassinated a year later by a radical, right-wing Israeli. The Clinton administration also played a central role in hammering out peace agreements in 1995 in war-torn former Yugoslavia—where armed conflict had broken out four years earlier among Serbs, Croats, Bosnian Muslims, and other factions and groups—and in 1998 in Northern Ireland.

Clinton recaptured the Democratic nomination without a serious challenge, while longtime GOP Senator Robert Dole of Kansas, the Senate majority leader, overcame several opponents but orchestrated a harmonious nominating convention with running mate Jack Kemp, a former New York congressman and Cabinet member. In November 1996, with most voters citing a healthy economy and the lack of an enticing alternative in Dole or the Reform Party's Perot, Clinton received 49 percent of the vote, becoming the first Democrat to be re-elected since FDR, in 1936. The GOP retained control of both houses of Congress.

Clinton, intent on mirroring the diversity of America in his Cabinet appointments, chose Hispanics Henry Cisneros (Housing and Urban Development) and Federico Peña (Transportation and, later, Energy), African Americans Ron Brown (Commerce) and Mike Espy (Agriculture), and women, including the nation's first woman attorney general, Janet Reno, and Madeleine Albright, the first woman secretary of state in U.S. history (Albright succeeded Warren Christopher, who served through Clinton's first term). Brown and 34 others on a trade mission died when his Air Force plane crashed in Croatia in April 1996. Cisneros and Espy both resigned under ethics clouds.

In 2000, Republican George W. Bush defeated Democrat Al Gore in a close and controversial election, with Bush receiving a majority of the electoral votes (after a decision by the Supreme Court to stop a third recount—essentially awarding Florida's electoral votes to him), but Gore receiving a majority of the popular vote. Eight months after being sworn in, the September 11th attacks occurred. In response to the attacks, President Bush declared a War on Terror, which led to the creation of a new cabinet level agency, the Department of Homeland Security, an invasion of Afghanistan, and an invasion of Iraq. On the domestic front, President Bush signed into law tax cuts, the No Child Left Behind Act, and Medicare prescription drug benefits for seniors.

After defeating Democrat John Kerry in the 2004 election, President Bush's second term was beset by scandals and criticism related to the War on Terror, Katrina and the perceived failure of the government's response, and an economy that went into recession. While extremely popular for much of his first term, his public approval ratings went from 90% approval to a low of 25% while finally rising to 34% as he left office. Only Harry Truman and Richard Nixon had lower ratings at the end of their presidencies.

The 2008 presidential election featured two Senators, Democrat Barack Obama from Illinois and Republican John McCain from Arizona. Senator Obama won and became the 44th president of the United States and its first African American president.

LATE 20TH CENTURY SOCIAL AND CULTURAL DEVELOPMENTS

AIDS: In 1981 scientists announced the discovery of Acquired Immune Deficiency Syndrome (AIDS), which was especially prevalent among homosexual males and intravenous drug users. Widespread fear resulted, including an upsurge in homophobia. The Centers for Disease Control and Prevention (CDC) and the National Cancer Institute, among others, pursued research on the disease. The Food and Drug Administration responded to calls for fast-tracking evaluation of drugs by approving the drug AZT in February 1991. With the revelation that a Florida dentist had infected three patients, there were calls for mandatory testing of healthcare workers. Supporters of testing argued before a House hearing in September 1991 that testing should be regarded as a public health, rather than a civil rights, issue. In early 1998, the CDC estimated that between 400,000 and 650,000 Americans were HIV-positive, meaning that they had the virus that causes AIDS.

Public health officials expressed concern about the difficulties in tracking the spread of AIDS, as the HIV infection was being reported to health agencies only when patients developed symptoms, which could be years after infection. New drug therapies, meanwhile, were preventing AIDS symptoms from ever appearing, creating the specter of growing numbers of people going unseen by public-health agencies as they spread the virus. These developments came against the backdrop of a marked change in the demographic makeup of the epidemic's victims—from mostly white homosexual males to African-Americans, Hispanics, and women, particularly those who were poor, intravenous drug users, or the sex partners of drug users.

Families: More than half the married women in the United States continued to hold jobs outside the home. Nearly one out of every two marriages was ending in divorce, and there was an increase in the number of unmarried couples living together, which contributed to a growing number of illegitimate births. So-called family values became a major theme in presidential politics, powered in part by the publication of leading conservative William J. Bennett's best-selling anthology *The Book of Virtues: A Treasury of Great Moral Stories.* Bennett had served as Bush's secretary of education and, later, as director of the Office of National Drug Control Policy, which the press shortened to "drug czar."

Terrorism Hits Home: While terrorist attacks continued to be a grim reality overseas through the 1980s and early 1990s, with Americans frequently targeted, such incidents had come to be perceived as something the United States wouldn't have to face on its own soil—until February 26, 1993, when a terrorist bomb ripped through the underground parking garage of the World Trade Center in New York City, killing six people and injuring more than 1,000. The blast shattered America's "myth of invulnerability," wrote foreign policy analyst Jeffrey D. Simon in his book *The Terrorist Trap.* Convicted and sentenced to 240 years each were four Islamic militants. On April 19, 1995, the Oklahoma City federal building was bombed: 168 people were killed and 500 injured. Timothy James McVeigh, a gun enthusiast involved in the American militia movement who had often expressed hatred toward the U.S. government and was particularly aggrieved over the government's assault two years earlier on a self-proclaimed prophet's compound in Waco, Texas, was convicted and sentenced to death in June 1997. A second defendant, Terry Nichols, was convicted of conspiracy. These attacks, however, were dwarfed by the September 11, 2001, attacks in which terrorists turned hijacked planes into missiles—two destroying the World Trade Center and one damaging the Pentagon. A fourth plane was brought down in Pennsylvania, apparently by passengers who overtook the hijackers. President Bush immediately cast suspicion upon Saudi exile Osama bin Laden and declared a "war on terrorism" that began with a military strike against Afghanistan, bin Laden's alleged base of operations.

Murder Trial a National Spectacle: In Los Angeles, former pro-football star, broadcaster, and actor O.J. Simpson was tried for the brutal murder in June 1994 of his ex-wife, Nicole Brown Simpson, and her friend Ronald Goldman. The nationally televised trial became a running spectacle for months. Simpson was found not guilty, but later, in a civil trial, would be found responsible for the slaying of Goldman and for committing battery against Nicole.

Crime and Politics: George H.W. Bush had won the presidency in 1988 on a strong anti-crime message, crystallized in a controversial TV spot that demonized Willie Horton, an African-American inmate in the Massachusetts jail system who was released while then-presidential candidate Michael Dukakis was the Democratic governor. Bill Clinton co-opted the traditional Republican crime issue by pushing through legislation for more community policing, an approach that, together with aggressive central management, was credited for the plummeting crime rate in New York City, for example.

U.S. Prisoner Count Grows: Between 1987 and 1997, the period spanning the Bush administration and Clinton's first term, the number of Americans in prison doubled, soaring from 800,000 to 1.6 million.

Drug Abuse Continues: Drug abuse continued to be widespread, with cocaine becoming more readily available, particularly in a cheaper, stronger form called "crack."

Labor: Labor union strength continued to ebb in the 1990s (though some observers pointed to the success of the 1997 Teamsters strike against United Parcel Service as a sign that labor was rebounding), with the U.S. Department of Labor's Bureau of Labor Statistics reporting that union membership dropped to 14.5 percent of wage and salary employment in 1996, down from 14.9 percent in 1995. In 1983, union members made up 20.1 percent of the work force. Unions continued to be responsible for higher wages for their members: organized workers reported median weekly earnings of $615, as against a median of $462 for non-union workers, according to the bureau.

Abortion and the High Court: In a July 1989 decision, *Webster v. Reproductive Health Services*, the U.S. Supreme Court upheld a Missouri law prohibiting public employees from performing abortions, unless the mother's life is threatened. With this decision came a shift in focus on the abortion issue from the courts to the state legislatures. Pro-life (anti-abortion rights) forces moved in several states to restrict the availability of abortions, but their results were mixed. Florida rejected abortion restrictions in October 1989, the governor of Louisiana vetoed similar legislation nine months later, and in early 1991 Maryland adopted a liberal abortion law. In contrast, Utah and Pennsylvania enacted strict curbs on abortion during the same period. At the national level, Bush in October 1989 vetoed funding for Medicaid abortions. The conflict between pro-choice (pro-abortion) and pro-life forces gained national attention through such events as a pro-life demonstration held in Washington in April 1990, and blockage of access to abortion clinics by Operation Rescue, a militant anti-abortion group, in the summer of 1991. Abortion clinics around the country continued to be the targets of protests and violence through the mid-1990s.

Gap Between Rich and Poor Widens: Kevin Phillips's *The Politics of Rich and Poor* (1990) argued that 40 million Americans in the bottom fifth of the population experienced a 1 percent decline in income between 1973 and 1979 and a 10 percent decline between 1979 and 1987. Meanwhile, the top fifth saw a rise of 7 percent and 16 percent during the same periods. The number of single-parent families living below the poverty line (annual income of $11,611 for a family of four) rose by 46 percent between 1979 and 1987. Nearly one-quarter of American children under age six were counted among the poor, said Phillips.

Censorship: The conservative leaning of the electorate in the late 20th century revealed its cultural dimension in a controversy that erupted over the National Endowment for the Arts in September 1989. Criticism of photographer Robert Mapplethorpe's homoerotic and masochistic pictures, among other artworks that had been funded by the Endowment, led Senator Jesse Helms of North Carolina to propose that grants for "obscene or indecent" projects, or those derogatory of religion, be cut off. Although the proposal ultimately failed, it raised questions about the government's role as a sponsor of art in an increasingly pluralistic society. The Mapplethorpe photographs also became an issue the following summer when Cincinnati's Contemporary Art Center was indicted on charges of obscenity when it exhibited the artist's work. A jury later struck down the charges. Meanwhile, in March 1990, the Recording Industry Association of America, in a move advocated by, among others, Tipper Gore, wife of Democratic Senator Al Gore of Tennessee (the man who would be elected vice-president in 1992), agreed to place new uniform warning labels on recordings that contained potentially offensive language.

Crisis in Education: The National Commission on Excellence in Education, appointed in 1981, argued in "A Nation at Risk" that a "rising tide of mediocrity" characterized the nation's schools. In the wake of the report, many states instituted reforms, including higher teacher salaries, competency tests for teachers, and an increase in required subjects for high school graduation. In September 1989 President Bush met with the nation's governors in Charlottesville, Virginia, to work on a plan to improve the schools. The governors issued a call for the establishment of national performance goals to be measured by achievement tests. In February 1990 the National Governors' Association adopted specific performance goals, stating that achievement tests should be administered in grades four, eight, and twelve. As the new millenium approached, however, signs began to emerge that the tide might be turning: a major global comparison found in June 1997 that America's 9- and 10-year-olds were among the world's best in science and also scored well above average in math.

Literary Trends: The 1980s and 1990s saw the emergence of writers who concentrated on marginal or regional aspects of national life. William Kennedy wrote a series of novels about Albany, New York, most notably *Ironweed* (1983). The small-town West attracted attention from Larry McMurtry, whose *Lonesome Dove* (1985) used myth to explore the history of the region. The immigrant experience gave rise to Amy Tan's *The Joy-Luck Club* (1989) and Oscar Hijuelos's *The Mambo Kings Play Songs of Love* (1990). Tom Wolfe satirized greed, and class and racial tensions in New York City in *The Bonfire of the Vanities* (1987). Toni Morrison's *Beloved* (1987) dramatized the African-American slavery experience.

REVIEW QUESTIONS

1. Which of the following statements is true of the Kansas-Nebraska Act?

   (A) It led to the disintegration of the Democratic party.
   (B) It was a measure that the South had been demanding for decades.
   (C) It led directly to the formation of the Republican party.
   (D) By applying "popular sovereignty" to territories formerly closed to slavery by the Missouri Compromise, it succeeded in maintaining the tenuous sectional peace that had been created by the Compromise of 1850.

2. All of the following were steps taken by the United States to aid Great Britain prior to U.S. entry into World War II EXCEPT

   (A) the sale of 50 destroyers to the British in exchange for 99-year leases on certain overseas naval bases.
   (B) gradual assumption by the U.S. Navy of an increasing role in patrolling the Atlantic against German submarines.
   (C) institution of the Lend-Lease Act for providing war supplies to Britain beyond its ability to pay.
   (D) the stationing of U.S. Marines in Scotland to protect it against possible German invasion.

3. Thomas Nast achieved fame and influence as a

   (A) radio commentator.
   (B) newspaper publisher.
   (C) photographer.
   (D) political cartoonist.

4. Which of the following is true of the Stamp Act Congress?

   (A) It was the first unified government for all the American colonies.
   (B) It provided an important opportunity for colonial stamp agents to discuss methods of enforcing the act.
   (C) It was attended only by Georgia, Virginia, and the Carolinas.
   (D) It provided an important opportunity for colonial leaders to meet and establish ties with one another.

5. The map below depicts the United States immediately after which of the following events?

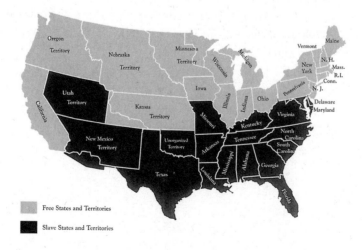

(A) Passage of the Compromise of 1850
(B) Negotiation of the Webster-Ashburton Treaty
(C) Passage of the Northwest Ordinance
(D) Settlement of the Mexican War

6. The principle of "popular sovereignty" was

(A) first conceived by Senator Stephen A. Douglas.
(B) applied as part of the Missouri Compromise.
(C) a central feature of the Kansas-Nebraska Act.
(D) a policy favored by the Whig party during the late 1840s and early 1850s.

7. In issuing the Emancipation Proclamation, one of Lincoln's goals was to

(A) gain the active aid of Britain and France in restoring the Union.
(B) stir up enthusiasm for the war in such border states as Maryland and Kentucky.
(C) please the Radicals in the North by abolishing slavery in areas of the South already under the control of Union armies.
(D) keep Britain and France from intervening on the side of the Confederacy.

8. Which of the following was not one of Hoover's responses to the Great Depression?

(A) He at first stressed the desirability of localism and private initiative rather than government intervention.
(B) He saw the Depression as akin to an act of nature, about which nothing could be done except to ride it out.
(C) He urged the nation's business leaders to maintain wages and full employment.
(D) His strategy for ending the Depression was a failure.

9. Which of the following statements is correct about the case of Whitaker Chambers and Alger Hiss?

(A) Hiss accused Chambers, an important mid-ranking government official, of being a Communist spy.
(B) The case gained national attention through the involvement of Senator Joseph R. McCarthy.
(C) Hiss was convicted of perjury for denying under oath that he had been a Communist agent.
(D) The case marked the beginning of American concern about Communist subversion.

10. Which of the following best characterizes the methods of Martin Luther King, Jr.?

(A) Nonviolent defiance of segregation
(B) Armed violence against police and troops
(C) Patience while developing the skills that would make blacks economically successful and gain them the respect of whites
(D) A series of petitions to Congress calling for correction of racial abuses

11. Which of the following best describes the agreement that ended the 1962 Cuban Missile Crisis?

(A) The Soviet Union agreed not to station troops in Cuba, and the United States agreed not to invade Cuba.
(B) The Soviet Union agreed to withdraw its missiles from Cuba, and the United States agreed not to invade Cuba.
(C) The Soviet Union agreed not to invade Turkey, and the United States agreed not to invade Cuba.
(D) The Soviet Union agreed to withdraw its missiles from Cuba, and the United States agreed not to invade Turkey.

12. The most common form of resistance on the part of black American slaves prior to the Civil War was

    (A) violent uprisings in which many persons were killed.
    (B) attempts to escape and reach Canada by means of the "Underground Railroad."
    (C) passive resistance, including breaking tools and slightly slowing the pace of work.
    (D) arson of plantation buildings and cotton gins.

13. Which of the following best describes the attitudes of Southern whites toward slavery during the mid-nineteenth century (ca. 1835–1865)?

    (A) Slavery was a necessary evil.
    (B) Slavery should be immediately abolished.
    (C) Slavery was a benefit to both whites and blacks.
    (D) Slavery should gradually be phased out and the freed slaves colonized to some place outside the United States.

14. For farmers and planters in the South, the 1850s was a period of

    (A) low prices for agricultural products.
    (B) rapid and violent fluctuations in crop prices.
    (C) high crop prices due to repeated crop failures.
    (D) high crop prices and sustained prosperity.

15. Immigrants coming to America from Eastern and Southern Europe during the late nineteenth century were most likely to

    (A) settle in large cities in the Northeast or Midwest.
    (B) settle on farms in the upper Midwest.
    (C) seek to file on homesteads on the Great Plains.
    (D) migrate to the South and Southwest.

16. Which of the following had the greatest effect in moving the United States toward participation in the First World War?

    (A) The German disregard of treaty obligations in violating Belgian neutrality
    (B) Germany's declaration of its intent to wage unrestricted submarine warfare
    (C) A German offer to reward Mexico with U.S. territory should it join Germany in a war against the United States
    (D) The beginning of the Russian Revolution

17. The Berlin Airlift was America's response to

    (A) the Soviet blockade of West Berlin from land communication with the rest of the western zone.
    (B) the acute war-time destruction of roads and railroads, making land transport almost impossible.
    (C) the unusually severe winter of 1947.
    (D) a widespread work stoppage by German transportation workers in protest of the allied occupation of Germany.

18. The economic theory of mercantilism would be consistent with which of the following statements?

    (A) Economies will prosper most when trade is restricted as little as possible.
    (B) A government should seek to direct the economy so as to maximize exports.
    (C) Colonies are of little economic importance to the mother country.
    (D) It is vital that a country imports more than it exports.

19. The primary American objection to the Stamp Act was that

(A) it was an internal tax, whereas Americans were prepared to accept only external taxes.

(B) it was the first tax of any kind ever imposed by Britain on the colonies.

(C) its proposed tax rates were so high that they would have crippled the colonial economy.

(D) it was a measure for raising revenue from the colonies but it had not been approved by the colonists through their representatives.

20. In seeking diplomatic recognition from foreign powers during the War for Independence, the American government found it necessary to

(A) make large financial payments to the governments of France, Spain, and Holland.

(B) promise to cede large tracts of American territory to France upon a victorious conclusion of the war.

(C) demonstrate its financial stability and self-sufficiency.

(D) demonstrate a determination and potential to win independence.

21. William Lloyd Garrison, in his publication *The Liberator,* was outspoken in calling for

(A) the gradual and compensated emancipation of slaves.

(B) colonization of slaves to some place outside the boundaries of the United States.

(C) repeal of the congressional "gag rule."

(D) immediate and uncompensated emancipation of slaves.

22. The Congressional "gag rule" stipulated that

(A) no law could be passed prohibiting slavery in the territories.

(B) no member of Congress could make statements or speeches outside of Congress pertaining to slavery.

(C) no antislavery materials could be sent through the mail to addresses in Southern states.

(D) no antislavery petitions would be formally received by Congress.

23. The main idea of Theodore Roosevelt's proposed "New Nationalism" was to

(A) make the federal government an instrument of domestic reform.

(B) undertake an aggressive new foreign policy.

(C) increase economic competition by breaking up all trusts and large business combinations.

(D) seek to establish a large overseas empire.

24. Franklin D. Roosevelt's New Deal program attempted or achieved all of the following EXCEPT

(A) Raised farm prices by paying farmers not to plant.

(B) Encouraged cooperation within industries so as to raise prices generally.

(C) Supported creation of the Reconstruction Finance Corporation.

(D) Invigorated the economy by lowering tariff barriers.

25. The Haymarket Incident involved

(A) a riot between striking workers and police.

(B) a scandal involving corruption within the Grant administration.

(C) allegations of corruption on the part of Republican presidential candidate James G. Blaine.

(D) a disastrous fire that called attention to the hazardous working conditions in some factories.

26. The "New Immigration" was made up primarily of

    (A) Europeans who came for economic rather than religious reasons.
    (B) Europeans who were better off financially than those of the "Old Immigration."
    (C) persons from Northern and Western Europe.
    (D) persons from Southern and Eastern Europe.

27. As a result of the Spanish-American War, the United States gained possession of Puerto Rico, Guam, and

    (A) the Philippines.
    (B) Cuba.
    (C) Bermuda.
    (D) the Panama Canal Zone.

28. The term "Long Hot Summers" refers to

    (A) major outdoor rock concerts during the late 1960s and early 1970s.
    (B) major Communist offensives against U.S. troops in Vietnam.
    (C) protests held in large American cities against the Vietnam War.
    (D) race riots in large American cities during the 1960s.

29. The immediate issue in dispute in Bacon's Rebellion was

    (A) the jailing of individuals or seizure of their property for failure to pay taxes during a time of economic hardship.
    (B) the under-representation of the back-country in Virginia's legislature.
    (C) the refusal of large planters to honor the terms of their contracts with former indentured servants.
    (D) the perceived failure of Virginia's governor to protect the colony's frontier area from the depredations of raiding Indians.

30. The Newburgh Conspiracy was concerned with

    (A) betrayal of the plans for the vital fort at West Point, New York.
    (B) the use of the Continental Army to create a more centralized Union of the states.
    (C) resistance to the collection of federal excise taxes in western Pennsylvania.
    (D) New England's threat to secede should the War of 1812 continue.

31. The Wilmot Proviso stipulated that

    (A) slavery should be prohibited in the lands acquired as a result of the Mexican War.
    (B) no lands should be annexed to the United States as a result of the Mexican War.
    (C) California should be a free state while the rest of the Mexican Cession should be reserved for the formation of slave states.
    (D) the status of slavery in the Mexican Cession should be decided on the basis of "Popular Sovereignty."

32. Which of the following was a goal of the Populist movement?

    (A) Free coinage of silver
    (B) Reform of child labor laws
    (C) Using modern science to solve social problems
    (D) Eliminating the electoral college as a method of choosing the nation's president

33. The settlement-house movement drew its workers primarily from which of the following groups?

    (A) Young, affluent, college-educated women
    (B) Poor Eastern European immigrants
    (C) Disabled veterans of the Spanish-American War
    (D) Idealistic young men who came to the city largely from rural areas

34. In its decision in the case of *Dred Scott v. Sandford,* the Supreme Court held that

    (A) separate facilities for different races were inherently unequal and therefore unconstitutional.
    (B) no black slave could be a citizen of the United States.
    (C) separate but equal facilities for different races were constitutional.
    (D) Affirmative Action programs were acceptable only when it could be proven that specific previous cases of discrimination had occurred within the institution or business in question.

35. The Whig party turned against President John Tyler because

    (A) he was felt to be ineffective in pushing the Whig agenda through Congress.
    (B) he spoke out in favor of the annexation of Texas.
    (C) he opposed the entire Whig legislative program.
    (D) he criticized Henry Clay's handling of the Nullification Crisis.

36. In coining the phrase "Manifest Destiny," journalist John L. O'Sullivan meant that

    (A) the struggle for racial equality was the ultimate goal of America's existence.
    (B) America was certain to become an independent country sooner or later.
    (C) it was the destiny of America to overspread the continent.
    (D) America must eventually become either all slave or all free.

37. All of the following were causes of the Mexican War EXCEPT

    (A) American desire for California.
    (B) Mexican failure to pay debts and damages owed to the U.S.

    (C) U.S. annexation of the formerly Mexican-held Republic of Texas.
    (D) Mexican desire to annex Louisiana.

38. The primary motive of those who founded the British colony in Virginia during the seventeenth century was the

    (A) desire for economic gain.
    (B) desire for religious freedom.
    (C) desire to create a perfect religious commonwealth as an example to the rest of the world.
    (D) desire to recreate in the New World the story of feudalistic society that was fading in the Old.

39. Which of the following is true of the Gulf of Tonkin incident?

    (A) It involved a clash of U.S. and Soviet warships.
    (B) In it, two North Vietnamese fighter-bombers were shot down as they neared U.S. Navy ships.
    (C) It involved the seizure, by North Vietnam, of a U.S. Navy intelligence ship in international waters.
    (D) It led to major U.S. involvement in the Vietnam War.

40. Which of the following statements is true of the SALT I treaty?

    (A) It brought sharp reductions in the number of ballistic missiles in both the U.S. and Soviet arsenals.
    (B) It was intended to encourage the deployment of defensive rather than offensive strategic weapons.
    (C) It indicated U.S. acceptance of the concept of Mutual Assured Destruction.
    (D) It was never ratified by the U.S. Senate.

ANSWER KEY

1.	(C)	11.	(B)	21.	(D)	31.	(A)
2.	(D)	12.	(C)	22.	(D)	32.	(A)
3.	(D)	13.	(C)	23.	(A)	33.	(A)
4.	(D)	14.	(D)	24.	(C)	34.	(B)
5.	(A)	15.	(A)	25.	(A)	35.	(C)
6.	(C)	16.	(B)	26.	(D)	36.	(C)
7.	(D)	17.	(A)	27.	(A)	37.	(D)
8.	(B)	18.	(B)	28.	(D)	38.	(A)
9.	(C)	19.	(D)	29.	(D)	39.	(D)
10.	(A)	20.	(D)	30.	(B)	40.	(C)

DETAILED EXPLANATIONS

1. **(C)** The Republican party came into being primarily out of the controversy stirred up by the Kansas-Nebraska Act. While this same controversy did cause a sizable splinter faction to leave the Democratic party and join the newly formed Republican party, it did not cause the disintegration of the Democratic party (A), which continued as a political force up to and beyond the Civil War. It is also true that the Kansas-Nebraska Act applied popular sovereignty to territory north of the Missouri Compromise line for the first time, but far from preserving the nation's fragile sectional harmony (D), it had quite the opposite effect. Although the South generally supported the Act, most Southerners had given the area little thought before Douglas introduced the issue (B).

2. **(D)** U.S. Marines were stationed in Iceland, not Scotland, to guard against possible German attack. Choice (C) may seem impossible, but the United States first instituted the Cash-and-Carry System and later began the Lend-Lease Act when British financial assets began to dwindle. The sale of destroyers to Britain (A) and the growing role of the U.S. Navy in the struggle to keep the Atlantic sea lanes open (B) were both steps taken by President Franklin D. Roosevelt prior to official U.S. entry into the war.

3. **(D)** Thomas Nast was a famous American political cartoonist of the late nineteenth century. He is remembered most of all for his criticism of the political machine of Wiliam M. "Boss" Tweed in New York City.

4. **(D)** One of the most important aspects of the Stamp Act Congress was the opportunity it provided for colonial leaders to meet and establish acquaintances with one another. Nine colonies—not merely Georgia, Virginia, and the Carolinas (C)—were represented at it, but far from being a unified government for all the American colonies (A), it simply passed mild resolutions protesting the Stamp Act. It was not, therefore, a vehicle for enforcing the act (B).

5. **(A)** The map depicts the United States after the Compromise of 1850. The states of Texas and California as well as the Utah and New Mexico Territories were not part of the United States at the time of the 1842 Webster-Ashburton Treaty (B), dealing with the Maine-New Brunswick boundary; and the 1787 Northwest Ordinance (C), organizing what was to become the states of Ohio, Indiana, Illinois, Michigan, and Wisconsin. California and the two territories were gained as a result of the Mexican War (D), but California statehood, as well as territorial status for Utah and New Mexico, had to await the Compromise of 1850.

6. **(C)** The principle of popular sovereignty was a central feature of the Kansas-Nebraska Act. Though championed by Senator Stephen A. Douglas (A), it had previously been put forward by 1848 Democratic presidential candidate Lewis Cass. A favorite policy of Democrats—not Whigs (D)—during the late 1840s and early 1850s, it proved a failure in solving the impasse over the status of slavery in the territories. It differed from the system of congressionally specified free and slave areas used in the Missouri Compromise (B).

7. **(D)** One of Lincoln's reasons for issuing the Emancipation Proclamation was to keep Britain and France from intervening on the side of the Confederacy. Lincoln neither needed, wanted, nor could have obtained the active aid of these countries in restoring the Union (A). The Radicals in the North would indeed have been pleased had Lincoln freed the slaves in areas of the South already under the control of Union armies (C), but it was precisely that which the Emancipation Proclamation did not do, largely out of concern for the more-or-less loyal slaveholding border states such as Maryland and Kentucky, who were not at all enthused about Lincoln's action even as it was (B).

8. **(B)** Hoover did *not* see the Depression as akin to an act of nature, about which nothing could be done. He did stress the desirability of localism and private initiative (A) and urged the nation's business leaders to maintain wages and full employment (C), but his efforts ended in failure (D).

9. **(C)** Hiss, a mid-ranking government official, was convicted of perjury for denying under oath that he had been a Communist agent, after being accused as such by admitted former Communist Whitaker Chambers, not the other way around (A). The case gained national attention through the involvement of young Congressman Richard Nixon, not Senator Joseph R. McCarthy (B), and while it did increase American concern about Communist subversion, it was by no means the beginning of such concern (D).

10. **(A)** Martin Luther King's methods were characterized by nonviolent defiance of segregation. While King and/or his supporters might make speeches or send petitions (D), civil disobedience gave his movement its urgency. Patience while developing the skills that would make blacks economically successful and gain them the respect of whites was the advice of late nineteenth century black leader Booker T. Washington (C), while armed violence was called for by King's more radical contemporaries of the 1960s (B).

11. **(B)** The agreement ending the Cuban Missile Crisis called for the Soviet Union to withdraw its missiles from Cuba while the United States agreed not to overthrow Castro's regime there. Turkey pertained to the matter involving Soviet's objections to U.S. missiles there, but it was not included in the agreement (C) and (D). The agreement also said nothing with regard to Soviet troops in Cuba (A).

12. **(C)** Blacks most commonly resisted slavery passively, if at all. The Underground Railroad (B), though celebrated in popular history, involved a relatively minute number of slaves. Arson (D) and violent uprising (A), though they did sometimes occur and were the subject of much fear on the part of white Southerners, were also relatively rare.

13. **(C)** During the period from 1835-1865 Southerners generally defended slavery as a positive benefit to society and even to the slaves themselves. That slavery was a necessary evil (A) and should be gradually phased out as the slaves were colonized outside the United States (D) was the attitude of an earlier generation of white Southerners, including Thomas Jefferson. That slavery should be immediately abolished (B) was the view of the Abolitionists, a minority even in the North during this period.

14. **(D)** Farmers and planters in the South enjoyed high crop prices and sustained prosperity during the 1850s. Crops were large (C) and prices were high and steady (A) and (B).

15. **(A)** For whatever reasons, immigrants of the "New Immigration" tended to settle in the large cities of the Northeast and Midwest. Very few of them settled on farms (B), filed on homesteads (C), or migrated to the South and Southwest (D).

16. **(B)** Germany's 1917 declaration of its intent to wage unrestricted submarine warfare was the most important factor in bringing the United States into World War I. German violation of Belgian neutrality in 1914 (A) did nothing to aid Germany's cause in America, and the revelation of Germany's suggestions to Mexico (C) was even more damaging, but neither of these had the impact of the U-boats. The fall of the Czar and beginning of the Russian Revolution (D) may or may not have had an influence on President Woodrow Wilson.

17. **(A)** The Berlin Airlift was Truman's response to the Soviet blockade of Berlin. Neither wartime destruction (B) nor a severe winter (C) would have necessitated such a measure and no such work stoppage (D) occurred.

18. **(B)** Mercantilists believed the government should seek to direct the economy so as to maximize exports. Mercantilists *did*, however, believe in government interference in the economy (A) and the possession of colonies (C). Exports, they asserted, must exceed imports, not the other way around (D).

19. **(D)** Americans' primary objection to the Stamp Act was its purpose of raising revenue from the Americans without the consent of their representatives. A few Americans and a future British prime minister mistook this for opposition to internal taxes only (A). The proposed tax rate was not ruinously high (C), and the British had previously imposed taxes on America (B).

20. **(D)** In order to gain foreign recognition during the War for Independence, it was necessary for the United States to demonstrate a determination and potential to win independence. The U.S. could not have demonstrated financial stability (C) at this time, nor could it have made financial payments (A). It did not prove necessary to make territorial concessions to France (B).

21. **(D)** Garrison called for the immediate and uncompensated emancipation of all slaves. He definitely opposed either gradualism or compensation (A). He also opposed colonization (B). Though he opposed the congressional gag rule (C), its repeal was not his main issue of concern.

22. **(D)** The congressional "gag rule" held that no antislavery petitions would be formally received by Congress. It did not directly govern the laws that could be considered (A) nor did it limit what a member could say outside of Congress (B). Anti-slavery materials sent through the mail would not be delivered to Southern addresses (C), but this was a separate matter.

23. **(A)** Roosevelt's New Nationalism pertained to domestic reform. Unrelated was the fact that Roosevelt always favored an aggressive foreign policy (B), including the establishment of an overseas empire (D). Though he gained a reputation as a trust-buster, Roosevelt was by no means in favor of breaking up all trusts and large business combinations (C).

24. **(C)** FDR's predecessor, Herbert Hoover, established the Reconstruction Finance Corporation in 1932. In doing so, he broke with many Republican leaders, including Secretary of the Treasury Andrew Mellon, who believed government had no choice but to let the business cycle run its course. Roosevelt's New Deal contained every other element listed.

25. **(A)** The Haymarket Incident involved the throwing of a bomb at Chicago police and a subsequent riot involving police and striking workers. There were plenty of scandals within the Grant administration (B), but this was not one of them. Allegations of corruption on the part of Republican presidential candidate James G. Blaine (C) were contained in the Mulligan Letters. The disastrous fire that pointed out the hazardous working conditions in some factories (D) was New York's Triangle Shirtwaist Company fire on March 25, 1911.

26. **(D)** The "New Immigration" was made up primarily of persons from Southern and Eastern Europe. Some, such as persecuted Russian Jews, came for religious reasons (A). The great majority were financially less well off (B) than those of the "Old Immigration," who came from Northern and Western Europe (C). Persons from Asia, Africa, and the Americas would not generally be considered part of the "New Immigration."

27. **(A)** The U.S. gained possession of the Philippines through the Spanish-American War. Cuba (B), though originally the primary issue of contention between Spain and the United States, was not annexed but rather granted its independence under the terms of the Platte Amendment. The Panama Canal Zone (D) was acquired within a few years of the Spanish-American War but in unrelated incidents and not from Spain. Bermuda (C) has never been acquired by the United States.

28. **(D)** The "Long Hot Summers" were filled with race rioting in America's large cities during the 1960s. Major outdoor rock concerts (A), such as the 1969 Woodstock concert, did occur during these years. The large Communist offensives against U.S. troops in Vietnam (B) went by the name Tet. The protests (C), which were numerous, were called anti-war protests.

29. **(D)** Bacon's followers were disgruntled at what they saw as the governor's refusal to protect their frontier area from Indian raids. The jailing of individuals or seizure of their property for failure to pay taxes during a time of economic hardship (A) was the source of Shays' Rebellion in 1786. The under-representation of the backcountry areas in colonial legislatures (B) was an ongoing source of irritation in the colonial South. The mistreatment of former indentured servants by large planters (C) and the favoritism of Virginia's Governor Berkeley to his clique of friends may have been underlying causes but were not the immediate issue in dispute in Bacon's Rebellion.

30. **(B)** The Newburgh Conspiracy was composed of army officers disgusted with a central government too weak to collect taxes to pay them and their troops. Betrayal of the plans for the fort at West Point (A) was Benedict Arnold's treason. Resistance to the collection of federal excise taxes in western Pennsylvania (C) took the form of the Whiskey Rebellion of 1791. New England's threat to secede should the War of 1812 continue (D) was made at the 1814 Hartford Convention.

31. **(A)** The Wilmot Proviso was intended to prohibit slavery in the area acquired through the Mexican War. Congress generally agreed that the United States would acquire some territory from the war (B). That California should be a free state while the rest of the Mexican Cession was reserved for slavery (C), and that the status of slavery in the Mexican Cession should be decided on the basis of "Popular Sovereignty" (D), were suggestions for a compromise that might calm the furor aroused by the Wilmot Proviso.

32. **(A)** The Populists desired free coinage of silver. They also desired direct election of U.S. Senators, not necessarily an end to the electoral college (D). The Progressive movement, which followed Populism, favored the reform of child labor laws (B) and the use of modern science to solve social problems (C).

33. **(A)** The settlement-house workers were often young, affluent, college-educated women such as Jane Addams. Poor immigrants (B) and disabled veterans (C) would have had less opportunity for such things. Idealistic young men (D) were apparently drawn to such enterprises in smaller numbers.

34. **(B)** In the 1857 case *Dred Scott v. Sandford* the Supreme Court held that no black slave could be a citizen of the United States. It was in the 1954 case *Brown v. Topeka Board of Education* that the court held separate facilities for the races to be unconstitutional (A). The reverse (C) was the court's holding in the 1896 case *Plessy v. Ferguson*. Affirmative Action was limited (D) in the 1970s and 1980s.

35. **(C)** The Whigs turned on Tyler because he opposed their entire legislative program. He did speak out in favor of Texas annexation (B), but this offense would have been relatively minor in Whig eyes by comparison.

36. **(C)**   O'Sullivan spoke of America's "manifest destiny to overspread the continent." The idea that America must eventually become either all slave or all free (D) was expressed by Lincoln in his "House Divided" speech and was called by William H. Seward the "Irrepressible Conflict." Racial equality (A) was still not a popular idea when O'Sullivan wrote in the first half of the nineteenth century. By that time, of course, America was already an independent country (B).

37. **(D)**   Mexico did expect to win the war, invade the U.S., and dictate a peace in Washington, but whatever desire, if any, the Mexicans may have had for the state of Louisiana was not a factor in the coming of the war. The U.S. did, however, desire to annex California (A) and did annex Texas (C); Mexico did refuse to pay its debts (B) and did claim Texas (C). All of these contributed to the coming of the war.

38. **(A)**   The colony at Jamestown was founded primarily for economic gain. Desire for religious freedom in some form (B) was the motivation of the settlers of Plymouth and some of those who settled Maryland and Pennsylvania. Desire to create a perfect religious commonwealth as an example to the rest of the world (C) was the motive for the Massachusetts Bay colony; and desire to recreate in the New World the sort of feudalistic society that was fading in the Old World (D) was probably a motive of some of the colonial proprietors such as those of the Carolinas.

39. **(D)**   The Gulf of Tonkin Incident led to major U.S. involvement in the Vietnam War. In the Gulf of Sidra during the 1980s, two clashes occurred involving the shooting down of Libyan, not Vietnamese, jets approaching U.S. ships (B). Off the coast of North Korea in 1968, North Korean, not Vietnamese, forces seized the U.S. Navy intelligence ship *USS Pueblo* (C).

40. **(C)**   The SALT I Treaty indicated U.S. acceptance of the concept of Mutual Assured Destruction. It was ratified by the U.S. Senate (D)—unlike the SALT II Treaty—but did not bring substantial reductions in the number of missiles on either side (A). It discouraged the deployment of defensive weapons (B).

PRACTICE TEST

CLEP Social Sciences and History

Also available at the REA Study Center (*www.rea.com/studycenter*)

This practice test is also offered online at the REA Study Center *(www.rea.com/studycenter)*. Since all CLEP exams are administered on computer, we recommend that you take the online version of this test to simulate test-day conditions and to receive these added benefits:

- **Timed testing conditions** – Gauge how much time you can spend on each question
- **Automatic scoring** – Find out how you did on the test, instantly
- **On-screen detailed explanations of answers** – Learn not just the correct answer, but also why the other answer choices are wrong
- **Diagnostic score reports** – Pinpoint where you're strongest and where you need to focus your study

Need more practice? Go to the REA Study Center and take Practice Test 2.

PRACTICE TEST

CLEP Social Sciences and History

Also available at the REA Study Center (*www.rea.com/studycenter*)

This practice test is also offered online at the REA Study Center *(www.rea.com/studycenter)*. Since all CLEP exams are administered on computer, we recommend that you take the online version of this test to simulate test-day conditions and to receive these added benefits:

- **Timed testing conditions** – Gauge how much time you can spend on each question
- **Automatic scoring** – Find out how you did on the test, instantly
- **On-screen detailed explanations of answers** – Learn not just the correct answer, but also why the other answer choices are wrong
- **Diagnostic score reports** – Pinpoint where you're strongest and where you need to focus your study

Need more practice? Go to the REA Study Center and take Practice Test 2.

3. "…there is no place for industry… no arts; no letters; no society; and which is the worst of all, continual fear, and danger of violent death; and the life of man, solitary, poor, nasty, brutish, and short." This quotation from Thomas Hobbes' *Leviathan* (1651) described the concept known as

   (A) natural rights
   (B) state of nature
   (C) social contract
   (D) reason of state (raison d'état)
   (E) nationalism

4. Which one of the following would most likely oppose *laissez-faire* policies in nineteenth century Europe?

   (A) A factory owner
   (B) A liberal
   (C) A free trader
   (D) A socialist
   (E) A middle-class businessman

5. The first time the Japanese people heard the voice of Emperor Hirohito on the radio was

   (A) during his coronation
   (B) when he announced his wedding
   (C) when he announced that Japanese troops were moving into Manchuria
   (D) when he announced Japan's surrender to the Allied Powers
   (E) when he declared war on the United States

6. Which was the first European power to seize control of African territories?

   (A) Portugal
   (B) Belgium
   (C) England
   (D) France
   (E) Germany

7. The ancient world leader who created the Persian Empire and who also freed the Jews from their Babylonian captivity was

   (A) Julius Caesar
   (B) Marc Antony
   (C) Augustus Caesar
   (D) Cyrus the Great
   (E) Pompey

8. The five pillars of faith require that Muslims do each of the following EXCEPT

   (A) acknowledge that there is only one God and that Mohammed is his prophet
   (B) pray five times per day
   (C) make a pilgrimage to Medina
   (D) fast during Ramadan
   (E) give alms to the poor

9. The ancient Athenians contributed all of the following to the subsequent development of Western Civilization EXCEPT

   (A) philosophy
   (B) geometry
   (C) monotheism
   (D) tragedy
   (E) the Olympic Games

10. During the 6th and 5th centuries BCE, a Chinese scholar by the name of _____ helped establish a better system of government by promoting various virtues among the ruling class. His teachings also led to the development of a civil service exam.

    (A) Wang Mang
    (B) Buddha
    (C) Kublai Kahn
    (D) Confucius
    (E) Shihuangdi

11. In his theory, Karl Marx explained that conflict between industrial workers and the owners of industry was

    (A) likely to decline in future years
    (B) usually harmful to social institutions
    (C) an inevitable consequence of capitalism
    (D) of little importance to social change
    (E) a rare occurrence in modern societies

12. When ratified by the original thirteen states in 1781, the weaknesses of the Articles of Confederation included the federal government's inability to levy taxes or regulate interstate commerce. Both weaknesses stemmed from a fear of

    (A) the Dutch Republic
    (B) the Spanish
    (C) the French
    (D) mobs
    (E) tyranny

13. The primary influence on the U.S. Constitution's separation of powers was derived from

    (A) Plato's *Apology*
    (B) Baron de Montesquieu's *The Spirit of the Laws*
    (C) Machiavelli's *The Prince*
    (D) Thomas Hobbes' *Leviathan*
    (E) Aristotle's *Politics*

14. Which of the following is used to effect the release of a person from improper imprisonment?

    (A) A writ of mandamus
    (B) A writ of habeas corpus
    (C) The Fourth Amendment requirement that police have probable cause in order to obtain a search warrant
    (D) The Supreme Court's decision in *Roe v. Wade*
    (E) The constitutional prohibition against *ex post facto* laws

15. When a member of the House of Representatives helps a citizen from his or her district receive some federal aid to which that citizen is entitled, the representative's action is referred to as

    (A) casework
    (B) pork barrel legislation
    (C) lobbying
    (D) logrolling
    (E) filibustering

16. One advantage incumbent members of Congress have over challengers in election campaigns is the use of

    (A) unlimited campaign funds
    (B) national party employees as campaign workers
    (C) the franking privilege
    (D) unlimited contributions from "fat cat" supporters
    (E) government-financed air time for commercials

QUESTIONS 17 to 18 refer to the table below.

GRAIN PRODUCERS				GRAIN IMPORTERS			
Grain	1st	2nd	3rd	Grain	1st	2nd	3rd
Corn	USA	China	Brazil	Corn	CIS	Japan	Spain
Wheat	CIS	USA	China	Wheat	China	CIS	Japan
Rice	China	India	Indonesia	Rice	Indonesia	Iran	CIS

17. Which nation—or group of nations—seems to have the LEAST efficient agricultural system?

    (A) Brazil
    (B) Indonesia
    (C) CIS
    (D) India
    (E) China

18. Which nation seems to have the MOST self-sufficient agricultural system?

    (A) USA
    (B) China
    (C) Brazil
    (D) Indonesia
    (E) India

19. Which is NOT a characteristic of American agriculture?

    (A) The rich ecosystem of North America
    (B) The use of mechanization
    (C) The diversity of climate and soil
    (D) Total free market capitalism
    (E) The trend toward agribusiness

20. All of the following are true of the Confederate war effort during the Civil War EXCEPT:

    (A) Confederate industry was never able to adequately supply Confederate soldiers with the armaments they needed to successfully fight the war.
    (B) Confederate agriculture was never able to adequately supply the people of the South with the food they needed.
    (C) Inflation became a major problem in the South as the Confederate government was forced to print more paper currency than it could support with gold or other tangible assets.
    (D) The inadequate railroad system of the South hindered movement of soldiers, supplies, and food from the places where they were stationed (or produced) to the places where they were most needed.
    (E) Tremendous resentment at the military draft developed among poor and middle-class Southerners because wealthy Southern males could pay to have a substitute take their place in the army.

21. What was the OVERALL U.S. unemployment rate during the worst periods of the Great Depression?

    (A) 10%
    (B) 25%
    (C) 40%
    (D) 60%
    (E) 90%

QUESTION 22 refers to the following.

22. The painting above by François Dubois, an eyewitness, describes the massacre on St. Bartholomew's Day of 1572 of

    (A) Dutch nobility
    (B) German peasants
    (C) French Calvinists
    (D) Spanish Catholics
    (E) English merchants

23. Which one of the following was a characteristic of the peace settlements at the end of World War I?

    (A) Division of Germany into two parts
    (B) Expansion of the territory of the Ottoman Empire
    (C) The emergence of the Soviet Union as a significant part of the European diplomatic system
    (D) The long-term stationing of American troops in Europe
    (E) Germany was not required to pay reparations.

24. Which of the following has NOT been a leader of an African country?

    (A) Kwame Nkrumah
    (B) Jomo Kenyatta
    (C) Aimé Césaire
    (D) Julius Nyerere
    (E) Patrice Lumumba

25. When Chinese students held a protest in Beijing's Tiananmen Square on May 4, 1989, they were commemorating the May 4 movement of what year?

    (A) 1919
    (B) 1911
    (C) 1901
    (D) 1895
    (E) 1969

26. A major difference between the early river valley civilization in Egypt and that of Mesopotamia is that the Egyptians

    (A) tended to believe in an afterlife, in part because of their relatively favorable geographical conditions and natural resources
    (B) were constantly under the threat of being attacked by various regional enemies
    (C) had a pessimistic view toward life, as reflected in the *Epic of Gilgamesh*
    (D) built many large structures called ziggurats
    (E) mostly did not believe in an afterlife

27. In a remarkable chain of events that linked together four famous figures from the ancient world, Socrates taught Plato, who in turn taught Aristotle, who then taught a Macedonian named _____, who later spread Greek learning throughout much of the then-known world.

    (A) Peter the Great
    (B) Alexander the Great
    (C) Alfred the Great
    (D) Charles the Great
    (E) Frederick the Great

28. Japan's Meiji Restoration led to the end of the Tokugawa Shogunate and a period of

    (A) increased power for the samurai class
    (B) rapid industrialization
    (C) greater reliance on farming as a driving force of the economy
    (D) increased acceptance of feudal practices
    (E) increased fear of foreigners

29. Today, most people in sub-Saharan Africa make their living based on

    (A) long-distance trade
    (B) light manufacturing
    (C) heavy manufacturing
    (D) subsistence farming
    (E) tourism

30. The Second Amendment to the U.S. Constitution was drafted to protect the right to

    (A) freedom of religion
    (B) freedom of speech
    (C) peaceably assemble
    (D) bear arms
    (E) a speedy trial

31. In *Federalist #10*, James Madison wrote: "The latent causes of faction are thus sown into the nature of man." In asserting this claim, he also argued that

    (A) "Men are born free, but everywhere they are in chains."
    (B) all levels of government must work together to restrict the rise of factions at all costs.
    (C) attempts by the government to restrict the organization of factions would be futile given the human tendency toward self-interest
    (D) the United States government should encourage factions by embracing the philosophy of "live and let live."
    (E) the United States government should ensure that each citizen has the right to bear arms, for, according to Madison, life in the state of nature is a "war of all against all."

32. In its 1920 census, the United States government showed the culmination of a long-term trend, where, for the first time, more people were living in

    (A) Texas than New York
    (B) Colorado than Pennsylvania
    (C) Nevada than Massachusetts
    (D) urban areas than rural areas
    (E) rural areas than urban areas

33. Major differences between procedures in the House of Representatives and the Senate would include:

    I. In the House, time for debate is limited, while in the Senate it is usually unlimited.
    II. In the House, the rules committee is very powerful, while in the Senate it is relatively weak.
    III. In the House, debate must be germane, while in the Senate it need not be.

    (A) I only
    (B) II only
    (C) III only
    (D) I and II only
    (E) I, II, and III

34. In the case *McCulloch v. Maryland* (1819), the Supreme Court

    (A) gave a broad interpretation to the First Amendment right of freedom of speech
    (B) claimed the power of judicial review
    (C) struck down a law of Congress for the first time
    (D) gave a broad interpretation to the "necessary and proper clause"
    (E) denied that the president has the right of executive privilege

35. Which of the following statements about the U.S. president's cabinet is FALSE?

    (A) It includes heads of the 15 executive departments.
    (B) It includes members of the House of Representatives.
    (C) Although not mentioned in the Constitution, the cabinet has been part of American government since the presidency of George Washington.
    (D) Presidents may appoint special advisors to the cabinet.
    (E) Senators may not serve in the cabinet.

QUESTIONS 36 and 37 refer to the following graph.

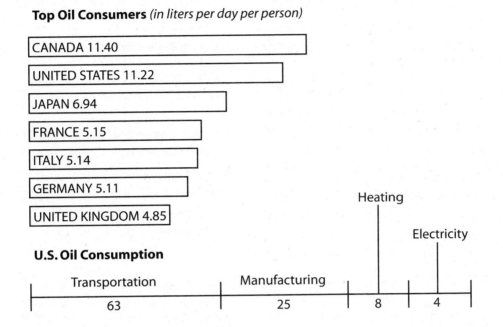

Top Oil Consumers *(in liters per day per person)*

CANADA 11.40
UNITED STATES 11.22
JAPAN 6.94
FRANCE 5.15
ITALY 5.14
GERMANY 5.11
UNITED KINGDOM 4.85

U.S. Oil Consumption

Transportation	Manufacturing	Heating	Electricity
63	25	8	4

36. Which is NOT a conclusion that can be drawn from the graphs?
   (A) Transportation takes up too high a proportion of U.S. oil usage
   (B) U.S. per capita consumption is over twice that of most European nations
   (C) North American oil demands are the highest
   (D) Manufacturing is a major consumer of oil
   (E) Heating needs take less than 10 percent of oil use

37. Which would be LEAST likely to explain the statistics in the graph?
   (A) The area size of a nation has a relationship to oil usage.
   (B) The European nations consume large quantities of oil.
   (C) The larger the population, the greater the usage.
   (D) Japan is the largest industrial power in Asia.
   (E) Industrial nations' people have lifestyles that use more oil.

38. Which is NOT true about the petroleum industry?
   (A) It is dealing with a nonrenewable resource.
   (B) It is essential to the plastics industry.
   (C) It reacts quickly to the law of supply and demand.
   (D) It is an example of a monopoly.
   (E) It is truly a multinational industry.

39. All of the following were main principles of the Navigation Acts EXCEPT:
   (A) Trade in the colonies was limited to only British or colonial merchants.
   (B) The laws prohibited the colonies from issuing their own paper currencies, greatly limiting their trading capabilities.
   (C) All foreign goods bound for the colonies had to be shipped through England where they were taxed with British import duties.
   (D) The colonists could not build or export products that directly competed with British export products.
   (E) Colonial enumerated goods could be sold only in England.

40. The reason slavery flourished in the Southern English colonies and not in New England is

(A) most New England farms were too small for slaves to be economically necessary or viable, whereas in the South the cultivation of staple crops such as rice and tobacco on large plantations necessitated the use of large numbers of indentured servants or slaves

(B) blacks from the tropical climate of Africa could not adapt to the harsh New England winters. Their high death rates made their use as slave laborers unprofitable

(C) a shortage of females in the Southern English colonies led to many female black Africans being imported as slaves and as potential wives for white planters in the region

(D) whereas New England religious groups such as the Puritans forbade slavery on moral grounds, the Anglican church, which dominated the Southern English colonies, encouraged the belief that blacks were inferior, and thus not deserving of equal status

(E) the Stono uprising in 1739 convinced New Englanders that the cost of controlling slaves was not worth their marginal economic benefits

41. All of the following are characteristics of Renaissance humanism EXCEPT:

(A) sanctity of the Latin texts of Scriptures
(B) belief that ancient Latin and Greek writers were inferior to later authors
(C) rejection of Christian principles
(D) it functioned as a primary cause of the Reformation.
(E) it accomplished scholarship in ancient languages

42. The October Manifesto of Czar Nicholas II promised all of the following EXCEPT:

(A) a Duma
(B) political reforms
(C) a Russian parliament
(D) a fair, democratic voting system
(E) full civil liberties

43. Which independent Asian nation did NOT exist before 1947?

(A) Thailand
(B) Pakistan
(C) India
(D) Korea
(E) Vietnam

44. All of the following were aspects of Britain's policy of indirect rule in colonial Africa EXCEPT

(A) subsidizing primary education for Africans
(B) the expectation of eventual self-government
(C) decentralized administration
(D) uniform government policy throughout the colonized territories
(E) incorporating traditional rulers into the government structure

45. The Glorious Revolution of 1688–89 resulted in all of the following EXCEPT

(A) the flight and abdication of James II
(B) an agreement that in the event of no heirs, the Hanover house would succeed the Stuarts
(C) the elevation of William III and Mary as the monarchs
(D) specification that all future monarchs must be members of the Church of England
(E) the passage of the Bill of Rights

46. Churchill gave his "Iron Curtain" speech in Missouri in 1946, and the Berlin Wall later became a manifestation of his dire warning. Construction of that wall began in

(A) 1948
(B) 1951
(C) 1955
(D) 1957
(E) 1961

47. After Asoka rose to power as Emperor of the Mauryan Empire in India in 268 BCE, he emphasized the practice of _____, which helped him promote a sense of unity among his diverse peoples.

(A) Buddhism
(B) Confucianism
(C) Catholicism
(D) Zoroastrianism
(E) Taoism

48. Although China had a much more impressive navy than any European nation by the early 1400s, during the Europe's Age of Exploration, the first country to take the lead in exploration was _____.

(A) England
(B) Portugal
(C) France
(D) Spain
(E) the Dutch Republic

49. The so-called Pax Romana was initiated during the reign of Augustus Caesar (27 BCE to 14 CE) and ended after the reign of _____, a man many historians believe to be the embodiment of Plato's concept of a philosopher-king.

(A) Tiberius
(B) Nero
(C) Constantine
(D) Justinian I
(E) Marcus Aurelius

50. John Marshall served as the U.S. Supreme Court Chief Justice from 1801-1835. With regard to what he considered to be the proper role of the federal government, he opposed each of the following presidents EXCEPT

(A) Thomas Jefferson
(B) James Madison
(C) James Monroe
(D) John Quincy Adams
(E) Andrew Jackson

51. In the study of economics, the Production Possibilities Curve is used to show a trade-off between

(A) two goods
(B) four goods
(C) eight goods
(D) ten goods
(E) as many goods as it takes to analyze a given problem

52. The major responsibility of the Federal Reserve Board is to

(A) implement monetary policy
(B) control government spending
(C) regulate commodity prices
(D) help the president run the executive branch
(E) keep records of troop strength in army reserve units across the country

53. Which of the following statements most accurately compares political parties in the United States with those in other Western democracies?

(A) Parties in the United States exert a greater influence over which candidates run for office.
(B) Parties are much more centralized in the United States.
(C) There are usually more political parties in other Western democracies.

(D) Party members in the national legislature are much freer to vote against the party line in other Western democracies.

(E) Party label is the principal criterion for voting for a candidate in the United States, whereas it is relatively unimportant in other Western democracies.

54. Which of the following is among the differences between a parliamentary and a presidential system?

I. In a parliamentary system, there is little or no separation of powers as in a presidential system.

II. In a parliamentary system, the chief executive officer is not chosen by a nationwide vote as in a presidential system.

III. In a presidential system, the chief executive officer may call elections for all members of the legislature at any time, unlike in a parliamentary system.

(A) I only
(B) II only
(C) III only
(D) I and II only
(E) I, II, and III

QUESTIONS 55 to 57 refer to the following.

• We must develop the vision to see that, in regard to the natural world, private and corporate ownership should be so limited as to preserve the interest of society and the integrity of the environment.

• We need greater awareness of our enormous powers, the fragility of the earth, and the consequent responsibility of men and governments for its preservation.

• We must redefine "progress" toward an emphasis on long-term quality rather than immediate quantity.

• We, therefore, resolve to act. We propose a revolution in conduct toward an environment which is rising in revolt against us. Granted that ideas and institutions long established are not easily changed; yet today is the first day of the rest of our life on this planet. We will begin anew.

55. Which group is NOT called upon to act in the statement?

(A) Private and corporate ownership
(B) Government
(C) Individuals
(D) Society
(E) Communities

56. What makes this quote relevant to economics?

(A) Ethical use of the environment
(B) Man as a member of the "community of all living things"
(C) Need for individual responsibility
(D) References to man's machines and past abuses
(E) Progress, in terms of quality of life

57. Which is NOT an example of how environmental concerns can become economic priorities?

(A) Recycling
(B) Reforestation
(C) Strip-mining restoration
(D) Greenhouse effect
(E) Coal-generated electricity to replace imported oil

58. Which battle was the turning point in the Pacific war between Japan and the United States?

(A) Leyte Gulf
(B) Pearl Harbor
(C) Coral Sea
(D) Midway
(E) Guadalcanal

59. The United States Supreme Court case of *Brown v. Board of Education of Topeka* was significant because it

(A) prohibited prayer in public schools on the grounds of separation of church and state

(B) legally upheld the doctrine of "separate but equal" educational facilities for blacks and whites

(C) clarified the constitutional rights of minors and restricted the rights of school administrators to set dress codes or otherwise infringe on students' rights

(D) upheld school districts' rights to use aptitude and psychological tests to "track" students and segregate them into "college prep" and "vocational" programs

(E) ordered the desegregation of public schools, prohibiting the practice of segregation via "separate but equal" schools for blacks and whites

60. Ferdinand and Isabella's policies of Spanish nationalism led to the expulsion, from Spain, of large numbers of Spanish

(A) Protestants
(B) Catholics
(C) Jews
(D) Calvinists
(E) Monks

61. During the Thirty Years' War, the Lutheran movement was saved from extinction by the military intervention of which foreign monarch?

(A) The French king, Philip the Fair
(B) The English king, Henry VIII
(C) The Swedish king, Gustavus Adolphus
(D) The Austrian emperor, Charles V
(E) The Spanish king, Philip II

62. In 1898, the United States took control of the Philippines from which country?

(A) China
(B) Japan
(C) England
(D) Spain
(E) Portugal

63. The following pairs of names are the names of African countries before and after achieving independence EXCEPT

(A) Bechuanaland – Botswana
(B) Dahomey – Benin
(C) Gold Coast – Ghana
(D) Swaziland – Malawi
(E) Angola – Angola

64. Between 1929 and 1933, the Federal Reserve Bank made the economic calamities associated with the Great Depression significantly worse by

(A) increasing the money supply
(B) decreasing the money supply
(C) leaving the money supply unchanged
(D) decreasing government spending
(E) increasing taxes

65. After the start of the Great Recession in 2007, the Federal Reserve Bank used a tactic known as _____ to significantly increase the money supply.

(A) going-for-broke
(B) beggar-thy-neighbor
(C) quantitative easing
(D) qualitative easing
(E) qualitative tightening

66. To protect the borders of their sprawling empire, the Romans built two defensive barricades in Britain during the 2nd century CE; one was called Antonine's Wall, while the other (more famous) wall became known as

    (A) Caesar's Wall
    (B) Augustus Caesar's Wall
    (C) Hadrian's Wall
    (D) Nero's Wall
    (E) the Great Wall of Britain

67. The Ural Mountains run through which of the following countries?

    (A) Switzerland
    (B) Finland
    (C) Germany
    (D) Hungary
    (E) Russia

68. With regard to fiscal policy, the federal government has two basic tools at its disposal: it can raise or lower

    (A) taxes and the money supply
    (B) government spending and interest rates
    (C) interest rates and the money supply
    (D) government spending and taxes
    (E) taxes and interest rates

69. In 1954, the Supreme Court ruled in *Brown v. Board of Education of Topeka* that, "We conclude that in the field of public education the doctrine of 'separate but equal' has no place. Separate educational facilities are inherently unequal." In doing so, this decision overturned the decision of the Supreme Court in the case of

    (A) *Dred Scott v. Sandford*
    (B) *Gibbons. v. Ogden*
    (C) *Griswold v. Connecticut*
    (D) *Plessy v. Ferguson*
    (E) *Gideon v. Wainwright*

70. Prior to Central and South America being conquered by the Spanish during the first half of the 16th century, the region contained two major empires. One was founded by the Aztecs, the other by the

    (A) Powhatan Confederacy
    (B) Incas
    (C) Iroquois Confederacy
    (D) Hopi
    (E) Huron

71. The statement "America has a pluralistic political system" means

    (A) there are many subcultures within American society
    (B) political power is divided between national and state governments
    (C) many interest groups compete in the political arena to influence public policy
    (D) rural interests are overrepresented in the national legislature
    (E) candidates for national office are usually elected by plurality vote

72. Which of the following best describes the relationship between educational background and participation in politics?

    (A) The more schooling one has, the more likely one is to vote.
    (B) The less schooling one has, the more likely one is to run for public office.
    (C) There is no relationship between educational background and participation in politics.
    (D) People with a high school education are more likely to vote than either those who did not finish high school or those with a college degree.
    (E) Those with no formal schooling have a greater personal interest in policy and tend to vote more often than those with high school diplomas.

73. All of the following are recognized functions of the major political parties EXCEPT

(A) recruiting candidates for public office
(B) aggregating interests into electoral alliances
(C) establishing channels of communication between public and government
(D) providing personnel to staff elections and run the government
(E) articulating interests

QUESTIONS 74 and 75 refer to the diagram below.

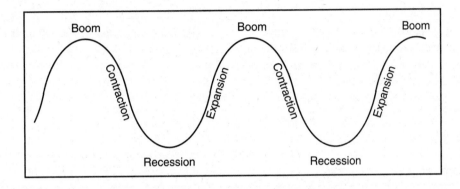

74. Which is the best title for the diagram above?

(A) Boom and Bust
(B) Causes of Economic Change
(C) The Business Cycle
(D) Causes of Recession
(E) The History of Business Activity

75. In referring to the stages of the cycle, depicted above, which would not be a factor considered by economists?

(A) Unemployment figures
(B) Manufacturing production
(C) Income levels
(D) War or peace
(E) Retail sales

76. Which is not a method used to encourage expansion during a recession?

(A) Political crisis, such as war
(B) Increased government spending
(C) Increased taxation
(D) Deregulation of industry
(E) Restriction of imports

77. The Great Awakening of the mid-eighteenth century refers to

(A) a series of religious revivals that swept through the English colonies spreading evangelistic fervor and challenging the control of traditional clerics over their congregations
(B) the intellectual revolution which served as a precursor to the Enlightenment and challenged orthodox religion's claims to knowledge of humankind and the universe
(C) the beginnings of the Industrial Revolution in England and its New World colonies
(D) the growing realization among English colonists that independence from England was only a matter of time and was the key to their future success
(E) the sudden awareness among North American Indians that their only chance for survival against the rapidly growing number of European colonists was to fight them before the Europeans grew any stronger

78. One of the major effects of the Industrial Revolution of the late nineteenth century in the United States was

    (A) an increased emphasis on worker health and safety issues
    (B) an increased emphasis on speed rather than quality of work
    (C) an increased emphasis on high-quality, error-free work
    (D) an increase in the number of small industrial facilities, which could operate more efficiently than larger, more costly industrial plants
    (E) a decrease in worker productivity as a result of continuous clashes between unions and management

79. All of the following were significant economic trends in Germany during the 1920s EXCEPT

    (A) large amounts of money leaving the country to pay reparations
    (B) periods of high inflation
    (C) a very stable currency (the mark)
    (D) periods of high unemployment
    (E) the German government placed large amounts of paper money in circulation

QUESTION 80 refers to the following.

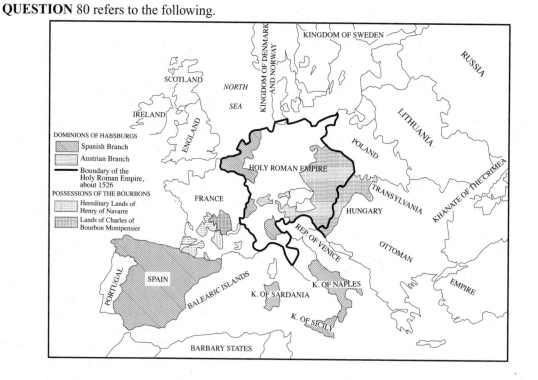

80. The map depicts Europe around

    (A) 1800
    (B) 1500
    (C) 1700
    (D) 1950
    (E) 1900

81. By 1914 which of the following countries was still an independent state not under colonial control?

   (A) Algeria
   (B) Congo
   (C) Angola
   (D) Egypt
   (E) Ethiopia

82. Thailand is bordered by which of the following countries?

   I. Myanmar
   II. Laos
   III. Vietnam
   IV. Cambodia

   (A) I, II, and III
   (B) I, II, and IV
   (C) I and II only
   (D) II and III only
   (E) IV only

83. During the Yalta Conference in February 1945, Joseph Stalin demanded a buffer zone to the west of Moscow, noting that this area was especially vulnerable to attack. Since 1800, the two most notable invasions that came from the west of Russia were: (1) the attack by the Nazis in 1941, known as Operation Barbarossa; and (2) the attack by the troops of _____, which took place in 1812.

   (A) the Duke of Wellington
   (B) Napoleon
   (C) Lord Nelson
   (D) Rochambeau
   (E) Lafayette

84. During the 1930s and 1940s, the main challenge to John Maynard Keynes' school of economic thought came from

   (A) Friedrich Hayek
   (B) Milton Friedman
   (C) Adam Smith
   (D) Arthur Laffer
   (E) John Kenneth Galbraith

85. In 1776, Adam Smith famously stated: "It is not from the benevolence of the butcher, the brewer, or the baker that we expect our dinner, but from their regard to their own _____."

   (A) hunger and appetites
   (B) tendency toward altruism
   (C) tendency toward greed
   (D) interest
   (E) foolish entrepreneurial spirit

86. When Thomas Jefferson completed the Louisiana Purchase in 1803, the western border of the United States shifted from the Mississippi River to the

   (A) Great Plains
   (B) Rocky Mountains
   (C) the Pacific Ocean
   (D) the western boundary of the Dakotas
   (E) the western boundary of Kansas

87. Which of the following accurately describes the European Union today?

   (A) An economic union that includes countries of roughly equal economic power.
   (B) A political union that includes countries of roughly equal political power.
   (C) An economic and political union that includes countries of roughly equal economic and political power.
   (D) An economic and political union that includes countries of unequal economic and political power.
   (E) An economic union that includes countries with varying degrees of economic power.

88. After the Berlin Conference of 1884-1885 and the subsequent "Scramble for Africa," the existing boundaries and tribal affiliations in Sub-Saharan Africa were

    (A) not modified
    (B) modified, but only to a limited extent
    (C) mostly ignored
    (D) ignored, but only by the British and French
    (E) ignored, but only by the Germans and Italians

89. Which of the following early river valley civilizations is matched incorrectly with the river(s) listed alongside of it?

    (A) Egypt / Nile River
    (B) Mesopotamia / Tigris and Volga Rivers
    (C) Chinese / Yellow and Yangtze Rivers
    (D) Indus / Indus River
    (E) Mesopotamia / Tigris and Euphrates Rivers

QUESTION 90 refers to the following.

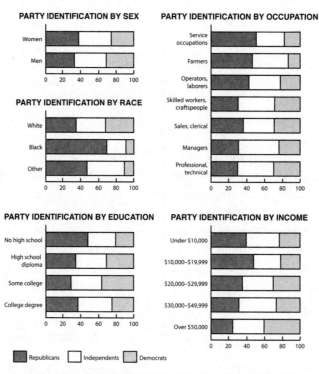

From Janda, Berry, Goldman, *The Challenge of Democracy*, 4th ed., 2001, p. 286. Copyright © 2001 Houghton Mifflin.

90. Based on the graphs above, which of the following were least likely to have voted for Franklin Roosevelt in 1940?

    (A) Southerners
    (B) White northern business leaders
    (C) Blue-collar workers
    (D) Racial minorities
    (E) Union members

91. The federal Constitution guarantees which of the following rights to persons arrested and charged with a serious crime?

I. To have an attorney appointed for them if they cannot afford to hire one
II. To remain silent
III. To compel witnesses in their favor to appear to testify if the case goes to court

(A) I only
(B) II only
(C) III only
(D) I and II only
(E) I, II, and III

92. The purpose of grandfather clauses and literacy tests, used in the southern states in the late 1800s and early 1900s, was to

(A) prevent illiterate whites from voting
(B) prevent recent immigrants from voting
(C) prevent Hispanics from running for public office
(D) prevent blacks from voting
(E) prevent "carpetbaggers" from running for public office

QUESTIONS 93 to 95 refer to the following passage.

Business functions by public consent, and its basic purpose is to serve constructively the needs of society – to the satisfaction of society.

"Historically, business has discharged this obligation mainly by supplying the needs and wants of people for goods and services, by providing jobs and purchasing power, and by producing most of the wealth of the nation. This has been what American society required of business, and business on the whole has done its job remarkably well...

"In generating... economic growth, American business has provided increasing employment, rising wages and salaries, employee benefit plans, and expanding career opportunities for a labor force....

"Most important, the rising standard of living of the average American family has enabled more and more citizens to develop their lives as they wish with less and less constraint imposed on them by economic need. Thus, most Americans have been able to afford better health, food, clothing, shelter, and education than the citizens of any other nation have ever achieved on such a large scale....

Source: U.S. Government report

93. Which statement best summarizes the attitude of the excerpt?

(A) Business has successfully met all the needs of society.
(B) Business has done a good job supplying the economic needs of society.
(C) Americans are best off with the least government.
(D) All Americans have benefited from the rising living standard.
(E) Government and business, in partnership, have created prosperity.

94. Which of the following organizations would be most likely to endorse this quote?

(A) Chamber of Commerce
(B) Department of Labor
(C) General Accounting Office
(D) Socialist Labor party
(E) AFL/CIO

95. Which of the following economic goals is not addressed by the quote?

    (A) Economic growth
    (B) Economic stability
    (C) Economic security
    (D) Economic justice
    (E) Economic freedom

96. Which is NOT one of the four basic economic activities of capitalism?

    (A) Production
    (B) Distribution
    (C) Manufacturing
    (D) Service
    (E) Labor

97. The key event that guaranteed Lincoln's re-election in 1864 was

    (A) the fall of Vicksburg to General Grant
    (B) the capture of New Orleans by Admiral Farragut
    (C) the defeat of Lee's army by General Meade at Gettysburg
    (D) the fall of Atlanta to General Sherman
    (E) the successful defense of Nashville by General Thomas against repeated Confederate counterattacks

98. The American Hostage Crisis in Iran was precipitated by which of the following?

    (A) The American government allowing the deposed Shah of Iran to come to the United States for cancer treatment.
    (B) President Jimmy Carter's involvement in arranging the Camp David accords between the Egyptians and the Israelis.
    (C) American air strikes against Iran's ally, Libya.
    (D) American support for Israel's 1980 invasion of southern Lebanon.
    (E) American attempts to overthrow the newly emplaced government of Ayatollah Khomeini.

99. During the era of European imperialism in Africa, 1870-1914, a "Cape to Cairo railway" was a project envisioned by

    (A) Italy
    (B) Britain
    (C) France
    (D) Germany
    (E) Spain

100. Which European nation failed to establish an African colony when its expeditionary force was overwhelmingly defeated by a native force at Adowa, Ethiopia, in 1896?

    (A) Italy
    (B) Belgium
    (C) Portugal
    (D) Britain
    (E) Austria

101. The Himalayan mountain range runs through which of the following Asian countries?

    I. China
    II. Nepal
    III. India
    IV. Bangladesh

    (A) I and II only
    (B) II and III only
    (C) I, II, and III only
    (D) I, III, and IV only
    (E) All of the above

102. Which of the following was the first European country to make the slave trade illegal?

    (A) Holland
    (B) Britain
    (C) France
    (D) Spain
    (E) Portugal

103. The Federal Deposit Insurance Corporation (FDIC) was created by

    (A) John F. Kennedy as part of his New Frontier

    (B) Franklin Delano Roosevelt as part of his New Deal

    (C) Theodore Roosevelt as part of his Square Deal

    (D) Harry Truman as part of his Fair Deal

    (E) Lyndon Johnson as part of his Great Society

104. Located in modern-day Israel, the city of Jerusalem is considered sacred to all of the following EXCEPT

    (A) Muslims
    (B) Catholics
    (C) Jews
    (D) Shintoists
    (E) Presbyterians

105. The Andes Mountain range (excluding its foothills) intersects with all of the following countries EXCEPT

    (A) Argentina
    (B) Chile
    (C) Uruguay
    (D) Colombia
    (E) Peru

106. To geographers, "CBD" stands for

    (A) Central Basin (of) Denmark
    (B) Central Business District
    (C) Central Baltic District
    (D) Central Basin District
    (E) Central Basin (of) Delhi

107. When considering the proper role of government, _____ believed that the average citizen would be easily swayed by demagogues and thus be prone to join mobs. As a consequence, he asserted that a strong central government was needed to control its citizenry.

    (A) Thomas Jefferson
    (B) James Madison
    (C) Alexander Hamilton
    (D) James Monroe
    (E) Andrew Jackson

108. During the 4th and 5th centuries CE, as the city of Rome continued to decline, the city of _____ continued to grow in terms of political and economic importance.

    (A) London
    (B) Moscow
    (C) Paris
    (D) Constantinople
    (E) Berlin

109. Which of the following rivers is associated with the incorrect city?

    (A) Rome / Arno River
    (B) London / Thames River
    (C) Prague / Vltava River
    (D) Paris / Seine River
    (E) Budapest / Danube River

110. Believing that he had landed in India in October, 1492, Columbus and his crew had actually landed in modern-day

    (A) Puerto Rico
    (B) Jamaica
    (C) Cuba
    (D) Haiti
    (E) Honduras

QUESTION 111 refers to the following excerpt from a Supreme Court decision.

It is emphatically the province and duty of the courts to say what the law is... If two laws conflict with each other, the courts must decide on the operation of each... If, then, the courts are to regard the Constitution, and the Constitution is superior to any ordinary act of the legislature, the Constitution and not such ordinary act, must govern the case to which they both apply.

111. This decision of the Supreme Court upheld the principle that

(A) a law contrary to the Constitution cannot be enforced by the courts
(B) Congress has the power to pass laws to carry out its constitutional duties
(C) interpretation of laws is a legislative function
(D) a law passed by Congress overrides a constitutional provision with which it conflicts
(E) courts are not equipped to decide questions of constitutional law

112. "Mark-up sessions," where revisions and additions are made to proposed legislation in Congress, usually occur in which setting?

(A) The majority leader's office
(B) On the floor of the legislative chamber
(C) In party caucuses
(D) In joint conference committees
(E) In committees or subcommittees

113. Which of the following has chief responsibility for assembling and analyzing the figures in the presidential budget submitted to Congress each year?

(A) Department of Commerce
(B) Department of Treasury
(C) Federal Reserve Board
(D) Office of Management and Budget
(E) Cabinet

QUESTIONS 114 to 118 refer to the charts below.

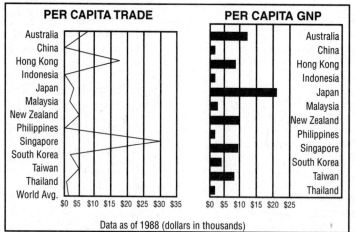

Data as of 1988 (dollars in thousands)

114. Comparing the two charts, the best conclusion is that

(A) there is a direct relationship between GNP and trade

(B) the nations all have increased their GNP

(C) they all exceeded the world average in trade

(D) Japan is the leader in both GNP and trade

(E) China ranks lowest in both categories

115. Which is NOT true about both charts?

(A) Both are figured per person
(B) Both are in thousands of dollars
(C) Both compare the same nations
(D) Both are the same type of graph
(E) Both use the same year's data

116. Which economic region of the world is reflected in the graphs?

(A) East Asia
(B) All Asia
(C) Northwest Asia
(D) All Pacific
(E) All ex-British colonies

117. According to the charts above, the nation that is increasing its prosperity the most is probably

(A) Australia
(B) Hong Kong
(C) Japan
(D) Singapore
(E) Taiwan

118. Which is the best way to describe the GNP?

(A) Total goods and services
(B) Total national production
(C) Greater national production
(D) Government natural production
(E) Gross national resources

119. The Compromise of 1877 resulted in

(A) the ascension of Republican Rutherford B. Hayes to the presidency in return for assurances that what was left of Reconstruction in the South would be ended.

(B) the division of the Dakota Territory into North Dakota and South Dakota.

(C) government financing for a Southern transcontinental railroad route in return for financial grants allowing the completion of the Great Northern Railroad from Minnesota to the Pacific Northwest.

(D) the ascension of Republican Rutherford B. Hayes to the presidency in return for the passage of an Amnesty Act which would pardon former Confederate soldiers, allowing them to regain their voting rights.

(E) the formal separation of Virginia and West Virginia and the official acceptance of statehood for West Virginia.

120. The Albany Congress of 1754 was convened for the major purpose of

(A) adding New York to the Dominion of New England

(B) getting the colonies to form a "grand council" to coordinate their western expansion and their common defense against Indians

(C) uniting the colonies under a "grand council" to resist British economic sanctions and coordinate activities against British tax officials

(D) cooperating with the French in their efforts to rid western New York and southern Canada of raiding Indian tribes

(E) writing a proclamation to be sent to King George in protest of the Stamp Act

ANSWER KEY

1.	(B)	31.	(C)	61.	(C)	91.	(E)
2.	(C)	32.	(D)	62.	(D)	92.	(D)
3.	(B)	33.	(E)	63.	(D)	93.	(B)
4.	(D)	34.	(D)	64.	(B)	94.	(A)
5.	(D)	35.	(B)	65.	(C)	95.	(D)
6.	(A)	36.	(A)	66.	(C)	96.	(E)
7.	(D)	37.	(C)	67.	(E)	97.	(D)
8.	(C)	38.	(D)	68.	(D)	98.	(A)
9.	(C)	39.	(B)	69.	(D)	99.	(B)
10.	(D)	40.	(A)	70.	(B)	100.	(A)
11.	(C)	41.	(E)	71.	(C)	101.	(C)
12.	(E)	42.	(D)	72.	(A)	102.	(B)
13.	(B)	43.	(B)	73.	(E)	103.	(B)
14.	(B)	44.	(D)	74.	(C)	104.	(D)
15.	(A)	45.	(B)	75.	(D)	105.	(C)
16.	(C)	46.	(E)	76.	(C)	106.	(B)
17.	(C)	47.	(A)	77.	(A)	107.	(C)
18.	(A)	48.	(B)	78.	(B)	108.	(D)
19.	(D)	49.	(E)	79.	(C)	109.	(A)
20.	(A)	50.	(D)	80.	(B)	110.	(D)
21.	(B)	51.	(A)	81.	(E)	111.	(A)
22.	(C)	52.	(A)	82.	(B)	112.	(E)
23.	(A)	53.	(C)	83.	(B)	113.	(D)
24.	(C)	54.	(D)	84.	(A)	114.	(E)
25.	(A)	55.	(A)	85.	(D)	115.	(D)
26.	(A)	56.	(D)	86.	(B)	116.	(A)
27.	(B)	57.	(E)	87.	(E)	117.	(D)
28.	(B)	58.	(D)	88.	(C)	118.	(A)
29.	(D)	59.	(E)	89.	(B)	119.	(A)
30.	(D)	60.	(C)	90.	(B)	120.	(B)

1. **(B)** Burr and Hamilton had never been close friends, and Hamilton made no secret of the fact that he did not trust Burr. During the congressional voting to resolve the outcome of the presidential election of 1800, when Burr might have become the third president of the United States, Hamilton had made attacks against Burr's personal character. In 1804, as Burr ran for governor of New York, Hamilton repeated and expanded those charges. When Burr lost the election, he blamed Hamilton, although there is no clear evidence that Hamilton's charges led to Burr's defeat. Burr demanded "satisfaction" through a duel and Hamilton accepted. Hamilton's death not only deprived the young nation of one of its premier thinkers and statesmen, but it ruined Burr's political career. He was charged with murder and forced to flee to avoid arrest. It was after this disaster that he began formulating his plan for an independent Western empire. Thus, choice (C) is incorrect.

2. **(C)** The question deals with the growth of the United States during President McKinley's tenure. President Madison was in office during the War of 1812. President Lincoln headed the government during the Civil War. President Wilson led the country during World War I. President F. D. Roosevelt was the leader during World War II. Thus, the correct answer is (C).

3. **(B)** Although "quotation" questions may ask the name of the author or the book title, this question requests more than factual recall. It requires an ability to recognize the main idea of the passage—to read the quotation and understand its philosophic implications. Knowledge of the terminology of seventeenth-century writers is also helpful. Hobbes' *Leviathan* described early human society (the "state of nature") as an anarchic "war of all against all." For self-protection, citizens agreed among themselves to form the first government, an agreement termed by Hobbes as the "social contract." It is especially important to read the quotation carefully, since two of the answers, (B) and (C), are from the *Leviathan*; you may be misled into choosing (C) because you have studied the *Leviathan* in a class and the "social contract" sounds familiar. If the correct answer is not apparent after a second reading of the quotation, it may at least be possible to eliminate the other two answers. The concept of natural rights, incorporated into the French Declaration of the Rights of Man and the Bill of Rights to the United States Constitution, was summarized by John Locke as the idea that human beings are born "free, equal, and independent." "Reason of state" was the justification used by French statesmen such as Cardinal Richelieu to defend measures to create a centralized absolute monarchy in France. Choice (E), nationalism, is not only incorrect but also irrelevant to this question.

4. **(D)** *Laissez-faire* (from the French *laissez-nous faire,* leave us alone) described the economic outlook of nineteenth-century liberals, many of whom were businessmen or industrialists who sought an end to government regulation of business. Proponents of *laissez-faire* envisioned an era of free economic activity in Europe without tariff barriers ("free trade"). Thus factory owners, liberals, and free traders were all supporters of *laissez-faire*. Not so with nineteenth-century socialists, who saw *laissez-faire* as an obstacle to even minimal measures to help the working class, such as government safety inspections of factories.

5. **(D)** On August 15, 1945, traffic came to a halt in Japan, as the nation listened to a prerecorded message in which Emperor Hirohito declared his acceptance of the Potsdam Declaration and Japan's defeat in the Second World War. This was the first time that the country had heard the emperor's voice. In the past, the emperor was considered to hold god-like status, and to allow his subjects to hear his voice, even for events and announcements like his coronation (A), his wedding (B), and declarations of war (C) and (E), would bring him down to the level of a human being. The fact that the emperor himself read the notice of surrender reinforced the completeness of Japan's defeat. They were no longer an imperial power, and their emperor was no longer a deity.

6. **(A)** In 1415 the Portuguese captured Ceuta, one of the first of a series of bases they were to take along the African coast. This marked the first incident of European colonial aggression on the African continent. Portugal's interests in Africa were to find a sea route to India, to explore trade possibilities in the continent (which later developed into transatlantic trade in slaves), to convert the people of Africa to Catholicism, and to assess the strength of the Muslim enemy. By 1640, when Ceuta passed to the Spanish, other European powers had already entered Africa for the same reasons as Portugal. While Belgium (B), England (C), France (D), and Germany (E) all eventually had colonial holdings in Africa, the door was opened up by Portugal (A).

7. **(D)** Prior to creating the Persian Empire, Cyrus the Great had been a shepherd, but he eventually became known as a fierce warrior and sagely leader. In addition to unifying various regional tribes to create the Persian Empire, he also had the reputation for treating his conquered foes fairly. The other answers—Julius Caesar, Marc Antony, Augustus Caesar, and Pompey—were all connected to the Roman Empire and therefore incorrect.

8. **(C)** Muslims are expected to make a pilgrimage to Mecca, not Medina. Although Medina is also considered a holy city (it is where Mohammed is buried), it ranks below Mecca in terms of importance. In addition to being the birthplace of Mohammed, Mecca serves as the center of the Islamic faith, as it contains the faith's most sacred shrine.

9. **(C)** Most historians attribute the concept of monotheism to the Israelites, and the figure of Abraham continues to be revered by the worshippers of three main monotheistic religions: Judaism, Christianity, and Islam. The other four answers all refer to legacies of the Greeks. The development of philosophy (A) is generally credited to Socrates (c. 469–399 BCE); geometry (B) to Euclid (c. 300–366 BCE); and tragedy (D) to Aeschylus (c. 525–466 BCE). The Greeks initiated the original Olympic games in 776 BCE.

10. **(D)** Confucius (551 to 479 BCE) was an extremely influential scholar and philosopher in China. Among other things, his teachings emphasized the importance of learning, humility, self-discipline, and concern for others. Wang Mang (A) ruled during the short-lived Xin Dynasty (9–23 CE) and was killed after his ambitious attempts at land reform failed badly. Buddha, or Siddhartha Gautama (563 – 479 BCE) was also a scholar, but he was from India. Like Confucius, his teachings had a profound influence on his followers who sought to find the best way to live, which he considered to be the "Middle Way." Kublai Kahn (C) was the grandson of Genghis Kahn and founded the Yuan Dynasty in China in 1271. Shihuangdi (E) founded the Qin Dynasty in 221 BCE. Known for his ruthless leadership tactics (including burning the books of Confucian scholars), he was the first person to unify China.

11. **(C)** Marx concluded that conflict between workers and owners was an intrinsic feature of capitalist societies. Since Marx saw this conflict as the principal reason for social change, (D) is incorrect. He also believed this conflict would intensify over time and result in a socialist revolution, so (A) is also incorrect. (B) is incorrect because Marx felt this conflict would ultimately benefit society instead of harming it.

12. **(E)** By the mid-1760s, after Britain's passage of the Proclamation of 1763, the Sugar Act, and the Stamp Act, America's colonial leaders increasingly became weary of the tyrannical nature of Britain's King George III and the British Parliament. These tensions rose to a crescendo after the passage of the Coercive Acts in 1774 (which, to be fair to the British, came after the willful destruction of British property in the Boston Tea Party in 1773). Given the foregoing, when the Articles of Confederation were finally ratified by all of the colonies in 1781, there existed an excessive fear of tyranny, which explains why the Articles provided the federal government with such a limited degree of power. Choices (A), (B), and (C) are incorrect because all three countries had become allies to the newly-born United States of America by the signing of the Treaty of Paris in 1783. Choice (D) is incorrect because fear of mobs (the viewpoint held by Alexander Hamilton) is the opposite of the fear of tyranny (the viewpoint held by Thomas Jefferson).

13. **(B)** Baron de Montesquieu's *The Spirit of the Laws*, published in 1748, provided a thoughtful defense for a country's constitution to include a clear separation of powers. James Madison was intimately familiar with Montesquieu's work when he helped draft the U.S. Constitution. The other four choices are all important works in terms of their contributions to the field of political philosophy, but it was Montesquieu who had the most influence on America's founders when they constructed their new constitution.

14. **(B)** A writ of habeas corpus is a court order which directs an official who is detaining someone to produce the person before the court so that the legality of the detention may be determined. The primary function of the writ is to effect the release of someone who has been imprisoned without due process of law. For example, if the police detained a suspect for an unreasonable time without officially charging the person with a crime, the person could seek relief from a court in the form of a writ of habeas corpus. (A) is incorrect because a writ of mandamus is a court order commanding an official to perform a legal duty of his or her office. It is not used to prevent persons from being improperly imprisoned. The Fourth Amendment requirement that police have probable cause in order to obtain a search warrant regulates police procedure. It is not itself a mechanism for effecting release of a person for improper imprisonment, so (C) is incorrect. Choice (D) is incorrect since the decision in *Roe v. Wade* dealt with a woman's right to have an abortion. It had nothing to do with improper imprisonment. Choice (E) is incorrect since the prohibition against ex post facto laws is not a mechanism for effecting the release of someone who is improperly imprisoned. Rather, it declares that changing the legal implications of an act, after the act has been committed, is improper.

15. **(A)** is the best answer since the term "casework" is used by political scientists to describe the activities of members of Congress on behalf of individual constituents. These activities might include helping an elderly person secure Social Security benefits, or helping a veteran obtain medical services. Most casework is actually done by congressional staff and may take as much as a third of the staff's time. Congresspersons supply this type of assistance for the good public relations it provides. Choice (B) fails because pork barrel legislation is rarely, if ever,

intended to help individual citizens. Pork barrel legislation authorizes federal spending for special projects, such as airports, roads, or dams, in the home state or district of a congressperson. It is meant to help the entire district or state. Also, there is no legal entitlement on the part of a citizen to a pork barrel project, such as there is with Social Security benefits. (C) is not the answer because lobbying is an activity directed toward congresspersons, not one done by congresspersons. A lobbyist attempts to get members of Congress to support legislation that will benefit the group which the lobbyist represents. Logrolling (D) is incorrect because it does not refer to congressional service for constituents. It refers instead to the congressional practice of trading votes on different bills. Congressperson A will vote for Congressperson B's pork barrel project and in return B will vote for A's pork barrel project. Filibustering (E) is incorrect. It is a technique used in the Senate to postpone a vote on a piece of legislation. The Senate has a tradition of unlimited debate and nongermane debate. This means that a senator may hold the floor for as long as (s)he likes and need not confine his/her remarks to the bill under consideration. Senators opposing a bill might get control of the floor and talk until the supporters agree to withdraw the bill from consideration.

16. **(C)** The franking privilege is the right of members of Congress to send mail to constituents at public expense. Challengers do not enjoy this privilege. Observers have noticed that the amount of free congressional mail increases during election years, as members try to keep their names before their constituents. Choice (A) is incorrect since incumbent congresspersons certainly do not have access to unlimited campaign funds. Congresspersons may spend as much of their own money as they wish, and they are free to raise money from contributors. But no candidate has unlimited personal funds, nor can incumbents raise unlimited funds from contributions. Choice (B) is incorrect because incumbents and challengers may both have access to national party employees as campaign workers. Both political parties have campaign committees for the House and Senate. All of the committees supply campaign managers, communications directors, and fund-raising experts to challengers and incumbents during election campaigns. (D) is incorrect because the Federal Election Campaign Act of 1974 placed a limit of $1,000 per election on individual contributions to political candidates. This put an end to so-called "fat cat" contributors who used to contribute vast sums to candidates. (E) is incorrect because the federal government does not finance any aspect of congressional campaigns.

17. **(C)** Despite the fact that it comprises leading wheat-producing regions, the former Soviet Union, or CIS, is the only entity that is in the top three in having to *import* extra grain in all three categories, including wheat.

18. **(A)** The United States is the only nation listed that does not import any of the grains but is listed in two categories as a top producer.

19. **(D)** The American farmer has traditionally had government assistance available in the form of loan programs, subsidies, price supports, and tariff protection. (A) and (C) are natural assets that American farmers have enjoyed. (B) and (E) have made American farms more efficient and cost effective.

20. **(A)** Contrary to myth, Confederate industry did a masterful job in producing weapons and ammunition for the Confederate military during the war. While it is true that the Confederates never had the abundance of weapons possessed by Union forces, particularly in artillery, it was only near the end of the war, when Union forces had overrun many production centers and totally destroyed the South's transportation network, that severe shortages of ammunition and weapons

developed. It is also true that at the start of the war, Confederate industry could not arm everyone who volunteered for military service; the Union had that same problem. Most Southerners had their own weapons so that despite the lack of government-produced weapons, there was no shortage of available weapons for soldiers. The biggest problem faced by the Confederate armies in regard to weapons and ammunition was a lack of uniformity for the vast array of "homegrown" weapons and ammunition used by their soldiers, not a shortage of weapons themselves.

21. **(B)** The national unemployment rate soared to approximately 25 percent of the workforce in early 1933. This meant that approximately 13 million workers were unemployed. While 25 percent was the national unemployment rate, in some cities the number of unemployed approached 90 percent. This was at a time when there were no welfare benefits or unemployment funds in most areas of the country. What made things worse was the sheer amount of time workers remained unemployed. By early 1937, unemployment had fallen to 14.3 percent, still representing 8 million unemployed workers. Then the recession of 1937 put an additional 2 million workers out of work again. The suffering of being unemployed as long as many of these workers is beyond description. Hobo camps and "Hoovervilles" popped up in virtually every American city. Worse, even for those who kept their jobs, poverty became widespread. Crop prices for farmers dropped by 60 percent. Wages, for workers who still had jobs, dropped 40 percent. Banks continued to collapse, taking the personal savings of depositors down with them, leaving depositors with no savings to help them through this period. So, while 25 percent may not sound catastrophic at first, combined with the collapse of wages and crop prices, as well as the collapse of banks and the sheer amount of time many people were out of work, the nation's economy was close to total collapse.

22. **(C)** The St. Bartholomew's Day Massacre in Paris of French Calvinists, often termed "Huguenots," led to a civil war in France (the War of the Three Henries) and the first Bourbon monarch (Henry IV). When dealing with questions based on illustrations (paintings or drawings), it is important to look for explicit details or other information in the question and in the illustration itself, since it is usually not possible to arrive at a correct answer by eliminating answers. The clues in this case are in the question rather than in the painting. If the primary clue is not sufficient ("St. Bartholomew's Day"), there is a secondary clue in the obviously French name of the painter. Do not be misled by the use of the term "French Calvinists" instead of the name "Huguenots," which is the term usually used by textbook writers; the use of the term "French Calvinists" is another detail testing your knowledge and understanding of European history.

23. **(A)** At first glance this question appears to test only the memorization of facts, but another look will show that it also requires understanding of the diplomatic situation in Europe around 1920. The correct answer may require some thought, since there was no political division of Germany into two governments, as happened at the end of World War II. The "division of Germany into two parts" refers to the "Polish Corridor," created by the peacemakers in order to give Poland an "outlet to the sea." The "Polish Corridor," a strip of formerly German land ceded to Poland in order to provide access to the port city of Danzig, isolated eastern Prussia from the remainder of Germany. It may be possible to arrive at the correct answer by analyzing the other four answers and eliminating them; each is untrue. The end of World War I brought the final collapse of the Ottoman Empire and its reduction to the borders of modern Turkey. The new Communist government of Russia, which came to power in 1917, was ostracized by the other great powers when the war ended. Choice (D) may be tempting because the United States left large numbers of troops in Europe after World War

II. This question refers to World War I, however. The United States withdrew from Europe both militarily and diplomatically after that war, preferring to return to "normalcy." Under the terms of the Treaty of Versailles, Germany was required to pay reparations.

24. **(C)** Aimé Césaire was a poet from Martinique (in the West Indies). Although poetry and political writing have been widely influential for writers and thinkers like Franz Fanon, Césaire has never been the leader of an African country. (A) Kwame Nkrumah was the prime minister of Ghana, (B) Jomo Kenyatta was president of Kenya, (D) Julius Nyerere was president of Tanzania, and (E) Patrice Lumumba was prime minister of the Congo.

25. **(A)** When Beijing students chose to hold a protest for the democracy movement in Tiananmen Square, they were making reference to the May 4 Movement of 1919. On this day, students in Beijing demonstrated in Tiananmen Square in protest of the Treaty of Versailles, ending World War I, which denied China all of its demands for return of territory held by foreigners. The demonstrations led to strikes by students and workers, and as a result, the Chinese delegation at Versailles refused to sign the treaty.

26. **(A)** Relative to the Mesopotamians, the Egyptians were blessed in terms of natural resources and geographical conditions. First, the Nile River overflowed on a regular basis, which made for predictable growing seasons. Second, Egypt had excellent natural boundaries that made it difficult to attack; these boundaries included the Sahara Desert, the Red Sea, and the Mediterranean Sea. Third, Egypt had excellent natural building materials, which allowed them to build impressive structures, including the pyramids. Choices (B), (C), and (E) are incorrect, because they all referred to conditions relevant to the Mesopotamians. Ziggurats (D) were buildings found in Mesopotamia, not in Egypt.

27. **(B)** During the 4th century BCE, Aristotle served as a private tutor for the future Alexander the Great. Choice (A), Peter the Great (1672–1725), was a Czar of Russia. Choice (C), Alfred the Great (c. 849–899), was a king of Wessex in the south of England. Choice (D), Charles the Great—also known as Charlemagne (1742–1814), was a legendary king of the Franks before being crowned as the Holy Roman Emperor in 1800. Answer (E), Frederick the Great (1712–1786), was a king of Prussia.

28. **(B)** While the Tokugawa Shoganate relied on an agricultural-based feudal structure and developed an insular nature, the Meiji Restoration, which began in 1868, embraced an outward-looking focus, and included the goal of modernizing Japan through rapid industrialization. As a result, the samurai class (A) lost power. In addition, there was a decreased emphasis on subsistence farming (C) and the previous feudal structure (D). Moreover, the xenophobia (E) that had been an integral component of the Tokugawa era slowly began to shift during the Meiji Restoration.

29. **(D)** In spite of a great deal of money being lent to and invested in various countries throughout Sub-Saharan Africa over the past six decades—most notably by the Chinese during the past ten years—this sub-continent mostly remains mired in corruption, poverty, and high infant mortality rates. As such, most people living in Sub-Saharan Africa do what they can to scratch out a living through subsistence agriculture.

30. **(D)** The Second Amendment concerns the right to bear arms. Choices (A), (B), and (C) are all protected by the First Amendment, while Choice (E) is protected by the Sixth Amendment.

31. **(C)** In *Federalist #10*, Madison gave a brilliant defense as to why a government could not prevent the creation of factions. His argument essentially came down to this: the "cure" (a police state that seeks to force the same opinions on all of its citizens) is worse than the "ailment" (factions may form and seek to harm others as well as influence political discourse). Choices (A) and (E) include famous quotations from Thomas Hobbes' *Leviathan*, a work that defends the need for a totalitarian state. Choice (B) is the antithesis of what Madison wrote. Choice (D) is incorrect because Madison certainly did not want the government to encourage the development of factions.

32. **(D)** America's industrial revolution began in earnest during the 1820s with the opening of the Lowell and Waltham textile mills outside of Boston. By the 1830s, a railroad boom had commenced as well. Over time, rapid industrialization and westward expansion led to a transportation revolution (roads, canals, and railroads) and a market revolution (selling goods to distant markets). As more factories opened up, more people left their family farms and moved to cities in search of work. This trend toward urbanization increased during the 1840s and 1850s, as large waves of German and Irish immigrants came to America, seeking jobs and a better life. Between 1890 and 1920, millions of new immigrants arrived in America, providing a steady source of cheap labor. Most of these immigrants came from southern and eastern Europe and were both poor and unskilled. As such, they were forced to accept low-paying factory jobs and live in tenement houses near their factories. Between 1820 and 1920, millions of struggling farmers and poor immigrants moved to American cities, mostly in the Northeast and Midwest. As a result, the 1920 census showed that more Americans were now living in urban areas rather than rural ones.

33. **(E)** The correct response is (E), since major differences between procedures in the House and Senate include all three of the features mentioned. Because the size of the House is fairly large, with 435 members, time for debate must be limited. If each member was allowed to speak as long as (s)he wanted on every bill, the House could not complete all of its business. Also, debate in the House must be germane. That is, when a member rises to speak, his/her comments must be related to the subject under consideration. This is another time-saving mechanism. The Senate has only 100 members and is not as rushed for time as the House. The Senate has traditionally allowed members to speak as long as they wish and does not force them to confine their remarks to the subject at hand. In the House, the rules committee is very powerful. No bill may get to the House floor without a rule from the rules committee. The rule gives the conditions for debate. The rule sets the time limit for debate and states whether and on what conditions the bill can be amended. The rules committee in the Senate has no such powers.

34. **(D)** In *McCulloch v. Maryland* (1819), the Supreme Court struck down a Maryland law which levied a tax on the Baltimore branch of the Bank of the United States. The Court's ruling was based on its interpretation of the "necessary and proper clause" of the Constitution. This clause may be found in Article I, section 8, of the Constitution. The Court ruled that the necessary and proper clause gives to Congress all powers which make it more convenient for Congress to carry out the enumerated powers of Article I, section 8. (Enumerated powers are those which are specifically mentioned.) The clause is also known as the "elastic clause" since the Court ruled that it gives unspecified powers to Congress. The Court's ruling gave the broadest possible interpretation to the clause, making it possible for Congress to do many things which are not specifically mentioned in the Constitution. By contrast, the Court could have ruled that the clause gave Congress only those powers which are absolutely indispensable to carrying out the enumerated powers. Such a narrow interpretation of the clause would have limited Congress to those activities without which it could

not possibly carry out the enumerated powers. (A) is incorrect since *McCulloch v. Maryland* did not deal with freedom of speech. Choice (B) fails because the power of judicial review (the right of the Court to strike down laws of Congress and to review the actions of the executive) was claimed by the Court in *Marbury v. Madison, 1803.* (C) is incorrect since the Court had previously struck down a law of Congress in *Marbury v. Madison.* Finally, (E) is incorrect because *McCulloch v. Maryland* had nothing to do with the question of executive privilege.

35. **(B)** The question asks which statement about the cabinet is false. Choice (B) is false, and, therefore, the correct answer. The Constitution states in Article I, section 6, that no person holding any office "under the United States" may be a member of Congress. Since cabinet positions are offices "under the United States," cabinet officials may not also be members of Congress. Choices (A) and (D) are true. The cabinet includes the heads of each of the 15 executive departments (State, Treasury, Interior, etc.) as stated in (A). In addition, the president may appoint any other high ranking official whom he wishes to the cabinet, as stated in (D). Choice (C) is true. President Washington was the first to hold cabinet meetings. Every president since Washington has used the cabinet as a tool for managing the federal bureaucracy. So choice (C) is not the correct answer. Choice (E) is not the correct choice. As we saw in the explanation for choice (B), the Constitution states that no one holding office "under the United States" may be a member of Congress. This means that senators may not be members of the cabinet.

36. **(A)** is not a proper conclusion because it is an opinion. The facts from the graph may be used to try to prove the need to cut transportation oil consumption, but the graph itself makes no conclusions. (B) This is true if the average of Germany, Italy, France, and Great Britain is used. (C) Since the United States and Canada top the chart, this is true. (D) This is true, with 25 percent. (E) is true, with about 8 percent.

37. **(C)** This cannot be a conclusion from the graphs, which are per person. Also, Canada, ranking second, has the smallest population on the list. (A) This could be a conclusion because the two largest nations are also the top two consumers. (B) Since four of the top seven consumers are European, this is true. (D) Japan is the only Asian nation listed. (E) This is a probable conclusion, especially when the quantity used for manufacturing in the United States is used as an indicator.

38. **(D)** This is no longer true. Today's industry is divided between many private and nationalized companies. (A) The supply of petroleum is limited and exhaustible. (B) Oil is the key ingredient in plastics. (C) Prices and supply are very sensitive to many conditions. (E) Oil supplies and prices are affected by conditions all over the world with many producers.

39. **(B)** The Navigation Acts were designed to force the colonies to trade exclusively with England and to give the British government extensive regulatory control over all colonial trade. All of the choices except choice (B) were major principles of these acts. The prohibition of the colonies from issuing paper currencies, while also having a major impact on colonial trade, was the focal point of the Currency Act of 1764 (approximately 100 years later than the Navigation Acts).

40. **(A)** Slavery never effectively established itself in New England, in large part because the economic system of the New England colonies and the large population of New England, which provided a large pool of workers, rendered the need for large numbers of slaves unnecessary. Most New England farms were relatively small, self-sufficient farms, and the members of farming communities depended on each other to keep their communities economically viable. In the Southern English colonies, there was less community cohesion among the colonists, there were

fewer people, and there was a constant demand for laborers to cultivate the cash crops necessary to keep the colonies economically afloat. At first this demand was met by the use of indentured servants, but after the 1660s the supply of potential servants dwindled and the only immediate replacement labor pool was imported slave labor.

41. **(E)** This question is partly knowledge-based, but it also requires an understanding of the principles of Christian Humanism and an ability to analyze what ideas they would disapprove, (A) and (C), and approve, (E). Renaissance Humanism, also known as Christian Humanism, combined studies of ancient languages with a zeal to make the Scriptures available in the local languages. Virtually all Christian Humanists translated portions of the Scriptures into European languages, using the Latin text which was the sole version available during the Middle Ages. Very few Christian Humanists were connected with the Reformation; the most famous of them, Erasmus of Rotterdam, criticized laxness within the Catholic church but refused to join with the Protestant reformers.

42. **(D)** Although the Czar's manifesto succeeded in calming and ending the Revolution of 1905, the document's promises of reforms contained a loophole: no mention was made of election procedures for the promised Duma, or parliament. When Nicholas II called the Duma into session after the revolution of 1905, he instituted voting procedures which gave considerably heavier representation to the wealthy and to districts around Moscow, which were considered the most loyal to the government.

43. **(B)** Pakistan, which includes parts of the Punjab, was carved from India in 1947. All of the other choices, Thailand (A), India (C), Korea (D), and Vietnam (E), existed as independent countries before 1947, though because of the partition, India's borders and political situation changed significantly after 1947. It is worthwhile to note that Pakistan, as created in 1947, was later split apart by the secession of Bangladesh in 1971.

44. **(D)** The British policy of indirect rule in Africa was designed to reduce tensions and minimize financial costs. It included flexibility and a minimum of direct British intervention. For this reason, the British tried to adapt their colonial policies to fit the wide variety of native systems in and between countries, and they did *not* want a tribal uniform policy (D), which would have been more rigid. Instead they modified the role of traditional rulers in local areas (E) and relied on a decentralized administration (C). The goal for these colonies was eventual self-rule (B), and for this reason they supported basic primary education for Africans which would equip them for this eventuality (A).

45. **(B)** The Glorious Revolution of 1688–89 did not result in an agreement that in the event of no heirs, the Hanover house would succeed the Stuarts. Such an arrangement was specified in the Act of Succession of 1701, a year before William III's death and the succession of Queen Anne. She outlived all her children. Upon her death in 1714, George I became the first Hanoverian King of England.

46. **(E)** In 1961, after John F. Kennedy gave his approval to overthrow Fidel Castro in what later became known as the Bay of Pigs fiasco, the Russian leader Nikita Khrushchev took advantage of Kennedy's vulnerability and went on the attack. He met with Kennedy in Vienna in June 1961 to address various Cold War-related issues, and after their meetings, Kennedy privately acknowledged that Khrushchev had "savaged him." By August 1961, construction of the Berlin Wall had already begun. In 1963, Kennedy gave a famous speech in West Berlin, where he pledged his solidarity with West Berliners by proclaiming, "Ich bin ein Berliner" ("I am a Berliner."). He also provided a poignant backdrop for his defense of democracy: "Freedom has many difficulties, and

democracy is not perfect, but we have never had to build a wall up to keep our people in." The Berlin Wall, the darkest and most enduring symbol of the Cold War, was torn down in 1989, two years before the dissolution of the Soviet Union.

47. **(A)** After experiencing a religious conversion after a brutal war against the Kalingans, where he adopted a firm belief in the teachings of Buddhism, Asoka sought to support his newfound belief system by building monasteries and sending out missionaries. The other answers were incorrect in that Confucianism (B) and Taoism (E) primarily took root in China, while Zoroastrianism (D) was an important religion in ancient Persia. Portuguese traders and missionaries did help establish a base for Catholicism (C) in the Indian port city of Goa in the early 1500s, but the Catholic faith did not spread extensively throughout the Indian subcontinent in the same manner that it did in other regions, such as South and Central America.

48. **(B)** Portugal's Prince Henry established a navigation school c. 1420, which helped propel his country to an early lead in the Age of Exploration. By 1498, for instance, Vasco da Gama had reached the coast of India. By the mid-1500s, however, Spain (D) had overtaken Portugal's lead in terms of colonization in the New World. England (A), France (C), and the Dutch Republic (E) were all much slower to devote the resources needed for exploration and colonization.

49. **(E)** The end of the *Pax Romana* (or the "Roman Peace") occurred at the end of the reign of Marcus Aurelius, who ruled from 161–180 CE Among his major accomplishments, he wrote a series of reflections entitled *Meditations*, a book that serves as an excellent example of stoic philosophy. Sadly, his son, Commodus, was a terrible leader, who ushered in a long period of decline for Rome. The remaining answers are incorrect in that Tiberius (A) ruled Rome from 14 to 37 CE; Nero (B) from 37 to 68; and Constantine (C) from 306 to 337. Justinian I (D) served as a legendary ruler of the Byzantine Empire from 527 to 565.

50. **(D)** Although Alexander Hamilton's Federalist Party had ceased to exist by the time John Quincy Adams was elected president in 1824, like John Marshall, Quincy Adams still embraced many of the principles that Hamilton had set forth. This included the need for an active federal government that used its influence and resources to build a strong national economy by supporting merchants and manufacturers. The other four choices—Jefferson, Madison, Monroe, and Jackson—all sought to minimize the rights of the federal government.

51. **(A)** The Production Possibilities Curve (or Frontier) is a basic economic model that shows the trade-off between two goods. The classic example is the trade-off that shows a society which must choose between producing guns (representing military goods) and butter (representing consumer goods). The reason these two items were first chosen remains unclear, but Nazi Herman Göring once stated, "Guns will make us powerful; butter will only make us fat."

52. **(A)** The Federal Reserve Board is a government agency consisting of seven members appointed for 14-year terms by the president, with the consent of the Senate. This board is at the head of the Federal Reserve System, which is comprised of member banks across the country. The primary function of the Federal Reserve Board is to implement monetary policy. The Federal Reserve Board has three methods of implementing monetary policy. First, it can change the reserve requirement, which is the amount of cash that member banks must keep on deposit in a regional Federal Reserve Bank. An increase in the requirement reduces the amount of cash a bank has on hand to loan. Second, the board can change the discount rate, which is the interest rate that member banks must pay to borrow money from a Federal Reserve Bank. A higher rate discourages a member bank

from borrowing and lending more money. Third, the board can buy and sell government securities. To increase the money supply, the board sells securities. To decrease the money supply, the board buys securities. Choice (B) is the most plausible alternative to (A), but fails because controlling government spending is a function of Congress and the president. Choice (C) is incorrect because the Federal Reserve Board has nothing to do with regulating commodity prices. Choice (D) is incorrect because the board does not help the president run the executive branch. Choice (E) is incorrect because the board does not keep records of troop strength in army reserve units.

53. **(C)**   The three largest countries of Western Europe—the United Kingdom, France, and the Federal Republic of Germany—have either a multi-party system or a two-plus party system. A multi-party system is one in which three or more major parties compete for seats in the national legislature, while a two-plus party system has two large parties and one or more small parties. The United Kingdom has a two-plus party system. There are two large parties, the Conservatives and Labour. The Liberals are a smaller third party and there are even smaller regional parties in Scotland, Northern Ireland, and Wales. France has a multi-party system. The Socialists, Neo-Gaullists, and Republicans are major parties, while the Communists and the National Front are small parties with few seats in parliament. The Federal Republic of Germany has a two-plus party system. The major parties are the Christian Democratic Union and the Social Democratic party. At the fringes of public life are the Greens and the Neo-Nazis. The United States, by contrast, has only two parties, which successfully compete on a national basis from one election to the next. These are, of course, the Democrats and the Republicans. Choice (A) is incorrect. In Western European countries, party leaders determine which persons will run for office under the party banner. In the United States, on the other hand, candidates for office are selected by the voters in primary elections. Sometimes in the United States a candidate whom the party leadership detests wins the primary, and thus the right to run for office under the party banner. In most Western European countries, political parties are much more centralized than in the United States; therefore, (B) is false. Choice (D) is false. Because the parties are centralized in Western Europe, and because party leaders select candidates for national office, a party member in the national legislature seldom votes against the party. If one did, party leaders would remove his or her name from the ballot in future elections. Choice (E) is incorrect. Since party members vote the party line almost all of the time in Western Europe, voters tend to not focus on the personalities of candidates, but rather on the party label. In the United States, where legislators vote their personal preference as often as the party line, party label is less important to voters. Voters in the United States tend to focus more on the personalities of candidates than European voters.

54. **(D)**   In a parliamentary system the chief executive, normally called the prime minister, is a member of parliament, the legislative body. The majority party in the lower house of the parliament selects its leader to be prime minister. The prime minister then selects a cabinet from among the members of the lower house who are in his/her party. The prime minister and cabinet are the highest executive officers of the country and are usually referred to as the government. There is no strict separation of powers, since the executive branch is made up of members of the legislature. In a presidential system, by contrast, the president is not a member of the legislature and is selected by popular, not by legislative vote. Cabinet members may not sit in the legislature. There is, then, a strict separation of powers, and thus Statement I is true. In a presidential system, the voters choose the president either by direct popular vote or through an electoral college. In a parliamentary system, the majority party in the lower house of parliament chooses one of its members as prime minister. The general public does not participate in choosing the prime minister. So Statement II is also true. In a parliamentary

system the prime minister may call special elections for the lower house of the legislature whenever (s)he wants. In a presidential system the president may not call a special election for members of the legislature, so III is false. The answer, then, is (D), I and II only.

55. **(A)** The first bulleted paragraph states that private and corporate ownership should be limited but they are not directly called upon to act. All other groups are called upon to band together to help the environment.

56. **(D)** These are obvious references to the past use of the environment for economic purposes rather than environmental concerns. (A) and (B) are moral statements, not economic ones. (C) This is a call to action. (E) This tries to redefine society's values.

57. **(E)** This is a political cost concern. Coal is more polluting than oil. (A) This is now used to sell products and is becoming profitable. (B) This is an attempt to replace trees as a renewable resource. (C) Repair and replacement of topsoil, erosion control, and replanting are attempts to reuse mined areas for agriculture. (D) Concern over this has changed products' chemical contents and created new laws to reduce airborne pollution.

58. **(D)** In early 1942, the Japanese high command, angered at air raids from American aircraft carriers, decided to force what was left of the American Pacific fleet into a decisive battle in which the American Navy and its carriers would be destroyed. They decided on an invasion of the American-held island of Midway. Midway was a logical choice. It was 1,100 miles northwest of Hawaii. More importantly, it had a seaplane base and an airstrip. In American hands it provided the United States with an observation post to monitor Japanese actions throughout the central Pacific. In Japanese hands, it would provide them with an airbase from which they could launch continuous air attacks on Pearl Harbor, making it unusable as an American base. If Japan invaded Midway, the Americans would have to send their fleet to defend it or face the loss of Pearl Harbor and Hawaii.

On paper, the plan seemed ideal. The Japanese could throw up to 10 aircraft carriers into the operation. They believed the Americans had only two available aircraft carriers (actually, the Americans had three usable carriers because the USS *Yorktown,* which the Japanese thought they had sunk at the Battle of Coral Sea, had survived and was repaired in time to fight at Midway). The Japanese had dozens of battleships and heavy cruisers. The Americans had only two battleships available, which they chose not to use, and only eight heavy cruisers. On paper, there seemed to be no way the Americans could win.

Unfortunately for the Japanese, the battle was not fought on paper. American cryptographers deciphered enough Japanese messages to uncover the plan. In addition, the overconfident Japanese, expecting to surprise a scattered American fleet, didn't concentrate their forces into an overwhelming single attack force. Instead they divided their fleet into four separate attack forces, each of which was vulnerable to American attack if caught off guard. When the Japanese arrived at Midway, a well-prepared, tightly concentrated American fleet was waiting. Despite a series of nearly catastrophic errors, the Americans caught the Japanese by surprise, sinking four of their largest aircraft carriers and killing 600 of Japan's best pilots. Without adequate air protection, the invasion was cancelled and the Japanese fleet returned to base. Midway was saved. At the time, American analysts thought they had just bought the United States some additional time until the Japanese regrouped and attacked again. In reality, the Japanese were so stunned by the defeat that they readjusted their war plans, switching to defensive operations. They never returned to Midway. With the Japanese now on the defensive, the United States was able to seize the initiative at Guadalcanal, beginning an island-hopping campaign that took America to Japan's outer islands. Midway was undoubtedly the turning point, as it marked the first significant American victory over the Japanese and the end of major Japanese offensive operations in the central Pacific.

59. **(E)** *Brown v. Board of Education of Topeka* was the first legal shot in the war to desegregate America's public schools. Up to this time, many school districts, particularly in the South, had segregated schools for black and white schoolchildren under the doctrine of "separate but equal" education. Sadly, most education facilities for black children were anything but equal. Blacks usually got dilapidated facilities, the worst teachers, and an inferior education. Frustrated black parents challenged the "separate but equal" doctrine in several states, and those challenges were consolidated into one case to be presented before the United States Supreme Court in 1954. Up until this case, previous civil rights cases had been heard before conservative Supreme Courts which had upheld the "separate but equal" doctrine. However, by 1954, the Court was a more liberal court, more sensitive to constitutional protections for all people.

60. **(C)** While this question calls for fact retention, it also requires an ability to analyze the implications of their policies—unless the answer is apparent upon first reading. The first monarchs of a united Spain, Ferdinand and Isabella, achieved that unity by gaining control of the remaining Muslim sections of southern Spain. In an effort to promote cultural unity and establish a national identity, they defined Spanish nationalism in terms of their understanding of orthodox Catholicism. Those not fitting their definition of orthodoxy were condemned as disloyal or subversive. Two particular groups, Jews and Muslims who had converted to Christianity but retained Muslim customs or dress, were forced into exile by Spanish authorities.

61. **(C)** The diversity of monarchs listed in the choices should indicate that guessing is a possibility. Two were devout Catholics (D) and (E), while a third (A) predates the Reformation by almost 200 years. During the Thirty Years' War, when Catholic forces from southern Germany and Austria were close to pushing Lutheran forces into the Baltic Sea, the Lutheran convert Gustavus Adolphus intervened in Germany, saving the Lutheran cause. Adolphus was himself killed during a key battle.

62. **(D)** As a result of the Spanish-American War in 1898, the United States gained control of the Philippines from Spain. The Philippines remained a U.S. territory until the Tydings-McDuffie Act of 1934 provided for its independence. This independence was not realized until 1945. Today, however, Spanish influence, mostly in the shape of religion, language, and culture, is still felt, as is America's presence in the form of popular culture.

63. **(D)** Swaziland, a former British colony, has been called Swaziland both before and after its independence. Malawi is a separate independent country, and the other choices, (A), (B), (C), and (E), are all the former and present names of countries in Africa.

64. **(B)** The Nobel-prize winning economist Milton Friedman asserted that the primary cause of the Great Depression was not the overconcentration of wealth, the overproduction of goods, or the overspeculation on stocks, but rather the Federal Reserve Bank allowing the money supply (as defined by M2) to fall by approximately one-third between 1929 and 1933. This errant policy decision starved the nation of credit, which in turn led to the closure of thousands of the nation's banks, wiping out the life savings of many Americans. While many economists dispute the singular focus of Friedman's analysis (arguing that a multitude of factors worked together to cause the Great Depression), virtually all economists agree that contracting the monetary policy during this time period was a major policy blunder that exacerbated a deep economic decline.

65. **(C)** Ben Bernanke, Chairman of the Federal Reserve Bank ("the Fed") from 2006 to 2014, is a Depression-era scholar who possesses an in-depth knowledge of the Fed's disastrous decision to contract the money supply during the first four years of the Great Depression (1929–1933). As a result, during the Great Recession of 2007–2009, Bernanke dramatically increased the money supply in a policy known as "quantitative easing." Many economists praised Bernanke's handling of monetary policy during this severe downturn, arguing that it kept the United States from another depression; others predicted that it would lead to massive inflation. By 2016, those who were worried about the development of another inflationary cycle looked to be in the wrong, as inflation has steadily remained below 2%.

66. **(C)** In 122 CE, after a visit to Britain, the Roman Emperor Hadrian began construction of a wall that would eventually bear his name. The barricade, which runs for roughly 80 miles near the English-Scottish border, stretches from the North Sea to the Irish Sea.

67. **(E)** The Ural Mountains, which are mainly located in Russia and sit to the east of Moscow, are generally considered to be the dividing line between Europe and Asia.

68. **(D)** The federal government has two primary tools to influence the economy: it can raise or lower taxes and it can raise or lower government spending. (The Federal Reserve Bank is the institution that can raise or lower interest rates and the money supply.) In 1936, during the worst economic crisis in modern history, economist John Maynard Keynes published his famous work *The General Theory of Employment, Interest and Money*, in which he argued that a country's federal government was the only institution big enough to "prime the pump" and thereby stimulate consumer and business demand. Keynes asserted that in a severe economic downturn the federal government should lower taxes and increase government spending; conversely, during an economic boom, he said the government should raise taxes and lower government spending. In making his argument, Keynes challenged the orthodox view of Adam Smith, who in 1776 argued that governments should take a *laissez-faire* (hands-off) approach to markets.

69. **(D)** The infamous decision rendered in the 1896 Supreme Court case *Plessy v. Ferguson* legitimized Jim Crow segregation laws with the phrase "separate but equal." The other four choices were all famous Supreme Court cases, but only the 1857 decision in *Dred Scott v. Sandford* involved the rights of African Americans. In that case, the Supreme Court, under Chief Justice Roger Taney, ruled that the institution of slavery was protected by the U.S. Constitution and that Congress lacked the power to alter that protection. That ruling was overturned in 1865 with the ratification of the Thirteenth Amendment.

70. **(B)** The Aztec Empire was based in modern-day Mexico in Central America, while the Incan Empire was based in modern-day Peru in South America. The Powhatan Confederacy (A), the Iroquois Confederacy (C), the Hopi (D), and the Huron (E) were all based in North America and none of them would have been considered empires.

71. **(C)** Political scientists use the term "pluralistic" to describe a political system in which innumerable groups of people share cultural, economic, religious, or ethnic interests. These groups organize and spend great amounts of time and money competing to influence government policy-making. The pluralistic concept of democracy is in contrast to the elitist model, which states that policy-making is dominated by elites such as wealthy industrialists, military leaders, or organizations such as the Trilateral Commission. Therefore, the answer is (C). Choice (A) fails because pluralism stresses not only cultural groups but economic, religious, and other types of groups. Also important to plural-

ism is the idea that the different groups do not merely exist but compete to influence public policy-making. Choice (B) fails because the term to describe a system in which political power is divided between national and state governments is "federalism." Choice (D) fails because to say that one group is overrepresented is more like an elitist view than a pluralistic view of politics. It is true that candidates for national office are elected by a plurality vote method (E). "Plurality vote" means that the candidate who gets the most votes, even if less than a majority, wins the election. However, the term "pluralism" does not refer to this method of election, so choice (E) is wrong.

72. **(A)** As the graph below shows, there is a direct correlation between voter turnout and educational level. Those with four years or more of college are more likely to vote than are those with one to three years of college. Those with one to three years of college are more likely to vote than are high school graduates. High school graduates are, in turn, more likely to vote than are those with less than a high school education. The answer is (A), the more schooling one has, the more likely one is to vote. Voting is only one form of political participation. Other forms are running for office, working in political campaigns, and contributing to campaigns. While it is difficult to find statistics which show the correlation between educational status and running for office, we do know that most people who are completely inactive (that is, do not participate in politics in any way) typically have little education and low incomes and are relatively young. Therefore, it is safe to conclude that the less education one has (B), the LESS likely one is to run for office; so (B) is not the answer. Choice (C) is clearly wrong, since many studies have shown a direct correlation between advanced educational status and political participation by voting. Choice (D) is wrong, as is clear from the graph on the next page. Those with a high school education are NOT more likely to vote than are those with a college degree. Choice (E) is wrong because, as the graph shows, the less education one has, the less likely one is to vote. It is logical to infer from this that those with no formal schooling are less likely to vote than are those with a high school education.

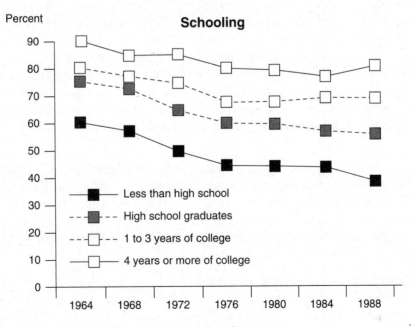

From James Q. Wilson, p. 130, *American Government*

73. **(E)** Articulating interests is generally thought of as the special task of interest groups. Parties, on the other hand, bring together or "aggregate" interests (B) in order to create a working majority to run government. Parties also play a significant role in recruiting candidates (A), serving as channels of communication (C), and staffing elections (D).

74. **(C)** Although the chart can be used for several of the choices, it is a simplified version of the business cycle. (A) The chart does not refer to "bust" or depression. (B) and (D) Changes are shown, but not causes. (E) If you added data, such as dates, it could be used to track historical fluctuations, but doesn't in this form.

75. **(D)** This may influence the other factors, but can have a variety of effects and is not part of the purely economic picture. (A) The number of people employed is used to define whether we are in a recession or not. (B) Obviously directly related to (A), it also shows prosperity, if products are in demand. (C) Personal earnings rise with an economic boom and help sustain it with spending. (E) This is an important indicator of income, production, and consumer confidence in the economy.

76. **(C)** Increased taxation is the most counterproductive to economic growth because it takes money out of spending circulation and reduces sales. (A) is usually not planned, but has been credited with helping the economy as a side effect because of the increased need for services and products. (B) Keynesian economics calls for "pump-priming" of the economy through government spending to employ people and increase production. (D) Supply-side economics contends that reducing government regulation frees up capital to create products and jobs. (E) This is often used as a short-term solution to help specific industries, such as the auto industry in the early 1980s. Long-term use may trigger international retaliation and create worse problems.

77. **(A)** The Great Awakening was a series of religious awakenings, or rebirths, centered primarily in New England but spread throughout the colonies, which changed the lives of English colonists. It challenged the old hierarchical religious order in which ordained clergy were deferred to and were believed to have knowledge based on extensive formal learning that the average member of a congregation lacked. It brought a much broader sense of community to colonists making them aware of others with similar questions and beliefs who lived outside their village or town. In many ways, it was the first of a series of events that helped to forge distinctively American regional identities, separate from their European heritage, among the North American colonists.

78. **(B)** There were many major changes resulting from the rapid industrial development in the United States from 1860 through 1900. First, there was a shift to building larger and larger industrial facilities to accommodate the new machine technologies coming into existence. Small factories could not absorb the cost of much of the machinery and did not produce enough to make the machinery profitable. So, contrary to choice (D), there was an increase in large industrial plants and a relative decline in small factories.

79. **(C)** Choices (B) and (C) are opposites; high inflation almost always affects the value of a country's currency. If you recognize this conflict, it will become apparent that one of these two answers is the correct answer. If necessary, it is worthwhile guessing, since your odds are 50 percent and only 0.25 point is deducted for an incorrect guess.

80. **(B)** On the map, several areas of Europe are depicted with dark shading. These areas are the lands controlled by the Hapsburgs in the sixteenth century. Choice (C) is incorrect, since Spain was lost by the Hapsburgs in the 1600s. A further clue: the large size of the Ottoman Empire, covering the entire Balkan peninsula, precludes any answer after about 1870.

81. **(E)** In 1914 only Ethiopia, along with Liberia, remained an independent state. Algeria (A) belonged to France; the Congo (B) was Belgian; Angola (C) was occupied by the Portuguese; and Egypt (D) was under British control.

82. **(B)** Thailand is bordered by Myanmar on the northwest, Laos on the north and east, and Cambodia on the southeast. Vietnam borders Laos and Cambodia on the east with China to its north and the South China Sea to its east. The "Golden Triangle," where Myanmar, Laos, and Thailand meet, is a notorious area for the growing and trafficking of drugs.

83. **(B)** Hitler, it appears, was not a very good history student, for he basically repeated the same blunders that Napoleon made in 1812, when his troops unsuccessfully invaded Russia. The armies of both men went down in defeat, in part because of the long supply lines and the brutal Russian winters. Stalin successfully negotiated his demand for a buffer zone with Franklin Roosevelt and Winston Churchill, who needed Russia's help to bring about a swift end to the war in Europe. In return, Stalin promised FDR and Churchill that he would hold free elections in Eastern Europe. He later betrayed that promise by holding rigged elections, thereby exacerbating the tensions between Russia and America at the outset of the Cold War.

84. **(A)** During the 1930s and 1940s, a great debate occurred between British economist John Maynard Keynes and Austrian economist Friedrich Hayek concerning the proper role of government in the economy. Keynes argued that governments should intervene during severe recessions or booming economies. Hayek, on the other hand, asserted that government involvement would eventually lead to a dependent people who, over time, would function much like the serfs did in a feudal society.

85. **(D)** In *The Wealth of Nations*, Adam Smith argued that human self-interest drives human behavior. The context for his quotation about the butcher, brewer, and baker is that if governments get involved in regulating markets, they will pervert individual incentives and cause market inefficiencies. As a result, Smith asserted that governments should keep their hands-off, noting that in the long-run markets always correct themselves.

86. **(B)** After Jefferson completed the Louisiana Purchase in 1803, the western boundary of the United States was located along the Rocky Mountains. This boundary did not reach the Pacific Ocean until 1848, after the signing of the Treaty of Guadalupe-Hidalgo at the conclusion of the Mexican-American War.

87. **(E)** Founded in 1993, the European Union (EU) is an economic union but not a political one, a fact that has caused a great deal of controversy, especially after Greece first began defaulting on its debts in 2010 and needed a bailout from stronger EU countries, such as Germany. In terms of economic power, the EU has a mixture of both strong and weak countries. As a result, many economists question the EU's long-term viability, especially after the 2016 vote in which the British decided to pull out of the EU.

88. **(C)** Manifesting a mindset that "might makes right," thirteen European powers carved up Sub-Saharan Africa with little regard for existing boundaries or tribal affiliations. An underlying motivation for the Berlin Conference was Otto von Bismarck's desire to enhance Germany's colonial

holdings so it could compete on the world stage with the likes of England and France. To justify carving up this vast region, the European powers relied on concepts such as "survival of the fittest," a term first coined by English sociologist Herbert Spencer (not Charles Darwin, as most people assume). Perhaps English industrialist Cecil Rhodes best summed up the prevailing European arrogance and racism of his era when he proclaimed that the Anglo-Saxon race was "the finest race in the world, and that the more of the world we inhabit, the better it is for the human race."

89. **(B)** The early river valley civilization in Mesopotamia was connected to the Tigris and Euphrates Rivers. The Volga River is the longest river in Europe and located in Russia.

90. **(B)** In 1932, Franklin Roosevelt was elected president in a landslide vote, ending a 12-year period of Republican domination of the presidency. This election is considered by political scientists a "realigning election." A realigning election is one in which a sharp, lasting change occurs in the coalition of voters which supports each of the parties. In the election of 1936, Roosevelt drew into the Democratic party a coalition of urban workers, blacks, southern whites, and Jews. Most of the urban workers were also union members. The coalition did not include large numbers of business interests, which continued to vote for the Republican party. This coalition continued to support the Democratic party until approximately 1968, when white southerners began to vote for the Republican candidate for president more often than for the Democratic candidate. The answer is (B), northern business leaders, since most of these voters supported the Republicans in each of the years Roosevelt ran for president (1932, 1936, 1940, and 1944). Choice (A) is wrong because most southerners, white and black alike, voted for Roosevelt each time he ran for president. Choice (C) is wrong because blue-collar workers heavily supported Roosevelt in each of his elections. Choice (D) is wrong because blacks and Jews, two prominent racial minorities, voted for Roosevelt. Choice (E) is false because union members, who were mostly blue-collar workers, heavily supported Roosevelt.

91. **(E)** The Fifth Amendment to the U.S. Constitution states, "No person shall be compelled in any criminal case to be a witness against himself...." The Supreme Court held in *Miranda v. Arizona,* 1966, that "In order to...permit a full opportunity to exercise the privilege against self-incrimination, the accused must be adequately and effectively apprised of his rights and the exercise of those rights must be fully honored." This means that when police apprehend a suspect in a criminal case they must immediately tell the person that (s)he has a right to remain silent. The Sixth Amendment to the U.S. Constitution states: "In all criminal prosecutions, the accused shall enjoy the right...to have compulsory process for obtaining witnesses in his favor, and to have Assistance of Counsel for his defense. The compulsory process clause means that the accused can subpoena witnesses in his/her favor to appear in court to testify for the defense. (A subpoena is a court order which commands a person to appear at a certain time and place to give testimony upon a certain matter.) The assistance of counsel clause of the Sixth Amendment was interpreted by the Supreme Court in *Argersinger v. Hamlin,* 1972, to mean that if the accused cannot afford an attorney, (s)he is entitled to have one appointed at government expense, in any felony or misdemeanor criminal case in which, if the accused is found guilty, (s)he may be sentenced to jail. It is clear from the above that the rights mentioned in statements I, II, and III are all guaranteed by the Constitution. Therefore, choice (E) is correct.

92. **(D)** Before the Civil War most blacks in the South were slaves. They were not citizens and had no civil or political rights. After the war, the Fourteenth and Fifteenth Amendments were added to the Constitution. The Fourteenth Amendment extended citizenship to blacks. The Fifteenth

Amendment stated that the "right of citizens of the United States to vote shall not be denied or abridged by the United States or by any state on account of race, color, or previous condition of servitude." Contrary to what one might assume, blacks did not immediately gain full voting rights. During the 1870s the Supreme Court held that the Fifteenth Amendment did not automatically confer the right to vote on anybody. States could not pass laws to prevent anyone from voting on the basis of race, but they could restrict persons from voting on other grounds. This interpretation of the Fifteenth Amendment allowed southern states to use several techniques to effectively exclude blacks from voting. Since most former slaves were illiterate, prospective voters were often required to pass literacy tests. Poll taxes were also levied, which kept blacks, who were mostly poor, from voting. Since many whites were also poor and illiterate, grandfather clauses were enacted to allow them to bypass the legal restrictions on voting. Grandfather clauses stated that if you or your ancestors had voted before 1867, you could vote without paying a poll tax or passing a literacy test. Choice (D) is correct because the purpose of grandfather clauses and literacy tests was to keep blacks from voting. Choice (A) is wrong because the purpose of the grandfather clause was to allow poor and illiterate whites to escape voting restrictions. Choice (B) is wrong because the intent of the restrictions was to prevent blacks, not immigrants, from voting. In addition, there was little immigration into the South during the time in question. Choices (C) and (E) are wrong because the measures were restrictions on the right to vote, not on the right to run for office.

93. **(B)** is the most specific statement because, although the first paragraph refers to the "needs of society," those needs are specified as economic in the rest of the quote. (A) Many of society's needs—legal rights, social needs, poverty – are not addressed. (C) This is not discussed. (D) The terms "average," "more" and "more," and "most" are used, not "all." (E) The government role is not discussed.

94. **(A)** The Chamber of Commerce represents U.S. businesspeople and this is definitely a pro-business statement. (B) The federal Department of Labor is not anti-business, but it is not its major concern to advocate pro-business stands. (C) The GAO is the auditing branch of the government and doesn't take a stand on pro- or anti-business statements. (D) The Socialist belief would probably be the opposite of the quote. (E) The union position would probably credit workers more and business less.

95. **(D)** Justice means fair treatment for all, sometimes enforced by government regulation. (A) This is specifically referred to in relation to employment, wages, etc. (B) This is indirectly referred to through rising living standards and growth which also provides security (C). (E) This is implied throughout and referred to as "less constraint."

96. **(E)** Labor is a factor in creating all of the others, which are the basic activities.

97. **(D)** In the autumn of 1864, a war-weary North faced a presidential election that offered them a clear choice. Abraham Lincoln ran on a platform of continuing the Civil War until the South was totally defeated. His opponent, former general George McClellan, ran on a platform calling for an armistice and recognition of the South as a separate nation. Early in the campaign, Lincoln looked to be in trouble. Although the Union had made deep penetrations into the western half of the Confederacy and had complete control of the Mississippi River, the Confederate armies in the East still fought valiantly on. It looked as if the Union armies could never destroy them and many people were questioning if it was worth the cost to try. The war had now been raging for $3\frac{1}{2}$ years. The

cost in human lives, time, and money had far surpassed everyone's worst fears. Many Northerners just wanted it to be over. Both Lincoln and Confederate President Jefferson Davis realized this. Accordingly, the Confederate strategy was to just hold on and deny the North any major victories before the election. Lincoln realized he needed a decisive victory before the election, pointing to a rapid defeat of the Confederacy, if he was to win. That victory occurred in September 1864 when Union forces under the command of William T. Sherman occupied Atlanta and followed up on this victory with his infamous "march to the sea." This victory pointed to the imminent destruction of the Confederacy. Finally, people could see a "light at the end of the tunnel" and desire to completely defeat the Confederates rose again in the North. The capture of Atlanta guaranteed Lincoln's reelection and sealed the fate of the Confederate States of America.

98. **(A)** After he was overthrown by revolutionary forces in 1978, the Shah of Iran fled, traveling to several countries. It was from Mexico that he asked for permission to enter the United States to receive cancer treatment. President Carter was warned that admitting the Shah to the United States, for any reason, would look to the Iranians like America still supported the Shah's regime and would lead to trouble. However, other advisors told Carter that the United States owed the Shah a large debt of gratitude for the favors he had done for America and also for the lack of decisive support from the United States when his government was overthrown. Carter had previously refused to grant the Shah exile in the United States, but when he was told of the Shah's need for cancer treatment, he decided to allow the Shah to enter the United States on humanitarian grounds. As predicted, the Iranians were infuriated by this. On November 4, 1979, young Iranian males, backed by their government and claiming to be students, seized the American embassy compound and took 76 hostages, 62 of whom were held for more than a year. It was the beginning of one of the worst nightmares in American foreign policy, and it helped ruin Carter's presidency.

99. **(B)** Here is a question that may be answered correctly even if, upon first reading, you are tempted to pass it by. The correct answer must be a country which had some degree of control over land in both Egypt and South Africa. If no answer comes to mind, you still may be able to remember the fact that the British had the largest colonial empire. After wrestling control of the Suez Canal in Egypt from its French builders and the Egyptian Khedive, the British government planned construction of a rail line linking Egypt with its recent acquisition of largely Dutch-settled land in South Africa. Typically, other European nations successfully moved to block the railroad by making claims to central African land along the route.

100. **(A)** The mention of Ethiopia may bring Italy to mind. If not, a possible guess is indicated if you are able to remember Mussolini's invasion of Ethiopia during the 1930s. The sole European nation to have its plans to establish an African colony in the late nineteenth century blocked by a native African force, Italy for some time regarded the incident a national humiliation. The incident was one of several reasons the Italian dictator Mussolini gave for his successful military takeover of Ethiopia in 1935.

101. **(C)** The Himalayan mountain range, the highest in the world, runs 1,500 miles from the northernmost tip of India, through Nepal, and along the southwest border of China. The Himalayas include Mt. Everest (Qomolongma), the tallest mountain in the world, and India's tallest mountain, Nanda Devi, which rises 25,645 feet. Bangladesh is almost completely surrounded by the northeastern border of India, facing the Bay of Bengal. It does have a small border with Burma on its southeast side.

102. **(B)** When Britain, bowing to internal abolitionist pressure, declared the slave trade illegal for its people in 1807, only Denmark, which made illegal the slave trade in 1805, had already outlawed the practice. The next to follow suit was Holland (A) in 1814, France (C) in 1818, and Spain (D) and Portugal (E) which restricted their slave trade to the seas south of the equator in 1815 and 1817, respectively.

103. **(B)** The Federal Deposit Insurance Corporation (FDIC) was an essential component of FDR's New Deal policies in 1933. Prior to its implementation, depositors risked losing their entire savings if a bank became insolvent. As a result of the FDIC, however, the federal government agreed to guaranty bank deposits for up to $5,000, but only in FDIC-approved banks. (Today that guaranty extends to deposits up to $250,000.)

104. **(D)** The Shinto religion is native to Japan and is a polytheistic faith that involves the worship of both nature and ancestors.

105. **(C)** The country of Uruguay is located on the Atlantic Ocean side of South America, whereas the Andes Mountain range runs along the Pacific Ocean side.

106. **(B)** Geographers use the designation "CBD" when referring to the Central Business District of a city. For example, Manhattan is considered the CBD of New York City.

107. **(C)** Unlike Thomas Jefferson, who defended his viewpoint toward a limited role for the federal government based upon his model citizen, the virtuous yeoman farmer, Alexander Hamilton had a rather jaundiced view of the common man. As a result, Hamilton greatly feared mobs and therefore sought a federal government that would swiftly put down rebellion. For example, he used Shays' Rebellion in western Massachusetts in 1786 to call for a convention of delegates in Philadelphia in 1787. At this gathering, Hamilton and James Madison led an assault against the ineffective Articles of Confederation, a document that was drafted based upon an excessive fear of tyranny.

108. **(D)** The modern-day city of Istanbul, Turkey, was known as Constantinople in 330 CE, after the Roman Emperor Constantine the Great made it the new capital of the Roman Empire. Strategically located on both sides of the Bosporus (a narrow straight that connects Europe to Asia), this city played an important role in three different empires: the Roman, Byzantine, and Ottoman. In what ranks as a key turning point in world history, the Ottoman Turks finally conquered this strategically-important city in 1453, putting an end to the last remnants of the formerly glorious Byzantine Empire.

109. **(A)** The Arno River runs through the city of Florence, not Rome. The primary river in Rome is the Tiber.

110. **(D)** On his first trip across the Atlantic Ocean, Columbus mistakenly thought he had reached India, but in fact he had landed in modern-day Haiti. Driven by various motives, including "God, Glory, and Gold," Columbus more or less died a failure, never finding the gold or the glory that he so desperately sought. With respect to God, although he maintained his Christian faith until his death in 1506, the interactions between Columbus and the native peoples that he encountered soon led to the forced coercion to Christianity for many, a tactic that clearly runs contrary to basic teachings in the Gospels.

111. **(A)** The passage is taken from the landmark case *Marbury v. Madison,* 1803. What the passage means, in everyday language, is:

1. Interpreting laws is a judicial function. 2. When two laws conflict, the courts must decide which will be enforced. 3. The Constitution is superior to laws passed by Congress or state legislatures (called statutory law). 4. Therefore, if a statute conflicts with the Constitution, the statute cannot be enforced by the courts.

Choice (B) is incorrect because the passage says nothing about Congress's right to pass laws to carry out its duties. Rather, the passage deals with a conflict between statutory and Constitutional law. Choice (C) is incorrect because it contradicts the main thesis of the passage. The passage clearly says that it is the duty of *courts*, not legislatures, to "say what the law is," which means the same as "interpretation of laws." Choice (D) is incorrect because the passage says when an act of the legislature and the Constitution conflict, the Constitution governs the case. Choice (E) is incorrect because the passage states specifically that if two laws conflict, the courts must decide the operation of each. It then posits a case where the two laws in conflict are an act of the legislature and the Constitution. The clear implication is that, in such a case, the courts must decide on the operation of the Constitution, which means deciding questions of Constitutional law.

112. **(E)** After a bill is introduced into either house of Congress, it is referred to the appropriate committee. The bill will then usually be referred by the committee to a subcommittee. After holding a hearing on the bill, the subcommittee will then have a mark-up session where revisions and additions are made to the bill. The bill is then referred back to the full committee, which may also hold a hearing and have a mark-up session. Choices (A), (B), and (C) are incorrect because mark-up sessions do not occur in the majority leader's office, on the floor of the legislative chambers, or in party caucuses. Choice (D) is the most plausible alternative to (E), because a joint conference committee is, after all, a committee. However, proposed legislation goes to a joint conference committee only after it has passed both houses of Congress. The Constitution requires that before a piece of legislation can become law, it must pass both houses in identical form. The purpose of the joint conference committee is to iron out differences in a bill that has passed one house in a different form than in the other. It is true that changes are made to such a bill in a joint conference committee, to satisfy members of both houses. However, the term "mark-up session" refers only to the activity of standing committees and subcommittees in Congress, not to joint conference committees.

113. **(D)** The Office of Management and Budget is the chief presidential staff agency. Its primary responsibility is to put together the budget that the president submits to Congress. Each agency and office of the executive branch must have its budget requests cleared by OMB before it gets into the president's budget. The OMB also studies the organization and operations of the executive branch, to ensure that each office and agency is carrying out its appropriate duty, as assigned by law. Choice (A) is incorrect because the Department of Commerce does not help the president to draw up his annual budget. The Department of Commerce was created in 1903 to protect the interests of businesspeople at home and abroad. Choice (B) is incorrect because the Department of Treasury is not involved in drawing up the president's budget. The functions of the Treasury Department include collecting taxes through the Internal Revenue Service, an administrative unit of the Department, administering the public debt, and coining money. Choice (C) is incorrect because the main responsibility of the Federal Reserve Board is the implementation of monetary policy. It has nothing to do with drawing up the president's annual budget. Choice (E) is incorrect

because the cabinet does not help the president draw up his budget. It advises the president on the administration of the executive departments.

114. **(E)**   (A) is not correct because there are some variances between nations high in GNP while not so high in trade. (B) is incorrect because there is no data comparing previous years. (C) is incorrect. Thailand, the Philippines, and Indonesia did not exceed the world average in trade. (D) is incorrect; Japan was not the leader in trade.

115. **(D)**   is not true. The trade graph is a line graph, and the GNP is a bar graph. All the others are true. (A) *Per capita* means per person.

116. **(A)**   is most accurate; all are on the eastern edge of Asia. (B) is incorrect because all of Asia is not represented, for example, India or the Persian Gulf. (C) is wrong; northwest Asia would be either the Persian Gulf area or Asian USSR. (D) is incorrect; Malaysia and Thailand are as close to the Indian Ocean as to the Pacific. (E) is wrong; only Australia, Hong Kong, Malaysia, New Zealand, and Singapore were ever British colonies. Japan and Thailand were never colonized by foreigners.

117. **(D)**   Singapore shows the greatest growth rate because its per capita trade is not only highest but exceeds its GNP, which means its people are producing exportable products which bring money back into the nation. Hong Kong is second.

118. **(A)**   GNP is the gross national product and is defined as the total goods and services produced by the nation in a given year. (B) is only partially correct because services are not specified. The other choices are not correct.

119. **(A)**   In the presidential election of 1876, Samuel Tilden defeated his Republican opponent, Rutherford B. Hayes, in the popular vote by 250,000 votes. However, there were 20 contested votes in the electoral college. If Hayes received all the contested electoral votes, he would win the election by one vote in the electoral college and he would gain the presidency. The matter was turned over to Congress, where a Republican-dominated commission awarded the disputed electoral votes to Hayes. The Senate ratified the commission's decision, but the Democrats in the House threatened to use political means to gain Tilden's victory through a House vote. Republicans negotiated the issue and the Compromise of 1877 was the result. Hayes won the presidency. Democrats received assurances that federal soldiers would be withdrawn from Southern states (effectively ending Reconstruction) and that blanket federal government support for Republicans in the South would end. This opened the door for Democrats to regain control in all the Southern states (they had already effectively regained control in all but three). None of the other choices listed in the question were in any way involved in the Compromise of 1877.

120. **(B)**   After the defeat of George Washington's Virginian forces at Fort Necessity by the French, it became clear that the colonies were too weak to individually tackle either the French or their various Indian allies. Benjamin Franklin perceived that united action by the colonies was the only hope of providing for their security. He called together the Albany Congress to discuss plans to enlist the aid of the various Iroquois tribes in colonial defense and to coordinate defense plans between the English colonies. It also called for the establishment of a "grand council" with representatives from each of the colonies to enact taxes and coordinate colonial economic activity. The plan is notable because it was the first to call for the individual colonies to act as a single, united entity. While the plan was visionary and ultimately necessary, the colonial legislatures ultimately rejected it.

PRACTICE TEST

ANSWER SHEET

1. Ⓐ Ⓑ Ⓒ Ⓓ Ⓔ	41. Ⓐ Ⓑ Ⓒ Ⓓ Ⓔ	81. Ⓐ Ⓑ Ⓒ Ⓓ Ⓔ
2. Ⓐ Ⓑ Ⓒ Ⓓ Ⓔ	42. Ⓐ Ⓑ Ⓒ Ⓓ Ⓔ	82. Ⓐ Ⓑ Ⓒ Ⓓ Ⓔ
3. Ⓐ Ⓑ Ⓒ Ⓓ Ⓔ	43. Ⓐ Ⓑ Ⓒ Ⓓ Ⓔ	83. Ⓐ Ⓑ Ⓒ Ⓓ Ⓔ
4. Ⓐ Ⓑ Ⓒ Ⓓ Ⓔ	44. Ⓐ Ⓑ Ⓒ Ⓓ Ⓔ	84. Ⓐ Ⓑ Ⓒ Ⓓ Ⓔ
5. Ⓐ Ⓑ Ⓒ Ⓓ Ⓔ	45. Ⓐ Ⓑ Ⓒ Ⓓ Ⓔ	85. Ⓐ Ⓑ Ⓒ Ⓓ Ⓔ
6. Ⓐ Ⓑ Ⓒ Ⓓ Ⓔ	46. Ⓐ Ⓑ Ⓒ Ⓓ Ⓔ	86. Ⓐ Ⓑ Ⓒ Ⓓ Ⓔ
7. Ⓐ Ⓑ Ⓒ Ⓓ Ⓔ	47. Ⓐ Ⓑ Ⓒ Ⓓ Ⓔ	87. Ⓐ Ⓑ Ⓒ Ⓓ Ⓔ
8. Ⓐ Ⓑ Ⓒ Ⓓ Ⓔ	48. Ⓐ Ⓑ Ⓒ Ⓓ Ⓔ	88. Ⓐ Ⓑ Ⓒ Ⓓ Ⓔ
9. Ⓐ Ⓑ Ⓒ Ⓓ Ⓔ	49. Ⓐ Ⓑ Ⓒ Ⓓ Ⓔ	89. Ⓐ Ⓑ Ⓒ Ⓓ Ⓔ
10. Ⓐ Ⓑ Ⓒ Ⓓ Ⓔ	50. Ⓐ Ⓑ Ⓒ Ⓓ Ⓔ	90. Ⓐ Ⓑ Ⓒ Ⓓ Ⓔ
11. Ⓐ Ⓑ Ⓒ Ⓓ Ⓔ	51. Ⓐ Ⓑ Ⓒ Ⓓ Ⓔ	91. Ⓐ Ⓑ Ⓒ Ⓓ Ⓔ
12. Ⓐ Ⓑ Ⓒ Ⓓ Ⓔ	52. Ⓐ Ⓑ Ⓒ Ⓓ Ⓔ	92. Ⓐ Ⓑ Ⓒ Ⓓ Ⓔ
13. Ⓐ Ⓑ Ⓒ Ⓓ Ⓔ	53. Ⓐ Ⓑ Ⓒ Ⓓ Ⓔ	93. Ⓐ Ⓑ Ⓒ Ⓓ Ⓔ
14. Ⓐ Ⓑ Ⓒ Ⓓ Ⓔ	54. Ⓐ Ⓑ Ⓒ Ⓓ Ⓔ	94. Ⓐ Ⓑ Ⓒ Ⓓ Ⓔ
15. Ⓐ Ⓑ Ⓒ Ⓓ Ⓔ	55. Ⓐ Ⓑ Ⓒ Ⓓ Ⓔ	95. Ⓐ Ⓑ Ⓒ Ⓓ Ⓔ
16. Ⓐ Ⓑ Ⓒ Ⓓ Ⓔ	56. Ⓐ Ⓑ Ⓒ Ⓓ Ⓔ	96. Ⓐ Ⓑ Ⓒ Ⓓ Ⓔ
17. Ⓐ Ⓑ Ⓒ Ⓓ Ⓔ	57. Ⓐ Ⓑ Ⓒ Ⓓ Ⓔ	97. Ⓐ Ⓑ Ⓒ Ⓓ Ⓔ
18. Ⓐ Ⓑ Ⓒ Ⓓ Ⓔ	58. Ⓐ Ⓑ Ⓒ Ⓓ Ⓔ	98. Ⓐ Ⓑ Ⓒ Ⓓ Ⓔ
19. Ⓐ Ⓑ Ⓒ Ⓓ Ⓔ	59. Ⓐ Ⓑ Ⓒ Ⓓ Ⓔ	99. Ⓐ Ⓑ Ⓒ Ⓓ Ⓔ
20. Ⓐ Ⓑ Ⓒ Ⓓ Ⓔ	60. Ⓐ Ⓑ Ⓒ Ⓓ Ⓔ	100. Ⓐ Ⓑ Ⓒ Ⓓ Ⓔ
21. Ⓐ Ⓑ Ⓒ Ⓓ Ⓔ	61. Ⓐ Ⓑ Ⓒ Ⓓ Ⓔ	101. Ⓐ Ⓑ Ⓒ Ⓓ Ⓔ
22. Ⓐ Ⓑ Ⓒ Ⓓ Ⓔ	62. Ⓐ Ⓑ Ⓒ Ⓓ Ⓔ	102. Ⓐ Ⓑ Ⓒ Ⓓ Ⓔ
23. Ⓐ Ⓑ Ⓒ Ⓓ Ⓔ	63. Ⓐ Ⓑ Ⓒ Ⓓ Ⓔ	103. Ⓐ Ⓑ Ⓒ Ⓓ Ⓔ
24. Ⓐ Ⓑ Ⓒ Ⓓ Ⓔ	64. Ⓐ Ⓑ Ⓒ Ⓓ Ⓔ	104. Ⓐ Ⓑ Ⓒ Ⓓ Ⓔ
25. Ⓐ Ⓑ Ⓒ Ⓓ Ⓔ	65. Ⓐ Ⓑ Ⓒ Ⓓ Ⓔ	105. Ⓐ Ⓑ Ⓒ Ⓓ Ⓔ
26. Ⓐ Ⓑ Ⓒ Ⓓ Ⓔ	66. Ⓐ Ⓑ Ⓒ Ⓓ Ⓔ	106. Ⓐ Ⓑ Ⓒ Ⓓ Ⓔ
27. Ⓐ Ⓑ Ⓒ Ⓓ Ⓔ	67. Ⓐ Ⓑ Ⓒ Ⓓ Ⓔ	107. Ⓐ Ⓑ Ⓒ Ⓓ Ⓔ
28. Ⓐ Ⓑ Ⓒ Ⓓ Ⓔ	68. Ⓐ Ⓑ Ⓒ Ⓓ Ⓔ	108. Ⓐ Ⓑ Ⓒ Ⓓ Ⓔ
29. Ⓐ Ⓑ Ⓒ Ⓓ Ⓔ	69. Ⓐ Ⓑ Ⓒ Ⓓ Ⓔ	109. Ⓐ Ⓑ Ⓒ Ⓓ Ⓔ
30. Ⓐ Ⓑ Ⓒ Ⓓ Ⓔ	70. Ⓐ Ⓑ Ⓒ Ⓓ Ⓔ	110. Ⓐ Ⓑ Ⓒ Ⓓ Ⓔ
31. Ⓐ Ⓑ Ⓒ Ⓓ Ⓔ	71. Ⓐ Ⓑ Ⓒ Ⓓ Ⓔ	111. Ⓐ Ⓑ Ⓒ Ⓓ Ⓔ
32. Ⓐ Ⓑ Ⓒ Ⓓ Ⓔ	72. Ⓐ Ⓑ Ⓒ Ⓓ Ⓔ	112. Ⓐ Ⓑ Ⓒ Ⓓ Ⓔ
33. Ⓐ Ⓑ Ⓒ Ⓓ Ⓔ	73. Ⓐ Ⓑ Ⓒ Ⓓ Ⓔ	113. Ⓐ Ⓑ Ⓒ Ⓓ Ⓔ
34. Ⓐ Ⓑ Ⓒ Ⓓ Ⓔ	74. Ⓐ Ⓑ Ⓒ Ⓓ Ⓔ	114. Ⓐ Ⓑ Ⓒ Ⓓ Ⓔ
35. Ⓐ Ⓑ Ⓒ Ⓓ Ⓔ	75. Ⓐ Ⓑ Ⓒ Ⓓ Ⓔ	115. Ⓐ Ⓑ Ⓒ Ⓓ Ⓔ
36. Ⓐ Ⓑ Ⓒ Ⓓ Ⓔ	76. Ⓐ Ⓑ Ⓒ Ⓓ Ⓔ	116. Ⓐ Ⓑ Ⓒ Ⓓ Ⓔ
37. Ⓐ Ⓑ Ⓒ Ⓓ Ⓔ	77. Ⓐ Ⓑ Ⓒ Ⓓ Ⓔ	117. Ⓐ Ⓑ Ⓒ Ⓓ Ⓔ
38. Ⓐ Ⓑ Ⓒ Ⓓ Ⓔ	78. Ⓐ Ⓑ Ⓒ Ⓓ Ⓔ	118. Ⓐ Ⓑ Ⓒ Ⓓ Ⓔ
39. Ⓐ Ⓑ Ⓒ Ⓓ Ⓔ	79. Ⓐ Ⓑ Ⓒ Ⓓ Ⓔ	119. Ⓐ Ⓑ Ⓒ Ⓓ Ⓔ
40. Ⓐ Ⓑ Ⓒ Ⓓ Ⓔ	80. Ⓐ Ⓑ Ⓒ Ⓓ Ⓔ	120. Ⓐ Ⓑ Ⓒ Ⓓ Ⓔ